GALE DIRECTORY OF PUBLICATIONS AND BROADCAST MEDIA

Update

ISSN 1048-7972

1993
GALE DIRECTORY OF PUBLICATIONS AND BROADCAST MEDIA
Update

An Interedition Service Providing 3,000 Updates
to Listings in the Main Volume and 2,000 New Listings

See Introduction for Details

Deborah M. Burek
Editor

Karen Troshynski-Thomas
Associate Editor

Gale Research Inc. • *DETROIT* • *WASHINGTON, D.C.* • *LONDON*

Editorial

Donald P. Boyden, *Senior Editor*

Deborah M. Burek, *Editor*

H. Diane Cooper, Holly M. Selden, and Karen Troshynski-Thomas, *Associate Editors*

Amy Lynn Emrich, Melanye K. Johnson, Madge Lockwood, and Michaela R. Ludwick, *Assistant Editors*

Karin E. Koek and Julie Winklepleck, *Contributing Editors*

Eric J. Restum, *Contributor*

Research

Victoria B. Cariappa, *Research Manager*

Gary J. Oudersluys, *Research Supervisor*

Tracie A. Wade, *Editorial Associate*

Andreia L. Earley, Kimberly D. Klaty, Phyllis S. Shepherd, and Barbara J. Thornton, *Editorial Assistants*

Computer Programming

Robert D. Aitchison, *Director Editorial Systems Administration and Development*

Theresa A. Rocklin, *Supervisor of Systems and Programming*

Lan Campeau, *Programmer*

Production

Mary Beth Trimper, *Production Manager*

Catherine Kemp, *External Production Assistant*

Data Entry

Benita L. Spight, *Data Entry Supervisor*

Gwendolyn S. Tucker, *Data Entry Group Leader*

LySandra C. Davis, Civie Ann Green, Nancy S. Jakubiak, and
Yolanda A. Johnson, *Data Entry Associates*

Art

Cynthia Baldwin, *Art Director*

C.J. Jonik, *Keyliner*

This book is printed on acid-free paper that meets the minimum requirements of American National Standard for Information Sciences—Permanence Paper for Printed Library Materials, ANSIZ39.48-1984. ∞™

♻ This book is printed on recycled paper that meets Environmental Protection Agency standards.

Printed in the United States of America
Published simultaneously in the United Kingdom
by Gale Research International Limited
(An affiliated company of Gale Research Inc.)

Contents

Introduction

Highlights

This *Update* to the *Gale Directory of Publications and Broadcast Media* (*GDPBM*, formerly the *Ayer Directory of Publications*) presents the latest industry information, including:

▶ 1,878 new listings
▶ 2,991 updated entries

Featuring 1,064 new publication listings and 814 new broadcast entries, the *Update* also includes major changes in information that directly affect the user's ability to contact 1,840 publication and 1,151 broadcast listees included in the main edition.

Preparation, Content, and Arrangement

Published midway between editions of *GDPBM*, this *Update* is sent free to all subscribers. Information presented is obtained from questionnaire responses, brochures, and catalogs, and is confirmed through telephone calls and audit bureau data.

Entries for newly established or newly identified media outlets are interfiled with revised listings. While new entries contain full text as in the main volume, updated listings use **boldface** type to highlight changes in the following categories:

- publication title/broadcast call letters or system name
- publisher
- address
- telephone number
- fax number
- publication or broadcast system status (defunct).

More detail regarding the scope and coverage of *GDPBM* listings is contained in the Sample Entries following this Introduction and in the introductory section to the main edition of *GDPBM*.

Acknowledgments

The staff is grateful to the many media professionals who responded to our requests for updated information and provided additional data by telephone or fax.

Comments and Suggestions Welcome

We invite comments and suggestions for improving *GDPBM* and ask our users to send us information on potential listings. Please contact:

Gale Directory of Publications and Broadcast Media
Gale Research Inc.
835 Penobscot Bldg.
Detroit, MI 48226-4094
Phone: (313)961-2242
Toll-free: 800-877-GALE
Facsimile: (313)961-6815

Sample Entries

The samples that follow are fabricated entries in which each numbered section designates information that might appear in a listing. The numbered items are explained in the descriptive paragraphs following each sample.

SAMPLE NEW PUBLICATION LISTING

[1] 📖 **222** **[2] American Computer Review**

[3] Jane Doe Publishing Company, Inc.

[4] 199 E. 49th St.
PO Box 724866
Salem, NY 10528-9129

[5] Phone: (518) 555-9277

[6] Fax: (518) 555-9288

[7] Magazine for users of Super Software Plus products. **[8] Subtitle:** The Programmer's Friend. **[9] Founded:** June 1979. **[10] Frequency:** Monthly (combined issue July/Aug.). **[11] Printing Method:** Offset. **[12] Trim Size:** 8½ x 11. **[13] Cols./Page:** 3. **[14] Col. Width:** 2 in. **Col. Depth:** 10 in. **[15] Key Personnel:** Susan Smith, Editor; James F. Newman, Publisher; Steve Jones, Advertising Mgr. **[16] ISSN:** 5151-6226. **[17] Subscription:** $25; $30 Canada. $2.50 single issue.

[18] Ad Rates: BW: $850
4C: $1,350

[19] Circulation: 25,000

[20] Formerly: Computer Software Review (1990). **Additional Contact Information:** Toll-free 800-282-9456.

---

[1] SYMBOL/ENTRY NUMBER. Each publication entry number is preceded by a symbol (a magazine or newspaper) representing the publishing industry. Entries are numbered sequentially. Entry numbers (rather than page numbers) are used in the index to refer to listings.

[2] PUBLICATION TITLE. Publication names are listed *as they appear on the masthead or title page*, as provided by respondents.

[3] PUBLISHING COMPANY. The name of a commercial publishing organization, an association, or an academic institution, as provided by respondents.

[4] ADDRESS. Full mailing address information is provided whenever possible. This may include: street address; post office box; city; state or province; and ZIP or postal code. ZIP plus-four numbers are provided when known.

[5] TELEPHONE NUMBER. Numbers listed in this section are usually the respondent's switchboard number. In some cases, phone numbers for specific personnel are provided in the Remarks section of the entries, under the subheading Additional Contact Information (see 20 below).

[6] FAX. Facsimile numbers are listed when provided.

[7] DESCRIPTION. Includes the type of publication (i.e., newspaper, magazine) as well as a brief statement of purpose, intended audience, or other relevant remarks.

[8] SUBTITLE. Included as provided by the listee.

[9] FOUNDED. Date the periodical was first published.

[10] FREQUENCY. Indicates how often the publication is issued— daily, weekly, monthly, quarterly, etc. Explanatory remarks sometimes accompany this information (e.g., for weekly titles, the day of issuance; for collegiate titles, whether publication is limited to the academic year; whether certain issues are combined).

11 PRINTING METHOD. Though offset is most common, other methods are listed as provided. This is distinguished from production method, listed under Remarks (see 20 below).

12 TRIM SIZE. Presented in inches unless otherwise noted.

13 NUMBER OF COLUMNS PER PAGE. Usually one figure, but some publications list two or more, indicating a variation in style.

14 COLUMN WIDTH AND COLUMN DEPTH. Column sizes are given exactly as supplied, whether measured in inches, picas (6 picas to an inch), nonpareils (each 6 points, 72 points to an inch), or agate lines (14 to an inch).

15 KEY PERSONNEL. Presents the names and titles of contacts at each publication.

16 INTERNATIONAL STANDARD SERIAL NUMBER (ISSN). Included when provided. Occasionally, United States Publications Serial (USPS) numbers are reported rather than ISSNs.

17 SUBSCRIPTION. Unless otherwise stated, prices shown in this section are the individual *annual* subscription rate. Other rates are listed when known, including multiyear rates, prices outside the United States, discount rates, library/institution rates, and single copy prices.

18 AD RATES. Respondents may provide non-contract (open) rates in any of six categories:

GLR = general line rate
BW = one-time black & white page rate
4C = one-time four-color page rate
SAU = standard advertising unit rate
CNU = Canadian newspaper advertising unit rate
PCI = per column inch rate.

Occasionally, explanatory information about other types of advertising appears in the Remarks section of the entries (see 20 below).

19 CIRCULATION. Figures represent *paid* circulation unless otherwise noted, and are accompanied by a symbol (except for sworn and estimated figures). Following are explanations of the nine circulation classifications used by *GDPBM*, accompanied by the appropriate symbol.

These audit bureaus are independent, nonprofit organizations that verify circulation rates. Interested users may contact the association for more information.

★ ABC: Audit Bureau of Circulations, 900 N. Meacham Rd., Schaumburg, IL 60173; (708) 605-0909.
△ BPA: Business Publications Audit of Circulations, 360 Park Ave. S., New York, NY 10010; (212) 532-6880.
◆ CAC: Certified Audit of Circulations, Inc., 155 Willowbrook Blvd., PO Box 379, Wayne, NJ 07474-0379; (201) 785-3000.
● CCAB: Canadian Circulations Audit Board, 188 Eglinton Ave. E., Ste. 304, Toronto, ON Canada M4P 2X7; (416) 487-2418.
□ VAC: Verified Audit Circulation, 13366 Beach Ave., Marina Del Rey, CA 90292; (213) 306-1577.

⊕ Post Office Statement: These figures are accompanied by a U.S. Post Office form verifying the rates.
  Sworn Statement: These figures are accompanied by the notarized signature of the editor, publisher, or other officer of the publication.
‡ Publisher's Report: These figures are accompanied by the signature of the editor, publisher, or other officer.
  Estimated Figures: These figures are the unverified report of the respondent.

The footer on every odd-numbered page contains a key to circulation and entry type symbols, as well as advertising abbreviations. Additionally, explanatory circulation comments may appear in the Remarks section of the entries (see 20 below).

20 REMARKS. Information listed in this section further explains that provided in the Ad Rates (see 18 above) or Circulation (see 19 above) sections, but also may include data not appropriate for standard entry headings, such as former titles, association memberships, or production method (desktop). The boldface subheading, **Additional Contact Information**, includes toll-free and telex numbers, as well as addresses and telephone numbers for off-site personnel (see 15 above).

SAMPLE UPDATED PUBLICATION LISTING

1 📖 222 **2** **American Computer Review**

3 Jane Doe Publishing Company, Inc.

4 199 E. 49th St.

PO Box 724866

Salem, NY **10528-9129**   **5** Phone: (518) 555-9277

7 **Former Title: Computer Software Review.**   **6** Fax: (518) 555-9288

8 **Ceased publication.**

1 through **6** are the same as described above under Sample New Publication Listing. Please note that item **2**, Publication Title, *always* appears in **boldface**, whether or not a title has changed.

7 FORMER TITLE. This portion of an updated entry appears only if the title has changed. If this type of notation is not shown beneath the address, there has been no change in title since the previous edition.

8 CEASED PUBLICATION. Notices of recent cessations are included.

Boldface highlighting in the Sample Updated Publication Listing indicates that the following portions of the entry have changed since last edition: PO Box number; ZIP code; and title. Other information is the same as that previously published; the note regarding cessation is provided for example only.

SAMPLE NEW BROADCAST LISTING

1 🎤 111 **2** **WROL-FM—105.1 & 106.1**

3 15376 Michigan Ave.   **4** Phone: (313) 555-1234

Dearborn, MI 48126   **5** Fax: (313) 555-8675

6 **Format:** Classical. **7** **Network(s):** Beethoven Satellite. **8** **Owner:** Renaissance Communications, Inc., 45 Rockefeller Plaza, New York, NY 10020; (212) 555-1234. **9** **Founded:** 1953. **10** **Formerly:** WNRD- FM (1965); WNHA-FM (1983). **11** **Operating Hours:** Continuous; 10% network, 90% local. **12** **ADI:** Detroit, MI; Lansing (Ann Arbor), MI. **13** **Key Personnel:** Katherine Kern, Pres.; Miranda Kern, V.P./Gen. Mgr.; Joel Park, Operations V.P.; Susan Penn, Gen. Systems Mgr.; Douglas Scherer, Promotions Mgr.; Sonny Cherold, Chief Engineer. **14** **Cities Served:** Allen Park, Dearborn, Dearborn Heights, Detroit, East Lansing, Lansing, and Taylor, MI. **15** **Local Programs:** *Who's Beethoven?* 6 p.m. Sun.; contact Clement Goebel. **16** **Wattage:** 5000. **17** **Ad Rates:** $120 for 30 seconds; $240 for 60 seconds. **18** **Additional Contact Information:** Toll-free (within Michigan) 800-999-1111.

1 SYMBOL/ENTRY NUMBER. Each broadcast or cable entry is preceded by a symbol (a microphone) representing the broadcasting industry. Entries are numbered sequentially. Entry numbers (rather than page numbers) are used in the index to refer to listings.

2 CALL LETTERS AND FREQUENCY/CHANNEL; OR CABLE COMPANY NAME. Occasionally two frequencies or channels are listed, indicating that the station is retransmitted to reach a larger area.

3 ADDRESS. Location and studio addresses appear as supplied by respondents. If provided, alternate addresses are listed in the Additional Contact Information section of the entries (see 18 below).

4 TELEPHONE NUMBER. Listed as supplied by respondents.

5 FAX. Facsimile numbers are listed when provided.

6 FORMAT. For television station entries, this subheading indicates whether the station is commercial or public. Radio station entries contain industry-defined (and, in some cases, station-defined) formats as indicated by respondents.

7 NETWORK(S). Notes national and regional networks with which a station is affiliated. The term "Independent" is used if noted by respondents.

8 OWNER. Lists the name of an individual or company, supplemented by the address and telephone number, when provided by listees.

9 FOUNDED. In most cases, the year the station began operating, regardless of changes in call letters and ownership.

10 FORMERLY. For radio and television stations, former call letters and the years in which they were changed are presented as provided by listees. Former cable company names are noted when available.

11 OPERATING HOURS. Lists on-air hours and often includes percentages of network and local programming.

12 ADI. Entries contain ADIs reported by respondents. The Area of Dominant Influence is a standard market region defined by Arbitron Ratings Company for U.S. television stations. Some respondents also list radio stations as part of ADIs.

13 KEY PERSONNEL. Presents the names and titles of contacts at each station or cable company.

14 CITIES SERVED. Although this heading is primarily found in cable system entries and provides information on channels and the number of subscribers, this category may also be included in entries where a radio or television station is received in various cities on different frequencies via a translator, or in remote areas through use of repeating transmitters.

15 LOCAL PROGRAMS. Lists names, air times, and contact personnel for up to three locally produced television shows. [Usually this item is not found in radio entries; it is provided here for example.]

16 WATTAGE. Applicable to radio stations, the wattage may differ for day and night in the case of AM stations. Occasionally a station's ERP (effective radiated power) is given in addition to, or instead of, actual licensed wattage.

17 AD RATES. Includes rates for 10, 15, 30, and 60 seconds (as provided by respondents). Some stations price advertisement spots "per unit," regardless of length; these units vary.

18 ADDITIONAL CONTACT INFORMATION. Includes toll-free and telex numbers, alternate telephone numbers, numbers for news lines and request lines, night numbers, alternate mailing addresses, electronic mail addresses, and/or any other means of contact provided by respondents.

SAMPLE UPDATED BROADCAST LISTING

1 ☎ 111 **2** WROL-FM—89.7 & 90.3
3 15376 Michigan Ave.
Dearborn, MI 48126

4 Phone: (313) 555-1234
5 Fax: (313) 555-8675

---

1 through **5** are the same as those described above under Sample New Broadcast Listing. Please note that item **2**, Call Letters, *always* appear in **boldface**, whether or not they have changed.

Boldface highlighting in the Sample Updated Broadcast Listing indicates that the following portions of the entry have changed since last edition: address; ZIP code; and fax number. Other information is the same as that previously published.

Entry information appearing in the Sample Entries portion of this directory has been fabricated. The entries named here do not, to the best of our knowledge, exist.

Index Notes

Following the main body of the *Update* is the Master Name and Keyword Index. Citations in this index are interfiled alphabetically regardless of media type.

Publication citations include the following:

- titles
- important keywords within titles
- titles of recent cessations
- former titles
- foreign language titles
- alternate titles.

Broadcast media citations include the following:

- station call letters
- cable company names
- former station call letters
- former cable company names.

Indexing is word-by-word rather than letter-by-letter; thus, "New York" is listed before "News." Current listings in the Index include geographic information and entry number.

INDEXING SAMPLE

[1] Administration in Mental Health [2] (New York, NY) **575**

[1] Allied Cable Systems [2] (Lancaster, NH) **876**

[3] Mental Health; Administration in (New York, NY) **575**

[4] Metro Tattler (Chicago, IL) ceased

[5] My I Svit/We and the World (Toronto, ON, Can.) **966**

We and the World/My I Svit (Toronto, ON, Can.) **966**

[6] WMDC-TV [7] **846**

[1] The full name (i.e., publication title, station call letters, or cable company name) of each entry is cited as it appears in the main body.

[2] Citations include in parentheses the city and state (or province and country for Canadian entries) in which the entry is located.

[3] Publications are also indexed by subject keywords and other important words within titles.

[4] Notices of recent cessations are included. (In cases where the editors have not been able to verify a cessation, citations appear in the index with the annotation "*Unable to locate.*")

[5] Foreign names are indexed in their respective languages, and in English, if the English translation is known.

[6] Former call letters are indexed (as are former publication or cable company names) without a geographic designation.

[7] References are to entry numbers rather than page numbers.

Abbreviations, Symbols, and Codes

Miscellaneous Abbreviations

&	And
4C	One-Time Four Color Page Rate
ABC	Audit Bureau of Circulations
Acad.	Academy
Act.	Acting
Adm.	Administrative, Administration
Admin.	Administrator
AFB	Air Force Base
AM	Amplitude Modulation
Amer.	American
APO	Army Post Office
Apt.	Apartment
Assn.	Association
Assoc.	Associate
Asst.	Assistant
Ave.	Avenue
Bldg.	Building
Blvd.	Boulevard
boul.	boulevard
BPA	Business Publications Audit of Circulations
BTA	Best Time Available
BW	One-time Black & White Page Rate
C	Central
CAC	Certified Audit of Circulations
CCAB	Canadian Circulations Audit Board
CEO	Chief Executive Officer
Chm.	Chairman
Chwm.	Chairwoman
CNU	Canadian Newspaper Advertising Unit Rate
c/o	Care of
Col.	Column
Coll.	College
Comm.	Committee
Co.	Company
COO	Chief Operating Officer
Coord.	Coordinator
Corp.	Corporation
Coun.	Council
CP	case postale
Ct.	Court
Dept.	Department
Dir.	Director
Div.	Division
Dr.	Doctor, Drive
E.	East
EC	East Central
ENE	East Northeast
ERP	Effective Radiated Power
ESE	East Southeast
Eve.	Evening
Exec.	Executive
Expy.	Expressway
Fed.	Federation
Fl.	Floor

FM	Frequency Modulation
FPO	Fleet Post Office
Fri.	Friday
Fwy.	Freeway
Gen.	General
GLR	General Line Rate
Hd.	Head
Hwy.	Highway
Inc.	Incorporated
Info.	Information
Inst.	Institute
Intl.	International
ISSN	International Standard Serial Number
Jr.	Junior
Libn.	Librarian
Ln.	Lane
Ltd.	Limited
Mgr.	Manager
mi.	miles
Mktg.	Marketing
Mng.	Managing
Mon.	Monday
Morn.	Morning
N.	North
NAS	Naval Air Station
Natl.	National
NC	North Central
NE	Northeast
NNE	North Northeast
NNW	North Northwest
No.	Number
NW	Northwest
Orgn.	Organization
PCI	Per Column Inch Rate
Pkwy.	Parkway
Pl.	Place
PO	Post Office
Pres.	President
Prof.	Professor
Rd.	Road
RFD	Rural Free Delivery
Rm.	Room
ROS	Run of Schedule
RR	Rural Route
Rte.	Route
S.	South
Sat.	Saturday
SAU	Standard Advertising Unit Rate
SC	South Central
SE	Southeast

Sec.	Secretary
Soc.	Society
Sq.	Square
Sr.	Senior
SSE	South Southeast
SSW	South Southwest
St.	Saint, Street
Sta.	Station
Ste.	Sainte, Suite
Sun.	Sunday
Supt.	Superintendent
SW	Southwest
Terr.	Terrace
Thurs.	Thursday
Tpke.	Turnpike
Treas.	Treasurer

Tues.	Tuesday
Univ.	University
USPS	United States Publications Serial
VAC	Verified Audit Circulation
V.P.	Vice President
W.	West
WC	West Central
Wed.	Wednesday
WNW	West Northwest
WSW	West Southwest
x/mo.	Times per Month
x/wk.	Times per Week
x/yr.	Times per Year

Circulation Symbols

★	ABC
△	BPA
◆	CAC
●	CCAB

□	VAC
⊕	Post Office Statement
‡	Publisher's Report

Entry Symbols

📖 .... Magazine, Newspaper, or Periodical Entry   🎤 .... Radio, Television, or Cable Entry

U.S. State and Territory Postal Codes

AK	Alaska
AL	Alabama
AR	Arkansas
AZ	Arizona
CA	California
CO	Colorado
CT	Connecticut
DC	District of Columbia
DE	Delaware
FL	Florida
GA	Georgia
HI	Hawaii
IA	Iowa
ID	Idaho
IL	Illinois
IN	Indiana
KS	Kansas
KY	Kentucky
LA	Louisiana
MA	Massachusetts
MD	Maryland
ME	Maine
MI	Michigan
MN	Minnesota
MO	Missouri
MS	Mississippi

MT	Montana
NC	North Carolina
ND	North Dakota
NE	Nebraska
NH	New Hampshire
NJ	New Jersey
NM	New Mexico
NV	Nevada
NY	New York
OH	Ohio
OK	Oklahoma
OR	Oregon
PA	Pennsylvania
PR	Puerto Rico
RI	Rhode Island
SC	South Carolina
SD	South Dakota
TN	Tennessee
TX	Texas
UT	Utah
VA	Virginia
VT	Vermont
WA	Washington
WI	Wisconsin
WV	West Virginia
WY	Wyoming

Canadian Province and Territory Postal Codes

AB .... Alberta
BC ....British Columbia
MB .... Manitoba
NB .... New Brunswick
NF .... Newfoundland
NS .... Nova Scotia

NT .... Northwest Territories
ON .... Ontario
PE .... Prince Edward Island
PQ .... Quebec
SK .... Saskatchewan
YT .... Yukon Territory

GALE DIRECTORY OF PUBLICATIONS AND BROADCAST MEDIA

Update

ALABAMA

ALEXANDER CITY

� 1 WSTH-FM - 106.1
1236 Broadway
PO Box 1640   Phone: (706)596-5100
Columbus, GA 31994   Fax: (706)596-5115

ANDALUSIA

☰ 2 WAAO-FM - 103.7
PO Box 987   Phone: (205)222-1166
Andalusia, AL 36420   **Fax: (205)222-1167**

☰ 3 WKYD-AM - 920
Hwy. 84 E.
PO Box 8   **Phone: (205)222-0920**
Andalusia, AL 36420   **Fax: (205)222-8641**

ANNISTON

☰ 4 Anniston NewChannels
620 Noble St.   Phone: (205)238-1144
Anniston, AL 36201   Fax: (205)236-4475
Owner: NewChannels Corp. **Founded:** 1960. **Cities Served:** Calhoun County, Talladega County, Fort McClellan, Hobson City, Jacksonville, Munford, Ohatchee, Oxford, and Weaver, AL.

ARAB

☰ 5 WCRQ-FM - 92.7
981 N. Parkway
PO Box 568   Phone: (205)586-9300
Arab, AL 35016   **Fax: (205)586-9301**

ASHLAND

☰ 6 WASZ-FM - 95.3
PO Box 395   **Phone: (205)354-4600**
Ashland, AL 36251   **Fax: (205)354-7224**

ATMORE

☰ 7 WGYJ-AM - 1590
PO Box 10   **Phone: (205)368-9495**
Atmore, AL 36502   **Fax: (205)368-1946**

AUBURN

▤ 8 Noise Control Engineer Journal
Institute of Noise Control Engineering
345 Ross Hall
Dept. of Mechanical Engineering   Phone: (205)844-3306
Auburn, AL 36849-3541   Fax: (205)844-3307

☰ 9 WAUD-AM - 1230
PO Box 3387   Phone: (205)887-3401
Auburn, AL 36830   **Fax: (205)887-7909**

BAY MINETTE

☰ 10 WBCA-AM - 1110
720 S. White Ave.
PO Box 426   Phone: (205)937-5596
Bay Minette, AL 36507   **Fax: (205)937-5597**

BESSEMER

☰ 11 Bessemer Cable
1025 Westlake Mall
Bessemer, AL 35020   Phone: (205)426-1971
Owner: American TV & Communications Corp. **Founded:** 1979. **Cities Served:** Jefferson County, Brigton, Brownvill, Lipscomb, and Roosevelt City, AL.

BIRMINGHAM

▤ 12 The Apostle
The Episcopal Diocese of Alabama
521 N. 20th St.   Phone: (205)328-8374
Birmingham, AL 35203   Fax: (205)328-9060

▤ 13 Dimension
Woman's Missionary Union
PO Box 830010   Phone: (205)991-8100
Birmingham, AL 35283-0010   Fax: (205)991-4990
Administrative magazine for general officers and directors of the Woman's Missionary Union. **Frequency:** Quarterly. **ISSN:** 0162-6825. **Subscription:** $10.95. $3.25 single issue.
                      Circulation: (Not Reported)
Advertising not accepted. The Woman's Missionary Union is an auxiliary to the Southern Baptist Convention.

Ad Rates: GLR = general line rate; BW = one-time black & white page rate; 4C = one-time four color page rate; SAU = standard advertising unit rate; CNU = Canadian newspaper advertising unit rate; PCI = per column inch rate.
Circulation: ★ = ABC; △ = BPA; ◆ = CAC; ● = CCAB; □ = VAC; ⊕ = PO Statement; ‡ = Publisher's Report; Boldface figures = sworn; Light figures = estimated.
Entry type: ▤ = Print; ☰ = Broadcast.

📖 **14 Kaleidoscope**
University of Alabama at Birmingham
Dept. of Student Publications
Box 76 University Center
University Sta.   Phone: (205)934-3354
Birmingham, AL 35294-1150   Fax: (205)934-8070

📖 **15 Southern Living**
Southern Living, Inc.
PO Box 523   Phone: (205)877-6000
Birmingham, AL 35201   Fax: (205)877-6700

🎤 **16 Birmingham Cable Communications**
6429 1st Ave. S.   Phone: (205)591-6880
Birmingham, AL 35212   Fax: (205)599-5641
Owner: Time Warner Cable. **Founded:** 1976. **Key Personnel:** Mike D'Ambra, Pres.; Julia Muscari, V.P. of Marketing; Tim Stout, Program Mgr.; Paul Bartlett, V.P. of Engineering; Rod Clark, V.P. of Ad. Sales. **Cities Served:** Jefferson County, Birmingham, Brighton, Brownville, Irondale, Lipscomb, and Roosevelt City, AL: 61,000 subscribing households; 50 channels; 1 community access channel; 49 hours per week of community access programming.

🎤 **17 WAPI-FM - 94.5**
2146 Highland Ave. S.   Phone: (205)933-9274
Birmingham, AL 35205   Fax: (205)933-2748

🎤 **18 WBIQ-TV - Channel 10**
2112 11th Ave. S., Ste. 400   Phone: (205)328-8756
Birmingham, AL 35256   Fax: (205)251-2192

🎤 **19 WBRC-TV - Channel 6**
Atop Red Mountain
Box 6   Phone: (205)322-6666
Birmingham, AL 35201   Fax: (205)583-4386

🎤 **20 WJLD-AM - 1400**
1449 Spaulding Ishkooda Rd.   Phone: (205)942-1776
Birmingham, AL 35211   Fax: (205)942-4814

BREWTON

🎤 **21 WKNU-FM - 106.3**
Ridge Rd.
Rte. 6, Box 468   Phone: (205)867-4824
Brewton, AL 36427   Fax: (205)867-7003

CAMDEN

🎤 **22 WCOX-AM - 1450**
Box 820   Phone: (205)682-9048
Camden, AL 36726   Fax: (205)682-4726
Format: Black Gospel; Religious; Talk. **Owner:** Down Home Broadcasting, Inc. **Operating Hours:** 5 a.m.-7 p.m. **Key Personnel:** Leroy T. Griffith, Gen. Mgr.; William Pompey, Pres.; Paul Johnson, Producer. **Wattage:** 1000. **Additional Contact Information:** Request line (205)682-4242.

🎤 **23 WCOX-FM - 102.3**
Box 820   Phone: (205)682-9048
Camden, AL 36726   Fax: (205)682-4726
Format: Black Gospel; Religious; Talk. **Owner:** Down Home Broadcasting, Inc. **Founded:** 1989. **Operating Hours:** 5 a.m.-midnight. **Key Personnel:** Leroy T. Griffith, Gen. Mgr.; William Pompey, Pres.; Paul Johnson, Producer. **Wattage:** 6000. **Additional Contact Information:** Request line (205)682-9898.

DEMOPOLIS

🎤 **24 WIIQ-TV - Channel 41**
c/o WBIQ-TV
2112 11th Ave. S., Ste. 400   Phone: (205)328-8756
Birmingham, AL 35256   Fax: (205)251-2192

DOTHAN

📖 **25 The Dothan Progress**
Freedom Newspapers, Inc.
226 Plaza 2
PO Box 1927   Phone: (205)793-9586
Dothan, AL 36302   Fax: (205)793-2040

🎤 **26 Cablevision Industries Corp.**
Box 8247
104 Woodburn Dr.   Phone: (205)793-1752
Dothan, AL 36301   Fax: (205)793-5667
Owner: Cablevision Industries, Inc. **Founded:** 1966. **Cities Served:** Dale, Geneva, and Houston counties, Clayhatchee, Dothan, Fort Rucker, Grimes, Level Plains, Malvem, Midland City, Napier Field, Newton, Pinckard, Rehobeth, and Taylor, AL.

🎤 **27 WVOB-FM - 91.3**
Box 1944   Phone: (205)793-3189
Dothan, AL 36302   Fax: (205)793-4344
Format: Educational; Religious. **Network(s):** USA Radio. **Owner:** Bethany Bible College and Bethany Theological Seminary, Inc. **Founded:** 1988. **Operating Hours:** 6 a.m.-10 p.m. **Key Personnel:** H.D. Shuemake, Gen. Mgr.; Steve A. Shuemake, Station Mgr. **Wattage:** 2500. **Ad Rates:** Noncommercial.

DOZIER

🎤 **28 WDIQ-TV - Channel 2**
c/o WBIQ-TV
2112 11th Ave. S., Ste. 400   Phone: (205)328-8756
Birmingham, AL 35256   Fax: (205)251-2192

EUTAW

📖 **29 Greene County Democrat**
Greene County Newspaper Co.
214 Boligee St.
PO Box 598   Phone: (205)372-3373
Eutaw, AL 35462   Fax: (205)372-2243

FAYETTE

🎤 **30 WLDX-AM - 990**
PO Box 189   Phone: (205)932-9539
Fayette, AL 35555   Fax: (205)932-3318

🎤 **31 WTXT-FM - 98.1**
PO Box 1109   Phone: (205)333-9800
Northport, AL 35476   Fax: (205)333-8834

FLORENCE

🎤 **32 WFIQ-TV - Channel 36**
c/o WBIQ-TV
2112 11th Ave. S., Ste. 400   Phone: (205)328-8756
Birmingham, AL 35256   Fax: (205)251-2192

FORT PAYNE

🎤 **33 WFPA-AM - 1400**
PO Box 155   Phone: (205)845-2111
Fort Payne, AL 35967   Fax: (205)845-0024

FULTONDALE

🎤 **34 Cencom Cable of Alabama, L.P.**
3524 Decatur Hwy.
PO Box 1108   Phone: (205)631-9681
Fultondale, AL 35068   Fax: (205)631-6609
Formerly: Insight Cablevision. **Key Personnel:** G.W. Booher, Gen. Mgr.; Richard Murphy, Operations Dir.; Arne Abel, Mktg. Dir.; Liz Donaldson, Personnel; Veronica Hambric, Customer Service Mgr. **Cities Served:** Fultondale, AL: 47,000 subscribing households. **Additional Contact Information:** (205)631-9555.

GUNTERSVILLE

◫ **35 The Advertiser-Gleam**
PO Box 190   Phone: (205)582-3232
Guntersville, AL 35976   **Fax: (205)582-3231**

HAMILTON

◉ **36 WERH-AM - 970**
PO Box 1119   Phone: (205)921-3481
Hamilton, AL 35570   **Fax: (205)921-3195**

HARTSELLE

◉ **37 WYAM-FM - 106.1**
809 N. Sparkman St.
Hartselle, AL 35640   Phone: (205)351-2345
Format: Contemporary Hit Radio (CHR). **Network(s):** Satellite Music. **Owner:** Gene Newman, at above address. **Founded:** 1991. **Operating Hours:** Continuous. **Key Personnel:** Gene Newman, Owner/Mgr. **Wattage:** 3000. **Ad Rates:** Available upon request. **Additional Contact Information:** Alt telephone (205)340-1490; (205)353-9230.

HOOVER

◉ **38 TCI Cablevision of Alabama, Inc.**
Box 360268
Hoover, AL 35216   Phone: (205)822-8731
Owner: Tele-Communications, Inc. **Founded:** 1967. **Cities Served:** Jefferson County, Shelby County, Bluff Park, Forest Brook, Green Valley, Homewood, Riverchase, Rocky Ridge, Shades Mountain, and Vestavia Hills, AL.

HUNTSVILLE

◉ **39 Comcast Cablevision**
2047 Max Luther Dr.   Phone: (205)859-7800
Huntsville, AL 35810   Fax: (205)852-5599
Owner: Comcast Corp. **Founded:** 1954. **Cities Served:** Madison County, AL.

◉ **40 WEUP-AM - 1600**
PO Box 11398   Phone: (205)837-9387
Huntsville, AL 35814   Fax: (205)837-9404
Format: Urban Contemporary. **Network(s):** American Urban Radio. **Owner:** Dr. Virginia Caples and Hundley Batts, Sr. **Founded:** 1958. **Operating Hours:** Continuous. **Key Personnel:** Virginia Caples, Gen. Mgr./Owner; Hundley Batts, Sr., Sales Coordinator/Owner; Dee Handley, Station Mgr.; Shirley Pride, Traffic Mgr.; Steve Murry, Program and Music Dir. **Wattage:** 5000 day; 500 night. **Ad Rates:** $18-$56 for 30 seconds; $22-$70 for 60 seconds.

◉ **41 WOCG-FM - 90.1**
Oakwood Rd. NW
Huntsville, AL 35896   Phone: (205)726-7418

◉ **42 WRSA-FM - 96.9**
PO Box 4144   Phone: (205)498-2634
Huntsville, AL 35802   Fax: (205)498-2791

JACKSON

◉ **43 WHOD-FM - 94.5**
4428 N. College Ave.
PO Box 518   Phone: (205)246-4431
Jackson, AL 36545   **Fax: (205)246-1980**

JASPER

◉ **44 WZPQ-AM - 1360**
9th Ave.
PO Box 622   Phone: (205)384-3461
Jasper, AL 35501   **Fax: (205)384-3462**

LAFAYETTE

◫ **45 Lafayette Sun**
PO Box 378   Phone: (205)864-8885
Lafayette, AL 36862   **Fax: (205)864-7775**

LANETT

◉ **46 WRLD-AM - 1490**
602 Cherry Dr.   Phone: (205)644-1179
Lanett, AL 36863   **Fax: (205)644-1490**

MARION

◉ **47 WAJO-AM - 1310**
PO Box 930   Phone: (205)683-6168
Marion, AL 36756   Fax: (205)683-9926
Format: Urban Contemporary. **Owner:** Marion Radio, Inc. **Founded:** 1984. **Formerly:** WJAM-AM. **Operating Hours:** Sunrise-sunset. **Key Personnel:** Elijah Rollins III, Station Mgr./Music Dir.; Quentin Rollins, Sales Rep.; Bill Bryant, Gospel Producer; Rev. Glenn King, Gospel Producer. **Wattage:** 5000. **Ad Rates:** $5 for 30 seconds; $8 for 60 seconds. **Additional Contact Information:** Request line: (205)683-6169.

MCCALLA

◉ **48 Twin County Cable TV, Inc.**
Box 483
McCalla, AL 35111   Phone: (205)477-6210
Owner: William H. Garner. **Founded:** 1988. **Cities Served:** Jefferson and Tuscaloosa Counties, Abernant, Bucksville, and Million Dollar Lake, AL.

MILLBROOK

◫ **49 The Community Press**
3440 Hwy. 14
PO Box 568   Phone: (205)285-6000
Millbrook, AL 36054   **Fax: (205)285-6001**

MOBILE

◫ **50 Negative Capability**
Negative Capability Press
62 Ridgelawn Dr. E.   **Phone: (205)343-6163**
Mobile, AL 36608   **Fax: (205)343-6163**

◉ **51 Enstar Cable of Mobile County**
6700-A Moffat Rd
Mobile, AL 36618   Phone: (205)649-4900
Owner: Falcon Cable TV. **Founded:** 1984. **Cities Served:** Mobile County, Mobile, and Prichard, AL.

◉ **52 MultiVision Cable TV**
6008 Clearview Rd.   Phone: (205)666-4070
Mobile, AL 36619-0469   Fax: (205)666-3988
Owner: MultiVision Cable TV Corp. **Founded:** 1981. **Cities Served:** Baldwin and Mobile counties, Theodore and Tillman's Corner, AL.

◉ **53 Partners in Communications-Alabama**
779-B Lakeside Dr.
Mobile, AL 36609   Phone: (205)661-1114
Owner: First Pic Cable TV. **Founded:** 1987. **Cities Served:** Mobile County and Dauphin Island, AL.

◉ **54 WBHY-AM - 840**
PO Box 1328
Mobile, AL 36633-1328   **Phone: (205)473-8488**

◉ **55 WBHY-FM - 88.5**
PO Box 1328
Mobile, AL 36633-1328   **Phone: (205)473-8488**

Ad Rates: GLR = general line rate; BW = one-time black & white page rate; 4C = one-time four color page rate; SAU = standard advertising unit rate; CNU = Canadian newspaper advertising unit rate; PCI = per column inch rate.
Circulation: ★ = ABC; △ = BPA; ◆ = CAC; ● = CCAB; □ = VAC; ⊕ = PO Statement; ‡ = Publisher's Report; Boldface figures = sworn; Light figures = estimated.
Entry type: ◫ = Print; ◉ = Broadcast.

3

♣ 56 WEIQ-TV - Channel 42
c/o WBIQ-TV
2112 11th Ave. S., Ste. 400   Phone: (205)328-8756
Birmingham, AL 35256   Fax: (205)251-2192

MONTEVALLO

▣ 57 The Alabamian
Selma Times Journal
Sta. 6336
Montevallo, AL 35115   Phone: (205)665-6228

MONTGOMERY

▣ 58 Airpower Journal
Bldg. 1400, Rm. 253, Maxwell Air
  Force Base   Phone: (205)953-5322
Montgomery, AL 36112-5532   Fax: (205)953-6739

▣ 59 Alabama Conservation
Alabama Dept. of Conservation and Natural Resources
64 N. Union St.   Phone: (205)242-3151
Montgomery, AL 36130-1901   Fax: (205)242-0999

▣ 60 Alabama School Journal
Alabama Education Assn.
422 Dexter Ave.   Phone: (205)834-9790
Montgomery, AL 36195   Fax: (205)262-8377

▣ 61 Neighbors
Alabama Farmers Federation
PO Box 11000   Phone: (205)288-3900
Montgomery, AL 36191-0001   Fax: (205)284-3957

♣ 62 WLBF-FM - 89.1
PO Box 210789
381 Mendel Pkwy. E.   Phone: (205)271-8900
Montgomery, AL 36121   Fax: (205)260-8926

MOUNTAIN BROOK

♣ 63 Mountain Brook Cablevision, Inc.
Box 75028
Mountain Brook, AL 35223   Phone: (205)879-5089
Owner: McDonald Investment. Founded: 1970. Key Personnel: Tom Walsh, Gen. Mgr. Cities Served: Shelby County, Mountain Brook, Vestania, and Hoover, AL: 17,500 subscribing households; 42 channels.

MUSCLE SHOALS

♣ 64 WLAY-FM - 105.5
620 E. 2nd St.   Phone: (205)383-2525
Muscle Shoals, AL 35660   Fax: (205)381-1450

NORTHPORT

♣ 65 CableSouth, Inc.
Box 778
Northport, AL 35476   Phone: (205)339-7972
Key Personnel: Tom Early, Gen. Mgr.; Jo Ann Bamberg, Office Mgr.; Tim Denton, Plant Mgr. Cities Served: Northport, AL: 6,000 subscribing households; 35 channels.

OPP

♣ 66 WAMI-FM - 102.3
Box 169
Opp, AL 36467   Phone: (205)493-3588
                                   Fax: (205)493-3588

OXFORD

♣ 67 WOXR-AM - 1580
PO Box 3770   Phone: (205)835-1580
Oxford, AL 36203   Fax: (205)831-1500

PIEDMONT

♣ 68 TCI Cablevision of Alabama
109 Seaboard Ave.   Phone: (205)447-7871
Piedmont, AL 36272   Fax: (205)447-8630
Owner: Tele-Communications, Inc. Key Personnel: Earl Hines, State Mgr.; Barry Kerr, Area Mgr.; Darrel Currier, Plant Mgr.; Cindy Smith, Office Mgr. Cities Served: Piedmont and Centre, AL; Cherokee, CO. 36 channels.

ROANOKE

♣ 69 Better Vision Cable Co.
Box 863   Phone: (205)863-8112
Roanoke, AL 36274   Fax: (205)863-2027

ROGERSVILLE

▣ 70 East Lauderdale News
PO Box 179   Phone: (205)247-5565
Rogersville, AL 35652   Fax: (205)247-1902

TALLADEGA

♣ 71 WEYY-FM - 92.7
PO Drawer 329   Phone: (205)362-8890
Talladega, AL 35160   Fax: (205)362-3440

TALLASSEE

♣ 72 WACQ-FM - 99.9
Rte. 4, Box 12
Tallassee, AL 36078   Phone: (205)283-6888
Format: Hot Adult Contemporary. Network(s): Alabama Radio (ALANET); USA Radio. Owner: Tiger Broadcasting, Inc., at above address. Operating Hours: Continuous. ADI: Montgomery-Selma, AL. Key Personnel: Fred Randall Hughey, Gen. Mgr./News Dir./Sports Dir.; Debra Hughey, Office Mgr./Public Service Dir.; Reid Spann, Program Dir.; Windle Jayrean, Music Dir. Wattage: 6000. Ad Rates: $10 for 30 seconds; $15 for 60 seconds.

TUSCALOOSA

▣ 73 Equipment World
Randall Publishing Co.
PO Box 2029   Phone: (205)349-2990
Tuscaloosa, AL 35403   Fax: (205)750-8070

▣ 74 The Senior Edition
6th St. & 20th Ave.
PO Box Drawer 1   Phone: (205)345-0505
Tuscaloosa, AL 35401   Fax: (205)349-0845
Newspaper for mature adults. Frequency: Monthly. Cols./Page: 5. Col. Width: 11.5 picas. Col. Depth: 13 in. Subscription: Free.
Ad Rates: BW: $471.25   Circulation: (Not Reported)
           4C: $611.25
           PCI: $7.25

▣ 75 South Atlantic Review
South Atlantic Modern Language Assn.
University of Alabama
Box 6109   Phone: (205)348-9067
Tuscaloosa, AL 35486   Fax: (205)348-5298

♣ 76 Comcast Cablevision of Tuscaloosa
700 Parkview Center   Phone: (205)345-0424
Tuscaloosa, AL 35402   Fax: (205)345-8223
Owner: Comcast Corp. Founded: 1957. Cities Served: Tuscaloosa County and Northport, AL.

VALLEY HEAD

♣ 77 WQRX-AM - 870
870 Jeff Cook Dr.   Phone: (205)635-6284
Valley Head, AL 35989   Fax: (205)845-0872

YORK

⬤ **78 WYLS-AM - 670**
11474 U.S. Hwy. 11   Phone: (205)392-5234
York, AL 36925   **Fax: (205)392-5234**

ALASKA

ANCHORAGE

79 Alaska Geographic
Alaska Geographic Society
PO Box 93370
Anchorage, AK 99509-3370
Phone: (907)562-0164
Fax: (907)562-0479

80 Barrow Sun
Rural Publications-Alaska
733 W. 4th Ave., Ste. 676
Anchorage, AK 99501
Phone: (907)277-2605
Fax: (907)563-2255

81 Bristol Bay News
Lindauer Newspapers
3709 Spenard Rd., Ste. 200
Anchorage, AK 99503
Ceased publication.
Phone: (907)562-4684
Fax: (907)563-4295

82 Sourdough Sentinel
Star Publishing Co.
16941 N. Eagle River Loop Rd.
Eagle River, AK 99577
Phone: (907)694-2727
Fax: (907)694-1545

83 KBRJ-FM - 104.1
11259 Tower Rd.
Anchorage, AK 99515
Phone: (907)522-3422
Fax: (907)349-3299

84 KDMD-TV - Channel 33 & 22
6921 Brayton Dr., No. 220
Anchorage, AK 99507-2488
Phone: (907)344-7758

85 KHAR-AM - 590
11259 Tower Rd.
Anchorage, AK 99515
Phone: (907)522-3422
Fax: (907)349-3299

86 KRUA-FM - 88.1
3211 Providence Dr.
Anchorage, AK 99508
Phone: (907)786-1077
Format: Alternative/Independent/Progressive. **Network(s):** American Public Radio (APR). **Owner:** UAA Board of Regents. **Formerly:** KMPS-FM. **Operating Hours:** 7 a.m.-1 a.m. **Key Personnel:** Suzi Pearson, Station Mgr.; Mitzi Ellis, Program Dir.; Shawn Campbell, Production Mgr.; Kamala Durry, Music Dir. **Wattage:** 100. **Ad Rates:** Noncommercial.

87 Prime Cable of Alaska, Inc.
5151 Fairbanks St.
Anchorage, AK 99503
Phone: (907)562-2400
Fax: (907)561-4396
Owner: Prime Cable Corp. **Founded:** 1980. **Cities Served:** Anchorage, Bethel, and Kenai Peninsula counties, Bethel, Chugiak, Eagle River, Elmendorf AFB, Fort Richardson, Kenai, Kenai Peninsula, Ridgeway, and Soldotna, AK.

BETHEL

88 KYUK-AM - 640
640 Radio St.
Pouch 468
Bethel, AK 99559
Phone: (907)543-3131
Fax: (907)543-3130

FAIRBANKS

89 Cooke Communications of Alaska
Box 1047
3990 S. Cushman St.
Fairbanks, AK 99701
Phone: (907)452-7191
Owner: Cooke Cablevision. **Founded:** 1979. **Cities Served:** Eielson AFB, Fairbanks County, Farmers Loop, Fort Greely, Fort Wainwright, and North Star Bourough, AK.

90 KTVF-TV - Channel 11
3528 International Way
Fairbanks, AK 99701
Phone: (907)452-5121
Fax: (907)452-5120

91 KXLR-FM - 95.9
3528 International Way
Fairbanks, AK 99701
Phone: (907)452-5121
Fax: (907)452-5120

JUNEAU

92 S.E. Alaska Business Journal
8365 Old Dairy Rd.
Juneau, AK 99801
Phone: (907)789-0829
Fax: (907)789-0829

93 Alaskan Cable Network Inc.
Ste. 1, 3161 Channel Dr.
Juneau, AK 99801
Phone: (907)586-3320
Fax: (907)463-3080
Owner: Alaskan Cable Network Inc. **Founded:** 1966. **Formerly:** Cooke Cablevision. **Key Personnel:** Jerry Parker, District Mgr.; Terry Dunlap, Plant Mgr.; Lea J. Ike, Marketing/Advertising Sales Mgr.; Dollie Jewell, Office Mgr. **Cities Served:** Juneau County and Douglas, AK: 7,900 subscribing households; 32 channels. **Additional Contact Information:** Alt. telephone (907)586-1200.

NAKNEK

94 KAKN-FM - 100.9
PO Box 214
Naknek, AK 99633
Phone: (907)246-7492
Fax: (907)246-7462

Ad Rates: GLR = general line rate; BW = one-time black & white page rate; 4C = one-time four color page rate; SAU = standard advertising unit rate; CNU = Canadian newspaper advertising unit rate; PCI = per column inch rate.
Circulation: ★ = ABC; △ = BPA; ◆ = CAC; ● = CCAB; □ = VAC; ⊕ = PO Statement; ‡ = Publisher's Report; Boldface figures = sworn; Light figures = estimated.
Entry type: ◫ = Print; ☚ = Broadcast.

7

NENANA

♣ 95 KIAM-AM - 630
Box 474   Phone: (907)832-5426
Nenana, AK 99760   Fax: (907)832-5450
Format: Religious. **Network(s):** USA Radio. **Owner:** Voice for Christ Ministries, Inc. **Founded:** 1985. **Operating Hours:** 7 a.m.-11 p.m. **Key Personnel:** Robert C. Eldridge, General Dir.; John Reese, Station Mgr./Field Coordinator; Brian Anderson, Music Dir. **Wattage:** 5000. **Ad Rates:** $2.80-$6 for 30 seconds; $3.75-$7.65 for 60 seconds.

SITKA

♣ 96 KCAW-FM - 104.7
2B Lincoln St.
Sitka, AK 99835   Phone: (907)747-5877
Format: Public Radio. **Network(s):** National Public Radio (NPR); American Public Radio (APR). **Owner:** Raven Radio Foundation. **Founded:** 1982. **Operating Hours:** Continuous. **Key Personnel:** Rich McClear, Gen. Mgr.; Jake Schumacher, Program Dir.; Jeb Sharp, News Dir.; Bill Prendergast, Chief Engineer. **Wattage:** 5000. **Ad Rates:** Noncommercial.

SKAGWAY

📖 97 The Skagway News
PO Box 1898   Phone: (907)983-2354
Skagway, AK 99840-0498   **Fax: (907)983-2356**

VALDEZ

♣ 98 KCHU-FM - 88.1
128 Pioneer Dr.
PO Box 467   Phone: (907)835-4665
Valdez, AK 99686   Fax: (907)835-2847
Format: Eclectic. **Network(s):** National Public Radio (NPR); American Public Radio (APR); Southern Educational Communication Association. **Owner:** Terminal Radio, Inc. **Founded:** 1984. **Operating Hours:** 5 a.m.-midnight. **Key Personnel:** James Winchester, Gen. Mgr.; David Perkins, Program Dir.; Bob Schmalfelt, News Dir. **Wattage:** 10,000. **Ad Rates:** Noncommercial.

ARIZONA

BISHBEE

♣ 99 Post-Newsweek Cable
99 Bisbee Rd.
Bisbee, AZ 85603

Phone: (602)432-4807
Fax: (602)432-7981

CLAYPOOL

♣ 100 KIKO-FM - 106.1
401 Broadway
Miami, AZ 85539

Phone: (602)425-4471
Fax: (602)425-9393

Format: Adult Contemporary; Classic Rock. **Network(s):** Unistar. **Owner:** Claypool Broadcasting Co. **Founded:** 1991. **Operating Hours:** 5 a.m.-midnight. **Key Personnel:** Willard Shoecraft, Pres./Gen. Mgr.; Tom Twynam, News Dir.; Steve Brandy, Sports Dir.; John Libynski, Program Mgr. **Wattage:** 6000. **Ad Rates:** $11 for 10 seconds; $14 for 60 seconds. **Additional Contact Information:** Alt. telephones: (602)254-9142; (602)425-7500; (602)425-4141.

COOLIDGE

♣ 101 KCKY-AM - 1150
PO Box 6
Coolidge, AZ 85228

Phone: (602)723-5448
Fax: (602)723-5961

DOUGLAS

▥ 102 The Argus
Cochise College
Hwy. 80 W
Douglas, AZ 85607

Phone: (602)364-0323
Fax: (602)364-0320

Former Title: The Apache

♣ 103 KAPR-AM - 930
Rte. 2, Box 243
Douglas, AZ 85607

Phone: (602)364-4495
Fax: (602)364-5277

♣ 104 KKRK-FM - 95.3
Rte. 2, Box 243
Douglas, AZ 85607

Phone: (602)364-4495
Fax: (602)364-5277

FLAGSTAFF

♣ 105 Warner Cable
1665 S. Plaza Way
Flagstaff, AZ 86001

Phone: (602)774-7141

Owner: Warner Cable Communications, Inc. **Founded:** 1954. **Key Personnel:** Mike Burns, Gen. Mgr.; Kim McReynolds, Office Mgr.; Dan Fessler, Technical Mgr.; Vicki Baugus, Sales & Marketing Supv. **Cities Served:** Coconino County, AZ: 12,000 subscribing households;

44 channels. **Additional Contact Information:** Alt. telephone (602)774-7143.

GREEN VALLEY

♣ 106 KGMS-FM - 97.1
3222 S. Richey Blvd.
Tucson, AZ 85713-5453

Phone: (602)790-2440
Fax: (602)790-2937

KINGMAN

♣ 107 KMOH-TV - Channel 6
4055 Stockton Hill Rd., No. 6
Kingman, AZ 86401

Phone: (602)757-7676
Fax: (602)758-8139

MESA

♣ 108 Cable America Corp.
350 E. 10th Dr.
Mesa, AZ 85202

Phone: (602)461-0715

Owner: Cable America Corp. **Founded:** 1989. **Cities Served:** Maricopa County, Queen Creek, and Williams AFB, AZ.

♣ 109 Mission Cable Co.
4323 E. Broadway, Ste. 107
Mesa, AZ 85206

Phone: (602)830-9877
Fax: (602)830-9889

NOGALES

♣ 110 KAYN-FM - 98.3
67 E. Baffert Dr., No. 6
Nogales, AZ 85621-9748

Phone: (602)761-1954
Fax: (602)761-3251

ORO VALLEY

♣ 111 KVOI-AM - 690
3222 S. Richey Blvd.
Tuscon, AZ 85713-5453

Phone: (602)790-2440
Fax: (602)790-2937

PEORIA

♣ 112 Insight Cablevision
13649 W. Northern Ave.
Peoria, AZ 85345

Phone: (602)935-4318
Fax: (602)582-9649

Owner: Insight Communications Co. **Cities Served:** Maricopa County, Cashion, El Mirage, Phoenix, and Tolleson, AZ.

PHOENIX

□ 113 Arizona Farm Bureau News
Arizona Farm Bureau Federation
3401 E. Elwood St.   Phone: (602)470-0088
Phoenix, AZ 85040-1625   **Fax: (602)470-0178**

□ 114 For Formulation Chemists Only
CITA International
PO Box 70   Phone: (602)234-2642
Phoenix, AZ 85001   Fax: (602)878-9616
Journal covering chemical industrial technology for technicians in the chemical specialty and consumer product industries. **Founded:** 1991. **Frequency:** 3x/yr. **Trim Size:** 7 x 10. **Cols./Page:** 2. **Key Personnel:** E. Morsy, Editor-in-Chief; R. Porte, Editor-in-Chief. **ISSN:** 0887-736X. **Subscription:** $285 North America; $300 Europe; $305 other countries. $170 single issue.
                 Circulation: 2,000
Advertising accepted; contact publisher for rates.

□ 115 Loud
Loud Magazine
PO Box 56425
Phoenix, AZ 85079
Magazine featuring reviews of records, videos, and concerts of heavy metal bands. **Frequency:** 6x/yr. **Key Personnel:** Joe Lopez, Editor. **Subscription:** $15. $2.95 single issue.
                 Circulation: (Not Reported)

□ 116 Paraplegia News
Paralyzed Veterans of America
2111 E. Highland Ave., Ste. 180   **Phone: (602)224-0500**
Phoenix, AZ 85016-4702   **Fax: (602)224-0507**

□ 117 Sports 'n Spokes
Paralyzed Veterans of America
2111 E. Highland Ave, Ste. 180   **Phone: (602)224-0500**
Phoenix, AZ 85016-4702   **Fax: (602)224-0507**

♣ 118 Insight Cablevision
21200 N. Black Canyon Hwy.   Phone: (602)582-8282
Phoenix, AZ 85027   Fax: (602)582-9649
Owner: Insight Communications Co. **Founded:** 1981. **Key Personnel:** Pam MacKenzie, Gen. Mgr.; Mike Williams, Operations Mgr.; Mark St. Cyr, Marketing Mgr. **Cities Served:** Phoenix (northwestern portion), Gilbert, Avondale, Tolleson, El Mirage, and Maricopa County, AZ: 21,000 subscribing households; 52 channels; 2 community access channels; 8 hours per week of community access programming. **Additional Contact Information:** (602)780-2222.

♣ 119 KDR-TV - Channel 64
5401 S. 39th St.   Phone: (602)470-0507
Phoenix, AZ 85040   Fax: (602)470-0810
Format: Hispanic. **Network(s):** Telemundo. **Owner:** Hispanic Broadcasters of Arizona, Inc. **Founded:** 1990. **Operating Hours:** 6 a.m.-12:30 a.m. **Key Personnel:** Jay S. Zucker, Pres./Gen. Mgr.; Patty Ruiz, Gen. Sales Mgr.; Juan Armenta, Production Dir.; Dale Taylor, Chief Engineer; Melinda Miranda, Program Dir. **Local Programs:** *Telenoticias.* **Ad Rates:** Available upon request.

♣ 120 KFLR-FM - 90.3
702 E. Thunderbird Rd.   **Phone: (602)978-0903**
Phoenix, AZ 85022   **Fax: (602)548-8089**

♣ 121 KPSN-FM - 96.9
3719 N. 32nd Ave.   Phone: (602)279-5577
Phoenix, AZ 85017   Fax: (602)230-2781

♣ 122 Post-Newsweek Cable
4742 N. 24th St., Ste. 270   Phone: (602)468-1177
Phoenix, AZ 85016   Fax: (602)468-9216

PRESCOTT

□ 123 Dick Tracy Adventures
Bruce Hamilton Publishing, Inc.
212 S. Montezuma
Prescott, AZ 86303
Magazine featuring Tracy strips in black and white. **Frequency:** 2x/

mo. **Key Personnel:** Bruce Hamilton, Publisher; Matt Masterson, Editor. **Subscription:** $3.95 single issue.
                 Circulation: (Not Reported)

□ 124 Dread of Night
Bruce Hamilton Publishing, Inc.
212 S. Montezuma
Prescott, AZ 86303
Magazine featuring horror stories. **Frequency:** 2x/mo. **Key Personnel:** Bruce Hamilton, Publisher; Leonard Clark, Editor. **Subscription:** $19.50. $3.95 single issue.
                 Circulation: (Not Reported)

□ 125 Grave Tales
Bruce Hamilton Publishing, Inc.
212 S. Montezuma
Prescott, AZ 86303
Magazine featuring tales of horror. **Frequency:** 2x/mo. **Key Personnel:** Bruce Hamilton, Editor and Publisher. **Subscription:** $19.50. $3.95 single issue.
                 Circulation: (Not Reported)

□ 126 Maggots
Bruce Hamilton Publishing, Inc.
212 S. Montezuma
Prescott, AZ 86303
Magazine features black and white horror comic book stories. **Frequency:** 2x/mo. **Key Personnel:** Bruce Hamilton, Editor and Publisher. **Subscription:** $19.95. $3.95 single issue.
                 Circulation: (Not Reported)

♣ 127 KNOT-AM - 1450
116 S. Alto St.
PO Box 151   Phone: (602)445-6880
Prescott, AZ 86302   **Fax: (602)445-6852**

RIVIERA

♣ 128 Dimension Cable TV Services
937 Marina Blvd.
Box 1119
Riviera, AZ 86442   Phone: (602)758-4844
Owner: Times Mirror Cable TV. **Founded:** 1974. **Cities Served:** Mohave County, AZ.

SAFFORD

♣ 129 KFMM-FM - 99.1
PO Box 1330   Phone: (602)428-0916
Safford, AZ 85548   Fax: (602)428-5396

SIERRA VISTA

□ 130 The Huachuca Scout
Five Star Publishing
PO Box 1119   Phone: (602)458-3340
Sierra Vista, AZ 85636   Fax: (602)458-9338

□ 131 The Paper
Five Star Publishing
PO Box 1119
1950 E. Fry Blvd.   Phone: (602)458-3340
Sierra Vista, AZ 85636   Fax: (602)458-9338
Former Title: The News Paper

□ 132 Tele Viewing
Five Star Publishing
PO Box 1119   Phone: (602)458-3340
Sierra Vista, AZ 85636   Fax: (602)458-9338

♣ 133 KFFN-FM - 100.9
2300 Busby Dr.   Phone: (602)458-4313
Sierra Vista, AZ 85635   Fax: (602)458-4317

♣ 134 KTAN-AM - 1420
2300 Busby Dr.   Phone: (602)458-4313
Sierra Vista, AZ 85635   **Fax: (602)458-4317**

TEMPE

📖 **135 KAET Magazine**
Arizona State University

Tempe, AZ 85287-1405   Phone: (602)965-3506
                                        Fax: (602)965-1000

THATCHER

📖 **136 The Gila Monster**
Eastern Arizona College

Thatcher, AZ 85552-0769   **Phone: (602)428-8321**
                                        Fax: (602)428-8462

TUCSON

📖 **137 Entertainment Magazine**
Southwest Alternatives Institute
PO Box 3355
Tucson, AZ 85722   Phone: (602)623-3733
Entertainment and dining guide for Arizona. **Founded:** 1977. **Frequency:** Monthly. **Printing Method:** Web offset. **Trim Size:** 10 1/2 x 13. **Cols./Page:** 4. **Col. Width:** 2 in. **Col. Depth:** 12 in. **Key Personnel:** Robert E. Zucker, Publisher. **ISSN:** 0742-9568. **Subscription:** $18; $30 other countries.

Ad Rates:	BW:	$599	**Circulation:** Non-paid 20,000
	4C:	$649	
	PCI:	$9.21	

📖 **138 Handball**
U.S. Handball Assn.
930 N. Benton Ave.
Tucson, AZ 85711   Phone: (602)795-0434
                                        Fax: (602)795-0465

📖 **139 Mineralogical Record**
PO Box 35565
Tucson, AZ 85740   Phone: (602)299-5702
                                        Fax: (602)544-0815

📖 **140 Passionate Parenting**
Passionate Parenthood Press
500 N. 4th Ave., Ste. 1
Tucson, AZ 85705
Magazine. Frequency: 4x/year. **Key Personnel:** Langdon Hill, Editor. **Subscription:** $13.96. $2.95 single issue.
                                        Circulation: (Not Reported)

📖 **141 Tucson Teen**
Southwest Alternatives Institute, Inc.
PO Box 3355
Tucson, AZ 85722   Phone: (602)623-3733
Periodical for and by youth. **Founded:** 1977. **Frequency:** Quarterly. **Printing Method:** Web offset. **Trim Size:** 10 1/2 x 13. **Cols./Page:** 4. **Col. Width:** 2 in. **Col. Depth:** 12 in. **Key Personnel:** Robert E. Zucker, Publisher. **ISSN:** 1044-954X. **Subscription:** $10.

Ad Rates:	BW:	$599	**Circulation:** Non-paid 15,000
	4C:	$699	
	PCI:	$9.21	

Formerly: "Youth Awareness Press".

📖 **142 Tucson Weekly**
Tucson Weekly Inc.
PO Box 2429
Tucson, AZ 85702   Phone: (602)792-3630
                                        Fax: (602)792-2096

🎙 **143 KHRR-TV - Channel 40**
2828 N. Country Club
Tucson, AZ 85716   Phone: (602)322-6888
                                        Fax: (602)881-7926
Format: Hispanic. **Network(s):** Telemundo. **Owner:** Hispanic Broadcasters of Arizona, Inc. **Founded:** 1989. **Formerly:** KHR-TV (1989-1992). **Operating Hours:** 6 a.m.-12:30 a.m. **Key Personnel:** Jay S. Zucker, Pres./Gen. Mgr.; Patty Ruiz, Gen. Sales Mgr.; Juan Armenta, Production Dir.; Dale Taylor, Chief Engineer; Melinda Miranda, Program Dir. **Local Programs:** *Telenoticias.* **Ad Rates:** Available upon request.

🎙 **144 KQTL-AM - 1210**
PO Box 1511   Phone: (602)628-1200
Tucson, AZ 85702   **Fax: (602)326-4927**

🎙 **145 KVOA-TV - Channel 4**
Box 5188   Phone: (602)792-2270
Tucson, AZ 85703   **Fax: (602)620-1309**

🎙 **146 Tucson Cablevision**
1440 E. 15th St.   Phone: (602)629-8410
Tucson, AZ 85719-6495   Fax: (602)624-5918
Owner: InterMedia Partners. **Founded:** 1982. **Cities Served:** Pima County, Davis-Monthan AFB, Foothills, Santos Thomas, and South Tucson, AZ.

WHITERIVER

🎙 **147 KNNB-FM - 88.1**
Hwy. 73, Skill Center Rd.
Box 310   Phone: (602)338-5229
Whiteriver, AZ 85941   **Fax: (602)338-1744**

WICKENBURG

🎙 **148 KFMA-FM - 93.7**
801 W. Wickenburg Way   Phone: (602)684-7804
Wickenburg, AZ 85358   Fax: (602)684-7805
Format: Alternative/Independent/Progressive (Rock). **Owner:** Harold R. Shumway. **Founded:** 1992. **Operating Hours:** Continuous. **Key Personnel:** Lloyd Melton, Gen. Mgr./Sales Mgr.; Ernesto Gladden, Operations Mgr.; Jonathan Rosen, Program Dir. **Wattage:** 6000. **Ad Rates:** $50-$70 per unit.

🎙 **149 KTIM-AM - 1250**
801 W. Wickenburg Way
Drawer Y   Phone: (602)684-7804
Wickenburg, AZ 85358   **Fax: (602)684-7805**

WINKELMAN

📖 **150 The Southwestern Sportsman Magazine**
HCR 3045
Winkelman, AZ 85292   Phone: (602)356-6049
Ceased publication.

ARKANSAS

ARKADELPHIA

♪ 151 KETG-TV - Channel 9
350 S. Donaghey
Conway, AR 72032
Phone: (501)682-2386
Fax: (501)682-4122
Format: Public TV. **Network(s):** Public Broadcasting Service (PBS).
Owner: Arkansas Educational Television Commission, at above
address. **Founded:** 1976. **Operating Hours:** 6 a.m.-11:30 p.m. week-
days; 7 a.m.-11:30 p.m. Sat.-Sun. **ADI:** Little Rock, AR. **Key
Personnel:** Susan Howarth, Exec. Dir.; Larry Foley, Assoc. Dir.; Kathy
Atkinson, Program Dir.; Ron Johnson, Communications Dir.; Carole
Adornetto, Production Dir.; Gary Schultz, Engineering Dir.; Amy
Oliver, Production Supv.; Jane Havens, Traffic Mgr. **Local Programs:**
Arkansas Week.; *Station Break.*; *Good Times PictureShow.* **Ad Rates:**
Noncommercial.

BENTONVILLE

▢ 152 Benton County Daily Record
209 NW A St.
PO Box 1049
Bentonville, AR 72712
Phone: (501)271-3700
Fax: (501)273-7777

♪ 153 TCA Cable TV
Box 489
Bentonville, AR 72712
Phone: (501)273-5644
Owner: TCA. **Key Personnel:** Dennis Yocum, Mgr. **Cities Served:**
Bentonville and Bella Vista, AR. 8,500 subscribing households. 35
channels; 1 community access channel.

BULL SHOALS

▢ 154 Lake River Times
Marion County Newspapers, Inc.
PO Box 599
Bull Shoals, AR 72619
Phone: (501)445-4275
Ceased publication.

CAMDEN

♪ 155 Cam-Tel Co.
113 Madison Ave.
Box 835
Camden, AR 71701
Phone: (501)836-8111
Owner: WEHCO-Video. **Founded:** 1963. **Formerly:** Cam-Telco. **Key
Personnel:** Jim Wilbanks, Executive V.P.; Charles Launius, Area
Manager. **Cities Served:** Camden, AR. 5683 subscribing households;
30 channels.

CONWAY

♪ 156 Conway Corp.
1319 Prairie St.
Box 99
Conway, AR 72032
Phone: (501)450-6000
Owner: Conway Corp. **Founded:** 1980. **Cities Served:** Faulkner Coun-
ty, AR.

♪ 157 KHDX-FM - 93.1
Hendrix College
Washington & Independence
Conway, AR 72032
Phone: (501)450-1339
Fax: (501)450-1200

DUMAS

▢ 158 Dumas Clarion
Clarion Publishing Co.
136 W. Waterman St.
PO Box 220
Dumas, AR 71639
Phone: (501)382-4925

EL DORADO

♪ 159 El Dorado Cablevision
1127 N. Madison
El Dorado, AR 71730
Phone: (501)862-1306
Owner: Douglas Communications Corp. II. **Founded:** 1964. **Cities
Served:** Union County and Old Union, AR.

FAYETTEVILLE

♪ 160 KAFT-TV - Channel 13
350 S. Donaghey
Conway, AR 72032
Phone: (501)682-2386
Fax: (501)682-4122
Format: Public TV. **Network(s):** Public Broadcasting Service (PBS).
Owner: Arkansas Educational Television Commission, at above
address. **Founded:** 1976. **Operating Hours:** 6 a.m.-11:30 p.m. week-
days; 7 a.m.-11:30 p.m. Sat.-Sun. **ADI:** Fort Smith, AR. **Key
Personnel:** Susan Howarth, Exec. Dir.; Larry Foley, Assoc. Dir.; Kathy
Atkinson, Program Dir.; Ron Johnson, Communications Dir.; Carole
Adornetto, Production Dir.; Gary Schultz, Engineering Dir.; Amy
Oliver, Production Supv.; Jane Havens, Traffic Mgr. **Local Programs:**
Arkansas Week.; *Station Break.*; *Good Times PictureShow.* **Ad Rates:**
Noncommercial.

♨ **161 Warner Cable Communications, Inc.**
125 W. Mountain St.
Box 1209   Phone: (501)521-7730
Fayetteville, AR 72702   Fax: (501)521-3825
Owner: Warner Cable Communications, Inc. **Founded:** 1953. **Cities Served:** Washington County, AR.

FORDYCE

♨ **162 KQEW-FM - 101.7**
303 Spring St.   Phone: (501)352-7137
Fordyce, AR 71742   **Fax: (501)352-7139**

FORREST CITY

♨ **163 East Arkansas Video, Inc.**
225 N. Washington
Box 1079
Forrest City, AR 72335   Phone: (501)633-8932
Owner: Weheo Video, Little Rock, AR. **Founded:** 1970. **Key Personnel:** Harold L. Kinnel, Gen. Mgr. **Cities Served:** Forrest City, Wynne, Marianna, and Brinkley, AR: 11,000 subscribing households; 35 channels; 8 community access channels.

FORT SMITH

♨ **164 TCI of Arkansas (CSI), Inc.**
Box 3408
Fort Smith, AR 72901-3898   Phone: (501)782-8941
Owner: Tele-Communications, Inc. **Founded:** 1961. **Cities Served:** Sebastian County, Bonanza, Greenwood, Hackett, Jenny Lind, Old Jenny Lind, and Sebastian Lakes, AR; Le Flore and Sequoyah Counties, Arkoma, Muldrow, and Roland, OK.

HARRISBURG

▯ **165 The Modern News**
PO Box 400
Harrisburg, AR 72432   Phone: (501)578-2121

HEBER SPRINGS

♨ **166 KAWW-AM - 1370**
422 W. Main St.
PO Box 324   Phone: (501)362-5863
Heber Springs, AR 72543   **Fax: (501)362-5864**

HELENA

♨ **167 KFFA-AM - 1360**
1360 Radio Dr.
Box 430
Helena, AR 72342   Phone: (501)338-8361
Format: Contemporary Country. **Owner:** Delta Broadcasting Inc. **Founded:** 1941. **Operating Hours:** Continuous. **Key Personnel:** J. M. Howe, Owner; Cynthia Able, Office Mgr.; Syl Huling, Operations Dir.; Lorie Smith, Music Dir. **Wattage:** 1000. **Ad Rates:** $5.50-$23.50 per unit. **Additional Contact Information:** (501)338-8331.

HOT SPRINGS

♨ **168 Resort TV Cable Co., Inc.**
1910 Albert Pike, Ste. N
Box 2770
Hot Springs, AR 71914   Phone: (501)624-5781
Owner: WEHCO Video, Inc. **Founded:** 1970. **Key Personnel:** Harvey Oxner, Gen. Mgr.; Wanda Ritter, Office Mgr.; John Minginas, Plant Mgr. **Cities Served:** Garland County and Mountain Pine, AR: 19,800 subscribing households; 36 channels; 1 community access channel; 6 hours per week of community access programming.

HOXIE

♨ **169 KHOX-FM - 105.3**
311 Andrews
Hoxie, AR 72433   Phone: (501)886-1350

LAKE VILLAGE

▯ **170 Eudora Enterprise**
PO Box 552   Phone: (501)265-2071
Lake Village, AR 71653   **Fax: (501)265-2807**

LINCOLN

▯ **171 The Westville Reporter**
The Cherokee Group
122 S. Williams
PO Box 550   Phone: (918)723-5445
Westville, OK 74965-0550   **Fax: (501)267-4290**

LITTLE ROCK

▯ **172 Farm Bureau Press**
Arkansas Farm Bureau Federation
10720 Kanis Rd.
PO Box 31   Phone: (501)224-4400
Little Rock, AR 72203-0031   **Fax: (501)228-1557**

♨ **173 KARN-AM - 920**
4021 W. 8th St.   Phone: (501)661-7500
Little Rock, AR 72204   **Fax: (501)661-7698**

♨ **174 KIPR-FM - 92.3**
415 N. McKinley, Ste. 920
Little Rock, AR 72205   Phone: (501)663-0092
Format: Urban Contemporary. **Network(s):** ABC. **Owner:** Cal Arnold. **Operating Hours:** Continuous. **Key Personnel:** Gordon Heiges, Gen. Mgr.; Joe Booker, Program Dir.; Mark Dillon, Music Dir.; Joe Rook, Sales Mgr. **Wattage:** 100,000.

♨ **175 Riverside Cable TV**
801 Scott St.   Phone: (501)376-5700
Little Rock, AR 72201   Fax: (501)375-1042
Owner: Storer Cable Communications. **Founded:** 1980. **Cities Served:** Pulaski and Saline Counties, Bryant, and Cammack Village, AR.

MAGNOLIA

♨ **176 KZHE-FM - 100.5**
909 E. Main   Phone: (501)234-7790
Magnolia, AR 71753   **Fax: (501)234-7791**

MARIANNA

▯ **177 Courier-Index**
Box 569   Phone: (501)295-2521
Marianna, AR 72360   **Fax: (501)295-9662**

MENA

♨ **178 KENA-AM - 1450**
1348 S. Reine St.
PO Box 1450   Phone: (501)394-1450
Mena, AR 71953   **Fax: (501)394-1459**

♨ **179 KENA-FM - 101.7**
1348 S. Reine St.
PO Box 1450   Phone: (501)394-1450
Mena, AR 71953   **Fax: (501)394-1459**

MONTICELLO

▯ **180 Drew County Shopper's Guide**
Times Printing Co., Inc.
314 N. Main St.   Phone: (501)367-5325
Monticello, AR 71655   Fax: (501)367-6612
Shopping guide. **Frequency:** Weekly. **Printing Method:** Web offset. **Cols./Page:** 6. **Col. Width:** 2 1/8 in. **Col. Width:** 21 1/2 in. **Key Personnel:** Betty Evans, Editor; Mary E. Jackson, Advertising Dir. **Subscription:** Free.
Ad Rates: PCI: $4.35   **Circulation:** 8,242

MORRILTON

📖 181 Conway County/Petit Jean Country Headlight
Headlight Newspapers, Inc.
PO Box 540
Morrilton, AR 72110   Phone: (501)354-2451
                                       Fax: **(501)354-4225**

MOUNTAIN VIEW

🎙 182 KEMV-TV - Channel 6
350 S. Donaghey   Phone: (501)682-2386
Conway, AR 72032   Fax: (501)682-4122
Format: Public TV. **Network(s):** Public Broadcasting Service (PBS).
Owner: Arkansas Educational Television Commission, at above
address. **Founded:** 1980. **Operating Hours:** 6 a.m.-11:30 p.m. week-
days; 7 a.m.-11:30 p.m. Sat.-Sun. **ADI:** Little Rock, AR. **Key
Personnel:** Susan Howarth, Exec. Dir.; Larry Foley, Assoc. Dir.; Kathy
Atkinson, Program Dir.; Ron Johnson, Communications Dir.; Carole
Adornetto, Production Dir.; Gary Schultz, Engineering Dir.; Amy
Oliver, Production Supv.; Jane Havens, Traffic Mgr. **Local Programs:**
Arkansas Week.; *Station Break.*; *Good Times PictureShow.* **Ad Rates:**
Noncommercial.

NORTH LITTLE ROCK

🎙 183 Storer Cable Communications
4609 Camp Robinson Rd.
Box 838   Phone: (501)758-3490
North Little Rock, AR 72118   Fax: (501)375-1042
Owner: Storer Cable Communications. **Founded:** 1973. **Cities Served:**
Pulaski County, Jacksonville, and Sherwood, AR.

OSCEOLA

📖 184 Citizen-Journal
Tennyson Publishing
Box 626   Phone: (501)563-3838
Osceola, AR 72370   Fax: (501)763-3462
Community newspaper. **Frequency:** Weekly. **Printing Method:** Offset.
Cols./Page: 6. **Col. Depth:** 21 in. **Key Personnel:** Sandra Brand, Editor;
Herb Smith, Advertising Mgr. **Subscription:** Free.
Ad Rates: BW: $326.34   **Circulation:** Free ‡7,000
                 PCI: $3.59

OZARK

🎙 185 KDYN-AM - 1540
Box 1086   Phone: (501)667-4567
Ozark, AR 72949   Fax: (501)667-5214
Format: Contemporary Country. **Network(s):** ABC; Arkansas Radio.
Owner: Ozark Communications Inc., at above address. **Formerly:**
KZRK-AM. **Operating Hours:** Sunrise-sunset. **Key Personnel:** Jerry V.
Dietz, Gen. Mgr./Sales Mgr./Owner; Marc Dietz, Program Dir.;
Marilyn Dietz, Office Mgr. **Wattage:** 500. **Ad Rates:** $3.50-$7 for 30
seconds; $5.10-$10 for 60 seconds.

PARAGOULD

🎙 186 KDRS-AM - 1490
Box 117   Phone: (501)236-7627
Paragould, AR 72451   Fax: (501)239-4583
Format: Contemporary Country. **Network(s):** NBC; Arkansas Radio;
Progressive Farmer. **Owner:** SAS Communications Inc. **Founded:**
1947. **Operating Hours:** 6 a.m.- midnight. **Key Personnel:** Jim Adkins,
Gen. Mgr.; Stephanie Burkhead, Advertising Coord.; Peggy Richard-
son, Sales Mgr.; Carol Hopper, Sales Mgr.; Diane Culver, Traffic
Mgr.; Mike Pruitt, Program Dir. **Wattage:** 1000. **Ad Rates:** $2.50-
$3.93 for 30 seconds; $4-$5.33 for 60 seconds. Combined rates
available with KLQZ-FM: $5-$7.86 for 30 seconds; $8-$10.66 for 60
seconds.

🎙 187 KLQZ-FM - 107.1
PO Box 117   Phone: (501)236-4583
Paragould, AR 72451   Fax: (501)239-4583
Format: Contemporary Country. **Owner:** SAS Communications Inc.
Operating Hours: 6 a.m.- 11 p.m. **Key Personnel:** Jim Adkins, Gen.
Mgr.; Terry Lee, Sales Mgr.; Peggy Richardson, Sales Mgr.; Carol
Hopper, Sales Mgr.; Diane Culver, Traffic Mgr. **Wattage:** 3000.

PERRYVILLE

📖 188 Perry County/Petit Jean Country Headlight
PO Box 540   Phone: (501)354-2451
Morrilton, AR 72110   Fax: **(501)354-4225**

PRAIRIE GROVE

📖 189 Prairie Grove Enterprise
The Cherokee Group
PO Box 650   Phone: (501)267-2002
Prairie Grove, AR 72753   Fax: **(501)267-4290**

🎙 190 KDAB-FM - 94.9
PO Box 949
Prairie Grove, AR 72753   Phone: (501)846-3653
Format: Southern Country Gospel. **Owner:** Joe Hart, at above address.
Founded: 1990. **Operating Hours:** Continuous. **Wattage:** 50,000. **Ad
Rates:** $4 for 30 seconds

SILOAM SPRINGS

📖 191 The Herald-Leader
Community Publishers, Inc.
101 N. Mount Olive
PO Box 370   Phone: (501)524-5144
Siloam Springs, AR 72761   Fax: **(501)524-3612**
Former Title: The Herald-Democrat

📖 192 Neighbor Shopper
Community Publishers, Inc.
PO Box 370   Phone: (501)524-5144
Siloam Springs, AR 72761   Fax: **(501)524-3612**
Former Title: Shopper News

WARREN

📖 193 Shoppers Guide Weekly
200 W. Cypress St.   Phone: (501)226-5831
Warren, AR 71671   Fax: **(501)226-6601**

WEST HELENA

🎙 194 KCLT-FM - 104.9
307 Hwy 49B
Box 2870   Phone: (501)572-9506
West Helena, AR 72390   Fax: (501)572-1845
Format: Urban Contemporary. **Network(s):** Southern Broadcasting;
American Urban Radio. **Owner:** West Helena Broadcasters Inc.
Founded: 1984. **Operating Hours:** Continuous. **Wattage:** 3000. **Addi-
tional Contact Information:** (501)572-3796.

WYNNE

📖 195 Shoppers News
Wynne Progress, Inc.
702 N. Falls Blvd.
PO Box 308   Phone: (501)238-2375
Wynne, AR 72396   Fax: **(501)238-4655**

📖 196 Wynne Progress
Wynne Progress, Inc.
702 N. Falls Blvd.
PO Box 308   Phone: (501)238-2375
Wynne, AR 72396   Fax: **(501)238-4655**

197 KWYN-FM - 92.5
Hwy. 64 W.
Wynne, AR 72396

Phone: (501)238-8141
Fax: **(501)238-5997**

CALIFORNIA

AGOURA HILLS

198 Biker
Paisano Publications, Inc.
28210 Dorothy Dr.　　　　Phone: (818)889-8740
Agoura Hills, CA 91301　　**Fax: (818)889-1252**

199 In the Wind
Paisano Publications, Inc.
28210 Dorothy Dr.　　　　Phone: (818)889-8740
Agoura Hills, CA 91301　　**Fax: (818)889-1252**

ALAMEDA

200 UAE
2061 Challenger Dr.
Alameda, CA 94501　　　　Phone: (415)865-2917
Owner: Tele-Communications, Inc. **Founded:** 1983. **Cities Served:** Alameda County, CA.

ALHAMBRA

201 Cencom Cable Television, Inc.
2215 Mission Rd.　　　　Phone: (818)300-6100
Alhambra, CA 91802　　　Fax: (818)300-3112
Owner: Gaylord Broadcasting Co.; Cencom Cable Assoc., Inc. **Founded:** 1981. **Cities Served:** Los Angeles County, Altadena, Azusa, Chapman Woods, City of Commerce, Covina, Huntington Park, La Canada-Flintridge, Monrovia, Montebello, Monterey Park, Norwalk, Pasadena, Rosemead, San Gabriel, South San Gabriel, Temple City, Walnut, and West Covina, CA.

ALTURAS

202 Modoc County Record
Box 531　　　　　　　　Phone: (913)233-2632
Alturas, CA 96101　　　　**Fax: (916)233-5113**

ANAHEIM

203 Classic Trucks
McMullen Publishing, Inc.
2145 W. LaPalma Ave.
Anaheim, CA 92801-1785
Magazine of classic American trucks from the 1950's and 1960's. **Frequency:** Quarterly. **Key Personnel:** Bob Clark, Editor; Tom McMullen, Publisher. **Subscription:** $3.50 single issue.
　　　　　　　　　　Circulation: (Not Reported)

204 Knives Illustrated
McMullen & Yee Publishing, Inc.
2145 W. La Palma Ave.　　Phone: (714)635-9040
Anaheim, CA 92801　　　　Fax: (714)533-9979

205 La Habra Star
Freedom Newspaper, Inc.
PO Box 70004　　　　　　**Phone: (714)634-1567**
Anaheim, CA 92825　　　**Fax: (714)704-3718**

206 Street Cruzin Magazine
McMullen Publishing, Inc.
2145 W. La Palma Ave.
Anaheim, CA 92801-1785
Magazine of cruising cars. **Frequency:** Quarterly. **Key Personnel:** Frank Hamilton, Editor; Tom McMullen, Publisher. **Subscription:** $2.95 single issue.
　　　　　　　　　　Circulation: (Not Reported)

207 MultiVision Cable TV
3041 E. Miraloma Ave.　　Phone: (714)632-9222
Anaheim, CA 92806　　　　Fax: (714)630-4353
Owner: MultiVision Cable TV Corp. **Founded:** 1980. **Cities Served:** Orange County and Villa Park, CA.

ANDERSON

208 The Valley Post
North Valley Newspapers, Inc.
2680 Gateway Dr.
PO Box 1148
Anderson, CA 96007　　　Phone: (916)365-2797

APPLE VALLEY

209 KAPL-AM - 1550
13470 Manhasset, No. 1　　Phone: (619)247-1111
Apple Valley, CA 92308　　Fax: (619)247-0884
Format: Middle-of-the-Road (MOR); Big Band/Nostalgia. **Network(s):** Satellite Music. **Owner:** KAPL Broadcasting, Inc., at above address. **Founded:** 1991. **Formerly:** KITH-AM. **Operating Hours:** Continuous. **Key Personnel:** Michael S. Norris, Gen. Mgr.; Cerrell T. Billups, Operations Dir.; Linda R. Fox, News Dir. **Wattage:** 5000 day; 500 night. **Ad Rates:** $3-$8 for 30 seconds; $4-$10 for 60 seconds.

AROMAS

210 The Rottweiler Quarterly
GRQ Publications
PO Box 900   Phone: (408)728-8461
Aromas, CA 95004   Fax: (408)728-4708
Magazine covering the training, breeding, health, and showing of rottweilers. **Founded:** 1987. **Frequency:** Quarterly. **Printing Method:** Sheet-fed offset. **Trim Size:** 8 1/4 x 10 3/4. **Cols./Page:** 3. **Col. Width:** 2 1/4 in. **Col. Depth:** 9 3/4 in. **Key Personnel:** Robin Stark, Editor; Tomi Edmiston, Publisher; Jill Kessler, Circulation Mgr. **ISSN:** 1040-8037. **Subscription:** $36; $44 other countries. $10 single issue.
Ad Rates: BW: $160   **Circulation:** ⊕**3,850**
                   4C: $580   Non-paid ⊕**250**

ARROYO GRANDE

211 KGLW-AM - 1340
PO Box 170
Arroyo Grande, CA 93421-0296   Phone: (805)489-5456
Format: Talk. **Network(s):** CBS; Talknet. **Owner:** Wischnia Communications Corp. **Formerly:** KATY-AM. **Operating Hours:** 8 a.m.-6 p.m. **Key Personnel:** Glo Rivera, Gen. Mgr.; Jeff Russinsky, Sales Mgr. **Wattage:** 1000. **Ad Rates:** $12-$14 for 30 seconds; $14-$16 for 60 seconds.

AZUSA

212 Azusa Herald
Highlander Newspapers
18383 E. Railroad St.   **Phone: (818)854-8100**
City of Industry, CA 91748   **Fax: (818)854-8719**

213 Clause
Azusa Pacific University
PO Box APU
Azusa, CA 91702   Phone: (818)969-3434
College newspaper. **Frequency:** Weekly. **Cols./Page:** 4. **Col. Width:** 2 1/2 in. **Col. Depth:** 16 in. **Key Personnel:** Elizabeth Langley, Editor. **Subscription:** Free.
Ad Rates: GLR: $5   **Circulation:** Non-paid 2,000
                   BW: $268
                   PCI: $14

BAKERSFIELD

214 KAFY-AM - 970
230 Truxton Ave.   Phone: (805)324-4411
Bakersfield, CA 93301-5312   **Fax: (805)327-9459**

215 KBCC-FM - 88.5
1801 Panorama Dr.   Phone: (805)395-4523
Bakersfield, CA 93305   Fax: (805)395-4241
Format: Alternative/Independent/Progressive. **Owner:** Bakersfield Community College. **Founded:** 1970. **Operating Hours:** 8 a.m.-10 p.m. Mon.-Thurs.; 8 a.m.-5 p.m. Fri. **Ad Rates:** $5 per unit.

216 KXEM-FM - 102.9
3701 Pegasus Dr., Ste. 102
Bakersfield, CA 93308-6842   **Phone: (805)393-0103**

217 Warner Cable
3600 N. Sillect Ave.   Phone: (805)327-8655
Bakersfield, CA 933089   Fax: (805)327-4074
Owner: Warner Cable Communications, Inc. **Founded:** 1966. **Cities Served:** Kern County, Delano, McFarland, Shafter, and Wasco, CA.

BANNING

218 TMC Wednesday
218 N. Murray St.
Banning, CA 92220   Fax: (714)849-2437
Former Title: This Week

BELLFLOWER

219 American Fire Journal
9072 E. Artesia Blvd., Ste. 7   Phone: (310)866-1664
Bellflower, CA 90706-6299   **Fax: (310)867-6434**

BERKELEY

220 Film Quarterly
University of California Press
2120 Berkeley of California Press   Phone: (510)642-4191
Berkeley, CA 94720   Fax: (510)643-7127
Journal covering all aspects of cinema. **Frequency:** Quarterly. **Printing Method:** Offset. **Trim Size:** 8 1/2 x 11. **Key Personnel:** Ann Martin, Editor; Rebecca R. Simon, Mktg. Mgr. **ISSN:** 0015-1386. **Subscription:** $19; $40 institutions. $5 single issue.
Ad Rates: BW: $375   **Circulation:** 3,000

221 Gesar
2425 Hillside Ave.
Berkeley, CA 94704   Phone: (510)548-5407
                                        Fax: (510)845-7540

222 Mountain Research and Development
University of California Press
2120 Berkeley Way   Phone: (510)642-7127
Berkeley, CA 94720   Fax: (510)643-7127
Journal concerned with the balance between mountain environments, development, and the well being of mountain people. **Frequency:** Quarterly. **Printing Method:** Offset. **Trim Size:** 8 1/2 x 11. **Key Personnel:** Jack D. Ives, Editor; Rebecca R. Simon, Mktg. Mgr. **ISSN:** 0276-4741. **Subscription:** $34; $21 students; $70 institutions. $9 single issue.
Ad Rates: BW: $250   **Circulation:** 960

223 The Public Historian
University of California Press
2120 Berkeley Way   Phone: (510)642-4191
Berkeley, CA 94720   Fax: (510)643-7127
Journal covering public history and policy. **Frequency:** Quarterly. **Printing Method:** Offset. **Trim Size:** 6 x 9. **Key Personnel:** Otis Graham, Jr., Editor; Rebecca R. Simon, Mktg. Mgr. **ISSN:** 0272-3433. **Subscription:** $37; $17 students; $49 institutions. $10 single issue.
Ad Rates: BW: $250   **Circulation:** 1,200

224 Rhitorica
University of California Press
2120 Berkeley Way   Phone: (510)642-4191
Berkeley, CA 94720   Fax: (510)643-7127
Journal covering the theory and practice of rhetoric in all aspects. **Frequency:** Quarterly. **Printing Method:** Offset. **Trim Size:** 6 x 9. **Key Personnel:** Michael Leff, Editor; Rebecca R. Simon, Mktg. Mgr. **ISSN:** 0734-8584. **Subscription:** $30; $15 students; $54 institutions. $8 single issue.
Ad Rates: BW: $250   **Circulation:** 950

225 Sacred River: Bay Area Women's Journal
PO Box 5131
Berkeley, CA 94705   Phone: (510)658-2182
Periodical focusing on local events, but includes articles and news of interest outside of California. **Frequency:** 6x/yr. **Printing Method:** Web press. **Trim Size:** 10 1/4 x 16 1/2. **Cols./Page:** 4. **Col. Width:** 2 1/2 in. **Key Personnel:** Becky Taber, Editor; Penny Leff, Editor; Carla Kondinsky, Editor. **Subscription:** $18.
Ad Rates: GLR: $5   **Circulation:** ‡150
                   BW: $800   Non-paid ‡10,000
                   PCI: $15
Color advertising not accepted.

226 Shmate
Box 4228
Berkeley, CA 94704
Ceased publication.

227 KPFA-FM - 94.1
1929 Martin Luther King Jr. Way   Phone: (415)848-6767
Berkeley, CA 94704   Fax: (415)848-3812

BEVERLY HILLS

228 American Premiere
8421 Wilshire Blvd.
Beverly Hills, CA 90211   Phone: (213)852-0434
Magazine covering the film industry. **Founded:** 1979. **Frequency:** 6x/

yr. **Printing Method:** Sheet fed offset. **Trim Size:** 8 3/8 x 10 7/8. **Cols./Page:** 3. **Subscription:** $16. $4 single issue.
Ad Rates: BW: $1,500   **Circulation:** (Not Reported)
4C: $2,200

229 Film Threat
L.F.P., Inc.
9171 Wilshire Blvd., Ste. 300   **Phone:** **(310)858-7155**
Beverly Hills, CA 90210   **Fax:** **(310)274-7985**

230 The Ideal Traveler
Publishing and Business Consultants
8530 Wilshire Blvd., Ste. 404E   Phone: (213)732-3477
Beverly Hills, CA 90211   **Fax:** **(213)SEC-3477**
Former Title: Vacation Overseas

231 Trading Cards
L.F.P., Inc.
9171 Wilshire Blvd., Ste. 300
Beverly Hills, CA 90210
Trading card magazine featuring key investment tips, player profiles, and industry news. **Frequency:** Monthly. **Key Personnel:** Chris Davidson, Editor. **Subscription:** $19.95. $2.95 single issue.
Circulation: (Not Reported)

BIG BEAR LAKE

232 Falcon Cablevision
41490 Big Bear Blvd.
Box 1771
Big Bear Lake, CA 91215   Phone: (714)866-3416
Owner: Falcon Cable TV. **Founded:** 1952. **Cities Served:** San Bernardino County, Big Bear City, Boulder Bay, Fawnskin, and Moonridge, CA.

BISHOP

233 Spectrum Newspapers Monthly, Contra Costa/Tri Valley
Spectrum Newspapers
11171 Sun Center Dr., Ste. 110   Phone: (916)852-6222
Rancho Cordova, CA 95670   Fax: (916)852-6397
Newspaper serving active senior citizens, 55 and older, in the Contra Costa and Tri Valley areas. **Founded:** 1975. **Frequency:** Monthly. **Printing Method:** Web offset. **Key Personnel:** Bob Carney, Editor; Jacqueline Lucido, Gen. Mgr.; Ridge Eagan, Advertising Dir. **USPS:** 980-481. **Subscription:** $12.
Circulation: 57,500

BREA

234 Brea Highlander
Orange County Register
625 N. Grand Ave.   **Phone:** **(714)835-1234**
Santa Ana, CA 92711   **Fax:** **(714)542-5037**

235 Century Cable of California
185 E. Alder St.
Box 547
Brea, CA 92621   Phone: (714)529-4918
Owner: Century Communications Corp. **Founded:** 1970. **Cities Served:** Los Angeles and Orange Counties, La Habra, and La Habra Heights, CA.

BURBANK

236 Disney's Colossal Comics Collection
Disney Comics, Inc.
500 S. Buena Vista St.   Phone: (818)567-5739
Burbank, CA 91521   Fax: (818)841-7235
Comics magazine for kids. **Founded:** 1991. **Frequency:** 6x/yr. **Printing Method:** Offset. **Subscription:** $1.95 single issue.
Ad Rates: BW: $4,950   **Circulation:** (Not Reported)

237 L.A. Parent/Parenting/San Diego Parent
L.A. Parent
PO Box 3204   Phone: (818)846-0400
Burbank, CA 91504   Fax: (818)841-4380
Magazine for parents. **Founded:** 1979. **Frequency:** Monthly. **Printing Method:** Offset. **Cols./Page:** 4. **Col. Width:** 15 picas. **Subscription:** $12.
Circulation: Free □209,038
Combined rate includes: L.A. Parent, Parenting, and San Diego Parent newspapers.

238 Paintball Magazine
CFW Enterprises, Inc.
4201 Vanowen Pl.
Burbank, CA 91505
Sports magazine featuring articles on pre-game preparations and equipment. The magazine also answers questions about paintball. **Frequency:** Monthly. **Key Personnel:** Jessica Sparks, Editor; Curtis Wong, Publisher. **Subscription:** $19.95. $3 single issue.
Circulation: (Not Reported)

BURLINGAME

239 Health World
1540 Gilbreth Rd.   Phone: (415)697-8038
Burlingame, CA 94010   Fax: (415)697-7937
Magazine focusing on nutrition and health. **Founded:** 1985. **Frequency:** 6x/yr. **Trim Size:** 8 1/2 x 11. **Subscription:** $12.50. $3 single issue.
Ad Rates: BW: $1,800   **Circulation:** (Not Reported)
4C: $2,500

240 San Francisco Peninsula Parent
Peninsula Parent Newspaper, Inc.
1131 Vancouver Ave.   Phone: (415)342-9203
Burlingame, CA 94010   Fax: (415)342-9276
Subtitle: Monthly Parenting Magazine. **Founded:** 1985. **Frequency:** Monthly. **Printing Method:** Web offset. **Trim Size:** 11 x 14. **Cols./Page:** 4. **Col. Width:** 2 7/8 in. **Col. Depth:** 13 in. **Subscription:** Free.
Ad Rates: BW: $1,632   **Circulation:** Free □52,819
4C: $2,082   Paid □123

CAMBRIA

241 The Cambrian
2442 Main St.
PO Drawer 67
Cambria, CA 93428   Phone: (805)927-8652

CANOGA PARK

242 Affordable Aircraft
Challenge Publications, Inc.
7950 Deering Ave.
Canoga Park, CA 91304
Magazine profiling airplanes pilots can fly without licenses. **Founded:** 1991. **Frequency:** Quarterly. **Key Personnel:** Norm Goyer, Editor; Edwin A. Schenpf, Publisher. **Subscription:** $5.95 single issue.
Circulation: (Not Reported)

243 Aviation Art
Challenge Publication, Inc.
7950 Deering Ave.
Canoga Park, CA 91304
Guide to aviation artists, galleries, and distributors. **Founded:** 1991. **Frequency:** Quarterly. **Key Personnel:** Michael O'Leary, Editor; Edwin A. Schepf, Publisher. **Subscription:** $23.95. $5.95 single issue.
Circulation: (Not Reported)

244 Battle of Britain
Challenge Publications, Inc.
7950 Deering Ave.
Canoga Park, CA 91304
Magazine commemorating the Battle of Britain. **Founded:** 1991.

Ad Rates: GLR = general line rate; BW = one-time black & white page rate; 4C = one-time four color page rate; SAU = standard advertising unit rate; CNU = Canadian newspaper advertising unit rate; PCI = per column inch rate.
Circulation: ★ = ABC; △ = BPA; ◆ = CAC; ● = CCAB; □ = VAC; ⊕ = PO Statement; ‡ = Publisher's Report; Boldface figures = sworn; Light figures = estimated.
Entry type: ◫ = Print; ♨ = Broadcast.

19

Frequency: Quarterly. **Key Personnel:** Michael O'Leary, Editor; Edwin Schnepf, Publisher. **Subscription:** $5.95 single issue.
Circulation: (Not Reported)

245 British Car
2D Publishing
22026 Gault St.   Phone: (818)710-1234
Canoga Park, CA 91303   Fax: (818)710-1877

246 Future War
Challenge Publications, Inc.
7950 Deering Ave.
Canoga Park, CA 91304
Magazine highlighting the Army, Navy, and Air Force roles in the Gulf War. **Founded:** 1991. **Frequency:** Quarterly. **Key Personnel:** Joe Poyer, Editor; Edwin Schnepf, Publisher. **Subscription:** $5.95 single issue.
Circulation: (Not Reported)

247 Navy Seals
Challenge Publications, Inc.
7950 Deering Ave.
Canoga Park, CA 91304
Magazine reporting on the activities of the Navy Seals. **Founded:** 1991. **Frequency:** Quarterly. **Key Personnel:** Edwin Schnepf, Editor and Publisher. **Subscription:** $3.95 single issue.
Circulation: (Not Reported)

248 Sport Cycling Freewheelin'
Challenge Publications, Inc.
7950 Deering Ave.
Canoga Park, CA 91304
Sports magazine featuring bike buying guide and safety gear. **Frequency:** Quarterly. **Key Personnel:** Brian Hemsworth, Editor; Ed Schnepf, Publisher. **Subscription:** $4.95 single issue.
Circulation: (Not Reported)

249 State Notary Bulletin
National Notary Assn.
8236 Remmet Ave.
PO Box 7184   Phone: (818)713-4000
Canoga Park, CA 91309-7184   Fax: (818)713-9061
Former Title: Notary Viewpoint

250 Street Rod Pickups
Challenge Publications, Inc.
7950 Deering Ave.
Canoga Park, CA 91304
Magazine covering vintage pickups. **Founded:** 1991. **Frequency:** Quarterly. **Key Personnel:** Eric Pierce, Editor; Edwin A. Schnepf, Publisher. **Subscription:** $9.95. $4.95 single issue.
Circulation: (Not Reported)

CANYON COUNTY

251 Western CATV Inc.
18356 Soledad Canyon Rd.
Canyon County, CA 91351   Phone: (802)252-2318
Owner: American TV & Communications Corp. **Founded:** 1963. **Cities Served:** Los Angeles County, Newhall, Santa Clarita, and Saugus, CA.

CARLSBAD

252 Daniels Cablevision
5720 W. Camino Real   Phone: (619)438-7741
Carlsbad, CA 92008   Fax: (619)438-8461
Owner: Tele-Communications, Inc. **Founded:** 1977. **Key Personnel:** Joni Odum, Gen. Mgr.; Valarie Brown, Local Program Dir.; Phil Urbina, Public Affairs Dir.; Sue Otto, Mktg. Dir.; Mike Canizaro, Sales Mgr. **Cities Served:** San Diego County, Del Mar, Encinitas, Fallbrook, Lake San Marcos, San Marcos, Solana Beach, Carlsbad, La Costa, Cardiff, and Vista, CA. 50,000 subscribing households; 54 channels; 1 community access channel; 25 hours per week of community access programming. **Additional Contact Information:** Alt. phone (619)931-7000.

CARPINTERIA

253 Freebies
Freebies Publishing Co.
1135 Eugenia Pl.
PO Box 5025   Phone: (805)566-1225
Carpinteria, CA 93014-5025   Fax: (805)566-0305

CERRITOS

254 Soccer International
WSL Holdings, Inc.
18000 Studebaker
Cerritos, CA 90701
Magazine featuring international soccer news. **Frequency:** Monthly. **Key Personnel:** Grahame L. Jones, Editor; Gary Hopkins, Publisher. **Subscription:** Free to qualified subscribers; $33. $2.75 single issue.
Circulation: (Not Reported)

CHATSWORTH

255 West Valley Cablevision
19749 Dearborn St.   Phone: (818)701-6500
Chatsworth, CA 91311   Fax: (818)701-3000
Owner: Cablevision Industries, Inc. **Founded:** 1981. **Cities Served:** Los Angeles County, Canoga Park, Chatsworth, Encino, Granada Hills, Lakeside Park, Northridge, Reseda, Sepulveda, Tarzana, Van Nuys, West Hills, Winnetka, and Woodland Hills, CA.

CHICO

256 Chico New Voice Newspaper
Cohasset Pond Publishing
119 Broadway
Chico, CA 95928   Phone: (916)894-7311
Newspaper of "news from a woman's view," with special features covering the city of Chico and northern California. **Founded:** 1991. **Frequency:** Monthly. **Printing Method:** Web offset. **Trim Size:** 11 1/2 x 13 3/4. **Cols./Page:** 5. **Col. Width:** 2 in. **Col. Depth:** 13 in. **Key Personnel:** Loretta J. Metcalf, Editor; Cathy Brooks, Assoc. Editor. **Subscription:** $25; $125 out of country.
Ad Rates: BW: $600   **Circulation:** Paid 200
4C: $1,000   Non-paid 9,800
Formerly: The New Voice.

257 The Orion
California State University
Dept of Journalism   Phone: (916)898-5751
Chico, CA 95929-0600   Fax: (916)898-4839

258 KCHH-FM - 103.5
PO Box 489   Phone: (916)893-8926
Chico, CA 95927   Fax: (916)893-8937

CITY OF INDUSTRY

259 United Artists Cable of Los Angeles County
15255 Salt Lake Ave.
City of Industry, CA 91745   Phone: (818)961-3622
Formerly: United Cable TV. **Key Personnel:** Kurt Taylor, Gen. Mgr.; Richard Olson, Engineering Mgr. **Cities Served:** Hacienda Heights, Valinda, Pico Rivera, South Wither and Baldwin Park, CA. 35,000 subscribing households; 63 channels; 1 community access channel; 24 hours per week of community access programming.

CLOVERDALE

260 Cloverdale Reveille
207 N. Cloverdale Blvd.
PO Box 157   Phone: (707)894-3339
Cloverdale, CA 95425   Fax: (707)894-3343

COACHELLA

261 KCLB-AM - 970
1694 6th St.   Phone: (619)398-2171
Coachella, CA 92236   Fax: (619)398-2739

🎙 **262 KCLB-FM - 93.7**
1694 6th St.   **Phone: (619)398-2171**
Coachella, CA 92236   Fax: (619)398-2739

CONCORD

🎙 **263 Concord Cable TV**
2450 Whitman Rd.
Concord, CA 94518   Phone: (510)685-2330
Owner: Western Communications. **Founded:** 1967. **Cities Served:**
Contra Costa County and Clayton, CA.

COSTA MESA

📖 **264 PTI Journal**
PTI Partnership
1666 Newport Blvd., Ste. 141   Phone: (714)752-1292
Costa Mesa, CA 92627   Fax: (714)752-9533

📖 **265 Rental Dealer News**
Rental Dealer News, Inc.
2900 Bristol St., Ste. J101   Phone: (714)755-1440
Costa Mesa, CA 92626   **Fax: (714)755-1450**

CULVER CITY

📖 **266 Library Mosaics**
Yenor, Inc.
Box 5171
Culver City, CA 90231   Phone: (310)410-1573
Magazine for and about library/media support staff. **Subtitle:** The
Magazine for Support Staff. **Founded:** 1989. **Frequency:** 6x/yr. **Key
Personnel:** Raymond G. Roney, Publisher. **ISSN:** 1054-9676. **Sub-
scription:** $20; $30 outside US. $3.50 single issue.
Ad Rates: BW: $125   **Circulation:** ⊕5,000

CUPERTINO

📖 **267 La Voz**
De Anza College
21250 Stevens Creek Blvd.   Phone: (408)864-8785
Cupertino, CA 95014   **Fax: (408)864-8603**

DESERT CENTER

🎙 **268 American Pacific Co.**
Box 246   Phone: (619)227-3245
Desert Center, CA 92239   **Fax: (619)227-3245**

DIAMOND BAR

📖 **269 Diamond Bar/Phillips Ranch Highlander**
Highlander Newspapers
18383 E. Railroad St.   **Phone: (818)854-8700**
City of Industry, CA 91748   **Fax: (818)854-8719**

DOWNEY

🎙 **270 Continental Cablevision**
10839 La Reina Ave.   Phone: (310)869-5301
Downey, CA 90241   Fax: (310)861-4522
Owner: Continental Cablevision, Inc. **Founded:** 1982. **Cities Served:**
Los Angeles County, Bellflower, Bell Gardens, La Miranda, Lynwood,
Maywood, Paramount, Santa Fe Springs, and South El Monte, CA.

DOWNIEVILLE

📖 **271 The Mountain Messenger**
Drawer A   Phone: (916)289-3262
Downieville, CA 95936-0395   **Fax: (916)289-3262**

DUBLIN

🎙 **272 Viacom Cablevision**
6640 Sierra Ln.
Dublin, CA 94568   Phone: (415)828-8510
Owner: Viacom Cable. **Founded:** 1963. **Cities Served:** Alameda
County, Contra Costa County, Dublin, Livermore, Pleasanton, San
Ramon, and Sunol, CA.

EL CAJON

📖 **273 Senior World of the Central Coast**
PO Box 1565
El Cajon, CA 92022   Phone: (619)442-4404
Ceased publication.

📖 **274 Senior World of Riverside/San Bernardino**
Californian Publishing Company
PO Box 1565   Phone: (619)593-2900
El Cajon, CA 92022   Fax: (619)442-4043
Magazine for mature adults. **Founded:** 1988. **Frequency:** Monthly.
Printing Method: Web offset. **Cols./Page:** 5. **Col. Width:** 11.6 picas.
Key Personnel: Resa Moreau, Gen. Mgr.; Laura Impastato, Exec.
Editor. **Subscription:** $30. $3 single issue.
Ad Rates: BW: $3,392   **Circulation: Paid** ▫617
            4C: $3,992   **Non-paid** ▫474,669
            PCI: $49
Additional Contact Information: Publisher's address: 1000 Pioneer
Way, El Cajon, CA 92020.

EL CENTRO

📖 **275 Imperial Valley Press**
Associated Desert Newspapers, Inc.
205 N. 8th St.
PO Box 2770   Phone: (619)337-3400
El Centro, CA 92244   Fax: (619)353-3003

ENCINO

📖 **276 On Production & Post-Production**
17337 Ventura Blvd., Ste. 226
Encino, CA 91316   Phone: (818)907-6682
Magazine covering production and post-production in corporate and
computer graphics, feature films, commercials, and television. **Found-
ed:** 1992. **Frequency:** Bimonthly. **Printing Method:** Sheetfed offset.
Trim Size: 8 3/8 x 10 7/8. **Cols./Page:** 3. **Col. Width:** 2 1/4 in. **Col.
Depth:** 10 in. **Key Personnel:** Howard Kunin, Editor and Publisher;
Denise Abbott, Feature Editor; Jim Fadden, Technical Editor. **ISSN:**
0044-7625. **Subscription:** $15; $23 other countries (surface mail); $32
other countries (airmail). $4 single issue.
Ad Rates: BW: $1,567   **Circulation: Paid** ‡2,000
            4C: $2,475   **Controlled** ‡14,000
Formerly: American Cinemeditor (1991).

ESCONDIDO

📖 **277 Fitness and Sports Review International**
Sports Training, Inc.
PO Box 460429   Phone: (619)480-0558
Escondido, CA 92046   Fax: (619)480-1277
International journal covering fitness and sports training. **Founded:**
1966. **Frequency:** 6x/yr. **Trim Size:** 8 1/2 x 11. **Cols./Page:** 2. **Col.
Width:** 3 1/2 in. **Key Personnel:** Dr. Michael Yessis, Editor. **ISSN:**
0275-598X. **Subscription:** $35. $6 single issue.
                                    Circulation: 600
Formerly: Soviet Sports Review (1992).

Ad Rates: GLR = general line rate; BW = one-time black & white page rate; 4C = one-time four color page rate; SAU = standard advertising unit rate;
CNU = Canadian newspaper advertising unit rate; PCI = per column inch rate.
Circulation: ★ = ABC; △ = BPA; ◆ = CAC; ● = CCAB; □ = VAC; ⊕ = PO Statement; ‡ = Publisher's Report; Boldface figures = sworn; Light figures = estimated.
Entry type: 📖 = Print; 🎙 = Broadcast.

21

EUREKA

⚏ 278 Tri-City Weekly
V & P Publishing, Inc.
527 D St.
PO Box 134   Phone: (707)443-8703
Eureka, CA 95501   Fax: (707)443-5022

FAIRFAX

⚏ 279 Procomm Enterprises Magazine
6 School St., Ste. 160   Phone: (415)459-4669
Fairfax, CA 94930   Fax: (415)459-4591

⚓ 280 Horizon Cable TV, Inc.
Box 937   Phone: (415)883-9251
Fairfax, CA 94978   Fax: (415)382-0814
Founded: 1987. **Key Personnel:** Kevin Daniel, Pres./Gen. Mgr.; Susan Daniel, Office Mgr. **Cities Served:** Novato, San Rafael, Point Reyes, Inverness, Olema, and Stinson Beach, CA. 2,300 subscribing households; 36 channels.

FALLBROOK

⚏ 281 Extraprize
PO Box 397   Phone: (619)728-5511
Fallbrook, CA 92028   Fax: (619)723-4967

FORT JONES

⚏ 282 The Lightbulb
M & M Associates
PO Box 1020
Fort Jones, CA 96032-9712   Phone: (805)388-3097
Former Title: Invent!

FRESNO

⚏ 283 The California Southern Baptist
California Southern Baptist Convention
678 E. Shaw Ave.   Phone: (209)229-9533
Fresno, CA 93710   Fax: (209)229-2824

⚏ 284 Journal of Pan African Studies
PO Box 13063
Fresno, CA 93794-3063   Phone: (209)266-2550
Journal. **Subtitle:** An International Medium of African Culture and Consciousness. **Founded:** 1987. **Frequency:** Quarterly. **Printing Method:** Offset. **Trim Size:** 8 1/2 x 11. **Cols./Page:** 4. **Key Personnel:** Itibari M. Zulu, Editor. **ISSN:** 0888-6601. **Subscription:** $12; $20 other. $4 single issue.

             Circulation: (Not Reported)

⚏ 285 Spectrum Newspapers Monthly, Fresno/Bakersfield
Spectrum Newspapers
11171 Sun Center Dr., Ste. 110   Phone: (916)852-6222
Rancho Cordova, CA 95670   Fax: (916)852-6397
Newspaper serving active senior citizens, 55 and older, in Fresno. **Founded:** 1975. **Frequency:** Monthly. **Printing Method:** Web offset. **Key Personnel:** Bob Carney, Editor; Jacqueline Lucido, Gen. Mgr.; Ridge Eagan, Advertising Dir. **USPS:** 980-481. **Subscription:** $12.
             Circulation: ‡49,500

⚓ 286 Continental Cablevision
1945 N. Helm Ave.   Phone: (209)252-8210
Fresno, CA 93727   Fax: (209)456-1544
Owner: Continental Cablevision, Inc. **Founded:** 1977. **Cities Served:** Fresno County, Madera County, Clovis, and Madera, CA.

⚓ 287 KBIF-AM - 900
2811 N. Wishon Ave.
Fresno, CA 93704-5572   Phone: (209)222-0900
Format: Religious. **Owner:** Cascade Broadcasting Corp. **Operating Hours:** 6 a.m.-midnight. **Key Personnel:** David M. Jack, Pres.; Linda Lopez, Mgr. **Wattage:** 1000. **Ad Rates:** Available upon request.

⚓ 288 KCML-FM - 107.5
5089 E. McKinley Ave.
Fresno, CA 93727   Phone: (209)255-5600
             Fax: (209)252-4522

⚓ 289 KSEE-TV - Channel 24
5035 E. McKinley   Phone: (209)454-2424
Fresno, CA 93727   Fax: (209)454-2485

FULLERTON

⚓ 290 Comcast Cablevision
1501 W. Commonwealth Ave.   Phone: (714)525-1191
Fullerton, CA 92633   Fax: (714)879-3232
Owner: Comcast Corp. **Founded:** 1981. **Cities Served:** Orange County, Buena Park, and Placentia, CA.

⚓ 291 KFCR-FM - 93.5
321 E. Chapman Ave.
Fullerton, CA 92632   Phone: (714)992-7264
Format: Alternative/Independent/Progressive. **Key Personnel:** Jeff Ryder, Music Dir. **Ad Rates:** Noncommercial.

GARDEN GROVE

⚓ 292 Paragon Cable TV
7441 Chapman Ave.   Phone: (714)895-6886
Garden Grove, CA 92641   Fax: (714)898-1524
Owner: KBLCOM, Inc. **Founded:** 1983. **Cities Served:** Orange County, Cypress, Fountain Valley, Garden Grove, Huntington Beach, Los Alamitos, Midway City, Rossmoor, Stanton, and Westminster, CA.

GILROY

⚓ 293 Falcon Cable Systems Co.
7630 Eigleberry St.
Gilroy, CA 95020   Phone: (408)842-5653
Owner: Falcon Cable. **Key Personnel:** Bruce Williams, Gen. Mgr.; Filomena Fagundes, Business Mgr.; William Kuhne, Plant Mgr. **Cities Served:** Gilroy, Hollister, Morgan Hill, King City, Soledad, Gonzales, Prundale and Carmel Highlands, CA. 30,800 subscribing households; 35 channels.

GLENDALE

⚓ 294 Sammons Communications
6246 San Fernando Rd.
Box 5104   Phone: (818)246-5581
Glendale, CA 91201   Fax: (818)242-9553
Owner: Sammons Communications, Inc. **Founded:** 1962. **Cities Served:** Los Angeles County, Burbank, La Canada, and La Crescenta, CA.

GLENDORA

⚏ 295 Glendora Press
Highlander Newspapers
18383 E. Railroad St.   Phone: (818)854-8700
City of Industry, CA 91748   Fax: (818)854-8719

GROVELAND

⚓ 296 Sun Country Cable
18638 Main St.
Box 435   Phone: (209)962-6373
Groveland, CA 95321   Fax: (209)962-4923
Founded: 1987. **Key Personnel:** Alan K. Banner, Mgr.; Kelly Kirkpatrick, Office Mgr. **Cities Served:** Groveland and Big Oak Flat, CA. 1700 subscribing households;   1 community access channel.

HAYWARD

⚏ 297 The Annals of Applied Probability
Institute of Mathematical Statistics
3401 Investment Blvd., Ste. 7   Phone: (510)783-8141
Hayward, CA 94545   Fax: (510)783-4131
Journal covering the applications of probability. **Founded:** 1991. **Frequency:** Quarterly. **Printing Method:** Offset. **Trim Size:** 7 x 10. **Cols./Page:** 1. **Col. Width:** 5 in. **Col. Depth:** 8 in. **Key Personnel:** J. Michael Steele, Editor. **ISSN:** 1050-5164. **Subscription:** $70 institutions.
Ad Rates: BW: $450   **Circulation:** 3,000

298 The Annals of Probability
Institute of Mathematical Statistics
3401 Investment Blvd., Ste. 7
Hayward, CA 94545   Phone: (510)783-8141
                                    Fax: (510)783-4131

299 The Annals of Statistics
Institute of Mathematical Statistics
3401 Investment Blvd., Ste. 7
Hayward, CA 94545   Phone: (510)783-8141
                                    Fax: (510)783-4131

300 The IMS Bulletin
Institute of Mathematical Statistics
3401 Investment Blvd., Ste. 7
Hayward, CA 94545   Phone: (510)783-8141
                                    Fax: (510)783-4131
Journal providing IMS news. **Founded:** 1972. **Frequency:** 6x/yr.
Printing Method: Offset. **Trim Size:** 7 x 10. **Cols./Page:** 1. **Col. Width:**
5 in. **Col. Depth:** 8 in. **Key Personnel:** Susan R. Wilson, Editor. **ISSN:**
0146-3942. **Subscription:** $50 institutions.
Ad Rates: BW: $250   **Circulation:** Paid 4,600

301 Statistical Science
Institute of Mathematical Statistics
3401 Investment Blvd., Ste. 7
Hayward, CA 94545   Phone: (510)783-8141
                                    Fax: (510)783-4131
Review journal of IMS. **Founded:** 1986. **Frequency:** Quarterly. **Print-
ing Method:** Offset. **Trim Size:** 8 1/2 x 10. **Cols./Page:** 1. **Col. Width:** 6
1/2 in. **Col. Depth:** 8 in. **Key Personnel:** Robert E. Kass, Exec. Editor.
ISSN: 0883-4237. **Subscription:** $75 institutions.
Ad Rates: BW: $450   **Circulation:** Paid 5,400

HOLLYWOOD

302 American Cinematographer
ASC Holding Corp.
PO Box 2230   **Phone: (213)969-4333**
Hollywood, CA 90078   Fax: (213)876-4973

303 Location Update
6922 Hollywood Blvd., No. 612   Phone: (213)461-8887
Hollywood, CA 90028   Fax: (213)469-3711
Magazine focusing on location filming. **Subtitle:** The Magazine of
Film and Video Production. **Founded:** 1986. **Frequency:** 9x/yr. **Print-
ing Method:** Web offset. **Key Personnel:** Lee Thomas, Editor; James
Thompson, Publisher. **ISSN:** 1058-3238. **Subscription:** $29.95; $39.95
Canada; $45.95 other countries. $3.95 single issue.
                                    Circulation: (Not Reported)
Advertising accepted; contact publisher for rates.

304 Metal Collectors Edition
Music Magazine Company
7080 Hollywood Blvd., Ste. 415
Hollywood, CA 90028
Magazine featuring articles and posters of heavy metal bands.
Founded: 1991. **Frequency:** Monthly. **Key Personnel:** Judy Wieder,
Editor; Arnold Levitt, Publisher. **Subscription:** $27. $3.95 single issue.
                                    Circulation: (Not Reported)

305 Spotlight Casting
Spotlight Casting Magazine
1605 N. Cahuenga, Ste. 207   Phone: (213)462-6775
Hollywood, CA 90028   Fax: (213)871-0234
Entertainment trade magazine. **Founded:** 1986. **Frequency:** Weekly.
Key Personnel: Claudine Sweeney, Editor; Susan Moore, Managing
Editor. **Subscription:** $55. $1.50 single issue.
Ad Rates: BW: $500   **Circulation:** Paid 5,000
           4C: $900   Non-paid 5,000
           PCI: $16

HUNTINGTON BEACH

306 Economic Inquiry
Western Economic Assn. Intl.
7400 Center Ave., Ste. 109
Huntington Beach, CA 92647-3039   Phone: (714)898-3222
Journal covering research in all areas of economics. **Founded:** 1962.

Frequency: Quarterly. **Printing Method:** Offset. **Trim Size:** 6 7/8 x 10.
Cols./Page: 2. **ISSN:** 0095-2583. **Subscription:** $50; $135 libraries;
$150 libraries outside of the Americas. $35 single issue.
Ad Rates: BW: $350   **Circulation:** Paid 3,300
                                              Non-paid 25

307 Huntington Beach/Fountain Valley Independent
Coast Community News
18682 Beach Blvd., Ste. 160   Phone: (714)965-3030
Huntington Beach, CA 92648   Fax: (714)965-7174
Former Title: Huntington Beach Independent

IRVINE

308 Ability Magazine
CRC Publishing
1682 Langley   Phone: (714)854-8700
Irvine, CA 92714   Fax: (714)261-8710
Subtitle: An Informative Resource on Disability Issues. **Founded:**
1991. **Frequency:** Bimonthly. **Printing Method:** Web heatset. **Trim
Size:** 8 1/2 x 11. **Cols./Page:** 3. **Key Personnel:** Ann Hampton, Editor;
Chet Cooper, contact. **ISSN:** 1062-5321. **Subscription:** $29.70.
                                    Circulation: (Not Reported)
Advertising accepted; contact publisher for rates.

309 News For Kids
D.M. Publishing, Inc.
19742 MacArthur Blvd.
Irvine, CA 92715
News magazine for kids 7 to 12 years of age. **Frequency:** Monthly. **Key
Personnel:** Fran Mulvania, Editor and Publisher. **Subscription:**
$18.95. $2.95 single issue.
                                    Circulation: (Not Reported)

310 Touring America
Fancy Publications, Inc.
3 Burroughs St.
Irvine, CA 92718
Travel magazine featuring ideas for trips in the United States,
Canada, and Mexico. **Frequency:** 6x/yr. **Key Personnel:** Gene Booth,
Editor; Norman Ridler, Publisher. **Subscription:** $15. $3.95 single
issue.
                                    Circulation: (Not Reported)

311 KUCI-FM - 88.9
PO Box 4362   Phone: (714)856-6868
Irvine, CA 92716-4362   **Fax: (714)856-8673**

LA JOLLA

312 Baja Explorer
ALTI Corporation
4180 La Jolla Village Dr., No. 520
La Jolla, CA 92037
Guide to hot spots and areas of interest for residents of Baja, CA.
Frequency: 6x/yr. **Key Personnel:** Landon Crumpton, Editor; Wayne
Hilbig, Publisher. **Subscription:** $16. $2.95 single issue.
                                    Circulation: (Not Reported)

LA MIRADA

313 Journal of Psychology and Theology
Rosemead School of Psychology
Biola University
13800 Biola Ave.   Phone: (310)903-4727
La Mirada, CA 90639   **Fax: (310)903-4748**

LA PUENTE

314 La Puente Highlander
Highlander Newspapers
18383 E. Railroad St.   **Phone: (818)854-8700**
City of Industry, CA 91748   **Fax: (818)854-8719**

Ad Rates: GLR = general line rate; BW = one-time black & white page rate; 4C = one-time four color page rate; SAU = standard advertising unit rate;
CNU = Canadian newspaper advertising unit rate; PCI = per column inch rate.
Circulation: ★ = ABC; △ = BPA; ◆ = CAC; ● = CCAB; □ = VAC; ⊕ = PO Statement; ‡ = Publisher's Report; Boldface figures = sworn; Light figures = estimated.
Entry type: ▥ = Print; ▟ = Broadcast.

LA QUINTA

♣ 315 KUNA-AM - 1400
PO Box 956   Phone: (619)568-6830
La Quinta, CA 92253-0956   Fax: (619)568-3984
Format: Ethnic (Spanish). **Owner:** Peninno Broadcasting. **Operating Hours:** Continuous. **Key Personnel:** Jay Scott, Gen. Mgr.; Jose Arpietta, Operations Mgr.; Mark Wright, Sales Mgr.; Melvin Oviva, Music Dir.; Rosa Rodreigez, Production Dir. **Wattage:** 1000.

LA VERNE

♣ 316 KULV-AM - 550
University of La Verne
1950 3rd St.
Student Center
La Verne, CA 91750   Phone: (714)596-1693
Format: Alternative/Independent/Progressive. **Key Personnel:** Eric Aronson, Music Dir. **Ad Rates:** Noncommercial.

LAGUNA BEACH

📖 317 This is Laguna
Laguna Press
PO Box 1568
Laguna Beach, CA 92652
Magazine profiling Laguna Beach, CA. **Frequency:** 6x/yr. **Key Personnel:** Pat Cochran, Editor and Publisher. **Subscription:** $10. $2 single issue.

Circulation: (Not Reported)

LAGUNA HILLS

📖 318 Professional Tool & Equipment News
Professional Tool & Equipment News, Inc.
23030 Lake Forest Dr., No. 201   Phone: (714)830-7520
Laguna Hills, CA 92653   Fax: (714)830-7523
Magazine for automotive shop owners and technicians. Reports on new tools and equipment. **Founded:** 1990. **Frequency:** 6x/yr. **Printing Method:** Web offset. **Trim Size:** 7 7/8 x 10 7/8. **Key Personnel:** Tom Carruthers, Editor; Robert H. Swenson, Associate Publisher/Advertising Rep. **Subscription:** Free for qualified individuals.
Ad Rates: BW: $5,275   **Circulation:** Non-paid ‡106,332
              4C: $6,925
Additional Contact Information: Editor's phone, (708)564-0677; fax, (708)564-2708.

LAKEWOOD

📖 319 Modern Maturity
American Assn. of Retired Persons
3200 E. Carson St.   Phone: (310)496-2277
Lakewood, CA 90712   **Fax: (310)496-4124**

LANCASTER

♣ 320 Jones Intercable, Inc.
41551 W. 10th St.   Phone: (805)273-1890
Palmdale, CA 93551   Fax: (805)273-6493
Owner: Jones Intercable, Inc. **Founded:** 1964. **Cities Served:** Kern County, Los Angeles County, California City, Elizabeth Lake, Green Valley, Leona Valley, Palmdale, and Quartz Hill, CA.

LEMOORE

♣ 321 KJOP-AM - 1240
15279 Hanford Armona Rd.   Phone: (209)584-5242
Lemoore, CA 93245   Fax: (209)584-0310
Format: Spanish Country. **Owner:** Radio Rey Inc. **Founded:** 1981. **Operating Hours:** 4 a.m.-11 p.m. **Key Personnel:** Jesus Larios, Gen. Mgr.; Federico Gomez, Program Dir.; Juan Rodriguez, News Dir.; Joe Hernandez, Sales Mgr.; John Pembroke, Owner. **Wattage:** 250 day; 1000 night. **Ad Rates:** $12-$32 for 30 seconds; $16-$36 for 60 seconds.

LINDEN

📖 322 California Odd Fellow and Rebekah
Linden Publications
19033 E. Main St.
PO Box 129   Phone: (209)887-3829
Linden, CA 95236-0129   **Fax: (209)887-3829**

LOMA LINDA

📖 323 University Scope
Loma Linda University
                                        Phone: (714)824-4526
Loma Linda, CA 92350   **Fax: (714)824-4181**

LOMPOC

📖 324 Record
Dontey Media Group
115 N. H St.   Phone: (805)736-2313
Lompoc, CA 93436   Fax: (805)736-5654
Newspaper. **Founded:** 1875. **Frequency:** Mon.-Sun. (morn.). **Printing Method:** Offset. **Cols./Page:** 6. **Key Personnel:** Rita Henning, Editor; David Stringer, Publisher; Dick Bausman, Advertising Mgr.
Ad Rates: GLR: $.73   **Circulation:** ★9,205
              4C: $1,344.75
              PCI: $8.58

LONG BEACH

📖 325 The Jazz Review and Collectors Discography
New Century Publishing
2005 Palo Verde Ave., Ste. 158
Long Beach, CA 90815
Magazine reporting on the jazz music industry. **Frequency:** Monthly. **Key Personnel:** Ken Borgers, Editor; Gary Wagner, Publisher. **Subscription:** $19.80./$2.75 single issue.

Circulation: (Not Reported)

♣ 326 CVI
2931 Redondo Ave.   Phone: (310)424-4657
Long Beach, CA 90806   Fax: (310)490-9981
Owner: Cablevision Industries. **Founded:** 1965. **Formerly:** Simmons Cable TV. **Key Personnel:** Frank McNellis, Gen. Mgr.; David Kydd, Program Dir.; John Craig, Marketing Mgr. **Cities Served:** Long Beach and Signal Hill, CA: 69,000 subscribing households; 53 channels; 1 community access channel.

♣ 327 KLBC-FM - 91
4901 E. Carson
Long Beach, CA 90808   Phone: (310)420-4312
Format: Alternative/Independent/Progressive. **Key Personnel:** M. Herbold, Music Dir. **Ad Rates:** Noncommercial.

LOS ALTOS

📖 328 Los Altos Town Crier
Peninsula Community Newspapers
138 Main St.
PO Drawer F   **Phone: (415)948-4489**
Los Altos, CA 94023   Fax: (415)948-6647

📖 329 RunCal
Pacific Association of the Athletics Congress
220 Main St., Ste. 205
PO Box 1621   Phone: (415)948-0618
Los Altos, CA 94023-1621   Fax: (415)949-2172
Magazine covering the sports of road running and track and field. **Founded:** 1987. **Frequency:** 6x/yr. **Printing Method:** Offset. **Trim Size:** 8 1/2 x 11. **Cols./Page:** 3. **Col. Width:** 2 1/2 in. **Col. Depth:** 10 in. **Key Personnel:** Mark Winitz, Editor-in-Chief. **Subscription:** $12. $2 single issue.
Ad Rates: BW: $400   **Circulation:** 7,000
              PCI: $25   Non-paid 1,000
Color advertising not accepted.

LOS ANGELES

□ 330 AdvocateMEN
Liberation Publications, Inc.
6922 Hollywood Blvd., 10th Fl.   Phone: (213)871-1225
Los Angeles, CA 90028   Fax: (213)467-6805
Magazine featuring gay, male erotica. **Founded:** 1984. **Frequency:**
Monthly. **Trim Size:** 8 x 10 7/8. **Key Personnel:** Jeff Yarbrough,
Editor. **ISSN:** 0742-4701. **Subscription:** $54. $5.95 single issue.
Ad Rates: BW: $2,265   **Circulation:** 45,000
              4C: $3,914

□ 331 Al Talib
Associated Students, U.C.L.A.
112 Kerckhoff Hall
308 Westwood Plaza
University of California, Los Angeles   Phone: (310)206-7877
Los Angeles, CA 90024   Fax: (310)206-0906
Community magazine for Muslim students. **Founded:** 1990. **Frequency:** Quarterly. **Key Personnel:** Mansur Kahn, Editor. **Subscription:** $16.

                            Circulation: Controlled 5,000
Advertising accepted; contact publisher for rates.

□ 332 Amerasia Journal
UCLA Asian American Studies Center
3230 Campbell Hall
405 Hilgard Ave.   Phone: (310)825-3415
Los Angeles, CA 90024-1546   Fax: (310)206-9844
Journal addressing intercultural interests. **Founded:** 1971. **Frequency:** 3x/yr. **Trim Size:** 9 x 6. **Cols./Page:** 1. **Key Personnel:** Russell C. Leong, Co-Editor; Glenn Omatsu, Co-Editor. **ISSN:** 0044-7471. **Subscription:** $18; $24 institutions. Subscription includes CrossCurrents Newsletter.
Ad Rates: BW: $160   **Circulation:** Paid 1,500
                                                   Non-paid 45
Additional Contact Information: Alternate phone: (310)825-2968.

□ 333 The American Senior
Publishing and Business Consultants
951 S. Oxford, Ste. 109   Phone: (213)732-3477
Los Angeles, CA 90006   **Fax: (213)SEC-3477**

□ 334 Black Lace
PO Box 83912
Los Angeles, CA 90083   Phone: (213)410-0808
Magazine published by and for African-American lesbians. Includes erotica and politically focused articles and analysis. **Frequency:** Quarterly.
                            Circulation: (Not Reported)

□ 335 Blitz
PO Box 48124
Los Angeles, CA 90048-0124   **Phone: (818)997-3294**

□ 336 Business Concepts
Publishing and Business Consultants
951 S. Oxford, Ste. 109   Phone: (213)732-3477
Los Angeles, CA 90006   **Fax: (213)SEC-3477**

□ 337 Californiai Magyarsag (California Hungarians)
207 S. Western Ave., Ste. 201   **Phone: (213)463-3473**
Los Angeles, CA 90004   Fax: (213)384-7642

□ 338 Central California Jewish Heritage
2130 S. Vermont Ave.   Phone: (213)737-2122
Los Angeles, CA 90007   **Fax: (213)737-1021**

□ 339 Credit & Finance
Publishing and Business Consultants
951 S. Oxford, Ste. 109   Phone: (213)732-3477
Los Angeles, CA 90006   **Fax: (213)SEC-3477**

□ 340 Current Employment
Publishing and Business Consultants
951 S. Oxford, Ste. 109   Phone: (213)732-3477
Los Angeles, CA 90006   **Fax: (213)SEC-3477**

□ 341 The Economic Home Owner
Publishing and Business Consultants
951 S. Oxford, Ste. 109   Phone: (213)732-3477
Los Angeles, CA 90006   **Fax: (213)SEC-3477**

□ 342 Explorer
Los Angeles Southwest College
1600 W. Imperial Hwy.
Los Angeles, CA 90047   Phone: (213)777-2225
Collegiate newspaper. **Founded:** 1965. **Frequency:** Every other week. **Cols./Page:** 5. **Col. Width:** 11.06 picas. **Key Personnel:** Javier Medina, Editor-in-Chief; Lee Burger, Managing Editor; Kay Gibbs, Advertising Mgr. **Subscription:** Free.
Ad Rates: BW: $250   **Circulation:** (Not Reported)
              PCI: $14

□ 343 Freshmen
Liberation Publications, Inc.
6922 Hollywood Blvd., 10th Fl.   Phone: (213)871-1225
Los Angeles, CA 90028   Fax: (213)467-6805
Magazine featuring gay, male erotica. **Founded:** 1991. **Frequency:** Monthly. **Trim Size:** 8 x 10 7/8. **ISSN:** 1060-5266. **Subscription:** $54. $5.95 single issue.
Ad Rates: BW: $1,866   **Circulation:** 12,000
              4C: $2,682

□ 344 Government Programs
Publishing and Business Consultants
951 S. Oxford, Ste. 109   Phone: (213)732-3477
Los Angeles, CA 90006   **Fax: (213)SEC-3477**

□ 345 Ha'Am
210C Kerckhoff Hall
Associated Students, U.C.L.A.   Phone: (213)825-6280
Los Angeles, CA 90024   Fax: (213)206-0906
News magazine. **Founded:** 1972. **Frequency:** 2x/trimester. **Subscription:** $16.
                            Circulation: (Not Reported)

□ 346 Health Diet & Nutrition
Publishing and Business Consultants
951 S. Oxford, Ste. 109   Phone: (213)732-3477
Los Angeles, CA 90006   **Fax: (213)SEC-3477**

□ 347 Herald Dispatch
4053 Marlton Ave.
PO Box 19027A   Phone: (213)291-9486
Los Angeles, CA 90008   Fax: (213)291-2123

□ 348 Innovation and Ideas
Publishing and Business Consultants
951 S. Oxford, Ste. 109   Phone: (213)732-3477
Los Angeles, CA 90006   **Fax: (213)SEC-3477**

□ 349 Intercambios Femeniles
National Network of Hispanic Women
12021 Wilshire Blvd., Ste. 353
Los Angeles, CA 90025   Phone: (213)225-9895
Magazine profiling career paths of successful Hispanic women. Includes career and resource information for professional and business women. **Frequency:** Quarterly.
                            Circulation: (Not Reported)

□ 350 International Documentary
International Documentary Association
1551 South Robertson Blvd.   Phone: (310)284-8422
Los Angeles, CA 90046   Fax: (310)785-9334
Journal promoting non-fiction film and video. **Subtitle:** News and Events of the International Documentary Association. **Frequency:**

Ad Rates: GLR = general line rate; BW = one-time black & white page rate; 4C = one-time four color page rate; SAU = standard advertising unit rate; CNU = Canadian newspaper advertising unit rate; PCI = per column inch rate.
Circulation: ★ = ABC; △ = BPA; ◆ = CAC; ● = CCAB; □ = VAC; ⊕ = PO Statement; ‡ = Publisher's Report; Boldface figures = sworn; Light figures = estimated.
Entry type: □ = Print; ▉ = Broadcast.

25

Monthly. **Cols./Page:** 3. **Key Personnel:** Nancy Wilkman, Editor; Carol Moore, Advertising Dir. **ISSN:** 0742-533X. **Subscription:** $35.
Ad Rates: BW: $275 **Circulation:** 1,300
Color advertising not accepted. **Additional Contact Information:** Advertising Dir. (310)459-0164.

351 Joong-Ang Daily News
690 Wilshire Pl.　　Phone: (213)389-2500
Los Angeles, CA 90017　　Fax: (213)389-8384
Newspaper published in Korean. **Founded:** 1965. **Frequency:** Daily. **Cols./Page:** 9. **Key Personnel:** Son Tae-Ik, Editor; Young-Sub Lee, Publisher. **Subscription:** $140.
Ad Rates: BW: $450 **Circulation:** Paid ★50,000
4C: $750 Free ★85,000

352 Model Call
Richard Poirier Model and Talent Agency
3575 Cahuenga Blvd. W., Ste. 254 Phone: (213)969-9990
Los Angeles, CA 90068-1341 Fax: (213)850-3382
Magazine focusing on the professional modeling industry. **Frequency:** Quarterly. **Printing Method:** Offset. **Trim Size:** 8 1/8 x 10 7/8. **Cols./Page:** 3. **Col. Width:** 2 1/4 in. **Col. Depth:** 10 in. **Key Personnel:** Richard Poirier, Publisher/Editor-in-Chief; Donny Poirier, Advertising Dir. **ISSN:** 1061-4737. **Subscription:** $14. $3.95 single issue.
Ad Rates: BW: $4,410 **Circulation:** 20,000
4C: $6,882

353 Motor World
Publishing and Business Consultants
951 S. Oxford, Ste. 109 Phone: (213)732-3477
Los Angeles, CA 90006 **Fax: (213)SEC-3477**

354 National Auctions and Sales
Publishing and Business Consultants
951 S. Oxford, Ste. 109 Phone: (213)732-3477
Los Angeles, CA 90006 **Fax: (213)SEC-3477**

355 NOMMO
Associated Students, U.C.L.A.
112 Kerckhoff Hall Phone: (310)825-3305
Los Angeles, CA 90024 Fax: (310)206-0906
Magazine for students. **Frequency:** Quarterly. **Subscription:** $16.
Circulation: (Not Reported)

356 Noticias del Mundo
1301 W. 2nd St. Phone: (213)482-9644
Los Angeles, CA 90026 Fax: (213)482-8602
Ceased publication.

357 Pacific Citizen
Japanese American Citizens League
941 E. 3rd St., No. 200 Phone: (213)626-6936
Los Angeles, CA 90013 Fax: (213)626-8213
Newspaper (tabloid). **Frequency:** 45x/yr. **Printing Method:** Offset. **USPS:** 30-8579. **Subscription:** $25.
Ad Rates: PCI: $20 **Circulation:** Paid ‡24,000
Free ‡100

358 Pacific Ties
Associated Students, U.C.L.A.
112 Kerckhoff Hall Phone: (310)825-1004
Los Angeles, CA 90024 Fax: (310)206-0906
Student magazine. **Frequency:** Quarterly. **Subscription:** $16.
Circulation: (Not Reported)

359 PBC Federal Tax Guide
Publishing & Business Consultants
951 S. Oxford, Ste. 109 Phone: (213)732-3477
Los Angeles, CA 90006 Fax: (213)732-3477
Magazine covering tax issues that affect individuals, seniors, and businesses. **Founded:** 1991. **Frequency:** Quarterly. **Printing Method:** Web offset. **Key Personnel:** Atia Napoleon, Editor and Publisher. **ISSN:** 1059-2032. **Subscription:** $26.99; $33.99 other countries.
Ad Rates: BW: $8,290 **Circulation:** (Not Reported)
4C: $9,750
Additional Contact Information: Mailing address: PO Box 75392, Los Angeles, CA 90005.

360 Psychological Perspectives
C. G. Jung Institute of Los Angeles
10349 W. Pico Blvd. Phone: (310)556-1193
Los Angeles, CA 90064 Fax: (310)556-2290
Journal of Jungian thought featuring articles, interviews, poetry, fiction, and book and film reviews. **Founded:** 1970. **Frequency:** 2x/yr. **Trim Size:** 6 x 9. **Cols./Page:** 1. **Col. Width:** 4.5 in. /CLD 7.5. **Key Personnel:** Ernest L. Rossi, Editor; Charlene M. Sieg, Managing Editor. **ISSN:** 0033-2925. **Subscription:** $12 single issue.
Ad Rates: BW: $300 **Circulation:** Paid 2,000
Non-paid 2,000

361 Reader
The Burnside Group, Inc.
5550 Wilshire Blvd., No. 301 Phone: (213)933-0161
Los Angeles, CA 90036 Fax: (213)933-0281
Urban alternative newspaper. **Subtitle:** Los Angeles' Free Weekly. **Founded:** 1978. **Frequency:** Weekly. **Printing Method:** Offset. **Trim Size:** 11 x 13 3/4. **Cols./Page:** 4. **Col. Width:** 14 picas. **Col. Depth:** 13 in. **Key Personnel:** James Vowell, Editor and Publisher. **ISSN:** 1046-2392. **Subscription:** $39.95.
Ad Rates: GLR: $1.80 **Circulation:** Paid ‡344
BW: $1,646 Non-paid ‡78,646
4C: $2,546
SAU: $25.32

362 Situations Digest
Publishing & Business Consultants
951 S. Oxford, Ste. 109 Phone: (213)732-3477
Los Angeles, CA 90006 Fax: (213)732-3477
Magazine covering societal situations. **Founded:** 1991. **Frequency:** Quarterly. **Printing Method:** Web offset. **Trim Size:** 8 1/2 X 11. **Key Personnel:** Atia Napoleon, Editor and Publisher. **ISSN:** 1059-1958. **Subscription:** $26.99; $33.99 other countries.
Ad Rates: BW: $8,290 **Circulation:** (Not Reported)
4C: $9,750
Additional Contact Information: Mailing address: PO Box 75392, Los Angeles, CA 90005.

363 Soldiers Today
Publishing & Business Consultants
951 S. Oxford, Ste. 109 Phone: (213)732-3477
Los Angeles, CA 90006 Fax: (213)732-3477
Magazine covering the social aspects of military life. **Founded:** 1991. **Frequency:** Quarterly. **Printing Method:** Web offset. **Trim Size:** 8 1/2 X 11. **Key Personnel:** Atia Napoleon, Editor and Publisher. **ISSN:** 1059-194X. **Subscription:** $26.99; $33.99 other countries.
Ad Rates: BW: $8,290 **Circulation:** (Not Reported)
4C: $9,750
Additional Contact Information: Mailing Address: PO Box 75392, Los Angeles, CA 90005.

364 The Tidings
1530 W. 9th St. Phone: (213)251-3360
Los Angeles, CA 90015 **Fax: (213)386-8667**

365 University Times
California State University
5151 State University Dr. Phone: (213)343-4215
Los Angeles, CA 90032 **Fax: (213)343-5337**

366 The World & Science
Publishing & Business Consultants
951 S. Oxford, Ste. 109 Phone: (213)732-3477
Los Angeles, CA 90006 Fax: (213)732-3477
Magazine featuring aspects of natural science relating to people and their environment. **Founded:** 1991. **Frequency:** Quarterly. **Printing Method:** Web offset. **Trim Size:** 8 1/2 X 11. **Key Personnel:** Atia Napoleon, Editor and Publisher. **ISSN:** 1059-9131. **Subscription:** $26.99; $33.99 other countries.
Ad Rates: BW: $8,290 **Circulation:** (Not Reported)
4C: $9,750

367 Zoo View
Greater Los Angeles Zoo Association
5333 Zoo Dr.
Los Angeles, CA 90027 Phone: (213)664-1100
Magazine for L.A. Zoo members. **Founded:** 1964. **Frequency:** Quarter-

ly. **Printing Method:** Web offset. **Trim Size:** 8 1/2 X 11. **Key Personnel:** Leslie Croyder, Editor. **Subscription:** $7. $2 single issue.

Circulation: Paid 50,000
Non-paid 1,000

Advertising not accepted.

☙ 368 American Cablesystems of South Central Los Angeles
2900 Crenshaw Blvd.   Phone: (310)730-9500
Los Angeles, CA 90016   Fax: (310)735-7424
Owner: Continental Cablevision, Inc. **Founded:** 1988. **Cities Served:** Los Angeles County and Inglewood, CA.

☙ 369 British-American Communications
6847 Foothill Blvd.   Phone: (818)951-3900
Los Angeles, CA 91042   Fax: (818)951-2951
Owner: British-American Communications. **Founded:** 1984. **Formerly:** British-Telecom, Inc.. **Key Personnel:** Michael K. Bridges, Pres.; Claude W. Bridges, Secretary; John Cheeseman, V.P./Chief Engineer. **Cities Served:** Los Angeles County, Century City, Marina Del Rey, Studio City, and West Los Angeles, CA. 3,100 subscribing households; 56 channels; 1 community access channel; 4 hours per week of community access programming. **Additional Contact Information:** Alt. telephone (213)385-1705.

☙ 370 Continental Cablevision
6314 Arizona Pl.   Phone: (310)216-3500
Los Angeles, CA 90045   Fax: (310)216-3535
Owner: Continental Cablevision, Inc. **Founded:** 1980. **Formerly:** American Cablesystems. **Key Personnel:** Matt McGuinnity, Gen. Mgr.; Steve Repech, Technical Operations Mgr.; April Franklin, Cust. Service Mgr.; Rosa Hill, Business Office Mgr.; Janet Evidon, Mktg. Mgr.; Bill Thornton, Community Program Mgr. **Cities Served:** Los Angeles County, Culver City, Hawthorn, Madera Heights, Marina Del Rey, Palms, Playa del Rey, Rancho Park, Venice, Westchester, Mar Vista, Cheviot Hills, Lennox, and Windsor Hills, CA. 69,000 subscribing households; 54 channels; 2 community access channel; 50 hours per week of community access programming.

☙ 371 KABC-AM - 790
3321 S. La Cienega Blvd.   Phone: (310)840-4958
Los Angeles, CA 90016   **Fax: (310)840-4977**

☙ 372 KCAL-TV - Channel 9
5515 Melrose Ave.   **Phone: (213)467-9999**
Los Angeles, CA 90038   Fax: (213)460-6265

☙ 373 KSCR-FM - 104.7
University of Southern California
Student Union 404
Los Angeles, CA 90089-0895   Phone: (213)740-5727
Format: Alternative/Independent/Progressive. **Key Personnel:** John Brinda, Music Dir. **Ad Rates:** Noncommercial.

LOS GATOS

📖 374 Bay Area Homestyle
Bay Area Publishing Group
455 Los Gatos Blvd., No. 103
Los Gatos, CA 95032   Phone: (408)358-4159
Ceased publication.

📖 375 Bay Area Parent
Bay Area Publishing Group
401 Alberto Way, Ste. A   Phone: (408)358-1414
Los Gatos, CA 95032   Fax: (408)356-4903
Founded: 1982. **Frequency:** Monthly. **Printing Method:** Web offset. **Trim Size:** 10 1/2 x 13 3/4. **Cols./Page:** 4. **Key Personnel:** Lynn Berardo, Editor-in-Chief; Mary Brence Martin, Mng. Editor; Sandy Moeckel, Publisher. **Subscription:** Free.
Ad Rates: BW: $1,780   **Circulation:** Free ▢70,000
4C: $2,180   Paid ▢809

📖 376 Los Gatos Weekly-Times
Metro Publishing Co.
245 Almendra Ave.   Phone: (408)298-8000
Los Gatos, CA 95030   Fax: (408)298-0602

MALIBU

📖 377 The Graphic Weekly
Pepperdine University
24255 Pacific Coast Hwy.   Phone: (310)456-4311
Malibu, CA 90263-4311   Fax: (310)456-4758
Student newspaper. **Founded:** 1937. **Frequency:** Weekly. **Cols./Page:** 6. **Col. Width:** 2 1/16 in. **Col. Depth:** 21 in. **Subscription:** Free; $12.50 (mail).
Ad Rates: PCI: $8   **Circulation:** Paid 100
Non-paid 2,900

📖 378 TRANSPACIFIC
TMI
23715 W. Malibu Rd., No. 390   Phone: (213)456-0790
Malibu, CA 90275   **Fax: (213)456-3724**

MAMMOTH LAKES

📖 379 Mammoth Times
New Times Publishing, Inc.
PO Box 3929   Phone: (619)934-3929
Mammoth Lakes, CA 93546   Fax: (619)934-3916
Weekly community newspaper. **Founded:** 1987. **Frequency:** Weekly. **Printing Method:** Web offset. **Trim Size:** 10 3/4 x 14 1/2. **Cols./Page:** 4. **Col. Width:** 2 1/4 in. **Col. Depth:** 13 1/4 in. **Key Personnel:** Wally Hofmann, Editor. **Subscription:** Free; $36 (mail).
Ad Rates: GLR: $1   **Circulation:** Free ▢8,729
BW: $398
4C: $598
SAU: $8.50

MANHATTAN BEACH

📖 380 Client Magazine
JB & ME Publishing
PO Box 3879
Manhattan Beach, CA 90266   Phone: (310)546-1255
Ceased publication.

MENLO PARK

📖 381 Sunset Magazine
Sunset Publishing Corp.
80 Willow Rd.   Phone: (415)321-3600
Menlo Park, CA 94025   **Fax: (415)328-6215**

MISSION VIEJO

📖 382 Aero Magazine
Fancy Publications, Inc.
PO Box 6050
Mission Viejo, CA 92690   Phone: (714)855-8822
Ceased publication.

MODESTO

📖 383 The Modesto Bee
McClatchy Newspapers, Inc.
14th & H
PO Box 3928   Phone: (209)578-2351
Modesto, CA 95352   Fax: (209)578-2271

📖 384 Spectrum Newspapers Monthly, Modesto
Spectrum Newspapers
11171 Sun Center Dr., Ste. 110   Phone: (916)852-6222
Rancho Cordova, CA 95670   Fax: (916)852-6397
Newspaper serving senior citizens, 55 and older, in Modesto. **Founded:** 1975. **Frequency:** Monthly. **Printing Method:** Web offset.

Key Personnel: Bob Carney, Editor; Jacqueline Lucido, Gen. Mgr.; Ridge Eagan, Advertising Dir. **USPS:** 980-481. **Subscription:** $12.

Circulation: ‡17,000

MONROVIA

📖 385 Partners
World Vision, Inc.
919 W. Huntington Dr.
Monrovia, CA 91016
Magazine featuring articles about people in other countries. **Frequency:** Quarterly. **Key Personnel:** Terry Madison, Editor; Robert Seiple, Publisher. **Subscription:** Free.

Circulation: (Not Reported)

MONTEREY

📻 386 KWAV-FM - 96.9
PO Box 1391   Phone: (408)649-0969
Monterey, CA 93942   **Fax: (408)649-0969**

📻 387 Monterey Peninsula Cable TV
2455 Henderson Way
Box 1711   Phone: (408)649-9100
Monterey, CA 93940   Fax: (408)649-8680
Owner: Western Communications. **Founded:** 1952. **Cities Served:** Monterey County, Carmel-by-the-Sea, Carmel Valley, Del Rey Oaks, Marina, Pacific Grove, Salinas, Sand City, and Seaside, CA.

MOUNT AUKUM

📖 388 Mt. Aukum Review
PO Box 483
Mount Aukum, CA 95656   Phone: (209)245-4016
Ceased publication.

NEEDLES

📻 389 KTOX-AM - 1340
PO Box 738
Needles, CA 92363-0738   **Phone: (619)326-2101**

NEWBURY PARK

📖 390 Abstracts in Social Gerontology
Sage Publications, Inc.
2455 Teller Rd.   Phone: (805)499-0721
Newbury Park, CA 91320   Fax: (805)499-0871

📖 391 Education Administration Quarterly
Corwin Press, Inc.
2455 Teller Rd.   Phone: (805)499-0721
Newbury Park, CA 91320   Fax: (805)499-0871

📖 392 Educational Policy
Corwin Press, Inc.
2455 Teller Rd.   Phone: (805)499-0721
Newbury Park, CA 91320   Fax: (805)499-0871
Journal covering research on educational policy and practice at local, national, and international levels. **Founded:** 1991. **Frequency:** Quarterly. **Trim Size:** 5 1/2 x 8 1/2. **Key Personnel:** Philip G. Altbach, Editor; Hugh G. Petrie, Editor. **Subscription:** $39; $110 institutions. $12.50 single issue; $30 single issue institutions.

Circulation: Paid 500
Non-paid 50
Additional Contact Information: Editorial address: Graduate School of Education, 430 Christopher Baldy Hall, SUNY-Buffalo, Buffalo, NY 14260; phone (716)636-2487. A division of Sage Publications Company.

📖 393 Evaluation Review
Sage Publications, Inc.
2455 Teller Rd.   Phone: (805)499-0721
Newbury Park, CA 91320   Fax: (805)499-0871
Journal exploring a range of methodological and conceptual approaches to evaluation. **Subtitle:** A Journal of Applied Social Research. **Frequency:** 6x/yr. **Printing Method:** Offset. **Trim Size:** 5 1/2 x 8 1/2. **Key Personnel:** Richard A. Berk, Editor; Howard E. Freeman, Editor; Sara Miller McGune, Publisher; Cristine Anderson, Circula-

tion Mgr. **ISSN:** 0193-841X. **Subscription:** $57; $159 institutions. $15 single issue; $30 single issue for institutions.
Ad Rates: BW: $250   **Circulation:** Paid 1,700
Formerly: Evaluation Practice.

📖 394 Journal of Management Inquiry
Sage Publications, Inc.
2455 Teller Rd.   Phone: (805)499-0721
Newbury Park, CA 91320   Fax: (805)499-0871
Journal providing non-traditional research and practice in management and organization. **Founded:** 1992. **Frequency:** Quarterly. **Printing Method:** Offset. **Trim Size:** 8 1/2 x 11. **Key Personnel:** Thomas G. Cummings, Editor; Sara Miller McGune, Publisher. **ISSN:** 1056-4926. **Subscription:** $42; $92 institutions. $15 single issue; $27 single issue for institutions.
Ad Rates: BW: $195   **Circulation:** Paid 800

📖 395 People and Education
Corwin Press, Inc.
2455 Teller Rd.   Phone: (805)499-0721
Newbury Park, CA 91320   Fax: (805)499-0871
Journal focusing on research and practice relating to the human element in education. **Subtitle:** The Human Side of Schools. **Founded:** March 1993. **Frequency:** Quarterly. **Key Personnel:** Janice L. Herman, Ph.D., Editor; Jerry J. Herman, Ph.D., Editor. **Subscription:** $35; $75 institutions. $10 single issue; $35 single issue institutions.
Circulation: (Not Reported)
Additional Contact Information: Editorial address: 4905 Lakehurst Dr., Northport, AL, 35476. (205)333-1243. A division of Sage Publications Company.

📖 396 Sociological Methods & Research
Sage Publications, Inc.
2455 Teller Rd.   Phone: (805)499-0721
Newbury Park, CA 91320   Fax: (805)499-0871
Journal covering quantitative research and methodology in the social sciences. **Founded:** 1971. **Frequency:** Quarterly. **Printing Method:** Offset. **Trim Size:** 5 1/2 x 8 1/2. **Cols./Page:** 1. **Col. Width:** 50 nonpareils. **Col. Depth:** 100 agate lines. **Key Personnel:** J. Scott Long, Editor; Sara Miller McGune, Publisher. **ISSN:** 0049-1241. **Subscription:** $53; $142 institutions. $18 single issue; $38 single issue for institutions.
Ad Rates: BW: $250   **Circulation:** Paid 1,550

📖 397 South Asia Journal
Sage Periodicals Press
2455 Teller Rd.   Phone: (805)499-0721
Newbury Park, CA 91320   Fax: (805)499-0871
Ceased publication.

NEWHALL

📖 398 The Signal
Box 877   Phone: (805)259-1234
Newhall, CA 91322   Fax: (805)254-8068
Newspaper. **Founded:** 1919. **Frequency:** Daily.
Circulation: (Not Reported)

NEWPORT BEACH

📖 399 Orange County Business Journal
4590 MacArthur Blvd., Ste. 100   Phone: (714)833-8373
Newport Beach, CA 92660   Fax: (714)833-8751

📖 400 Technology Business
Strategy Network Corporation
4667 MacArthur Blvd., No. 200
Newport Beach, CA 92660   **Phone: (714)852-9115**
Ceased publication.

📖 401 Truck Sales & Leasing
Newport Communications
PO Box W   Phone: (714)261-1636
Newport Beach, CA 92658-8910   **Fax: (714)261-2904**
Former Title: Heavy Truck Salesman

📖 402 Truckers News
Newport Communications
PO Box W   Phone: (714)261-1636
Newport Beach, CA 92658-8910   **Fax: (714)261-2904**

📖 **403 Truckstop World**
Newport Communications
PO Box W
Newport Beach, CA 92658

Phone: (714)261-1636
Fax: (714)261-2904

📖 **404 Viva Petites!**
USA Petites
537 Newport Dr.
Fashion Island
Newport Beach, CA 92660

Phone: (714)643-5008
Fax: (714)362-3013

Fashion magazine for petite women. **Frequency:** Monthly. **Subscription:** $18.

Circulation: (Not Reported)

📡 **405 Comcast Cablevision of Newport Beach**
901 W. 16th St.
Newport Beach, CA 92663

Phone: (714)642-7276

Owner: Comcast Corp. **Founded:** 1969. **Cities Served:** Orange County, CA.

NORTH HOLLYWOOD

📖 **406 Entertainment Connection**
6350 Laurel Canyon Blvd.
North Hollywood, CA 91606

Phone: (213)466-1511
Fax: (818)763-1930

Entertainment magazine. **Founded:** 1988. **Frequency:** Monthly. **Printing Method:** Sheetfed lithography. **Trim Size:** 8 1/2 x 11. **Cols./Page:** 3. **Col. Width:** 2 1/2 in. **Key Personnel:** Janie Bradford, Editor and Publisher; Donna Y. Caldwell, Mng. Editor; T. Hall, Advertising Mgr. **Subscription:** $30. $2.75 single issue.

Ad Rates:	BW:	$1,200	Circulation: Paid ‡24,750
	4C:	$1,900	Non-paid ‡250
	PCI:	$45	

NORTHRIDGE

📖 **407 Nous**
Nous Publications
California State University
Dept. of Philosophy
18111 Nordhoff St.
Northridge, CA 91330

Phone: (812)855-5676
Fax: (812)855-5678

📡 **408 KCSN-FM - 88.5**
18111 Nordhoff St.
Northridge, CA 91330

Phone: (818)885-3089
Fax: (818)885-3069

OAKLAND

📖 **409 The Black Scholar**
Black World Foundation
PO Box 2869
Oakland, CA 94609

Phone: (510)547-6633
Fax: (510)547-6679

📖 **410 California Agriculture**
University of California
Office of the Vice President
Agriculture & Natural Resources
300 Lakeside Dr., 6th Fl.
Oakland, CA 94612-3560

Phone: (510)987-0044
Fax: (510)465-2659

📖 **411 CALUnderwriter**
California Assn. of Life Underwriters
70 Washington St., No. 325
Oakland, CA **94607**

Phone: (510)834-2258
Fax: (510)834-1453

📖 **412 The Catholic Voice**
2918 Lakeshore Ave.
Oakland, CA 94610-3614

Phone: (510)893-4711
Fax: (510)893-4734

📖 **413 Creation Spirituality Magazine**
Friends of Creation Spirituality
PO Box 19216
Oakland, CA 94619

Phone: (510)482-4984
Fax: (510)482-0387

Magazine. **Subtitle:** A Magazine of Earthly Wisdom for an Evolving

Planet. **Frequency:** 6x/yr. **Printing Method:** Offset. **Trim Size:** 8 1/8 x 10 3/4. **Cols./Page:** 3. **Key Personnel:** Matthew Fox, Editor-in-Chief; Dan Turner, Editor; John Mabry, Managing Editor; Mary Kay Hunyady, Asst. Editor; Julie Fretzin, Marketing Dir. **ISSN:** 1053-9891. **Subscription:** $24. $4 single issue.

Ad Rates: BW: $400   **Circulation:** Paid ⊕**12,844**
                                              Non-paid ⊕**1,661**

📖 **414 Snake Power: A Journal of Contemporary Female Shamanism**
5856 College Ave.
PO Box 138
Oakland, CA 94118

Phone: (415)658-7033

Ceased publication.

📖 **415 Third World Resources**
Third World Resources
464 19th St.
Oakland, CA 94612

Phone: (510)835-4692
Fax: (510)835-3017

Review of resources from and about the Third World. **Founded:** 1985. **Frequency:** Quarterly. **Printing Method:** Sheetfed offset. **Trim Size:** 8 1/2 x 11. **Cols./Page:** 3. **Col. Width:** 2 1/2 in. **Col. Depth:** 10 in. **Key Personnel:** Tom Fenton, Editor; Mary Heffron, Editor. **ISSN:** 8755-8831. **Subscription:** $35 two years; $35 institutions; $50 two years other countries; $50 institutions other countries. $4 single issue.

Ad Rates: BW: $450   **Circulation:** Paid ‡250
                                              Non-paid ‡1,750

📖 **416 The Wise Woman**
2441 Cordova St.
Oakland, CA 94602

Phone: (510)536-3174

Magazine focusing on feminist issues, goddess lore, and feminist spirituality and witchcraft. Contains original research on witch hunts, women's heritage, and women today. **Founded:** 1980. **Frequency:** Quarterly. **Printing Method:** Offset. **Key Personnel:** Ann Forfreedom, Publisher. **ISSN:** 0883-119X. **Subscription:** $15. $4 single issue.

Ad Rates: BW: $40   **Circulation:** (Not Reported)

OCEANSIDE

📖 **417 International Gymnast**
Sundbysports, Inc.
225 Brooks
PO Box 2450
Oceanside, CA 92051

Phone: (619)722-0030
Fax: (619)722-6208

ORANGE

📡 **418 KNAB-AM - 830**
University of Chapman
333 N. Glassell St.
Orange, CA 92666

Phone: (714)744-7020

Format: Alternative/Independent/Progressive. **Ad Rates:** Noncommercial.

📡 **419 KNAB-FM - 90.1**
University of Chapman
333 N. Glassell St.
Orange, CA 92666

Phone: (714)744-7020

Format: Alternative/Independent/Progressive. **Ad Rates:** Noncommercial.

OROVILLE

📖 **420 The Digger Shopper & News**
2057 Mitchell Ave.
PO Box 5006
Oroville, CA 95966

Phone: (916)533-2170
Fax: (916)533-2181

Former Title: The Digger

OXNARD

421 KOXR-AM - 910
418 W. 3rd St.
Oxnard, CA 93030

Phone: (805)487-0444
Fax: (805)487-2117

PALM DESERT

422 Kitchen and Bath Design Ideas
Kasmar Publications, Inc.
PO Box 12638
Palm Desert, CA 92255
Magazine focusing on professionally designed kitchens and bathrooms. **Frequency:** Bimonthly. **Key Personnel:** Jage Paroline, Editor; Kasnea Martin, Publisher. **Subscription:** $3.50 single issue.

Circulation: (Not Reported)

PALM SPRINGS

423 International Fine Art/Collector
Global-Art Link, Inc.
33 N. Palm Canyon Dr., Ste 206
Palm Springs, CA 92262
Magazine reporting on art and auction news. Includes interviews with artists, dealers, and collectors. **Frequency:** Monthly. **Key Personnel:** Wanda Tucker, Editor; William E. Freckleton, Publisher. **Subscription:** $59.95. $10 single issue.

Circulation: (Not Reported)

424 KPSC-FM - 88.7
Box 77913
Los Angeles, CA 90007

Phone: (213)743-5872
Fax: (213)743-5853

425 KWXY-AM - 1340
68700 Dinah Shore Dr.
Palm Springs, CA 92264

Phone: (619)328-1104
Fax: (619)328-7814

PALO ALTO

426 U.S.-Japan Women's Journal: A Journal for the International Exchange of Gender Studies
U.S.-Japan Women's Center
926 Bautista Ct.
Palo Alto, CA 94303

Phone: (415)857-9049
Fax: (415)494-8160

Publication with English supplement for international exchange on women and gender. **Frequency:** 2x/yr. **Trim Size:** 7 1/8 x 10 1/8. **Cols./Page:** 1. **Col. Width:** 5 1/2 in. **Col. Depth:** 8 1/2 in. **Key Personnel:** Yoko Kawashima, Editor. **ISSN:** 1059-9770. **Subscription:** $50; $100 institutions. $10 single issue.
Ad Rates: BW: $200

Circulation: (Not Reported)

PASADENA

427 Firsts: Collecting Modern First Editions
The Lucerne Group
1879 E. Orange Blvd.
Pasadena, CA 91104
Magazine for collectors of first editions of modern books. **Frequency:** Monthly. **Key Personnel:** Brad Munson, Publisher; Robin H. Smiley, Editor. **Subscription:** $35.

Circulation: (Not Reported)

428 Iniquities: The Magazine of Great Wickedness and Wonders
Iniquities Publications
167 Sierra Bonita Ave.
Pasadena, CA 91106
Magazine covering horror fiction. **Frequency:** Quarterly. **Key Personnel:** Buddy Martinez, Editor and Publisher. **Subscription:** $19.95. $4.95 single issue.

Circulation: (Not Reported)

429 KAZN-AM - 1300
800 Sierra Madre Villa Ave.
Pasadena, CA 91107

Phone: (818)388-1300
Fax: (818)351-4204

Format: Ethnic (Asian). **Owner:** Pan Asia Broadcasting, Inc. **Founded:** 1989. **Operating Hours:** 5 a.m.-1 a.m. **Key Personnel:** Shirley S. Price, V.P./Station Mgr. **Wattage:** 5000 day; 1000 night.

430 Kinneloa Television Systems
2267 E. Washington Blvd.
Pasadena, CA 91104

Phone: (818)798-6298
Fax: (818)798-2832

PASO ROBLES

431 Country News
Berwick Communications, Inc.
77 Marquita Ave.
Paso Robles, CA 93446

Phone: (805)237-6060
Fax: (805)237-6066

Community newspaper. **Founded:** 1976. **Frequency:** Weekly. **Printing Method:** Offset. **Trim Size:** 10 1/2 x 16. **Key Personnel:** Sheena Berwick, Editor/Sales Mgr.; Keith Berwick, Pres.; Lois Toft, Circ. Supervisor. **USPS:** 485-790. **Subscription:** $12; $26 (mail).
Ad Rates: BW: $671.20 **Circulation:** Controlled □18,093
4C: $1,159.20
PCI: $8.39

PENN VALLEY

432 Valley Voice
17404 Penn Valley Dr.
PO Box 967
Penn Valley, CA 95946

Phone: (916)432-4935
Fax: (916)273-1854

PETALUMA

433 Wilderness Trails
Trans-Pacific
712 Sartoric Dr.
Petaluma, CA 94954
Magazine for outdoor activists. **Frequency:** Quarterly. **Key Personnel:** Palani Velloo, Editor and Publisher. **Subscription:** $12.74. $3.50 single issue.

Circulation: (Not Reported)

PLACENTIA

434 Mustang Illustrated
McMullen & Yee Publishing, Inc.
7745 Placentia Ave.
Placentia, CA 92670

Phone: (714)572-2255
Fax: (714)572-1864

435 Placentia Highlander
Orange County Register
625 N. Grand Ave.
Santa Ana, CA 92711

Phone: (714)835-1234
Fax: (714)542-5037

PLATINA

436 The Orthodox Word
Saint Herman of Alaska Brotherhood
PO Box 70
Platina, CA 96076-0070

Phone: (916)343-2859
Fax: (916)628-5323

PLEASANTON

437 RV West Magazine
PresComm Media, Inc.
4133 Mohr Ave., Ste. I
Pleasanton, CA 94566-4750

Phone: (510)426-3200
Fax: (510)426-1422

POINT ARENA

438 Sagewoman Magazine
PO Box 641
Point Arena, CA 95468

Phone: (707)882-2052
Fax: (707)882-2793

Periodical focusing on women's spirituality. **Founded:** 1986. **Frequency:** Quarterly. **Printing Method:** Offset. **Trim Size:** 8 1/2 x 11. **Subscription:** $18; $30 outside U.S.
Ad Rates: BW: $400 **Circulation:** Paid ‡5,500
Non-paid ‡100

PORTERVILLE

439 KOJJ-FM - 100.5
165 North D, Ste. 3
Porterville, CA 93257

Phone: (202)785-2720

RANCHO CORDOVA

440 Spectrum Newspapers Weekly, Sacramento
Spectrum Newspapers
11171 Sun Center Dr.
PO Box 1030   Phone: (916)852-6222
Rancho Cordova, CA 95741-1030   Fax: (916)852-6397

RED BLUFF

441 Quality Digest
QCI Intl.
PO Box 882
1350 Vista Way   Phone: (916)527-8875
Red Bluff, CA 96080-0882   Fax: (916)527-6983

REDLANDS

442 San Bernardino County Museum Assn. Quarterly
San Bernardino County Museum Assn.
2024 Orange Tree Ln.   Phone: (909)798-8570
Redlands, CA 92374   Fax: (909)798-8585
Journal on regional history and natural history. **Founded:** 1956.
Frequency: Quarterly. **Printing Method:** Offset. **Trim Size:** 8 1/2 x 11.
Key Personnel: Jennifer Reynolds, Editor. **Subscription:** $40. $15
single issue.

                                      Circulation: Paid 500
                                                  Non-paid 25

Advertising not accepted.

REDONDO BEACH

443 School Bus Fleet
Bobit Publishing
2512 Artesia Blvd.   Phone: (310)376-8788
Redondo Beach, CA 90278   **Fax: (310)376-9043**

REDWOOD CITY

444 Longitude 122
650 Bair Island Rd., Ste. 106   Phone: (415)306-0122
Redwood City, CA 94063   Fax: (415)306-0120
Subtitle: California's Boating Newspaper. **Founded:** 1983. **Frequency:**
Monthly. **Printing Method:** Web offset. **Key Personnel:** Bob Koczor,
Editor and Publisher. **Subscription:** $25.

                                      Circulation: ‡1,375
                                                Free ‡27,500

445 Outlook
The California Society of Certified Public Accountants
275 Shoreline Dr.   **Phone: (415)802-2600**
Redwood City, CA 94065   **Fax: (415)802-2225**

RICHMOND

446 Bay Cablevision
2900 Technology Ct.   Phone: (510)262-1825
Richmond, CA 94806   Fax: (510)262-1838
Owner: The Henfest Group, Pottstown, PA. **Key Personnel:** Dahlia
Moodie, Operations Mgr. **Cities Served:** Berkeley, Richmond, Hercu-
les, El Cerrito, and El Sobrante, CA. **Additional Contact Information:**
Customer Service (510)262-1800.

RIVERBANK

447 The Riverbank News
Live Oak Publishing
122 S. 3rd   Phone: (209)847-3021
Oakdale, CA 95361   **Fax: (209)847-9750**

RIVERSIDE

448 Cinefex
PO Box 20027   Phone: (714)788-9828
Riverside, CA 92516   Fax: (714)788-1793
Journal covering motion picture special effects. **Subtitle:** The Journal
of Cinematic Illusions. **Founded:** 1980. **Frequency:** Quarterly. **Printing
Method:** Sheetfed offset. **Trim Size:** 8 x 9. **Cols./Page:** 2. **Key
Personnel:** Jody Dunran, Editor; Jon Shay, Publisher. **ISSN:** 0198-
1056. **Subscription:** $22. $6.95 single issue.
Ad Rates: BW: $1,700   **Circulation:** Paid 20,000
                 4C: $2,500   Non-paid 1,000

449 Choice TV
6680 View Park Ct.   Phone: (714)687-2721
Riverside, CA 92503   Fax: (714)353-1228
Owner: Gaylord Broadcasting Co.; Cencom Cable Assoc., Inc. **Found-
ed:** 1980. **Cities Served:** Riverside West County, Home Gardens,
Jurupa Hills, Mira Loma, Norco, Rubidoux, and Sunnyslope, CA.

ROHNERT PARK

450 KSUN-FM - 91
1801 E. Cotati Ave.
Rohnert Park, CA 94928   Phone: (707)664-2621
Format: Alternative/Independent/Progressive. **Key Personnel:** Brigette
Chelberg, Music Dir. **Ad Rates:** Noncommercial.

ROSAMOND

451 KAVC-FM - 105.5
2997 Desert, No. 4
PO Box 2069
Rosamond, CA 93560   **Phone: (805)256-3448**

ROWLAND HEIGHTS

452 Rowland Heights Highlander
Highlander Newspapers
18383 E. Railroad St.   **Phone: (818)854-8700**
City of Industry, CA 91748   **Fax: (818)854-8719**

SACRAMENTO

453 CALIFORNIA GEOLOGY Magazine
California Dept. of Conservation
Division of Mines & Geology
Geologic Information & Publications
801 K St., MS 14-33   Phone: (916)445-0514
Sacramento, CA 95814-3532   Fax: (916)327-1853

454 California Grange News
California State Grange
2101 Stockton Blvd.   Phone: (916)454-5805
Sacramento, CA 95817   **Fax: (916)739-8189**

455 California Journal
Information for Public Affairs, Inc.
1714 Capitol Ave.   Phone: (916)444-2840
Sacramento, CA 95814   **Fax: (916)444-2339**

456 Catholic Herald
5890 Newman Ct.   Phone: (916)452-3344
Sacramento, CA 95819   **Fax: (916)452-2945**

457 CDA Journal of the California Dental Association
California Dental Association
PO Box 13749   Phone: (916)443-0505
Sacramento, CA 95853   Fax: (916)443-2943
Journal covering scientific, legislative, and news topics of interest to
dentists. **Frequency:** Monthly. **Printing Method:** Sheet fed offset. **Trim
Size:** 8 3/8 x 10 7/8. **Cols./Page:** 3. **Col. Width:** 2 1/4 in. **Col. Depth:** 10
in. **Key Personnel:** Dr. Jack F. Conley, Editor; Douglas K. Curley,

Mng. Editor; Sue Hummel, Advertising Mgr. **ISSN: 0746-424X.**
Subscription: $12; $24 nonmembers; $60 institutions.
Ad Rates: BW: $1,430   **Circulation:** (Not Reported)
          4C: $2,180
Additional Contact Information: Advertising Mgr. (916)443-3382 ext.
4610.

📖 **458 The Journal of Risk and Insurance**
American Risk and Insurance Assn.
California State University, Sacramento
School of Business
6000 J St.   Phone: (916)278-6609
Sacramento, CA **95819-6088**   **Fax: (916)278-5437**

📖 **459 Sacramento City College Express**
Sacramento City College
3835 Freeport Blvd.
Sacramento, CA 95822   **Phone: (916)558-2561**

📖 **460 Senior Citizens Today**
1924 Alhambra Blvd.
PO Box 163270
Sacramento, CA 95816   Phone: (916)455-0723
Ceased publication.

📖 **461 Senior Spectrum Monthly, Alameda**
Senior Spectrum Monthly
9261 Folsom Blvd., Ste. 401
Sacramento, CA 95813   Phone: (916)364-5454
Ceased publication.

📖 **462 Senior Spectrum Monthly, Bakersfield**
Senior Spectrum Monthly
9261 Folsome Blvd., Ste. 401
Sacramento, CA 95813   Phone: (916)364-5454
Ceased publication.

📖 **463 Senior Spectrum Monthly, Marin**
Senior Spectrum Monthly
9261 Folsome Blvd., Ste. 401
Sacramento, CA 95813   Phone: (916)364-5454
Ceased publication.

📖 **464 Senior Spectrum Monthly, North Santa Clara**
Senior Spectrum Monthly
9261 Folsome Blvd., Ste. 401
Sacramento, CA 95813   Phone: (916)364-5454
Ceased publication.

📖 **465 Senior Spectrum Monthly, Salinas/Monterey**
Senior Spectrum Monthly
9261 Folsome Blvd., Ste. 401
Sacramento, CA 95813   Phone: (916)364-5454
Ceased publication.

📖 **466 Senior Spectrum Monthly, San Mateo**
Senior Spectrum Monthly
9261 Folsome Blvd., Ste. 401
Sacramento, CA 95813   Phone: (916)364-5454
Ceased publication.

📖 **467 Senior Spectrum Monthly, Solano**
Senior Spectrum Monthly
9261 Folsome Blvd., Ste. 401
Sacramento, CA 95813   Phone: (916)364-5454
Ceased publication.

📖 **468 Spectrum Newspapers Monthly, Greater Sacramento**
Spectrum Newspapers
11171 Sun Center Dr., Ste. 110   Phone: (916)852-6222
Rancho Cordova, CA 95670   Fax: (916)852-6397
Newspaper serving active senior citizens, 55 and older, in the greater
Sacramento area. **Founded:** 1975. **Frequency:** Monthly. **Key Personnel:**
Bob Carney, Editor; Jacqueline Lucido, Gen. Mgr.; Ridge Eagan,
Natl. Advertising Dir. **USPS:** 980-481. **Subscription:** $12.
                              Circulation: ‡31,000

🎙 **469 KCMY-TV - Channel 29**
1029 K St., Ste. 23   Phone: (916)443-2929
Sacramento, CA 95814   **Fax: (916)442-6414**

🎙 **470 KEBR-FM - 89.3**
3108 Fulton Ave.   Phone: (916)481-9191
Sacramento, CA 95821   Fax: (916)481-0410
Format: Religious. **Network(s):** Family Stations Radio. **Owner:** Family
Stations, at above address. **Founded:** 1992. **Operating Hours:** Continu-
ous. **Key Personnel:** Peggy Renschler, Production Dir.; Carl Auel,
Station Mgr. **Wattage:** 3100. **Ad Rates:** Noncommercial.

🎙 **471 KEDG-AM - 530**
California State University
c/o AFI Business Office
6000 J St.
Sacramento, CA 95819-6011   Phone: (916)278-5882
Format: Alternative/Independent/Progressive. **Key Personnel:** Karen
Misener, Music Dir. **Ad Rates:** Noncommercial.

🎙 **472 KSEG-FM - 96.9**
620 Bercut Dr.   Phone: (916)446-5769
Sacramento, CA 95814   **Fax: (916)446-3588**

🎙 **473 Pacific West Cable Co.**
1513 Sports Dr., No. 9
Sacramento, CA 95834   Phone: (916)928-2500
Owner: Pacific West Cable Co. **Founded:** 1988. **Cities Served:** Sacramento County and Arden-Arcade, CA.

SALINAS

📖 **474 American Squaredance**
661 Middlefield Rd.   Phone: (408)443-0761
Salinas, CA 93906   **Fax: (408)443-6902**

📖 **475 Moves**
Decision Games
PO Box 1289
Salinas, CA 93902-1289
Tactical magazine for wargamers. **Frequency:** 7x/yr. **Key Personnel:**
Callie Cummins, Editor. **Subscription:** $25. $5.50 single issue.
                              Circulation: (Not Reported)

📖 **476 Vacation Rentals Magazine**
American Publishing
PO Box 10189
Salinas, CA 93912   Phone: (408)753-2414
Magazine featuring vacation homes for consumers and the rental
industry. **Founded:** 1992. **Frequency:** 6x/yr. **Printing Method:** Web
offset. **Trim Size:** 8 1/2 x 11. **Cols./Page:** 3. **ISSN:** 1059-3845.
Subscription: $28. $4 single issue.
                              Circulation: Paid 22,310
Advertising accepted; contact publisher for rates.

🎙 **477 KDON-FM - 102.5**
55 Plaza Circle   Phone: (408)422-5363
Salinas, CA **93901**   Fax: (408)758-1890

🎙 **478 KLAU-AM - 1540**
1188 Padre Dr., Ste. 202   **Phone: (408)655-4100**
Salinas, CA 93901-2261   **Fax: (408)655-1710**

🎙 **479 KMBY-FM - 107.1**
1188 Padre Dr., Ste. 202   **Phone: (408)655-4100**
Salinas, CA 93901-2261   **Fax: (408)655-1710**

SAN ANSELMO

📖 **480 STRINGS**
The String Letter Press, Publishers
412 Red Hill Ave., Ste. 15   Phone: (415)485-6946
San Anselmo, CA **94960**   Fax: (415)485-0831

SAN BERNARDINO

🎙 **481 Comcast Cablevision of San Bernardino**
2090 N. D St.   Phone: (714)883-0831
San Bernardino, CA 92405   Fax: (714)881-4657
Owner: Comcast Corp. **Founded:** 1968. **Cities Served:** San Bernardino
County, Bloomington, Fontana, Highland, and Loma Linda, CA.

♦ **482 KHTX-FM - 97.5**
Box 50005   Phone: **(714)384-9750**
San Bernardino, CA 92412   Fax: **(714)884-5844**

♦ **483 KRSO-AM - 590**
Box 50005   Phone: **(714)384-9750**
San Bernardino, CA 92412   Fax: **(714)884-5844**

SAN DIEGO

▥ **484 Adolescence**
Libra Publishers, Inc.
3089C Clairemont Dr., Ste. 383
San Diego, CA 92117   , Phone: **(619)571-1414**

▥ **485 Beach & Bay Press**
Mannis Communications, Inc.
2204 Garnet   Phone: (619)270-3103
San Diego, CA 92109   Fax: (619)270-9325
Community newspaper. **Founded:** 1988. **Frequency:** Weekly. **Printing Method:** Offset. **Cols./Page:** 4. **Col. Width:** 2 1/4 in. **Col. Depth:** 15 3/4 in. **Key Personnel:** Julie and David Mannis, Publishers; John Gregory, Editor. **Subscription:** Free.
Ad Rates: BW: $1.092   **Circulation:** Free ▢**22,121**
                4C: $1,492   Paid ▢**55**
                PCI: $17

▥ **486 Books**
San Diego Union-Tribune
PO Box 191   Phone: **(619)293-1531**
San Diego, CA 92112   Fax: **(619)293-2432**
Former Title: Currents in Books

▥ **487 Consciousness and Cognition: An International Journal**
Academic Press
1250 6th Ave.
San Diego, CA 92101   Phone: (619)699-6825
Journal focusing on a natural science approach to consciousness, voluntary control, and self. **Founded:** 1992. **Frequency:** Quarterly. **Trim Size:** 6 7/8 x 10. **Key Personnel:** Bernard J. Baars, Editor; William P. Banks, Editor. **ISSN:** 1053-8100. **Subscription:** $122.
Ad Rates: BW: $660   **Circulation:** (Not Reported)

▥ **488 Continental Newstime**
Continental Features/Continental News Service
341 W. Broadway, Ste. 265
San Diego, CA 92101   Phone: (619)492-8696

▥ **489 CVGIP: Graphical Models and Image Processing**
Academic Press, Inc.
1250 Sixth Ave.
San Diego, CA 92101   Phone: (619)699-6825
Journal focusing on the computational models underlying computer generated or -processed imagery. **Frequency:** 6x/yr. **Trim Size:** 8 1/2 x 11. **Key Personnel:** Linda Shapiro, Editor-in-Chief. **Subscription:** $302.
Ad Rates: BW: $660   **Circulation:** (Not Reported)

▥ **490 CVGIP: Image Understanding**
Academic Press, Inc.
1250 Sixth Ave.
San Diego, CA 92101   Phone: (619)699-6825
Journal focusing on the computer analysis of pictorial information. **Frequency:** 6x/yr. **Trim Size:** 8 1/2 x 11. **Key Personnel:** Linda Shapiro, Editor-in-Chief. **Subscription:** $302.
Ad Rates: BW: $660   **Circulation:** (Not Reported)

▥ **491 Environmental Research**
Academic Press, Inc.
1250 Sixth Ave.
San Diego, CA 92101   Phone: (619)699-6825
Journal covering the toxic effects of environmental agents in humans and animals. **Frequency:** 8x/yr. **Trim Size:** 6 7/8 x 10. **Key Personnel:** Philip J. Landrigan, Editor-in-Chief. **Subscription:** $640.
Ad Rates: BW: $780   **Circulation:** (Not Reported)

▥ **492 Family Therapy**
Libra Publishers, Inc.
3089C Claremont Dr., Ste. 383   Phone: (619)581-9449
San Diego, CA 92117   Fax: **(619)571-1414**

▥ **493 International Spectrum Tech**
IDBMA, Inc.
10675 Treena St., Ste. 103   Phone: (619)578-3152
San Diego, CA 92131   Fax: (619)271-1032
Ceased publication.

▥ **494 Journal of the American College of Dentists**
American College of Dentists
4403 Marlborough Ave.   Phone: (619)283-2203
San Diego, CA 92116   Fax: **(301)977-3330**

▥ **495 Journal of Structural Biology**
Academic Press, Inc.
1250 Sixth Ave.
San Diego, CA 92101   Phone: (619)699-6825
Journal covering the structural analysis of biological matter. **Frequency:** 6x/yr. **Trim Size:** 8 1/2 x 11. **Key Personnel:** Neli Albi, Editor-in-Chief; Robert Glaeser, Assoc. Editor. **Subscription:** $236.
Ad Rates: BW: $780   **Circulation:** (Not Reported)
Formerly: Journal of Ultrasound and Molecular Structure Research.

▥ **496 Peninsula Beacon**
Mannis Communications, Inc.
2204 Garnet   Phone: (619)270-3103
San Diego, CA 92109   Fax: (619)270-9325
Community newspaper. **Founded:** 1979. **Frequency:** Weekly. **Printing Method:** Offset. **Cols./Page:** 4. **Col. Width:** 2 1/2 in. **Col. Depth:** 15 3/4 in. **Key Personnel:** John Gregory, Editor; Julie Mannis, Publisher; David Mannis, Publisher. **Subscription:** Free.
Ad Rates: BW: $1,092   **Circulation:** Controlled ▢**20,617**
                4C: $1,492   Paid ▢**50**
                PCI: $17

▥ **497 San Diego Home/Garden**
Westward Communications
445 G St.   Phone: (619)233-4567
San Diego, CA 92101   Fax: (619)233-1004
Magazine featuring interior and exterior designs for homes in the San Diego area. **Founded:** 1979. **Frequency:** Monthly. **Printing Method:** Web offset. **Trim Size:** 8 1/8 x 10 7/8. **Cols./Page:** 3. **Col. Depth:** 10 in. **Key Personnel:** Peter Jensen, Editor; Lawrence Bame, Publisher; Coolley Carley, Advertising Dir.; Anna Holstine, Circulation Dir. **ISSN:** 0274-483X. **Subscription:** $16. $2.25 single issue.
Ad Rates: BW: $2,450   **Circulation:** Paid ★**31,047**
                4C: $3,685
Additional Contact Information: Mailing address: PO Box 1471, San Diego, CA 92112-1471.

▥ **498 San Diego Independent**
Mannis Communications, Inc.
2204 Garnet
SAN Diego, CA 92109   Phone: **(619)270-3103**
Ceased publication.

▥ **499 The San Diego Union-Tribune**
Union-Tribune Publishing Co.
PO Box 191   Phone: (619)299-3131
San Diego, CA 92112-4106   Fax: **(619)293-2333**

▥ **500 San Diego Woman Magazine**
4186 Sorrento Valley Blvd., Ste. N
San Diego, CA 92121   Phone: (619)452-2900
Magazine containing articles and information for women on professional and personal growth. **Founded:** 1984. **Frequency:** Monthly. **Printing Method:** Web offset. **Trim Size:** 8 x 10 7/8. **Cols./Page:** 3. Col.

Width: 2 1/4 in. Col. Depth: 10 in. Key Personnel: Vicki Elzner, Advertising Mgr. Subscription: $15; $25 out of area.

| Ad Rates: | BW: | $1,595 | Circulation: Paid ‡1,000 |
| | 4C: | $1,985 | Non-paid ‡25,000 |

📖 **501 University City Light**
3202 Governor Dr., Ste. 204   Phone: (619)554-0991
San Diego, CA 92122   Fax: (619)554-0186

📖 **502 Women's Times**
930 W. Washington St., Suite 14   Phone: (619)294-9918
San Diego, CA 92103   Fax: (619)294-2183
Newspaper of San Diego County. Founded: 1991. Frequency: Monthly. Trim Size: 11 x 15. Cols./Page: 4. Subscription: $15.

| Ad Rates: | BW: | $1,565 | Circulation: Free ⊕25,000 |
| | 4C: | $3,200 | Paid ⊕5,000 |

🎤 **503 KCBQ-FM - 105.3**
Box 1053   Phone: (619)286-1170
San Diego, CA 92112   Fax: (619)449-8548

🎤 **504 KIFM-FM - 98.1**
3655 Nobel Dr., No. 470   Phone: (619)560-9800
San Diego, CA 92122-1005   Fax: (619)581-4628

🎤 **505 KPBS-FM - 89.5**
    Phone: (619)594-8100
San Diego, CA 92182   Fax: (619)265-6478

🎤 **506 Southwestern Cable TV/San Diego Division**
8949 Ware Ct.   Phone: (619)695-3110
San Diego, CA 92121   Fax: (619)566-6248
Owner: American TV & Communications Corp. Founded: 1963. Cities Served: San Diego County, Clairemont, Del Mar Heights, La Jolla, Linda Vista, Mira Mesa, Mission Beach, North Poway, Pacific Beach, Poway, Tierrasanta, and University City, CA.

SAN FRANCISCO

📖 **507 Broomstick**
3543 18th St., No. 3
San Francisco, CA 94110
Feminist political journal by, for, and about women over 40. Frequency: Quarterly. Subscription: $30; $35 in Canada; $40 other countries. $5 single issue. Free to incarcerated women over 40.
Circulation: (Not Reported)

📖 **508 California Republic**
Daily Journal Corp.
915 E. 1st St.   Phone: (213)229-5300
Los Angeles, CA 90012-1820   Fax: (213)680-3682
Ceased publication.

📖 **509 Computer Language**
Miller Freeman Inc.
600 Harrison Ave.
San Francisco, CA 94107   Phone: (415)905-2200

📖 **510 Culture Concrete**
Culture Concrete Inc.
2141-C Mission St., Ste. 305
San Francisco, CA 94110
Magazine containing book, movie, music, and theatre reviews, short stories, and cartoons. Frequency: Quarterly. Key Personnel: C.E. Petroni, Editor and Publisher. Subscription: $16. $5 single issue.
Circulation: (Not Reported)

📖 **511 DENEUVE**
FRS Enterprises
2336 Market St., No. 15   Phone: (415)863-6538
San Francisco, CA 94114   Fax: (415)863-1609
National lesbian magazine covering news, politics, sports, arts, entertainment, and trends. Includes fiction, poetry, and profiles. Subtitle: Lesbian Magazine. Founded: 1991. Frequency: 6x/yr. Printing Method: Web press. Trim Size: 8 1/2 x 11. Cols./Page: 3. Col. Width: 2 1/2 in. Col. Depth: 7 1/2 in. Key Personnel: Frances Stevens, Publisher/Editor-in-Chief; Katie Brown, Managing Editor; Wendy

York, Advertising Mgr.; Victoria Turner, Circulation Mgr. Subscription: $24. $4 single issue.

Ad Rates:	BW:	$720	Circulation: Paid 32,000
	4C:	$1,320	Non-paid 100
	PCI:	$25	

📖 **512 Educational Foundations**
Caddo Gap Press
3145 Geary Blvd., Ste. 275   Phone: (415)750-9978
San Francisco, CA 94118   Fax: (415)751-0947

📖 **513 France Today**
France Press, Inc.
1051 Divisadero   Phone: (415)921-5100
San Francisco, CA 94115   Fax: (415)921-0213
Magazine covering contemporary issues, events, trends, and travel in France. Founded: 1985. Frequency: 10x/yr. Subscription: $27.

| Ad Rates: | BW: | $500 | Circulation: ‡8,000 |

📖 **514 Grandmasters**
China Direct Publishing, Inc.
PO Box 31578
San Francisco, CA 94131
Sports magazine featuring 48 of the most famous masters andgrandmasters of martial arts. Frequency: Quarterly. Key Personnel: Chin Wing Kong, Editor; Roger D. Hagood, Publisher. Subscription: $19. $4.95 single issue.
Circulation: (Not Reported)

📖 **515 Health**
Hippocrates Partners
301 Howard St., 28th Fl.   Phone: (415)512-9100
San Francisco, CA 94105-2241   Fax: (415)512-9600
Former Title: In Health

📖 **516 Multimedia World**
501 Second St.   Phone: (415)281-8650
San Francisco, CA 94107   Fax: (415)281-3915
Magazine covering computer multimedia hardware and software. Founded: 1991. Frequency: 6x/yr. Key Personnel: Craig Lagrow, Editor-in-Chief.
Circulation: 100,000
Advertising accepted; contact publisher for rates. Formerly: MPC World.

📖 **517 NextWorld**
Intergrated Media, Inc.
501 2nd St.
San Francisco, CA 94107
Magazine explores the symbiotic relationship of people to the computer. Frequency: 2x/mo. Key Personnel: Michael Miley, Publisher; Gordon Haight, Editor. Subscription: $39.90. $4.95 single issue.
Circulation: (Not Reported)

📖 **518 Nonprofit Management and Leadership**
Jossey-Bass Publishers
350 Sansome St.   Phone: (415)433-1740
San Francisco, CA 94104   Fax: (415)433-0499
Journal specializing in the theory and practice of nonprofit management. Founded: 1990. Frequency: Quarterly. Subscription: $45; $72 institutions.
Circulation: (Not Reported)

📖 **519 Northern California Jewish Bulletin**
88 1st St., Ste. 300   Phone: (415)957-9340
San Francisco, CA 94105   Fax: (415)957-0266

📖 **520 Nuclear Tracks and Radiation Measurements**
Pergamon Press
University of San Francisco
Department of Physics   Phone: (415)666-6281
San Francisco, CA 94117   Fax: (415)666-2469
Scientific journal. Frequency: Quarterly. Cols./Page: 2. Col. Width: 7.1 cm. Col. Depth: 23 cm. ISSN: 0735-245X. Subscription: $435 institutions.
Circulation: (Not Reported)
Advertising accepted; contact publisher for rates. Publisher's address: 660 White Plains Rd., Tarrytown, NY 10591-5153; ph one (914)524-9200.

📖 **521 On Our Backs**
526 Castro St.
San Francisco, CA 94114   Phone: (415)861-4723
Entertainment periodical for lesbians containing fiction, features, columns, and pictorials. **Subtitle:** Entertainment For The Adventurous Lesbian. **Founded:** 1984. **Frequency:** 6x/yr. **Printing Method:** Web offset. **Trim Size:** 8 3/8 x 10 7/8. **Cols./Page:** 3. **Col. Width:** 2 3/8 in. **Col. Depth:** 9 1/2 in. **Key Personnel:** Debi Sundahl, Editor; Nan Kinney, Assoc. Publisher; Marnie DeBois, Advertising Mgr. **ISSN:** 0890-2224. **Subscription:** $34.95. $7 single issue.
Ad Rates: BW: $1,400   **Circulation:** ⊕10,000
            4C: $2,200

📖 **522 Public Productivity & Management Review**
Jossey-Bass Publishers
350 Sansome St.   Phone: (415)433-1740
San Francisco, CA 94104   Fax: (415)433-0499
Magazine covering productivity and management improvements. **Founded:** 1976. **Frequency:** Quarterly. **Key Personnel:** Marc Holzer, Editor-in-Chief. **Subscription:** $52; $82 institutions.
                          Circulation: (Not Reported)

📖 **523 Qigong**
China Direct Publishing, Inc.
PO Box 31578
San Francisco, CA 94131
Magazine featuring ancient Chinese holistic exercise for the body, mind, and breath. **Frequency:** Quarterly. **Key Personnel:** Ching Wing Kong, Editor; Roger D. Hagood, Publisher. **Subscription:** $19.80. $4.95 single issue.
                          Circulation: (Not Reported)

📖 **524 Small Business Exchange**
PO Box 422609
San Francisco, CA 94142-2609   Phone: (415)255-6411
Trade newspaper. **Founded:** 1985. **Frequency:** 2x/mo. **Cols./Page:** 5. **Col. Width:** 2 in. **Col. Depth:** 16 in. **Key Personnel:** Gerald W. Johnson, Managing Editor. **ISSN:** 0892-5992. **Subscription:** $92.50-$220. $3-$5 single issue.
Ad Rates: BW: **Circulation:** (Not Reported)
            $2,361.15
            PCI: $41.98
Formerly: Northern California Construction Journal; Southern California Construction Journal; Products & Services Journal; Arizonia Contract Journal.

📖 **525 Spectrum Newspapers Monthly, San Francisco/ Marin/San Mateo**
Spectrum Newspapers
11171 Sun Center Dr., Ste. 110   Phone: (916)852-6222
Rancho Cordova, CA 95670   Fax: (916)852-6397
Newspaper serving active senior citizens, age 55 and older, in San Francisco, San Mateo, and Marin County. **Founded:** 1975. **Frequency:** Monthly. **Printing Method:** Web offset. **Key Personnel:** Bob Carney, Editor; Jacqueline Lucido, Gen. Mgr.; Ridge Eagan, Advertising Dir. **USPS:** 980-481. **Subscription:** $12.
                          Circulation: ‡62,000

📖 **526 Summer Fun**
Time Publishing Ventures, Inc.
501 2nd St.
San Francisco, CA 94107
Magazine features articles on family travel, nutrition, health, and fitness. **Frequency:** 4x/yr. **Key Personnel:** David Markus, Editor; Carol A. Smith, Publisher. **Subscription:** $12. $2.50 single issue.
                          Circulation: (Not Reported)

📖 **527 Sunworld**
Integrated Media, Inc.
501 Second St.   Phone: (415)243-4188
San Francisco, CA 94107   Fax: (415)267-1732
Technical magazine for users of Sun Microsystems computers. **Founded:** 1987. **Frequency:** Monthly. **Printing Method:** Web offset. **Trim Size:** 8 x 10 3/4 in. **Cols./Page:** 3. **Col. Width:** 13 picas. **Col. Depth:** 55.5 picas. **Key Personnel:** Gordon Haight, Publisher; Michael

McCarthy, Editor-in-Chief; Mark Cappel, Exec. Editor; Kane Scarlett, Managing Editor. **ISSN:** 1046-5456.
Ad Rates: BW: $7,575   **Circulation:** 70,000
            4C: $9,395
Formerly: Suntech Journal.

📖 **528 Teacher Education Quarterly**
Caddo Gap Press
3145 Geary Blvd., Ste. 275   Phone: (415)750-9978
San Francisco, CA 94118   Fax: (415)751-0947

🎙 **529 KALW-FM - 91.7**
2576 Harrison St.
San Francisco, CA 94110   Phone: (415)695-5740

🎙 **530 KMTP-TV - Channel 32**
1311 Sutter St., Ste. 200
San Francisco, CA 94109   Phone: (415)394-5687

🎙 **531 KOFY-AM - 1050**
2500 Marin St.   Phone: (415)821-2020
San Francisco, CA 94124   Fax: (415)641-1163

🎙 **532 KOIT-AM - 1260**
400 2nd St.   Phone: (415)777-0965
San Francisco, CA 94107   Fax: (415)896-0965

🎙 **533 KOIT-FM - 96.5**
400 2nd. St.   Phone: (415)777-0965
San Francisco, CA 94107   Fax: (415)896-0965

🎙 **534 Viacom Cablevision of San Francisco**
2055 Folsum St.   Phone: (415)863-8500
San Francisco, CA 94110   Fax: (415)863-1659
Owner: Viacom Cable. **Founded:** 1953. **Cities Served:** San Francisco County.

SAN JOSE

📖 **535 Austin-Healey Magazine**
Austin-Healey Club
Box 6197   Phone: (415)349-9812
San Jose, CA 95150   Fax: (415)349-3750

📖 **536 Khang Chien Magazine**
PO Box 7826   Phone: (408)363-1078
San Jose, CA 95150   Fax: (408)363-1178
Vietnamese-language magazine covering events and developments in Vietnam. **Founded:** 1982 **Frequency:** Monthly. **Key Personnel:** Vu Quang Vinh, Distributing Mgr. **ISSN:** 0892-7588. **Subscription:** $22; $26 Canada; $42 other countries.
                          Circulation: Paid 7,000
                                       Non-paid 2,000
Advertising accepted; contact publisher for rates.

📖 **537 San Jose Post-Record**
Daily Journal Corp.
90 N. 1st St., Ste 100   Phone: (408)292-7833
San Jose, CA 95113   Fax: (408)287-2544

📖 **538 Senior Times**
S.T. Publications
42 E. Santa Clara, Ste. 213   Phone: (408)288-5771
San Jose, CA 95113   Fax: (408)288-5794

🎙 **539 Coast Cable**
2502 Stevens Creek Blvd.   Phone: (408)944-9100
San Jose, CA 95128   Fax: (408)456-0842
Owner: Coast Cable Partners. **Founded:** 1990. **Cities Served:** Santa Clara County East, CA.

540 Heritage Communications, Inc.
234 E. Gish Rd.
Box 114   Phone: (408)452-9100
San Jose, CA 95103-0114   Fax: (408)452-5720
Owner: Tele-Communications, Inc. **Founded:** 1968. **Cities Served:**
Santa Clara West County, Campbell, Cupertino, and Los Gatos, CA.

541 KBAY-FM - 100.3
PO Box 6616   Phone: (408)370-7377
San Jose, CA 95150   **Fax: (408)364-4545**

542 KICU-TV - Channel 36
1585 Schallenberg Rd.   Phone: (408)298-3636
San Jose, CA 95131   **Fax: (408)298-1353**

SAN JUAN CAPISTRANO

543 Dimension Cable Services
26181 Avenido Aeropuerto   Phone: (714)240-1212
San Juan Capistrano, CA 92675   Fax: (714)661-7297
Owner: Times Mirror Cable TV. **Cities Served:** Orange County, San
Diego County, Capistrano Beach, Cota De Caza, El Toro, Emerald
Bay, Laguna Beach, Mission Viejo, Modjeska, San Clemente, San
Juan Capistrano, San Onofre, Silverado, South Laguna, Trabuco
Canyon, and Tustin, CA.

SAN LUIS OBISPO

544 Command Magazine
XTR Corp.
3547-D S. Higuera   Phone: (805)546-9596
San Luis Obispo, CA 93401   Fax: (805)546-0570
Magazine profiling military strategies, analysis, and concepts. **Subtitle:** Military History, Strategy & Analysis. **Founded:** 1989. **Frequency:**
6x/yr. **Trim Size:** 8 1/2 x 11. **Cols./Page:** 3. **Col. Width:** 18 picas. **Col.
Depth:** 9 in. **Key Personnel:** Ty Bomba, Editor; Amiee Stahl,
Advertising Dir.; Chris Perello, Assoc. Editor/Business Mgr. **ISSN:**
1059-5651. **Subscription:** $17.95. $3.95 single issue.
     Circulation: ‡13,000
     Non-paid ‡100
Advertising accepted; contact publisher for rates.

545 KCBX-FM - 90.1
4100 Vachell Ln.
San Luis Obispo, CA 93401   Phone: (805)781-3020
Format: Classical; Jazz; News; Information. **Owner:** KCBX Inc.;
(805)781-3020. **Founded:** 1974. **Operating Hours:** 5:30 a.m.-1 a.m.
Key Personnel: Frank Lanzone, Gen. Mgr. **Wattage:** 5600.

546 KKUS-FM - 98.1
396 Buckley Rd.   Phone: (805)541-8798
San Luis Obispo, CA 93401   **Fax: (805)541-9331**

SAN MARCOS

547 Dimension Cable TV
2790 Business Park Dr.
Vista, CA 92083   Phone: (619)598-6666
Owner: Times Mirror Cable TV. **Founded:** 1972. **Cities Served:** San
Diego County, Bonsall, Cardiff-by-the-Sea, Encinitas, Escondido,
Leucadia, Oceanside, Ramona, Rancho Santa Fe, San Dieguito,
Solana Beach, Vista, and Whispering Palms, CA.

SAN MATEO

548 Coastside Chronicle
San Mateo Times Newspaper Group
PO Box 5400   Phone: (415)340-4100
San Mateo, CA 94402   **Fax: (415)348-4446**

549 New Media
Hyper Media Communications, Inc.
901 Mariner's Island Blvd., Ste. 365
San Mateo, CA 94404
Magazine for the creators, producers, and deliverers of computer-generated presentations and multimedia business and educational
products. **Frequency:** 2x/mo. **Key Personnel:** David Bunnell, Publisher; Bechy Waring, Editor. **Subscription:** $24. $3.95 single issue.
     Circulation: (Not Reported)

550 The Pullman Herald
PO Box 1491
San Mateo, CA 94401-0872
Ceased publication.

SAN PABLO

551 The Advocate
Contra Costa College
2600 Mission Bell Dr.   **Phone: (510)235-7800**
San Pablo, CA 94806   **Fax: (510)236-6768**

SAN RAFAEL

552 Grocers Report
Super Markets Productions Ltd.
PO Box 6124   Phone: (415)479-0211
San Rafael, CA 94903   **Fax: (415)479-0211**

553 Marin County Court Reporter
4380 Redwood Hwy., Ste B-10   **Phone: (415)479-4311**
San Rafael, CA 94903   **Fax: (415)479-4314**

554 Viacom Cablevision of Marion County
1111 Anderson Dr.
San Rafael, CA 94901   Phone: (415)457-9100
Owner: Viacom Cable. **Cities Served:** Marin County, Belvedere, Corte
Madera, Fairfax, Kentfield, Lagunitas, Marin City, San Anselmo, San
Geronimo, San Rafael, Sausalito, Tuburon, and Woodacre, CA.

SAN RAMON

**555 Ed, The Official Publication of USDLA (United
States Distance Learning Association)**
Box 5106   Phone: (415)820-5563
San Ramon, CA 94583-0906   Fax: (415)820-5894
Journal covering applications of teleconferencing to education.
Founded: 1985. **Frequency:** Monthly. **Trim Size:** 8 1/2 x 11. **Cols./
Page:** 2. **Key Personnel:** Renee Wilmeth, Publisher/Dir.; Pam Parks,
Sales Mgr. **Subscription:** $100.
     Circulation: (Not Reported)
Advertising accepted; contact publisher for rates.

556 The Nooner Magazine
2491 San Ramon Valley Blve., Ste. 1-
355   Phone: (510)833-2578
San Ramon, CA 94583   Fax: (510)833-8404
Magazine containing information on entertainment, leisure, community, and business events in the San Ramon, CA area. **Subtitle:** Fun
Reading for Valley Business. **Founded:** 1989. **Frequency:** Monthly.
Printing Method: Web offset. **Trim Size:** 11 x 17. **Cols./Page:** 4. **Col.
Width:** 2 1/4 in. **Col. Depth:** 15 1/4 in. **Key Personnel:** Karen Fagen,
Editor and Publisher; Sam Williams, Publisher; Rob Fagen, Circulation Mgr. **Subscription:** $12.99. $1.09 single issue.
Ad Rates: PCI: $27.50   **Circulation:** Paid 11
     Non-paid 15,000

SANGER

557 El Sol Del Valle
718 N St.   Phone: (209)875-8771
Sanger, CA 93657   **Fax: (209)875-6455**

SANTA ANA

558 Anaheim Hills Highlander
Orange County Register
625 N. Grand Ave.   **Phone: (714)835-1234**
Santa Ana, CA 92711   **Fax: (714)542-5037**

559 Orange County Reporter
Daily Journal Corporation
915 E. 1st St.   Phone: (213)229-5300
Los Angeles, CA **90012**-4042   Fax: (213)680-3682

SANTA BARBARA

📖 560 Buyouts & Acquisitions
5290 Overpass Rd.
Santa Barbara, CA 93111   Phone: (805)964-7841
Ceased publication.

📖 561 Companion Animal Practice
Veterinary Practice Publishing Co.
PO Box 4457
Santa Barbara, CA 93103   Phone: (805)965-1028
Ceased publication.

📖 562 Feline Practice
Veterinary Practice Publishing Co.
PO Box 4457   Phone: (805)965-1028
Santa Barbara, CA 93140-4457   Fax: (805)965-0722
Journal covering feline medicine and surgery. **Founded:** 1971. **Frequency:** 6x/yr. **Key Personnel:** Nancy A. Bull, Publisher. **ISSN:** 1057-6614. **Subscription:** $28; $50 other countries.
Ad Rates: BW: $1,295   **Circulation:** 6,500
           4C: $2,120

📖 563 The Journal of Services Marketing
Journal of Services Marketing, Inc.
108 Loma Media Rd.   Phone: (805)564-1313
Santa Barbara, CA 93103   Fax: (805)564-8800
Academic journal edited for practitioners. **Founded:** 1987. **Frequency:** Quarterly. **ISSN:** 0887-6045. **Subscription:** $60; $95 institutions; $100 other countries. $25 single issue.
                        Circulation: (Not Reported)

📖 564 Veterinary Practice Staff
Veterinary Practice Publishing Co.
PO Box 4457   Phone: (805)965-1028
Santa Barbara, CA 93140-4457   Fax: (805)965-0722
Professional magazine covering current ideas and new information in veterinary medicine. **Founded:** 1989. **Frequency:** 6x/yr. **ISSN:** 1047-8639. **Subscription:** $28; $45 foreign.
Ad Rates: BW: $1,295   **Circulation:** 11,000
           4C: $2,120

🎙 565 Cox Cable Santa Barbara
22 S. Fairview Ave.   Phone: (805)683-7751
Santa Barbara, CA 93117   Fax: (805)964-6069
Owner: Cox Cable Communications. **Founded:** 1962. **Cities Served:** Santa Barbara County, Carpinteria, Goleta, Isla Vista, Mission Canyon, and Montecito, CA.

🎙 566 KCQR-FM - 94.5
4141 State St., Ste. E-9   Phone: (805)964-7670
Santa Barbara, CA 93110   Fax: (805)683-2753
Format: Classic Rock. **Owner:** South Coast Broadcasting Inc. **Founded:** 1989. **Operating Hours:** Continuous. **Key Personnel:** Sue Romaine, Gen. Mgr.; Greg Bryce, Operations Mgr.; Tom Van Sant, Program Dir.; Dave Hefferman, Promotions Dir.

SANTA CLARA

📖 567 Spectrum Newspapers Monthly, Santa Clara/ Monterey
Spectrum Newspapers
11171 Sun Center Dr., Ste. 110   Phone: (916)852-6222
Rancho Cordova, CA 95670   Fax: (916)852-6397
Newspaper serving active senior citizens, 55 and older, in Santa Clara and Monterey. **Founded:** 1975. **Frequency:** Monthly. **Printing Method:** Web offset. **Key Personnel:** Bob Carney, Editor; Jacqueline Lucido, Gen. Mgr.; Ridge Eagan, Advertising Dir. **USPS:** 980-481. **Subscription:** $12.
                        Circulation: ‡70,000

🎙 568 KSCU-FM - 103.3
500 El Camino Real – 3207
Santa Clara University   Phone: (408)554-4413
Santa Clara, CA 95053-3207   Fax: (408)554-5544

SANTA CLARITA

📖 569 MA Training
Rainbow Publications, Inc.
24715 Rockefeller
PO Box 918   Phone: (805)257-4066
Santa Clarita, CA 91355-9018   Fax: (805)257-3028

SANTA CRUZ

📖 570 Matrix Women's Newsmagazine
108 Locust St., No. 14
Santa Cruz, CA 95060   Phone: (408)429-1238
Periodical for feminists in the central coast and Bay Area regions of California. **Frequency:** Monthly. **Subscription:** $14.
                        Circulation: (Not Reported)

🎙 571 KUSP-FM - 88.9
PO Box 423
203 8th Ave.   Phone: (408)476-2800
Santa Cruz, CA 95061   Fax: (408)476-2800

🎙 572 United Artists Entertainment Co.
420 May Ave.
Box 1910   Phone: (408)439-5099
Santa Cruz, CA 95060   Fax: (408)439-5065
Owner: Tele-Communications, Inc. **Founded:** 1989. **Cities Served:** Santa Cruz County, Apto, Ben Lomond, and Scotts Valley, CA.

SANTA MONICA

📖 573 Chocolate and Nut World
Lott Publishing Co.
PO Box 1107
Santa Monica, CA 90406   **Phone: (310)397-4217**

📖 574 Computer Publishing Magazine
Pacific Magazine Group
513 Wilshire Blvd., Ste. 344
Santa Monica, CA 90401   Phone: (213)455-1414
Ceased publication.

📖 575 Cracker/Snack World
Lott Publishing Co.
PO Box 1107
Santa Monica, CA 90406   Phone: (310)397-4217
Trade news about cracker and snack industries. **Founded:** 1988. **Frequency:** Quarterly. **Key Personnel:** Dave Lotz, Editor and Publisher. **Subscription:** $24. $6 single issue.
Ad Rates: BW: $198   **Circulation:** Paid 300
                                     Non-paid 1,700

📖 576 On Montana
PO Box 1077   Phone: (310)319-1680
Santa Monica, CA 90406   Fax: (310)393-4750
Community newspaper. **Founded:** 1984. **Frequency:** Monthly. **Cols./Page:** 5. **Col. Depth:** 13 in. **Subscription:** $9.
                        Circulation: (Not Reported)
Advertising accepted; contact publisher for rates.

🎙 577 Century Southwest Cable
2939 Nebraska Ave.
Santa Monica, CA 90404   Phone: (310)829-7079
Owner: Century Communications Corp. **Founded:** 1967. **Cities Served:** Los Angeles and San Bernadino South Counties, Alta Loma, Bel Air, Bel Canyon, Beverly Crest, Beverly Hills, Boyle Heights, Cucamonga, Eagle Rock, El Segundo, El Sereno, Elysian Park, Glassell, Griffith Park, Highland Park, Hollywood, Lincoln Heights, Marina Del Ray, Mount Washington, Pacific Palisades, Santa Monica, Sherman Oaks, West Hollywood, West Los Angeles, and Westwood, CA.

Ad Rates: GLR = general line rate; BW = one-time black & white page rate; 4C = one-time four color page rate; SAU = standard advertising unit rate; CNU = Canadian newspaper advertising unit rate; PCI = per column inch rate.
Circulation: ★ = ABC; △ = BPA; ◆ = CAC; ● = CCAB; □ = VAC; ⊕ = PO Statement; ‡ = Publisher's Report; Boldface figures = sworn; Light figures = estimated.
Entry type: 📖 = Print; 🎙 = Broadcast.

37

SANTA ROSA

578 Sonoma County Women's Voices
PO Box 4448
Santa Rosa, CA 95402   Phone: (707)575-5654
Periodical addressing issues and concerns of women in Sonoma County, CA. Includes calendar of events, news, features, poetry, and review. **Founded:** 1980. **Frequency:** Monthly. **Printing Method:** Web offset. **Cols./Page:** 3. **Col. Width:** 3 1/4 in. **Col. Depth:** 16 in. **Subscription:** $10.

Ad Rates:	BW:	$430	Circulation:	300
	PCI:	$10	Non-paid	3,700

579 KHTT-FM - 92.9
Box 1598   Phone: (707)545-3313
Santa Rosa, CA 95402   **Fax: (707)545-0124**

580 KSRO-AM - 1350
Box 1598   Phone: (707)545-3313
Santa Rosa, CA 95402   **Fax: (707)545-0124**

SANTEE

581 Wishing Well Magazine
Laddie's Ventures II
PO Box 713090
Santee, CA 92072-3090   Phone: (619)443-4818
Confidential correspondence/meeting service for women who love women. **Founded:** 1974. **Frequency:** 6x/yr. **Printing Method:** Offset. **Trim Size:** 7 x 8 1/2. **Cols./Page:** 2. **Col. Width:** 3 in. **Col. Depth:** 7 1/2 in. **Key Personnel:** Laddie Holser, Editor and Publisher. **Subscription:** $25. $5 single issue.

Ad Rates:	BW:	$100	Circulation:	Paid ‡4,500
	PCI:	$10		Non-paid ‡500

SAUSALITO

582 Whole Earth Review
Point Foundation
27 Gate 5 Rd.   Phone: (415)332-1716
Sausalito, CA 94965   **Fax: (415)332-2416**

SIGNAL HILL

583 The Signal
Signal Hill Publishing Co.
2107 Cherry Ave., Ste. B   Phone: (310)498-0707
Signal Hill, CA 90806   Fax: (310)498-7847
Community newspaper. **Founded:** 1990. **Frequency:** Weekly. **Printing Method:** Web offset. **Cols./Page:** 5. **Col. Width:** 11 picas. **Col. Depth:** 87 picas. **Key Personnel:** Thomas K. Allen, Publisher. **Subscription:** Free.

Ad Rates:	BW:	$637.50	Circulation: Free □21,014
	PCI:	$10	

SONOMA

584 Spectrum Newspapers Monthly, Sonoma
Spectrum Newspapers
11171 Sun Center Dr., Ste. 110   Phone: (916)852-6222
Rancho Cordova, CA 95670   Fax: (916)852-6397
Newspaper serving active senior citizens, 55 and older, in Sonoma. **Founded:** 1975. **Frequency:** Monthly. **Printing Method:** Web offset. **Key Personnel:** Bob Carney, Editor; Jacqueline Lucido, Gen. Mgr.; Ridge Eagan, Advertising Dir. **USPS:** 980-481. **Subscription:** $12.
Circulation: ‡29,500

SOQUEL

585 Paddle Sports
Paddle Sports Magazine
PO Box 1388
Soquel, CA 95073
Sports magazine covering a complete range of paddling activities. **Frequency:** Quarterly. **Key Personnel:** Joseph Grassadonia, Editor; Penny Wells, Publisher. **Subscription:** $7.95. $2.95 single issue.
Circulation: (Not Reported)

SOUTH LAKE TAHOE

586 Tahoe Action
Tahoe Daily Tribune, Inc.
PO Box 1358   Phone: (916)541-3880
South Lake Tahoe, CA 96151   Fax: (916)541-0373
Lake Tahoe's entertainment guide. **Frequency:** Weekly. **Trim Size:** 11 3/8 X 14. **Cols./Page:** 5. **Col. Depth:** 13 in. **Key Personnel:** John Sloan, Mng. Editor; Ron Stewart, Publisher. **Subscription:** Free.
Circulation: Paid ‡10,000
Free ‡32,000
Advertising accepted; contact publisher for rates.

SPRING VALLEY

587 Waves
Windate Enterprises, Inc.
PO Box 368   Phone: (619)660-0402
Spring Valley, CA 91976   Fax: (619)660-0408
International ocean technology newsmagazine. **Founded:** 1981. **Frequency:** 6x/yr.
Circulation: (Not Reported)
Advertising accepted; contact publisher for rates.

STANFORD

588 Montage
Stanford University
PO Box 9476
Stanford, CA 94309
Bilingual magazine addressing student issues in the U.S. and Commonwealth of Independent States. **Frequency:** Quarterly. **Key Personnel:** Mark McKean, Editor; Susan Weiner, Publisher. **Subscription:** $20. $4 single issue.
Circulation: (Not Reported)

STOCKTON

589 Spectrum Newspapers Weekly, Stockton
Spectrum Newspapers
11171 Sun Center Dr., Ste. 110   Phone: (916)852-6222
Rancho Cordova, CA 95670   Fax: (916)852-6397
Newspaper serving active senior citizens, 55 and older, in the Stockton area. **Founded:** 1975. **Frequency:** Weekly. **Printing Method:** Web offset. **Key Personnel:** Bob Carney, Editor; Jacqueline Lucido, Gen. Mgr.; Ridge Eagan, Natl. Advertising Dir. **USPS:** 980-481. **Subscription:** $18.32.
Circulation: ‡12,750

590 Continental Cablevision
6505 Tam O'Shanter   Phone: (209)473-4955
Stockton, CA 95210   Fax: (209)473-8177
Owner: Continental Cablevision, Inc. **Founded:** 1973. **Cities Served:** San Joaquin County, French Camp, Lathrop, Lincoln Village West, Linden, and Manteca, CA.

591 KJAX-AM - 1280
110 N. El Dorado   Phone: (209)948-5569
Stockton, CA 95202   **Fax: (209)464-9999**

592 KJOY-FM - 99.3
110 N. El Dorado St.   Phone: (209)948-5569
Stockton, CA 95202   **Fax: (209)464-9999**

TORRANCE

593 Chiropractic Products
Novicom, Inc.
3510 Torrance Blvd., No. 315   Phone: (310)316-8112
Torrance, CA 90503   Fax: (310)316-8422
Magazine featuring new products and services available in the chiropractic field. **Founded:** 1985. **Frequency:** 8x/yr. **Printing Method:** Web offset. **Trim Size:** 8 3/8 x 10 7/8. **Cols./Page:** 3. **Key Personnel:** Julie Craig, Editor; Marvin Rosenfeld, Publisher; George Ross, Advertising Mgr. **ISSN:** 1041-2360. **Subscription:** $16. $2 single issue.

Ad Rates:	BW:	$1,470	Circulation: Controlled 35,000
	4C:	$2,070	

◫ **594 Contemporary Podiatric Physician**
Novicom, Inc.
3510 Torrance Blvd., No. 315   Phone: (310)316-8112
Torrance, CA 90503   Fax: (310)316-8422
Magazine featuring articles pertaining to primary care. **Founded:**
1991. **Frequency:** 6x/yr. **Printing Method:** Web offset. **Trim Size:** 8 3/8
x 10 7/8. **Cols./Page:** 3. **Key Personnel:** Nancy Girardini, Editor;
Marvin Rosenfeld, Publisher; George Ross, Advertising Mgr. **Sub-
scription:** $12. $2 single issue.
Ad Rates: BW: $1,090   **Circulation:** Controlled 10,000
          4C: $1,690

◫ **595 Orthopedic Products**
Novicom, Inc.
3510 Torrance Blvd., No. 315   Phone: (310)316-8112
Torrance, CA 90503   Fax: (310)316-8422
Magazine featuring new products and services available in the
orthopedic field. **Founded:** 1992. **Frequency:** 6x/yr. **Printing Method:**
Web offset. **Trim Size:** 8 3/8 x 10 7/8. **Cols./Page:** 3. **Key Personnel:**
Susan Fennell, Editor; Marvin Rosenfeld, Publisher; George Ross,
Advertising Mgr. **Subscription:** $12. $2 single issue.
Ad Rates: BW: $1,200   **Circulation:** Controlled 18,000
          4C: $1,800

◫ **596 Physical Therapy Products**
Novicom, Inc.
3510 Torrance Blvd., No. 315   Phone: (310)316-8112
Torrance, CA 90503   Fax: (310)316-8422
Magazine featuring new products and services available in the
physical therapy field. **Founded:** 1989. **Frequency:** 6x/yr. **Printing
Method:** Web offset. **Trim Size:** 8 3/8 x 10 7/8. **Cols./Page:** 3. **Key
Personnel:** Julie Craig, Editor; Marvin Rosenfeld, Publisher; George
Ross, Advertising Mgr. **ISSN:** 1059-096X. **Subscription:** $12. $2
single issue.
Ad Rates: BW: $1,595   **Circulation:** Controlled 40,000
          4C: $2,295

◫ **597 Plastic Surgery Products**
Novicom Inc.
3510 Torrance Blvd., No. 315   Phone: (310)316-8112
Torrance, CA 90503   Fax: (310)316-8422
Magazine featuring new products and services available in the plastic
surgery field. **Founded:** 1991. **Frequency:** 6x/yr. **Printing Method:** Web
offset. **Trim Size:** 8 3/8 x 10 7/8. **Key Personnel:** Sue Fennell, Editor;
George Ross, Advertising Mgr.; Marvin Rosenfeld, Publisher. **Sub-
scription:** $12. $2 single issue.
Ad Rates: BW: $1,040   **Circulation:** Controlled 18,000
          4C: $1,640

◫ **598 Podiatric Products**
Novicom, Inc.
3510 Torrance Blvd., No. 315   Phone: (310)316-8112
Torrance, CA 90503   Fax: (310)316-8422
Magazine featuring new products and services available in the
podiatric field. **Founded:** 1984. **Frequency:** 6x/yr. **Printing Method:**
Web offset. **Trim Size:** 8 3/8 x 10 7/8. **Cols./Page:** 3. **Key Personnel:**
Nancy Girardini, Editor; Marvin Rosenfeld, Publisher; George Ross,
Advertising Mgr. **ISSN:** 0890-3972. **Subscription:** $12. $2 single issue.
Ad Rates: BW: $1,040   **Circulation:** Controlled 13,000
          4C: $1,640

🎙 **599 Paragon Communications**
1511 Cravens Ave.   Phone: (310)618-9496
Torrance, CA 90501   Fax: (310)328-7628
Owner: Paragon Communications. **Founded:** 1983. **Cities Served:** Los
Angeles County, El Segundo, Gerdena, Hawthorne, Lawndale, and
North Torrance, CA.

TUJUNGA

🎙 **600 Colony Communications, Inc.**
10000 Commerce Ave.   Phone: (818)352-8621
Tujunga, CA 90142   Fax: (818)352-7745
Owner: Colony Communications, Inc. **Founded:** 1957. **Cities Served:**

Los Angeles County, Kagel Canyon, Lakeview Terrace, Pacoima, Sun
Valley, Sunland, Sylmar, and Tujunga, CA.

TWENTY-NINE PALMS

◫ **601 The Lesbian News**
PO Box 1430   Phone: (619)367-3386
Twenty-nine Palms, CA 92277   Fax: (619)367-3386
Magazine of lesbian and gay-oriented articles, features, and cartoons.
Founded: 1975. **Frequency:** Monthly. **Printing Method:** Web offset.
Trim Size: 10 1/2 x 14 1/4. **Cols./Page:** 3. **Col. Width:** 3 1/4 in. **Col.
Depth:** 14 in. **Key Personnel:** Deborah Bergman, Editor and Publisher;
Karen Hight, Advertising Dir. **Subscription:** $35; $15 students. $5
single issue.
Ad Rates: BW: $495   **Circulation:** ‡27,000
          4C: $745
Available on cassette. **Additional Contact Information:** Toll-free 800-
237-0277.

UKIAH

◫ **602 Ukiah Daily Journal**
590 S. School St.
PO Box 749   **Phone: (707)468-3500**
Ukiah, CA 95482   **Fax: (707)468-5780**

UNIVERSAL CITY

◫ **603 Pratfall**
PO Box 8341
Universal City, CA 91608   Phone: (818)985-2713
Magazine featuring Laurel and Hardy. **Founded:** 1969. **Frequency:**
Irregular. **Printing Method:** Litho. **Trim Size:** 8 1/2 x 11. **Subscription:**
$2 single issue.
          Circulation: 1,500
Advertising not accepted.

VALENCIA

◫ **604 Traveling Times**
Traveling Times, Inc.
25115 W. Ave. Stanford   Phone: (805)295-1250
Valencia, CA 91355   Fax: (805)295-8558
Travel magazine. **Founded:** 1973. **Frequency:** Quarterly. **Printing
Method:** Web offset. **Key Personnel:** Mirko A. Ilich, Editor-in-Chief/
Publisher.
          Circulation: ‡1,650,000
Advertising not accepted.

VALLEJO

🎙 **605 KNBA-AM - 1190**
3267 Sonoma Blvd.   Phone: (707)644-8944
Vallejo, CA 94590   **Fax: (707)644-3736**

VAN NUYS

◫ **606 NAILpro**
Creative Age Publications, Inc.
7628 Densmore Ave.   Phone: (818)782-7328
Van Nuys, CA 91406   Fax: (818)782-7450
Magazine for nail salon owners and manicurists. **Founded:** 1990.
Frequency: Monthly. **Printing Method:** Web offset. **Trim Size:** 8 x 10
3/4. **Cols./Page:** 3. **Key Personnel:** Barbara Feiner, Exec. Editor;
Deborah Carver, Publisher; Carol Summer, Publisher. **ISSN:** 1049-
4553. **Subscription:** $31. $5 single issue.
Ad Rates: BW: $2,772   **Circulation:** Paid ‡4,200
          4C: $3,652   Non-paid ‡29,300
Formerly: The Magazine for Nail Professionals.

Ad Rates: GLR = general line rate; BW = one-time black & white page rate; 4C = one-time four color page rate; SAU = standard advertising unit rate;
CNU = Canadian newspaper advertising unit rate; PCI = per column inch rate.
Circulation: ★ = ABC; △ = BPA; ◆ = CAC; ● = CCAB; □ = VAC; ⊕ = PO Statement; ‡ = Publisher's Report; Boldface figures = sworn; Light figures = estimated.
Entry type: ◫ = Print; 🎙 = Broadcast.

📖 **607 West Coast Lifestyle Magazine**
14148 Burbank Blvd., Ste. 7
Van Nuys, CA 91401
Phone: (818)780-8400
Fax: (818)780-8979
Lifestyle magazine. **Founded:** 1984. **Frequency:** 6x/yr. **Key Personnel:** W. Bill Golding, Editor and Publisher.
Circulation: Paid ★75,000
Advertising accepted; contact publisher for rates. **Formerly:** L.A. Lifestyle; DBA West Coast Lifestyle.

🎙 **608 UAE**
15055 Oxnard St.
Van Nuys, CA 91411
Phone: (818)785-9090
Fax: (818)376-9090
Owner: Tele-Communications, Inc. **Founded:** 1986. **Cities Served:** Los Angeles County, North Hollywood, San Fernando, and Sherman Oaks, CA.

VISTA

📖 **609 Mobile Homes Courier**
A & M Publishers
425 W. Vista Way
Vista, CA 92083
Phone: (619)724-7161
Fax: (619)726-3064

WALNUT CREEK

📖 **610 Contra Costa News Register**
601 N. Main St., Ste. 107
PO Box 4779
Walnut Creek, CA 94596
Phone: (510)934-2780
Fax: (510)934-2532

📖 **611 Contra Costa Times**
2640 Shadelands Dr.
PO Box 5088
Walnut Creek, CA 94596-1087
Phone: (510)935-2525
Fax: (510)943-8362

📖 **612 Rossmoor News**
Golden Rain Foundation
PO Box 2190
Walnut Creek, CA 94595
Phone: (510)939-0622
Fax: (510)935-8348

WEST COVINA

📖 **613 West Covina Highlander**
Highlander Newspapers
18383 E. Railroad St.
City of Industry, CA 91748
Phone: (818)854-8700
Fax: (818)854-8719

WEST HILLS

📖 **614 Golden Isis Magazine**
Bldg. 105, Box 137
23233 Saticoy St.
West Hills, CA 91304
Journal focusing on mystical surrealism and the occult, especially goddess-inspired. **Founded:** 1980. **Frequency:** Quarterly. **Trim Size:** 5 1/2 x 8.1/2. **Key Personnel:** Gerina Dunwich, Editor and Publisher. **Subscription:** $15. $3.95 single issue.
Circulation: (Not Reported)
Advertising accepted; contact publisher for rates.

WEST SACRAMENTO

📖 **615 Stage Directions**
SMW Communications Inc.
3020 Beacon Blvd.
West Sacramento, CA 95691-3436
Phone: (916)373-0201
Fax: (916)373-0232
Publication for and about community, regional and academic theater. **Founded:** 1988. **Frequency:** 10x/yr. **Printing Method:** Offset. **Trim Size:** 8 1/2 x 11. **Cols./Page:** 3. **Key Personnel:** Stephen Peithman, Editor; Susan Wershing, Publisher. **ISSN:** 1047-1901. **Subscription:** $26. $3.50 single issue.

Ad Rates:	BW:	$575	Circulation: ‡2,200
	4C:	$858	Non-paid ‡300
	PCI:	$60	

WESTLAKE VILLAGE

🎙 **616 Ventura County Cablevision**
2645 Townsgate Rd., Ste. 200
Westlake Village, CA 91361
Phone: (805)379-5300
Fax: (805)379-5321
Founded: 1963. **Key Personnel:** Alexander Zwissler, Pres.; Dan Deutsch, V.P.; Charles Schrum, Dir. of Engineering; Richard N. Velen, Dir. of Marketing; Pat Palmer, Dir. of Customer Service. **Cities Served:** Los Angeles County, Ventura County, Calabasas, Camarillo, Fillmore, Meiners Oaks, Moorpark, Newbury Park, Ojai, Piru, Santa Paula, Thousand Oaks, and Westlake Village, CA: 86,500 subscribing households; 37 channels; 3 community access channels; 42 hours per week of community access programming.

WILLITS

🎙 **617 KLLK-AM - 1250**
12 W. Valley St.
Willits, CA 95490
Phone: (707)459-1250
Fax: (707)459-1251

WILLOWS

🎙 **618 KIQS-AM - 1560**
118 W. Sycamore
PO Box 7
Willows, CA 95988
Phone: (916)934-4654
Fax: (916)934-4656
Format: Spanish. **Network(s):** ABC. **Owner:** Margaret Ann Rusnak, at above address. **Founded:** 1961. **Operating Hours:** Sunrise-sunset. **Key Personnel:** Anthony Rusnak, Gen. Mgr./Owner; Peggy Rusnak, Office Mgr. and Program Dir.; Norm Gardner, Sports and Music Dir. **Wattage:** 250. **Ad Rates:** $3.35 for 10 seconds; $3.75-$5.95 for 30 seconds; $4.70-$7.60 for 60 seconds. **Additional Contact Information:** Alternate telephone (916)934-5054.

🎙 **619 KIQS-FM - 105.5**
118 W. Sycamore
PO Box 7
Willows, CA 95988
Phone: (916)934-4654
Fax: (916)934-4656
Format: Adult Contemporary; Contemporary Country. **Network(s):** ABC. **Owner:** Margaret Ann Rusnak, at above address. **Founded:** 1961. **Operating Hours:** 6 a.m.-10 p.m. **Key Personnel:** Anthony Rusnak, Gen. Mgr./Owner; Peggy Rusnak, Office Mgr. and Program Dir.; Norm Gardner, Sports and Music Dir. **Wattage:** 5400. **Ad Rates:** Combined rates available with KIQS-AM: $5.25 for 10 seconds; $6.20-$9.30 for 30 seconds; $7.80-$11.85 for 60 seconds. **Additional Contact Information:** Alternate telephone (916)934-5054.

WOODLAND

📖 **620 For Patients Only**
20335 Ventura Blvd., No. 400
Woodland, CA 91364
Phone: (818)704-5555
Fax: (818)704-6500
Lifestyle magazine for dialysis and kidney transplantation patients. **Founded:** 1989. **Frequency:** Bimonthly. **Printing Method:** Sheetfed offset. **Trim Size:** 8 3/8 x 11. **Cols./Page:** 3. **Col. Width:** 2 1/8 in. **Col. Depth:** 10 in. **Key Personnel:** Loren Frank, Editor; Susan Sommer, Asst. Publisher; Joan Harrison, Advertising Mgr. **ISSN:** 0899-837X. **USPS:** 558-790. **Subscription:** $15.

Ad Rates:	BW:	$1,715	Circulation: (Not Reported)
	4C:	$2,540	
	PCI:	$100	

WOODLAND HILLS

📖 **621 Bus World**
Stauss Publications
PO Box 39
Woodland Hills, CA **91365**
Phone: (818)710-0208
Fax: (818)710-0208

📖 **622 Men's Fitness**
Weider Publications
21100 Erwin St.
Woodland Hills, CA 91367
Phone: (818)884-6800
Fax: (818)704)5734

📖 **623 Mobile Office**
CurtCo Publishing
21800 Oxnard St., No. 250
Woodland Hills, CA 91367
Phone: (818)593-6100
Fax: (818)593-6153

📖 **624 Mobile Office Magazine's Quarterly Cellular Buyers' Guide**
CurtCo Publishing
21800 Oxnard St., No. 250   Phone: (818)593-6100
Woodland Hills, CA 91367   Fax: (818)593-6153

📖 **625 Portable Computing**
Curtco Publishing
21800 Oxnard St., Ste. 250
Woodland Hills, CA 91367   Phone: (818)593-6106

YORBA LINDA

📖 **626 Yorba Linda Star**
Orange County Register
625 N. Grand Ave.
PO Box 11626   Phone: (714)835-1234
Santa Ana, CA 92711   Fax: (714)542-5037

COLORADO

ALAMOSA

627 The Alamosa News
SLV Publishing
410 San Juan Ave.   Phone: (719)589-5424
Alamosa, CO 81101   Fax: (719)589-3387
Newspaper. **Founded:** 1990. **Frequency:** Weekly (Wed.). **Printing Method:** Offset. **Trim Size:** 10 1/2 x 16. **Cols./Page:** 5. **Key Personnel:** Steve Haynes, Publisher/Advertising Mgr. **USPS:** 007-952. **Subscription:** $16.95; $25.95 other countries.
Ad Rates: BW: $396   **Circulation:** Paid ⊕**401**
          PCI: $4.95   Non-paid ⊕**6**
Additional Contact Information: Mail ad material to: Steve Haynes, SLV Publishing, 229 Adams S t., Monte Vista, CO 81144.

ARVADA

628 Cattle Guard
Colorado Cattlemen's Assn.
8833 Ralston Rd.   **Phone: (303)431-6422**
Arvada, CO 80002-2839   **Fax: (303)431-6446**

AURORA

629 KDEN-AM - 1340
10600 E. Exposition Ave., Ste. B
Aurora, CO 80012-2107

BERTHOUD

630 The Old Berthoud Recorder
344 Mountain Ave.
PO Box J   Phone: (303)532-3715
Berthoud, CO 80513   **Fax: (303)532-3918**

BOULDER

631 Blues Access
1514 North St.   Phone: (303)443-7245
Boulder, CO 80304   Fax: (303)939-9729
Magazine providing articles and information on blues musicians. **Founded:** 1990. **Frequency:** Quarterly. **Printing Method:** Web offset. **Trim Size:** 8 1/8 x 10 5/8. **Key Personnel:** Cary Wolfson, Editor and Publisher. **Subscription:** $12.
Ad Rates: BW: $450   **Circulation:** ‡1,700
                                       Non-paid ‡10,300

632 Practical Survial
Mountain Star International
1750 30th St., Ste. 498
Boulder, CO 80301
Magazine profiling natural lifestyles. **Frequency:** 6x/year. **Key Personnel:** Tom Slizewski, Editor; J. Lynn Brown, Publisher. **Subscription:** $18. $3.95 single issue.
                                Circulation: (Not Reported)

633 Women's Sports & Fitness
Sports & Fitness, Inc.
2025 Pearl St.   Phone: (303)440-5111
Boulder, CO 80302   Fax: (303)440-3313

634 KBOL-AM - 1490
3085 Bluff St.
PO Box 146   Phone: (303)444-1490
Boulder, CO 80306   **Fax: (303)442-5265**

635 KUCB-AM - 530
UMC
Campus Box 27
Boulder, CO 80309   Phone: (303)492-5031
Format: Alternative/Independent/Progressive. **Key Personnel:** Kim McCleskey, Music Dir. **Ad Rates:** Noncommercial.

636 TCI Cablevision of Colorado
Box 17610
Boulder, CO 80301-2514   Phone: (303)443-6836
Owner: Tele-Communications, Inc. **Founded:** 1965. **Cities Served:** Boulder County, CO.

CENTER

637 Center Post-Dispatch
SLV Publishing
PO Box 1059   Phone: (719)754-3172
Center, CO 81125-1059   Fax: (719)852-3387

COLORADO SPRINGS

638 American Hockey Magazine
The Publishing Group, Inc.
4965 North 30th St.   Phone: (719)599-5500
Colorado Springs, CO 80919   Fax: (719)599-5994

639 Discipleship Journal
Nav Press
PO Box 35004   Phone: (719)531-3529
Colorado Springs, CO 80935   Fax: (719)598-7128

Ad Rates: GLR = general line rate; BW = one-time black & white page rate; 4C = one-time four color page rate; SAU = standard advertising unit rate; CNU = Canadian newspaper advertising unit rate; PCI = per column inch rate.
Circulation: ★ = ABC; △ = BPA; ◆ = CAC; ● = CCAB; □ = VAC; ⊕ = PO Statement; ‡ = Publisher's Report; Boldface figures = sworn; Light figures = estimated.
Entry type: ▣ = Print; ♣ = Broadcast.

640 Focus on the Family Magazine
Focus on the Family
420 N. Cascade   Phone: (719)531-3400
Colorado Springs, CO 80903   Fax: (719)531-3499
Magazine containing marriage and parenting articles from a Christian perspective. **Founded:** 1982. **Frequency:** Monthly **Printing Method:** Web offset. **Trim Size:** 8 x 10 3/4. **Cols./Page:** 3. **Col. Width:** 13 picas. **Key Personnel:** James C. Dobson, Pres./Publisher; Mike Yorkey, Editor; Rolf Zettersten, Exec.V.P.; Sydna Hawthorne-Masse, Circulation Mgr. **ISSN:** 0894-3346. **Subscription:** Free to members.
    Circulation: Free 1,800,000

Advertising not accepted.

641 The Olympian
U.S. Olympic Committee
One Olympic Plaza   **Phone: (719)578-4529**
Colorado Springs, CO 80909   Fax: (719)578-4677

642 Colorado Springs Cablevision
213 N. Union Blvd.   Phone: (719)633-6616
Colorado Springs, CO 80909-5705   Fax: (719)633-0932
Owner: American TV & Communications Corp. **Founded:** 1969. **Key Personnel:** Jeffrey B. Tarbert, Gen. Mgr.; Kevin Hyman, Operations Dir.; Becky Hurley, Research & Development. **Cities Served:** El Paso County, Cascade, Chipita Park, Fountain, Green Mountain Falls, Manitou Springs, Pleasant View, and Rockrimmon, CO. 85,000 subscribing households; 60 channels; 1 community access channel; 20-30 hours per week of community access programming.

643 KAFA-FM - 104.5
PO Box 6066
USAFA
Colorado Springs, CO 80841   Phone: (719)472-5233
Format: Alternative/Independent/Progressive. **Key Personnel:** Chris Friefeld, Music Dir. **Ad Rates:** Noncommercial.

644 KHII-FM - 105.5
PO Box 1055
Colorado Springs, CO **80901**   Phone: (719)578-1055
    Fax: (719)520-9374

645 KILO-FM - 93.9
Box 2080   Phone: (719)634-4896
Colorado Springs, CO 80901   **Fax: (719)634-5837**

646 KKFM-FM - 98.1
Penthouse Ste.
411 Lakewood Circle   Phone: (719)596-5536
Colorado Springs, CO 80910   **Fax: (719)596-6718**

647 KRDO-TV - Channel 13
399 S. 8th St.   Phone: (719)632-1515
Colorado Springs, CO 809051   **Fax: (719)475-0815**

648 KSPZ-FM - 92.9
2864 S. Circle Dr., Ste. 150   Phone: (719)632-3536
Colorado Springs, CO 80906   **Fax: (719)579-0881**

649 KTLF-FM - 90.5
1802 Chapel Hills Dr., Ste. A   Phone: (719)593-0600
Colorado Springs, CO 80920   **Fax: (719)593-2399**

DENVER

650 Friendly Woman
PO Box 100838
Denver, CO 80250-0838   Phone: (303)761-6649
Journal focusing on the ideas, feelings, hopes, and experiences of Quaker women. **Founded:** 1976. **Frequency:** Quarterly. **Trim Size:** 8 1/2 x 11. **Cols./Page:** 3. **ISSN:** 0740-5618. **Subscription:** $12. $3 single issue.
    Circulation: Paid ‡800

Advertising not accepted.

651 Media Memo
4585 Wolff St.   Phone: (303)455-9125
Denver, CO 80212   **Fax: (303)455-9125**

652 The Metropolitan
Metropolitan State College of Denver
Board of Publications
955 Lawrence St., Rm. 156
PO Box 173362, Campus Box 57   Phone: (303)556-8361
Denver, CO 80217-3362   Fax: (303)556-2596

653 Radio Resource
Pandata Corp.
PO Box 24768   Phone: (303)771-8616
Denver, CO 80224-0768   Fax: (303)771-8605
Magazine for mobile radio system end users. **Subtitle:** System Solutions for Mobile Communications. **Founded:** 1987. **Frequency:** 6x/yr. **Key Personnel:** Rikki T. Lee, Editor; Paulla Nelson-Shira, Publisher; David Gillespie, Sales Mgr.; Mary Capps, Production Coordinator.
    Circulation: (Not Reported)

Advertising accepted; contact publisher for rates.

654 Rocky Mountain Oyster
Mountaintop Publishing, Inc.
PO Box 27467   Phone: (303)985-3034
Denver, CO 80227   Fax: (303)986-5664
Titillating publication on love, romance, and sex for people over 21. **Founded:** 1976. **Frequency:** Weekly. **Printing Method:** Web press. **Trim Size:** 11 1/2 x 17. **Cols./Page:** 4 and 6. **Col. Width:** 14 picas. **Col. Depth:** 15 1/4 in. **Key Personnel:** Elaine Leass, Publisher; Gary Schen, Advertising Mgr. **Subscription:** $82.

Ad Rates:	GLR:	$2	**Circulation:** Paid 11,374
	BW:	$698	Non-paid 30,541
	4C:	$1,098	
	PCI:	$35	

655 Spectrum Newspapers Monthly, Denver
Spectrum Newspapers
11171 Sun Center Dr., Ste. 110   Phone: (916)852-6222
Rancho Cordova, CA 95670   Fax: (916)852-6397
Newspaper serving active senior citizens, 55 and older, in Denver. **Founded:** 1975. **Frequency:** Monthly. **Printing Method:** Web offset. **Key Personnel:** Bob Carney, Editor; Jacqueline Lucido, Gen. Mgr.; Ridge Eagan, Natl. Advertising Dir. **USPS:** 980-481. **Subscription:** $12.
    Circulation: ‡47,000

656 Viltis
1337 Marion St.
Denver, CO 80218   Phone: (303)839-1589

657 KBNO-AM - 1220
2727 Bryant St., No. 100   Phone: (303)292-5266
Denver, CO 80211   **Fax: (303)433-1330**

658 KJME-AM - 1390
828 Santa Fe Dr.
Denver, CO 80204-4345   Phone: (303)623-1390
Format: Hispanic/Ethnic. **Owner:** Jo-Mor Communications. **Operating Hours:** Continuous. **Key Personnel:** Andres Neidig, Gen. Mgr.; Tony Guerrero, Program Dir.; Esther Sedillos, Office Mgr. **Wattage:** 5000. **Ad Rates:** $25 for 30 seconds;$35 for 60 seconds.

659 KLZ-AM - 560
2150 W. 29th Ave., Ste. 400   **Phone: (303)433-5500**
Denver, CO 80211   **Fax: (303)433-6560**

660 KOA-AM - 850
1380 Lawrence St., Ste. 1300   Phone: (303)893-8500
Denver, CO 80204   **Fax: (303)595-0850**

661 KRXY-FM - 107.5
7075 W. Hampden Ave.   Phone: (303)989-1075
Denver, CO 80227   **Fax: (303)989-9081**

662 KUSA-TV - Channel 9
500 Speer Blvd.   **Phone: (303)871-9999**
Denver, CO 80203   **Fax: (303)871-1819**

663 KXKL-AM - 1280
1560 Broadway, Ste. 1100   Phone: (303)832-5665
Denver, CO 80202   **Fax: (303)832-7000**

♨ 664　Mile Hi Cablevision Associates Ltd.
1617 S. Acoma St.　　　　　　　　Phone: (303)778-2978
Denver, CO 80223-3624　　　　　　Fax: (303)778-2912
Owner: Mile Hi Cablevision Associates Ltd. **Founded:** 1983. **Cities Served:** Arapahoe County, Denver County, and Glendale, CO.

♨ 665　Mount Evans Cable and Video
1873 S. Belleair St., Ste. 1550
Denver, CO 80222　　　　　　　**Phone: (303)756-5600**

DURANGO

📖 666　Bullish On Crafts
P & R Publications, Inc.
PO Box 5077
Durango, CO 81301
Crafts magazine. **Frequency:** 2x/mo. **Key Personnel:** Pam Bono, Editor. **Subscription:** $21. $3.50 single issue.
　　　　　　　　　　　Circulation: (Not Reported)

♨ 667　KDGO-AM - 1240
1315 Main Ave., No. 308　　　　　Phone: (303)247-1240
Durango, CO 81301-5156　　　　　**Fax: (303)247-2771**

♨ 668　KDUR-FM - 91.9
CUB 239
College Union Bldg.　　　　　　　Phone: (303)247-7261
Durango, CO 81301　　　　　　　　**Fax: (303)259-1774**

♨ 669　KREZ-TV - Channel 6
170 Turner Dr.
PO Box 2508　　　　　　　　　　Phone: (303)259-6666
Durango, CO 81302　　　　　　　　**Fax: (303)247-8472**

EATON

📖 670　North Weld Herald
PO Box 38　　　　　　　　　　　Phone: (303)454-3466
Eaton, CO 80615　　　　　　　　　**Fax: (303)454-3467**

ENGLEWOOD

📖 671　Colorado Business Magazine
Wiesner Publishing
7009 S. Potomac　　　　　　　　Phone: (303)397-7600
Englewood, CO 80112　　　　　　　Fax: (303)397-7619

📖 672　Southern Pharmacy Journal
333 W. Hampden Ave., Ste. 1050　　**Phone: (303)761-8818**
Englewood, CO 80110-2340　　　　　Fax: (303)761-2440

📖 673　Telocator Magazine
The Business Word Inc.
5300 S. Roselyn, Ste. 400　　　　　**Phone: (303)290-8500**
Englewood, CO 80111　　　　　　　**Fax: (800)328-3211**

♨ 674　KHIH-FM - 94.7
7880 E. Berry　　　　　　　　　　Phone: (303)779-8797
Englewood, CO 80111　　　　　　　**Fax: (303)740-9019**

♨ 675　UAE
6850 S. Tucson Way
Englewood, CO 80112　　　　　　　Phone: (303)790-0386
Owner: Tele-Communications, Inc. **Cities Served:** Boardwalk, Brandy Chase, Cherry Creek Greens, and The Lodge, CO.

FORT MORGAN

♨ 676　KBRU-FM - 102
PO Box 430　　　　　　　　　　Phone: (303)867-5674
Fort Morgan, CO 80701　　　　　　**Fax: (303)867-5675**

GLENWOOD SPRINGS

♨ 677　KGLN-AM - 980
Box 1028　　　　　　　　　　　Phone: (303)945-9124
Glenwood Springs, CO 81602　　　　Fax: (303)945-5409
Format: Oldies. **Network(s):** CNN Radio. **Owner:** Colorado West Broadcasting Inc. **Founded:** 1951. **Operating Hours:** 6 a.m.-midnight. **Key Personnel:** Allen Bell, Pres./Gen. Mgr. **Wattage:** 1000. **Ad Rates:** $10-$18 for 30 seconds; $15-$23 for 60 seconds. Combined rates available with KTMS-FM.

GRANBY

♨ 678　KRKY-AM - 930
Box 1030　　　　　　　　　　　Phone: (303)887-2566
Granby, CO 80446　　　　　　　　**Fax: (303)887-3295**

GRAND JUNCTION

♨ 679　KEKB-FM - 99.9
315 Kennedy Ave.　　　　　　　　**Phone: (303)243-3699**
Grand Junction, CO 81501　　　　　Fax: (303)243-0567

♨ 680　KMSA-FM - 91.3
1175 Texas Ave.
Grand Junction, CO 81502　　　　　Phone: (303)248-1240
Format: Alternative/Independent/Progressive. **Key Personnel:** Eric Watson, Music Dir. **Ad Rates:** Noncommercial.

GREENWOOD VILLAGE

📖 681　The Villager
8933 E. Union, Ste. 230　　　　　Phone: (303)773-8313
Greenwood Village, CO 80111　　　Fax: (303)773-8456

HAXTUN

📖 682　The Haxtun Herald
PO Box 128　　　　　　　　　　Phone: (303)774-6118
Haxtun, CO 80731　　　　　　　　**Fax: (303)774-6437**

IGNACIO

♨ 683　Rural Route Video
PO Box 640
Ignacio, CO 81137-0640　　　　　Phone: (303)563-9593

LA JARA

📖 684　The Conejos County Citizen
SLV Publishing
PO Box 79
517 Main St.　　　　　　　　　　Phone: (719)274-4192
La Jara, CO 81140　　　　　　　　Fax: (719)852-3387
Newspaper. Founded: 1892. **Frequency:** Weekly (Thurs.). **Printing Method:** Offset. **Trim Size:** 10 1/2 x 16. **Cols./Page:** 5. **Col. Width:** 2 in. **Key Personnel:** Ray James, Editor; Steve Haynes, Publisher/Advertising Mgr. **USPS:** 308-760. **Subscription:** $14; $21 other countries.
Ad Rates:　BW:　$484　　　　**Circulation:** Paid ⊕700
　　　　　　　PCI:　$6.05　　　　　　　　　　　Free ⊕7
Additional Contact Information: Mail ad material to: Steve Haynes, SLV Publishing, 229 Adam s St., Monte Vista, CO 81144.

LA JUNTA

♨ 685　Heritage Cablevision
Lincoln Sq. Professional Bldg., Ste. 103
2218 San Juan
Box 877　　　　　　　　　　　Phone: (719)384-5487
La Junta, CO 81050　　　　　　　Fax: (719)384-4596
Owner: TCI. **Key Personnel:** Joe Stackhouse, System Mgr.; Jeannie Barber, Office Mgr.; Randy Pace, Chief Technician. **Cities Served:**

Lamar, La Junta, Swink, Rockyford, Fowler, Colorado City, Rye, and Walsenburg, CO:8,700 subscribing households; 4 community access channel.

LAKEWOOD

686 The Air Pollution Consultant
McCoy and Associates, Inc.
13701 W. Jewell Ave., Ste. 202
Lakewood, CO 80228　　　Phone: (303)987-0333
Journal covering air pollution issues. **Founded:** 1991. **Frequency:** Bimonthly. **Trim Size:** 8 1/2 x 11. **Cols./Page:** 3. **Col. Width:** 2.32 in. **Col. Depth:** 9.38 in. **Key Personnel:** Eric J. Weber, Editor; Drew E. McCoy, Pres. **ISSN:** 1058-6628. **Subscription:** $375.
　　　　　　　　　　Circulation: (Not Reported)
Advertising not accepted.

687 Trends Magazine
American Animal Hospital Assn.
12575 W. Bayaud Ave.　　　Phone: (303)986-2800
Lakewood, CO 80228　　　Fax: (303)986-1700

LAMAR

688 KSEC-FM - 93.3
Box 890　　　　　　　Phone: (719)336-2206
Lamar, CO 81052　　　　Fax: (719)336-7973

LIMON

689 KLIM-AM - 1120
165 E. Ave.
Box 87
Limon, CO 80828　　　　Phone: (303)775-2572
Format: Country. **Network(s):** AP. **Owner:** Green-Harris Broadcasting Corp., at above address. **Founded:** 1984. **Key Personnel:** Larry Green, Pres.; Ramona Harris, Gen. Mgr. **Wattage:** 250.

MONTE VISTA

690 SLV Midweek
SLV Publishing
229 Adams St.　　　　　Phone: (719)852-3531
Monte Vista, CO 81144　　Fax: (719)852-3387
Community newspaper. **Founded:** 1978. **Frequency:** Weekly (Wed.). **Printing Method:** Offset. **Trim Size:** 10 1/2 x 16. **Cols./Page:** 5. **Col. Width:** 2 in. **Key Personnel:** Steve Haynes, Publisher. **Subscription:** Free.
Ad Rates:　BW:　$820　　**Circulation:** Free ‡17,500
　　　　　SAU:　$10.25

691 SLV Saturday Want Ads
SLV Publishing
229 Adams St.　　　　　Phone: (719)852-3531
Monte Vista, CO 81144　　Fax: (719)852-3387
Community newspaper. **Founded:** 1990. **Frequency:** Weekly (Saturday). **Printing Method:** Offset. **Trim Size:** 10 1/2 x 16. **Cols./Page:** 5. **Col. Width:** 2 in. **Key Personnel:** Steve Haynes, Publisher. **Subscription:** Free.
Ad Rates:　BW:　$820　　**Circulation:** Free ‡11,588
　　　　　SAU:　$10.25

MONTROSE

692 KKXK-FM - 94.1
Box 970　　　　　　　Phone: (303)249-4546
Montrose, CO 81402　　　Fax: (303)249-2229

693 KSTR-FM - 96.1
600 Rood Ave.　　　　　Phone: (303)242-5787
Grand Junction, CO 81501　Fax: (303)245-6585

PUEBLO

694 The Colorado Tribune
Colorado Printing of Pueblo
447 Park Dr.　　　　　　Phone: (719)561-4008
Pueblo, CO 81005　　　　Fax: (719)561-4007

695 KERP-FM - 91.9
4227 Plane View St.　　　Phone: (719)561-8784
Pueblo, CO 81005　　　　Fax: (719)561-8784

696 KTSC-TV - Channel 8
2200 Bonforte Blvd.　　　Phone: (719)543-8800
Pueblo, CO 81001-4901　　Fax: (719)549-2208

697 TCI Cablevision of Colorado
Box 576
Pueblo, CO 81003-2203　　Phone: (719)546-1090
Owner: Tele-Communications, Inc. **Founded:** 1970. **Cities Served:** Pueblo County.

SALIDA

698 KVRH-AM - 1340
7600 County Rd. 120　　　Phone: (719)539-2575
Salida, CO 81201　　　　Fax: (719)539-4851

699 KVRH-FM - 92
7600 County Rd. 120　　　Phone: (719)539-2575
Salida, CO 81201　　　　Fax: (719)539-4851

STEAMBOAT SPRINGS

700 The Steamboat Whistle
Raljon Publishing, Inc.
1041 Lincoln Ave.
PO Box 4827　　　　　　Phone: (303)879-1502
Steamboat Springs, CO 80477　Fax: (303)879-2888

STRASBURG

701 Eastern Colorado News
Town & Country Publications, Inc.
1522 Main St.　　　　　Phone: (303)622-4417
Strasburg, CO 80136-0555　Fax: (303)622-9716

THORNTON

702 American Cablevision
2190 E. 104th Ave.
Thornton, CO 80233　　　Phone: (303)450-2200
Owner: American TV & Communications Corp. **Cities Served:** Adams County, Arapahoe County, Douglas County, Jefferson County, North Glenn, Littleton, Thornton, and Wheat Ridge, CO.

TRINIDAD

703 KCRT-AM - 1240
100 Fisher Dr.　　　　　Phone: (719)846-3355
Trinidad, CO 81082　　　Fax: (719)846-4711

704 KCRT-FM - 92.7
100 Fisher Dr.　　　　　Phone: (719)846-3355
Trinidad, CO 81082　　　Fax: (719)846-4711

VAIL

705 KQMT-FM - 101.5
1000 Lionsridge Loop　　　Phone: (303)476-7444
Vail, CO 81657　　　　　Fax: (303)476-8211

WHEAT RIDGE

706 Akita World
Hoflin Publishing Ltd.
4401 Zephyr St.　　　　　Phone: (303)402-2222
Wheat Ridge, CO 80033-3299　Fax: (303)422-7000
Frequency: Bimonthly. **Key Personnel:** Donald R. Hoflin, Mng. Editor and Publisher; Cynthia L. Kersteins, Editor. **Subscription:** $42; $51 other countries. $9 single issue.
Ad Rates:　BW:　$100　　**Circulation:** Paid 1,668
　　　　　4C:　$400　　　　　　Non-paid 301

☐ 707 The Borzoi Quarterly
Hoflin Publishing Ltd.
4401 Zephyr St.   Phone: (303)420-2222
Wheat Ridge, CO 80033-3299   Fax: (303)422-7000
Frequency: Quarterly. **Key Personnel:** Donald R. Hoflin, Mng. Editor
and Publisher; Judy E. Mears, Editor. **Subscription:** $36; $40 other
countries. $10 single issue.
Ad Rates: BW: $100   **Circulation:** Paid 473
                4C: $400   Non-paid 290

☐ 708 The Boston Quarterly
Hoflin Publishing Ltd.
4401 Zephyr St.   Phone: (303)420-2222
Wheat Ridge, CO 80033-3299   Fax: (303)422-7000
Frequency: Quarterly. **Key Personnel:** Donald R. Hoflin, Mng. Editor
and Publisher; Cynthia L. Kersteins, Editor. **Subscription:** $36; $40
other countries. $10 single issue.
Ad Rates: BW: $100   **Circulation:** Paid 479
                4C: $400   Non-paid 256

☐ 709 Brittany World
Hoflin Publishing Ltd.
4401 Zephyr St.
Wheat Ridge, CO 80033-3299   Phone: (303)402-2222
Ceased publication.

☐ 710 The Bull Terrier Quarterly
Hoflin Publishing Ltd.
4401 Zephyr St.   Phone: (303)420-2222
Wheat Ridge, CO 80033-3299   Fax: (303)422-7000
Frequency: Quarterly. **Key Personnel:** Donald R. Hoflin, Mng. Editor
and Publisher; Pamela Geer, Editor. **Subscription:** $32; $36 other
countries. $9 single issue.
Ad Rates: BW: $100   **Circulation:** Paid 328
                4C: $400   Non-paid 195

☐ 711 Collie Variety
Hoflin Publishing Ltd.
4401 Zephyr St.
Wheat Ridge, CO 80033-3299   Phone: (303)420-2222
Ceased publication.

☐ 712 The Corgi Quarterly
Hoflin Publishing Ltd.
4401 Zephyr St.   Phone: (303)420-2222
Wheat Ridge, CO 80033-3299   Fax: (303)422-7000
Frequency: Quarterly. **Key Personnel:** Donald R. Hoflin, Mng. Editor
and Publisher; Judy E. Mears, Editor. **Subscription:** $36; $40 other
countries. $10 single issue.
Ad Rates: BW: $100   **Circulation:** Paid 639
                4C: $400   Non-paid 282

☐ 713 The Dalmation Quarterly
Hoflin Publishing Ltd.
4401 Zephyr St.   Phone: (303)420-2222
Wheat Ridge, CO 80033-3299   Fax: (303)422-7000
Frequency: Quarterly. **Key Personnel:** Donald R. Hoflin, Mng. Editor
and Publisher; Judy E. Mears, Editor. **Subscription:** $36; $40 other
countries. $10 single issue.
Ad Rates: BW: $100   **Circulation:** Paid 562
                4C: $400   Non-paid 293

☐ 714 Doberman World
Hoflin Publishing Ltd.
4401 Zephyr St.   Phone: (303)420-2222
Wheat Ridge, CO 80033-3299   Fax: (303)422-7000
Frequency: Quarterly. **Key Personnel:** Donald R. Hoflin, Mng. Editor
and Publisher; Judy E. Mears, Editor. **Subscription:** $36; $40 other
countries. $10 single issue.
Ad Rates: BW: $100   **Circulation:** Paid 913
                4C: $400   Non-paid 411
Formerly: The Doberman Quarterly.

☐ 715 The Elkhound Quarterly
Hoflin Publishing Ltd.
4401 Zephyr St.   Phone: (303)420-2222
Wheat Ridge, CO 80033-3299   Fax: (303)422-7000
Frequency: Quarterly. **Key Personnel:** Donald R. Hoflin, Mng. Editor
and Publisher; Judy E. Mears, Editor. **Subscription:** $36; $40 other
countries. $10 single issue.
Ad Rates: BW: $100   **Circulation:** Paid 242
                4C: $400   Non-paid 216

☐ 716 The English Cocker Quarterly
Hoflin Publishing Ltd.
4401 Zephyr St.   Phone: (303)420-2222
Wheat Ridge, CO 80033-3299   Fax: (303)422-7000
Frequency: Quarterly. **Key Personnel:** Donald R. Hoflin, Mng. Editor
and Publisher; Judy E. Mears, Editor. **Subscription:** $36; $40 other
countries. $10 single issue.
Ad Rates: BW: $100   **Circulation:** Paid 666
                4C: $400   Non-paid 289

☐ 717 The German Shepherd Quarterly
Hoflin Publishing Ltd.
4401 Zephyr St.   Phone: (303)420-2222
Wheat Ridge, CO 80033-3299   Fax: (303)422-7000
Magazine for German Shepherd owners and enthusiasts. **Frequency:**
Quarterly. **Key Personnel:** Donald R. Hoflin, Mng. Editor and
Publisher; Cynthia L. Kersteins, Editor. **Subscription:** $36; $40 other
countries. $10 single issue.
Ad Rates: BW: $100   **Circulation:** Paid ‡1,301
                4C: $400   Non-paid ‡382

☐ 718 Golden Retriever World
Hoflin Publishing Ltd.
4401 Zephyr St.   Phone: (303)420-2222
Wheat Ridge, CO 80033-3299   Fax: (303)422-7000
Magazine for golden retriever owners and enthusiasts. **Frequency:**
Quarterly. **Key Personnel:** Donald R. Hoflin, Mng. Editor and
Publisher; Judy E. Mears, Editor. **Subscription:** $36; $40 other
countries. $10 single issue.
Ad Rates: BW: $100   **Circulation:** Paid ‡472
                4C: $400   Non-paid ‡290

☐ 719 The Gordon Quarterly
Hoflin Publishing Ltd.
4401 Zephyr St.   Phone: (303)420-2222
Wheat Ridge, CO 80033-3299   Fax: (303)422-7000
Frequency: Quarterly. **Key Personnel:** Donald R. Hoflin, Mng. Editor
and Publisher; Judy E. Mears, Editor. **Subscription:** $36; $40 other
countries. $10 single issue.
Ad Rates: BW: $100   **Circulation:** Paid 253
                4C: $400   Non-paid 235

☐ 720 The Irish Wolfhound Quarterly
Hoflin Publishing Ltd.
4401 Zephyr St.   Phone: (303)420-2222
Wheat Ridge, CO 80033-3299   Fax: (303)422-7000
Magazine for Irish Wolfhound owners and enthusiasts. **Frequency:**
Quarterly. **Key Personnel:** Donald R. Hoflin, Mng. Editor and
Publisher; Cynthia L. Kersteins, Editor. **Subscription:** $36; $40 other
countries. $10 single issue.
Ad Rates: BW: $100   **Circulation:** Paid ‡674
                4C: $400   Non-paid ‡269

☐ 721 The Labrador Quarterly
Hoflin Publishing Ltd.
4401 Zephyr St.   Phone: (303)420-2222
Wheat Ridge, CO 80033-3299   Fax: (303)422-7000
Magazine for Labrador retriever owners and enthusiasts. **Frequency:**
Quarterly. **Key Personnel:** Donald R. Hoflin, Mng. Editor and
Publisher; Judy E. Mears, Editor. **Subscription:** $36; $40 other
countries. $10 single issue.
Ad Rates: BW: $100   **Circulation:** Paid ‡1,817
                4C: $400   Non-paid ‡292

Ad Rates: GLR = general line rate; BW = one-time black & white page rate; 4C = one-time four color page rate; SAU = standard advertising unit rate;
CNU = Canadian newspaper advertising unit rate; PCI = per column inch rate.
Circulation: ★ = ABC; △ = BPA; ◆ = CAC; ● = CCAB; □ = VAC; ⊕ = PO Statement; ‡ = Publisher's Report; Boldface figures = sworn; Light figures = estimated.
Entry type: ☐ = Print; ☙ = Broadcast.

📖 **722 The Malamute Quarterly**
Hoflin Publishing Ltd.
4401 Zephyr St.   Phone: (303)420-2222
Wheat Ridge, CO 80033-3299   Fax: (303)422-7000
Magazine for Malamute dog owners and enthusiasts. **Frequency:**
Quarterly. **Key Personnel:** Donald R. Hoflin, Editor and Publisher;
Judy E. Mears, Editor. **Subscription:** $36; $40 other countries. $10
single issue.
Ad Rates: BW: $100   **Circulation:** Paid ‡545
               4C: $400   Non-paid ‡338

📖 **723 The Persian Quarterly**
Hoflin Publishing Ltd.
4401 Zephyr St.
Wheat Ridge, CO 80033-3299   Phone: (303)420-2222
Ceased publication.

📖 **724 Quilter's Newsletter Magazine**
Leman Publications, Inc.
6700 W. 44th Ave.   Phone: (303)420-4272
Wheat Ridge, CO **80034**   Fax: (303)420-7358

📖 **725 The Rhodesian Ridgeback Quarterly**
Hoflin Publishing Ltd.
4401 Zephyr St.   Phone: (303)420-2222
Wheat Ridge, CO 80033-3299   Fax: (303)422-7000
Frequency: Quarterly. **Key Personnel:** Donald R. Hoflin, Mng. Editor
and Publisher; Laura D. Neufeld, Editor. **Subscription:** $36; $40 other
countries. $10 SNG.
Ad Rates: BW: $100   **Circulation:** Paid 363
               4C: $400   Non-paid 240

📖 **726 The Saint Bernard Quarterly**
Hoflin Publishing Ltd.
4401 Zephyr St.
Wheat Ridge, CO 80033-3299   Phone: (303)420-2222
Ceased publication.

📖 **727 The Samoyed Quarterly**
Hoflin Publishing Ltd.
4401 Zephyr St.   Phone: (303)420-2222
Wheat Ridge, CO 80033-3299   Fax: (303)422-7000
Frequency: Quarterly. **Key Personnel:** Donald R. Hoflin, Mng. Editor
and Publisher; Cynthia L. Kerstiens, Editor. **Subscription:** $36; $40
other countries. $10 single issue.
Ad Rates: BW: $90   **Circulation:** Paid 669
               4C: $390   Non-paid 330

📖 **728 The Siberian Quarterly**
Hoflin Publishing Ltd.
4401 Zephyr St.   Phone: (303)420-2222
Wheat Ridge, CO 80033-3299   Fax: (303)422-7000
Frequency: Quarterly. **Key Personnel:** Donald R. Hoflin, Mng. Editor
and Publisher; Judy E. Mears, Editor. **Subscription:** $36; $40 other
countries. $10 single issue.
Ad Rates: BW: $100   **Circulation:** Paid 990
               4C: $400   Controlled 345

📖 **729 The Windhound**
Hoflin Publishing Ltd.
4401 Zephyr St.
Wheat Ridge, CO 80033-3299   Phone: (303)420-2222
Ceased publication.

CONNECTICUT

BLOOMFIELD

730 WLVX-AM - 1550
2 Wintonbury Mall
Bloomfield, CT 06002

Phone: (203)243-1550
Fax: (203)286-0004

BOLTON

731 Eastern Connecticut Television Corporation
200 Boston Tpke.
PO Box 9171
Bolton, CT 06043

Phone: (203)645-1454

Founded: 1991. **Key Personnel:** Sandra Sprague, Executive Dir. **Cities Served:** Andover, Bolton, Ellington, Hebron, Marlborough, Tolland, and Vernon, CT: 20,000 subscribing households; 2 community access channels; 25 hours per week of community access programming.

BRANFORD

732 Heritage Communications, Inc.
Box 667
Branford, CT 06405-0667

Phone: (203)488-7042
Fax: (203)776-0594

Owner: Tele-Communications, Inc. **Founded:** 1975. **Cities Served:** New Haven County, East Haven, Guilford, Madison, North Branford, Northford, North Haven, and Wallingford, CT.

BRIDGEPORT

733 Hysteria
PO Box 8581, Brewster Sta.
Bridgeport, CT 06605

Phone: (203)333-9399

Women's humor magazine. **Subtitle:** Feminism, Humor, and Social Change. **Founded:** 1993. **Frequency:** Quarterly. **Printing Method:** Offset. **Trim Size:** 8 1/2 x 11. **Cols./Page:** 3. **Col. Width:** 2 1/4 in. **Key Personnel:** Deborah Werksman, Editor and Publisher.

Ad Rates: BW: $500   **Circulation:** ‡10,000
PCI: $25

734 The Quayle Quarterly
PO Box 8593, Brewster Sta.
Bridgeport, CT 06605

Phone: (203)333-9399

Ceased publication.

735 Cablevision of Southern Connecticut
122 River St.
Bridgeport, CT 06604

Phone: (203)846-4700
Fax: (203)333-5883

Owner: Cablevision Systems Corp. **Founded:** 1977. **Key Personnel:** Irene Tripodi, Gen. Mgr.; Maryce Cunningham, Program Dir.; Tom Appleby, News Dir. **Cities Served:** Fairfield County, New Haven County, Milford, Orange, Stratford, Woodbridge, and Bridgeport, CT:

81,000 subscribing households; 45 channels; 1 community access channel; 67 hours per week of community access programming.

736 WEBE-FM - 107.9
2 Lafayette Sq.
Bridgeport, CT 06604

Phone: (203)333-9108
Fax: (203)333-9107

DERBY

737 Song Hits' Superstars
Charlton Publications, Inc.
60 Division St.
Derby, CT 06418

Magazine containing interviews and photos of popular musicians. **Frequency:** 6x/yr. **Key Personnel:** Mary Jane Canetti, Editor; John Santangelo, Publisher. **Subscription:** $20. $2.50 single issue.

Circulation: (Not Reported)

EAST HARTFORD

738 Precision Shooting
37 Burnham St.
East Hartford, CT 06108

Phone: (203)249-6811
Fax: (203)727-9690

FARMINGTON

739 Developmental Brain Dysfunction
S. Karger Publishers, Inc.
26 W. Avon Rd.
PO Box 529
Farmington, CT 06085-0529

Phone: (203)675-7834
Fax: (203)675-7302

Former Title: Brain Dysfunction

740 European Journal of Human Genetics
S. Karger Publishers, Inc.
26 W. Avon Rd.
PO Box 529
Farmington, CT 06085

Phone: (203)675-7834
Fax: (203)675-7302

Official journal of the European Society of Human Genetics. **Frequency:** Quarterly. **Printing Method:** Offset. **Trim Size:** 7 x 9 7/8. **Key Personnel:** G. Romeo, Editor-in-Chief; M. Devoto, Asst. Editor. **ISSN:** 1018-4813. **Subscription:** $142.10; $203 institutions.

Ad Rates: BW: $755   **Circulation:** (Not Reported)

741 Experimental Nephrology
S. Karger Publishers, Inc.
26 W. Avon Rd.
PO Box 529
Farmington, CT 06085

Phone: (203)675-7834
Fax: (203)675-7302

Journal focusing on the biology of the kidney and renal diseases. Includes clinical studies. **Founded:** 1993. **Frequency:** 6x/yr. **Printing**

Method: Offset. **Trim Size:** 8 1/4 x 11. **Key Personnel:** Prof. L. G. Fine, Editor-in-Chief; G. Remuzzi Bergamo, Deputy Editor. **ISSN:** 1018-7782. **Subscription:** $182.25; $405 institutions.
Ad Rates: BW: $755   **Circulation:** (Not Reported)

📖 **742 Indoor Environment**
S. Karger Publishers, Inc.
26 W. Avon Rd.
PO Box 529   Phone: (203)675-7834
Farmington, CT 06085-0529   Fax: (203)675-7302
Scientific journal. **Subtitle:** The Journal of Indoor Air International. **Founded:** 1992. **Frequency:** 6x/yr. **Printing Method:** Offset. **Trim Size:** 210 x 280 mm. **Cols./Page:** 1. **Col. Width:** 99 nonpareils. **Key Personnel:** D.F. Weetman, Editor-in-Chief. **ISSN:** 1016-4901. **Subscription:** $146.50; $293 institutions.
Circulation: 1,000
Advertising accepted; contact publisher for rates. **Additional Contact Information:** S. Karger AG, PO Box CH-4009 Basel, Switzerland.

GREENWICH

♣ **743 United Video Cablevision, Inc.**
PO Box 6710   Phone: (203)661-1166
Greenwich, CT 06836   Fax: (203)661-1475

GUILFORD

📖 **744 Wire Journal International**
Wire Assn. Intl.
1570 Boston Post Rd.
PO Box H   Phone: (203)453-2777
Guilford, CT 06437   Fax: (203)453-8384

HAMDEN

♣ **745 WPLR-FM - 99.1**
1191 Dixwell Ave.   Phone: (203)287-9070
Hamden, CT 06514   Fax: (203)287-8997

MADISON

📖 **746 Israel Journal of Psychiatry and Related Sciences**
International Universities Press, Inc.
59 Boston Post Rd.
PO Box 1524   Phone: (203)245-4000
Madison, CT 06443-1524   Fax: (203)245-0775
International psychiatric journal. **Subtitle:** Official Journal of the Israel Psychiatric Association. **Founded:** 1964. **Frequency:** Quarterly. **Key Personnel:** E.L. Edelstein M.D., Editor. **Subscription:** $65; $75 institutions; $85 other countries; $95 institutions other countries.
Circulation: (Not Reported)
Advertising accepted; contact publisher for rates.

MANCHESTER

♣ **747 Cox Cable Greater Hartford, Inc.**
801 Parker St.   Phone: (203)646-6400
Manchester, CT 06040   Fax: (203)643-4041
Owner: Cox Cable Communications. **Founded:** 1975. **Cities Served:** Hartford County, Glastonbury, Newington, Rocky Hill, South Windsor, and Wethersfoeld, CT.

MIDDLETOWN

♣ **748 Comcast Cablevision of Middletown**
19 Tuttle Pl.
Middletown, CT 06457   Phone: (203)632-1139
Key Personnel: Thomas Coughlin, Gen. Mgr.; Rebecca Usenia, Advertising Sales Mgr. **Cities Served:** Middletown, Cromwell, Portland, Middlefield, and East Hampton, CT: 22,000 subscribing households; 38 channels; 1 community access channel; 20 hours per week of community access programming.

NEW HAVEN

📖 **749 Destination Magazine**
MacClaren Press, Inc.
PO Box 580
New Haven, CT 06513-0580   Phone: (203)782-1420
Frequency: 2x/year. **Key Personnel:** Joel MacClaren, Publisher; Roberta Kaufman, Sr. Account Exec.; Molly Phinney, Editorial Asst.
Circulation: (Not Reported)

📖 **750 Exclusively Connecticut**
315 Peck St.
New Haven, CT 06513-0580   Phone: (203)782-1420
Periodical for women living and working in New Haven, Fairfield, and Hartford Counties, CT. **Frequency:** Monthly. **Key Personnel:** Joel MacClaren, Editor and Publisher; Molly Phinney, Editorial Asst.; Risa Hozer, Account Exec. **Subscription:** $13.
Circulation: (Not Reported)
Formerly: New Haven County Woman; Exclusively Women.

📖 **751 Inner-City**
2 Eld St.   Phone: (203)773-0688
New Haven, CT 06511   Fax: (203)787-5067

📖 **752 Real Estate Quarterly**
MacClaren Press, Inc.
PO Box 580
New Haven, CT 06513-1580   Phone: (203)721-7455
Ceased publication.

📖 **753 Yale Journal of Law and Feminism**
Box 401A Yale Sta.   Phone: (203)432-4056
New Haven, CT 06520   Fax: (203)432-2592
Journal serving as a forum for the analysis of women's experience as affected by the law. **Founded:** 1989. **Frequency:** 2x/yr. **Printing Method:** Offset. **Cols./Page:** 1. **ISSN:** 1043-9366. **Subscription:** $16; $12 students; $28 institutions.
Ad Rates: BW: $75   **Circulation:** Paid 900
Non-paid 200
Advertising, one time, inside back cover $125.

♣ **754 Storer Cable TV of Connecticut, Inc.**
190 Whalley Ave.
New Haven, CT 06511   Phone: (203)865-0429
Owner: Storer Cable Communications. **Founded:** 1964. **Cities Served:** New Haven County, Hamden, and West Haven, CT.

NEW MILFORD

📖 **755 The Woodworker's Journal**
517 Litchfield Rd.
PO Box 1629   Phone: (203)355-2694
New Milford, CT 06776   Fax: (203)350-2165

NORWALK

📖 **756 American Iron Magazine**
TAM Communications, Inc.
6 Prowitt St.   Phone: (203)855-0008
Norwalk, CT 06855   Fax: (203)852-9980
Subtitle: "For People Who Love Harley-Davidsons". **Founded:** 1989. **Frequency:** Monthly. **Printing Method:** Web offset. **Key Personnel:** Buzz Kanter, Publisher; Tony Perrone   **Subscription:** $25. $2.95 single issue.
Circulation: (Not Reported)
Advertising accepted; contact publisher for rates. Circulation data is also available upon request.

📖 **757 Easy & Fun Word Seek Puzzles**
Penny Press
6 Prowitt St.
Norwalk, CT 06855
Magazine containing 63 word seek puzzles with solutions in back. **Frequency:** 6x/yr. **Key Personnel:** Fran Danon, Editor. **Subscription:** $5.88. $.99 single issue.
Circulation: (Not Reported)

📖 **758 Family Word Seek Puzzles**
Penny Press, Inc.
6 Prowitt St.
Norwalk, CT 06855
Magazine containing over 100 large-type puzzles and primary word seek puzzles. **Frequency:** Quarterly. **Key Personnel:** Don Loiacano, Editor. **Subscription:** $7.47. $1.99 single issue.
Circulation: (Not Reported)

📖 **759 Favorite Variety Puzzles and Games**
Penny Press, Inc.
6 Prowitt St.
Norwalk, CT 06855
Magazine containing over 250 puzzles including Double Trouble, Alphabet Soup, Flower Power, and more. **Frequency:** Quarterly. **Key Personnel:** Fran Danon, Editor. **Subscription:** $7.47. $1.99 single issue.
Circulation: (Not Reported)

📖 **760 Favorite Word Seek Puzzles**
Penny Press, Inc.
6 Porwitt St.
Norwalk, CT 06855
Magazine containing Word Seek and other puzzles. **Frequency:** 6x/yr. **Key Personnel:** Don Loiacano, Editor. **Subscription:** $5.88. $.99 single issue.
Circulation: (Not Reported)

🔊 **761 Cablevision of Connecticut LP**
28 Cross St.   Phone: (203)846-4700
Norwalk, CT 06851   Fax: (203)846-9412
Owner: Cablevision Systems Corp. **Founded:** 1982. **Cities Served:** Fairfield County, Darien, Easton, Greenwich, New Canaan, Norwalk, Redding, Stamford, Weston, Westport, and Wilton, CT.

PORTLAND

📖 **762 New England Entertainment Digest**
Taylor Publishing
PO Box 313   Phone: (203)342-4730
Portland, CT 06480   Fax: (203)342-5368
Publication containing news and features about the entertainment industry. **Founded:** 1979. **Frequency:** Monthly. **Printing Method:** Offset. **Trim Size:** 11 1/2 x 17. **Cols./Page:** 6. **Col. Width:** 1 5/8 in. **Col. Depth:** 16 in. **Key Personnel:** Bob Taylor, Editor and Publisher. **ISSN:** 0896-1506. **Subscription:** $15. $1.50 single issue.
Ad Rates: BW: $525   **Circulation:** ‡5,000
              PCI: $12

PROSPECT

📖 **763 Job Shop Technology**
Edwards Publishing Co.
16 Waterbury Rd.
PO Box 7193   Phone: (203)758-4474
Prospect, CT 06712   Fax: (203)758-4475

PUTNAM

📖 **764 Eglute**
Sisters of Immaculate Conception
Putnam, CT 06260   Phone: (203)928-7955
Ceased publication.

SOUTH NORWALK

📖 **765 Full Effect**
Pilot Communications
29 Haviland St.
South Norwalk, CT 06854
Magazine featuring interviews and photos of R&B and hiphop artists. **Frequency:** 6x/yr. **Key Personnel:** Crystal Brown, Editor; Roger Munford, Publisher. **Subscription:** $2.95 single issue.
Circulation: (Not Reported)

SOUTH WINDSOR

📖 **766 The Commercial Record**
435 Buckland Rd.   Phone: (203)644-3489
South Windsor, CT 06074-0902   Fax: (203)644-7363

STAMFORD

📖 **767 Bodybuilding Lifestyles**
Titan Sports, Inc.
1055 Summer St.
Stamford, CT 06905
Sports magazine. **Frequency:** Monthly. **Key Personnel:** Rochelle Larkin, Editor; Tom W. Emanuel, Publisher. **Subscription:** $19.95. $3.50 single issue.
Circulation: (Not Reported)

📖 **768 Curriculum Product News**
Educational Media, Inc.
992 High Ridge Rd.   Phone: (203)322-1300
Stamford, CT 06905   Fax: (203)329-9177

TORRINGTON

🔊 **769 Laurel Cablevision**
RR 3, Box 323
Torrington-Litchfield Rd.   Phone: (203)567-3103
Torrington, CT 06759   Fax: (203)567-8531
Owner: Time-Warner. **Founded:** 1972. **Key Personnel:** Joshua L. Jamison, Gen. Mgr.; Robert Bailey, Technical Mgr.; Pamela Little, Business and Operations Mgr.; Edward Guinea, Public Relations and Program Mgr. **Cities Served:** Litchfield, Torrington, Watertown, Thomaston, Morris, and Warren, CT.

WATERBURY

🔊 **770 Sammons Communications**
695 Huntingdon Ave.
Waterbury, CT 06708   Phone: (203)755-1178
Owner: Sammons Communications, Inc. **Founded:** 1975. **Cities Served:** Litchfield County, New Haven County, Middlebury, Platts Mills, Plymouth, Prospect, Terryville, and Wolcott, CT.

WEST HARTFORD

📖 **771 ConnStruction**
McHugh Design, Advertising & Publishing
62 Lasalle Rd., Ste. 211   Phone: (203)523-7518
West Hartford, CT 06107   Fax: (203)231-8808

📖 **772 The Hartford Automobiler**
AAA Automobile Club of Hartford
815 Farmington Ave.   Phone: (203)236-3261
West Hartford, CT 06119   Fax: (203)523-7688

📖 **773 Windsor Locks Journal**
Imprint, Inc.
20 Isham Rd.   Phone: (203)236-3571
West Hartford, CT 06127-1800   Fax: (203)236-4188

🔊 **774 United Cable TV Corp.**
91 Shield St.
West Hartford, CT 06110   Phone: (203)677-9599
Owner: Tele-Communications, Inc. **Founded:** 1975. **Cities Served:** Hartford County, Bloomfield, East Hartford, Simsbury, West Hartford, and Windsor, CT.

🔊 **775 WWUH-FM - 91.3**
200 Bloomfield Ave.   Phone: (203)768-4703
West Hartford, CT 06117   Fax: (203)768-5016

Ad Rates: GLR = general line rate; BW = one-time black & white page rate; 4C = one-time four color page rate; SAU = standard advertising unit rate; CNU = Canadian newspaper advertising unit rate; PCI = per column inch rate.
Circulation: ★ = ABC; △ = BPA; ◆ = CAC; ● = CCAB; □ = VAC; ⊕ = PO Statement; ‡ = Publisher's Report; Boldface figures = sworn; Light figures = estimated.
Entry type: 📖 = Print; 🔊 = Broadcast.

51

WESTON

776 The Weston Forum
Acorn Press, Inc.
16 Bailey Ave.
PO Box 1019   Phone: (203)438-6544
Ridgefield, CT 06877   Fax: (203)438-3395
Community newspaper. **Frequency:** Weekly. **Cols./Page:** 6. **Col. Depth:** 2 1/16 in. **Col. Depth:** 21 in. **Key Personnel:** Sybil Blau, Editor; Thomas B. Nash, Publisher; James DeFillipo, Advertising Dir. **Subscription:** $30.
Ad Rates: BW: $882   **Circulation:** Paid ◆**3,660**
                4C: $1,282
                PCI: $7

WESTPORT

777 Bulletin of Bibliography
Greenwood Publishing Group
PO Box 5007   Phone: (203)226-3571
Westport, CT 06881   **Fax: (203)222-1502**

778 MultiCultural Review
Greenwood Publishing Group, Inc.
88 Post Rd. W.   Phone: (203)226-3571
Westport, CT 06881-9990   Fax: (203)222-1502
Magazine providing collection information to librarians and educators. **Subtitle:** Dedicated to a Better Understanding of Ethnic, Racial, & Religious Diversity. **Founded:** 1992. **Frequency:** Quarterly. **Printing Method:** Offset. **Trim Size:** 8 1/2 x 11. **Cols./Page:** 3. **Key Personnel:** Brenda Mitchell-Powell, Editor-in-Chief. **ISSN:** 1058-9236. **Subscription:** $59; $79 other countries. $25 single issue.
Ad Rates: BW: $750   **Circulation:** (Not Reported)
                4C: $1,500
Additional Contact Information: Advertising contact: Garrance, Inc. (914)834-7070.

WILTON

779 Running Times
Air Age Fitness Group, Inc.
251 Danbury Rd.   Phone: (203)834-2900
Wilton, CT 06897   Fax: (203)762-9803
Sports magazine. **Founded:** 1977. **Frequency:** Monthly. **Trim Size:** 8 1/2 x 11. **Cols./Page:** 3. **Key Personnel:** James O'Brien, Editor; Louis V. DeFrancesco, Jr., Publisher. **Subscription:** Free to qualified subscribers; $17.70. $2.95 single issue.
                                   Circulation: Paid 77,545
                                                    Non-paid 16,943
Advertising accepted; contact publisher for rates.

DELAWARE

GEORGETOWN

♣ 780 WDTS-AM - 620
Delaware Tech
PO Box 610
Georgetown, DE 19947   Phone: (302)856-5400
Format: Alternative/Independent/Progressive. **Key Personnel:** Tamera
Postles, Music Dir. **Ad Rates:** Noncommercial.

♣ 781 WZBH-FM - 93.5
701 N. Dupont Hwy.
PO Box 111   Phone: (302)856-2567
Georgetown, DE 19947   **Fax: (302)856-6839**

HARRINGTON

♣ 782 Simmons Cabel TV of Midshore
Rd.4
PO Box 225
Harrington, DE 19952   Phone: (302)398-4714
Owner: Simmons Communications Co. L.P. **Key Personnel:** Scott
Vosbury, Gen. Mgr.; Ron Carroll, Plant Manager. **Cities Served:**
Central Deleware and southeastern Maryland. 16,000 subscribing
households; 33 channels.

MILFORD

♣ 783 WXPZ-FM - 101.3
626 County Rd.
PO Box K   Phone: (302)424-1013
Milford, DE 19963   Fax: (302)424-2358

MILLSBORO

♣ 784 Simmons Cable TV of Lower Delaware
305 W. DuPont Hwy.
Millsboro, DE 19966   Phone: (302)732-6600
Owner: Simmons Communications, Inc. **Founded:** 1968. **Cities Served:**
Sussex County, Bethany Beach, Clarksville, Dagsboro, Frankford,
Millville, Ocean View, Omar, Roxana, Selbyville, and Slaughter
Beach, DE; Worcester County and Bishopville, MD.

NEW CASTLE

♣ 785 TCI Cablevision of New Castle County
4008 N. DuPont Hwy.   Phone: (302)652-1454
New Castle, DE 19720-6325   Fax: (302)655-0774
Owner: Tele-Communications, Inc. **Founded:** 1969. **Key Personnel:**
Miles McNamee, Dir. of Marketing & Sales; Jon Danielsen, Gen.
Mgr.; Denise Troise, Dir. of Customer Service; Don Pittman, Plant
Mgr.; Mike Williams, Program Mgr.; Bruce Meisterman, Dir. of
Advertising Sales; Joanne Courtney, Accounting Mgr. **Cities Served:**
New Castle County, Arden, Ardencroft, Ardentown, Bellefonte,
Elsmere, Newark, New Castle, and Newport, DE: 126,699 subscribing
households; 51 channels; 1 community access channel; 57 hours per
week of community access programming.

NEWARK

▥ 786 The Review
University of Delaware
B1 Student Center   Phone: (302)831-2771
Newark, DE 19716-6184   **Fax: (302)831-1396**

REHOBOTH BEACH

▥ 787 Delaware Beachcomber
Atlantic Publications, Inc.
PO Box 309   Phone: (302)227-9466
Rehoboth Beach, DE 19971   Fax: (302)227-9469
Shopping guide. **Founded:** 1966. **Frequency:** Weekly. **Printing Method:**
Web offset. **Key Personnel:** Jane Meleady, Gen. Mgr.
Ad Rates: PCI: $9   **Circulation:** Free ‡20,000

▥ 788 Delaware Coast Press
Atlantic Publications, Inc.
PO Box 309   Phone: (302)227-9466
Rehoboth Beach, DE 19971   **Fax: (302)227-9469**

WILMINGTON

▥ 789 Delaware Art Museum Quarterly
Delaware Art Museum
2301 Kentmere Pkwy.   Phone: (302)571-9590
Wilmington, DE 19806   **Fax: (302)571-0220**

▥ 790 Delaware Medical Journal
Medical Society of Delaware
1925 Lovering Ave.   Phone: (302)658-3957
Wilmington, DE 19806-2166   **Fax: (302)658-9669**

▥ 791 Family Times
Family Times, Inc.
1900 Superfine Ln.   Phone: (302)575-0935
Wilmington, DE 19802   Fax: (302)575-0933
Parenting magazine. **Founded:** 1991. **Frequency:** Monthly. **Printing
Method:** Web press. **Trim Size:** 10 x 14. **Cols./Page:** 4. **Col. Width:** 2 3/
8 in. **Key Personnel:** Alison Garber, Editor and Publisher. **Subscrip-
tion:** $12.
Ad Rates: BW: $1,200   **Circulation:** Free ☐50,000
              4C: $1,600   Paid ☐42
Additional Contact Information: Toll-free (800)969-2666.

DISTRICT OF COLUMBIA

WASHINGTON

792 A Better Tomorrow
Thomas Nelson, Inc.
5301 Wisconsin Ave. NW, Ste. 620   Phone: (202)364-8000
Washington, DC 20015   Fax: (202)364-8910
Magazine focusing on issues and concerns of senior citizens. **Subtitle:** The Magazine for Seniors With A Future. **Founded:** 1992. **Frequency:** Quarterly. **Printing Method:** Offset. **Trim Size:** 8 1/2 x 10 7/8. **Key Personnel:** Bruce Barbour, Publisher; Dale Hanson Bourke, Editor; Leslie Nunn, Circulation and Advertising Dir.; Carol Kristen, Circulation Mgr. **Subscription:** $19.80.
Ad Rates: BW: $2,195   **Circulation:** Combined 100,000
                         4C: $2,965
Additional Contact Information: Alternate address PO Box 141000, Nashville, TN 37214-1000

793 ABC Today
Associated Builders and Contractors, Inc.
729 15th St. NW   Phone: (202)637-8800
Washington, DC 20005   **Fax: (202)347-1121**

794 American Bankers Association Banking Literature Index
American Bankers Association
1120 Connecticut Ave. NW   Phone: (202)663-5000
Washington, DC 20036   Fax: (202)828-4535
Index of articles on banking trends, topics, issues, and operations. **Founded:** 1982. **Frequency:** Monthly. **Trim Size:** 8 1/2 x 11. **Cols./Page:** 2. **Key Personnel:** Aubrey Hamilton, Editor; Joan Gervino, Publisher. **ISSN:** 0736-5659. **Subscription:** $105; $155 non-members. $14 single issue; $18 single issue non-members.
                                     Circulation: Paid ⊕410
                                                            Non-paid ⊕20
Advertising not accepted.

795 American Journal of Addictions
American Psychiatric Press
1400 K St. NW   Phone: (202)682-6310
Washington, DC 20005   Fax: (202)789-2648
Journal covering all scientific and clinical aspects of alcohol and drug addictions. **Founded:** 1992. **Frequency:** Quarterly. **Key Personnel:** Sheldon Miller, Editor. **ISSN:** 1055-0496. **Subscription:** $99.
                                     Circulation: Paid 1,400
                                                            Non-paid 25
Advertising accepted; contact publisher for rates.

796 American Pharmacy
American Pharmaceutical Assn.
2215 Constitution Ave. NW   Phone: (202)628-4410
Washington, DC 20037   **Fax: (202)783-2351**

797 Anthropology and Humanism Quarterly
Soc. for Humanistic Anthropology
American Anthropological Assn.
1703 New Hampshire Ave. NW   **Phone: (202)232-8800**
Washington, DC 20009   **Fax: (202)667-5345**

798 Arts Education Policy Review
Heldref Publications
Helen Dwight Reid Educational Foundation
1319 18th St. NW   Phone: (202)296-6267
Washington, DC 20036-1802   Fax: (202)296-5149
Former Title: Design for Arts in Education

799 Asian Affairs: An American Review
Heldref Publications
Helen Dwight Reid Educational Foundation
1319 18th St. NW   Phone: (202)296-6267
Washington, DC 20036-1802   Fax: (202)296-5149

800 The Brookings Review
The Brookings Institution
1775 Massachusetts Ave. NW   Phone: (202)797-6257
Washington, DC 20036   **Fax: (202)797-6195**

801 Career Opportunities Bulletin
Women's Bar Association of DC
1819 H St. NW, Ste. 1205   Phone: (202)785-1540
Washington, DC 20006   Fax: (202)293-3388
Periodical featuring articles and events related to law. Includes updates on job listings. **Frequency:** 9x/yr.
                                             Circulation: (Not Reported)

802 Catholic University Law Review
Columbus School of Law - Catholic
    University of America
Leahy Hall Rm. 1
620 Michigan Ave. NE
Washington, DC 20064   Phone: (202)319-5157

803 Children's Voice
Child Welfare League of America
440 First St. NW, Ste. 310   Phone: (202)638-2952
Washington, DC 20001-2085   Fax: (202)638-4004
Magazine providing information on child welfare programs and policy developments. **Founded:** 1985. **Frequency:** Quarterly. **Printing**

Ad Rates: GLR = general line rate; BW = one-time black & white page rate; 4C = one-time four color page rate; SAU = standard advertising unit rate; CNU = Canadian newspaper advertising unit rate; PCI = per column inch rate.
Circulation: ★ = ABC; △ = BPA; ◆ = CAC; ● = CCAB; □ = VAC; ⊕ = PO Statement; ‡ = Publisher's Report; Boldface figures = sworn; Light figures = estimated.
Entry type: ▣ = Print; ▮ = Broadcast.

55

Method: Sheetfed. **Trim Size:** 8 1/2 x 11. **Cols./Page:** 3. **Key Personnel:** Mary Liepold, Editor; Cathye Thomas, Advertising Mgr. **ISSN:** 1057-736X. **Subscription:** $35; $50 institutions.
Ad Rates: BW: $850 **Circulation:** 10,000
Formerly: Child Welfare League Newsletter: Children's Voice (1991).

804 City & Society
American Anthropological Assn.
1703 New Hampshire Ave., NW Phone: (202)232-8800
Washington, DC 20009 Fax: (202)667-5345
Publication of the American Anthropological Assn. **Frequency:** 2x/mo. **Key Personnel:** Constance P. deRoche, Editor.
Circulation: (Not Reported)

Advertising not accepted.

805 Coastal Management
Taylor & Francis
1101 Vermont Ave. NW, Ste. 200 Phone: (202)289-2174
Washington, DC 20005 Fax: (202)289-3665

806 College Teaching
Heldref Publications
Helen Dwight Reid Educational
Foundation
1319 18th St. NW Phone: (202)296-6267
Washington, DC 20036-1802 **Fax: (202)296-5149**

807 Communio-International Catholic Review
PO Box 4557
Washington, DC 20017 **Phone: (202)526-0251**

808 Congressional Digest
3231 P St. NW Phone: (202)333-7332
Washington, DC 20007 **Fax: (202)625-6670**

809 Construction & Modernization Report
American Hotel & Motel Association
1201 New York Ave. NW Phone: (202)289-3100
Washington, DC 20005 Fax: (202)289-3158
Lists new hotel/motel construction and renovation projects throughout the US and Canada. **Frequency:** Monthly. **Key Personnel:** Jo Bonnie Kaplan, Editor; Sally Brasse, Dir. **Subscription:** Membership only.
Circulation: (Not Reported)

Advertising not accepted.

810 CONSTRUCTOR
Associated General Contractors Information
1957 E St. NW Phone: (202)393-2040
Washington, DC 20006-5199 Fax: (202)347-4004

811 Crisis Magazine
The Brownson Institute
1511 K St. NW, No. 525
Washington, DC 20005 Phone: (202)347-7411

812 Critique: Studies in Contemporary Fiction
Heldref Publications
Helen Dwight Reid Educational
Foundation
1319 18th St. NW Phone: (202)296-6267
Washington, DC 20036-1802 **Fax: (202)296-5149**

813 Educational Gerontology: An International Journal
Taylor & Francis
1101 Vermont Ave. NW, No. 200 Phone: (202)289-2174
Washington, DC 20005 Fax: (202)289-3665

814 Energy Sources
Taylor & Francis
1101 Vermont Ave. NW, Ste. 200 Phone: (202)289-2174
Washington, DC 20005 Fax: (202)289-3665

815 Energy Systems and Policy
Taylor & Francis
1101 Vermont Ave. NW, Ste. 200 Phone: (202)289-2174
Washington, DC 20005 Fax: (202)289-3665

816 Experimental Aging Research
Taylor & Francis
1101 Vermont Ave., Ste. 200 Phone: (202)289-2174
Washington, DC 20005 Fax: (202)289-3665
International journal devoted to the scientific study of the aging process. **Founded:** 1974. **Frequency:** Quarterly. **Printing Method:** Web offset. **Trim Size:** 6 x 9. **Cols./Page:** 1. **Col. Width:** 4 1/2 in. **Col. Depth:** 7 1/2 in. **Key Personnel:** Merrill Elias, Editor-in-Chief. **Subscription:** $35; $135 other countries.
Ad Rates: BW: $400 **Circulation:** 1,000

817 Fiber and Integrated Optics
Taylor & Francis
1101 Vermont Ave. NW, Ste. 200 Phone: (202)289-2174
Washington, DC 20005 Fax: (202)289-3665

818 Foundation News
Council on Foundations
1828 L St NW **Phone: (202)466-6512**
Washington, DC 20036 **Fax: (202)785-3926**

819 Geomicrobiology Journal
Taylor & Francis
1101 Vermont Ave. NW, Ste. 200 Phone: (202)289-2174
Washington, DC 20005 Fax: (202)289-3665

820 The GW Hatchet
George Washington University
800 21st St. NW, Ste. 434 Phone: (202)994-7079
Washington, DC 20052 Fax: (202)994-1309

821 Hospital & Community Psychiatry
American Psychiatric Assn.
1400 K St. NW Phone: (202)682-6070
Washington, DC 20005 **Fax: (202)682-6114**

822 The Information Society
Taylor & Francis
1101 Vermont Ave. NW, Ste. 200 **Phone: (202)289-2174**
Washington, DC 20005 **Fax: (202)289-3665**

823 Initiatives: Journal of NAWE
National Association of Women in Education
1325 18th St. NW, Ste. 210
Washington, DC 20036-6511 Phone: (202)659-9330
Journal focusing on education and the personal and professional development of women. **Frequency:** Quarterly. **ISSN:** 0094-3460. **Subscription:** $40; $50 other countries. $13 single issue.
Circulation: (Not Reported)

824 Inter-American Review of Bibliography
Organization of American States
1889 F St. NW **Phone: (202)458-3242**
Washington, DC 20006 **Fax: (202)458-6115**

825 The International Economy
The International Economy Publications, Inc.
1133 Connecticut Ave. NW, Ste. 901 Phone: (202)861-0791
Washington, DC 20006 Fax: (202)861-0790
Magazine. **Subtitle:** The Magazine of International Economic Policy. **Founded:** 1987. **Frequency:** 6x/yr. **Printing Method:** Web offset. **Trim Size:** 8 1/4 x 10 7/8. **Cols./Page:** 3. **Key Personnel:** Noelle McGlynn, Associate Publisher. **ISSN:** 0898-4336. **Subscription:** $72. $12 single issue.
Circulation: (Not Reported)
Advertising accepted; contact publisher for rates.

826 International Journal of Personal Construct Psychology
Taylor & Francis
1101 Vermont Ave., Ste. 200 Phone: (202)289-2174
Washington, DC 20005 Fax: (202)289-3665

827 The Internist: Health Policy in Practice
American Society of Internal Medicine
2011 Pennsylvania Ave. NW, Ste. 800 **Phone: (202)835-2746**
Washington, DC 20006-1808 **Fax: (202)835-0441**

828   Issues in Comprehensive Pediatric Nursing
Taylor & Francis
1101 Vermont Ave. NW, No. 200   Phone: (202)289-2174
Washington, DC 20005   Fax: (202)289-3665

829   Issues in Mental Health Nursing
Taylor & Francis
1101 Vermont Ave. NW, No. 200   Phone: (202)289-2174
Washington, DC 20005   Fax: (202)289-3665

830   The Journal of Arts Management, Law, and Society
Heldref Publications
Helen Dwight Reid Educational
   Foundation
1319 18th St. NW   Phone: (202)296-6267
Washington, DC 20036-1082   Fax: (202)296-5149
Former Title: Journal of Arts Management & Law

831   Journal of Family Psychology
American Psychological Association
750 First St., NE
Washington, DC 20002-4242   Phone: (202)336-5571

832   The Journal of Legal Medicine
Taylor & Francis
1101 Vermont Ave., Ste. 200   Phone: (202)289-2174
Washington, DC 20005-3521   Fax: (202)289-3665

833   The Journal of Organic Chemistry
American Chemical Society
1155 16th St. NW   Phone: (202)872-4600
Washington, DC 20036   Fax: (202)872-4615

834   Journal of Psychotherapy Practice and Research
American Psychiatric Press
1400 K St. NW   Phone: (202)682-6336
Washington, DC 20005   Fax: (202)789-2648
Journal for practicing and research psychotherapists. **Founded:** 1992.
Frequency: Quarterly. **Key Personnel:** Jerald Kay M.D., Editor. **ISSN:**
1055-050X. **Subscription:** $135.

                                    Circulation: Paid 1,600
                                                  Non-paid 25
Advertising accepted; contact publisher for rates.

835   Journal of Toxicology and Environmental Health
Taylor & Francis
1101 Vermont Ave. NW, No. 200   Phone: (202)289-2174
Washington, DC 20005   Fax: (202)289-3665

836   LAN Life Association News
National Assn. of Life Underwriters
1922 F St. NW   Phone: (202)331-6070
Washington, DC 20006-4387   Fax: (202)331-2179

837   Law Briefs
Office of General Counsel
U.S. Catholic Conference
3211 Fourth St. NE   Phone: (202)541-3300
Washington, DC 20017   Fax: (202)541-3337

838   Marine Geodesy
Taylor & Francis
1101 Vermont Ave. NW, Ste. 200   Phone: (202)289-2174
Washington, DC 20005   Fax: (202)289-3665

839   Medical Anthropology Quarterly
American Anthropological Assn.
1703 New Hampshire Ave., NW   Phone: (202)232-8800
Washington, DC 20009   Fax: (202)667-5345
Journal of the American Anthrolopological Assn. **Frequency:** Quarter-
ly. **Key Personnel:** Ann V. Millard, Editor.
                                    Circulation: (Not Reported)
Advertising accepted; contact publisher for rates.

840   Military Forum
1730 M St. NW
Washington, DC 20036   Phone: (202)857-1400
Ceased publication.

841   Minerals Today
Bureau of Mines
810 Seventh St. NW
Mail Stop 5201   Phone: (202)501-9358
Washington, DC 20241   Fax: (202)501-9958

842   National Geographic
National Geographic Society
Beck Rm. 370
1145 17th St. NW   Phone: (202)857-7000
Washington, DC 20036   Fax: (202)828-5658

843   National NOW Times
National Organization for Women, Inc.
1000 16th St. NW, Ste. 700   Phone: (202)331-0066
Washington, DC 20036   Fax: (202)785-8576

844   The New Teamster
International Brotherhood of Teamsters
25 Louisiana Ave. NW   Phone: (202)624-6800
Washington, DC 20001-2198   Fax: (202)624-6918
Former Title: The International Teamster

845   The Northwest Current
The Current Newspapers
5125 MacArthur Blvd. NW, Suite 10
Washington, DC 20016   Phone: (202)244-7223

846   Nucleonics Week
McGraw-Hill, Inc.
1200 G St. NW, Ste. 1100   Phone: (202)463-1651
Washington, DC 20005   Fax: (202)463-1611

847   Ocean Development and International Law
Taylor & Francis
1101 Vermont Ave. NW, Ste. 200   Phone: (202)289-2174
Washington, DC 20005   Fax: (202)289-3665

848   Proceedings of the Entomological Society of
      Washington
Entomological Soc. of Washington
Smithsonian Institution
Dept. of Entomology NHB 168
Washington, DC 20560   Phone: (202)382-1780

849   Psychological Assessment
American Psychological Assn.
750 First St., NE
Washington, DC 20002-4242   Phone: (202)336-5571

850   PsycSCAN: PSYCHOANALYSIS
American Psychological Assn.
750 First St., NE   Phone: (202)336-5571
Washington, DC 20002-4242   Fax: (202)336-5633

851   The Public Employee Magazine
American Federation of State, County & Municipal Employees
1625 L St. NW   Phone: (202)429-1144
Washington, DC 20036-5687   Fax: (202)429-1084

852   Public Power
American Public Power Association
2301 M St. NW
Washington, DC 20037   Phone: (202)467-2948

853   Reading Psychology: An International Quarterly
Taylor & Francis
1101 Vermont Ave. NW, No. 200   Phone: (202)289-2174
Washington, DC 20005   Fax: (202)289-3665

📖 **854 Reading and Writing Quarterly: Overcoming Learning Difficulties**
Taylor & Francis
1101 Vermont Ave. NW, No. 200   Phone: (202)289-2174
Washington, DC 20005   Fax: (202)289-3665

📖 **855 Real Estate Finance Today**
Mortgage Bankers Assn.
1125 15th St. NW   Phone: (202)861-6500
Washington, DC 20005   **Fax: (202)429-9524**

📖 **856 Realtor News (All Member Issue)**
National Assn. of Realtors
777 14th St, NW
Washington, DC 20005   Fax: (202)383-1231

📖 **857 Research News Reporter**
Institute for Women's Policy Research
1400 20th St. NW, Ste. 104
Washington, DC 20036   Phone: (202)785-5100
Periodical of reprinted newspaper articles from the New York Times, Wall Street Journal, and Washington Post on: work and education; poverty and income; politics and society; family life; health and reproductive issues. **Frequency:** 6x/yr. **Subscription:** $150; $195 non-profit organizations; $295 corporations.
                                       Circulation: (Not Reported)

📖 **858 Sculpture**
International Sculpture Center
1050 17th St. NW, Ste. 250   Phone: (202)965-6066
Washington, DC 20036   Fax: (202)965-7318

📖 **859 Skylines**
Building Owners and Managers Assn. (BOMA) International
1201 New York Ave.   **Phone: (202)408-2686**
Washington, DC 20005   Fax: (202)371-0181

📖 **860 Social Work**
National Assn. of Social Workers
750 First St. NE, Ste. 700   Phone: (202)408-8600
Washington, DC 20002-4241   Fax: (202)336-8312

📖 **861 Society & Natural Resources**
Taylor & Francis
1101 Vermont Ave. NW, Ste. 200   **Phone: (202)289-2174**
Washington, DC 20005   **Fax: (202)289-3665**

📖 **862 Sociological Spectrum: The Official Journal of the Mid-South Sociological Association**
Taylor & Francis
1101 Vermont Ave. NW, No. 200   Phone: (202)289-2174
Washington, DC 20005   Fax: (202)289-3665

📖 **863 Spiritual Life**
Washington Province of Discalced Carmelite Friars, Inc.
2131 Lincoln Rd. NE   **Phone: (202)832-8489**
Washington, DC 20002   Fax: (302)832-8967

📖 **864 Theory and Research in Social Education**
National Council for the Social Studies
3501 Newark St., NW   Phone: (202)966-7840
Washington, DC 20016   Fax: (202)966-2061
Scholarly journal. **Founded:** 1973. **Frequency:** Quarterly. **Printing Method:** Offset. **Trim Size:** 6 x 9. **Cols./Page:** 1. **Key Personnel:** Jack R. Jaenkel, Editor. **ISSN:** 0093-3104. **Subscription:** $35. $10 single issue.
Ad Rates: BW: $250   **Circulation:** ⊕750

📖 **865 Today's Better Life**
5301 Wisconsin Ave. NW, Ste. 620   Phone: (202)364-8000
Washington, DC 20015   Fax: (202)364-8910
A magazine promoting spiritual, physical, and emotional health. **Founded:** 1991. **Frequency:** Quarterly. **Printing Method:** Web offset. **Trim Size:** 8 1/2 x 10 7/8. **Key Personnel:** Dr. Frank Minirth, Editor; Dr. Paul Meier, Editor; Dale Hanson Bourke, Publisher. **Subscription:** $19.80. $4.95 single issue.
Ad Rates: BW: $1,995   **Circulation:** Combined 100,000
            4C: $2,695
Formerly: Christian Psychology for Today.

📖 **866 21st Century Science & Technology**
21st Century Science Associates, Inc.
PO Box 16285   Phone: (703)777-7473
Washington, DC 20041   Fax: (703)777-8853
Science magazine. **Founded:** 1988. **Frequency:** Quarterly. **Printing Method:** Offset. **Trim Size:** 8 1/4 x 10 1/2. **Cols./Page:** 2 or 3. 20 or 13 picas. **Col. Depth:** 9 in. **Key Personnel:** Marjorie Mazel Hecht, Mng. Editor. **ISSN:** 0895-6420. **Subscription:** $20. $3 single issue.
Ad Rates: BW: $1,000   **Circulation:** ⊕45,309
                                       Non-paid ⊕2,382
4C: $1,500 (cover only).

📖 **867 Ultrastructural Pathology**
Taylor & Francis
1101 Vermont Ave. NW, No. 200   Phone: (202)289-2174
Washington, DC 20005   Fax: (202)289-3665

📖 **868 U.S. News & World Report**
2400 N St. NW   Phone: (202)955-2000
Washington, DC 20037   **Fax: (202)955-2049**

📖 **869 Urban Forests**
American Forests
PO Box 2000   Phone: (202)667-3300
Washington, DC 20013-2000   Fax: (202)667-7751
Magazine covering the planting and maintenance of urban trees to better the environment. **Subtitle:** The Magazine of Community Trees. **Founded:** June/July, 1990. **Frequency:** Bimonthly. **Key Personnel:** Gerald Fox, Sr. Editor; Michelle Robbins, Managing Editor. **ISSN:** 1052-2484. **Subscription:** Free; $18 other countries.
                                       Circulation: (Not Reported)

📖 **870 The Volta Review**
Alexander Graham Bell Assn. for the Deaf
3417 Volta Pl. NW   Phone: (202)337-5220
Washington, DC 20007-2778   **Fax: (202)337-8314**

📖 **871 The Washington Blade**
1408 U St. NW, 2nd Fl.   **Phone: (202)797-7000**
Washington, DC 20009   **Fax: (202)797-7040**

📖 **872 The Wheat Grower**
National Association of Wheat Growers
415 2nd St. NE, Ste. 300   Phone: (202)547-7800
Washington, DC 20002-4993   Fax: (202)546-2638

📖 **873 Youth Today**
American Youth Work Center
1751 N St. NW   Phone: (202)785-0764
Washington, DC 20036   Fax: (202)728-0657
National newspaper focused on out-of-school programs and services in operation in the U.S. Reports on news, policy formulation, decision-making, and emerging technology affecting youth-serving agencies. **Frequency:** 6x/yr. **Key Personnel:** Bill Treanor, Publisher; Bill Howard, Editor.
                                       Circulation: Controlled 10,000
Additional Contact Information: Advertising office Judy Solomon Associates, 7910 Woodmont Ave., Ste. 916, Bethesda, MD 20814, (301)652-8862.

📖 **874 YSB**
Paige Publications, Inc.
3109 M St., NW
Washington, DC 20007
Magazine discussing the interest and concerns of African-American youth. **Frequency:** 10x/yr. **Key Personnel:** Frank Dexter Brown, Editor; Debra L. Lee, Publisher. **Subscription:** $11.95. $1.95 single issue.
                                       Circulation: (Not Reported)

📡 **875 District Cablevision, Inc.**
1328 Florida Ave. NW
Washington, DC 20009   Phone: (202)332-7000
Owner: District Cablevision, Inc. and Telecomunications, Inc. **Founded:** 1985. **Key Personnel:** Betty Palumbo, Gen. Mgr.; Rodney Bagley, Assistant Gen. Mgr.; Thomas McGrath, Operations Dir.; Diane Smith, Accounting Mgr.; Donnie Fritzgerald, Plant Mgr. **Cities Served:** Washington, DC: 79,000 subscribing households; 58 channels. **Additional Contact Information:** (202)332-8777.

♣ 876 WDCA-TV - Channel 20
5202 River Rd.   Phone: (301)986-9322
Bethesda, MD 20816   Fax: (301)654-3517

♣ 877 WPGC-AM - 1580
6301 Ivy Ln., Ste. 800   Phone: (301)441-3500
Greenbelt, MD 20770   Fax: (301)345-9505

FLORIDA

APALACHICOLA

878 Carrabelle Times
PO Box 820
Apalachicola, FL 32329

Phone: (904)653-8868
Fax: (904)653-8036

879 WOYS-FM - 100.9
Box 527
Eastpoint, FL 32328

Phone: (904)670-8450
Fax: (904)670-8450

ARCADIA

880 WKGF-AM - 1480
201 W. Asbury St.
PO Box 632
Arcadia, FL 33821

Phone: (813)494-2427
Fax: (813)494-9444

AVON PARK

881 WKHF-AM - 1390
PO Box 29
Avon Park, FL 33825

Phone: (813)453-9543

Format: Religious (Contemporary Christian). Simulcasts WKGF-AM.
Network(s): ABC; Florida Radio. **Owner:** Gulf Dunes Broadcasting, at
above address. **Operating Hours:** Continuous; 95% network, 5% local.
Ad Rates: $6-$20 for 30 seconds; $7-$21 for 60 seconds.

BARTOW

882 WWBF-AM - 1130
1130 Radio Rd.
Bartow, FL 33830

Phone: (813)533-0744
Fax: (813)533-8546

BOCA RATON

883 La Florida Magazine
Florida City Group, Inc.
3350 NW 2nd Ave.
Boca Raton, FL 33431
Magazine featuring articles on topics of interest to individuals living
in Florida. **Frequency:** 5x/yr. **Key Personnel:** David Davidiou, Editor
and Publisher. **Subscription:** $15. $3.50 single issue.

Circulation: (Not Reported)

BONITA SPRINGS

884 WEVU-TV - Channel 26

Phone: (813)495-
WEVU
3451 Bonita Bay Blvd.
Bonita Springs, FL 33923

Fax: (813)947-1722

BRADENTON

885 Paragon Communications
3301 14th St. W.
Box J
Bradenton, FL 34206

Phone: (813)748-1822

Owner: Universal Cablevision, Inc. **Founded:** 1969. **Cities Served:**
Manatee County, Anna Maria, Bradenton Beach, and Holmes Beach,
FL.

BUNNELL

886 Flagler/Palm Coast News-Tribune
901 6th St.
PO Box 2831
Daytona Beach, FL 33120-2831

Phone: (904)252-1511
Fax: (904)437-0139

CALLAWAY

887 WDRK-FM - 103.5
5620 Cherry St., Ste. C
Panama City, FL 32404

Phone: (904)769-1377
Fax: (904)763-0186

CASSELBERRY

888 WONQ-AM - 1140
1033 Semoran Blvd., No. 253
Casselberry, FL 32707-5758

Phone: (407)830-0800
Fax: (407)260-6100

CHIEFLAND

889 WLQH-FM - 97.3
PO Box 99
Chiefland, FL 32626

Phone: (904)493-4940
Fax: (904)493-9943

Format: Country. **Network(s):** AP; Florida Radio. **Owner:** White
Construction, at above address. **Founded:** 1992. **Operating Hours:** 6
a.m.-midnight. **Key Personnel:** Norma Schessler, Gen. Mgr.; Bob
Moody, Program Dir.; Jesse Miller, Music Dir. **Wattage:** 6000. **Ad
Rates:** $5.50 for 30 seconds; $7.50 for 60 seconds. **Additional Contact
Information:** Business line (904)493-4011.

CLERMONT

890 South Lake Press
Republic Newspapers, Inc.
PO Box 120868
Clermont, FL 34712

Phone: (904)394-2183
Fax: (904)394-8001

Ad Rates: GLR = general line rate; BW = one-time black & white page rate; 4C = one-time four color page rate; SAU = standard advertising unit rate;
CNU = Canadian newspaper advertising unit rate; PCI = per column inch rate.
Circulation: ★ = ABC; △ = BPA; ◆ = CAC; ● = CCAB; □ = VAC; ⊕ = PO Statement; ‡ = Publisher's Report; Boldface figures = sworn; Light figures = estimated.
Entry type: ▯ = Print; ▮ = Broadcast.

61

COCOA

♨ 891 WWKO-AM - 860
200 Burnett Rd.   Phone: (407)636-8600
Cocoa, FL 32926   Fax: (407)636-1993

CORAL GABLES

📖 892 Cavalier
Dugent Publishing Co.
2600 Douglas Rd., No. 600   Phone: (305)443-2378
Coral Gables, FL 33134   Fax: (305)443-1191
Ceased publication.

📖 893 Journal of Interamerican Studies and World Affairs
University of Miami/North-South
Center Pub.
Graduate School of International
Studies
PO Box 248205   Phone: (305)284-8967
Coral Gables, FL 33124-3027   Fax: (305)284-6370

📖 894 NAFAC News
National Assn. for Ambulatory Care
2333 Ponce De Leon Blvd., No. 511   Phone: (305)441-2421
Coral Gables, FL 33134-5407   Fax: (305)441-0108

📖 895 Tecnologia del Plastico
C.C. International Publishing, Inc.
901 Ponce de Leon Blvd., Ste. 901   Phone: (305)448-6875
Coral Gables, FL 33134   Fax: (305)448-9942

CORAL SPRINGS

📖 896 Bachelor Book Magazine
Bachelor International Enterprises, Inc.
8222 Wiles Rd., Ste. 111   Phone: (305)341-8801
Coral Springs, FL 33067   Fax: (305)341-8982

📖 897 Plants Sites & Parks
Pocral, Inc.
10100 W. Sample Rd. No.201   Phone: (305)753-2660
Coral Springs, FL 33065   Fax: (305)755-7048

DANIA

♨ 898 WNKR-FM - 101.1
3301 College Ave.
Dania, FL 33142   Phone: (305)475-7419
Format: Alternative/Independent/Progressive. **Key Personnel:** Gregg
Weiner, Music Dir. **Ad Rates:** Noncommercial.

DAYTONA BEACH

📖 899 Our World
Our World Publishing Corp.
1104 N. Nova Rd., Ste. 251   Phone: (904)441-5367
Daytona Beach, FL 32117   Fax: (904)441-5604
Travel magazine. **Subtitle:** The International Gay Travel Magazine.
Founded: 1989. **Frequency:** 10x/mo. **Printing Method:** Web offset.
Trim Size: 8 x 10 3/4. **Cols./Page:** 3. **Col. Width:** 2 1/4 in. **Col. Depth:**
9 3/4 in. **Key Personnel:** Richard Valdmanis, Sales Mgr. **ISSN:** 1044-
6699. **Subscription:** $44; $52 other countries. $4.95 single issue.
Ad Rates: BW: $585   **Circulation:** ‡17,000
4C: $950

♨ 900 TCI Cablevision of Florida
Box 2100
Daytona Beach, FL 32114   Phone: (904)253-6503
Owner: Tele-Communications, Inc. **Founded:** 1968. **Cities Served:**
Volusia County, Daytona Beach Shores, Ponce Inlet, Port Orange,
Daytona Beach, and Spruce Creek, FL.

DE FUNIAK SPRINGS

♨ 901 WGTX-AM - 1280
Box 627   Phone: (904)892-3158
De Funiak Springs, FL 32433   Fax: (904)892-4642

DE LAND

📖 902 Skydiving
1725 N. Lexington Ave.   Phone: (904)736-4793
De Land, FL 32724   Fax: (904)736-9786

📖 903 Sun News
111 S. Alabama Ave.
Box 1119   Phone: (904)734-3661
De Land, FL 32721-1119   Fax: (904)736-8972
Ceased publication.

DEERFIELD BEACH

📖 904 Changes Magazine
U.S. Journal, Inc.
3201 SW 15th St.   Phone: (305)360-0909
Deerfield Beach, FL 33442   Fax: (305)360-0034
Self-help and recovery magazine. **Founded:** 1986. **Frequency:** Bi-
monthly. **Key Personnel:** Jeffrey Laign, Mng. Editor. **Subscription:**
$20; $40 other countries. $3.75 single issue.
Ad Rates: BW: $1,710   **Circulation:** Paid ★29,640
4C: $2,110   Non-paid ★8,360
Additional Contact Information: Toll-free (800)851-9100.

📖 905 Palm Beach Jewish Journal North
The South Florida Newspaper Network
601 Fairway Dr.   Phone: (305)698-6397
Deerfield Beach, FL 33441   Fax: (305)698-6719
Former Title: Palm Beach Jewish Journal

📖 906 South Florida Home Buyer's Guide
Real Estate Magazine
2151 W. Hillsboro Blvd., Ste. 300   Phone: (305)428-5602
Deerfield Beach, FL 33442   Fax: (305)426-4750
Ceased publication.

DESTIN

📖 907 The Beach Breeze
PO Box 6160   Phone: (904)267-1262
Destin, FL 32541   Fax: (904)267-1262
Community newspaper. **Founded:** 1990. **Frequency:** Weekly. **Printing
Method:** Offset. **Trim Size:** 14 x 23. **Cols./Page:** 6. **Col. Width:** 12
picas. **Col. Depth:** 21 in. **Key Personnel:** John P. Jones, Editor; Julie
McCoy, Mng. Editor; Gary Woodham, Publisher; Cindy Woodham,
Publisher; Brenda Peters, Advertising Mgr. **Subscription:** $12.72; $15
(outside Florida).
Ad Rates: BW: $476.28   **Circulation:** Paid ⊕877
PCI: $3.78   Free ⊕3,500
Additional Contact Information: Alt. phone (904)267-3883.

DUNNELLON

📖 908 Biocontrol Science and Technology
Carfax Publishing Co.
PO Box 2025
Dunnellon, FL 34430-2025
Journal covering research in the fields of biological pest, disease, and
weed control. **Founded:** 1991. **Frequency:** Quarterly. **Key Personnel:**
C.C. Payne, Editor-in-Chief; M.G. Solomon, Editor; J.W. Deacon,
Editor. **ISSN:** 0958-3157. **Subscription:** $280; $77 single issue.
Circulation: (Not Reported)
Advertising accepted; contact publisher for rates. **Additional Contact
Information:** Editorial address Editor-in-Chief, Horticulture Research
International, Wellesbourne, Warwick Cv35 9EF, UK; subscriptions
and advertising department address Carfax Publishing Co., PO Box
25, Abingdon, Oxfordshire OX14 3UE, UK.

📖 909 Contemporary South Asia
Carfax Publishing Co.
PO Box 2025
Dunnellon, FL 34430-2025
Journal covering policy issues and historical articles on South Asia.
Founded: 1992. **Frequency:** 3x/yr. **Key Personnel:** Gowher Rizvi,
Editor; Robert Cassen, Editor; Subrata Mitra, Review Editor; Tom
Jannuzi, Consulting Editor; Iftikhar Malik, Regional Editor; Kazi
Shahidullah, Regional Editor; Bishnu Mohapatra, Regional Editor;

Sridhar K. Khatri, Regional Editor. **ISSN:** 0958-4935. **Subscription:** $150. $66 single issue.

Circulation: (Not Reported)
Advertising accepted; contact publisher for rates. **Additional Contact Information:** Editorial address Nuffield College, University of Oxford, Oxford, OX1 1NF, UK; subscription and advertising departments Carfax Publishing Co., PO Box 25, Abingdon, Oxfordshire, OX14 3UE, UK.

📖 **910 Nanobiology: Journal of Research in Nanoscale Living**
Carfax Publishing Co.
PO Box 2025
Dunnellon, FL 34430-2025
Journal covering all aspects of cellular systems in coherence. Emphasizes processes acting on nanomechanisms, such as repair, replication, and where the cytoskeleton acts as an operator. **Frequency:** Quarterly.
Key Personnel: Per Anders Hansson, Editor-in-Chief; Hirokazu Hotani, Co-Editor; Stuart R. Hameroff, Co-Editor; P.I. Lazarev, Co-Editor; W.R. Adey, Assoc. Editor; Antonio Lazcano, Assoc. Editor; Vladimir Kislov, Assoc. Editor; Steen Rasmussen, Assoc. Editor. **ISSN:** 0958-3165. **Subscription:** $280.
Circulation: (Not Reported)
Additional Contact Information: For subscriptions and advertisements PO Box 25, Abingdon, Oxfordshire, OX14 3UE, UK.

FORT LAUDERDALE

📖 **911 Broward Review**
Review Publications, Inc.
PO Box 14366   **Phone:** (305)468-2600
Fort Lauderdale, FL 33302   **Fax:** (305)468-2630

📖 **912 Sun-Sentinel**
News and Sun-Sentinel Co.
200 E. Las Olas   **Phone:** (305)356-4000
Fort Lauderdale, FL 33301-2293 **Fax:** (305)356-4559

📖 **913 Weekly Scene**
1750 Commercial Blvd., No. 3   **Phone:** (305)561-0568
Fort Lauderdale, FL 33334   **Fax:** (305)561-0568

🎙 **914 Selkirk Communications, Inc.**
644 S. Andrews Ave.   **Phone:** (305)527-6620
Fort Lauderdale, FL 33301   **Fax:** (305)527-4039
Owner: Cablevision Industries, Inc. **Founded:** 1979. **Cities Served:** Broward County, Lauderdale-by-the-Sea, Oakland Park, and Sea Ranch Lakes, FL.

FORT MYERS

🎙 **915 Jones Intercable, Inc.**
2212 McGregor Blvd.
Box 1360   **Phone:** (813)334-8055
Fort Myers, FL 33902   **Fax:** (813)334-7023
Owner: Jones Intercable, Inc. **Founded:** 1962. **Cities Served:** Lee County, Cypress Lake, Fort Meyers, Fort Meyers Shores, and Iona Gardens, FL.

🎙 **916 WAYJ-FM - 88.7**
1860 Boy Scout Dr., Ste. 202   **Phone:** (813)936-1929
Fort Myers, FL 33907   **Fax:** (813)936-5433

🎙 **917 WCRM-AM - 1350**
3448 Canal St.
Fort Myers, FL 33916   **Phone:** (813)332-1350

🎙 **918 WSFP-FM - 90.1**
University of South Florida
8111 College Pkwy., Areca, No.216   **Phone:** (813)432-5580
Fort Myers, FL 33919   **Fax:** (813)432-5585

FORT WALTON BEACH

🎙 **919 Emerald Coast Cable Television**
784 N. Beal Pkwy.
Drawer 2827   **Phone:** (904)862-4142
Fort Walton Beach, FL 32549   **Fax:** (904)862-1708
Owner: Cox Cable Communications/Warner Cable Communications. **Founded:** 1963. **Key Personnel:** Michelle Oswalt, Customer Services Mgr. **Cities Served:** Okaloosa County, Walton County, Choctaw Beach, Destin, Okaloosa Island, Shalimar, and Villa Tasso, FL: 58,300 subscribing households; 45 channels; 1 community access channel; 10 hours per week of community access programming.

GAINESVILLE

📖 **920 Business & Professional Ethics Journal**
University of Florida
Center for Applied Philosophy
332 Griffin-Floyd Hall
Gainesville, FL 32611   **Phone:** (904)392-2084

📖 **921 Florida Leader For High School Students**
Oxendine Publishing, Inc.
PO Box 14081   **Phone:** (904)373-6907
Gainesville, FL 32604-2081   **Fax:** (904)373-8120
Educational magazine for students. **Founded:** 1991. **Frequency:** Quarterly. **Printing Method:** Offset. **Trim Size:** 8 1/2 x 11. **Cols./Page:** 3. **Key Personnel:** W.H. Oxendine, Jr., Publisher. **Subscription:** $20. $3.50 single issue.
Circulation: 100
Non-paid 40,000
Advertising accepted; contact publisher for rates.

📖 **922 Florida Living**
North Florida Publishing, Inc.
102 NE 10th Ave., Ste. 6   **Phone:** (904)372-8865
Gainesville, FL 32601   **Fax:** (904)372-3453

📖 **923 FloridAgriculture**
Florida Farm Bureau Federation
PO Box 147030   **Phone:** (904)374-1523
Gainesville, FL **32614-7030** Fax: (904)374-1501

📖 **924 The Gainesville Iguana**
PO Box 14712
Gainesville, FL 32604   **Phone:** (904)378-5655
Journal focused on feminist, anti-racist, labor, and progressive local news. **Founded:** October 1986. **Frequency:** Monthly. **Printing Method:** Web offset. **Trim Size:** 8 3/8 x 10 7/8. **Cols./Page:** 3. **Col. Width:** 2 1/4 in. **Col. Depth:** 9 1/8. **Key Personnel:** Joe Courter, Co-Editor; Jenny Brown, Co-Editor; Pete Self, Photo Editor. **Subscription:** Free; $10 (mail).
Ad Rates: BW: $80   **Circulation:** Paid 700
PCI: $5   Non-paid 3,000

📖 **925 Professional Ethics: A Multidisciplinary Journal**
University of Florida
Center for Applied Philosophy
332 Griffin-Floyd Hall
Gainesville, FL 32611   **Phone:** (904)392-2084
Interdisciplinary journal on professional ethics. **Founded:** 1992. **Frequency:** Quarterly. **Trim Size:** 6 x 9. **Cols./Page:** 1. **Col. Width:** 4 in. **Col. Depth:** 7 in. **Key Personnel:** Robert J. Baum, Editor. **ISSN:** 1063-6579. **Subscription:** $20; $40 institutions.
Ad Rates: BW: $200   **Circulation:** (Not Reported)

📖 **926 The Record Farmer and Ranch-Statewide**
PO Box 806
620 N. Main St.   **Phone:** (904)377-2444
Gainesville, FL 32602   **Fax:** (904)338-1986
Community newspaper with statewide agricultural publications. **Founded:** 1965. **Frequency:** Weekly. **Printing Method:** Offset. **Cols./Page:** 5. **Col. Width:** 1 7/8 in. **Col. Depth:** 15 in. **Key Personnel:** G.B.

Crawford, Editor; Connie Rowe, Co-Publisher; Ben Rowe, Co-Publisher. **USPS:** 086-430. **Subscription:** $16; $18 out of state.
Ad Rates: GLR: $.66   **Circulation:** ‡5,000
                BW: $691.50
                4C: $991.50
                PCI: $9.22
Formerly: Independent Farm and Ranch.

☐ 927   The Record-Local
PO Box 806
620 N. Main St.   Phone: (904)377-2444
Gainesville, FL 32602   Fax: (904)338-1986
Community and business newspaper. **Founded:** 1989. **Frequency:**
Weekly. **Printing Method:** Offset, **Cols./Page:** 5. **Col. Width:** 1 7/8 in.
Col. Depth: 15 in. **Key Personnel:** G.B. Crawford, Editor; Connie
Rowe, Co-Publisher; Ben Rowe, Co-Publisher. **USPS:** 086-430.
Subscription: $16; $18 out of state.
Ad Rates: GLR: $.41   **Circulation:** ‡5,000
                BW: $432.40
                4C: $732.40
                PCI: $6.96
Formerly: Independent Farmer and Rancher.

☐ 928   University of Florida Today Magazine
University of Florida National Alumni Association
355 Tigert Hall   Phone: (904)392-0186
Gainesville, FL 32611   Fax: (904)392-3358

♣ 929   Cox Cable-University City
1115 NW 4th St.   Phone: (904)377-1741
Gainesville, FL 32601   Fax: (904)378-2790
Owner: Cox Cable Communications. **Founded:** 1965. **Cities Served:**
Alachua County, FL.

♣ 930   WUFT-FM - 89.1
University of Florida, Gainesville
2206 Weimer Hall   Phone: (904)392-5200
Gainesville, FL 32611   **Fax: (904)392-5731**

HAINES CITY

♣ 931   WLVF-AM - 930
110 W. Scenic Hwy.
Haines City, FL 33844   **Phone: (813)422-9583**

HERNANDO

♣ 932   WRZN-AM - 720
3988 N. Roscoe Rd.   Phone: (904)726-7221
Hernando, FL 32642   **Fax: (904)726-3172**

HIALEAH

♣ 933   Dynamic Cablevision of Florida
2151 W. 62nd St.   Phone: (305)558-2112
Hialeah, FL 33016-2624   Fax: (305)828-4418
Owner: Colony Communications, Inc. **Founded:** 1978. **Cities Served:**
Dade County, Coral Gables, Hialeah gardens, Medley, Miami
Springs, Sweetwater, Virginia Gardens, and West Miami, FL.

HOLLYWOOD

☐ 934   Davie/Cooper City Sun
6491 Taft St.   Phone: (305)929-8100
Hollywood, FL 33024-4110   Fax: (305)929-8169
Ceased publication.

☐ 935   EDI World
EDI World, Inc.
2021 Coolidge St.   Phone: (305)925-5900
Hollywood, FL 33020   Fax: (305)925-7533
Former Title: Production & Inventory Management

☐ 936   Miramar
6491 Taft St.   Phone: (305)929-8100
Hollywood, FL 33024-4110   Fax: (305)929-8169
Ceased publication.

☐ 937   Pembroke Pines Sun
6491 Taft St.   Phone: (305)929-8100
Hollywood, FL 33024-4110   Fax: (305)929-8169
Ceased publication.

♣ 938   Hollywood Cablevision
3000 N. 29th Ct.
Box 2368   Phone: (305)921-1770
Hollywood, FL 33022   Fax: (305)925-8178
Owner: P.D.Q. Cable TV, Inc. **Founded:** 1980. **Cities Served:** Broward
County, FL.

HUDSON

♣ 939   WYFE-FM - 88.9
16310-1 U.S. Hwy. 19
Hudson, FL 34674-6060   **Phone: (813)862-9323**

INVERNESS

♣ 940   WINV-AM - 1560
1541 S. Hillock Terrace   Phone: (904)726-1560
Inverness, FL **34452**   **Fax: (904)637-3223**

JACKSONVILLE

☐ 941   Kalliope: A Journal of Women's Art
Florida Community College at Jacksonville
3939 Roosevelt Blvd.
Jacksonville, FL 32205   Phone: (904)381-3511
Journal containing women's poetry, fiction, interviews, reviews, and
artwork. **Founded:** 1978. **Frequency:** 3x/yr. **Printing Method:** Offset.
Trim Size: 7 1/4 x 8 1/2. **Cols./Page:** 1. **Key Personnel:** Mary Sue
Koeppel, Editor. **ISSN:** 0735-7885. **Subscription:** $10.50; $16.50
other countries; $18 institutions; $24 institutions other countries. $7
single issue.
                                   Circulation: Paid 900
                                                 Non-paid 100
Advertising not accepted.

♣ 942   Continental Cablevision
5934 Richard St.
Box 17613
Jacksonville, FL 32245-8810   Phone: (904)731-7700
Owner: Continental Cablevision, Inc. **Founded:** 1979. **Cities Served:**
Duval County, St. Johns County, Jacksonville Naval Air Station, and
Mayport Naval Air Station, FL.

♣ 943   WFIN-AM - 650
2800 University Blvd. N
Jacksonville, FL 32211   Phone: (904)744-3950
Format: Alternative/Independent/Progressive. **Key Personnel:** Steve
Krueger, Music Dir. **Ad Rates:** Noncommercial.

♣ 944   WJCT-TV - Channel 7
100 Festival Park Ave.   Phone: (904)353-7770
Jacksonville, FL 32202-1397   **Fax: (904)354-6846**

♣ 945   WROS-AM - 1050
5590 Rio Grande Ave.
Jacksonville, FL 32205   **Phone: (904)353-1050**

♣ 946   WVOJ-AM - 970
2427 University Blvd. N.   Phone: (904)743-6970
Jacksonville, FL 32211   **Fax: (904)743-6975**

KEY LARGO

☐ 947   Gibbons-Humm's Guide to the Florida Keys
Gibbons Publishing
PO Box 2921   Phone: (305)451-4429
Key Largo, FL 33037   Fax: (305)451-5201
Former Title: Humm's Guide to the Florida Keys

KEY WEST

♣ 948   WIIS-FM - 107.1
517 Eaton St.   **Phone: (305)292-1133**
Key West, FL 33040   **Fax: (305)292-6936**

♣ **949　WOZN-FM - 98.7**
Box 1874　　　　　　　　　　Phone: (305)293-9898
Tallahassee, FL 32302　　　　　Fax: (305)293-9654
Format: Classic Rock. **Owner:** Key West Communications Inc.
Founded: 1986. **Operating Hours:** Continuous. **Key Personnel:** B.F.J.
Timm, Pres.; Larry Blocher, Gen. Mgr.; Tonie Blocher, Sales Mgr.
Wattage: 100,000.

KISSIMMEE

▣ **950　Florida Cattleman and Livestock Journal**
Florida Cattleman's Assn.
PO Box 421403　　　　　　　**Phone: (407)846-8025**
Kissimmee, FL 34742-1403　　　**Fax: (407)933-8209**

LAKE MARY

▣ **951　Inside Music**
Strang Communications
600 Rinehart Rd.　　　　　　　Phone: (407)333-0600
Lake Mary, FL 32746　　　　　　Fax: (407)333-9753
Christian music magazine. **Founded:** 1990. **Frequency:** 6x/yr. **Key
Personnel:** Ana Gascon, Editor; Tim Gilmour, Publisher; Lori Slough,
Account Exec.
　　　　　　　　　Circulation: Non-paid ‡100,000
Advertising accepted; contact publisher for rates.

LAKELAND

♣ **952　Cablevision of Central Florida**
5735 S. Florida Ave.
Box 6220
Lakeland, FL 33807　　　　　　Phone: (813)644-6149
Owner: American TV & Communications Corp. **Founded:** 1983.
Cities Served: Pinellas County, FL.

LAND O LAKES

▣ **953　The Laker**
Republic Newspapers, Inc.
PO Box 1199　　　　　　　　Phone: (813)949-5796
Land O Lakes, FL 34639　　　　**Fax: (813)949-9435**

LANTANA

▣ **954　Soap Opera Magazine**
Soap Opera Magazine, Inc.
600 SE Coast Ave.
Lantana, FL 33462
Magazine reporting on daytime television soap operas. **Frequency:**
Weekly **Key Personnel:** Joseph Polecy, Editor; Barbara Marks, Pub-
lisher. **Subscription:** $35. $.79 single issue.
　　　　　　　　　Circulation: (Not Reported)

LEESBURG

♣ **955　Lake County Cablevision**
1310 Marion St.　　　　　　　Phone: (904)787-7875
Leesburg, FL 34749-0919　　　　Fax: (904)365-6279
Owner: Scripps Howard Cable Co. **Founded:** 1968. **Cities Served:** Lake
County, Eustis, Fruitland Park, Howey-in-the-Hills, Lady Lake,
Montverde, Mount Dora, Mount Plymouth, Sorrento, Tavares, and
Umatilla, FL.

LIVE OAK

♣ **956　WQHL-AM - 1250**
Box 130　　　　　　　　　　Phone: (904)362-1250
Live Oak, FL 32060　　　　　　**Fax: (904)364-3504**

♣ **957　WQHL-FM - 98.1**
1305 E. Helvenston St.
PO Box 130　　　　　　　　　Phone: (904)362-1250
Live Oak, FL 32060　　　　　　**Fax: (904)364-3504**

MARATHON SHORES

▣ **958　The Keys Advertiser**
8907 O/S Hwy.
PO Box 523358　　　　　　　Phone: (305)743-8766
Marathon Shores, FL 33052-3358　Fax: (305)743-9977
Shopping guide. **Founded:** 1990. **Frequency:** Weekly. **Subscription:**
Free.
Ad Rates:　BW:　$390　　　　**Circulation:** Free 9,000
　　　　　　4C:　$590
　　　　　　PCI:　$6

MARGATE

▣ **959　The Voice of Florida**
5150 W. Copans Rd., Ste. 1130　Phone: (305)972-3307
Margate, FL 33063　　　　　　Fax: (305)968-3588
Former Title: The Voice

MARIANNA

▣ **960　Marianna Jackson County Floridan**
4403 Constitution Ln.　　　　　Phone: (904)526-3614
Marianna, FL 32446　　　　　　**Fax: (904)482-4470**

♣ **961　WJAQ-FM - 100.9**
140 W. Lafayette St., Ste. A
PO Box 569　　　　　　　　　Phone: (904)482-3046
Marianna, FL 32446　　　　　　**Fax: (904)526-7702**

♣ **962　WJNF-FM - 91.1**
PO Box 450　　　　　　　　　Phone: (904)526-4477
Marianna, FL 32446　　　　　　**Fax: (904)526-1832**

♣ **963　WTOT-AM - 980**
140 W. Lafayette St., Ste. A
PO Box 569　　　　　　　　　Phone: (904)482-3046
Marianna, FL 32446　　　　　　**Fax: (904)526-7702**

MIAMI

▣ **964　El Nuevo Herald**
Miami Herald Publishing Co.
1 Herald Plaza　　　　　　　Phone: (305)376-3535
Miami, FL 33132　　　　　　　**Fax: (305)376-2099**

▣ **965　New Times of Miami**
PO Box 011591　　　　　　　Phone: (305)372-0004
Miami, FL 33101　　　　　　　Fax: (305)372-3446
Community newspaper. **Frequency:** Weekly (Tues.). **Key Personnel:**
Jim Mullin, Editor; Tom Finkel, Managing Editor. **Subscription:** Free.
　　　　　　　　　Circulation: Free □78,934
　　　　　　　　　　　　　　　Paid □39
Advertising accepted; contact publisher for rates.

▣ **966　Offshore Worldwide**
Offshore Worldwide, Inc.
2000 S. Dixie Hwy., Ste. 206-C
Miami, FL 33133
Magazine profiling international offshore powerboat racing. **Founded:**
1991. **Frequency:** 10/year. **Key Personnel:** J.D. Berg, Editor. **Subscrip-
tion:** $40. $6 single issue.
　　　　　　　　　Circulation: (Not Reported)

♣ **967　Dade Cable TV**
9825 SW 72nd St.　　　　　　Phone: (305)595-0924
Miami, FL 33173　　　　　　　Fax: (305)598-3944
Owner: Storer Cable Communications. **Founded:** 1979. **Cities Served:**
Dade County, FL.

📶 968 Miami Tele-Communications, Inc.
Box 011791
Miami, FL 33136   Phone: (305)326-1574
Owner: Tele-Communications, Inc. **Founded:** 1984. **Cities Served:**
Dade County and Opa-Locka, FL.

📶 969 Storer Cable TV of Florida
18601 NW 2nd Ave.   Phone: (305)652-9900
Miami, FL 33169   Fax: (305)645-6718
Owner: Storer Cable Communications. **Founded:** 1978. **Cities Served:**
Broward County, Dade County, Biscayne Park, El Portal, Miramar,
Miami Shores, Miami Beach, and Pembroke Park, FL.

📶 970 TCI of Florida
18601 NW 2nd Ave.
Miami, FL 33169   **Phone: (305)653-5541**

MIAMI SHORES

📖 971 The Flame
Barry University
11300 NE 2nd Ave.   Phone: (305)899-3187
Miami Shores, FL 33161   Fax: (305)899-3186

MONTICELLO

📶 972 WJPH-FM - 101.9
1275 S. Jefferson St.   **Phone: (904)997-3536**
Monticello, FL 32344   **Fax: (904)997-6813**

NAPLES

📶 973 Palmer Cablevision
Box 413018   Phone: (813)793-9600
Naples, FL 33941-3018   Fax: (813)793-1317
Owner: Palmer Communications, Inc. **Founded:** 1967. **Cities Served:**
Collier County, Naples, Lely, Marco Island, and Marco Shores, FL.

📶 974 WAVV-FM - 101.1
11800 Tamiami Trail E.   Phone: (813)775-9288
Naples, FL 33962   **Fax: (813)793-7000**

NOKOMIS

📖 975 EE Evaluation Engineering
Nelson Publishing
Nelson Bldg.
2504 N. Tamiami Trail   Phone: (813)966-9521
Nokomis, FL 34275   Fax: (813)966-2590

NORTH BAY VILLAGE

📶 976 Gold Coast Cablevision
1681 79th St., Causeway   Phone: (305)864-7824
North Bay Village, FL 33141   Fax: (305)861-9165
Owner: Rifkin & Assoc. **Founded:** 1980. **Key Personnel:** Kevin D.
Grossman, Gen. Mgr.; Jay Abbazia, Mktg. Dir.; Marty Mohr, Chief
Engineer; Dave Floberg, Controller; Angela Winslow, Cust. Service
Dir. **Cities Served:** Dade County, Bal Harbor, Bay Harbor Islands,
Golden Beach, North Bay Village, Miami Beach, and Surfside, FL:
45,000 subscribing households; 52 channels; 3 community access
channels. **Additional Contact Information:** Alt. phone (305)861-8069.

NORTH MIAMI

📖 977 Pleasure Boatings Caribbean Sports & Travel
  Magazine
GRAPHCOM PUBLISHING, INC.
1995 NE 150 St., Ste. 107   Phone: (305)945-7403
North Miami, FL 33181   Fax: (305)947-6410
Former Title: Pleasure Boating Magazine

OAKLAND PARK

📖 978 Haut Decor
Haut Decor, Inc.
3290 NE 12th Ave.   Phone: (305)568-9444
Oakland Park, FL 33334   Fax: (305)568-9445
Subtitle: The Voice of the Florida Design Community. **Founded:** 1990.

Frequency: 2x/mo. **Trim Size:** 11 x 14 3/4. **Cols./Page:** 4. **Col. Width:** 2
1/4 in. **Col. Depth:** 13 3/4 in. **Key Personnel:** Janet Verdeguer, Editor-
in-Chief; Manuel Verdeguer, Publisher. **Subscription:** $2 single issue.
Ad Rates: BW: $1,600   **Circulation:** 15,000
            4C: $1,920

OCALA

📖 979 Horsemen's Journal
American Equine Publishers, Inc.
PO Box 2106
Ocala, FL 34478-2106

📖 980 Sporting Guns
U.S. Gun Distributors, Inc.
2395 SW College Rd.
Ocala, FL 32674
Magazine includes gun reviews and NRA hunting seasons and fees.
Frequency: Quarterly. **Key Personnel:** Dwayne Victory, Editor; Edwin
Gallagher, Publisher. **Subscription:** $24.95. $5.95 single issue.
                              Circulation: (Not Reported)

📶 981 WTMC-AM - 1290
3621 NW 10th St.   **Phone: (904)629-7400**
Ocala, FL 34475   **Fax: (904)629-2139**

OCOEE

📶 982 WGTO-AM - 540
821 Marshall Farms Rd.   **Phone: (407)656-5440**
Ocoee, FL 34761   **Fax: (407)656-5492**

ORANGE PARK

📶 983 WPDQ-AM - 690
3651 US Hwy. 17 S.   **Phone: (904)278-4949**
Orange Park, FL 32073-7113   **Fax: (904)269-3299**

ORLANDO

📖 984 Racing Collectibles Price Guide
Sportstars, Inc.
PO Box 607785   Phone: (407)578-7850
Orlando, FL 32860-7785   Fax: (407)290-6745
Magazine featuring the "Stock Car Racing Collectors Guide to the
Current Value of Collector Cards" and diecast memorabilia. **Founded:**
1988. **Frequency:** Monthly. **Printing Method:** Web offset. **Trim Size:** 8
3/8 x 10 7/8. **Cols./Page:** 3. **Key Personnel:** Dane Turner, Editor-in-
Chief. **Subscription:** $32. $3 single issue.
                              Circulation: Combined 50,000

📶 985 Cablevision of Central Florida
3767 All American Blvd.
Orlando, FL 32810   Phone: (407)295-9119
Owner: Time Warner Entertainment Company. **Founded:** 1985. **Key
Personnel:** David Spencer, V.P. of Operations; Tammy Wiley,
Program Mgr. **Cities Served:** Orange County, Osceola County, and
Seminole County; Apopka, Belle Isle, Casselberry, Eatonville, Edgewood, Kissimmee, Longwood, Maitland, Sanford, Windemere, Winter Park, and Winter Springs, FL: 200,000 subscribing households; 42
channels; 1 community access channel; 25 hours per week of
community access programming.

📶 986 WACX-TV - Channel 55
4520 Parkbreeze Ct.
Orlando, FL 32808   **Phone: (407)298-5555**

📶 987 WAJL-AM - 1190
Box 547068
Orlando, FL 32854-7068   Phone: (407)841-9255
Format: Religious (Contemporary Christian). **Network(s):** Christian
Broadcasting (CBN). **Owner:** Alleluia Ministries Inc. **Founded:** 1977.
Operating Hours: Sunrise-sunset. **Key Personnel:** Albert H. Chubb,
Pres./Gen. Mgr.; Carolyn Bernhardt, Sales Mgr.; Carla Camelin,
Public Service Dir.; Graham Barnard, Production Supervisor. **Watt-
age:** 5000.

♨ 988 WUCF-FM - 89.9
PO Box 162199   Phone: (407)823-2133
Orlando, FL 32816-2199   Fax: (407)823-6364
Format: Alternative/Independent/Progressive; Classical; Jazz. **Network(s):** American Public Radio (APR). **Owner:** University of Central Florida, at above address. **Founded:** 1977. **Operating Hours:** Continuous. **Key Personnel:** Jeffery Ross, Music Dir.; Dr. Jose Maunez-Cuadra, Gen. Mgr.; Rafael Gonzalez, Mktg. Dir.; Bill Fries, Program Dir.; Peter Carroll, Cultural and Classical. **Wattage:** 8000. **Ad Rates:** Noncommercial. Underwriting available. **Additional Contact Information:** Gen. Mgr. (407)823-5162, Mktg. Dir. (407)823-5906.

♨ 989 WWNZ-AM - 740
PO Box 740   **Phone: (407)299-7400**
Orlando, FL 32808   Fax: (407)290-2879

♨ 990 WWNZ-FM - 104.1
3500 W. Colonial
PO Box 740   **Phone: (407)299-7400**
Orlando, FL 32808   Fax: (407)290-2879

PALATKA

▥ 991 Consumer Extra
1825 St. Johns Ave.
PO Box 777   Phone: (904)328-2721
Palatka, FL 32078   Fax: (904)325-0663
Ceased publication.

PANAMA CITY

▥ 992 The Journal of Ideas
Institute for Memetic Research, Inc.
PO Box 16327
Panama City, FL 32406-1327
Journal covering the evolution of ideas, discovery of creative processes, memetics, and abstract evolution. **Founded:** 1990. **Frequency:** Quarterly. **Printing Method:** Offset. **Trim Size:** 8 1/2 x 11. **Cols./Page:** 2. **Col. Width:** 2 3/4 in. **Col. Depth:** 9 in. **Key Personnel:** Dr. Elan Moritz, Editor. **ISSN:** 1049-6335. **Subscription:** $46; $138 institutions. $26 single issue.

                                       Circulation: ‡200

Advertising not accepted.

♨ 993 WFSG-TV - Channel 56
c/o WFSU-TV
2565 Pottsdamer St.
Tallahassee, FL 32304   **Phone: (904)487-3170**

PENSACOLA

▥ 994 Perido Pelican
Gulf Breeze Publishing Co.
Box 34257   Phone: (904)934-1200
Pensacola, FL 32507   Fax: (904)932-8765
Community newspaper. **Founded:** 1989. **Frequency:** 2x/mo. **Printing Method:** Offset. **Trim Size:** 11 3/8 x 13 1/2. **Cols./Page:** 5. **Col. Width:** 12 picas. **Key Personnel:** Fran Thompson, Editor and Publisher.
Ad Rates: GLR: $9   **Circulation:** Non-paid ★8,000

♨ 995 Cox Cable TV of Pensacola
2205 La Vista Ave.   Phone: (904)477-2695
Pensacola, FL 32504   Fax: (904)479-3912
Owner: Cox Cable Communications. **Founded:** 1969. **Cities Served:** Escambia County, FL.

PERRY

♨ 996 WNFK-FM - 105.5
PO Box 779   Phone: (904)584-2972
Perry, FL 32347   Fax: (904)584-4616
Format: Country. Simulcasts WPRY-AM. **Network(s):** NBC; Florida Radio. **Owner:** RAHU Broadcasting, Inc., 1 Broadcast Pl., Hwy. 27 E., Perry, FL 32347. **Founded:** 1990. **Operating Hours:** 6 a.m.-midnight.

Key Personnel: Don W. Hughes, V.P./Gen. Mgr.; Bill Stephens, Sales Mgr.; Linda Thurman, Traffic Mgr./Bookkeeping; Amy Hughes, Program Mgr. **Wattage:** 3000. **Ad Rates:** $3-$6 for 15 seconds; $4-$7 for 30 seconds; $5-$9 for 60 seconds.

♨ 997 WPRY-AM - 1400
PO Box 779   Phone: (904)584-2972
Perry, FL 32347   Fax: (904)584-4616
Format: Country. Simulcasts WNFK-FM. **Network(s):** NBC; Florida Radio. **Owner:** RAHU Broadcasting, Inc., 1 Broadcast Pl., Hwy. 27 E., Perry, FL 32347. **Founded:** 1953. **Operating Hours:** 6 a.m.-midnight. **Key Personnel:** Don W. Hughes, V.P./Gen. Mgr.; Bill Stephens, Sales Mgr.; Linda Thurman, Traffic Mgr./Bookkeeping; Amy Hughes, Program Mgr. **Wattage:** 1000. **Ad Rates:** $2-$4 for 15 seconds; $2.50-$5 for 30 seconds; $3-$6 for 60 seconds.

POMPANO BEACH

▥ 998 The Observer
Broward Community College
North Campus
1000 Coconut Creek Blvd.   Phone: (305)973-2237
Pompano Beach, FL 33066   Fax: (305)973-2389

♨ 999 Continental Cablevision
141 NW 16th St.
Box 1689   Phone: (305)946-7011
Pompano Beach, FL 33061   Fax: (305)946-7000
Owner: Continental Cablevision, Inc. **Founded:** 1975. **Cities Served:** Broward County, FL.

PORT ST. LUCIE

▥ 1000 Conversion and Empaque Magazine
Coast Publishing, Inc.
Zedcoast Center
1680 SW Bayshore Blvd.   Phone: (407)879-6666
Port St. Lucie, FL 34984   Fax: (407)879-7388
Magazine. **Subtitle:** The Converting and Packaging Magazine for all of Latin America. **Founded:** 1992. **Frequency:** 6x/yr. **Printing Method:** Web offset. **Trim Size:** 8 1/8 x 10 7/8. **Key Personnel:** Miguel Garzon, Editor; Juan Carlos Gayoso, Intl. Sales Dir. **Subscription:** $40. $10 single issue.
Ad Rates: BW: $2,225   **Circulation:** Non-paid △14,071
               4C: $3,045
               PCI: $60

▥ 1001 Copy Imaging and Reproduction
Coast Publishing
ZedCoast Center
1680 SW Bayshore Blvd.   Phone: (407)879-6666
Port Saint Lucie, FL 34984   Fax: (407)879-7388
Trade magazine. **Founded:** 1980. **Frequency:** Bimonthly. **Printing Method:** Web offset. **Trim Size:** 8 1/2 x 10 7/8. **Cols./Page:** 3. **Col. Width:** 13 picas. **Key Personnel:** Karen Lowery, Editor; Cyndi Schulman, Publisher; Jeff Macharyas, Art Dir.; Bonnie deCuba, Circulation Mgr.; Karen Seymour, Sales Mgr.; Betsy Eichelberger, Marketing Mgr. **ISSN:** 0897-9405. **Subscription:** $21.
Ad Rates: BW: $3,400   **Circulation:** Paid 100
               4C: $4,250   Non-paid 25,000
               PCI: $65

PRINCETON

♨ 1002 Adelphia Cable Associates-South Dade
Box 4082   Phone: (305)238-7960
Princeton, FL 33032   Fax: (305)238-3770
Owner: Adelphia Communications Corp. **Founded:** 1971. **Cities Served:** Dade County, Cutler Ridge, Florida City, Goulds, Homestead, Kendall, Kings Bay, Leisure City, Naranja Lakes, Perrine, and South Miami Heights, FL.

Ad Rates: GLR = general line rate; BW = one-time black & white page rate; 4C = one-time four color page rate; SAU = standard advertising unit rate;
CNU = Canadian newspaper advertising unit rate; PCI = per column inch rate.
Circulation: ★ = ABC; △ = BPA; ◆ = CAC; ● = CCAB; □ = VAC; ⊕ = PO Statement; ‡ = Publisher's Report; Boldface figures = sworn; Light figures = estimated.
Entry type: ▥ = Print; ♨ = Broadcast.

67

PUNTA GORDA

📖 **1003 Charlotte Shopping Guide**
128 W. Charlotte Ave.   Phone: (813)639-1136
Punta Gorda, FL 33950   **Fax: (813)639-4832**

RIVIERA BEACH

🎤 **1004 Adelphia Communications**
2129 Congress Ave.   Phone: (407)863-5701
Riviera Beach, FL 33404   Fax: (407)845-7709
Owner: Adelphia Communications Corp. **Founded:** 1967. **Cities Served:** Martin and Palm Beach North counties, FL.

RUSKIN

📖 **1005 Shopper Observer News**
100 E. Shell Point Rd.   Phone: (813)645-3111
Ruskin, FL 33570   Fax: (813)645-4118
Shopping guide. **Founded:** 1958. **Frequency:** Weekly (Wed.). **Printing Method:** Offset. **Trim Size:** 11 3/8 x 13 3/4. **Cols./Page:** 6. **Col. Width:** 2 1/16 in. **Key Personnel:** Stephen Mixon, Publisher; Sherri Cole, Editor. **Subscription:** Free.
Ad Rates: BW: $400   **Circulation: Free 18,200**
         4C: $500
         PCI: $8

SAINT PETERSBURG

📖 **1006 Auto Racing Memories**
PO Box 12226   Phone: (813)895-3482
Saint Petersburg, FL 33733   **Fax: (813)895-3389**

📖 **1007 Florida Underwriter**
National Underwriter Co.
9887 Gandy Blvd. N., Ste. 213   Phone: (813)576-1101
St. Petersburg, FL 33702   **Fax: (813)577-4002**

📖 **1008 Sailaway**
Travel Agents International, Inc.
111 2nd Ave. NE, 15th Fl.
PO Box 31005   **Phone: (813)895-8241**
St. Petersburg, FL 33731-8905   **Fax: (813)894-6318**
Ceased publication.

🎤 **1009 WECR-AM - 550**
Campus Box D
4200 54th Ave. S.
St. Petersburg, FL 33711   Phone: (813)864-8419
Format: Alternative/Independent/Progressive. **Ad Rates:** Noncommercial.

🎤 **1010 WRXB-AM - 1590**
1700 34th St. S.   **Phone: (813)327-9792**
Saint Petersburg, FL 33711   **Fax: (813)321-3025**

SANFORD

🎤 **1011 WTRR-AM - 1400**
PO Box 1448   Phone: (407)322-1400
Sanford, FL 32772-1448   Fax: (407)330-7571

SANIBEL

📖 **1012 Sanibel/Captiva Islander**
Breeze Publishing Co.
2407 Periwinkle Dr.   Phone: (813)472-5185
Sanibel, FL 33957   **Fax: (813)472-5302**

SARASOTA

📖 **1013 Pelican Press**
230 Avenida Madera   Phone: (813)349-4949
Sarasota, FL 34242   **Fax: (813)349-4968**

🎤 **1014 Storer Cable TV of Florida, Inc.**
5205 Fruitville Rd.
Box 1178   Phone: (813)371-4444
Sarasota, FL 34232   Fax: (813)371-5097
Owner: Storer Cable Communications. **Founded:** 1962. **Cities Served:** Manatee and Sarasota counties, FL.

🎤 **1015 WKXY-AM - 930**
2500 10th St.
Sarasota, FL **34237**   Phone: (813)366-4422

🎤 **1016 WSPB-AM - 1450**
PO Box 2618   **Phone: (813)388-2966**
Sarasota, FL 34230-2618   **Fax: (813)388-3204**

SOUTH DAYTONA

📖 **1017 APCO BULLETIN**
APCO, Inc.
2040 S. Ridgewood   Phone: (904)322-2500
South Daytona, FL 32119   **Fax: (904)322-2501**

STUART

📖 **1018 Charter Industry**
PO Box 375
Stuart, FL **34995-0375**   Phone: (407)288-1066

📖 **1019 Flashes Shopping Guide**
Flashes, Inc.
17 W. Flagler Ave.   Phone: (407)287-0650
Stuart, FL 34994   **Fax: (407)283-5090**

SUNRISE

📖 **1020 The Broward Informer**
PO Box 130207
Sunrise, FL 33313   Phone: (305)370-6009
Former Title: The Broward-Sunrise Informer

TALLAHASSEE

📖 **1021 The Academy of Florida Trial Lawyers Journal**
218 S. Monroe St.   Phone: (904)224-9403
Tallahassee, FL 32301   Fax: (904)224-4254
Frequency: Monthly. **Cols./Page:** 2. **Col. Width:** 20 picas. **Col. Depth:** 53 picas. **Subscription:** $300. $10 single issue.
Ad Rates: BW: $350   **Circulation:** Paid ⊕**3,106**
                              Non-paid ⊕**853**

📖 **1022 Capital Outlook**
417 N. Duval St.   **Phone: (904)681-1852**
Tallahassee, FL 32301   **Fax: (904)681-1093**

📖 **1023 Financial Management**
Financial Management Assn.
Florida State University
College of Business
Dept. of Finance   Phone: (904)644-6512
Tallahassee, FL 32306-1042   **Fax: (904)644-7671**

📖 **1024 Florida Market Bulletin**
Florida Dept. of Agriculture & Consumer Services
280 Conner Bldg.
Tallahassee, FL 32399-1650   **Phone: (904)488-7000**

📖 **1025 Florida Music Director**
Florida Music Educators Assn.
207 Office Plaza Dr.   **Phone: (904)878-6844**
Tallahassee, FL 32301   **Fax: (904)942-1793**

📖 **1026 Quality Cities**
Florida League of Cities
201 Park Ave. W.
PO Box 1757   Phone: (904)222-9684
Tallahassee, FL 32302-1757   Fax: (904)222-3806
Former Title: Quality Cities '91

♣ **1027 WANM-AM - 1070**
300 W. Tennessee   Phone: (904)222-1070
Tallahassee, FL 32301   **Fax: (904)561-3645**

♣ **1028 WFSQ-FM - 91.5**
2561 Pottsdammer St.   Phone: (904)487-3086
Tallahassee, FL 32310   Fax: (904)487-3293
Format: Classical (Fine arts and entertainment). **Network(s):** National
Public Radio (NPR). **Founded:** 1990. **Formerly:** WFSU-FM. **Operating
Hours:** Continuous. **Key Personnel:** Caroline Austin, Station Mgr.;
Sally Spener, News Dir.; Marc Gaspard, Music Dir. **Wattage:** 100,000.
Ad Rates: Noncommercial.

♣ **1029 WFSU-TV - Channel 11**
2565 Pottsdamer St.   Phone: (904)487-3170
Tallahassee, FL 32310   **Fax: (904)487-3093**

♣ **1030 WHBX-FM - 96.1**
109-B Ridgeland Rd.   **Phone: (904)385-1156**
Tallahassee, FL 32312   **Fax: (904)224-8329**

TAMPA

📖 **1031 El Sol de la Florida**
El Sol Publishers, Inc.
PO Box 5928   **Phone: (813)251-4229**
Tampa, FL 33675-5928   **Fax: (813)254-1494**

📖 **1032 Hypatia**
University of South Florida
Soc. 107   Phone: (813)974-5531
Tampa, FL 33620-8100   Fax: (813)974-2668
Subtitle: A Journal of Feminist Philosophy. **Founded:** 1983. **Frequen-
cy:** Quarterly. **Key Personnel:** Linda Lopez McAlister, Editor. **ISSN:**
0887-5367.**Subscription:** $32.50; $45 other countries; $50 institu-
tions; $52.50 institutions in other countries.
                                          Circulation: 1,300

📖 **1033 Multi-Images Magazine**
Association for Multi-Image International
10008 N. Dale Mabry Hwy., No. 113   Phone: (813)960-1692
Tampa, FL 33618-4424   Fax: (813)962-7911
Journal covering multimedia events and presentation media technolo-
gies. **Subtitle:** The Journal of the Association for Multi-Image
International, Inc. **Founded:** 1974. **Frequency:** 6x/yr. **Printing Method:**
Sheet-fed. **Trim Size:** 8 1/2 x 11. **Key Personnel:** Charles E. Morrison,
Editor/Creative Dir.; Steven A. Fasnacht, Art Dir. **ISSN:** 0893-5440.
Subscription: $40. $6.25 single issue.
Ad Rates: BW: $990   **Circulation:** Paid ‡2,000
                4C: $1,665

♣ **1034 Jones Intercable, Inc.**
4400 W. Buffalo   Phone: (813)877-6805
Tampa, FL 33607   Fax: (813)875-2507
Owner: Jones Intercable, Inc. **Founded:** 1983. **Cities Served:** Hillsborough County, FL.

♣ **1035 WTMP-AM - 1150**
5207 Washington Blvd.   Phone: (813)626-4108
Tampa, FL 33619   Fax: (813)621-0616

♣ **1036 WTTA-TV - Channel 38**
5510 Gray St.   **Phone: (813)289-3838**
Tampa, FL 33609   **Fax: (813)289-0000**

♣ **1037 WUTZ-AM - 1075**
University of Tampa
401 W. Kennedy Blvd.
Tampa, FL 33606   Phone: (813)253-3333
Format: Alternative/Independent/Progressive. **Ad Rates:** Noncom-
mercial.

TARPON SPRINGS

📖 **1038 Tarpon Springs**
11 E. Orange St.   Phone: (813)942-6933
Tarpon Springs, FL 34689   **Fax: (813)937-7109**

TAVERNIER

♣ **1039 WFKZ-FM - 103.1**
93351 Overseas Hwy.
Tavernier, FL 33070   Fax: (305)852-5586
Format: Adult Contemporary. **Owner:** Key Chain, Inc., at above
address; (305)852-9085. **Founded:** 1983. **Operating Hours:** Continuous. **Key Personnel:** K.C. Stewart, Program Dir.; Jack Niedbalski,
Gen. Mgr. and Sales Mgr. **Wattage:** 6000. **Ad Rates:** $11-$16 for 30
seconds; $13-$20 for 60 seconds.

TEMPLE TERRACE

📖 **1040 Human Organization**
Society for Applied Anthropology
5205 E. Fowler Ave., Ste. 310   **Phone: (813)985-7816**
Temple Terrace, FL 33617   Fax: (813)989-1505

TITUSVILLE

📖 **1041 PhotoPro**
Patch Communications
5211 S. Washington Ave.
PO Box F   Phone: (407)268-5010
Titusville, FL 32780   Fax: (407)267-7216

WEST PALM BEACH

📖 **1042 Palm Beach Illustrated**
Palm Beach Media Group
1016 N. Dixie Hwy.
PO Box 3344   Phone: (407)659-0210
West Palm Beach, FL 33401   Fax: (407)659-1736

📖 **1043 Palm Beach Jewish Journal South**
The South Florida Newspaper Network
601 Fairway Dr.   **Phone: (305)698-6397**
Deerfield Beach, FL 33441   **Fax: (305)698-6719**
Former Title: Palm Beach Jewish Journal

♣ **1044 Tele-Media Corporation**
2200 N. Florida Mango Rd., Ste. 302
West Palm Beach, FL 33409   Phone: (407)683-1414

WINTER PARK

📖 **1045 WaterSki Magazine**
World Publications, Inc.
PO Box 2456   Phone: (407)628-4802
Winter Park, FL 32790   **Fax: (407)628-7061**

ZEPHYRHILLS

📖 **1046 East Pasco Weekend Shopping Guide**
Republic Newspapers, Inc.
38333 State Rd., 5th Ave.
PO Box 638   Phone: (831)782-1558
Zephyrhills, FL 33541   Fax: (813)788-7987
Shopping guide. **Frequency:** Weekly. **Subscription:** $14.
Ad Rates: PCI: $8   **Circulation:** Free ‡24,500

📖 **1047 Zephyrhills News**
Republic Newspapers, Inc.
PO Box 638   Phone: (813)782-1558
Zephyrhills, FL 33539   **Fax: (813)788-7987**

Ad Rates: GLR = general line rate; BW = one-time black & white page rate; 4C = one-time four color page rate; SAU = standard advertising unit rate;
CNU = Canadian newspaper advertising unit rate; PCI = per column inch rate.
Circulation: ★ = ABC; △ = BPA; ◆ = CAC; ● = CCAB; □ = VAC; ⊕ = PO Statement; ‡ = Publisher's Report; Boldface figures = sworn; Light figures = estimated.
Entry type: 📖 = Print; ♣ = Broadcast.

GEORGIA

ACWORTH

📖 **1048 Food People**
Olson Publications, Inc.
5805 Bells Ferry Rd.
Acworth, GA 30101   Phone: (404)928-8994

ADEL

📖 **1049 Adel News-Tribune**
PO Box 312   Phone: (912)896-2233
Adel, GA 31620   **Fax: (912)896-2233**

ALMA

📖 **1050 Alma Times-Statesman**
PO Box 428   Phone: (912)632-7201
Alma, GA 31510-0428   **Fax: (912)632-4156**

ATHENS

📖 **1051 Flagpole Magazine**
PO Box 1027   Phone: (706)549-9523
Athens, GA 30603   Fax: (706)548-8981
Magazine covering the arts, entertainment, politics, and news in
Athens, GA; also reports on the international music scene. **Founded:**
1987. **Frequency:** Weekly. **Printing Method:** Web press. **Trim Size:** 11
3/8 x 15. **Cols./Page:** 4. **Col. Width:** 2 3/8 in. **Col. Depth:** 13 in. **Key
Personnel:** Stephen Crawford, Editor; Dennis Greenia, Publisher;
Dana Taylor, Advertising Mgr. **Subscription:** $38. $1.50 single issue.
Ad Rates: BW: $720   **Circulation:** ⊕**16,000**
                4C: $845

📖 **1052 Georgia Historical Quarterly**
Georgia Historical Society
203 LeConte Hall
University of Georgia   **Phone: (706)542-6300**
Athens, GA 30602   **Fax: (706)542-2455**

🎙 **1053 TCI Cablevision of Georgia**
495 Hawthorne Ave., Ste. 102
Athens, GA 30606   Phone: (706)543-6585
Owner: Tele-Communications, Inc. **Founded:** 1964. **Cities Served:**
Clarke, Madison, and Oconee counties, GA.

🎙 **1054 WPUP-FM - 103.7**
255 S. Milledge Ave.   Phone: (706)549-6222
Athens, GA 30605-1045   **Fax: (706)353-1967**

🎙 **1055 WRFC-AM - 960**
255 S. Milledge Ave.   Phone: (706)549-6222
Athens, GA 30605-1045   **Fax: (706)353-1967**

ATLANTA

📖 **1056 Adhesives Age**
Communication Channels, Inc.
6151 Powers Ferry Rd.   **Phone: (404)955-2500**
Atlanta, GA 30339   **Fax: (404)955-0400**

📖 **1057 Air Cargo World**
Communication Channels, Inc.
6151 Powers Ferry Rd. NW   **Phone: (404)955-2500**
Atlanta, GA 30339-2941   **Fax: (404)955-0400**

📖 **1058 Arthritis Care & Research**
Arthritis Health Professionals
1314 Spring St. NW
Atlanta, GA 30309

📖 **1059 Atlanta Homes and Lifestyles**
Wiesner Inc.
5775-B Glenridge Dr.   **Phone: (404)252-6670**
Atlanta, GA 30328   **Fax: (404)252-6673**

📖 **1060 Atlanta Parent**
Capers for Kids Publications
1135 Sheridan Rd. NE, No. 4   Phone: (404)325-1763
Atlanta, GA 30324   Fax: (404)325-4386
Parenting magazine. **Founded:** 1983. **Frequency:** Monthly. **Printing
Method:** Web offset. **Trim Size:** 11 1/4 x 15. **Cols./Page:** 4. **Col. Width:**
2 1/4 in. **Col. Depth:** 13 in. **Key Personnel:** Liz White, Editor and
Publisher. **Subscription:** Free.
Ad Rates: BW: $1,518   **Circulation:** Free □**44,768**
                4C: $1,968   Paid □**200**
                PCI: $41.40

📖 **1061 The Atlanta Small Business Monthly**
2342 Perimeter Park Dr., Ste. 200
Atlanta, GA 30341   Phone: (404)986-0447

📖 **1062 Bank Financial Management International**
Lafferty Publications
1422 W. Peachtree St.   Phone: (404)874-5120
Atlanta, GA 30309   Fax: (404)874-5123
Worldwide trends in bank profitability, capital, and regulation.
Frequency: Monthly. **Key Personnel:** Tom LaFreniere, Editor. **Sub-
scription:** $595 (10 issues).
                                        Circulation: (Not Reported)

1063 Biblical Archaeologist
Scholars Press
819 Houston Mill Rd.   Phone: (404)636-4757
Atlanta, GA 30329   Fax: (404)636-8301

1064 Bulletin of the American Society of Papyrologists
Scholars Press
PO Box 15399   Phone: (404)636-4757
Atlanta, GA 30333-0399   Fax: (404)636-8301

1065 Cards International
Lafferty Publications
1422 W. Peachtree St.   Phone: (404)874-5120
Atlanta, GA 30309   Fax: (404)874-5123
The worldwide briefing on the plastic card industry. **Frequency:** 2x/mo. **Key Personnel:** Tom Murphy, U.S. Editor. **Subscription:** $545 (23 issues).
                                         Circulation: (Not Reported)

1066 The Christian Index
Georgia Baptist Convention
2930 Flowers Rd. S.   Phone: (404)936-5312
Atlanta, GA 30341   Fax: (404)936-5260

1067 Commuter Air International
6151 Powers Ferry Rd., NW   **Phone: (404)955-2500**
Atlanta, GA 30339-2941   **Fax: (404)955-0400**

1068 Corporate Accounting International
Lafferty Publications
1422 W. Peachtree St.   Phone: (404)874-5120
Atlanta, GA 30309   Fax: (404)874-5123
The international accounting, reporting, and auditing source. **Frequency:** Monthly. **Key Personnel:** Lisa Gandy-Wargo, Editor. **Subscription:** $445 (10 issues).
                                         Circulation: (Not Reported)

1069 Electronic Payments International
Lafferty Publications
1422 W. Peachtree St.   Phone: (404)874-5120
Atlanta, GA 30309   Fax: (404)874-5123
Global intelligence on the electronic payments industry, covering marketplace and technology developments in retail EFT services, EDI, homebanking, and interbank payment systems. **Frequency:** Monthly. **Key Personnel:** Tom Murphy, Editor. **Subscription:** $495 (10 issues).
                                         Circulation: (Not Reported)

1070 Farmers & Consumers Market Bulletin
Georgia Dept. of Agriculture
Agriculture Bldg., Capitol Sq., Rm. 226
19 Martin Luther King Jr. Dr.   Phone: (404)656-3682
Atlanta, GA 30334   **Fax: (404)651-7957**

1071 International Accounting Bulletin
Lafferty Publications
1422 W. Peachtree St.   Phone: (404)874-5120
Atlanta, GA 30309   Fax: (404)874-5123
The business briefing for international accountants. **Frequency:** Monthly. **Key Personnel:** Tom LaFreniere, Editor. **Subscription:** $495 (10 issues).
                                         Circulation: (Not Reported)

1072 Journal of Biblical Literature
Scholars Press
PO Box 15399   Phone: (404)636-4757
Atlanta, GA 30333-0399   Fax: (404)636-8301

1073 Journal of Film and Video
Dept. of Communication
University Plaza
Georgia State Univ.   Phone: (404)651-3200
Atlanta, GA 30303   Fax: (404)651-1409

1074 Journal of Negro History
Assn. for the Study of Afro-American Life and History
Morehouse College
Box 20
Atlanta, GA 30314   Phone: (404)681-2650

1075 Management Consultant International
Lafferty Publications
1422 W. Peachtree St.   Phone: (404)874-5120
Atlanta, GA 30309   Fax: (404)874-5123
Worldwide news and trends in the consultancy industry. **Frequency:** Monthly. **Key Personnel:** Lisa Gandy-Wargo, Editor. **Subscription:** $495 (10 issues).
                                         Circulation: (Not Reported)

1076 Openings
Scholars Press
PO Box 15399   Phone: (404)636-4757
Atlanta, GA 30333-0399   Fax: (404)636-8301
Tabloid of professional job listings for religious scholars. **Founded:** 1985. **Frequency:** 6x/yr. **Printing Method:** Web offset. **Cols./Page:** 4. **Key Personnel:** Jeff C. Andrews, Editor. **Subscription:** $22; $12 student member; $30 nonmember and institutions; $25 Canada and Mexico; $15 student member Canada and Mexico; $33 nonmember and institutions Canada and Mexico; $34 other countries; $24 student member other countries; $42 nonmember and institutions in other countries.
                                         Circulation: 2,500
Additional Contact Information: Publishers address 819 Houston Mill Rd., Atlanta, GA 30329.

1077 Plumb
Rice Printing Co.
3183 Shallowford Rd.   Phone: (404)458-4414
Atlanta, GA 30341   **Fax: (404)457-3893**

1078 Sage: A Scholarly Journal on Black Women
SAGE Women's Educational Press, Inc.
PO Box 42741   Phone: (404)223-7528
Atlanta, GA 30311-0741   Fax: (404)753-8383
Journal for African-American women. Contains articles, interviews, profiles, documents, book reviews, and bibliographies. **Founded:** 1984. **Frequency:** 2x/yr. **ISSN:** 0741-8639. **Subscription:** $15; $21 outside U.S.; $25 institutions; $31 institutions outside U.S.
                                         Circulation: Paid 1,000
                                                          Non-paid 800
Advertising accepted; contact publisher for rates.

1079 Semeia
Scholars Press
PO Box 15399   Phone: (404)636-4757
Atlanta, GA 30333-0399   Fax: (404)636-8301

1080 The Technique
Georgia Institute of Technology
Student services Bldg.
Mail Code 0290   Phone: (404)894-2830
Atlanta, GA 30332-0290   **Fax: (404)853-9928**

1081 Textile World
Maclean Hunter Publishing Co.
4170 Ashford Dunwoody Rd., Ste. 420   Phone: (404)847-2770
Atlanta, GA 30319   Fax: (404)252-6150

1082 Trusts and Estates
Communications Channels, Inc.
6151 Powers Ferry Rd. NW   **Phone: (404)955-2500**
Atlanta, GA 30339-2941   **Fax: (404)955-0400**

1083 WHERE Magazine
WHERE Magazine International
1293 Peachtree St. NE, Ste. 720   Phone: (404)876-5566
Atlanta, GA 30309-3531   Fax: (404)876-6157
Magazine providing visitor information, including city map and a list of attractions, shopping areas, restaurants, and special events. **Founded:** August 1966. **Frequency:** Monthly. **Printing Method:** Offset. **Trim Size:** 8 1/2 x 11. **Cols./Page:** 3. **Col. Width:** 13 picas. **Col. Depth:** 57.5 picas. **Key Personnel:** Kathy Roberts, Editor; Lea Sullivan, Advertising Mgr. **Subscription:** $25.
Ad Rates: BW: $2,310   **Circulation:** Paid ‡300
               4C: $2,760   Non-paid ‡40,000

1084 MetroVision Inc.
115 Perimeter Center Pl. NE, Ste. 550   Phone: (404)394-8837
Atlanta, GA 30346-1238   **Fax: (404)698-0228**

& **1085 WAFS-AM - 920**
1447 Peachtree St., NE, Ste. 600
Atlanta, GA 30309　　　　　　　Phone: (404)888-0920
Format: Religious. **Owner:** Moody Bible Institute of Chicago. **Founded:** 1989. **Operating Hours:** Continuous. **Key Personnel:** Joe Emert, Gen. Mgr.; Teresa Pakiz, Asst. Mgr.; DeLain Roberts, News Dir.; Donna Boyd, Administrative Assistant. **Wattage:** 5000 day; 1000 night.

& **1086 WPBA-TV - Channel 30**
740 Bismarck Rd. NE　　　　　　Phone: (404)827-8900
Atlanta, GA 30324　　　　　　　**Fax: (404)827-8956**

& **1087 WREK-FM - 91.1**
Georgia Institue of Technology
165 8th St. NW　　　　　　　　Phone: (404)894-2468
Atlanta, GA 30332　　　　　　　**Fax: (404)853-3066**

& **1088 WXIA-TV - Channel 11**
1611 W. Peachtree St. NE　　　　Phone: (404)892-1611
Atlanta, GA 30309　　　　　　　**Fax: (404)882-0182**

AUGUSTA

⬚ **1089 Gray's Sporting Journal**
PO Box 1207
Augusta, GA 30903-1207　　　　**Phone: (706)722-6060**

⬚ **1090 The Metro Courier**
PO Box 2385　　　　　　　　　Phone: (404)724-6556
Augusta, GA 30903　　　　　　　Fax: (404)722-7104
Former Title: Metro County Courier

& **1091 WBBQ-FM - 104.3**
PO Box 2066　　　　　　　　　Phone: (803)279-6610
Augusta, GA 30903-2066　　　　　Fax: (802)279-0220

& **1092 WFAM-AM - 1050**
552 Laney-Walker Ext.　　　　　Phone: (706)722-6077
Augusta, GA 30901　　　　　　　**Fax: (706)722-7066**

BAINBRIDGE

& **1093 WJAD-FM - 97.3**
1609 E. Shotwell St.　　　　　　Phone: (912)246-1650
Bainbridge, GA 31717　　　　　　**Fax: (912)248-0975**

& **1094 WMGR-AM - 930**
1609 E. Shotwell St.　　　　　　Phone: (912)246-1650
Bainbridge, GA 31717　　　　　　**Fax: (912)248-0975**

BAXLEY

& **1095 WBYZ-FM - 94.5**
Box 389　　　　　　　　　　　Phone: (912)367-3000
Baxley, GA 31513　　　　　　　Fax: (912)367-9779
Format: Contemporary Country. **Network(s):** ABC. **Owner:** South Georgia Broadcasters. **Founded:** 1982. **Operating Hours:** Continuous. **Key Personnel:** Peggy Miles, Gen. Mgr. **Wattage:** 100,000. **Ad Rates:** $7.50 for 30 seconds; $9.50 for 60 seconds. **Additional Contact Information:** Alt. phone (912)367-3001.

BLACKSHEAR

& **1096 WGIA-AM - 1350**
245 E. Main St.
PO Box 619　　　　　　　　　Phone: (912)449-3442
Blackshear, GA 31516　　　　　　**Fax: (912)449-1266**

BREMEN

⬚ **1097 The Haralson Gateway Beacon**
Worrell Enterprises, Inc.
222 Tallapoosa St.
PO Box 685　　　　　　　　**Phone: (706)537-2434**
Bremen, GA 30110　　　　　　　**Fax: (706)537-0826**

& **1098 WBKI-AM - 1440**
613 Tallapoosa St.
Bremen, GA 30110　　　　　　　Phone: (404)537-0840

BUENA VISTA

⬚ **1099 Patriot-Citizen**
Box 108
Buena Vista, GA 31803　　　　　**Phone: (706)846-3188**

CARTERSVILLE

& **1100 Prestige Cable TV**
156 Morningside Dr.
Box 785
Cartersville, GA 30120　　　　　**Phone: (404)382-0531**

COLUMBUS

⬚ **1101 The National Environmental Journal**
Campbell Publishing Co.
PO Box 2567　　　　　　　　　Phone: (706)324-6746
Columbus, GA 31902　　　　　　Fax: (706)324-1177
Trade publication for environmental and pollution control professionals. **Founded:** September 1991. **Frequency:** 6x/yr. **Printing Method:** Web offset. **Trim Size:** 8 1/8 x 10 7/8. /CPP 2 or 3. **Key Personnel:** Chris Bryon Campbell, Publisher; Paul Cheremisinoff, Editor; Lisa Foskey, Circulation Mgr. **Subscription:** $38; $70 other countries; $90 other countries airmail. $6 single issue.
Ad Rates:　BW:　$4,165　　**Circulation:** Paid ‡100
　　　　　　4C:　$5,230　　　　Non-paid ‡54,000
　　　　　　PCI:　$90

& **1102 TCI Cablevision of Georgia**
Box 1678
Columbus, GA 31906　　　　　　Phone: (706)324-2288
Owner: Tele-Communications, Inc. **Founded:** 1970. **Cities Served:** Harris County, Muscogee County, and Bibb City, GA.

& **1103 TeleCable of Columbus, Inc.**
3650 Buena Vista Rd.
Box 6449
Columbus, GA 31995　　　　　　Phone: (706)687-1158
Owner: TeleCable Corp. **Founded:** 1970. **Cities Served:** Muscogee County, GA.

CONYERS

& **1104 WEXA Cable, Inc.**
1359 Iris Dr.　　　　　　　　Phone: (404)483-0010
Conyers, GA 30208　　　　　　Fax: (404)483-8305
Key Personnel: Ed Dunbar, Gen. Mgr./V.P.; J.C. Kirkland, Plant Mgr.; Cindy Hewatt, Business Mgr.; Sandi Mace, Mktg. Mgr. **Cities Served:** Conyers, Rockdale County and Newton County, GA. 12,400 subscribing households; 48 channels; 1 community access channel.

CORNELIA

& **1105 WCON-FM - 99.3**
540 N. Main St.
PO Box 100　　　　　　　　　**Phone: (706)778-2241**
Cornelia, GA 30531　　　　　　**Fax: (706)778-0576**

COVINGTON

1106 City of Covington CATV
2111 Conyers St.
PO Box 1527   Phone: (706)787-4444
Covington, GA 30209   **Fax: (706)787-7463**

CUMMING

1107 WHNE-AM - 1170
1107 Atlanta Hwy.   Phone: (404)887-3136
Cumming, GA 30130   **Fax: (404)887-3333**

DAWSON

1108 The Dawson News
139 W. Lee St.
PO Box 350   Phone: (912)995-2175
Dawson, GA 31742   **Fax: (912)995-3713**

1109 Southern Connection
PO Box 754
Dawson, GA 31742   Phone: 800-824-3917
Shopping guide. **Founded:** 1990. **Frequency:** Weekly. **Printing Method:** Web offset. **Cols./Page:** 7. **Col. Width:** 8 picas. **Col. Depth:** 15 in. **Key Personnel:** Diane Waters, Publisher. **Subscription:** Free.
                 Circulation: Free ‡12,898
Advertising accepted; contact publisher for rates. **Formerly:** Dawson Buyers Guide.

DECATUR

1110 The DeKalb Sun
Decatur News Publishing Co., Inc.
739 DeKalb Industrial Way   Phone: (404)292-3536
Decatur, GA 30033   Fax: (404)299-3218
Former Title: DeKalb News-Sun

DEMOREST

1111 The American Genealogist
PO Box 398
Demorest, GA 30535-0398   **Phone: (706)865-6440**

DOUGLAS

1112 Douglas News
313 N. Peterson Ave.   Phone: (912)384-9112
Douglas, GA 31533-0923   Fax: (912)384-4220
Community newspaper. **Founded:** October 10, 1990. **Frequency:** Weekly (Saturday). **Printing Method:** Offset. **Trim Size:** 10 1/2 x 15. **Cols./Page:** 6. **Col. Width:** 9 picas. **Key Personnel:** William H. Kibbey, Editor; Carlene S. Phelps, Publisher; Elaine Fox, Advertising Mgr.

Ad Rates:	GLR:	$1	Circulation: Free ‡16,000
	BW:	$380	Paid ‡48
	4C:	$530	
	PCI:	$4	

1113 WDMG-AM - 860
PO Box 860   Phone: (912)384-3250
Douglas, GA 31533   **Fax: (912)383-8552**

DULUTH

1114 Gwinnett Daily News
The News Co., Inc.
200 Hampton Green
PO Box 956789   Phone: (404)381-8535
Duluth, GA 30136   Fax: (404)963-2271
Ceased publication.

1115 Gwinnett Plus
The News Co., Inc.
200 Hampton Green
Duluth, GA 30136   Phone: (404)381-8535
Ceased publication.

EATONTON

1116 Southern Cable View
PO Box 3668   Phone: (404)485-2288
Eatonton, GA 31024   Fax: (404)485-0118
Formerly: GEM Communications. **Key Personnel:** Jim Brown, Gen. Mgr.; Anthony Black, Plant Mgr.; Staci Farrow, Office Mgr.

ELBERTON

1117 WWRK-FM - 92.1
Box 638   **Phone: (706)283-1400**
Elberton, GA 30635   **Fax: (706)283-8710**

FORT BENNING

1118 Infantry
U.S. Army Infantry School
PO Box 2005   Phone: (404)545-2350
Fort Benning, GA 31905-0605   **Fax: (706)545-7838**

FORT VALLEY

1119 The Camellia Journal
American Camellia Society
Massee Lane Gardens
1 Massee Ln.   Phone: (912)967-2358
Fort Valley, GA 31030   **Fax: (912)967-2083**

GAINESVILLE

1120 WBCX-FM - 89.1
Brenau College
1 Centennial Circle   Phone: (706)534-6185
Gainesville, GA 30501   **Fax: (706)534-6114**

1121 WGGA-AM - 1240
305 A Green St.
PO Box 1318   **Phone: (706)532-6211**
Gainesville, GA 30503   Fax: (404)532-1314

1122 WGGA-FM - 101.9
305 A Green St.   **Phone: (706)532-6211**
Gainesville, GA 30503   Fax: (404)532-1314

GORDON

1123 Wilkinson County News
Box 205   Phone: (912)946-2218
Irwinton, GA 31042   **Fax: (912)946-2218**

HARTWELL

1124 WKLY-AM - 980
PO Box 636   Phone: (404)376-2233
Hartwell, GA 30643   **Fax: (404)376-3100**

HOMERVILLE

1125 WBTY-FM - 105.5
Box 577
Homerville, GA 31634   Phone: (912)487-3414
Format: Classic Rock. **Owner:** Southern Broadcasting and Investments. **Founded:** 1979. **Operating Hours:** Continuous. **Key Personnel:** Nancy Strickland, Mgr.; Jane Hill, Operations Mgr. **Wattage:** 3000. **Ad Rates:** $2.50 for 30 seconds; $4.75 for 60 seconds.

JONESBORO

1126 Wometco Cable
6435 Tara Blvd., Ste. 22   Phone: (404)478-0010
Jonesboro, GA 30236   Fax: (404)471-6639
Owner: Wometco Cable Corp. **Cities Served:** Clayton, Fulton, and Henry counties, GA.

LA GRANGE

🎙 1127 WTRP-AM - 620
806 Franklin Rd.
PO Box 1203　　　　　　　　　　Phone: (706)884-8611
La Grange, GA 30241　　　　　　Fax: (706)884-8612

LAKELAND

📖 1128 Lanier County News
Cook Publishing Co.
PO Box 278　　　　　　　　　　　Phone: (912)482-3367
Lakeland, GA 31635　　　　　　　Fax: (912)896-2233

LOUISVILLE

📖 1129 Louisville News & Farmer & Wadley Herald
Jefferson Press, Inc.
PO Box 487　　　　　　　　　　　Phone: (912)625-7722
Louisville, GA 30434　　　　　　　Fax: (912)625-8128

MACON

📖 1130 Perspectives in Religious Studies
National Assn. of Baptist Professors of Religion
Mercer University
Macon, GA 31207　　　　　　　Phone: (912)752-2759

🎙 1131 WIBB-AM - 1280
369 2nd St.
PO Box 4527
Macon, GA 31208　　　　　　　Phone: (912)742-2505
Format: Urban Contemporary/Gospel. **Owner:** Davis Broadcasting
Co., Inc. **Key Personnel:** Albert E. Smith, Gen. Mgr.; Patricia Glass,
Gen. Sales Mgr.; Jess Branson, Sales Mgr.; George Threatt, Opera-
tions Mgr. **Wattage:** 5000.

🎙 1132 WMAZ-TV - Channel 13
1314 Gray Hwy.　　　　　　　　Phone: (912)752-1313
Macon, GA 31211　　　　　　　　Fax: (912)752-1331

MILLEDGEVILLE

📖 1133 Georgia College Connection
Georgia College Alumni Assn., Inc.
517 Hancock St.
PO Box 98　　　　　　　　　　　Phone: (912)453-5400
Milledgeville, GA 31061　　　　　　Fax: (912)453-5744
Former Title: Georgia College Alumni News Quarterly

🎙 1134 WKGQ-AM - 1060
PO Box 832　　　　　　　　　　　Phone: (912)453-9406
Milledgeville, GA 31061-0832　　　Fax: (912)453-3298

🎙 1135 WMVG-AM - 1450
1250 W. Charlton St.
PO Box 519　　　　　　　　　　　Phone: (912)452-0586
Milledgeville, GA 31061　　　　　　Fax: (912)452-5886

MOULTRIE

🎙 1136 WMGA-AM - 580
Box 1380　　　　　　　　　　　　Phone: (912)985-0580
Moultrie, GA 31776　　　　　　　Fax: (912)890-8609

MOUNTAIN CITY

🎙 1137 WALH-AM - 1340
Box F　　　　　　　　　　　　　Phone: (706)746-2256
Mountain City, GA 30562　　　　　Fax: (706)746-2259
Format: Gospel; Contemporary Country; Bluegrass. **Network(s):** Sun
Radio. **Owner:** W.L. Savage and Hugh Walden. **Founded:** 1986.
Operating Hours: 6 a.m.-11 p.m. **Key Personnel:** W.L. Savage, Gen.
Mgr./Sales and News Dir.; Lorraine Savage, Sales Mgr.; W.P.

Franklin, Music Dir. **Wattage:** 1000. **Ad Rates:** $2.75-$3.50 for 30
seconds; $3.75-$4.50 for 60 seconds.

NORCROSS

📖 1138 Better Crops with Plant Food
Potash & Phosphate Institute
655 Engineering Dr., Ste 110　　　Phone: (404)447-0335
Norcross, GA 30092-2821　　　　Fax: (404)448-0439

📖 1139 IIE Transactions
Institute of Industrial Engineers
25 Technology Park/Atlanta　　　　Phone: (404)449-0461
Norcross, GA 30092　　　　　　　Fax: (404)263-8532

📖 1140 Industrial Engineering
Institute of Industrial Engineers
25 Technology Park/Atlanta　　　　Phone: (404)449-0461
Norcross, GA 30092　　　　　　　Fax: (404)263-8532

📖 1141 Unlimited Concepts
756 Holcomb Bridge Rd.
Bldg. 6　　　　　　　　　　　　Phone: (404)446-8334
Norcross, GA 30071　　　　　　　Fax: (404)448-5357
Community magazine. **Founded:** 1991. **Frequency:** Weekly. **Printing
Method:** Rotogravure. **Trim Size:** 10 x 11 1/2. **Cols./Page:** 3. **Col.
Width:** 3 1/8 in. **Col. Depth:** 11 1/4 in. **Key Personnel:** Gladstone
Owens, Editor; Lisa Reese, Publisher.
Ad Rates:　BW:　$32,759　　　**Circulation:** Paid 120,000
　　　　　　4C:　$42,950　　　　　　　　Non-paid 50,000
　　　　　　PCI:
　　　　　　$1,231.30

ROCHELLE

🎙 1142 WMCG-FM - 104.9
Box 1049
Rochelle, GA 31079　　　　　　　Phone: (912)362-4108

ROCKMART

📖 1143 Rockmart Journal
News Publishing Co.
PO Box 1633　　　　　　　　　　Phone: (404)290-5330
Rome, GA 30162-1633　　　　　　Fax: (706)232-9632

ROSWELL

📖 1144 Miata Magazine
Miata Club of America
PO Box 767127　　　　　　　　　Phone: (404)998-4766
Roswell, GA 30076　　　　　　　　Fax: (404)998-4767
Association magazine for Miata owners. **Founded:** 1989. **Frequency:**
Quarterly. **Printing Method:** Web offset. **Trim Size:** 8 1/8 x 10 7/8.
Key Personnel: Norman H. Garrett III, Editor. **Subscription:** $25.
Ad Rates:　BW:　$1,750　　　**Circulation:** Paid 28,000
　　　　　　4C:　$3,540　　　　　　　　Non-paid 10,000

ROYSTON

📖 1145 The News Leader
PO Box 26　　　　　　　　　　　Phone: (706)245-7351
Royston, GA 30662-0006　　　　　Fax: (706)245-5991

SAINT MARY'S

🎙 1146 WECC-AM - 1190
2101 Hwy. 40 E.
PO Box 1190　　　　　　　　　　Phone: (912)882-1190
Saint Mary's, GA 31558　　　　　Fax: (912)882-9322

SAVANNAH

1147 Savannah Cablevision
5515 Abercom St.
Box 22907   Phone: (912)354-2813
Savannah, GA 31405   Fax: (912)353-6045
Owner: American TV & Communications Corp. **Founded:** 1965.
Cities Served: Bryan County, Chatham County, Effinham County,
and Liberty County; Bloomingdale, Garden City, Midway, Pooler,
Port Wentworth, Rincon, Springfield, Thunderbolt, and Vernonburg,
GA; Hampton County, Brunson, and Varnville, SC.

1148 WJCL-TV - Channel 22
PO Box 61268   Phone: (912)925-0022
Savannah, GA 31420-1268   **Fax: (912)925-8621**

SNELLVILLE

1149 Wometco of Gwinnett
Box 1049   Phone: (404)921-0010
Snellville, GA 30278   Fax: (404)979-0101
Owner: Wometco Cable Corp. **Founded:** 1979. **Cities Served:** Gwinnett
County, GA.

SUMMERVILLE

1150 Chattooga Press
News Publishing Co.
PO Box 485   Phone: (706)290-5330
Summerville, GA 30747   Fax: (706)232-9632
Newspaper. **Founded:** 1982. **Frequency:** Weekly. **Printing Method:**
Offset. **Cols./Page:** 6. **Col. Width:** 2 1/16 in. **Col. Depth:** 21 1/4 in. **Key
Personnel:** B.H. Mooney, III, Publisher. **Subscription:** Free.
Ad Rates: GLR: $4.65   **Circulation:** Free 10,200
                  BW: $592.88

1151 The Summerville News
PO Box 310   **Phone: (706)857-2494**
Summerville, GA 30747   **Fax: (706)857-2393**

1152 WGTA-AM - 950
State Hwy. 100
PO Box 200   **Phone: (706)857-2466**
Summerville, GA 30747   **Fax: (706)857-3652**

SUWANEE

1153 NE Gwinnett Cablevision
3580-F Hwy. 317   Phone: (404)932-0084
Suwanee, GA 30174   Fax: (404)932-8423
Owner: Rifkin & Associates. **Founded:** 1979. **Cities Served:** Cherokee,
Fulton, Gwinnett, and Hall counties, GA.

SWAINSBORO

1154 WJAT-AM - 800
PO Box 289   Phone: (912)237-2011
Swainsboro, GA 30401   **Fax: (912)237-2011**

1155 WJAT-FM - 98.1
PO Box 289   Phone: (912)237-2011
Swainsboro, GA 30401   **Fax: (912)237-2011**

THOMASTON

1156 WTGA-FM - 95.3
208 S. Center St.   **Phone: (706)647-7121**
Thomaston, GA 30286   **Fax: (706)647-7122**

THOMSON

1157 McDuffie Progress
PO Box 1090
101 Church St.   Phone: (706)595-1601
Thomson, GA 30824   **Fax: (706)595-1601**

TIFTON

1158 WSGY-FM - 100.3
PO Box 1466   **Phone: (912)382-1100**
Tifton, GA 31794   Fax: (912)436-9100

TUCKER

1159 GEORGIA Magazine
Georgia Electric Membership Corp.
PO Box 1707
2100 E. Exchange Pl.   **Phone: (404)270-6950**
Tucker, GA 30085   **Fax: (404)270-6995**

WARNER ROBINS

1160 WRCC-AM - 1600
2052 Watson Blvd.
Box 5051   Phone: (912)922-2222
Warner Robins, GA 31099   Fax: (912)922-2224
Format: Country. **Network(s):** Satellite Music. **Owner:** Televiewers
Inc. **Operating Hours:** Continuous. **Key Personnel:** Vernon Arnold,
Gen. Mgr.; Janiz Arnold, Sales Mgr. **Wattage:** 2500 day; 500 night. **Ad
Rates:** $5-$14 for 30 seconds; $7-$18 for 60 seconds. **Additional
Contact Information:** Alt. telephone (912)929-HITS.

1161 WRCC-FM - 101.7
2052 Watson Blvd.
Box 5051   Phone: (912)922-2222
Warner Robins, GA 31099   **Fax: (912)929-4487**

HAWAII

CAPTAIN COOK

1162 Loving More
Pep Publishing
PO Box 6306   Phone: (808)929-9691
Captain Cook, HI 96704-6306   Fax: (808)929-9831
Magazine focusing on group marriage. **Founded:** 1983. **Frequency:** Quarterly. **Key Personnel:** Ryam Nearing, Editor. **Subscription:** $25. $4 single issue.

Circulation: ‡600

Advertising accepted; contact publisher for rates. **Formerly:** Pep Talk - Group Marriage News.

HAWI

1163 Kamehameha Cablevision
Box 174
Hawi, HI 96719   Phone: (808)889-5868

HONOLULU

1164 Building Management Hawaii
Trade Publsihing Co.
287 Mokauea St.
Honolulu, HI 98819   Phone: (808)848-0711
Magazine covering maintenance and building management. **Founded:** 1983. **Frequency:** Monthly. **Cols./Page:** 3. **Col. Width:** 13 picas. **Col. Depth:** 57 picas. **Key Personnel:** Pearl Page, Mng. Editor; John Black, Exec. Editor.

Circulation: Non-paid 5,000

1165 Hawaii Bar Journal
Hawaii State Bar Association
1136 Union Mall, PH1   Phone: (808)537-1868
Honolulu, HI 96813   Fax: (808)521-7936
Legal journal containing Hawaii State Bar news and articles for Hawaii attorneys. **Founded:** 1968. **Frequency:** 6x/yr. **Printing Method:** Offset. **Trim Size:** 8 1/8 x 10 7/8. **Cols./Page:** 3. **Col. Width:** 2.5 in. **Col. Depth:** 8 in. **Key Personnel:** Karen Yoshida, Managing Editor; Carol K. Muranaka, Editor-in-Chief. **Subscription:** $30; $60 other countries. $2 single issue.
Ad Rates: GLR: $6   **Circulation:** Paid ⊕4,142
           BW: $635   Non-paid ⊕983
           4C: $1,130
Formerly: Hawaii Bar News.

1166 Hawaii CPA News
Crossroads Press, Inc.
PO Box 833   Phone: (808)521-0021
Honolulu, HI 96808   Fax: (808)528-2325
Publication for accountants. **Founded:** 1966. **Frequency:** Monthly.

Printing Method: Photo offset. **Trim Size:** 8 1/8 x 10 7/8. **Cols./Page:** 3. **Col. Width:** 2 1/4 in. **Col. Depth:** 10 in. **Key Personnel:** Stephen S. Lent, Publisher. **Subscription:** Free to qualified subscribers.
Ad Rates: GLR: $7.45   **Circulation:** Paid 1,750
           BW: $480
           4C: $1,060
Formerly: The Balance Sheet.

1167 Hawaii Dental Journal
Crossroads Press, Inc.
PO Box 833   Phone: (808)521-0021
Honolulu, HI 96808   Fax: (808)528-2325
Dental journal. **Founded:** 1967. **Frequency:** Bimonthly. **Printing Method:** Photo offset. **Trim Size:** 8 1/8 x 10 7/8. **Cols./Page:** 3. **Col. Width:** 2 1/4 in. **Col. Depth:** 10 in. **Key Personnel:** Stephen S. Lent, Publisher.
Ad Rates: GLR: $7.45   **Circulation:** Paid 1,100
           BW: $480
           4C: $1,060

1168 Hawaii Hospitality
Trade Publishing Co.
287 Mokauea St.   Phone: (808)848-0711
Honolulu, HI 98819   Fax: (808)841-3053
Hotel management newsmagazine in Hawaii. **Founded:** 1983. **Frequency:** Bimonthly. **Printing Method:** Offset. **Trim Size:** 8 1/8 x 10 7/8. **Key Personnel:** John M. Black, Editor; Carl Hebenstreit, Publisher. **Subscription:** $18.
Ad Rates: BW: $1,170   **Circulation:** Non-paid ‡2,800
           4C: $1,765

1169 Hawaii Medical Journal
Crossroads Press, Inc.
863 Halekauwila   **Phone: (808)521-0021**
Honolulu, HI 96814   **Fax: (808)528-2325**

1170 Hawaiian Airlines Magazine
Becker Communications
1188 Bishop St., Ste. 2708   Phone: (808)533-4165
Honolulu, HI 96813   Fax: (808)537-4990
Subtitle: Hawaiian Airlines In Flight. **Founded:** 1990. **Frequency:** Monthly. **Printing Method:** Web offset. **Trim Size:** 8 1/8 x 10 7/8. **Cols./Page:** 3. **Col. Width:** 13 agate lines. **Col. Depth:** 10 in. **Key Personnel:** George Engebretson, Editor; Ruth Ann Becker, Publisher. **Subscription:** $35. $6 single issue.

Circulation: 82,000

1171 Vintage News
PO Box 853   Phone: (808)591-0049
Honolulu, HI 96808   Fax: (808)591-0038
Magazine. **Founded:** 1988. **Frequency:** 6x/yr. **Trim Size:** 10 1/4 x 15.

Key Personnel: Campbell Mansfield, Editor and Publisher; Lorraine Walters, Advertising Mgr. **Subscription:** $6.
Ad Rates: BW: $700 **Circulation:** Non-paid 10,000

⚓ 1172 KIPO-FM - 89.3
738 Kaheka St., No. 101 Phone: (808)955-8821
Honolulu, HI 96814 **Fax: (808)942-5477**

⚓ 1173 KWHE-TV - Channel 14
1188 Bishop St., Ste. 502 Phone: (808)538-1414
Honolulu, HI 96813 Fax: (808)526-0326

LAHAINA

⚓ 1174 KPOA-FM - 93.5
505 Front St., No. 215 Phone: (808)667-9110
Lahaina, HI 96761 **Fax: (808)661-8850**

⚓ 1175 UAE
910 Honoapiilani Hwy.
No. 6 W. Maui Center
Lahaina, HI 96740 Phone: (808)661-0972
Owner: Tele-Communications, Inc. **Founded:** 1968. **Cities Served:** Maui County, Honokowai, Kaanapali, Kahana, Kapalua, Lahaina, Mahinahina, and Napili, HI.

LIHUE

⚓ 1176 KFMN-FM - 96.9
PO Box 1566 Phone: (808)246-1197
Lihue, HI 96766-5566 **Fax: (808)246-9697**

MILILANI TOWN

⚓ 1177 Oceanic Cablevision, Inc.
200 Akamainui St. Phone: (808)625-2100
Mililani Town, HI 96789 Fax: (808)625-5888
Owner: TimeWarner Cable. **Founded:** 1968. **Key Personnel:** Don Carroll, Pres.; Kit Beuret, Dir. of Public Affairs. **Cities Served:** Honolulu, HI, and surrounding communities: 230,000 subscribing households; 45 channels; 2 community access channels.

PEARL CITY

⚓ 1178 KIPO-AM - 1380
738 Kaheka St., No. 101 Phone: (808)955-8821
Honolulu, HI 96814 **Fax: (808)942-5477**

PUHI

⚓ 1179 Kauai CableVision
Box 2116 Phone: (808)245-7720
Puhi, HI 96766 Fax: (808)245-5221
Owner: InterMedia Partners. **Founded:** 1981. **Cities Served:** Kauai County and Barking Sands Naval Base, HI.

IDAHO

BOISE

📖 **1180 Gunfighter**
Graphic Art Publishing
5325 Kendall
Boise, ID 83706   **Phone: (208)375-1010**
Former Title: Wing Spread

📖 **1181 Miner's News**
PO Box 5694
7289 Franklin Rd.   Phone: (208)375-3680
Boise, ID 83705   Fax: (208)375-0975
Mining newspaper. **Founded:** 1985. **Frequency:** 6x/yr. **Printing Method:** Web offset. **Trim Size:** 11 x 16 1/2. **Cols./Page:** 5. **Col. Width:** 2 in. **Col. Depth:** 14 1/2 in. **Key Personnel:** Gary White, Publisher. **ISSN:** 0890-6157. **Subscription:** $25; $30 Canada.
Ad Rates: BW: $1,695   **Circulation:** Paid ‡1,488
           4C: $2,245   Non-paid ‡5,855

🎙 **1182 KBSU-FM - 90.3**
Boise State University
1910 University Dr.
Boise, ID 83725   Phone: (208)385-3663

🎙 **1183 KHEZ-FM - 103.3**
3050 N. Lakeharbor, Ste. 120   Phone: (208)384-1033
Boise, ID 83703   Fax: (208)343-2103

🎙 **1184 KIZN-FM - 92.3**
9400 Fairview   **Phone: (208)378-9200**
Boise, ID 83704   **Fax: (208)375-2707**

🎙 **1185 UAE**
8400 Westpark St.   Phone: (208)377-2941
Boise, ID 83704   Fax: (208)377-7500
Owner: Tele-Communications, Inc. **Founded:** 1979. **Cities Served:** Ada County and Canyon County, Eagle, Garden City, Kuna, Meridian, and Nampa, ID.

COEUR D'ALENE

🎙 **1186 Kootenai Cable Inc.**
108 Indiana Ave.   Phone: (208)667-5521
Coeur d'Alene, ID 83814   Fax: (208)667-4804
Owner: Rock Associates. **Founded:** 1970. **Cities Served:** Kootenai County, ID.

GARDEN VALLEY

📖 **1187 The Idaho World**
World Publishing Company, Inc.
PO Box 99   Phone: (208)392-4989
Garden Valley, ID 83622   **Fax: (208)462-3487**

IDAHO FALLS

📖 **1188 Cable Scene**
Pioneer Publications
PO Box 3838
Idaho Falls, ID 83403   Phone: (208)523-7777

📖 **1189 Houseboat Magazine**
Harris Publishing, Inc.
520 Park Ave.
Idaho Falls, ID 83402
Magazine for houseboating in America. **Frequency:** 6x/yr. **Key Personnel:** Rex Thomas, Editor; Darryl Harris, Publisher. **Subscription:** $11.95 Free to qualified subscribers; $16.95. $2.95 single issue.
                   Circulation: (Not Reported)

🎙 **1190 KID-AM - 590**
1655 S. Woodruff Ave., Ste. A   Phone: (208)524-5900
Idaho Falls, ID 83404   **Fax: (208)522-9696**

🎙 **1191 KID-FM - 96.1**
1655 S. Woodruff Ave., Ste. A   Phone: (208)524-5900
Idaho Falls, ID 83404   **Fax: (208)522-9696**

LEWISTON

🎙 **1192 KMOK-FM - 106.9**
805 Stewart Ave.   Phone: (208)746-5056
Lewiston, ID 83501   **Fax: (208)743-4440**

🎙 **1193 KRLC-AM - 1350**
805 Stewart Ave.   Phone: (208)743-1551
Lewiston, ID 83501   **Fax: (208)743-4440**

MONTPELIER

📖 **1194 The Bear Laker**
Citizen Publishing Co. - The News Examiner
847 Washington
PO Box 278
Montpelier, ID 83254   Phone: (208)847-0552

Ad Rates: GLR = general line rate; BW = one-time black & white page rate; 4C = one-time four color page rate; SAU = standard advertising unit rate; CNU = Canadian newspaper advertising unit rate; PCI = per column inch rate.
Circulation: ★ = ABC; △ = BPA; ◆ = CAC; ● = CCAB; □ = VAC; ⊕ = PO Statement; ‡ = Publisher's Report; Boldface figures = sworn; Light figures = estimated.
Entry type: 📖 = Print; 🎙 = Broadcast.

79

MOSCOW

1195 Women in Natural Resources
University of Idaho
Bowers Laboratory
Moscow, ID 83843　　　　　　Phone: (208)885-6754
Periodical for women in forestry, wildlife, range, fisheries, recreation, and related social sciences. **Frequency:** Quarterly.
　　　　　　　　　　Circulation: (Not Reported)

1196 KUOI-FM - 89.3
University of Idaho
Student Union Bldg.　　　　　Phone: (208)885-6433
Moscow, ID 83843　　　　　　**Fax: (208)885-5543**

MOUNTAIN HOME

1197 Pipeline
PO Box 1330　　　　　　　Phone: (208)587-3331
Mountain Home, ID 83647　　　Fax: (208)587-9205
Community newspaper. **Founded:** 1992. **Frequency:** Weekly. **Cols./Page:** 4. **Col. Width:** 28 nonpareils. **Col. Width:** 210 agate lines. **Key Personnel:** Kelly Everitt, Editor; Coleen W. Swenson, Publisher; Debra Shoemaker, Advertising Mgr. **Subscription:** $20.
Ad Rates: PCI:　　$4　　　　**Circulation:** Free 4,200

OLDTOWN

1198 KMJY-FM - 104.9
PO Box 1740
Oldtown, ID 83822　　　　　Phone: (208)437-5331
Format: Contemporary Country; Oldies. **Network(s):** CNN Radio. **Owner:** James Stargel, at above address. **Founded:** 1986. **Operating Hours:** 6 a.m.-10 p.m. **Key Personnel:** James Stargel, Mgr.; Julianne Chambers, News Dir. **Ad Rates:** $3-$5 for 15 seconds; $5-$7 for 30 seconds; $7-$10 for 60 seconds. **Additional Contact Information:** Alt. phones (208)437-5887; (208)448-1604.

POCATELLO

1199 KRCD-AM - 1490
811 W. Cedar
Pocatello, ID 83201　　　　　**Phone: (208)232-0010**

1200 TCI Cablevision of Idaho
Box 2469　　　　　　　　Phone: (208)232-1784
Pocatello, ID 83201　　　　　Fax: (208)234-4756
Owner: Tele-Communications, Inc. **Founded:** 1954. **Key Personnel:** Sue Parker, Mgr.; Jerry Ransbottom, Plant Mgr.; Mike Waldron, Office Mgr. **Cities Served:** Bannock County, Chubbock, Pocatello, and Inkom, ID: 54 channels; 2 community access channel; 252 hours per week of community access programming.

SHELLEY

1201 The Shelley Pioneer
Pioneer Publications
PO Box P
Shelley, ID 83274　　　　　Phone: (208)357-7661
Former Title: The Pioneer

WEISER

1202 Falcon Video Communications
24 W. Idaho St.　　　　　　Phone: (208)549-3040
Weiser, ID 83672　　　　　　Fax: (208)549-3328
Owner: Falcon Cable TV, 10866 Wilshire Blvd., Ste. 500, Los Angeles, CA 90024. **Formerly:** Snake River Valley Cablevision (1992). **Key Personnel:** John West, System Mgr.; Peggy Harvey, Office Mgr.; Carla Roberts, Office Mgr. **Cities Served:** Weiser, Emmett, McCall, New Meadows, Council, Cascade, and Donnelly, ID; Halfway, OR: 4,930 subscribing households.

1203 KWEI-FM - 99.3
PO Box 791
Weiser, ID 83672　　　　　　**Phone: (208)549-2241**

ILLINOIS

ABINGDON

📖 **1204 Abingdon Argus**
Acklin Newspaper Group
103 S. Main St.
PO Box 32
Abingdon, IL 61410

Phone: (309)462-5758
Fax: (309)462-3221

ALBION

📖 **1205 Journal-Register**
19 W. Main St.
PO Box 10
Albion, IL 62806

Phone: (618)445-2355
Fax: (618)445-3459

ALEDO

📖 **1206 The Gun Report**
World Wide Gun Report, Inc.
110 S. College
PO Box 38
Aledo, IL 61231

Phone: (309)582-5311
Fax: (309)582-5555

ASHLAND

📖 **1207 Ashland Sentinel**
116 N. Hardin
PO Box 418
Ashland, IL 62612-0418

Phone: (217)476-3332
Fax: (217)476-3356

ATKINSON

📖 **1208 Atkinson-Annawan News**
Kenawee Star Courier
113 W. Exchange
PO Box 727
Atkinson, IL 61235

Phone: (309)936-7741
Fax: (309)936-7150

AURORA

🎤 **1209 Jones Intercable, Inc.**
8 E. Galena
Aurora, IL 60505

Phone: (708)897-2288
Fax: (708)897-3187

Owner: Jones Intercable, Inc. **Founded:** 1971. **Cities Served:** Du Page County, Kane County, and Kendall County; Boulder Hill, Montgomery, North Aurora, and Oswego, IL.

AVON

📖 **1210 Avon Sentinel**
Acklin Newspaper Group
Box H
Avon, IL 61415

Phone: (309)462-5758
Fax: (309)462-3221

BERWYN

📖 **1211 American Sokol Publication**
The American Sokol Organization
6424 W. Cermak Rd.
Berwyn, IL 60402

Phone: (708)795-6671
Fax: (708)795-0539

📖 **1212 Nedelni Hlasatel**
6426 W. Cermak
Berwyn, IL 60402

Phone: (708)749-1891
Fax: (708)749-1935

Czech and Slovak language newspaper. **Subtitle:** Czechoslovak Daily Herald. **Founded:** 1891. **Frequency:** 2x/wk. **Printing Method:** Web offset. **Trim Size:** 10 3/16 x 16. **Cols./Page:** 4. **Col. Width:** 2 3/8 in. **Key Personnel:** Josef Kucera, Pres. **Subscription:** $50.

Ad Rates: BW: $400   **Circulation:** 10,000
            PCI: $10

BLOOMINGDALE

📖 **1213 Bloomingdale Press**
Press Publications
1645 Bloomingdale Rd.
Bloomingdale, IL 60108

Phone: (708)307-1101
Fax: (708)307-1190

BLOOMINGTON

📖 **1214 FarmWeek**
Illinois Agricultural Assn.
1701 Towanda Ave.
Bloomington, IL 61701

Phone: (309)557-3140
Fax: (800)998-6090

📖 **1215 The McLean County Community News**
106 Oak Creek Plaza
PO Box 1625
Bloomington, IL 61701

Phone: (309)827-8555
Fax: (309)829-6926

🎤 **1216 TeleCable of Bloomington-Normal**
1202 W. Division St.
Box 1386
Bloomington, IL 61702-1386

Phone: (309)454-3350

Owner: TeleCable Corp. **Founded:** 1969. **Cities Served:** McLean County, IL.

1217 WIHN-FM - 96.7
PO Box 610
Bloomington, IL 61702-0610

Phone: (309)888-4496
Fax: (309)452-9677

BRIDGEVIEW

1218 Palos Hills-Hickory Hills Reporter
Regional Publishing Corp.
12243 S. Harlem Ave.
Palos Heights, IL 60463

Phone: (708)448-6161

Former Title: Bridgeview-Hills Reporter

CAIRO

1219 WKRO-AM - 1490
Rte. 1, US-51
Box 311
Cairo, IL 62914

Phone: (618)734-1490
Fax: (618)734-0884

CANTON

1220 WBYS-AM - 1560
1000 E. Linn St.
Box 600
Canton, IL 61520

Phone: (309)647-1560
Fax: (309)647-1563

Format: News/Agricultural/Information/Sports/Eclectic. Network(s): ABC; Tribune Radio; Illinois News. Owner: Fulton County Broadcasting Co. Founded: 1947. Operating Hours: Sunrise-sunset. Key Personnel: Charles E. Wright, Gen. Mgr.; Kevin Stephenson, Sales Mgr./Sports Dir.; Leon Groover, Program Dir.; Phil Miller, News Dir.; Pat Taylor, Traffic Dir. Wattage: 250. Ad Rates: $3.45-$6.95 for 15 seconds;$4.90-$9.90 for 30 seconds;$7.05-$14.10.

1221 WBYS-FM - 98.3
1000 E. Linn St.
Box 600
Canton, IL 61520

Phone: (309)647-1560
Fax: (309)674-1563

Format: News/Agricultural/Information/Sports/Eclectic. Network(s): ABC; Tribune Radio; Illinois News. Owner: Fulton County Broadcasting Co. Operating Hours: 5:30 a.m.-midnight weekdays; 5:30-11 Sat.-Sun. Key Personnel: Charles E. Wright, Gen. Mgr.; Kevin Stephenson, Sales Mgr./Sports Dir.; Leon Groover, Program Dir.; Phil Miller, News Dir.; Natalie Orwig, Traffic Dir. Wattage: 3000. Ad Rates: $3.45-$6.95 for 15 seconds;$4.90-$9.90 for 30 seconds;$7.05-$14.10 for 60 seconds.

CARBONDALE

1222 WOOZ-FM - 99.9
1025 E. Main
Carbondale, IL 62902

Phone: (618)549-3243
Fax: (618)549-2455

CARLINVILLE

1223 Macoupin County Enquirer
125 E. Main St.
PO Box 200
Carlinville, IL 62626

Phone: (217)854-2534
Fax: (217)854-2535

1224 WCNL-FM - 96.7
No. 55 Carlinville Plaza
Carlinville, IL 62626

Phone: (217)854-3131
Fax: (217)854-3416

CARMI

1225 Angus Topics
Angus Topics, Inc.
3 Smith St.
Carmi, IL 62821

Phone: (618)382-8553
Fax: (618)382-3436

CAROL STREAM

1226 Assembly
Hitchcock Publishing Co.
191 S. Gary Ave.
Carol Stream, IL 60188

Phone: (708)665-1000
Fax: (708)462-2225

Former Title: Assembly Engineering

1227 Your Church
CTi Publications
465 Gundersen Dr.
Carol Stream, IL 60188

Phone: (708)260-6200
Fax: (708)260-0114

CARROLLTON

1228 Greene County Shopper
PO Box 231
Carrollton, IL 62016

Phone: (217)942-3626
Fax: (217)942-3699

1229 Jersey County Shopper
PO Box 231
Carrollton, IL 62016

Phone: (217)942-3626
Fax: (217)942-3699

CARTHAGE

1230 WCAZ-AM - 990
84 S. Madison
Carthage, IL 62321

Phone: (217)357-3128
Fax: (217)357-2014

1231 WCAZ-FM - 92.1
84 S. Madison
Carthage, IL 62321

Phone: (217)357-3128
Fax: (217)357-2014

CARY

1232 Utility Construction and Maintenance
Practical Communications, Inc.
321 Cary Point Dr.
PO Box 183
Cary, IL 60013

Phone: (708)639-2200
Fax: (708)639-9542

Magazine for equipment managers, maintenance supervisors, and utilities and CATV's municipalities and contractors. Subtitle: The Equipment Magazine. Founded: 1990. Frequency: Quarterly. Trim Size: 8 1/8 x 10 7/8. Key Personnel: Alan Richter, Editor; Bob Lanham, Publisher. Subscription: $11. $5 single issue.

Ad Rates:	BW:	$2,996	Circulation: Paid 251
	4C:	$3,946	Non-paid 25,249
	PCI:	$107	

CERRO GORDO

1233 The News-Record
221 E. South
PO Box 49
Cerro Gordo, IL 61818-0049

Phone: (217)763-3541
Fax: (217)763-5001

CHAMPAIGN

1234 American Journal of Psychology
University of Illinois Press
54 E. Gregory Dr.
Champaign, IL 61820

Phone: (217)333-8935
Fax: (217)244-8082

1235 American Music
University of Illinois Press
54 E. Gregory Dr.
Champaign, IL 61820

Phone: (217)333-8935
Fax: (217)244-8082

1236 The Bulletin of the Center for Children's Books
University of Illinois Press
54 E. Gregory Dr.
Champaign, IL 61820

Phone: (217)333-0950
Fax: (217)244-8082

1237 The Daily Illini
Illini Media Co.
57 E. Green St.
Champaign, IL 61820

Phone: (217)333-3733
Fax: (217)244-6616

1238 Illinois Journal of Mathematics
University of Illinois Press
54 E. Gregory Dr.
Champaign, IL 61820

Phone: (217)333-8935
Fax: (217)244-8082

1239 The Journal of Aesthetic Education
University of Illinois Press
54 E. Gregory Dr.
Champaign, IL 61820

Phone: (217)333-8935
Fax: (217)244-8082

Ⅲ **1240 The Quarterly Review of Economics and Finance**
JAI Press Inc.
University of Illinois
428 Commerce W.
1206 S. 6th St.   Phone: (217)333-2330
Champaign, IL 61820   Fax: (217)244-3118

Ⅲ **1241 Rehabilitation Education**
Georgia Southern Press
University of Illinois at Urbana-
  Champaign
Rehabilitation Education Programs
1207 South Oak St.   Phone: (217)333-6688
Champaign, IL 61820   Fax: (217)244-6784
Scholarly journal. **Founded:** 1987. **Frequency:** Quarterly. **Trim Size:** 6
1/2 x 9 1/2. **Cols./Page:** 1. **Key Personnel:** C.S. Geist, Editor-in-Chief,
Tim Field, Publisher. **ISSN:** 0889-7018. **Subscription:** $100. $27
single issue.
Ad Rates: BW: $300   **Circulation:** Paid ‡500
                                                    Non-paid ‡20

CHICAGO

Ⅲ **1242 ABA Journal**
American Bar Assn.
750 N. Lake Shore Dr.   **Phone: (312)988-5999**
Chicago, IL 60611   Fax: (312)988-6014

Ⅲ **1243 Administrative Law Review**
American Bar Association
750 N. Lake Shore Dr.   Phone: (312)988-6068
Chicago, IL 60611-4497   Fax: (312)988-6281
Scholarly legal journal on developments in the field of administrative
law and regulatory practice. **Founded:** 1974. **Frequency:** Quarterly.
Printing Method: Typeset. **ISSN:** 0001-8368. **Subscription:** $35; $40
other countries. $10 single issue.
                                        Circulation: (Not Reported)
Advertising not accepted.

Ⅲ **1244 American Journal of Education**
University of Chicago Press
5720 S. Woodlawn Ave.   Phone: (312)702-7600
Chicago, IL 60637   **Fax: (312)702-0172**

Ⅲ **1245 The Appraisal Journal**
Appraisal Institute
875 N. Michigan Ave., Ste. 2400   **Phone: (312)335-4100**
Chicago, IL 60611-1980   Fax: (312)335-4400

Ⅲ **1246 Assessment Digest**
International Assn. of Assessing Officers
1313 E. 60th St.   **Phone: (312)947-2045**
Chicago, IL 60637-2892   Fax: (312)363-2246

Ⅲ **1247 Black Books Bulletin: Words Work**
7524 S. Cottage Grove Ave.   Phone: (312)651-0700
Chicago, IL 60619   Fax: (312)651-7286
Consumer magazine. **Frequency:** Quarterly. **Subscription:** $2.95 single
issue.
                                        Circulation: (Not Reported)
Advertising accepted; contact publisher for rates.

Ⅲ **1248 Book Links: Connections Books, Libraries, and
       Classrooms**
American Library Assn.
50 E. Huron St.   Phone: (312)280-5718
Chicago, IL 60611-9969   Fax: (312)337-6787
Magazine featuring themed bibliographies of children's books to
support literature-based curriculum. **Founded:** 1991. **Frequency:** 6x/yr.
Trim Size: 8 3/8 x 10 7/8. **Key Personnel:** Barbara Elleman, Editor.
ISSN: 1055-4742. **Subscription:** $18; $24 (airmail). $3.50 single issue.
Ad Rates: BW: $1,670   **Circulation:** Paid 26,000
               4C: $3,020   Non-paid 14,000

Ⅲ **1249 Bridgeport/Back of the Yards EXTRA**
EXTRA Publications, Inc.
3918 W. North Ave.
Chicago, IL 60647   Phone: (312)252-3534
Community newspaper. **Frequency:** Weekly (Thurs). **Key Personnel:**
Mila Tellez, Publisher; Mary Montgomery, Exec. Editor; Miguel Alba,
Mng. Editor; Don Pringle, Advertising Mgr.

                                        Circulation: □7,231

Ⅲ **1250 Bulletin of the Atomic Scientists**
Educational Foundation for Nuclear Science
6042 S. Kimbark Ave.   Phone: (312)702-2555
Chicago, IL 60637   Fax: (312)702-0725

Ⅲ **1251 Business Insurance**
Crain Communications, Inc.
740 N. Rush St.   Phone: (312)649-5286
Chicago, IL 60611-2590   **Fax: (312)280-3174**

Ⅲ **1252 Chicago Computers & Users**
KB Communications
1412 N. Halsted St.   Phone: (312)944-0100
Chicago, IL 60622   Fax: (312)915-5906
Computer magazine. **Frequency:** Monthly. **Subscription:** $12.
Ad Rates: BW: $1,175   **Circulation:** 25,000
               4C: $2,075
               PCI: $55

Ⅲ **1253 China Law Reporter**
American Bar Association
750 N. Lake Shore Dr.   Phone: (312)988-6101
Chicago, IL 60611-4497   Fax: (312)988-6281
Practical journal on issues facing lawyers and scholars who deal with
business and law in the People's Republic of China. **Founded:** 1984.
Frequency: Quarterly. **Trim Size:** 6 x 9. **Cols./Page:** 1. **Col. Width:** 4 1/
2 in. **Col. Depth:** 7 in. **Subscription:** $43; $53 other countries. $20
single issue.
                                        Circulation: (Not Reported)

Ⅲ **1254 Clinical Infectious Diseases**
University of Chicago Press
5720 S. Woodlawn Ave.   Phone: (312)702-7600
Chicago, IL 60637   **Fax: (312)702-0172**

Ⅲ **1255 Comparative Education Review**
The University of Chicago Press
5720 S. Woodlawn Ave.   Phone: (312)702-7600
Chicago, IL 60637   **Fax: (312)702-0172**

Ⅲ **1256 Computerized Investing**
American Assn. of Individual Investors
625 N. Michigan Ave., Ste. 1900   Phone: (312)280-0170
Chicago, IL 60611   **Fax: (312)280-1625**

Ⅲ **1257 Corporate Legal Times**
222 Merchandise Mart Plaza, Ste. 1513   Phone: (312)644-4378
Chicago, IL 60654   Fax: (312)644-0765
Subtitle: Managing In-House Law Departments and Outside Law
Firms. **Founded:** 1991. **Frequency:** Monthly (Tues.). **Printing Method:**
Web offset. **Trim Size:** 11 x 17. **Cols./Page:** 4. **Col. Width:** 2 3/8 in.
Col. Depth: 13 1/2 in. **Key Personnel:** Thomas L. Goodman, Publish-
er; Charles H. Carman, Editor-in-Chief; Bruce Rubenstein, Managing
Editor. **ISSN:** 1063-3006. **Subscription:** $95. $10 single issue.
Ad Rates: BW: $5,823   **Circulation:** ‡45,000
               4C: $6,623
               PCI: $185

Ⅲ **1258 Criminal Justice**
American Bar Association Section of Criminal Justice
750 N. Lake Shore Dr.   Phone: (312)988-6046
Chicago, IL 60611-4497   Fax: (312)988-6281
Magazine providing practical treatment of aspects of criminal law.
Founded: 1986. **Frequency:** Quarterly. **Printing Method:** Web offset.
Trim Size: 8 3/8 x 10 7/8. **Cols./Page:** 3. **Col. Width:** 2 3/16 in. **Col.
Depth:** 9 1/2 in. **Key Personnel:** Carole Smith, Editor; Nora Whitford,

Advertising Mgr. **ISSN:** 0887-7785. **Subscription:** $33; $38 other countries. $8.50 single issue.
Ad Rates: BW: $890   **Circulation:** Paid **8,603**
4C: $1,690   Non-paid **1,252**
Additional Contact Information: Fax numbers: (312)988-6282; (312)988-6283.

📖 **1259 Energy Focus**
Palmer Publishing Co.
651 W. Washington St., No. 300   Phone: (312)993-0929
Chicago, IL 60601   Fax: (312)993-0960
Trade magazine. **Frequency:** 6x/yr. **Key Personnel:** Phillip Palmer, Publisher; Steve Read, Editorial Dir.; Stacy Mueller, Mng. Editor. **Subscription:** $15. $6 single issue.
Ad Rates: BW: $4,200   **Circulation:** 25,000
4C: $4,800

📖 **1260 Family Law Quarterly**
American Bar Association
750 N. Lake Shore Dr.   Phone: (312)988-6068
Chicago, IL 60611-4497   Fax: (312)988-6281
Journal including regular coverage of judicial decisions, legislation, taxation, summaries of state and local bar association projects, and book reviews. **Founded:** 1967. **Frequency:** Quarterly. **Key Personnel:** Cie Brown, Mng. Editor. **ISSN:** 0014-729X. **Subscription:** $34; $39 other countries. $8.50 single issue.
     Circulation: (Not Reported)
Advertising not accepted.

📖 **1261 FDM (Furniture Design & Manufactuing)**
Delta Communications Inc.
455 N. Cityfront Plaza Dr.   Phone: (312)222-2000
Chicago, IL **60611-5503**   Fax: (312)222-2026

📖 **1262 Gas Abstracts**
Institute of Gas Technology
3424 S. State St.   **Phone: (312)949-3810**
Chicago, IL 60616   **Fax: (312)949-5298**

📖 **1263 Groom & Board**
H.H. Backer Associates, Inc.
20 E. Jackson Blvd.   Phone: (312)663-4040
Chicago, IL 60604   Fax: (312)663-5676

📖 **1264 HOT WIRE: The Journal of Women's Music and Culture**
5210 Wayne   Phone: (312)769-9009
Chicago, IL 60640   Fax: (312)728-7002
Journal covering women's music and culture, theater, and film festivals. Each issue includes a stereo recording, interviews, and feature and how-to articles. **Founded:** 1987. **Frequency:** 3x/yr. **Trim Size:** 8 1/2 x 11. **Cols./Page:** 3. **Col. Width:** 2.5 in. **Col. Depth:** 9 in. **Key Personnel:** Tom Armstrong, Jr., Editor/Publisher; Lynn Siniscalchi, Business Mgr. **ISSN:** 0747-8887. **Subscription:** $17.
     Circulation: Paid 2,000
     Non-paid 10,000
Advertising accepted; contact publisher for rates.

📖 **1265 Illinois Banker**
Illinois Bankers Assn.
111 N. Canal St., Ste. 111   Phone: (312)876-9900
Chicago, IL 60606   Fax: (312)876-3826

📖 **1266 Illinois CPA Insight**
Illinois CPA Society
222 S. Riverside Plaza, 16th Fl.   Phone: (312)993-0393
Chicago, IL 60606   **Fax: (312)993-7713**
Former Title: Insight

📖 **1267 Inside Gold Coast**
Inside Publications
4710 N. Lincoln   Phone: (312)878-7333
Chicago, IL 60625   Fax: (312)878-0959
Community newspaper. **Founded:** 1989. **Frequency:** Weekly (Wed.). **Printing Method:** Web offset. **Cols./Page:** 5. **Col. Width:** 2 in. **Col.**

Depth: 13 1/2 in. **Key Personnel:** Larry Roenigk, Advertising Coordinator.
Ad Rates: GLR: $2.50   **Circulation:** Free ‡15,000
BW: $874.80
4C: $1,474.80
PCI: $20

📖 **1268 Inside Lake View**
Inside Publications
4710 N. Lincoln   Phone: (312)878-7333
Chicago, IL 60625   Fax: (312)878-0959
Community newspaper. **Founded:** 1992. **Frequency:** Weekly (Wed.). **Printing Method:** Web offset. **Cols./Page:** 5. **Col. Width:** 2 in. **Col. Depth:** 13 1/2 in. **Key Personnel:** Larry Roenigk, Advertising Coordinator.
Ad Rates: GLR: $2.50   **Circulation:** Free ‡20,000
BW: $874.80
4C: $1,474.80
PCI: $20

📖 **1269 Inside Ravenswood**
Inside Publications
4710 N. Lincoln   Phone: (312)878-7333
Chicago, IL 60625   Fax: (312)878-0959
Community newspaper. **Founded:** 1967. **Frequency:** Weekly (Wed.). **Printing Method:** Web offset. **Cols./Page:** 5. **Col. Width:** 2 in. **Col. Depth:** 13 1/2 in. **Key Personnel:** Larry Roenigk, Advertising Coordinator.
Ad Rates: GLR: $2.50   **Circulation:** Free ‡20,000
BW: $874.80
4C: $1,474.80
PCI: $20

📖 **1270 Journal of AHIMA**
American Health Information Management Association
919 N. Michigan Ave., Ste. 1400   Phone: (312)787-2672
Chicago, IL 60611   **Fax: (312)787-9793**

📖 **1271 Journal of Consumer Research**
The University of Chicago Press
5720 S. Woodlawn Ave.
PO Box 37005   Phone: (312)702-7600
Chicago, IL 60637   **Fax: (312)702-0172**

📖 **1272 Journal of the History of Sexuality**
The University of Chicago Press
5720 S. Woodlawn Ave.
Chicago, IL 60637   Phone: (312)702-7600
     Fax: (312)702-0172

📖 **1273 Kaleidoscope Music**
Kaleidoscope Music Inc.
1422 W. Belle Plaine, No. 2W
Chicago, IL 60613   Phone: (312)281-9174
Magazine promoting alternative and college radio music. **Founded:** 1993. **Frequency:** Quarterly. **Key Personnel:** John H. Mallory, Editor; Todd Brocker, Publisher; Jill Larson, Advertising Dir. **Subscription:** $10 single issue.
     Circulation: Paid 500
     Non-paid 500

📖 **1274 Kolping Banner**
Catholic Kolping Society of America
PO Box 46252   Phone: (312)763-5511
Chicago, IL **60646-0252**   **Fax: (312)763-5511**

📖 **1275 LAMPlighter**
The American Bar Association
750 N. Lake Shore Dr.   Phone: (312)988-6101
Chicago, IL 60611-4497   Fax: (312)988-6281
Journal providing useful information to armed forces legal assistance officers and other interested parties. **Subtitle:** Legal Assistance for Military Personel (LAMP). **Founded:** 1988. **Frequency:** Quarterly. **Trim Size:** 8 1/2 x 11. **Cols./Page:** 3. **Col. Width:** 2 1/4 in. **Col. Depth:** 8 1/2 in. **ISSN:** 1044-8756. **Subscription:** Free.
     Circulation: (Not Reported)

1276 Law & Social Inquiry
The University of Chicago Press
5720 S. Woodlawn Ave.
PO Box 37005   Phone: (312)702-7600
Chicago, IL 60637   Fax: (312)702-0172

1277 Library Administration & Management
American Library Assn., Library Administration & Mgmt. Assn.
50 E. Huron St.   Phone: (312)944-6780
Chicago, IL 60611   Fax: (312)280-3257

1278 Materials Management in Health Care
American Hospital Publishing, Inc.
737 N. Michigan Ave., No. 700   Phone: (312)440-6800
Chicago, IL 60611-2615   Fax: (312)951-8491
Trade magazine for purchasers, managers, and manufacturers of health care equipment and supplies. **Founded:** 1992. **Frequency:** Monthly. **Printing Method:** Web offset. **Trim Size:** 8 1/8 x 10 7/8. **Cols./Page:** 3. **Key Personnel:** Laura Souhrada, Editor. **Subscription:** $30; $50 other countries. $3 single issue.

Ad Rates:	GLR:	$14.60	Circulation: Non-paid 25,382
	BW:	$2,455	
	4C:	$3,455	
	PCI:	$126	

1279 Metro EXTRA
EXTRA Publications, Inc.
3918 W. North Ave.
Chicago, IL 60647   Phone: (312)252-3534
Community newspaper. **Frequency:** Weekly (Thurs). **Key Personnel:** Mila Tellez, Publisher; Mary Montgomery, Exec. Editor; Miguel Alba, Mng. Editor; Don Pringle, Advertising Mgr.

Circulation: □4,709

1280 Modern Metals
Delta Communications Inc.
455 N. Cityfront Plaza Dr.   Phone: (312)222-2000
Chicago, IL 60611-5503   Fax: (312)222-2026

1281 Monographs of the Society for Research in Child Development
University of Chicago Press
5720 S. Woodlawn Ave.   Phone: (312)702-7600
Chicago, IL 60637   Fax: (312)702-0172

1282 National Security Law Report
The American Bar Association
750 N. Lake Shore Dr.   Phone: (312)988-6101
Chicago, IL 60611-4497   Fax: (312)988-6281
Contains cases, articles, legislation, regulations, and other materials concerning national security. **Founded:** 1978. **Frequency:** Monthly. **Printing Method:** Offset. **Trim Size:** 8 1/2 x 11. **Cols./Page:** 2. **Col. Width:** 3 1/4 in. **ISSN:** 0736-2773. **Subscription:** Free.
Circulation: (Not Reported)

1283 The Neighborhood Works
Center for Neighborhood Technology
2125 W. North Ave.   Phone: (312)278-4800
Chicago, IL 60647   Fax: (312)278-3840
Technical magazine. **Subtitle:** Building Alternative Visions for the City. **Founded:** 1978. **Frequency:** 6x/yr. **Trim Size:** 8 1/2 x 11. **Cols./Page:** 3. **Key Personnel:** Mary O'Connell, Editor; Patti Wolter, Managing Editor; Bridget Torres, Circulation Mgr. **Subscription:** $30; $40 institutions. $3 single issue.
Circulation: Paid 1,200
Non-paid 400
Advertising accepted; contact publisher for rates.

1284 Neon
Adams Communications
414 N. Orleans St., Ste. 800   Phone: (312)222-8999
Chicago, IL 60610   Fax: (312)222-0699
Ceased publication.

1285 Outside
Mariah Publications Corp.
1165 N. Clark St.   Phone: (312)951-0990
Chicago, IL 60610   Fax: (312)664-5397

1286 Perspectives in Biology and Medicine
University of Chicago Press
5720 S. Woodlawn Ave.   Phone: (312)702-7600
Chicago, IL 60637   Fax: (312)702-0172

1287 Perspectives on Science
University of Chicago Press
5720 S. Woodlawn Ave.   Phone: (312)702-6000
Chicago, IL 60637   Fax: (312)702-0172
Journal featuring studies on the sciences that integrate historical, philosophical, and sociological perspectives. **Subtitle:** Historical, Philosophical, Social. **Founded:** 1993. **Frequency:** Quarterly. **Printing Method:** Offset. **Trim Size:** 6 x 9. **Cols./Page:** 1. **Key Personnel:** Joseph C. Pitt, Editor; Cheryl Jones, Advertising Mgr. **ISSN:** 1063-6145. **Subscription:** $35; $70 institutions; $25 students.
Circulation: (Not Reported)
Advertising accepted; contact publisher for rates.

1288 Pilsen/Little Village/Cicero/Berwyn EXTRA
EXTRA Publications, Inc.
3918 W. North Ave.
Chicago, IL 60647   Phone: (312)252-3534
Community newspaper. **Frequency:** Weekly (Thurs.). **Key Personnel:** Mila Telez, Publisher; Mary Montgomery, Exec. Editor; Miguel Alba, Mng. Editor; Don Pringle, Advertising Mgr.
Ad Rates: SAU: $15   **Circulation:** □13,297
SAU rate is sold in combination with Bridgeport/Back of the Yards EXTRA and Southwest EXTRA.

1289 Plant Services
Putman Publishing Co., Inc.
301 E. Erie St.   Phone: (312)644-2020
Chicago, IL 60611   Fax: (312)644-6709

1290 Plumbing Heating Piping
Delta Communications, Inc.
455 N. Cityfront Plaza Dr.   Phone: (312)222-2000
Chicago, IL 60611   Fax: (312)222-2026

1291 Probe
National Assembly of Religious Women
529 S. Wabash, Rm. 404   Phone: (312)663-1980
Chicago, IL 60605   Fax: (312)663-9161

1292 The Professional Lawyer
The American Bar Association
541 N. Fairbanks Ct.   Phone: (312)988-5307
Chicago, IL 60611-3314   Fax: (312)988-5491
Magazine providing a forum for the exchange of views and ideas on professionalism and ethics issues for bar leaders, lawyers, law school educators, and others. **Founded:** 1989. **Frequency:** Quarterly. **Trim Size:** 8 1/2 x 11. **Cols./Page:** 3. **Col. Width:** 2 1/4 in. **Col. Depth:** 9 1/2 in. **Key Personnel:** Jill Nicholson, Editor. **ISSN:** 1042-5675. **Subscription:** $20; $15 ABA members. $5 single issue.
Circulation: Paid 250
Non-paid 100
Advertising not accepted.

1293 Public Contract Law Journal
The American Bar Association
750 N. Lake Shore Dr.   Phone: (312)988-6090
Chicago, IL 60611-4497   Fax: (312)988-6281
Contains articles on all phases of federal, state, and local procurement and grant law. **Frequency:** Quarterly. **Trim Size:** 6 x 9. **Cols./Page:** 1. **ISSN:** 0033-3341. **Subscription:** $20. $5 single issue.
Circulation: (Not Reported)
Advertising not accepted.

Ad Rates: GLR = general line rate; BW = one-time black & white page rate; 4C = one-time four color page rate; SAU = standard advertising unit rate; CNU = Canadian newspaper advertising unit rate; PCI = per column inch rate.
Circulation: ★ = ABC; △ = BPA; ◆ = CAC; ● = CCAB; □ = VAC; ⊕ = PO Statement; ‡ = Publisher's Report; Boldface figures = sworn; Light figures = estimated.
Entry type: ▢ = Print; ▮ = Broadcast.

85

📖 1294 Public Opinion Quarterly
The University of Chicago Press
5720 S. Woodlawn Ave.   Phone: (312)702-7600
Chicago, IL 60637   **Fax: (312)702-0172**

📖 1295 Southwest EXTRA
EXTRA Publications, Inc.
3918 W. North Ave.
Chicago, IL 60647   Phone: (312)252-3534
Community newspaper. **Frequency:** Weekly (Thurs.). **Key Personnel:**
Mila Tellez, Publisher; Mary Montgomery, Exec. Editor; Miguel Alba,
Mng. Editor; Don Pringle, Advertising Mgr.
                                         Circulation: ☐4,926

📖 1296 Stagebill Group
B & B Enterprises Inc.
500 N. Michigan Ave., Ste. 1530   Phone: (312)565-0890
Chicago, IL 60611   **Fax: (312)685-3911**

📖 1297 Student Lawyer
American Bar Assn.
750 N. Lake Shore Dr.
Chicago, IL 60611   Phone: (312)988-5000

📖 1298 SV Entertainment
SV Entertainment
680 N. Lake Shore Dr.
Chicago, IL 60611
Ceased publication.

📖 1299 Tort & Insurance Law Journal
The American Bar Association
750 N. Lake Shore Dr.   Phone: (312)988-6090
Chicago, IL 60611-4497   Fax: (312)988-6281
Scholarly journal on current or emerging issues of national scope in
the fields of tort and insurance law. **Frequency:** Quarterly. **Trim Size:** 6
x 9. **Cols./Page:** 1. **ISSN:** 0015-8356. **Subscription:** $23; $28 other
countries. $5 single issue.
                                         Circulation: (Not Reported)
Advertising not accepted. **Formerly:** The Forum.

📖 1300 Truck Blue Book Residual Values
Maclean Hunter Market Reports, Inc.
29 N. Wacker Dr.   Phone: (312)726-2802
Chicago, IL 60606   Fax: (312)726-2574
Book covering residual value projections for medium and heavy-duty
trucks. **Frequency:** Quarterly. **Key Personnel:** George C. Stanton,
Publisher. **Subscription:** $65; $75 other countries. $30 single issue.
                                         Circulation: (Not Reported)
Advertising not accepted. **Formerly:** Truck Blue Book Lease Guide.

📖 1301 udm/Upholstery Design and Manufacturing
Delta Communications, Inc.
455 N. Cityfront Plaza Dr.   Phone: (312)222-2000
Chicago, IL 60611-5503   Fax: (312)222-2026

📖 1302 The Urban Lawyer
The American Bar Association
750 N. Lake Shore Dr.   Phone: (312)988-6083
Chicago, IL 60611-4497   Fax: (312)988-6281
Articles on various areas of urban, state, and local government law.
Founded: 1969. **Frequency:** Quarterly. **Printing Method:** Offset. **Trim
Size:** 6 x 9. **Cols./Page:** 1. **Key Personnel:** Richard W. Bright, Mng.
Editor. **ISSN:** 0042-0905. **Subscription:** $36; $40.50 other countries.
$12 single issue.
                                         Circulation: Paid 6,200
                                                        Non-paid 300

📖 1303 Van Conversion Blue Book
Maclean Hunter Market Reports, Inc.
29 N. Wacker Dr.   Phone: (312)726-2802
Chicago, IL 60606   Fax: (312)726-2574
Book covering valuations on used van conversions. **Frequency:**
Quarterly. **Key Personnel:** George C. Stanton, Publisher. **ISSN:** 0884-
7231.
                                         Circulation: (Not Reported)
Advertising not accepted.

📖 1304 Van Conversion Lease Guide
Maclean Hunter Market Reports, Inc.
29 N. Wacker Dr.   Phone: (312)726-2802
Chicago, IL 60606   Fax: (312)726-2574
Auto guide. **Frequency:** Quarterly.
                                         Circulation: (Not Reported)

📖 1305 The Wholesaler
Delta Communications
455 N. Cityfront Plaza   Phone: (312)222-2000
Chicago, IL 60611   Fax: (312)222-2026

📖 1306 Winterthur Portfolio
Univeristy of Chicago Press
5720 S. Woodlawn Ave.   Phone: (312)702-6000
Chicago, IL 60637   Fax: (312)702-0172
Journal covering the history of American art and artifacts. **Subtitle:** A
Journal of American Material Culture. **Founded:** 1964. **Frequency:** 3x/
yr. **Printing Method:** Offset. **Trim Size:** 8 1/2 x 11. **Cols./Page:** 2. **Key
Personnel:** Catherine Hutchins, Editor; Cheryl Jones, Advertising
Mgr. **ISSN:** 0084-0416. **Subscription:** $30; $64 institutions; $38
individual other countries; $72 institutions other countries. $10 single
issue. $21.50 single issue for institutions.
Ad Rates: BW: $220   **Circulation:** Paid ‡1,600

📖 1307 Women Lawyers Journal
National Association of Women Lawyers
750 N. Lake Shore Dr.
Chicago, IL 60611   Phone: (312)988-6186
Professional journal for attorneys in the U.S. and abroad. **Frequency:**
Quarterly. **Subscription:** $12.
                                         Circulation: (Not Reported)

🎤 1308 Chicago Cable TV
1931 W. Diversey Blvd.
Chicago, IL 60614   Phone: (312)525-8653
Owner: Tele-Communications, Inc. **Founded:** 1986. **Cities Served:**
Cook County, IL.

🎤 1309 Group W Cable of Chicago, Inc.
3970 N. Milwaukee Ave.   Phone: (312)794-2080
Chicago, IL 60641   Fax: (312)794-2291
Owner: Prime Cable Corp. **Founded:** 1984. **Cities Served:** Cook
County, IL.

🎤 1310 WCRW-AM - 1240
5625 N. Milwaukee Ave
Chicago, IL 60646-6218   **Phone: (312)763-8250**

🎤 1311 WCRX-FM - 88.1
600 S. Michigan
Chicago, IL 60605   Phone: (312)663-1693
Format: Alternative/Independent/Progressive. **Key Personnel:** Tom
Joyce, Music Dir. **Ad Rates:** Noncommercial.

🎤 1312 WGCI-AM - 1390
332 S. Michigan Ave., Ste. 600   Phone: (312)427-4800
Chicago, IL 60604   **Fax: (312)987-4453**

🎤 1313 WSCR-AM - 820
4949 W. Belmont Ave.
Chicago, IL 60641   Phone: (312)777-1700
Format: Sports. **Network(s):** AP. **Owner:** Diamond Broadcasting, at
above address. **Founded:** 1992. **Formerly:** WPNT-AM; WAIT-AM.
Operating Hours: Sunrise-sunset. **Key Personnel:** Seth Mason, V.P.;
Harvey Wells, Gen. Mgr.; Ron Gleason, Program and Sports Dir.;
Abby Polonsky, Senior Producer; Henry Henderson, Coordinating
Producer. **Wattage:** 5000.

🎤 1314 WVAZ-FM - 102.7
800 S. Wells, Ste. 250   **Phone: (312)360-9000**
Chicago, IL 60607   **Fax: (312)360-9070**

🎤 1315 WXAV-FM - 88.3
3700 W. 100 3rd St.
Chicago, IL 60655   Phone: (312)779-9858
Format: Alternative/Independent/Progressive. **Key Personnel:** Devin
Curnow, Music Dir. **Ad Rates:** Noncommercial.

DANVILLE

🎙 **1316 Warner Cable of Danville**
806 1/2 E. Main St., Ste. A
Danville, IL 61832   Phone: (217)443-2941
Owner: Time-Warner Entertainment Group. **Key Personnel:** Mary
Ann Perkins, Gen. Mgr.; Jennifer Munro, Office Mgr.; Stephen
Schneider, Technical Mgr. **Cities Served:** Danville, IL: 16,000 sub-
scribing households; 29 channels; 1 community access channel; 60
hours per week of community access programming.

DARIEN

📖 **1317 The Carmelite Review**
Canadian-American Province of Carmelite Order
8433 Bailey Rd.   **Phone: (708)969-4141**
Darien, IL **60561-5305**   Fax: (708)968-9542

DE KALB

📖 **1318 Thresholds in Education**
Thresholds in Education Foundation
PO Box 771   Phone: (815)753-9357
De Kalb, IL 60115   **Fax: (815)753-2100**

🎙 **1319 Warner Cable of De Kalb**
1430 Sycamore Rd.
Box 786
De Kalb, IL 60115   Phone: (815)758-3401
Owner: Time-Warner Communications, Inc. **Key Personnel:** Andrew
Bast, Gen. Mgr. **Cities Served:** De Kalb, Sycamore, Rochelle, Creston,
and Hillcrest: IL. 37 channels; 1 community access channel; 10 hours
per week of community access programming.

DECATUR

🎙 **1320 UAE**
1275 N. Water St.   Phone: (217)424-8455
Decatur, IL 62521   Fax: (217)429-0170
Owner: Tele-Communications, Inc. **Founded:** 1972. **Cities Served:**
Macon County, Forsyth, Long Creek, and Mount Zion, IL.

DES PLAINES

📖 **1321 Construction Products**
Cahners Publishing Co.
1350 E. Touhy Ave.
PO Box 5080   Phone: (708)635-8800
Des Plaines, IL 60017-5080   **Fax: (708)390-2690**
Former Title: Highway and Heavy Construction Products

📖 **1322 Contractor Magazine**
Cahners Publishing Co.
1350 E. Touhy Ave.   **Phone: (708)390-2678**
Des Plaines, IL 60018   **Fax: (708)390-2690**

📖 **1323 Professional Builder & Remodeler**
Cahners Publishing Co.
1350 E. Touhy Ave.   Phone: (708)635-8800
Des Plaines, IL 60018   **Fax: (708)635-9950**
Former Title: Professional Builder

📖 **1324 SECURITY**
Cahners Publishing Co.
1350 E. Touhy Ave.
PO Box 5080   Phone: (708)635-8800
Des Plaines, IL 60018   **Fax: (708)635-9950**

📖 **1325 Semiconductor International**
Cahners Publishing Company
1350 E. Touhy Ave.   Phone: (708)635-8800
Des Plaines, IL 60018   Fax: (708)390-2770
Magazine profiling the semiconductor industry. **Subtitle:** The Indus-
try's Source Book. **Founded:** 1978. **Frequency:** Monthly. **Trim Size:** 8 x

10 3/4. **Cols./Page:** 3. **Key Personnel:** Robert Compton, Editor.
Subscription: Free to qualified subscribers.
Ad Rates: BW: $4,480   Circulation: Paid △1,015
                4C: $5,750   Non-paid △45,541
                PCI: $195

ELGIN

📖 **1326 The Courier News**
Copley Press, Inc.
300 Lake St.   **Phone: (708)888-7800**
Elgin, IL 60120   Fax: (708)888-7714

ELK GROVE VILLAGE

🎙 **1327 WYLL-FM - 106.7**
25 Northwest Point   Phone: (708)956-5030
Elk Grove Village, IL **60007**   Fax: (708)956-5040

ELMHURST

📖 **1328 Elmhurst Press**
Press Publications
112 S. York St.   Phone: (708)834-0900
Elmhurst, IL 60126   **Fax: (708)834-0910**

📖 **1329 Up Beat Daily**
Maher Publications, Inc.
180 W. Park Ave.   Phone: (708)941-2030
Elmhurst, IL 60126   **Fax: (708)941-3210**

ELMWOOD PARK

📖 **1330 Elm Leaves**
Pioneer Press Newspapers
1232 Central Ave.   Phone: (708)251-4300
Wilmette, IL 60091   **Fax: (708)251-7606**

EVANSTON

📖 **1331 The Complete Smoker**
The Complete Smoker, Ltd. Publications
PO Box 7036
Evanston, IL 60204
Magazine featuring tobacco pipes, cigars, tobacco, and its history.
Frequency: Quarterly. **Key Personnel:** Theodore Gage, Editor and
Publisher. **Subscription:** $17.50. $4.95 single issue.
                                   Circulation: (Not Reported)

📖 **1332 Inside Hollywood**
World Publishing Company
990 Grove St.
Evanston, IL 60201-4370
Entertainment magazine. **Frequency:** 6x/yr. **Key Personnel:** Robert
Meyers, Editor; Norman Jacobs, Publisher. **Subscription:** $22. $2.50
single issue.
                                   Circulation: (Not Reported)

📖 **1333 Movie Marketplace**
World Publishing Co.
990 Grove St., 4th Fl.
Evanston, IL 60201-4370   Phone: (708)491-6440
Founded: 1987. **Frequency:** Bimonthly. **Trim Size:** 5 1/2 x 7 1/2. **Cols./
Page:** 2. **Col. Width:** 13.6 picas. **Col. Depth:** 41 picas. **Key Personnel:**
Robert Meyers, Editor-in-Chief. **ISSN:** 1051-5488. **USPS:** 003-376.
Subscription: $19.94. $2.95 single issue.
                                   Circulation: Paid ★112,524
                                   Non-paid ★18,838
Advertising accepted; contact publisher for rates. **Formerly:** Video
Marketplace.

⚓ 1334 WNUR-FM - 89.6
1905 Sheridan Rd.
Evanston, IL 60208-2260   Phone: (708)491-7101
Format: Alternative/Independent/Progressive. **Owner:** Northwestern University, at above address. **Operating Hours:** Continuous. **Key Personnel:** Adam Walker, Music Dir.; Shane Grahm, Music Dir.; Cari Shoda, Gen. Mgr.; Jeremy Lehrer, Program Dir.; Robbie Upson, Operations Dir.; Philane Patterson, Promotions Dir. **Wattage:** 7200. **Ad Rates:** Noncommercial. **Additional Contact Information:** News line: (708)491-2234.

FLOSSMOOR

⚓ 1335 WHFH-FM - 88.5
999 Kedzie Ave.   Phone: (708)798-9434
Flossmoor, IL 60422   **Fax: (708)799-3142**

FORD HEIGHTS

⚓ 1336 WCFJ-AM - 1470
1000 Lincoln Hwy.   Phone: (708)758-8600
Ford Heights, IL 60411   **Fax: (708)758-8602**

FRANKLIN PARK

📖 1337 Franklin Park Herald-Journal
Pioneer Press Newspapers
1232 Central Ave.   Phone: (708)251-4300
Wilmette, IL 60091   **Fax: (708)251-7606**

GLEN ELLYN

📖 1338 Control Ambiental Magazine
Tower Publishing
Bldg. B, Ste. 104
800 Roosevelt Rd.   Phone: (708)469-0788
Glen Ellyn, IL 60137   Fax: (708)469-0191
Spanish trade publication for environmental and hazardous materials management professionals. **Frequency:** 9x/year (combined issues in Jan./Feb., July/Aug., and Nov./Dec.) **Key Personnel:** Stephanie Riley, Assoc. Editor; Deborah Folga, Sales Mgr.
         Circulation: (Not Reported)

HAMPSHIRE

📖 1339 Hampshire Register News
Northwest Newspaper Group
193 N. State St.   Phone: (708)683-2627
Hampshire, IL 60140   **Fax: (708)683-4955**

ITASCA

📖 1340 Family Safety & Health
National Safety Council
1121 Spring Lake Dr.   **Phone: (708)285-1121**
Itasca, IL 60143-3201   **Fax: (708)285-1315**

📖 1341 Safety & Health
National Safety Council
1121 Spring Lake Dr.   Phone: (708)285-1121
Itasca, IL 60143   Fax: (708)285-9114
Publication focusing on safety and health issues. **Founded:** 1919. **Frequency:** Monthly. **Printing Method:** Offset. **Trim Size:** 8 1/8 x 10 7/8. **Cols./Page:** 3. **Col. Width:** 2 1/8 in. **Col. Depth:** 10 in. **Key Personnel:** Kevin Axe, Publisher; Joel Wakitsch, Advertising Mgr. **Subscription:** $56. $5 single issue.
Ad Rates: BW: $3,100   **Circulation:** Paid ‡36,665
          4C: $4,050

📖 1342 Today's Supervisor
National Safety Council
1121 Spring Lake Dr.   Phone: (708)285-1121
Itasca, IL 60143-3201   **Fax: (708)775-2285**

LA FAYETTE

📖 1343 Prairie Shopper
McGirgan Productions
101 Jefferson
PO Box 27   Phone: (309)995-3877
La Fayette, IL 61449-9927   Fax: (309)995-3975
Newspaper with shopping guide. **Founded:** 1981. **Frequency:** Weekly (Wed.). **Printing Method:** Offset. **Cols./Page:** 6. **Col. Width:** 19 nonpareils. **Col. Depth:** 224 agate lines. **Key Personnel:** Lowell E. McKirgan, Publisher. **Subscription:** $20.
Ad Rates: GLR: $.25   **Circulation:** Free 5,900
          BW: $268.80
          SAU: $4.20
          PCI: $2.80

LAKE FOREST

📖 1344 Camp-orama
Woodall Publishing Co.
PO Box 5000   Phone: (708)362-6700
Lake Forest, IL 60045-5000   Fax: (708)362-8776
Magazine covering the RV industry and camping destinations. **Subtitle:** The RV'ers Guide to Florida. **Founded:** 1974. **Frequency:** Monthly. **Cols./Page:** 4. **Col. Width:** 14 picas. **Col. Depth:** 84 picas. **Key Personnel:** Ann Emerson, Editor; Lori Nielsen, Production Dir. **Subscription:** $15. $2.50 single issue.
Ad Rates: BW: $1,002   **Circulation:** 32,000
          4C: $1,502

📖 1345 Camperways
Woodall Publishing Co.
PO Box 5000   Phone: (708)362-6700
Lake Forest, IL 60045-5000   Fax: (708)362-8776
Magazine covering the RV industry and camping destinations. **Subtitle:** The Middle Atlantic RV Lifestyle source. **Founded:** 1979. **Frequency:** Monthly. **Cols./Page:** 4. **Col. Width:** 14 picas. **Col. Depth:** 84 picas. **Key Personnel:** Ann Emerson, Mng. Editor; Lori Nielsen, Production Dir. **Subscription:** $15. $2.50 single issue.
Ad Rates: BW: $1,053   **Circulation:** 40,000
          4C: $1,553

📖 1346 Trails-A-Way
Woodall Publishing Company
PO Box 5000   Phone: (708)362-6700
Lake Forest, IL 60045-5000   Fax: (708)362-8776
Magazine covering the RV industry and camping destinations. **Subtitle:** The RV Guide to the Midwest. **Founded:** 1971. **Frequency:** Monthly. **Cols./Page:** 4. **Col. Width:** 14 picas. **Col. Depth:** 84 picas. **Key Personnel:** Ann Emerson, Mng. Editor; Lori Nielsen, Production Dir. **Subscription:** $15. $2.50 single issue.
Ad Rates: BW: $1,053   **Circulation:** 40,000
          4C: $1,553

LINCOLNSHIRE

📖 1347 Visions
Vance Publishing Corp.
400 Knightsbridge Pkwy.
PO Box 1400   Phone: (708)634-2600
Lincolnshire, IL 60069   Fax: (708)634-4379
Ceased publication.

LISLE

📖 1348 Walker's Estimating & Construction Journal
Frank R. Walker Co.
PO Box 3180   Phone: (708)971-8989
Lisle, IL 60532   Fax: (708)971-0586

LOMBARD

📖 1349 Computer Game Review
Sendai Publications, Inc.
1920 Highland Ave.
Lombard, IL 60148
Magazine featuring the latest developments in computer games.

Frequency: Quarterly. **Key Personnel:** Steve Harris, Publisher; Mike Riley, Editor. **Subscription:** $3.50 single issue.

Circulation: (Not Reported)

◫ 1350 Super Gaming
Sendai Publications, Inc.
1920 Highland Ave.
Lombard, IL 60148
Magazine features the latest news in international electronic gaming. **Frequency:** Quarterly. **Key Personnel:** Steve Harris, Publisher; Mike Riley, Editor. **Subscription:** $9.95. $2.95 single issue.

Circulation: (Not Reported)

MACOMB

⬤ 1351 WMEC-TV - Channel 22
c/o CONVOCOM
PO Box 6248   Phone: (217)786-6647
Springfield, IL 62708   **Fax: (217)786-7286**

MARION

⬤ 1352 WBVN-FM - 104.5
PO Box 1126   Phone: (618)997-1500
Marion, IL 62959   **Fax: (618)997-3194**

MARYVILLE

⬤ 1353 Cencom Cable Associates
200 W. Division St.   Phone: (618)345-8121
Maryville, IL 62062   Fax: (618)345-6234
Owner: Cencom Cable Associates. **Founded:** 1986. **Formerly:** South-Western Cable TV, Ltd.. **Key Personnel:** Dave Miller, System Mgr.; Monica Foster, Office Mgr. **Cities Served:** Sorento, New Douglas, Hamel, Marine, Alhambra, Worden, Madison, Venice, Pontoon Beach, Highland, Troy, Columbia, Waterloo, Dupo, Millstadt, Glen Carbon, Saint Jacob, Maryville, Collinsville, Caseyville, Edwardsville, and Granite City, IL: 36,500 subscribing households; 37 channels; 1 community access channel; 10 hours per week of community access programming.

MAYWOOD

◫ 1354 Maywood Herald
Pioneer Press Newspapers
1232 Central Ave.   Phone: (708)251-4300
Wilmette, IL 60091   **Fax: (708)251-7606**

MELROSE PARK

◫ 1355 Melrose Park Herald
Pioneer Press Newspapers
1232 Central Ave.   Phone: (708)251-4300
Wilmette, IL 60091   **Fax: (708)251-7606**

◫ 1356 Snips Magazine
1949 Cornell Ave.   Phone: (708)544-3870
Melrose Park, IL 60160-9953   Fax: (708)544-3884

MOLINE

◫ 1357 The Gold Book
Moline Dispatch Publishing Co.
                      Phone: (319)322-
1720 Fifth Ave.   GOLD
Moline, IL 61265   Fax: (309)797-0311
Magazine covering the Quad-cities. **Founded:** 1985. **Frequency:** Weekly. **Printing Method:** Offset. **Cols./Page:** 2. **Key Personnel:** Jan Heintz, Editor/Manager. **Subscription:** $12.

Circulation: (Not Reported)

Advertising accepted; contact publisher for rates. Member of The Small Newspapers Group, Inc. **Additional Contact Information:** Alternate phone number (309)764-4344, ext. 259.

⬤ 1358 Cox Cable Quint-Cities
3900 26th Ave.   Phone: (309)797-2580
Moline, IL 61265   Fax: (309)797-2414
Owner: Cox Cable Communications. **Founded:** 1972. **Cities Served:** Rock Island County, East Moline, Hampton, and Silvis, IL; Scott County, Bettendorf, Davenport, Eldridge, Long Grove, Mount Joy, Panorama Park, Pleasant Valley, and Riverdale, IA.

MONMOUTH

⬤ 1359 WMCR-AM - 640
Monmouth College
Monmouth, IL 61462   Phone: (309)457-2155
Format: Alternative/Independent/Progressive. **Key Personnel:** Eric Ostermeier, Music Dir. **Ad Rates:** Noncommercial.

MORTON

⬤ 1360 WTAZ-FM - 102.3
332 Detroit Ave.
Morton, IL 61550-1846   Phone: (309)263-0102

MORTON GROVE

◫ 1361 Morton Grove Champion
Pioneer Press Newspapers
1232 Central Ave.   Phone: (708)251-4300
Wilmette, IL 60091   **Fax: (708)251-7606**

MOUNT CARMEL

⬤ 1362 WRBT-FM - 94.9
PO Box 490   **Phone: (618)263-6567**
Mount Carmel, IL 62863   **Fax: (618)263-3220**

MUNDELEIN

◫ 1363 Mundelein Review
Pioneer Press Newspapers
1232 Central Ave.   Phone: (708)251-4300
Wilmette, IL 60091   **Fax: (708)251-7606**

NEWTON

⬤ 1364 WIKK-FM - 103.5
Hwy 33 W.
PO Box 304   Phone: (618)783-8000
Newton, IL 62448   Fax: (618)783-4040
Format: Adult Contemporary. **Network(s):** Mutual Broadcasting System. **Owner:** S. Kent Lankford. **Founded:** 1992. **Operating Hours:** 5 a.m.-midnight; 9% network, 91% local. **Key Personnel:** S. Kent Lankford, Owner/Gen. Mgr.; Mike Brady, Sales Mgr.; Chris Stevens, Program Dir.; April Burry, News Dir. **Wattage:** 25,000. **Ad Rates:** $6-$10 for 30 seconds; $8-$12 for 60 seconds.

NILES

◫ 1365 Craftrends/Sew Business
Century Communications Inc.
6201 Howard St.   **Phone: (708)647-1200**
Niles, IL 60714   **Fax: (708)647-7055**
Former Title: Craftrends

◫ 1366 Journal of Chromatographic Science
Preston Publications
Preston Industries, Inc.
PO Box 48312   Phone: (708)965-0566
Niles, IL 60714   Fax: (708)965-7639

◫ 1367 Niles Spectator
Pioneer Press Newspapers
1232 Central Ave.   Phone: (708)251-4300
Wilmette, IL 60091   **Fax: (708)251-7606**

1368 **Plate World**
Plate World, Ltd.
9200 N. Maryland Ave.   Phone: (708)581-8310
Niles, IL **60714**   **Fax: (708)966-9463**

NORTHFIELD

1369 **Clavier**
Instrumentalist Co.
200 Northfield Rd.   Phone: (708)446-5000
Northfield, IL 60093-3390   Fax: (708)446-6263

1370 **Floral & Nursery Times**
XXX Publishing Enterprises Ltd.
436 W. Frontage Rd.   **Phone: (708)441-0300**
Northfield, IL 60093   **Fax: (708)441-0308**

OAK BROOK

1371 **OAG Business Travel Planner, North American Edition**
Official Airlines Guides, Inc.
2000 Clearwater Dr.   Phone: (708)574-6000
Oak Brook, IL 60521   **Fax: (708)574-6667**
Former Title: OAG Travel Planner Hotel & Motel Redbook (North American Edition)

1372 **OAG Travel Planner, European Edition**
Official Airline Guides
2000 Clearwater Dr.   Phone: (708)574-6000
Oak Brook, IL 60521   Fax: (708)574-6667
Former Title: European Edition OAG Travel Planner Hotel & Motel Redbook

1373 **OAG Travel Planner - Pacific/Asia Edition**
Official Airline Guides
2000 Clearwater Dr.   Phone: (708)574-6000
Oak Brook, IL 60521   Fax: (708)574-6667
Former Title: Pacific/Asia Edition OAG Travel Planner Hotel & Motel RedBook

OAK PARK

1374 **Forest Park Review**
Wednesday Journal Inc.
141 S. Oak Park Ave.   Phone: (708)366-0600
Oak Park, IL 60302   Fax: (708)524-0447

1375 **Oak Leaves**
Pioneer Press Newspapers
1232 Central Ave.   Phone: (708)251-4300
Wilmette, IL 60091   **Fax: (708)251-7606**

1376 **Cablevision of Chicago**
820 W. Madison St.
Oak Park, IL 60302   Phone: (312)383-9110
Owner: Cablevision Systems Corp. **Founded:** 1979. **Cities Served:** Cook and DuPage counties, IL.

OLNEY

1377 **Olney Daily Mail**
206 Whittle Ave.
PO Box 340   Phone: (618)393-2931
Olney, IL 62450   **Fax: (618)392-2953**

OSWEGO

1378 **The SDC Bulletin: Turning Wheels**
Studebaker Drivers Club, Inc.
PO Box 1040   Phone: 800-527-3452
Oswego, IL 60543   **Fax: (209)634-2163**

PALATINE

1379 **Fleet Equipment**
Maple Publishing Co.
134 W. Slade St.   Phone: (708)359-6100
Palatine, IL 60067-1696   **Fax: (708)359-6420**

PEKIN

1380 **WBNH-FM - 88.5**
Box 1132
Pekin, IL 61555   Phone: (309)347-8850
Format: Religious. **Network(s):** Moody Broadcasting. **Owner:** Central Illinois Radio Fellowship Inc. **Operating Hours:** Continuous. **Key Personnel:** Scott Krus, Station Mgr. **Wattage:** 4300.

1381 **WCIC-FM - 91.5**
3263 Court St.   Phone: (309)353-9191
Pekin, IL 61554   Fax: (309)355-1141
Format: Adult Contemporary. **Owner:** Illinois Bible Institute, PO Box 140, Carlinville, IL 62626. **Founded:** 1983. **Operating Hours:** Continuous. **Key Personnel:** Dave Brooks, Station Mgr.; Chuck Pryor, Program and Music Dir.; Connie Card, Production Dir. **Wattage:** 35,000. **Ad Rates:** Noncommercial; listener-supported.

PEORIA

1382 **TCI Cablevision of Central Illinois**
3517 N. Dries Ln.   Phone: (309)686-2600
Peoria, IL 61604   Fax: (309)688-9828
Owner: Tele-Communications, Inc. **Founded:** 1973. **Formerly:** United Artists Entertainment. **Key Personnel:** Tom Clark, Gen. Mgr.; Michelle Heap, Marketing Mgr. **Cities Served:** Tazewell County, Peoria County, and Woodford County; Bartonville, Bellevue, Creve Coeur, East Peoria, Norwood, Peoria Heights, and Washington, IL: 55,383 subscribing households; 1 community access channel; 30 hours per week of community access programming.

PROVISO

1383 **West Proviso Herald**
Pioneer Press Newspapers
1232 Central Ave.   Phone: (708)251-4300
Wilmette, IL 60091   **Fax: (708)251-7606**

QUINCY

1384 **WQCY-FM - 99.5**
Box 731
Quincy, IL 62306   Phone: (217)228-2800
                                   Fax: (717)228-1031

1385 **WQEC-TV - Channel 27**
c/o CONVOCOM
PO Box 6248   Phone: (217)786-6647
Springfield, IL 62708   **Fax: (217)786-7286**

1386 **WTAD-AM - 930**
Box 731
Quincy, IL 62306   Phone: (217)228-2800
                                   Fax: (217)228-1031

RIVER FOREST

1387 **Forest Leaves**
Pioneer Press Newspapers
1232 Central Ave.   Phone: (708)251-4300
Wilmette, IL 60091   **Fax: (708)251-7606**

ROCHELLE

1388 **Leader**
211 Hwy. 38 E.
Box 46
Rochelle, IL 61068   Phone: (815)562-4171

ROCK ISLAND

1389 **The Observer**
Augustana College
Box 208
Rock Island, IL 61201   Phone: (309)794-7485

ROCKFORD

📖 1390 Rockford Magazine
Gannett
99 E. State St.   Phone: (815)961-2400
Rockford, IL 61104   Fax: (815)961-2279
Magazine highlighting the city of Rockford. **Founded:** 1986. **Frequency:** Monthly. **Printing Method:** Web offset. **Trim Size:** 8 x 10 3/4. **Cols./Page:** 3. **Col. Width:** 2 1/4 in. **Col. Depth:** 9 3/4 in. **Key Personnel:** Eileen S. Townsend, Editor; Scott Clark, Gen. Mgr.; Kelli Hobel, Circulation Mgr. **Subscription:** $17.95. $2.95 single issue.
Ad Rates: BW: $1,995   **Circulation:** Paid ‡8,000
              4C: $2,695   Non-paid ‡7,000

🎙 1391 A-R Cable Services, Inc.
227 N. Wyman St.   Phone: (815)962-4400
Rockford, IL 61101   Fax: voice act.
Owner: Cablevision Systems Corp. **Founded:** 1973. **Key Personnel:** Wiley Jones, Gen. Mgr.; K.C. McWilliams, Operations Mgr.; Chuck Gelazus, Chief Engineer. **Cities Served:** Winnebago County, Cherry Valley, Loves Park, Machesney Park, New Milford, and Rockford, IL: 59,000 subscribing households; 35 channels; 3 community access channels; 50 hours per week of community access programming.
Additional Contact Information: telephone (815)987-4510.

🎙 1392 WIFR-TV - Channel 23
PO Box 123
2523 N. Meridian Rd.   Phone: (815)987-5300
Rockford, IL 61105   **Fax: (815)965-0981**

🎙 1393 WLUV-AM - 1520
2272 Elmwood
PO Box 2616   Phone: (815)877-9588
Rockford, IL 61103   **Fax: (815)877-9649**

🎙 1394 WLUV-FM - 96.7
2272 Elmwood   Phone: (815)877-9588
Rockford, IL 61103   **Fax: (815)877-9649**

🎙 1395 WNIJ-FM - 90.5
711 N. Main St.   **Phone: (815)753-9000**
Rockford, IL 61103-6999   Fax: (815)753-9938

🎙 1396 WXXQ-FM - 98.5
483 N. Mulford Rd.   Phone: (815)235-4113
Rockford, IL 61107   Fax: (815)235-9377

ROLLING MEADOWS

🎙 1397 Continental Cablevision
1575 Rohlwing Rd.   Phone: (708)530-4477
Rolling Meadows, IL 60009   Fax: (708)530-8654
Owner: Continental Cablevision, Inc. **Founded:** 1982. **Key Personnel:** Rebecca R. Cianci, Program Mgr. **Cities Served:** Rolling Meadows, Hoffman Estates, Palatine, Elk Grove Village, and Buffalo Grove, IL: 50,000 subscribing households; 2 channels; 1 community access channel; 25 hours per week of community access programming.

ST. CHARLES

📖 1398 Cross Stitch Sampler
NKS Publications
707 Kantz Rd.
St. Charles, IL 60174
Needleworks magazine. **Frequency:** Quarterly. **Key Personnel:** Debbie Novak, Editor. **Subscription:** $12. $3.95 single issue.
                          Circulation: (Not Reported)
Formerly: Needlewords, Cross Stitch Sampler.

📖 1399 Fox Valley Living
Sampler Publications, Inc.
107 W. Main St.   Phone: (708)377-7570
Saint Charles, IL 60174   **Fax: (708)377-8065**

SALEM

🎙 1400 WJBD-AM - 1350
PO Box 70   Phone: (618)548-2000
Salem, IL 62881   **Fax: (618)548-2079**

🎙 1401 WJBD-FM - 100.1
PO Box 70   Phone: (618)548-2000
Salem, IL 62881   **Fax: (618)548-2079**

SCHILLER PARK

📖 1402 Living The Word
J.S. Paluch Co., Inc.
3825 N. Willow Rd.
PO Box 2703   Phone: (708)678-9300
Schiller Park, IL 60176   Fax: (708)671-5715
Inspirational commentary and scripture readings. **Subtitle:** Not Only On Sunday. **Founded:** 1986. **Frequency:** 7x/yr. **Printing Method:** Web offset. **Trim Size:** 5 3/8 x 8 3/8. **Cols./Page:** 1 and 2. **Col. Width:** 26.5 and 12.5 picas. **Col. Depth:** 43 picas. **Key Personnel:** Dolores J. Orzel, Editor; Dan McGuire, Mng. Editor. **Subscription:** $9.95.
                                  Circulation: ‡22,000
Advertising not accepted.

📖 1403 Schiller Park Independent
Pioneer Press Newspapers
1232 Central Ave.   Phone: (708)251-4300
Wilmette, IL 60091   **Fax: (708)251-7606**

SKOKIE

📖 1404 Collegiate Insider
Innate Graphics, Inc.
4124 Oakton St.   Phone: (708)673-3458
Skokie, IL 60076   Fax: (708)675-0591
Magazine focusing on entertainment and careers for the college student. **Founded:** 1983. **Frequency:** 11x/yr. **Printing Method:** Web offset. **Trim Size:** 8 3/8 x 10 7/8. **Cols./Page:** 3. **Key Personnel:** Mark Jansen, Editor. **Subscription:** $19.99.
Ad Rates: BW: $29,910   **Circulation:** Paid △1,013,350
              4C: $36,910   Non-paid △6,000
              PCI: $479
Formerly: Insider Magazine, T & B.

📖 1405 Computer Listing Service's Machinery & Equipment Guide
Wineberg Publications
7842 N. Lincoln   Phone: (708)676-1900
Skokie, IL 60077   **Fax: (708)676-0063**

📖 1406 Dental Lab Products
MEDEC Dental Communications
7400 Skokie Blvd.   Phone: (708)674-0110
Skokie, IL 60077-3339   Fax: (708)674-2991

📖 1407 Dental Products Report
MEDEC Dental Communications
7400 Skokie Blvd.   Phone: (708)674-0110
Skokie, IL 60077-3339   Fax: (708)674-2991

📖 1408 Skokie Review
Pioneer Press Newspapers
1232 Central Ave.   Phone: (708)251-4300
Wilmette, IL 60091   **Fax: (708)251-7606**

SOUTH HOLLAND

📖 1409 The Prepress Bulletin
International Prepress Assn.
552 W. 167th St.   **Phone: (708)596-5110**
South Holland, IL 60473   Fax: (708)596-5112

SPRING VALLEY

1410 Spring Valley's Bureau County Republican
106 E. St. Paul St.
PO Box 147   Phone: (815)664-4321
Spring Valley, IL 61362   **Fax: (815)663-1451**

SPRINGFIELD

1411 Times Mirror Cable TV of Springfield
711 S. Dirksen Pkwy.
Box 3066
Springfield, IL 62708   Phone: (217)788-5666
Owner: Times Mirror Cable TV. **Founded:** 1967. **Cities Served:**
Sangamon County, Grandview, Jerome, Leland Grove, Rochester,
Southern View, and Springfield, IL.

1412 WSEC-TV - Channel 14/65
c/o CONVOCOM
PO Box 6248   Phone: (217)786-6647
Springfield, IL 62708   **Fax: (217)786-7286**

STREAMWOOD

1413 Harley Women Magazine
Asphalt Angels Publications, Inc.
PO Box 374   Phone: (708)888-2645
Streamwood, IL 60107   **Fax: (708)888-2954**

SYCAMORE

1414 Dekalb Edition
2425 Bethany Rd.   Phone: (815)748-5153
Sycamore, IL 60118   Fax: (815)748-5184
Community newspaper serving DeKalb County, IL. **Founded:** 1992.
Frequency: Weekly. **Cols./Page:** 6. **Col. Width:** 2 in. **Col. Depth:** 2 in.
Key Personnel: Kim Kubiak, Editor.
                              Circulation: Non-paid 22,000
Advertising accepted; contact publisher for rates.

TAYLORVILLE

1415 WTIM-AM - 1410
111 W. Main Cross
PO Box 169   **Phone: (217)824-9846**
Taylorville, IL 62568   Fax: (217)824-3301

TECHNY

1416 Divine Word Missionaries
Divine Word Missionary Society
1835 Waukegan Rd.   Phone: (708)272-7600
Techny, IL 60082   **Fax: (708)272-8572**

TRENTON

1417 Sun
PO Box 118   Phone: (618)224-9422
Trenton, IL 62293-0118   **Fax: (618)224-9422**

URBANA

1418 Disc Golf Journal
Disc-Connection
1801 Richardson Dr., No. 6
Urbana, IL 61801   Phone: (217)344-3552
Magazine for the sport of disc golf. **Subtitle:** "The World's Finest Disc
Golf Publication." **Founded:** 1991. **Frequency:** Bimonthly. **Printing
Method:** Offset. **Trim Size:** 11 3/4 x 16. **Cols./Page:** 4. **Col. Width:** 2 1/
2 in. **Col. Depth:** 14 3/4 in. **Key Personnel:** Tom Schlueter, Publisher;
Kathy Ignowski, Managing Editor. **ISSN:** 1055-4785. **Subscription:**
$18. $4 single issue.
Ad Rates: BW: $100   **Circulation:** Paid ‡1,500
                                              Free ‡500

VERNON HILLS

1419 Vernon Hills Review
Pioneer Press Newspapers
1232 Central Ave.   Phone: (708)251-4300
Wilmette, IL 60091   **Fax: (708)251-7606**

VIRDEN

1420 Girard Gazette
169 W. Jackson St.   Phone: (217)965-3355
Virden, IL 62690   **Fax: (217)965-4512**

VIRGINIA

1421 Virginia Gazette
Beardstown Newspapers, Inc.
117 E. Springfield St.   **Phone: (217)452-3513**
Virginia, IL 62691   **Fax: (217)452-3382**
Former Title: Virginia Gazette of Cass County

WESTCHESTER

1422 Westchester Herald
Pioneer Press Newspapers
1232 Central Ave.   Phone: (708)251-4300
Wilmette, IL 60091   **Fax: (708)251-7606**

WHITE HALL

1423 Greene Prairie Press
112 E. Sherman   Phone: (217)742-3313
White Hall, IL 62092   **Fax: (217)742-3313**

INDIANA

ANDERSON

⚘ 1424 UAE
633 Jackson St.   Phone: (317)649-0407
Anderson, IN 46016   Fax: (317)649-1532
Owner: Tele-Communications, Inc. **Founded:** 1972. **Cities Served:**
Madison County, IN.

⚘ 1425 WAXT-FM - 96.7
PO Box 610   Phone: (317)644-7791
Anderson, IN 46015-0610   **Fax: (317)641-2383**

AUBURN

📖 1426 The Evening Star
Kendallville Publishing Co., Inc.
Box 431   Phone: (219)925-2611
Auburn, IN 46706-0431   Fax: (219)925-2625

BEECH GROVE

📖 1427 The Perry Township Weekly
Reporter-Times, Inc.
PO Box 187   Phone: (317)787-3291
Beech Grove, IN 46107   Fax: (317)787-3325
Former Title: Township Weekly

BERNE

📖 1428 Cross-Stitch Plus
House of White Birches
306 E. Parr Rd.   Phone: (219)589-8741
Berne, IN 46711   **Fax: (219)589-8093**
Former Title: Women's Circle Counted Cross-Stitch

📖 1429 Desserts!
House of White Birches
306 E. Parr Rd.
Berne, IN 46711
Magazine profiling homemade desserts. **Frequency:** 6x/yr. **Key Personnel:** Judi K. Merkel, Editor; Carl H. Muselman, Publisher; Arthur K. Muselman, Publisher. **Subscription:** $9.95. $1.95 single issue.
Circulation: (Not Reported)

📖 1430 Doll World
House of White Birches
306 E. Parr Rd.   Phone: (219)589-8741
Berne, IN 46711   **Fax: (219)589-8093**
Former Title: National Doll World

📖 1431 International Doll World Collector's Price Guide
House of White Birches
306 E. Parr Rd.
Berne, IN 46711
Magazine featuring answers to questions collectors need to know.
Frequency: Quarterly **Key Personnel:** Carl H. Muselman, Publisher; Arthur K. Muselman, Publisher; Rebekah Montgomery, Editor.
Subscription: $12.97. $2.95 single issue.
Circulation: (Not Reported)

BLOOMINGTON

📖 1432 Differences: A Journal of Feminist Cultural Studies
Indiana University Press
601 N. Morton   Phone: (812)855-9449
Bloomington, IN 47404   Fax: (812)855-7931
Journal focusing on cultural studies and feminism. **Frequency:** 3x/yr.
Printing Method: Offset. **Trim Size:** 7 3/4 x 9. **ISSN:** 1040-7391.
Subscription: $28; $48 institutions; $38 other countries; $58 institutions other countries. $10 single issue.
Ad Rates: GLR: $200   **Circulation:** 1,200

📖 1433 Educational Horizons
Pi Lambda Theta
4101 E. 3rd St.   Phone: (812)339-3411
Bloomington, IN 47407   Fax: (812)339-3462
Journal for professionals in education. **Frequency:** Quarterly.
Circulation: (Not Reported)

📖 1434 Journal of the Experimental Analysis of Behavior
Society for the Experimental Analysis of Behavior
Indiana University
Psychology Dept.
Bloomington, IN 47405-1301   **Phone: (812)339-4718**

📖 1435 The Journal of Women's History
Indiana University
History Dept.
742 Ballantine Hall   Phone: (812)855-1320
Bloomington, IN 47405   Fax: (812)855-5678
Feminist journal on women's history. **Founded:** 1989. **Frequency:** 3x/yr. **Trim Size:** 6 x 9. **Cols./Page:** 1. **Col. Width:** 4 1/2 in. **Col. Depth:** 8 in. **Key Personnel:** Joan Hoff, Co-Editor; Christie Farnham, Co-Editor; Beth Olson, Managing Editor; Georg'ann Cattelona, Book Review Editor. **ISSN:** 1042-7961. **Subscription:** $25; $45 institutions; $55 institutions other countries. $10 single issue.
Ad Rates: BW: $200   **Circulation:** Paid ‡1,108
                                               Non-paid ‡50

♣ **1436 TCI of Indiana, Inc.**
Box 729
Bloomington, IN 47401   Phone: (812)332-9486
Owner: Tele-Communications, Inc. **Founded:** 1966. **Cities Served:**
Bloomington County, IN.

♣ **1437 WBWB-FM - 96.7**
PO Box 7797
304 State Rd. 446
Bloomington, IN 47407   Phone: (812)336-8000
                    Fax: (812)336-7000

♣ **1438 WIUS-FM - 95**
815 E. 8th St.
Bloomington, IN 47406   Phone: (812)855-6552
Format: Alternative/Independent/Progressive. **Key Personnel:** Gary
Schoenwetter, Music Dir. **Ad Rates:** Noncommercial.

CAYUGA

▭ **1439 Herald News**
Box 158
Cayuga, IN **47928-0158**   Phone: (317)492-4401

COLUMBUS

♣ **1440 WCSI-AM - 1010**
3212 Washington St.   Phone: (812)372-4448
Columbus, IN 47203   Fax: (812)372-1061
Format: News; Talk; Middle-of-the-Road (MOR). **Network(s):** Mutual
Broadcasting System; AP; Talknet. **Owner:** White River Broadcasting
Co. **Founded:** 1957. **Operating Hours:** 5 a.m.-10 p.m. **Key Personnel:**
Ernest Caldemone, Station and Sales Mgr.; Kurt Heminger, Business
Mgr.; Dave Peach, Program Dir.; Brook Steed, News Dir.; Sam
Simmermaker, Sports Dir. **Wattage:** 500 day. 19 night.

CRAWFORDSVILLE

♣ **1441 WCVL-AM - 1550**
1880 N. Rd. 200 W.
PO Box 603   Phone: (317)362-8200
Crawfordsville, IN 47933   **Fax: (317)364-1550**

CROWN POINT

▭ **1442 Crown Point Shopping News**
Crown Point Shopping News
111 Hack Ct.
Crown Point, IN 46307   Phone: (219)663-5330
Shopping guide. **Frequency:** Weekly (Wed.). **Cols./Page:** 6. **Col. Width:**
1 3/8 in. **Subscription:** Free.
Ad Rates: BW: $565
         4C: $2,000
         PCI: $5.95   **Circulation:** Free ▢18,500

DANVILLE

▭ **1443 The Republican**
Hendricks County Republican, Inc.
6 E. Main St.
PO Box 149
Danville, IN 46122   Phone: (317)745-2777

DELPHI

▭ **1444 Sun-Journal**
Jones Community Newspapers, Inc.
211 S. Washington St.
PO Box 236   Phone: (317)564-2010
Delphi, IN 46923-0236   Fax: (317)564-3889

ELKHART

▭ **1445 RV Trade Digest**
Continental Publishing Co. of Indiana, Inc.
PO Box 1805   Phone: (219)295-1962
Elkhart, IN 46515   **Fax: (219)295-7574**

♣ **1446 WVPE-FM - 88.1**
2424 California Rd.
Elkhart, IN 46514   Phone: (219)262-5660
            Fax: (719)262-5700

EVANSVILLE

♣ **1447 UAE**
1900 N. Fares Ave.
Box 4658   Phone: (812)428-2462
Evansville, IN 47711   Fax: (812)428-2427
Owner: Tele-Communications, Inc. **Founded:** 1979. **Cities Served:**
Vanderburgh County, and Darmstadt, IN.

♣ **1448 WGBF-FM - 103.1**
PO Box 297   **Phone: (502)831-2982**
Evansville, IN 47702-0297   **Fax: (502)831-2977**

♣ **1449 WPSR-FM - 90.7**
5400 1st Ave.   **Phone: (812)465-8241**
Evansville, IN 47710   **Fax: (812)465-8241**

♣ **1450 WTVW-TV - Channel 7**
477 Carpenter St.
PO Box 7   **Phone: (812)424-7777**
Evansville, IN 47701-0007   Fax: (812)421-4040

♣ **1451 WWOK-AM - 1280**
PO Box 297   **Phone: (502)831-2982**
Evansville, IN 47702   **Fax: (502)831-2977**

FORT WAYNE

♣ **1452 Comcast Cablevision**
720 Taylor St.   Phone: (219)456-9000
Fort Wayne, IN 46802   Fax: (219)456-8879
Owner: Comcast Corp. **Founded:** 1979. **Cities Served:** Allen County,
Huntington County, Noble County, Wells County, and Whitley
County; Avilla, Canterbury Green, Huntertown, New Haven, and
Roanoke, IN.

♣ **1453 WFFT-TV - Channel 55**
3707 Hillegas Rd.   **Phone: (219)471-5555**
Fort Wayne, IN 46808   Fax: (219)484-4331

♣ **1454 WMEE-FM - 97.3**
2915 Maples Rd.   Phone: (219)447-5511
Fort Wayne, IN 46816   **Fax: (219)447-7546**

FRENCH LICK

♣ **1455 WFLQ-FM - 100.1**
PO Box 100   Phone: (812)936-9100
French Lick, IN 47432   **Fax: (812)936-9100**

GARY

♣ **1456 Cablevision Associates of Gary**
925 Kentucky
Box M 869
Gary, IN 46402   Phone: (219)882-9700
Owner: Tele-Communications, Inc. **Founded:** 1981. **Cities Served:**
Lake County, IN.

GEIST

▭ **1457 The Good Life**
Publications Unlimited, Inc.
622 S. Rangeline Rd.
Carmel, IN 46032   **Phone: (317)843-2993**

GOSHEN

▭ **1458 The Mennonite Quarterly Review**
Mennonite Historical Society
Goshen College   Phone: (219)535-7111
Goshen, IN 46526-9988   **Fax: (219)535-7438**

♣ 1459 WGCS-FM - 91.1
Goshen College
1700 S. Main St.
Goshen, IN 46526   Phone: (219)535-7488

GRANGER

♣ 1460 WRBR-FM - 103.9
6910 Gumwood Rd., No. 12   Phone: (219)273-1836
Granger, IN 46530   Fax: (219)271-5555

GREENCASTLE

♣ 1461 WGRE-FM - 91.5
Depauw University
609 S. Locust St.
Greencastle, IN 46135   Phone: (317)658-4642

GREENFIELD

▯ 1462 Ad News
Ad News - Indy East
119 W. North St.
PO Box 602   Phone: (317)462-7368
Greenfield, IN 46140   Fax: (317)462-7779

▯ 1463 Indy East News
Ad News - Indy East
119 W. North St.
PO Box 602   Phone: (317)462-7368
Greenfield, IN 46140   Fax: (317)462-7779

▯ 1464 Westside Enterprise
Ad News - Indy East
119 W. North St.
PO Box 602   Phone: (317)462-7368
Greenfield, IN 46140   Fax: (317)462-7779
Former Title: West Side

HAMMOND

♣ 1465 UAE
844 169th St.
Hammond, IN 46324   Phone: (219)932-4711
Owner: Tele-Communications, Inc. **Founded:** 1980. **Cities Served:**
Lake County, IN.

HUNTINGTON

▯ 1466 The Pope Speaks: The Church Documents
Bimonthly
Our Sunday Visitor, Inc.
200 Noll Plaza   Phone: (219)356-8400
Huntington, IN 46750   **Fax: (219)356-8472**

♣ 1467 WPDJ-AM - 1300
1600 E. Taylor St.
PO Box 367
Huntington, IN 46750   Phone: (219)358-0718

INDIANAPOLIS

▯ 1468 Allegheny Trucker
Allied Publications
7355 Woodland Dr.   Phone: (317)297-5500
Indianapolis, IN 46278   Fax: (317)299-1356
Truck trader magazine. Part of the Allied Network. **Frequency:**
Monthly. **Printing Method:** Offset. **Trim Size:** 8 x 10 3/4. **Cols./Page:**
3. **Col. Width:** 2 5/16 in. **Col. Depth:** 9 3/4 in. **Key Personnel:** James
Bellin, Publisher. **Subscription:** $18. $2 single issue.
Ad Rates: BW: $615   **Circulation:** Paid ‡18,245
        4C: $1,210   Non-paid ‡434,518
Circulation figures are combined with all other Allied Trader
Magazine Network publications.

▯ 1469 Badger Trucker
Allied Publications
7355 Woodland Dr.   Phone: (317)297-5500
Indianapolis, IN 46278   Fax: (317)299-1356
Truck trader magazine. Part of the Allied Network. **Frequency:**
Monthly. **Printing Method:** Offset. **Trim Size:** 8 x 10 3/4. **Cols./Page:**
3. **Col. Width:** 2 5/16 in. **Col. Depth:** 9 3/4 in. **Key Personnel:** James
Bellin, Publisher. **Subscription:** $18. $2 single issue.
Ad Rates: BW: $615   **Circulation:** Paid ‡18,245
        4C: $1,210   Non-paid ‡434,518
Circulation figures are combined with all other Allied Trader
Magazine Network publications.

▯ 1470 California Trucker
Allied Publications
7355 Woodland Dr.   Phone: (317)297-5500
Indianapolis, IN 46278   Fax: (317)299-1356
Truck trader magazine. Part of the Allied Network. **Frequency:**
Monthly. **Printing Method:** Offset. **Trim Size:** 8 x 10 3/4. **Cols./Page:**
3. **Col. Width:** 2 5/16 in. **Col. Depth:** 9 3/4 in. **Key Personnel:** James
Bellin, Publisher. **Subscription:** $18. $2 single issue.
Ad Rates: BW: $770   **Circulation:** Paid ‡18,245
        4C: $1,365   Non-paid ‡434,518
Circulation figures are combined with all other Allied Trader
Magazine Network publications.

▯ 1471 Carolina Trucker
Allied Publications
7355 Woodland Dr.   Phone: (317)297-5500
Indianapolis, IN 46278   Fax: (317)299-1356
Truck trader magazine. **Frequency:** Monthly. **Printing Method:** Offset.
Trim Size: 8 x 10 3/4. **Cols./Page:** 3. **Col. Width:** 2 5/16 in. **Col. Depth:**
9 3/4 in. **Key Personnel:** James Bellin, Publisher. **Subscription:** $18. $2
single issue.
Ad Rates: BW: $615   **Circulation:** Paid ‡18,245
        4C: $1,210   Non-paid ‡434,518
Circulation figures are combined with all other Allied Trader
Magazine Network publications.

▯ 1472 Cascade Trucker
Allied Publications
7355 Woodland Dr.   Phone: (317)297-5500
Indianapolis, IN 46278   Fax: (317)299-1356
Truck trader magazine. Part of the Allied Network. **Frequency:**
Monthly. **Printing Method:** Offset. **Trim Size:** 8 x 10 3/4. **Cols./Page:**
3. **Col. Width:** 2 5/16 in. **Col. Depth:** 9 3/4 in. **Key Personnel:** James
Bellin, Publisher. **Subscription:** $18. $2 single issue.
Ad Rates: BW: $670   **Circulation:** Paid ‡18,245
        4C: $1,265   Non-paid ‡434,518
Circulation figures are combined with all other Allied Trader
Magazine Network publications.

▯ 1473 Central States Trucker
Allied Publications
7355 Woodland Dr.   Phone: (317)297-5500
Indianapolis, IN 46278   Fax: (317)299-1356
Truck trader magazine. Part of the Allied Network. **Frequency:**
Monthly. **Printing Method:** Offset. **Trim Size:** 8 x 10 3/4. **Cols./Page:**
3. **Col. Width:** 2 5/16 in. **Col. Depth:** 9 3/4 in. **Key Personnel:** James
Bellin, Publisher. **Subscription:** $18. $2 single issue.
Ad Rates: BW: $605   **Circulation:** Paid ‡18,245
        4C: $1,200   Non-paid ‡434,518
Circulation figures are combined with all other Allied Trader
Magazine Network publications.

▯ 1474 Children's Digest
Children's Better Health Institute
1100 Waterway Blvd.
PO Box 567   Phone: (317)636-8881
Indianapolis, IN **46206**   Fax: (317)637-0126

Ad Rates: GLR = general line rate; BW = one-time black & white page rate; 4C = one-time four color page rate; SAU = standard advertising unit rate;
CNU = Canadian newspaper advertising unit rate; PCI = per column inch rate.
Circulation: ★ = ABC; △ = BPA; ◆ = CAC; ● = CCAB; □ = VAC; ⊕ = PO Statement; ‡ = Publisher's Report; Boldface figures = sworn; Light figures = estimated.
Entry type: ▯ = Print; ♣ = Broadcast.

1475 Indy's Child
Indy's Child, Inc.
8900 Keystone Crossing, No. 538
Indianapolis, IN 46240   Phone: (317)843-1494
Magazine covering parenting news. **Founded:** 1984. **Frequency:**
Monthly. **Printing Method:** Web press. **Trim Size:** 11 x 13 1/2. **Cols./**
Page: 4. **Col. Width:** 2 7/8 in. **Col. Depth:** 12 3/8 in. **Key Personnel:**
Mary Wynne Cox, Editor/Business Mgr.; Barbara S. Wynne, Publish-
er. **Subscription:** $15.
Ad Rates:	BW:	$1,200	Circulation:	Free □41,755
	4C:	$1,500		Paid □322
	PCI:	$27.50		

1476 Keystone/Jersey Truck Exchange
Allied Publications
7355 Woodland Dr.   Phone: (317)297-5500
Indianapolis, IN 46278   Fax: (317)299-1356
Truck trader magazine. Part of the Allied Network. **Frequency:**
Monthly. **Printing Method:** Offset. **Trim Size:** 8 x 10 3/4. **Cols./Page:**
3. **Col. Width:** 2 5/16 in. **Col. Depth:** 9 3/4 in. **Key Personnel:** James
Bellin, Publisher. **Subscription:** $18. $2 single issue.
| Ad Rates: | BW: | $730 | Circulation: | Paid ‡18,245 |
| | 4C: | $1,325 | | Non-paid ‡434,518 |
Circulation figures are combined with all other Allied Trader
Magazine Network publications.

1477 The Lion of Alpha Epsilon Pi
8815 Wesleyan Rd.   Phone: (317)876-1913
Indianapolis, IN 46268-1185   **Fax: (317)876-1057**

1478 Michigan Truck Exchange
Allied Publications
7355 Woodland Dr.   Phone: (317)297-5500
Indianapolis, IN 46278   Fax: (317)299-1356
Truck trader magazine. Part of the Allied Network. **Frequency:**
Monthly. **Printing Method:** Offset. **Trim Size:** 8 x 10 3/4. **Cols./Page:**
3. **Col. Width:** 2 5/16 in. **Col. Depth:** 9 3/4 in. **Key Personnel:** James
Bellin, Publisher. **Subscription:** $18. $2 single issue.
| Ad Rates: | BW: | $425 | Circulation: | Paid ‡18,245 |
| | 4C: | $1,020 | | Non-paid ‡434,518 |
Circulation figures are combined with all other Allied Trader
Magazine Network publications.

1479 Minn/Dakota Truck Merchandiser
Allied Publications
7355 Woodland Dr.   Phone: (317)297-5500
Indianapolis, IN 46278   Fax: (317)299-1356
Truck trader magazine. **Frequency:** Monthly. **Printing Method:** Offset.
Trim Size: 8 x 10 3/4. **Cols./Page:** 3. **Col. Width:** 2 5/16 in. **Col. Depth:**
9 3/4 in. **Key Personnel:** James Bellin, Publisher. **Subscription:** $18. $2
single issue.
| Ad Rates: | BW: | $615 | Circulation: | Paid ‡18,245 |
| | 4C: | $1,210 | | Non-paid ‡434,518 |
Circulation figures are combined with all other Allied Trader
Magazine Network publications.

1480 Mountain America Truck Trader
Allied Publications
7355 Woodland Dr.   Phone: (317)297-5500
Indianapolis, IN 46278   Fax: (317)299-1356
Truck trader magazine. Part of the Allied Network. **Frequency:**
Monthly. **Printing Method:** Offset. **Trim Size:** 8 x 10 3/4. **Cols./Page:**
3. **Col. Width:** 2 5/16 in. **Col. Depth:** 9 3/4 in. **Key Personnel:** James
Bellin, Publisher. **Subscription:** $18. $2 single issue.
| Ad Rates: | BW: | $730 | Circulation: | Paid ‡18,245 |
| | 4C: | $1,325 | | Non-paid ‡434,518 |
Circulation figures are combined with all other Allied Trader
Magazine Network publications.

1481 New England Truck Exchange
Allied Publications
7355 Woodland Dr.   Phone: (317)297-5500
Indianapolis, IN 46278   Fax: (317)299-1356
Truck trader magazine. Part of the Allied Network. **Frequency:**
Monthly. **Printing Method:** Offset. **Trim Size:** 8 x 10 3/4. **Cols./Page:**
3. **Col. Width:** 2 5/16 in. **Col. Depth:** 9 3/4 in. **Key Personnel:** James
Bellin, Publisher. **Subscription:** $18. $2 single issue.
| Ad Rates: | BW: | $730 | Circulation: | Paid ‡18,245 |
| | 4C: | $1,325 | | Non-paid ‡434,518 |

Circulation figures are combined with all other Allied Trader
Magazine publications.

1482 New York Truck Exchange
Allied Publications
7355 Woodland Dr.   Phone: (317)297-5500
Indianapolis, IN 46278   Fax: (317)299-1356
Truck trader magazine. Part of the Allied Network. **Frequency:**
Monthly. **Printing Method:** Offset. **Trim Size:** 8 x 10 3/4. **Cols./Page:**
3. **Col. Width:** 2 5/16 in. **Col. Depth:** 9 3/4 in. **Key Personnel:** James
Bellin, Publisher. **Subscription:** $18. $2 single issue.
| Ad Rates: | BW: | $800 | Circulation: | Paid ‡18,245 |
| | 4C: | $1,395 | | Non-paid ‡434,518 |
Circulation figures are combined with all other Allied Trader
Magazine Network publications.

1483 Texas Trucker
Allied Publications
7355 Woodland Dr.   Phone: (317)297-5500
Indianapolis, IN 46278   Fax: (317)299-1356
Truck trader magazine. **Frequency:** Monthly. **Printing Method:** Offset.
Trim Size: 8 x 10 3/4. **Cols./Page:** 3. **Col. Width:** 2 5/16 in. **Col. Depth:**
9 3/4 in. **Key Personnel:** James Bellin, Publisher. **Subscription:** $18. $2
single issue.
| Ad Rates: | BW: | $615 | Circulation: | Paid ‡18,245 |
| | 4C: | $1,210 | | Non-paid ‡434,518 |
Circulation figures are combined with all other Allied Trader
Magazine Network publications.

1484 U.S. Kids
PO Box 567   Phone: (317)636-8881
Indianapolis, IN 46206   Fax: (317)637-0126
Magazine featuring stories and activities geared for children. /**FRQ**
8x/yr. **Printing Method:** Web Offset. **Trim Size:** 8 1/8 x 10 7/8. **Key**
Personnel: Marta Partington, Editor. **Subscription:** $14.95; $21.95
other countries.
| Ad Rates: | 4C: | $5,000 | Circulation: | Paid ‡200,000 |
| | | | | Non-paid ‡2,000 |

1485 The Wesleyan Advocate
The Wesleyan Publishing House
PO Box 50434   **Phone: (317)576-8156**
Indianapolis, IN 46250-0434   **Fax: (317)577-4397**

1486 American Cablevision
3030 Roosevelt Ave.
Indianapolis, IN 46218   Phone: (317)632-2288
Owner: American TV & Communications Corp. **Founded:** 1981.
Cities Served: Hendricks County and Marion County, Brownsburg,
and Danville, IN.

1487 Comcast Cablevision of Indiana
5330 E. 65th St.   Phone: (317)353-2225
Indianapolis, IN 46220   Fax: (317)842-5143
Owner: Comcast Corp. **Founded:** 1979. **Cities Served:** Hamilton
County, Hancock County, Hendricks County, Marion County, Mor-
gan County, and Shelby County; Beech Grove, Clemont, Crows Nest,
Cumberland, Homecroft, Lawrence, Meridian Hills, Mooresville,
North Crows Nest, Plainfield, Ravenswood, Southport, Speedway,
Warren Park, Williams Creek, and Wynnedale, IN.

1488 WHHH-FM - 96.3
6264 LaPas Trail
Indianapolis, IN 46268   Phone: (317)239-9696
Format: Contemporary Hit Radio (CHR). **Owner:** William S. Poor-
man. **Founded:** 1991. **Operating Hours:** Continuous. **Key Personnel:**
Bill Shirk, Gen. Mgr.; Scott Wheeler, Program Dir. **Wattage:** 3000.

1489 WICR-FM - 88.7
1400 E. Hanna Ave.   **Phone: (317)788-3280**
Indianapolis, IN 46227   **Fax: (317)788-3490**

1490 WNDE-AM - 1260
6161 Fall Creek Rd.   Phone: (317)257-7565
Indianapolis, IN 46220   **Fax: (317)254-9619**

1491 WTTV-TV - Channel 4
3490 Bluff Rd.   **Phone: (317)782-4444**
Indianapolis, IN 46217   **Fax: (317)780-5464**

🎙 1492 WXIN-TV - Channel 59
1440 N. Meridian St.   Phone: (317)632-5900
Indianapolis, IN 46202   Fax: (317)687-6531

🎙 1493 WXXP-FM - 97.9
PO Box 50-2098
Indianapolis, IN 45250   Phone: (317)776-0090

JASPER

🎙 1494 WBDC-FM - 100.9
PO Box 1009   Phone: (812)683-4144
Jasper, IN 47547-1009   Fax: (812)683-5891

JEFFERSONVILLE

🎙 1495 WZCC-AM - 1570
220 Potters Ln.   **Phone: (812)941-1570**
Jeffersonville, IN 47129   Fax: (812)944-7782

LAWRENCEBURG

📖 1496 Harrison Press
Register Publications
126 W. High St.
PO Box 328   Phone: (812)926-0063
Lawrenceburg, IN 47025   Fax: (812)537-5576
Community newspaper. **Frequency:** Weekly. **Printing Method:** Offset.
Trim Size: 14 1/2 x 22 3/4. **Cols./Page:** 6. **Col. Width:** 13 in. **Col.
Depth:** 21 in. **Key Personnel:** John Retniger, Publisher; Ollie Roehm,
Editor; Joe Awad, Managing Editor. **USPS:** 236-100. **Subscription:**
$9.50; $11 out of area.
Ad Rates:	GLR:	$.29	Circulation: Paid ⊕5,279
	BW:	$567	Non-paid ⊕40
	4C:	$993	
	PCI:	$4.10	

LIGONIER

📖 1497 Advance Leader
PO Box 30   Phone: (219)894-3102
Ligonier, IN 46767   Fax: (219)894-3104

MADISON

🎙 1498 Simmons Cable TV of Kentucky/Indiana
108 E. 2nd St.   Phone: (812)265-4922
Madison, IN 47250   Fax: (812)265-6095
Owner: Simmons Communications, Stamford, CT 06901. **Founded:**
1962. **Formerly:** Ohio Valley Cable (1980); Centel Cable (1989). **Key
Personnel:** Joan Taylor, Office Mgr.; Bonnie Burkhardt, Advertising
Mgr. **Cities Served:** Rowan, Montgomery, Laurel, Boyle, Mercer,
Anderson, Madison, Garrard, Estill, Jessamine, Woodford, Scott,
Bourbon, Nicholas, and Clark counties, KY, and Jefferson County,
IN. 75,100 subscribing households; 35 channels; 1 community access
channel. **Ad Rates:** $4-$25 for 30 seconds. **Additional Contact
Information:** Advertising address: 1617 Foxhaven Dr., Richmond, KY
40475; ph. (606)624-9666, (812)265-2029, or (800)289-5152, fax
(606)624-0060.

MARION

🎙 1499 Marion Cable TV, Inc.
2923 W. Western Ave.
Box 1568
Marion, IN 46953   Phone: (317)662-0071
Owner: American TV & Communications Corp. **Founded:** 1966.
Cities Served: Grant County, IN.

🎙 1500 WBAT-AM - 1400
120 N. Miller Ave.
Box 839   Phone: (317)664-6239
Marion, IN 46952   Fax: (317)662-0730
Format: Adult Contemporary. **Network(s):** CBS. **Owner:** Mid-America

Radio Group. **Founded:** 1947. **Operating Hours:** Continuous. **Key
Personnel:** Carolyn Bush, Office Mgr.; Jim Brunner, Sales Mgr.; Mark
Metzner, Program Dir.; Tim Rush, News Dir.; David Poehler, Gen.
Mgr. **Wattage:** 1000. **Ad Rates:** $12-$18.25 for 30 seconds; $16-$22.50
for 60 seconds. **Additional Contact Information:** Alt. phone (317)662-
1400.

🎙 1501 WCJC-FM - 99.3
120 N. Miller Ave.
Box 839   Phone: (317)664-6239
Marion, IN 46952   Fax: (317)662-0730
Format: Contemporary Country. **Network(s):** Satellite Radio. **Owner:**
Mid-American Radio Group Inc. **Founded:** 1989. **Operating Hours:**
Continuous. **Key Personnel:** David Poehler, Gen. Mgr.; Jim Brunner,
Sales Mgr.; Mark Metzner, Program Dir.; Tim Rush, News Dir.;
Carolyn Bush, Office Mgr. **Wattage:** 3000. **Ad Rates:** $9.50-$14.25 for
30 seconds; $11.75-$17.50 for 60 seconds.

MERRILLVILLE

🎙 1502 U.S. Cable of Northern Indiana
6161 Cleveland St.   Phone: (219)887-6008
Merrillville, IN 46410   Fax: (219)887-3070
Owner: U.S. Cable Corp. **Founded:** 1981. **Cities Served:** Lake County,
IN and Cook and Will counties, IL.

MIDDLEBURY

📖 1503 Middlebury Independent
Largrange Publishing Co., Inc.
PO Box 68   Phone: (219)825-9112
Middlebury, IN 46540   Fax: (219)463-2734

MISHAWAKA

🎙 1504 Heritage Cablevision Associates
Box 6248
Mishawaka, IN 46545
Owner: Tele-Communications, Inc. **Founded:** 1971. **Cities Served:**
Marshall County, St. Joseph County, Mishawaka, Osceola, Plymouth,
and Roseland, IN.

MUNCIE

🎙 1505 WCRD-AM - 540
8C216 Ball State University
Muncie, IN 47303   Phone: (317)285-1467
Format: Alternative/Independent/Progressive. **Key Personnel:** Paul
Nelson, Music Dir.

NEW CASTLE

🎙 1506 WMDH-FM - 102.5
PO Box 690   Phone: (317)529-2600
New Castle, IN 47362   Fax: (317)529-1688

NEWBURGH

🎙 1507 WGAB-AM - 1180
1180 Maple Ln.
Newburgh, IN 47630   **Phone: (812)451-2422**

🎙 1508 WJPS-FM - 106.1
1180 Maple Ln.   Phone: (812)451-2422
Newburgh, IN 47630   Fax: (812)424-8284

NORTH MANCHESTER

🎙 1509 WBKE-FM - 89.5
Manchester College
Box 88   Phone: (219)982-5272
North Manchester, IN 46962   Fax: (219)982-6868
Format: Educational. **Owner:** Manchester College. **Founded:** 1968.
Operating Hours: Continuous. **Key Personnel:** Lisa White, Station

Mgr.; Julie Cutlip, Program Dir.; Walter Patton, Business Mgr.; Jennifer DuMond, News Dir.; Jennifer Savage-Haines, Music Dir. **Wattage:** 3000.

NOTRE DAME

📖 **1510 Review of Politics**
Box B
Notre Dame, IN 46556

Phone: (219)239-6623
Fax: (219)239-8609

📖 **1511 Scholastic Magazine**
University of Notre Dame
La Fortune Center
Notre Dame, IN 46556

Phone: (219)239-7569

PERU

📖 **1512 The Shopper News**
179 N. Miami
Peru, IN 46970

Phone: (317)472-3984
Fax: (317)472-1299

Shopping guide. **Founded:** 1966. **Frequency:** Weekly (Wed.). **Printing Method:** Offset. **Subscription:** Free.
Ad Rates: BW: $432   **Circulation:** Free ☐14,577
            SAU: $4.50

PORTAGE

🎙 **1513 WNDZ-AM - 750**
2576 Portage Mall
Portage, IN 46368-3006

Phone: (219)763-2750
Fax: (219)762-0539

REMINGTON

📖 **1514 Remington Press**
PO Box 129
Remington, IN 47977

Phone: (219)261-3577
Fax: (219)866-3775

ROCHESTER

📖 **1515 The Compass**
The Sentinel Corp.
118 E. 8th
Rochester, IN 46975

Phone: (219)223-2111
Fax: (219)223-5782

Shopping guide. **Frequency:** Weekly. **Printing Method:** Web offset. **Cols./Page:** 6. **Col. Width:** 13 picas. **Col. Depth:** 21 1/2 in. **Key Personnel:** Arthur Hoffman, Advertising Mgr. **Subscription:** Free.
Circulation: Free 6,530

📖 **1516 Shopping Guide News**
Shopping Guide News
PO Box 229
Rochester, IN 46975

Phone: (219)223-5417
Fax: (219)223-8330

Shopping guide. **Frequency:** Weekly (Wed.). **Printing Method:** Web offset. **Trim Size:** 10 1/4 x 15. **Cols./Page:** 6. **Col. Width:** 9 1/2 picas. **Key Personnel:** Don Towle, Publisher; Betty Foster, Advertising Mgr. **Subscription:** Free.
Ad Rates: BW: $337.50   **Circulation:** Free ☐9,108
            PCI: $4.25   Paid ☐67

🎙 **1517 WROI-FM - 92.1**
100 W. 9th St., Ste. 306
Rochester, IN 46975

Phone: (219)223-6059
Fax: (219)223-2238

SAINT MEINRAD

📖 **1518 Marriage and Family**
Abbey Press
Hill Dr.
Saint Meinrad, IN 47577

Phone: (812)357-8011

Ceased publication.

SHERIDAN

🎙 **1519 Concept Cablevision**
106 Main St.
Box 71
Sheridan, IN 46069

Phone: (317)758-4474

Owner: Helen P. Belisle. **Key Personnel:** Randall L. Warrick, Mgr. **Cities Served:** Oxford, Advance, New Ross, Jamestown, Whitestown,

Kirklin, Terhune, Worthington, Sheridan, North Salem, Lapel, Frankton, Summitville, Darlington, Ladoga, Lake Holiday, New Market, Waynetown, Montezuma and Roachdale, IN. 4649 subscribing households; 18 channels.

SOUTH BEND

📖 **1520 South Bend Tribune**
225 W. Colfax Ave.
South Bend, IN 46626

Phone: (219)235-6161
Fax: (219)236-1765

🎙 **1521 WETL-FM - 91.7**
635 S. Main St.
South Bend, IN 46601

Phone: (219)282-4076
Fax: (219)282-4122

TERRE HAUTE

📖 **1522 The Weekly Terre Haute**
1301 Ohio St.
PO Box 1019
Terre Haute, IN 47808

Phone: (812)238-1691

Ceased publication.

🎙 **1523 American Cablevision**
1605 Wabash Ave.
Terre Haute, IN 47807

Phone: (812)232-5013
Fax: (812)232-7453

Owner: American TV & Communications Corp. **Founded:** 1966. **Cities Served:** Vigo County, Riley, and West Terre Haute, IN.

🎙 **1524 WISU-FM - 89.7**
Indiana State University
217 N. 6th St.
Terre Haute, IN 47809

Phone: (812)237-3248
Fax: (812)237-3241

VALPARAISO

📖 **1525 Extra**
The Vidette Messenger
1111 Glendale Blvd.
Valparaiso, IN 46383

Phone: (219)462-5151
Fax: (219)465-7298

Shopper. **Founded:** 1986. **Frequency:** Weekly (Wed.). **Printing Method:** Offset. **Subscription:** Free.
Ad Rates: GLR: $.126   **Circulation:** Free ‡9,400
            BW: $227.04
            4C: $461.04
            PCI: $1.76
Formerly: Buyer's Guide.

WABASH

📖 **1526 Plain Dealer**
123 W. Canal St.
Box 379
Wabash, IN 46992

Phone: (219)563-2131
Fax: (219)563-0816

🎙 **1527 WAYT-AM - 1510**
1360 S. Wabash St.
Wabash, IN 46992

Phone: (219)563-1161

Format: Adult Contemporary. **Network(s):** Mutual Broadcasting System. **Owner:** Conway Communications Corp., at above address. **Operating Hours:** Sunrise-sunset. **Key Personnel:** Roderick E. Schram, Gen. Mgr. **Wattage:** 250. **Ad Rates:** $8.05-$9.78 for 30 seconds.

WEST LAFAYETTE

📖 **1528 The Woman Conductor**
Women Band Directors National Association
345 Overlook Dr.
West Lafayette, IN 47906

Phone: (317)463-1738

Journal reporting on career improvement, conducting techniques, and association news. **Founded:** 1984 **Frequency:** 3x/yr. **Printing Method:** Desktop.

Circulation: (Not Reported)

Advertising not accepted.

WEST TERRE HAUTE

🎙 **1529 WWVR-FM - 105.5**
3438 S. Whitcomb Pl.
PO Box 207
West Terre Haute, IN **47885-0207**   Phone: (812)533-1663

WOLCOTT

📖 **1530 The New Wolcott Enterprise**
125 W. Market St.
PO Box 78   Phone: (219)279-2167
Wolcott, IN 47995   **Fax: (219)279-2167**

IOWA

AMES

1531 The Advertiser
Van Drie Enterprises, Inc.
508 Kellogg
PO Box 904 Phone: (515)233-1251
Ames, IA 50010 **Fax: (515)233-1244**

1532 Modern Logic: International Journal of the History of Mathematical Logic, Set Theory, and Foundation of Mathematics
Modern Logic Publishing
Box 1036, Welch Ave. Sta.
Ames, IA 50010-1036 Phone: (515)292-7499
Journal covering historical studies of 19th- and 20th-century mathematics. **Founded:** 1990. **Frequency:** Quarterly. **Printing Method:** Offset. **Trim Size:** 8 1/2 x 11. **Cols./Page:** 1. **Key Personnel:** Irving H. Anellis, Editor and Publisher. **ISSN:** 1047-5982. **Subscription:** $100.
Ad Rates: GLR: $6 **Circulation:** Paid 65
BW: $50 Non-paid 20

ARMSTRONG

1533 The Ringsted Dispatch
PO Box 285
Armstrong, IA 50514 Phone: (712)864-3460
Former Title: Dispatch

BATTLE CREEK

1534 The Battle Creek Times
Cow Pasture Studio
Box 28
Battle Creek, IA 51006 Phone: (712)365-4460
Ceased publication.

BELLE PLAINE

1535 South Benton Star-Press
MPC Publishing Co.
PO Box 208 Phone: (319)444-2520
Belle Plaine, IA 52208 **Fax: (319)444-2522**

BLOOMFIELD

1536 KXOF-FM - 106.3
PO Box 186 Phone: (515)664-3721
Bloomfield, IA 52537 **Fax: (515)664-3721**

BURLINGTON

1537 WestMarc Cable
Box 519
Burlington, IA 52601-6571 Phone: (319)753-6571
Owner: Tele-Communications, Inc. **Founded:** 1979. **Cities Served:** Des Moines County, IA.

CEDAR FALLS

1538 Northern Iowan
University of Northern Iowa
112 Maucker Union Phone: (319)273-2157
Cedar Falls, IA 50614-0166 **Fax: (319)273-5931**

1539 KHKE-FM - 89.5
University of Northern Iowa **Phone: (319)273-6400**
Cedar Falls, IA 50614-0359 **Fax: (319)273-2682**

1540 KRNI-AM - 1010
University of Northern Iowa **Phone: (319)273-6400**
Cedar Falls, IA 50614-0359 **Fax: (319)273-6282**

CEDAR RAPIDS

1541 Buildings
Stamats Communications, Inc.
427 6th Ave. SE
PO Box 1888 Phone: (319)364-6167
Cedar Rapids, IA 52406 **Fax: (319)364-4278**

1542 Iowa Farmer Today
501 2nd Ave. SE **Phone: (319)398-8461**
Cedar Rapids, IA 52401-5279 **Fax: (319)398-8482**

1543 Cox Cable Cedar Rapids, Inc.
6300 Council St., NE, Ste. A Phone: (319)395-9699
Cedar Rapids, IA 52402 Fax: (319)393-7017
Owner: Cox Enterprises, PO Box 105349, Atlanta, GA 30348. **Founded:** 1979. **Key Personnel:** Mike Horan, V.P./Gen. Mgr.; Denis Martel, Engineering Operations Mgr.; Carol Painter, Controller; Arlene Heck, Mktg. Mgr.; Andy Gann, Customer Operations Mgr. **Cities Served:** Linn County, Hiawatha, Marion, and Toddville, IA: 41,800 subscribing households; 35 channels; 1 community access channel; 114 hours per week of community access programming.

1544 KCCK-FM - 88.3
6301 Kirkwood Blvd. SW Phone: (319)398-5446
Cedar Rapids, IA 52406 **Fax: (319)398-5492**

Ad Rates: GLR = general line rate; BW = one-time black & white page rate; 4C = one-time four color page rate; SAU = standard advertising unit rate; CNU = Canadian newspaper advertising unit rate; PCI = per column inch rate.
Circulation: ★ = ABC; △ = BPA; ◆ = CAC; ● = CCAB; □ = VAC; ⊕ = PO Statement; ‡ = Publisher's Report; Boldface figures = sworn; Light figures = estimated.
Entry type: 📖 = Print; 🎙 = Broadcast.

🎙 **1545 KMRY-AM - 1450**
1957 Blairsferry Rd. NE
Cedar Rapids, IA 52402   Phone: (319)393-1450
     Fax: (319)393-5080

CENTERVILLE

🎙 **1546 KCOG-AM - 1400**
402 N. 12th St.
Centerville, IA 52544   Phone: (515)437-4242
Format: Adult Contemporary. **Network(s):** USA Radio. **Owner:** KCOG Inc. **Founded:** 1949. **Operating Hours:** 5 a.m.-midnight. **Key Personnel:** Fred Jenkins, Gen. Mgr. **Wattage:** 500 day; 1000 night.

CHARLES CITY

🎙 **1547 KCHA-AM - 1580**
207 N. Main St.   **Phone: (515)228-1000**
Charles City, IA 50616   Fax: (515)228-1200

🎙 **1548 KCHA-FM - 95.9**
207 N. Main St.   **Phone: (515)228-1000**
Charles City, IA 50616   Fax: (515)228-1200

🎙 **1549 KCZE-FM - 95.1**
207 N. Main St.
Charles City, IA 50616   Phone: (515)228-1000
Format: Adult Contemporary. **Owner:** Mega Media Ltd. **Founded:** 1993. **Operating Hours:** 18 hours daily. **Key Personnel:** Jim Hebel, Pres. **Wattage:** 5500.

🎙 **1550 KCZQ-FM - 102.3**
207 N. Main St.
Charles City, IA 50616   Phone: (515)228-1000
Format: Adult Contemporary. **Owner:** Mego Media Ltd. **Founded:** 1991. **Operating Hours:** 18 hours daily. **Key Personnel:** Jim Hebel, Pres. **Wattage:** 3000.

CLINTON

📖 **1551 The Gallery**
Clinton Community College
     Phone: (319)242-6841
Clinton, IA 52732   **Fax: (319)242-7868**

🎙 **1552 Heritage Cablevision**
Box 47   Phone: (319)243-6350
Clinton, IA 52732-4115   Fax: (319)243-7146
Owner: Tele-Communications, Inc. **Founded:** 1974. **Cities Served:** Clinton, Jackson, and Scott counties, IA and Carroll and Whiteside counties, IL.

DAVENPORT

📖 **1553 The Catholic Messenger**
736 Federal St.
PO Box 460   Phone: (319)323-9959
Davenport, IA 52805-0460   **Fax: (319)323-6612**

🎙 **1554 KQCS-FM - 93.5**
5315 Tremont Ave., Ste. B   **Phone: (319)391-0712**
Davenport, IA 52807   **Fax: (319)391-0620**

DAYTON

📖 **1555 Dayton Review**
Main & Skillet
Box 6   Phone: (515)547-2811
Dayton, IA 50530   Fax: (515)547-2203

DECORAH

📖 **1556 Public Opinion**
Box 350
107 E. Water St.   Phone: (319)382-4221
Decorah, IA 52101   **Fax: (319)382-5949**

DES MOINES

📖 **1557 Better Homes and Gardens Decorative Woodcrafts**
Meredith Corp.
1716 Locust St.   Phone: (515)284-3439
Des Moines, IA 50336   Fax: (515)284-3343
Magazine containing information and special projects for decorative painting on wood. **Founded:** 1991. **Frequency:** 6x/yr. **Printing Method:** Offset. **Trim Size:** 8 x 10 1/2. **Key Personnel:** Beverly Rivers, Editor; William R. Reed, Publisher; Chris Schraft, Advertising Dir. **Subscription:** $29.97. $4.95 single issue.
Ad Rates: BW: $4,375   **Circulation:** Paid ‡250,000
            4C: $6,250

📖 **1558 Country Home**
Meredith Corp.
1716 Locust St.   Phone: (515)284-2015
Des Moines, IA 50309-3023   **Fax: (515)284-3684**

📖 **1559 Golden State Beverage Times**
Diamond Publications
744 Twelve Oaks Ctr.
15500 Wayzata Blvd.   Phone: (612)449-9446
Wayzata, MN 55391-1416   Fax: (612)449-9447
Former Title: Beverage Journal of Spirits, Wine and Beer Marketing in Iowa

📖 **1560 Parent's Digest**
Meredith Corporation
1716 Locust St.
Des Moines, IA 50380-0886
Magazine includes information on family relationships and children's health and emotional development. **Frequency:** 4x/year. **Key Personnel:** Mary Hohler, Editor; Myrna Blyth, Publisher. **Subscription:** $5.99. $2.95 single issue.
     Circulation: (Not Reported)

🎙 **1561 Heritage Communications, Inc.**
2205 Ingersoll Ave.   Phone: (515)246-1555
Des Moines, IA 50312-5289   Fax: (515)246-8504
Owner: Tele-Communications, Inc. **Founded:** 1974. **Cities Served:** Polk County, Warren County, Altoona, Ankeny, Bondurant, Carlisle, Clive, Grimes, Johnston, Lakewood, Norwalk, Pleasant Hill, Saylorville, Urbandale, West Des Moines, and Windsor Heights, IA.

🎙 **1562 KLYF-FM - 100.3**
1801 Grand Ave.   Phone: (515)242-3500
Des Moines, IA 50309-3362   **Fax: (515)242-3798**

🎙 **1563 KSMG-FM - 90.7**
108 3rd St., Ste. 103
Des Moines, IA 50309   Phone: (515)282-1033
Format: Alternative/Independent/Progressive. **Key Personnel:** Ron Sorenson, Music Dir.

DUBUQUE

🎙 **1564 KLCR-FM - 96.9**
Loras College
1450 Arta Visa Rd.
PO Box 50
Dubuque, IA 52004-0178   Phone: (319)588-7172
Format: Alternative/Independent/Progressive. **Key Personnel:** Shawn Alexander, Music Dir. **Ad Rates:** Noncommercial.

🎙 **1565 TCI of Iowa**
Box 119
Dubuque, IA 52004-0119   Phone: (319)557-8020
Owner: Tele-Communications, Inc. **Founded:** 1954. **Cities Served:** Dubuque County, IA.

DUMONT

🎙 **1566 Dumont Cablevision**
506 Pine St.   Phone: (515)857-3213
Dumont, IA 50625   Fax: (515)857-3300
Owner: Dumont Telephone Co. **Key Personnel:** William R. Blakley, Mgr.; Carryl Uhlenhopp, Office Mgr.; Terry Arenhoz, Technician. **Cities Served:** Dumont, Bristow and Geneva, IA. 388 subscribing households; 26 channels; 1 community access channel.

DUNLAP

☐ **1567 The Dunlap Reporter**
114 Iowa Ave.   Phone: (712)643-5380
Dunlap, IA 51529   **Fax: (712)643-2173**

EAGLE GROVE

☐ **1568 Wright County Shopper's Guide**
Mid-America Publishing Corp.
314 W. Broadway
PO Box 6   Phone: (515)448-4745
Eagle Grove, IA 50533-0006   Fax: (515)448-3182
Shopper. **Founded:** 1980. **Frequency:** Weekly. **Printing Method:** Offset. **Cols./Page:** 6. **Col. Width:** 2 1/8 in. **Col. Depth:** 21 in. **Key Personnel:** Gary L. Milks, Publisher. **Subscription:** Free.
Ad Rates: PCI: $3.70   **Circulation:** Free ‡4,000

☖ **1569 TVIQ Inc.**
214 W. Broadway
Box 453
Eagle Grove, IA 50533   Phone: (515)448-4725

ELKADER

☐ **1570 The Clayton County Register**
Griffith Press, Inc.
PO Box 130   Phone: (319)245-1311
Elkader, IA 52043-0130   **Fax: (319)245-1312**

FAIRFIELD

☐ **1571 Book Marketing Update**
Open Horizons
PO Box 205   **Phone: (515)472-6130**
Fairfield, IA 52556-0205   Fax: (515)472-3186

FORT DODGE

☐ **1572 Aviators Hot Line**
Heartland Communications Group
1003 Central Ave.
PO Box 958
Fort Dodge, IA 50501   Phone: (800)247-2000
Subtitle: Total Market Coverage For Active Buyers and Sellers of Corporate and General Aircraft, Parts, and Services. **Founded:** 1978. **Frequency:** Monthly. **Printing Method:** Offset. **Trim Size:** 7 5/8 x 10 3/4. **Cols./Page:** 4. **Col. Width:** 1 5/8 in. **Key Personnel:** Linda Belew-Conaway, Publication Mgr. **Subscription:** $21.95; $69 other countries. $2 single issue.
Ad Rates: BW: $570   **Circulation:** Paid ‡3,100
               4C: $1,000   Non-paid ‡40,000
               PCI: $30

☐ **1573 Business Air Today**
Heartland Communications Group, Inc.
1003 Central Ave.
PO Box 1052
Fort Dodge, IA 50501   Phone: (800)247-2000
Subtitle: The Premiere Source For Corporate Aviation Acquisitions. **Founded:** 1992. **Frequency:** Bimonthly. **Printing Method:** Offset. **Trim Size:** 7 3/4 x 10 3/4. **Key Personnel:** Marty Anderson, Nat'l. Sales Mgr. **Subscription:** $21.95; $69 other countries. $2 single issue.
Ad Rates: 4C: $1,200   **Circulation:** Non-paid ‡23,000

☐ **1574 Contractors Hot Line**
Heartland Communications Group, Inc.
1003 Central Ave.
Fort Dodge, IA 50501   Phone: (515)955-1600
Buy-sell-trade catalog serving the heavy construction market. **Founded:** 1966. **Frequency:** Weekly. **Printing Method:** Offset. **Trim Size:** 7 7/8 x 10 3/4. **Cols./Page:** 4. **Col. Depth:** 10 in. **Key Personnel:** Robert B.

Howe, Publisher; David J. Bradley, Nat'l. Mktg. Mgr. **ISSN:** 0192-6330. **Subscription:** $89. $2.25 single issue; $2.75 single issue Canada.
Ad Rates: BW: $600   **Circulation:** Paid ‡5,030
               PCI: $20   Non-paid ‡9,978
Additional Contact Information: Toll-free (800)247-2000.

☐ **1575 Farm Equipment Guide**
Heartland Communications Group, Inc.
1003 Central Ave.
PO Box 1052
Fort Dodge, IA 50501   Phone: (515)955-1600
Publication with farm machinery prices and brokers. **Founded:** 1981. **Frequency:** Monthly. **Trim Size:** 7 5/8 x 10 3/4. **Cols./Page:** 4. **Col. Width:** 39.6 picas. **Col. Depth:** 59 picas. **Key Personnel:** Lisa Ziems, Publisher; Jane A. Messenger, Editor. **ISSN:** 1047-725X. **Subscription:** $49.95.
Ad Rates: BW: $500   **Circulation:** Paid ‡9,012
                                             Non-paid ‡3,240
Additional Contact Information: Toll-free (800)247-2000. Fax ext. 1904.

☐ **1576 Farmers Hot Line**
Heartland Communications Group, Inc.
1003 Central Ave.
PO Box 1115
Fort Dodge, IA 50501   Phone: (515)955-1600
Trade magazine. **Subtitle:** Your Guide to the Newest and Latest Farm Products. **Founded:** 1975. **Frequency:** Bimonthly. **Trim Size:** 7 5/8 x 10 3/4. **Cols./Page:** 4. **Col. Width:** 42 picas. **Col. Depth:** 59 picas. **Key Personnel:** Sandra J. Simonson, Publisher; Wayne L. Venter, Assoc. Publisher; Patricia A. Woodall, V.P. **ISSN:** 0192-6322. **Subscription:** $19.95 (all state edition); $9.95 (manufacturers' edition; single state edition).
Ad Rates: BW: $500   **Circulation:** Paid ‡47,540
               4C: $1,010   Non-paid ‡1,660
               PCI: $20
Additional Contact Information: Toll-free (800)247-2000. Fax ext. 1904.

☐ **1577 Hot Line Construction Equipment Monthly Update**
Heartland Communications Group, Inc.
1003 Central Ave.
Fort Dodge, IA 50501   Phone: (515)995-1600
Subtitle: The One-Of-A-Kind Locating and Pricing Guide for Construction Equipment. **Founded:** 1988. **Frequency:** Monthly. **Printing Method:** Offset. **Trim Size:** 7 7/8 x 10 3/4. **Cols./Page:** 4. **Col. Width:** 1 5/8 in. **Col. Depth:** 10 in. **Key Personnel:** Robert B. Howe, Publisher. **Subscription:** $39.95. $7.50 single issue.
                                          Circulation: (Not Reported)
Additional Contact Information: Toll-free (800)247-2000. Advertising accepted; contact publisher for rates.

☐ **1578 Industrial Machine Trader**
Heartland Communications Group, Inc.
1003 Central Ave.
PO Box 1415   Phone: (515)955-1600
Fort Dodge, IA 50501   Fax: (515)955-3753
Subtitle: The Only Weekly Nationwide Publication That Links Active Buyers And Sellers Of New And Used Industrial Machinery. **Founded:** 1983. **Frequency:** Weekly. **Printing Method:** Offset. **Trim Size:** 7 5/8 x 10 3/4. **Cols./Page:** 4. **Col. Width:** 1 5/8 in. **Key Personnel:** Steve Scanlan, Publisher. **ISSN:** 1047-4374. **Subscription:** $79. $2.25 single issue; $2.75 single issue Canada.
Ad Rates: BW: $450   **Circulation:** Paid ‡800
               4C: $1,100   Controlled ‡10,000
               PCI: $15
Additional Contact Information: Toll-free (800)247-2000.

☐ **1579 Land and Water**
Trolley Center
900 Central Ave., Ste. 21
PO Box 1197   Phone: (515)576-3191
Fort Dodge, IA 50501   **Fax: (515)576-2606**

Ad Rates: GLR = general line rate; BW = one-time black & white page rate; 4C = one-time four color page rate; SAU = standard advertising unit rate; CNU = Canadian newspaper advertising unit rate; PCI = per column inch rate.
Circulation: ★ = ABC; △ = BPA; ◆ = CAC; ● = CCAB; □ = VAC; ⊕ = PO Statement; ‡ = Publisher's Report; Boldface figures = sworn; Light figures = estimated.
Entry type: ☐ = Print; ☖ = Broadcast.

103

📖 **1580 Mid-America Weekly Trucking**
Heartland Communication Group, Inc.
1003 Central Ave.
PO Box 1052
Fort Dodge, IA 50501   Phone: (515)955-1600
Magazine serving all segments of America's largest regional trucking market. **Founded:** 1972. **Frequency:** Weekly. **Trim Size:** 8 x 10 3/4. **Cols./Page:** 4. **Col. Width:** 1 13/16 in. **Col. Depth:** 10 in. **Key Personnel:** Beth Buehlar, Editor; Denise McLellan, Publisher; Cindy Youngquist, Advertising Mgr. **ISSN:** 1047-4366. **Subscription:** $59.
Ad Rates: BW: $400   **Circulation:** Non-paid 100,000
          4C: $600
          PCI: $30
Additional Contact Information: Toll-free (800)247-2000. Fax ext. 1440. **Formerly:** National Truck Trader, Midwest Truck Trader.

📖 **1581 Our California Environment**
Rte. 3, PO Box 1197   Phone: (515)576-3191
Fort Dodge, IA 50501   Fax: (515)576-5675
Ceased publication.

📖 **1582 Plastics Hot Line**
PH Publishing
1003 Central Ave.
Fort Dodge, IA 50501   Phone: (515)955-1600
                     Fax: (515)955-3753
Trade magazine. **Subtitle:** The Nation's Marketplace for Plastics Processing Equipment & Materials, Business and Employment Opportunities. **Founded:** 1990. **Frequency:** Weekly. **Printing Method:** Offset. **Trim Size:** 7 3/8 x 10 3/4. **Cols./Page:** 4. **Col. Width:** 1 5/8 in. **Col. Depth:** 1 in. **Key Personnel:** Steve Scanlan, Publisher. **Subscription:** $59.
Ad Rates: BW: $475   **Circulation:** Controlled ‡6,000
          4C: $800
          PCI: $20

📖 **1583 Printers Hot Line**
Heartland Communications Group, Inc.
1003 Central Ave.
Fort Dodge, IA 50501   Phone: (515)955-1600
Trade periodical reporting information on new and used printing equipment. **Founded:** 1978. **Frequency:** Weekly. **Printing Method:** Web offset. **Trim Size:** 7 5/8 x 10 3/4. **Cols./Page:** 4. **Col. Width:** 1 5/8 in. **Col. Depth:** 9 3/4 in. **Key Personnel:** Richard C. Thomas, Publisher. **Subscription:** $89 single issue.
Ad Rates: BW: $688   **Circulation:** Paid ‡4,000
          4C: $850   Non-paid ‡110,000
          PCI: $20
Additional Contact Information: Fax extension: 1467.

🎙 **1584 KTPR-FM - 91.1**
330 Ave. M   Phone: (515)955-5877
Fort Dodge, IA 50501   Fax: (515)576-7206

GLENWOOD

📖 **1585 Glenwood Opinion Tribune**
Landmark Communications, Inc.
PO Box 191   Phone: (712)527-3191
Glenwood, IA 51534   Fax: (712)527-3193

GOWRIE

📖 **1586 The Gowrie News**
Box 473   Phone: (515)352-3325
Gowrie, IA 50543   Fax: (515)352-3309

HARLAN

📖 **1587 Harlan PennySaver**
1114 7th St.
PO Box 721   Phone: (712)755-3111
Harlan, IA 51537-0721   Fax: (712)755-3324
Shopper. **Frequency:** Weekly. **Printing Method:** Offset. **Cols./Page:** 6. **Col. Width:** 10 1/2 picas. **Key Personnel:** Alan Mores, Publisher. **Subscription:** Free.
Ad Rates: GLR: $3.06   **Circulation:** Free ‡10,500
          BW: $261

HOLSTEIN

📖 **1588 The Advance**
The ADVANCE Inc.
116 N. Main
PO Box 550
Holstein, IA 51025   Phone: (712)368-4368
Former Title: Holstein Advance

HUDSON

📖 **1589 Hudson Herald**
Box 210   Phone: (319)988-3855
Hudson, IA 50643   Fax: (319)988-3855

IDA GROVE

📖 **1590 Ida County Pioneer-Record**
PO Box 31   Phone: (712)364-2022
Ida Grove, IA 51445   Fax: (712)364-2044

IOWA CITY

📖 **1591 Common Lives/Lesbian Lives**
PO Box 1553
Iowa City, IA 52244   Phone: (319)353-6265
Magazine focusing on the lives of lesbians. Includes lesbian history, biography, correspondence, journal entries, fiction, poetry, and visual art. **Frequency:** Quarterly.
                         Circulation: (Not Reported)

📖 **1592 Iowa Law Review**
University of Iowa
College of Law   Phone: (319)335-9132
Iowa City, IA 52242-1113   Fax: (319)335-9019

📖 **1593 Legislative Studies Quarterly**
Comparative Legislative Research Center
University of Iowa
349 Schaeffer Hall   Phone: (319)335-2361
Iowa City, IA 52242   Fax: (319)335-3211

🎙 **1594 Heritage Communications, Inc.**
Box 4500
Iowa City, IA 52240-4453   Phone: (319)351-3670
Owner: Tele-Communications, Inc. **Founded:** 1980. **Cities Served:** Johnston County, Coralville, and University Heights, IA.

KEOKUK

🎙 **1595 KOKX-AM - 1310**
PO Box 427   Phone: (319)524-5410
Keokuk, IA 52632-0427   Fax: (319)524-7275

KEYSTONE

🎙 **1596 South Benton Cablevision, Inc.**
86 Main St.   Phone: (319)442-3243
Keystone, IA 52249-0277   Fax: (319)442-3210
Owner: Keystone Farmers Cooperative Telephone Co., at above address. **Key Personnel:** John C. Brady, Mgr. **Cities Served:** Keystone, Garrison, and Elberon, IA: 363 subscribing households; 23 channels; 1 community access channel; 168 hours per week of community access programming.

LAKE PARK

📖 **1597 News**
PO Box 157   Phone: (712)832-3131
Lake Park, IA 51347   Fax: (712)832-3131

LOGAN

📖 **1598 Logan Herald-Observer**
Bloom Publishing Co. 112 S. 4th Ave.
PO Box 148   Phone: (712)644-2705
Logan, IA 51546-0148   Fax: (712)647-3081

LYNNVILLE

1599 NASDA Quarterly
North American South Devon Association
Box 68   Phone: (515)527-2437
Lynnville, IA 50163   Fax: (515)594-4498
Trade magazine. **Founded:** 1978. **Frequency:** Quarterly. **Cols./Page:** 3.
Key Personnel: Dr. T.E. Fitzpatrick, Exec.Sec. **Subscription:** $4. $1
single issue.
                                          Circulation: 4,000
Advertising accepted; contact publisher for rates.

MARSHALLTOWN

1600 Pennysaver
507 E. Anson
Box 246   Phone: (515)752-6630
Marshalltown, IA 50158   **Fax: (515)752-7073**

MASON CITY

1601 The Mason City Shopper
Lee Enterprises
938 N. Federal
Box 1506   Phone: (515)424-3044
Mason City, IA 50401   Fax: (515)424-6786

MISSOURI VALLEY

1602 Missouri Valley Merchandiser
501 E. Erie   Phone: (712)642-2791
Missouri Valley, IA 51555   **Fax: (712)642-2595**

OSAGE

1603 KCZY-FM - 92.7
200 N. 7th St.   **Phone: (515)228-1000**
Osage, IA 50461   **Fax: (515)228-1200**

OSKALOOSA

1604 KBOE-FM - 104.9
PO Box 380   Phone: (515)673-3493
Oskaloosa, IA 52577-0380   Fax: (515)673-3495
Format: Contemporary Country. **Network(s):** ABC. **Owner:** Jomast
Corp., at above address. **Founded:** 1969. **Formerly:** KOSK-FM (1991).
Operating Hours: 5 a.m.-midnight. **ADI:** Des Moines, IA. **Key
Personnel:** Scott Ewing, Gen. Mgr./Sales Mgr.; Holly Toom, Assistant
and Office Mgr.; Gary Engel, News Dir.; Doug Broek, Sports Dir.
Wattage: 50,000. **Ad Rates:** $9.60 for 30 seconds; $11.60 for 60
seconds. **Additional Contact Information:** Toll-free: 800-728-5868.

PERRY

1605 Chiefland Shopper
Chief Printing Co.
1323 2nd St.
PO Box 98   Phone: (515)465-4666
Perry, IA 50220   **Fax: (515)465-3087**

1606 Chiefland's Central Iowa Farm Magazine
PO Box 98   Phone: (515)465-4666
Perry, IA 50220   **Fax: (515)465-3087**

POCAHONTAS

1607 Pocahontas County Advertiser
218 N. Main   Phone: (712)335-3553
Pocahontas, IA 50574   **Fax: (712)335-3554**

1608 Pocahontas Record Democrat
218 N. Main   Phone: (712)335-3553
Pocahontas, IA 50574   **Fax: (712)335-3554**

POSTVILLE

1609 The Postville Herald-Leader
PO Box 100   **Phone: (319)864-3333**
Postville, IA 52162-0580   **Fax: (319)864-3400**

SCHLESWIG

1610 Schleswig Leader
105 1/2 Second St.
PO Box 70   Phone: (712)676-3414
Schleswig, IA 51461   **Fax: (712)882-1206**

SHELDON

1611 KIWA-FM - 105.5
411 9th St.   Phone: (712)324-2597
Sheldon, IA 51201   Fax: (712)324-2340

SIOUX CENTER

1612 Sioux Center Shopper
67 3rd St. NE   Phone: (712)722-0511
Sioux Center, IA 51250   **Fax: (712)722-0507**

SIOUX CITY

1613 Folkart Treasures
Forkart Treasures
2740 S. Paxton
Sioux City, IA 51106
Magazine focuses on country living products. **Frequency:** Quarterly.
Key Personnel: Jennifer Winquist, Editor. **Subscription:** $19.95. $4
single issue.
                                          Circulation: (Not Reported)

1614 Sooland Cablecom Corp.
900 Steuben St.   Phone: (712)233-2000
Sioux City, IA 51101   Fax: (712)233-2235
Owner: Post-Newsweek Cable, Inc. **Founded:** 1979. **Cities Served:**
Woodbury County, and Sergeant Bluff, IA; Union County, Dakota
Dunes, and North Sioux City, SD.

THOMPSON

1615 The Thompson Courier-Rake Register
PO Box 318   Phone: (515)584-2770
Thompson, IA 50478-0318   Fax: (515)582-4442
Former Title: Thompson Courier

TIPTON

1616 Clarence-Lowden Sun News
Conservative Publishing Co.
Box 271   Phone: (319)886-2131
Tipton, IA 52772   Fax: (319)886-6466
Rural newspaper. **Founded:** 1879. **Frequency:** Weekly. **Printing Meth-
od:** Offset. **Cols./Page:** 6. **Col. Width:** 10 in. **Col. Depth:** 16 in. **Key
Personnel:** Pat Kroemer, Editor; Sally Taylor, Publisher; L. Miller,
Advertising Mgr. **Subscription:** $14; $17 out of area.
Ad Rates: GLR: $.18   **Circulation:** ‡1,212
               BW: $218
               4C: $348
               PCI: $2.52

WALNUT

1617 Tradition Magazine
National Traditional Country Music Assn.
PO Box 438   Phone: (712)784-3001
Walnut, IA 51557   **Fax: (712)784-2010**

WAPELLO

1618 Richland Plainsman-Clarion
Louisa Publishing Co. Ltd.
Wapello, IA 52653   Fax: (319)523-8167
Newspaper. **Frequency:** Daily. **Key Personnel:** Michael Hodger, Editor. **USPS:** 986-780. **Subscription:** $16; $18 out of county; $23 out of state.
Ad Rates: SAU: $3.63   **Circulation:** 1,378
                PCI: $3.08

WATERLOO

1619 KFMW-FM - 107.9
514 Jefferson St.   Phone: (319)234-2200
Waterloo, IA 50701   Fax: (319)234-9999
Format: Contemporary Hit Radio (CHR). **Network(s):** Unistar. **Owner:** Park Radio of Iowa, Inc./ Park Communications Group. **Formerly:** KWWL-FM. **Operating Hours:** Continuous. **Key Personnel:** Don Morehead, Gen. Mgr.; Fred Hendrickson, Sales Mgr.; Mark Hansen, Program Dir.; Kathy Flynn, News Dir.; Dolly Fortier, Public Service Dir. **Wattage:** 100,000.

1620 WestMarc Cable TV
Box 2457
Waterloo, IA 50702-6118   Phone: (319)232-8800
Owner: Tele-Communications, Inc. **Founded:** 1979. **Cities Served:** Black Hawk County, IA.

WEST BRANCH

1621 West Branch Times
Sun Dog Press, Inc.
PO Box 368   Phone: (319)643-2131
West Branch, IA 52358   **Fax: (319)643-2848**

WINTHROP

1622 The Winthrop News
Box A   Phone: (319)935-3027
Winthrop, IA 50682   **Fax: (319)935-3082**

KANSAS

ABILENE

📖 **1623 Central Marketplace**
Reflector Chronicle Publishing Corp.
303 N. Broadway
PO Box 8
Abilene, KS 67410
Phone: (913)263-1000
Fax: (913)263-1645

ALTA VISTA

📖 **1624 Alta Vista Journal**
White City Printing Co.
PO Box 278
Alta Vista, KS 66834
Phone: (913)349-5516
Fax: (913)349-5516

ANDOVER

📖 **1625 The Andover Journal Advocate**
The Andover Journal Publishing, Inc.
324 W. Central, No. D
PO Box 271
Andover, KS 67002
Phone: (316)733-2002

ATWOOD

🎙 **1626 Atwood Cable Systems Inc.**
423 State St.
Atwood, KS 67730
Phone: (913)626-3261
Fax: (913)626-9005

CALDWELL

📖 **1627 The Caldwell Messenger**
PO Box 313
Caldwell, KS 67022
Phone: (316)845-2320
Fax: (316)845-6461

CHANUTE

🎙 **1628 KKOY-FM - 105.5**
Box 788
Chanute, KS 66720
Phone: (316)431-3700
Fax: (316)431-4643

COFFEYVILLE

📖 **1629 Arabian Horse Express**
PO Box 845
Coffeyville, KS 67337
Phone: (316)251-7340
Fax: (316)251-4717

DERBY

🎙 **1630 KYFW-FM - 88.3**
243 Harrel St.
Derby, KS 67037-2628
Phone: (316)788-7883
Format: Religious. **Owner:** Bible Broadcasting Network Inc., Charlotte, NC. **Founded:** 1988. **Formerly:** KCEV-FM (1990). **Operating Hours:** Continuous. **Key Personnel:** Matt Johnson, Station Mgr. **Wattage:** 17,000.

ELLSWORTH

📖 **1631 Rice County Monitor-Journal**
Ellsworth Reporter
PO Box 7
Ellsworth, KS 67439
Phone: (913)472-3103
Fax: (913)472-3268
Community newspaper. **Frequency:** Weekly. **Printing Method:** Offset. **Cols./Page:** 6. **Col. Width:** 12 picas. **Key Personnel:** Phyllis Whiteman, Editor; Kami K. Gaston, Publisher. **Subscription:** $14.74.
Ad Rates: GLR: $.18
BW: $225
PCI: $2.64
Circulation: 718

EMPORIA

🎙 **1632 KEGS-FM - 101.7**
322 Commercial
Emporia, KS 66801
Phone: (316)343-8525
Fax: (316)343-8528

FORT LEAVENWORTH

📖 **1633 Military Review**
USACGSC
ATTN: ATZL-SWM-R
Fort Leavenworth, KS 66027-6910
Phone: (913)684-5642
Fax: (913)684-2448

GARDEN CITY

🎙 **1634 KBUF-AM - 1030**
1309 E. Fulton St.
Garden City, KS 67846
Phone: (316)276-2366
Fax: (316)276-3568

🎙 **1635 KWKR-FM - 99.9**
308 N. 7th St.
PO Box 878
Garden City, KS 67846
Phone: (316)276-3251
Fax: (316)276-3649
Format: Classic Rock. **Network(s):** Unistar. **Owner:** Threjay, Inc., at above address. **Founded:** 1983. **Operating Hours:** 5 a.m.-1 a.m. **Key Personnel:** Ronald C. Isham, Pres.; Judith Isham, V.P.; Doug Wagner, Sales Mgr.; Scott Roberts, Operations Mgr.; Donald Brintnall, Chief

Ad Rates: GLR = general line rate; BW = one-time black & white page rate; 4C = one-time four color page rate; SAU = standard advertising unit rate; CNU = Canadian newspaper advertising unit rate; PCI = per column inch rate.
Circulation: ★ = ABC; △ = BPA; ◆ = CAC; ● = CCAB; □ = VAC; ⊕ = PO Statement; ‡ = Publisher's Report; Boldface figures = sworn; Light figures = estimated.
Entry type: 📖 = Print; 🎙 = Broadcast.

107

Engineer. **Wattage:** 99,000. **Ad Rates:** $6-$27 for 30 seconds; $9-$40.50 for 60 seconds.

GARDNER

📖 **1636 The Spring Hill New Era**
Tri-County Newspapers
PO Box 303　　　　　　　　　　　Phone: (913)884-7615
Gardner, KS 66030　　　　　　　　Fax: (913)884-6707
Newspaper. **Founded:** 1893. **Frequency:** Weekly. **Key Personnel:** Janet Swanson, Editor. **Subscription:** $17; $20 out of state.
　　　　　　　　　　　　　　Circulation: Paid 1,000
　　　　　　　　　　　　　　　　　　　　Free 1,800

Advertising accepted; contact publisher for rates.

GOODLAND

🎙 **1637 KKCI-FM - 102.5**
Box 569
Broadcast Plaza　　　　　　　　　Phone: (913)899-2309
Goodland, KS 67735　　　　　　　**Fax: (913)899-3138**

🎙 **1638 KLOE-AM - 730**
Box 569
Broadcast Plaza　　　　　　　　　Phone: (913)899-2309
Goodland, KS 67735　　　　　　　**Fax: (913)899-3138**

GREAT BEND

🎙 **1639 KVGB-AM - 1590**
PO Box 609
Great Bend, KS 67530　　　　　　Phone: (316)792-4317
Format: Contemporary Country. **Owner:** Forward of Kansas, Inc. **Operating Hours:** Continuous. **Key Personnel:** George Donley, V.P./Gen. Mgr.; Michael Carson, Traffic and Program Dir.; Mark Springfeldt, Music Dir.; J. Schaeffer, News Dir. **Wattage:** 5000.

🎙 **1640 KVGB-FM - 104.3**
PO Box 609
Great Bend, KS 67530　　　　　　Phone: (316)792-4317
Format: Contemporary Country. **Owner:** Forward of Kansas, Inc. **Founded:** 1937. **Operating Hours:** Continuous. **Key Personnel:** George Donley, V.P./Gen. Mgr.; Micheal Carson, Traffic and Program Dir.; Mark Springfeldt, Music Dir.; J. Schaefer, News Dir.; George Donley, V.P./Gen. Mgr.; Michael Carson, Program and Traffic Dir.; Mark Springfeldt, Music Dir.; J. Schaefer, News Dir. **Wattage:** 10,000.

HAYS

🎙 **1641 Hays Cable TV Co.**
2300 Hall St.　　　　　　　　　　Phone: (913)625-5910
Hays, KS 67601　　　　　　　　　**Fax: (913)625-8030**

🎙 **1642 KJLS-FM - 103.3**
107 W. 13th
Box 364　　　　　　　　　　　　Phone: (913)628-1064
Hays, KS 67601　　　　　　　　　**Fax: (913)628-1822**

HUTCHINSON

🎙 **1643 KSKU-FM - 106.1**
106 N. Main　　　　　　　　　　Phone: (316)665-5758
Hutchinson, KS 67501　　　　　　**Fax: (316)665-6655**

🎙 **1644 KWHK-AM - 1260**
106 W. 43rd Ave.　　　　　　　　Phone: (316)663-4461
Hutchinson, KS 67502　　　　　　**Fax: (316)662-1481**

JUNCTION CITY

🎙 **1645 Tristar Cable, Inc.**
Box 1829
Junction City, KS 66441　　　　　Phone: (913)238-3099

LA CROSSE

📖 **1646 The Rush County News**
PO Box 39　　　　　　　　　　　Phone: (913)222-2555
La Crosse, KS 67548　　　　　　　**Fax: (913)222-2460**

LARNED

🎙 **1647 KANS-AM - 1510**
200 E. 8th　　　　　　　　　　　Phone: (316)285-2127
Larned, KS 67550　　　　　　　　Fax: (316)285-2101
Format: Adult Contemporary. **Network(s):** Satellite Network News; Kansas Information; Kansas Agriculture. **Owner:** C and C Consulting, 1713 Clark Ave., Emporia, KS 66801; (316)342-7375. **Operating Hours:** 6 a.m.-midnight. **Key Personnel:** R.D. Carter, Gen. Mgr.; Danny Stevens, Program Dir. **Wattage:** 1000.

🎙 **1648 KQDF-FM - 96.7**
200 E. 8th　　　　　　　　　　　Phone: (316)285-2127
Larned, KS 67550　　　　　　　　Fax: (316)285-2101
Format: Adult Contemporary. **Network(s):** Kansas Information; Kansas Agriculture. **Owner:** C and C Consulting. **Operating Hours:** 6 a.m.-midnight. **Key Personnel:** Dan Gilkey, Operations Mgr.; R.D. Carter, Contact. **Wattage:** 3000. **Ad Rates:** $6.50-$8 for 30 seconds; $7.50-$9.50 for 60 seconds. Combined rates available with KANS-AM.

LAWRENCE

📖 **1649 The C Users Journal**
R & D Publications
1601 W. 23rd St., Ste. 200　　　　Phone: (913)841-1631
Lawrence, KS 66046-0127　　　　Fax: (913)841-2624
Magazine providing advanced information for C and C developers worldwide. **Founded:** 1987. **Frequency:** Monthly. **Printing Method:** Web offset. **Trim Size:** 8 1/4 x 10 7/8. **Cols./Page:** 3. **Col. Width:** 13 picas. **Col. Depth:** 54 picas. **Key Personnel:** Robert Ward, Publisher; Diane Thomas, Managing Editor; P.J. Planger, Senior Editor. **ISSN:** 0898-9788. **Subscription:** $29.95. $4.50 single issue.
Ad Rates:　BW:　$1,630　　　**Circulation:** Paid ★35,679
　　　　　　　4C:　$2,060　　　　　　　Non-paid ★1,881

📖 **1650 Ethnicity & Disease**
International Society for Hypertension in Blacks
PO Box 1897　　　　　　　　　　Phone: (913)843-1221
Lawrence, KS 66044-8897　　　　Fax: (913)843-1274
Journal devoted to studying population differences in disease patterns. **Founded:** 1991. **Frequency:** Quarterly. **Key Personnel:** Richard S. Cooper, Editor. **ISSN:** 1049-510X. **Subscription:** $90; $98 foreign.
　　　　　　　　　　　　　　Circulation: (Not Reported)

📖 **1651 Modelling of Geo-Biosphere Processes**
Catena Verlag
PO Box 1897　　　　　　　　　　Phone: (913)843-1221
Lawrence, KS 66044-8897　　　　Fax: (913)843-1274
Journal concerning the modelling of the micro- and macroscale processes in the systems of the geo-biosphere. **Founded:** 1991. **Frequency:** Quarterly. **Key Personnel:** Y. Mualem, Editor. **ISSN:** 0938-9563. **Subscription:** $132.
　　　　　　　　　　　　　　Circulation: (Not Reported)

MANHATTAN

📖 **1652 Jazz Educators Journal**
International Assn. of Jazz Educators
PO Box 724　　　　　　　　　　　Phone: (913)776-8744
Manhattan, KS 66502　　　　　　**Fax: (913)776-6190**

📖 **1653 Kansas Quarterly**
Kansas State University
English Department　　　　　　　　Phone: (913)532-6716
Manhattan, KS 66506　　　　　　**Fax: (913) 532-7004**

📖 **1654 Literary Magazine Review**
English Dept.
Kansas State University　　　　　　Phone: (913)532-6716
Manhattan, KS 66506　　　　　　**Fax: (913) 532-7004**

🎙 **1655 TCI of Kansas, Inc.**
Box 788
Manhattan, KS 66502-6083　　　　Phone: (913)776-9239
Owner: Tele-Communications, Inc. **Founded:** 1961. **Cities Served:** Pottawatomie and Riley counties, KS.

MARYSVILLE

◻ **1656 The Marysville Advocate**
107 S. 9th
Box 271
Marysville, KS 66508-0271   Phone: (913)562-2317

MCPHERSON

🎙 **1657 KBBE-FM - 101.7**
Box 1069   Phone: (316)241-1504
McPherson, KS 67460   Fax: (316)241-3078
Format: Adult Contemporary; Contemporary Country. **Owner:** Davies Communications Inc. **Founded:** 1974. **Operating Hours:** 6 a.m.-midnight. **Key Personnel:** Jerry Davies, General and Sales Mgr.; Diane Davies, Program Dir.; Jon Chelesnik, News and Sports Dir.; Wanda Morris, Office Mgr. **Wattage:** 3000.

🎙 **1658 Multimedia Cablevision of McPherson**
322 N. Main
Box 887
McPherson, KS 67460   Phone: (316)241-6880
Owner: Multimedia Cablevision, Inc. **Founded:** 1981. **Formerly:** McPherson Cablevision. **Key Personnel:** Susan Cooper, Office Mgr.; Steve Lies, System Mgr. **Cities Served:** McPherson, KS; 3600 subscribing households; 29 channels; 2 community access channel; 24 hours per week of community access programming.

MINNEAPOLIS

🎙 **1659 Cablevision of Miltonvale**
302 W. 2nd St.
PO Box 150
Minneapolis, KS 67467   Phone: (913)392-3505
Owner: Cablevision of Texas, at above address. **Cities Served:** Miltonvale,KS. 186 subscribing households.

🎙 **1660 Cablevision of Minneapolis**
100 N. Concord
PO Box 150
Minneapolis, KS 67467   Phone: (913)392-3505
Owner: Cablevision of Texas, PO Box 310, Lockney, TX 79241. **Cities Served:** Minneapolis, KS. 620 subscribing households; 24 channels. 1 community access channel; 2 hours per week of community access programming.

🎙 **1661 Cablevision of Texas**
PO Box 150
Minneapolis, KS 67467   Phone: (913)392-3505
Owner: Cablevision of Texas, PO Box 310, Lockney, TX 79241. **Cities Served:** 30. 500 subscribing households.

MONTEZUMA

◻ **1662 Montezuma Press**
200 Aztec
PO Box 188   Phone: (316)846-2312
Montezuma, KS 67867   **Fax: (316)846-2312**

NEWTON

🎙 **1663 TCI of Kansas**
206 W. 6th St.
Box 684   Phone: (316)283-7270
Newton, KS 67114   Fax: (316)283-7622
Owner: Tele-Communications, Inc. **Founded:** 1976. **Formerly:** Newton Cable TV; Crest Communications. **Key Personnel:** Ray Hubbard, System Mgr.; Troy Boaz, Chief Technician; Marilyn Lundblade, Office Mgr. **Cities Served:** Newton and North Newton, KS: 33 channels. Halstead, Valley Center, Peabody, Park City, Buhler, Nickerson, Sedgwick, Hesston, Maize, Haven, and Inman: 24 channels. All systems: 1 community access channel; 168 hours per week of community access programming.

NORTH NEWTON

🎙 **1664 KBCU-FM - 88.1**
300 E. 27th St.   Phone: (316)284-5228
North Newton, KS 67117   Fax: (316)284-5286

OSAGE CITY

◻ **1665 Osage County Chronicle**
403 Market St.
PO Box 248   Phone: (913)528-3215
Osage City, KS 66523   Fax: (913)528-3210

◻ **1666 Osage County Journal**
Osage County Publishing Co., Inc.
403 Market St.
Osage City, KS 66523   Phone: (913)528-3215
Ceased publication.

OTTAWA

🎙 **1667 KOFO-AM - 1220**
PO Box 16
Ottawa, KS 66067   Phone: (913)242-1220

🎙 **1668 KTJO-FM - 88.9**
Ottawa University
1001 S. Cedar
PO Box 10   Phone: (913)242-5200
Ottawa, KS 66067-3399   **Fax: (913)242-7429**

OVERLAND PARK

◻ **1669 Beverages**
International Beverage Publishers, Inc.
10741 El Monte
PO Box 7406   Phone: (913)341-0020
Overland Park, KS 66211   Fax: (913)341-3025
Ceased publication.

◻ **1670 Equine Veterinary Journal**
Veterinary Learning Systems
10950 Grandview Dr., No. 458   Phone: (913)451-3475
Overland Park, KS 66210   Fax: (913)451-3929
Ceased publication.

◻ **1671 R.E.P.**
Intertec Publishing Corp.
9800 Metcalf   Phone: (913)341-1300
Overland Park, KS 66212-2215   Fax: (913)967-1898
Ceased publication.

🎙 **1672 KJLA-AM - 1190**
8826 Santa Fe Dr., No. 300   Phone: (913)341-5552
Overland Park, KS 66212-3672   **Fax: (913)341-0811**

🎙 **1673 TeleCable of Overland Park, Inc.**
8221 W. 119th St.
Box 12922
Overland Park, KS 66213   Phone: (913)451-5858
Owner: TeleCable Corp. **Founded:** 1971. **Cities Served:** Johnson County, KS.

PITTSBURG

🎙 **1674 KKOW-FM - 96.9**
Rte. 5, Box 45   Phone: (316)231-7200
Pittsburg, KS 66762   **Fax: (316)231-3321**

🎙 **1675 KOAM-TV - Channel 7**
Box 659   **Phone: (417)624-0233**
Pittsburg, KS 66762   **Fax: (417)624-3115**

⬥ **1676 KSEK-AM - 1340**
1340 E. Quincy   Phone: (316)232-1340
Pittsburg, KS 66762   **Fax: (316)232-6341**

SAINT MARYS

📖 **1677 St. Marys Star**
517 W. Bertrand
PO Box 190   Phone: (913)437-2935
Saint Marys, KS 66536-0190   **Fax: (913)437-2095**

SALINA

⬥ **1678 KHCD-FM - 89.5**
815 N. Walnut, Ste. 300   Phone: (316)665-3555
Hutchinson, KS 67501   **Fax: (316)662-6740**

⬥ **1679 TCI of Kansas, Inc.**
Box 1577
Salina, KS 67401-2640   Phone: (913)825-7175
Owner: Tele-Communications, Inc. **Founded:** 1962. **Cities Served:**
Saline County, KS.

SCOTT CITY

📖 **1680 News Chronicle**
News Chronicle Printing Co., Inc.
PO Box 218   Phone: (316)872-2114
Scott City, KS 67871   **Fax: (316)872-3672**

⬥ **1681 KFLA-AM - 1310**
Rte. 1, Box 14   Phone: (316)872-5345
Scott City, KS 67871   Fax: (316)872-5346
Format: Religious. **Network(s):** USA Radio; Kansas Information;
Kansas Agriculture. **Owner:** West Jewell Management, Inc., 6535 W.
Jewell Ave., Denver, CO 80226. **Founded:** 1962. **Operating Hours:** 6
a.m.-11 p.m. **Key Personnel:** Everet M. Green, Station Mgr. **Wattage:**
500 day. **Ad Rates:** $5.25 for 30 seconds;$6.30 for 60 seconds.

SENECA

⬥ **1682 Cablevision Inc.**
522 Main St.
Box 127
Seneca, KS 66538   Phone: (913)336-6157
Owner: James Doucette. **Key Personnel:** Mark Heideman, Gen. Mgr.
Cities Served: Seneca, Sabetha, Onaga, Havensville, Blue Rapids, and
Barnes, KS: 2,506 subscribing households; 2 community access
channels. **Additional Contact Information:** Toll-free: 800-530-4384.

STERLING

📖 **1683 Sterling Bulletin**
105 S. Broadway
PO Box 97   Phone: (316)278-2114
Sterling, KS 67579   **Fax: (316)278-2114**

TOPEKA

📖 **1684 Kansas Monthly Employment Review**
Kansas Dept. of Human Resources-Labor Market Information
  Services
401 SW Topeka Blvd.   Phone: (913)296-5058
Topeka, KS 66603-3182   **Fax: (913)296-5286**

⬥ **1685 KTWU-TV - Channel 11**
301 N. Wanamaker Rd.   Phone: (913)272-8181
Topeka, KS 66606-9601   **Fax: (913)271-2850**

⬥ **1686 TCI of Kansas, Inc.**
1615 Washburn Ave.
Topeka, KS 66604-2880   Phone: (913)233-5081
Owner: Tele-Communications, Inc. **Founded:** 1977. **Cities Served:**
Shawnee County, KS.

ULYSSES

⬥ **1687 KFXX-FM - 106.7**
PO Box 1067   Phone: (316)356-1420
Ulysses, KS 67880   **Fax: (316)356-3635**

⬥ **1688 KULY-AM - 1420**
PO Box 1067   Phone: (316)356-1420
Ulysses, KS 67880   **Fax: (316)356-3635**

WHITE CITY

📖 **1689 White City Reporter**
PO Box 278   Phone: (913)349-5516
White City, KS 66872   **Fax: (913)349-5516**

WICHITA

📖 **1690 Active Aging**
Friends University
1910 University   Phone: (316)264-7353
Wichita, KS 67213   **Fax: (316)264-0127**

📖 **1691 Heart of the City**
Finney Communications Inc.
PO Box 48479
Wichita, KS 67201   Phone: (316)652-0036
Subtitle: Magazine Celebrating Wichita's African American Lifestyle.
Founded: 1990. **Frequency:** 6x/yr. **Printing Method:** Web offset. **Trim
Size:** 8 1/4 x 11. **Key Personnel:** G. Finney-Knight, Publisher; Brenda
Gray, Editor. **ISSN:** 1060-667X. **Subscription:** $7.95.
                              Circulation: Paid ‡4,000
Advertising accepted; contact publisher for rates. **Additional Contact
Information:** Publisher, (316)684-4361.

⬥ **1692 AirCapital Cablevision, Inc.**
701 E. Douglas
Box 3027   Phone: (316)262-4270
Wichita, KS 67201   Fax: (316)252-2309
Owner: Multimedia Cablevision, Inc. **Founded:** 1979. **Cities Served:**
Sedgwick County, Bel Aire, Eastborough, Kechi, and Park City, KS.

⬥ **1693 KEYN-FM - 103.7**
2829 Salina Ave.   Phone: (316)838-7744
Wichita, KS 67204   **Fax: (316)832-0061**

⬥ **1694 KMUW-FM - 89.1**
3317 E. 17th St.   Phone: (316)682-5737
Wichita, KS 67208   **Fax: (316)689-3946**

KENTUCKY

ASHLAND

♨ **1695 Dimension Cable**
225 Russell Rd., US 23 N.
Box 1357
Ashland, KY 41160   Phone: (606)329-2990
Owner: Times Mirror Cable TV. **Founded:** 1970. **Cities Served:**
Ashland and Boyd counties, KY.

BENTON

▥ **1696 Leisure Scene**
PO Box 410   Phone: (502)527-3162
Benton, KY 42025   Fax: (502)527-3925
Summer tourist magazine. **Founded:** 1970. **Frequency:** Weekly (summer only). **Printing Method:** Offset. **Cols./Page:** 6. **Col. Depth:** 13 in.
Key Personnel: Greg Travis, Editor; Terri Dunnigan, Advertising Mgr.
Subscription: Free.
Ad Rates: BW: $234   **Circulation:** Free ‡20,000
            4C: $384
            PCI: $3

BEREA

♨ **1697 WKXO-FM - 106.7**
406 Chestnut St.
Box 307   Phone: (606)986-9321
Berea, KY 40403   **Fax: (606)986-8675**

BOWLING GREEN

▥ **1698 Country Peddler**
PO Box 492   Phone: (502)842-3314
Bowling Green, KY 42102   Fax: (502)782-1625

▥ **1699 The Journal of Coal Quality**
The Society for Applied Coal Science
Western Kentucky University
313 TCNW   Phone: (502)745-6244
Bowling Green, KY 42101   **Fax: (502)745-6244**

♨ **1700 Storer Cable Communications of Southern Kentucky**
515 Double Springs Rd.
PO Box 659   Phone: (502)782-0903
Bowling Green, KY 42102-0659   Fax: (502)782-8355
Owner: Storer Cable Communications. **Founded:** 1981. **Key Personnel:**
Sarah Glenn Grise, Gen. Mgr.; Rick Williams, Mktg. Mgr.; Sheryl
Morris, Program Coordinator; Don Jones, Technical Mgr.; Jean
Secrest, Sales Mgr. **Cities Served:** Bowling Green, Oakland, Smiths
Grove, Woodburn, Plum Springs, and the unincorporated areas of
Warren County, KY: 19,000 subscribing households; 40 channels; 5

community access channels; 20 hours per week of community access
programming.

BRANDENBURG

♨ **1701 WMMG-AM - 1140**
1715 By-Pass Rd.   Phone: (502)422-3961
Brandenburg, KY 40108   **Fax: (502)422-3464**

♨ **1702 WMMG-FM - 93.5**
1715 By-Pass Rd.   Phone: (502)422-3961
Brandenburg, KY 40108   **Fax: (502)422-3464**

CLINTON

▥ **1703 Hickman County Gazette**
Hwy. 51 S.
PO Box 100   Phone: (502)653-3381
Clinton, KY 42031   **Fax: (502)653-2583**

COVINGTON

♨ **1704 Storer Communications**
717 Madison Ave.
Covington, KY 41012   Phone: (616)431-0300
Owner: Storer Cable Communications. **Founded:** 1981. **Cities Served:**
Boone County, Campbell County, Kenton County, Alexandria, Bellvue, Bromley, Burlington, Camp Springs, Claryville, Cold Spring,
Constance, Crescent Park, Crescent Springs, Crestview Hills, Crittenden, Edgewood, Elsmere, Erlanger, Fairview, Florence, Fort Mitchell,
Fort Thomas, Fort Wright, Hebron, Highland Heights, Independence,
Lakeside Park, Latonia Lakes, Ludlow, Melbourne, Morning View,
Park Hills, Ridgeview Heights, Ryland Heights, Silver Grove, Southgate, Taylor Mill, Union, Villa Hills, Visalia, Walton, Wilder, and
Woodlawn, KY.

EDMONTON

♨ **1705 WKNK-FM - 99.1**
PO Box 457   Phone: (502)651-6050
Glasgow, KY 42142-0457   Fax: (502)651-7666
Format: Country. **Network(s):** KyNet. **Owner:** Newberry Broadcasting,
Inc., at above address. **Founded:** 1990. **Operating Hours:** Continuous.
ADI: Nashville (Cookeville), TN. **Key Personnel:** Steven W. Newberry, Pres.; Vickie Hatchett, Gen. Mgr.; Dale Thornhill, Operations
Mgr.; Tim Hurst, Gen. Sales Mgr. **Wattage:** 3000. **Ad Rates:** $4-$8 for
30 seconds; $5-$9 for 60 seconds. Combined rates available with
WHHT-FM.

ELIZABETHTOWN

1706 TeleScripps Cable Co.
2919 Ring Rd.   Phone: (502)737-4200
Elizabethtown, KY 42701   Fax: (502)737-3379
Owner: Howard Scripps Cable Co. **Founded:** 1965. **Cities Served:**
Hardin County, KY.

ELKTON

1707 Todd County Standard
PO Box 308
Public Sq.   **Phone: (502)265-2439**
Elkton, KY 42220   Fax: (502)265-2571

FALMOUTH

1708 The Falmouth Outlook
Cynthiana Democrat
210 Main St.   Phone: (606)654-3333
Falmouth, KY 41040   **Fax: (606)654-4365**

1709 The Shopper's Outlook
The Falmouth Outlook
210 Main St.   Phone: (606)654-3333
Falmouth, KY 41040   **Fax: (606)654-4365**

FRANKFORT

1710 Kentucky Beverage Journal
Midway Publications, Inc.
PO Box 346   **Phone: (606)846-5231**
Frankfort, KY 40347   **Fax: (606)846-4378**

1711 Frankfort Electric & Water Plant Board
315 W. 2nd St.
Frankfort, KY 40301   Phone: (502)223-3401
Owner: Community Cable Service. **Founded:** 1952. **Cities Served:**
Franklin and Shelby counties, KY.

GRAYSON

1712 WKCC-FM - 96.7
617 N. Carol Malone Blvd.
Grayson, KY 41143-1199   **Phone: (606)474-3257**

1713 WUGO-FM - 102.3
US-60 W.   Phone: (606)474-5144
Grayson, KY 41143   Fax: (606)474-7777
Format: Adult Contemporary. **Network(s):** CBS. **Owner:** Carter Coun-
ty Broadcasting Co., Inc., PO Box 487, Grayson, KY 41143;
(606)474-5144. **Founded:** 1967. **Operating Hours:** 6 a.m.-midnight.
Key Personnel: Francis Nash, Mgr.; Jim Phillips, News Dir.; Terry
Kidd, Music Dir.; Jeff Roe, Traffic Dir. **Wattage:** 4800. **Ad Rates:**
$2.20-$3.50 for 15 seconds; $3.20-$4.80 for 30 seconds; $4-$6 for 60
seconds.

GREENSBURG

1714 WAKY-AM - 1550
Box 246   Phone: (502)932-7401
Greensburg, KY 42743   Fax: (502)932-7402
Format: Oldies. **Owner:** Veer Broadcasting. **Founded:** 1972. **Formerly:**
WGRK-AM. **Operating Hours:** Sunrise-sunset. **Key Personnel:** Mi-
chael R. Wilson, V.P./Gen. Mgr.; Joy Wilson, Sales Mgr. **Wattage:**
1000. **Additional Contact Information:** (502)789-1464.

HINDMAN

1715 Troublesome Creek Times
Knott County Publishing Co., Inc.
PO Box 700   Phone: (606)785-5134
Hindman, KY 41822-0700   Fax: (606)785-0105

JENKINS

1716 Letcher County Community News-Press
Superior Printing and Publishing
PO Box 156, Rte. 805   Phone: (606)855-4541
Cromona, KY 41810   **Fax: (606)855-9290**

LEXINGTON

1717 The Coal Journal
301 E. Main, Ste. 1110   Phone: (606)233-0092
Lexington, KY 40508   Fax: (606)255-9138

1718 The Kentucky Journal
Kentucky Center for Public Issues
167 W. Main St., Ste. 904   Phone: (606)255-5361
Lexington, KY 40507   Fax: (606)233-0760
Community newspaper. **Frequency:** 6x/yr. **Trim Size:** 8 1/2 x 11. **Key
Personnel:** David Mudel, Editor; Bob Sexton, Publisher. **ISSN:** 1063-
9357. **Subscription:** $20. $3.50 single issue.
Ad Rates: BW: $500   **Circulation:** Paid 1,450
                                                    Non-paid 400

1719 Southern Folklore Quarterly
University Press of Kentucky
663 S. Limestone St.
Lexington, KY 40506-0336

1720 TeleCable of Lexington, Inc.
2544 Palumbo Dr.
Lexington, KY 40509   Phone: (606)268-1123
Owner: TeleCable Corp. **Founded:** 1980. **Cities Served:** Fayette
County, KY.

1721 WCGW-AM - 770
Box 24776   Phone: (606)885-9119
Lexington, KY 40524   Fax: (606)885-9129

1722 WUKY-FM - 91.3
University of Kentucky
340 McVey Hall   Phone: (606)257-3221
Lexington, KY 40506-0045   **Fax: (606)257-6291**

LONDON

1723 The Sentinel-Echo
Park Newspapers of Kentucky, Inc.
PO Box 830   Phone: (606)878-7400
London, KY 40743-0830   **Fax: (606)878-7404**

1724 WFTG-AM - 1400
F.T.G. Broadcasting Inc.
534 Tobacco Rd.   Phone: (606)864-2148
London, KY 40741   Fax: (606)864-0645

1725 WMAK-AM - 980
PO Box 195
Pittsburg, KY 40755   **Phone: (606)878-0980**

1726 WWEL-FM - 104
534 Tobacco Rd.   Phone: (606)864-2148
London, KY 40741   Fax: (606)864-0645
Format: Hot Contemporary Country. **Owner:** Key Broadcasting.
Founded: 1980. **Operating Hours:** Continuous. **Key Personnel:** Francis
Wilholt, Gen. Mgr.; Drew Taylor, Operations Dir./Program Dir.
Wattage: 3000. **Ad Rates:** Noncommercial. **Additional Contact Infor-
mation:** (606)864-2048.

LOUISVILLE

1727 Church & Society
Social Justice and Peacemaking Unit PCUSA
100 Witherspoon St.   Phone: (502)569-5804
Louisville, KY 40202-1396   **Fax: (502)569-8034**

1728 The Disability Rag
PO Box 145
Louisville, KY 40201   Phone: (502)459-5343
Newspaper on women's disability rights. **Frequency:** 6x/yr. **Subscription:** $12.

Circulation: (Not Reported)

1729 Health Watch
Heath Watch Magazine, Inc.
455 S. 4th Ave., Ste. 908
Louisville, KY 40202-2511
Magazine for health care consumers. **Frequency:** Bimonthly. **Key Personnel:** Mollie Vento, Editor; Bobby C. Baker, M.D., Publisher. **Subscription:** $14.95. $2.95 single issue.

Circulation: (Not Reported)

1730 Horizons
Presbyterian Women in the Presbyterian Church
100 Witherspoon St.   Phone: (502)569-5366
Louisville, KY 40202-1396   Fax: (502)569-8085
Magazine for Presbyterian women. **Founded:** 1988. **Frequency:** 6x/yr. **Key Personnel:** Barbara Roche, Editor. **ISSN:** 1040-0087. **Subscription:** $12; $14 other countries.

Circulation: Paid 28,000
Non-paid 1,000

Advertising not accepted.

1731 Inside PFS First Publisher
The Cobb Group
9420 Bunsen Pkwy., Ste. 300   Phone: 1-800-223-8720
Louisville, KY 40220   Fax: (502)491-4200
Ceased publication.

1732 Inside ToolBook
The Cobb Group
9420 Bunsen Pkwy., Ste. 300   Phone: 1-800-223-8720
Louisville, KY 40220   Fax: (502)491-4200
Ceased publication.

1733 Inside Turbo C
The Cobb Group
9420 Bunsen Pkwy., Ste. 300   Phone: 1-800-223-8720
Louisville, KY 40220   Fax: (502)491-4200
Ceased publication.

1734 The Louisville Cardinal
University of Louisville
Old Student Center, Ste. 305   Phone: (502)588-6727
Louisville, KY 40292   **Fax: (502)588-0700**

1735 Microsoft Networking Journal
The Cobb Group
9420 Bunsen Pkwy., Ste. 300   Phone: 1-800-223-8720
Louisville, KY 40220   Fax: (502)491-4200
Ceased publication.

1736 The Symphony User's Journal
The Cobb Group, Inc.
9420 Bunsen Pkwy., Ste. 300   Phone: (502)491-1900
Louisville, KY 40220   Fax: (502)491-4200
Ceased publication.

1737 Storer Communications of Jefferson County
1536 Story Ave.   Phone: (502)584-6111
Louisville, KY 40206   Fax: (502)584-1401
Owner: Storer Cable Communications. **Founded:** 1979. **Key Personnel:** Charles King, Gen. Mgr.; Chris Bowling, Ad Sales Mgr.; Jeffrey Landers, Production Mgr./Program Dir.; Doug McKenzie, Business Mgr.; John Pait, Operations Mgr. **Cities Served:** Jefferson County, Oldham County, Anchorage, Audubon Park, Bankcroft, Barboumeade, Beechwood Village, Bellermeade, Bellwood, Briarwood, Broadfields, Broeck Point, Brownsboro Village, Cambridge, Cherrywood Village, Creekside, Crossgate, Devondale, Douglass Hills, Glenview Hills, Glenview Manor, Goose Creek, Graymoor, Green Spring, Hickory Hill, Hills and Dales, Hollow Creek, Hollyvilla,

Hurtsbourne Acres, Indian Hills, Jeffersontown, Keeneland, Kingsley, Lincolnshire, Lyndon, Lynnview, Manor Creek, Maryhill Estates, Meadow Vale, Meadowbrook Estates, Middletown, Minor Lane Heights, Mockingbird Valley, Moorland, Norbourne Estates, Northfield, Norwood, Parkway Village, Pewee Valley, Plantation, Prospect, Richlawn, River Bluff, Riverwood, Robinswood, Rolling Fields, Rolling Hills, St. Matthews, St. Regis Park, Seneca Gardens, Shively, South Park View, Springlee, Strathmoor Gardens, Strathmoor Manor, Strathmore Village, Sycamore, Thornhill, Watterson Park, Wellington, West Buechel, West Point, Westwood, Wildwood, Winding Falls, Windy Hill, Woodland Hills, and Woodlawn Park, KY: 180,000 subscribing households; 42 channels; 2 community access channels; 50 hours per week of community access programming.

LUDLOW

1738 Ecumenical Trends
Graymoor Ecumenical Institute
Box 16136   **Phone: (606)581-6216**
Ludlow, KY 41016   Fax: (212)870-2001

MAYFIELD

1739 WNGO-AM - 1320
PO Box 679   Phone: (502)247-5122
Mayfield, KY 42066   **Fax: (502)247-4207**

META

1740 Mountain Cable TV
590 Upper Johns Creek Rd.
Meta, KY 41501   Phone: (606)437-6193
Owner: Mountain Cable Systems, Inc. **Founded:** 1966. **Formerly:** Blackburn Cable TV. **Cities Served:** Meta, KY: 50 subscribing households; 12 channels.

MIDWAY

1741 WKLU-AM - 920
PO Box 4550
Midway, KY 40347
Owner: Hughes Companies. **Wattage:** 500.

MONTICELLO

1742 WFLW-AM - 1360
Worsham Ln.
PO Box 427   Phone: (606)348-8427
Monticello, KY 42633   **Fax: (606)348-3867**

1743 WKYM-FM - 101.7
150 Worsham Ln.
PO Box 427   Phone: (606)348-7083
Monticello, KY 42633   Fax: (606)348-3867
Format: Top 40; Oldies. **Network(s):** Westwood One Radio; KyNet. **Owner:** Regional Broadcasting Co. **Founded:** 1965. **Formerly:** WFLW-FM (1974). **Operating Hours:** 5 a.m.-midnight. **Key Personnel:** Stephen W. Staples, Owner/Gen. Mgr./Music Dir.; Debbie Brown, Promotions Mgr. **Wattage:** 6000. **Ad Rates:** $3-$8 for 30 seconds; $4-$10 for 60 seconds. Combined rates available with WFLW-AM. **Additional Contact Information:** Alt. telephone (606)348-HITS.

MORGANFIELD

1744 Union CATV Inc.
Rte. 5
Box 2C
Morganfield, KY 42437-1275   Phone: (502)389-1818
                                              Fax: (502)389-2459

MURRAY

1745 WBLN-FM - 103.7
1500 Diuquid   Phone: (502)753-2400
Murray, KY 42071   **Fax: (502)753-9434**

Ad Rates: GLR = general line rate; BW = one-time black & white page rate; 4C = one-time four color page rate; SAU = standard advertising unit rate; CNU = Canadian newspaper advertising unit rate; PCI = per column inch rate.
Circulation: ★ = ABC; △ = BPA; ◆ = CAC; ● = CCAB; □ = VAC; ⊕ = PO Statement; ‡ = Publisher's Report; Boldface figures = sworn; Light figures = estimated.
Entry type: ▢ = Print; ✆ = Broadcast.

113

OWENSBORO

♨ **1746　Owensboro Cablevision**
1 Industrial Dr.
Box 1798　　　　　　　　　　　Phone: (502)685-2991
Owensboro, KY 42302　　　　　　Fax: (502)685-0854
Owner: Century Communications Corp. **Founded:** 1967. **Cities Served:**
Daviess County, KY.

PADUCAH

♨ **1747　Comcast Cablevision of Paducah**
800 Broadway　　　　　　　　　Phone: (502)442-6382
Paducah, KY 42001　　　　　　　Fax: (502)442-4071
Owner: Comcast Corp. **Founded:** 1978. **Cities Served:** Graves, Livingston, Marshall and McCracken counties, KY and Massac County, IL.

♨ **1748　WKYQ-FM - 93.3**
6000 WKYQ Rd.　　　　　　　Phone: (502)554-0093
Paducah, KY 42003　　　　　　　Fax: (502)554-5468

PAINTSVILLE

♨ **1749　Big Sandy TV Cable, Inc.**
PO Box 956　　　　　　　　　　Phone: (606)789-3455
Paintsville, KY 41240　　　　　　**Fax: (606)789-5362**

PINEVILLE

♨ **1750　WANO-AM - 1230**
HC 84
Box 1　　　　　　　　　　　　　Phone: (606)337-2100
Pineville, KY 40977　　　　　　　**Fax: (606)337-5900**

♨ **1751　WZKO-FM - 106.3**
HC 84
Box 1　　　　　　　　　　　　　**Phone: (606)337-2100**
Pineville, KY 40977　　　　　　　**Fax: (606)337-5900**

SMITHLAND

▥ **1752　The Livingston Ledger**
Kentucky Publishing, Inc.
PO Box 129　　　　　　　　　　Phone: (502)928-2128
Smithland, KY 42081　　　　　　**Fax: (502)442-5220**

VANCLEVE

♨ **1753　WMTC-AM - 730**
1003 KY 541
Box 8　　　　　　　　　　　　　Phone: (606)666-5006
Vancleve, KY 41385　　　　　　　**Fax: (606)666-4612**

♨ **1754　WMTC-FM - 99.9**
1003 KY 541
Box 8　　　　　　　　　　　　　Phone: (606)666-5006
Vancleve, KY 41385　　　　　　　**Fax: (606)666-4612**

WEST LIBERTY

♨ **1755　WLKS-AM - 1450**
129 College St.　　　　　　　　**Phone: (606)743-3145**
West Liberty, KY 41472　　　　　**Fax: (606)743-7792**

WICKLIFFE

♨ **1756　WGKY-FM - 95.9**
Box 500
Hwy. 286　　　　　　　　　　　Phone: (502)335-3696
Wickliffe, KY 42087　　　　　　　**Fax: (502)335-3698**

WILLIAMSTOWN

▥ **1757　Grant County News**
151 N. Main
PO Box 247　　　　　　　　　　Phone: (606)824-3344
Williamstown, KY 41097　　　　　Fax: (606)824-5888

♨ **1758　City of Williamstown Cable**
TV Department
400 N. Main St.　　　　　　　　**Phone: (606)824-3633**
Williamstown, KY 41097　　　　　Fax: (606)824-3246

LOUISIANA

ABBEVILLE

♣ 1759 KROF-AM - 960
Highway 167 N.
Box 610
Abbeville, LA 70511-0610

Phone: (318)893-2531
Fax: (318)893-2569

♣ 1760 KROF-FM - 105.1
Box 610
Highway 167 N.
Abbeville, LA 70511-0610

Phone: (318)893-2531
Fax: (318)893-2569

ALEXANDRIA

♣ 1761 KALB-AM - 580
Box 471
Alexandria, LA 71301

Phone: (318)443-2543
Fax: (318)443-7306

Format: Oldies. **Network(s):** Satellite Music. **Owner:** Alexandria Broadcasting Co. **Founded:** 1935. **Operating Hours:** Continuous. **Key Personnel:** Bob May, Gen. Sales Mgr.; Terry Menning, Program Dir. **Wattage:** 5000. **Ad Rates:** $12-$19 for 30 seconds; $18-$25 for 60 seconds. Combined rates available with KZMZ-FM.

♣ 1762 KICR-FM - 98.7
PO Box 8798
Alexandria, LA 71306-1798

Phone: (318)473-0098
Fax: (318)473-9929

AMITE

♣ 1763 WABL-AM - 1570
Bankston Rd.
PO Box 787
Amite, LA 70422

Phone: (504)748-8385
Fax: (504)748-3918

BAKER

♣ 1764 WQCK-FM - 92.7
5280 Groom Rd.
Baker, LA 70714

Phone: (504)774-7780
Fax: (504)774-7785

BATON ROUGE

▢ 1765 The Evangelist
Jimmy Swaggart Ministries
PO Box 2550
Baton Rouge, LA 70821

Phone: (504)768-8300
Fax: (504)769-2244

▢ 1766 Louisiana Agriculture
Louisiana Agricultural Experiment Station
PO Box 25100
Baton Rouge, LA 70804-5100

Phone: (504)388-2263
Fax: (504)388-2478

♣ 1767 UAE
5428 Florida Blvd.
Baton Rouge, LA 70896

Phone: (504)923-0256
Fax: (504)925-1668

Owner: Tele-Communications, Inc. **Founded:** 1975. **Cities Served:** East Baton Rouge County, Central and East Baton Rouge Parish, LA.

♣ 1768 WNDC-AM - 910
3000 Tecumseh St.
Baton Rouge, LA 70805

Phone: (504)357-4571
Fax: (504)356-7784

♣ 1769 WTGE-FM - 100.7
5220 Essen Lane
Baton Rouge, LA 70809

Phone: (504)766-3233
Fax: (504)766-4112

BELLE CHASSE

♣ 1770 KMEZ-FM - 102.9
401 Whitney Ave., Ste. 160
Gretna, LA 70056

Phone: (504)364-1212
Fax: (504)367-8024

BOSSIER CITY

♣ 1771 UAE
725 Benton Rd.
Bossier City, LA 71111

Phone: (318)747-1666
Fax: (318)746-2186

Owner: Tele-Communications, Inc. **Founded:** 1978. **Cities Served:** Bossier County, LA.

BOUTTE

▢ 1772 Le Bon Temps
PO Box 1199
Boutte, LA 70039

Phone: (504)758-2795
Fax: (504)758-7000

▢ 1773 River Parishes Guide
PO Box 1199
Boutte, LA 70039

Phone: (504)758-2796
Fax: (504)758-7000

COLFAX

♣ 1774 Galaxy Cablevision
210 Webb Smith Dr.
PO Box 228
Colfax, LA 71417

Phone: (318)627-3215

Owner: Galaxy Cablevision, L.P. **Founded:** 1980. **Cities Served:** Colfax, Boyce, Cotton Port, Lecompte, Cheneyville, Simmersport, Moreauville,Krotz Springs, Natchez, Woodworth, Kolin, St. Joseph, Newellton, Water Proof, Clayton, and Montgomery, LA. 8700 subscribing households; 25 channels.

COLUMBIA

☙ 1775 KCTO-AM - 1540
Box 1319
Columbia, LA 71418　　　　　Phone: (318)649-2756
Format: Gospel. **Network(s):** Progressive Farmer; Louisiana; Unistar.
Owner: KCTO Broadcasting Co. **Founded:** 1973. **Operating Hours:**
Sunrise-sunset. **Key Personnel:** Tom Gay, Owner/Station Mgr.; Niles
Laborde, Operations Mgr. **Wattage:** 1000. **Ad Rates:** $2.50 for 30
seconds; $5 for 60 seconds.

CROWLEY

☐ 1776 Remnant Christian Magazine
PO Drawer C　　　　　Phone: (318)783-1560
Crowley, LA 70527　　　　　Fax: (318)783-1674
Christian magazine. **Founded:** 1989. **Frequency:** Monthly. **Cols./Page:**
4. **Col. Width:** 2 1/4 in. **Col. Depth:** 12 1/2 in. **Key Personnel:** Chip
Bailey, Editor and Publisher. **ISSN:** 1047-6431. **Subscription:** $15.
　　　　　Circulation: ‡150
　　　　　Non-paid ‡15,000
Advertising accepted; contact publisher for rates.

☙ 1777 Crowley Cable TV
PO Box 274
Crowley, LA 70526　　　　　Phone: (318)783-5931
Key Personnel: Ray Mayo, Mgr. **Cities Served:** Crowley and Rayne,
LA: 6,958 subscribing households; 29 channels.

DENHAM SPRINGS

☐ 1778 Louisiana Baptist Builder
Baptist Missionary Assn. of Louisiana
PO Box 1297
Denham Springs, LA 70727-1297

☙ 1779 KRVE-FM - 96.1
601 Hatchel Ln.
PO Box 68
Denham Springs, LA 70727　　　　　Phone: (504)665-5154
　　　　　Fax: (504)499-9696

DONALDSONVILLE

☙ 1780 KKAY-AM - 1590
3365 Hwy. 1 S.
Donaldsonville, LA 70346　　　　　Phone: (504)473-5764

EUNICE

☙ 1781 KBAZ-FM - 102.1
109 S. 2nd St.
Eunice, LA 70535　　　　　Phone: (318)457-3543
Format: Country; Cajun & Zydeco. **Network(s):** Satellite Music.
Owner: Nezpique Communications Ltd. **Founded:** 1990. **Operating
Hours:** Continuous. **Key Personnel:** Robert L. Fontenot, Mgr./Sales
Mgr.; Jocelyn Bradley, Traffic Mgr.; Missy B. Benoit, Program and
Promotions Dir.; Edna Poullard, Sales. **Wattage:** 25,000. **Ad Rates:**
$4.30-$5.75 for 30 seconds; $6.45-$8.60 for 60 seconds.

GRETNA

☙ 1782 KKNO-AM - 750
16 Westbank Expy, Ste. 204
Gretna, LA 70053　　　　　Phone: (504)366-5505

HAMMOND

☙ 1783 KSLU-FM - 90.9
Box 783, University Sta.　　　　　Phone: (504)549-2330
Hammond, LA 70402　　　　　**Fax: (504)549-5014**

HARAHAN

☙ 1784 Cox Cable Jefferson Parish
338 Edwards Ave.　　　　　Phone: (504)733-5680
Harahan, LA 70123　　　　　Fax: (504)734-0869
Owner: Cox Cable Communications. **Founded:** 1979. **Cities Served:**
Jefferson and Plaquemines counties, Gretna, Harahan, Jean Lafitte,
Kenner Plaquemines Parish, and Westwego, LA.

HOMER

☐ 1785 The Advertiser
PO Box 117　　　　　Phone: (318)927-3721
Homer, LA 71038　　　　　Fax: (318)263-8897
Community newspaper. **Frequency:** Weekly. **Printing Method:** Offset.
Cols./Page: 6. **Col. Width:** 2 1/16 in. **Col. Depth:** 21 in. **Key Personnel:**
Jerry Pye, Publisher; Kathy Compton, Advertising Mgr. **Subscription:**
Free.
　　　　　Circulation: Free 8,549
Advertising accepted; contact publisher for rates.

HOUMA

☙ 1786 KCIL-FM - 107.5
906 Belanger
Box 2068　　　　　Phone: (504)851-1020
Houma, LA 70361　　　　　Fax: (504)872-4403
Format: Contemporary Country. **Network(s):** Unistar; Louisiana.
Owner: Guaranty Broadcasting. **Founded:** 1946. **Operating Hours:**
Continuous. **Key Personnel:** Michael Stone, Program Dir./Assistant
Gen. Mgr.; Michael Adams, Gen. Mgr.; Don Thomas, Production
Dir.; Virginia Childs, News Dir. **Wattage:** 100,000. **Ad Rates:** $20-$32
for 30 seconds; $24-$46 for 60 seconds.

LAFAYETTE

☐ 1787 Creole Magazine
PO Box 91496　　　　　Phone: (318)269-1956
Lafayette, LA 70509　　　　　Fax: (318)332-4775
Community magazine discussing the cultural heritage, customs,
music, cuisine, and language of southwest Louisiana. **Subtitle:** "Serv-
ing Southwestern Louisiana and the World." **Founded:** 1990. **Frequen-
cy:** Monthly. **Trim Size:** 8 1/4 x 10 1/2. **Cols./Page:** 3. **Col. Width:** 3 3/
4 in. and 2 1/2 in. **Col. Depth:** 9 1/2 in. **Key Personnel:** Ruth Foote,
Editor and Publisher; Emmette J. Jacob, Jr., Exec. Publisher; Dianne
Dupas, Advertising Dir. **Subscription:** Free; $15 out of distribution
area; $30 other countries. $1.50 single issue.
Ad Rates: 　BW: 　$250　　　**Circulation:** Paid ‡200
　　　　PCI: 　$14　　　　Non-paid ‡9,700
Additional Contact Information: Toll-free 800-421-0197.

☐ 1788 Gait Way
Gait Way Publications, Inc.
PO Box 31306
Lafayette, LA 70593
Magazine chronicling horse breeds with smaller registries. **Frequency:**
Monthly. **Key Personnel:** Tissa Porter, Publisher. **Subscription:**
$23.95. $5 single issue.
　　　　　Circulation: (Not Reported)

LAKE CHARLES

☙ 1789 TCI of Louisiana
Box 5365
Lake Charles, LA 70601-8506　　　　　Phone: (318)477-9674
Owner: Tele-Communications, Inc. **Founded:** 1967. **Cities Served:**
Calcasieu County, LA.

MANY

☙ 1790 KWLV-FM - 107.1
605 San Antonio Ave.
Box 1005
Many, LA 71449　　　　　Phone: (318)256-5924

MORGAN CITY

☙ 1791 KBJ-TV - Channel 39
608 Michigan St.　　　　　Phone: (504)384-6960
Morgan City, LA 70380　　　　　**Fax: (504)385-1916**

NATCHITOCHES

☙ 1792 KNWD-FM - 91.7
Northwestern State University
PO Box 3038　　　　　Phone: (318)357-5693
Natchitoches, LA 71497　　　　　**Fax: (318)357-6564**

NEW IBERIA

♣ 1793 KANE-AM - 1240
2316 E. Main St.
New Iberia, LA 70560

Phone: (318)365-3434
Fax: (318)367-5385

NEW ORLEANS

♤ 1794 Dialogue Newsjournal
Box 71221
New Orleans, LA 70172   Phone: (504)581-3336
Journal supporting alternative politics and culture. **Subtitle:** New Orleans' Progressive Community Journal. **Founded:** 1981. **Frequency:** 6x/yr. **Printing Method:** Offset. **Cols./Page:** 2. **Col. Width:** 2 1/2 in. **Col. Depth:** 7 1/2 in. **Key Personnel:** Brad Ott, Publisher. **Subscription:** $5. Free single issue.

Circulation: Paid 350
Non-paid 1,650

Advertising accepted; contact publisher for rates.

♤ 1795 Gambit
Firststar Communications of Louisiana
4141 Bienville St.   Phone: (504)486-5900
New Orleans, LA 70119   Fax: (504)488-7263
Publication exploring politics, dining, and entertainment in New Orleans. **Founded:** 1980. **Frequency:** Weekly. **Cols./Page:** 4. **Col. Width:** 14.5 picas. **Col. Depth:** 87 picas.

Circulation: Free □35,589

Advertising accepted; contact publisher for rates.

♤ 1796 Peptides
Pergamon Press
University of New Orleans
Tulane School of Medicine
1601 Perdido St.   Phone: (504)568-0811
New Orleans, LA 70146   Fax: (504)522-8559
Scientific journal. **Subtitle:** Peptides: An International Journal. **Founded:** 1980. **Frequency:** Quarterly. **Trim Size:** 7 x 9. **Cols./Page:** 2. **Col. Width:** 3 3/8 in. **Key Personnel:** Abba J. Kastin, M.D., Editor-in-Chief. **ISSN:** 0196-9781. **Subscription:** $115; $845 institutions.

Circulation: (Not Reported)

Publisher's address: 660 White Plains Rd., Tarrytown, NY 10591-5153; phone (914)524-9200.

♣ 1797 Cox Cable of New Orleans
2120 Canal St.   Phone: (504)522-3838
New Orleans, LA 70112   Fax: (504)529-2394
Owner: Cox Cable Communications. **Founded:** 1982. **Cities Served:** Orleans County and Parish, LA.

♣ 1798 WBSN-FM - 89.1
3939 Gentilly Blvd.
New Orleans, LA 70126   Phone: (504)286-3600
Format: Adult Contemporary; Religious (christian). **Owner:** New Orleans Baptist Theological Seminary. **Founded:** 1978. **Operating Hours:** Continuous. **Key Personnel:** Rick Funderburk, Gen. Mgr.; Stan Watts, Program Dir.; Brian Sanders, Development Dir. **Wattage:** 10,000. **Ad Rates:** Noncommercial.

♣ 1799 WLAE-TV - Channel 32
2929 S. Carrollton Ave.   Phone: (504)866-7411
New Orleans, LA 70118   Fax: (504)861-5186

♣ 1800 WWNO-FM - 89.9
University of New Orleans   Phone: (504)286-7000
New Orleans, LA 70148   Fax: (504)286-7317

PORT ALLEN

♤ 1801 The Louisiana Cattleman
Louisiana Cattlemen's Assn.
4921 I-10 Frontage Rd.   Phone: (504)343-3491
Port Allen, LA 70767   Fax: (504)336-0002
Former Title: The Louisiana Cattleman/The Louisiana Diaryman

SHREVEPORT

♣ 1802 Cablevision of Shreveport
6529 Quilen Rd.   Phone: (318)631-3060
Shreveport, LA 71108   Fax: (318)631-1027
Owner: American TV & Communications Corp. **Founded:** 1976. **Cities Served:** Caddo County, De Soto County, Bethany, and Greenwood, LA; Harrison County and Waskom, TX.

♣ 1803 KOKA-AM - 980
PO Box 103   Phone: (318)222-3122
Shreveport, LA 71161   Fax: (318)221-9802

SLIDELL

♣ 1804 Cablevision Industries of Saint Tammany
37356 Ben Thomas Rd.
Box 890   Phone: (504)626-1188
Slidell, LA 70459   Fax: (504)649-3250
Owner: Cablevision Industries, Inc. **Founded:** 1979. **Cities Served:** Saint Tammany County, Lacombe, Pearl River, and Saint Tammany Parish, LA. **Additional Contact Information:** Alternate telephone, (504)882-6888.

SULPHUR

♣ 1805 Carlyss Cablevision, Inc.
Box 222   Phone: (318)583-4973
Sulphur, LA 70664-0222   Fax: (318)583-2063
Owner: John Allen Henning. **Founded:** 1982. **Key Personnel:** Raymond Henagan, Mgr.; Ray Ebersole, Chief Engineer; Lonnie Lormand, Mktg. **Cities Served:** Carlyss, LA: 1,333 subscribing households; 30 channels; 1 community access channel. **Additional Contact Information:** (318)583-2111.

THIBODAUX

♣ 1806 Lafourche Communications
1306 Ridgefield Rd.
Box 5178   Phone: (504)446-8444
Thibodaux, LA 70301   Fax: (504)446-9849
Owner: Cablevision Industries, Inc. **Founded:** 1970. **Cities Served:** Thibodaux, Raceland, Paulina, Labadieville, Napoleonville, and Vacherie, LA.

VILLE PLATTE

♣ 1807 KVPI-FM - 92.5
809 W. LaSalle St.
PO Drawer J   Phone: (318)363-2124
Ville Platte, LA 70586   Fax: (318)363-3574

VINTON

♤ 1808 The Vinton News
News Leader, Inc.
716 E. Napoleon
PO Box 1999   Phone: (318)589-7650
Sulphur, LA 70664   Fax: (318)528-3044

VIVIAN

♣ 1809 KNCB-AM - 1320
PO Box 1072   Phone: (318)375-3278
Vivian, LA 71082   Fax: (318)375-3329

WESTLAKE

♤ 1810 Builder News Extra
News Leader, Inc.
PO Box 127
Westlake, LA 70669   Phone: (318)436-0583
Former Title: Westlake/Moss Bluff News Buyer's Guide

☙ 1811　KAOK-AM - 1400
801 Columbia Southern Rd.　　　　Phone: (318)882-0243
Westlake, LA 70669　　　　　　　　Fax: (318)882-6731

WINNFIELD

☙ 1812　KVCL-AM - 1270
No. 1 KVCL Rd.
PO Box 548　　　　　　　　　　　Phone: (318)628-5822
Winnfield, LA 71483-0548　　　　　Fax: (318)628-7355

☙ 1813　KVCL-FM - 92.1
No. 1 KVCL Rd.
PO Box 548　　　　　　　　　　　Phone: (318)628-5822
Winnfield, LA 71483　　　　　　　　Fax: (318)628-7355

MAINE

AUBURN

♠ 1814 A-R Cable Services, Inc.
121 Mill St.   Phone: (207)783-2023
Auburn, ME 04210   · Fax: (207)786-2563
Owner: Cablevision Systems Corp. **Founded:** 1966. **Cities Served:** Androscoggin County, Oxford County, Auburn, Lisbon, Lisbon Falls, Mechanic Falls, Oxford, and Sabattus, ME. **Additional Contact Information:** Toll-free: 800-492-0757.

BANGOR

♠ 1815 A-R Cable Services, Inc.
278 Florida Ave.
Box 1405   Phone: (207)942-4661
Bangor, ME 04401   Fax: (207)942-5426
Owner: Cablevision Systems Corp. **Founded:** 1971. **Key Personnel:** William Fay, Gen. Mgr.; Robert Jones, Engineering Mgr.; Deborah Chapman, Marketing and Sales Mgr.; Patti Rollins, Customer Service Mgr. **Cities Served:** Hancock County, Penobscot County, Piscataquis County, Waldo County, Bar Harbor, Bass Harbor, Belfast, Bernard, Bradley, Brewer, Bucksport, Corinna, Dexter, Dover-Foxcroft, Eddington, Ellsworth, Hampden, Holden, Indian Island, Lincoln, Manset, Milford, Newport, Old Town, Orono, Orrington, Searsport, Southwest Harbor, Tremont, Veazie, Verona, and Winterport, ME: 24,300 subscribing households; 36 channels; 1 community access channel.

BATH

♠ 1816 WKRH-FM - 105.9
PO Box 308   Phone: (207)443-6671
Bath, ME 04530-0308   Fax: (207)443-8610
Format: Adult Contemporary. **Network(s):** Satellite Radio. **Owner:** Kaleidoscope, Inc., at above address. **Formerly:** WIGY-FM (1989). **Operating Hours:** Continuous. **Key Personnel:** J. Frank Burke, Pres./Gen. Mgr.; Susan M. Burke, Asst. Gen. Mgr.; Rick Reilly, Sales Mgr. **Wattage:** 50,000. **Ad Rates:** $12-$14 per unit.

BELFAST

▥ 1817 The Republican Journal
Courier Publications
4 Main St.
Box 327   Phone: (207)338-3333
Belfast, ME 04915-0327   **Fax: (207)338-5498**

BOOTHBAY HARBOR

▥ 1818 Boothbay Register
95 Townsend Ave.   Phone: (207)633-4620
Boothbay Harbor, ME 04538   **Fax: (207)633-7123**

CALAIS

▥ 1819 The Calais Advertiser
Advertiser Publishing Co.
Box 660   Phone: (207)454-3561
Calais, ME 04619-0660   **Fax: (207)454-3458**

CAMDEN

▥ 1820 High Color
Imagetech Publications
21 Elm St., 3rd Fl.   Phone: (207)236-6267
Camden, ME 04843   Fax: (207)236-6018
Subtitle: The Magazine of PC Graphics & Video. **Founded:** April 1992. **Frequency:** 6x/yr. **Printing Method:** Offset. **Trim Size:** 8 1/8 x 10 7/8. **Cols./Page:** 3. **Key Personnel:** Michael Forcillo, Publisher. **ISSN:** 1060-5282. **Subscription:** $14.95; $28 other countries. $3.95 single issue.

Ad Rates: BW: $6,245   **Circulation:** (Not Reported)
            4C: $7,295

▥ 1821 Resolution
Imagetech Publications
21 Elm St., 3rd Fl.   Phone: (207)236-6267
Camden, ME 04843   Fax: (207)236-6018
Ceased publication.

DOVER-FOXCROFT

▥ 1822 The Price Buster
County Wide Communications, Inc.
78 River St.
Dover-Foxcroft, ME 04426   Phone: (207)564-7548
Shopper. **Founded:** 1979. **Frequency:** Weekly. **Trim Size:** 10 x 15. **Cols./Page:** 5. **Col. Width:** 11 picas. **Col. Depth:** 15 in. **USPS:** 566-530 **Subscription:** $24; $32 out of area.
Ad Rates: BW: $300   **Circulation:** Non-paid ‡6,000
            SAU: $4
Formerly: County Wide Shopper's Guide.

FARMINGTON

1823 Livermore Falls Advertiser
Mt. Blue Publishing Co., Inc.
PO Box 750   Phone: (207)897-4321
Farmington, ME 04938   Fax: (207)778-6970

1824 WKTJ-FM - 99.3
PO Box 590
Farmington, ME 04938   Phone: (207)778-3400

GUILFORD

1825 Guilford Journal
County Wide Communications, Inc.
PO Box 772
Guilford, ME 04443   Phone: (207)564-7548
Community newspaper. **Founded:** 1991. **Frequency:** Weekly. **Printing Method:** Web offset. **Trim Size:** 11 x 17. **Cols./Page:** 5. **Col. Width:** 11 picas. **Col. Depth:** 15 in. **Key Personnel:** Lester J. Reynolds, Editor; Bob Benta, Publisher. **USPS:** 566-530. **Subscription:** $24. $1 single issue.
Ad Rates: GLR: $3   **Circulation:** Paid ‡1,600
                BW: $200   Non-paid ‡500

HOULTON

1826 Mattawamkeag Cablevision
Box 38
Houlton, ME 04730   Phone: (207)532-4451
Owner: Don Dee. **Founded:** 1988. **Cities Served:** Mattawamkeag and Winn, ME. 317 subscribing households; 13 channels.

LEWISTON

1827 WCBB-TV - Channel 10
1450 Lisbon St.   Phone: (207)783-9101
Lewiston, ME 04240   Fax: (207)783-5193

MILO

1828 United Video Cablevision
17 Park St.   Phone: (207)943-7953
Milo, ME 04463   Fax: (207)943-2784
Key Personnel: Peter W. Hamlin, System Mgr.

OLD TOWN

1829 Old Town-Orono Times
Box 568   Phone: (207)827-4451
Old Town, ME 04468   Fax: (207)827-2280

ORONO

1830 American Potato Journal
Potato Assn. of America
Public Affairs
University of Maine
Orono, ME 04469   Phone: (207)942-9273

PORTLAND

1831 Evening Express
The Portland Newpapers
PO Box 1460   Phone: (207)780-9000
Portland, ME 04104   Fax: (207)780-9499
Ceased publication.

1832 Public Cable Co.
188 Johnson Rd.
Box 8180   Phone: (207)775-3431
Portland, ME 04104   Fax: (207)775-6422
Owner: American TV & Communications Corp; New England Cablevision, Inc. **Founded:** 1975. **Cities Served:** Cumberland County, Cape Elizabeth, Casco, Cumberland, Falmouth, Gorham, Gray, New Gloucester, North Yarmouth, Pownal, South Portland, West Pownal, Westbrook, Windham, and Yarmouth, ME.

READFIELD

1833 Maine Water Utilities Association Journal
Maine Water Utilities Assn.
PO Box 120   Phone: (207)685-4334
Readfield, ME 04355   Fax: (207)685-4324

ROCKLAND

1834 United Video Cablevision of Maine
400 Old County Rd.
Rockland, ME 04841   Phone: (207)596-6622
Owner: Larry Flinn. **Founded:** 1972. **Key Personnel:** Brian Gasser, Gen. Mgr.; Valerie Winchenbach, Office Mgr.; David Winchenbach, Chief Technician. **Cities Served:** Knox County, Booth Bay region, Mt. Desert area, Hanrock, and Calais, ME. 18,000 subscribing households.

SANFORD

1835 WCDQ-FM - 92.1
Box 631   Phone: (207)324-7271
Sanford, ME 04073   Fax: (207)324-2464
Format: Classic Rock. **Owner:** WSME, Inc. **Founded:** 1985. **Formerly:** WEBI-FM. **Operating Hours:** Continuous. **Key Personnel:** Donald Crown, Gen. Mgr.; Timothy Maxfield, Sales Mgr.; Russ Dumont, Program Dir.; Jonathan Smith, News Dir.; Becky Brown, Business Mgr. **Wattage:** 3000. **Ad Rates:** $22-$40 per unit. Combined rates available with WSME-AM.

1836 WSME-AM - 1220
Box 631   Phone: (207)324-7271
Sanford, ME 04073   Fax: (207)324-2464
Format: News; Talk. **Network(s):** For The People. **Owner:** WSME Inc. **Operating Hours:** Continuous. **Key Personnel:** Don Crown, Owner; Tim Maxfield, Sales Mgr.; Russ Dumont, Program Dir. **Wattage:** 1000. **Ad Rates:** $12-$30 per unit. Combined rates available with WCDQ-FM.

SCARBOROUGH

1837 WPKM-FM - 106.3
551 U.S. Rte. 1
PO Box 610   Phone: (207)883-9596
Scarborough, ME 04074   Fax: (207)883-9530

WEST FARMINGTON

1838 WKTJ-AM - 1380
Voter Hill Rd.
West Farmington, ME 04992   Phone: (207)778-3400
Format: Adult Contemporary; Oldies; Country. **Owner:** Franklin Broadcasting Corp., PO Box 590, Farmington, ME 04938; (207)778-3000. **Founded:** 1959. **Operating Hours:** 5:30 a.m.-midnight; 10% network, 90% local. **Key Personnel:** Russ Nutt, Music Dir.; Alfredo Ibarguen, Pres./Engineer; Claire Taylor, Station Mgr.; Stephen R. Bull, Sales Mgr./Program Dir.; Russell Nut, News Dir. **Wattage:** 1000. **Ad Rates:** $4.70-$12.10 for 30 seconds; $5.30-$13.40 for 60 seconds.

MARYLAND

ANNAPOLIS

⚟ **1839 Maryland Register**
Division of State Documents
PO Box 2249   Phone: (410)974-2486
Annapolis, MD 21404-2249   Fax: (410)974-2546

⚟ **1840 Shipmate**
U.S. Naval Academy Alumni Assn.
Alumni House
247 King George St.
Annapolis, MD 21402   Phone: (410)263-4469

🎙 **1841 WHVY-FM - 103.1**
112 Main St.   Phone: (410)626-0103
Annapolis, MD 21401   Fax: (410)267-7634

🎙 **1842 WNAV-AM - 1430**
Admiral Dr.
PO Box 829   Phone: (401)263-1430
Annapolis, MD 21401   Fax: (410)268-5360

BALTIMORE

⚟ **1843 Anesthesia & Analgesia**
Williams & Wilkins
428 E. Preston St.   **Phone: (301)528-4000**
Baltimore, MD 21202   **Fax: (301)528-8597**

⚟ **1844 Arethusa**
The Johns Hopkins University Press
701 W. 40th St., Ste. 275   Phone: (410)516-6982
Baltimore, MD 21211   Fax: (410)516-6998
Journal on literary and cultural classics. **Founded:** 1969. **Frequency:** 3x/yr. **Printing Method:** Offset. **Trim Size:** 6 x 9. **Cols./Page:** 1. **Col. Width:** 26 picas. **Col. Depth:** 7 in. **Key Personnel:** John Peradotto, Editor; Tara Dorai-Berry, Advertising Mgr. **Subscription:** $16; $27 institutions.

Circulation: ‡620
Advertising accepted; contact publisher for rates.

⚟ **1845 The Baltimore Sun**
501 N. Calvert St.   Phone: (410)332-6000
Baltimore, MD 21278-0001   Fax: (410)332-6670
Newspaper. **Frequency:** Daily (morn.), Sun. (eve.). **Printing Method:** Offset. **Cols./Page:** 6. **Col. Width:** 2 1/16 in. **Col. Depth:** 21 in. **Key Personnel:** John Carroll, Sr. V.P. and Editor; Kathryn Christensen, Mng. Editor; Michael Davies, Publisher.
Circulation: Daily ★391,952
Sun. ★488,506

⚟ **1846 Configurations**
The Johns Hopkins University Press
701 W. 40th St., Ste. 275   Phone: (410)516-6982
Baltimore, MD 21211   Fax: (410)516-6982
Journal on the humanities. **Frequency:** 3x/yr. **Printing Method:** Offset. **Trim Size:** 6 x 9. **Cols./Page:** 1. **Col. Width:** 26 picas. **Col. Depth:** 7 in. **Key Personnel:** Jim Bono; Wiida Anderson; Ken Knoespel. **Subscription:** $21; $47 institutions.
Ad Rates: BW: $190   **Circulation:** (Not Reported)
Advertising accepted; contact publisher for rates.

⚟ **1847 Eighteenth-Century Life**
The Johns Hopkins University Press
701 W. 40th St., Ste. 275   Phone: (410)516-6982
Baltimore, MD 21211   Fax: (410)516-6998
Journal on the 18th century. **Frequency:** 3x/yr. **Printing Method:** Offset. **Trim Size:** 6 x 9. **Cols./Page:** 1. **Col. Width:** 26 picas. **Col. Depth:** 7 in. **Key Personnel:** Robert P. MacCobbin, Editor; Tara Dorai-Berry, Advertising Mgr. **Subscription:** $19; $37 institutions.
Ad Rates: BW: $185   **Circulation:** 940

⚟ **1848 The Greyhound**
Loyola College
100 W. Coldspring Ln. T4W
Baltimore, MD 21210-2352   **Phone: (410)617-2282**

⚟ **1849 Henry James Review**
The Johns Hopkins University Press
701 W. 40th St., Ste. 275   Phone: (410)516-6982
Baltimore, MD 21211   Fax: (410)516-6998
Literary journal. **Frequency:** 3x/yr. **Printing Method:** Offset. **Trim Size:** 7 x 10. **Cols./Page:** 1. **Col. Width:** 26 picas. **Col. Depth:** 7 in. **Key Personnel:** Daniel Mark Fogel, Editor; Tara Dorai-Berry, Advertising Mgr. **Subscription:** $22; $37 institutions.
Ad Rates: BW: $185   **Circulation:** ‡840

⚟ **1850 ICSID Review**
The Johns Hopkins University Press
701 W. 40th St., Ste. 275   Phone: (410)516-6982
Baltimore, MD 21211   Fax: (410)516-6998
Social and political science journal focusing on foreign policy studies. **Frequency:** 2x/yr. **Printing Method:** Offset. **Trim Size:** 7 x 10. **Cols./Page:** 1. **Col. Width:** 26 picas. **Col. Depth:** 7 in. **Key Personnel:** Ibrahim F. I. Shihata, Editor; Tara Dorai-Berry, Advertising Mgr. **Subscription:** $50.
Ad Rates: BW: $175   **Circulation:** ‡470

⚟ **1851 The Jerusalem Journal of International Relations**
The Johns Hopkins University Press
701 W. 40th St., Ste. 275   Phone: (410)62-6982
Baltimore, MD 21211   Fax: (410)516-6998
Ceased publication.

ᛤ **1852 Journal of Democracy**
The JohnS Hopkins University Press
701 W. 40th St. Ste. 275   Phone: (410)516-6982
Baltimore, MD 21211   Fax: (410)516-6998
Journal covering democratic regimes and movements around the world. **Frequency:** Quarterly. **Trim Size:** 6 x 9. **Key Personnel:** Marc F. Plattner, Editor; Tara Dorai-Berry, Advertising Mgr. **Subscription:** $24; $48 institutions.
Ad Rates: BW: $215   **Circulation:** 1,000

ᛤ **1853 Journal of Modern Greek Studies**
The Johns Hopkins University Press
701 W. 40th St., Ste. 275   Phone: (410)516-6982
Baltimore, MD 21211   Fax: (410)516-6998
Journal focusing on modern Greek studies. **Frequency:** 2x/yr. **Printing Method:** Offset. **Trim Size:** 6 x 9. **Cols./Page:** 1. **Col. Width:** 26 picas. **Col. Depth:** 7 in. **Key Personnel:** Peter Bien, Editor; Tara Dorai-Berry, Advertising Mgr. **Subscription:** $19; $42.50 institutions.
Ad Rates: BW: $180   **Circulation:** ‡700

ᛤ **1854 Kennedy Institute of Ethics Journal**
The Johns Hopkins University Press
701 W. 40th. St. Ste. 275   Phone: (410)516-6982
Baltimore, MD 21211   Fax: (410)516-6998
Journal featuring opinions and analysis of bioethics. **Founded:** 1991. **Frequency:** Quarterly. **Trim Size:** 6 3/4 x 10. **Cols./Page:** 1. **Col. Width:** 4 3/4 in. **Col. Depth:** 7 1/2 in. **Key Personnel:** Robert M. Veatch, Sr. Editor; Renie Schapiro, Editor; Carol Mason Spicer, Managing Editor. **ISSN:** 1054-6863. **Subscription:** $45; $65 institutions; $20 students.
Ad Rates: BW: $215   **Circulation:** 1,685

ᛤ **1855 The Lion and the Unicorn**
The Johns Hopkins University Press
701 W. 40th St., Ste. 275   Phone: (410)516-6982
Baltimore, MD 21211   Fax: (410)516-6998
Literary studies journal. **Frequency:** 2x/yr. **Printing Method:** Offset. **Trim Size:** 6 x 9. **Cols./Page:** 1. **Col. Width:** 26 picas. **Col. Depth:** 7 in. **Key Personnel:** Jack Zipes, Co-Editor; Louisa Smith, Co-Editor; Tara Dorai-Berry, Advertising Mgr. **Subscription:** $19; $34 institutions.
Ad Rates: BW: $200   **Circulation:** ‡1,500

ᛤ **1856 Literature and Medicine**
The Johns Hopkins University Press
701 W. 40th St., Ste. 275   Phone: (410)516-6982
Baltimore, MD 21211   Fax: (410)516-6998
Journal. **Frequency:** 2x/yr. **Printing Method:** Offset. **Trim Size:** 6 x 9. **Cols./Page:** 1. **Col. Width:** 26 picas. **Col. Depth:** 7 in. **Key Personnel:** Anne Hudson Jones, Editor; Tara Dorai-Berry, Advertising Mgr. **Subscription:** $19; $34 institutions.
Ad Rates: BW: $200   **Circulation:** 700

ᛤ **1857 Maryland Family Magazine**
Maryland Family, Inc.
104 Water St.
Baltimore, MD 21202
Magazine provides information on local events and topics of interest to individuals living in Maryland. **Frequency:** Monthly. **Key Personnel:** Rudy Miller, Editor. **Subscription:** $12.
     Circulation: (Not Reported)

ᛤ **1858 Modern Judaism**
The Johns Hopkins University Press
701 W. 40th St., Ste. 275   Phone: (410)516-6982
Baltimore, MD 21211   Fax: (410)516-6998
Journal on Judaism. **Frequency:** 3x/yr. **Printing Method:** Offset. **Trim Size:** 6 x 9. **Cols./Page:** 1. **Col. Width:** 26 picas. **Col. Depth:** 7 in. **Key Personnel:** Steven Katz, Editor; Tara Dorai-Berry, Advertising Mgr. **Subscription:** $28; $50 institutions.
Ad Rates: BW: $190   **Circulation:** ‡700

ᛤ **1859 Performing Arts Journal**
The Johns Hopkins University Press
701 W. 40th St., Ste. 275   Phone: (410)516-6982
Baltimore, MD 21211   Fax: (410)516-6998
Journal. **Frequency:** 3x/yr. **Printing Method:** Offset. **Trim Size:** 6 x 9. **Cols./Page:** 1. **Col. Width:** 26 picas. **Col. Depth:** 7 in. **Key Personnel:** Bonnie Marranca, Co-Editor; Gautam Dasgupta, Co-Editor; Tara Dorai-Berry, Advertising Mgr. **Subscription:** $18; $37 institutions.
Ad Rates: BW: $290   **Circulation:** ‡1,350

ᛤ **1860 Philosophy and Literature**
The Johns Hopkins University Press
701 W. 40th St., Ste. 275   Phone: (410)516-6982
Baltimore, MD 21211   Fax: (410)516-6998
Journal. **Frequency:** 2x/yr. **Printing Method:** Offset. **Trim Size:** 6 x 9. **Cols./Page:** 1. **Col. Width:** 26 picas. **Col. Depth:** 7 in. **Key Personnel:** Denis Dutton, Co-Editor; Patrick Henry, Co-Editor; Tara Dorai-Berry, Advertising Mgr. **Subscription:** $19; $38 institutions.
Ad Rates: BW: $235   **Circulation:** ‡1,100

ᛤ **1861 Port of Baltimore**
Maryland Port Administration
World Trade Center   **Phone: (410)385-4480**
Baltimore, MD 21202   Fax: (410)333-1126

ᛤ **1862 Proof Texts**
The Johns Hopkins University Press
701 W. 40th St., Ste. 275   Phone: (410)516-6982
Baltimore, MD 21211   Fax: (410)516-6998
Journal. **Frequency:** 3x/yr. **Printing Method:** Offset. **Trim Size:** 6 x 9. **Cols./Page:** 1. **Col. Width:** 26 picas. **Col. Depth:** 7 in. **Key Personnel:** Alan Mintz, Co-Editor; David G. Roskies, Co-Editor; Tara Dorai-Berry, Advertising Mgr. **Subscription:** $20; $47 institutions.
Ad Rates: BW: $190   **Circulation:** ‡900

ᛤ **1863 Theatre Topics**
The Johns Hopkins University Press
701 W. 40th St., Ste. 275   Phone: (410)516-6982
Baltimore, MD 21211   Fax: (410)516-6998
Journal covering all aspects of the theater. Published in cooperation with the Association for Theatre in Higher Education. **Frequency:** 2x/year. **Key Personnel:** Beverley Byers-Pevitts, Editor; Tara Dorai-Berry, Advertising Mgr. **Subscription:** $15.50; $24 institutions.
Ad Rates: BW: $215   **Circulation:** 1,900

ᛤ **1864 Urban Profile Magazine**
Urban Frofile Communications, Inc.
729 E. Pratt St., Ste. 504   Phone: (410)244-7101
Baltimore, MD 21202   Fax: (410)752-1837
Magazine covering African-American student interests. **Founded:** 1988. **Frequency:** Monthly. **Key Personnel:** Keith T. Clinkscales, Publisher/Editor-In-Chief; Leonard E. Burnett, Jr., Exec. Dir. **ISSN:** 1049-9695. **Subscription:** $10; $18 two years.
Ad Rates: BW: $3,700   **Circulation:** (Not Reported)
     4C: $4,800
     PCI: $200

ᛤ **1865 Vegetarian Journal**
Vegetarian Resource Group
PO Box 1463
Baltimore, MD 21203   Phone: (410)366-8343
Journal with recipes and news related to vegetarianism. **Founded:** 1982. **Frequency:** 6x/yr. **Trim Size:** 8 1/2 x 11. **Cols./Page:** 2 and 3. **Key Personnel:** Debra Wasserman, Editor; Reed Mangels, Nutrition Editor; Ziona Swigart, Circulation Mgr. **ISSN:** 0885-7636. **Subscription:** $20; $30 Canada; $40 other countries. $3 single issue.
     Circulation: 24,000
Advertising not accepted.

♟ **1866 UAE**
2525 Kirk Ave.   Phone: (301)366-7469
Baltimore, MD 21218   Fax: (301)366-7469
Owner: Tele-Communications, Inc. **Founded:** 1986. **Cities Served:** Baltimore County, MD.

♟ **1867 WBAL-TV - Channel 11**
3800 Hooper Ave.
Baltimore, MD 21211   **Phone: (410)467-3000**

♟ **1868 WBGR-AM - 860**
3000 Druid Park Dr.   **Phone: (410)367-7773**
Baltimore, MD 21215   **Fax: (410)367-4702**

♟ **1869 WEAA-FM - 88.9**
Hillen Rd. & Coldspring Ln.
Baltimore, MD 21239   **Phone: (410)319-3564**

♟ **1870 WLIF-FM - 101.9**
1570 Hart Rd.   **Phone: (410)823-1570**
Baltimore, MD 21286   **Fax: (410)821-5482**

� 1871 WNUV-TV - Channel 54
3001 Druid Park Dr.   Phone: (410)462-5400
Baltimore, MD 21215   Fax: (410)523-4319

☀ 1872 WQSR-FM - 105.7
305 Washington Ave., 4th Fl.   Phone: (410)825-1000
Baltimore, MD 21204-4715   Fax: (410)825-2442

☀ 1873 WXYV-FM - 102.7
1829 Reistertown Rd.   Phone: (410)653-2200
Baltimore, MD 21208   Fax: (410)486-8057

BEL AIR

☀ 1874 Clearview CATV Inc.
2242 Conwingo Rd.
Bel Air, MD 21015   Phone: (717)258-3746
Founded: 1988. **Key Personnel:** William Domurad, Pres.; Douglas
Nace, Gen. Mgr. **Cities Served:** Harford County, MD: 4,700 subscrib-
ing households; 37 channels.

BERLIN

☐ 1875 Maryland Coast Dispatch
PO Box 467   Phone: (410)641-4561
Berlin, MD 21811   Fax: (410)641-0966
Tabloid. **Founded:** 1970. **Frequency:** Weekly. **Trim Size:** 10 x 13 1/2.
Cols./Page: 4. **Col. Width:** 2 3/4 in. **Col. Depth:** 13 1/2in.
Ad Rates: BW: $607.95   **Circulation:** Paid ‡25,000
            4C: $907.95
            SAU: $11

BETHESDA

☐ 1876 ASFA Marine Biotechnology Abstracts
Cambridge Scientific Abstracts
7200 Wisconsin Ave.   Phone: (301)961-6750
Bethesda, MD 20814   Fax: (301)961-6720
Journal covering the application of molecular biology and molecular
genetics to aquatic organisms. **Founded:** 1989. **Frequency:** Quarterly.
Key Personnel: Darrel Stover, Editor; Angela Hitti, Mng. Editor; Ted
Caris, Publisher; Bart De Castro, Mktg. Dir. **ISSN:** 1043-8971.
Subscription: $185; $195 other countries.
                              Circulation: (Not Reported)
Cambridge Scientific Abstracts is a division of the Cambridge
Information Group.**Additional Contact Information:** Angela Hitti:
(301)961-6744. Published in cooperation with four U.N. agencies.
Advertising not accepted.

**☐ 1877 ASFA Part 3: Aquatic Pollution & Environmental
Quality**
Cambridge Scientific Abstracts
7200 Wisconsin Ave.   Phone: (301)961-6750
Bethesda, MD 20814   Fax: (301)961-6720
Journal covering worldwide literature on pollution and conservation
of fresh and salt water environments. **Founded:** 1990. **Frequency:**
Bimonthly. **Key Personnel:** Jonathan Sears, Editor; Angela Hitti, Mng.
Editor; Ted Caris, Publisher; Bart De Castro, Mktg. Dir. **ISSN:** 1045-
6031. **Subscription:** $230; $240 other countries.
                              Circulation: (Not Reported)
Cambridge Scientific Abstracts is a divison of the Cambridge
Information Group. **Additional Contact Information:** Angela Hitti:
(301)961-6744. Published in cooperation with four U.N. agencies.
Advertising not accepted.

☐ 1878 Association Trends
Martineau Corp.
7910 Woodmont Ave., Ste. 1150   Phone: (301)652-8666
Bethesda, MD 20814   Fax: (301)656-8654

☐ 1879 EIS: Digests of Environmental Impact Statements
Cambridge Scientific Abstracts
7200 Wisconsin Ave.   Phone: (301)961-6750
Bethesda, MD 20814   Fax: (301)961-6720
Journal abstracting government environmental impact statements.
Founded: 1970. **Frequency:** Bimonthly. **Key Personnel:** Stuart Stern,
Editor; Edward Reid, Editor; Angela Hitti, Mng. Editor; Ted Caris,
Publisher. **ISSN:** 0364-1074. **Subscription:** $490; $525 other coun-
tries.
                              Circulation: (Not Reported)
Cambridge Scientific Abstracts is a divison of the Cambridge
Information Group. **Additional Contact Information:** Angela Hitti:
(301)961-6744. Advertising not accepted.

☐ 1880 Future Survey
World Future Society
7910 Woodmont Ave., Ste. 450   Phone: (301)656-8274
Bethesda, MD 20814-3032   Fax: (301)951-0394
Publication featuring books, articles, and reports concerning the
future. **Frequency:** Monthly. **Printing Method:** Offset. **Trim Size:** 8 1/2
x 11. **Cols./Page:** 2. **Col. Width:** 20 picas. **Col. Depth:** 136 agate lines.
Key Personnel: Michael Marien, Editor. **ISSN:** 0190-3241. **Subscrip-
tion:** $75; $115 institutions.
                              Circulation: Paid 2,100
Advertising not accepted.

☐ 1881 Futures Research Quarterly
World Future Society
7910 Woodmont Ave., Ste. 450   Phone: (301)656-8274
Bethesda, MD 20814   Fax: (301)951-0394

☐ 1882 The Futurist
World Future Society
7910 Woodmont Ave., Ste. 450   Phone: (301)656-8274
Bethesda, MD 20814   Fax: (301)951-0394

☐ 1883 Human Genome Abstracts
Cambridge Scientific Abstracts
7200 Wisconsin Ave.   Phone: (301)961-6750
Bethesda, MD 20814   Fax: (301)961-6720
Journal covering molecular biology and genetics research. **Subtitle:**
Basic Research and Clinical Applications. **Founded:** 1990. **Frequency:**
Bimonthly. **Key Personnel:** Wilma Ek, Editor; Angela Hitti, Mng.
Editor; Ted Caris, Publisher; Bart DeCastro, Mktg. Dir. **ISSN:** 1045-
4470. **Subscription:** $195; $215 other countries.
                              Circulation: (Not Reported)
Cambridge Scientific Abstracts is a divison of the Cambridge
Information Group. **Additional Contact Information:** Angela Hitti:
(301)961-6744. Advertising not accepted.

☐ 1884 Oncogenes & Growth Factors Abstracts
Cambridge Scientific Abstracts
7200 Wisconsin Ave.   Phone: (301)961-6750
Bethesda, MD 20814   Fax: (301)961-6720
Journal covering the mechanisms that cause cancerous cell growth.
Founded: 1989. **Frequency:** Quarterly. **Key Personnel:** Fred Spangler,
Editor; Angela Hitti, Mng. Editor; Ted Caris, Publisher; Bart DeCas-
tro, Mktg. Dir. **ISSN:** 1043-8963. **Subscription:** $190; $200 other
countries.
                              Circulation: (Not Reported)
Cambridge Scientific Abstracts is a divison of the Cambridge
Information Group. **Additional Contact Information:** Angela Hitti:
(301)961-6744. Advertising not accepted.

☐ 1885 Risk Abstracts
Cambridge Scientific Abstracts
7200 Wisconsin Ave.   Phone: (301)961-6750
Bethesda, MD 20814   Fax: (301)961-6720
Journal covering the assessment and management of risk. **Founded:**
1984. **Frequency:** Quarterly. **Key Personnel:** Niels C. Lind, Editor;
Jatin Nathwani, Editor; Angela Hitti, Mng. Editor. **ISSN:** 0824-3336.
Subscription: $145; $155 other countries.
                              Circulation: (Not Reported)
Cambridge Scientific Abstracts is a divison of the Cambridge
Information Group. **Additional Contact Information:** Angela Hitti:

Ad Rates: GLR = general line rate; BW = one-time black & white page rate; 4C = one-time four color page rate; SAU = standard advertising unit rate;
CNU = Canadian newspaper advertising unit rate; PCI = per column inch rate.
Circulation: ★ = ABC; △ = BPA; ◆ = CAC; ● = CCAB; ☐ = VAC; ⊕ = PO Statement; ‡ = Publisher's Report; Boldface figures = sworn; Light figures = estimated.
Entry type: ☐ = Print; ☀ = Broadcast.

123

(301)961-6744. Published in cooperation with the Institute for Risk Research, University of Waterloo, Ontario, Canada. Advertising not accepted.

BURTONSVILLE

1886 Decoy Magazine
Decoy Magazine
PO Box 277
Burtonsville, MD 20866   Phone: (301)890-0262
Magazine for decoy collectors and enthusiasts. **Founded:** 1979. **Frequency:** 6x/yr. **Trim Size:** 8 1/2 x 11. **Cols./Page:** 3. **Col. Width:** 2 7/16 in. **Col. Depth:** 9 11/16 in. **Key Personnel:** Joe Engers, Publisher. **ISSN:** 1055-0364. **Subscription:** $30; $35 Canada; $60 other countries. $6 single issue.
Ad Rates: BW: $450   **Circulation:** Paid ‡2,500
                4C: $685   Non-paid ‡100

CATONSVILLE

1887 Arbutus Times
Patuxent Publishing
405 Frederick Rd., Ste. 7   Phone: (410)788-4500
Catonsville, MD 21228   Fax: (410)788-4103
Community newspaper. **Founded:** 1956. **Frequency:** Weekly. **Printing Method:** Web offset. **Trim Size:** 11 x 16. **Cols./Page:** 5. **Col. Width:** 1 13/16 in. **Col. Depth:** 15 in. **Key Personnel:** Pete Kerzel, Editor; S. Zeke Orzinsky, Publisher. **Subscription:** $12; $14 out of area; $22 out of state.
Ad Rates: BW: $832   **Circulation:** ◆3,715
                                                Free ◆266

1888 Catonsville Times
Patuxent Publishing
7 Frederick Rd., Ste. 7   Phone: (410)788-4500
Catonsville, MD 21228   Fax: (410)788-4103
Community newspaper. **Founded:** 1881. **Frequency:** Weekly. **Printing Method:** Web offset. **Trim Size:** 11 x 16. **Cols./Page:** 5. **Col. Width:** 1 13/16 in. **Col. Depth:** 15 in. **Key Personnel:** Pete Kerzel, Editor; S. Zeke Orzinsky, Publisher. **Subscription:** $16; $18 out of area; $22 out of state.
Ad Rates: BW: $1,015   **Circulation:** Paid ◆6,923
                                                Free ◆488

1889 WUMD-FM - 560
5401 Willkin Ave.
Catonsville, MD 21228   Phone: (301)455-3192
Format: Alternative/Independent/Progressive. **Key Personnel:** Rob Thornton, Music Dir. **Ad Rates:** Noncommercial.

CHESTERTOWN

1890 Kent County News
PO Box 30   Phone: (301)778-2011
Chestertown, MD 21620   **Fax: (301)778-6522**

COLLEGE PARK

1891 Feminist Studies
University of Maryland
Women's Studies Program
College Park, MD 20742   Phone: (301)405-7415
Scholarly journal discussing women's studies issues. **Founded:** 1972. **Frequency:** 3x/year. **Key Personnel:** Claire G. Moses, Editor. **ISSN:** 0046-3663. **Subscription:** $25; $55 institutions. $10 single issue.
Ad Rates: BW: $250   **Circulation:** 7,500
Color advertising not accepted.

COLUMBIA

1892 Columbia Magazine
Patuxent Publishing, Co.
10750 Little Patuxent Pkwy.   Phone: (301)730-3620
Columbia, MD 21044   **Fax: (301)730-7053**

1893 N.E. Times Reporter
Patuxent Publishing Co.
10750 Little Patuxent Pkwy.   Phone: (301)730-3620
Columbia, MD 21044   Fax: (301)730-7053
Community newspaper. **Founded:** 1945. **Frequency:** Weekly (Wed.). **Printing Method:** Web offset. **Trim Size:** 11 x 16. **Cols./Page:** 5. **Col. Width:** 11 picas. **Col. Depth:** 15 in. **Key Personnel:** S. Zeke Orlinsky, Publisher; B. Willis, Editor. **Subscription:** Free; $104 (First Class mail).
Ad Rates: BW: $847   **Circulation:** Paid ‡17
                4C: $1,297   Free ‡16,560

CRISFIELD

1894 Crisfield Times
PO Box 230   **Phone: (410)968-1188**
Crisfield, MD 21817   **Fax: (410)968-1197**

CUMBERLAND

1895 Vintage Fashions
Hobby House Press
900 Frederick St.   Phone: (301)759-3770
Cumberland, MD 21502   Fax: (301)759-4940
Ceased publication.

DAMASCUS

1896 Damascus Courier-Gazette
The Gazette Newspapers
PO Caller, No. 6006   **Phone: (301)253-0911**
Gaithersburg, MD 20877   **Fax: (301)670-7183**

EASTON

1897 Star-Democrat
Chesapeake Publishing Corp.
1 Airport Dr.   **Phone: (410)822-1500**
Easton, MD 21602   **Fax: (410)820-6519**

ELLICOTT CITY

1898 Howard Cable TV Assoc. Inc.
3417 Plumtree Dr.
Ellicott City, MD 21042   Phone: (410)461-1156

FREDERICK

1899 AOPA Pilot
421 Aviation Way   **Phone: (301)695-2350**
Frederick, MD 21701   **Fax: (301)695-2180**

FROSTBURG

1900 WFWM-FM - 91.7
Frostburg State University
Compton Hall   Phone: (301)689-4143
Frostburg, MD 21532   **Fax: (301)689-4069**

1901 WLIC-FM - 97.1
He's Alive Corp. Offices
34 Springs Rd.
PO Box 540   Phone: (301)895-3292
Grantsville, MD 21536   **Fax: (301)895-3293**

GAITHERSBURG

1902 Sports Focus Magazine
Capital Sports Focus, Inc.
316 E. Diamond Ave., Ste. 103   Phone: (301)670-6717
Gaithersburg, MD 20877   Fax: (301)670-9043
Sports magazine. **Founded:** 1988. **Frequency:** Monthly. **Printing Method:** Web offset. **Trim Size:** 10 1/8 x 14. **Cols./Page:** 4. **Col. Width:** 2 1/4 in. **Col. Depth:** 13 1/8 in. **Key Personnel:** Manny Rosenberg, Publisher. **Subscription:** $15.95.
Ad Rates: BW: $3,300   **Circulation:** Controlled ‡100,000
                4C: $4,050
Additional Contact Information: In Philadelphia call (215)925-4514.

GAMBRILLS

♣ 1903 Jones Intercable, Inc.
815 Rte. 3
Box 267   Phone: (301)987-3900
Gambrills, MD 21054   Fax: (301)923-3568
Owner: Jones Intercable, Inc. **Founded:** 1983. **Cities Served:** Anne Arundel and Prince Georges counties, MD.

GERMANTOWN

▢ 1904 Journal of Parametrics
International Society of Parametric Analysts
PO Box 1056   **Phone: (301)670-8925**
Germantown, MD 20875-1056   **Fax: (301)670-1942**

HAGERSTOWN

▢ 1905 The Winner
The Health Connection
55 W. Oak Ridge Dr.
Hagerstown, MD 21740   Phone: (301)790-9735
Magazine for 4th-6th graders that focuses on health issues, including substance abuse. **Founded:** 1956. **Frequency:** Monthly (during academic year). **Printing Method:** Offset. **Trim Size:** 8 x 10 5/8. **Key Personnel:** Gerald Wheeler, Editor. **Subscription:** $8.95.
Circulation: Paid 23,000
Advertising not accepted.

HANOVER

▢ 1906 Pennysaver
Pennysaver Group of Maryland
1342 Charwood Rd.   Phone: (410)684-2600
Hanover, MD 21076   Fax: (410)684-2065
Shopping guide. **Founded:** 1979. **Frequency:** Weekly. **Printing Method:** Web offset. **Trim Size:** 7 1/2 x 11. **Cols./Page:** 2. **Col. Depth:** 10 in. **Key Personnel:** Mike Onorato, Sales Dir. **Subscription:** Free.
Circulation: Controlled ▢505,000
Advertising accepted; contact publisher for rates.

HOLLYWOOD

♣ 1907 American Cable TV of St. Marys County
10 Airport View Dr.   Phone: (301)373-3201
Hollywood, MD 20636   Fax: (301)373-3757
Owner: American Cable TV Investors 5, Ltd. **Formerly:** Simmons Cable TV. **Key Personnel:** Phil Spindt, Gen. Mgr.; Jerry Orris, Plant Mgr. **Cities Served:** Patuxent River, Leonardtown, St. Mary's County, North Beach, and Chesapeake Beach, MD; 15,700 subscribing households; 40 channels.

LANHAM

♣ 1908 MultiVision Cable TV
9609 Anapolis Rd.   Phone: (301)731-5560
Lanham, MD 20706   Fax: (301)731-7822
Owner: MultiVision Cable TV Corp. **Founded:** 1980. **Key Personnel:** Jeffrey Patrick, Production Mgr. **Cities Served:** Prince Georges County, MD; 75,000 subscribing households; 73 channels. **Additional Contact Information:** (301)306-5700.

LEONARDTOWN

♣ 1909 WKIK-AM - 1370
PO Box 510
Leonardtown, MD 20650   Phone: (301)475-9545
Format: Contemporary Country. **Network(s):** Satellite Music. **Owner:** JBJ Communications, Inc., at above address. **Founded:** 1953. **Operating Hours:** Continuous. **ADI:** Washington, DC. **Key Personnel:** Robert E. Johnson, Pres./Gen. Mgr.; Sharon C. Johnson, Program Dir. **Wattage:** 1000. **Ad Rates:** Available upon request.

MIDDLETOWN

▢ 1910 The Middletown Valley Citizen
Citizen Communications, Inc.
1220 Marker Rd.
Middletown, MD 21769   Phone: (301)371-9399
Community newspaper. **Founded:** 1990. **Frequency:** Weekly. **Printing Method:** Offset. **Cols./Page:** 5. **Col. Width:** 2 in. **Col. Depth:** 14 in. **Key Personnel:** Julie Maynard, Co-Editor; Scott Edie, Co-Editor. **ISSN:** 1056-7674. **Subscription:** $12; $17 out of area.
Ad Rates: PCI: $4.25   **Circulation:** Paid ‡1,010
                                                 Non-paid ‡35
Additional Contact Information: Alternate phone: (301)834-7722.

♣ 1911 WAFY-FM - 103.1
4707 Schley Ave.
PO Box 600   Phone: (301)371-7900
Braddock Heights, MD 21714   Fax: (301)371-7901

MILLERSVILLE

♣ 1912 Acton Corp. North Arundel CATV
406 Headquarters Dr., Ste. 201   Phone: (410)987-8400
Millersville, MD 21108   Fax: (410)987-4890
Owner: Acton Corp. **Founded:** 1979. **Key Personnel:** Robert Salem, V.P.; Richard Oldenburg, Regional Mgr.; Charles Ingrao, Marketing Coordinator; Craig Malang, Corporate Engineer; Patricia Archibald, Office Mgr. **Cities Served:** Northern Anne Arundel County, MD: 42,004 subscribing households; 54 channels; 2 community access channels; 168 hours per week of community access programming.

MONTGOMERY

♣ 1913 Cable TV of Montgomery
20 W. Gude Dr.   Phone: (301)294-7600
Rockville, MD 20850-1151   Fax: (301)294-7697
Owner: Hauser Communications. **Founded:** 1984. **Cities Served:** Montgomery County, Prince Georges County, Barnesville, Battery Park, Bethesda, Boyds, Brookville, Burtonsville, Chevy Chase, Damascus, Derwood, Friendship Heights, Gaithersburg, Garrett Park, Germantown, Glen Echo, Kensington, North White Oak, Oakmont, Olney, Poolesville, Potomac, Rockville, Silver Spring, Somerset, South White Oak, Tacoma Park, Washington Grove, and West Bethesda, MD.

NEW CARROLLTON

▢ 1914 Logistics Spectrum
Society of Logistics Engineers
8100 Professional Pl., No. 211   **Phone: (301)459-8446**
New Carrollton, MD 20785-2283   **Fax: (301)459-1522**

NORTH POTOMAC

▢ 1915 Belles Lettres: A Review of Books by Women
11151 Captain's Walk Ct.   Phone: (301)294-0278
North Potomac, MD 20878   Fax: (301)294-0023

OAKLAND

♣ 1916 WMSG-AM - 1050
PO Box 271   Phone: (301)334-3800
Oakland, MD 21550   Fax: (301)334-5800

♣ 1917 WXIE-FM - 92.3
PO Box 271   **Phone: (301)334-1100**
Oakland, MD 21550   **Fax: (301)334-5800**

Ad Rates: GLR = general line rate; BW = one-time black & white page rate; 4C = one-time four color page rate; SAU = standard advertising unit rate; CNU = Canadian newspaper advertising unit rate; PCI = per column inch rate.
Circulation: ★ = ABC; △ = BPA; ♦ = CAC; ● = CCAB; □ = VAC; ⊕ = PO Statement; ‡ = Publisher's Report; Boldface figures = sworn; Light figures = estimated.
Entry type: ▢ = Print; ♣ = Broadcast.

125

OCEAN CITY

1918 Beachcomber
Atlantic Publications, Inc.
3316 Coastal Hwy., Box 479   Phone: (401)289-6834
Ocean City, MD 21842   Fax: (401)289-6838
Entertainment newspaper. **Founded:** 1962. **Frequency:** Weekly (Fri.).
Key Personnel: Stewart Dobson, Editor and Publisher; Tammy
Goldsmith, Circulation Mgr.; Sue Lalhbury, Advertising Mgr. **Subscription:** Free.
Ad Rates: BW: $728
          4C: $1,133   **Circulation:** Free 18,000
          PCI: $11.20

1919 Oceana Magazine
PO Box 1943   Phone: (410)250-5512
Ocean City, MD 21842-1943   Fax: (302)539-6815
Magazine. **Founded:** 1978. **Frequency:** Weekly. **Printing Method:** Web
offset. **Trim Size:** 10 x 15. **Cols./Page:** 4. **Col. Width:** 14 picas. **Col.
Depth:** 84 picas. **Key Personnel:** Elizabeth Brownell, Editor. **Subscription:** $55 for 42 issues.
          Circulation: Non-paid ‡27,000
Advertising accepted; contact publisher for rates.

OWINGS MILLS

1920 Amazon Times
PO Box 135
Owings Mills, MD 21117
Publication featuring dialogue on all topics of interest to lesbians.
Founded: 1990. **Frequency:** Quarterly. **Key Personnel:** Charlotte Zinser, Editor. **Subscription:** $20; $25 institutions.
          Circulation: (Not Reported)
Advertising not accepted. Available on audio cassette.

1921 Community Times
Landmark Community Newspaper of MD, Inc.
PO Box 346   Phone: (301)876-4670
Westminster, MD 21158-0346   Fax: (301)857-1176
Former Title: Randallstown News

OXON HILL

1922 Resurrection Magazine
Jackson & Jackson
PO Box 004   Phone: (301)297-5803
Oxon Hill, MD 20750   Fax: (301)297-7538
Christian non-denominational magazine. **Subtitle:** The Magazine For
the Family of Believers. **Founded:** 1989. **Frequency:** Quarterly. **Trim
Size:** 8 1/2 x 11. **Key Personnel:** Sandra L. Jackson, Editor. **ISSN:**
1044-8586. **Subscription:** $18. $4 single issue.
Ad Rates: BW: $275   **Circulation:** Paid ‡200
          Controlled ‡300

POTOMAC

1923 Avionics Magazine
Phillips Business Information, Inc.
7811 Montrose Rd.   Phone: (301)340-2100
Potomac, MD 20854   Fax: (301)340-0542

**1924 International Journal of Micrographics & Optical
Technology**
Avedon Associates
14 Accord Ct.   Phone: (301)983-0604
Potomac, MD 20854   Fax: (301)983-0113
Journal covering electronic imaging and micrographics. **Subtitle:**
Including all aspects of Electronic Information Transfer. **Founded:**
1983. **Frequency:** Quarterly. **Trim Size:** 185 mm x 245 mm. **Cols./
Page:** 2. **Col. Width:** 75 mm. **Col. Depth:** 200 mm. **Key Personnel:** Don
Avedon, Editor. **ISSN:** 0743-9636. **Subscription:** $175.
          Circulation: Paid 2,000
          Non-paid 100
Advertising accepted; contact publisher for rates.

ROCKVILLE

1925 411
United Communications Group
11300 Rockville Pike, Ste. 1100   Phone: (301)816-8950
Rockville, MD 20852-3030   **Fax: (301)816-8945**

1926 Petroleum Marketer
GCI Publishing Co.
1801 Rockville Pike, No. 330   **Phone: (301)984-7333**
Rockville, MD 20852   **Fax: (301)984-7340**

SALISBURY

1927 Salisbury News & Advertiser
Independent Newspapers, Inc.
27 Court Plaza   Phone: (410)749-0272
Salisbury, MD 21801   Fax: (410)749-5073

SILVER SPRING

1928 Executive Suite Magazine
10169 New Hampshire Ave., No. 171   Phone: (301)439-7750
Silver Spring, MD 20903   Fax: (301)439-7885
Black-oriented business guide for the metropolitan Baltimore and
Washington D.C. areas. **Subtitle:** Keeping Business In The Black.
Founded: 1991. **Frequency:** Monthly. **Printing Method:** Web offset.
Trim Size: 8 1/4 x 10 3/4. **Cols./Page:** 3. **Col. Width:** 2 1/4 in. **Col.
Depth:** 9 1/2 in. **Key Personnel:** James Eric, Publisher. **Subscription:**
$24.
Ad Rates: BW: $600   **Circulation:** Paid ‡200
          4C: $750   Controlled ‡9,800

1929 Labor's Heritage
The George Meany Memorial Archives
10000 New Hampshire Ave.   **Phone: (301)431-6400**
Silver Spring, MD 20903   Fax: (301)434-0371

1930 The Nautilus
Trophon Corp.
PO Box 7279   Phone: (202)786-2073
Silver Spring, MD 20907-7279   **Fax: (202)357-2343**

1931 WWRC-AM - 980
8121 Georgia Ave.   Phone: (301)587-4900
Silver Spring, MD 20910   **Fax: (301)589-9461**

TIMONIUM

1932 Comcast Cablevision of Baltimore County
1830 York Rd.   Phone: (301)252-1012
Timonium, MD 21093   Fax: (301)252-1728
Owner: Comcast Corp. **Founded:** 1978. **Key Personnel:** Stephen Burch,
Regional V.P.; Curt Pendleton, Gen. Mgr.; Paul Chiamulera, Marketing Dir.; Bill Sievers, Operations Dir.; Tom Gorman, Engineering Dir.
Cities Served: Baltimore County, Arbutus, Catonsville, Cockeysville,
Dundalk, Ellicott City, Essex, Lansdowne-Baltimore Highlands, Middle River, Overlea, Owings-Mills, Parkville, Pikesville, Randallstown,
Reisterstown, Rosedale, Timonium-Lutherville, Towson, and Woodlawn, MD.

TOWSON

1933 WFEL-AM - 1570
1550 Hart Rd.   Phone: (410)823-5357
Towson, MD 21286   Fax: (410)337-9179

WESTMINSTER

1934 The Phoenix
Western Maryland College
2 College Hill   **Phone: (410)751-8600**
Westminster, MD 21157   Fax: (410)857-2729

MASSACHUSETTS

ALLSTON

☙ 1935 Cablevision of Boston
28 Travis St.
Allston, MA 02134   Phone: (617)787-6600
Owner: Cablevision Systems Corp. **Founded:** 1982. **Cities Served:**
Suffolk County, Allston, Black Bay, Beacon Hill, Brighton, Charlestown, Chinatown, Dorchester, East Boston, Fenway, Hyde Park, Jamaica Plain, Mattapan, North End, Roslindale, Roxbury, South Boston, South End, and West Roxbury, MA.

AMHERST

◫ 1936 Massachusetts Magazine
University of Massachusetts
Munson Hall
Amherst, MA 01003   **Phone: (413)545-0155**

ARLINGTON

◫ 1937 The Arlington Advocate
Century Newspapers
5 Water St.   Phone: (617)643-7901
Arlington, MA 02174   Fax: (617)648-4913

AYER

◫ 1938 Montachusett Times
Nashoba Publications, Inc.
69 Fitchburg Rd.
PO Box 362   Phone: (508)772-0777
Ayer, MA 01432   Fax: (508)772-4012
Ceased publication.

BOSTON

◫ 1939 American Journal of Law & Medicine
American Soc. of Law & Medicine, Inc.
765 Commonwealth Ave., Ste. 1634   **Phone: (617)262-4990**
Boston, MA 02215   Fax: (617)437-7596

◫ 1940 Business History Review
Harvard Business School, Cotting 100
Soldiers Field   Phone: (617)495-6154
Boston, MA 02163   Fax: (617)495-6001

◫ 1941 Foodservice East
The Newbury Street Group, Inc.
76 Summer St.
Boston, MA 02110   **Phone: (617)695-9080**

◫ 1942 Inner HORIZONS
The Daughters of St. Paul
50 St. Paul's Ave.
Jamaica Plain   Phone: (617)522-8911
Boston, MA 02130   Fax: (617)522-4081
Ceased publication.

◫ 1943 Journal for Experimental Mathematics
Jones and Bartlett Publishers
1 Exeter Plaza, Ste. 1435   Phone: (617)859-3900
Boston, MA 02116   Fax: (617)859-7675
Journal devoted to developing mathematical theory and insight.
Founded: 1992. **Frequency:** Quarterly. **Key Personnel:** David B.A.
Epstein, Editor. **ISSN:** 1058-6458. **Subscription:** $130. $40 single
issue.
                    Circulation: (Not Reported)
Advertising accepted; contact publisher for rates. **Additional Contact**
Information: Toll-free number, (800)832-0034.

◫ 1944 New England Economic Indicators
Federal Reserve Bank of Boston
PO Box 2076   Phone: (617)973-3543
Boston, MA 02106-2076   Fax: (617)973-3957
Statistical publication. **Frequency:** Monthly. **Trim Size:** 8 1/2 x 11. **Key**
Personnel: Thomas Miles, Editor. **Subscription:** Free.
                    Circulation: (Not Reported)
Advertising not accepted.

◫ 1945 Teen Voices Magazine
Women Express, Inc.
PO Box 6009 JFK
Boston, MA 02114   Phone: (617)227-4557
Subtitle: The Original Magazine For, By and About Teenage and
Young Adult Women. **Founded:** 1989. **Frequency:** Quarterly. **Trim**
Size: 10 x 14. **Key Personnel:** Alison Amoroso, Editor/Exec. Dir.;
Sherrie Green, Managing Editor. **Subscription:** $20.
Ad Rates: BW: $800   **Circulation:** Paid 2,000
                    Non-paid 8,000

◫ 1946 The World
Unitarian Universalist Assn.
25 Beacon St.   Phone: (617)742-2100
Boston, MA 02108   **Fax: (617)367-3237**

☙ 1947 WBIV-AM - 1060
1105 Commonwealth Ave., Ste. 204   Phone: (617)562-0620
Boston, MA 02215   **Fax: (617)254-0670**

☙ 1948 WBUR-FM - 90.9
630 Commonwealth Ave.   Phone: (617)353-2790
Boston, MA 02215   Fax: (617)353-4747
Format: News; Information; Eclectic. **Network(s):** National Public

Radio (NPR); American Public Radio (APR). **Owner:** The Trustees of Boston University. **Founded:** 1950. **Operating Hours:** Continuous. **Key Personnel:** Jane Christo, Gen. Mgr.; George Boosey, Mng. News and Program Dir.; George Preston, Music Dir.; James McIlniney, Business Mgr.; Sam Fleming, News Dir.; Bianca Bator, Corporate Underwriting; Jay Clayton, Mktg. Mgr.; Steve Elman, Asst. Gen. Mgr. **Wattage:** 7200. **Ad Rates:** Noncommercial.

⚓ 1949 WGBH-FM - 89.7
125 Western Ave.   Phone: (617)492-2777
Boston, MA 02134   Fax: (617)864-7927

⚓ 1950 WHDH-AM - 850
7 Bulfinch Pl.   Phone: (617)248-5501
Boston, MA 02114-2913   Fax: (617)742-8827

⚓ 1951 WZLX-FM - 100.7
200 Clarendon St.   Phone: (617)267-0123
Boston, MA 02116   Fax: (617)421-9305

BREWSTER

⚓ 1952 WFCC-FM - 107.5
Box 2090
Brewster, MA 02631   Phone: (508)896-9322

BRIGHTON

📖 1953 New Age Journal
Rising Star Associates
342 Western Ave.   Phone: (617)787-2005
Brighton, MA 02135   Fax: (617)787-2879

BROCKTON

⚓ 1954 Continental Cablevision
4 Main St.   Phone: (508)588-2434
Brockton, MA 02401   Fax: (508)588-5168
Owner: Continental Cablevision, Inc. **Founded:** 1983. **Key Personnel:** Richard Donaghue, Gen. Mgr.; Lou Russo, Community Program Mgr.; T.J. Lacey, Mktg. Mgr.; Jack Orpen, Technical Operations Mgr.; Renea Jeffers, Cust. Service Mgr. **Cities Served:** Norfolk County, Plymouth County, East Bridgewater, Hanson, Holbrook, West Bridgewater, Brockton, Stoughton, Aron, Easton, Raynham, and Whitman, MA: 34,500 subscribing households; 70 channels; 3 community access channels; 13 hours per week of community access programming. **Additional Contact Information:** Alt. phone (508)588-9290.

CAMBRIDGE

📖 1955 Bad Attitude
PO Box 390110
Cambridge, MA 02139   Phone: (508)372-6247
Journal for women who are interested in lesbian lifestyles. Features erotic fiction. **Founded:** 1984. **Frequency:** 6x/yr. **Key Personnel:** Jasmine Sterling, Editor.
                Circulation: (Not Reported)
Advertising accepted; contact publisher for rates.

📖 1956 Cultural Survival Quarterly
Cultural Survival, Inc.
215 1st St.   Phone: (617)374-1650
Cambridge, MA 02142   Fax: (617)621-3814

📖 1957 Growing Without Schooling
Holt Associates
2269 Massachusetts Ave.   Phone: (617)864-3100
Cambridge, MA 02140   Fax: (617)864-9235

📖 1958 Harvard Crimson
The Harvard Crimson, Inc.
14 Plympton St.   Phone: (617)495-7890
Cambridge, MA 02138-6606   Fax: (617)495-8193

📖 1959 The Harvard Salient
PO Box 1053
Cambridge, MA 02238   Phone: (617)496-5674
Founded: 1981. **Frequency:** 2x/mo. **Printing Method:** Offset. **Cols./Page:** 4. **Col. Width:** 2 1/4 in. **Col. Depth:** 15 in. **Key Personnel:**

Dianne Reeder, Editor; Sarena Lin, Business Mgr. **Subscription:** $20; $30 other countries.
Ad Rates: BW: $200   **Circulation:** 4,500
        PCI: $8

📖 1960 Mathematical Finance
Blackwell Publishers
238 Main St.
Cambridge, MA 02142
Journal. **Subtitle:** An International Journal of Mathematics, Statistics, and Financial Economics. **Founded:** 1991. **Frequency:** Quarterly. **Trim Size:** 9 3/4 x 6 3/4. **Key Personnel:** Stanley R. Pliska, Editor. **ISSN:** 0960-1627. **Subscription:** $141.
Ad Rates: BW: $300   **Circulation:** ‡700

📖 1961 New Liberation News Service
PO Box 41, MIT Branch
Cambridge, MA 02139   Phone: (617)253-0399
Alternative media news service. **Subtitle:** Uncensored and Free. **Founded:** 1990. **Frequency:** Monthly. **Printing Method:** Offset. **ISSN:** 1060-4227. **Subscription:** $45.
                Circulation: (Not Reported)
Advertising not accepted.

📖 1962 Nucleus
Union of Concerned Scientists
26 Church St.   Phone: (617)547-5552
Cambridge, MA 02238   Fax: (617)864-9405
Magazine covering issues concerning science and scientists. **Subtitle:** The Magazine of the Union of Concerned Scientists. **Frequency:** Quarterly. **Trim Size:** 8 1/2 x 11. **Key Personnel:** Janet S. Wagner, Editor. **ISSN:** 0888-5729. **Subscription:** $15. single issue Free.
                Circulation: (Not Reported)
Advertising not accepted.

📖 1963 Radical Teacher
PO Box 102
Cambridge, MA 02142   Phone: (617)492-3468
Periodical containing articles, photos, interviews, and book reviews on radical feminist theory and practice in education. **Founded:** 1975. **Frequency:** 3x/yr. **Key Personnel:** Susan O'Malley, Editor; Louis Kampf, Circulation Mgr. **ISSN:** 0191-4847. **Subscription:** $10.
                Circulation: 3,000

⚓ 1964 Continental Cablevision
88 Sherman St.   Phone: (617)876-5005
Cambridge, MA 02140   Fax: (617)876-8613
Owner: Continental Cablevision, Inc. **Founded:** 1985. **Cities Served:** Middlesex County, and Arlington, MA.

CONCORD

📖 1965 PageMarker In-Depth
Mindcraft Publishing Corp.
52 Domino Dr.
Concord, MA 01742
A what- and how-to computer magazine. **Frequency:** Monthly. **Key Personnel:** Andrew Maddox, Publisher; Mike Harvey, Editor. **Subscription:** $69. $7.50 single issue.
                Circulation: (Not Reported)

DEDHAM

📖 1966 Daily Transcript
Harte-Hanks Community Newspapers
580 Winter St.   Phone: (617)487-7200
Waltham, MA 02154   Fax: (617)326-9675

DORCHESTER

📖 1967 Dorchester Argus-Citizen
South Boston Tribune
395 W. Broadway
PO Box 6
South Boston, MA 02127   Phone: (617)268-3440

FALL RIVER

⬤ 1968 Greater Fall River Cable TV
800 Warren St.
Box 671   Phone: (508)675-1171
Fall River, MA 02722   Fax: (508)679-5662
Owner: Colony Communications, Inc. **Founded:** 1979. **Cities Served:**
Bristol County, MA.

⬤ 1969 WHTB-AM - 1400
130 Rock St.   Phone: (508)677-0505
Fall River, MA 02720   Fax: (508)672-6784

FOXBORO

⬤ 1970 CVI-Cablevision Industries
85 E. Belcher Rd.   Phone: (508)543-8650
Foxboro, MA 02035   Fax: (508)543-7936
Owner: Cablevision Industries, Inc. **Founded:** 1983. **Cities Served:**
Bristol, Middlesex, Norfolk, Plymouth, and Worcester counties, MA.

FRAMINGHAM

📖 1971 CIO
CIO Publishing
492 Old Connecticut Path
PO Box 9208   Phone: (508)872-8200
Framingham, MA 01701-9208   Fax: (508)872-0618
Publication for Chief Information Officers (CIOs) and other senior
executives. **Subtitle:** The Magazine For Information Executives.
Founded: 1987. **Frequency:** 18x/yr. **Printing Method:** Web offset. **Trim
Size:** 8 1/8 x 10 3/4. **Cols./Page:** 3. **Key Personnel:** Marcia Blumenthal,
Editor-in-Chief; Joe Levy, Publisher. **ISSN:** 0894-9301. **Subscription:**
$59. $7 single issue.
Ad Rates: BW: $11,950   **Circulation:** Paid △2,075
4C: $17,950   Controlled △65,026

FRANKLIN

📖 1972 Wheel, 7463 Newspaper for Dealers
Kruza Kaleidoscopix, Inc.
PO Box 389
Franklin, MA 02038-0389   Phone: (508)528-6211
Publication for automobile dealers. **Founded:** 1985. **Frequency:** Quar-
terly. **Printing Method:** Offset. **Trim Size:** 11 x 17. **Cols./Page:** 4. **Col.
Width:** 13 picas. **Col. Depth:** 15 in. **Key Personnel:** J.A. Kroza, Editor.
Subscription: $96.
Ad Rates: BW: $1,600   **Circulation:** Paid ‡7,500
Controlled ‡1,500

GREAT BARRINGTON

📖 1973 Hikane: The Capable Womon
PO Box 841
Great Barrington, MA 01230
Magazine serving as a networking/grassroots tool for disabled lesbians
and their "wimmin" allies. Available in print, cassette, and braille.
Founded: 1989. **Frequency:** Quarterly. **Printing Method:** Offset. **Trim
Size:** 8 1/2 x 11. **Subscription:** $14; $24 institution.
Circulation: (Not Reported)

HYDE PARK

📖 1974 The Waybill
Mystic Valley Railroad Society
PO Box 486
Hyde Park, MA 02136   Phone: (617)361-4445
Tabloid covering railroad related items and events. **Founded:** 1970.
Frequency: Quarterly. **Printing Method:** Web offset. **Trim Size:** 11 x
17. **Cols./Page:** 4. **Col. Width:** 2 1/2 in. **Key Personnel:** W. Russel
Rylko, Contact. **ISSN:** 0897-7577. **Subscription:** Included with mem-
bership.
Ad Rates: BW: $200   **Circulation:** Paid ‡6,000
PCI: $6   Free ‡8,000

Color advertising not accepted.

LITTLETON

📖 1975 Meteorological & Geoastrophysical Abstracts
American Meteorological Society
c/o Inforonics
550 Newtown Rd.
PO Box 458   Phone: (508)486-8976
Littleton, MA 01460   Fax: (508)486-0027

LOWELL

⬤ 1976 Lowell Cable TV Co., Inc.
12 Washer St.
Box 1121   Phone: (508)459-3313
Lowell, MA 01853   Fax: (508)454-6910
Owner: Colony Communications, Inc. **Founded:** 1979. **Cities Served:**
Middlesex County, Chelmsford, and Tewksbury, MA.

LYNN

⬤ 1977 Warner Cable Communications, Inc.
26 Tremont St.
Lynn, MA 01902   Phone: (617)599-5801
Owner: Warner Cable Communications, Inc. **Founded:** 1980. **Cities
Served:** Essex County, MA.

MEDFORD

📖 1978 New England Performer Magazine
11 Riverside Ave., Ste. 4   Phone: (617)395-7055
Medford, MA 02155   Fax: (617)391-8252
Trade magazine for musicians. **Founded:** 1988. **Frequency:** Monthly.
Printing Method: Web offset. **Trim Size:** 8 1/4 x 10 3/4. **Cols./Page:** 3.
Key Personnel: Rick Schettino, Editor; David Ridgley, Publisher;
William House, Advertising Mgr. **Subscription:** $20. $2 single issue.
Ad Rates: BW: $490   **Circulation:** Paid 2,000
4C: $1,190   Non-paid 15,000
Formerly: Musicians Only Magazine.

⬤ 1979 Warner Cable Communications, Inc.
278 Mystic Ave.   Phone: (617)397-2600
Medford, MA 02155   Fax: (617)397-0211
Owner: Warner Cable Communications, Inc. **Founded:** 1972. **Cities
Served:** Middlesex and Suffolk counties, MA.

MIDDLEBORO

📖 1980 Eastern/Western Quarter Horse Journal
Eastern/Western Publishing
Box 690
Middleboro, MA 02346   Phone: (508)947-6831
Ceased publication.

NEEDHAM

📖 1981 Needham Chronicle
Hart-Hanks Community Newspapers
580 Winter St.   Phone: (617)487-7200
Waltham, MA 02154   Fax: (617)487-7377

⬤ 1982 Continental Cablevision of Massachusetts, Inc.
95 Wexford St.
Needham, MA 02194   Phone: (617)455-8693
Owner: Continental Cablevision, Inc. **Founded:** 1981. **Cities Served:**
Middlesex and Norfolk counties, MA.

Ad Rates: GLR = general line rate; BW = one-time black & white page rate; 4C = one-time four color page rate; SAU = standard advertising unit rate;
CNU = Canadian newspaper advertising unit rate; PCI = per column inch rate.
Circulation: ★ = ABC; △ = BPA; ◆ = CAC; ● = CCAB; □ = VAC; ⊕ = PO Statement; ‡ = Publisher's Report; Boldface figures = sworn; Light figures = estimated.
Entry type: 📖 = Print; ⬤ = Broadcast.

129

NEW BEDFORD

⚓ 1983 Whaling City Cable TV
700 Kempton St.   Phone: (508)999-1390
New Bedford, MA 02740   Fax: (508)992-7365
Owner: Colony Communications, Inc. **Founded:** 1975. **Cities Served:**
Bristol County and Dartmouth, MA.

NEWTON

📖 1984 Advanced Systems News
Cahners Publishing Co.
275 Washington St.
Newton, MA 02158   Phone: (617)964-3030
Ceased publication.

📖 1985 Datamation
Cahners Publishing Assoc., L.P.
275 Washington St.   Phone: (617)964-3030
Newton, MA 02158-1630   **Fax: (617)558-4506**

📖 1986 EDN Products and Careers
Cahners Publishing Co.
275 Washington St.   Phone: (617)964-3030
Newton, MA 02158-1630   **Fax: (617)558-4470**
Former Title: EDN News Edition

📖 1987 Electronics Purchasing
Cahners Publishing Co.
275 Washington St.   **Phone: (617)558-4723**
Newton, MA 02158-1630   **Fax: (617)558-4327**

📖 1988 Musical Merchandise Review
Larkin Publications
100 Wells Ave.   Phone: (617)964-5100
Newton, MA 02159-9103   **Fax: (617)964-2752**

📖 1989 R & D Magazine
Cahners Publishing Company
275 Washington St.   Phone: (708)635-8800
Newton, MA 02158   Fax: (708)390-2618
Magazine covering the field of applied research and development.
Founded: 1959. **Frequency:** Monthly. **Printing Method:** Web offset.
Trim Size: 8 x 10 3/4. **Cols./Page:** 3. **Col. Width:** 2 1/8 in. **Col. Depth:**
10 in. **Key Personnel:** Rob Cassidy, Editor-in-Chief. **ISSN:** 0746-
9179. **Subscription:** $69.95. $20 single issue.
Ad Rates: BW: $7,750   **Circulation:** Paid △1,703
        4C: $9,535   Non-paid △108,500
Formerly: Industrial Research and Development.

📖 1990 Test & Measurement World
Cahners Publishing Co.
275 Washington St.   Phone: (617)964-3030
Newton, MA 02158-1630   **Fax: (617)558-4470**

NORTH EASTON

📖 1991 The Summit
Stonehill College
    Phone: (508)238-1081
North Easton, MA 02356   **Fax: (508)230-8268**

NORTH READING

📖 1992 North Reading Transcript
Great Oak Publications
PO Box 7
North Reading, MA 01864   Phone: (508)664-4761
    Fax: (508)664-4954

ORANGE

⚓ 1993 WCAT-FM - 99.9
660 E. Main St.
Orange, MA 01364   Phone: (508)544-2321
Format: Young Adult Contemporary. **Network(s):** Satellite Music.
Owner: P & S Broadcasting, Inc., at above address. **Founded:** 1956.
Operating Hours: Continuous. **Key Personnel:** Richard W. Partridge,
Pres./Gen. Mgr.; Jean S. Partridge, Station Mgr. **Wattage:** 3000. **Ad**

Rates: $7-$10 for 30 seconds; $8-$12 for 60 seconds; Combined rates
available with WCAT-AM.

ORLEANS

📖 1994 Woman of Power
Woman of Power, Inc.
PO Box 2785
Orleans, MA 02653   Phone: (508)240-7877
Magazine containing articles, interviews, profiles, art, poetry, and
photographs. **Subtitle:** A Magazine of Feminism, Spirituality, and
Politics. **Founded:** 1984. **Frequency:** Quarterly. **Printing Method:** Web
offset. **Trim Size:** 8 3/8 x 10 7/8. **Cols./Page:** 2. **Col. Width:** 20 picas.
Key Personnel: Charlene McKee, Editor. **ISSN:** 0743-2356. **Subscription:** $30. $8 single issue.
Ad Rates: BW: $785   **Circulation:** Paid 6,000
            Non-paid 14,000
Color advertising not accepted.

QUINCY

⚓ 1995 Continental Cablevision
81 School St.   Phone: (617)471-3200
Quincy, MA 02169   Fax: (617)472-7350
Owner: Continental Cablevision, Inc. **Founded:** 1982. **Cities Served:**
Norfolk County, MA.

SOMERVILLE

📖 1996 Radical America
Alternative Education Project
1 Summer St.
Somerville, MA 02143   Phone: (617)628-6585

SOUTH DARTMOUTH

📖 1997 The Chronicle
Hathaway Publishing Corp.
45 Slocum Rd.
PO Box 80268   Phone: (508)992-1522
South Dartmouth, MA 02748-0268   Fax: (508)992-1620

SOUTH HADLEY

📖 1998 Mount Holyoke Alumnae Quarterly
Mount Holyoke Alumnae Association
303 Mary E. Woolley Hall   Phone: (413)538-2251
South Hadley, MA 01075   Fax: (413)538-2254

SPRINGFIELD

⚓ 1999 Continental Cablevision, Inc. of Springfield
3303 Main St.   Phone: (413)733-5121
Springfield, MA 01107   Fax: voice act.
Owner: Continental Cablevision, Inc. **Founded:** 1982. **Cities Served:**
Hampden County, MA.

⚓ 2000 WNEK-FM - 105.1
Western New England College
1215 Wibraham Rd.   Phone: (413)782-1582
Springfield, MA 01119   **Fax: (413)796-2008**

STONEHAM

📖 2001 Melrose News Weekender
377 Main St.   Phone: (617)438-1660
Stoneham, MA 02180   **Fax: (617)438-6762**
Former Title: Melrose Saugus Shopper News

📖 2002 The Stoneham Independent
377 Main St.   Phone: (617)438-1660
Stoneham, MA 02180   **Fax: (617)438-6762**

📖 2003 Stoneham News Weekender
377 Main St.   Phone: (617)438-1660
Stoneham, MA 02180   **Fax: (617)438-6762**
Former Title: Stoneham Shopper News

SUDBURY

◻ **2004 Bonsai Today**
Stone Lantern Publishing Co.
PO Box 816   Phone: (508)443-7110
Sudbury, MA 01776   **Fax: (508)443-9115**

◻ **2005 WHEELS, ETC.**
Want Ad Publications, Inc.
740 Boston Post Rd.   Phone: (508)443-4100
Sudbury, MA 01776-3330   Fax: (508)443-5281
Automobile classified ad magazine containing photos. **Founded:** 1984.
Frequency: Weekly (Tues.) **Printing Method:** Offset. **Trim Size:** 8 1/4 x
11. **Cols./Page:** 2. **Col. Width:** 3 1/2 in. **Col. Depth:** 10 in. **Key
Personnel:** Patricia Halter, Editor; Pam McLain, Circulation Mgr.
Subscription: $120. $1.25 single issue.
                                        Circulation: ‡10,000
Advertising accepted; contact publisher for rates. **Formerly:** Wheels
and Keels.

SWAMPSCOTT

◻ **2006 Swampscott Reporter**
North Shore Weeklies, Inc.
40 South St.   **Phone: (617)631-7700**
Marblehead, MA 01945   **Fax: (617)639-2830**

WALTHAM

◻ **2007 Forced Exposure**
PO Box 9102   Phone: (617)562-0507
Waltham, MA 02254-9102   Fax: (617)562-0533

◻ **2008 Justice**
Brandeis University
PO Box 9110   **Phone: (617)736-3750**
Waltham, MA 02254-9110   **Fax: (617)736-3756**

WARE

◻ **2009 New England Antiques Journal**
Turley Publications
4 Church St.
PO Box 120   Phone: (413)967-3505
Ware, MA 01082   Fax: (413)967-6009

WEBSTER

♣ **2010 WGFP-AM - 940**
Douglas Rd.   Phone: (508)943-9400
Webster, MA 01570   **Fax: (508)943-0405**

WELLESLEY

◻ **2011 Wellesley Magazine**
Wellesley College
106 Central St.   **Phone: (617)283-2331**
Wellesley, MA 02181-8201   **Fax: (617)283-3638**
Former Title: Alumnae Magazine

◻ **2012 The Women's Review of Books**
Wellesley College   **Phone: (617)283-2087**
Wellesley, MA 02181   **Fax: (617)283-3645**

WELLESLEY HILLS

◻ **2013 Contingency Planning and Recovery Journal (CPR-
J)**
Management Advisory Publications
Contingency Planning & Recovery
  Institute
57 Greylock Rd.
PO Box 81151   Phone: (617)235-2895
Wellesley Hills, MA 02181-0001   **Fax: (617)235-5446**

WESTFIELD

♣ **2014 Continental Cablevision**
1110 E. Mountain Rd.   Phone: (413)562-9923
Westfield, MA 01085   Fax: (413)568-6625
Owner: Continental Cablevision, Inc. **Founded:** 1970. **Cities Served:**
Hampden and Hampshire counties, MA.

WESTFORD

◻ **2015 Color Publishing**
PennWell Publishing Co.
1 Technology Park Dr.
PO Box 987   Phone: (508)692-0700
Westford, MA 01886   Fax: (508)692-7806
Magazine covering electronic color publishing industry. **Founded:**
1991. **Frequency:** 6x/yr. **Printing Method:** Web offset. **Trim Size:** 8 x
10 7/8. **Key Personnel:** Robert P. Hulton, Publisher; Frank Romano,
Editor-in-Chief; Tom McMillan, Editor. **ISSN:** 1055-9701. **Subscrip-
tion:** $19.90; $28.90 foreign. $5 single issue.
Ad Rates: BW: $3,875   **Circulation:** 24,000
                 4C: $5,170
Additional Contact Information: Sales and Marketing offices 1 Technology Park Dr., PO Box 987, Westford, MA 01886, phone (508)392-
2168, fax (508)692-7806; for insertion orders and materials contact
Sue Mullarkey, phone (508)392-2196, fax (508)692-8349.

◻ **2016 Computer Artist**
PennWell Publishing Co.
1 Technology Park Dr.
PO Box 987   Phone: (508)692-0700
Westford, MA 01886   Fax: (508)692-7806
Magazine for creative professionals who use computers in art, design,
and illustration. **Founded:** 1992. **Frequency:** 6x/yr. **Printing Method:**
Web offset. **Trim Size:** 8 X 10 7/8. **Key Personnel:** Robert Holton,
Publisher; Tom McMillan, Editor. **ISSN:** 1063-312X. **Subscription:**
$19.95. $5.95 single issue.
Ad Rates: BW: $6,500   **Circulation:** Non-paid **40,000**
                 4C: $8,475
For insertion orders and materials contact Sue Mullarkey, phone
(508)392-2196, fax (508)692-8349.

◻ **2017 Lightwave**
PennWell Publishing
1 Technology Park Dr.
PO Box 992   Phone: (508)692-0700
Westford, MA 01886   Fax: (508)692-8391

WILLIAMSTOWN

◻ **2018 The Advocate**
Berkshire Advocate, Inc.
38 Spring St.
PO Box 95   Phone: (413)458-9000
Williamstown, MA 01267   Fax: (413)458-5715

WILMINGTON

◻ **2019 Wilmington Town Crier**
Wilmington News Co., Inc.
104 Lowell St.
PO Box 460   Phone: (508)658-2346
Wilmington, MA 01887-0660   Fax: (508)658-2266
Community newspaper. **Founded:** 1955. **Frequency:** Weekly. **Printing
Method:** Offset. **Cols./Page:** 6. **Col. Width:** 12 picas. **Col. Depth:** 21
picas. **Key Personnel:** Larz F. Neilson, Editor; C. Stuart Neilson,
Advertising Mgr. **Subscription:** $18; $22 out of area. $.50 single issue.
Ad Rates: GLR: $.375   **Circulation:** Paid ◆**5,310**
                 PCI: $5.25   Free ◆**130**

WOBURN

⊞ 2020 Aboriginal Science Fiction
Second Renaissance Foundation Inc.
PO Box 2449
Woburn, MA 01888-0849   Phone: (617)935-9326
Science fiction literary magazine. **Subtitle:** Tales of the Human Kind.
Founded: 1986. **Frequency:** Quarterly. **Printing Method:** Web offset.
Trim Size: 8 3/8 x 10 7/8. **Cols./Page:** 2 and 3. **Col. Width:** 3 1/4 and 2
1/8 in. **Col. Depth:** 10 in. **Key Personnel:** Charles C. Ryan, Editor.
ISSN: 0895-3198. **Subscription:** $18. $3.95 single issue.
Ad Rates: BW: $750   **Circulation:** Paid ⊕**23,121**
              4C: $1,200   Non-paid ⊕**197**
              PCI: $30

WORCESTER

⊞ 2021 Centrum Guide
Worcester County Newspapers
PO Box 1000   Phone: (508)799-0511
Worcester, MA 01614   Fax: (508)832-2431
Ceased publication.

⊞ 2022 Economic Geography
Clark University
950 Main St.   Phone: (508)793-7311
Worcester, MA 01610   **Fax: (508)793-8881**

⊞ 2023 Newspeak
Worcester Polytechnic Institute
Box 2700   Phone: (508)831-5464
Worcester, MA 01609   **Fax: (508)831-5721**

⊞ 2024 Strange Days
Broken Arrow Publishing
PO Box 564
Worcester, MA 01613   Phone: (508)865-5891
Magazine profiles writers specializing in the bizarre. **Founded:** 1990.
Frequency: Quarterly. **Printing Method:** Offset. **Trim Size:** 8 1/2 x 11.
Key Personnel: Peter Bianca, Editor. **Subscription:** $16.95. $4.95
single issue.
Ad Rates: BW: $100   **Circulation:** Paid 1,200
              4C: $250

⬤ 2025 Greater Worcester Cablevision
95 Higgins St.   Phone: (508)853-1515
Worcester, MA 01606-1913   Fax: (508)854-5042
Owner: Greater Media, Inc. **Founded:** 1969. **Key Personnel:** Richard
Tuthill, V.P./Gen. Mgr.; Art Goody, Marketing Mgr.; Allan Eisenberg,
Dir. of Ad Sales; Brian Bedard, Technical Mgr. **Cities Served:** Auburn,
Boylston, Dudley, Grafton, Holden, Leicester, Millbury, Northbor-
ough, Northbridge, Oxford, Paxton, Southborough, Southbridge,
Spencer, Sturbridge, Upton, Webster, West Boylston, West Brook-
field, Westborough, and Worcester, MA: 110,000 subscribing house-
holds; 58 channels; 3 community access channels.

⬤ 2026 WCHC-FM - 89.1
Holy Cross College
Box G
Worcester, MA 01610   Phone: (508)793-2475
Format: Alternative/Independent/Progressive; Rap. **Owner:** Trustees
of the College of the Holy Cross. **Operating Hours:** 7 a.m.-2 a.m. **Key
Personnel:** Paul K. Connolly, Gen. Mgr.; John Schultz, Announcing
Dir.; Myron Michalski, Asst. Mgr.; Jason Alexander, Music Dir.
Wattage: 100. **Additional Contact Information:** (508)793-2471;
(508)793-2474.

⬤ 2027 WICN-FM - 90.5
6 Chatham St.
Worcester, MA 01609   Phone: (508)752-0700

MICHIGAN

ADRIAN

🎙 **2028 WVAC-FM - 107.9**
Adrian College
110 S. Madison St.
Adrian, MI 49221
Phone: (517)265-5161
Fax: (517)264-3331

ALLEGAN

📖 **2029 Tri-Cities Flashes**
Flashes Publishers, Inc.
595 Jenner Dr.
Allegan, MI 49010
Phone: (616)673-2141
Fax: (616)673-4761

ANN ARBOR

📖 **2030 The Ann Arbor News**
340 E. Huron St.
Ann Arbor, MI 48104
Phone: (313)994-6989
Fax: (313)994-6879

📖 **2031 The Education Digest**
Prakken Publications, Inc.
PO Box 8623
Ann Arbor, MI 48107-8623
Phone: (313)769-1211
Fax: (313)769-8383

📖 **2032 New Covenant**
PO Box 7009
Ann Arbor, MI 48107
Phone: (313)668-4896
Fax: (313)668-6104

📖 **2033 Reference Services Review**
Pierian Press
PO Box 1808
Ann Arbor, MI 48106
Phone: (313)434-5530
Fax: (313)434-6409

📖 **2034 Serials Review**
Pierian Press
PO Box 1808
Ann Arbor, MI 48106
Phone: (313)434-5530
Fax: (313)434-6409

BAD AXE

📖 **2035 The Business Blanket**
c/o The Thumb Blanket
47 Westland Dr., Box 237
Bad Axe, MI 48413-0237
Phone: (517)269-9918
Fax: (517)269-8109
Magazine for Michigan businesses in the Bad Axe, MI area. **Founded:** January, 1991. **Frequency:** Monthly. **Printing Method:** Web offset.

Trim Size: 11 1/4 x 14. **Cols./Page:** 4. **Col. Depth:** 2 1/2 in. **Col. Depth:** 13 in. **Key Personnel:** Mark W. Rummel, Editor. **Subscription:** Free.
Ad Rates:

GLR:	$.714	**Circulation:** Non-paid ‡1,972
BW:	$225	
4C:	$552	
PCI:	$10	

BATTLE CREEK

📖 **2036 Children's Literature Association Quarterly**
Children's Literature Assn.
PO Box 138
Battle Creek, MI **49016**
Phone: (616)965-8180

🎙 **2037 WBXX-FM - 95.3**
Box 3495
Battle Creek, MI 49016
Phone: (616)963-5555
Fax: (616)963-5185
Format: Contemporary Hit Radio (CHR). **Owner:** Liggett Broadcasting. **Founded:** 1976. **Formerly:** WMJC. **Operating Hours:** Continuous. **Key Personnel:** Joe Dawson, Operations Mgr.; Sharon Croner, Sales Mgr.; James Jensen, Pres. **Wattage:** 3000. **Ad Rates:** $41.

🎙 **2038 WOLY-AM - 1500**
15074 6 1/2 Mile Rd.
Battle Creek, MI 49017
Phone: (616)965-1515
Fax: (616)965-1315

BELLAIRE

📖 **2039 Antrim County News**
Up North Publications, Inc.
PO Box 337
Bellaire, MI 49615
Phone: (616)533-8523

📖 **2040 The Town Meeting**
Up North Publications, Inc.
PO Box 337
Bellaire, MI 49615
Phone: (616)264-9711
Community newspaper. **Founded:** 1974. **Frequency:** Weekly. **Printing Method:** Offset. **Key Personnel:** Mary Hockstad, Contact. **Subscription:** $22; $25 out of area.

Circulation: (Not Reported)

BENTON HARBOR

📖 **2041 REMark**
Heath/Zenith Users' Group
PO Box 217
Benton Harbor, MI 49023-0217
Phone: (616)982-3463
Fax: (616)982-3330
Ceased publication.

BEULAH

2042 Ad-Visor
PO Box 797   Phone: (616)882-9613
Beulah, MI 49617   **Fax: (616)882-9615**

BLOOMFIELD HILLS

2043 International Journal of Systems Automation:
 Research & Applications (SARA)
SARA Institute
PO Box 781   Phone: (313)492-0551
Bloomfield Hills, MI 48303-0731   Fax: (313)661-8333
Journal covering the interrelationship among engineering, design,
data management, robotics, artificial intelligence, and manufacturing.
Subtitle: Systems Engineering, Concurrent Engineering. **Founded:**
1991. **Frequency:** Quarterly. **Key Personnel:** Biren Prasad, Editor-in-
Chief; H. Barry Bebb, Co-Editor; V.M. Ponomaryov, Co-Editor;
Pierre Haren, Co-Editor. **ISSN:** 1055-8462. **Subscription:** $105.
Ad Rates: GLR: $4   **Circulation:** Paid ‡417
       BW: $750   Non-paid ‡892
       4C: $1,500

2044 WBFH-FM - 88.1
4200 Andover Rd.   Phone: (313)645-4740
Bloomfield Hills, MI 48302   Fax: (313)645-4744
Format: Album-Oriented Rock (AOR) (Educational). **Owner:** Board of
Education of Bloomfield Hills School District. **Founded:** 1976.
Operating Hours: 10:15 a.m.-10 p.m. **Key Personnel:** Pete Bowers,
Gen. Mgr.; Ron Wittebols, Asst. Mgr. **Wattage:** 360. **Ad Rates:**
Noncommercial.

BOYNE CITY

2045 Outstate Business
Harbor House Publishers, Inc.
221 Water St.   Phone: (616)582-2814
Boyne City, MI 49712   Fax: (616)582-3392
Former Title: North Force

CAMDEN

2046 The Farmers' Advance
Suburban Communications Corp.
Box 8   **Phone: (517)368-0365**
Camden, MI 49232   Fax: (517)368-5131

CHARLOTTE

2047 Charlotte Shopping Guide and Eaton County News
Community Newspapers
239 S. Cochran   **Phone: (517)643-3113**
Charlotte, MI **48813**   Fax: (517)543-3677

2048 WNNY-AM - 1390
PO Box 338   Phone: (517)543-8200
Charlotte, MI 48813   **Fax: (517)543-7779**

CLINTON TOWNSHIP

2049 PIME World
PIME Missionaries
35750 Moravian Dr.   Phone: (313)791-2100
Clinton Township, MI **48035-2138**   Fax: (313)791-8204

DE WITT

2050 WQHH-FM - 96.5
101 Northcrest Rd., Ste. 4   Phone: (517)484-9600
Lansing, MI 48906-1262   Fax: (517)484-9699
Format: Adult Urban Contemporary. **Owner:** Mid Michigan/Diamond
Broadcasters. **Founded:** 1980. **Operating Hours:** Continuous. **Key
Personnel:** Helena Dubose, Pres./Gen. Mgr. **Wattage:** 3000. **Ad Rates:**
$10-$50 per unit. Combined rates available with WXLA-AM.

DEARBORN

2051 Journal of Manufacturing Systems
Society of Manufacturing Engineers
1 SME Dr.
PO Box 930   Phone: (313)271-1500
Dearborn, MI 48121-0930   Fax: (313)271-2861

2052 Manufacturing Engineering
Society of Manufacturing Engineers
1 SME Dr.
PO Box 930   Phone: (313)271-1500
Dearborn, MI 48121   Fax: (313)271-2861

DEARBORN HEIGHTS

2053 Continental Cablevision
2800 S. Gulley Rd.   Phone: (313)277-1050
Dearborn Heights, MI 48125   Fax: (313)277-1796
Owner: Continental Cablevision, Inc. **Founded:** 1984. **Cities Served:**
Wayne County and Westland, MI.

DETROIT

2054 American-Arab Message
17514 Woodward   Phone: (313)868-2266
Detroit, MI 48203   **Fax: (313)868-2267**

2055 Automotive Reports
Wards Communications, Inc.
28 W. Adams   Phone: (313)962-4433
Detroit, MI 48226   Fax: (313)962-4456
Periodical containing news and statistics on the auto industry.
Founded: 1924. **Frequency:** Weekly. **Printing Method:** Offset. **Trim
Size:** 8 1/2 x 11. **Cols./Page:** 2. **Col. Width:** 20 picas. **Key Personnel:**
David E. Zoia, Editor; David C. Smith, Publisher. **Subscription:** $910.
                                    Circulation: (Not Reported)
Advertising not accepted.

2056 The Detroit Lawyer
Detroit Bar Assn.
2380 Penobscot Bldg.   Phone: (313)961-6120
Detroit, MI 48226-4811   **Fax: (313)965-0842**

2057 Oakland Life
Crain Communications, Inc.
1400 Woodbridge   Phone: (313)446-0300
Detroit, MI 48207-3187   Fax: (313)446-1687
Metropolitan magazine. **Founded:** 1991. **Frequency:** Monthly. **Printing
Method:** Offset. **Trim Size:** 8 x 10 3/4. **Cols./Page:** 3. **Col. Width:** 2 1/4
in. **Col. Depth:** 10 in. **Key Personnel:** John Barron, Editor.
Ad Rates: BW: $4,550   **Circulation:** Controlled 42,000
        4C: $6,175

2058 Varsity News
University of Detroit-Mercy
4001 W. McNichols   Phone: (313)993-3300
Detroit, MI 48221   Fax: (313)993-1011
College newspaper. **Founded:** 1918. **Frequency:** Weekly (September-
April). **Printing Method:** Offset. **Cols./Page:** 5. **Col. Width:** 11 picas.
Col. Depth: 13 in. **Key Personnel:** D. Chug Abramowitz, Editor-in-
Chief; Shawn Lawrence, News Editor. **Subscription:** Free.
Ad Rates: BW: $386   **Circulation:** Free ‡4,000
        PCI: $9

2059 The Witness
The Episcopal Church Publishing Co.
1249 Washington Blvd., Ste. 3115   Phone: (313)962-2650
Detroit, MI 48226-1868   **Fax: (313)962-1012**

2060 WJLB-FM - 97.9
645 Griswold St., Suite 633   Phone: (313)965-2000
Detroit, MI 48226-4177   **Fax: (313)965-1729**

2061 WRIF-FM - 101.1
26500 Northwestern Hwy., No. 203   Phone: (313)827-1111
Southfield, MI **48034**   Fax: (313)827-9538

🎙 **2062 WXON-TV - Channel 20**
27777 Franklin Rd., No. 1220
Southfield, MI 48034

Phone: (313)355-2020
Fax: (313)355-0368

EAST JORDAN

📖 **2063 Michigan Snowmobiler**
01615 Advance-East Jordan Rd.
PO Box 417
East Jordan, MI 49727

Phone: (616)536-2371
Fax: (616)536-7691

EAST LANSING

📖 **2064 MEA Voice**
Michigan Education Assn.
1216 Kendale Blvd.
Box 2573
East Lansing, MI 48826-2573
Former Title: Voice

Phone: (517)332-6551
Fax: (517)337-5414

📖 **2065 The State News**
State News, Inc.
345 Student Service Bldg.
East Lansing, MI 48824-1113

Phone: (517)355-8252
Fax: (517)353-2599

ELSIE

🎙 **2066 WOES-FM - 91.3**
8989 Colony Rd.
Elsie, MI 48831

Phone: (517)862-4237
Fax: (517)862-4463

ESCANABA

🎙 **2067 WJMN-TV - Channel 3**
c/o CBS, Inc.
PO Box 19055
Green Bay, WI 54307-9055

Phone: (414)437-5411
Fax: (414)437-4576

FARMINGTON

📖 **2068 Stone Through the Ages**
Marble Institute of America
33505 State St.
Farmington, MI 48335
Ceased publication.

Phone: (313)476-5558
Fax: (313)476-1630

FARMINGTON HILLS

🎙 **2069 MetroVision of Oakland County**
37635 Enterprise Court
Farmington Hills, MI 48018

Phone: (313)553-7300
Fax: (313)553-4829

Owner: MetroVision, Inc. **Founded:** 1983. **Cities Served:** Oakland County, MI.

🎙 **2070 WORB-FM - 90.3**
27055 Orchard Lake Rd.
Farmington Hills, MI 48018

Phone: (313)471-7718

Format: Alternative/Independent/Progressive; Eclectic. **Owner:** Oakland Community College. **Founded:** 1975. **Operating Hours:** 8 a.m.-10 p.m. weekdays; 8 a.m.-5:30 p.m. Sat.-Sun. **Key Personnel:** Ronald Burda, Faculty Advisor; Jonathan Moshier, Station Mgr.; Alex Stoherine, Program Dir.; Rich Stringfellow, Music Dir. **Wattage:** 10. **Ad Rates:** Noncommercial.

FLINT

🎙 **2071 Comcast Cablevision of Flint**
3008 Airpark Dr. S.
Flint, MI 48507

Phone: (313)235-9200
Fax: (313)235-9205

Owner: Comcast Corp. **Founded:** 1966. **Cities Served:** Genesee County, Oakland County, Burton, Clio, Flint Twp., Flushing, Grand Blanc, Holly Village, Mount Morris, Swartz Creek, and Vienna Twp., MI.

🎙 **2072 WCRZ-FM - 107.9**
3338 E. Bristol Rd.
Flint, MI 48501

Phone: (313)743-1080
Fax: (313)742-5170

🎙 **2073 WKMF-AM - 1470**
3338 E. Bristol Rd.
PO Box 1470
Flint, MI 48501

Phone: (313)742-1470
Fax: (313)742-5170

FRANKENMUTH

🎙 **2074 WGMZ-FM - 101.7**
306 W. Genesee St.
Frankenmuth, MI 48734

Phone: (517)652-3265

Format: News; Easy Listening. **Network(s):** AP. **Owner:** Radiocom Ltd. **Founded:** 1987. **Operating Hours:** Continuous. **Key Personnel:** Linda Trestrail, Bus. Mgr./Promotions Dir.; Joe Pratt, News Dir.; Chip Birch, Sports. **Wattage:** 3000. **Ad Rates:** $7.50-$20 for 30 seconds; $14-$28 for 60 seconds.

FREMONT

🎙 **2075 WSHN-AM - 1550**
PO Box 190
Fremont, MI 49412

Phone: (616)924-4700
Fax: (616)924-9746

🎙 **2076 WSHN-FM - 100.1**
PO Box 190
Fremont, MI 49412

Phone: (616)924-4700
Fax: (616)924-9746

GRAND RAPIDS

📖 **2077 Cadence**
Valley Media, Inc.
705 Bagley SE
Grand Rapids, MI 49506

Phone: (616)454-9456
Fax: (616)454-4666

📖 **2078 Chimes**
Calvin College
3201 Burton SE
Grand Rapids, MI **49546**

Phone: (616)957-7031

📖 **2079 Missionary Monthly**
Missionary Monthly, Inc.
c/o I.D.E.A. Ministries
4595 Broadmoor Ave. SE
Grand Rapids, MI 49512

Phone: (616)698-8393
Fax: (616)698-3080

🎙 **2080 UAE**
955 Century Ave., SW
Grand Rapids, MI 49503

Phone: (616)247-0575
Fax: (616)247-0932

Owner: Tele-Communications, Inc. **Founded:** 1976. **Cities Served:** Allegan County, Kent County, Ottowa County, Ada, Cascade, East Grand Rapids, Grandville, Kentwood, and Wyoming, MI.

🎙 **2081 WGRD-FM - 97.9**
38 W. Fulton, Ste. 200
Grand Rapids, MI 49503

Phone: (616)459-4111

🎙 **2082 WGVK-TV - Channel 52**
301 W. Fulton
Grand Rapids, MI 49504-6492

Phone: (616)771-6666
Fax: (616)771-6625

🎙 **2083 WGVU-AM - 1480**
301 W. Fulton
Grand Rapids, MI 49504-6492

Phone: (616)771-6666

Format: News; Information. **Network(s):** AP; American Public Radio (APR); National Public Radio (NPR). **Owner:** Grand Valley State University. **Founded:** 1954. **Formerly:** WMAX-AM. **Operating Hours:** Continuous. **Key Personnel:** Michael T. Walenta, Gen. Mgr.; Scott Hanley, Asst. Gen. Mgr.; Rob Willey, Program Dir.; David Moore, News Dir.; Robert Lumbert, Chief Engineer. **Wattage:** 5000. **Ad Rates:** Noncommercial. Underwriting available. **Additional Contact Information:** News line (616)771-6716.

♪ 2084 WGVU-FM - 88.5
301 W. Fulton
Grand Rapids, MI 49504-6492
Phone: (616)771-6666
Fax: **(616)771-6625**

♪ 2085 WGVU-TV - Channel 35
301 W. Fulton
Grand Rapids, MI 49504-6492
Phone: (616)771-6666
Fax: **(616)771-6625**

♪ 2086 WLAV-FM - 96.9
50 Louis NW
Grand Rapids, MI 49503
Phone: (616)456-5461
Fax: **(616)451-3299**

♪ 2087 WOOD-FM - EZ-105.7
180 N. Division
Grand Rapids, MI 49503
Phone: (616)459-1919
Fax: **(616)732-3330**

GRAYLING

📖 2088 Crawford County Avalanche
100 Michigan Ave.
PO Box 490
Grayling, MI 49738
Phone: (517)348-6811
Fax: **(517)348-6806**

♪ 2089 WGRY-AM - 1230
6514 Old Lake Rd.
Grayling, MI 49738
Phone: (517)348-6171
Fax: **(517)348-6181**

♪ 2090 WGRY-FM - 101.1
6514 Old Lake Rd.
Grayling, MI 49738
Phone: (517)348-6171
Fax: **(517)348-6181**

HARRISON

♪ 2091 WDEE-AM - 1500
715 Dailey Dr. (200th Ave. S)
PO Box 549
Harrison, MI 48625
Phone: (517)539-7105
Format: Country. Simulcasts WKKM-FM, Harrison, MI. **Network(s):** ABC. **Owner:** David A. Carmine, 209 E. Spruce, PO Box 549, Harrison, MI 48625. **Founded:** 1981. **Operating Hours:** Sunrise-sunset; 5% network, 95% local. **Key Personnel:** David A. Carmine, Owner/Mgr. **Wattage:** 250. **Ad Rates:** Available upon request.

HASTINGS

♪ 2092 WBCH-AM - 1220
119 W. State St.
PO Box 88
Hastings, MI 49058
Phone: (616)945-3414
Fax: **(616)945-3470**

♪ 2093 WBCH-FM - 100.1
PO Box 88
Hastings, MI 49058
Phone: (616)945-3414
Fax: **(616)945-3470**

HOUGHTON

♪ 2094 WOLF-FM - 97.7
313 E. Montezuma Ave.
Houghton, MI 49931
Phone: (906)482-7700
Format: Adult Contemporary. **Network(s):** ABC. **Owner:** Harvey L. Desnick, 142 Woodland, Laurium, MI 49931; (906)337-7751. **Founded:** 1981. **Formerly:** WHUH-FM (1989). **Operating Hours:** Continuous. **Key Personnel:** Dick Storm, News Dir.; Kevin Ericson, Program Dir.; Norm Koski, Sports Dir.; Ed Janisse, Promotions Dir. **Wattage:** 3500. **Ad Rates:** $10-$16.50 for 60 seconds.

HOWELL

♪ 2095 WHMI-FM - 93.5
1372 W. Grand River
PO Box 935
Howell, MI 48843
Phone: (517)546-0860
Fax: **(517)546-1758**

KALAMAZOO

📖 2096 Comparative Drama
Western Michigan University
Dept. of English
Kalamazoo, MI 49008-3899
Phone: (616)387-2579
Fax: **(616)387-8750**

📖 2097 Journal of Sociology and Social Welfare
Western Michigan University
School of Social Work
Kalamazoo, MI 49008-5034
Phone: **(616)387-3918**
Fax: **(616)387-3217**

♪ 2098 Cablevision 7 Michigan, Inc.
7851 S. Westnedge
Kalamazoo, MI 49002
Phone: (616)323-2236
Fax: (616)323-0580
Owner: Cablevision Systems Corp. **Founded:** 1966. **Cities Served:** Kalamazoo County, MI.

♪ 2099 WKDS-FM - 89.9
606 E. Kilgore
Kalamazoo, MI 49001
Phone: **(616)337-0899**
Fax: **(616)337-0251**

♪ 2100 WMUK-FM - 102.1
Western Michigan University
Kalamazoo, MI 49008
Phone: (616)387-5715
Fax: (616)387-4630
Format: Classical; News; Jazz; Public Radio; Bluegrass. **Network(s):** National Public Radio (NPR); Michigan Public Radio. **Owner:** Western Michigan University, at above address. **Founded:** 1951. **Formerly:** WMCR-FM. **Operating Hours:** 5:30 a.m.-12 a.m. Sun.-Thurs.; 5:30 a.m.-1 a.m. Fri.-Sat. **Key Personnel:** Garrard Macleod, Gen. Mgr.; Richard Atwell, Assoc. Gen. Mgr.; Floyd Pientka, Music Dir.; Tony Griffin, News Dir.; Mark Tomlonson, Chief Engineer. **Wattage:** 50,000. **Ad Rates:** Noncommercial.

♪ 2101 WQLR-FM - 106.5
4200 W. Main St.
Kalamazoo, MI 49006
Phone: (616)345-7121
Fax: (616)345-1430
Format: Adult Contemporary. **Owner:** Fairfield Broadcasting Co. **Founded:** 1972. **Operating Hours:** Continuous. **Key Personnel:** Stephen Trivers, Pres./Station Mgr.; William Wertz, V.P./Music Dir.; Dennis Martin, Sales Mgr.; Kenneth Lanphear, Operations Mgr./Sports Dir.; Jodi Victor, News Dir. **Wattage:** 33,000.

LAKE ODESSA

📖 2102 Lakewood News
J-Ad Graphics, Inc.
1952 N. Broadway
PO Box 188
Hastings, MI 49058
Phone: (616)945-9554
Fax: (616)945-5192
Local paper of Lake Odessa, Woodland, Sunfield, Mulliken, and Clarksville Freeport. **Founded:** 1988. **Frequency:** Weekly. **Printing Method:** Web offset. **Cols./Page:** 6. **Col. Width:** 1 5/8 in. **Col. Depth:** 16 in. **Subscription:** Free; $16 (mail).

Ad Rates:	BW:	$254.40	Circulation: Paid 70
	4C:	$454.40	Free 6,000
	PCI:	$3.50	

LANSING

📖 2103 Michigan Banker
PO Box 12236
Lansing, MI 48901-2236
Phone: (517)332-7800
Fax: **(517)332-7806**

📖 2104 Michigan Farm News
Michigan Farm Bureau
7373 W. Saginaw Hwy.
PO Box 30960
Lansing, MI 48909-8460
Phone: (317)849-6110
Fax: (317)576-5859
Agribusiness publication for Michigan farmers. **Founded:** 1928. **Frequency:** 2x/mo. **Printing Method:** Web offset. **Trim Size:** 11 x 17. **Cols./Page:** 4. **Col. Width:** 2 3/8 in. **Col. Depth:** 10 in. **Key Personnel:** Dennis Rudat, Editor; Susan Snyder, Advertising Mgr.

| Ad Rates: | BW: | $1,900 | Circulation: ‡47,829 |
| | 4C: | $2,300 | |

📖 2105 Michigan Hospitals
Michigan Hospital Assn.
6215 W. St. Joseph Hwy.
Lansing, MI 48917
Phone: (517)323-3443
Fax: (517)323-0946
Trade magazine for Michigan hospital leaders and healthcare policy makers. **Founded:** 1965. **Frequency:** Bimonthly. **Printing Method:** Offset. **Trim Size:** 8 1/2 x 11. **Cols./Page:** 2 and 3. **Col. Width:** 4 7/8 in. and 3 1/4 in. **Key Personnel:** Karel Juhl, Editor; Pat Horan,

Advertising Mgr. **ISSN:** 0026-220X. **Subscription:** $18; $65 other countries.
Ad Rates: GLR: $.45   **Circulation:** ‡1,750
                BW: $400
                4C: $1,300

📖 2106 Michigan Overseas Veteran
Dept. of Michigan Veterans of Foreign Wars
924 N. Washington   **Phone:** (517)485-9456
Lansing, MI 48901   **Fax:** (517)485-6432

📡 2107 Continental Cablevision
333 Washington Sq. N.   **Phone:** (517)485-8100
Lansing, MI 48933   **Fax:** (517)485-5940
Owner: Continental Cablevision, Inc. **Founded:** 1976. **Cities Served:** Clinton County, Eaton County, Ingham County, De Witt, Eaton Rapids, Grand Ledge, Lansing Twp., and Watertown Twp., MI.

📡 2108 WLCC-AM - 640
Lansing Community College
PO Box 40010
Lansing, MI 48901-7210   **Phone:** (517)483-1710
Format: Alternative/Independent/Progressive. **Key Personnel:** Tony Hicks, Music Dir. **Ad Rates:** Noncommercial.

LESLIE

📖 2109 Leslie Local Independent
S. & G. Publications
109 Carney
Box 617   **Phone:** (517)589-8228
Leslie, MI 49251   **Fax:** (517)589-8228

LIVONIA

📖 2110 Miniature Collector
Scott Publications
30595 8 Mile Rd.   **Phone:** (313)477-6650
Livonia, MI 48152   **Fax:** (313)477-6795

📡 2111 MetroVision of Livonia, Inc.
Box CN3305   **Phone:** (313)422-2810
Livonia, MI 48151   **Fax:** (313)422-2239
Owner: MetroVision, Inc. **Founded:** 1984. **Cities Served:** Wayne County, MI.

LUDINGTON

📡 2112 WKLA-FM - 106.3
5941 W. U.S. 10   **Phone:** (616)843-3438
Ludington, MI 49431-2447   **Fax:** (616)843-1886
Format: Adult Contemporary. **Network(s):** ABC. **Owner:** John E. Chickering, at above address. **Founded:** 1971. **Operating Hours:** 5 a.m.-1 a.m. **Key Personnel:** John E. Chickering, Gen. Mgr./Owner; David A. Hawley, Business Mgr.; Robert E. Engblade, Chief Engineer; James A. Frost, Sales Mgr.; John W. DeMint, Production Mgr.; Ray Cummins, News Dir. **Wattage:** 6000. **Ad Rates:** $6.60-$12 for 30 seconds; $8.25-$15 for 60 seconds. Combined rates available with WKLA-AM.

MANCHESTER

📖 2113 Manchester Enterprise
109 E. Main
PO Box 37
Manchester, MI 48158   **Phone:** (313)428-8173

MANISTEE

📡 2114 WMTE-FM - 97.7
359 River St.
Manistee, MI 49660   **Phone:** (616)723-9906
Format: Album-Oriented Rock (AOR)/Classic Rock. **Network(s):** NBC; Mutual Broadcasting System; Westwood One Radio. **Owner:**

Manistee Broadcasting, Inc. **Formerly:** WRRK-FM. **Operating Hours:** 5 a.m.-1 a.m. **Key Personnel:** Laurie Foster, Gen. Mgr.; Suzanne Stevens, Sales Mgr.; Bernie Schroeder, News Dir. **Wattage:** 3000. **Ad Rates:** $4-$8 for 30 seconds; $5-$9 for 60 seconds.

MANISTIQUE

📡 2115 WCMM-FM - 94.7
1501 Deer St.
PO Box 220   **Phone:** (906)341-8444
Manistique, MI 49854   **Fax:** (906)341-6222
Format: Country. **Network(s):** ABC. **Owner:** WSHN Inc., PO Box 190, Fremont, MI 49412; (616)924-4700. **Founded:** 1992. **Operating Hours:** Continuous. **Key Personnel:** Stuart Noordyk, Pres.; Todd Noordyk, Corporate Mgr.; Don Noordyk, Gen. Mgr.; Annette Cox, Traffic and Billing. **Wattage:** 100,000. **Ad Rates:** $6.60-$12 for 30 seconds; $8.25-$15 for 60 seconds. **Additional Contact Information:** Toll-free: 800-947-9266; 8764 CC County Rd., Rapid River, MI, 49878.

MAYVILLE

📖 2116 Mayville Monitor
6071 Fulton St.   **Phone:** (517)843-6441
Mayville, MI 48744-0299   **Fax:** (517)843-6441

MENOMINEE

📡 2117 WHYB-FM - 103.9
413 10th Ave.
PO Box 365   **Phone:** (906)863-5551
Menominee, MI 49858   **Fax:** (906)863-5679

MILFORD

📖 2118 Hometown Newpapers
Suburban Communications Corp.
453 N. Main St.
PO Box 339   **Phone:** (313)685-1507
Milford, MI 48381   **Fax:** (313)437-9460

MONROE

📡 2119 WEJY-FM - 97.5
1275 N. Macomb St.
Monroe, MI 48161   **Phone:** (313)241-1491

MORENCI

📖 2120 The Morenci Observer
120 North St.   **Phone:** (517)458-6811
Morenci, MI 49256   **Fax:** (517)458-6811

MOUNT CLEMENS

📖 2121 Macomb County Legal News
Macomb Publishing Co.
67 Cass Ave.   **Phone:** (313)469-4510
Mount Clemens, MI 48043   **Fax:** (313)469-2892

MOUNT PLEASANT

📖 2122 Sun
Central Michigan Newspapers, Inc.
PO Box 447   **Phone:** (517)772-2971
Mount Pleasant, MI 48804-0447   **Fax:** (517)773-0382

📡 2123 WABX-AM - 990
1 Energy Pl., Ste. 311
5805 Pickard
Mount Pleasant, MI 48858   **Phone:** (517)772-4173

Ad Rates: GLR = general line rate; BW = one-time black & white page rate; 4C = one-time four color page rate; SAU = standard advertising unit rate; CNU = Canadian newspaper advertising unit rate; PCI = per column inch rate.
Circulation: ★ = ABC; △ = BPA; ◆ = CAC; ● = CCAB; □ = VAC; ⊕ = PO Statement; ‡ = Publisher's Report; Boldface figures = sworn; Light figures = estimated.
Entry type: 📖 = Print; 📡 = Broadcast.

MUNISING

2124 WHCH-FM - 98.3
110 W. Onota St.
Munising, MI 49862   Phone: (906)387-4000
                                      Fax: (906)387-5161

2125 WQXO-AM - 1400
110 W. Onota St.
PO Box 100
Munising, MI 49862   Phone: (906)387-4000
                                      Fax: (906)387-5161

MUSKEGON

2126 WestMarc Cable
Box 978   Phone: (616)733-0818
Muskegon, MI 49443   Fax: (616)733-0426
Owner: Tele-Communications, Inc. **Founded:** 1966. **Cities Served:** Muskegon, Newaygo, and Ottawa counties, MI.

2127 WQWQ-AM - 1520
6083 Martin Rd.   Phone: (616)798-2245
Muskegon, MI 49444-9746   Fax: (616)798-3819

NEW BALTIMORE

2128 The Voice
Voice Communications Corp.
PO Box 760   Phone: (313)949-7900
New Baltimore, MI 48047   Fax: (313)949-2217
Community newspaper. **Founded:** April 1983. **Frequency:** Weekly. **Printing Method:** Offset. **Cols./Page:** 5. **Col. Width:** 2 in. **Col. Depth:** 15 in. **Subscription:** $21.
Ad Rates: PCI: $26.80   **Circulation:** Free 53,542

NILES

2129 Hometown News
314 E. Main St.   **Phone: (616)684-8844**
Niles, MI 49120   **Fax: (616)684-6115**

ONTONAGON

2130 WOAS-FM - 88.5
701 Parker   Phone: (906)884-4422
Ontonagon, MI 49953   **Fax: (906)884-2942**

OTISVILLE

2131 Yesterdaze Toys
275 S. State Rd.   Phone: (313)631-4593
Otisville, MI 48463   Fax: (313)631-4567
Ceased publication.

PARMA

2132 The Parma News
PO Box 279   Phone: (517)531-4542
Parma, MI 49269   **Fax: (517)531-3576**

PETOSKEY

2133 The Graphic
319 State St.
PO Box 528   Phone: (616)347-2544
Petoskey, MI 49770-0528   Fax: (616)347-6833
Entertainment resort newspaper. **Founded:** 1960. **Frequency:** Weekly. **Printing Method:** Offset. **Trim Size:** 11 3/8 x 14. **Cols./Page:** 5. **Col. Width:** 5 in. **Col. Depth:** 12 in. **Key Personnel:** Ken Winter, Editor; Kirk Schaller, Publisher; Tori Calouffe, Advertising Mgr. **Subscription:** Free.
                                      Circulation: Free 17,000

PORT HURON

2134 WSGR-FM - 91.3
323 Erie St.
Port Huron, MI 48061-5015   **Phone: (313)984-5064**

PORTAGE

2135 Ambiance
Ambiance Inc.
1310 Sussex
Portage, MI 49002-2625   Phone: (616)327-4769
International journal featuring articles, short stories, poetry, and original graphic art. **Founded:** 1992. **Frequency:** 3x/yr. **Printing Method:** Offset. **Trim Size:** 8 1/2 x 11. **Cols./Page:** 3. **Col. Width:** 2 in. **Col. Depth:** 8 in. **Key Personnel:** Lynne Parcells, Editor and Publisher. **Subscription:** Free.
                                      Circulation: Non-paid ‡5,600
Advertising not accepted.

2136 Devachan
American Mensa Ltd.
1310 Sussex
Portage, MI 49002-2625   **Phone: (616)327-4769**
Ceased publication.

ROCHESTER

2137 WOUX-FM - 90.1
Oakland University
65 Oakland Center
Rochester, MI 48309   Phone: (313)370-4272
Format: Alternative/Independent/Progressive. **Key Personnel:** Scott Berry, Music Dir. **Ad Rates:** Noncommercial.

ROYAL OAK

2138 UAE
4500 Delemere Blvd.   Phone: (313)549-2100
Royal Oak, MI 48073   Fax: (313)549-6289
Owner: Tele-Communications, Inc. **Founded:** 1983. **Cities Served:** Oakland County, MI.

SAGINAW

2139 Cox Cable Saginaw
720 N. Bates St.   Phone: (517)799-8030
Saginaw, MI 48602   Fax: (517)799-7829
Owner: Cox Cable Communications. **Founded:** 1973. **Cities Served:** Saginaw County, Buena Vista Township, Carrollton Township, Saginaw Township, Spaulding Township, and Zilwaukee, MI.

2140 WAQP-TV - Channel 49
707 Federal Ave.   Phone: (517)754-1038
Saginaw, MI 48607   **Fax: (517)754-8668**

2141 WIOG-FM - 102.5
1795 Tittabawassee   Phone: (517)752-3456
Saginaw, MI 48605   **Fax: (517)754-5046**

SAINT JOHNS

2142 The Clinton County News
Community Newspapers, Inc.
215 N. Clinton   **Phone: (517)224-2361**
Saint Johns, MI 48879   **Fax: (517)224-4452**

SAUGATUCK

2143 WEVS-FM - 92.7
3676 63rd St.
PO Box 927
Saugatuck, MI 49453   Phone: (616)857-1721

SOUTHFIELD

2144 Detroit Metropolitan Woman
North Park Plaza
17117 W. 9 Mile Rd., Ste. 1115   Phone: (313)443-6500
Southfield, MI 48075-4517   Fax: (313)443-6501
Magazine containing news, features, and information for women in the metropolitan Detroit area. **Founded:** 1991. **Frequency:** Monthly. **Printing Method:** Web press. **Trim Size:** 8 x 10 3/4. **Cols./Page:** 3. **Key**

Personnel: Patricia Peart, Editor; Alice F. Sieloff, Publisher. Subscription: $15. $2 single issue.

Ad Rates: BW: $2,375   **Circulation:** Paid ‡10,000
 4C: $2,520   Non-paid ‡20,000

♣ 2145 Continental Cablevision
27800 Franklin Rd.   Phone: (313)353-3905
Southfield, MI 48034   Fax: (313)353-0141
Owner: Continental Cablevision, Inc. **Founded:** 1982. **Cities Served:** Oakland County, Keego Harbor, Lathrup Village, Oak Park, Orchard Lake, Royal Oak Township, Sylvan Lake, and West Bloomfield Township, MI.

♣ 2146 WKBD-TV - Channel 50
26905 W. 11 Mile Rd.   Phone: (313)350-5050
Southfield, MI 48034   Fax: (313)355-2692

♣ 2147 WXYT-AM - 1270
15600 W. 12 Mile Rd.
Southfield, MI 48076   Phone: (313)569-8000

STERLING HEIGHTS

♣ 2148 WUFL-AM - 1030
42669 Garfield Rd., Ste. 328   Phone: (313)263-1030
Clinton Township, MI 48038   Fax: (313)228-1030

TAYLOR

♣ 2149 Maclean Hunter Cable TV
24744 Eureka Rd.   Phone: (313)946-6010
Taylor, MI 48180   Fax: (313)946-4421
Owner: Maclean Hunter Cable TV. **Founded:** 1980. **Cities Served:** Monroe and Wayne counties, MI.

THREE OAKS

▯ 2150 The Other Side of the Lake
Artistic Energy Group, Inc.
505 W. Locust
PO Box 303   Phone: (616)756-2421
Three Oaks, MI 49128   Fax: (616)796-7220
Newspaper for second homeowners and tourists. **Founded:** 1988. **Frequency:** Monthly (9x/yr). **Printing Method:** Web offset. **Trim Size:** 11 3/8 x 15. **Cols./Page:** 6. **Col. Width:** 9.5 picas. **Col. Depth:** 14 in. **Key Personnel:** Michael Hojnacki, Editor/Publisher. **Subscription:** $11.

Ad Rates: BW: $840   **Circulation:** Free 10,000
 4C: $1,650
 PCI: $10

TROY

▯ 2151 Link
Yellow Pages Publishers Association
340 E. Big Beaver Rd.   Phone: (313)244-6211
Troy, MI 48083   Fax: (313)244-6230
Trade magazine. **Founded:** 1989. **Frequency:** 10x/yr. **Printing Method:** Offset. **Trim Size:** 8 x 10 7/8. **Cols./Page:** 3. **Key Personnel:** Larry Small, Assoc. Publisher; Barbara Beck, Promotions Mgr. **Subscription:** $60. $6 single issue.

Ad Rates: BW: $1,705   **Circulation:** Paid △2,022
 4C: $3,040   Non-paid △9,971

UNIVERSITY CENTER

♣ 2152 WUCM-TV - Channel 19
Delta Rd.
University Center   Phone: (517)686-9350
University Center, MI 48710   Fax: (517)686-8736

♣ 2153 WUCX-TV - Channel 35
University Center, Delta Rd.   Phone: (517)686-9350
University Center, MI 48710   Fax: (517)686-8736

VICKSBURG

▯ 2154 The Broadcast
Vicksburg Publications, Inc.
109 S. Main
Box 154   Phone: (616)649-2333
Vicksburg, MI 49097   Fax: (616)649-2335
Shopping guide. **Founded:** 1936. **Frequency:** Weekly. **Printing Method:** Web offset. **Cols./Page:** 6. **Key Personnel:** Jackie Lawrence, Publisher. **Subscription:** Free.

Ad Rates: PCI: $3.60   **Circulation:** Free ‡10,500

WARREN

▯ 2155 The Megarian
The Mega Society
4177 Garrick Ave.
Warren, MI 48091   Phone: (313)757-4177

♣ 2156 WPHS-FM - 89.1
30333 Hoover Rd.   Phone: (313)751-3689
Warren, MI 48093   Fax: (313)574-3062

WHITEHALL

♣ 2157 WEFG-AM - 1490
PO Box 158   Phone: (616)893-2247
Whitehall, MI 49461   Fax: (616)893-2147

♣ 2158 WEFG-FM - 97.5
PO Box 158   Phone: (616)893-2247
Whitehall, MI 49461   Fax: (616)893-2147

YPSILANTI

♣ 2159 WEMU-FM - 89.1
426 King Hall
Eastern Michigan University   Phone: (313)487-2229
Ypsilanti, MI 48197   Fax: (313)487-1015

MINNESOTA

ADRIAN

📖 **2160 Nobles County Review**
PO Box 160
Adrian, MN 56110

Phone: (507)483-2213
Fax: (507)425-2501

ALBERT LEA

📻 **2161 KATE-AM - 1450**
305 S. 1st Ave.
Albert Lea, MN 56007   Phone: (507)373-2338
Format: Middle-of-the-Road (MOR); News. **Network(s):** ABC. **Owner:** Communications Properties Inc. **Founded:** 1937. **Operating Hours:** Continuous. **Key Personnel:** Dennis Martin, V.P./Gen. Mgr.; Vern Rassmusen, Sales Mgr.; Bill Elliott, News Dir.; Al Carstens, Farm Dir. **Wattage:** 1000. **Ad Rates:** $54-$66 per unit.

📻 **2162 KRGR-FM - 95.3**
305 S. 1st Ave.
Albert Lea, MN 56007   Phone: (507)373-2338
Format: Oldies; Adult Contemporary. **Owner:** Communications Properties, Inc. **Founded:** 1974. **Formerly:** KCPI-FM. **Operating Hours:** Continuous. **Key Personnel:** Dennis Martin, V.P./Gen. Mgr.; Vern Rasmussen, Sales Mgr.; Bill Elliott, News Dir.; Al Carstens, Farm Dir.; Mike Sullivan, Sports Dir.; Dave Lesch, Program Dir. **Wattage:** 3000. **Ad Rates:** $25-$29 per unit.

ALEXANDRIA

📖 **2163 The Echo/Press**
Alexandria Printing Co.
121 5th Ave. W.
PO Box 549   Phone: (612)763-3133
Alexandria, MN 56308   Fax: (612)763-3258
Former Title: Lake Region Echo/Press

📻 **2164 KIKV-FM - 100.7**
604 Third Ave. W.
Box 1024   Phone: (612)762-2154
Alexandria, MN 56308   **Fax: (612)762-2156**

APPLETON

📻 **2165 KWCM-TV - Channel 10**
120 W. Schlieman   Phone: (612)289-2622
Appleton, MN 56208   **Fax: (612)289-2634**

BROOKLYN PARK

📻 **2166 Colony Communications, Inc.**
6901 Winnetka Ave. N.   Phone: (612)533-8347
Brooklyn Park, MN 55428   Fax: (612)531-4445
Owner: Colony Communications, Inc. **Founded:** 1982. **Cities Served:** Hennepin County, MN.

📻 **2167 KBCW-AM - 1470**
5820 74th Ave. N.   Phone: (612)561-6766
Brooklyn Park, MN 55443   **Fax: (612)560-6350**

BROWNTON

📖 **2168 The Bulletin**
McLeod Publishing
134 4th Ave. N.
PO Box 309
Brownton, MN 55312   Phone: (612)328-4444
Former Title: Brownton Bulletin

CHASKA

📖 **2169 Business Ethics**
Mavis Publications, Inc.
1107 Hazeltine Blvd., Ste. 530
Chaska, MN 55318   Phone: (612)448-8864
Business magazine. **Subtitle:** The Magazine of Socially Responsible Business. **Founded:** 1987. **Frequency:** Bimonthly. **Cols./Page:** 3. **Key Personnel:** Marjorie Kelly, Editor and Publisher. **Subscription:** $49. $5 single issue.
Ad Rates: BW: $1,170   **Circulation:** Paid 5,000
              4C: $1,550   Non-paid 7,000

CIRCLE PINES

📖 **2170 Circulating Pines**
Circulating Pines, Inc.
9201 Lexington Ave. N.
PO Box 97
Circle Pines, MN 55014   Phone: (612)784-3090

CLEARWATER

📻 **2171 WTCN-AM - 1220**
RR 1, Box 141
Clearwater, MN 55320-9731   Phone: (612)439-1220
Format: Eclectic. **Network(s):** Independent. **Owner:** AB Communications. **Founded:** 1949. **Operating Hours:** Continuous. **Key Personnel:** John McCoolley, Gen. Mgr. **Wattage:** 5000 day; 250 night.

Ad Rates: GLR = general line rate; BW = one-time black & white page rate; 4C = one-time four color page rate; SAU = standard advertising unit rate; CNU = Canadian newspaper advertising unit rate; PCI = per column inch rate.
Circulation: ★ = ABC; △ = BPA; ◆ = CAC; ● = CCAB; □ = VAC; ⊕ = PO Statement; ‡ = Publisher's Report; Boldface figures = sworn; Light figures = estimated. **Entry type:** 📖 = Print; 📻 = Broadcast.

141

CLOQUET

♣ 2172 WKLK-FM - 96.5
807 Cloquet Ave.
Cloquet, MN 55720   Phone: (218)879-4534
Format: Oldies. **Network(s):** Satellite Music. **Owner:** Alan R. Quarnstrom. **Founded:** 1992. **Operating Hours:** Continuous. **ADI:** Duluth, MN-Superior, WI. **Key Personnel:** Alan R. Quarnstrom, Gen. Mgr. **Wattage:** 6000. **Ad Rates:** $6-$11 for 30 seconds; $8.50-$15.50 for 60 seconds.

COLLEGEVILLE

⚏ 2173 Sisters Today
The Liturgical Press
St. John's Abbey   Phone: (612)363-7065
Collegeville, MN 56321-7500   **Fax: (612)363-3299**

♣ 2174 KJNB-FM Cable - 99.9
St. Johns University
Box 1255   Phone: (612)363-3380
Collegeville, MN 56321   **Fax: (612)363-2504**

COTTONWOOD

⚏ 2175 Tri-County News
78 W. 1st St.
PO Box 76   Phone: (507)423-6239
Cottonwood, MN 56229   **Fax: (507)423-6230**

DULUTH

⚏ 2176 The Duluthian
Duluth Chamber of Commerce
118 E. Superior St.   Phone: (218)722-5501
Duluth, MN 55802   Fax: (218)722-3223

EAGAN

⚏ 2177 Bodywise Magazine
Russ Moore & Assoc.
4151 Knob Dr., Ste. 200   Phone: (612)452-0571
Eagan, MN 55122   Fax: (612)454-5791
Fitness, health and preventive medicine magazine for young women. **Frequency:** Weekly. **Printing Method:** Offset. **Trim Size:** 8 1/4 x 10 3/4. **Key Personnel:** Judy Surmano, Editor; Russell Moore, Publisher.
Ad Rates: BW: $2,935   **Circulation:** Paid ‡200,000
              4C: $3,730

⚏ 2178 Textile Care
Russ Moore & Assoc.
4151 Knob Dr., Ste. 200   Phone: (612)452-0571
Eagan, MN 55122   Fax: (612)454-5791
Professional laundry review. **Founded:** 1986. **Frequency:** Quarterly. **Printing Method:** Offset. **Trim Size:** 8 1/4 x 10 3/4. **Key Personnel:** Russell Moore, Publisher. **Subscription:** Free.
Circulation: Non-paid 11,251

EAGLE BEND

⚏ 2179 Independent News Herald
Box 248   Phone: (218)738-2532
Eagle Bend, MN 56446   **Fax: (218)738-2533**

EDEN PRAIRIE

⚏ 2180 Eden Prairie News
Southwest Suburban Publishing
327 S. Marshall Rd.
PO Box 8   Phone: (612)445-3333
Shakopee, MN 55379   Fax: (612)445-3333
Community newspaper. **Frequency:** Weekly. **Printing Method:** Offset. **Cols./Page:** 6. **Col. Width:** 2 in. **Col. Depth:** 21 in. **Key Personnel:** Mark Weber, Publisher; Gary Klatt, Advertising Dir.; Ruby Mohlin, Circulation Mgr. **Subscription:** $15; $25 out of area.
Ad Rates: PCI: $9.35   **Circulation:** Paid ⊕7,247
                                                Free ⊕3,841
Additional Contact Information: Editorial address: 7901 Flying Cloud

Dr., Ste. 150, Eden Prairie, MN 55344; phone (612)829-0917; fax (612)829-0917.

♣ 2181 KMSP-TV - Channel 9
11358 Viking Dr.   **Phone: (612)944-9999**
Eden Prairie, MN 55344-7258   **Fax: (612)942-0286**

ELY

⚏ 2182 North Country Angler
Milestones, Inc.
2 E. Sheridan   Phone: (218)365-3141
Ely, MN 55731   Fax: (218)365-3142
Summer fishing newspaper. **Founded:** 1975. **Frequency:** Weekly (summer only). **Printing Method:** Web offset. **Trim Size:** Tabloid. **Cols./Page:** 4. **Col. Width:** 2 1/4 in. **Col. Depth:** 13 in. **Key Personnel:** Bob Cary, Editor. **Subscription:** $10; $12 out of area.
Ad Rates: BW: $260   **Circulation:** Free ‡6,000
              PCI: $5

EXCELSIOR

⚏ 2183 Supertrax Magazine
Supertrax Publishing USA, Inc.
19285 Hwy. 7, Ste. 4
Excelsior, MN 55331   **Phone: (612)470-0600**

FAIRFAX

⚏ 2184 Fairfax Standard
102 SE 1st
Box 589   Phone: (507)426-7235
Fairfax, MN 55332   Fax: (507)426-7235

FAIRMONT

⚏ 2185 Fairmont Photo Press
112 E. 1st St.
PO Box 973   Phone: (507)238-9456
Fairmont, MN 56031-2899   **Fax: (507)238-9457**

FERGUS FALLS

⚏ 2186 Faith and Fellowship
Faith and Fellowship Press
Box 655   **Phone: (218)739-3336**
Fergus Falls, MN 56537   Fax: (218)739-5514

♣ 2187 KBRF-AM - 1250
728 Western Ave. N.   Phone: (218)736-7596
Fergus Falls, MN 56537   **Fax: (218)736-2836**

FOSSTON

♣ 2188 KKCQ-AM - 1480
Hwy. 2 E.
PO Box 606   Phone: (218)435-1919
Fosston, MN 56542-0606   **Fax: (218)435-1480**

♣ 2189 KKCQ-FM - 107.1
Hwy. 2 E.
PO Box 606   Phone: (218)435-1919
Fosston, MN 56542-0606   **Fax: (218)435-1480**

GRANITE FALLS

⚏ 2190 The Advocate-Tribune
138 8th Ave.   Phone: (612)669-7449
Granite Falls, MN 56241   **Fax: (612)564-4293**

HALLOCK

⚏ 2191 Kittson County Enterprise
Northern Media
109 3rd St. S.
PO Box 730
Hallock, MN 56728   Phone: (218)843-2868

HANSKA

☐ **2192 The Hanska Herald**
PO Box 45
Hanska, MN **56041-0045**   Phone: (507)439-6214

HASTINGS

♣ **2193 KDWA-AM - 1460**
PO Box 215
1718 Vermillion St.
Hastings, MN 55033   Phone: (612)437-1460

HOWARD LAKE

☐ **2194 Howard Lake Herald**
PO Box 190   Phone: (612)543-2131
Howard Lake, MN 55349   Fax: **(612)543-2135**

☐ **2195 Laker Shopper**
PO Box 190   Phone: (612)543-2131
Howard Lake, MN 55349   Fax: **(612)543-2135**

LAKE ELMO

☐ **2196 Indigenous Woman**
Indigenous Women's Network
PO Box 174
Lake Elmo, MN 55042   Phone: (612)770-3861
Magazine dedicated to the issues and concerns of indigenous women of the Americas and Pacific Islands. Produced by a collective. **Founded:** 1991. **Frequency:** 1-3x/yr. **Key Personnel:** Lisa Bellanger, Contributor; Lea Foushee, Contributor. **Subscription:** $10 (two issues); $20 other countries (two issues). $5.33 single issue.
          Circulation: 3,000
          Non-paid 1,000
Advertising accepted; contact publisher for rates and conditions.

LONG PRAIRIE

♣ **2197 KEYL-AM - 1400**
PO Box 187
221 Lake St. S.   Phone: (612)732-2164
Long Prairie, MN 56347   Fax: **(612)732-2284**

LUVERNE

♣ **2198 KLQL-FM - 101.1**
PO Box H
Hwy. 16 E   Phone: (507)283-4444
Luverne, MN 56156   Fax: (507)283-4445

MADISON

♣ **2199 KLQP-FM - 92.1**
PO Box 70   Phone: (612)598-7301
Madison, MN 56256   Fax: **(612)598-7955**

MANKATO

☐ **2200 The Land**
PO Box 3169
Mankato, MN 56002   Phone: (507)345-4523

♣ **2201 Cable Network, Inc.**
PO Box 3248   Phone: (507)387-1151
Mankato, MN **56002**   Fax: **(507)625-1266**

MINNEAPOLIS

☐ **2202 Decision**
The Billy Graham Evangelistic Assn.
PO Box 779   Phone: (612)338-0500
Minneapolis, MN 55440   Fax: **(612)335-1299**

☐ **2203 Freeway News**
Skyway Publications, Inc.
33 S. 5th St.   Phone: (612)375-9222
Minneapolis, MN **55402**   Fax: **(612)375-9208**

☐ **2204 The James White Review**
PO Box 3356, Butler Qtr. Sta.
Minneapolis, MN 55403   Phone: **(612)339-8317**

☐ **2205 Low and Inside**
PO Box 290228
Minneapolis, MN 55429   Phone: (612)535-3931
Subtitle: The National Publication Looking At Baseball From A Different Angle. **Founded:** 1988. **Frequency:** Monthly. **Printing Method:** Offset. **Trim Size:** 7 1/2 x 11. **Cols./Page:** 2. **Col. Width:** 3 1/8 in. **Col. Depth:** 9 3/4 in. **Key Personnel:** Nick Vetter, Editor; Scott Mahlmann, Co-Editor/Photographer. **Subscription:** $15. $2.50 single issue.
Ad Rates: BW: $310   **Circulation:** (Not Reported)
Additional Contact Information: Co-Editor's phone: (612)571-0993.

☐ **2206 Maize, A Lesbian Country Magazine**
Word Weavers
PO Box 8742
Minneapolis, MN 55408
Magazine focusing on the rural lesbian experience and strategies for economic survival and community building. Topics include food, shelter, agriculture, environmental issues, and healing arts. Contains essays, news, book reviews, interviews, and how-to articles. **Frequency:** Quarterly. **Subscription:** $10.
          Circulation: (Not Reported)

☐ **2207 (Minneapolis) Northeaster**
3964 Central Ave., NE   Phone: (612)788-9003
Minneapolis, MN 55421   Fax: (612)788-9003
Community newspaper. **Founded:** 1978. **Frequency:** 2x/mo. **Printing Method:** Web offset. **Cols./Page:** 5. **Col. Width:** 5 picas. **Col. Depth:** 15 in. **Key Personnel:** Kerry Ashmore, Publisher.
Ad Rates: PCI: $16.25   **Circulation:** Non-paid ‡30,000

☐ **2208 Minnesota**
University of Minnesota Alumni Assn.
University of Minnesota
501 Coffman Memorial Union
300 Washington Ave. SE   Phone: (612)624-2323
Minneapolis, MN 55455-0396   Fax: (612)626-8167

☐ **2209 MIS Quarterly**
MIS Research Center
University of Minnesota
Carlson School of Management
271 19th Ave. S.   Phone: **(612)624-7803**
Minneapolis, MN 55455   Fax: (612)626-1316

☐ **2210 Music and Dance News**
Dot Publications, Inc.
10600 University Ave. NW   Phone: (612)757-4414
Minneapolis, MN **55448-6166**   Fax: (612)757-6605
Former Title: Entertainment Bits

☐ **2211 Northwestern Financial Review**
NFR Communications
2850 Metro Dr., Ste. 524   Phone: (612)854-2177
Minneapolis, MN 55425   Fax: (612)854-2627

2212 NST: Nature, Society and Thought
University of Minnesota
116 Church St. SE
Minneapolis, MN 55455-0112   Phone: (612)922-7993
Subtitle: A Journal of Dialectical and Historical Materialism. **Founded:** 1987. **Frequency:** Quarterly. **Printing Method:** Photo offset. **Trim Size:** 5 1/2 x 8 1/2. **Cols./Page:** 1. **Col. Width:** 4 in. **Col. Depth:** 7 in. **Key Personnel:** Erwin Marquit, Editor; Leo Auerbach, Manuscript Editor. **ISSN:** 0890-6130. **Subscription:** $15; $28 institutions. $5 single issue; $10 single issue for institutions.
                    Circulation: (Not Reported)

2213 Quirk's Marketing Research Review
Quirk Enterprises, Inc.
PO Box 23536   Phone: (612)861-8051
Minneapolis, MN 55423   Fax: (612)861-8051
Frequency: 10x/yr. (June/July, Aug./Sept.). **Printing Method:** Sheet fed. **Trim Size:** 8 x 10 7/8. **Cols./Page:** 2 and 3. **Key Personnel:** Joseph Rydholm, Editor; Tom Quirk, Publisher. **ISSN:** 0893-7451. **Subscription:** $40. $10 single issue.
Ad Rates: BW: $1,650   **Circulation:** Non-paid 15,500
           4C: $2,275

2214 U.S. Art
Adams Publishing of Minneapolis/St. Paul, Inc
12 S. 16th St., Ste. 400   Phone: (612)339-7571
Minneapolis, MN 55402   Fax: (612)339-5806
Magazine providing collectors with news on art and artists. **Subtitle:** The Magazine for America's Print Buyers. **Frequency:** 9x/yr. **Printing Method:** Web offset. **Trim Size:** 10 x 12. **Key Personnel:** Frank Sisser, Editor and Publisher; Gloria Gaddis, Advertising Dir. **ISSN:** 0899-1782. **Subscription:** $24.95. $4.25 single issue.
Ad Rates: BW: $2,230   **Circulation:** Paid 8,000
                          Non-paid 57,000

2215 Woodswomen News
Woodswomen, Inc.
25 W. Diamond Lake Rd.   Phone: (612)822-3809
Minneapolis, MN 55419   Fax: (612)822-3814
Newspaper offering learning opportunities for women interested in outdoor and wilderness travel experiences. **Frequency:** Quarterly. **Trim Size:** 11 1/4 x 17 1/4. **Cols./Page:** 4. **Col. Width:** 2 3/8 in. **Col. Depth:** 14 1/4 in. **Key Personnel:** Jane Eastwood, Editor. **Subscription:** $20; Free to members.
                    Circulation: (Not Reported)
Advertising accepted; contact publisher for rates. **Additional Contact Information:** Toll-free (800)279-0555.

2216 KQQL-FM - 107.9
100 Washington Sq., Ste. 1319   Phone: (612)333-8118
Minneapolis, MN 55401-2107   Fax: (612)333-1616
Format: Oldies. **Owner:** Trumper Communications, Inc., 900 Oakmont Ln., Ste. 210, Westmont, IL 60559. **Founded:** 1988. **Operating Hours:** Continuous. **Key Personnel:** Kevin McCarthy, V.P./Gen. Mgr.; Shelly Malecha, Gen. Sales Mgr.; Kevin Metheny, Program Mgr.; Ann Licater, Promotions Mgr.; Greg Kern, Chief Engineer; John Szaynowski, Business Mgr. **Wattage:** 100,000.

2217 Paragon Cable
801 Plymouth Ave.   Phone: (612)522-5200
Minneapolis, MN 55411   Fax: (612)521-7626
Owner: KBLCOM, Inc. **Founded:** 1983. **Cities Served:** Hennepin County, Eden Prairie, Edina, Hopkins, Minnetonka, and Richfield, MN.

2218 WMMR-FM - 96.3
328 Coffman Union
300 Washington Ave. SE
Minneapolis, MN 55455   Phone: (612)625-5926
Format: Alternative/Independent/Progressive; modern Album-Oriented Rock (AOR). **Network(s):** ABC. **Founded:** 1942. **Operating Hours:** Continuous. **Key Personnel:** Jim Musil, Gen. Mgr.; Steve Nelson, Program Dir.; Robin Edgerton, Music Dir.; Steve Ebel, Sales Mgr. **Ad Rates:** $3-$10 for 30 seconds; $6-$11.50 for 60 seconds.

MINNETONKA

2219 Archery Business
Ehlert Publishing, Inc.
601 Lakeshore Pkwy., Ste. 600   Phone: (612)476-2200
Minnetonka, MN 55305-5215   Fax: (612)476-8065

2220 Bowhunting World
Ehlert Publishing Group
601 Lakeshore Pkwy., Ste. 600   Phone: (612)476-2200
Minnetonka, MN 55305-5215   Fax: (612)476-8065

2221 Farm Store
Miller Publishing Co.
12400 Whitewater Dr., Ste. 1600   Phone: (612)931-0211
Minnetonka, MN 55343   Fax: (612)938-1832

2222 Feedstuffs Cattle Supplement
The Miller Publishing Company
12400 Whitewater Drive
Minnetonka, MN 55343   Phone: (612)931-0211
Ceased publication.

2223 Snow Week
Ehlert Publishing Group
601 Lakeshore Pkwy., Ste. 600   Phone: (612)476-2200
Minnetonka, MN 55305-5215   Fax: (612)476-8065

2224 Snowmobile Business
Ehlert Publishing Group
601 Lakeshore Pkwy., Ste. 600   Phone: (612)476-2200
Minnetonka, MN 55305-5215   Fax: (612)476-8065

MOORHEAD

2225 KCCM-FM - 91.1
Concordia College
901 S. 8th St.   Phone: (218)299-3666
Moorhead, MN 56562   Fax: (218)299-3418

MOOSE LAKE

2226 Star-Gazette
308 Elm St.
Box 449   Phone: (218)485-4406
Moose Lake, MN 55767   Fax: (218)485-4190

MORA

2227 Advertiser
Karabee Publications
106 NW Railroad Ave.
PO Box 5   Phone: (612)679-2661
Mora, MN 55051-0003   Fax: (612)679-2663
Former Title: Mora Advertiser

NEW PRAGUE

2228 KCHK-AM - 1350
PO Box 251   Phone: (612)758-2571
New Prague, MN 56071   Fax: (612)758-3170

NEW ULM

2229 Journal
303 N. Minnesota St.
Box 487   Phone: (507)359-2911
New Ulm, MN 56073   Fax: (507)359-7362

NORTH ST. PAUL

2230 North Shopping Bulletin
Lillie Suburban Newspapers
2515 E. Seventh Ave.   Phone: (612)777-8800
North St. Paul, MN 55109   Fax: (612)777-8288
Ceased publication.

NORTHFIELD

🎙 **2231 WCAL-FM - 89.3**
1520 St. Olaf Ave.
Northfield, MN 55057   Phone: (507)646-3071

PARK RAPIDS

🎙 **2232 KDKK-FM - 97.5**
Box 49   Phone: (218)732-3306
Park Rapids, MN 56470   Fax: (218)732-3307

🎙 **2233 KPRM-AM - 870**
Box 49   Phone: (218)732-3306
Park Rapids, MN 56470   Fax: (218)732-3307

PRESTON

🎙 **2234 KFIL-FM - 103.1**
Box 377   Phone: (507)765-3856
Preston, MN 55965   Fax: (507)765-2738

🎙 **2235 Midwest CableVision**
218 Main St. SW
PO Box 34
Preston, MN 55965   Phone: (507)765-2712

PRIOR LAKE

📖 **2236 Prior Lake American**
Southwest Suburban Publishing
327 S. Marshall Rd.
PO Box 8   Phone: (612)445-3333
Shakopee, MN 55379   Fax: (612)445-3333

RED LAKE FALLS

📖 **2237 Gazette**
PO Box 370   Phone: (218)253-2594
Red Lake Falls, MN 56750   Fax: (218)253-4114

ROCHESTER

📖 **2238 Gastroenterology**
Mayo Foundation
200 1st St. SW   Phone: (507)284-9019
Rochester, MN 55905   Fax: (507)284-9184

📖 **2239 Journal of Neurosurgery**
Mayo Clinic   Phone: (507)284-1441
Rochester, MN 55905   Fax: (507)284-5206

🎙 **2240 WestMarc Cable**
Box 69
Rochester, MN 55904-1611   Phone: (507)289-1611
Owner: Tele-Communications, Inc. **Founded:** 1958. **Cities Served:** Dodge County, Goodhue County, Olmsted County, Byron, Eyota, Kasson, Stewartville, and Zumbrota, MN.

RUSHFORD

📖 **2241 Tri-County Record**
Tri-County Publishing, Inc.
Box 429
Rushford, MN 55971   Phone: (507)864-7700

📖 **2242 Tri-County Record Special Edition**
Tri-County Publishing, Inc.
PO Box 429
Rushford, MN 55971   Phone: (507)864-7700
Shopper. **Frequency:** Monthly. **Trim Size:** 14 x 22 1/2. **Cols./Page:** 6. **Col. Width:** 2 3/16 in. **Col. Depth:** 21 1/2 in. **Subscription:** Free.
Ad Rates: PCI: $4.83   **Circulation:** Free 3,400

ST. JAMES

📖 **2243 Lewisville Spotlight**
St. James Publishing Co., Inc.
604 1st Ave., S.
PO Box 67   Phone: (507)375-3161
St. James, MN 56081   **Fax: (507)375-3221**

📖 **2244 Plaindealer**
St. James Publishing Co., Inc.
604 1st Ave. S.
PO Box 67   Phone: (507)375-3161
Saint James, MN 56081   **Fax: (507)375-3221**

📖 **2245 Watonwan County Shoppers Guide**
St. James Publishing Co., Inc.
604 1st Ave. S.
PO Box 67   Phone: (507)375-3161
Saint James, MN 56081   **Fax: (507)375-3221**

SAINT PAUL

📖 **2246 Gobbles**
Minnesota Turkey Growers Assn.
2380 Wycliff St.   Phone: (612)646-4553
Saint Paul, MN 55114   Fax: (612)646-4554

📖 **2247 God's Word Today**
PO Box 64088   **Phone: (612)647-5284**
Saint Paul, MN 55164   **Fax: (612)647-4346**

📖 **2248 Hungry Mind Review: Children's Book Supplement**
Hungry Mind Review
1648 Grand Ave.   Phone: (612)699-2610
St. Paul, MN 55105   Fax: (612)699-0970
Magazine for children's literature. **Founded:** 1991. **Frequency:** Quarterly. **Cols./Page:** 4. **Col. Width:** 2 1/4 in. **Col. Depth:** 15 in. **Key Personnel:** Bart Schneider, Editor; R. David Unowsky, Publisher. **Subscription:** $12.
Ad Rates: BW: $1,350   **Circulation:** Paid 2,000
          PCI: $45   Non-paid 50,000

📖 **2249 Llewellyn's New Worlds of Mind and Spirit**
Llewellyn Publications
PO Box 64383   Phone: (612)291-1970
Saint Paul, MN 55164-0383   Fax: (612)291-1908
Former Title: The Llewellyn New Times

📖 **2250 Melpomene: A Journal for Women's Health Research**
Melpomene Institute
1010 University Ave. W.   Phone: (612)642-1951
St. Paul, MN 55104-4706   Fax: (612)642-1871
Periodical on research and education of the relationship between health and physical activity. **Founded:** 1982. **Frequency:** 3x/yr. **Cols./Page:** 3. **Col. Width:** 2 3/8 in. **Col. Depth:** 7 in. **Key Personnel:** Judy Remington, Editor. **ISSN:** 1043-8734. **Subscription:** $32; $20 students; $35 Canada; $38 other countries; $50 institutions; $250 corporations. $5 single issue.

          Circulation: Paid 1,496
          Non-paid 173
Advertising not accepted.

📖 **2251 Minnesota Cities**
League of Minnesota Cities
3490 Lexington Ave. N   **Phone: (612)490-5600**
Saint Paul, MN 55126   **Fax: (612)490-0072**

📖 **2252 Minnesota History**
Minnesota Historical Society
345 Kellogg Blvd.   Phone: (612)297-4462
Saint Paul, MN 55102-1906   Fax: (612)297-1345

☐ **2253 Minnesota Legionnaire**
Minnesota American Legion Publishing Co.
State Veterans Service Bldg.   Phone: (612)291-1800
Saint Paul, MN 55155   **Fax: (612)291-1057**

☐ **2254 Minnesota Women's Press**
Minnesota Women's Press, Inc.
771 Raymond Ave.   Phone: (612)646-3968
Saint Paul, MN 55114-1522   **Fax: (612)646-2186**

♣ **2255 Continental Cablevision**
214 E. 4th St.
Union Depot Pl.   Phone: (612)224-2697
Saint Paul, MN 55101   Fax: (612)298-9520
Owner: Continental Cablevision, Inc. **Founded:** 1985. **Cities Served:**
Dakota County, Ramsey County, Inver Grove Heights, South Saint
Paul, Sunfish Lake, and West Saint Paul, MN.

♣ **2256 KNOW-FM - 91.1**
45 E. 7th St.   Phone: (612)290-1500
St. Paul, MN 55101   **Fax: (612)290-1258**

SAINT PETER

☐ **2257 St. Peter Herald**
Box 520   Phone: (507)931-4520
Saint Peter, MN 56082   **Fax: (507)931-4522**

SPRINGFIELD

☐ **2258 Springfield Advance-Press**
13 S. Marshall Ave.
PO Box 78   Phone: (507)723-4225
Springfield, MN 56087   **Fax: (507)723-4400**

STAPLES

☐ **2259 Sunday Square Shooter**
Devlin Newspapers, Inc.
Box 100
224 4th St. N.   Phone: (218)894-1112
Staples, MN 56479   Fax: (218)894-3570
Shopping guide. **Frequency:** Weekly. **Printing Method:** Offset. **Cols./**
Page: 6. **Col. Width:** 12 picas. **Col. Depth:** 21 1/2 in. **Key Personnel:**
Brenda Halvorson, Gen. Mgr. **Subscription:** Free.
Ad Rates: BW: $606.30   **Circulation:** Free ‡8,500
              PCI: $4.70

THIEF RIVER FALLS

☐ **2260 The Times**
Thief River Falls Times, Inc.
324 N. Main Ave.   Phone: (218)681-4450
Thief River Falls, MN 56701   **Fax: voice act.**

♣ **2261 KSRQ-FM - 90.1**
1301 Hwy. 1 E.
Northwest Technical College   Phone: (218)681-6364
Thief River Falls, MN 56701   Fax: (218)681-5519

TOWER

☐ **2262 The Timberjay**
The Timberjay, Inc.
Tower Municipal Bldg.   Phone: (218)753-2950
Tower, MN 55790   **Fax: (218)757-3322**

VERNON CENTER

☐ **2263 Favorite Westerns & Serial World**
Rte. 1, Box 103
Vernon Center, MN 56090   Phone: (507)549-3677
Magazine for fans of old westerns and serial movies. **Founded:** 1974.
Frequency: Quarterly. **Printing Method:** Web offset. **Trim Size:** 8 1/2 x
11. **Cols./Page:** 3. **Col. Width:** 12 picas. **Col. Depth:** 10 in. **Key**
Personnel: Norman Kieter, Editor. **Subscription:** $16; $20 other
countries. $5 single issue.
Ad Rates: BW: $75   **Circulation:** 2,000

WARREN

☐ **2264 Sheaf**
127 W. Johnson Ave.
Box 45   Phone: (218)745-5174
Warren, MN 56762   **Fax: (218)745-5175**

WAYZATA

☐ **2265 Marine Store Merchandising**
RCM Enterprises, Inc.
PO Box 720
Twelve Oaks Center 922   Phone: (612)473-5088
Wayzata, MN 55391   **Fax: (612)473-7068**

☐ **2266 Sports Spectrum**
Discovery House Publishers
Box 3566
Wayzata, MN 55391
Christian magazine discussing sport and life issues. **Frequency:** 6x/yr.
Key Personnel: Dave Branon, Editor; Dave Bunham, Publisher.
Subscription: $15. $2.50 single issue.
                                      Circulation: (Not Reported)

WINONA

☐ **2267 The Cardinal**
St. Mary's College
700 Terrace Hgts., No. 36   Phone: (507)457-1630
Winona, MN 55987   **Fax: (507)457-1633**

♣ **2268 KHME-FM - 101.1**
360 Vila St.   Phone: (507)454-4663
Winona, MN 55987   Fax: (507)454-1463
Format: Adult Contemporary. **Network(s):** CNN Radio. **Owner:** Bud
Baechler. **Founded:** 1992. **Operating Hours:** 4:55 a.m.-12:30 a.m. **Key**
Personnel: Bill Withers, Gen. Mgr.; Connie Hawkinson, Sales Mgr.;
Patty Fitzpatrick, Business Mgr.; David Dicke, Program Dir.; David
Welshhons, Information Dir. **Wattage:** 6000. **Ad Rates:** $4.50 for 15
seconds; $4.30-$7.45 for 30 seconds; $6.60-$10.05 for 60 seconds.

♣ **2269 KSMR-FM - 92.5**
St. Mary's College, No. 29
700 Terrace Hgts.   Phone: (507)457-1613
Winona, MN 55987   **Fax: (507)457-6930**

WINSTED

☐ **2270 Winsted Lester Prairie Journal**
Winsted Publishing, Inc.
Box 129   Phone: (612)485-2535
Winsted, MN 55395   **Fax: (612)543-2135**

MISSISSIPPI

AMORY

♣ 2271 WAFM-FM - 95.3
Box 458
Amory, MS 38821
Phone: (601)256-9726
Fax: (601)256-8512
Format: Adult Contemporary. **Network(s):** Unistar. **Owner:** Ed Stanford, 900 Rose Ln., Amory, MS 38821; (601)256-8419. **Founded:** 1974. **Operating Hours:** 5:30 a.m.-11 p.m. **Key Personnel:** Ed Stanford, Mgr.; Ken Wardlaw, Sales Mgr.; Clara Kennedy, Traffic Mgr./Secretary. **Wattage:** 3000. **Ad Rates:** $5 for 30 seconds; $6 for 60 seconds.

BELZONI

♣ 2272 WELZ-AM - 1460
PO Box 299
Belzoni, MS 39038
Phone: (601)247-1744
Fax: (601)247-1744

♣ 2273 WVRD-FM - 107.1
PO Box 299
Belzoni, MS 39038
Phone: (601)247-1744
Fax: (601)247-1744

BILOXI

♣ 2274 UAE Cable, Mississippi Gulf Coast
786 W. Washington Loop
Box 10
Biloxi, MS 39530
Phone: (601)374-5900
Fax: (601)435-3939
Owner: Tele-Communications, Inc. **Founded:** 1963. **Cities Served:** Harrison County, Jackson County, D'Iberville, and Ocean Springs, MS.

BROOKHAVEN

♣ 2275 WBKN-FM - 92.1
203 E. Monticello St.
PO Box 711
Brookhaven, MS 39601
Phone: (601)833-6221
Fax: (601)833-6221

♣ 2276 WCHJ-AM - 1470
203 E. Monticello St.
PO Box 711
Brookhaven, MS 39601
Phone: (601)833-6221
Fax: (601)833-6221

CALHOUN CITY

▥ 2277 The Monitor-Herald
Murphree Bros. and Co., Inc.
PO Box 69
Calhoun City, MS 38916-0069
Phone: (601)628-5241
Fax: (601)628-8423

CLARKSDALE

▥ 2278 Delta Farm Press
Farm Press Publications, Inc.
PO Box 1420
14920 U.S. Hwy. 61
Clarksdale, MS 38614
Phone: (601)624-8503
Fax: (601)627-1977

♣ 2279 WAID-FM - 106
20 E. 2nd St.
Box 668
Clarksdale, MS 38614
Phone: (601)627-2281
Format: Oldies. **Owner:** Radio Cleveland Inc. **Founded:** 1977. **Operating Hours:** Continuous. **Key Personnel:** Greg C. Shurden, Gen. Mgr.; Christy McBrayer, Operations Mgr. **Wattage:** 3000. **Ad Rates:** $3.95-$6.05 for 30 seconds; $5.20-$7.50 for 60 seconds.

♣ 2280 WROX-AM - 1450
Central Bldg., Ste. 222
125 3rd St.
Clarksdale, MS 38614
Phone: (601)627-7343
Fax: (601)627-1000

COLLINS

▥ 2281 The News-Commercial
104 1st St. S
PO Box 1299
Collins, MS 39428
Phone: (601)765-8275
Fax: (601)765-6952

COLUMBUS

♣ 2282 WACR-FM - 103.9 & 95.7
1910 14th Ave. N.
PO Box 1078
Columbus, MS 39703
Phone: (601)328-1050
Fax: (601)328-1054
Format: Urban Contemporary. **Owner:** T & W Communications, Inc., PO Box 312, West Point, MS 39773. **Operating Hours:** Continuous. **ADI:** Columbus-Tupelo (West Point), MS. **Key Personnel:** Danny Byrd, Gen. Mgr.; Sherwinn Prescott, Gen. Sales Mgr.; Jerold Jackson, Program Dir. **Wattage:** 3000. **Ad Rates:** $25 per unit.

CORINTH

♣ 2283 WADI-FM - 95.3
1608 S. John St.
Corinth, MS 38834
Phone: (601)287-3101
Fax: (601)287-9262
Format: Contemporary Country. **Owner:** Joe Taylor Jobe. **Operating Hours:** Continuous. **Key Personnel:** Joe Taylor Jobe, Owner/Pres./Gen. Mgr.; Joan Jobe, Commercial Mgr./Program and Music Dir. **Wattage:** 4200. **Ad Rates:** $4 for 30 seconds; $5 for 60 seconds.

GLOSTER

2284 Wilk-Amite Record
243 Main St.
Gloster, MS 39638

Phone: (601)225-4531
Fax: (601)384-2276

GREENVILLE

2285 TCA Cable TV
318 Main St.
Box 1278
Greenville, MS 38701   Phone: (601)332-0518
Owner: TCA Cable TV, Inc. **Founded:** 1954. **Cities Served:** Washington County and Swiftwater, MS.

2286 WBAQ-FM - 97.9
PO Box 656   Phone: (601)335-3383
Greenville, MS 38702-0656   **Fax: (601)335-3383**

GREENWOOD

2287 Staplreview
Staplcton
PO Box 547   Phone: (601)453-6231
Greenwood, MS 38930   **Fax: (601)453-6274**

2288 WABG-AM - 960
PO Box 408
Greenwood, MS 38930   Phone: (601)453-7822
Format: Contemporary Country. **Network(s):** Satellite Music. **Owner:** Greenwood Broadcasting Co. Inc. **Founded:** 1950. **Operating Hours:** 6 a.m.-10 p.m. **Key Personnel:** James Chick, Gen. Mgr. **Wattage:** 1000 day; 500 night. **Ad Rates:** $13-$16.50 for 30 seconds; $15.50-$19.50 for 60 seconds.

GULFPORT

2289 Gulf Coast Horizon
1417 24th Ave.
Gulfport, MS 39501-2068
Ceased publication.

2290 Post-Newsweek Cable
3415 Hewes Ave.   Phone: (601)864-1506
Gulfport, MS 39507   Fax: (601)865-9476
Owner: Post-Newsweek Cable, Inc. **Founded:** 1958. **Cities Served:** Harrison County, MS.

HATTIESBURG

2291 Cablesystems of Mississippi
2100 Lincoln Rd.
Hattiesburg, MS 39402   Phone: (601)268-1188
Owner: American TV & Communications Corp. **Founded:** 1954. **Cities Served:** Forrest County, Greene County, Jones County, Lamar County, Perry County, Lake Serene, Leakesville, Oak Grove, Petal, Purvis, Rawls Springs, Richton, and Sumrall, MS.

HERNANDO

2292 WVIM-FM - 95.3
PO Box 487   **Phone: (601)429-4465**
Hernando, MS 38632   **Fax: (601)276-0361**

HOLLY SPRINGS

2293 WKRA-AM - 1110
1400-B E. Salem Ave.
PO Box 398
Holly Springs, MS 38635   **Phone: (601)252-1110**

JACKSON

2294 Mississippi Pharmacist
Mississippi Pharmacists Assn.
341 Edgewood Terrace Dr.   Phone: (601)981-0416
Jackson, MS 39206-6299   **Fax: (601)981-0451**

2295 Capital Cablevision
5375 Executive Pl.
Box 9426   Phone: (601)982-0922
Jackson, MS 39286   Fax: (601)982-9532
Owner: Time Warner Cable. **Founded:** 1972. **Key Personnel:** Steve McMahon, Pres.; Elmo Roebuck, V.P. of Engineering; Bruce Corkern, V.P. of Finance; Frances Smith, Dir. of Public Affairs; Paul Hardin, Dir. of Marketing. **Cities Served:** Hinds County, Madison County, Rankin County, Cleary Heights, Clinton, Florence, Madison, Richland, Jackson, Ridgeland, Raymond, Bolton, Edwards, and Deerfield, MS.

2296 WJXN-AM - 1450
Box 786   Phone: (601)352-6673
Jackson, MS 39205   **Fax: (601)948-6052**

2297 WSLI-AM - 930
PO Box 222   **Phone: (601)925-3458**
Jackson, MS 39205   **Fax: (601)995-9632**

MAGEE

2298 The Simpson Shopper
Simpson Publishing Co.
PO Box 338   Phone: (601)849-3434
Magee, MS 39111-0338   Fax: (601)849-6828
Shopping guide. **Founded:** 1986. **Frequency:** Weekly. **Printing Method:** Offset. **Trim Size:** 11 1/2 x 16. **Cols./Page:** 6. **Col. Width:** 9 picas. **Col. Depth:** 15 in. **Key Personnel:** Owen Lusk, Editor/Publisher. **Subscription:** Free.
Ad Rates: BW: $682.20   **Circulation:** (Not Reported)
             4C: $887.20
             PCI: $7.58
Combined advertising rates available with the Magee Courier and the Simpson County News.

MATHISTON

2299 The Breeze
Wood Junior College
Rt. 2   Phone: (601)263-4964
Mathiston, MS 39752   Fax: (601)263-4964

2300 Chips-O-Wood
Wood Junior College
Rte. 2   Phone: (601)263-8128
Mathiston, MS 39752   Fax: (601)263-4964

MERIDIAN

2301 Comcast Cablevision of Meridian
909 24th Ave.   Phone: (601)693-2366
Meridian, MS 39301   Fax: (601)693-2278
Owner: Comcast Corp. **Founded:** 1964. **Cities Served:** Lauderdale County, MS.

2302 WMER-AM - 1390
208 5th Ave.
Meridian, MS 39301   Phone: (601)693-1414

MISSISSIPPI STATE

2303 Mississippi State University Alumnus
Mississippi State University
Box 5328   **Phone: (601)325-3442**
Mississippi State, MS 39762   **Fax: (601)325-7455**

OLIVE BRANCH

2304 Home Market Magazine
8885 Goodman
PO Box 486   Phone: (601)895-6220
Olive Branch, MS 38654   Fax: (601)895-4377
Publication of real estate listings. **Founded:** 1981. **Frequency:** Monthly. **Printing Method:** Web press. **Trim Size:** 10 1/2 x 13 1/4. **Cols./Page:** 4. **Key Personnel:** Susan Hanna, Marketing Dir. **Subscription:** Free.
                              Circulation: Free ‡16,000
Advertising accepted; contact publisher for rates.

OXFORD

📖 **2305 Night Club & Bar Magazine**
Oxford Publishing, Inc.
307 W. Jackson Ave.   Phone: (601)236-5510
Oxford, MS 38655   Fax: (601)236-5541

PASCAGOULA

🎙 **2306 Sammons Communications of Mississippi, Inc.**
5100 McPhelah Rd.
Box 1818
Pascagoula, MS 39567   Phone: (601)769-1221
Owner: Sammons Communications, Inc. **Founded:** 1971. **Cities Served:** Jackson County, MS.

🎙 **2307 WZZJ-AM - 1580**
3113 Telephone Rd.
Pascagoula, MS 39567   **Phone: (601)762-5683**

QUITMAN

🎙 **2308 WBFN-AM - 1500**
Drawer 70   Phone: (601)776-2931
Quitman, MS 39355   Fax: (601)776-5484
Format: Contemporary Country. **Owner:** Quitman Broadcasting Co.
Operating Hours: Sunrise-sunset. **Key Personnel:** Herman Kelly, Pres.;
Terry Bonner, V.P./Gen. Mgr.; Micheal Fairchild, Program Dir./
Music Dir.; Margaret Loften, Sales Mgr. **Wattage:** 1000.

🎙 **2309 WYKK-FM - 98.3**
Drawer 70   Phone: (601)776-2931
Quitman, MS 39355   Fax: (601)776-5484
Format: Urban Contemporary. **Owner:** Quitman Broadcasting Co.
Operating Hours: Continuous. **Key Personnel:** Herman Kelly, Pres.;
Terry Bonner, V.P./Gen. Mgr.; Micheal Fairchild, Program Dir./
Music Dir.; Margaret Lofton, Sales Mgr. **Wattage:** 3000.

TUPELO

🎙 **2310 WLOV-TV - Channel 27**
PO Box 350
Beech Springs Rd.   **Phone: (601)842-7620**
Tupelo, MS 38802   **Fax: (601)844-7061**

🎙 **2311 WZLQ-FM - 98.5**
PO Box 410   Phone: (601)842-7658
Tupelo, MS 38802   Fax: (601)842-0197

WESSON

🎙 **2312 WCLL-FM - 90.7**
Box 649   **Phone: (601)643-8384**
Wesson, MS 39191-0649   Fax: (601)643-2366

Ad Rates: GLR = general line rate; BW = one-time black & white page rate; 4C = one-time four color page rate; SAU = standard advertising unit rate;
CNU = Canadian newspaper advertising unit rate; PCI = per column inch rate.
Circulation: ★ = ABC; △ = BPA; ◆ = CAC; ● = CCAB; □ = VAC; ⊕ = PO Statement; ‡ = Publisher's Report; Boldface figures = sworn; Light figures = estimated.
Entry type: 📖 = Print; 🎙 = Broadcast.

149

MISSOURI

BETHANY

📖 **2313 Bethany Republican-Clipper**
Bethany Printing Co.
PO Box 351   Phone: (816)425-6325
Bethany, MO 64424   **Fax: (816)425-3441**

📖 **2314 Pony Express**
Bethany Printing Co.
PO Box 351   Phone: (816)425-6325
Bethany, MO 64424   **Fax: (816)425-3441**

BIRCH TREE

🎙 **2315 KBMV-FM - 107.1**
Box 215
Birch Tree, MO 65438   Phone: (314)292-3821

BUTLER

🎙 **2316 KMAM-AM - 1530**
800 E. Nursery St.   Phone: (816)679-4191
Butler, MO 64730   **Fax: (816)679-4193**

🎙 **2317 KMOE-FM - 92.1**
800 E. Nursery St.   Phone: (816)679-4191
Butler, MO 64730   **Fax: (816)679-4193**

CAPE GIRARDEAU

🎙 **2318 KRCU-FM - 90.9**
1 University Plaza
Cape Girardeau, MO 63701   **Phone: (314)651-5070**

CARTHAGE

🎙 **2319 KMXL-FM - 95.1**
221 E. 4th St.
PO Box 426   Phone: (417)358-6054
Carthage, MO 64836   Fax: (417)358-1278
Format: Soft Adult Contemporary. **Owner:** Ronald L. Petersen. **Founded:** 1972. **Formerly:** KRGK-FM (1990). **Operating Hours:** Continuous. **Key Personnel:** Ronald L. Petersen, Pres./Gen. Mgr.; Mark Danielson, News Dir.; Bob Kassi, Gen. Sales Mgr. **Wattage:** 50,000. **Ad Rates:** $8-$17 for 30 seconds; $10-$19 for 60 seconds.

CARUTHERSVILLE

🎙 **2320 KLOW-FM - 103.1**
Hwy. 84 W.
PO Box 909   Phone: (314)333-1370
Caruthersville, MO 63830   Fax: (314)333-1370
Format: Adult Contemporary. **Network(s):** Mutual Broadcasting System; Brownfield. **Owner:** Pemiscot Broadcasting, Inc. **Founded:** 1975. **Formerly:** KCRV-FM. **Operating Hours:** 5:30 a.m.-midnight. **Key Personnel:** Cleat Stanfill, Gen. Mgr.; Ed DeLisle, Sales Mgr.; Danny Nelson, Music Dir.; Palmer Johnson, Engineer. **Wattage:** 3000. **Ad Rates:** $4-$7 for 30 seconds; $6-$9 for 60 seconds.

CASSVILLE

📖 **2321 Cassville Barry County Advertiser**
PO Box 488   Phone: (417)847-4475
Cassville, MO 65625   Fax: (417)847-4523
Community newspaper. **Founded:** 1967. **Frequency:** Weekly. **Printing Method:** Offset. **Trim Size:** 13 3/4 x 17 1/2. **Cols./Page:** 6. **Col. Width:** 1 3/4 in. **Col. Depth:** 17 in. **Key Personnel:** Irene Horner, Editor; Jean Melton, Publisher. **Subscription:** Free; $20 out of county.
Ad Rates: BW: $280   **Circulation:** Paid ‡300
           SAU: $5.45   Non-paid ‡10,000
           PCI: $4.20

CLARK

📖 **2322 Small Farm Today**
Missouri Farm Publishing, Inc.
c/o Ridgetop Ranch
3903 W. Ridge Trail Rd.   Phone: (314)687-3525
Clark, MO 65243   **Fax: (314)687-3148**
Former Title: Missouri Farm

CLAYTON

📖 **2323 Franklin County Watchman**
200 S. Bemiston, Ste. 201
Clayton, MO 63105   Phone: (314)725-1515
Weekly community newspaper containing legal and public notices. **Founded:** 1952. **Frequency:** Weekly. **Printing Method:** Offset. **Key Personnel:** Gabriela Bethke, Editor; R. W. Kuper, Publisher. **USPS:** 217-720. **Subscription:** $25.
Ad Rates: GLR: $1   **Circulation:** Combined ‡20,000
           BW: $100
           SAU: $6

□ **2324 Saint Charles Watchman**
200 S. Bemiston, Ste. 201
Clayton, MO 63105   Phone: (314)725-1515
Newspaper containing legal and public notices. **Founded:** 1984.
Frequency: Daily. **Cols./Page:** 5. **Col. Width:** 2 in. **Col. Depth:** 22 in.
Key Personnel: Gabriela Bethke, Editor; R. W. Kuper, Publisher.
Subscription: $75.
Ad Rates: GLR: $1   **Circulation:** Combined ‡20,000
                BW: $100
                SAU: $6

COLE CAMP

□ **2325 Benton County Shopper**
PO Box 280
Cole Camp, MO 65325   Phone: (816)668-4418
Shopping guide. **Frequency:** Weekly. **Cols./Page:** 5. **Col. Width:** 1 1/2
in. **Col. Depth:** 13 in. **Key Personnel:** Diana Kreisel, Contact.
Subscription: Free.
Ad Rates: PCI: $2.65   **Circulation:** Free 5,800

COLUMBIA

□ **2326 Mid-Missouri Business**
Network Publishing Corporation
312 Nebraska, Ste. C   Phone: (314)443-1311
Columbia, MO 65201   Fax: (314)875-1149
Magazine providing business information on central Missouri. **Found-
ed:** April, 1992. **Frequency:** Monthly. **Printing Method:** Offset. **Trim
Size:** 11 1/4 X 14 1/2. **Cols./Page:** 4. **Col. Width:** 2 7/16 in. **Col. Depth:**
13 in. **Key Personnel:** Bruce Q. Mackey, Editor and Publisher.
Subscription: $9.95. $.95 single issue.
Ad Rates: BW: $700   **Circulation:** (Not Reported)
                4C: $900

□ **2327 Missouri Historical Review**
State Historical Society of Missouri
1020 Lowry St.   Phone: (314)882-7083
Columbia, MO 65201   **Fax: (314)884-4950**

□ **2328 Missourian**
Missourian Publishing Assn., Inc.
301 S. 9th St.
PO Box 917   Phone: (314)442-3161
Columbia, MO 65205   Fax: (314)882-5702
Former Title: Missourian Weekly

□ **2329 Prison Life**
Scott Magazines
111 S. Main St.   Phone: (314)449-3291
Columbia, MO 65201   Fax: (314)449-4085
Magazine focusing on the prison population. **Founded:** December
1992. **Frequency:** 6x/yr. **Printing Method:** Offset. **Trim Size:** 8 1/8 x 11
1/8. **Key Personnel:** Shan Rodgers, Editor; Joe Strahl, Publisher.
Subscription: $19.95. $3.95 single issue.
Ad Rates: BW: $3,040   **Circulation:** (Not Reported)
                4C: $3,650
Additional Contact Information: Toll-free 800-395-8627. Prisoners call
collect (314)449-3291. Publisher's address: 519 8th Ave., New York,
NY 10018; phone (212)967-6262.

♣ **2330 KFRU-AM - 1400**
503 Old 63 North   Phone: (314)449-4141
Columbia, MO 65201   **Fax: (314)449-7770**

♣ **2331 TCI Cablevision of Missouri**
Box 757
Columbia, MO 65291-4267   Phone: (314)443-1535
Owner: Tele-Communications, Inc. **Founded:** 1977. **Cities Served:**
Boone County, MO.

DEXTER

♣ **2332 KDEX-AM - 1590**
Hwy. 114 E.
PO Box 249   Phone: (314)624-3545
Dexter, MO 63841   **Fax: (314)624-3545**

DREXEL

□ **2333 Drexel Star**
130 Main St.
PO Box 378   Phone: (816)657-2222
Drexel, MO 64742   Fax: (816)657-2045

EL DORADO SPRINGS

♣ **2334 KESM-AM - 1580**
200 Radio Lane
El Dorado Springs, MO 64744   Phone: (418)876-2741
Format: Country; Album-Oriented Rock (AOR). **Network(s):** NBC.
Owner: Wildwood Communications Inc. **Operating Hours:** Sunrise-
sunset; some nights. **Key Personnel:** Donald Kahn, Gen. Mgr.; Susan
Kahn, Station Mgr./Sales Mgr.; Rhonda Corbin, News Dir. **Wattage:**
500.

EXCELSIOR SPRINGS

♣ **2335 KEXS-AM - 1090**
201 Industrial Park Rd.
Industrial Park Rd.   Phone: (816)637-6061
Excelsior Springs, MO 64024   **Fax: (816)637-6061**

FAIRFAX

□ **2336 The Fairfax Forum**
PO Box 17
Fairfax, MO 64446-0017   Phone: (816)686-2741

FLORISSANT

♣ **2337 Cencom of Saint Louis**
3300 Sunswept Park Dr.
Florissant, MO 63033
Owner: Concom Cable Assoc., Inc. **Founded:** 1982. **Cities Served:**
Black Jack, MO and St. Louis County (northern part).

GENEVIEVE

□ **2338 Perryville Sun Times**
PO Box 428
Genevieve, MO 63670   Phone: (314)883-2980
Community newspaper. **Founded:** 1989. **Frequency:** Weekly.
Ad Rates: PCI: $4.25   **Circulation:** ‡2,600

HANNIBAL

♣ **2339 KHMO-AM - 1070**
119 N. Third St.   Phone: (314)221-3450
Hannibal, MO 63401   Fax: (314)221-5331
Format: Middle-of-the-Road (MOR). **Network(s):** CNN Radio. **Owner:** Bick Broadcasting. **Founded:** 1941. **Operating Hours:** 5 a.m.-
midnight. **Key Personnel:** Ed Foxall, Gen. Mgr.; Joel Sampson,
Program Dir.; Jon Hanvelt, News Dir. **Wattage:** 5000.

INDEPENDENCE

□ **2340 Saints Herald**
Herald Publishing House
3225 S. Noland Rd.
PO Box 1770   Phone: (816)252-5010
Independence, MO 64055   Fax: (816)252-3976

♣ **2341 Landmark Cablevision**
4700 Selsa Rd.
Box 2000
Independence, MO 64055   Phone: (816)795-8377
Owner: Douglas Communications Corp. **Founded:** 1973. **Cities Served:**
Johnson County, Baldwin Park, Blue Springs, Blue Summit, Grain
Valley, Greenwood, Lake Lotawana, Lake Tapawingo, Lake Winneba-
go, Peculiar, Pleasant Hill, Raytown, and Sugar Creek, MO; Cass
County, Clay County, Jackson County, and Olathe, KS.

JEFFERSON CITY

2342 Missouri Lawyers Weekly
223 Madison   Phone: (800)635-5297
Jefferson City, MO 65101   Fax: (314)634-2287
Newspaper for lawyers. **Founded:** 1987. **Frequency:** Weekly. **Printing Method:** Offset. **Trim Size:** 11 1/2 x 17 1/2. **Cols./Page:** 4. **Col. Width:** 2 3/8 in. **Col. Depth:** 16 in. **Key Personnel:** Milton B. Garber, Publisher; Bryan L. Hettenbach; Karen Antweiler, Production Mgr.; J. Edward Pawlick, Editor-in-Chief. **USPS:** 002-425. **Subscription:** $195. $4.50 single issue.
Ad Rates:	GLR:	$5	Circulation: Paid ⊕2,365
	BW:	$1,300	Non-paid ⊕131
	4C:	$1,465	
	PCI:	$25	

2343 Rural Missouri
Assn. of Missouri Electric Cooperatives, Inc.
2722 E. McCarty St.   Phone: (314)635-6857
Jefferson City, MO 65101   **Fax: (314)635-2511**

2344 KJMO-FM - 100.1
3109 S. 10 Mile Dr.   Phone: (314)893-5100
Jefferson City, MO 65109   **Fax: (314)893-4137**

2345 KRCG-TV - Channel 13
PO Box 659   Phone: (314)896-5144
Jefferson City, MO 65102   **Fax: (314)896-5193**

JOPLIN

2346 JIT
Circuit Equipment
PO Box 48
Joplin, MO 64802-0048
Ceased publication.

2347 The Pentecostal Messenger
Pentecostal Church of God
4901 Pennsylvania
PO Box 850   Phone: (417)624-7050
Joplin, MO 64802-0850   **Fax: (417)624-7102**

KANSAS CITY

2348 American Family Physician
American Academy of Family Physicians
8880 Ward Pkwy.   Phone: (816)333-9700
Kansas City, MO 64114   **Fax: (816)333-0303**

2349 Celebration
National Catholic Reporter Publishing Co.
Celebration Publications
PO Box 419493   Phone: (816)531-0538
Kansas City, MO 64141   **Fax: (816)931-5082**

2350 Economic Review
Federal Reserve Bank of Kansas City
925 Grand Ave.   Phone: (816)881-2683
Kansas City, MO **64198-0001**   Fax: (816)881-2569

2351 Family Records, TODAY
The American Family Records Assn.
311 E. 12th St.
PO Box 15505
Kansas City, MO 64106   **Phone: (816)373-6570**

2352 Journal of Insurance Regulation
National Association of Insurance Commissioners
120 W. 12th St., Ste. 1100   Phone: (816)842-3600
Kansas City, MO 64105-1925   Fax: (816)471-7004
Professional journal focusing on insurance regulatory issues. **Founded:** 1982. **Frequency:** Quarterly. **Trim Size:** 6 x 9. **Cols./Page:** 1. **Col. Width:** 4 3/8 in. **Col. Depth:** 6 3/4 in. **Key Personnel:** Barbara P.

Heaney, Editor; Karen Montalto, Asst. Publications Mgr. **ISSN:** 0736-248X. **Subscription:** $15 single issue.
Circulation: Paid ‡1,807
Non-paid ‡20
Advertising not accepted.

2353 Workbench
KC Publishing, Inc.
700 W. 47th St., Ste. 310   Phone: (816)531-5730
Kansas City, MO **64112**   Fax: (816)531-3873

2354 American Cablevision
800 101 Terr., Ste. 100
Box 5454   Phone: (816)358-5360
Kansas City, MO 64131   Fax: (816)941-0164
Owner: Kansas City Cable Partners. **Founded:** 1980. **Cities Served:** Johnson County, Mission Hills, Mission Woods, Westwood, and Westwood Hills, KS; Clay County, Jackson County, Platte County, Avondale, Claycomo, Gladstone, Glenaire, Houston Lake, Lake Waukomis, Liberty, North Kansas City, Northmoor, Oaks, Oakview, Oakwood, Oakwood Manor, Oakwood Park, Platte Woods, Pleasant Valley, Riverside, Smithville, Village of the Oaks, and Weatherby Lake, MO.

2355 KPRT-AM - 1590
1131 Colorado   **Phone: (816)763-2040**
Kansas City, MO 64130   **Fax: (816)966-1055**

LANCASTER

2356 The Excelsior
Excelsior Newspaper, Inc.
Box 250   Phone: (816)457-3707
Lancaster, MO 63548-0250   **Fax: (816)457-3707**

MALDEN

2357 The Delta News
American Publishing Co.
Box 486
127 W. Main   Phone: (314)276-5148
Malden, MO 63863   Fax: (314)276-3687
Newspaper. **Founded:** 1977. **Frequency:** Weekly. **Key Personnel:** Lorraine Heiser, Editor; Gina Stoverink, Gen. Mgr.; Steve Puryear, Advertising Mgr.; Carolyn James, Office Mgr.
Ad Rates:	BW:	$598.50	Circulation: Paid 226
	4C:	$798.50	Free 10,700
	PCI:	$4.75	

MARYVILLE

2358 KDLX-FM - 106
800 University Dr.
Maryville, MO 64468   Phone: (816)562-1163
Format: Alternative/Independent/Progressive. **Key Personnel:** Jeffery Brown, Music Dir. **Ad Rates:** Noncommercial.

MONTGOMERY CITY

2359 KMCR-FM - 103.9
PO Box 189   Phone: (314)564-2275
Montgomery City, MO 63361   **Fax: (314)564-2275**

MOUND CITY

2360 Mound City News-Independent
511 State St.
PO Box 175   Phone: (816)442-5423
Mound City, MO 64470   **Fax: (816)442-5423**

Ad Rates: GLR = general line rate; BW = one-time black & white page rate; 4C = one-time four color page rate; SAU = standard advertising unit rate; CNU = Canadian newspaper advertising unit rate; PCI = per column inch rate.
Circulation: ★ = ABC; △ = BPA; ◆ = CAC; ● = CCAB; □ = VAC; ⊕ = PO Statement; ‡ = Publisher's Report; Boldface figures = sworn; Light figures = estimated.
Entry type: ◫ = Print; ✇ = Broadcast.

153

NEOSHO

🎙 2361 KBTN-AM - 1420
216 W. Spring
PO Box K   Phone: (417)451-1420
Neosho, MO 64850   **Fax: (417)451-2526**

NORTH KANSAS CITY

📖 2362 Foundation Contractor
R.W. Nielsen Co.
320 Armour Rd., Ste. 215   Phone: (816)471-0980
North Kansas City, MO 64116   Fax: (816)471-0982
Subtitle: The Magazine of Commercial and Residential Concrete Foundation Construction. **Founded:** 1989. **Frequency:** 6x/yr. **Printing Method:** Sheetfed offset. **Trim Size:** 8 x 10 3/4. **Cols./Page:** 3. **Key Personnel:** Roger W. Nielsen, Editor and Publisher; Carolyn Nielsen, Assoc. Editor. **Subscription:** $20; $40 other countries. $3 single issue.
Ad Rates: BW: $1,660   **Circulation:** (Not Reported)
       4C: $2,010
Formerly: The Concrete Foundation Contractor.

📖 2363 TILT-UP
R.W. Nielsen Co.
320 Armour Rd. Ste. 215   Phone: (816)471-0980
North Kansas City, MO 64116   Fax: (816)471-0982
Magazine for contractors, developers, architects, and engineers interested in tilt-up construction. **Subtitle:** The Voice of the Tilt-Up Concrete Industry. **Founded:** 1991. **Frequency:** Quarterly. **Trim Size:** 8 x 10 3/4. **Cols./Page:** 3. **Key Personnel:** Rodger Nielsen, Editor and Publisher; Carolyn Nielsen, Assoc. Editor. **ISSN:** 1064-4865. **Subscription:** $25; $35 other countries. $3 single issue.
Ad Rates: BW: $1,660   **Circulation:** (Not Reported)
       4C: $2,010

OVERLAND

🎙 2364 Continental Cablevision of Saint Louis County, Inc.
2411 Verona
Overland, MO 63114   Phone: (314)428-0915
Owner: Continental Cablevision, Inc. **Founded:** 1980. **Cities Served:** Saint Louis County, Breckenridge Hills, Brentwood, Chesterfield, and Clayton, MO.

OWENSVILLE

📖 2365 Free Shopper
Warden Publishing Co.
106 E. Washington
PO Box 540   Phone: (314)437-2323
Owensville, MO 65066-0540   Fax: (314)437-3033
Community newspaper and shopper. **Founded:** 1982. **Frequency:** Weekly. **Printing Method:** Offset. **Trim Size:** 14 x 22. **Cols./Page:** 6. **Col. Depth:** 21 1/2 in. **Key Personnel:** Don Warden, Editor; Tom Warden, Editor. **Subscription:** Free.
Ad Rates: BW: $387   **Circulation:** Free ‡5,656
       SAU: $3

PARKVILLE

📖 2366 Dive Training
Dive Training Ltd.
405 Main St.   Phone: (816)741-5151
Parkville, MO 64152   Fax: (816)741-6458
Diving magazine promoting training and safety. **Subtitle:** The New Divers Magazine. **Founded:** 1991. **Frequency:** Monthly. **Printing Method:** Offset. **Trim Size:** 7 7/8 x 10 1/2. **Cols./Page:** 3. **Key Personnel:** Gary S. Worden, Editor and Publisher. **ISSN:** 1061-3323. **Subscription:** $20. $2.95 single issue.
Ad Rates: BW: $4,150   **Circulation:** Paid ‡6,000
       4C: $6,020   Non-paid ‡70,000

PERRYVILLE

🎙 2367 KBDZ-FM - 93.1
PO Box 344
Perry Plaza, No. 10
Perryville, MO 63775   **Phone: (314)547-8005**

PETERS

🎙 2368 TCI Cablevision of Missouri
4160 Old Mill Pkwy.
Peters, MO 63376-9979   Phone: (314)441-7737
Owner: Tele-Communications, Inc. **Founded:** 1980. **Cities Served:** St. Charles County, MO.

PIEDMONT

🎙 2369 KPWB-FM - 104.9
Hwy. HH
Rte. 3, Box 3202   Phone: (314)223-4218
Piedmont, MO 63957   Fax: (314)223-2351
Format: Country. **Network(s):** ABC; Satellite Music. **Owner:** Hunt Broadcasting Group, at above address. **Operating Hours:** Continuous. **Key Personnel:** Timothy D. Dodson, Operations Mgr./News Dir.; Mark Miles, Program Dir.; Gaylord Harvey, Sales Mgr. **Wattage:** 3000. **Ad Rates:** $3.50-$6 for 30 seconds; $5-$8 for 60 seconds.

PITTSBURG

📖 2370 Writer's Guidelines Magazine
Writers Guidelines, Inc.
HC 77, Box 608
Pittsburg, MO 65724   Phone: (417)993-5544

POPLAR BLUFF

🎙 2371 KAHR-FM - 96.7
PO Box 1275   Phone: (314)686-3700
Poplar Bluff, MO 63901-1275   Fax: (314)686-1713
Format: Oldies. **Network(s):** Satellite Music. **Owner:** Gerald Hunt. **Operating Hours:** Continuous. **Key Personnel:** Jim Borders, Station Mgr.; Robbie Frish, Operations Mgr.; Craig Meador, Engineering. **Wattage:** 3000.

🎙 2372 KLID-AM - 1340
KLID Bldg.
102 N. 11th
Poplar Bluff, MO 63901   **Phone: (314)686-1600**

ROCK PORT

📖 2373 The Atchison County Mail
300 S. Main St.
PO Box 40   Phone: (816)744-6245
Rock Port, MO 64482-0040   **Fax: (816)744-2645**

ROLLA

📖 2374 The Weekly
American Publishing Co.
915 N. Southwest Blvd.
PO Box 808
Rolla, MO 65401-0808
Ceased publication.

ST. JOSEPH

🎙 2375 KSFT-AM - 1550
PO Box 8550   Phone: (816)279-6346
St. Joseph, MO 64506   **Fax: (816)279-8280**

ST. LOUIS

📖 2376 Allan Kaye's Sports Cards News & Price Guides
Allan Kaye Publications, Inc.
10300 Watson Rd.
St. Louis, MO 63127
Combination price and information guide with feature stories from top dealers. **Frequency:** 2x/mo. **Key Personnel:** Allan Kaye, Editor and Publisher. **Subscription:** $24.95. $3.95 single issue.
                 Circulation: (Not Reported)

📖 2377 American Agent & Broker
Commerce Publishing Co.
330 N. 4th St.   Phone: (314)421-5445
Saint Louis, MO 63102   Fax: (314)421-1070

2378 The American Muslim
American Muslim Support Group
PO Box 5670
Saint Louis, MO 63121   Fax: (314)291-3711
Founded: 1989. Frequency: Quarterly. Key Personnel: Sheila Musaji, Editor. Subscription: $15; $30 other countries; $5 prisoners.
                                     Circulation: 1,000
Advertising accepted; contact publisher for rates.

2379 Analytical and Quantitative Cytology and Histology
Science Printers and Publishers, Inc.
PO Drawer 12425
8342 Olive Blvd.   Phone: (314)991-4588
St. Louis, MO 63132   Fax: (314)991-4654
Journal covering analytical and quantitative cytology and histology. Founded: 1979. Frequency: 6x/yr. Printing Method: Offset. Trim Size: 8 x 10 3/4. Cols./Page: 2. Col. Width: 3 3/8 in. Col. Depth: 10 in. Key Personnel: George L. Wied, M.D., Editor-in-Chief; Donna Kessel, Publisher. ISSN: 0884-6812. Subscription: $196; $279 institutions. $50 single issue.
Ad Rates: BW: $862   Circulation: Paid ‡2,804
           4C: $1,728   Non-paid ‡30

2380 Cadenza
Washington University
Campus Box 1039   Phone: (314)935-5941
Saint Louis, MO 63130   Fax: (314)935-5938
Community newspaper. Frequency: Weekly (Fri.). Printing Method: Offset. Cols./Page: 4. Col. Width: 2 3/8 in. Col. Depth: 12 in. Key Personnel: Dale Wiley, Editor. Subscription: Free; $29 out of area.
Ad Rates: BW: $501.41   Circulation: Non-paid ‡9,000
           PCI: $10.15

2381 Facts and Comparisons
111 W. Port Plaza, Ste. 423   Phone: (314)878-2515
Saint Louis, MO 63146   Fax: (314)878-5563
Drug information organized by therapeutic category. Founded: 1945. Frequency: Monthly. Printing Method: Web offset. Trim Size: 5 1/2 x 8 1/2. Key Personnel: C.S. Sewster, Publisher; Barb Wright, Circulation Mgr. ISSN: 0014-6617. Subscription: $165; $80 student. $95.50 single issue.
                                     Circulation: (Not Reported)
Advertising not accepted.

2382 Gastrointestinal Endoscopy
Mosby-Year Book, Inc.
11830 Westline Industrial Dr.   Phone: (314)872-8370
St. Louis, MO 63146   Fax: (314)432-1380

2383 Gateway Heritage
Missouri Historical Society
PO Box 11940   Phone: (314)746-4559
Saint Louis, MO 63112-0040   Fax: (314)746-4548

2384 Geriatric Nursing
Mosby-Year Book, Inc.
11830 Westline Industrial Dr.   Phone: (314)872-8370
St. Louis, MO 63146   Fax: (314)432-1380

2385 Happy Times
Concordia Publishing House
3558 S. Jefferson Ave.
Saint Louis, MO 63118   Phone: (314)268-1076

2386 Healing Words
Creative Communications for the Parish
10300 Watson Rd.   Phone: (314)821-1363
Saint Louis, MO 63127   Fax: (314)821-9031
Devotional magazine for hospital patients. Subtitle: Spiritual Resources For Your Hospital Stay. Founded: 1988. Frequency: Quarterly. Printing Method: Offset. Trim Size: 5 3/8 x 8 3/8. Cols./Page: 1. Col. Width: 3 7/8 in. Col. Depth: 7 in. Key Personnel: Larry Neeb, Publisher; Arden Mead, Editor.
                                     Circulation: ‡36,000
Advertising not accepted.

2387 Journal of Policy History
Saint Louis University
256 DuBourg Hall
221 N. Grand Blvd.
St. Louis, MO 63103   Phone: (314)658-2339

2388 Lutheran Witness
Board for Communication Services The Lutheran Church-Missouri Synod
1333 S. Kirkwood Rd.   Phone: (314)965-9917
Saint Louis, MO 63122-7295   Fax: (314)822-8307

2389 Nursing Outlook
Mosby-Year Book, Inc.
11830 Westline Industrial Dr.   Phone: (314)872-8370
St. Louis, MO 63146   Fax: (314)872-9164

2390 Optometric Economics
American Optometric Assn.
243 N. Lindbergh Blvd.   Phone: (314)991-4100
Saint Louis, MO 63141   Fax: (314)991-4101
Marketing magazine for optometrists. Founded: 1991. Frequency: Monthly. Printing Method: Offset. Trim Size: 8 1/8 x 10 7/8. Key Personnel: Jack Runninger, Editor; Gene Mitchell, Mng. Editor; Joel Raeber, Advertising Mgr. ISSN: 1052-7346. Subscription: $12 member; $30 non-member.
Ad Rates: BW: $3,000   Circulation: Paid △23,000
           4C: $4,150   Non-paid △6,000

2391 Review for Religious
3601 Lindell Blvd., Rm. 428   Phone: (314)535-3048
Saint Louis, MO 63108   Fax: (314)535-0601

2392 St. Louis Advertising
Advertising Club of Greater St. Louis
305 N. Broadway   Phone: (314)231-4185
Saint Louis, MO 63102   Fax: (314)231-4188
Former Title: Ad/Mag

2393 Schutzhund USA
United Schutzhund Clubs of America
3704 Lemay Ferry Rd.   Phone: (314)894-3431
Saint Louis, MO 63125   Fax: (314)894-0358
Subtitle: The Official Publication of the United Schutzhund Clubs of America. Frequency: 6x/yr. Printing Method: Sheetfed offset. Trim Size: 8 1/2 x 10 3/8. Cols./Page: 2 or 3. Col. Depth: 7 in. Key Personnel: Mark Hess, Editor. ISSN: 0194-5033. Subscription: $42. $5 single issue.
Ad Rates: BW: $125   Circulation: Paid 3,500
           4C: $700   Non-paid 500
Advertising not accepted for vicious looking or biting dogs.

2394 South County Times
Webster-Kirkwood Times, Inc.
122-A W. Lockwood Ave.   Phone: (314)968-2699
Saint Louis, MO 63119   Fax: (314)968-2961
Former Title: South County News-Times

2395 STL
St. Louis Regional Educational Television-KETC
6996 Millbrook Blvd.   Phone: (314)726-7685
Saint Louis, MO 63130   Fax: (314)726-0677

2396 Student Life
Washington University
Campus Box 1039   Phone: (314)889-5920
Saint Louis, MO 63130   Fax: (314)935-5938

2397 Studies in the Spirituality of Jesuits
Seminar on Jesuit Spirituality
3700 W. Pine Blvd.   Phone: (314)652-5737
Saint Louis, MO 63108   Fax: (314)652-0810

Ad Rates: GLR = general line rate; BW = one-time black & white page rate; 4C = one-time four color page rate; SAU = standard advertising unit rate; CNU = Canadian newspaper advertising unit rate; PCI = per column inch rate.
Circulation: ★ = ABC; △ = BPA; ♦ = CAC; ● = CCAB; □ = VAC; ⊕ = PO Statement; ‡ = Publisher's Report; Boldface figures = sworn; Light figures = estimated.
Entry type: ▣ = Print; ♨ = Broadcast.

155

⚲ 2398 West County Journal
Suburban Newspapers of Greater St. Louis
1714 Deer Track Trail　　　　　　　　Phone: (314)821-2462
Saint Louis, MO 63131　　　　　　　　**Fax: (314)821-3408**

⚲ 2399 Cencom of Saint Louis
9358 Dielman Industrial Dr.　　　　　Phone: (314)997-7570
Saint Louis, MO 63132　　　　　　　　Fax: (314)997-4109
Owner: Cencom Cable Assoc., Inc. **Founded:** 1981. **Cities Served:**
Ballwin, Bridgeton, Bridgeton Terrace, Charlack, Ellisville, Glendale,
Hanley Hills, Manchester, Oakland, Rock Hill, Shrewsbury, St. John,
Sycamore Hills, Vinita Park, Warson Woods, Webster Groves,
Winchester, Woodson Terrace, MO.

⚲ 2400 KPLR-TV - Channel 11
4935 Lindell Blvd.　　　　　　　　　Phone: (314)367-7211
St. Louis, MO 63108-1587　　　　　　**Fax: (314)454-6488**

⚲ 2401 KWUR-FM - 90.3
Washington University
Box 1182　　　　　　　　　　　　　Phone: (314)935-5952
Saint Louis, MO 63130　　　　　　　　**Fax: (314)935-8516**

⚲ 2402 Saint Louis Tele-Communications
4940 Delmar Blvd.
Saint Louis, MO 63108-1659　　　　　Phone: (314)361-7300
Owner: Tele-Communications, Inc. **Founded:** 1985. **Cities Served:**
Saint Louis, MO.

SEDALIA

⚲ 2403 KSDL-FM - 92.1
Box 1056
Sedalia, MO 65301　　　　　　　　　Phone: (816)826-1050
Format: Hot Adult Contemporary. **Owner:** Bick Broadcasting Co.
Formerly: KCBW-FM. **Operating Hours:** 5 a.m.-midnight. **Key Personnel:** Dennis Polk, Gen. Mgr. **Wattage:** 3000. **Ad Rates:** Combination rates with KSIS-AM: $7.80-$14.30 for 30 seconds.

SMITHVILLE

⚲ 2404 The Smithville Lake Democrat-Herald
110 N. Bridge
PO Box 269　　　　　　　　　　　　Phone: (816)532-4444
Smithville, MO 64089-0269　　　　　　**Fax: (816)532-4918**

SPRINGFIELD

⚲ 2405 Memos
General Council of the Assemblies of God Gospel Publishing
　House
1445 Boonville Ave.
Springfield, MO 65802-1894　　　　　Phone: (417)862-2781

⚲ 2406 Missouri Grocer
Missouri Grocers' Assn.
PO Box 10223　　　　　　　　　　　Phone: (417)831-6667
Springfield, MO 65808　　　　　　　　**Fax: (417)831-3907**

⚲ 2407 Springfield Business Journal
209 E. Walnut St.　　　　　　　　　Phone: (417)831-3238
Springfield, MO 65806　　　　　　　　Fax: (417)831-5478
Business newspaper. **Founded:** 1980. **Frequency:** Weekly. **Printing
Method:** Web offset. **Key Personnel:** Dianne Elizabeth, Editor and
Publisher. **Subscription:** $36. $1 single issue.
Ad Rates: BW:　　$756　　　　　**Circulation:** ⊕2,384
　　　　　　4C:　　$1,206　　　　　Non-paid ⊕2,473

⚲ 2408 Springfield Parent
PO Box 4732　　　　　　　　　　　Phone: (417)881-4411
Springfield, MO 65808　　　　　　　　Fax: (417)881-7516
Parenting publication. **Founded:** 1987. **Frequency:** Monthly. **Subscription:** Free.
Ad Rates: BW:　　$750　　　　　**Circulation:** Free □27,571
　　　　　　　　　　　　　　　　　　Paid □39

⚲ 2409 The Standard
Southwest Missouri State University
901 S. National　　　　　　　　　　Phone: (417)836-5272
Springfield, MO 65804　　　　　　　　**Fax: (417)836-6583**

⚱ 2410 KADI-FM - 99.5
1701 W. Sunshine, Ste. H
Springfield, MO 65807　　　　　　　　Phone: (417)831-0995
Format: Religious (Contemporary Christian). **Network(s):** CNN Radio. **Owner:** Snowmen Broadcasting, Inc. **Founded:** 1990. **Operating
Hours:** Continuous. **Key Personnel:** R.C. Amex, Gen. Mgr. **Wattage:**
6000.

⚱ 2411 KGBX-AM - 1400
840 S. Glenstone
Broadcast Plaza　　　　　　　　　　Phone: (417)869-1059
Springfield, MO 65802　　　　　　　　Fax: (417)869-1000
Format: Adult Contemporary. **Owner:** Sunburst II, Inc. **Operating
Hours:** Continuous. **Key Personnel:** John Borders, Pres.; Bob May,
V.P. **Wattage:** 50,000.

⚱ 2412 KGBX-FM - 105.9
840 S. Glenstone
Broadcast Plaza　　　　　　　　　　Phone: (417)869-1059
Springfield, MO 65802　　　　　　　　Fax: (417)869-1000
Format: Country. **Owner:** Sunburst II, Inc. **Operating Hours:** Continuous. **Key Personnel:** John Borders, Pres.; Bob May, V.P. **Wattage:**
50,000.

⚱ 2413 TeleCable of Springfield
1533 S. Enterprise　　　　　　　　　Phone: (417)883-7557
Springfield, MO 65804　　　　　　　　Fax: (417)883-0265
Owner: TeleCable Corp, 999 Waterside Dr., Dominion Tower,
Norfolk, VA 23501. **Founded:** 1979. **Key Personnel:** Jerry Rutherford,
V.P./Gen. Mgr.; Judy Dean, Office Mgr.; Rick Pool, Technical Mgr.;
Bob Herzog, Sales Mgr.; Stan Melton, Asst. Mgr. **Cities Served:** Green
County and Battlefield, MO: 46,900 subscribing households; 57
channels; 4 community access channels; 83 hours per week of
community access programming.

STOVER

⚲ 2414 Morgan County Press
Vernon Publishing Inc.
PO Box 130　　　　　　　　　　　　Phone: (314)377-4616
Stover, MO 65078　　　　　　　　　　Fax: (314)377-4512

TARKIO

⚱ 2415 KTRX-FM - 93.5
Box 162-A　　　　　　　　　　　　Phone: (816)736-4127
Tarkio, MO 64491　　　　　　　　　　Fax: (816)736-4127
Format: Country. **Network(s):** ABC. **Owner:** KANZA, Inc., 102 N.
Mason, Carrollton, MO 64633. **Founded:** 1977. **Operating Hours:**
Continuous. **Key Personnel:** Mike L. Carter, Pres.; Roger Houts,
Operations Mgr.; Mary Kay Ryan, Office Mgr.; Wayne Combs, News
Dir.; Jay Truitt, Dir. **Wattage:** 6000. **Ad Rates:** $56-$72 for 30
seconds; $70-$90 for 60 seconds.

TRENTON

⚱ 2416 KTTN-AM - 1600
PO Box 307　　　　　　　　　　　　Phone: (816)359-2261
Trenton, MO 64683　　　　　　　　　**Fax: (816)359-4126**

⚱ 2417 KTTN-FM - 92.1
PO Box 307　　　　　　　　　　　　Phone: (816)359-2261
Trenton, MO 64683　　　　　　　　　**Fax: (816)359-4126**

UNION

⚲ 2418 Cornerstone
East Central Junior College
Hwy. 50
PO Box 529　　　　　　　　　　　　**Phone: (314)583-5195**
Union, MO 63084　　　　　　　　　　**Fax: (314)583-6637**

UNIONVILLE

⚲ 2419 Unionville Republican & Putnam County Journal
Black Bird Creek Printing Co.
PO Box 365　　　　　　　　　　　　Phone: (816)947-2222
Unionville, MO 63565　　　　　　　　Fax: (816)947-2223

WASHINGTON

♪ **2420 KGNV-FM - 89.9**
PO Box 87
Washington, MO 63090

Phone: (314)239-0400
Fax: (314)583-5975

MONTANA

BELGRADE

🎙 2421 KGVW-AM - 640
2050 Amsterdam Rd.
Belgrade, MT 59714   Phone: (406)388-4281
Format: Religious; Gospel; Talk. **Network(s):** Ambassador Inspirational Radio; SkyLight Satellite; Montana News. **Owner:** Enterprise Network. **Operating Hours:** 6 a.m.-11 p.m. **ADI:** Helena, MT. **Key Personnel:** Mark Brashear, Gen. Mgr.; C.J. Swoboda, Program Dir.; Dale Heidner, Chief Engineer; Julia Evans Christian, Office Mgr. **Wattage:** 10,000 day; 1000 night. **Ad Rates:** $5-$6 for 30 seconds; $6-$7.50 for 60 seconds.

🎙 2422 KGVW-FM - 96.7
2050 Amsterdam Rd.
Belgrade, MT 59714   Phone: (406)388-4281
Format: Adult Contemporary; Religious. **Network(s):** SkyLight Satellite; Ambassador Inspirational Radio. **Owner:** Enterprise Network. **ADI:** Helena, MT. **Key Personnel:** Mark Brashear, Gen. Mgr.; C.J. Swoboda, Program Dir.; Dale Heidner, Chief Engineer; Julia Evans Christian, Office Mgr. **Ad Rates:** $6-$7 for 30 seconds; $8-$9 for 60 seconds.

BIG SANDY

📖 2423 Big Sandy Mountaineer
PO Box 529   Phone: (406)378-2176
Big Sandy, MT 59520   Fax: (406)378-2176

BIGFORK

📖 2424 Bigfork Eagle
PO Box 406   Phone: (406)837-5131
Bigfork, MT 59911   Fax: (406)837-5460

BILLINGS

🎙 2425 Billings TCI/TCI Cablevision of Montana
Box 20497
Billings, MT 59102-4152   Phone: (406)245-3051
Owner: Tele-Communications, Inc. **Founded:** 1968. **Cities Served:** Yellowstone County, MT.

🎙 2426 Premiere Cable Services, Inc.
180 Cook St., No. 209
Denver, CO 80206-5312   Phone: (208)664-3370
Owner: Premiere Cable I & II Ltd. **Founded:** 1988. **Cities Served:** Yellowstone County, MT.

BOZEMAN

🎙 2427 KBOZ-AM - 1090
5445 Johnson Rd.
Box 20   Phone: (406)586-5466
Bozeman, MT 59715   Fax: (406)587-8201
Format: Country. **Network(s):** ABC. **Owner:** Citadel Associates Ltd. Partnership. **Founded:** 1975. **Operating Hours:** Continuous. **Key Personnel:** John Brandt, Gen. Mgr.; Dan Davis, Program Dir.; Mark Allen, Music Dir. **Wattage:** 5000.

🎙 2428 KBOZ-FM - 93.7
5445 Johnson Rd.
Box 20   Phone: (406)586-5466
Bozeman, MT 59715   Fax: (406)587-8201
Format: Adult Contemporary. **Network(s):** ABC. **Owner:** Citadel Communications. **Operating Hours:** Continuous. **Key Personnel:** John Brandt, Gen. Mgr.; Vicki Mann, Gen. Sales Mgr. **Wattage:** 100,000. **Ad Rates:** Available upon request.

CIRCLE

🎙 2429 Cable and Communications Corp.
Box 280
Circle, MT 59215   **Phone: (406)485-3301**

GLASGOW

🎙 2430 KLTZ-AM - 1240
504 2nd Ave. S.
PO Box 671   Phone: (406)228-9336
Glasgow, MT 59230   **Fax: (406)228-9338**

GLENDIVE

🎙 2431 KGLE-AM - 590
Box 931   Phone: (406)365-3331
Glendive, MT 59330   Fax: (406)365-3332
Format: Gospel. **Network(s):** Christian Broadcasting (CBN); Ambassador Inspirational Radio; Moody Broadcasting. **Owner:** Christian Enterprise Inc. **Founded:** 1962. **Operating Hours:** Sunrise-sunset. **Key Personnel:** Jim McBride, Station Mgr. **Wattage:** 1000. **Ad Rates:** $2.25-$3.25 for 30 seconds; $3.50-$4.50 for 60 seconds.

GREAT FALLS

🎙 2432 TCI Cablevision of Great Falls
Box 6410
Great Falls, MT 59403   Phone: (406)727-8881
Owner: Tele-Communications, Inc. **Founded:** 1958. **Cities Served:** Cascade County, MT.

HARLOWTON

2433 Times-Clarion
111 S. Central
PO Box 307
Harlowton, MT 59036-0307
Phone: (406)632-5633
Fax: **(406)632-5644**

2434 Cable TV of Harlo Corp.
Box 242
Harlowton, MT 59036-0242
Phone: (406)632-4300
Fax: **(406)632-5644**

HAVRE

2435 Triangle Cable TV
Box 1230
Havre, MT 59501
Phone: (406)265-7807
Fax: **(406)265-7801**

HELENA

2436 AERO Sun-Times
44 N. Last Chance Gulch, No. 9
Helena, MT 59601
Phone: (406)443-7272
Fax: **(406)442-9120**

2437 KHKR-FM - 104.1
Box 4111
Helena, MT 59604
Phone: (406)449-4251
Fax: (406)449-3553
Format: Contemporary Country. **Network(s):** Satellite Music. **Owner:** Big Sky Communications Inc. **Founded:** 1988. **Operating Hours:** Continuous. **Key Personnel:** Kurt Kittelson, Operations Mgr. **Wattage:** 3000. **Ad Rates:** $6-$7.50 for 30 seconds; $8.50-$10 for 60 seconds. **Additional Contact Information:** Sales Dept. telephone (406)442-0400.

2438 KVCM-AM - 680
Box 4111
Helena, MT 59604
Phone: (406)449-4251
Fax: (406)449-3553
Format: Religious (Christian). **Network(s):** UPI; SkyLight Satellite. **Owner:** Big Sky Communications Inc. **Founded:** 1988. **Formerly:** KHKR-AM (June 1991). **Operating Hours:** 6 a.m.- midnight. **Key Personnel:** Kurt Kittelson, Operations Mgr.; Ed Matter, Gen. Mgr. **Wattage:** 3000. **Ad Rates:** Noncommercial. **Additional Contact Information:** Alt. phone (406)265-5845.

2439 TCI Cablevision of Montana
Box 5509
Helena, MT 59604-5509
Phone: (406)443-3401
Owner: Tele-Communications, Inc. **Founded:** 1955. **Cities Served:** Lewis and Clark County and East Helena, MT.

KALISPELL

2440 The Daily Inter Lake
Inter Lake Publishing Co.
727 E. Idaho
PO Box 7610
Kalispell, MT **59904**
Phone: (406)755-7000
Fax: (406)752-6114

MISSOULA

2441 Montana Kaimin
University of Montana
Journalism Bldg., Rm. 206
Missoula, MT 59812
Phone: (406)243-6541
Fax: **(406)243-5475**

2442 KDXT-FM - 93.3
1608 S. 3rd St. W., Ste. 200
Missoula, MT **59801**
Phone: **(406)728-9399**
Fax: (406)721-3020

RONAN

2443 Lake County Leader
C.P.A., Inc.
123 Main St. SW.
Ronan, MT 59864
Phone: (406)676-3800
Fax: **(406)883-4349**

WHITEFISH

2444 Kinesis
Kinesis Partnership, Ltd.
PO Box 4007
Whitefish, MT 59937
Magazine for writers, poets, and artists. **Founded:** 1991. **Frequency:** 6x/yr. **Subscription:** $10. $2 single issue.
Circulation: (Not Reported)

NEBRASKA

BELLEVUE

♣ 2445 UAE
1500 Wall St.
Bellevue, NE 68005
Phone: (402)292-3460
Fax: (402)292-9366
Owner: Tele-Communications, Inc. **Founded:** 1980. **Cities Served:** Sarpy County, NE.

BLAIR

▥ 2446 Clipper Shopper
Enterprise Publishing Corp.
16th & Front St.
PO Box 328
Blair, NE 68008
Phone: (402)426-2121
Fax: (402)426-2227

♣ 2447 KBWH-FM - 106.3
1570 Washington St.
PO Box 366
Blair, NE 68008-0366
Phone: (402)533-2777
Fax: (402)533-2778
Format: Adult Contemporary. **Network(s):** CNN Radio. **Owner:** Sunrise Broadcasting of Nebraska, Inc., at above address; (402)533-2777. **Founded:** 1990. **Operating Hours:** Continuous. **Key Personnel:** Kevin Van Grouw, Gen. Mgr.; Walter Keller, Sales Mgr.; Thom Morrow, News Dir.; Bobbi Anderson, Office Mgr. **Wattage:** 3000. **Ad Rates:** $3-$6.60 for 10 seconds;$4-$8.25 for 30 seconds;$5.50-$11 for 60 seconds.

CHADRON

▥ 2448 The Eagle
Chadron State College
259 Administration Bldg.
Chadron, NE 69337
Phone: (308)432-6303
Fax: (308)432-6464

♣ 2449 KCSR-AM - 610
226 Bondeaux
PO Box 931
Chadron, NE 69337
Phone: (308)432-5545
Fax: (308)432-2960

CROOKSTON

♣ 2450 KINI-FM - 96.1
PO Box 419
Saint Francis, SD 57572
Phone: (605)747-2291
Fax: (605)747-5057

FREMONT

▥ 2451 The Fremonter
R & D Publishing, Inc.
854 E. 23rd St.
PO Box 1056
Fremont, NE 68025
Phone: (402)721-1030
Fax: (402)721-5276
Shopper. **Founded:** 1987. **Frequency:** Weekly. **Cols./Page:** 6. **Col. Width:** 1 1/2 in. **Col. Depth:** 16 in. **Key Personnel:** Robb Harmon, Gen. Mgr.
Ad Rates: SAU: $6.50   Circulation: (Not Reported)

GIBBON

▥ 2452 The Gibbon Reporter
PO Box 820
Gibbon, NE 68840-0820
Phone: (308)468-5393
Former Title: Reporter

HARDY

♣ 2453 KSNB-TV - Channel 4
Rte. 1, Box 121
Hardy, NE 68943
Phone: (402)226-2011
Fax: (402)226-2011

IMPERIAL

▥ 2454 Grant Tribune Sentinel
Johnson Publications, Inc.
622 Broadway
Imperial, NE 69033-0727
Phone: (308)882-4453
Community newspaper. **Frequency:** Weekly. **Printing Method:** Offset. **Cols./Page:** 6. **Col. Width:** 12.375 picas. **Col. Depth:** 21 1/2 in. **Key Personnel:** Loral Johnson, Co-Publisher; Elna Johnson, Co-Publisher; Dennis Morgan, Editor. **Subscription:** $13.50; $15 out of area; $17.50 out of state.
Ad Rates: SAU: $3.27   Circulation: Paid ⊕1,760
                                            Non-paid ⊕10

▥ 2455 Holyoke Enterprise
Johnson Publications, Inc.
622 Broadway
Imperial, NE 69033-0727
Phone: (308)882-4453
Community newspaper. **Founded:** 1900. **Frequency:** Weekly (Thurs. morn.). **Cols./Page:** 6. **Col. Width:** 12.375 picas. **Col. Depth:** 21 1/2 in. **Key Personnel:** Loral Johnson, Co-Publisher; Elna Johnson, Co-Publisher; Brenda Brandt, Mng. Editor; Connie Hoffman, Advertising Mgr. **Subscription:** $13.50; $26 two years; $14.50 out of area; $17 out of state.
Ad Rates: SAU: $4   Circulation: (Not Reported)

KEARNEY

2456 KKPR-AM - 1460
PO Box 130
Kearney, NE 68848   **Phone: (308)236-9900**

2457 KKPR-FM - 98.9
PO Box 130
Kearney, NE 68848   **Phone: (308)236-9900**

LINCOLN

2458 Journal of Vision Rehabilitation
Media Periodicals
2444 'O' St., Ste. 202   Phone: (402)474-2676
Lincoln, NE 68510   Fax: (402)474-5104

2459 Nebraska History
Nebraska State Historical Soc.
1500 R St.
Box 82554   Phone: (402)471-4747
Lincoln, NE 68501   **Fax: (402)471-3100**

2460 Nebraska Medical Journal
Nebraska Medical Assn.
233 S. 13th St., Ste. 1512
Lincoln, NE 68508   Phone: (402)474-4472
     Fax: (402)474-2198

2461 Photochemistry and Photobiology
American Society for Photobiology
Department of Chemistry
University of Nebraska   Phone: (402)273-2733
Lincoln, NE 68588-0376   Fax: (402)472-2044
Journal covering the effects of light on chemical and biological processes.**Founded:** 1962. **Frequency:** Monthly. **Trim Size:** 8 1/2 x 11. **Cols./Page:** 2. **Col. Width:** 3 3/4 in. **Col. Depth:** 9 1/4 in. **Key Personnel:** Dr. Pill-Soon Song, Editor-in-Chief; Gene Kean, Advertising Dir. **ISSN:** 0031-8655. **Subscription:** Free (members); $525 institutions.

     Circulation: 815
     Non-paid 1,600
Advertising accepted; contact publisher for rates. **Additional Contact Information:** Advertising Dir. phone (913)843-1235, fax (913)843-1274. Publisher's address PO Box 3271, Agusta, GA 30914; phone (706)721-2601, fax (706)721-3048.

2462 Southern Nebraska Register
PO Box 80329
Lincoln, NE 68506   Phone: (402)488-0090

2463 KFGE-FM - 105.3
4343 O St.
Lincoln, NE 68510   Phone: (402)475-4567
Format: Hot Country. **Founded:** 1992. **Operating Hours:** Continuous. **Key Personnel:** Lisa Warner, Gen. Mgr.; Brenda Farrington, Sales Mgr.; Jonathan Taylor, Program Dir.; Jill Thomas, Promotions Mgr. **Wattage:** 3000.

2464 Lincoln Cablevision
5400 S. 16th St.
Lincoln, NE 68512   Phone: (402)421-0330
Owner: MetroVision, Inc. **Founded:** 1968. **Key Personnel:** Richard Bates, Gen. Mgr.; Richard Kiolbasa, Asst. Mgr. **Cities Served:** Lancaster County, Saline County, and Crete, NE: 72,000 subscribing households; 78 channels; 5 community access channels.

MINDEN

2465 The Minden Courier
C D Publishing Inc.
PO Box 379   Phone: (308)832-2220
Minden, NE 68959-0379   **Fax: (308)832-1526**

NORFOLK

2466 KXNE-TV - Channel 19
c/o KUON-TV
Box 83111   Phone: (402)472-3611
Lincoln, NE 68501   **Fax: (402)472-1785**

O'NEILL

2467 KBRX-AM - 1350
Box 150   Phone: (402)336-1612
O'Neill, NE 68763   **Fax: (402)336-3585**

2468 KBRX-FM - 102.9
Box 150   Phone: (402)336-1612
O'Neill, NE 68763   **Fax: (402)336-3585**

OMAHA

2469 The Catholic Voice
The Catholic Voice Publishing Co.
6060 NW Radial
PO Box 4010   Phone: (402)558-6611
Omaha, NE 68104   **Fax: (402)558-6614**

2470 Creightonian
Creighton University
Dept. of Journalism & Mass
  Communication
California at 24th St.   Phone: (402)280-4060
Omaha, NE 68178-0119   **Fax: (402)280-4730**

2471 Kids, Kids, Kidz
J & J Publications, Inc.
PO Box 24032   Phone: (402)391-0441
Omaha, NE 68124-0032   **Fax: (402)399-9797**

2472 Cox Cable of Omaha
11505 W. Dodge Rd.
Omaha, NE 68154   Phone: (402)330-6770
Owner: Cox Cable Communications. **Founded:** 1981. **Cities Served:** Douglas County, NE; Pottawattamie County and Carter Lake, IA. **Additional Contact Information:** telephone (402)330-6528.

2473 Douglas County Cablevision
2312 S. 156th Circle   Phone: (402)333-6484
Omaha, NE 68130   Fax: (402)333-5752
Owner: MetroVision, Inc. **Founded:** 1981. **Cities Served:** Douglas County, NE and Pottawattamie County, IA.

2474 KBLZ-FM - 89.9
MBSC 128
University of Nebraska at Omaha
Omaha, NE 68182-0296   Phone: (402)554-2957
Format: Alternative/Independent/Progressive. **Key Personnel:** Beth Rigatuso, Music Dir. **Ad Rates:** Noncommercial.

2475 KVNO-FM - 90.7
     Phone: (402)559-
60th & Dodge St., Engg-202   KVNO
Omaha, NE 68182-0234   **Fax: (402)554-2440**

PLAINVIEW

2476 Plainview News
Box 9   Phone: (402)582-4921
Plainview, NE 68769-0009   **Fax: (402)582-4922**

RED CLOUD

2477 Red Cloud Chief
309 N. Webster
Box 466
Red Cloud, NE 68970   Phone: (402)746-3700

SCOTIA

2478 The Scotia Register
PO Box 306
Scotia, NE 68875-0306   **Phone: (308)245-4125**

SEWARD

📖 **2479 The Weekender**
129 S. 6th St.
Box 449   Phone: (402)643-3676
Seward, NE 68434   Fax: (402)643-3678
Shopping guide. **Frequency:** Weekly. **Printing Method:** Offset. **Cols./
Page:** 7. **Col. Width:** 12.2 picas. **Col. Depth:** 22 in. **Key Personnel:** Lori
Shriner, Editor; Mark Rhoades, Publisher; Lynn Dance, Advertising
Mgr. **Subscription:** Free.
Ad Rates: SAU: $4.77   **Circulation:** Free ‡4,500

SHELTON

📖 **2480 The Shelton Clipper**
Clipper Publishing Co.
Box 520
Shelton, NE 68876-0520   Phone: (308)647-5158
Former Title: Clipper

SUTHERLAND

📖 **2481 Courier-Times**
Box 367   Phone: (308)386-4617
Sutherland, NE 69165   **Fax: (308)386-2426**

WAHOO

📖 **2482 Wahoo Newspaper**
Saunders County Publishing Inc.
564 N. Broadway   Phone: (402)443-4162
Wahoo, NE 68066   **Fax: (402)443-4459**

YORK

🎙 **2483 KAWL-AM - 1370**
RR 4, Box 121A
York, NE 68467-9804   Phone: (402)362-4433
Format: Country; Talk; Full Service. **Network(s):** NBC; Talknet.
Owner: KAWL-AM/FM. **Founded:** 1954. **Operating Hours:** Continu-
ous. **Key Personnel:** Tom Robson, Gen. Mgr. **Wattage:** 500. **Ad Rates:**
$4-$8 for 30 seconds; $8-$12 for 60 seconds.

🎙 **2484 KTMX-FM - 104.9**
RR 4, Box 121A
York, NE 68467-9804   Phone: (402)362-4433
Format: Oldies; Adult Contemporary. **Network(s):** NBC. **Owner:**
KAWL-AM/FM. **Founded:** 1971. **Formerly:** KAWL-FM (1991). **Oper-
ating Hours:** Continuous. **Key Personnel:** Tom Robson, Gen. Mgr.
Wattage: 25,000. **Ad Rates:** $6-$12 for 30 seconds; $12-$16 for 60
seconds.

NEVADA

CARSON CITY

♣ 2485 TCI Cablevision of Nevada, Inc.
Box 2068
Carson City, NV 89702   Phone: (702)882-2136
Owner: Tele-Communications, Inc. **Founded:** 1962. **Cities Served:**
Carson City County, NV.

ELKO

▥ 2486 Elko Daily Free Press
3720 Idaho St.   Phone: (702)738-3118
Elko, NV **89801**   Fax: (702)738-2215

LAS VEGAS

▥ 2487 Nevada Senior World
M & S Publishing
3100 W. Sahara, Ste. 207   Phone: (702)367-6709
Las Vegas, NV 89102   Fax: (702)367-6883
Former Title: The Senior Times

▥ 2488 Spectrum Newspapers Monthly, Las Vegas
Spectrum Newspapers
11171 Sun Center Dr., Ste. 110   Phone: (916)852-6222
Rancho Cordova, CA 95670   Fax: (916)852-6397
Newspaper serving senior citizens, 55 and older, in Las Vegas.
Founded: 1975. **Frequency:** Monthly. **Printing Method:** Web offset.
Key Personnel: Bob Carney, Editor; Jacqueline Lucido, Gen. Mgr.;
Ridge Eagan, Advertising Dir. USPS: 980-481. Subscription: $12.
          Circulation: ‡41,000

♣ 2489 KRLR-TV - Channel 21
920 S. Commerce   Phone: (702)382-2121
Las Vegas, NV **89106**   Fax: (702)382-1351

♣ 2490 Prime Cable of Las Vegas
900 S. Commerce   Phone: (702)384-8084
Las Vegas, NV 89106   Fax: (702)383-0614
Owner: G.C. Associates; Prime Cable Corp. **Founded:** 1980. **Cities
Served:** Clark County, Boulder City, Green Valley, Henderson, and
North Las Vegas, NV.

RENO

▥ 2491 Spectrum Newspapers Monthly, Reno
Spectrum Newspapers
11171 Sun Center Dr., Ste. 110   Phone: (916)852-6222
Rancho Cordova, CA 95670   Fax: (916)852-6397
Newspaper serving active senior citizens, 55 and older, in Reno.
Founded: 1975. **Frequency:** Monthly. **Printing Method:** Web offset.

Key Personnel: Bob Carney, Editor; Jacqueline Lucido, Gen. Mgr.;
Ridge Eagan, Natl. Advertising Dir. USPS: 980-481. Subscription:
$12.
          Circulation: ‡20,000

▥ 2492 Western Roofing/Insulation/Siding
Dodson Publications, Inc.
546 Court St.   Phone: (702)333-1080
Reno, NV 89501   **Fax: (702)333-1081**

♣ 2493 KOLO-TV - Channel 8
4850 Ampere Dr.
PO Box 10000   **Phone: (702)858-8888**
Reno, NV 89510-0005   **Fax: (702)858-8855**

♣ 2494 KTVN-TV - Channel 2
4925 Energy Way   **Phone: (702)858-2222**
Reno, NV 89502   **Fax: (702)858-2345**

♣ 2495 TCI of Nevada, Inc.
1250 Terminal Way
Reno, NV 89502   Phone: (702)329-9695
Owner: Tele-Communications, Inc. **Founded:** 1953. **Cities Served:**
Sierra County and Peavine, CA; Washoe County, Cold Springs Valley,
Mogul, Reno Cascade, Sierra Royal, Spanish Springs Valley, Verdi,
and Wadsworth, NV.

TONOPAH

♣ 2496 KHWK-FM - 92.7
Box 1669   Phone: (702)482-5724
Tonopah, NV 89049   **Fax: (702)482-3238**

NEW HAMPSHIRE

BERLIN

🎙 2497 Warner Cable Communications
219 Main St. Phone: (603)752-4330
Berlin, NH 03570 **Fax: (603)752-3940**

CHARLESTOWN

📖 2498 Earth Work
Student Conservation Association
PO Box 550 Phone: (603)543-1700
Charlestown, NH 03603 Fax: (603)543-1828
Magazine offering career advice and a nationwide listing of natural resources and environmental jobs for students and professionals. **Founded:** February, 1991. **Frequency:** Monthly. **Printing Method:** Offset. **Trim Size:** 8 1/2 x 11. **Cols./Page:** 3. **Col. Width:** 2 3/8 in. **Col. Depth:** 9 5/8 in. **Key Personnel:** Joan Moody, Editor. **ISSN:** 1060-5053. **Subscription:** $29.95. $6 single issue.

Ad Rates:	GLR	$150	Circulation: Paid 5,500
	BW	$650	
	4C	$1,000	
	PCI	$30	

Formerly: Job Scan.

CLAREMONT

🎙 2499 WXXK-FM - 101.7
25 Pine St. **Phone: (603)543-1511**
Claremont, NH 03743-2686 **Fax: (603)543-1706**

COLEBROOK

📖 2500 The News and Sentinel
1 Bridge St.
Box 39 Phone: (603)237-5501
Colebrook, NH 03576 **Fax: (603)237-5060**

CONCORD

📖 2501 WomenWise
Concord Feminist Health Center
38 S. Main St.
Concord, NH 03301 Phone: (603)225-2739
Journal covering all aspects of women's health. **Founded:** 1978. **Frequency:** Quarterly. **Key Personnel:** Carol Anderson Porter, Editor. **ISSN:** 0890-9695. **Subscription:** $10; $25 institutions. $2.95 single issue.

Circulation: Paid 600
Non-paid 1,400

Advertising accepted; contact publisher for rates.

🎙 2502 Continental Cablevision
8 Commercial St. Phone: (603)224-1984
Concord, NH 03301 Fax: (603)226-0764
Owner: Continental Cablevision, Inc. **Founded:** 1970. **Formerly:** TeleCable, Inc.. **Key Personnel:** Mary J. Colletti, Gen. Mgr.; John E. Dowd, Technical Mgr.; Jeff Vandeberghe, Mktg. Mgr. **Cities Served:** Belknap County, Grafton County, Hillsborough County, Merrimack County, Alexandria, Allenstown, Antrim, Boscawen, Bow, Bridgewater, Bristol, Canterbury, Chichester, Deering, Hebron, Henniker, Hillsboro, Hopkinton, New Hampton, Pembroke, Suncook, and Weare, NH: 26,000 subscribing households; 49 channels; 4 community access channels; 40 hours per week of community access programming.

DERRY

📖 2503 Derry News
Derry Publishing Co.
46 W. Broadway
PO Box 307 Phone: (603)437-7000
Derry, NH 03038-0307 **Fax: (603)432-4510**

🎙 2504 WDER-AM - 1320
8 Lawrence Rd.
Box 465 Phone: (603)434-9302
Derry, NH 03038 **Fax: (603)434-1035**

DURHAM

📖 2505 NWSA Journal
National Women's Studies Association
University of New Hampshire
Dept. of English Phone: (603)862-1313
Durham, NH 03824 Fax: (603)862-2030
Periodical containing feminist scholarship. **Subtitle:** A Publication of the National Women's Studies Association. **Founded:** 1988. **Frequency:** 3x/yr. **Printing Method:** Offset. **Cols./Page:** 1. **Col. Width:** 5 in. **Col. Depth:** 8 in. **Key Personnel:** Patrocinio Schweickart, Editor; Susan D. Franzosa, Assoc. Editor. **ISSN:** 1040-0656. **Subscription:** $39.50; $24 member; $105 institutions.
Ad Rates: BW: $200 Circulation: ‡1,300
Color advertising not accepted. Published by Ablex Publishing Corp. **Additional Contact Information:** Publisher's address: 355 Chestnut St., Norwood, NJ 07648; (201)767-8450.

EXETER

🎙 2506 Grassroots Cable Systems
PO Box 280 Phone: (603)772-4600
Exeter, NH 03833-0280 Fax: (603)772-4650
Key Personnel: W. Robert Felder, Pres.; Marsha B. Felder, V.P./

Ad Rates: GLR = general line rate; BW = one-time black & white page rate; 4C = one-time four color page rate; SAU = standard advertising unit rate; CNU = Canadian newspaper advertising unit rate; PCI = per column inch rate.
Circulation: ★ = ABC; △ = BPA; ◆ = CAC; ● = CCAB; □ = VAC; ⊕ = PO Statement; ‡ = Publisher's Report; Boldface figures = sworn; Light figures = estimated.
Entry type: 📖 = Print; 🎙 = Broadcast.

167

Business Operations Mgr.; Keith Felder, V.P./Engineering; Kristi Perlham, V.P./Accounting. **Cities Served:** Exeter, NH: 6,300 subscribing households; 29 channels.

GREENLAND

2507 Dateline New England
Dateline New England
PO Box 800   Phone: (603)433-3020
Greenland, NH 03840   Fax: (603)427-2099
Publication for singles. **Founded:** 1988. **Frequency:** Monthly. **Trim Size:** 8 1/4 x 10 7/8. **Cols./Page:** 2. **Col. Width:** 3 3/4 in. **Col. Depth:** 7 3/4 in. **Key Personnel:** Nancy B. Stone, Publisher. **Subscription:** $12.
     Circulation: Free □15,153
Advertising accepted; contact publisher for rates. **Formerly:** Dateline New Hampshire.

HANOVER

2508 Dartmouth Alumni Magazine
Dartmouth College
38 N. Main St.   Phone: (603)646-2256
Hanover, NH 03755-3762   Fax: (603)646-1209

2509 WDCR-AM - 1340
PO Box 957   **Phone: (603)646-3313**
Hanover, NH 03755   Fax: (603)643-7655

KEENE

2510 WKNE-AM - 1290
PO Box 466   Phone: (603)352-9230
Keene, NH 03431   **Fax: (603)357-3926**

2511 WKNE-FM - 103.7
PO Box 466   Phone: (603)352-9230
Keene, NH 03431   **Fax: (603)357-3926**

LACONIA

2512 Citizen
Citizen Publishing Co.
171 Fair St.   Phone: (603)524-3800
Laconia, NH 03247   Fax: (603)524-6702

2513 WEMJ-AM - 1490
Box 1490   Phone: (603)524-6050
Laconia, NH 03247   **Fax: (603)528-6397**

LITTLETON

2514 WLTN-FM - 96.7
20 Main St.
Littleton, NH 03561   Phone: (603)444-3911
Format: Oldies. **Network(s):** ABC. **Owner:** Peter Aydelott, at above address. **Founded:** 1991. **Operating Hours:** Continuous. **Key Personnel:** Peter Aydelott, Gen. Mgr.; Bradford S. Bailey, Sales and Station Mgr.; Ellen Cronin, News Dir.; Judith Aydelott, Business Mgr.; Jackie Hoverman, Production Dir.; Vicky McKay, Office and Traffic Mgr. **Wattage:** 3000. **Ad Rates:** $6.70-$8.70 for 30 seconds; $9-$11.70 for 60 seconds; Combined rates available with WLTN-AM.

LONDONDERRY

2515 Harron Cablevision
184-A Rockingham Rd.   Phone: (603)432-0382
Londonderry, NH 03053   Fax: (603)432-7428
Owner: Harron Communications Corp. **Founded:** 1984. **Cities Served:** Hillsborough and Rockingham counties, NH.

NASHUA

2516 Warner Cable of Nashua
3 Bud Way
Nashua, NH 03063   Phone: (603)882-4415
Owner: Warner Cable Communications, Inc. **Founded:** 1967. **Cities Served:** Hillsborough County, NH.

NEW LONDON

2517 WNTK-FM - 100.5
250 Newport Rd.
PO Box 2295   Phone: (603)526-9464
New London, NH 03257   **Fax: (603)526-9464**

PETERBOROUGH

2518 Calliope
Cobblestone Publishing, Inc.
7 School St.   Phone: (603)924-7209
Peterborough, NH 03458   Fax: (603)924-7380

2519 Cobblestone
Cobblestone Publishing, Inc.
7 School St.   Phone: (603)924-7209
Peterborough, NH 03458   Fax: (603)924-7380

2520 DOS Resource Guide
IDG Communications/Peterborough Inc.
80 Elm St.
Peterborough, NH 03458
Magazine focuses on setting up and maintaining DOS systems. **Frequency:** Monthly. **Key Personnel:** Jeff DeTroy, Publisher; Roger Murphy, Editor. **Subscription:** $4.95 single issue.
     Circulation: (Not Reported)

2521 PC Games
A+ Publishing, Inc.
80 Elm St.   Phone: (603)924-0100
Peterborough, NH 03458   **Fax: (603)924-9384**

2522 Video Event
Connell Communications, Inc.
86 Elm St.   Phone: (603)924-7271
Peterborough, NH 03458   **Fax: (603)924-7013**

2523 Video PROphiles
IDG Communications/Peterborough, Inc.
80 Elm St.
Peterborough, NH 03458
Magazine for the serious video user. **Frequency:** 6x/yr. **Key Personnel:** Marjorie Costello, Editor; Gregory P. Fagan, Publisher. **Subscription:** $14.97. $2.95 single issue
     Circulation: (Not Reported)

PLYMOUTH

2524 WPCR-FM - 91.7
CUBANNEX
Plymouth State College   Phone: (603)535-2242
Plymouth, NH 03264   Fax: (603)535-2783

PORTSMOUTH

2525 Continental Cablevision of New Hampshire, Inc.
150 Greenleaf Ave.   Phone: (603)436-6050
Portsmouth, NH 03801   Fax: (603)431-0083
Owner: Continental Cablevision, Inc. **Founded:** 1971. **Cities Served:** Portsmouth, NH and York, ME.

RINDGE

2526 WFPR-AM - 640
Franklin Pierce College
College Rd.
PO Box 60
Rindge, NH 03461-0060   Phone: (603)899-4100
Format: Alternative/Independent/Progressive. **Key Personnel:** Mike Waterbury, Music Dir. **Ad Rates:** Noncommercial.

ROCHESTER

2527 New England Cablevision Inc.
PO Box 1450
22 Farmington Rd.   Phone: (603)332-5466
Rochester, NH 03867   **Fax: (603)335-4106**

SALEM

📖 **2528　Electronic Publishing & Typeworld**
Pennwell Publishing Co.
PO Box 170　　　　　　　　　　Phone: (603)898-2822
Salem, NH 03079　　　　　　　　Fax: (603)898-3393
Former Title: Typeworld

🎙 **2529　Continental Cablevision of New England, Inc.**
8 E. Industrial Dr.　　　　　　　Phone: (603)893-1648
Salem, NH 03079　　　　　　　　Fax: (603)894-4899
Owner: Continental Cablevision, Inc. **Founded:** 1973. **Cities Served:**
Rockingham County, NH.

WOLFEBORO

📖 **2530　Railroad Information**
Railroad Information
RR 2, PO Box 500　　　　　　　　Phone: (603)569-4870
Wolfeboro, NH 03894　　　　　　　Fax: (603)569-4870
Publication providing a listing for model railroad shows, tourist
railroad schedules, and rail excursions. **Subtitle:** A Compendium of
Railroad Related Events in the Eastern United States and Canada.
Founded: 1977. **Frequency:** Quarterly. **Trim Size:** 5 1/2 x 8. **Cols./Page:**
1. **Col. Width:** 4 1/2 in. **Col. Depth:** 7 1/2 in. **Subscription:** $24. $2.50
single issue.
Ad Rates:　BW:　　$35　　　　　　**Circulation:** Paid ‡600
　　　　　　　　　　　　　　　　　　　　　　Non-paid ‡25

Ad Rates:　GLR = general line rate; BW = one-time black & white page rate; 4C = one-time four color page rate; SAU = standard advertising unit rate;
CNU = Canadian newspaper advertising unit rate; PCI = per column inch rate.
Circulation: ★ = ABC; △ = BPA; ◆ = CAC; ● = CCAB; □ = VAC; ⊕ = PO Statement; ‡ = Publisher's Report; Boldface figures = sworn; Light figures = estimated.
Entry type: 📖 = Print; 🎙 = Broadcast.

169

NEW JERSEY

BELLE MEAD

◻ **2531 Anesthesiology Review**
CORE Publishing Division, Excerpta Medica, Inc.
105 Raider Bvd.   **Phone: (908)874-8550**
Belle Mead, NJ 08502   Fax: (908)874-0707

BELMAR

◉ **2532 Monmouth Cablevision Associates**
Box 58   **Phone: (201)681-3400**
Belmar, NJ 07719-0058   Fax: (201)681-5458
Owner: Monmouth Cablevision Associates. **Founded:** 1979. **Cities Served:** Monmouth County, NJ.

BERGENFIELD

◻ **2533 NJW Magazine (New Jersey Woman)**
27 McDermott Pl.
Bergenfield, NJ 07621   Phone: (201)384-0201
Magazine emphasizing women's accomplishments and regional pride.
Founded: 1979. **Frequency:** 7x/yr. **Trim Size:** 8 3/8 x 10 7/8. **Cols./Page:** 3. **Col. Width:** 14 picas. **Col. Depth:** 10 in. **Key Personnel:** Louise B. Hofesh, Editor. **ISSN:** 0197-4610. **Subscription:** $24.
Ad Rates: BW: $1,796   **Circulation:** Paid 15,000
            4C: $2,496   Non-paid 30,000
            PCI: $175

BLOOMFIELD

◻ **2534 The Independent Press**
Worral Community Newspapers
266 Liberty St.
PO Box 110   Phone: (201)743-4040
Bloomfield, NJ 07003-0110   Fax: (201)680-8848

BORDENTOWN

◻ **2535 The Leader**
Lorraine Publishing, Inc.
137 Farnsworth Ave.
PO Box 189
Bordentown, NJ 08505   Phone: (609)298-7111
Ceased publication.

BRIDGETON

◉ **2536 WSNJ-FM - 107.7**
1969 Old Burlington Rd.
PO Box 69   Phone: (609)451-2930
Bridgeton, NJ 08302   **Fax: (609)453-9440**

BRIDGEWATER

◻ **2537 Strictly Somerset**
Courier News
1201 Rte. 22 W.   Phone: (908)722-8800
Bridgewater, NJ 08807   **Fax: (908)707-3252**

BUTLER

◻ **2538 Today Newspapers**
North Jersey Newspapers, Co.
10 Park Place   **Phone: (201)492-3509**
Butler, NJ 07405   **Fax: (201)838-1495**
Former Title: Sunday Journal

CAMDEN

◻ **2539 Criminal Law Forum**
Rutgers University School of Law   Phone: (609)757-6352
Camden, NJ 08102   Fax: (609)757-6487
Peer-review journal dedicated to the advancement of criminal law theory, practice, and reform throughout the world. **Subtitle:** An International Journal. **Founded:** Autumn 1989. **Frequency:** 3x/yr. (during the academic year). **Trim Size:** 6 x 9. **Cols./Page:** 1. **Col. Width:** 4.5 in. **Col. Depth:** 7.5 in. **Key Personnel:** Professor Roger S. Clark, Editor-in-Chief; Professor Isabel Grant, Book Review Editor. **ISSN:** 1046-8374. **Subscription:** $36 U.S. and Canada; $45 other countries. $15 single issue; $20 single issue other countries.
                              Circulation: Paid 210
                                          Non-paid 50

Advertising not accepted.

CAPE MAY COURT HOUSE

◉ **2540 WBNJ-FM - 105.5**
223 N. Main St.   **Phone: (609)465-2044**
Cape May Court House, NJ 08210   **Fax: (609)465-2241**

CEDAR KNOLLS

◉ **2541 WDHA-FM - 105.5**
55 Horsehill Rd.   **Phone: (201)455-1055**
Cedar Knolls, NJ 07927   Fax: (201)538-3060

CHATHAM

◻ **2542 Automatic I.D. News**
Advanstar Communications, Inc.
466 Southern Blvd.
PO Box 448   Phone: (201)514-1422
Chatham, NJ 07928   Fax: (201)514-1404

CHERRY HILL

⚓ **2543 Garden State Cable TV**
1250 Haddonfield-Berlin Rd.
Box 5025   Phone: (609)354-1880
Cherry Hill, NJ 08034   Fax: (609)354-1459
Owner: Comcast Corp. **Founded:** 1975. **Cities Served:** Burlington County, Camden County, Gloucester County, Ocean County, Salem County, Audubon, Audubon Park, Barrington, Bellmawr, Berlin, Camden, Carneys Point, Chesterfield, Clementon, Collingswood, Easthampton, Fieldsboro, Florence, Fort Dix, Gibbsboro, Haddon Heights, Haddonfield, Hainesport, Hi-Nella, Laurel Springs, Lawnside, Lindenwold, Lumberton, Magnolia, Medford Lakes, Merchantville, Moorestown, Mount Holly, Mount Laurel, Oaklyn, Pemberton, Pennsauken, Pine Hill, Pitman, Runnemede, Somerdale, Stratford, Tavistock, Woodlynne, and Wrightstown, NJ.

CRESSKILL

⚓ **2544 Cablevision of New Jersey, Inc.**
5 Legion Dr.   Phone: (201)569-3720
Cresskill, NJ 07626   Fax: (201)569-3082
Owner: Cablevision Systems Corp. **Founded:** 1976. **Key Personnel:** Richard N. Rasmus, Gen. Mgr. **Cities Served:** Bergen County, NJ: 47,000 subscribing households; 40 channels; 1 community access channel.

DENVILLE

◻ **2545 Tricycle: The Buddhist Review**
The Buddhist Ray, Inc.
Tri Box 3000
Denville, NJ 07834
Magazine for members of the Buddhist community. **Frequency:** Quarterly. **Key Personnel:** Helen Tworkov, Editor. **Subscription:** $20. $5.50 single issue.
Circulation: (Not Reported)

◻ **2546 The X Journal**
COOT, Inc.
PO Box 3000
Denville, NJ 07834-9795
Magazine for developers and users to share related X information. **Frequency:** 2x/mo. **Key Personnel:** Jerry Smith, Publisher; Richard Friedman, Editor. **Subscription:** $39. $6.50 single issue.
Circulation: (Not Reported)

DEPTFORD

⚓ **2547 WNJC-AM - 1360**
Box 5500   Phone: (609)582-1360
Deptford, NJ 08012   Fax: (609)582-1518

DOVER

⚓ **2548 Sammons Communications of New Jersey, Inc.**
160 E. Blackwell St.   Phone: (201)361-6955
Dover, NJ 07801   Fax: (201)361-4879
Owner: Sammons Communications, Inc. **Founded:** 1972. **Cities Served:** Morris and Sussex counties, NJ.

EAST BRUNSWICK

◻ **2549 Recorder**
Greater Media Newspapers
Edgeboro Rd.   Phone: (908)254-7000
East Brunswick, NJ 08816   Fax: (908)254-0256
Ceased publication.

EAST ORANGE

◻ **2550 East Orange Record**
Worrall Community Newspapers, Inc.
425 Main St., 2nd Fl.   Phone: (201)674-8000
Orange, NJ 07051-0849   **Fax: (201)674-2038**

⚓ **2551 Suburban Cablevision**
43 E. Prospect St.   Phone: (201)672-3033
East Orange, NJ 07017   Fax: (201)672-7511
Owner: Maclean Hunter Cable TV. **Founded:** 1975. **Cities Served:** Essex County, Hudson County, Middlesex County, Union County, Cadwell, Carteret, Essex Fells, Fairfield, Fanwood, Garwood, Glen Ridge, Harrison, Irvington, Kenilworth, Linden, Mountainside, New Providence, Orange, Perth Amboy, Rahway, Roseland, Roselle, Roselle Park, South River, Springfield, Summit, Verona, West Cadwell, West Orange, Winfield, and Woodbridge, NJ.

EATONTOWN

⚓ **2552 Storer Cable**
403 South St.
Box 598
Eatontown, NJ 07724   Phone: (908)542-8107
Owner: Storer Cable Communications. **Founded:** 1972. **Cities Served:** Monmouth County, NJ.

ELIZABETH

◻ **2553 One Church**
Patriarchal Parishes of the Russian Orthodox Church
158 Stiles St.
Elizabeth, NJ 07208   **Phone: (201)352-1192**

◻ **2554 The Pet Dealer**
Howmark Publishing Corp.
567 Morris Ave.   **Phone: (908)353-7373**
Elizabeth, NJ 07208   **Fax: (908)353-8221**

⚓ **2555 TKR Cable**
536 N. Broad St.   Phone: (908)353-0472
Elizabeth, NJ 07208   Fax: (908)289-5895
Owner: TKR Cable Co. **Founded:** 1972. **Cities Served:** Union County, NJ.

FAIRFIELD

◻ **2556 Laser Views**
3A Oak Rd.   Phone: (800)899-4116
Fairfield, NJ 07004   Fax: (201)575-3505
Magazine featuring articles on and reviews of laser discs. **Subtitle:** America's Laser Disc Magazine. **Founded:** 1985. **Frequency:** 6x/yr. **Printing Method:** Web offset. **Trim Size:** 8 1/2 x 11. **Cols./Page:** 3. **Col. Width:** 2 1/3 in. **Col. Depth:** 10 in. **Key Personnel:** David Goodman, Editor and Publisher. **Subscription:** $15. $2.50 single issue.
Ad Rates: BW: $2,640   **Circulation:** 26,000
             4C: $3,300

FLORHAM PARK

◻ **2557 Driving**
AAA New Jersey Automobile Club
1 Hanover Rd.
Florham Park, NJ 07932   Phone: (201)377-7200
AAA membership newspaper. **Founded:** 1924. **Frequency:** 6x/yr. **Printing Method:** Web offset. **Trim Size:** 10 1/2 x 13 3/4. **Cols./Page:** 4. **Col. Width:** 2 1/4 in. **Col. Depth:** 13 1/16 in. **Key Personnel:** Pamela S. Fischer, Editor. **USPS:** 161-380. **Subscription:** $4. $1 single issue.
Ad Rates: BW: $4,400   **Circulation:** Free ‡157,000
             4C: $5,475
Formerly: NJ Auto-ist (1969).

GLASSBORO

⚓ **2558 WGLS-FM - 89.7**
Rowan College of New Jersey   Phone: (609)863-7336
Glassboro, NJ 08028   **Fax: (609)863-5020**

HOBOKEN

🕮 **2559 The Stute**
Stevens Institute of Technology
Phone: (201)659-0143
Hoboken, NJ 07030 **Fax: (201)216-8341**

♆ **2560 Riverview Cablevision**
360 1st St. Phone: (201)798-1614
Hoboken, NJ 07030 Fax: (201)798-4163
Owner: Sutton Capital Group. **Founded:** 1970. **Key Personnel:** Gregory Arnold, Gen. Mgr.; Tina Segali, Mktg. Dir.; Greg Maugeri, Sales Mgr.; Mike Lo Tompio, Plant Mgr.; Dawn Clark-Wright, L.O. Dir. **Cities Served:** Hoboken, North Bergen, Union City, West Hankon, and West New York. 44,500 subscribing households; 39 channels; 1 community access channel; 85 hours per week of community access programming.

HOPE

🕮 **2561 Pocono World**
Pocono World Magazine
PO Box 443
Hope, NJ 07844-0443
Magazine featuring articles on sports, culture, and developments in the Pocono region. **Frequency:** Quarterly. **Key Personnel:** Brian Hineline, Editor; L.A. Popp, Publisher. **Subscription:** $8. $2.95 single issue.
Circulation: (Not Reported)

ISELIN

🕮 **2562 NAFA Fleet Executive**
National Assn. of Fleet Administrators, Inc.
120 Wood Ave. S., Ste. 615 Phone: (908)494-8100
Iselin, NJ 08830-2709 Fax: (908)494-6789

JERSEY CITY

♆ **2563 Cable TV of Jersey City**
2121 Kennedy Blvd. Phone: (201)915-0508
Jersey City, NJ 07305 Fax: (201)434-5870
Owner: Maclean Hunter Cable TV. **Founded:** 1987. **Cities Served:** Hudson County, NJ.

♆ **2564 WGKR-AM - 540**
Jersey City State College
2039 Kennedy Blvd.
Jersey City, NJ 07305 Phone: (201)200-3556
Format: Alternative/Independent/Progressive. **Key Personnel:** Richard Cirminello, Music Dir. **Ad Rates:** Noncommercial.

LINCROFT

♆ **2565 WBJB-FM - 90.5**
Brookdale Community College
Lincroft, NJ 07738 **Phone: (908)224-2252**

MADISON

🕮 **2566 The Literary Review**
Fairleigh Dickinson University
285 Madison Ave. Phone: (201)593-8564
Madison, NJ 07940 **Fax: (201)593-8510**

MANALAPAN

🕮 **2567 Hobby Merchandiser**
Hobby Publications Inc.
Box 420 Phone: (908)446-4900
Manalapan, NJ 07726 Fax: (908)446-5488

MORRIS PLAINS

🕮 **2568 Aerospace Products**
Gordon Publications, Inc.
301 Gibraltar Dr.
Box 650 Phone: (201)292-5100
Morris Plains, NJ 07950-0650 **Fax: (201)898-9281**

🕮 **2569 Fiberoptic Product News**
Gordon Publications
301 Gibraltar Dr.
PO Box 650 Phone: (201)292-5100
Morris Plains, NJ 07950 **Fax: (201)292-0783**

🕮 **2570 Reseller Management**
Elsevier Communications
301 Gilbraltar Dr.
PO Box 650 Phone: (201)292-5100
Morris Plains, NJ 07950 **Fax: (201)292-0783**

MORRISTOWN

🕮 **2571 Art Culinaire**
40 Mills St. **Phone: (201)993-5500**
Morristown, NJ 07960 Fax: (201)822-8437

MOUNT LAUREL

🕮 **2572 BBS Callers Digest**
Callers Digest, Inc.
PO Box 416
Mount Laurel, NJ 08054
Magazine featuring bulletin board systems. **Frequency:** Monthly **Key Personnel:** Richard Paquette, Publisher; Bruce Pempek, Editor. **Subscription:** $25. $3.50 single issue.
Circulation: (Not Reported)

NEW BRUNSWICK

🕮 **2573 Academic Questions**
Transaction Periodicals Consortium
Rutgers - The State University of New Jersey
Dept. 3092 **Phone: (908)932-2280**
New Brunswick, NJ 08903 **Fax: (908)932-3138**

🕮 **2574 The American Sociologist**
Transaction Periodicals Consortium
Rutgers - The State University of New Jersey
Dept. 3092 **Phone: (908)932-2280**
New Brunswick, NJ 08903 **Fax: (908)932-3138**

🕮 **2575 The Caellian**
Douglass College
DPO 153
New Brunswick, NJ 08903 Phone: (908)846-7871

🕮 **2576 Child Welfare**
Transaction Periodicals Consortium
Rutgers - The State University of New Jersey
Dept. 3092 **Phone: (908)932-2280**
New Brunswick, NJ 08903 **Fax: (908)932-3138**

🕮 **2577 Current Psychology**
Transaction Periodicals Consortium
Rutgers - The State University of New Jersey
Dept. 3092 **Phone: (908)932-2280**
New Brunswick, NJ 08903 **Fax: (908)932-3138**

Ad Rates: GLR = general line rate; BW = one-time black & white page rate; 4C = one-time four color page rate; SAU = standard advertising unit rate; CNU = Canadian newspaper advertising unit rate; PCI = per column inch rate.
Circulation: ★ = ABC; △ = BPA; ◆ = CAC; ● = CCAB; □ = VAC; ⊕ = PO Statement; ‡ = Publisher's Report; Boldface figures = sworn; Light figures = estimated.
Entry type: 🕮 = Print; ♆ = Broadcast.

⚟ **2578 Information Processing & Management**
Pergamon Press
School of Communication, Information
& Library Studies
Rutgers, the State University of New
Jersey
4 Huntington St.   Phone: (908)932-8017
New Brunswick, NJ 08903   Fax: (908)932-6916
International journal. **Frequency:** 6x/yr. **Key Personnel:** Tefko Sara-
cevic, PhD., Editor-in-Chief; Harold Borko, Associate Editor; W.
Bruce Croft, Associate Editor; C.J. van Rijsbergen, Associate Editor
(Europe); Trudi Bellardo, Associate Editor. **ISSN:** 0306-4573. **Sub-
scription:** $465 institutions.
                        Circulation: (Not Reported)
Advertising accepted; contact publisher for rates. **Additional Contact
Information:** Publishing, subscription, and advertising offices 660
White Plains Rd., Tarrytown, NY 10591-5153.

⚟ **2579 Intereconomics**
Transaction Periodicals Consortium
Rutgers - The State University of New
Jersey
Dept. 3092   **Phone: (908)932-2280**
New Brunswick, NJ 08903   **Fax: (908)932-3138**

⚟ **2580 Intergrative Physiological and Behavioral Science**
Transaction Periodicals Consortium
Dept. 3093
Rutgers-The State University of New
Jersey   Phone: (908)932-2280
New Brunswick, NJ 08903   Fax: (908)932-3138
Journal dedicated to the advancement of biological sciences. **Founded:**
1965. **Frequency:** Quarterly. **Trim Size:** 6 x 9. **Key Personnel:** Stewart
G. Wolf, Editor. **ISSN:** 0093-2213. **Subscription:** $98; $168 institu-
tions.
Ad Rates: BW: $200   **Circulation:** Paid ‡500
Formerly: The Pavlovian Journal of Biological Science.

⚟ **2581 International Journal of Insect Morphalogy &
Embryology**
Pergamon Press
Rutgers University
Department of Entomelogy   Phone: (908)932-9459
New Brunswick, NJ 08903-0231   Fax: (908)932-7229
Journal covering the morphology and developmental biology of
insects. **Founded:** 1971. **Frequency:** Quarterly. **Trim Size:** 7 1/2 x 9 3/4.
Cols./Page: 1. **Col. Width:** 5 1/4 in. **Col. Depth:** 7 3/4 in. **Key
Personnel:** Ayodhya P. Gupta, Editor-in-Chief. **ISSN:** 0020-7322.
Subscription: $415 institutions.
                        Circulation: (Not Reported)
Advertising accepted; contact publisher for rates. Publisher's address:
660 White Plains Rd., Tarrytown, NY 10591-5153; phone (914)524-
9200.

⚟ **2582 Journal of American Ethnic History**
Transaction Periodicals Consortium
Rutgers - The State University of New
Jersey
Dept. 3092   **Phone: (908)932-2280**
New Brunswick, NJ 08903   **Fax: (908)932-3138**

⚟ **2583 Journal of Northeast Asian Studies**
Transaction Periodicals Consortium
Rutgers - The State University of New
Jersey
Dept. 3092   **Phone: (908)932-2280**
New Brunswick, NJ 08903   **Fax: (908)932-3138**

⚟ **2584 Knowledge and Policy**
Transaction Periodicals Consortium
Rutgers - The State University of New
Jersey
Dept. 3092   **Phone: (908)932-2280**
New Brunswick, NJ 08903   **Fax: (908)932-3138**

⚟ **2585 Labor Studies Journal**
Transaction Periodicals Consortium
Rutgers - The State University of New
Jersey
Dept. 3092   **Phone: (908)932-2280**
New Brunswick, NJ 08903   **Fax: (908)932-3138**

⚟ **2586 North-South**
Transaction Publishers
Department 3091
Rutgers-The State University of New
Jersey
New Brunswick, NJ 08903   Phone: (201)932-2280
Subtitle: The Magazine of the Americas. **Frequency:** Quarterly.
Subscription: $30; $60 institutions.
                        Circulation: (Not Reported)

⚟ **2587 Plant Molecular Biology Reporter**
Transaction Periodicals Consortium
Rutgers - The State University of New
Jersey
Dept. 3092   **Phone: (908)932-2280**
New Brunswick, NJ 08903   **Fax: (908)932-3138**

⚟ **2588 Public Budgeting and Finance**
Transaction Periodicals Consortium
Rutgers - The State University of New
Jersey
Dept. 3092   **Phone: (908)932-2280**
New Brunswick, NJ 08903   **Fax: (908)932-3138**

⚟ **2589 The Review of Black Political Economy**
Transaction Periodicals Consortium
Rutgers - The State University of New
Jersey
Dept. 3092   **Phone: (908)932-2280**
New Brunswick, NJ 08903   **Fax: (908)932-3138**

⚟ **2590 Society**
Transaction Periodicals Consortium
Rutgers - The State University of New
Jersey
Dept. 3092   **Phone: (908)932-2280**
New Brunswick, NJ 08903   **Fax: (908)932-3138**

⚟ **2591 Studies in Comparative International Development**
Transaction Periodicals Consortium
Rutgers - The State University of New
Jersey
Dept. 3092   **Phone: (908)932-2280**
New Brunswick, NJ 08903   **Fax: (908)932-3138**

⚟ **2592 Transafrica Forum**
Transaction Periodicals Consortium
Rutgers - The State University of New
Jersey
Dept. 3092   **Phone: (908)932-2280**
New Brunswick, NJ 08903   **Fax: (908)932-3138**

⚟ **2593 Women's Studies Abstracts**
Transaction Periodicals and Consortium
Rutgers University   Phone: (908)932-2280
New Brunswick, NJ 08903   Fax: (908)932-3138
Periodical containing abstracts and listings of articles and book
reviews. Covers education, socialization, prejudice, interpersonal
relations, and the women's movement. Also available on CD-ROM.
Frequency: Quarterly. **Subscription:** $124.
                        Circulation: (Not Reported)

NEWARK

⚟ **2594 The Observer**
Newark College of Arts and Sciences
Rutgers University
350 Dr. Martin Luther King Jr. Blvd.   **Phone: (201)648-5358**
Newark, NJ 07102   Fax: (201)648-1333

♣ **2595 Gateway Cable TV**
360 Central Ave.   Phone: (201)622-1727
Newark, NJ 07103   Fax: (201)642-2221
Owner: Gilbert Media. **Founded:** 1982. **Cities Served:** Essex County and South Orange, NJ.

NEWTON

⊞ **2596 Doll Life**
All American Crafts, Inc.
243 Newton-Sparta Rd.
Newton, NJ 07860
Magazine featuring antique Victorian dolls. **Frequency:** Quarterly. **Key Personnel:** Jerry Cohen, Publisher; Michele M. Epstein, Editor. **Subscription:** $15.80. $3.95 single issue.
                              Circulation: (Not Reported)

⊞ **2597 Paint Works**
All American Crafts, Inc.
243 Newton-Sparta Rd.
Newton, NJ 07860
Magazine featuring multimedia arts and crafts projects for all skill levels. **Frequency:** 2x/mo. **Key Personnel:** Jerry Cohen, Publisher; Matthew Jones, Editor. **Subscription:** $23.70. $3.95 single issue.
                              Circulation: (Not Reported)

NORWOOD

⊞ **2598 International Journal of Computer Simulation**
Ablex Publishing Corp.
355 Chestnut St.   Phone: (314)341-4836
Norwood, NJ 07648   Fax: (314)341-4150
Journal covering research and development, product development, and tutorials in computer simulation. **Founded:** 1991. **Frequency:** Quarterly. **Key Personnel:** George W. Zobrist, Editor. **ISSN:** 1055-8470. **Subscription:** $95.
                              Circulation: (Not Reported)

OAKLAND

♣ **2599 United Artists Cable of New Jersey**
7 Fir Ct.   Phone: (201)337-1550
Oakland, NJ 07436   Fax: (201)337-9126
Owner: Tele-Communications, Inc. **Founded:** 1966. **Cities Served:** Bergen, Essex, Morris, and Passaic counties, NJ.

OCEAN CITY

♣ **2600 WKTU-FM - 98.3**
618 West Ave.   **Phone: (609)398-7600**
Ocean City, NJ 08226   **Fax: (609)398-4311**

ORADELL

⊞ **2601 Tile World**
Tradelink Publishing Co., Inc.
320 Kinderkamack Rd.   Phone: (201)599-0136
Oradell, NJ 07649-2101   Fax: (201)599-2378
Magazine for producers and users of tile and tile-related products. **Founded:** 1987. **Frequency:** 6x/yr. **Printing Method:** Web. **Trim Size:** 8 1/8 x 10 7/8. **Cols./Page:** 3. **Col. Width:** 2 1/4 in. **Col. Depth:** 10 in. **Key Personnel:** John Sailer, Editor; Mike Lench, Publisher; David Lench, Business Mgr. **Subscription:** $38. $7 single issue.
Ad Rates: BW: $1,875   **Circulation:** Paid ‡458
              4C: $2,760   Non-paid ‡15,951
              PCI: $96

ORANGE

⊞ **2602 Orange Transcript**
Worrall Community Newspapers
425 Main St., 2nd Fl.
PO Box 849   Phone: (201)674-8000
Orange, NJ 07051-0849   Fax: (201)674-2038

⊞ **2603 West Orange Chronicle**
Worrall Community Newspapers, Inc.
PO Box 849   Phone: (201)674-8000
Orange, NJ 07051   **Fax: (201)674-2038**

PENNSAUKEN

⊞ **2604 DataWorld**
Faulkner Information Services
114 Cooper Center
7905 Browning Rd.   Phone: (609)662-2070
Pennsauken, NJ 08109-4374   Fax: (609)662-3380

⊞ **2605 Telecommunications World**
Faulkner Information Services
114 Cooper Center
7905 Browning Rd.   Phone: (609)662-2070
Pennsauken, NJ 08109-4319   Fax: (609)662-3380

PISCATAWAY

♣ **2606 TKR Cable Co. Tri-System**
275 Centennial Ave.   Phone: (908)356-1013
Piscataway, NJ 08854   Fax: (908)356-6657
Owner: TKR Cable Co. **Founded:** 1977. **Cities Served:** Middlesex, Monmouth, and Somerset counties, NJ.

PRINCETON

⊞ **2607 The Gallup Poll Monthly**
Gallup Organization
47 Hulfish St.
PO Box 628   **Phone: (609)924-9600**
Princeton, NJ 08542   **Fax: (609)924-2584**

⊞ **2608 Journal of Exposure Analysis and Environmental Epidemiology**
Princeton Scientific Publishing
PO Box 2155
Princeton, NJ 08543-2155   Phone: (609)683-4750
Subtitle: The Official Organ of the International Society of Exposure Analysis. **Founded:** 1991. **Frequency:** Quarterly. **Trim Size:** 7 x 10. **Cols./Page:** 1. **Key Personnel:** Edo Pellizzari, Editor. **ISSN:** 1053-4245. **Subscription:** $160.
                              Circulation: 450
                              Non-paid 100
Advertising accepted; contact publisher for rates.

⊞ **2609 Princeton Alumni Weekly**
Princeton Alumni Publications
194 Nassau St   Phone: (609)258-4885
Princeton, NJ 08542   **Fax: (609)258-2247**

⊞ **2610 The Princeton Engineer**
Princeton University
ACE 23 Engineering Quadrangle
Princeton, NJ 08544   Phone: (609)258-1643
Ceased publication.

PRINCETON JUNCTION

♣ **2611 WWPH-FM - 107.9**
346 Clarksville Rd.
Princeton Junction, NJ 08550   **Phone: (609)799-3209**

RANDOLPH

♣ **2612 WCCM-AM - 820**
214 Centergrove Rd.
Randolph, NJ 07869   Phone: (201)328-5215
Format: Alternative/Independent/Progressive. **Key Personnel:** Gene Fitzpatrick, Music Dir. **Ad Rates:** Noncommercial.

RIDGEWOOD

2613 Town News
North Jersey Newspapers
75 N. Maple Ave.   **Phone: (201)368-0100**
Ridgewood, NJ 07450   **Fax: (301)368-0706**

RINGWOOD

2614 Soundtrack
Journal of the Independent Music Association
317 Skyline Lake Dr.   **Phone: (201)831-1317**
Ringwood, NJ 07456   **Fax: (201)831-8672**
Journal containing marketing information for independent record labels. **Subtitle:** Journal of the Independent Music Association. **Founded:** 1989. **Frequency:** Bimonthly. **Trim Size:** 8 1/2 x 11. **Cols./Page:** 3. **Col. Width:** 2 1/4 in. **Col. Depth:** 9 3/4 in. **Key Personnel:** Don Kulak, Exec. Editor and Publisher. **ISSN:** 1042-0649. **Subscription:** $75; $80 Canada and Mexico. $5.50 single issue.
Ad Rates: BW: $395   **Circulation:** Paid 1,600
              4C: $450   Controlled 1,000

RIVER EDGE

2615 Asia-Pacific Engineering Journal Part A: Electrical Engineering
World Scientific Publishing Co., Inc.
1060 Main St., Ste. 1B   **Phone: (201)487-9655**
River Edge, NJ 07661   **Fax: (201)487-9656**
Journal focusing on microelectronics, communications engineering, and computer engineering. **Founded:** 1991. **Frequency:** Quarterly. **Trim Size:** 6 1/2 x 9 3/4. **Cols./Page:** 1. **Col. Width:** 5 in. **Col. Depth:** 8 in. **Key Personnel:** M.S. Leong, Editor; S. Selvalingam, Asst. Managing Editor. **ISSN:** 0129-5411. **Subscription:** $80.
                                   Circulation: (Not Reported)
Advertising accepted; contact publisher for rates.

2616 International Journal on Artificial Intelligence Tools
World Scientific Publishing
1060 Main St., Ste. 1B   **Phone: (201)487-9655**
River Edge, NJ 07661   **Fax: (201)487-9656**
Journal covering design, development, and testing of AI tools. **Founded:** 1992. **Frequency:** Quarterly. **Trim Size:** 6 1/2 x 9 3/4. **Cols./Page:** 1. **Col. Width:** 5 in. **Col. Depth:** 8 in. **Key Personnel:** Nikolaos G. Bourbakis, Editor-in-Chief. **ISSN:** 0218-2130. **Subscription:** $160.
                                   Circulation: (Not Reported)
Advertising accepted; contact publisher for rates.

2617 International Journal of Genome Research
World Scientific Publishing Co., Inc.
1060 Main St., Ste. 1B   **Phone: (201)487-9655**
River Edge, NJ 07661   **Fax: (201)487-9656**
Journal covering human genome research. **Founded:** 1991. **Frequency:** Bimonthly. **Trim Size:** 6 1/2 x 9 3/4. **Cols./Page:** 1. **Col. Width:** 5 in. **Col. Depth:** 8 in. **Key Personnel:** H.A. Lim, Managing Editor; W. Ansorge, Managing Editor; M. Frank-Kamenetskii, Managing Editor; H. Lehrach, Managing Editor; A.D. Mirzabekov, Managing Editor; N. Shimizu, Managing Editor; C. Smith, Managing Editor. **ISSN:** 0218-1932. **Subscription:** $240.
                                   Circulation: (Not Reported)
Advertising accepted; contact publisher for rates.

2618 International Journal of High Speed Electronics
World Scientific Publishing
1060 Main St., Ste. 1B   **Phone: (201)487-9655**
River Edge, NJ 07661   **Fax: (201)487-9656**
Journal covering topics related to high speed devices, circuits, and systems. **Founded:** 1990. **Frequency:** Quarterly. **Trim Size:** 6 1/2 x 9 3/4. **Cols./Page:** 1. **Col. Width:** 5 in. **Col. Depth:** 8 in. **Key Personnel:** P.K. Tien, Editor-in-Chief; E.S. Kuh, Co-Editor-in-Chief. **ISSN:** 0129-1564. **Subscription:** $195.
                                   Circulation: (Not Reported)
Advertising accepted; contact publisher for rates.

2619 International Journal of Intelligent and Cooperative Information Systems
World Scientific Publishing Co., Inc.
1060 Main St., Ste. 1B   **Phone: (201)487-9655**
River Edge, NJ 07661   **Fax: (201)487-9656**
Journal covering the potential roles and nature of the emerging notion of ICIS. **Founded:** 1992. **Frequency:** Quarterly. **Trim Size:** 6 1/2 x 9 3/4. **Cols./Page:** 1 **Col. Width:** 5 in. **Col. Depth:** 8 in. **Key Personnel:** Mike P. Papazoglou, Editor-in-Chief; Timos K. Sellis, Editor-in-Chief. **ISSN:** 0218-2157. **Subscription:** $220.
                                   Circulation: (Not Reported)
Advertising accepted; contact publisher for rates.

2620 International Journal of Nonlinear Optical Physics
World Scientific Publishing
1060 Main St., 1B   **Phone: (201)487-9655**
River Edge, NJ 07661   **Fax: (201)487-9656**
Journal devoted to nonlinear interactions of light with matter. **Founded:** 1992. **Frequency:** Quarterly. **Trim Size:** 6 1/2 x 9 3/4. **Cols./Page:** 1. **Col. Width:** 5 in. **Col. Depth:** 8 in. **Key Personnel:** Iam-Choon Khoo, Editor-in-Chief. **ISSN:** 0218-1991. **Subscription:** $275.
                                   Circulation: (Not Reported)
Advertising accepted; contact publisher for rates.

2621 International Journal of PIXE
World Scientific Publishing
1060 Main St., Ste. 1B   **Phone: (201)487-9655**
River Edge, NJ 07661   **Fax: (201)487-9656**
Journal covering techniques and applications of particle-induced X-ray emmision (PIXE). **Founded:** 1991. **Frequency:** Quarterly. **Trim Size:** 6 1/2 x 9 3/4. **Cols./Page:** 1. **Col. Width:** 5 in. **Col. Depth:** 8 in. **Key Personnel:** S. Morita, Editor-in-Chief. **ISSN:** 0219-1835. **Subscription:** $240.
                                   Circulation: (Not Reported)
Advertising accepted; contact publisher for rates.

2622 Journal of Knot Theory and Its Ramifications
World Scientific Publishing Co., Inc.
1060 Main St., Ste. 1B   **Phone: (201)487-9655**
River Edge, NJ 07661   **Fax: (201)487-9656**
Journal covering developments in knot theory and ramifications in math and other sciences. **Founded:** 1992. **Frequency:** Quarterly. **Trim Size:** 6 1/2 x 9 3/4. **Cols./Page:** 1. **Col. Width:** 5 in. **Col. Depth:** 8 in. **Key Personnel:** Louis Kaufman, Managing Editor; W.B.R. Lickorish, Managing Editor; M. Wadati, Managing Editor. **ISSN:** 0218-2165. **Subscription:** $185.
                                   Circulation: (Not Reported)
Advertising accepted; contact publisher for rates.

2623 Vanilla Ice and Today's Top Teen Stars
MM Publications, Inc.
63 Grand Ave., Ste 115
River Edge, NJ 07661
Magazine featuring articles and interviews on teen musicians. **Frequency:** 6x/yr. **Key Personnel:** Anne M. Raso, Editor. **Subscription:** $3.50 single issue.
                                   Circulation: (Not Reported)

SALEM

2624 The Sampler
Gannett Co., Inc.
304 Harding Hwy.
Rte. 48, Bldg. 2   **Phone: (609)299-1900**
Carneys Point, NJ 08069   **Fax: (609)299-1908**

SCOTCH PLAINS

2625 The Times
Foster Publishing Co.
1600 E. 2nd St.
PO Box 368   **Phone: (908)322-5266**
Scotch Plains, NJ 07076   **Fax: (908)322-6117**

SOMERVILLE

2626 TeeVee Moneysaver (Edition 1)
TeeVee Moneysaver, Inc., Publications
52 West St.
PO Box 954   **Phone: (908)722-6270**
Somerville, NJ 08876   **Fax: (908)722-7303**

SOUTH ORANGE

📖 **2627 Biblical Theology Bulletin**
Biblical Theology Bulletin, Inc.
Seton Hall University
South Orange, NJ 07079   Phone: (201)761-9770

TEANECK

📖 **2628 FAMA**
Fama Publications, Inc.
105 Copley Ave.
Teaneck, NJ 07666
Latin-American entertainment magazine. **Frequency:** Monthly. **Key Personnel:** Carlos Vega, Editor and Publisher. **Subscription:** $30. $1.95 single issue.

Circulation: (Not Reported)

THOROFARE

📖 **2629 The American Journal of Knee Surgery**
Slack, Medical Publishing, Inc.
6900 Grove Rd.   Phone: (609)848-1000
Thorofare, NJ 08086-9447   Fax: (609)853-5991

📖 **2630 Journal of the National Medical Association**
Slack, Inc.
6900 Grove Rd.   **Phone: (609)848-1000**
Thorofare, NJ 08086-9447   Fax: (609)853-5991

TOMS RIVER

🎤 **2631 Clear TV Cable**
830 Rte. 37 W.
Box 847   Phone: (201)286-2971
Toms River, NJ 08754   Fax: (201)286-2914
Owner: Adelphia Communications Corp. **Founded:** 1971. **Cities Served:** Ocean County, NJ.

TRENTON

🎤 **2632 Comcast Cablevision of Mercer County**
940 Prospect St.
Box 7600
Trenton, NJ 08628   Phone: (609)394-8587
Owner: Comcast Corp. **Founded:** 1981. **Cities Served:** Mercer County, Ewing Twp., Lawrenceville, and Pennington Borough, NJ.

WALDWICK

📖 **2633 Family Process**
Family Process, Inc.
29 Walter Hammond Pl., Ste. A.   Phone: (201)612-9868
Waldwick, NJ 07463   Fax: (201)612-9892

WASHINGTON

📖 **2634 Compressed Air**
253 E. Washington Ave.
Washington, NJ 07882-2495   **Phone: (908)850-7818**

WAYNE

🎤 **2635 WPSC-FM - 88.7**
300 Pompton Rd.   Phone: (201)595-3331
Wayne, NJ 07470   **Fax: (201)595-2483**

WHIPPANY

📖 **2636 MetroWest Jewish News**
901 Rte. 10   **Phone: (201)887-3900**
Whippany, NJ 07981-1157   Fax: (201)887-4152

NEW MEXICO

ALBUQUERQUE

◻ 2637 The Adobe Journal: Traditions Southwest
The Adobe Foundation
PO Box 7725
Albuquerque, NM 87194   Phone: (505)243-7801
Magazine featuring adobe architecture in the American southwest and the world. **Founded:** September, 1989. **Frequency:** Quarterly. **Printing Method:** Web offset. **Trim Size:** 11 x 14. **Key Personnel:** Michael Moguin, Editor. **Subscription:** $15. $4 single issue.
Ad Rates: BW: $500   **Circulation:** Paid 1,100
                                   Non-paid 3,400

◻ 2638 Albuquerque Woman
Duval Publications
PO Box 6133
Albuquerque, NM 87197   Phone: (505)247-9195
Periodical for women in the Albuquerque, NM area. Includes articles on business and career issues. **Founded:** 1989. **Frequency:** 6x/yr. **Trim Size:** 8 1/2 x 11. **Cols./Page:** 3. **Col. Width:** 2 1/4 in. **Col. Depth:** 10 in. **Subscription:** $11.50. $2.75 single issue.
Ad Rates: BW: $695   **Circulation:** Paid ‡1,000
            4C: $869   Non-paid ‡4,500

◻ 2639 Health City Sun
PO Box 1517
Albuquerque, NM 87103   Phone: (505)242-3010
                               Fax: (505)842-5464

◻ 2640 Journal of Anthropological Research
University of New Mexico
Dept. of Anthropology   Phone: (505)277-3027
Albuquerque, NM 87131-1561   **Fax: (505)277-0874**

◻ 2641 New Mexico Engineering Quarterly
New Mexico Society of Professional Engineers
1615 University Blvd. NE
Albuquerque, NM 87102   Phone: (505)247-9181
Ceased publication.

◻ 2642 The Resource Center Bulletin
Inter-Hemispheric Education Resource Center
PO Box 4506   Phone: (505)842-8288
Albuquerque, NM 87196   Fax: (505)246-1601
Magazine provides research and analysis on current international issues, especially U.S. foreign policy in the Third World. **Founded:** 1985. **Frequency:** Quarterly. **Key Personnel:** John Hawley, Contact. **ISSN:** 0891-2688. **Subscription:** $5; $7.50 other countries.
                           Circulation: Paid 2,000
                               Non-paid 1,500
Advertising not accepted.

◻ 2643 Review of International Affairs
PO Box 4526
Albuquerque, NM 87106-4526   Phone: (505)296-2320

♪ 2644 Jones Intercable Inc.
4611 Montbel Pl., NE   Phone: (505)761-6200
Albuquerque, NM 87107   Fax: (505)761-6273
Owner: Jones Intercable, Inc. **Founded:** 1978. **Key Personnel:** Kevin Bethke, Gen. Mgr.; Brian Throop, Chief Engineer; Lynne Lofton, Operations Mgr. **Cities Served:** Bernalilo County, Sandoval County, Valencia County, Bernalilo, Bosque Farms, Corrales, Los Ranchos de Albuquerque, North Valley, Paradise Hills, Peralta, and South Valley, NM: 90,000 subscribing households; 44 channels; 2 community access channelS.

♪ 2645 KOLT-FM - 105.9
3700 Rio Granda Blvd.NW, Ste.2   **Phone: (505)345-2399**
Albuquerque, NM 87106   **Fax: (505)345-3199**

ANGEL FIRE

♪ 2646 KAFR-FM - 99.1
Box 520   Phone: (505)377-2597
Angel Fire, NM 87710   Fax: (505)377-3578
Format: Album-Oriented Rock (AOR)/Adult Contemporary. **Owner:** Moreno Valley Broadcasting. **Founded:** 1992. **Operating Hours:** Continuous. **Key Personnel:** Francis O'Connell, Gen. Mgr.; Brian Elund, Program Dir.; Jimmie Joynt, Engineer; Ken Lamson, Engineer. **Wattage:** 50,000. **Ad Rates:** $12-$15 for 30 seconds; $15-$18 for 60 seconds.

AZTEC

♪ 2647 KCQL-AM - 1340
303 Ash   Phone: (505)334-7558
Aztec, NM 87410   Fax: (505)334-7557
Format: Oldies. **Network(s):** Unistar. **Owner:** J. Thomas Development, at above address. **Founded:** 1959. **Formerly:** KNDE-AM (1962); KHAP-AM (1976); KKBK-AM (1987); KCEM-AM (1992). **Operating Hours:** Continuous. **Key Personnel:** Jeff Thomas, Gen. Mgr.; John Lockmiller, Gen. Mgr.; Dan Kelley, Operations and Program Dir. **Wattage:** 1000. **Ad Rates:** Available upon request.

♪ 2648 KKFG-FM - 104.5
303 Ash   Phone: (505)334-7558
Aztec, NM 87410   Fax: (505)334-7557
Format: Hot Country. **Network(s):** Unistar. **Owner:** J. Thomas Development, at above address. **Founded:** 1987. **Formerly:** KMYO-FM (1988); KCEM-FM (1992). **Operating Hours:** Continuous. **Key Personnel:** Jeff Thomas, Gen. Mgr.; John Lockmiller, Gen. Mgr.; Dan

Kelley, Operation and Program Dir. **Wattage:** 100,000. **Ad Rates:** Available upon request.

EUNICE

📖 **2649 Eunice Press**
Golden West Free Press, Inc.
1007 Main
PO Box 1207   Phone: (505)394-3296
Eunice, NM 88231   **Fax: (915)586-2562**

FARMINGTON

🎤 **2650 KNMI-FM - 88.9**
2103 W. Main St.
Box 1230   Phone: (505)327-4357
Farmington, NM 87401   **Fax: (505)325-9035**

🎤 **2651 TCI Cable of New Mexico**
1911 N. Butler St.   Phone: (505)327-6143
Farmington, NM 87401-9909   Fax: (505)325-3457
Owner: Tele-Communications, Inc. **Founded:** 1954. **Cities Served:** San Juan County, NM.

GALLUP

📖 **2652 The Voice of the Southwest**
PO Box 1338   Phone: (505)863-4406
Gallup, NM 87301   **Fax: (505)722-9131**

🎤 **2653 KKOR-FM - 94.5**
405-407 S. 2nd St.
Gallup, NM 87301   Phone: (505)863-6851
                                     Fax: (505)863-2429

🎤 **2654 KYVA-AM - 1230**
405-407 S. 2nd St.
Gallup, NM 87301   Phone: (505)863-6851
                                     Fax: (505)863-2429

LAS CRUCES

🎤 **2655 KRWG-FM - 90.7**
PO Box 3000   Phone: (505)646-4525
Las Cruces, NM 88003   **Fax: (505)646-1924**

🎤 **2656 KRWG-TV - Channel 22**
Box 30001
Dept. TV 22   **Phone: (505)646-2222**
Las Cruces, NM 88003   **Fax: (505)646-1924**

🎤 **2657 Las Cruces TV Cable**
110 E. Idaho
Box J   Phone: (505)523-2531
Las Cruces, NM 88004   Fax: (505)521-7208
Owner: Western Communications. **Founded:** 1971. **Key Personnel:** John Chrisopher, Pres.; Kim Wright Ray, Ad Dir.; Paula Angell, Mktg. Dir.; Bud Heimat, Engineering Dir.; Ruth Clark, Cust. Service Dir. **Cities Served:** Dona Ana County, Mesilla Park, Mesilla, and Las Cruces, NM: 24,000 subscribing households; 40 channels; 1 community access channel; 20 hours per week of community access programming. **Additional Contact Information:** Alt. phone (505)523-9322.

LAS VEGAS

🎤 **2658 KFUN-AM - 1230**
Box 710
Las Vegas, NM 87701   Phone: (505)425-6766
Format: Contemporary Country and Spanish. **Network(s):** ABC. **Owner:** KFUN/KLVF, Inc. **Founded:** 1941. **Operating Hours:** 6 a.m.-10 p.m. **Key Personnel:** nis Mitchell, Pres. **Wattage:** 1000. **Ad Rates:** $4.50-$5 for 30 seconds; $5.50-$6 for 60 seconds; Combined rates available with KLVF.

ROSWELL

🎤 **2659 KBIM-TV - Channel 10**
214 N. Main St.   Phone: (505)622-2120
Roswell, NM 88201   **Fax: (505)623-6606**

🎤 **2660 KCRX-AM - 1430**
905 Avenida Del Sumbre
PO Box 2052   Phone: (505)622-7677
Roswell, NM 88202-2052   **Fax: (505)622-7677**

🎤 **2661 KOBR-TV - Channel 8**
124 E. 4th St.   Phone: (505)625-8888
Roswell, NM 88201   **Fax: (505)625-8866**

SANTA FE

📖 **2662 The Santa Fe New Mexican**
PO Box 2048   Phone: (505)983-3303
Santa Fe, NM 87504   Fax: (505)986-9147

📖 **2663 The Santa Fean Magazine**
The Santa Fean Magazine and Publishing Company
1440 A St. Francis Dr.   Phone: (505)983-8914
Santa Fe, NM 87501   Fax: (505)983-8013
Magazine covering art, museums, restaurants, personalities, history, events, and natural attractions in Santa Fe. **Founded:** 1972. **Frequency:** Monthly (except Feb.). **Trim Size:** 8 1/2 x 11. **Cols./Page:** 2 and 3. **Col. Width:** 18 picas and 14 picas. **Col. Depth:** 60 picas. **Key Personnel:** Betty Bauer, Publisher; Marian Love, Publisher. **ISSN:** 1046-2708. **Subscription:** $19.35; $45 Canada.
Ad Rates: BW: $2,435   **Circulation: Paid □10,877**
              4C: $2,735   Controlled □3,680

🎤 **2664 UAE**
1414 Luisa St.   Phone: (505)982-4379
Santa Fe, NM 87501   Fax: (505)983-4088
Owner: Tele-Communications, Inc. **Founded:** 1970. **Cities Served:** Santa Fe County, NM.

SANTA ROSA

🎤 **2665 KSSR-AM - 1340**
PO Box 427
Santa Rosa, NM 88435   **Phone: (505)472-5777**

TAOS

📖 **2666 Taos Magazine**
Whitney Publishing Co., Inc.
Box 1380
Taos, NM 87571   **Phone: (505)758-5404**

TORREON

📖 **2667 Tantra: The Magazine**
PO Box 79
Torreon, NM 87061-0079   Phone: (505)384-2292
Magazine containing articles on tantric practices, history, teachers, art, music, and lifestyles. **Founded:** 1991. **Frequency:** 4x/yr. **Printing Method:** Sheetfed offset. **Trim Size:** 8 1/4 x 10 3/4. **Cols./Page:** 3. **Key Personnel:** Susana Andrews, Editor; Alan Verdegraal, Publisher. **ISSN:** 1064-0584. **Subscription:** $18. $4.50 single issue.
Ad Rates: BW: $240   **Circulation: Paid ‡2,150**
              4C: $540   Non-paid ‡5,000
              PCI: $22

TRUTH OR CONSEQUENCES

📖 **2668 Chaparral Guide**
Herald Publishing Co. Inc.
1204 N. Date St.
PO Box 752   Phone: (505)894-2143
Truth or Consequences, NM 87901   Fax: (505)894-7824
Newspaper containing tourist information about and history of Sierra County, MN. **Founded:** 1967. **Frequency:** Monthly. **Printing Method:** Offset. **Trim Size:** 15 x 11 1/4. **Cols./Page:** 3. **Col. Width:** 18.5 picas. **Col. Depth:** 80.5 picas. **Key Personnel:** Jim Streicher, Editor; Bob Tooley, Publisher; Mike Tooley, Publisher. **Subscription:** Free.
Ad Rates: BW: $126   **Circulation: Free 6,000**
              PCI: $3

NEW YORK

ALBANY

📖 **2669 Capital District Business Review**
PO Box 15081   Phone: (518)437-9855
Albany, NY 12212-5081   Fax: (518)437-0764

📖 **2670 Legislative Gazette**
State University of New York
PO Box 7023   Phone: (518)473-9739
Albany, NY 12225   Fax: (518)486-6609
Magazine for and about state government. **Founded:** 1978. **Frequency:** Weekly. **Printing Method:** Offset. **Trim Size:** 10 x 16. **Cols./Page:** 6. **Col. Width:** 9.5 picas. **Key Personnel:** Alan Chartock, Publisher; Glenn Doty, Editor. **Subscription:** $99.
Ad Rates: GLR: $.52   **Circulation:** Paid ⊕**385**
          BW: $696   Non-paid ⊕**18,200**
          4C: $1,096
          PCI: $7.25

🎤 **2671 Capital Cablevision Systems, Inc.**
130 Washington Ave.
Albany, NY 12203   Phone: (518)869-5500
Owner: American TV & Communications Corp. **Founded:** 1974. **Cities Served:** Albany County, Altamont, Colonie, Green Island, Guilderland, Menands, and Watervliet, NY.

🎤 **2672 WABY-AM - 1400**
Box 12521   Phone: (518)456-6101
Albany, NY 12212   Fax: (518)456-6377

AMITYVILLE

📖 **2673 Journal of Individual Employment Rights**
Baywood Publishing, Inc.
26 Austin Ave.   Phone: (516)691-1270
Amityville, NY 11701   Fax: (516)691-1770
Journal covering employee rights. **Founded:** 1992. **Frequency:** Quarterly. **Key Personnel:** Kurt H. Decker, Editor; Harry Kershen, Editor. **ISSN:** 1055-7521. **Subscription:** $40.50; $99.50 institutions; $45.35 other countries; $104.35 institutions in other countries.
                            Circulation: (Not Reported)
Advertising accepted; contact publisher for rates.

ANNADALE-ON-HUDSON

🎤 **2674 WXBC-AM - 540**
Box College
Annadale-On-Hudson, NY 12504   Phone: (914)758-6822
Format: Alternative/Independent/Progressive. **Key Personnel:** Matthew Schickele, Music Dir. **Ad Rates:** Noncommercial.

ARMONK

📖 **2675 Anthropology & Archeology of Eurasia**
M.E. Sharpe, Inc.
80 Business Park Dr.
Armonk, NY 10504   Phone: (914)273-1800
                         Fax: (914)273-2106
Former Title: Soviet Anthropology & Archeology

📖 **2676 Chinese Education & Society**
M.E. Sharpe, Inc.
80 Business Park Dr.
Armonk, NY 10504   Phone: (914)273-1800
                         Fax: (914)273-2106
Former Title: Chinese Education

📖 **2677 Journal of Russian and East European Psychiatry**
M.E. Sharpe, Inc.
80 Business Park Dr.
Armonk, NY 10504   Phone: (914)273-1800
                         Fax: (914)273-2106
Former Title: Soviet Neurology & Psychiatry

📖 **2678 Journal of Russian and East European Psychology**
M.E. Sharpe, Inc.
80 Business Park Dr.
Armonk, NY 10504   Phone: (914)273-1800
                         Fax: (914)273-2106
Former Title: Soviet Psychology

📖 **2679 Problems of Economic Transition**
M.E. Sharpe, Inc.
80 Business Park Dr.
Armonk, NY 10504   Phone: (914)273-1800
                         Fax: (914)273-2106
Former Title: Problems of Economics

📖 **2680 Russian and Eastern European Finance and Trade**
M.E. Sharpe, Inc.
80 Business Park Dr.
Armonk, NY 10504   Phone: (914)273-1800
                         Fax: (914)273-2106
Former Title: Soviet & Eastern European Foreign Trade

📖 **2681 Russian Education and Society**
M.E. Sharpe, Inc.
80 Business Park Dr.
Armonk, NY 10504   Phone: (914)273-1800
                         Fax: (914)273-2106
Former Title: Soviet Education

📖 **2682 Russian Politics and Law**
M.E. Sharpe, Inc.
80 Business Park Dr.
Armonk, NY 10504   Phone: (914)273-1800
                         Fax: (914)273-2106
Former Title: Soviet Law and Government

⊕ 2683　Russian Social Science Review
M.E. Sharpe, Inc.
80 Business Park Dr.　　　　　　Phone: (914)273-1800
Armonk, NY 10504　　　　　　　Fax: (914)273-2106
Former Title: Soviet Review

⊕ 2684　Russian Studies in History
M.E. Sharpe, Inc.
80 Business Park Dr.　　　　　　Phone: (914)273-1800
Armonk, NY 10504　　　　　　　Fax: (914)273-2106
Former Title: Soviet Studies in History

⊕ 2685　Russian Studies in Literature
M.E. Sharpe, Inc.
80 Business Park Dr.　　　　　　Phone: (914)273-1800
Armonk, NY 10504　　　　　　　Fax: (914)273-2106
Former Title: Soviet Studies in Literature

⊕ 2686　Russian Studies in Philosophy
M.E. Sharpe, Inc.
80 Business Park Dr.　　　　　　Phone: (914)273-1800
Armonk, NY 10504　　　　　　　Fax: (914)273-2106
Former Title: Soviet Studies in Philosopy

⊕ 2687　Sociological Research
M.E. Sharpe, Inc.
80 Business Park Dr.　　　　　　Phone: (914)273-1800
Armonk, NY 10504　　　　　　　Fax: (914)273-2106
Former Title: Soviet Sociology

⊕ 2688　Statutes and Decisions: Laws of the USSR and Its Successor States
M.E. Sharpe, Inc.
80 Business Park Dr.　　　　　　Phone: (914)273-1800
Armonk, NY 10504　　　　　　　Fax: (914)273-2106
Former Title: Soviet Statutes and Decisions

BATAVIA

⊕ 2689　Ag Focus
Cooperative Extension Assn.
420 E. Main St.　　　　　　　　Phone: (716)343-3040
Batavia, NY 14020　　　　　　　Fax: (716)343-1275
Former Title: Ag Impact

BAYSIDE

⊕ 2690　The Flushing Times
Queens Publishing Corp.
214-11 41st St.　　　　　　　　Phone: (718)299-0300
Bayside, NY 11361　　　　　　　Fax: (718)225-7117
Local newspaper. **Founded:** 1992. **Frequency:** Weekly. **Printing Method:** Offset. **Cols./Page:** 5. **Col. Width:** 24 nonpareils. **Col. Depth:** 200 agate lines. **Key Personnel:** Steven Blank, Editor and Publisher. **USPS:** 008-034. **Subscription:** $10; $15 two years.
Ad Rates:　PCI:　　$28　　　**Circulation:** Paid 4,000
　　　　　　　　　　　　　　　　　　　　　　　　Non-paid 500
Space sold in combination with The Little Neck Ledger and The Bayside Times.

BINGHAMTON

⊕ 2691　Activities, Adaptation and Aging
The Haworth Press, Inc.
10 Alice St.
Binghamton, NY 13904-1580　　　Fax: (607)722-1424
Subtitle: The Gerontological Journal of Activities. **Founded:** 1980. **Frequency:** Quarterly. **Key Personnel:** Phyllis M. Foster, ACC, Editor; Bill Cohen, Publisher. **ISSN:** 0192-4788. **Subscription:** $32; $75 institutions; $160 libraries.
Ad Rates:　BW:　　$300　　　　**Circulation:** 383
Additional Contact Information: Editor's address: Activities Program Consultant, 6549 S. Lincoln St., Littleton, CO 80121. Toll-free (800)342-9678.

⊕ 2692　Health Marketing Quarterly
The Haworth Press, Inc.
10 Alice St.　　　　　　　　　　Phone: 800-342-9678
Binghamton, NY 13904-1580　　　Fax: (607)722-1424
Journal for marketing health and human services. **Founded:** 1983.

Frequency: Quarterly. **Key Personnel:** William J. Winston, Editor; Bill Cohen, Publisher. **ISSN:** 0735-9683. **Subscription:** $45; $95 institutions; $200 libraries.
Ad Rates:　BW:　　$300　　　**Circulation:** (Not Reported)
Formerly: Health Medical Care Services Review. **Additional Contact Information:** Editor's address: Managing & Marketing Consultant, PO Box 8566, Berkeley, CA 94707.

⊕ 2693　The Hospice Journal
The Haworth Press, Inc.
10 Alice St.
Binghamton, NY 13904-1580　　　Fax: (607)722-1424
Founded: 1985. **Frequency:** Quarterly. **Key Personnel:** Madalon O'Rawe Amenta, RN, DPH, EDT, Editor; Bill Cohen, Publisher. **ISSN:** 0742-969X. **Subscription:** $35; $60 institutions; $105 libraries.
Ad Rates:　BW:　　$300　　　　**Circulation:** 2,906
Additional Contact Information: Editor's address: 5512 Northumberland St., Pittsburgh, PA 15217. Toll-free (800)342-9678.

⊕ 2694　Journal of Aging and Social Policy
The Haworth Press, Inc.
10 Alice St.
Binghamton, NY 13904-1580　　　Fax: (607)722-1424
Founded: 1989. **Frequency:** Quarterly. **Key Personnel:** Scott Bass, Ph.D., Editor; Robert Morris, DSW, Editor; Bill Cohen, Publisher. **Subscription:** $28; $32 institutions; $75 libraries.
Ad Rates:　BW:　　$300　　　　**Circulation:** 336
Additional Contact Information: Editor's address: c/o Scott A. Bass, Ph.D., Gerontology Institute, University of Massachussetts, Boston, MA 02125. Toll-free (800)342-9678.

⊕ 2695　Journal of Aquatic Food Product Technology
The Haworth Press, Inc.
10 Alice St.
Binghamton, NY 13904-1580　　　Fax: (607)722-1424
Founded: 1991. **Frequency:** Quarterly. **Key Personnel:** Dr. George Pitgott, Editor; Bill Cohen, Publisher. **ISSN:** 1049-8850. **Subscription:** $24; $36 institutions; $48 libraries.
Ad Rates:　BW:　　$300　　　**Circulation:** (Not Reported)
Additional Contact Information: Editor's address: Institute of Food Science and Technology, University of Washington, 3707 Brooklyn Ave. NE, Seattle, WA 98195. Toll-free (800)342-9678.

⊕ 2696　Journal of Asia-Pacific Business
The Haworth Press, Inc.
10 Alice St.　　　　　　　　　　Phone: (607)722-5857
Binghamton, NY 13904-1580　　　Fax: (607)722-1424
Journal featuring managerially oriented as well as academic articles centered on the Asia-Pacific region. **Founded:** Spring 1993. **Frequency:** Quarterly. **Key Personnel:** Zahir A. Quraeshi, Editor; Bill Cohen, Publisher. **ISSN:** 1059-9231. **Subscription:** $24; $48 institutions; $75 libraries.
Ad Rates:　BW:　　$300　　　**Circulation:** (Not Reported)
Additional Contact Information: Editorial address: Dept. of Marketing, Haworth College of Business, Western Michigan University, Kalamazoo, MI 49008. Toll-free for orders 800-3-HAWORTH.

⊕ 2697　Journal of Business-to-Business Marketing
The Haworth Press, Inc.
10 Alice St.
Binghamton, NY 13904-1580　　　Fax: (607)722-1424
Founded: 1991. **Frequency:** Quarterly. **Key Personnel:** David Wilson, Ph.D., Editor; Bill Cohen, Publisher. **ISSN:** 1051-712X. **Subscription:** $24; $36 institutions; $48 libraries.
Ad Rates:　BW:　　$300　　　**Circulation:** (Not Reported)
Additional Contact Information: Toll-free (800)342-9678. Editor's address: Dept. of Business Administration, 707-D Business Administration Bldg., Pennsylvania State University, University Park, PA 16802.

⊕ 2698　Journal of College Student Psychotherapy
The Haworth Press, Inc.
10 Alice St.
Binghamton, NY 13904-1580　　　Fax: (607)722-1424
Founded: 1986. **Frequency:** Quarterly. **Key Personnel:** Leighton Whitaker, Ph.D., Editor; Bill Cohen, Publisher. **ISSN:** 8756-8225. **Subscription:** $32; $45 institutions; $105 libraries.
Ad Rates:　BW:　　$330　　　　**Circulation:** 346
Additional Contact Information: Editor's address: Psychological Ser-

vices, Swarthmore College, Swarthmore, PA 19081. Toll-free (800)342-9678.

2699 Journal of Divorce and Remarriage
The Haworth Press, Inc.
10 Alice St.   Phone: (800)342-9678
Binghamton, NY 13904-1580   Fax: (607)722-1424
Journal containing clinical studies and research in family therapy, mediation, studies, and law. **Founded:** 1990. **Frequency:** Quarterly. **Key Personnel:** Craig A. Everett, Ph.D., Editor; Bill Cohen, Publisher. **ISSN:** 1050-2556. **Subscription:** $45; $125 institutions; $200 libraries.
Ad Rates: BW: $300   **Circulation:** 483
Formerly: Journal of Divorce. **Additional Contact Information:** Editor's address: Arizona Institute of Family Therapy, Sonora Desert Professional Blvd., Ste. 150, 6060 N. Fountain Plaza Dr., Tucson, AZ 85704.

2700 Journal of East-West Business
The Haworth Press, Inc.
10 Alice St.   Phone: (800)342-9678
Binghamton, NY 13904   Fax: (607)722-1424
Journal dealing with contemporary and emerging topics of business studies, strategies, development, and practice relating to Eastern Europe and Asia. **Founded:** Spring 1993. **Frequency:** Quarterly. **Key Personnel:** Stan Paliwoda, Editor; Bill Cohen, Publisher. **Subscription:** $18; $24 institutions; $32 libraries.
Ad Rates: BW: $300   **Circulation:** (Not Reported)
Additional Contact Information: Editorial address: Professor and Faculty of Management, University of Calgary, Calgary, AB, Canada T2N 1N4.

2701 Journal of Elder Abuse and Neglect
The Haworth Press, Inc.
10 Alice St.
Binghamton, NY 13904-1580   Fax: (607)722-1424
Founded: 1988. **Frequency:** Quarterly. **Key Personnel:** Rosalie S. Wolf, Ph.D., Editor; Suzan McMurray-Anderson, Ph.D., Editor; Bill Cohen, Publisher. **ISSN:** 0894-6566. **Subscription:** $24; $32 institutions; $90 libraries.
Ad Rates: BW: $300   **Circulation:** 637
Additional Contact Information: Dr. Wolf: Institute on Aging, The Medical Center of Central Massachussetts, 119 Belmont St., Worchester, MA 01605; Dr. McMurray-Anderson: 12 Hawden Rd., Worchester, MA 01602. Toll-free (800)342-9678.

2702 Journal of Euromarketing
The Haworth Press, Inc.
10 Alice St.
Binghamton, NY 13904-1580   Fax: (607)722-1424
Founded: 1991. **Frequency:** Quarterly. **Key Personnel:** Erderner Kaynak, Ph.D., Editor; Bill Cohen, Publisher. **ISSN:** 1049-6483. **Subscription:** $24; $32 institutions; $42 libraries.
Ad Rates: BW: $300   **Circulation:** (Not Reported)
Additional Contact Information: Editor's address: International Business Press, PO Box 231, Middletown, PA 17057. Toll-free (800)342-9678.

2703 Journal of Family Psychotherapy
The Haworth Press, Inc.
10 Alice St.   Phone: 8003-342-9678
Binghamton, NY 13904-1580   Fax: (607)722-1424
Journal includes case studies, treatment reports, and strategies in clinical practice for psychotherapists. **Subtitle:** The Quarterly Journal of Case Studies, Treatment Reports, and Strategies in Clinical Practice. **Founded:** 1990. **Frequency:** Quarterly. **Key Personnel:** Terry Trepper, Ph.D., Director, Editor; Bill Cohen, Publisher. **ISSN:** 0897-5353. **Subscription:** $32; $42 institutions; $90 libraries.
Ad Rates: BW: $300   **Circulation:** 316
Additional Contact Information: Editor's address: Family Studies Center, Purdue University-Calumet, Hammond, IN 46323-2094. **Formerly:** Journal of Psychotherapy and the Family.

2704 Journal of Family Social Work
The Haworth Press, Inc.
10 Alice St.   Phone: 800-342-9678
Binghamton, NY 13904-1580   Fax: (607)722-1424
Journal serves as a forum for family practitioners, scholars, and educators in the field of social work. **Founded:** 1992. **Frequency:** Quarterly. **Key Personnel:** Tom Smith, Ph.D., Editor; Bill Cohen, Publisher. **ISSN:** 1052-2158. **Subscription:** $30; $75 institutions; $95 libraries.
Ad Rates: BW: $300   **Circulation:** (Not Reported)
Additional Contact Information: Editorial Address: School of Social Work, Family Studies Center, Florida State University, Tallahassee, FL 32306. **Formerly:** Journal of Social Work and Human Sexuality.

2705 Journal of Feminist Family Therapy
The Haworth Press, Inc.
10 Alice St.   Phone: 800-342-9678
Binghamton, NY 13904-1580   Fax: (607)722-1424
Journal exploring the relationship between feminist theory and family therapy practice and theory. **Founded:** 1989. **Frequency:** Quarterly. **Key Personnel:** Lois Braverman, ACSW, Editor; Bill Cohen, Publisher. **ISSN:** 0895-2833. **Subscription:** $24; $40 institutions; $105 libraries.
Ad Rates: BW: $300   **Circulation:** (Not Reported)
Additional Contact Information: Editor's address: 3833 Woods Dr., Des Moines, IA 50312.

2706 Journal of Food Products Marketing
The Haworth Press, Inc.
10 Alice St.   Phone: 800-342-9678
Binghamton, NY 13904-1580   Fax: (607)722-1424
Journal profiling the food marketing industry, including food promotion and advertising, and new food product development. **Subtitle:** Innovations In Food Advertising, Food Promotion, Food Publicity, and Food Sales Promotion Management. **Founded:** 1991. **Frequency:** Quarterly. **Key Personnel:** John Stanton, Ph.D., Editor; Bill Cohen, Publisher. **ISSN:** 1045-4446. **Subscription:** $28; $48 institutions; $75 libraries.
Ad Rates: BW: $300   **Circulation:** (Not Reported)
Additional Contact Information: Editor's contact address: C.J. McNutt, Chair of Food King, St. Joseph's University, 5600 City Ave., Philadelphia, PA 19131.

2707 Journal of Gay and Lesbian Psychotherapy
The Haworth Press, Inc.
10 Alice St.
Binghamton, NY 13904-1580   Fax: (607)722-1424
Founded: 1988. **Frequency:** Quarterly. **Key Personnel:** David Scasta, M.D., Editor; Bill Cohen, Publisher. **ISSN:** 0891-7140. **Subscription:** $24; $45 institutions; $75 libraries.
Ad Rates: BW: $300   **Circulation:** 1,018
Additional Contact Information: Editor's address: 1439 Pineville Rd., New Hope, PA 18938. Toll-free (800)342-9678.

2708 Journal of Geriatric Drug Therapy
The Haworth Press, Inc.
10 Alice St.
Binghamton, NY 13904-1580   Fax: (607)722-1424
Founded: 1987. **Frequency:** Quarterly. **Key Personnel:** James Cooper, Ph.D., FCP, Editor; Bill Cohen, Publisher. **ISSN:** 8756-4629. **Subscription:** $40; $60 institutions; $125 libraries.
Ad Rates: BW: $300   **Circulation:** 175
Additional Contact Information: Editor's address: University of Georgia, College of Pharmacy, Dept. of Pharmacy Practice, Athens, GA 30602. Toll-free (800)342-9678.

2709 Journal of Gerontological Social Work
The Haworth Press, Inc.
10 Alice St.
Binghamton, NY 13904-1580   Fax: (607)722-1424
Founded: 1978. **Frequency:** Quarterly. **Key Personnel:** Rose Dobrof, DSW, Editor; Bill Cohen, Publisher. **ISSN:** 0163-4372. **Subscription:** $35; $85 institutions; $175 libraries.
Ad Rates: BW: $300   **Circulation:** 748
Additional Contact Information: Editor's address: Hunter College,

School of Social Work, Brookdale Center on Aging, 440 E. 26th St., New York, NY 10010. Toll-free (800)342-9678.

2710 Journal of Herbs, Spices, and Medicinal Plants
The Haworth Press, Inc.
10 Alice St.
Binghamton, NY 13904-1580   Fax: (602)722-1424
Founded: 1991. **Frequency:** Quarterly. **Key Personnel:** Lyle Cracker, Ph.D., Editor; Bill Cohen, Publisher. **ISSN:** 1049-6475. **Subscription:** $24; $32 institutions; $42 libraries.
Ad Rates: BW: $300   **Circulation:** (Not Reported)
Additional Contact Information: Editor's address: University of Massachussetts, Department of Plant and Soil Sciences, Amherst, MA 01003. Toll-free (800)342-9678.

2711 Journal of Independent Social Work
The Haworth Press, Inc.
10 Alice St.   Phone: 800-342-9678
Binghamton, NY 13904-1580   Fax: (607)722-1424
Journal provides analyses of the economic, social, and professional trends, affecting independent social workers. **Subtitle:** Innovations in Professional Services & Private Practice. **Founded:** 1987. **Frequency:** Quarterly. **Key Personnel:** Dr. Robert Barker, LCSW, Editor; Bill Cohen, Publisher. **ISSN:** 0883-7562. **Subscription:** $30; $45 institutions; $95 library.
Ad Rates: BW: $300   **Circulation:** 171
Additional Contact Information: Editor's address: 501 N. 10th St., Tacoma, WA 98402.

2712 Journal of International Financial Markets, Institutions and Money
International Business Press/The Haworth Press, Inc.
10 Alice St.
Binghamton, NY 13904-1580   Fax: (607)722-1424
Founded: 1991. **Frequency:** Quarterly. **Key Personnel:** Ike Mathur, Ph.D., Editor; Bill Cohen, Publisher. **ISSN:** 0897-4438. **Subscription:** $50; $75 institutions.
Ad Rates: BW: $300   **Circulation:** (Not Reported)
Additional Contact Information: Editor's contact address: Chrmn., Dept. of Finance, Southern Illinois University at Carbondale, College of Business and Administration, Carbondale, IL 62901. Toll-free (800)342-9678.

2713 Journal of Marketing Channels
The Haworth Press, Inc.
10 Alice St.   Phone: 800-342-9678
Binghamton, NY 13904-1580   Fax: (607)722-1424
Journal for marketing executives profiling distribution systems, strategies, and management. **Subtitle:** Distribution Systems, Strategy, & Management. **Founded:** 1991. **Frequency:** Quarterly. **Key Personnel:** Bert Rosenbloom, Ph.D., Editor; Bill Cohen, Publisher. **ISSN:** 1046-669X. **Subscription:** $32; $48 institutions; $75 libraries.
Ad Rates: BW: $300   **Circulation:** (Not Reported)
Additional Contact Information: Editor's addresss: Drexel University, College of Business and Administration, 32nd and Market Streets, Philadelphia, PA 19104.

2714 Journal of Multicultural Social Work
The Haworth Press, Inc.
10 Alice St.   Phone: 800-342-9678
Binghamton, NY 13904-1580   Fax: (607)722-1424
Journal examines multicultural social issues related to social work policy, research, theory, and practice. **Founded:** 1991. **Frequency:** Quarterly. **Key Personnel:** Paul Keys, Ph.D., Editor; Bill Cohen, Publisher. **ISSN:** 1042-8224. **Subscription:** $28; $32 institutions; $48 libraries.
Ad Rates: BW: $300   **Circulation:** 158
Additional Contact Information: Editor's address: Hunter College, School of Social Work, 129 E. 79th St., New York, NY 10021.

2715 Journal of Multinational Financial Management
International Business Press/The Haworth Press, Inc.
10 Alice St.
Binghamton, NY 13904-1580   Fax: (607)722-1424
Founded: 1990. **Frequency:** Quarterly. **Key Personnel:** Ike Mathur, Ph.D., Editor; Bill Cohen, Publisher. **ISSN:** 1042-444X. **Subscription:** $50; $75 institutions.
Ad Rates: BW: $300   **Circulation:** 85
Additional Contact Information: Editor's contact address: Chairman, Dept. of Finance, College of Business and Administration, Southern

Illinois University at Carbondale, Carbondale, IL 62901-4626. Toll-free (800)342-9678.

2716 Journal of Nonprofit and Public Sector Marketing
The Haworth Press, Inc.
10 Alice St.   Phone: 800-342-9678
Binghamton, NY 13904-1580   Fax: (607)722-1424
Journal provides forum for the development of marketing thought and the dissemination of marketing information to the nonprofit, public sector. **Founded:** 1992. **Frequency:** Quarterly. **Key Personnel:** Donald Self, Ph.D., Editor; Bill Cohen, Publisher. **ISSN:** 1049-5142. **Subscription:** $28; $48 institutions; $75 libraries.
Ad Rates: BW: $300   **Circulation:** (Not Reported)
Additional Contact Information: Editor's address: Dept. of Marketing, Auburn University, Montgomery, AL 36193. **Formerly:** Journal of Marketing for Mental Health.

2717 Journal of Nutritional Immunology
The Haworth Press, Inc.
10 Alice St.   Phone: 800-342-9678
Binghamton, NY 13904-1580   Fax: (607)722-1424
Journal providing a forum for research scientists interested in how nutrition affects immunology. **Founded:** 1992. **Frequency:** Quarterly. **Key Personnel:** Jullian E. Spallholz, Ph.D., Editor; Bill Cohen, Publisher. **ISSN:** 1049-5150. **Subscription:** $32; $48 institutions; $75 libraries.
Ad Rates: BW: $300   **Circulation:** (Not Reported)
Additional Contact Information: Editor's address: 507 Food Science Bldg., PO Box 4170, Texas Tech University, Lubbock, TX 79409.

2718 Journal of Offender Rehabilitation
The Haworth Press, Inc.
10 Alice St.
Binghamton, NY 13904-1580   Fax: (607)722-1424
Founded: 1990. **Frequency:** Quarterly. **Key Personnel:** Nathaniel J. Pallone, Ph.D., Editor; Bill Cohen, Publisher. **ISSN:** 1050-9674. **Subscription:** $40; $75 institutions, $165 libraries.
Ad Rates: BW: $300   **Circulation:** 195
Additional Contact Information: Editor's address: Rutgers–The State University of New Jersey, Livingston College Campus, 133 A Lucy Stone Hall, New Brunswick, NJ 08903. Toll-free (800)342-9678. **Formerly:** Journal of Offender Counseling, Services, and Rehabilitation.

2719 Journal of Pharmacoepidemiology
The Haworth Press, Inc.
10 Alice St.   Phone: 800-342-9678
Binghamton, NY 13904-1580   Fax: (607)722-1424
Journal assessing the drug therapy industry. **Subtitle:** Innovations in Pharmaceutical Research and Practice. **Founded:** 1989. **Frequency:** Quarterly. **Key Personnel:** Jack E. Fincham, Ph.D., Editor; Bill Cohen, Publisher. **ISSN:** 0896-6966. **Subscription:** $24; $32 institutions; $48 libraries.
Ad Rates: BW: $300   **Circulation:** 204
Additional Contact Information: Editor's address: Assoc. Dean for Academic Affairs, Samford University, School of Pharmacy, Birmingham, AL 35229.

2720 Journal of Promotion Management
The Haworth Press, Inc.
10 Alice St.   Phone: 800-342-9678
Binghamton, NY 13904-1580   Fax: (607)722-1424
Journal providing information and research findings on the field of promotion management. **Subtitle:** Innovations in Planning and Applied Research for Advertising, Sales Promotion, Personal Selling, Public Relations, and Re-Seller Support. **Founded:** Fall 1991. **Frequency:** Quarterly. **Key Personnel:** Dr. Fred Crane, Editor; Bill Cohen, Publisher. **ISSN:** 1049-6491. **Subscription:** $24; $36 institutions; $48 libraries.
Ad Rates: BW: $300   **Circulation:** (Not Reported)
Additional Contact Information: Editor's address: School of Business, Dalhousie University, 6152 Coburg Rd., Halifax, Nova Scotia, Canada B3H 1Z5.

2721 Journal of Psychology and Human Sexuality
The Haworth Press, Inc.
10 Alice St.
Binghamton, NY 13904-1580   Fax: (607)722-1424
Founded: 1988. **Frequency:** Quarterly. **Key Personnel:** Eli Coleman,

Ph.D., Editor; Bill Cohen, Publisher. **ISSN:** 0890-7064. **Subscription:** $24; $35 institutions; $95 libraries.
Ad Rates: BW: $300 **Circulation:** 226
Additional Contact Information: Editor's address: Program in Human Sexuality, 1300 S. 2nd St., Minneapolis, MN 55414-1092. Toll-free (800)342-9678.

⊞ 2722 Journal of Religion in Psychotherapy
The Haworth Press, Inc.
10 Alice St. Phone: 800-342-9678
Binghamton, NY 13904-1580 Fax: (607)722-1424
Journal exploring the role of religion in psychotherapy. **Founded:** 1990. **Frequency:** Quarterly. **Key Personnel:** William M. Clements, Ph.D., Editor; Bill Cohen, Publisher. **ISSN:** 1045-5876. **Subscription:** $24; $32 institutions; $60 libraries.
Ad Rates: BW: $300 **Circulation:** (Not Reported)
Additional Contact Information: Editor's address: Dir. of Behavioral Science, The Medical Center, Dept. of Family Practice, PO Box 951, 710 Center St., Columbus, GA 31994-2299. **Formerly:** Journal of Pastoral Psychotherapy.

⊞ 2723 Journal of Religious Gerontology
The Haworth Press, Inc.
10 Alice St.
Binghamton, NY 13904-1580 Fax: (607)722-1424
Founded: 1990. **Frequency:** Quarterly. **Key Personnel:** William M. Clements, Editor; Bill Cohen, Publisher. **ISSN:** 1050-2289. **Subscription:** $32; $40 institutions; $95 libraries.
Ad Rates: BW: $300 **Circulation:** 803
Additional Contact Information: Editor's address: Professor, Pastor Care and Counseling, School of Theology at Claremont, 1325 N. College Ave., Claremont, CA 91711. Toll-free (800)342-9678.

⊞ 2724 Journal of Small Fruit and Viticulture
Food Products Press
10 Alice St. Phone: 800-342-9678
Binghamton, NY 13904-1580 Fax: (607)722-1424
Journal covering technologies in management and marketing of berries, kiwi, and other small fruit. **Founded:** 1992. **Frequency:** Quarterly. **Key Personnel:** Robert E. Gough, Editor; Bill Cohen, Publisher. **ISSN:** 1052-0015. **Subscription:** $15; $24 institutions; $36 libraries.
Circulation: (Not Reported)
Additional Contact Information: Editor's address: PO Box 100, Ridge Rd., Oakfield, ME 04763.

⊞ 2725 Journal of Social Service Research
The Haworth Press, Inc.
10 Alice St. Phone: 800-342-9678
Binghamton, NY 13904-1580 Fax: (607)722-1424
Journal addressing issues of design, delivery, and management of social services. **Founded:** 1977. **Frequency:** Quarterly. **Key Personnel:** Shanti K. Khinduka, Editor; Bill Cohen, Publisher. **ISSN:** 0148-8376. **Subscription:** $40; $125 institutions; $200 libraries.
Ad Rates: BW: $300 **Circulation:** 441
Additional Contact Information: Editor's address: George Warren Brown School of Social Work, Washington University, PO Box 1196, St. Louis, MO 63130.

⊞ 2726 Journal of Sustainable Forestry
Haworth Press
10 Alice St. Phone: (800)342-9678
Binghamton, NY 13904-1580 Fax: (607)722-1424
Journal covering topics in biotechnology, physiology, silviculture, wood science, economics, and forest management. **Founded:** Fall, 1992. **Frequency:** Quarterly. **Key Personnel:** Graeme P. Berlyn, Ph.D., Editor; Bill Cohen, Publisher. **ISSN:** 1054-9811. **Subscription:** $24; $36 institutions; $48 libraries.
Ad Rates: BW: $300 **Circulation:** (Not Reported)
Additional Contact Information: Editor's address; Prof. of Forestry and Environmental Studies, Yale University School of Forestry & Environmental Studies, Greeley Memorial Lab, 370 Prospect St., New Haven, CT 06511.

⊞ 2727 Journal of Teaching in International Business
International Business Press/The Haworth Press, Inc.
10 Alice St.
Binghamton, NY 13904-1580 Fax: (607)722-1424
Founded: 1989. **Frequency:** Quarterly. **Key Personnel:** Erdener Kaynak, Ph.D., Editor; Bill Cohen, Publisher. **ISSN:** 0897-5930. **Subscription:** $24; $32 institutions; $48 libraries.
Ad Rates: BW: $300 **Circulation:** 245
Additional Contact Information: Editorial contact address: Exec. Editor, International Business Press, PO Box 231, Middletown, PA 17057. Toll-free (800)342-9678.

⊞ 2728 Journal of Vegetable Crop Production
The Haworth Press, Inc.
10 Alice St.
Binghamton, NY 13904-1580 Fax: (607)722-1424
Founded: 1993. **Frequency:** Quarterly. **Key Personnel:** I.L. Nonnecke, Editor; Bill Cohen, Publisher. **ISSN:** 1049-6467. **Subscription:** $24; $32 institutions; $42 libraries.
Ad Rates: BW: $300 **Circulation:** (Not Reported)
Additional Contact Information: Editor's address: Nonnecke & Associates, 160 Woolwich St., Guelph, ON, Canada N1H 3V3. Toll-free (800)342-9678.

⊞ 2729 Journal of Women and Aging
The Haworth Press, Inc.
10 Alice St.
Binghamton, NY 13904-1580 Fax: (607)722-1424
Founded: 1989. **Frequency:** Quarterly. **Key Personnel:** J. Dianne Garner, DSW; Editor; Bill Cohen, Publisher. **ISSN:** 0895-2841. **Subscription:** $28; $38 institutions; $75 libraries.
Ad Rates: BW: $300 **Circulation:** 383
Additional Contact Information: Editor's address: Department of Social Work, Washburn University, Topeka, KS 66621. Toll-free (800)342-9678.

⊞ 2730 Loss, Grief and Care
The Haworth Press, Inc.
10 Alice St.
Binghamton, NY 13904-1580 Fax: (607)722-1242
Founded: 1986. **Frequency:** Quarterly. **Key Personnel:** Austin Kutscher, M.D., Editor; Bill Cohen, Publisher. **ISSN:** 8756-4610. **Subscription:** $32; $45 institutions; $75 libraries.
Circulation: (Not Reported)
Additional Contact Information: Editor's address: Foundation of Thanatology, 630 W. 168th St., New York, NY 10032. Toll-free (800)342-9678.

⊞ 2731 Occupational Therapy in Health Care
The Haworth Press, Inc.
10 Alice St. Phone: 800-342-9678
Binghamton, NY 13904-1580 Fax: (607)722-1424
Journal for occupational therapists. **Subtitle:** A Journal of Contemproary Practice. **Founded:** 1984. **Frequency:** Quarterly. **Key Personnel:** Susan Cook Merrill, MS, OTR, Editor; Bill Cohen, Publisher. **ISSN:** 0738-0577. **Subscription:** $36; $48 institutions; $95 libraries.
Ad Rates: BW: $300 **Circulation:** 399
Additional Contact Information: Editor's address: Phillips Academy, Andover, MD 01810.

⊞ 2732 Occupational Therapy in Mental Health
The Haworth Press, Inc.
10 Alice St. Phone: 800-342-9678
Binghamton, NY 13904-1580 Fax: (607)772-1424
Journal for occupational therapists working in the mental health field. **Subtitle:** A Journal of Psychosocial Practice and Research. **Founded:** 1980. **Frequency:** Quarterly. **Key Personnel:** Diane Gibson, MS, OTR, Editor/Dir.; Bill Cohen, Publisher. **ISSN:** 0164-212X. **Subscription:** $36; $90 institutions; $165 library.
Ad Rates: BW: $300 **Circulation:** 725
Additional Contact Information: Editor's address: Activity Therapy Dept., The Sheppard and Enoch Pratt Hospital, PO Box 6815, Towson, MD 21204.

◫ **2733 Physical Therapy in Health Care**
The Haworth Press, Inc.
10 Alice St.   Phone: 800-342-9678
Binghamton, NY 13904-1580   Fax: (607)722-1424
Journal provides information on the management of problems encountered in physical therapy and health care. **Subtitle:** The Contempory Journal of Clinical Practice. **Founded:** 1986. **Frequency:** Quarterly. **Key Personnel:** Mary Singleton, Ph.D., Co-Editor; Eleanor R. Branch, Ph.D., Co-Editor; Bill Cohen, Publisher. **ISSN:** 0742-9711. **Subscription:** $25; $32 institutions; $60 libraries.
Ad Rates: BW: $300   **Circulation:** 134
Additional Contact Information: Editors' address: c/o Eleanor Branch, Dept of Physical Therapy, PO Box 3405, Duke Univ. Medical Ctr., Durham, NC 27710.

◫ **2734 Primary Sources & Original Works**
The Haworth Press, Inc.
10 Alice St.   Phone: 800-342-9678
Binghamton, NY 13904-1580   Fax: (607)722-1424
Journal contains articles, reports, reviews, columns, mini forums, collector and collection profiles and discussions of current issues and challenges of handling primary sources in institutions. **Founded:** Spring 1991. **Frequency:** Quarterly. **Key Personnel:** Larry McCrank, Editor; Bill Cohen, Publisher. **ISSN:** 1042-8216. **Subscription:** $25; $45 institutions and libraries.
Ad Rates: BW: $300   **Circulation:** (Not Reported)
Formerly: Special Collections. **Additional Contact Information:** Editorial Address: Library & Instructional Services, Ferris State University, Big Rapids, MI 49307.

◫ **2735 The Psychotherapy Patient**
The Haworth Press, Inc.
10 Alice St.   Phone: 800-342-9678
Binghamton, NY 13904-1580   Fax: (607)722-1424
Journal for professional psychotherapists. **Subtitle:** A Journal of Attribute-Focused Practice. **Founded:** 1984. **Frequency:** Quarterly. **Key Personnel:** E. Mark Stern, Ph.D., Editor; Bill Cohen, Publisher. **ISSN:** 0738-6176. **Subscription:** $36; $75 institutions; $125 libraries.
Ad Rates: BW: $300   **Circulation:** 199
Additional Contact Information: Editor's address: 215 E. 11th St., New York, NY 10003.

◫ **2736 Psychotherapy in Private Practice**
The Haworth Press, Inc.
10 Alice St.   Phone: 800-342-9678
Binghamton, NY 13904-1580   Fax: (607)722-1424
Journal for private practice psychotherapists. **Subtitle:** Innovations In Clinical Methods and Assessment, Consultation and Practice Management. **Founded:** 1983. **Frequency:** Quarterly. **Key Personnel:** Robert Weitz, Ph.D., Editor; Bill Cohen, Publisher. **ISSN:** 0731-7158. **Subscription:** $32; $60 institutions; $135 libraries.
Ad Rates: BW: $300   **Circulation:** 399
Additional Contact Information: Editor's address: 7566 Martinique Blvd., Boca Raton, FL 33433.

◫ **2737 Social Work in Health Care**
The Haworth Press, Inc.
10 Alice St.
Binghamton, NY 13904-1580   Fax: (607)722-1424
Founded: 1975. **Frequency:** Quarterly. **Key Personnel:** Sylvia Clarke, MSW, ACSW, Editor; Bill Cohen, Publisher. **ISSN:** 0098-1389. **Subscription:** $36; $85 institutions; $145 libraries.
Ad Rates: BW: $300   **Circulation:** 1,567
Additional Contact Information: Editor's address: Dept. of Social Work, The Mount Sinai Hospital, 1 Gustave L. Levy Place, New York, NY 10029. Toll-free (800)342-9678.

◫ **2738 Social Work With Groups**
The Haworth Press, Inc.
10 Alice St.   Phone: 800-342-9678
Binghamton, NY 13904-1580   Fax: (607)722-1424
Journal for social workers focusing on groups and groupwork in psychiatric, rehabilitation, and multipurpose social work. **Subtitle:** A Journal of Community and Clinical Practice. **Founded:** 1978. **Frequency:** Quarterly. **Key Personnel:** Roselle Kurland, Editor; Bill Cohen, Publisher. **ISSN:** 0160-9513. **Subscription:** $36; $95 institutions; $175 libraries.
Ad Rates: BW: $300   **Circulation:** 837
Additional Contact Information: Editorial Address: Hunter College, School of Social Work, 129 E. 79th St., New York, NY 10021.

◫ **2739 Women and Therapy**
.The Haworth Press, Inc.
10 Alice St.   Phone: 800-342-9678
Binghamton, NY 13904-1580   Fax: (607)722-1424
Journal focusing on women and therapy. Explores all aspects of the therapeutic process. **Founded:** 1982. **Frequency:** Quarterly. **Key Personnel:** Ellen Cole, Ph.D., Co-Editor; Esther D. Rothblum, Ph.D., Co-Editor; Bill Cohen, Publisher. **ISSN:** 0270-3149. **Subscription:** $36; $75 institutions; $150 libraries.
Ad Rates: BW: $300   **Circulation:** Paid ‡1,400
Additional Contact Information: Editors' addresses: Ellen Cole, Ph.D.: Prescott College, 220 Grove Ave., Prescott, AZ 86301; Esther D. Rothblum, Ph.D.: Dept. of Psychology, John Dewey Hall, Univ. of Vermont, Burlington, VT 05405.

BRONX

◫ **2740 Bulletin of the Torrey Botanical Club**
Torrey Botanical Club
c/o New York Botanical Garden
Scientific Publications Dept.   Phone: (212)220-8721
Bronx, NY 10458-5126   Fax: (212)220-6504

◫ **2741 Current Biography**
The H.W. Wilson Co.
950 University Ave.   Phone: (718)588-8400
Bronx, NY 10452   Fax: (718)590-1617

◫ **2742 International Philosophical Quarterly**
Foundation for International Philosophical Exchange
Fordham University   Phone: (718)579-2057
Bronx, NY 10458   Fax: (718)579-2321

◫ **2743 Wilson Library Bulletin**
The H.W. Wilson Co.
950 University Ave.   Phone: (718)588-8400
Bronx, NY 10452   Fax: (718)590-1617

🎙 **2744 Cablevision of New York City**
930 Southview Ave.
Bronx, NY 10473   Phone: (212)991-6000
Owner: Cablevision Systems Corp. **Founded:** 1988. **Cities Served:** Bronx County, NY.

BROOKLYN

◫ **2745 Harmony Magazine**
PO Box 81, Pratt Sta.
Brooklyn, NY 11205   Phone: (718)875-7448
Former Title: Network Africa

◫ **2746 Kashrus Faxletter**
Yeshiva Birkas Reuven
PO Box 204
Brooklyn, NY 11204   Phone: (718)336-8544
Jewish faxletter. **Founded:** 1991. **Frequency:** Monthly. **Trim Size:** 8 1/2 x 11. **Cols./Page:** 2. **Col. Width:** 21 picas. **Col. Depth:** 10 in. **Key Personnel:** Rabbi Yosef Wikler, Editor. **Subscription:** $30.
Ad Rates: BW: $200   **Circulation:** ‡100

◫ **2747 Women and Health**
117 St. John's Pl.   Phone: (212)305-3724
Brooklyn, NY 11217   Fax: (212)305-6832
Ceased publication.

🎙 **2748 WKRB-FM - 90.9**
201 Oriental Blvd.
Brooklyn, NY 11235   Phone: (718)368-5816
Format: Contemporary Hit Radio (CHR) (dance). **Key Personnel:** Rob Burdi, Music Dir. **Ad Rates:** Noncommercial.

BUFFALO

◫ **2749 The Spectrum**
Spectrum Student Periodical, Inc.
State University of NY. at Buffalo
132 Student Union   Phone: (716)645-2468
Buffalo, NY 14260   Fax: (716)645-2766

2750 Western New York Health Magazine and Hospital News
25 Boxwood Ln.
PO Box 211   Phone: (716)668-5223
Buffalo, NY 14225   Fax: (716)668-0364
Former Title: Hospital News of Western New York

2751 Women and Guns
Second Amendment Foundation
267 Linwood Ave.
PO Box 488, Sta. C   Phone: (716)885-6408
Buffalo, NY 14209   Fax: (716)884-4471
Magazine for women gun owners. **Founded:** 1989. **Frequency:** Monthly. **Printing Method:** Web offset. **Trim Size:** 8 1/2 x 11. **Col. Width:** 2 1/4 in. **Col. Depth:** 7 in. **Key Personnel:** Peggy Tartaro, Exec. Editor; Sonny Jones, Editor. **Subscription:** $24; $72 other countries. $3 single issue.
Ad Rates: BW: $450   **Circulation:** ‡18,000
            4C: $1,100
            PCI: $25

2752 TCI of New York
2585 Main St.
Buffalo, NY 14214-2080   Phone: (716)862-4600
Owner: Tele-Communications, Inc. **Founded:** 1966. **Cities Served:** Erie County, NY.

2753 WBFO-FM - 88.7
3435 Main St.   Phone: (716)829-2555
Buffalo, NY 14214   Fax: (716)829-2277

CAMBRIDGE

2754 The Eagle
PO Box 36   Phone: (518)677-5158
Cambridge, NY 12816   Fax: (518)677-2319

CANTON

2755 WVNC-FM - 96.7
PO Box 136   Phone: (315)379-9777
Canton, NY 13617   Fax: (315)379-9778

CHESTER

2756 Heaven Bone
Heaven Bone Press
PO Box 486   Phone: (914)469-9018
Chester, NY 10918   Fax: (914)469-7880

CHITTENANGO

2757 Chittenango Bridgeport Times
Eagle Newspapers
PO Box 65   Phone: (315)637-3121
Fayetteville, NY 13066-0099   Fax: (315)637-3124

COBLESKILL

2758 Daily Editor
Lee Publications, Inc.
59 E. Main St.
PO Box 170   Phone: (518)234-4368
Cobleskill, NY 12043   Fax: (518)673-8849

COLD SPRING HARBOR

2759 PCR Methods and Applications
Cold Spring Harbor Laboratory
1 Bungtown Rd.   Phone: (516)367-8492
Cold Spring Harbor, NY 11724   Fax: (516)367-8532
Journal covering polymerase chain reaction PCR methodology and techniques. **Founded:** 1991. **Frequency:** Quarterly. **Printing Method:** Offset. **Trim Size:** 8 1/2 x 11. **Cols./Page:** 3. **Col. Width:** 2 1/4 in. **Col.**

Depth: 9 1/2 in. **Key Personnel:** Judy Cuddihy, Editor; Nancy Kuhle, Advertising Mgr. **ISSN:** 1054-9803. **Subscription:** $55; $170 institutions.
Ad Rates: BW: $3,900   **Circulation:** (Not Reported)
            4C: $5,000

CONKLIN

2760 The Vestal Town Crier
Masthead Publications, Inc.
PO Box 208   Phone: (607)775-0472
Conklin, NY 13748   Fax: (607)775-5863
Newspaper. **Founded:** 1989. **Frequency:** Weekly. **Cols./Page:** 6. **Col. Width:** 1 1/2 in. **Col. Depth:** 16 in. **Key Personnel:** Don Einstein, Publisher; Elizabeth Einstein, Managing Editor. **Subscription:** $16; $18 out of county.
Ad Rates: PCI: $4.50   **Circulation:** ⊕1,150
Additional Contact Information: Owner's address: 1035 Conklin Rd., Conklin, NY 13748.

COOPERSTOWN

2761 New York History
New York State Historical Assn.
Lake Rd.
PO Box 800   Phone: (607)547-2508
Cooperstown, NY 13326   Fax: (607)547-5384

CORTLAND

2762 The Dragon Chronicle
State University of New York College at Cortland
Corey Union, Rm. 111   Phone: (607)753-2803
Cortland, NY 13045   Fax: (607)753-2807

EAST AURORA

2763 Farm News of Erie and Wyoming Counties
Cooperative Extension Assns. of Erie and Wyoming Counties
21 S. Grove St.   Phone: (716)652-5401
East Aurora, NY 14052   Fax: (716)652-5073

EAST ROCHESTER

2764 WRQI-FM - 95.1 & 95.5
349 W. Commercial St., Ste. 2695   Phone: (716)586-2263
East Rochester, NY 14445   Fax: (716)586-0098

ELMIRA

2765 WECW-FM - 95.5
Elmira College
Elmira, NY 14901   Phone: (607)735-1885

ELMSFORD

2766 Progress in Surface Science
Pergamon Press Inc.
395 Saw Mill River Rd.
Elmsford, NY 10523
Journal profiling research and findings in the field of surface science. **Frequency:** Monthly. **Cols./Page:** 1. **Col. Width:** 7 in. **Col. Depth:** 10 in. **Key Personnel:** Dr. Sydney G. Davison, Editor. **ISSN:** 0079-6816.
                                        Circulation: (Not Reported)
Advertising accepted; contact publisher for rates. **Additional Contact Information:** Editor's address: Dr. Sydney G. Davison, University of Waterloo, Applied Mathematics Dept., Waterloo, ON, Canada N2L 2G1; Phone (519)888-4533, fax (519)746-6530.

2767 Reproductive and Genetic Engineering
Pergamon Press/Maxwell House
Farfield Park   Phone: (914)345-6425
Elmsford, NY 10523   Fax: (914)592-3625
Former Title:

Ad Rates: GLR = general line rate; BW = one-time black & white page rate; 4C = one-time four color page rate; SAU = standard advertising unit rate; CNU = Canadian newspaper advertising unit rate; PCI = per column inch rate.
Circulation: ★ = ABC; △ = BPA; ◆ = CAC; ● = CCAB; □ = VAC; ⊕ = PO Statement; ‡ = Publisher's Report; Boldface figures = sworn; Light figures = estimated.
Entry type: ◫ = Print; ♣ = Broadcast.

187

📖 **2768 Spectrochimica Acta**
Pergamon Press
395 Saw Mill River Rd.
Elmsford, NY 10523
Professional journal providing manuscripts on experimental and theoretical aspects of molecular spectroscopy and its application in chemical problems. **Subtitle:** Part A: Molecular Spectrocopsy. **Founded:** 1939. **Frequency:** Monthly. **Key Personnel:** Prof. Jeffrey Steinfeld, Editor. **ISSN:** 0584-8539. **Subscription:** $895 institutions.
　　　　　　　　　　　　　　　　Circulation: (Not Reported)
Additional Contact Information: Editorial address Dept. of Chemistry, Massachusetts Institute of Technology, Cambridge, MA 02139; phone (617)253-4525, fax (617)253-7030.

FAIRPORT

📖 **2769 Fairport Perinton Herald Mail**
A & P Publishing Co.
PO Box 506　　　　　　　　　**Phone: (716)264-4690**
Pittsford, NY 14534　　　　　　**Fax: (716)264-9779**

FARMINGDALE

📖 **2770 Electronics Now**
Gernsback Publications, Inc.
500-B Bi-County Blvd.　　　　　Phone: (516)293-3000
Farmingdale, NY 11735　　　　　Fax: (516)293-3115
Former Title: Radio-Electronics

FAYETTEVILLE

📖 **2771 Fayetteville Eagle-Bulletin**
Eagle Newspapers
Box 65　　　　　　　　　　　　Phone: (315)637-3121
Fayetteville, NY 13066　　　　　Fax: (315)637-3124

FLORAL PARK

📖 **2772 The Gateway**
PO Box 227
Floral Park, NY 11002　　　　　Phone: (516)775-2700

FLUSHING

⚓ **2773 American Cablevision of Queens**
4161 Kissena Blvd.　　　　　　Phone: (718)358-0900
Flushing, NY 11355-3189　　　　Fax: (718)204-8578
Owner: American TV & Communications Corp. **Founded:** 1986. **Cities Served:** Queens County, Astoria, Corona, East Elmhurst, Glendale, Jackson Heights, Long Island City, Maspeth, Middle Village, Ridgewood, and Woodside, NY.

⚓ **2774 Brooklyn-Queens Cable TV**
4161 Kissena Blvd.　　　　　　Phone: (718)463-4100
Flushing, NY 11355-3189　　　　Fax: (718)961-5120
Owner: Warner Cable Communications. **Founded:** 1985. **Cities Served:** Kings County, Nassau County, Queens County, Auburndale, Bay Ridge, Bay Terrace, Bayside, Beechhurst, Bellerose, Boerum Hill, Bowne Park, Briarwood, Brooklyn Heights, Brookville, Cambria Heights, Carrol Gardens, Clearview, Clinton Hill, Cobble Hill, College Hill, Douglaston, Dyker Heights, East Flushing, Farragut, Floral Park, Flushing, Flushing South, Forest Hills, Fort Greene, Fresh Meadows, Glen Oaks, Gowanus, Greenpoint, Hillcrest, Hollis, Jamaica, Jamaica Hills, Laurelton, Linden Hill, Little Neck, Malba, Murray Hill, New Hyde Park, Oakland Gardens, Pomonok, Queens Village, Queensboro Hill, Rego Park, Rosedale, South Brooklyn, Springfield Gardens, Sunset Park, Utopia, Whitestone, Willets Point, and Williamsburg, NY.

FOREST HILLS

📖 **2775 Nursing Abstracts**
Nursing Abstracts Co., Inc.
PO Box 295
Forest Hills, NY 11375　　　　　**Fax: (718)268-8872**

FULTON

📖 **2776 The Valley Shopper**
Fulton Newspapers, Inc.
2nd and Oneida Sts.
Fulton, NY 13069　　　　　　　Phone: (315)598-6397

GENEVA

⚓ **2777 Cablevision Industries, Inc.**
3518 Sutton Rd.
Geneva, NY 14456　　　　　　　Fax: (315)253-2455
Owner: Cablevision Industries, Inc. **Founded:** 1972. **Cities Served:** Ontario and Seneca counties, NY. **Additional Contact Information:** Toll-free: 800-253-2455.

GLEN FALLS

⚓ **2778 WBZA-AM - 1230**
Everts Ave.
Box 928
Glen Falls, NY 12801　　　　　Phone: (518)792-2151
Format: Middle-of-the-Road (MOR). **Network(s):** Mutual Broadcasting System. **Owner:** Northway Broadcasting Inc. **Founded:** 1986. **Operating Hours:** Continuous. **Key Personnel:** Clay Ashworth, Gen. Mgr.; Janey Ashworth, Operations Mgr.; Steve Willet, Program Dir.; Debbie Hoy, News Dir. **Wattage:** 1000. **Ad Rates:** $30 per unit.

GLENMONT

📖 **2779 Professional Insurance Agents**
PIA Management Services Inc.
25 Chamberlain St.
PO Box 997　　　　　　　　　Phone: (518)434-3111
Glenmont, NY 12077-0997　　　Fax: (518)434-2342

GRAND ISLAND

⚓ **2780 WHLD-AM - 1270**
2692 Staley Rd.　　　　　　　Phone: (716)773-1270
Grand Island, NY 14072　　　　**Fax: (716)773-1498**

GREAT NECK

📖 **2781 Making It! Careers Newsmagazine**
Workstyles, Inc.
5 Rose Ave.
Great Neck, NY 11021　　　　　Phone: (516)829-8829

GREENE

📖 **2782 Chenango American, Whitney Point Reporter, and Oxford Review Times**
PO Box 566　　　　　　　　　Phone: (607)656-4511
Greene, NY 13778　　　　　　　**Fax: (607)563-7118**

HAMBURG

📖 **2783 Hamburg Penny Saver**
H & K Publications, Inc.
50 Buffalo St.　　　　　　　　Phone: (716)649-4413
Hamburg, NY 14075　　　　　　**Fax: (716)649-6374**

HAUPPAUGE

⚓ **2784 Cablevision Systems Corp.**
1600 Motor Pkwy.
Box 1600　　　　　　　　　　Phone: (516)348-6800
Hauppauge, NY 11788　　　　　Fax: (516)348-6872
Owner: Cablevision Systems Corp. **Founded:** 1966. **Cities Served:** Suffolk County, NY.

HAWTHORNE

📖 **2785 Fairfield County Business Journal**
Westfair Communications, Inc.
22 Saw Mill River Rd.　　　　　**Phone: (914)347-5200**
Hawthorne, NY 10532　　　　　**Fax: (914)347-5576**

◫ **2786 International Journal of Cultural Property**
Walter de Gruyter, Inc.
200 Saw Mill River Rd.
Hawthorne, NY 10532
Journal covering all disciplines which concern cultural property.
Founded: 1992. **Frequency:** Quarterly. **Printing Method:** Photo typeset.
Trim Size: 6 1/2 x 9 1/2. **Key Personnel:** Prof. Norman E. Palmer,
Editor-in-Chief. **ISSN:** 0940-7391. **Subscription:** $138.
Circulation: (Not Reported)

◫ **2787 Westchester County Business Journal**
Westfair Communications, Inc.
22 Saw Mill River Rd.   **Phone:** (914)347-5200
Hawthorne, NY 10532   **Fax:** (914)347-5576

HORNELL

◫ **2788 Stamps Auction News**
American Publishing Co.
85 Canisteo St.   **Phone:** (607)324-2212
Hornell, NY 14843   **Fax:** (607)324-1753
Financial journal of the stamp market. **Frequency:** Monthly. **Printing
Method:** Web offset. **Trim Size:** 8 x 10 3/4. **Cols./Page:** 4. **Col. Width:**
6 3/4 in. **Col. Depth:** 10 in. **Key Personnel:** Denise Axtell, Editor; John
MicGlire, Publisher; Cathi Kenton, Advertising Mgr. **Subscription:**
$29. $4 single issue.
Ad Rates: BW: $220   **Circulation:** Paid ‡750
              4C: $470   Non-paid ‡500
              PCI: $9.50

♣ **2789 WLEA-AM - 1480**
RD, No. 1   **Phone:** (607)324-1480
Hornell, NY 14843   **Fax:** (607)324-5415

ITHACA

◫ **2790 The Cornell Hotel and Restaurant Administration
Quarterly**
Cornell School of Hotel Administration
Statler Hall   **Phone:** (607)255-5093
Ithaca, NY 14853   **Fax:** (607)257-1204

◫ **2791 Ithaca Pennysaver**
Tri-Village Pennysaver, Inc.
15 Geneva St.
PO Box 416   **Phone:** (607)273-1611
Interlaken, NY 14847   **Fax:** (607)273-6248

◫ **2792 Philosophical Review**
Sage School of Philosophy
Cornell University
327 Goldwin Smith Hall   **Phone:** (607)255-6817
Ithaca, NY 14853-3201   **Fax:** (607)255-1454

♣ **2793 American Community Cablevision**
519 W. State St.   **Phone:** (607)272-3456
Ithaca, NY 14850   **Fax:** (607)277-5404
Owner: Time Warner Cable. **Founded:** 1952. **Cities Served:** Tiaga and
Tompkins counties.

♣ **2794 WHCU-AM - 870**
1751 Hanshaw Rd.   **Phone:** (607)257-6400
Ithaca, NY 14850   **Fax:** (607)257-6497

♣ **2795 WVIV-FM - 105.9**
Roy H. Parks School of
  Communication
Ithaca College
Ithaca, NY 14850   **Phone:** (607)274-1040
Format: Album-Oriented Rock (AOR) (heavy metal). **Ad Rates:**
Noncommercial.

♣ **2796 WYXL-FM - 97.3**
1751 Hanshaw Rd.   **Phone:** (607)257-6400
Ithaca, NY 14850   **Fax:** (607)257-6497

JAMAICA

◫ **2797 Airport Press**
P.A.T.I., Inc.
PO Box 879   **Phone:** (718)244-6788
Jamaica, NY 11430-0879   **Fax:** (718)995-3432

JAMESTOWN

◫ **2798 The Post-Journal**
15 W. 20
Box 190   **Phone:** (716)487-1111
Jamestown, NY 14701   **Fax:** (716)664-3119

JOHNSTOWN

♣ **2799 WIZR-AM - 930**
178 E. State St.
PO Box 146   **Phone:** (518)762-4631
Johnstown, NY 12095   **Fax:** (518)762-0105

♣ **2800 WSRD-FM - 104.9**
178 E. State St.
PO Box 146   **Phone:** (518)762-4631
Johnstown, NY 12095   **Fax:** (518)762-0105

KINGSTON

♣ **2801 WBPM-FM - 94.3**
82 John St.   **Phone:** (914)331-8200
Kingston, NY 12401   **Fax:** (914)331-8292

♣ **2802 WGHQ-AM - 920**
82 John St.
PO Box 1880   **Phone:** (914)331-8200
Kingston, NY 12401   **Fax:** (914)321-8292

LAKE PLACID

◫ **2803 The Lake Placid News**
Ogden Newspapers, Inc.
Mill Hill, Box 111   **Phone:** (518)523-4401
Lake Placid, NY 12946   **Fax:** (518)523-1351

♣ **2804 WIRD-AM - 920**
PO Box 831   **Phone:** (518)523-3341
Lake Placid, NY 12946   **Fax:** (518)523-1349

♣ **2805 WLPW-FM - 105.5**
PO Box 831   **Phone:** (518)523-3341
Lake Placid, NY 12946   **Fax:** (518)523-1349

LANCASTER

♣ **2806 WXRL-AM - 1300**
PO Box 170
5426 William St.
Lancaster, NY 14086   **Phone:** (716)681-1313

LEWISBORO

◫ **2807 The Lewisboro Ledger**
Acorn Press, Inc.
PO Box 188   **Phone:** (914)763-8821
Cross River, NY 10518   **Fax:** (203)438-3395

LEWISTON

◫ **2808 The Scottish Banner**
755 Center St.   **Phone:** (716)754-4507
Lewiston, NY 14092   **Fax:** (716)754-9020

Ad Rates: GLR = general line rate; BW = one-time black & white page rate; 4C = one-time four color page rate; SAU = standard advertising unit rate;
CNU = Canadian newspaper advertising unit rate; PCI = per column inch rate.
Circulation: ★ = ABC; △ = BPA; ♦ = CAC; ● = CCAB; □ = VAC; ⊕ = PO Statement; ‡ = Publisher's Report; Boldface figures = sworn; Light figures = estimated.
Entry type: ◫ = Print; ♣ = Broadcast.

LIVERPOOL

📖 **2809 The Review**
The Eagle Newspapers
7-9-11 Genesee St.
PO Box 270
Baldwinsville, NY 13027   Phone: (315)635-3921
                                 Fax: (315)635-3914

🎤 **2810 WRHP-FM - 107.9**
620 Old Liverpool Rd.   Phone: (315)457-6110
Liverpool, NY 13088   **Fax: (315)457-1610**

LOCUST VALLEY

📖 **2811 Leader**
Locust Valley Publishing Co., Inc.
160 Birch Hill Rd.
PO Box 468   Phone: (516)676-1434
Locust Valley, NY 11560   **Fax: (516)671-7442**

LOUDONVILLE

📖 **2812 The Promethean**
Siena College
                     Phone: (518)783-2560
Loudonville, NY 12211   **Fax: (518)783-2493**

MAMARONECK

🎤 **2813 UAE**
609 Center Ave.   Phone: (914)899-9000
Mamaroneck, NY 10543   Fax: (914)381-5650
Owner: Tele-Communications, Inc. **Founded:** 1977. **Cities Served:** Westchester County, NY.

MANHASSET

📖 **2814 Journal of Substance Abuse Treatment**
North Shore University Hospital
Cornell University Medical College
400 Community Dr.   Phone: (516)562-3015
Manhasset, NY 11030   Fax: (516)562-3996
Medical journal. **Founded:** 1984. **Frequency:** 6x/yr. **Printing Method:** Offset. **Trim Size:** 8 1/2 x 11. **Key Personnel:** John E. Imhof, Ph.D, Editor-in-Chief. **ISSN:** 0740-5472. **Subscription:** $110; $219 institutions.
                 Circulation: (Not Reported)
Advertising accepted; contact publisher for rates. Published by Pergamon Press.

📖 **2815 Tour & Travel News**
CMP Publications, Inc.
600 Community Dr.   **Phone: (516)562-5000**
Manhasset, NY 11030   Fax: (516)562-5472

📖 **2816 Windows**
CMP Publications
600 Community Dr.   Phone: (516)562-5000
Manhasset, NY 11030-3847   Fax: (516)562-5101
Magazine on Windows software. **Subtitle:** The World's Number One Source of Windows Information. **Founded:** 1990. **Frequency:** Monthly. **Trim Size:** 8 x 10 3/4. **Key Personnel:** E. Drake Lundell, Publishing Dir.; Frederic S. Langa, Editorial Dir.; Scott Wolf, Publisher; David Dix, Sr. Editor; Mike Elgan, Mng. Editor. **Subscription:** $24.94. $2.95 single issue; $3.95 single issue Canada.
Ad Rates: BW: $11,000   **Circulation:** ‡275,000
           4C: $13,975
Formerly: OS/2 Magazine; OS/2 and Windows Magazine; Windows and OS/2; Windows Magazine.

MARYKNOLL

📖 **2817 Maryknoll Magazine**
Maryknoll Fathers and Brothers
                 Phone: (914)941-7590
Maryknoll, NY 10545   **Fax: (914)945-0670**

MASSAPEQUA

📖 **2818 New York Update**
M.M.B. Inc.
5550 Merrick Rd.
Massapequa, NY 11758-6216
Magazine featuring stories about people in the film and music industry. **Frequency:** Monthly. **Key Personnel:** Cheryl Meglio, Editor; Steve Marshall, Publisher. SBR $20. $2.25 single issue.
                 Circulation: (Not Reported)

MEDINA

📖 **2819 Medina Daily Journal-Register–Eastern Niagara Edition**
Medina Daily Journal-Register, Inc.
409-13 Main St.   Phone: (716)798-1400
Medina, NY 14103   Fax: (716)798-0290
Community newspaper. **Founded:** 1976. **Frequency:** Weekly. **Printing Method:** Offset. **Cols./Page:** 6. **Col. Width:** 2 in. **Col. Depth:** 21 in. **Key Personnel:** Owen Toale, Gen. Mgr.; Greg Kerth, Advertising Mgr. **Subscription:** Free.
Ad Rates: BW: $201.60   **Circulation:** Free 2,300
           PCI: $1.60

📖 **2820 Medina Penny Saver**
Medina Daily Journal-Register, Inc.
409-13 Main St.   Phone: (716)798-0290
Medina, NY 14103   Fax: (716)798-0290
Shopping guide. **Frequency:** Weekly. **Printing Method:** Offset. **Cols./Page:** 5. **Col. Width:** 2 in. **Col. Depth:** 13 in. **Key Personnel:** Owen Toale, Gen. Mgr.; Greg Kerth, Advertising Mgr. **Subscription:** Free.
Ad Rates: BW: $291.85   **Circulation:** Free 13,800
           PCI: $4.49

MIDDLETOWN

🎤 **2821 CVI-Cablevision Industries**
25 Industrial Dr.   Phone: (914)692-6794
Middletown, NY 10940   Fax: (914)692-0778
Owner: Cablevision Industries, Inc., Wierk Ave., Liberty, NY 12754; (914)292-7550. **Founded:** 1956. **Key Personnel:** William V. Jensen, Gen. Mgr. **Cities Served:** Blooming Grove, Crawford, Deerpark, Gardiner, Goshen, Hamptonburgh, Highland, Lloyd, Montgomery, Mount Hope, New Paltz, Newburgh, Plattekill, Walkill, Bloomingburg, Goshen, Highland Falls, Maybrook, Otisville, Walden, Washingtonville, Wurtsboro, Middletown, Port Jervis, and West Point, NY: 47,500 subscribing households; 37 channels; 3 community access channels; 272 hours per week of community access programming. **Additional Contact Information:** Toll-free: 800-431-8878.

MOUNT KISCO

🎤 **2822 WVIP-FM - 106.3**
Radio Circle
Mount Kisco, NY 10549   Phone: (914)241-1310
                 Fax: (914)666-7508

NANUET

🎤 **2823 TKR Cable Co. of Rockland**
25 Smith St.   Phone: (914)624-8200
Nanuet, NY 10945   Fax: (914)623-5619
Owner: TKR Cable Co. **Founded:** 1980. **Key Personnel:** Jim Helfgott, Gen. Mgr.; Frank LoBueno, Program Mgr.; Kevin Hewitt, Technical Mgr.; Laura Bachat, Marketing Mgr.; Kathie Farrington, Customer Service Mgr.; Sharon Francis, Community Relations Mgr.; Lucille Celli, Business Mgr. **Cities Served:** Rockland County, NY and Montvale, NJ: 45,000 subscribing households; 54 channels; 3 community access channel; 20 hours per week of community access programming.

NEW PALTZ

📖 **2824 The Oracle**
State University College
Sub. 419
New Paltz, NY 12561   **Phone: (914)257-3030**
                 Fax: (914)257-3031

🎙 2825 WFNP-FM - 88.7
State University of New York
SUB, Rm. 413   Phone: (914)257-3099
New Paltz, NY 12561   Fax: (914(257-3099

NEW WINDSOR

📖 2826 Schoolmates
United States Chess Federation
186 Rt. 9 W.   Phone: (914)562-8350
New Windsor, NY 12550   Fax: (914)561-2437
Chess for youth. **Founded:** 1985. **Frequency:** Bimonthly. **ISSN:** 1040-7707. **Subscription:** $7; $12 Canada; $15.12 Canada airmail; $22 other countries; $14 two years; $19 two years Canada; $22.12 two years Canada airmail; $29 two years other countries. $2.25 single issue.

                                      Circulation: (Not Reported)

NEW YORK

📖 2827 A. Magazine
Metro East Publications, Inc.
296 Elizabeth St., Ste. 2F   Phone: (212)505-1416
New York, NY 10012   Fax: (212)505-2077
Magazine reporting on Asian American life, culture, and art. **Subtitle:** The Asian American Quarterly. **Founded:** 1992. **Frequency:** Quarterly. **Printing Method:** Web offset. **Trim Size:** 8 1/8 x 10 7/8. **Key Personnel:** Phoebe Eng, Publisher; Jeff Yang, Editor-in-Chief. **Subscription:** $10. $3 single issue.

                                      Circulation: 20,000

Advertising accepted; contact publisher for rates.

📖 2828 Access! Manhattan
PO Box 319, Gracie Sta.
New York, NY 10028   Phone: (212)737-9358
Guide to Manhattan's public access cable TV. **Founded:** 1991. **Frequency:** 6x/yr. **Printing Method:** Offset. **Trim Size:** 8 1/2 x 11. **Cols./Page:** 2. **Col. Width:** 3 1/2 in. **Col. Depth:** 10 in. **Key Personnel:** L. French, Editor and Publisher. **Subscription:** $12. $1.50 single issue.
Ad Rates: BW: $500   **Circulation:** (Not Reported)
Color advertising not accepted.

📖 2829 Accounting Today
425 Park Ave.   Phone: (212)756-5155
New York, NY 10022   Fax: (212)756-5175
Business magazine profiling the tax and accounting industries. **Founded:** 1987. **Frequency:** 2x/mo. **Subscription:** $69. $4.50 single issue.

                          Circulation: Paid △25,000
                                      Non-paid △5,000

Advertising accepted; contact publisher for rates.

📖 2830 ACM Computing Surveys
Assn. for Computing Machinery
1515 Broadway, 17th Fl.   Phone: (212)869-7440
New York, NY 10036-9998   Fax: (212)944-1318

📖 2831 ACM Transactions on Database Systems
Assn. for Computing Machinery
1515 Broadway, 17th Fl.   Phone: (212)869-7440
New York, NY 10036   Fax: (212)944-1318

📖 2832 ACM Transactions on Graphics
Assn. for Computing Machinery
1515 Broadway, 17th Fl.   Phone: (212)869-7440
New York, NY 10036-9998   Fax: (212)944-1318

📖 2833 ACM Transactions on Information Systems
Assn. for Computing Machinery
1515 Broadway, 17th Fl.   Phone: (212)869-7440
New York, NY 10036-9998   Fax: (212)944-1318

📖 2834 ACM Transactions on Mathematical Software
Assn. for Computing Machinery
1515 Broadway, 17th Fl.   Phone: (212)869-7440
New York, NY 10036-9998   Fax: (212)944-1318

📖 2835 ACM Transactions on Programming Languages and Systems
Assn. for Computing Machinery
1515 Broadway, 17th Fl.   Phone: (212)869-7440
New York, NY 10036-9998   Fax: (212)944-1318

📖 2836 Acoustical Physics
American Institute of Physics
335 E. 45th St.   Phone: (516)576-2460
New York, NY 10017   Fax: (516)576-2488
Former Title: Soviet Physics-Acoustics

📖 2837 Across the Board
The Conference Board, Inc.
845 3rd Ave.   Phone: (212)339-0451
New York, NY 10022   Fax: (212)980-7014

📖 2838 Advertising Age
Crain Communications, Inc.
220 E. 42nd St.   Phone: (212)210-0168
New York, NY 10017   Fax: (212)210-0111

📖 2839 Afn Shvel
League for Yiddish, Inc.
200 W. 72nd St., Ste. 40   Phone: (212)787-6675
New York, NY 10023   Fax: (212)769-2820

📖 2840 AICHE Journal
American Insitute of Chemical Engineers
345 E. 47th St.   Phone: (212)705-7649
New York, NY 10017   Fax: (212)752-3294
Journal with articles on chemical engineering research and development, stressing the immediate and potential values in engineering. **Subtitle:** Chemical Engineering Research and Development. **Founded:** 1955. **Frequency:** Monthly. **Trim Size:** 10 3/4 x 8. **Cols./Page:** 2. **Col. Width:** 20 picas. **Col. Depth:** 56 picas. **Key Personnel:** Dr. Matthew V. Tirrell, Editor; Haeja L. Han, Mng. Editor. **ISSN:** 0001-1541. **Subscription:** $60 members; $349 non-members. $35 single issue.
Ad Rates: BW: $790   **Circulation:** Paid ‡3,300
                                      Controlled ‡3,950

📖 2841 Alzheimer Disease and Associated Disorders
Raven Press
1185 Avenue of the Americas
Mail Stop 3B   Phone: (212)930-9500
New York, NY 10036   Fax: (212)869-3495
An international forum for groundbreaking advances in basic science and clinical research of Alzheimer's Disease. **Founded:** 1987. **Frequency:** Quarterly. **Printing Method:** Sheetfed offset. **Trim Size:** 6 7/8 x 10. **Key Personnel:** Rita Scheman, Publisher; Antoinette Cimino, Editorial Mgr.; Phyllis C. Noyes, Advertising Mgr. **Subscription:** $82; $100 other countries; $105 institutions; $125 institutions other countries. $32 single issue.
Ad Rates: BW: $650   **Circulation:** 1,000
               4C: $750
A Wolters Kluwer Company.

📖 2842 American Country Collectibles
GCR Publishing Group, Inc.
1700 Broadway
New York, NY 10019
Magazine featuring how, where, and which collectibles to buy. **Frequency:** Quarterly. **Key Personnel:** Charles Goodman, Publisher; Florine McCain, Editor. **Subscription:** $3.50 single issue.
                                      Circulation: (Not Reported)

2843 American Journal of Clinical Oncology
Raven Press
1185 Avenue of the Americas
Mail Stop 3B   Phone: (212)930-9500
New York, NY 10036   Fax: (212)869-3495
Journal covering ongoing research in cancer treatment. **Founded:** 1978. **Frequency:** Bimonthly. **Printing Method:** Web offset. **Trim Size:** 8 1/4 x 10 7/8. **Key Personnel:** Rita Scheman, Publisher; Luther W. Brady, M.D., Editor-in-Chief; Phyllis C. Noyes, Advertising Mgr. **Subscription:** $124; $156 other countries; $158 institutions; $198 institutions other countries. $33 single issue.
Ad Rates: BW: $795   **Circulation:** 2,500
              4C: $1,055
A Wolters Kluwer Company.

2844 The American Journal of Dermatopathology
Raven Press
1185 Avenue of the Americas
Mail Stop 3B   Phone: (212)930-9500
New York, NY 10036   Fax: (212)869-3495
Journal offering state-of-the-art coverage of the rapid progress in studying skin diseases. **Subtitle:** Official Publication of the Society for Dermatopathology. **Founded:** 1979. **Frequency:** Bimonthly. **Trim Size:** 8 1/4 x 11. **Key Personnel:** Rita Scheman, Publisher; Clifton R. White, Jr. M.D., Editor-in-Chief; Phyllis C. Noyes, Advertising Mgr. **Subscription:** $124; $161 other countries; $168 institutions; $205 institutions other countries. $34 single issue.
Ad Rates: BW: $785   **Circulation:** 2,500
              4C: $900
A Wolters Kluwer Company.

2845 The American Journal of Forensic Medicine and Pathology
Raven Press
1185 Avenue of the Americas
Mail Stop 3B   Phone: (212)930-9500
New York, NY 10036   Fax: (212)869-3495
Journal presenting up-to-date coverage of forensic medical practices worldwide. **Subtitle:** Official Publication of the National Association of Medical Examiners. **Founded:** 1980. **Frequency:** Quarterly. **Printing Method:** Sheetfed offset. **Trim Size:** 8 1/4 x 11. **Key Personnel:** Rita Scheman, Publisher; Vincent J.M. DiMaio, M.D., Editor-in-Chief; Phyllis C. Noyes, Advertising Mgr. **Subscription:** $116; $150 other countries; $160 institutions; $198 institutions other countries. $50 single issue.
Ad Rates: BW: $800   **Circulation:** 2,500
              4C: $995
A Wolters Kluwer Company.

2846 The American Journal of Pediatric Hematology/ Oncology
Raven Press
1185 Avenue of the Americas
Mail Stop 3B   Phone: (212)930-9500
New York, NY 10036   Fax: (212)869-3495
Journal with reports on major advances in the diagnosis and treatment of cancer and blood diseases in children. **Subtitle:** Official Publication of the American Society of Pediatric Hematology/Oncology. **Founded:** 1979. **Frequency:** Quarterly. **Printing Method:** Sheetfed offset. **Trim Size:** 8 1/4 x 11. **Key Personnel:** Rita Scheman, Publisher; Carl Pochedly, M.D., Editor-in-Chief; Phyllis C. Noyes, Advertising Mgr. **Subscription:** $116; $150 other countries; $160 institutions; $198 institutions other countries. $50 single issue.
                              Circulation: (Not Reported)
A Wolters Kluwer Company.

2847 The American Patriot
Proud Publishing Co. Inc.
475 Park Ave. S., Ste. 2201
New York, NY 10016
Magazine reporting on all aspects of the U.S. military. **Frequency:** Quarterly. **Key Personnel:** Ted Newson, Editor; David Zenter, Publisher. **Subscription:** $2.95 single issue.
                              Circulation: (Not Reported)

2848 American Voice
Kentucky Foundation for Women
The Waldorf Astoria
301 Park Ave.   Phone: (212)755-2539
New York, NY 10022   Fax: (212)755-2539
Journal containing fiction, poetry, essays, and photographs. **Frequency:** Quarterly.
                              Circulation: (Not Reported)

2849 Analog Science Fiction & Fact
Dell Magazines
380 Lexington Ave.   **Phone: (212)856-6400**
New York, NY 10168-0035   **Fax: (212)697-1567**

2850 Annals of Epidemiology
Elsevier Science Publishing Co. Inc.
655 Avenue of the Americas   Phone: (212)989-5800
New York, NY 10010   Fax: (212)633-3990
Subtitle: Official Journal of the American College of Epidemiology. **Founded:** 1990. **Frequency:** 6x/yr. **Printing Method:** Offset. **Trim Size:** 8 1/4 x 11. **Cols./Page:** 2. **Key Personnel:** Julie Buring, Editor; Charles Hennekens, Editor. **ISSN:** 1047-2729. **Subscription:** $195 institutions; $225 other countries.
Ad Rates: BW: $625   **Circulation:** Paid 1,100
              4C: $995   Non-paid 100

2851 The Annals of Thoracic Surgery
Elsevier Science Publishing Co., Inc.
655 Avenue of the Americas   Phone: (212)633-3977
New York, NY 10010   **Fax: (212)633-3820**

2852 Art & Antiques
919 3rd Ave.   **Phone: (212)752-5557**
New York, NY 10022   **Fax: (212)752-7147**

2853 Arthroscopy
Raven Press
1185 Avenue of the Americas
Mail Stop 3B   Phone: (212)930-9500
New York, NY 10036   Fax: (212)869-3495
Journal exploring the current trends and latest innovations in both diagnostic and operative arthroscopy. **Subtitle:** Official Journal of the Arthroscopy Association of North America and the International Arthroscopy Association. **Founded:** 1985. **Frequency:** Quarterly. **Printing Method:** Sheetfed offset. **Trim Size:** 8 1/4 x 11. **Key Personnel:** Rita Scheman, Publisher; Gary G. Poehling, M.D., Editor-in-Chief; Phyllis C. Noyes, Advertising Mgr. **Subscription:** $118; $155 other countries; $160 institutions; $200 institutions other countries. $50 single issue.
Ad Rates: BW: $935   **Circulation:** 6,500
              4C: $1,410
A Wolters Kluwer Company.

2854 Astronomy Reports
American Institute of Physics
335 E. 45th St.   Phone: (516)576-2460
New York, NY 10017   **Fax: (516)576-2488**
Former Title: Soviet Astronomy

2855 Auditions U.S.A.
The King Network
150 5th Ave.
New York, NY 10011   Phone: (212)645-8400
Journal providing audition information for people in show business. **Founded:** 1992. **Frequency:** Monthly. **Trim Size:** 11 x 17. **Cols./Page:** 4. **Key Personnel:** John King, Publisher. **Subscription:** $10 for 14 issues. $2 single issue.
Ad Rates: BW: $1,000   **Circulation:** Paid ‡80,000
              4C: $1,800   Non-paid ‡25,000
              PCI: $35

2856 Bank Technology News
Faulkner & Gray, Inc.
11 Penn Plaza   **Phone: (212)967-7000**
New York, NY 10001   **Fax: (212)467-7155**
Former Title: Bank New Product News

2857 Banking Law Review
Faulkner & Gray, Inc.
106 Fulton St., Ste. 200   Phone: (212)766-5794
New York, NY 10038   Fax: (212)406-8131
Ceased publication.

2858 Beverage Media
161 Avenue of the Americas   Phone: (212)620-0100
New York, NY 10013   Fax: (212)620-0473

2859 Body Fashions/Intimate Apparel (BFIA)
Advanstar Communications
270 Madison Ave.   Phone: (212)951-6600
New York, NY 10016   Fax: (212)481-6563

2860 Breakthrough
Global Education Associates
475 Riverside Dr., Ste. 1848   Phone: (212)870-3290
New York, NY 10115   Fax: (212)870-2055
Journal. **Frequency:** Periodic.

Circulation: (Not Reported)

2861 Business & Society Review
200 W. 57th St., 15th Fl.   Phone: (212)399-1088
New York, NY 10019   Fax: (212)245-1973

2862 Butterick Make It!
Butterick Company, Inc.
161 6th Ave.   Phone: (212)620-2500
New York, NY 10013   Fax: (212)620-2746
Magazine designed to inspire creativity in the fashion industry.
Frequency: Quarterly. **Key Personnel:** Barbara Fimbel, Editor; Art
Joinnides, Publisher. **Subscription:** $9.95. $2.95 single issue.
Circulation: (Not Reported)
Advertising accepted; contact publisher for rates.

2863 Car Stereo Review
Hachette Magazines, Inc.
1633 Broadway, 45th Fl.   Phone: (212)767-6020
New York, NY 10019   Fax: (212)767-5615

2864 Casting News
The King Network
150 5th Ave   Phone: (212)645-8400
New York, NY 10011   Fax: (212)674-4002
Trade magazine featuring news of television, film, print, video,
fashion and stage castings. **Founded:** 1991. **Frequency:** Monthly. **Trim
Size:** 11 x 17. **Cols./Page:** 6. **Key Personnel:** John King, Publisher.
Subscription: $35; $45 out of city.
Ad Rates: BW: $1,200   Circulation: Paid 10,000
              PCI: $35   Non-paid 8,000

2865 Cerebrovascular and Brain Metabolism Reviews
Raven Press
1185 Avenue of the Americas
Mail Stop 3B   Phone: (212)930-9500
New York, NY 10036   Fax: (212)869-3495
Journal that scrutinizes the clinical aspects of cerebrovascular disor-
ders, evaluates methods for assessing cerebral circulatory and brain
metablism changes, and details relevant progress in neuropharmacol-
ogy, neurophysiology, and neuropathology. **Founded:** 1989. **Frequency:**
Quarterly. **Printing Method:** Sheetfed offset. **Trim Size:** 6 7/8 x 10.
Key Personnel: Rita Scheman, Publisher; A. Murray Harper, M.D.,
Editor; Phyllis C. Noyes, Advertising Mgr. **Subscription:** $98; $120
other countries; $120 institutions; $145 institutions other countries.
$36 single issue.
Ad Rates: BW: $470   Circulation: 1,000
              4C: $650
A Wolters Kluwer Company.

2866 Chief Information Officer Journal
Faulkner & Gray, Inc.
11 Penn Plaza   Phone: (212)967-7000
New York, NY 10001   Fax: (212)967-7155

2867 CHILD
The New York Times Co. Women's Magazines
110 5th Ave., 3rd Fl.   Phone: (212)463-1000
New York, NY 10011   Fax: (212)463-1383

2868 Chinese Physics
American Institute of Physics
335 E. 45th St.   Phone: (516)576-2460
New York, NY 10017   Fax: (516)576-2488

2869 Chronobiology International
Raven Press
1185 Avenue of the Americas
Mail Stop 3B   Phone: (212)930-9500
New York, NY 10036   Fax: (212)869-3495
Subtitle: A Journal of Basic and Applied Biologial Rhythm Research.
Founded: 1984. **Frequency:** Bimonthly. **Printing Method:** Sheetfed
offset. **Trim Size:** 6 7/8 x 10. **Key Personnel:** Rita Scheman, Publisher;
Alain Reinberg, M.D., Ph.D., Editor; Michael Smolensky, Ph.D.,
Editor; Phyllis C. Noyes, Advertising Mgr. **Subscription:** $110; $129
other countries; $250 institutions; $281 institutions other countries.
$47 single issue.
Ad Rates: BW: $590   Circulation: 2,000
              4C: $800
A Wolters Kluwer Company.

2870 Civil War Chronicles
American Heritage, Inc.
Forbes Bldg.
60 5th Ave.
New York, NY 10010
Magazine chronicling the Civil War. **Frequency:** Quarterly. **Key
Personnel:** Richard Snow, Editor; Malcolm S. Forbes, Jr., Publisher.
Subscription: $10. $2.95 single issue.
Circulation: (Not Reported)

2871 The Clinical Journal of Pain
Raven Press
1185 Avenue of the Americas
Mail Stop 3B   Phone: (212)930-9500
New York, NY 10036   Fax: (212)869-3495
Journal presenting timely coverage of clinically relevant topics in pain
management with special emphasis on diagnostic and treatment of
dilemmas, pharmacologic management, and psychosocial aspects.
Subtitle: Official Journal of the American Academy of Pain Medicine.
Founded: 1985. **Frequency:** Quarterly. **Printing Method:** Sheetfed
offset. **Trim Size:** 8 1/4 x 11. **Key Personnel:** Rita Scheman, Publisher;
Peter Wilson, M.B., B.S., Ph.D., Editor; Phyllis C. Noyes, Advertising
Mgr. **Subscription:** $84; $105 other countries; $125 institutions; $150
institutions other countries. $38 single issue.
Ad Rates: BW: $840   Circulation: 2,500
              4C: $995
A Wolters Kluwer Company.

2872 Clinical Journal of Sport Medicine
Raven Press
1185 Avenue of the Americas
Mail Stop 3B   Phone: (212)930-9500
New York, NY 10036   Fax: (212)869-3495
Journal presenting expert clinical guidance and ongoing research
activities in the diagnosis, treatment, and rehabilitation of sport- and
exercise-related injuries. **Founded:** 1991. **Frequency:** Quarterly. **Print-
ing Method:** Sheetfed offset. **Trim Size:** 8 1/4 x 11. **Key Personnel:**
Rita Scheman, Publisher; Gordon O. Matheson, M.D., Ph.D., Editor-
in-Chief; Phyllis C. Noyes, Advertising Mgr. **Subscription:** $85; $95
other countries; $100 institutions; $132 institutions other countries.
$33 single issue.
Ad Rates: BW: $750   Circulation: 2,000
              4C: $1,010
A Wolters Kluwer Company.

Ad Rates: GLR = general line rate; BW = one-time black & white page rate; 4C = one-time four color page rate; SAU = standard advertising unit rate;
CNU = Canadian newspaper advertising unit rate; PCI = per column inch rate.
Circulation: ★ = ABC; △ = BPA; ◆ = CAC; ● = CCAB; □ = VAC; ⊕ = PO Statement; ‡ = Publisher's Report; Boldface figures = sworn; Light figures = estimated.
Entry type: ▢ = Print; ▮ = Broadcast.

193

📖 **2873 Clinical Neuropharmacology**
Raven Press
1185 Avenue of the Americas
Mail Stop 3B   Phone: (212)930-9500
New York, NY 10036   Fax: (212)869-3495
Journal featuring both classic neurologic disorders as well as those disorders often called psychiatric. **Founded:** 1978. **Frequency:** Bimonthly. **Printing Method:** Sheetfed offset. **Trim Size:** 6 7/8 x 10. **Key Personnel:** Rita Scheman, Publisher; Harold L. Klawans, M.D., Editor-in-Chief; Phyllis C. Noyes, Advertising Mgr. **Subscription:** $113; $146 other countries; $164 institutions; $199 institutions other countries. $33 single issue.
Ad Rates: BW: $565   **Circulation:** 1,500
              4C: $995
A Wolters Kluwer Company.

📖 **2874 The Collectors Club Philatelist**
22 E. 35th St.   Phone: (212)685-0559
New York, NY 10016-3806   **Fax: (212)481-1269**

📖 **2875 Conference Board Briefing Charts**
The Conference Board
845 3rd Ave   Phone: (212)399-0317
New York, NY 10022   Fax: (212)980-7014
Features chart studies. **Frequency:** Quarterly. **Trim Size:** 8 1/2 x 11. **Key Personnel:** Lucie Blau, Editor; Chuck Tow, Editor. **Subscription:** $100; $150 nonmember. $25 single issue; $37.50 nonmember single issue.
                                      Circulation: Paid 150
                                                   Non-paid 2
Advertising not accepted.

📖 **2876 Conservative Judaism**
The Rabbinical Assembly
3080 Broadway   Phone: (212)678-8060
New York, NY 10027   Fax: (212)749-9166

📖 **2877 Contemporary Management in Critical Care**
Churchill Livingstone, Inc.
1560 Broadway
New York, NY 10036   **Phone: (212)819-5400**
Ceased publication.

📖 **2878 Contemporary Management in Internal Medicine**
Churchill Livingstone, Inc.
1560 Broadway
New York, NY 10036   **Phone: (212)819-5400**
Ceased publication.

📖 **2879 Contemporary Management in Obstetrics and Gynecology**
Churchill Livingstone, Inc.
1560 Broadway
New York, NY 10036   **Phone: (212)819-5400**
Ceased publication.

📖 **2880 Contemporary Management in Otolaryngology**
Churchill Livingstone, Inc
1560 Broadway
New York, NY 10036   **Phone: (212)819-5400**
Ceased publication.

📖 **2881 The Contemporary Management Series**
Churchill Livingstone, Inc.
1560 Broadway
New York, NY 10036   **Phone: (212)819-5400**
Ceased publication.

📖 **2882 Convulsive Therapy**
Raven Press
1185 Avenue of the Americas
Mail Stop 3B   Phone: (212)930-9500
New York, NY 10036   Fax: (212)869-3495
Journal covering all aspects of contemporary ECT, reporting on major clinical and research developments worldwide. **Founded:** 1985. **Frequency:** Quarterly. **Printing Method:** Sheetfed offset. **Trim Size:** 6 7/8 x 10. **Key Personnel:** Rita Scheman, Publisher; Max Fink, M.D., Editor; Phyllis C. Noyes, Advertising Mgr. **Subscription:** $99; $125

other countries; $145 institutions; $175 institutions other countries. $44 single issue.
Ad Rates: BW: $635   **Circulation:** 1,000
              4C: $910
A Wolters Kluwer Company.

📖 **2883 Cornea**
Raven Press
1185 Avenue of the Americas
Mail Stop 3B   Phone: (212)930-9500
New York, NY 10036   Fax: (212)869-3495
Journal offering the latest clinical and basic researh on the cornea and the anterior segment of the eye. **Founded:** 1982. **Frequency:** Bimonthly. **Printing Method:** Sheetfed offset. **Trim Size:** 8 1/4 x 11. **Key Personnel:** Rita Scheman, Publisher; H. Dwight Cavanagh, M.D., Ph.D., Editor-in-Chief; Phyllis C. Noyes, Advertising Mgr. **Subscription:** $132; $170 other countries; $174 institutions; $212 institutions other countries. $35 single issue.
Ad Rates: BW: $800   **Circulation:** 1,500
              4C: $1,190
A Wolters Kluwer Company.

📖 **2884 Crime Beat**
54 Corporation
10 E. 39th St.   Phone: (212)683-1017
New York, NY 10016   Fax: (212)532-4428
Newsmagazine. **Founded:** 1991. **Frequency:** Monthly. **Trim Size:** 9 7/8 x 11. **Key Personnel:** T.E.D. Klein, Editor; Nils A. Shapiro, Publisher. **ISSN:** 1058-529X. **Subscription:** $19.95. $2.50 single issue.
Ad Rates: BW: $1,500   **Circulation:** 100,000
              4C: $2,000

📖 **2885 Crystallography Reports**
American Institute of Physics
335 E. 45th St.   Phone: (516)576-2460
New York, NY 10017   **Fax: (516)576-2488**
Former Title: Soviet Physics-Crystallography

📖 **2886 Curator**
American Museum of Natural History
Central Park W. at 79th St.   **Phone: (212)769-5500**
New York, NY 10024   Fax: (212)769-5511

📖 **2887 Current Literature in Family Planning**
Katharine Dexter McCormick Library
Planned Parenthood Federation of
   America.
810 7th Ave.   **Phone: (212)261-4637**
New York, NY 10019   Fax: (212)245-1845

📖 **2888 Designer Specifier**
North American Publishing Co.
322 8th Ave.   Phone: (212)620-7330
New York, NY 10001   Fax: (212)620-7335
Ceased publication.

📖 **2889 Development Business**
United Nations Div. for Economic and Social Information
1 United Nation Plaza
DCI Bldg., Rm. 560   Phone: (212)963-8065
New York, NY 10017   **Fax: (212)963-1381**

📖 **2890 Diagnostic Molecular Pathology**
Raven Press
1185 Avenue of the Americas
Mail Stop 3B   Phone: (212)930-9500
New York, NY 10036   Fax: (212)869-3495
Journal featuring practical reports on the use of molecular techniques for more accurate diagnosis and improved treatment recommendations in surgical pathology. **Founded:** 1991. **Frequency:** Quarterly. **Printing Method:** Sheetfed offset. **Trim Size:** 8 1/4 x 11. **Key Personnel:** Rita Scheman, Publisher; Ronald A. DeLellis, M.D., Editor-in-Chief; Hubert J. Wolfe, M.D., Editor-in-Chief; Phyllis C. Noyes, Advertising Mgr. **Subscription:** $75; $85 other countries; $85 institutions; $95 institutions other countries. $24 single issue.
Ad Rates: BW: $750   **Circulation:** 3,000
              4C: $920
A Wolters Kluwer Company.

⚏ 2891 Do It Yourself Hairstyles and Makeovers
GCR Publishing Group, Inc.
1700 Broadway
New York, NY 10019
Magazine. **Frequency:** Quarterly. **Key Personnel:** Florine McCain,
Editor; Charles Goodman, Publisher. **Subscription:** $3.50 single issue.
                              Circulation: (Not Reported)

⚏ 2892 Drug & Cosmetic Industry
Advanstar Communications, Inc.
270 Madison Ave.   **Phone: (212)951-6719**
New York, NY 10016   **Fax: (212)981-6562**

⚏ 2893 Editorials On File
Facts On File, Inc.
460 Park Ave. S.   **Phone: (212)683-2244**
New York, NY 10016   **Fax: (212)683-3633**

⚏ 2894 Elle
Hachette Magazines, Inc.
1633 Broadway   **Phone: (212)767-5800**
New York, NY 10019   **Fax: (2120489-4216**

⚏ 2895 Embarazo (Pregnancy)
Gruner & Jahr USA Publishing
685 3rd Ave.   **Phone: (212)878-8700**
New York, NY 10017   **Fax: (212)986-4449**
Magazine educating Hispanic mothers-to-be about pregnancy and
birth. **Founded:** 1990. **Frequency:** 2x/yr. **Printing Method:** Offset. **Trim
Size:** 5 3/8 x 7 1/2. /CPP 2. **Key Personnel:** Dean Sanderson,
Publisher; Sam Pagan, Assoc. Publisher; Elvia Delgado, Editor-in-
Chief.
Ad Rates: BW: $7,480   **Circulation:** Non-paid ‡200,400
            4C: $9,970

⚏ 2896 Essence
Essence Communications, Inc.
1500 Broadway 6th fl.   **Phone: (212)642-0600**
New York, NY 10036   **Fax: (212)921-5173**

⚏ 2897 Family Fun
Blue Waters Communication, Inc.
599 Lexington Ave.
New York, NY 10022
Magazine promoting family unity. **Frequency:** 10x/year. **Key Personnel:** Jake Winebaum Editor and Publisher. **Subscription:** $9.97. $1.95
single issue.
                         Circulation: (Not Reported)

⚏ 2898 Field & Stream
Times Mirror Magazines, Inc.
2 Park Ave.   **Phone: (212)779-5000**
New York, NY 10016   **Fax: (212)725-3836**

⚏ 2899 Financial Technology News
150 Nassau St.   **Phone: (212)267-7707**
New York, NY 10038   **Fax: (212)267-7726**
Ceased publication.

⚏ 2900 Food & Wine
American Express Publishing Corp.
1120 Avenue of the Americas
New York, NY 10036   **Phone: (212)382-5600**
                          Fax: (212)768-1573

⚏ 2901 For the Bride by Demetrios
DJE Publications Ltd.
222 W. 37th St.   **Phone: (212)967-0750**
New York, NY 10018   **Fax: (212)947-7024**
Consumer magazine. **Founded:** 1991. **Frequency:** Quarterly. **Printing
Method:** Web offset. **Trim Size:** 8 1/8 x 10 13/16. **Key Personnel:**
Patricia Daly, Advertising Dir. **Subscription:** $4.50 single issue.
Ad Rates: BW: $6,400   **Circulation:** 150,000
            4C: $8,000

⚏ 2902 Foreign Affairs
Council on Foreign Relations
58 E. 68th St.   **Phone: (212)734-0400**
New York, NY 10021   **Fax: (212)861-2759**

⚏ 2903 Freedom Review
Freedom House
120 Wall St.   **Phone: (212)514-8040**
New York, NY **10005-4001**   **Fax: (212)514-8050**

⚏ 2904 Friends of Financial History
Museum of American Financial History
26 Broadway   Phone: (212)908-4519
New York, NY 10004   Fax: (212)908-4600
Magazine dedicated to the issues, individuals, and institutions of
America's financial development. **Founded:** 1978. **Frequency:** Quarter-
ly. **Printing Method:** Offset. **Trim Size:** 8 1/8 x 10 7/8. **Cols./Page:** 3.
Col. Width: 2 1/8 in. **Col. Depth:** 9 1/4. **Key Personnel:** Jason Zweig,
Editor; Anne T. Keane, Mng. Editor. **ISSN:** 0278-8861. **Subscription:**
$25 U.S. and Canada; $30 Europe. $7 single issue.
Ad Rates: GLR: $5   **Circulation:** Paid ‡480
            BW: $300   Non-paid ‡2,500
            4C: $900
Published 1978-1990 by R.M. Smythe & Co., Inc.

⚏ 2905 Frontiers In Neuronendocrinology
Raven Press
1185 Avenue of the Americas
Mail Stop 3B   Phone: (212)930-9500
New York, NY 10036   Fax: (212)869-3495
Journal providing outstanding coverage of major developments in
neuroendocrinology. **Founded:** 1980. **Frequency:** Quarterly. **Printing
Method:** Sheetfed offset. **Trim Size:** 6 7/8 x 10. **Key Personnel:** Rita
Scheman, Publisher; William F. Ganong, M.D., Co-Editor; Luciano
Martini, M.D., Co-Editor; Phyllis C. Noyes, Advertising Mgr. **Sub-
scription:** $150; $175 other countries; $195 institutions; $235 institu-
tions other countries. $59 single issue.
Ad Rates: BW: $495   **Circulation:** 1,000
            4C: $650
A Wolters Kluwer Company.

⚏ 2906 Garfield Magazine
Welsh Publishing Group, Inc.
300 Madison Ave.
New York, NY 10017
Children's magazine. **Frequency:** Quarterly. **Key Personnel:** Michael
Teitelbaum, Editor; Donald E. Welsh, Publisher. **Subscription:** $7.80.
$1.95 single issue.
                         Circulation: (Not Reported)

⚏ 2907 Gift Reporter
GLM Publications
215 Lexington Ave., Ste. 1901   **Phone: (212)532-0651**
New York, NY 10016   **Fax: (212)532-2128**
Ceased publication.

⚏ 2908 Gift & Stationery Business
Miller Freeman, Inc.
1515 Broadway, 34th Fl.   **Phone: (212)869-1300**
New York, NY 10036   **Fax: (212)768-0002**

⚏ 2909 Girl Scout Leader
Girl Scouts of the U.S.A.
420 Fifth Ave.   **Phone: (212)852-8000**
New York, NY 10018-2702   **Fax: (212)852-6511**

⚏ 2910 Glamour
Conde Nast Publications, Inc.
350 Madison Ave.   Phone: (212)880-8800
New York, NY 10017   **Fax: (212)880-6922**

2911 Hair Cut and Style
Harris Publications
1115 Broadway
New York, NY 10010
Fashion magazine featuring hair and make-up tips and trends.
Frequency: Quarterly. **Key Personnel:** Mary Greenberg, Editor; Stanley R. Harris, Publisher. **Subscription:** $2.95 single issue.
                                        Circulation: (Not Reported)

2912 Heavy Metal Thunder
Starlog Communications International, Inc.
475 Park Ave. S.
New York, NY 10016
Magazine reporting on the heavy metal music scene. **Frequency:**
Quarterly. **Key Personnel:** Chris Botta, Editor; Norman Jacobs,
Publisher. **Subscription:** $3.95 single issue.
                                        Circulation: (Not Reported)

2913 Heresies: A Feminist Publication on Art & Politics
Heresies Collective, Inc.
280 Broadway, Ste. 412
New York, NY 10013   Phone: (212)227-2108
Periodical containing essays, poetry, short fiction, satire, criticism,
letters, interviews, page art, photography, and visual art. **Founded:**
1977. **Frequency:** 1-2/yr. **Trim Size:** 8 1/2 x 11. **ISSN:** 0146-3411.
Subscription: $23; $33 institutions. $6.75 single issue.
                                        Circulation: Paid ‡15,000

2914 Hippocampus
Churchill Livingstone, Inc.
650 Avenue of the Americas   Phone: (212)206-5000
New York, NY 10011   Fax: (212)727-7808
Neurobiological journal focusing on the hippocampus brain region.
Frequency: Quarterly. **Key Personnel:** David G. Amaral, Editor;
Menno P. Witter, Editor. **Subscription:** $95; $60 graduate student;
$175 institutions; $112 other countries; $77 graduate student in other
countries; $192 institutions in other countries; $127 other countries
(airmail); $92 graduate student in other countries (airmail); $207
institutions in other countries (airmail).
Ad Rates: BW: $500   **Circulation:** Paid ‡4,000
                4C: $650

2915 House Beautiful's Houses and Plans
Hearst Corp.
959 8th Ave., 1st Fl.
New York, NY 10019-5970   Phone: (212)649-2094
Magazine. **Frequency:** 5x/yr.
                                        Circulation: (Not Reported)

2916 HR Focus
American Management Assn.
135 W. 50th St.   Phone: (212)903-8389
New York, NY 10020   **Fax: (212)903-8083**

2917 The Hudson Review
The Hudson Review, Inc.
684 Park Ave.   Phone: (212)650-0020
New York, NY 10021   **Fax: (212)734-4177**

2918 The Human Resources Professional
Faulkner & Gray, Inc.
11 Penn Plaza   **Phone: (212)967-7000**
New York, NY **10001**   **Fax: (212)967-7155**

2919 Income Opportunities
IO Publications, Inc.
1500 Broadway   **Phone: (212)642-0600**
New York, NY **10036-4015**   **Fax: (212)302-8269**

2920 Independent Power Report's Avoided-Cost Quarterly
1221 Avenue of the Americas   Phone: (212)512-2905
New York, NY 10020-1095   Fax: (212)512-2723
Founded: 1986. **Frequency:** Quarterly. **Cols./Page:** 2. **Col. Width:** 3 1/2
in. **Col. Depth:** 9 3/4 in. **Key Personnel:** Richard Schwartz, Editor.
Subscription: $475.
                                        Circulation: (Not Reported)
Advertising not accepted.

2921 Infectious Agents and Disease
Raven Press
1185 Avenue of the Americas
Mail Stop 3B   Phone: (212)930-9500
New York, NY 10036   Fax: (212)869-3495
Journal providing a unique new look at the molecular biology and
clinical aspects of infectious disease. **Founded:** 1992. **Frequency:**
Bimonthly. **Printing Method:** Sheetfed offset. **Trim Size:** 8 1/4 x 11.
Key Personnel: Rita Scheman, Publisher; Bernard Roizman, Sc.D.,
Editor-in-Chief; Phyllis C. Noyes, Advertising Mgr. **Subscription:** $85;
$103 other countries; $119 institutions; $149 institutions other
countries. $37 single issue.
Ad Rates: BW: $700   **Circulation:** 1,200
                4C: $995
A Wolters Kluwer Company.

2922 Inside Media
470 Park Ave. S., 7th Fl. N.   Phone: (212)683-3540
New York, NY 10016   Fax: (212)683-3986

2923 Insurance Review
Journal of Commerce
2 World Trade Center, Ste. 2750   **Phone: (212)837-7090**
New York, NY 10048   Fax: (212)837-7035

2924 International Archive
915 Broadway   Phone: (212)673-6600
New York, NY 10010   Fax: (212)673-9795
Magazine covering television, film, and print ad campaigns worldwide. **Founded:** 1984. **Frequency:** 6x/yr. **ISSN:** 0893-0260. **Subscription:** $43.97. $9.25 single issue.
Ad Rates: BW: $1,600   **Circulation:** Paid 7,000
                4C: $2,300   Non-paid 400

2925 International Journal of Gynecological Pathology
Raven Press
1185 Avenue of the Americas
Mail Stop 3B   Phone: (212)930-9500
New York, NY 10036   Fax: (212)869-3495
Journal investigating human disorders, mainly in the field of anatomic pathology. **Subtitle:** Official Journal of the International Society of
Gynecological Pathologists. **Founded:** 1982. **Frequency:** Quarterly.
Printing Method: Sheetfed offset. **Trim Size:** 8 1/4 x 11. **Key
Personnel:** Rita Scheman, Publisher; Henry J. Norris, M.D., Editor-in-Chief; Phyllis C. Noyes, Advertising Mgr. **Subscription:** $135; $169
other countries; $190 institutions; $232 institutions other countries.
$58 single issue.
Ad Rates: BW: $650   **Circulation:** 1,500
                4C: $1,010
A Wolters Kluwer Company.

2926 Investing Licensing & Trading Conditions Abroad
Economist Intelligence Unit
215 Park Ave. S., 15th Fl.   Phone: (212)460-0600
New York, NY 10003   Fax: (212)995-8837

2927 The Jerusalem Quarterly
Institute on the Middle East, Inc.
300 E. 42nd St.   Phone: (212)972-7045
New York, NY 10017   Fax: (212)986-2907
Ceased publication.

2928 JETP
American Institute of Physics
335 E. 45th St.   Phone: (516)576-2460
New York, NY 10017   **Fax: (516)576-2488**
Former Title: Soviet Physics-JETP

2929 JETP Letters
American Institute of Physics
335 E. 45th St.   Phone: (516)576-2460
New York, NY 10017   **Fax: (516)576-2488**

2930 Jewish Currents
Assn. for Promotion of Jewish Secularism, Inc.
22 E. 17th St., Ste. 601
New York, NY **10003-1919**   Phone: (212)924-5740

2931 Journal of Advertising Research
Advertising Research Foundation, Inc.
641 Lexington Ave.   Phone: (212)751-5656
New York, NY 10022   Fax: (212)319-5265

2932 Journal of the Association for Computing Machinery
Assn. for Computing Machinery
1515 Broadway, 17th fl.   Phone: (212)869-7440
New York, NY 10036   **Fax: (212)944-1318**

2933 The Journal of Bank Accounting and Auditing
Faulkner & Gray, Inc.
106 Fulton St., Ste. 200   Phone: (212)766-8000
New York, NY 10038   Fax: (212)766-8131
Ceased publication.

2934 Journal of Biopharmaceutical Statistics
Marcel Dekker
270 Madison Ave.   Phone: (212)696-9000
New York, NY 10016   Fax: (212)685-4540
Journal covering applications of statistics in biopharmaceutical research. **Founded:** 1991. **Frequency:** 2x/yr. **Trim Size:** 7 x 10. **Key Personnel:** Karl E. Peace, Editor; Janet McClain, Advertising Rep. **ISSN:** 1054-3406. **Subscription:** $35; $165 institutions.
Ad Rates: BW: $640   **Circulation:** (Not Reported)
              4C: $1,401

2935 Journal of Cardiovascular Pharmacology
Raven Press
1185 Avenue of the Americas
Mail Stop 3B   Phone: (212)930-9500
New York, NY 10036   Fax: (212)869-3495
Journal discloses new information about cardiovascular drugs from research workers and the clinicians who use these drugs in therapy. **Founded:** 1979. **Frequency:** Monthly. **Printing Method:** Sheetfed offset. **Trim Size:** 8 1/4 x 11. **Key Personnel:** Rita Scheman, Publisher; Jan Koch-Weser, M.D., Co-Editor-in-Chief; Paul M. Vanhoutte, M.D., Ph.D., Co-Editor-in-Chief; Phyllis C. Noyes, Advertising Mgr. **Subscription:** $260; $330 other countries; $460 institutions; $564 institutions other countries. $47 single issue.
Ad Rates: BW: $680   **Circulation:** 2,500
              4C: $995
A Wolters Kluwer Company.

2936 The Journal of Case Management
Springer Publishing Co.
536 Broadway   Phone: (212)431-4370
New York, NY 10012-3955   Fax: (212)941-7842
Journal. **Subtitle:** New Developments in Case Management Practice. **Founded:** 1992. **Frequency:** Quarterly. **Printing Method:** Offset. **Trim Size:** 8 1/2 x 11. **Cols./Page:** 2. **Col. Width:** 3 1/2 in. **Col. Depth:** 9 in. **Key Personnel:** Joan Quinn, Editor; Matt Fenton, Mng. Editor; Linda Mapplefad, Advertising Mgr. **Subscription:** $38; $78 institutions; $44 other countries. $12 single issue.
Ad Rates: BW: $300   **Circulation:** Paid ‡600
                                                      Non-paid ‡100

2937 Journal of Cerebral Blood Flow and Metabolism
Raven Press
1185 Avenue of the Americas
Mail Stop 3B   Phone: (212)930-9500
New York, NY 10036   Fax: (212)869-3495
Journal that gathers new information on experimental, theoretical, and clinical aspects of brain circulation and metabolism. **Subtitle:** Official Journal of the International Society of Cerebral Blood Flow and Metabolism. **Founded:** 1981. **Frequency:** Bimonthly. **Printing Method:** Sheetfed offset. **Trim Size:** 8 1/4 x 11. **Key Personnel:** Rita Scheman, Publisher; Myron D. Ginsberg, M.D., Editor-in-Chief; Phyllis C. Noyes, Advertising Mgr. **Subscription:** $271; $329 other countries; $424 institutions; $492 institutions other countries. $82 single issue.
Ad Rates: BW: $785   **Circulation:** 2,000
              4C: $1,100
A Wolters Kluwer Company.

2938 Journal of Clinical Gastroenterology
Raven Press
1185 Avenue of the Americas
Mail Stop 3B   Phone: (212)930-9500
New York, NY 10036   Fax: (212)869-3495
Journal featuring original articles on the diagnosis of digestive diseases, treatment modalities, and surgical intervention. **Founded:** 1979. **Frequency:** 8x/yr. **Printing Method:** Sheetfed offset. **Trim Size:** 8 1/4 x 11. **Key Personnel:** Rita Scheman, Publisher; Howard M. Spiro, M.D., Editor-in-Chief; Phyllis C. Noyes, Advertising Mgr. **Subscription:** $106; $148 other countries; $170 institutions; $202 institutions other countries. $30 single issue.
Ad Rates: BW: $685   **Circulation:** 2,500
              4C: $985
A Wolters Kluwer Company.

2939 Journal of Clinical Neuro-opthalmology
Raven Press
1185 Avenue of the Americas
Mail Stop 3B   Phone: (212)930-9500
New York, NY 10036   Fax: (212)869-3495
Journal reporting on recent developments in diagnosing and treating opthalmologic, neurologic, endocrinologic, inflammatory, and neoplastic conditions affecting the motor and the visual systems. **Founded:** 1981. **Frequency:** Quarterly. **Printing Method:** Sheetfed offset. **Trim Size:** 8 1/4 x 11. **Key Personnel:** Rita Scheman, Publisher; J. Lawton Smith, M.D., Editor-in-Chief; Phyllis C. Noyes, Advertising Mgr. **Subscription:** $104; $134 other countries; $145 institutions; $174 institutions other countries. $44 single issue.
Ad Rates: BW: $735   **Circulation:** 1,200
              4C: $920
A Wolters Kluwer Company.

2940 The Journal of Consumer Lending
Faulkner & Gray, Inc.
106 Fulton St., Ste. 200   Phone: (212)766-8000
New York, NY 10038   Fax: (212)766-8131
Ceased publication.

2941 Journal of Corporate Taxation
Warren Gorham, Lamont Inc.
1 Penn Plaza, 40th Fl.   Phone: (212)971-5194
New York, NY 10119   Fax: (212)971-5025

2942 Journal of Diabetes and Its Complications
Elsevier Science Publishing Co., Inc.
655 Avenue of the Americas   **Phone: (212)989-5800**
New York, NY 10010   Fax: (212)633-3990

2943 Journal of Electrocardiology
Churchill Livingstone, Inc.
1560 Broadway
New York, NY 10035   **Phone: (212)819-5440**

2944 Journal of Electromyography and Kinesiology
Raven Press
1185 Avenue of the Americas
Mail Stop 3B   Phone: (212)930-9500
New York, NY 10036   Fax: (212)869-3495
Journal with laboratory and clinical research and specialized reports from scientists worldwide. **Subtitle:** Official Journal of the International Society of Electrophysical Kinesiology. **Founded:** 1991. **Frequency:** Quarterly. **Printing Method:** Sheetfed offset. **Trim Size:** 8 1/4 x 11. **Key Personnel:** Rita Scheman, Publisher; Carlo J. DeLuca, Ph.D., Editor-in-Chief, Phyllis C. Noyes, Advertising Mgr. **Subscription:** $98; $110 other countries; $130 institutions; $150 institutions other countries. $38 single issue.
Ad Rates: BW: $550   **Circulation:** 1,000
              4C: $750
A Wolters Kluwer Company.

2945 The Journal of European Business
Faulkner & Gray, Inc.
11 Penn Plaza   **Phone: (212)967-7000**
New York, NY 10001   **Fax: (212)967-7155**

⌑ 2946 The Journal of General Physiology
The Rockefeller University Press
222 E. 70th St.   Phone: (212)327-8527
New York, NY 10021   Fax: (212)327-8513

⌑ 2947 Journal of Glaucoma
Raven Press
1185 Avenue of the Americas
Mail Stop 3B   Phone: (212)930-9500
New York, NY 10036   Fax: (212)869-3495
Journal addressing the spectrum of issues affecting definition, diagnosis, and management of the glaucomas. **Founded:** 1992. **Frequency:** Quarterly. **Printing Method:** Sheetfed offset. **Trim Size:** 8 1/4 x 11. **Key Personnel:** Rita Scheman, Publisher; E. Michael Van Buskirt, M.D., Editor-in-Chief; Phyllis C. Noyes, Advertising Mgr. **Subscription:** $85; $100 other countries; $105 institutions; $120 institutions other countries. $30 single issue.
Ad Rates: BW: $570   **Circulation:** 1,000
               4C: $750
A Wolters Kluwer Company.

⌑ 2948 Journal of Immunotherapy
Raven Press
1185 Avenue of the Americas
Mail Stop 3B   Phone: (212)930-9500
New York, NY 10036   Fax: (212)869-3495
Journal featuring rapid publication of articles on immunomodulators, lymphokines, antibodies, cells, and cell products in cancer biology and therapy. **Subtitle:** Official Journal of the Society for Biological Therapy. **Founded:** 1982. **Frequency:** 8x/yr. **Printing Method:** Sheetfed offset. **Trim Size:** 8 1/4 x 11. **Key Personnel:** Rita Scheman, Publisher; Steven A. Rosenberg, M.D., Editor-in-Chief; Phyllis C. Noyes, Advertising Mgr. **Subscription:** $176; $226 other countries; $306 institutions; $384 institutions other countries. $48 single issue.
Ad Rates: BW: $655   **Circulation:** 1,500
               4C: $1,025
Formerly: Journal of Biological Response Modifiers. A Wolters Kluwer Company.

⌑ 2949 The Journal of Investigative Dermatology
Elsevier Science Publishing Co., Inc.
655 Avenue of the Americas   Phone: (212)989-5800
New York, NY 10010   Fax: (212)633-3820

⌑ 2950 Journal of Neurochemistry
Raven Press
1185 Avenue of the Americas
Mail Stop 3B   Phone: (212)930-9500
New York, NY 10036   Fax: (212)869-3495
Journal providing coverage of significant advances in neurochemistry and molecular and cellular biology. **Subtitle:** Official Journal of the International Society for Neurochemistry. **Founded:** 1956. **Frequency:** Monthly. **Printing Method:** Web offset. **Trim Size:** 8 1/4 x 10 7/8. **Key Personnel:** Rita Scheman, Publisher; A.A. Boulton, Editor-in-Chief; K.F. Tipton, Editor-in-Chief; Phyllis C. Noyes, Advertising Mgr. **Subscription:** $319; $1,057 institutions. $88 single issue.
Ad Rates: BW: $705   **Circulation:** 2,500
               4C: $995
A Wolters Kluwer Company.

⌑ 2951 Journal of Neurosurgical Anesthesiology
Raven Press
1185 Avenue of the Americas
Mail Stop 3B   Phone: (212)930-9500
New York, NY 10036   Fax: (212)869-3495
Journal with reports on improvements in intraoperative and postoperative management, new drugs, and details on new equipment and technologies. **Founded:** 1989. **Frequency:** Quarterly. **Printing Method:** Sheetfed offset. **Trim Size:** 8 1/4 x 11. **Key Personnel:** Rita Scheman, Publisher; James E. Cottrell, M.D., Editor-in-Chief; Phyllis C. Noyes, Advertising Mgr. **Subscription:** $120; $140 other countries; $140 institutions; $160 institutions other countries. $40 single issue.
Ad Rates: BW: $690   **Circulation:** 2,000
               4C: $1,070
A Wolters Kluwer Company.

⌑ 2952 Journal of Orthopaedic Trauma
Raven Press
1185 Avenue of the Americas
Mail Stop 3B   Phone: (212)930-9500
New York, NY 10036   Fax: (212)869-3495
Journal devoted exclusively to the diagnosis and management of hard and soft tissue trauma, including injuried to bone, muscle, ligaments, tendons, and the spinal cord. **Subtitle:** Official Publication: Orthopaedic Trauma Association. **Founded:** 1987. **Frequency:** Quarterly. **Printing Method:** Sheetfed offset. **Trim Size:** 8 1/4 x 11. **Key Personnel:** Rita Scheman, Publisher; Phillip G. Spiegel, M.D., Editor-in-Chief; Phyllis C. Noyes, Advertising Mgr. **Subscription:** $94; $120 other countries; $110 institutions; $140 institutions other countries. $35 single issue.
Ad Rates: BW: $770   **Circulation:** 2,000
               4C: $1,120
A Wolters Kluwer Company.

⌑ 2953 Journal of Pharmacological and Toxicological Methods
Elsevier Science Publishing Co., Inc.
655 Avenue of the Americas   Phone: (212)989-5800
New York, NY 10010   Fax: (212)633-3990
Former Title: Journal of Pharmacological Methods

⌑ 2954 The Journal of Pricing Management
Faulkner & Gray, Inc.
106 Fulton St., Ste. 200   Phone: (212)766-8000
New York, NY 10038   Fax: (212)766-8131
Ceased publication.

⌑ 2955 Journal of Real Estate Taxation
Warren Gorham, Lamont Inc.
1 Penn Plaza, 40th Fl.   Phone: (212)971-5194
New York, NY 10119   Fax: (212)971-5025

⌑ 2956 Journal of Retailing
New York University
8-176 Management Education Centre
44 W. 4th St.   Phone: (212)998-0550
New York, NY 10012-1126   Fax: (212)995-4211

⌑ 2957 Journal of Spinal Disorders
Raven Press
1185 Avenue of the Americas
Mail Stop 3B   Phone: (212)930-9500
New York, NY 10036   Fax: (212)869-3495
Journal presenting thoroughly documented case reports and carefully selected literature review articles. **Founded:** 1985. **Frequency:** Quarterly. **Printing Method:** Sheetfed offset. **Trim Size:** 8 1/4 x 11. **Key Personnel:** Rita Scheman, Publisher; Dan M. Spengler, M.D., Editor-in-Chief; Thomas B. Ducker, M.D., Editor-in-Chief; Phyllis C. Noyes, Advertising Mgr. **Subscription:** $89; $110 other countries; $106 institutions; $128 institutions other countries. $32 single issue.
Ad Rates: BW: $895   **Circulation:** 2,000
               4C: $1,050
A Wolters Kluwer Company.

⌑ 2958 Journal of Water Resources Planning and Management
American Society of Civil Engineers
345 E. 47th St.   Phone: (212)705-7288
New York, NY 10017-2398   Fax: (212)980-4681
Professional journal examining social, economic, environmental, and administrative concerns relating to the use and conservation of water. **Frequency:** 6x/yr. **Key Personnel:** William W.G. Yeh, Editor; David R. Dawdy, Assoc. Editor; David T. Ford, Assoc. Editor; Augustine J. Fredrich, Assoc. Editor; Mohammad Karamouz, Assoc. Editor; Richard N. Palmer, Assoc. Editor; Christopher G. Uchrin, Assoc. Editor. **ISSN:** 0733-9496. **Subscription:** $25; $104 nonmembers; $36 other countries; $115 nonmembers in other countries.
                                        Circulation: (Not Reported)
Advertising not accepted.

⌑ 2959 Labor Arbitration in Government
American Arbitration Assn.
140 W. 51st St.   Phone: (212)484-4011
New York, NY 10020-1203   Fax: (212)541-4841

◫ **2960 Ladies' Home Journal**
Meredith Publishing
100 Park Ave.   Phone: (212)953-7070
New York, NY 10017   **Fax: (212)351-3650**

◫ **2961 Lens and Eye Toxicity Research**
Marcel Dekker, Inc.
270 Madison Ave.   Phone: (212)696-9000
New York, NY 10016   Fax: (212)685-4540
Ceased publication.

◫ **2962 Lies Of Our Times**
Sheridan Square Press, Inc.
145 W. 4th St.   Phone: (212)254-1061
New York, NY 10012-1052   Fax: (212)254-9598
Magazine focusing on misinformation in the New York Times and
other major media. **Founded:** 1990. **Frequency:** 10x/yr. **Printing
Method:** Web offset. **Trim Size:** 8 1/2 x 11. **Cols./Page:** 2. **Key
Personnel:** Ellen Ray, Exec. Editor; William H. Schaap, Mng. Editor;
Edward S. Herman, Editor. **Subscription:** $24.
                                     Circulation: Paid 8,000
                                                      Non-paid 100
Advertising not accepted.

◫ **2963 Links: Health and Development Report**
National Central America Health Rights Network
PO Box 202
New York, NY 10276   Phone: (212)732-4790
Journal covering international health policy and social justice issues.
Founded: 1984. **Frequency:** Quarterly. **Key Personnel:** Tom Frieden,
Editor; Debreh Gilbert, Managing Editor. **ISSN:** 0894-3036. **Sub-
scription:** $15; $25 foreign and institutions. $3.75 single issue.
Ad Rates: BW: $350   **Circulation:** Paid 3,000
                                                  Non-paid 2,000
Additional Contact Information: 11 Maiden Ln., No. 10D, New York,
NY 10038.

◫ **2964 Live Wire**
J.Q. Adams Productions, Inc.
519 8th Ave.
New York, NY 10018
Magazine reports on hard rock musicians. **Frequency:** 6x/yr. **Key
Personnel:** Mike Smith, Editor; Henry McQueeney, Publisher. **Sub-
scription:** $2.95 single issue.
                                     Circulation: (Not Reported)

◫ **2965 Low Temperature Physics**
American Institute of Physics
335 E. 45th St.   Phone: (516)576-2460
New York, NY 10017   **Fax: (516)576-2488**
Former Title: Soviet Journal of Low Temperature Physics

◫ **2966 M inc.**
Fairchild Publications, Inc.
W. 34th St.   Phone: (212)630-4000
New York, NY 10001   Fax: (212)630-4837
Ceased publication.

◫ **2967 Madre**
121 W. 27th St., Rm. 301   Phone: (212)627-0444
New York, NY 10001   Fax: (212)675-3704
Periodical containing a multi-cultural perspective on political and
social issues affecting women and children in the United States and
the Middle East. **Frequency:** Quarterly.
                                     Circulation: (Not Reported)

◫ **2968 Management Review**
American Management Assn.
135 W. 50th St., 15th Fl.   **Phone: (212)903-8393**
New York, NY 10020-1201   **Fax: (212)903-8083**

◫ **2969 Manhattan Spirit**
363 7th Ave., 12th Fl.   Phone: (212)268-8600
New York, NY 10001-3904   Fax: (212)594-0719
Community newspaper. **Founded:** 1985. **Frequency:** Weekly (Tues.).

Printing Method: Web offset. **Trim Size:** 11 3/8 x 15. **Cols./Page:** 6.
Col. Width: 9 picas. **Col. Depth:** 14 in. **Key Personnel:** Tom Allon,
Editor-in-Chief/Publisher. **Subscription:** Free.
Ad Rates: BW: $2,900   **Circulation:** Free ‡76,000
              4C: $3,200
              SAU: $50.75
              PCI: $36.91
Circulation audited by CPVS.

◫ **2970 Meeting News**
Miller Freeman, Inc.
1515 Broadway   Phone: (212)869-1300
New York, NY 10036   Fax: (212)302-6273

◫ **2971 Model News**
The King Network
150 5th Ave., Ste. 831
New York, NY 10011   **Phone: (212)645-8400**

◫ **2972 Motor Boating & Sailing**
Hearst Magazines
250 W. 55th St.   Phone: (212)649-3068
New York, NY 10019   **Fax: (212)489-9258**

◫ **2973 Movement Disorders**
Raven Press
1185 Avenue of the Americas
Mail Stop 3B   Phone: (212)930-9500
New York, NY 10036   Fax: (212)869-3495
Journal that brings together peer-reviewed articles that further the
understanding of motor control mechanisms in disease. **Subtitle:**
Official Journal of the Movement Disorder Society. **Founded:** 1986.
Frequency: Quarterly. **Printing Method:** Sheetfed offset. **Trim Size:** 8
1/4 x 11. **Key Personnel:** Rita Scheman, Publisher; Stanley Fahn,
M.D., Editor-in-Chief; C. David Marsden, D. Sc., F.R.C.P., F.R.S.,
Editor-in-Chief; Phyllis C. Noyes, Advertising Mgr. **Subscription:**
$177; $229 other countries; $223 institutions; $289 institutions other
countries. $72 single issue.
Ad Rates: BW: $730   **Circulation:** 1,500
              4C: $1,145
A Wolters Kluwer Company.

◫ **2974 N.Y. Habitat Magazine**
The Carol Group, Ltd.
928 Broadway   Phone: (212)505-2030
New York, NY 10010   Fax: (212)254-6795

◫ **2975 National Farm Finance News**
Dorset Group, Inc.
212 W. 35th St., 13th floor   Phone: (212)563-4405
New York, NY 10001   Fax: (212)564-8879
Ceased publication.

◫ **2976 National Home Center News**
Lebhar-Friedman, Inc.
425 Park Ave.   **Phone: (212)756-5151**
New York, NY 10022   **Fax: (212)756-5295**

◫ **2977 NCJW Journal**
National Council of Jewish Women
53 W. 23rd St.   Phone: (212)645-4048
New York, NY 10010   Fax: (212)645-7466
Periodical reporting issues of interest to NCJW members. **Frequency:**
Quarterly. **Printing Method:** Web offset. **Trim Size:** 8 1/2 x 11. **Cols./
Page:** 3. **Col. Width:** 2 6/8 in. **Col. Depth:** 9 in. **Key Personnel:** Lauren
Schwartz, Editor. **ISSN:** 0161-2115.
Ad Rates: BW: $1,000   **Circulation:** Paid 100,000
              4C: $4,000
              PCI: $60

Ad Rates: GLR = general line rate; BW = one-time black & white page rate; 4C = one-time four color page rate; SAU = standard advertising unit rate;
CNU = Canadian newspaper advertising unit rate; PCI = per column inch rate.
Circulation: ★ = ABC; △ = BPA; ◆ = CAC; ● = CCAB; □ = VAC; ⊕ = PO Statement; ‡ = Publisher's Report; Boldface figures = sworn; Light figures = estimated.
Entry type: ◫ = Print; ◢ = Broadcast.

199

📖 **2978 Neuropsychiatry, Neuropsychology, and Behavioral Neurology**
Raven Press
1185 Avenue of the Americas
Mail Stop 3B　　　　　　　　　　Phone: (212)930-9500
New York, NY 10036　　　　　　　Fax: (212)869-3495
Journal featuring original research articles, review articles, and brief reports covering diagnostic, theraputic, and research work in areas such as pharmacotherapy, somatics, imaging, and EEG. **Founded:** 1989. **Frequency:** Quarterly. **Printing Method:** Sheetfed offset. **Trim Size:** 8 1/4 x 11. **Key Personnel:** Rita Scheman, Publisher; Michael Alan Taylor, M.D., Editor-in-Chief; Phyllis C. Noyes, Advertising Mgr. **Subscription:** $89; $119 other countries; $119 institutions; $149 institutions other countries. $37 single issue.
Ad Rates:　BW:　　$550　　　　　**Circulation:** 1,500
　　　　　　　4C:　　$950
A Wolters Kluwer Company.

📖 **2979 Neurosurgery Quarterly**
Raven Press
1185 Avenue of the Americas
Mail Stop 3B　　　　　　　　　　Phone: (212)930-9500
New York, NY 10036　　　　　　　Fax: (212)869-3495
Journal with worldwide developments in the diagnosis, management, and surgical treatment of neurological disorders. **Founded:** 1991. **Frequency:** Quarterly. **Printing Method:** Sheetfed offset. **Trim Size:** 8 1/4 x 11. **Key Personnel:** Rita Scheman, Publisher; Donlin M. Long, M.D., Ph.D., Editor-in-Chief; Phyllis C. Noyes, Advertising Mgr. **Subscription:** $89; $118 other countries; $112 institutions; $136 institutions other countries. $34 single issue.
Ad Rates:　BW:　　$615　　　　　**Circulation:** 1,000
　　　　　　　4C:　　$1,030
A Wolters Kluwer Company.

📖 **2980 New Body's Eat Light**
GCR Publishing Group, Inc.
1700 Broadway
New York, NY 10019
Magazine includes diet-conscious eating tips. **Frequency:** Quarterly. **Key Personnel:** Marilyn Hansen, Editor; Charles Goodman, Publisher. **Subscription:** $2.95 single issue.
　　　　　　　　　　　　　Circulation: (Not Reported)

📖 **2981 New Choices For Retirement Living**
Retirement Living Publishing Co., Inc.
28 W. 23rd St.　　　　　　　　　Phone: (212)366-8800
New York, NY 10010-5204　　　　**Fax: (212)366-8899**

📖 **2982 New York Press**
New York Press, Inc.
295 Lafayette St.　　　　　　　　Phone: (212)679-1234
New York, NY 10012-2794　　　　Fax: (212)941-7824
Newspaper. **Founded:** 1988. **Frequency:** Weekly (Wed.). **Printing Method:** Offset. **Cols./Page:** 6. **Col. Width:** 1 1/2 in. **Key Personnel:** Russ Smith, Editor. **Subscription:** Free.
Ad Rates:　BW:　　$1,885　　　**Circulation:** Free ☐75,000
　　　　　　　4C:　　$3,085
　　　　　　　PCI:　　$29.75
Additional Contact Information: Alternate telephone: (212)941-1130.

📖 **2983 New York University Alumni News Magazine**
New York University
25 W. 4th St., No. 604　　　　　Phone: (212)998-6846
New York, NY 10012　　　　　　Fax: (212)995-4021
Ceased publication.

📖 **2984 NY: The City Journal**
Manhattan Institute
42 E. 71st St.
New York, NY 10021
Magazine addressing the issues and concerns facing New York City. **Frequency:** Quarterly. **Key Personnel:** Richard Vigilante, Editor; William Hammett, Publisher. **Subscription:** $25. $6.95 single issue.
　　　　　　　　　　　　　Circulation: (Not Reported)

📖 **2985 NYC/New Youth Connections**
Youth Communication
144 W. 27th St., 8th Fl.　　　　Phone: (212)242-3270
New York, NY **10001**　　　　　　Fax: (212)242-7057

📖 **2986 Ob Gyn News**
International Medical News Group
770 Lexington Ave.　　　　　　　**Phone: (212)888-3232**
New York, NY 10021　　　　　　　**Fax: (212)421-0106**

📖 **2987 Object**
COOT, Inc.
588 Broadway, Ste. 604
New York, NY 1012
A how-to computer magazine. **Frequency:** 2x/mo. **Key Personnel:** Marie A. Lenzi, Publisher; Richard P. Friedman, Editor. **Subscription:** $25. $4.50 single issue.
　　　　　　　　　　　　　Circulation: (Not Reported)

📖 **2988 The Official Beverly Hills, 90210 Magazine**
Welsh Publishing Group, Inc.
300 Madison Ave.
New York, NY 10017
Magazine featuring articles about and interviews with the stars of the T.V. series Beverly Hills 90210. **Frequency:** 6x/yr. **Key Personnel:** Sheryl Kahn, Editor; Donald E. Welsh, Publisher. **Subscription:** $2.50 single issue.
　　　　　　　　　　　　　Circulation: (Not Reported)

📖 **2989 Ophthalmic Plastic and Reconstructive Surgery**
Raven Press
1185 Avenue of the Americas
Mail Stop 3B　　　　　　　　　　Phone: (212)930-9500
New York, NY 10036　　　　　　　Fax: (212)869-3495
Journal devoted exclusively to reconstructive surgery, trauma, congenital malformations, functional disorders, cosmetic deformities, and other maladies of the orbital region. **Subtitle:** Official Publication of the The American Society of Ophthalmic Plastic and Reconstructive Surgery. **Founded:** 1985. **Frequency:** Quarterly. **Printing Method:** Sheetfed offset. **Trim Size:** 8 1/4 x 11. **Key Personnel:** Rita Scheman, Publisher; Bernice Z. Brown, M.D., Co-Editor-in-Chief; Richard K. Dortzbach, M.D., Co-Editor-in-Chief; Phyllis C. Noyes, Advertising Mgr. **Subscription:** $104; $126 other countries; $150 institutions; $176 institutions other countries. $44 single issue.
Ad Rates:　BW:　　$695　　　　　**Circulation:** 1,500
　　　　　　　4C:　　$940
A Wolters Kluwer Company.

📖 **2990 Optics and Spectroscopy**
American Institute of Physics
335 E. 45th St.　　　　　　　　　Phone: (516)576-2460
New York, NY 10017　　　　　　　**Fax: (516)576-2488**

📖 **2991 Our Right to Know**
Fund for Open Information and Accountability, Inc.
145 W. 4th St.
New York, NY 10012
Ceased publication.

📖 **2992 Out**
110 Greene St., Ste. 800
New York, NY 10012-3812
General interest magazine for homosexuals and lesbians. Features articles on culture, people, and current issues of concern to the gay community. **Frequency:** 6x/yr. **Subscription:** $19.95; $26 in Canada; $32 other countries. $4.95 single issue.
　　　　　　　　　　　　　Circulation: (Not Reported)

📖 **2993 Outweek Magazine**
159 W. 25th St.
New York, NY 10010　　　　　　　Phone: (212)337-1200
Lesbian and gay magazine covering national and international news, reviews of media, on health, arts and entertainment, cartoons, humor and satire, and extensive New York City listings. **Frequency:** Weekly. **Subscription:** $59.95.
　　　　　　　　　　　　　Circulation: (Not Reported)

📖 **2994 Pancreas**
Raven Press
1185 Avenue of the Americas
Mail Stop 3B　　　　　　　　　　Phone: (212)930-9500
New York, NY 10036　　　　　　　Fax: (212)869-3495
Journal providing a central forum for communication of original works involving both basic and clinical research on the exocrine and endocrine pancreas and their interrelationship and consequences in

disease states. **Subtitle:** Official Journal of the American Pancreatic Association. **Founded:** 1986. **Frequency:** Bimonthly. **Printing Method:** Sheetfed offset. **Trim Size:** 8 1/4 x 11. **Key Personnel:** Rita Scheman, Publisher; Vay Liang Go, M.D., Editor-in-Chief; Phyllis Noyes, Advertising Mgr. **Subscription:** $234; $286 other countries; $358 institutions; $410 institutions other countries. $68 single issue.
Ad Rates: BW: $655   **Circulation:** 1,500
           4C: $1,025
A Wolters Kluwer Company.

⚹ 2995   Physics of Atomic Nuclei
American Institute of Physics
335 E. 45th St.   **Phone:** (516)576-2460
New York, NY 10017   **Fax: (516)576-2488**
Former Title: Soviet Journal of Nuclear Physics

⚹ 2996   Physics-Doklady
American Institute of Physics
335 E. 45th St.   **Phone:** (516)576-2460
New York, NY 10017   **Fax: (516)576-2488**
Former Title: Soviet Physics-Doklady

⚹ 2997   Physics of Particles and Nuclei
American Institute of Physics
335 E. 45th St.   **Phone:** (516)576-2460
New York, NY 10017   **Fax: (516)576-2488**
Former Title: Soviet Journal of Particles and Nuclei

⚹ 2998   Physics of the Solid State
American Institute of Physics
335 E. 45th St.   **Phone:** (516)576-2460
New York, NY 10017   **Fax: (516)576-2488**
Former Title: Soviet Physics-Solid State

⚹ 2999   Physics-Uspekhi
American Institute of Physics
335 E. 45th St.   **Phone:** (516)516-2460
New York, NY 10017   **Fax: (516)576-2488**
Former Title: Soviet Physics (Uspekhi)

⚹ 3000   Pixel Vision
Pixel Vision
154 W. 57th St., No. 826
New York, NY 10019   **Phone:** (212)581-3000
The English/French computer magazine. **Subtitle:** The Computer Image Magazine. **Founded:** 1986. **Frequency:** 5x/yr. **Printing Method:** Offset. **Trim Size:** 8 x 12. **Key Personnel:** Joel Laroche, Publisher; Judson Rosebush, Editor. **Subscription:** $35.
Ad Rates: 4C: $2,500   **Circulation:** (Not Reported)

⚹ 3001   Plasma Physics Reports
American Institute of Physics
335 E. 45th St.   **Phone:** (516)576-2460
New York, NY 10017   **Fax: (516)576-2488**
Former Title: Soviet Journal of Plasma Physics

⚹ 3002   Playgirl
Playgirl, Inc.
801 2nd Ave.   **Phone:** (212)986-5100
New York, NY 10017   **Fax: (212)697-6343**

⚹ 3003   Politics and Probe: the intelligence journal of the workers left
National Alliance, Inc.
500 Greenwich St., Ste 202   **Phone:** (212)941-9400
New York, NY 10013   **Fax:** (212)941-8340
Ceased publication.

⚹ 3004   Polymers for Advanced Technologies
John Wiley & Sons
506 3rd Ave.
New York, NY 10158
Journal. **Founded:** 1990. **Frequency:** 8x/year. **Printing Method:** Offset

lithograph. **Cols./Page:** 2. **Key Personnel:** Menachem Lewin, Editor. **ISSN:** 1042-7147.
                Circulation: (Not Reported)
Advertising accepted; contact publisher for rates. **Additional Contact Information:** Baffins Lane, Chichester, Sussex PO19 1UD, UK.

⚹ 3005   Population and Development Review
The Population Council
1 Dag Hammarskjold Plaza, 44th Fl.   **Phone: (212)339-0500**
New York, NY 10017   **Fax:** (212)755-6052

⚹ 3006   Poskinolt Press
Tiger Press
JAF Sta.
Box 7415
New York, NY 10116-4630
Contemporary poetry and prose magazine. **Founded:** 1989. **Frequency:** Quarterly. **Trim Size:** 5 1/2 x 8 1/2. **Key Personnel:** Patricia D. Coscia, Editor; Ed Janz, Co-Editor. **Subscription:** $2 single issue.
                Circulation: (Not Reported)
Advertising accepted; contact publisher for rates. **Production Method:** Desktop.

⚹ 3007   Public Budgeting and Financial Management
Marcel Dekker, Inc.
270 Madison Ave.   **Phone:** (212)696-9000
New York, NY 10016   **Fax:** (212)685-4540
Subtitle: An International Journal. **Frequency:** 3x/yr. **Trim Size:** 5 1/8 x 9. **Key Personnel:** Jack Rabin, Editor; Janet McClain, Ad. Rep. **ISSN:** 1042-4741. **Subscription:** $137.50; $275 institutions.
Ad Rates: BW: $640   **Circulation:** Non-paid 300
           4C: $1,401

⚹ 3008   Quantum Electronics
American Institute of Physics
335 E. 45th St.   **Phone:** (516)576-2460
New York, NY 10017   **Fax: (516)576-2488**
Former Title: Soviet Journal of Quantum Electronics

⚹ 3009   Quilt Craft
Lopez Publications, Inc.
111 E. 35th St.
New York, NY 10016
Quilting magazine. **Frequency:** Quarterly. **Key Personnel:** Adrian B. Lopez, Publisher; Karen O'Dowd, Editor. **Subscription:** $9.95. $3.95 single issue.
                Circulation: (Not Reported)

⚹ 3010   The Racing Times
315 Hudson St.   **Phone:** (212)366-7600
New York, NY 10013   **Fax:** (212)366-7738
Racing newspaper. **Founded:** 1991. **Frequency:** Mon.-Sun. **Printing Method:** Offset. **Trim Size:** 14 x 21. **Cols./Page:** 7. **Key Personnel:** Dan Ferguson, Advertising Dir.
Ad Rates: PCI: $17.20   **Circulation:** Paid 18,000
                                   Free 2,500

⚹ 3011   The Radio Ranks
Bethlehem Publishing Co.
322 E. 50th   **Phone:** (212)832-7170
New York, NY 10022   **Fax:** (212)826-3169
Former Title: The Radio Sweep

⚹ 3012   Railway Track & Structures
Simmons-Boardman Publishing Corp.
345 Hudson   **Phone:** (212)620-7200
New York, NY 10014   **Fax:** (212)633-1165

⚹ 3013   RCDA
Research Center for Religion and Human Rights in Closed Societies, Ltd.
475 Riverside Dr., Ste. 448
New York, NY 10115   **Phone:** (212)870-2481
Former Title: RCDA-Religion in Communist Dominated Areas

3014 Report on Urologic Techniques
Churchill Livingstone, Inc
1560 Broadway
New York, NY 10036   Phone: (212)819-5400
Ceased publication.

3015 The Review of Financial Studies
Oxford University Press
200 Madison Ave.
New York, NY 10016
Journal. Founded: 1988. Frequency: Quarterly. Trim Size: 6 x 9. ISSN:
0893-9454. Subscription: $65; $75 other countries; $160 institutions;
$170 institutions other countries. $19.50 single issue; $22.50 single
issue other countries; $48 single issue institutions; $51 single issue
institutions other countries.
                              Circulation: (Not Reported)

3016 Right On!
Sterling Macfadden Partnership
355 Lexington Ave.   Phone: (212)973-3200
New York, NY 10017   Fax: (212)986-5926

3017 Rock on Tour
Tempo Publishing Company, Inc.
475 Park Ave. S., Ste. 2201
New York, NY 10016
Magazine profiling rock bands. Frequency: Quarterly. Key Personnel:
Beth R. Nussbaum, Editor; David Zentner, Publisher. Subscription:
$3.95 single issue.
                              Circulation: (Not Reported)

3018 Semiconductors
American Institute of Physics
335 E. 45th St.   Phone: (516)576-2460
New York, NY 10017   Fax: (516)576-2488
Former Title: Soviet Physics-Semiconductors

3019 Ser Padres (Being Parents)
Gruner & Jahr USA Publishing
685 3rd Ave.   Phone: (212)878-8700
New York, NY 10017   Fax: (212)986-4449
Hispanic magazine providing information on parenting.Founded:
1990. Frequency: Bimonthly. Printing Method: Offset. Trim Size: 7 7/
8 x 10 1/2. Col. Width: 3. Key Personnel: Elvia Delgado, Editor-in-
Chief; Sam Pagan, Assoc. Publisher; Dean Sanderson, Publisher.
Subscription: $6 single issue.
Ad Rates: BW: $11,240   Circulation: Paid △2,678
            4C: $14,990   Controlled △273,169

3020 Sex Roles: A Journal of Research
Center for the Study of Wopmen and Society
33 W. 42nd St.   Phone: (212)642-2954
New York, NY 10036   Fax: (212)642-1987
Periodical containing empirical research on sex roles and book
reviews. Founded: 1975. Frequency: Monthly. Key Personnel: Sue
Rosenberg Zalk, Editor; Ayala Gabriel, Assoc. Editor; Nancy Kutner,
Assoc. Editor. ISSN: 0360-0025. Subscription: $31; $37.50 other
countries; $197.50 institutions; $230 institutions other countries.
                              Circulation: (Not Reported)
Additional Contact Information: Contact advertising sales representative for rates: Daniel S. Lipner, Weston Media Associates, PO Box
1110, Greens Farms, CT 06436; phone, (203)261-2500; fax (203)261-
0101.

3021 Short Fiction by Women
Box 1276, Stuyvesant Sta.
New York, NY 10009
Periodical containing original fiction by women writers. Founded:
1991. Frequency: 3x/yr. Trim Size: 5 1/2 x 8 1/2. Key Personnel:
Rachel Whalen, Editor. Subscription: $18.
                              Circulation: 1,000
Advertising not accepted.

3022 Shout
JQ Adams Productions, Inc.
519 8th Ave.
New York, NY 10018
Magazine profiling rock musicians. Frequency: 6x/yr. Key Personnel:

Mike Smith, Editor; Henry M. McQueeney, Publisher. Subscription:
$2.95 single issue.
                              Circulation: (Not Reported)

3023 Show Biz News
The King Network
150 5th Ave., Ste. 831
New York, NY 10011   Phone: (212)645-8400
Former Title: Models & Talent

3024 16 Magazine
16 Magazine, Inc.
233 Park Ave. S.   Phone: (212)979-4932
New York, NY 10003   Fax: (212)979-7507

3025 Ski
Times Mirror Magazines, Inc.
2 Park Ave.   Phone: (212)779-5000
New York, NY 10016   Fax: (212)481-9261

3026 Skin Art
Outlaw Biker Enterprises, Inc.
450 7th Ave., Ste. 2305
New York, NY 10123
Magazine illustrating tattoos. Founded: 1991. Frequency: Quarterly.
Key Personnel: Casey Exton, Editor and Publisher. Subscription:
$4.95 single issue.
                              Circulation: (Not Reported)

3027 Slim Fast Magazine
Welsh Publishing Group, Inc.
300 Madison Ave.
New York, NY 10017
Magazine including low-fat, low-calorie recipes. Frequency: Quarterly.
Key Personnel: Margot Gilman, Editor; Donald Welsh, Publisher.
Subscription: $7.80. $1.95 single issue.
                              Circulation: (Not Reported)

3028 Small Business Reports
American Management Assn.
135 W. 50th St.   Phone: (212)903-8160
New York, NY 10020   Fax: (212)903-8083

3029 The Source
Source Publications, Inc.
594 Broadway, Ste. 510   Phone: (212)274-0464
New York, NY 10012   Fax: (212)274-8334
Magazine profiling the hip-hop music scene. Subtitle: The Magazine
of Hip-Hop Music, Culture, and Politics. Founded: 1988. Frequency:
Monthly. Printing Method: Web offset. Trim Size: 8 1/2 x 10 7/8. Key
Personnel: Jon Shecter, Editor; David Mays, Publisher; H. Edward
Young, Jr. Associate Publisher; James Bernard, Senior Editor. ISSN:
1063-2085. Subscription: $19.95. $2.95 single issue.
Ad Rates: BW: $2,730   Circulation: Paid 65,000
            4C: $3,640   Non-paid 1,500

3030 Soviet Journal of Optical Technology
American Institute of Physics
335 E. 45th St.   Phone: (516)576-2460
New York, NY 10017   Fax: (516)576-2488

3031 Sporting Goods Dealer
Times Mirror Magazines
2 Park Ave.   Phone: (212)779-5000
New York, NY 10016   Fax: (212)213-3540

3032 Standard Corporation Records
Standard & Poor's Corp.
25 Broadway   Phone: (212)208-8364
New York, NY 10004   Fax: (212)412-0459

3033 Summary of Labor Arbitration Awards
American Arbitration Assn.
140 W. 51st St.   Phone: (212)484-4011
New York, NY 10020-1203   Fax: (212)541-4841

3034 Super Easy-To-Do
Modern Day Periodicals, Inc.
1115 Broadway
New York, NY 10010
Magazine containing large-type puzzles. Frequency: 6x/yr. Key Per-

sonnel: Jerry Cunliffe, Editor; Stanley R. Harris, Publisher. **Subscription:** $1.25 single issue.

Circulation: (Not Reported)

3035 Super Stars
16 Magazines, Inc.
157 W. 57th St.
New York, NY 10019   Phone: (212)489-7220
Magazine with exclusive features of the most popular young performers on today's youth-oriented entertainment scene. **Founded:** 1957. **Frequency:** Quarterly. **Printing Method:** Web offset. **Trim Size:** 8 x 10 7/8. **Key Personnel:** K. Hall, Publisher. **ISSN:** 1044-0836. **USPS:** 699-940. **Subscription:** $3.50 single issue.
Ad Rates: BW: $1,475   **Circulation:** Paid ★300,000
            4C: $3,770

3036 Superfly
Crash Productions Inc.
250 W. 57th St., Ste 2315
New York, NY 10019
Magazine reporting on the rock music scene. **Frequency:** 6x/yr. **Key Personnel:** Diana Willis, Editor; Gloria F. Goldwater, Publisher. **Subscription:** $13.50. $2.95 single issue.
Circulation: (Not Reported)

3037 Surgical Laparoscopy & Endoscopy
Raven Press
1185 Avenue of the Americas
Mail Stop 3B   Phone: (212)930-9500
New York, NY 10036   Fax: (212)869-3495
Journal focusing on the diagnostic and therapeutic uses of laparoscopy and endoscopy in areas such as gastrointestinal surgery, urologic surgery, as well as gynecologic surgery. **Founded:** 1991. **Frequency:** Quarterly. **Printing Method:** Sheetfed offset. **Trim Size:** 8 1/4 x 11. **Key Personnel:** Rita Scheman, Publisher; Karl A. Zucker, M.D., Editor; Phyllis C. Noyes, Advertising Mgr. **Subscription:** $85; $100 other countries; $116 institutions; $133 institutions other countries. $33 single issue.
Ad Rates: BW: $685   **Circulation:** 4,500
            4C: $920
A Wolters Kluwer Company.

3038 Taxation for Accountants
Warren Gorham Lamont, Inc.
1 Penn Plaza, 40th Fl.   Phone: (212)971-5000
New York, NY 10119   Fax: (212)971-5025

3039 Taxation for Lawyers
Warren Gorham Lamont, Inc.
1 Penn Plaza, 40th Fl.   Phone: (212)971-5000
New York, NY 10119   Fax: (212)971-5025

3040 Technical Physics
American Institute of Physics
335 E. 45th St.   Phone: (516)576-2460
New York, NY 10017   **Fax: (516)576-2488**
Former Title: Soviet Physics-Technical Physics

3041 Tennis Illustrated
Family Media, Inc.
3 Park Ave.
New York, NY 10016
Tennis magazine featuring articles about the players, game, instruction, and equipment. **Frequency:** 10x/yr. **Key Personnel:** Bud Collins, Editor; Stephen McEnvoy, Publisher. **Subscription:** $9.97 Free to qualified subscribers; $15.94. $2.50 single issue.
Circulation: (Not Reported)

3042 Therapeutic Drug Monitoring
Raven Press
1185 Avenue of the Americas
Mail Stop 3B   Phone: (212)930-9500
New York, NY 10036   Fax: (212)869-3495
Subtitle: A Journal Devoted to Therapeutic Drug Monitoring and Clinical Drug Toxicology. **Founded:** 1979. **Frequency:** Bimonthly.

Printing Method: Sheetfed offset. **Trim Size:** 8 1/4 x 11. **Key Personnel:** Rita Scheman, Publisher; Steven J. Soldin, Ph.D., Editor-in-Chief; Folke Sjoqvist, M.D., Editor-in-Chief; Phyllis C. Noyes, Advertising Mgr. **Subscription:** $160; $198 other countries; $260 institutions; $325 institutions other countries. $54 single issue.
Ad Rates: BW: $695   **Circulation:** 2,000
            4C: $975
A Wolters Kluwer Company.

3043 30 Days to a Better Body
GCR Publishing Group Inc.
1700 Broadway
New York, NY 10019
Magazine includes exercise tips. **Founded:** 1991. **Frequency:** Quarterly. **Key Personnel:** Shelly Dawson, Editor; Charles Goodman, Publisher. **Subscription:** $2.95 single issue.

Circulation: (Not Reported)

3044 Tiger Beat Magazine
The Sterling/Macfadden Partnership
355 Lexington Ave., Ste. FL-13   Phone: (212)973-3200
New York, NY 10017-6603   Fax: (212)986-5926

3045 Toxicology Methods
Raven Press
1185 Avenue of the Americas
Mail Stop 3B   Phone: (212)930-9500
New York, NY 10036   Fax: (212)869-3495
Journal covering all areas of toxicology. **Founded:** 1991. **Frequency:** Quarterly. **Printing Method:** Sheetfed offset. **Trim Size:** 6 7/8 x 10. **Key Personnel:** Rita Scheman, Publisher; Shayne C. Gad, Ph.D., Editor-in-Chief; Phyllis Noyes, Advertising Mgr. **Subscription:** $84; $97 other countries; $137 institutions; $158 institutions other countries. $40 single issue.
Ad Rates: BW: $510   **Circulation:** 1,000
            4C: $695
A Wolters Kluwer Company.

3046 Toy and Hobby World
A4 Publications (USA), Inc.
41 Madison Ave. 5th Fl.   Phone: (212)685-0404
New York, NY 10010   Fax: (212)685-0483

3047 Transition
Oxford University Press
200 Madison Ave.   Phone: (212)679-7300
New York, NY 10016   Fax: (212)725-2972
Magazine on African and African-American issues. **Founded:** 1961. **Frequency:** Quarterly. **Trim Size:** 6 7/8 x 9 3/4. **Cols./Page:** 2. **Col. Width:** 2 1/2 in. **Col. Depth:** 7 13/16 in. **Key Personnel:** Henry Louis Gates, Jr., Editor; Kwame Anthony Appiah, Editor. **Subscription:** $24. $8.95 single issue.
Ad Rates: BW: $200   **Circulation:** (Not Reported)
Additional Contact Information: Telex 6859654.

3048 Treasury and Risk Management Magazine
The Economist Bldg.
111 W. 57th St.   Phone: (212)541-0512
New York, NY 10019   Fax: (212)459-3007
Magazine for corporate treasurers. **Founded:** 1991. **Frequency:** Quarterly. **Trim Size:** 7 x 10. **Key Personnel:** Lissa Short, Advertising Mgr. **Subscription:** $60.
Ad Rates: BW: $7,000   **Circulation:** 46,000
            4C: $8,900

3049 Trends in Cardiovascular Medicine
Elsevier Science Publishing Co., Inc.
655 Avenue of the Americas   Phone: (212)989-5800
New York, NY 10010   Fax: (212)633-3990
Research and clinical review journal. **Founded:** 1991. **Frequency:** 6x/yr. **Trim Size:** 8 1/2 x 11. **Cols./Page:** 3. **Key Personnel:** Kenneth R. Chien, Editor-in-Chief; Linda Gruner, Managing Editor; Richard

Geyer, Advertising Mgr. **ISSN:** 1050-1738. **Subscription:** $73; $145 institutions; $96 other countries; $171 institutions in other countries.
Ad Rates: BW: $590   **Circulation:** Paid 1,000
          4C: $900   Non-paid 1,100

3050 Trends Update
Book Industry Study Group, Inc.
160 5th Ave.
New York, NY 10010
Ceased publication.

3051 TWICE
Cahners Publishing
245 W. 17th St.   Phone: (212)645-0067
New York, NY 10010   **Fax: (212)337-7066**

3052 UFO Universe
Charlotte Magazine Corp.
1700 Broadway
New York, NY 10019
Magazine reporting on UFO sightings and issues. **Frequency:** 6x/yr.
Key Personnel: Timothy Green Beckley, Editor; Charles Goodman, Publisher. **Subscription:** $18. $3.50 single issue.
                        Circulation: (Not Reported)

3053 Ultrasound Quarterly
Raven Press
1185 Avenue of the Americas
Mail Stop 3B   Phone: (212)930-9500
New York, NY 10036   Fax: (212)869-3495
Journal with coverage of the newest, most sophisticated ultrasound techniques as well as in-depth analyses of important developments in the field. **Founded:** 1983. **Frequency:** Quarterly. **Printing Method:** Sheetfed offset. **Trim Size:** 6 7/8 x 10. **Key Personnel:** Rita Scheman, Publisher; Roger C. Sanders, M.D., Editor-in-Chief; Phyllis C. Noyes, Advertising Mgr. **Subscription:** $98; $122 other countries; $118 institutions; $140 institutions other countries. $35 single issue.
Ad Rates: BW: $595   **Circulation:** 2,000
          4C: $950
A Wolters Kluwer Company.

3054 UN Chronicle
United Nations, Rm. DC1-0530   Phone: (212)963-8262
New York, NY 10017   **Fax: (212)963-8013**

3055 United States Banker
Kalo Communications, Inc.
60 E. 42nd St., Ste. 3810
New York, NY 10165   **Phone: (212)599-3310**

3056 Urologic Radiology
Springer-Verlag New York, Inc.
175 5th Ave.   Phone: (212)460-1500
New York, NY 10010   Fax: (212)473-6272
Ceased publication.

3057 USA Today Crosswords
Hachette Magazines, Inc.
1633 Broadway
New York, NY 10019
Ceased publication.

3058 Video Shopper
Reese Communications, Inc.
460 W. 34th St.
New York, NY 10001
Video magazine featuring how-to's, new products, and much more.
Frequency: 6x/yr. **Key Personnel:** Jay Rosenfield, Editor; Eric C. Schwartz, Publisher. **Subscription:** $13.50. $2.50 single issue.
                        Circulation: (Not Reported)

3059 Visionaire
Visionaire Publishing
55 W. 11th. St.   Phone: (212)691-0282
New York, NY 10011   Fax: (212)691-0282
Magazine covering all aspects of art and fashion. **Founded:** 1991.
Frequency: Quarterly. **Key Personnel:** Stephen Gan, Editor. **Subscription:** $100; $150 other countries.
                        Circulation: (Not Reported)
Advertising not accepted.

3060 Vogue Knitting Magazine
Butterick Co., Inc.
161 6th Ave.   Phone: (212)620-2500
New York, NY 10013   Fax: (212)620-2746
Fashion magazine for knitters. **Founded:** 1982. **Frequency:** 3x/yr. **Key Personnel:** Nancy J. Thomas, Editor; Art Joinnides, Publisher.
                        Circulation: (Not Reported)
Advertising accepted; contact publisher for rates.

3061 WBAI Folio
Pacifica-WBAI Radio
505 8th Ave.   Phone: (212)279-0707
New York, NY 10018   Fax: (212)564-5359
Radio publication. **Frequency:** 11x/yr. **Key Personnel:** Valerie van Isler, Station and Gen. Mgr. **ISSN:** 0005-272X. **Subscription:** $50; $25 students and seniors.
Ad Rates: BW: $450   **Circulation:** 14,000
          PCI: $45

3062 Woman Entrepreneur
American Woman's Economic Development Corporation
641 Lexington Ave., 9th Fl.   Phone: (212)688-1900
New York, NY 10022   Fax: (212)668-2718
Magazine for women in business. **Frequency:** Monthly.
                        Circulation: (Not Reported)

3063 Womanews
PO Box 220, Village Sta.
New York, NY 10014   Phone: (212)674-1698
New York City feminist newspaper. Includes calendar of events and issues of national interest to women. **Frequency:** Monthly. **Subscription:** $1.25 single issue.
                        Circulation: (Not Reported)

3064 Woman's Day Crosswords
Hachette Publications, Inc.
1633 Broadway
New York, NY 10019   Phone: (212)767-6000
Ceased publication.

3065 Women's Health Issues
Elsevier Science Publishing Co., Inc.
655 Avenue of the Americas   Phone: (212)989-5800
New York, NY 10010   Fax: (212)633-3990
Journal containing original articles and expert commentary on medical, social, legal, ethical, and public policy issues, especially relating to women. **Frequency:** Quarterly. **Printing Method:** Offset. **Trim Size:** 8 1/2 x 11. **ISSN:** 1049-3867. **Subscription:** $42; $84.
                    Circulation: Paid 2,500
Advertising accepted; contact publisher for rates.

3066 World Wrestling Federation Battlemania
Voyager Communications, Inc.
132 W. 21st St.
New York, NY 10011
Magazine features Texas Tornado vs. Mr. Perfect. **Frequency:** Monthly. **Key Personnel:** James Shooter, Publisher; Laura Hitchcock, Editor. **Subscription:** $30. $2.50 single issue.
                        Circulation: (Not Reported)

3067 WREE-View
Women for Racial and Economic Quality
198 Broadway, No. 608
New York, NY 10036   Phone: (212)385-1103
Journal focusing on the problems of working and working-class women. **Frequency:** 3-4x/yr. **Subscription:** $6.
                        Circulation: (Not Reported)

3068 Wrestling Confidential
Dojo Publishing, Inc.
300 W. 43rd St.
New York, NY 10036
Wrestling magazine. **Frequency:** 6x/yr. **Key Personnel:** Michael Ottara, Editor; Joseph David, Publisher. **Subscription:** $2.50 single issue.
                        Circulation: (Not Reported)

♣ **3069 Manhattan Cable TV, Inc.**
120 E. 23rd St.   Phone: (212)598-7200
New York, NY 10010   Fax: (212)529-3591
Owner: American TV & Communications Corp. **Founded:** 1967.
Cities Served: New York County and Roosevelt Island, NY.

♣ **3070 Paragon Cable Manhattan**
5120 Broadway   Phone: (212)304-3000
New York, NY 10034   Fax: (212)304-3199
Owner: Paragon Communications. **Founded:** 1966. **Cities Served:** New
York County, NY.

♣ **3071 WBAI-FM - 95.5**
505 8th Ave.   Phone: (212)279-0707
New York, NY 10018   Fax: (212)564-5359
Format: Eclectic; Educational. **Network(s):** Pacifica. **Owner:** Pacifica
Foundation. **Founded:** 1948. **Operating Hours:** Continuous. **Key
Personnel:** Jennie Bourne, News Dir.; Andrew Phillips, Program Dir.;
Mario Murillo, Public Affairs Dir.; George Wellington, Operations
Dir.; Amy Goodman, News Dir.; Valerie van Isher, Gen. Mgr.
Wattage: 50,000. **Ad Rates:** Advertising not accepted. Advertising
available through the station's program guide, WBAI Folio.

♣ **3072 WBMB-AM - 590**
155 E. 24th St.
New York, NY 10010   Phone: (212)447-3019
Format: Alternative/Independent/Progressive. **Key Personnel:** Holly
Schmidt, Music Dir. **Ad Rates:** Noncommercial.

♣ **3073 WFIT-AM - 530**
230 W. 27th St.
New York, NY 10001   Phone: (212)760-7876
Format: Alternative/Independent/Progressive. **Key Personnel:** Tim
Shaw, Music Dir. **Ad Rates:** Noncommercial.

♣ **3074 WHCR-FM - 90.3**
City College of New York
138th & Convent Ave.
New York, NY 10031   **Phone: (212)650-7481**

♣ **3075 WLTW-FM - 106.7**
1515 Broadway, 40th Fl.   Phone: (212)258-7000
New York, NY 10036   **Fax: (212)764-2734**

♣ **3076 WNYU-FM - 89.1**
721 Broadway
New York, NY 10003   Phone: (212)998-1660
Format: Alternative/Independent/Progressive. **Key Personnel:** Kristin
Carney, Music Dir. **Ad Rates:** Noncommercial.

♣ **3077 WPIX-TV - Channel 11**
220 E. 42nd St.   Phone: (212)949-1100
New York, NY 10017   **Fax: (212)986-1032**

♣ **3078 WPUB-AM - 640**
41 Park Rd.
New York, NY 10038   Phone: (212)346-1270
Format: Alternative/Independent/Progressive. **Key Personnel:** Marilee
Berberabe, Music Dir. **Ad Rates:** Noncommercial.

NIAGARA FALLS

▢ **3079 Turtle Quarterly**
Native American Center for the Living Arts, Inc.
25 Rainbow Blvd. S.
Niagara Falls, NY 14303   Phone: (716)284-2427
Magazine offering features by and about Native Americans concern-
ing both ancient and contemporary issues. **Founded:** 1986. **Frequency:**
Quarterly. **Printing Method:** Offset. **Trim Size:** 8 1/2 x 11. **Cols./Page:**
3. **Col. Width:** 2 1/4 in. **Col. Depth:** 10 in. **Key Personnel:** Millie
Knapp, Editor. **Subscription:** $15; $21 Canada; $38 other countries.
$4 single issue. $4.75 single issue in Canada.
Ad Rates: BW: $135   **Circulation:** Paid 1,100
             4C: $285   Non-paid 3,000

♣ **3080 Adelphia Cable Communications of Niagara**
2604 Seneca Ave.
Niagara Falls, NY 14305   Phone: (716)297-6900
Owner: Adelphia Communications Corp. **Founded:** 1970. **Cities
Served:** Lewiston, Niagara, Sandborn, and Niagara County, NY.

NIAGARA UNIVERSITY

▢ **3081 Journal of Interlibrary Loan and Information Supply**
The Haworth Press, Inc.
Niagara University Library   **Phone: (716)286-8001**
Niagara University, NY 14109-2200   **Fax: (716)286-8030**

NORTH GREECE

♣ **3082 WGMC-FM - 90.1**
Box 300   **Phone: (716)621-9233**
North Greece, NY 14515   **Fax: (716)621-8692**

OGDENSBURG

▢ **3083 North Country Catholic**
Diocese of Ogdensburg
308 Isabella St.
PO Box 326   Phone: (315)393-2540
Ogdensburg, NY 13669   **Fax: (315)393-5108**

OLD WESTBURY

♣ **3084 WNYT-AM - 550**
268 Wheatly Rd.
Old Westbury, NY 11568-1037   Phone: (516)686-7577
Format: Alternative/Independent/Progressive. **Key Personnel:** Russel
Lord, Music Dir. **Ad Rates:** Noncommercial.

ONEIDA

▢ **3085 Pennysaver (Oneida Edition)**
Oneida Newspapers, Inc.
718 Genesse St.
PO Box 297   Phone: (315)697-2969
Oneida, NY 13421   Fax: (315)363-3115
Shopping guide. **Founded:** 1957. **Frequency:** Weekly (Tues.). **Printing
Method:** Photo offset. **Trim Size:** 10 3/8 x 16. **Cols./Page:** 6. **Col.
Width:** 1 5/8 in. **Col. Depth:** 16 in. **Key Personnel:** Jeanne R. Moon,
Gen. Mgr.; Cyndi Tarry, Circulation Mgr. **Subscription:** Free.
Ad Rates: BW: $388.80   **Circulation:** Free ◆15,500
             SAU: $4.13
Additional Contact Information: (315)697-2969. Combined advertis-
ing rates available with Pennysaver (Chittenago Edition).

OSWEGO

▢ **3086 Lake Effect**
Lake County Writers Group, Inc.
PO Box 59
Oswego, NY 13126   Phone: (315)635-5714
Ceased publication.

PEARL RIVER

▢ **3087 Our Town**
Community Media Inc.
25 W. Central Ave.   **Phone: (914)732-8200**
Pearl River, NY 10965   **Fax: (914)732-9214**

PERU

♣ **3088 WGFB-FM - 99.9**
RD 2, Box 157
Peru, NY 12972   Phone: (518)561-0960

PITTSFORD

3089 Pittsford This Week
PO Box 506   Phone: (716)264-4692
Pittsford, NY 14534   Fax: (716)264-9779
Shopping guide/Community newspaper. Founded: 1962. Frequency: Weekly. Printing Method: Web offset. Trim Size: 11 x 17. Cols./Page: 6. Col. Width: 6 1/2 picas. Col. Depth: 16 in. Key Personnel: Ed Sorenson, Publisher; Mike Sorenson, Publisher. Subscription: Free.
Circulation: Free 13,000
Advertising accepted; contact publisher for rates. Formerly: Brighton-Pittsford Shopper.

PLATTSBURGH

3090 WCFE-FM - 91.9
1 Sesame St.   Phone: (518)563-9770
Plattsburgh, NY 12901   Fax: (518)561-1928

3091 WPLT-FM - 93.9
110 Angell College Ctr.
Office of Campus Life   Phone: (518)564-2727
Plattsburgh, NY 12901   Fax: (518)564-7827

PLEASANTVILLE

3092 Straight Talk: A Magazine for Teens
The Learning Partnership
PO Box 199   Phone: (914)769-0055
Pleasantville, NY 10570   Fax: (914)769-5676
Health magazine for teens. Founded: 1991. Frequency: Quarterly. Printing Method: Web offset. Trim Size: 8 x 10 3/4. Cols./Page: 3. Col. Width: 2 1/8 in. Col. Depth: 9 5/16 in. Key Personnel: Rita Fisher, Editor-in-Chief. ISSN: 1062-0095. Subscription: $14.30.
Circulation: (Not Reported)
Advertising not accepted. Formerly: Rodale's Straight Talk.

POTSDAM

3093 North Country This Week
PO Box 975   Phone: (315)265-2068
Potsdam, NY 13676   Fax: (315)268-8701

3094 Northern New York Business Journal
North Country This Week
PO Box 975   Phone: (315)265-2068
Potsdam, NY 13676   Fax: (315)268-8701
Business journal servicing business owners, managers, and professionals in St. Lawrence County, NY. Founded: 1991. Frequency: 6x/yr. Trim Size: 11 1/2 x 13 1/2. Cols./Page: 4. Col. Width: 2 1/2 in. Col. Depth: 13 in. Key Personnel: Bill Shumuray, Editor and Publisher; Carol Adler-Jacoby, Advertising Mgr. Subscription: $7.50.
Ad Rates: BW: $460   Circulation: 5,000
Color advertising not accepted.

3095 WPDM-AM - 1470
Potsdam-Canton Rd.
PO Box 348   Phone: (315)265-5510
Potsdam, NY 13676   Fax: (315)265-4040

3096 WSNN-FM - 99.3
Potsdam-Canton Rd.
PO Box 348   Phone: (315)265-5510
Potsdam, NY 13676   Fax: (315)265-4040

POUGHKEEPSIE

3097 FIRST DAYS
American First Day Cover Society
PO Box 2879
Poughkeepsie, NY 12603   Phone: (914)473-2925

3098 WKIP-FM - 96.9
PO Box 1450   Phone: (914)471-2300
Poughkeepsie, NY 12602   Fax: (914)471-2683
Format: News; Talk. Simulcasts WKIP-AM. Network(s): ABC; NBC. Owner: Richard Novik. Operating Hours: Continuous; 42% network, 58% local. Key Personnel: Steven Berner, Gen. Mgr./Natl. Sales Mgr.;

Joseph Ryan, Program Dir.; Mary Kay Dolan, News Dir. Wattage: 3000. Ad Rates: $30-$43 for 30 seconds; $32-$45 for 60 seconds.

QUEENS

3099 Queens Inner Unity Cable Systems
133-19 Atlantic Ave.
Richmond Hill
Queens, NY 11417   Phone: (718)670-6550
Owner: Percy Sutton; Unity Broadcasting Network. Founded: 1988. Cities Served: Queens County, NY.

QUEENSBURY

3100 WGFR-FM - 92.1
Adirondack Community College   Phone: (518)793-4491
Queensbury, NY 12804   Fax: (518)745-1433

ROCHESTER

3101 Environmental & Experimental Botany
Department of Radiation Biology and Biophysics
The University of Rochester
School of Medicine and Dentistry   Phone: (716)275-3634
Rochester, NY 14642   Fax: (716)275-6007
Scientific journal. Founded: 1961. Frequency: Quarterly. Printing Method: Typeset. Trim Size: 7 1/8 x 9 7/8. Cols./Page: 2. Col. Width: 2 7/8 in. Col. Depth: 7 3/8 in. Key Personnel: Morion W. Miller, Editor-in-Chief. ISSN: 0098-8472. Subscription: $305 institutions.
Circulation: 800
Advertising not accepted.

3102 Jewish Ledger
2535 Brighton Henrietta Town Line
Rd.   Phone: (716)427-2434
Rochester, NY 14623-2711   Fax: (716)427-8521

3103 Northwest Pennysaver
Suburban Circle Publications, Inc.
2808 Dewey Ave.   Phone: (716)663-0068
Rochester, NY 14616   Fax: (716)663-0146
Ceased publication.

3104 Rochester Golf Week Newspaper
2535 Brighton Henrietta Town Line
Rd.   Phone: (716)427-2434
Rochester, NY 14623-2711   Fax: (716)427-8521

3105 Greater Rochester Cablevision, Inc.
71 Mount Hope Ave.   Phone: (716)325-1111
Rochester, NY 14620   Fax: (716)987-6300
Owner: American TV & Communications Corp. Cities Served: Genesee County, Monroe County, Orleans County, Brighton, Brockport, Byron, Chili, Clarendon, Clarkson, East Rochester, Fairport, Gates, Greece, Hamlin, Henrietta, Hilton, Holley, Irondequoit, Murray, Ogden, Parman, Penfield, Perinton, Pittsford, Riga, Spencerport, Sweden, and Webster, NY.

3106 WITR-FM - 89.7
Rochester Institute of Technology
1 Lomb Memorial Dr.
PO Box 20563   Phone: (716)475-2000
Rochester, NY 14602-0563   Fax: (716)475-5817

3107 WVOR-FM - 100.5
PO Box 40400   Phone: (716)454-3942
Rochester, NY 14604   Fax: (716)454-5010

ROCKVILLE

3108 Rockville Centre Herald
Richner Publicatons, Inc.
143 E. Park Ave.   Phone: (516)431-3400
Long Beach, NY 11561-3522   Fax: (516)889-4419
Community newspaper. Founded: 1990. Frequency: Weekly (Wed.). Cols./Page: 6. Col. Depth: 200 agate lines. Key Personnel: Jeff Kluewer, Editor; Clifford Richner, Publisher; Stuart Richner, Publish-

er; Barbara Klein, Advertising Mgr. **USPS:** 398-610. **Subscription:** $12; $20 two years.

Ad Rates:

GLR:	$.64	**Circulation:** Paid ‡3,160
BW:	$768	Non-paid ‡2,011
SAU:	$12.32	
PCI:	$8.96	

ROCKVILLE CENTRE

3109 The Heavyweight Champions: Ring Special
The Ring Magazine, Inc.
PO Box 768
Rockville Centre, NY 11571-9905
Boxing magazine featuring the heavyweight champions of the world. **Frequency:** Quarterly. **Key Personnel:** Steven Farhood, Editor; Stanley Weston, Publisher. **Subscription:** $3.95 single issue.
Circulation: (Not Reported)

3110 WCW Magazine
G.C. London Publishing Enterprises, Inc.
55 Maple Ave.
Rockville Centre, NY 11570
Wrestling magazine. **Frequency:** Monthly. **Key Personnel:** Craig Peters, Editor; Stanley Weston, Publisher. **Subscription:** $24.95. $2.95 single issue.
Circulation: (Not Reported)

ROME

3111 WZLB-AM - 1450
549 S. Jay St.
RD 6, Box 22   Phone: (315)336-7700
Rome, NY 13440   Fax: (315)336-1447

ROOSEVELTOWN

3112 CKON-FM - 97.3
PO Box 140   Phone: (518)358-3426
Rooseveltown, NY 13683   Fax: (613)575-2064
Format: Album-Oriented Rock (AOR) (heavy metal). **Key Personnel:** Bill Henry Reidy, Music Dir.

ROSENDALE

3113 Binnewater Tides
Women's Studio Workshop
PO Box 489
Rosendale, NY 12472   Phone: (914)658-9133
Newspaper for women artists, including writers and photographers. **Founded:** 1987. **Frequency:** Quarterly. **Printing Method:** Offset. **Key Personnel:** Ann Kalmbach, Editor. **Subscription:** $10; $18 other.
Circulation: Paid ‡1,000
Non-paid ‡6,000
$55/business card ad.

ROTTERDAM

3114 WTRY-FM - 98.3
316 Canal Sq.
Schenectady, NY 12305   **Phone: (518)786-3623**

SALAMANCA

3115 Security News
Terra Publishing, Inc.
PO Box 460   Phone: (716)945-3488
Salamanca, NY 14779   Fax: (716)945-5238
Subtitle: The News Source for the Security Industry. **Founded:** 1990. **Frequency:** Monthly. **Printing Method:** Web offset. **Trim Size:** 10 1/2 x 17. **Cols./Page:** 4. **Key Personnel:** Timothy Jackson, Editor and Publisher; Richard Hahn, Advertising Mgr. **USPS:** 001-171.

Ad Rates:

BW:	$2,250	**Circulation:** Paid ⊕19,220
4C:	$2,875	Non-paid ⊕150

SCHENECTADY

3116 WMHT-FM - 89.1
Box 17   Phone: (518)356-1700
Schenectady, NY 12301   Fax: (518)356-0173
Format: Public Radio; Classical. **Owner:** WMHT Educational Telecommunications, Inc. **Founded:** 1990. **Operating Hours:** Continuous. **Key Personnel:** W. Donn Rogosin, Pres./Gen. Mgr.; Marianna Cunningham, Dir.; Karen Perretta, Program Dir. **Wattage:** 11,000. **Ad Rates:** Noncommercial.

3117 WRHV-FM - 88.7
Box 17   **Phone: (518)356-1700**
Schenectady, NY 12301   **Fax: (518)356-0173**

3118 WVKZ-AM - 1240
433 State St.   **Phone: (518)382-5400**
Schenectady, NY 12305   **Fax: (518)370-5394**

3119 WWCP-FM - 96.7
433 State St., Ste. 123   **Phone: (518)382-5400**
Schenectady, NY 12305   **Fax: (518)370-5394**

3120 WZRQ-FM - 102.3
316 Canal Sq.   **Phone: (518)381-1180**
Schenectady, NY 12305   **Fax: (518)393-0316**

SENECA FALLS

3121 WSFW-AM - 1110
1 Water St.   Phone: (315)568-9888
Seneca Falls, NY 13148-0608   **Fax: (315)568-9889**

3122 WSFW-FM - 99.3
1 Water St.   Phone: (315)568-9888
Seneca Falls, NY 13148-0608   **Fax: (315)568-9889**

SKANEATELES

3123 Skaneateles Press
Eagle Newspapers
Box 6   Phone: (315)637-3121
Fayetteville, NY **13066**   Fax: (315)637-3124

SOUTHAMPTON

3124 Southampton Press
Southampton Town Newspapers
135 Windmill Ln.
PO Box 1207   Phone: (516)283-4100
Southampton, NY 11968   **Fax: (516)283-4927**

STATEN ISLAND

3125 Staten Island Cable
100 Cable Way   Phone: (718)447-7000
Staten Island, NY 10303   Fax: (718)816-8433
Owner: Cox Cable Communications/Time Warner Communications. **Founded:** 1986. **Key Personnel:** Stephen Pagano, Gen. Mgr./Pres.; Chris Van Name, V.P. of Marketing; Roy Menton, Program & Production Mgr.; Josh Caplan, Advertising Sales Mgr.; Henry Schwab, Plant Operations Mgr. **Cities Served:** Richmond County, NY: 74,000 subscribing households; 77 channels; 4 community access channelS; 136 hours per week of community access programming.

STUYVESANT STATION

3126 Seconds
Seconds Magazine
PO Box 2553
Stuyvesant Station, NY 10009
Magazine profiling underground and alternative music. **Founded:**

Ad Rates: GLR = general line rate; BW = one-time black & white page rate; 4C = one-time four color page rate; SAU = standard advertising unit rate;
CNU = Canadian newspaper advertising unit rate; PCI = per column inch rate.
Circulation: ★ = ABC; △ = BPA; ◆ = CAC; ● = CCAB; □ = VAC; ⊕ = PO Statement; ‡ = Publisher's Report; Boldface figures = sworn; Light figures = estimated.
Entry type: ▣ = Print; ▇ = Broadcast.

207

1991. **Frequency:** 6x/yr. **Key Personnel:** S. Barrymore Blush, Editor. **Subscription:** $15. $2.50 single issue.

Circulation: (Not Reported)

SYOSSET

♣ 3127 WKWZ-FM - 88.5
Southwoods Rd.   Phone: (516)364-5745
Syosset, NY 11791   **Fax: (516)921-6032**

SYRACUSE

⌘ 3128 The Dolphin
LeMoyne College
16 Loyola Hall   Phone: (315)445-4542
Syracuse, NY 13214-1399   **Fax: (315)445-4520**

♣ 3129 Cooke Cablevision
500 S. Salina St.   Phone: (315)471-1911
Syracuse, NY 13202   Fax: (315)471-1502
Owner: Adelphia Communications Corp. **Founded:** 1979. **Cities Served:** Onondaga County, NY.

♣ 3130 Syracuse NewChannels Corp.
6154 Thompson Rd.
Box 4791
Syracuse, NY 13221   Phone: (315)437-1401
Owner: NewChannels Corp. **Founded:** 1974. **Key Personnel:** Mark Ganley, V.P./Gen. Mgr.; Terry Brennan, Marketing Mgr.; Mike Kennedy, Technical Mgr.; Mary Cotter, V.P. **Cities Served:** Cayuga County, Onondaga County, Oswego County, Brutus, Camillus, Cato, Cicero, Clay, De Witt, East Syracuse, Elbridge, Fayetteville, Geddes, Ira, Jordan, La Fayette, Liverpool, Lysander, Manlius, Marcellus, Mentz, Meridian, Minoa, North Syracuse, Onondaga, Otisco, Phoenix, Pompey, Port Byron, Salina, Skaneateles, Solvay, Tully, Van Buren, and Weedsport, NY: 80,000 subscribing households; 50 channels; 1 community access channel; 25 hours per week of community access programming.

♣ 3131 WMHR-FM - 102.9
4044 Makyes Rd.   Phone: (315)469-5051
Syracuse, NY 13215   **Fax: (315)469-4066**

TARRYTOWN

⌘ 3132 Accounting, Management and Information Technologies
Pergamon Press
660 White Plains Rd.
Tarrytown, NY 10591-5153   Phone: (914)524-9200
Journal covering the interrelations of management and accounting. **Founded:** 1991. **Frequency:** Quarterly. **Key Personnel:** Richard J. Boland, Editor. **ISSN:** 0959-8022. **Subscription:** $296.

Circulation: (Not Reported)

⌘ 3133 American Bookseller
560 White Plains Rd.   Phone: (914)631-7800
Tarrytown, NY 10591   **Fax: (914)631-8391**

⌘ 3134 Applied Mathematics Letters
Pergamon Press
660 White Plains Rd.   Phone: (914)524-9200
Tarrytown, NY 10591-5153   Fax: (914)333-2444
Scientific journal. **Subtitle:** An International Journal of Rapid Publication. **Founded:** 1988. **Frequency:** 6x/yr. **Key Personnel:** E. Y. Rodin, Editor. **ISSN:** 0893-9659.

Circulation: Non-paid 700
Advertising accepted; contact publisher for rates.

⌘ 3135 Biomass & Bioenergy
Pergamon Press
660 White Plains Rd.
Tarrytown, NY 10591-5153   Phone: (914)524-9200
Journal covering all aspects of biomass and bioenergy research. **Frequency:** Monthly. **Key Personnel:** J. Coombs, Editor. **ISSN:** 0961-9534. **Subscription:** $589.

Circulation: (Not Reported)

⌘ 3136 Chaos, Solitons, and Fractals
Pergamon
660 White Plains Rd.
Tarrytown, NY 10591-5153   Phone: (914)524-9200
Journal covering bifurcation and singularity theory; deterministic chaos and fractals. **Frequency:** Bimonthly. **Key Personnel:** M.S. El Naschie, Editor. **ISSN:** 0960-0779. **Subscription:** $608.

Circulation: (Not Reported)

⌘ 3137 Children and Youth Services Review
Pergamon Press, Inc.
660 White Plains Rd.   Phone: (914)524-9200
Tarrytown, NY 10591-5153   Fax: (914)333-2444

⌘ 3138 Chromatographia
Pergamon Press, Inc.
660 White Plains Rd.   Phone: (914)524-9200
Tarrytown, NY 10591-5153   Fax: (914)333-2444

⌘ 3139 Clinical Hemorheology
Pergamon Press, Inc.
660 White Plains Rd.   Phone: (914)524-9200
Tarrytown, NY 10591-5153   Fax: (914)333-2444

⌘ 3140 Clinical Psychology Review
Pergamon Press Inc.
660 White Plains Rd.
Tarrytown, NY 10591-5153
Official journal of the Division of Clinical Psychology of the American Psychological Association. Contains papers on clinical psychology and related topics. **Founded:** 1980. **Frequency:** 8x/yr. **Trim Size:** 7 x 10. **Cols./Page:** 1. **Key Personnel:** Alan S. Bellack, Co-Editor; Michel Hersen, Co-Editor; Peggie Mahon, Editorial Asst.; Burt Bolton, Editorial Asst. **ISSN:** 0272-7358. **Subscription:** $94; $375 institutions; $712.50 institutions/two years.

Circulation: (Not Reported)
Advertising accepted; contact publisher for rates. **Additional Contact Information:** Editorial offices: Medical College of Pennsylvania at EPPI, 3200 Henry Ave., Philadelphia, PA 19129.

⌘ 3141 Comparative Biochemistry and Physiology: Part A: Comparative Physiology
Pergamon Press, Inc.
660 White Plains Rd.   Phone: (914)524-9200
Tarrytown, NY 10591-5153   Fax: (914)333-2444

⌘ 3142 Comparative Immunology, Microbiology and Infectious Diseases
Pergamon Press, Inc.
660 White Plains Rd.   Phone: (914)524-9200
Tarrytown, NY 10591-5153   Fax: (914)333-2444

⌘ 3143 Computer Languages
Pergamon Press, Inc.
660 White Plains Rd.   Phone: (914)524-9200
Tarrytown, NY 10591-5153   Fax: (914)333-2444

⌘ 3144 Computerized Medical Imaging and Graphics
Pergamon Press, Inc.
660 White Plains Rd.   Phone: (914)524-9200
Tarrytown, NY 10591-5153   Fax: (914)333-2444

⌘ 3145 Computers in Biology and Medicine
Pergamon Press, Inc.
660 White Plains Rd.   Phone: (914)524-9200
Tarrytown, NY 10591-5153   Fax: (914)333-2444

⌘ 3146 Computers & Chemical Engineering
Pergamon Press, Inc.
660 White Plains Rd.   Phone: (914)524-9200
Tarrytown, NY 10591-5153   Fax: (914)333-2444

⌘ 3147 Computers & Chemistry
Pergamon Press, Inc.
660 White Plains Rd.   Phone: (914)524-9200
Tarrytown, NY 10591-5153   Fax: (914)333-2444

⌘ 3148 Computers & Education
Pergamon Press, Inc.
660 White Plains Rd.   Phone: (914)524-9200
Tarrytown, NY 10591-5153   Fax: (914)333-2444

📖 **3149 Computers & Electrical Engineering**
Pergamon Press, Inc.
660 White Plains Rd.   Phone: (914)524-9200
Tarrytown, NY 10591-5153   Fax: (914)333-2444

📖 **3150 Computers & Fluids**
Pergamon Press, Inc.
660 White Plains Rd.   Phone: (914)524-9200
Tarrytown, NY 10591-5153   Fax: (914)333-2444

📖 **3151 Computers & Geosciences**
Pergamon Press, Inc.
660 White Plains Rd.   Phone: (914)524-9200
Tarrytown, NY 10591-5153   Fax: (914)333-2444

📖 **3152 Computers & Graphics**
Pergamon Press, Inc.
660 White Plains Rd.   Phone: (914)524-9200
Tarrytown, NY 10591-5153   Fax: (914)333-2444

📖 **3153 Computers & Industrial Engineering**
Pergamon Press, Inc.
660 White Plains Rd.   Phone: (914)524-9200
Tarrytown, NY 10591-5153   Fax: (914)333-2444

📖 **3154 Computers & Mathematics with Applications**
Pergamon Press, Inc.
660 White Plains Rd.   Phone: (914)524-9200
Tarrytown, NY 10591-5153   Fax: (914)333-2444

📖 **3155 Computers & Operations Research**
Pergamon Press, Inc.
660 White Plains Rd.   Phone: (914)524-9200
Tarrytown, NY 10591-5153   Fax: (914)333-2444

📖 **3156 Computers & Structures**
Pergamon Press, Inc.
660 White Plains Rd.   Phone: (914)524-9200
Tarrytown, NY 10591-5153   Fax: (914)333-2444

📖 **3157 Drug Information Journal**
Pergamon Press, Inc.
660 White Plains Rd.   Phone: (914)524-9200
Tarrytown, NY 10591-5153   Fax: (914)333-2444

📖 **3158 Environmental Toxicology and Chemistry**
Pergamon Press
660 White Plains Rd.   Phone: (914)524-9200
Tarrytown, NY 10591-5153   Fax: (914)333-2444
Official journal of the Society of Environmental Toxicology and
Chemistry; contains research in environmental chemistry and toxicol-
ogy and hazard assessment. **Subtitle:** An International Journal.
Founded: 1982. **Frequency:** Monthly. **Trim Size:** 6 3/4 X 9. **Cols./Page:**
2. **Col. Width:** 2 5/8 in. **Col. Depth:** 8 1/4 in. **Key Personnel:** C. H.
Ward, Editor-in-Chief. **ISSN:** 0730-7268. **Subscription:** $30 students;
$90; $495 institutions.
Ad Rates: BW: $600   **Circulation:** Paid 3,100
Additional Contact Information: Editorial address: Rice University,
Dept. of Environmental Science and Engineering, Houston, TX
77251, ph: (713)527-8101, ext. 2603, fax: (713)285-5203.

📖 **3159 Evaluation and Program Planning**
Pergamon Press, Inc.
660 White Plains Rd.   Phone: (914)524-9200
Tarrytown, NY 10591-5153   Fax: (914)333-2444

📖 **3160 Experimental Gerontology**
Pergamon Press
660 White Plains Rd.
Tarrytown, NY 10591-5153   Phone: (714)524-9200
Journal of scientific reports on gerontology. **Founded:** 1972. **Frequen-
cy:** 2x/mo. **Key Personnel:** Dr. Leonard Hayflick, Editor.
                              Circulation: (Not Reported)
Additional Contact Information: Editorial office: PO Box 89, The Sea
Ranch, CA 95497, phone: (707)785-3181, fax: (707)785-3809.

📖 **3161 Expert Systems With Applications: An International Journal**
Pergamon Press
660 White Plains Rd.
Tarrytown, NY 10591-5153   Phone: (914)524-9200
Journal covering expert systems technology and applications in a wide
array of areas. **Frequency:** Quarterly. **Key Personnel:** Jay Liebowitz,
Editor. **ISSN:** 0957-4174. **Subscription:** $437.
                              Circulation: (Not Reported)

📖 **3162 Free Radical Biology & Medicine**
Pergamon Press
660 White Plains Rd.
Tarrytown, NY 10591-5153   Phone: (914)524-9200
Founded: 1987. **Frequency:** Monthly. **Key Personnel:** Dr. William A.
Pryor, Co-Editor-in-Chief; Dr. Kelvin J.A. Davies, Co-Editor-in-
Chief.
                              Circulation: (Not Reported)
Advertising accepted; contact publisher for rates. Formed by merger
of Advances in Free Radical Biology & Medicine and Free Radicals in
Biology & Medicine (1987). **Additional Contact Information:** Editorial
address: Louisianna State University, 711 Choppin, Baton Rouge, LA
70803-1800; phone (504)388-2063, fax (504)388-4936.

📖 **3163 Government Publications Review**
Pergamon Press, Inc.
660 White Plains Rd.   Phone: (914)524-9200
Tarrytown, NY 10591-5153   Fax: (914)333-2444

📖 **3164 Habitat International**
Pergamon Press, Inc.
660 White Plains Rd.   Phone: (914)524-9200
Tarrytown, NY 10591-5153   Fax: (914)333-2444

📖 **3165 International Communications in Heat and Mass Transfer**
Pergamon Press, Inc.
660 White Plains Rd.   Phone: (914)524-9200
Tarrytown, NY 10591-5153   Fax: (914)333-2444

📖 **3166 Journal of Aerosol Science**
Pergamon Press, Inc.
660 White Plains Rd.   Phone: (914)524-9200
Tarrytown, NY 10591-5153   Fax: (914)333-2444

📖 **3167 Journal of Insect Physiology**
Pergamon Press, Inc.
660 White Plains Road   Phone: (914)524-9200
Tarrytown, NY 10591-5153   Fax: (914)333-2444

📖 **3168 Journal of Physics and Chemistry of Solids**
Pergamon Press, Inc.
660 White House Plains   Phone: (914)524-9200
Tarrytown, NY 10591-5153   Fax: (914)333-2444

📖 **3169 The Journal of Steroid Biochemistry and Molecular Biology**
Pergamon Press, Inc.
660 White Plains Road   Phone: (914)524-9200
Tarrytown, NY 10591-5153   Fax: (914)333-2444

📖 **3170 Journal of Terramechanics**
Pergamon Press, Inc.
660 White Plains Road   Phone: (914)524-9200
Tarrytown, NY 10591-5153   Fax: (914)333-2444

📖 **3171 Journal of Thermal Biology**
Pergamon Press, Inc.
660 White Plains Road   Phone: (914)524-9200
Tarrytown, NY 10591-5153   Fax: (914)333-2444

🕮 3172 Journal of Vestibular Research
Pergamon Press
660 White Plains Rd.
Tarrytown, NY 10591-5153   Phone: (914)524-9200
Journal covering the neurophysiology of the vestibular and related visual function. **Frequency:** Quarterly. **Key Personnel:** Ralph M. Jell, Editor; Desmond J. Ireland, Editor. **ISSN:** 0957-4271. **Subscription:** $190.

         Circulation: (Not Reported)

🕮 3173 Learning and Instruction: The Journal of the European Association for Research on Learning and Instruction
Pergamon Press
660 White Plains Rd.
Tarrytown, NY 10591-5153   Phone: (914)524-9200
Journal covering learning, development, instruction, and teaching. **Founded:** 1991. **Frequency:** Quarterly. **Key Personnel:** Erik De Corte, Editor. **ISSN:** 0959-4752. **Subscription:** $179.80.
         Circulation: (Not Reported)

🕮 3174 Leonardo
Pergamon Press, Inc.
660 White Plains Road   Phone: (914)524-9200
Tarrytown, NY 10591   Fax: (914)333-2444

🕮 3175 Mathematical and Computer Modelling
Pergamon Press
660 White Plains Rd.   Phone: (914)524-9200
Tarrytown, NY 10591-5153   Fax: (914)333-2444
Scientific journal. **Subtitle:** An International Journal. **Founded:** 1980. **Frequency:** Monthly. **Key Personnel:** E. Y. Rodin, Editor. **ISSN:** 0895-7177.
         Circulation: Non-paid 1,000
Advertising accepted; contact publisher for rates.

🕮 3176 Microgravity Quarterly
Pergamon Press
660 White Plains Rd.
Tarrytown, NY 10591-5153   Phone: (914)524-9200
Journal seeking to promote the culture of microgravity environment. **Frequency:** Quarterly. **Key Personnel:** L.G. Napolitano, contact. **ISSN:** 0958-5036. **Subscription:** $266.
         Circulation: (Not Reported)

🕮 3177 Progress in Solid State Chemistry
Pergamon Press, Inc.
660 White Plains Rd.   Phone: (914)524-9200
Tarrytown, NY 10591   Fax: (914)333-2444

🕮 3178 Renewable Energy: An International Journal
Pergamon Press
660 White Plains Rd.
Tarrytown, NY 10591-5153   Phone: (914)524-9200
Journal covering new developments in renewable energy. **Frequency:** Bimonthly. **Key Personnel:** A.A. Sayigh, Editor. **ISSN:** 0960-1481. **Subscription:** $561.
         Circulation: (Not Reported)

🕮 3179 Swimsuit Spectacular
Star Editorial, Inc.
660 White Plains Rd.
Tarrytown, NY 10591
Fashion magazine featuring celebrities and readers from STAR. **Frequency:** 5x/yr. **Key Personnel:** Anne Eaton, Editor. **Subscription:** $1.95 single issue.
         Circulation: (Not Reported)

TICONDEROGA

🎙 3180 WANC-FM - 103.9
c/o WAMC-FM
318 Central Ave.   Phone: (518)465-5233
Albany, NY 12206   Fax: (518)432-0991

TONAWANDA

🕮 3181 ELF: Eclectic Literary Forum
ELF Associates Inc.
PO Box 392
Tonawanda, NY 14150   Phone: (716)693-7006
Magazine profiling literary works. **Founded:** 1991. **Frequency:** Quarterly. **Printing Method:** Offset. **Trim Size:** 8 1/2 x 11. **Cols./Page:** 1 or 2. **Col. Depth:** 8 3/4. **Key Personnel:** C.K. Erbes, Editor; S.J. DiChristina, Assoc. Editor; Suzanne Neubauer, Publisher. **ISSN:** 1054-3376. **Subscription:** $12; $20 other countries; $24 institutions. $4 single issue.
         Circulation: Paid ‡2,500
         Non-paid ‡2,800
Advertising accepted; contact publisher for rates.

TROY

🎙 3182 TroyNewChannels
59 Leversee Rd.   Phone: (518)237-3740
Troy, NY 12182   Fax: (518)237-1217
Owner: NewChannels Corp. **Founded:** 1972. **Cities Served:** Albany, Rensselaer, and Saratoga counties, NY.

TUPPER LAKE

🎙 3183 WRGR-FM - 102.3
Box 1030
Tupper Lake, NY 12986   **Phone: (518)359-9747**

UTICA

🎙 3184 Harron Cable of New York
Box 105   Phone: (315)797-8111
Utica, NY 13503   Fax: (315)797-9722
Owner: Harron Communications Group. **Founded:** 1964. **Cities Served:** Herkimer and Oneida East counties, NY.

🎙 3185 WOWB-FM - 105.5
PO Box 4490   Phone: (315)823-1230
Utica, NY 13504-4490   **Fax: (315)823-1231**

VICTOR

🕮 3186 Victor This Week
A & P Publishing Co.
PO Box 506   **Phone: (716)264-4690**
Pittsford, NY 14534   **Fax: (716)264-9779**
Former Title: Victor-Farmington Herald

WALDEN

🕮 3187 Wallkill Valley Times
23 E. Main St.
PO Box 446   Phone: (914)778-2181
Walden, NY 12586   **Fax: (914)778-1196**

WEST NYACK

🕮 3188 Rockland Review
55 Virginia Ave.
PO Box 211   Phone: (914)358-0222
West Nyack, NY 10994-0211   **Fax: (914)358-1162**

WEST SENECA

🎙 3189 Adelphia Cable
789 Indian Church Rd.   Phone: (716)827-9444
West Seneca, NY 14224   Fax: (716)827-3890
Owner: Adelphia Communications Corp. **Founded:** 1965. **Cities Served:** Erie County, Niagara County, Amherst, Blasdell, Boston, Cheektowaga, Depew, Eden, Hamburg, Kenmore, Lackawanna, North Tonawanda, West Seneca, Wheatfield, and Williamsville, NY.

WHITE HALL

♣ 3190 WNYV-FM - 94.1
Box 141
White Hall, NY 12887   Phone: (802)287-9031
Format: Oldies; Adult Contemporary; Contemporary Country. **Owner:** Pine Tree Broadcasting Co. **Founded:** 1990. **Operating Hours:** 5:30 a.m.-midnight. **Key Personnel:** Judith E. Leech, Gen. Mgr./Sales Mgr.; Joel W. Williams, News Dir.; Chris McCormack, Program Dir.; Keith Harrington, Sports Dir.; Helen Willis, Public Service Dir. **Wattage:** 3000. **Ad Rates:** Combined rates available with WVNR-AM: $6.75-$9.50 for 30 seconds; $8.25-$11 for 60 seconds. **Additional Contact Information:** Alt. telephone (802)287-9030.

WHITE PLAINS

▢ 3191 Aviation Monthly
Peter Katz Productions, Inc.
PO Box 831
White Plains, NY 10602-0831   **Phone: (914)949-7443**

▢ 3192 Interactive Media Business
Knowledge Industry Publications, Inc.
701 Westchester Ave.   Phone: (914)328-9157
White Plains, NY 10604   Fax: (914)328-9093
Subtitle: For Publishers and Developers of Interactive Media. **Founded:** 1992. **Frequency:** Monthly. **Printing Method:** Offset. **Trim Size:** 8 1/2 x 11. **Cols./Page:** 3. **Key Personnel:** Howard Millman, Editor; Barbara Stockwell, Publisher. **ISSN:** 1065-299X. **Subscription:** $65; $115 other countries. $9.75 single issue.
Ad Rates: BW: $1,700   **Circulation:** (Not Reported)
         4C: $2,375

▢ 3193 NTSB Reporter
Peter Katz Productions, Inc.
PO Box 831
White Plains, NY 10602-0831   **Phone: (914)949-7443**

WILLIAMSVILLE

▢ 3194 Northstar
Erie Community College
6205 Main St.   **Phone: (716)851-1597**
Williamsville, NY 14221   **Fax: (716)851-1335**

♣ 3195 WNUC-FM - 107.7
5500 Main St.   Phone: (716)626-1077
Williamsville, NY 14221   Fax: (716)626-1395

WINGDALE

♣ 3196 Cablevision of Dutchess
Rte. 22, RR 1
Box 133   Phone: (914)832-3350
Wingdale, NY 12594   Fax: (914)832-3129

YONKERS

▢ 3197 The Pelham Sun
Martinelli Publications
40 Larkin Pl.   Phone: (914)965-4000
Yonkers, NY 10701   Fax: (914)965-4026

▢ 3198 Zillions
Consumers Union of U.S., Inc.
101 Truman Ave.   Phone: (914)378-2000
Yonkers, NY 10703   **Fax: (914)378-2904**

♣ 3199 Cablevision Systems Corp.
1150 Yonkers Ave.   Phone: (914)237-1600
Yonkers, NY 10704   Fax: (919)237-0454
Owner: Cablevision Systems Corp. **Founded:** 1977. **Cities Served:** Westchester County, NY.

Ad Rates: GLR = general line rate; BW = one-time black & white page rate; 4C = one-time four color page rate; SAU = standard advertising unit rate; CNU = Canadian newspaper advertising unit rate; PCI = per column inch rate.
Circulation: ★ = ABC; △ = BPA; ◆ = CAC; ● = CCAB; □ = VAC; ⊕ = PO Statement; ‡ = Publisher's Report; Boldface figures = sworn; Light figures = estimated.
Entry type: ▢ = Print; ♣ = Broadcast.

211

NORTH CAROLINA

ANDREWS

📖 **3200 The Andrews Journal**
Community Newspapers, Inc.
PO Box 250   Phone: (704)321-4271
Andrews, NC 28901   **Fax: (704)321-5890**

ASHEVILLE

📖 **3201 Asheville Citizen-Times**
Asheville Citizen-Times Publishing Co.
14 O. Henry Ave.
PO Box 2090   Phone: (704)252-5611
Asheville, NC 28801   Fax: (704)251-0585
Former Title: Ashville Citizen

🎙 **3202 WCQS-FM - 88.1**
73 Broadway   Phone: (704)253-6875
Asheville, NC 28801   **Fax: (704)253-6700**

🎙 **3203 WFQS-FM - 91.3**
73 Broadway   Phone: (704)253-6875
Asheville, NC 28801   **Fax: (704)253-6700**

BEAUFORT

🎙 **3204 WBTB-AM - 1400**
PO Box 940   Phone: (919)247-6343
Beaufort, NC 28516   Fax: (919)247-7343

BELHAVEN

🎙 **3205 Belhaven Cable TV**
PO Box 8   Phone: (919)943-3736
Belhaven, NC 27810   **Fax: (919)943-3738**

BLACK MOUNTAIN

🎙 **3206 WAVJ-AM - 1350**
PO Box 1360
Black Mountain, NC 28711   **Phone: (704)669-5683**

BOONE

📖 **3207 Albion: A Quarterly Journal Concerned with British Studies**
Dept. of History
Appalachian State University   Phone: (704)262-6004
Boone, NC 28608   Fax: (704)262-2592
Founded: 1968. **Frequency:** Quarterly. **Trim Size:** 6 x 9. **Key Personnel:**

Michael J. Moore, Editor. **ISSN:** 0095-1390. **Subscription:** $40; $55 institutions.
Ad Rates: BW: $150   **Circulation:** Paid ‡1,503
       Non-paid ‡34

📖 **3208 Trophy Striper**
The Fishing Report, Inc.
PO Box 386
Boone, NC 28607
Fishing magazine. **Frequency:** 6x/yr. **Key Personnel:** R.D. Hodges, Editor. **Subscription:** $15. $2.95 single issue.
       Circulation: (Not Reported)

BRYSON CITY

🎙 **3209 WBHN-AM - 1590**
Bennett Hill Rd.
PO Box 1309   Phone: (204)488-2682
Bryson City, NC 28713   **Fax: (704)488-3594**

BURLINGTON

📖 **3210 City-County Magazine**
PO Box 517   Phone: (919)226-8436
Burlington, NC 27216   **Fax: (919)226-8437**

BURNSVILLE

📖 **3211 The Yancey Journal**
PO Drawer 280   Phone: (704)682-2120
Burnsville, NC 28714   **Fax: (704)682-9421**

CARY

📖 **3212 Behavioral Ecology**
Oxford University Press
2001 Evans Rd.   Phone: 800-852-7323
Cary, NC 27513   Fax: (919)677-1714
Founded: 1990. **Frequency:** Quarterly. **Printing Method:** Offset. **Trim Size:** 8 1/2 x 11. **Key Personnel:** Donald L. Kramer, Editor; Staffan Ulfstrand, Editor. **Subscription:** $120.
Ad Rates: BW: $300   **Circulation:** Paid 1,125
       Non-paid 32

CHAPEL HILL

📖 **3213 The Triangle Comic Review**
PO Box 2896   Phone: (919)968-4244
Chapel Hill, NC 27515-2896   **Fax: (919)968-3700**

3214 WXYC-FM - 89.3
PO Box 51, Carolina Union
Chapel Hill, NC 27599   Phone: (919)962-7768
Format: Alternative/Independent/Progressive. Key Personnel: Randy Bullock, Music Dir. Ad Rates: Noncommercial.

CHARLOTTE

3215 GO Magazine
AAA Carolina Motor Club
PO Box 30008   Phone: (704)377-3600
Charlotte, NC 28230   Fax: (704)358-1585
Former Title: GO

3216 Hosiery News
Natl. Assn. of Hosiery Manufacturers
200 N. Sharon Amity Rd.   Phone: (704)365-0913
Charlotte, NC 28211   Fax: (704)362-2056

3217 Star & Lamp
Pi Kappa Phi Fraternity
PO Box 240526   Phone: (704)523-6000
Charlotte, NC 28224   Fax: (704)521-8962
Former Title: The Star & Lamp of Pi Kappa Phi

3218 Cablevision of Charlotte
316 E. Morehead   Phone: (704)377-2228
Charlotte, NC 28202   Fax: (704)332-4550
Owner: American TV & Communications Corp. Founded: 1967. Cities Served: Mecklenburg County and Matthews, NC.

DURHAM

3219 Baseball America
Baseball America, Inc.
PO Box 2089   Phone: (919)682-9635
Durham, NC 27702   Fax: (919)682-2880

3220 The Independent
PO Box 2690   Phone: (919)286-1972
Durham, NC 27715   Fax: (919)286-4274

3221 Journal of Parapsychology
Parapsychology Press
Box 6847, College Sta.   Phone: (919)688-8241
Durham, NC 27708   Fax: (919)683-4338

3222 The Old-Time Herald
Old-Time Music Group, Inc.
1812 House Ave.   Phone: (919)490-6578
Durham, NC 27707   Fax: (919)490-6578
Magazine discussing folk music, bluegrass, cabin songs, and ballads. Subtitle: A Magazine Dedicated to Old-Time Music. Founded: 1989. Frequency: Quarterly. Key Personnel: Alice Gerrard, Editor; Bill Hicks, Assoc. Editor. USPS: 002-672. Subscription: $15; $18 other countries; $21 institutions/libraries.
    Circulation: (Not Reported)
Advertising accepted; contact publisher for rates.

3223 The South Atlantic Quarterly
Duke University Press
104 Art Museum Bldg.   Phone: (919)684-2540
Durham, NC 27708   Fax: (919)684-8644

3224 Southern Exposure
Institute for Southern Studies
PO Box 531
Durham, NC 27702   Phone: (919)419-8311

3225 Durham Cablevision
708 E. Club Blvd.
Durham, NC 27704   Phone: (919)477-3599
Owner: American TV & Communications Corp. Founded: 1977. Cities Served: Durham County, NC.

EDEN

3226 WLOE-AM - 1490
PO Box 488   Phone: (919)548-9207
Eden, NC 27288   Fax: (919)548-4636

EDENTON

3227 WBXB-FM - 100.1
Box 0   Phone: (919)482-2224
Edenton, NC 27932   Fax: (919)482-5290
Format: Gospel. Network(s): American Urban Radio; American Urban Radio. Owner: Edenton Christian Radio. Founded: 1986. Operating Hours: Continuous. Key Personnel: William L. Bonner, Station Mgr. Wattage: 50,000. Ad Rates: $4-$13 for 30 seconds; $5-$15 for 60 seconds. Additional Contact Information: (919)482-3200; (919)482-7679.

3228 WERX-FM - 102.3
PO Box 95   Phone: (919)482-2103
Edenton, NC 27932   Fax: (919)482-5591

ELIZABETH CITY

3229 WCNC-AM - 1240
PO Box 1246   Phone: (919)335-4379
Elizabeth City, NC 27906-1246   Fax: (919)338-1561

3230 WKJX-FM - 96.7
903 Halstead Blvd.   Phone: (919)338-0196
Elizabeth City, NC 27909   Fax: (919)338-0197

FARMVILLE

3231 Farmville Enterprise
Box 247   Phone: (919)753-4126
Farmville, NC 27828   Fax: (919)753-4127

FAYETTEVILLE

3232 Cablevision of Fayetteville
Box 40508   Phone: (919)864-2004
Fayetteville, NC 28309   Fax: (919)864-8878
Owner: American TV & Communications Corp. Founded: 1963. Cities Served: Cumberland, Harnett, Robeson, and Sampson counties, NC.

FOREST CITY

3233 WAGY-AM - 1320
1110 Oak St.
PO Box 280   Phone: (704)245-9887
Forest City, NC 28043   Fax: (704)287-2429

FRANKLIN

3234 WRFR-FM - 96.7
Radio Hill Rd.
PO Box 470   Phone: (704)524-4418
Franklin, NC 28734   Fax: (704)369-8070

GASTONIA

3235 WGNC-AM - 1450
PO Box 1884   Phone: (704)868-8222
Gastonia, NC 28053-1884   Fax: (704)482-4680

GOLDSBORO

3236 Goldsboro TIMES
PO Box 1659   Phone: (919)734-0302
Goldsboro, NC 27533   Fax: (919)734-2792
Former Title: Metro Times

GREENSBORO

3237 Game Players Sega Guide
GP Publications, Inc.
300-A S Westgate Dr.   Phone: (919)852-6711
Greensboro, NC 24707   Fax: (919)632-1165
Magazine contains reviews of Sega Genesis, Game Gear, and CD-ROM games. Founded: 1992. Frequency: 6x/yr. Printing Method: Web

offset. **Trim Size:** 7 7/8 x 10 3/4. **Key Personnel:** Selby Bateman, Exec. Editor; Mike Romano, Publisher. **Subscription:** $3.95 single issue.
Ad Rates: BW: $3,795   **Circulation:** (Not Reported)
              4C: $4,740

📖 **3238 News & Record**
PO Box 20848   Phone: (919)373-7000
Greensboro, NC 27420   Fax: (919)373-7043
Former Title: Greensboro News & Record

📖 **3239 Omni**
Omni Publications International Ltd.
324 W. Wendover Ave., Ste. 205   **Phone: (919)275-9809**
Greensboro, NC 27408   Fax: (919)378-1862

📖 **3240 People & Places (High Point Edition)**
1312 Long St., Ste. 104
PO Box 51458
High Point, NC 27262   Phone: (919)877-8430
Insert to the Greensboro News & Record. **Founded:** 1988. **Frequency:** Weekly. **Cols./Page:** 5. **Col. Width:** 12 picas. **Key Personnel:** Bob Burchette, Editor.
                              Circulation: (Not Reported)
Advertising accepted; contact publisher for rates.

📖 **3241 Southern Plumbing, Heating, Cooling**
Southern Trade Publications, Inc.
Box 18343
Greensboro, NC 27419   **Phone: (919)454-3516**

📖 **3242 Triad Business News**
High Point Enterprises, Inc.
5601 Roanne Way, Ste. 113
Greensboro, NC 27409   Phone: (919)854-30001
Business publication. **Founded:** 1986. **Frequency:** Weekly. **Printing Method:** Offset. **Key Personnel:** F. Dale Howard, Gen. Mgr. **Subscription:** $9.88; $42 out of state.
Ad Rates: BW: $1,792   **Circulation:** ‡15,539
              4C: $2,242

📖 **3243 United Hemispheres**
Pace Communications, Inc.
1301 Carolina St.   Phone: (919)378-6065
Greensboro, NC 27401   Fax: (919)275-2864
In flight magazine for United Airlines passengers. **Subtitle:** The World Brought to You by United Arlines. **Founded:** 1987. **Frequency:** Monthly. **Printing Method:** Web offset. **Trim Size:** 8 x 10 7/8. **Cols./Page:** 3. **Key Personnel:** Kate Greer, Editor; Bonnie McElveen-Hunter, Publisher; Gail Story, Assoc. Publisher. **Subscription:** $28. $5 single issue.
Ad Rates: BW: $23,580   **Circulation:** Non-paid △463,182
              4C: $33,690

🎙 **3244 Alert Cable TV**
5615 Sapp Rd.
Box 8549   Phone: (919)854-1200
Greensboro, NC 27409   Fax: (919)294-7957
Owner: Cablevision Industries, Inc. **Founded:** 1982. **Key Personnel:** A. Wayne Wright, Gen. Mgr. **Cities Served:** Guilford County, Rockingham County, Greensboro, and High Point, NC: 25,000 subscribing households; 44 channels; 1 community access channel.

🎙 **3245 Cablevision of Greensboro**
1813 Spring Garden St.
Box 5487   Phone: (919)379-0200
Greensboro, NC 27403   Fax: (919)274-9609
Owner: American TV & Communications Corp. **Founded:** 1968. **Cities Served:** Guilford County, NC.

🎙 **3246 WKZL-FM - 107.5**
192 E. Lewis St.   **Phone: (919)274-8042**
Greensboro, NC 27406   **Fax: (919)274-1629**

🎙 **3247 WUAG-FM - 103.1**
Taylor Bldg.
UNCG Campus
Greensboro, NC 27413   Phone: (919)334-5470
Format: Alternative/Independent/Progressive. **Key Personnel:** Eric Shepherd, Music Dir. **Ad Rates:** Noncommercial.

GREENVILLE

📖 **3248 Alcohol**
Pergamon Press
East Carolina University School of
  Medicine
Departments of Pharmacology &
  Psychiatric Medicine   Phone: (919)551-2735
Greenville, NC 27858   Fax: (919)551-3203
Biomedical research journal. **Founded:** 1984. **Frequency:** 6x/yr. **Cols./Page:** 2. **Col. Width:** 3 1/4 in. **Col. Depth:** 10 in. **Key Personnel:** R.D. Meyers, Editor. SBR $510.
                              Circulation: (Not Reported)
Advertising not accepted. Publisher's address: 660 White Plains Rd., Tarrytown, NY 10591-5153; phone (914)524-9200.

📖 **3249 The East Carolinian**
East Carolina University
Student Publications Bldg.   Phone: (919)757-6366
Greenville, NC 27858-4353   **Fax: (919)757-6558**

📖 **3250 The 'M' Voice Newspaper**
PO Box 8361   Phone: (919)757-0365
Greenville, NC 27834   **Fax: (919)757-1793**

HICKORY

🎙 **3251 Catawba Valley CATV**
1121 Lenoir-Rhyne Blvd.
Box 2989   Phone: (704)322-3875
Hickory, NC 28601   Fax: (704)322-5492
Owner: Prime Cable Corp. **Founded:** 1976. **Cities Served:** Catawba County, NC: 31,000 subscribing households; 38 channels; 1 community access channel; 8 hours per week of community access programming.

🎙 **3252 WIRC-AM - 630**
PO Box 938   **Phone: (919)322-4130**
Hickory, NC 28603   Fax: (919)324-WFAX

KINGS MOUNTAIN

🎙 **3253 WKMT-AM - 1220**
1215 Cleveland Ave.
Kings Mountain, NC 28086   Phone: (704)739-1220

KINSTON

🎙 **3254 WELS-AM - 1010**
313 N. Queen St.   Phone: (919)523-5151
Kinston, NC 28501-4931   **Fax: (919)523-9357**

🎙 **3255 WKGK-FM - 102.9**
313 N. Queen St.   Phone: (919)523-5151
Kinston, NC 28501-4931   **Fax: (919)523-9357**

LAURINBURG

🎙 **3256 WEWO-AM - 1460**
Hwy. 74 E.
Box 529   **Phone: (919)276-1460**
Laurinburg, NC 28553   Fax: (919)276-9787

Ad Rates: GLR = general line rate; BW = one-time black & white page rate; 4C = one-time four color page rate; SAU = standard advertising unit rate; CNU = Canadian newspaper advertising unit rate; PCI = per column inch rate.
Circulation: ★ = ABC; △ = BPA; ◆ = CAC; ● = CCAB; □ = VAC; ⊕ = PO Statement; ‡ = Publisher's Report; Boldface figures = sworn; Light figures = estimated.
Entry type: 📖 = Print; 🎙 = Broadcast.

215

LIBERTY

▢ **3257 The Liberty News**
PO Box 69   Phone: (919)622-4781
Liberty, NC 27298   **Fax: (919)622-4944**

LILLINGTON

▢ **3258 Harnett County News**
PO Box 939   Phone: (919)893-5121
Lillington, NC 27546   **Fax: (919)893-6128**

MADISON

▢ **3259 The Big Reel**
Empire Publishing, Inc.
3130 U.S. 220   Phone: (919)427-5850
Madison, NC 27025   Fax: (919)427-7372

♨ **3260 WMYN-AM - 1420**
PO Box 311   Phone: (919)548-9207
Madison, NC 27025   **Fax: (919)548-4636**

MATTHEWS

♨ **3261 Vision Cable of North Carolina**
4606 Margaret Wallace Rd.   Phone: (704)545-0136
Matthews, NC 28105   Fax: (704)545-1460
Owner: Vision Cable Communications, Inc. **Founded:** 1982. **Cities Served:** Lancaster County, SC and Mecklenburg and Union counties, NC.

MOCKSVILLE

♨ **3262 WDSL-AM - 1520**
PO Box 1123   Phone: (704)634-2177
Mocksville, NC 27028-2582   Fax: (704)634-5025

MONROE

♨ **3263 WDEX-AM - 1430**
PO Box 1050   Phone: (704)289-9444
Monroe, NC 28110   **Fax: (704)282-0011**

MOREHEAD CITY

♨ **3264 WKQT-FM - 103.3**
Hwy. 70 E   Phone: (919)247-6343
Morehead City, NC 28570   **Fax: (919)247-7068**

♨ **3265 WMBL-AM - 740**
Rt. 2, Box 601   **Phone: (919)240-0740**
Morehead City, NC 28557   Fax: (919)726-3188

MORGANTON

♨ **3266 WQXX-FM - 92.1**
1103 N. Green St.
PO Drawer 969   Phone: (704)437-0521
Morganton, NC 28680-0969   **Fax: (704)433-8855**

MOUNT AIRY

♨ **3267 WSYD-AM - 1300**
Box 1126   Phone: (919)786-2147
Mount Airy, NC 27030   Fax: (919)789-9858
Format: Oldies; Country; Gospel. **Owner:** E.F. Poore, 237 Main St., Mount Airy, NC 27030. **Founded:** 1951. **Operating Hours:** Continuous. **Key Personnel:** Mike Poore, Gen. Mgr.; Linda Wright, Office Mgr.; Ronald Johnson, News Dir. **Wattage:** 5000 day; 1000 night.

MOUNTAIN HOME

▢ **3268 Back Home**
Words Worth Communications, Inc.
PO Box 370   Phone: (704)696-3838
Mountain Home, NC 28758   Fax: (704)696-0700
Home magazine about rural living. **Subtitle:** HANDS-ON & DOWN-TO-EARTH. **Founded:** 1990. **Frequency:** Quarterly. **Printing Method:** Full web offset. **Trim Size:** 8 3/8 x 10 3/4. **Cols./Page:** 3. **Col. Width:** 13.5 picas. **Col. Depth:** 55 picas. **Key Personnel:** Terry Krautwurst, Editor; Richard Freudenberger, Advertising Mgr.; Liz Brennan, Circulation Mgr. **ISSN:** 1051-323X. **Subscription:** $16. $4 single issue.
Ad Rates: BW: $915   **Circulation:** ‡16,000
              4C: $1,485

NEW BERN

♨ **3269 WSFL-FM - 106.5**
Box 3436   Phone: (919)633-2406
New Bern, NC 28564   **Fax: (919)633-6546**

PLEASANT GARDEN

▢ **3270 The Short Line**
PO Box 607
Pleasant Garden, NC 27313   Phone: (919)674-2168
Journal covering current events and the history of the Shortline railroad. **Subtitle:** The Journal of Research on Shortline and Industrial Railroads. **Founded:** 1973. **Frequency:** Bimonthly. **Printing Method:** Offset. **Trim Size:** 8 1/2 x 11. **Cols./Page:** 3. **Col. Width:** 3 in. **Col. Depth:** 9 1/2 in. **Key Personnel:** Garreth M. McDonald, Editor and Publisher. **ISSN:** 0199-4050. **USPS:** 130-330. **Subscription:** $17; $21 other countries. $3 single issue.
                                        Circulation: Paid ⊕1,444
                                                       Non-paid ⊕20
Advertising not accepted.

RALEIGH

▢ **3271 Great Expeditions**
PO Box 18036   **Phone: (919)846-3600**
Raleigh, NC 27619   **Fax: (919)847-0780**

▢ **3272 North Carolina Insight**
North Carolina Center for Public Policy Research
PO Box 430
Raleigh, NC 27602   Phone: (919)832-2839
Journal. **Subtitle:** A Quarterly Journal Addressing Issues of Concern to North Carolina Citizens**Founded:** 1978. **Frequency:** Quarterly. **Trim Size:** 7 x 10. **Key Personnel:** Mike McLaughlin, Editor; Tom Mather, Associate Editor. **Subscription:** $36.
                                        Circulation: Paid ‡1,200
                                                       Non-paid ‡600

▢ **3273 North Carolina Lawyers Weekly**
107 Fayetville St. Mall   Phone: (919)829-9333
Raleigh, NC 27602   Fax: (919)829-8088
Magazine publishing statewide court decisions. **Founded:** 1988. **Frequency:** Weekly. **Printing Method:** Offset. **Trim Size:** 10 x 16. **Cols./Page:** 4. **Col. Width:** 13.5 picas. **Key Personnel:** Michael Dayton, Editor; David Blackwell, Publisher; Samantha McGakey, Advertising Mgr. **ISSN:** 1041-1747.
Ad Rates: GLR: $5.25   **Circulation:** Paid △2,958
              BW: $1,122   Non-paid △76
              4C: $1,362
              PCI: $26.75

▢ **3274 Tarheel Banker**
NC Bankers Assn.
PO Box 30609   Phone: (919)782-6960
Raleigh, NC 27622-0609   **Fax: (919)782-6701**

▢ **3275 Triangle Business Journal**
PO Box 95143   **Phone: (919)878-0010**
Raleigh, NC 27625   **Fax: (919)790-6885**

♨ **3276 Cablevision of Raleigh**
2505 Atlantic Ave.   Phone: (919)821-7925
Raleigh, NC 27604   Fax: (919)829-2670
Owner: American TV & Communications Corp. **Founded:** 1968. **Cities Served:** Wake County, NC.

♨ **3277 WQDR-FM - 94.7**
3012 Highwoods Blvd., Ste. 201   **Phone: (919)876-6464**
Raleigh, NC 27604   Fax: (919)790-6457

ROCKINGHAM

☐ **3278 Rockingham Ledger**
Greensboro News Co.
200 E. Market St.
PO Box 20848
Greensboro, NC 27420-5667   Phone: (919)373-7111
Shopping guide. **Frequency:** 2x/wk. **Subscription:** Free.
                                   Circulation: (Not Reported)
Advertising accepted; contact publisher for rates.

SHELBY

☐ **3279 Satellite Retailer**
Triple D Publishing, Inc.
1300 S. Dekalb St.   Phone: (704)482-9673
Shelby, NC 28150   Fax: (704)484-8558
Technical, service, and market information on satellite TV. **Subtitle:**
The Magazine for the Serious Satellite Dealer. **Founded:** 1985.
Frequency: Monthly. **Printing Method:** Web offset. **Trim Size:** 10 7/8 x
8 1/4. **Cols./Page:** 3. **Col. Width:** 2 1/4 in. **Col. Depth:** 8 1/2 in. **Key
Personnel:** David B. Melton, Editor; Donna B. Hovis, Advertising
Mgr. ISSN: 0890-1252. USPS: 001-824. **Subscription:** $12. $2.50
single issue.
Ad Rates: BW: $1,936   **Circulation:** Paid ⊕**8,182**
               4C: $2,596   Non-paid ⊕**2,553**

SOUTHERN PINES

🎙 **3280 WEEB-AM - 990**
Box 1855   Phone: (919)692-7440
Southern Pines, NC 28388   **Fax: (919)692-7372**

🎙 **3281 WIOZ-AM - 550**
Box 1677   Phone: (919)692-2107
Southern Pines, NC 28388   **Fax: (919)692-6849**

🎙 **3282 WIOZ-FM - 106.9**
Box 1677   Phone: (919)692-2107
Southern Pines, NC 28388   **Fax: (919)692-6849**

SPARTA

☐ **3283 The Alleghany News**
Alleghany News, Inc.
PO Box 8   Phone: (919)372-8999
Sparta, NC 28675   **Fax: (919)372-5707**

SPRUCE PINE

☐ **3284 Mitchell News Journal**
401 Locust Ave.
PO Box 339   Phone: (704)765-2071
Spruce Pine, NC 28777   Fax: (704)765-1616

SYLVA

☐ **3285 The Sylva Herald & Ruralite**
24 E. Main St.
PO Box 307   Phone: (704)586-2611
Sylva, NC 28779-0307   **Fax: (704)586-2637**

TARBORO

🎙 **3286 WCPS-AM - 760**
3403 Main St.
PO Box 100   **Phone: (919)823-2191**
Tarboro, NC 27886   Fax: (919)823-2043

WAYNESVILLE

🎙 **3287 WQNS-FM - 104.9**
PO Box 659   Phone: (704)456-8661
Waynesville, NC 28786   **Fax: (704)456-4316**

WILMINGTON

☐ **3288 UNCW Magazine**
The University of North Carolina at
  Wilmington   Phone: (919)395-3751
Wilmington, NC 28403-3297   Fax: (919)395-3847
College publication. **Founded:** 1990. **Frequency:** Quarterly. **Trim Size:**
8 1/2 x 11. **Cols./Page:** 3. **Col. Width:** 2 7/8 in. **Col. Depth:** 9 3/4 in.
Key Personnel: Mary Ellen Polson, Editor. **Subscription:** $25.
                                   Circulation: Paid 5,500
                                       Non-paid 12,000
Advertising not accepted. **Formerly:** UNCW Today.

🎙 **3289 WJKA-TV - Channel 26**
PO Box 2626   Phone: (919)343-8826
Wilmington, NC 28402   **Fax: (919)251-0978**

🎙 **3290 WMFD-AM - 630**
716 Princess St.
PO Box 1751   Phone: (919)763-6363
Wilmington, NC **28402**   **Fax: (919)251-0534**

WINDSOR

🎙 **3291 WDRP-FM - 98.9**
PO Box 567
Windsor, NC 27983-0567   **Phone: (919)794-3130**

WINSTON-SALEM

☐ **3292 Winston-Salem Chronicle**
617 N. Liberty St.
PO Box 1636   Phone: (919)722-8624
Winston-Salem, NC 27102   **Fax: (919)723-9173**

☐ **3293 Winston-Salem Magazine**
Forsyth Communications, Inc.
231 W. 5th St.
Winston-Salem, NC **27101**   Phone: (919)722-8706

🎙 **3294 Summit Cable Services**
1410 Trade Mart Blvd.   Phone: (919)785-3390
Winston-Salem, NC 27127   Fax: (919)785-9899
Owner: Summit Communications Group, Inc. **Founded:** 1970. **Cities
Served:** Davie County, Forsyth County, Bermuda Run, Clemmons,
Kernersville, and Walkertown, NC.

🎙 **3295 WAKE-FM - 89.5**
Wake Forest University
512 Benson Center
Winston-Salem, NC 27109   Phone: (919)759-4894
Format: Alternative/Independent/Progressive. **Key Personnel:** Greg
Carmicheal, Music Dir. **Ad Rates:** Noncommercial.

🎙 **3296 WSGH-AM - 1040**
Box 25368   Phone: (919)773-0869
Winston-Salem, NC 27114   **Fax: (919)699-3645**

YADKINVILLE

☐ **3297 Yadkin Ripple**
PO Box 7   Phone: (919)679-2341
Yadkinville, NC 27055   **Fax: (919)679-2340**

NORTH DAKOTA

BELCOURT

🎙 **3298 KEYA-FM - 88.5**
PO Box 190
Belcourt, ND 58316

Phone: (701)477-5686
Fax: (701)477-3252

BEULAH

📖 **3299 Beulah Beacon**
BHG, Inc.
PO Box 609
Beulah, ND 58523-0609
Community newspaper. **Frequency:** Weekly. **Printing Method:** Offset.
Cols./Page: 6. **Col. Width:** 2 in. **Col. Depth:** 21 1/2 in. **Key Personnel:**
Bob Link, Editor; Ken Beauchamp, Mng. Editor. **Subscription:** $20;
$23 out of area; $30 out of state.

Ad Rates: 4C: $200
SAU: $4.50
Local advertising rates: 4C: $165.

Circulation: Paid ⊕**2,398**
Free ⊕**39**

🎙 **3300 KHOL-AM - 1410**
Hwy. 21
Box 819
Beulah, ND 58523

Phone: (701)873-2215
Fax: (701)873-2363

BISMARCK

📖 **3301 Dakota Catholic Action**
520 N. Washington St.
PO Box 1137
Bismarck, ND 58502

Phone: (701)222-3035
Fax: (701)223-3693

📖 **3302 North Dakota Outdoors**
North Dakota Game and Fish Dept.
100 N. Bismarck Expressway
Bismarck, ND 58501-5095

Phone: (701)221-6300
Fax: (701)221-6352

🎙 **3303 KBME-TV - Channel 3**
c/o Prairie Public Broadcasting
PO Box 3240
Fargo, ND 58108-3240

Phone: (701)241-6900
Fax: (701)239-7650

🎙 **3304 KCND-FM - 90.5**
c/o Prairie Public Radio
1814 N. 15th St.
Bismarck, ND 58501

Phone: (701)224-1700
Fax: (701)224-0555

🎙 **3305 KDPR-FM - 89.9**
c/o Prairie Public Radio
1814 N. 15th St.
Bismarck, ND 58501

Phone: (701)224-1700
Fax: (701)224-0555

🎙 **3306 KXUM-AM - 670**
University of Mary
7500 University Dr.
Bismarck, ND 58504

Phone: (701)255-7500

Format: Alternative/Independent/Progressive. **Key Personnel:** John
Baker, Music Dir. **Ad Rates:** Noncommercial.

CARRINGTON

🎙 **3307 KDAK-AM - 1600**
859 Main St.
Box 50
Carrington, ND 58421

Phone: (701)652-3151
Fax: (701)652-2916

DICKINSON

🎙 **3308 KDSE-TV - Channel 9**
c/o Prairie Public Broadcasting
207 N. 5th St.
PO Box 3240
Fargo, ND 58108-3240

Phone: (701)241-6900
Fax: (701)239-7650

ELLENDALE

🎙 **3309 Dickey Rural Services**
Hwy. 281 N
PO Box 69
Ellendale, ND 58436

Phone: (701)349-3687

🎙 **3310 KJRE-TV - Channel 19**
c/o Prairie Public Broadcasting
PO Box 3240
Fargo, ND 58108-3240

Phone: (701)241-6900
Fax: (701)239-7650

Format: Public TV. Satellite of KFME-TV Fargo, ND. **Network(s):**
Public Broadcasting Service (PBS). **Owner:** Prairie Public Broadcast-
ing, at above address. **Operating Hours:** 6:45 a.m.-midnight. **ADI:**
Fargo, ND. **Key Personnel:** Dennis Falk, Pres.; Michael Trosman,
Production Mgr.; Larry White, Television Mgr. **Local Programs:**
Prairie News Journal. Prairie Town Meetings. **Ad Rates:** Noncommer-
cial.

FARGO

🎙 **3311 Cablecom of Fargo**
10624 Page Dr.
Box 2421
Fargo, ND 58106

Phone: (701)280-0033
Fax: (701)280-0094

Owner: Post-Neweek Cable, Inc. **Founded:** 1979. **Cities Served:** Cass
County, Briarwood, Frontier, and Prairie Rose, ND.

🔊 **3312 KFME-TV - Channel 13**
c/o Prairie Public Broadcasting
PO Box 3240
Fargo, ND 58108-3240   Phone: (701)241-6900
       Fax: (701)239-7650

🔊 **3313 KLTA-FM - 105.1**
2501 13th Ave S.W., Ste. 201   Phone: (701)237-4500
Fargo, ND 58103   Fax: (701)235-9082

GRAND FORKS

📖 **3314 PLAINSWOMAN**
Plainswoman, Inc.
PO Box 8027
Grand Forks, ND 58202   Phone: (701)777-8043
Ceased publication.

🔊 **3315 KGFE-TV - Channel 2**
c/o Prairie Public Broadcasting
PO Box 3240
Fargo, ND 58108-3240   Phone: (701)241-6900
       Fax: (701)239-7650

🔊 **3316 TCI of North Dakota, Inc.**
1302 N. 4th Ave.
Box 6005
Grand Forks, ND 58203-3143   Phone: (701)746-1345
Owner: Tele-Communicatons, Inc. **Founded:** 1970. **Cities Served:** Grand Forks, ND; Polk County and East Grand Forks, MN.

HARVEY

🔊 **3317 KHND-AM - 1470**
718 Lincoln Ave.
Harvey, ND 58341   Phone: (701)324-4848
Format: Contemporary Country. **Network(s):** ABC; American Ag Net. **Owner:** Prairie Communications Inc. **Founded:** 1981. **Operating Hours:** 6 a.m.-9 p.m. **Key Personnel:** Todd Lewis, Station Mgr.; Clarence Coneliusen, Program Dir.; Rusty Nichols, Music Dir.; Cyndy Medberry, Sales Mgr. **Wattage:** 1000. **Ad Rates:** $.45-$1 for 5 seconds; $2.70-$6 for 30 seconds.

HEBRON

📖 **3318 Hebron Herald**
PO Box 9
Hebron, ND 58638   Phone: (701)878-4494
       Fax: (701)878-4494

HETTINGER

📖 **3319 Obesity & Health**
Healthy Living Institute
RR 2, Box 905
Hettinger, ND 59639   Phone: (701)567-2845
       Fax: (701)567-2443
Journal covering research on all aspects of obesity. **Subtitle:** Current Research and Related Issues. **Founded:** 1986. **Frequency:** 6x/yr. **Trim Size:** 8 1/2 x 11. **Key Personnel:** Francis M. Berg, Editor and Publisher. **ISSN:** 1044-1522. **Subscription:** $59; $27 student; $60 Canada; $68 other countries.

      Circulation: Paid ⊕**1,500**
           Non-paid ⊕**50**
Advertising accepted; contact publisher for rates. **Additional Contact Information:** Francis Berg, (701)567-2646; editorial office 402 S. 14th St., Hettinger, ND 58639.

JAMESTOWN

🔊 **3320 KSJB-AM - 600**
212 1st Ave. S.
PO Box 1840   Phone: (701)252-3570
Jamestown, ND **58402-1840**   **Fax: (701)252-1277**

🔊 **3321 KSJZ-FM - 93.3**
212 1st Ave. S.
PO Box 1840   Phone: (701)252-3570
Jamestown, ND **58402-1840**   **Fax: (701)252-1277**

MINOT

🔊 **3322 KMPR-FM - 88.9**
c/o Prairie Public Radio
1814 N. 15th St.
Bismarck, ND 58501   Phone: (701)224-1700
       Fax: (701)224-0555

🔊 **3323 KMSU-AM - 790**
500 University Ave. W.
Minot, ND 58707   Phone: (701)357-3829
Format: Alternative/Independent/Progressive. **Key Personnel:** Chris Peterson, Music Dir. **Ad Rates:** Noncommercial.

🔊 **3324 TCI of North Dakota**
1919 2nd St. SE
Minot, ND 58701   Phone: (701)852-0376
Owner: Tele-Communications, Inc. **Founded:** 1974. **Cities Served:** Ward County, ND.

VALLEY CITY

🔊 **3325 KOVC-AM - 1490**
232 3rd St. NE
Box 994   Phone: (701)845-1490
Valley City, ND 58072   Fax: (701)845-2903
Format: Country. **Owner:** Ingstad Broadcasting Inc. **Founded:** 1936. **Key Personnel:** Tim Ost, Gen. Mgr.; Dave Reed, Program Dir.; Jason Hunt, Music Dir.; Paul Titchenal, Chief Engineer. **Wattage:** 1000.

WILLISTON

🔊 **3326 KPPR-FM - 89.5**
c/o Prairie Public Radio
1814 N. 15th St.
Bismarck, ND 58501   Phone: (701)224-1700
       Fax: (701)224-0555

🔊 **3327 KWSE-TV - Channel 6**
c/o Prairie Public Broadcasting
PO Box 3240
Fargo, ND 58108-3240   Phone: (701)241-6900
       Fax: (701)239-7650

WISHEK

📖 **3328 The Wishek Star**
511 Beaver Ave.
Box 275   Phone: (701)452-2331
Wishek, ND 58495   **Fax: (701)452-2340**

OHIO

AKRON

📖 **3329 The United Rubber Worker**
United Rubber, Cork, Linoleum & Plastic Workers of America, AFL-CIO, CLC
570 White Pond Dr. **Phone: (216)869-0320**
Akron, OH **44320-1156** **Fax: (216)869-5627**

🎙 **3330 Warner Cable Communications, Inc.**
1655 Brittain Rd. Phone: (216)633-9203
Akron, OH 44310 Fax: (216)633-7970
Owner: Warner Cable Communications, Inc. **Founded:** 1969. **Cities Served:** Medina, Portage, Summit, and Wayne counties, Barberton, Cuyahoga Falls, Doylestown, Fairlawn, Lakemore, Mogadore, Munroe Falls, Norton, Silver Lake, Stow, Tallmadge, and Wadsworth, OH.

ARCHBOLD

📖 **3331 Farmland News**
104 Depot St.
PO Box 240 Phone: (419)445-9456
Archbold, OH 43502-0240 **Fax: (419)445-4444**

ASHLAND

🎙 **3332 WRDL-FM - 88.9**
401 College Ave.
Ashland, OH 44805 Phone: (419)289-5139

ATHENS

🎙 **3333 WLDH-AM - 850**
E. Green Office
Athens, OH 45071 Phone: (614)597-9759
Format: Alternative/Independent/Progressive. **Key Personnel:** Neal Schmitt, Music Dir. **Ad Rates:** Noncommercial.

AURORA

📖 **3334 Aurora Advocate**
Record Publishing Co.
1619 Commerce Dr.
PO Box 1549 Phone: (216)688-0088
Stow, OH 44224-0549 **Fax: (216)688-1588**

BEREA

📖 **3335 The Exponent**
Baldwin-Wallace College
275 Eastland Rd. Phone: (216)826-2272
Berea, OH **44017-2088** Fax: (216)826-2388

📖 **3336 New Cleveland Woman**
104 E. Bridge St.
Berea, OH 44017 **Phone: (216)243-3740**
Ceased publication.

BROOKLYN HEIGHTS

🎙 **3337 Metroten Cablevision, Inc.**
1250 Granger Rd.
Brooklyn Heights, OH 44131 Phone: (216)749-7000
Owner: Metropolitan Satellite. **Founded:** 1985. **Cities Served:** Cuyahoga County, Brook Park, Brooklyn, Brooklyn Heights, and Newburgh Heights, OH.

CAMBRIDGE

🎙 **3338 WWKC-FM - 104.9**
4988 Skyline Dr.
PO Box 338
Cambridge, OH 43725 **Phone: (614)732-5777**

CANFIELD

📖 **3339 Pastoral Life**
Society of St. Paul
Phone: (216)533-5503
Canfield, OH 44406 **Fax: (216)533-1076**

CANTON

🎙 **3340 Warner Cable of Canton**
Box 8559 Phone: (216)494-9200
Canton, OH 44711 Fax: (216)497-6397
Owner: Warner Cable Communications, Inc. **Founded:** 1966. **Cities Served:** Carroll, Mahoning, Stark, and Tuscarawas counties, OH.

CHILLICOTHE

🎙 **3341 WCHI-AM - 1350**
45 W. Main St. Phone: (614)773-3000
Chillicothe, OH 45601 Fax: (614)774-4494
Format: News/Oldies/Sports. **Owner:** Wyandot Radio. **Founded:** 1950. **Operating Hours:** Continuous. **Key Personnel:** Dave Smith, Pres.; Bob

Ad Rates: GLR = general line rate; BW = one-time black & white page rate; 4C = one-time four color page rate; SAU = standard advertising unit rate; CNU = Canadian newspaper advertising unit rate; PCI = per column inch rate.
Circulation: ★ = ABC; △ = BPA; ◆ = CAC; ● = CCAB; □ = VAC; ⊕ = PO Statement; ‡ = Publisher's Report; Boldface figures = sworn; Light figures = estimated.
Entry type: 📖 = Print; 🎙 = Broadcast.

Neal, Program Dir.; John Rose, Sports Dir. **Wattage:** 1000. **Ad Rates:** $15-$20 per unit.

CINCINNATI

☐ 3342 AIPE Facilities
American Institute of Plant Engineers
8180 Corporate Park Dr., Ste. 305   Phone: (513)489-2473
Cincinnati, OH **45242**   Fax: (513)247-7422

☐ 3343 All About Kids
All About Kids, Inc.
1077 Celestial, Ste. 101   Phone: (513)684-0501
Cincinnati, OH 45202   Fax: (513)684-0507
Magazine provides information on parenting issues. **Subtitle:** A Monthly Parenting Paper. **Founded:** 1988. **Frequency:** Monthly. **Printing Method:** Web offset. **Trim Size:** 11 3/8 x 13 3/4. **Cols./Page:** 4. **Col. Width:** 2 3/8 in. **Col. Depth:** 13 in. **Subscription:** Free.
Ad Rates: BW: $1,100   **Circulation: Free ☐62,000**
                   4C: $1,750

☐ 3344 Dia a Dia
Forward Movement Publications
412 Sycamore St.   Phone: (513)721-6659
Cincinnati, OH 45202   Fax: (513)421-0315
A daily devotional (Spanish). **Frequency:** Quarterly. **Printing Method:** Offset. **Trim Size:** 3 1/2 x 5 1/2. **Cols./Page:** 1. **Col. Width:** 33 nonpareils. **Col. Depth:** 70 agate lines. **Key Personnel:** Rev. Charles H. Long, Editor/Dir. **ISSN:** 1059-1370. **Subscription:** $6 two years; $8 two years other countries. $.50 single issue.
Circulation: Paid 6,000
Advertising not accepted. **Formerly:** Dia por Dia.

☐ 3345 Eastern Hills Journal-Press
Press Community Newspapers
Northeast Newspaper Group
9121 Union Cemetary   Phone: (513)683-5115
Cincinnati, OH **45249**   Fax: (513)677-4690

☐ 3346 The Greater Cincinnati Business Record
Paige Marom Corp.
708 Walnut St., Ste. 400   Phone: (513)421-9300
Cincinnati, OH 45202   Fax: (513)421-9212

☐ 3347 HOW
F&W Publications, Inc.
1507 Dana Ave.   Phone: (513)531-2222
Cincinnati, OH 45207   Fax: (513)531-2902

☐ 3348 The Journal for Quality and Participation
Assn. for Quality and Participation
801-B W. 8th St., No. 501   Phone: (513)381-1959
Cincinnati, OH 45203   Fax: (513)381-0070

☐ 3349 Northeast Suburban Life Press
Press Community Newspapers
Northeast Newspaper Group
9121 Union Cemetary Rd.   Phone: (513)683-5115
Cincinnati, OH **45249**   Fax: (513)677-4690

☐ 3350 Spark!
F&W Publication, Inc.
1507 Dana Ave.   Phone: (513)531-2222
Cincinnati, OH 45207   Fax: (513)531-1843
Creative writing and art projects for kids. **Subtitle:** Creative Fun for Kids. **Founded:** 1991. **Frequency:** 9x/yr. **Trim Size:** 8 x 10 7/8. **Key Personnel:** Jeffry Lapin, Publisher; Michael Ward, Editor. **ISSN:** 1057-5227. **Subscription:** $19.95. $2.95 single issue.
Ad Rates: BW: $1,850   **Circulation: Paid 85,000**
                   4C: $2,645   Non-paid 10,000

☐ 3351 Suburban Life-Press
Press Community Newspapers
Northeast Newspaper Group
9121 Union Cemetary Rd.   Phone: (513)683-5115
Cincinnati, OH **45249**   Fax: (513)677-4690

☐ 3352 Teaching Theatre
Educational Theatre Association
3368 Central Pkwy.   Phone: (513)559-1996
Cincinnati, OH 45225   Fax: (513)559-0012
Journal for theater teachers. **Founded:** 1989. **Frequency:** Quarterly. **Printing Method:** Offset. **Trim Size:** 8 1/2 x 11. **Cols./Page:** 2. **Col. Width:** 22 picas. **Col. Depth:** 10 in. **Key Personnel:** James Palmarini, Editor. **Subscription:** $2 single issue.
Circulation: 1,500
Advertising not accepted.

☐ 3353 VIDEO WATCHDOG
PO Box 5283
Cincinnati, OH 45205-0283   **Phone: (513)471-8989**

♣ 3354 Warner Cable Communications, Inc.
11252 Cornell Park Dr.   Phone: (513)489-5000
Cincinnati, OH 45242   Fax: (513)489-5043
Owner: Warner Cable Communications, Inc. **Founded:** 1980. **Cities Served:** Butler County, Clemont County, Hamilton County, Warren County, Arlington Heights, Blue Ash, Deer Park, Elmwood Place, Evendale, Fairfax, Forest Park, Glendale, Goshen, Greenhills, Harrison, Indian Hill, Lebanon, Lincoln Heights, Lockland, Loveland, Madeira, Maineville, Mariemont, Mason, Milford, Montgomery, Mount Healthy, Newtown, North College Hill, Norwood, Reading, Sharonville, Silverton, South Lebanon, Springdale, Terrace Park, West Harrison, Woodlawn, and Wyoming, OH.

♣ 3355 WEBN-FM - 102.7
1111 St. Gregory   Phone: (513)621-9326
Cincinnati, OH 45202   **Fax: (513)784-1249**

♣ 3356 WMLX-AM - 1180
250 W. Court St., No. 312 E   Phone: (513)241-1180
Cincinnati, OH 45202   **Fax: (513)381-1160**

♣ 3357 WTSJ-AM - 1050
800 Compton Rd., No. 33   Phone: (513)931-8080
Cincinnati, OH 45231   **Fax: (513)931-8108**

♣ 3358 WVXU-FM - 91.7
Xavier University
3800 Victory Pkwy.   Phone: (513)731-9898
Cincinnati, OH 45207-7211   **Fax: (513)745-1004**

CLEVELAND

☐ 3359 Aftermarket Business
Advanstar Communications, Inc.
7500 Old Oak Blvd.   **Phone: (216)891-2604**
Cleveland, OH 44130   **Fax: (216)891-2625**

☐ 3360 Alternative Press
1451 W. 112th St., No. 1   Phone: (216)529-0005
Cleveland, OH 44102-2350   Fax: (216)529-9239
Magazine focusing on new music and independent and college radio. **Subtitle:** New Music Now. **Founded:** 1985. **Frequency:** 10x/yr. **Printing Method:** Web offset. **Trim Size:** 10 x 12. **Cols./Page:** 3 and 4. **Col. Depth:** 9 3/4 in. **Key Personnel:** Mike Shea, Publisher; Joe Banks, Editor; Mike Shea, Advertising Mgr.; Dawn Burns, Circulation Mgr. **Subscription:** $24.95; $33 Canada and Mexico; $56 other countries (air mail). $3 single issue.
Ad Rates: BW: $1,900   **Circulation: Paid ‡12,548**
                   4C: $3,400   Non-paid ‡1,614

☐ 3361 American Machinist
Penton Publishing
1100 Superior Ave.
Cleveland, OH 44114   **Phone: (216)696-7000**

☐ 3362 Beverage Industry
Advanstar Communications, Inc.
7500 Old Oak Blvd.   Phone: (216)243-8100
Cleveland, OH 44130   **Fax: (216)891-2651**

☐ 3363 Candy Marketer
Advanstar Communications, Inc.
7500 Old Oak Blvd.   **Phone: (216)826-2850**
Cleveland, OH 44130   **Fax: (216)891-2683**

3364 Catholic Universe Bulletin
Catholic Universe Bulletin Publishing Co., Inc.
1027 Superior Ave.   Phone: (216)696-6525
Cleveland, OH 44114-2556   **Fax: (216)696-6519**

3365 City Reports
812 Huron Rd., No. 712   Phone: (216)621-7800
Cleveland, OH 44115   Fax: (216)621-7927
Newspaper. **Founded:** 1992. **Frequency:** Weekly. **Printing Method:**
Offset. **Trim Size:** 14 X 22 3/4. **Cols./Page:** 4. **Col. Width:** 3 in. **Col.**
Depth: 21.5 in. **Subscription:** $13.
Ad Rates: BW: $2,425   **Circulation:** Non-paid 47,000

3366 Cleveland Clinic Journal of Medicine
The Cleveland Clinic Educational Foundation
9500 Euclid Ave., E3-70   **Phone: (216)444-2661**
Cleveland, OH 44195-5058   Fax: (216)444-9385

3367 Computer-Aided Engineering
Penton Publishing
1100 Superior Ave.   Phone: (216)696-7000
Cleveland, OH 44114   **Fax: (216)696-1309**

3368 Corporate Cleveland Magazine
Business Journal Publishing Co.
1720 Euclid Ave., Ste. 300
Cleveland, OH 44115   Phone: (216)621-1644
Former Title: Ohio Business

3369 Economic Commentary
Federal Reserve Bank of Cleveland
PO Box 6387   Phone: (800)543-3489
Cleveland, OH 44101   Fax: (216)579-3050
Periodical applying economic theory to current events and long-term
policy issues. **Founded:** 1948. **Frequency:** 2x/mo. **Printing Method:**
Offset lithography. **Trim Size:** 8 1/2 x 11. **Cols./Page:** 3. **Col. Width:**
12 picas. **Col. Depth:** 54 picas. **Key Personnel:** Robin Ratliff, Co-
Editor; Tess Ferg, Co-Editor. **ISSN:** 0428-1276. **Subscription:** Free.
                                     Circulation: Non-paid ‡11,500

Advertising not accepted.

3370 Economic Trends
Federal Reserve Bank of Cleveland
PO Box 6387   Phone: (800)543-3489
Cleveland, OH 44101   Fax: (216)579-3050
Periodical analyzing current economic developments. **Founded:** 1979.
Frequency: Monthly. **Printing Method:** Offset lithography. **Trim Size:**
8 1/2 x 11. **Cols./Page:** 3. **Col. Width:** 11.5 picas. **Col. Depth:** 13.5
picas. **Key Personnel:** Robin Ratliff, Co-Editor; Tess Ferg, Co-Editor.
ISSN: 0748-2922. **Subscription:** Free.
                                     Circulation: Non-paid 14,500
Advertising not accepted.

3371 Emmanuel
Congregation of Blessed Sacrament
5384 Wilson Mills Rd.   Phone: (216)449-2103
Cleveland, OH 44143-3092   **Fax: (216)449-3862**

3372 Food & Drug Packaging
Advanstar Communications, Inc.
7500 Old Oak Blvd.   Phone: (216)243-8100
Cleveland, OH 44130   **Fax: (216)891-2651**

3373 Geriatrics
Advanstar Communications, Inc.
7500 Old Oak Blvd.   **Phone: (216)243-8100**
Cleveland, OH 44130   **Fax: (216)891-2735**

3374 Hospital Formulary
Advanstar Communications Inc.
7500 Old Oak Blvd.   **Phone: (216)891-2689**
Cleveland, OH 44130   **Fax: (216)891-2735**

3375 Landscape Management
Advanstar Communications, Inc.
7500 Old Oak Blvd.   Phone: (216)243-8100
Cleveland, OH 44130   **Fax: (216)891-2675**

3376 Locomotive Engineers Journal
Brotherhood of Locomotive Engineers
1370 Ontario St.   Phone: (216)241-2630
Cleveland, OH 44113-1702   Fax: (216)861-0932

3377 The Observer
Case Western Reserve University
11111 Euclid Ave.   **Phone: (216)368-2916**
Cleveland, OH 44106   **Fax: (216)368-2914**

3378 Pest Control
Advanstar Communications, Inc.
7500 Old Oak Blvd.   Phone: (216)243-8100
Cleveland, OH 44130   **Fax: (216)891-2675**

3379 Pit & Quarry
Advanstar Communications, Inc.
7500 Old Oak Blvd.   Phone: (216)243-8100
Cleveland, OH 44130   **Fax: (216)891-2675**

3380 Riveting News
Hard Hatted Women
PO Box 93384
Cleveland, OH 44101   Phone: (216)961-4449
Newspaper on racism, affirmative action, child care, the environment,
housing, and other issues relating to women. Contains book reviews.
Frequency: Quarterly. **Subscription:** $7.
                                     Circulation: (Not Reported)

3381 School and College
1100 Superior Ave.   **Phone: (216)696-1777**
Cleveland, OH 44114   **Fax: (216)696-1606**

3382 33 Metal Producing–Nonferrous Edition
Penton Publishing
1100 Superior Ave.   Phone: (216)696-7000
Cleveland, OH 44140   Fax: (216)696-7658
Trade magazine. **Founded:** 1990. **Frequency:** Quarterly. **Key Personnel:**
W.D. Huskonen, Editor; James Forthoter, Publisher.
                                     Circulation: Controlled ‡5,000

3383 Transportation & Distribution
Penton Publishing
1100 Superior Ave.   Phone: (216)696-7000
Cleveland, OH 44114-2543   **Fax: (216)696-4135**

3384 WGAR-FM - 99.5
5005 Rockside Rd., Ste. 530   Phone: (216)328-9950
Cleveland, OH **44131**   **Fax: (216)328-9951**

3385 WRDZ-AM - 1260
8200 Snowville Rd.   Phone: (216)526-8989
Cleveland, OH 44114   **Fax: (216)526-9781**

CLYDE

3386 WNGG-FM - 100.9
PO Box 66   Phone: (419)547-8742
Clyde, OH 43410   Fax: (419)547-6649
Format: Oldies. **Network(s):** Satellite Music. **Owner:** S & S Communi-
cations Group, Inc. **Founded:** 1980. **Formerly:** WMEX-FM (1988);
WLLO-FM (1991). **Operating Hours:** Continuous. **Key Personnel:**
Kent D. Smith, Chairman; David L. Searfoss, Pres.; Maria L. Smith,
Operations Mgr.; Jim Dee, Program Dir. **Wattage:** 3000.

COLUMBUS

3387 Office Leasing Guide
200 E. Rich St.
Columbus, OH 43215
Phone: (614)461-4040
Fax: (614)365-2980
Publication listing commercial/industrial space for lease. **Founded:**
1986. **Frequency:** Quarterly. **Trim Size:** 8 1/2 x 11. **Key Personnel:**
James Brecher, Editor; Richard T. Brown, Sales Mgr. **Subscription:**
Included in subscription to Business First.

| Ad Rates: | BW: | $2,365 | Circulation: | 10,450 |
| | 4C: | $2,965 | | |

3388 Ohio Woodlands
The Ohio Forestry Assn., Inc.
1335 Dublin Rd., Ste. 203D
Columbus, OH 43215
Phone: (614)486-6767
Fax: (614)486-6769

3389 Rinksider
Target Publishing Co.
2470 E. Main St.
Columbus, OH 43209
Phone: (614)235-1022
Fax: (614)235-3584
Trade newspaper for roller rink operators. **Founded:** 1958. **Frequency:**
6x/yr. **Printing Method:** Web offset. **Trim Size:** 11 x 15. **Cols./Page:** 4.
Col. Width: 2 1/4 in. **Col. Depth:** 13 1/2 in. **Key Personnel:** Linda
Katz, Publisher. **Subscription:** $20.

| Ad Rates: | BW: | $700 | Circulation: | Paid ‡250 |
| | 4C: | $1,050 | | Non-paid ‡1,750 |

3390 Theory Into Practice
The College of Education
Ohio State University
146 Arps Hall
1945 N. High St.
Columbus, OH 43210
Phone: (614)292-3407

3391 All-American Cablevision
1980 Alum Creek Dr.
Columbus, OH 43207
Phone: (614)445-7141
Owner: American TV & Communications Corp. **Founded:** 1973.
Cities Served: Delaware County, Franklin County, Bexley, Groveport,
Obetz, and Westerville, OH.

3392 Warner Cable of Columbus
1266 Dublin Rd.
Columbus, OH 43215
Phone: (614)481-5000
Fax: (614)481-5044
Owner: Warner Cable Communications, Inc. **Founded:** 1971. **Cities**
Served: Delaware and Franklin counties, OH.

CUYAHOGA FALLS

3393 WBNX-TV - Channel 55
2690 State Rd.
Cuyahoga Falls, OH 44223
Phone: (216)928-5711
Fax: (216)929-2410

DAYTON

3394 Acquisition of Greater Dayton
Hannover Publishing Co. Inc.
6356 Far Hills Ave.
Dayton, OH 45459
Phone: (513)436-2342
Fax: (513)436-3426
Publication covering regional commercial real estate and economic
development. **Founded:** 1985. **Frequency:** Monthly. **Printing Method:**
Web. **Trim Size:** 11 3/8 x 15. **Cols./Page:** 4. **Col. Width:** 2 3/8 in. **Col.**
Depth: 14 in. **Key Personnel:** Gene Fox, Editor; Thomas G. Thoms,
Publisher. **ISSN:** 1063-3405.

Ad Rates:	BW:	$1,834	Circulation:	Non-paid ‡10,500
	4C:	$2,184		
	PCI:	$43.82		

3395 Amalgam
PO Box 88-WBB
Dayton, OH 45409
Phone: (513)228-7310
Magazine featuring alternative and entertainment coverage, includes
fiction. **Founded:** 1992. **Frequency:** 6x/yr. **Cols./Page:** 3. **Col. Width:** 2
in. **Col. Depth:** 9 1/4 in. **Key Personnel:** Joseph Procopio, Co-Editor;
Kevin Amorim, Co-Editor. **Subscription:** $12. $1 single issue.

| Ad Rates: | BW: | $276 | Circulation: | Non-paid 2,500 |
| | PCI: | $4.25 | | |

3396 Dayton Business Reporter
Hannover Publishing Co., Inc.
6356 Far Hills Ave.
Dayton, OH 45459-2782
Phone: (513)436-2342
Fax: (513)436-3426
Publication providing regional business to business information.
Founded: 1991. **Frequency:** Monthly. **Printing Method:** Web offset.
Trim Size: 11 3/8 x 15. **Cols./Page:** 4. **Col. Width:** 2 3/8 in. **Col. Depth:**
14 in. **Key Personnel:** Gene Fox, Editor; Thomas G. Thoms,
Publisher. **ISSN:** 1063-3413. **Subscription:** $18.

Ad Rates:	BW:	$1,834	Circulation:	Non-paid ‡10,500
	4C:	$2,184		
	PCI:	$43.82		

3397 Dayton Daily News
Dayton Newspapers Inc.
45 S. Ludlow St.
Dayton, OH 45402
Phone: (513)225-2335
Fax: (513)225-2489

3398 Executive Speeches
PO Box 292437
Dayton, OH 45429
Phone: (513)294-8493
Fax: (513)294-6044
Magazine covering speeches of interest to CEOs. **Founded:** 1986.
Frequency: 6x/yr. **Printing Method:** Offset. **Trim Size:** 8 1/2 x 11.
Cols./Page: 2. **Key Personnel:** Robert O. Skovgard, Editor. **ISSN:**
0888-4110. **Subscription:** $60.

Circulation: (Not Reported)
Advertising not accepted.

3399 Miami Valley Business News
1438 Wayne Ave.
Dayton, OH 45410
Phone: (513)256-1919
Fax: (513)256-6366
Magazine containing news for business owners and company leaders
in the Dayton, OH area. **Subtitle:** Metro Dayton's Leading Business
Journal. **Founded:** 1990. **Frequency:** Monthly. **Printing Method:** Web
offset. **Trim Size:** 11 3/8 x 13 3/4. **Cols./Page:** 5. **Col. Width:** 1 7/8 in.
Subscription: $15. $1.50 single issue.

Circulation: Paid ‡1,500
Non-paid ‡12,500
Advertising accepted; contact publisher for rates. **Formerly:** Miami
Valley's New Business.

3400 Today's Catholic Teacher
Peter Li Education Group
330 Progress Rd..
Dayton, OH 45439
Phone: (513)847-5900
Fax: (513)847-5910

3401 Continental Cablevision
4166 Little York Rd.
Dayton, OH 45414
Phone: (513)890-4300
Owner: Continental Cablevision, Inc. **Founded:** 1977. **Cities Served:**
Montgomery County, OH.

3402 Viacom Cablevision of Dayton
275 Leo St.
Box 213
Dayton, OH 45404
Phone: (513)223-4077
Owner: Viacom Cable. **Founded:** 1976. **Cities Served:** Montgomery
County, OH.

3403 WPTD-TV - Channel 16
110 S. Jefferson St.
Dayton, OH 45402-2402
Phone: (513)220-1600
Fax: (513)220-1642

DELPHOS

3404 WDOH-FM - 107.1
111 E. 2nd St.
PO Box 100
Delphos, OH 45833
Phone: (419)692-3963
Fax: (419)692-5896

DRESDEN

3405 Dresden Village News
17 E. 9th St.
PO Box 105
Dresden, OH 43821-0105
Phone: (614)754-1608
Fax: (614)754-1609

DUBLIN

3406 Dublin Villager
CNS/ThisWeek
PO Box 636
94 N. High St., Ste. 20
Dublin, OH 43017
Phone: (614)889-5733
Fax: (614)889-9555

3407 Water Well Journal
Ground Water Publishing Co.
6375 Riverside Dr.
Dublin, OH 43017
Phone: (614)761-3222
Fax: (614)761-3446

EATON

3408 Vantage Cable Associates, L.P.
2708 Grand Ave.
Des Moines, IA 50312
Phone: (515)243-2441

FOSTORIA

3409 WFOB-AM - 1430
PO Box W.
Fostoria, OH 44830
Phone: (419)435-5666
Fax: (419)435-6611

FREDERICKTOWN

3410 The Knox County Citizen
Knox County Printing Co.
Box 240
Fredericktown, OH 43019
Phone: (614)694-4016
Fax: (614)694-4555

3411 The Times Advertiser
Knox County Printing Co.
Box 240
Fredericktown, OH 43019
Phone: (614)694-4016
Fax: (614)694-4555

3412 WWBK-FM - 98.3
155 N. Main St.
Fredericktown, OH 43019
Phone: (614)694-1577
Fax: (614)694-1518

GAHANNA

3413 Rocky Fork Enterprise
Lagemann Publications, Inc.
110 N. High St.
PO Box 30769
Gahanna, OH 43230
Phone: (614)471-1600
Fax: (614)471-1764

3414 The Single Scene
Columbus Single Scene
Box 30856
Gahanna, OH 43230
Phone: (614)476-8802

3415 WCVO-FM - 104.9
4400 Reynoldsburg-New Albany Rd.
PO Box 7
New Albany, OH 43054
Phone: (614)855-9171
Fax: (614)855-9280

GENEVA

3416 WATJ-AM - 1560
95 W. Main St.
Geneva, OH 44041
Phone: (216)286-1560
Fax: (216)286-7445

3417 WKKY-FM - 104.9
95 W. Main St.
Geneva, OH 44041
Phone: (216)466-1049
Fax: (216)466-3138

GRANVILLE

3418 The Denisonian
Denison University
Slayter Hall
Granville, OH 43023
Phone: (614)587-6378
Fax: (614)587-6417
Student newspaper serving Denison University. **Founded:** 1857. **Frequency:** Weekly (Thurs.). **Trim Size:** 96 x 61.5 picas. **Cols./Page:** 5. **Col. Width:** 11.5 picas. **Col. Depth:** 96 picas. **Subscription:** $16 semester; $30 academic year.
Ad Rates: PCI: $4.50
Circulation: ‡2,500

HURON

3419 Erie County Reporter
PO Box 128
Huron, OH 44839
Phone: (419)433-5983
Fax: (419)433-6643

3420 The Voice & The Reporter
212 Cleveland
Huron, OH 44839
Phone: (419)433-5983
Fax: (216)967-2535
Ceased publication.

KENT

3421 WKSU-FM - 89.7
1613 E. Summit St.
Kent, OH 44242
Phone: (216)672-3114
Fax: (216)672-4107

KETTERING

3422 Continental Cablevision
4333 Display Ln.
Kettering, OH 45429
Phone: (513)294-6800
Owner: Continental Cablevision, Inc. **Founded:** 1978.

LANCASTER

3423 WHOK-FM - 95.5
1660 Columbus-Lancaster Rd. NW
Lancaster, OH 43130
Phone: (614)341-9595
Fax: (614)653-0702

LOGAN

3424 WLGN-FM - 98.3
1 Radio Ln.
Box 429
Logan, OH 43138
Phone: (614)385-2151
Fax: (614)385-4022
Format: Hot Country. **Network(s):** Ray Sports. **Owner:** Logan Broadcasting, at above address. **Founded:** 1965. **Operating Hours:** 5:30 a.m.-10 p.m. Mon.-Sat; Sunrise-sunset Sun. **ADI:** Columbus (Chillicothe), OH. **Key Personnel:** Roger Hinerman, Owner/Mgr.; Bob Nair, News Dir.; Mike Diamond, Program Dir. **Wattage:** 3000. **Ad Rates:** $6.75-$8.50 for 30 seconds; $7.75-$9.50 for 60 seconds.

LOVELAND

3425 Loveland Herald-Press
Press Community Newspapers
Northeast Newspaper Group
9121 Union Cemetary Rd.
Cincinnati, OH **45249**
Phone: (513)683-5115
Fax: (513)677-4690

MANSFIELD

3426 WRGM-AM - 1440
2900 Park Ave. W.
Mansfield, OH 44906
Phone: (419)529-5900
Fax: (419)529-2319

3427 WVMC-FM - 90.7
500 Logan Rd.
Mansfield, OH 44907
Phone: (419)756-5651
Fax: (419)756-7470

Ad Rates: GLR = general line rate; BW = one-time black & white page rate; 4C = one-time four color page rate; SAU = standard advertising unit rate; CNU = Canadian newspaper advertising unit rate; PCI = per column inch rate.
Circulation: ★ = ABC; △ = BPA; ◆ = CAC; ● = CCAB; □ = VAC; ⊕ = PO Statement; ‡ = Publisher's Report; Boldface figures = sworn; Light figures = estimated.
Entry type: 🕮 = Print; ♆ = Broadcast.

3428 WVNO-FM - 106.1
2900 Park Ave. W.
Phone: (419)529-5900
Mansfield, OH 44906
Fax: (419)529-2319
Format: Soft Rock. **Owner:** Johnny Appleseed Broadcasting Co.
Founded: 1961. **Operating Hours:** Continuous. **Key Personnel:** Gunther Meisse, Pres./Gen. Mgr.; Glenn Cheesman, Gen. Sales Mgr.; Steve Nelson, News Dir.; James Holmes, Operations Mgr.; Wayne Fick, Chief Engineer. **Wattage:** 50,000.

MARIETTA

3429 The Marcolian
Marietta College
Box A20
Phone: (614)374-4809
Marietta, OH 45750
Fax: (614)374-4896

MASSILLON

3430 Massillon Cable TV Inc.
814 Cable Ct. NW
PO Box 814
Phone: (216)833-4134
Massillon, OH 44648-0814
Fax: (216)833-7522

NEW PHILADELPHIA

3431 WTUZ-FM - 99.9
2695 Possom Hollow Rd. SE
Phone: (216)339-2222
New Philadelphia, OH 44663
Fax: (216)339-5441

NEWARK

3432 On Target
Public Affairs Office
Newark Air Force Base
831 Irving-Wick Dr. W.
Phone: (614)522-7779
Newark, OH 43057-0031
Fax: (614)522-7449

NEWCOMERSTOWN

3433 The Newcomerstown News
PO Box 30
Phone: (614)498-7117
Newcomerstown, OH 43832
Fax: (614)432-6219

NILES

3434 The Niles Times
35 W. State St.
Phone: (216)652-5841
Niles, OH 44446
Fax: (216)652-3948
Former Title: Niles Daily Times

PARMA

3435 Cox Cable Cleveland Area, Inc.
12221 Plaza Dr.
Phone: (216)676-8300
Parma, OH 44130
Fax: (216)676-8689
Owner: Cox Cable Communications. **Founded:** 1980. **Cities Served:** Cuyahoga County, Broadview Heights, Fairview Park, Lakewood, Olmsted Falls, Parma Heights, Rocky River, and Seven Hills, OH.

PORT CLINTON

3436 Ohio's Outdoor Beacon
Outdoor Beacon, Inc.
PO Box 87
Phone: (419)732-3474
Port Clinton, OH 43452
Fax: (419)734-5382

RAVENNA

3437 Record-Courier
126 N. Chestnut St.
PO Box 1201
Phone: (216)296-9657
Ravenna, OH 44266
Fax: (216)296-2698

RITTMAN

3438 The Trading Post
Trogdon Publishing, Inc.
12555 Benner Rd.
PO Box 45
Phone: (216)925-3040
Rittman, OH 44270
Fax: (216)927-6890

SALEM

3439 Tele-media Company
427 E. State St.
Phone: (216)332-1527
Salem, OH 44460
Fax: (216)332-5391

SHAKER HEIGHTS

3440 WBZR-AM
c/o 2909 Weymouth Ave.
Shaker Heights, OH 44120

SIDNEY

3441 WMVR-AM - 1080
2929 Russell Rd.
Box 889
Phone: (513)498-1055
Sidney, OH 45365
Fax: (513)498-2277

TOLEDO

3442 Junior Chronicle
Catholic Chronicle, Inc.
2130 Madison Ave.
PO Box 1866
Phone: (419)243-4178
Toledo, OH 43624
Fax: (419)243-4235
Ceased publication.

3443 Warship International
International Naval Research Orgn.
5905 Reinwood Dr.
Toledo, OH 43613-5605
Phone: (419)472-1331

WARREN

3444 TCI Cablevision of Ohio
2650 Weir Rd. NE
Warren, OH 44483-2520
Phone: (216)544-0416
Owner: Tele-Communications, Inc. **Founded:** 1974. **Cities Served:** Trumbull County, OH.

WELLSTON

3445 The Wellston Telegram
12 S. Ohio Ave.
PO Box 111
Phone: (614)384-6102
Wellston, OH 45692
Fax: (614)286-8438

WILMINGTON

3446 WSWO-FM - 102.3
Box 1
Phone: (513)382-1023
Wilmington, OH 45177
Fax: (513)382-1665

WOOSTER

3447 Ohio News
Ohio Holstein Assn.
1375 Heyl Rd.
PO Box 459
Phone: (216)264-9088
Wooster, OH 44691
Fax: (216)263-1653

3448 Clear Picture Inc.
444 W. Miltown Rd.
PO Box 897
Phone: (216)345-8114
Wooster, OH 44691
Fax: (216)345-5265

YOUNGSTOWN

📖 **3449   Catholic Exponent**
Catholic Exponent, Inc.
PO Box 6787-44501
144 W. Wood St.   Phone: (216)744-5251
Youngstown, OH 44503   **Fax: (216)744-8451**

♣ **3450   Warner Cable Communications, Inc.**
755 Wick Ave.
Box 6220   Phone: (216)747-2550
Youngstown, OH 44501   Fax: (216)747-5003
Owner: Warner Cable Communications, Inc. **Founded:** 1980. **Cities Served:** Mahoning County and Trumbull County, OH.

OKLAHOMA

ALVA

3451 Northwestern News
Northwestern Oklahoma State University
Jesse Dunn Annex, Rm. 232 — Phone: (405)327-1700
Alva, OK 73717 — **Fax: (405)327-1881**

BARTLESVILLE

3452 Donrey Media Group
4127 Nowata Rd. SE
Bartlesville, OK 74006 — **Phone: (918)335-0123**

CHANDLER

3453 The Lincoln County News
Lincoln County Publishing Co., Inc.
718 Manvel
Box 248 — Phone: (405)258-1818
Chandler, OK 74834-0248 — **Fax: (405)258-1824**

CHICKASHA

3454 KWCO-AM - 1560
PO Box 1268 — Phone: (405)224-1560
Chickasha, OK 73023-1268 — **Fax: (405)224-2890**

3455 KXXK-FM - 105.5
PO Box 1268 — Phone: (405)224-1560
Chickasha, OK 73023-1268 — **Fax: (405)224-2890**

CLINTON

3456 The Clinton Daily News
Clinton Daily News Co.
522 Avant Ave. — Phone: (405)323-5151
Clinton, OK 73601 — **Fax: (405)323-5154**

DURANT

3457 KHIB-FM - 91.9
Southeastern State University
Box 4129, Sta. A
Durant, OK 74701 — **Phone: (405)924-0121**

EDMOND

3458 KCSC-FM - 90.1
University of Central Oklahoma
100 N. University Dr. — Phone: (405)341-2980
Edmond, OK 73034 — **Fax: (405)341-4964**

ELK CITY

3459 KADS-AM - 1240
Box 949 — Phone: (405)243-5237
Elk City, OK 73648 — Fax: (405)225-0463
Format: Oldies; Agricultural. **Network(s):** ABC; Oklahoma News. **Owner:** Kenneth E. Martin, at above address. **Founded:** 1932. **Operating Hours:** Continuous. **Key Personnel:** Kenneth E. Martin, Pres.; Jack Palmore, Music Gen. Mgr. and Dir.; Cheryl Baker, Gen. Sales Mgr.; Pat Gilbreth, Chief Engineer; Kenneth E. Martin, Gen. Mgr.; Cheryl Baker, Office Mgr.; News, Sports, and Program Dir.; Georgia Martin, Sales Mgr.; Pat Gilbreth, Chief Engineer. **Wattage:** 1000. **Ad Rates:** $3.70-$5.50 for 30 seconds;$4.70-$6.50 for 60 seconds.

ENID

3460 KGWA-AM - 960
Box 960 — Phone: (405)234-4230
Enid, OK 73702 — **Fax: (405)237-3233**

3461 TCI Cablevision of Oklahoma
131 E. Main
Enid, OK 73701-5741 — Phone: (405)237-7373
Owner: Tele-Communications, Inc. **Founded:** 1966. **Cities Served:** Garfield County, OK.

FORT GIBSON

3462 Mission Cable Co.
102 N. Lee
PO Box 970 — **Phone: (918)478-2100**
Fort Gibson, OK 74434 — **Fax: (918)478-2355**

HOBART

3463 Hobart Democrat-Chief
407 S. Main
PO Box 432 — Phone: (405)726-3333
Hobart, OK 73651 — **Fax: (405)726-3431**

Ad Rates: GLR = general line rate; BW = one-time black & white page rate; 4C = one-time four color page rate; SAU = standard advertising unit rate; CNU = Canadian newspaper advertising unit rate; PCI = per column inch rate.
Circulation: ★ = ABC; △ = BPA; ◆ = CAC; ● = CCAB; □ = VAC; ⊕ = PO Statement; ‡ = Publisher's Report; Boldface figures = sworn; Light figures = estimated.
Entry type: 🕮 = Print; 🎙 = Broadcast.

KINGFISHER

📖 **3464 Kingfisher Times and Free Press**
PO Box 209   Phone: (405)375-3220
Kingfisher, OK 73750   Fax: **(405)375-3222**

LAWTON

📖 **3465 The Lawton Constitution**
Lawton Publishing Co.
PO Box 2069   Phone: (405)353-0620
Lawton, OK 73502   Fax: **(405)585-5140**
Former Title: The Constitution AM & PM

🎙 **3466 KCCU-FM - 89.3**
Administration Bldg.
2800 West Gore Blvd.   Phone: (405)581-2425
Lawton, OK 73505   Fax: **(405)581-2867**

MARLOW

🎙 **3467 KFXT-FM - 100.9**
1101 Hwy. 81 N.
Marlow, OK 73055   Phone: **(405)658-9292**

MAYSVILLE

📖 **3468 The Maysville News**
Box 617
Maysville, OK 73057-0617   Phone: (405)867-4457

NORMAN

📖 **3469 The Norman Transcript**
PO Drawer 1058   Phone: (405)321-1800
Norman, OK 73070-1058   Fax: **(405)366-3520**

🎙 **3470 KNOR-AM - 1400**
115 W. Gray   Phone: (405)321-1400
Norman, OK 73069   Fax: **(405)321-6820**

🎙 **3471 Norman Cable TV**
1023 N. Flood St.
Norman, OK 73069   Phone: (405)321-3740
Owner: Multimedia Cablevision, Inc. Founded: 1975. Cities Served:
Cleveland County, OK.

OKLAHOMA CITY

📖 **3472 Oklahoma Living**
Oklahoma Assn. of Electric Cooperatives
PO Box 11047   Phone: (405)478-1455
Oklahoma City, OK 73136   Fax: **(405)478-0246**
Former Title: Oklahoma Rural News

📖 **3473 PSA Journal**
Photographic Society of America
3000 United Founders Blvd., No. 103   Phone: (405)843-1437
Oklahoma City, OK 73112   Fax: **(405)843-1438**

🎙 **3474 Cox Cable Oklahoma City**
2312 NW 10th St.   Phone: (405)525-2771
Oklahoma City, OK 73107   Fax: (405)525-8030
Owner: Cox Cable Communications. Founded: 1980. Cities Served:
Canadian County, Cleveland County, McClain County, and Oklahoma County, OK.

🎙 **3475 KOMA-AM - 1520**
PO Box 6000   Phone: (405)794-4000
Oklahoma City, OK 75153   Fax: (405)793-0514
Format: Oldies. Network(s): CBS. Owner: WSBC Broadcasting Co.
Founded: 1922. Operating Hours: Continuous. Key Personnel: Vance
Harrison, Jr., V.P./Gen. Mgr.; Cliff Wilson, Gen. Sales Mgr.; Kent
Jones, Program Dir.; Michael Dean, Music Dir.; Steve Bennet, News
Dir. Wattage: 50,000.

OWASSO

🎙 **3476 KQLL-FM - 106.1**
9909 E. 106th St. N.   Phone: (918)272-6999
Owasso, OK 74055   Fax: **(918)272-4450**

PAULS VALLEY

🎙 **3477 KGOK-FM - 97.7**
Box 610   Phone: (405)238-3314
Pauls Valley, OK 73075   Fax: **(405)238-5959**

SAYRE

🎙 **3478 KVIJ-TV - Channel 8**
c/o Marsh Media
1 Broadcast Center
Amarillo, TX 79101   Phone: (806)373-1787
Format: Commercial TV. Simulcasts KVII-TV Amarillo, TX. Network(s): ABC. Owner: Marsh Media Ltd., at above address. ADI:
Oklahoma City, OK.

SHAWNEE

📖 **3479 CPA Software News**
Software News Publishing
1105 N. Beard, Ste. 200   Phone: (405)275-3100
Shawnee, OK 74801   Fax: (405)275-3101
Magazine featuring articles intended to assist CPAs with computer
software purchase, use, and maintenance. Subtitle: The Independent
Voice for Accountants Software. Founded: 1991. Frequency: 6x/yr.
Printing Method: Web offset. Trim Size: 11 1/2 x 14. Cols./Page: 4 or
5. Key Personnel: Allen Rose, Publisher; Angie Greenfield Rose,
Advertising Dir. Subscription: $25. $8 single issue.
Ad Rates: BW: $2,000   Circulation: Controlled ‡50,000
             4C: $3,000

STILLWATER

🎙 **3480 KSPI-AM - 780**
PO Box 2288
Stillwater, OK 74076   Phone: (405)372-7800

TAFT

🎙 **3481 KHJM-FM - 100.3**
215 State St., Ste. 910
PO Box 2416
Muskogee, OK 74402   Phone: (918)682-2233
Format: Religious; Country (Christian). Network(s): USA Radio.
Owner: Taft Broadcasting, Inc. Founded: 1990. Operating Hours:
Continuous. Key Personnel: Bryant W. Ellis, Pres.; Roy Davis,
Program Mgr. Wattage: 6000.

TAHLEQUAH

📖 **3482 Cherokee Advocate**
Cherokee Nation
PO Box 948   Phone: (918)456-0671
Tahlequah, OK 74465   Fax: (918)456-6485

TULSA

📖 **3483 Dental Economics**
PennWell Publishing Co.
PO Box 3408   Phone: (918)835-3161
Tulsa, OK 74101   Fax: **(918)831-9804**

📖 **3484 James Joyce Quarterly**
600 S. College
University of Tulsa   Phone: (918)631-2501
Tulsa, OK 74104-3189   Fax: (918)631-2033

📖 **3485 Journal of Sedimentary Petrology**
SEPM (Society for Sedimentary Geology)
PO Box 4756   Phone: (617)253-3397
Tulsa, OK 74131   Fax: **(405)743-2498**

3486 Tulsa Studies in Women's Literature
Tulsa Studies in Women's Literature, The University of Tulsa
600 S. College Ave.   Phone: (918)631-2503
Tulsa, OK 74104   Fax: (918)631-2033
Periodical containing articles, reviews, notes, and queries from
scholars on women's literature, including those reading in a language
other than English. **Founded:** 1982. **Frequency:** 2x/yr. **Subscription:**
$12; $10 student; $14 institutions. $7 single issue; $8 single issue
outside U.S.
Ad Rates: BW: $150   **Circulation:** 500

3487 KCMA-FM - 92.1
2021 S. Lewis Ave.   Phone: (918)747-9999
Tulsa, OK 74104-5715   Fax: (918)747-7345

3488 KTUL-TV - Channel 8
Box 8   **Phone: (918)445-8888**
Tulsa, OK 74101   Fax: (918)445-9316

3489 UAE
6650 E. 44th St.   Phone: (918)665-1990
Tulsa, OK 74145   Fax: (918)665-0590
Owner: Tele-Communications, Inc. **Founded:** 1974. **Cities Served:**
Creek County, Okmulgee County, Osage County, Rogers County,
Tulsa County, Wagoner County, Broken Arrow, Catoosa, Chelsea,
Glenpool, Jenks, Kiefer, Owasso, Rolling Hills, Sand Springs, and
Sapulpa, OK.

Ad Rates: GLR = general line rate; BW = one-time black & white page rate; 4C = one-time four color page rate; SAU = standard advertising unit rate;
CNU = Canadian newspaper advertising unit rate; PCI = per column inch rate.
Circulation: ★ = ABC; △ = BPA; ◆ = CAC; ● = CCAB; □ = VAC; ⊕ = PO Statement; ‡ = Publisher's Report; Boldface figures = sworn; Light figures = estimated.
Entry type: ▥ = Print; ▮ = Broadcast.

231

OREGON

ASHLAND

📖 **3490 Backwoods Home Magazine**
Backwoods Home Magazine, Inc.
1257 Siskiyou Blvd., No. 213   Phone: (503)488-2053
Ashland, OR 97520   Fax: (503)488-2063
Magazine profiling independent, self sufficient lifestyles. **Subtitle:** A Practical Journal of Self Reliance. **Founded:** 1989. **Frequency:** 6x/yr. **Trim Size:** Web press. **Trim Size:** 8 1/2 x 11. **Cols./Page:** 3. **Key Personnel:** Dave Duffy, Editor and Publisher. **ISSN:** 1050-9712. **Subscription:** $16.95. $3.50 single issue.
Ad Rates: BW: $1,500   **Circulation:** ‡23,000
         4C: $1,800

ASTORIA

🔊 **3491 KVAS-AM - 1230**
1490 Marine Dr.   Phone: (503)325-6221
Astoria, OR 97103   **Fax: (503)325-6145**

BAKER

📖 **3492 The Record-Courier**
1718 Main St.
PO Box 70
Baker, OR 97814-0070   **Phone: (503)523-5353**

🔊 **3493 KCMB-FM - 104.7**
2405 2nd St.   Phone: (503)523-3400
Baker, OR 97814-2507   Fax: (503)523-5481
Format: Contemporary Country. **Network(s):** ABC. **Owner:** Clare M. Ferguson-Capps. **Founded:** 1988. **Operating Hours:** Continuous. **Key Personnel:** Randy McKone, Gen. Mgr. **Wattage:** 1000. **Additional Contact Information:** Alt. phone (503)963-3405; Alt. fax (503)963-9451.

BURNS

🔊 **3494 TCI Cablevision of Oregon, Inc.**
85 E. B St.   Phone: (503)573-2941
Burns, OR 97720   **Fax: (503)573-3115**

COOS BAY

🔊 **3495 KHSN-AM - 1230**
Box 180
Coos Bay, OR 97420   Phone: (503)267-2121
Format: Big Band/Nostalgia; Middle-of-the-Road (MOR). **Network(s):** ABC. **Owner:** Laurence Goodman, at above address. **Founded:** 1928. **Operating Hours:** Continuous. **Key Personnel:** Craig Finley, Gen. Mgr.; Bill McGuire, Sales Mgr.; Mike Chaves, Program Dir. **Wattage:**

1000. **Ad Rates:** Combined rates available with KOOS-FM: $5-$15 for 30 seconds; $6.50-$16.50 for 60 seconds.

🔊 **3496 KYNG-AM - 1420**
Box 4303
Coos Bay, OR 97420   Phone: (503)267-7055
Format: News; Talk. **Network(s):** ABC. **Owner:** Ray Sparks, at above address. **Founded:** 1956. **Wattage:** 1000.

🔊 **3497 KYNG-FM - 106.5**
Box 4303
Coos Bay, OR 97420   Phone: (503)267-7055
Format: Top 40. **Network(s):** ABC. **Owner:** Ray Sparks, at above address. **Founded:** 1979. **Key Personnel:** James Baker, Pres./Gen. Mgr.; Diane Whitson, Gen. Sales Mgr.; J.J. Jensen, Program Dir./Music Dir./News Dir.; Tim Hishizer, Chief Engineer. **Wattage:** 3000.

🔊 **3498 KYTT-FM - 98.7**
455 N. Broadway   Phone: (503)269-2022
Coos Bay, OR 97420   **Fax: (503)267-0114**

CORVALLIS

📖 **3499 CALYX: A Journal of Art and Literature by Women**
CALYX, Inc.
PO Box B   Phone: (503)753-9384
Corvallis, OR 9739   Fax: (503)753-0515
Journal containing poetry, prose, art and book review, translations, and photography of women artists and writers. **Founded:** 1976. **Frequency:** 2x/yr. **Printing Method:** Offset. **Trim Size:** 7 x 8. **Subscription:** $18; $22.50 institutions; $30 Canada; $36 other countries. $8 single issue.
Ad Rates: GLR: $.75   **Circulation:** (Not Reported)
         BW: $550
Color advertising not accepted.

📖 **3500 Ornamentals Northwest**
Cooper Extension Service
Oregon State University
Cordley Hall 2042   **Phone: (503)737-5452**
Corvallis, OR 97331-2911   Fax: (503)737-3479

EUGENE

📖 **3501 Rain Magazine**
Rain, Inc.
PO Box 30097
Eugene, OR 97403
Magazine concerning ecology and sustainable living. **Founded:** October 1974. **Frequency:** Quarterly. **Printing Method:** Offset. **Trim Size:** 8

Ad Rates: GLR = general line rate; BW = one-time black & white page rate; 4C = one-time four color page rate; SAU = standard advertising unit rate; CNU = Canadian newspaper advertising unit rate; PCI = per column inch rate.
Circulation: ★ = ABC; △ = BPA; ◆ = CAC; ● = CCAB; □ = VAC; ⊕ = PO Statement; ‡ = Publisher's Report; Boldface figures = sworn; Light figures = estimated.
Entry type: 📖 = Print; 🔊 = Broadcast.

1/2 x 11. **Cols./Page:** 2. **Key Personnel:** Danielle Janes, Co-Editor; Greg Bryant, Co-Editor. **ISSN:** 0739-621X. **Subscription:** $20. $5 single issue.

Circulation: 700
Non-paid 1,300

Advertising not accepted.

3502 Womyn's Press
Womyn's Press Collective
PO Box 562
Eugene, OR 97440　　　　　　Phone: (503)689-3974
Eclectic feminist journal. **Founded:** 1970. **Frequency:** Bimonthly. **Trim Size:** 11 x 17. **Cols./Page:** 3. **Col. Width:** 3 in. **Subscription:** Free; $8-$30 out of state; $18 institutions; Free to prisoners.
Ad Rates:　BW:　$360　　　　　　**Circulation:** 300
　　　　PCI:　$8　　　　　　Non-paid 1,700
Color advertising not accepted.

3503 KEZI-TV - Channel 9
2225 Coburg Rd.
PO Box 7009　　　　　　Phone: (503)485-5611
Eugene, OR 97401-0009　　　　**Fax: (503)342-1568**

3504 KLCC-FM - 89.7
4000 E. 30th Ave.　　　　　　Phone: (503)726-2224
Eugene, OR 97405　　　　　　**Fax: (503)747-3962**

3505 KRVM-FM - 91.9
200 N. Monroe St.　　　　　　Phone: (503)687-3370
Eugene, OR 97402　　　　　　**Fax: (503)484-9863**

3506 KZEL-FM - 96.1
270 Oakway Ctr.　　　　　　Phone: (503)342-7096
Eugene, OR 97401　　　　　　Fax: (503)484-6397

3507 TCI Cablevision of Oregon
990 Garfield St.
Box 2500
Eugene, OR 97402-1369　　　　Phone: (503)484-3000
Owner: Tele-Communications, Inc. **Founded:** 1954. **Key Personnel:** Michael White, Gen. Mgr.; Jacquelene Johnson, Mktg. Mgr.; Todd Wylie, Advertising Sales Mgr.; Eleanor Logan, Office Mgr.; Darrell Linklater, Plant Mgr. **Cities Served:** Lane and Linn counties, Alvadore, Eugene, Glenwood, Harrisburg, Junction City, Santa Clara, and Springfield, OR: 52,000 subscribing households; 36 channels; 2 community access channelS; 40 hours per week of community access programming.

FLORENCE

3508 KCST-AM - 1250
1231 18th St.
Box 20000
Florence, OR 97439　　　　　　Phone: (503)997-9136
Format: Middle-of-the-Road (MOR). **Network(s):** ABC. **Owner:** Coast Broadcasting Co. **Operating Hours:** 5:30 a.m.-10:30 p.m. **Key Personnel:** Jon Thompson, Gen. Mgr.; Debbie Phelps, Office Mgr.

FOREST GROVE

3509 KPUR-FM - 94.5
Student Service
2043 College Way
Forest Grove, OR 97116　　　　Phone: (503)359-2200
Format: Alternative/Independent/Progressive. **Key Personnel:** Steve Klein, Music Dir. **Ad Rates:** Noncommercial.

HILLSBORO

3510 KUIK-AM - 1360
3355 NE Cornell Rd.
PO Box 566　　　　　　Phone: (503)640-1360
Hillsboro, OR 97124　　　　　　**Fax: (503)640-6108**

KLAMATH FALLS

3511 Herald and News
Klamath Publishing
1301 Esplanade St.
PO Box 788　　　　　　Phone: (503)885-4410
Klamath Falls, OR 97601　　　　**Fax: (503)883-4007**

3512 TCI Cablevision of Oregon
300 E. Main St.
Box 8
Klamath Falls, OR 97601-3795　　Phone: (503)882-5533
Owner: Tele-Communications, Inc. **Founded:** 1953. **Cities Served:** Klamath County, OR.

LA GRANDE

3513 The Eastern Beacon
Eastern Oregon State College
1410 L. Ave.　　　　　　**Phone: (503)962-3386**
La Grande, OR 97850-2899　　　Fax: (503)962-3335

LINCOLN CITY

3514 KBCH-AM - 1400
Box 820　　　　　　Phone: (503)994-2181
Lincoln City, OR 97367　　　　Fax: (503)994-2004
Format: Easy Listening. **Owner:** Oceanlake Broadcasting, Lincoln City, OR. **Founded:** 1930. **Operating Hours:** Continuous. **Key Personnel:** Hal Fowler, Gen. Mgr./Operations and Sports Dir.; Eleanor Phillips, Public Affairs Dir.; Tim King, News Dir.; Terry McKevilly, Sales Mgr.; Bruce Holt, Operations Dir. **Wattage:** 1000.

3515 KCRF-FM - 96.7
Box 820
Lincoln City, OR 97367　　　　Phone: (503)994-5273
Format: Classic Rock. **Owner:** Oceanlake Broadcasting, Lincoln City, OR. **Founded:** 1980. **Operating Hours:** Continuous. **Key Personnel:** Hal Fowler, Gen. Mgr./Operations and Sports Dir.; Tim King, News Dir.; Eleanor Phillips, Public Affairs Dir.; Terry McKevilly, Sales Mgr.; Bruce Holt, Operations. **Wattage:** 3000.

MEDFORD

3516 KBOY-FM - 95.7
2729 Jacksonville Hwy.　　　　Phone: (503)779-2244
Medford, OR 97501　　　　　　Fax: (503)772-6282

3517 KRVC-AM - 730
2729 Jacksonville Hwy
Medford, OR 97501　　　　　　**Phone: (503)779-2244**

3518 TCI Cablevision of Oregon
926 S. Grape St.
Box 399
Medford, OR 97501　　　　　　Phone: (503)779-1851
Owner: Tele-Communications, Inc. **Founded:** 1958. **Cities Served:** Jackson County, OR.

MILTON-FREEWATER

3519 KTEL-AM - 1490
112 NE 5th Ave.　　　　　　**Phone: (503)938-6688**
Milton-Freewater, OR 97862　　**Fax: (503)938-6689**

3520 KTEL-FM - 93.3
112 NE 5th Ave.　　　　　　**Phone: (503)938-6688**
Milton-Freewater, OR 97862　　Fax: (503)938-6689

MILWAUKIE

3521 The Digger
Oregon Association of Nurserymen, Inc.
2780 SE Harrison, No. 102　　　Phone: (503)653-8733
Milwaukie, OR 97222　　　　　**Fax: (503)653-1528**

ONTARIO

⚫ 3522 Jackpot Antenna-Vision, Inc.
Box 516
Ontario, OR 97914   Phone: (503)889-2418
Owner: Lee Smith. **Founded:** 1974. **Key Personnel:** Dave Smith, V.P.; Ed Aronson, Mgr. **Cities Served:** Jackpot, NV: 300 subscribing households; 22 channels; 1 community access channel.

OREGON CITY

▭ 3523 Enterprise Courier
10th & Main St.
Oregon City, OR 97045   Phone: (503)656-1911
Ceased publication.

PORTLAND

▭ 3524 Mailers Review
MR Publishing
7850 SE Stark St.   Phone: (503)257-0764
Portland, OR 97215-2380   Fax: (503)257-7935
Magazine profiling international mailing, document processing, and shipping processes. **Subtitle:** The Only International Monthly Mailing Document Processing/Shipping Publication. **Founded:** 1989. **Frequency:** Monthly **Printing Method:** Web offset. **Trim Size:** 10 3/4 x 13 1/2. **Cols./Page:** 3. **Col. Width:** 3 5/16 in. **Col. Depth:** 11 11/16 in. **Key Personnel:** Deborah A. Griffin, Publisher; Michael Roeper, CEO; Richard W. Pavely, Consulting Editor; Randy Moniot, General Mgr. **Subscription:** $39. $5 single issue.
Ad Rates: BW: $2,147   **Circulation:** 1,200
           4C: $2,947   Non-paid 33,800

▭ 3525 Oregon Historical Quarterly
Oregon Historical Society
1200 SW Park Ave.   Phone: (503)222-1741
Portland, OR 97205-2483   Fax: (503)221-2035

▭ 3526 Primroses
American Primrose Society
9705 SW Spring Crest Dr.
Portland, OR 97225

▭ 3527 Reference & Research Book News
Book News, Inc.
5600 NE Hassalo St.   Phone: (503)281-9230
Portland, OR 92713   Fax: (503)284-8859
Journal containing reviews of scholarly and research books of interest to libraries. **Subtitle:** Annotations and Reviews of New Books. **Founded:** 1986. **Frequency:** 8x/yr. **Printing Method:** Offset. **Trim Size:** 8 1/2 x 11. CPP 2. **Key Personnel:** Fred Gullette, Publisher; Jane Erskine, Editor. **ISSN:** 0887-3763. **Subscription:** $40; $52 other countries; $58 institutions; $70 institutions in other countries.
           Circulation: (Not Reported)

▭ 3528 Sci Tech Book News
Book News, Inc.
5600 NE Hassalo St.   Phone: (503)281-9230
Portland, OR 92713   Fax: (503)284-8859
Magazine containing reviews and annotations of new books in science, technology, and medicine. **Subtitle:** The Annotated Bibliography of New Books in Science, Technology, and Medicine. **Founded:** 1977. **Frequency:** 10x/yr. **Printing Method:** Offset. **Trim Size:** 8 1/2 x 11. **Cols./Page:** 2. **Key Personnel:** Fred Gillette, Publisher; Jane Erskine, Editor. **ISSN:** 0196-6006. **Subscription:** $45; $60 other countries; $65 institutions; $80 institutions in other countries.
           Circulation: (Not Reported)

▭ 3529 Spectrum Newspapers Monthly, Portland
Spectrum Newspapers
11171 Sun Center Dr., Ste. 110   Phone: (916)852-6222
Rancho Cordova, CA 95670   Fax: (916)852-6397
Newspaper serving active senior citizens, 55 and older, in Portland. **Founded:** 1975. **Frequency:** Monthly. **Printing Method:** Web offset.

Key Personnel: Bob Carney, Editor; Jacqueline Lucido, Gen. Mgr.; Ridge Eagan, Advertising Dir. **USPS:** 980-481. **Subscription:** $12.
           Circulation: ‡75,000

⚫ 3530 KATU-TV - Channel 2
2153 NE Sandy Blvd.   Phone: (503)231-4222
Portland, OR 97232   **Fax:** (503)236-0952

⚫ 3531 KBMS-AM - 1480
510 SW 3rd Ave., Ste. 100
Portland, OR 97204   Phone: (206)699-1881
Format: Urban Contemporary. **Owner:** Christopher H. Bennett Broadcasting Washington. **Founded:** 1955. **Formerly:** KAAR-AM. **Operating Hours:** Continuous. **Key Personnel:** Christopher H. Bennett, Owner/Gen. Mgr.; Angela Jenkins, Station Mgr./Program and Music Dir.; Johnny Jordan, Asst. Production Mgr.; Sheryl Doyle, Account Exec. **Wattage:** 1000 day; 2500 night. **Ad Rates:** $32 for 30 seconds; $42 for 60 seconds.

⚫ 3532 KBPS-AM - 1450
515 NE 15th Ave.
Portland, OR 97232   Phone: (503)280-5828

⚫ 3533 KBPS-FM - 89.9
515 NE 15th
Portland, OR 97232   Phone: (503)280-5828

⚫ 3534 KDUP-AM - 860
5000 N. Willanette
Portland, OR 97203   Phone: (503)283-7121
Format: Alternative/Independent/Progressive. **Key Personnel:** John Bauccio, Music Dir. **Ad Rates:** Noncommercial.

⚫ 3535 KPHP-AM - 1290
4700 SW Macadam St., No. 102   **Phone: (503)242-1950**
Portland, OR 97201   **Fax: (503)242-0155**

⚫ 3536 Paragon Cable
3075 NE Sandy Blvd.   Phone: (503)230-2099
Portland, OR 97232   Fax: (503)230-2218
Owner: KBLCOM, Inc. **Founded:** 1982. **Cities Served:** Clackamas County, Multnomah County, Corbett, Fairview, Gresham, Happy Valley, Linnton, Maywood Park, Orient, Springdale, Troutdale, and Wood Village, OR.

⚫ 3537 TCI Cablevision of Oregon
3500 SW Bond St.
Portland, OR 97201   Phone: (503)222-2253
Owner: Tele-Communications, Inc. **Founded:** 1952. **Cities Served:** Multnomah County, Washington County, Dunthorpe, Riverdale, and Sylvan, OR.

PRINEVILLE

▭ 3538 X-TRA
Eagle Newspapers, Inc.
558 N. Main St.   Phone: (503)447-6205
Prineville, OR 97754   Fax: (503)447-1754
Shopper. **Founded:** 1991. **Frequency:** Weekly. **Printing Method:** Offset. **Trim Size:** 14 x 21 3/4. **Cols./Page:** 6. **Col. Width:** 2 1/16 in. **Col. Depth:** 21 in. **Key Personnel:** Bill Schaffer, Gen. Mgr. **Subscription:** Free.
           Circulation: Free 1,900
Advertising rate of $1 per column inch available in combination with the Central Oregonian.

⚫ 3539 KIJK-FM - 95.1
Box K
Prineville, OR 97754   Phone: (503)447-6239
           Fax: (503)447-4724

⚫ 3540 KRCO-AM - 690
Box K
Prineville, OR 97754   Phone: (503)447-6239
           Fax: (503)447-4724
Format: Hot Country. Simulcasts KIJK-FM. **Network(s):** Mutual Broadcasting System. **Owner:** High Lakes Broadcasting, at above

Ad Rates: GLR = general line rate; BW = one-time black & white page rate; 4C = one-time four color page rate; SAU = standard advertising unit rate; CNU = Canadian newspaper advertising unit rate; PCI = per column inch rate.
Circulation: ★ = ABC; △ = BPA; ◆ = CAC; ⚫ = CCAB; ▭ = VAC; ⊕ = PO Statement; ‡ = Publisher's Report; Boldface figures = sworn; Light figures = estimated.
Entry type: ▭ = Print; ⚫ = Broadcast.

235

address. **Operating Hours:** 6 p.m.-midnight. **Key Personnel:** John Kendall, Owner/Mgr. **Wattage:** 1,000. **Ad Rates:** $10 for 30 seconds; $14 for 60 seconds. Combined rates available with KIJK-FM.

SALEM

3541 Science Fiction Review
SFR Publications
PO Box 20340
Salem, OR 97407
Magazine includes reviews of fiction and science fiction. **Frequency:** Monthly. **Key Personnel:** Elton Elliott, Editor and Publisher. **Subscription:** $35. $3.95 single issue.

Circulation: (Not Reported)

3542 KSLM-AM - 1390
PO Box 631   **Phone:** (503)363-1390
Salem, OR 97308   **Fax:** (503)363-5688

3543 Mill Creek Cable TV, Inc.
3100 Turner Rd. SE
Salem, OR 97302   Phone: (503)363-7717
Owner: John Poole. **Founded:** 1984. **Cities Served:** Marion County, OR.

3544 Viacom Cablevision
1710 Salem Industrial Dr.   Phone: (503)370-2770
Salem, OR 97303   Fax: (503)370-2571
Owner: Viacom Cablevision. **Founded:** 1969. **Cities Served:** Marion County, Polk County, Yamhill County, Amity, and Keizer, OR.

SPRINGFIELD

3545 KMTR-TV - Channel 16
3825 International Ct.   Phone: (503)746-1600
Springfield, OR 97477   **Fax: (503)747-0866**

WALDPORT

3546 KBBM-AM
235 SW Arrow, Ste. 3
Box 1419
Waldport, OR 97394   Phone: (503)563-5115

PENNSYLVANIA

ALLENTOWN

3547 Lehigh Law Journal
Bar Association of Lehigh County
1114 Walnut St.
Allentown, PA **18102**

Phone: (215)433-6204
Fax: (215)770-9826

3548 Twin County Cable TV, Inc.
3925 Airport Rd.
Allentown, PA 18103

Phone: (215)262-6100
Fax: (215)261-5099

Owner: Twin County Cable TV. **Founded:** 1963. **Cities Served:** Lehigh and Northampton counties, PA.

ALTOONA

3549 Warner Cable Communications, Inc. of Altoona
2200 Beale Ave.
Box 2330
Altoona, PA 16601

Phone: (814)946-5491
Fax: (814)943-1721

Owner: Warner Cable Communications, Inc. **Founded:** 1962. **Cities Served:** Blair County, PA.

AMBLER

3550 All Crosswords Special
Stavrolex Publications, Inc.
7002 West Butler Pke.
Ambler, PA 19002
Magazine for crossword puzzle solvers. **Frequency:** 6x/yr. **Key Personnel:** Janis Weiner, Editor; Karla Kirby, Publisher. **Subscription:** $10.40. $1.99 single issue.

Circulation: (Not Reported)

3551 All Number-Finds
Official Publications, Inc.
7002 W. Butler Pke.
Ambler, PA 19002
Magazine of number puzzles. **Frequency:** 6x/yr. **Key Personnel:** Douglas Heller, Editor; Des McNulty, Publisher. **Subscription:** $6.30. $1.25 single issue.

Circulation: (Not Reported)

3552 Cinema, Video & Cable Movie Digest
Movie Digest, Inc.
7002 W. Butler, No. 100
Ambler, PA 19002
Entertainment magazine featuring the best movies and videos for the month ahead. **Frequency:** Monthly. **Key Personnel:** Michelle Amot, Editor and Publisher. **Subscription:** $23.40. $1.95 single issue.

Circulation: (Not Reported)

3553 Crossword Corner
Stavrolex Publications, Inc.
7002 W. Butler Pke.
Ambler, PA 19002
Crossword puzzle magazine. **Frequency:** 6x/yr. **Key Personnel:** Jamis Weiner, Editor; Karla Kirby, Publisher. **Subscription:** $8. $1.50 single issue.

Circulation: (Not Reported)

3554 Cryptograms Plus
Stavrolex Publications
7002 W. Butler Pke.
Ambler, PA 19002
Magazine featuring secret messages to be decoded by the reader. **Frequency:** 6x/yr. **Key Personnel:** Janis Weiner, Editor; Karla Kirby, Publisher. **Subscription:** $6.75. $1.25 single issue.

Circulation: (Not Reported)

3555 Easy Fill-Ins
Harle Publications, Inc.
7002 W. Butler Pke.
Ambler, PA 19002
Crossword puzzle magazine providing the answers; the reader fills in the diagram. **Frequency:** 6x/yr. **Key Personnel:** Janis Weiner, Editor; Karla Kirby, Publisher. **Subscription:** $8. $1.50 single issue.

Circulation: (Not Reported)

3556 Superior Fill-Ins
Stavrolex Publications, Inc.
7002 W. Butler Pke.
Ambler, PA 19002
Magazine containing Fill-In puzzles. The answers are provided and the reader must fill in the diagram. **Frequency:** 6x/yr. **Key Personnel:** Douglas Heller, Editor; Karla Kirby, Publisher. **Subscription:** $5.40. $1 single issue.

Circulation: (Not Reported)

BEAVER FALLS

3557 WGEV-FM - 88.3
Geneva College
Beaver Falls, PA 15010

Phone: (412)847-6671
Fax: (412)847-6672

BENSALEM

3558 Bensalem Express
Metropolitan Media Enterprises Inc.
PO Box 129
Bensalem, PA 19020

Phone: (215)943-7077
Fax: (215)943-7135

Community newspaper. **Founded:** 1990. **Frequency:** Weekly. **Printing Method:** Offset. **Trim Size:** 15 x 22. **Cols./Page:** 6. **Col. Width:** 2 in.

Ad Rates: GLR = general line rate; BW = one-time black & white page rate; 4C = one-time four color page rate; SAU = standard advertising unit rate; CNU = Canadian newspaper advertising unit rate; PCI = per column inch rate.
Circulation: ★ = ABC; △ = BPA; ◆ = CAC; ● = CCAB; □ = VAC; ⊕ = PO Statement; ‡ = Publisher's Report; Boldface figures = sworn; Light figures = estimated.
Entry type: ▭ = Print; ♣ = Broadcast.

Col. Depth: 21 in. Key Personnel: David R. Vasquez, Editor and Publisher. Subscription: $40.
Ad Rates: BW: $976.50   Circulation: Free ‡20,000
         SAU: $7.75
Color advertising not accepted.

BETHLEHEM

♣ 3559 Service Electric Cable TV
2260 Ave. A   Phone: (215)865-9100
Bethlehem, PA 18017   Fax: (215)865-5031
Owner: Service Electric Cable TV, Inc. Founded: 1951. Cities Served: Berks County, Bucks County, Lehigh County, Northampton County, Alburtis, Bangor, Bath Bethlehem, Catasauqua, Coopersburg, Coplay, East Bangor, Fountain Hill, Freemansburg, Hellertown, Nazareth, Nockamixon, North Catasauqua, Pen Argyl, Portland, Riegelsville, Roseto, Tatmy, and Wind Gap, PA.

♣ 3560 WLVR-FM - 91.3
Lehigh University
29 Trembley Dr.   Phone: (215)758-4187
Bethlehem, PA 18015-3066   **Fax: (215)758-4186**

BLAIRSVILLE

♣ 3561 WLCY-FM - 106.3
Rtes. 22 & 19   Phone: (412)459-8888
Blairsville, PA 15717   Fax: (412)459-8980

BOILING SPRINGS

⬚ 3562 The Herb Quarterly
Long Mountain Press, Inc.
PO Box 548   Phone: (717)245-2764
Boiling Springs, PA 17007   **Fax: (717)245-2764**

BRADFORD

⬚ 3563 McKean County Miner
265 South Ave.
PO Box 17
Bradford, PA 16701   Phone: (814)362-6563

BROOMALL

⬚ 3564 Gray Areas
Gray Areas, Inc.
PO Box 808
Broomall, PA 19008-0808   Phone: (215)353-8238
Magazine profiling alternative lifestyles and music. Subtitle: Examining the Gray Areas of Life. Frequency: Quarterly. Printing Method: Web offset. Trim Size: 8 1/8 x 10 7/8. Cols./Page: 2 or 3. Key Personnel: Netta Gilboa, Publisher ISSN: 1062-5712. Subscription: $18; $26 other countries. $4.50 single issue.
Ad Rates: BW: $600   Circulation: Paid ‡10,000
         4C: $1,200

BRYN ATHYN

⬚ 3565 New Church Life
General Church of the New Jerusalem
PO Box 277   Phone: (215)947-6225
Bryn Athyn, PA 19009   **Fax: (215)947-3078**

BUTLER

♣ 3566 WBUT-AM - 1050
1768 N. Main St.
Box 1645
Butler, PA 16001-1645   Phone: (412)287-5778
         Fax: (412)282-9188
Format: Adult Contemporary; Full Service. Network(s): Mutual Broadcasting System. Owner: WBUT-FM. Founded: 1949. Operating Hours: 6 a.m.-10 p.m. Key Personnel: Robert C. Brandon, Pres. and Gen. Mgr. Wattage: 500. Ad Rates: $7.75-$11.75 for 30 seconds;$9-$15 for 60 seconds.

CARLISLE

⬚ 3567 Dickinson Law Review
Dickinson School of Law
150 S. College St.   Phone: (717)243-4611
Carlisle, PA 17013   **Fax: (717)243-4443**

CHESTER

♣ 3568 WDNR-FM - 89.5
PO Box 1000
1 University   Phone: (215)499-4439
Chester, PA 19013   Fax: (215)876-9751

CHESTER SPRINGS

⬚ 3569 Bible Standard and Herald of Christ's Kingdom
Laymen's Home Missionary Movement
1156 St. Matthews Rd.
PO Box 67
Chester Springs, PA 19425-0067   Phone: (215)827-7665

⬚ 3570 Present Truth and Herald of Christ's Epiphany
Laymen's Home Missionary Movement
1156 St. Matthews Rd.
PO Box 67
Chester Springs, PA 19425-0067   Phone: (215)827-7665

CLARION

♣ 3571 WCCB-AM - 640
263 Gamle
Clarion, PA 16214   Phone: (814)226-2479
Format: Alternative/Independent/Progressive. Key Personnel: Dave Bellard, Music Dir. Ad Rates: Noncommercial.

♣ 3572 WWCH-AM - 1300
725 Wood St.
PO Box 688   Phone: (814)226-4500
Clarion, PA 16214   **Fax: (814)226-5898**

CLEARFIELD

♣ 3573 WOKW-FM - 102.9
Rr. Old Town Rd.
PO Box 589   Phone: (814)765-4955
Clearfield, PA 16830   Fax: (814)765-7038
Format: Adult Contemporary. Network(s): Satellite Music. Owner: Raymark Broadcasting Co., Inc., PO Box 73, Clearfield, PA 16830. Founded: 1989. Operating Hours: Continuous; 75% network, 25% local. Key Personnel: Mark Harley, Pres./Gen. Mgr.; Dan Litten, News Dir. Wattage: 3000. Ad Rates: $5.60-$9 for 30 seconds; $7-$11 for 60 seconds.

COATESVILLE

♣ 3574 Suburban Cable TV
Rte. 82 at Monacy Rd.   Phone: (215)383-4383
Coatesville, PA 19320   Fax: (215)384-3804
Owner: Lenfest Communications, Inc. Founded: 1968. Cities Served: Chester and Delaware counties, PA.

COUDERSPORT

♣ 3575 Coudersport TV Cable Co.
14 S. Main St.
Coudersport, PA 16915   **Fax: (814)274-8642**

DELMONT

♣ 3576 Cable-Scope of Glenns Ferry
PO Box 406   Phone: (412)668-2194
Delmont, PA 15626   Fax: (412)668-7703
Founded: 1980. Key Personnel: David M. Kass, Pres. Cities Served: Glenns Ferry, ID.

EAST STROUDSBURG

♨ 3577 WESS-FM - 90.3
East Stroudsburg University
Box 198
East Stroudsburg, PA 18301   **Phone: (717)424-3134**

EMMAUS

📖 3578 Backpacker
Rodale Press, Inc.
33 E. Minor St.   **Phone: (215)967-8650**
Emmaus, PA 18098   Fax: (215)967-8960

📖 3579 Men's Health
Rodale Press, Inc.
33 E. Minor St.   Phone: (215)967-5171
Emmaus, PA 18098   **Fax: (215)967-8956**

📖 3580 The New Farm
Rodale Institute
222 Main St.   **Phone: (215)967-8405**
Emmaus, PA 18098   **Fax: (215)967-8959**

📖 3581 Organic Gardening
Rodale Press, Inc.
33 E. Minor St.   Phone: (215)967-5171
Emmaus, PA 18098   **Fax: (215)967-8963**

ERIE

📖 3582 Weekender
Times Publishing Co.
205 W. 12th St.   Phone: (814)870-1600
Erie, PA 16534   **Fax: (814)870-1808**

♨ 3583 Erie Cablevision
823 Peach St.   Phone: (814)453-4553
Erie, PA 16501   Fax: (814)456-5162
Owner: American TV & Communications Corp. **Founded:** 1981.
Cities Served: Erie County, PA.

♨ 3584 WRIE-AM - 1260
471 Robison Rd.   Phone: (814)868-5355
Erie, PA 16509   **Fax: (814)868-1876**

♨ 3585 WXKC-FM - 99.9
471 Robison Rd.   Phone: (814)868-5355
Erie, PA 16509   **Fax: (814)868-1876**

GETTYSBURG

♨ 3586 WGTY-FM - 107.7
775 Old Harrisburg Rd.
PO Box 3179   Phone: (717)334-3101
Gettysburg, PA 17325   Fax: (717)334-5822

GIBSONIA

📖 3587 Pittsburgh's Child
Honey Hill Publishing
10742 Babcock Blvd.
PO Box 418   Phone: (412)443-1891
Gibsonia, PA 15044-0418   Fax: (412)443-1877
Newspaper on parenting. **Subtitle:** Pittsburgh's Preference for Parent-
ing News. **Founded:** 1988. **Frequency:** Monthly. **Printing Method:** Web
offset. **Trim Size:** 11 1/2 x 14. **Cols./Page:** 4. **Col. Width:** 2 5/16 in.
Col. Depth: 12 3/8 in. **Subscription:** $9.
Ad Rates: BW: $1,340   **Circulation:** Free □43,692
          SAU: $30
4 color rates available upon request.

GREENSBURG

♨ 3588 TCI of Greensburg
Box 1167
Greensburg, PA 15601-2225   Phone: (412)834-6990
Owner: Tele-Communications, Inc. **Founded:** 1966. **Cities Served:**
Allegheny and Westmoreland counties, PA.

HAMBURG

📖 3589 Item
3rd & State Sts.   Phone: (215)562-7515
Hamburg, PA 19526   **Fax: (215)562-7516**

HARRISBURG

📖 3590 Central Penn Business Journal
Journal Publications, Inc.
1500 N. Second St.   Phone: (717)236-4300
Harrisburg, PA 17102   Fax: (717)236-6803

📖 3591 The VOICE for Education
Pennsylvania State Education Assn.
400 N. 3rd St.
PO Box 1724   Phone: (717)255-7134
Harrisburg, PA 17105   **Fax: (717)255-7124**

📖 3592 Wildfowl Carving and Collecting
Stackpole Publishing
PO Box 1831   Phone: (717)234-5091
Harrisburg, PA 17105   Fax: (717)234-1359

♨ 3593 Sammons Communications
4601 Smith St.
Harrisburg, PA 17109-1597   Phone: (717)540-8900
Owner: Sammons Communications, Inc. **Founded:** 1965. **Cities
Served:** Cumberland, Dauphin, Perry, and York counties, PA.

♨ 3594 WHP-TV - Channel 21
3300 N. 6th St.   Phone: (717)238-2100
Harrisburg, PA 17110   **Fax: (717)238-0196**

HERSHEY

♨ 3595 SRW Inc.
71 Cedar Ave.   **Phone: (717)533-3322**
Hershey, PA 17033-1419   **Fax: (717)533-3344**

HUGHESVILLE

📖 3596 East Lycoming Shopper and News
Division of Sun-Gazette
RD 3, Box 14-A   Phone: (717)584-2134
Hughesville, PA 17737   **Fax: (717)584-5399**

HUNTINGDON

♨ 3597 WHUN-AM - 1150
400 Washington St.
PO Box 404   Phone: (814)643-3340
Huntingdon, PA 16652   **Fax: (814)643-7379**

♨ 3598 WLAK-FM - 103.5
400 Washington St.
PO Box 404   Phone: (814)643-3340
Huntingdon, PA 16652   **Fax: (814)643-7379**

INDIANA

♨ 3599 WDAD-AM - 1450
21 N. 5th St.   Phone: (412)349-1450
Indiana, PA 15701   Fax: (412)349-6842
Format: Adult Contemporary. **Network(s):** CBS. **Owner:** RMS Media
Management Inc. **Operating Hours:** Continuous. **Key Personnel:** Dick

Ad Rates: GLR = general line rate; BW = one-time black & white page rate; 4C = one-time four color page rate; SAU = standard advertising unit rate;
CNU = Canadian newspaper advertising unit rate; PCI = per column inch rate.
Circulation: ★ = ABC; △ = BPA; ◆ = CAC; ● = CCAB; □ = VAC; ⊕ = PO Statement; ‡ = Publisher's Report; Boldface figures = sworn; Light figures = estimated.
Entry type: 📖 = Print; ♨ = Broadcast.

239

Sherry, Mgr.; Todd Marino, Operations Mgr.; Chauncey Ross, News Dir. **Wattage:** 1000.

JERSEY SHORE

🎤 3600 WJSA-AM - 1600
262 Allegheny St.   Phone: (717)398-7200
Jersey Shore, PA 11740   **Fax: (717)398-7201**

JOHNSTOWN

📖 3601 Tribune-Democrat
425 Locust St.   **Phone: (814)532-5150**
Johnstown, PA 15901   Fax: (814)539-1409

KIMBERTON

📖 3602 Biodynamics
Biodynamic Farming & Gardening Association
PO Box 550   Phone: (215)935-7797
Kimberton, PA 19442-0550   **Fax: (215)983-3196**

LANCASTER

🎤 3603 Suburban Cable TV
528 W. Orange St.
Lancaster, PA 17603   Phone: (717)291-3000
Owner: Lenfest Communications, Inc. **Founded:** 1966. **Cities Served:** Lancaster County, PA.

LARKSVILLE

📖 3604 Moneytalk
334 Highlark Dr.   Phone: (717)287-6498
Larksville, PA 18704   **Fax: (717)287-9718**

LAVEROCK

📖 3605 Woman's Art Journal
1711 Harris Rd.
Laverock, PA 19118
Journal containing articles and reviews on art history and other topics pertaining to women in the visual arts. **Founded:** 1980. **Frequency:** 2x/yr. **Printing Method:** Offset. **Trim Size:** 8 1/2 x 11. **Cols./Page:** 2 and 3. **Col. Width:** 3 3/4 in. and 2 1/2 in. **Key Personnel:** Elsa H. Fine, Contact. **ISSN:** 0270-7993. **Subscription:** $14; $20 institutions.
                                    Circulation: Combined ‡2,100
Advertising accepted; contact publisher for rates.

LEVITTOWN

📖 3606 Levittown Express
Metropolitan Media Enterprises Inc.
PO Box 823   Phone: (215)943-7077
Levittown, PA 19058   Fax: (215)943-7135
Community newspaper. **Founded:** 1989. **Frequency:** Weekly. **Printing Method:** Offset. **Trim Size:** 15 x 22. **Cols./Page:** 6. **Col. Width:** 2 in. **Col. Depth:** 21 1/2 in. **Key Personnel:** David R. Vasquez, Editor and Publisher. **Subscription:** $40.
Ad Rates: BW: $976.50   **Circulation:** Free ‡26,500
             SAU: $7.75
Color advertising not accepted.

LEWISBURG

📖 3607 The Valley Trader
Oberdorf Publishing
21 N. 3rd St.   Phone: (717)524-9850
Lewisburg, PA 17837   Fax: (717)524-4048
Shopper. **Founded:** 1980. **Frequency:** Weekly (Wed.). **Printing Method:** Web offset. **Trim Size:** 11 x 16. **Cols./Page:** 6. **Col. Width:** 9.5 picas. **Col. Depth:** 15 in. **Key Personnel:** Max Oberdorf, Publisher; James Ginn-Railey, Advertising Mgr. **Subscription:** Free.
Ad Rates: GLR: $.39   **Circulation:** Paid ◆25
             BW: $495   Free ◆16,775
             4C: $1,100
             PCI: $5.50
Additional Contact Information: 800-800-4047.

MARIETTA

📖 3608 Old News
Susquehanna Times & Magazine, Inc.
400 Stackstown Rd.
Marietta, PA 17547-9300   Phone: (717)426-2212
Magazine (tabloid) featuring biographical history. **Founded:** 1989. **Frequency:** Monthly (not published in August). **Printing Method:** Web offset. **Trim Size:** 11 x 17. **Cols./Page:** 4. **Col. Width:** 2 5/8 in. **Col. Depth:** 15 1/2 in. **Key Personnel:** Rick Bromer, Editor; Nancy Bromer, Publisher. **ISSN:** 1047-3068. **Subscription:** $14. $2 single issue.
                                        Circulation: ‡20,000
Advertising not accepted.

MARS

📖 3609 Cranberry Eagle/The News Weekly
Eagle Printing Co., Inc.
Gigliotti Plaza, Ste. 201
20120 Rte. 19
Cranberry Township   **Phone: (412)452-5912**
Mars, PA 16046   **Fax: (412)452-4768**

MASONTOWN

🎤 3610 WRIJ-FM - 106.9
He's Alive Corp. Offices
34 Springs Rd.
PO Box 540   Phone: (301)895-3292
Grantsville, MD 21536   **Fax: (301)895-3293**

MEDIA

🎤 3611 WKSZ-FM - 100.3
1001 Baltimore Pike   Phone: (215)565-8900
Media, PA 19063   **Fax: (215)565-6024**

MIFFLINBURG

📖 3612 Mifflinburg Telegraph
358 Walnut St.   Phone: (717)966-2255
Mifflinburg, PA 17844-0189   **Fax: (717)966-9706**

MONTROSE

📖 3613 Miniature Quilts
Chitra Publications
2 Public Ave.   Phone: (717)278-1984
Montrose, PA 18801   Fax: (717)278-2223
Magazine focusing on minature quilts. **Founded:** 1991. **Frequency:** Quarterly. **Printing Method:** Web offset. **Trim Size:** 8 3/8 x 10 7/8. **Key Personnel:** Christiane Meunier, Publisher; Patti Bacheldor, Editor. **ISSN:** 1065-0245. **Subscription:** $9.95. $3.50 single issue.
Ad Rates: BW: $820   **Circulation:** Paid ‡85,000
             4C: $1,175

📖 3614 Vegetarial Gourmet
Chitra Publications
2 Public Ave.   Phone: (717)278-1984
Montrose, PA 18801   Fax: (717)278-2223
Vegetarian cooking magazine. **Founded:** 1992. **Frequency:** Quarterly. **Printing Method:** Web offset. **Trim Size:** 8 3/8 x 10 7/8. **Key Personnel:** Christian Meunier, Publisher; Jessie Dubey, Editor. **Subscription:** $9.95. $3.50 single issue.
Ad Rates: BW: $950   **Circulation:** Paid ‡70,000
             4C: $1,450

MOUNT JEWETT

📖 3615 Bradford Journal/Miner
PO Box 17
Bradford, PA 16701   Phone: (814)362-6563
Former Title: Bradford Journal

MOUNT JOY

◻ 3616 Antiques & Auction News
Engle Publishing Co.
PO Box 500, Rte. 230 W   **Phone: (717)653-4300**
Mount Joy, PA 17552   **Fax: (717)653-6165**

◻ 3617 P.A.C.
Engle Publishing Co.
Rte. 230 W
PO Box 500   **Phone: (717)653-4300**
Mount Joy, PA 17552   **Fax: (717)653-6165**
Publication for paper and advertising collectors. **Frequency:** Monthly.
Circulation: (Not Reported)
Advertising accepted; contact publisher for rates. **Additional Contact
Information:** Toll-free 800-482-2886.

MOUNT POCONO

♣ 3618 WPMR-AM - 960
PO Box 132   **Phone: (717)839-3939**
Mount Pocono, PA 18344   **Fax: (717)837-7625**

NARBERTH

◻ 3619 Physicians News Digest
Physicians News Digest, Inc.
230 Windsor Ave.   **Phone: (215)668-1040**
Narberth, PA 19072   **Fax: (215)668-9177**
Non-clinical medical magazine providing local medical news and
practice management advice. **Founded:** 1987. **Frequency:** Monthly.
Printing Method: Web offset. **Trim Size:** 11 x 17. **Cols./Page:** 4. **Col.
Width:** 2 3/8 in. **Col. Depth:** 10 1/4 in. **Key Personnel:** Jeffrey Barg,
Editor and Publisher; Paula Lipp, Mng. Editor; Peter A. Heiman,
Sales and Mktg. Dir. **Subscription:** $35. $3.50 single issue.
Ad Rates: BW: $1,535   **Circulation:** Paid ‡85
             4C: $2,235   Controlled ‡31,336
             PCI: $45

NAZARETH

◻ 3620 O Gauge Railroading
Myron J. Biggar Group, Inc.
PO Box 239
Brandywine Rd.   **Phone: (215)759-0406**
Nazareth, PA 18064   **Fax: (215)759-0406**

NEW PROVIDENCE

♣ 3621 WDAC-FM - 94.5
683 Lancaster Pike   **Phone: (717)284-4123**
New Providence, PA 17560   **Fax: (717)284-2300**

NEW WILMINGTON

♣ 3622 New Wilmington Borough Cable Dept.
140 W. Neshannock Ave.   **Phone: (412)946-8167**
New Wilmington, PA 16142   **Fax: (412)946-8841**

NEWPORT

◻ 3623 The News-Sun
19 S. 2nd St.
Box 128   **Phone: (717)567-6226**
Newport, PA 17074   **Fax: (717)582-7933**

NEWTOWN

◻ 3624 Convenience Store Decisions
Donohue-Meehan Publishing
6 Penns Trail, No. 205   **Phone: (215)579-9770**
Newtown, PA 18940-1889   **Fax: (215)579-9773**

◻ 3625 Delaware River and The Water Front
Z Dock Publications
PO Box 159   **Phone: (215)860-8577**
Newtown, PA 18940-0159   **Fax: (215)579-2524**
Ceased publication.

NORTHAMPTON

♣ 3626 Twin County Trans Video Inc.
5508 Nor-Bath Blvd.   **Phone: (215)262-6100**
Northampton, PA 18067   **Fax: (215)261-5099**

OXFORD

◻ 3627 Chronicle News Magazine
AD Pro, Inc.
PO Box 520   **Phone: (215)932-2444**
Oxford, PA 19363-0520   **Fax: (215)932-2246**

PAOLI

◻ 3628 Philadelphia Golf Magazine
Philadelphia Golf Publishing Co.
1583 Maple Ave.   **Phone: (215)989-9700**
Paoli, PA 19301   **Fax: (215)254-8958**

PHILADELPHIA

◻ 3629 AAA Delaware Motorist
AAA Mid-Atlantic, Inc.
2040 Market St.   **Phone: (215)864-5455**
Philadelphia, PA 19103-3302   **Fax: (215)568-1153**
Auto club publication featuring automotive, travel, and insurance
stories. **Frequency:** 6x/yr. **Printing Method:** Web offset. **Trim Size:** 10
1/2 x 12 1/2. **Cols./Page:** 4. **Col. Width:** 2 3/8 in. **Key Personnel:** John
C. Moyer, Editor. **USPS:** 152-080. **Subscription:** Free to members.
Circulation: 50,000
Advertising accepted; contact publisher for rates. **Formerly:** Delaware
Keystone Motorist.

◻ 3630 AAA Maryland Motorist
AAA Mid-Atlantic, Inc.
2040 Market St.   **Phone: (215)864-5455**
Philadelphia, PA 19103-3302   **Fax: (215)568-1153**
Auto club publication featuring auto, travel, and insurance stories.
Frequency: 6x/yr. **Printing Method:** Web offset. **Trim Size:** 10 1/2 x 12
1/2. **Cols./Page:** 4. **Col. Width:** 2 3/8 in. **Key Personnel:** John C.
Moyer, Editor. **USPS:** 331-960. **Subscription:** Free to members.
Circulation: 243,000
Advertising accepted; contact publisher for rates.

◻ 3631 Business Documents
North American Publishing Co.
401 N. Broad St.   **Phone: (215)238-5300**
Philadelphia, PA 19108   **Fax: (215)238-5457**
Former Title: Forms and Label Purchasing

◻ 3632 Business Review
Dept. of Research, Federal Reserve Bank of Philadelphia
10 Independence Mall   **Phone: (215)574-6428**
Philadelphia, PA 19106   **Fax: (215)574-4364**

◻ 3633 Friends Journal
1501 Cherry St.   **Phone: (215)241-7277**
Philadelphia, PA 19102   **Fax: (215)568-1377**

◻ 3634 High End
High End Publishing
8895 Alton St.
Philadelphia, PA 19115
Magazine features news, reviews, and video game information.
Frequency: 2x/mo. **Key Personnel:** Ralph Capriotti, Publisher; Todd
Capriotti, Editor. **Subscription:** $9.95. $2.95 single issue.
Circulation: (Not Reported)

☐ **3635 Labyrinth**
4722 Baltimore Ave.
Philadelphia, PA 19143   Phone: (215)724-6181
Feminist newspaper for women in the Philadelphia, PA area.
Frequency: Monthly. **Subscription:** $15.
Circulation: (Not Reported)

☐ **3636 The Legal Intelligencer**
Packard Press
1617 JFK Blvd. Ste, 1245   Phone: (215)563-2700
Philadelphia, PA 19103   Fax: (215)563-4911

☐ **3637 Metrokids Magazine**
2101 Spruce St.   Phone: (215)735-7035
Philadelphia, PA 19103   Fax: (215)735-1547
Regional magazine for families. **Founded:** 1990. **Frequency:** Monthly.
Printing Method: Web offset. **Trim Size:** 10 x 13. **Cols./Page:** 4. **Col.
Width:** 2 1/4 in. **Col. Depth:** 11 1/4 in. **Key Personnel:** Nancy Lisagor,
Editor; Joan M. Horvarth, Mng. Editor. **Subscription:** $15. Free single
issue.
Ad Rates: BW: $1,350   **Circulation:** Free ☐**70,000**
           4C: $2,150

☐ **3638 Parents Express**
PO Box 12900
Philadelphia, PA 19108   Phone: (215)789-2277
Parenting publication. **Founded:** 1989. **Frequency:** Monthly. **Printing
Method:** Web offset. **Key Personnel:** Cynthia Roberts, Co-Editor and
Publisher; Sharon Sexton, Co-Publisher/Editor. **Subscription:** $10.
Ad Rates: BW: $1,300   **Circulation:** ‡63,000
           4C: $1,775
Formerly: Skip.

☐ **3639 Showcase Magazine**
718 Arch St., Ste. 6N
Philadelphia, PA 19106-1505   Phone: (215)238-1450
Ceased publication.

☐ **3640 The Soroptimists of the Americas**
Soroptimist International
1616 Walnut St., Ste. 700   Phone: (215)732-0512
Philadelphia, PA 19103   Fax: (212)732-7508
Publication for members of Soroptimist International, a service
organization for executive and professional women. **Frequency:** 6x/yr.
Circulation: (Not Reported)

☐ **3641 South Philadelphia American**
1215 Garritt St.
Philadelphia, PA 19147-4922   Phone: (215)467-2713
Founded: 1937. **Frequency:** Weekly. **Printing Method:** Offset. **Cols./
Page:** 5. **Col. Width:** 2 in. **Col. Depth:** 16 in. **Key Personnel:** Fred
Trombetta, Publisher; Roger Barone, Photo Editor. **Subscription:**
Free.
Ad Rates: BW: $250   **Circulation:** Free ‡20,000
           PCI: $3.50
Color advertising not accepted.

🕭 **3642 Comcast Cablevision of Philadelphia**
11400 Northeast Ave.   Phone: (215)961-3800
Philadelphia, PA 19116   Fax: (215)961-3875
Owner: Comcast Corp. **Founded:** 1986. **Cities Served:** Philadelphia
County, PA.

🕭 **3643 Greater Philadelphia Cablevision, Inc.**
1351 S. Delaware Ave.   Phone: (215)463-1100
Philadelphia, PA 19147   Fax: (215)463-2330
Owner: Greater Media, Inc. **Founded:** 1972. **Cities Served:** Philadelphia County, PA.

🕭 **3644 Wade Cablevision**
170 N. 49th St.   Phone: (215)871-7870
Philadelphia, PA 19131   Fax: (215)482-8170
Owner: Wade Communications, Inc. **Founded:** 1987. **Cities Served:**
Philadelphia County, PA.

🕭 **3645 WCAU-TV - Channel 10**
City Ave. & Monument Rd.   Phone: (215)668-5510
Philadelphia, PA 19131   Fax: (215)668-5532

🕭 **3646 WMMR-FM - 93.3**
Independence Mall E.   Phone: (215)238-8000
Philadelphia, PA **19106**   **Fax: (215)238-4737**

PITTSBURGH

☐ **3647 American Skating World**
Business Communications, Inc.
1816 Brownsville Rd.   Phone: (412)885-7600
Pittsburgh, PA 15210   Fax: (412)885-7617
Tabloid covering all phases of figure skating. **Founded:** 1981. **Frequen-
cy:** Monthly. **Printing Method:** Web offset. **Trim Size:** 11 x 14. **Cols./
Page:** 4. **Col. Width:** 2 3/8 in. **Col. Depth:** 12 7/8 in. **Key Personnel:**
Michael E. Romanus, Jr., Publisher; Robert A. Mock, Editor; H.
Kermit Jackson, Mng. Editor. **ISSN:** 0744-1363. **Subscription:** $19.95.
$2.95 single issue.
Ad Rates: BW: $934.93   **Circulation:** Paid ⊕**3,241**
           4C: $1,334.93   Non-paid ⊕**459**

☐ **3648 American Srbobran**
Serb National Federation
One Fifth Ave., 7th Fl.   **Phone: (412)642-7372**
Pittsburgh, PA 15222   **Fax: (412)642-1372**

☐ **3649 Chiropractic History**
207 Grandview Dr. S.   Phone: (412)237-4554
Pittsburgh, PA 15215   Fax: (412)237-4512
Journal. **Subtitle:** The Archives and Journal of the Association for the
History of Chiropractic. **Founded:** 1981. **Frequency:** 2x/yr. **Printing
Method:** Offset. **Trim Size:** 8 1/2 x 11. **Cols./Page:** 2. **Col. Width:** 3 1/2
in. **Col. Depth:** 9 1/2 in. **Key Personnel:** Russell W. Gibbons, Editor.
ISSN: 0736-4377. **Subscription:** $35. $17.50 single issue.
Ad Rates: BW: $150   **Circulation:** Paid ‡523
                     Non-paid ‡250

☐ **3650 Community News South**
Group Publications, Ltd.
1816 Brownsville Rd.   Phone: (412)885-7600
Pittsburgh, PA 15210-3908   Fax: (412)885-7617
Community newspaper. **Founded:** 1980. **Frequency:** Every other week.
Printing Method: Web offset. **Trim Size:** 10 1/4 x 13. **Cols./Page:** 5.
Col. Width: 2 in. **Key Personnel:** Betty Koefflen, Exec. Editor; Michael
E. Romenus, Publisher.
Ad Rates: BW: $667.15   **Circulation:** Free 10,000
           PCI: $10.26
Color advertising not accepted. **Formerly:** Community Action Press.

☐ **3651 Ethnology**
Dept. of Anthropology
University of Pittsburgh   Phone: (412)648-7503
Pittsburgh, PA 15260   **Fax: (412)648-7535**

☐ **3652 Pittsburgh City Paper**
1 Library Pl., G2   Phone: (412)469-3080
Duquesne, PA 15110   Fax: (412)469-3099
City newspaper. **Founded:** 1991. **Frequency:** Weekly (Wed.). **Printing
Method:** Web offset. **Trim Size:** 11 3/8 x 14. **Cols./Page:** 8. **Col. Width:**
1 1/8 in. **Col. Depth:** 13 in. **Key Personnel:** Andy March, Publisher.
Subscription: Free; $35 (mail).
Ad Rates: GLR: $1.75   **Circulation:** Free **50,000**
           BW: $1,050   Paid **5**
           4C: $1,350
           PCI: $17.50

☐ **3653 Progress in Energy and Combustion Science**
Pergamon Press
Carnegie Mellon University
Department of Mechanical Engineering   Phone: (412)268-2498
Pittsburgh, PA 15213-3890   Fax: (412)268-3348
Journal reviewing technical information in the fields of energy and
combustion science. **Founded:** 1975. **Frequency:** 6x/yr. **Cols./Page:** 2.
Col. Width: 2 3/4 in. **Col. Depth:** 9 1/4 in. **Key Personnel:** Prof.
Norman Chigier, Editor. **Subscription:** $109; $545 institutions.
Circulation: (Not Reported)
Advertising not accepted.

☐ **3654 The Server Pennsylvania**
Group Publications, Ltd.
1816 Brownsville Rd.   Phone: (412)885-7600
Pittsburgh, PA **15210**-3908   Fax: (412)885-7617

□ **3655 Shooting Star Review**
Shooting Star Productions Inc.
7123 Race St.
Pittsburgh, PA 15208-1424   **Phone: (412)731-7464**

□ **3656 South Hills Record**
Gateway Publications
3623 Brownsville Rd.   **Phone: (412)884-3111**
Pittsburgh, PA 15227   **Fax: (412)884-3113**

□ **3657 Steelabor**
United Steelworkers of America
5 Gateway Ctr.   **Phone: (412)562-2442**
Pittsburgh, PA 15222   **Fax: (412)562-2445**

♣ **3658 TCI of Pennsylvania, Inc.**
300 Corliss St.
Pittsburgh, PA 15220-4815   Phone: (412)771-8100
Owner: Tele-Communications, Inc. **Founded:** 1984. **Cities Served:** Allegheny County, PA.

♣ **3659 WMVB-AM - 890**
526 Pama Ave.
Pittsburgh, PA 15222   Phone: (412)263-6600
Format: Alternative/Independent/Progressive. **Key Personnel:** Greg Maitland, Music Dir. **Ad Rates:** Noncommercial.

♣ **3660 WPLW-AM - 1590**
201 Ewing Rd.   Phone: (412)922-0550
Pittsburgh, PA 15205   **Fax: (412)922-0553**

♣ **3661 WPPJ-AM - 670**
201 Wood St.
PO Box 262
Pittsburgh, PA 15222   Phone: (412)392-4725
Format: Alternative/Independent/Progressive. **Ad Rates:** Noncommercial.

PITTSTON

♣ **3662 WVIA-FM - 89.9**
70 Old Boston Rd.   Phone: (717)826-6144
Pittston, PA 18640-9606   Fax: (717)655-1180
Format: Eclectic; Classical; Jazz; New Age; Bluegrass; News. **Network(s):** National Public Radio (NPR); American Public Radio (APR). **Founded:** 1973. **Operating Hours:** Continuous. **Key Personnel:** A. William Kelly, Pres./CEO; Erica Funke, Station Mgr.; George Graham, Contemporary Arts Dir.; Larry Vojtko, Operations Dir.; Ray Boyle, Development Dir.; Rory Giovannucci, Corporate Communications Dir.; William L. Myers, Engineering Dir.; Ronald Stravinsky, Bus. Mgr. **Wattage:** 50,000. **Ad Rates:** Noncommercial. **Additional Contact Information:** (717)655-2808.

POTTSVILLE

□ **3663 Reptile & Amphibian Magazine**
NG Publishing, Inc.
RD. 3, Box 3709-A   Phone: (717)662-6050
Pottsville, PA 17901   Fax: (717)622-5838
Magazine for herpetologists and pet owners. **Founded:** November/December, 1989. **Frequency:** 6x/yr. **Printing Method:** Offset. **Trim Size:** 5 1/2 x 8 1/2. **Cols./Page:** 2. **Col. Width:** 2 1/4 in. **Col. Depth:** 7 3/4 in. **Key Personnel:** Norman Frank, Editor and Publisher. **ISSN:** 1059-0668. **Subscription:** $12; $22 two years; $15 Canada; $37 other countries.
Ad Rates: BW: $397   **Circulation:** Paid ⊕7,396
          4C: $680   Non-paid ⊕382

RADNOR

□ **3664 ECN (Electronic Component News)**
Chilton Co.
Chilton Way   Phone: (215)964-4347
Radnor, PA 19089   **Fax: (215)964-4348**

□ **3665 Energy User News**
Chilton Co.
Chilton Way   Phone: (215)964-4000
Radnor, PA 19089   **Fax: (215)964-4647**

□ **3666 Industrial Safety and Hygiene News**
Chilton Co.
Chilton Way   **Phone: (215)964-4055**
Radnor, PA 19089   **Fax: (215)964-4273**

□ **3667 Jewelers' Circular-Keystone**
Chilton Co.
Chilton Way   Phone: (215)964-4000
Radnor, PA 19089   **Fax: (215)964-4481**

READING

□ **3668 Salon Today Management Magazine**
People-Media, Inc.
320 Morgantown Rd.
PO Box 91   Phone: (215)376-0500
Reading, PA 19603   **Fax: (215)376-5943**

SCRANTON

□ **3669 Lackawanna Jurist**
Lackawanna Bar Assn.
205 1 Pyramid Center
204 Wyoming Ave.   Phone: (717)969-9161
Scranton, PA 18503   Fax: (717)969-9162

♣ **3670 Verto Cable TV**
Box 918
Scranton, PA 18503   Phone: (717)342-0285
Owner: Verto Cable TV. **Founded:** 1973. **Key Personnel:** Joseph Pagnotti, Pres.; Marlene Miller, Mgr.; James Peters, Engineer. **Cities Served:** Lackawanna County, Luzerne County, Avoca, Dickson City, Exeter, Forty Fort, Luzerne, Moosic, Nanticoke, Old Forge, Plymouth, Scranton, Swoyersville, Taylor, Throop, West Wyoming, and Wyoming, PA: 54,000 subscribing households; 35 channels; 1 community access channel.

♣ **3671 WUSR-AM - 550**
301 Jefferson Hall
Linden-Jefferson St.
Scranton, PA 18510   Phone: (717)941-7648
Format: Alternative/Independent/Progressive. **Key Personnel:** Gail Hamlin, Music Dir. **Ad Rates:** Noncommercial.

♣ **3672 WUSR-FM - 107.9**
301 Jefferson Hall
Linden-Jefferson St.
Scranton, PA 18510   Phone: (717)941-7648
Format: Alternative/Independent/Progressive. **Key Personnel:** Gail Hamlin, Music Dir. **Ad Rates:** Noncommercial.

SHIPPENSBURG

♣ **3673 WSYC-FM - 88.7**
Cumberland Union Bldg.
Shippensburg University   Phone: (717)532-6006
Shippensburg, PA 17257   **Fax: (717)532-1636**

SOMERSET

□ **3674 Somerset County Shopper**
Somerset Newspapers, Inc.
334 W. Main St.
PO Box 638   Phone: (814)445-9621
Somerset, PA 15501   **Fax: (814)445-2935**

Ad Rates: GLR = general line rate; BW = one-time black & white page rate; 4C = one-time four color page rate; SAU = standard advertising unit rate;
CNU = Canadian newspaper advertising unit rate; PCI = per column inch rate.
Circulation: ★ = ABC; △ = BPA; ◆ = CAC; ● = CCAB; □ = VAC; ⊕ = PO Statement; ‡ = Publisher's Report; Boldface figures = sworn; Light figures = estimated.
Entry type: □ = Print; ♣ = Broadcast.

SPANGLER

🎙 3675 WCCZ-FM - 97.3
PO Box 400   Phone: (814)948-
Spangler, PA 15775   GOLD
Format: Oldies. **Network(s):** USA Radio; Jones Satellite. **Owner:** Raymark Broadcasting Co., Inc., PO Box 73, Clearfield, PA 16830; (814)765-4955. **Founded:** 1991. **Operating Hours:** Continuous; 75% network, 25% local. **Key Personnel:** Mark E. Harley, Pres./Gen. Mgr. **Wattage:** 3000. **Ad Rates:** $5.10-$8 for 30 seconds; $6.40-$10 for 60 seconds.

SPRINGFIELD

📖 3676 Phillies Report
Sports Press, Inc.
PO Box 157   Phone: (215)543-4077
Springfield, PA 19064   **Fax: (215)544-4013**

STATE COLLEGE

📖 3677 The Daily Collegian
Penn State University
123 S. Burrowes St.   **Phone: (814)865-1828**
University Park, PA 16801   **Fax: (814)865-3848**

🎙 3678 WBHV-FM - 103.1
Box 888   Phone: (814)237-4959
State College, PA 16804   Fax: (814)234-1659
Format: Contemporary Hit Radio (CHR). **Owner:** Nittany Broadcasting Co., at above address. **Founded:** 1963. **Formerly:** WXLR-FM (1988). **Operating Hours:** Continuous. **Key Personnel:** John Fredrickson, Gen. Mgr.; Nick Galli, Pres.; Mike Maze, Program Dir.; Dana Schulte, Gen. Sales Mgr.; Paul Kraimer, Music Dir. **Wattage:** 3000. **Ad Rates:** $9-$24 per unit. Combined rates available with WMAJ-AM: $12-$27 per unit.

🎙 3679 WRSC-AM - 1390
160 Clearview Ave.   **Phone: (814)238-5085**
State College, PA 16801   Fax: (814)238-8993

STROUDSBURG

📖 3680 The Woman's Pulpit
International Association of Women Ministers
579 Main St.
Stroudsburg, PA 18360   Phone: (717)421-7751
Periodical reporting on issues of interest to women in Christian ministry. **Frequency:** Quarterly. **Subscription:** $15.
     Circulation: 450

SWARTHMORE

📖 3681 The Phoenix
Swarthmore College
Swarthmore, PA 19081   **Phone: (215)328-8173**

TITUSVILLE

🎙 3682 WTIV-AM - 1230
Box 184   Phone: (814)827-3651
Titusville, PA 16354-0184   **Fax: (814)827-1679**

TOWANDA

🎙 3683 WTTC-AM - 1550
214 Main St.   Phone: (717)265-2165
Towanda, PA 18848   **Fax: (717)265-8665**

TROY

🎙 3684 WHGL-AM - 1310
170 Redington Ave.   Phone: (717)297-0100
Troy, PA 16947   **Fax: (717)297-3193**

UNIVERSITY PARK

📖 3685 The Journal of Speculative Philosophy
Penn State University Press
Penn State University
240 Sparks   **Phone: (814)865-1512**
University Park, PA 16802   **Fax: (814)863-7986**

UPPER DARBY

🎙 3686 Suburban Cable TV
503 S. Cedar Ln.   Phone: (215)853-2200
Upper Darby, PA 19082   Fax: (215)853-1185
Owner: Lenfest Communications, Inc. **Founded:** 1976. **Cities Served:** Delaware County, Aldan, Clifton Heights, East Lansdowne, Lansdowne, Millbourne, and Yeadon, PA.

VALLEY FORGE

📖 3687 U.S. Tech
Mid-Atlantic Tech Publications Inc.
Valley Forge Office Colony, Bldg. 2-100
PO Box 957   Phone: (215)783-6100
Valley Forge, PA 19481   Fax: (215)783-0317
Magazine for electronics engineers, production managers, and purchasing agents. **Founded:** 1986. **Frequency:** Monthly. **Printing Method:** Web offset. **Trim Size:** 10 7/8 x 14 3/4. **Key Personnel:** Jacob Fattal, Publisher/Pres.; Walter Salm, Editor; Elizabeth Salm, Assoc. Editor; George Pachter, V.P. of Sales.
Ad Rates: BW: $2,935   **Circulation:** 50,000
             4C: $3,435
Formerly: Atlantic Tech; Pacific Tech; Mid-Atlantic Tech.

WASHINGTON

📖 3688 W & J Magazine
Washington and Jefferson College
     Phone: (412)223-6074
Washington, PA 15301   **Fax: (412)223-6108**

WAYNESBORO

🎙 3689 WEEO-AM - 1130
Box 309   Phone: (717)762-7171
Waynesboro, PA 17268   Fax: (717)762-9111
Format: Christian Contemporary. **Network(s):** Mutual Broadcasting System. **Owner:** Marbobben, Inc. **Founded:** 1971. **Operating Hours:** Sunrise-sunset. **Key Personnel:** Bob Thomas, Gen. Mgr.; Roy Summers, Operations Mgr. **Wattage:** 1000. **Ad Rates:** $5.50-$10.65 for 30 seconds; $6.90-$13.30 for 60 seconds.

WEST CHESTER

📖 3690 The Homes Magazine
Daily Local News Co.
250 N. Bradford Ave.   Phone: (215)430-1134
West Chester, PA 19382   Fax: (215)430-1180
Real estate magazine. **Founded:** 1988. **Frequency:** 2x/mo. **Key Personnel:** J. Peter Lindquist, Advertising Mgr.
     Circulation: (Not Reported)
Advertising accepted; contact publisher for rates. **Formerly:** The Chester County Homes.

WESTFIELD

📖 3691 Free Press-Courier
Tioga Printing Corp.
Box 127
Westfield, PA 16950   Phone: (814)367-2230

WESTTOWN

📖 3692 Medical Malpractice-OB/GYN Litigation Reporter
Andrews Publications
Box 1000   Phone: (215)399-6600
Westtown, PA 19395   Fax: (215)399-6610
Former Title: Medical Malpractice Litigation Reporter

WILLIAMSPORT

🎤 **3693 WKSB-FM - 102.7**
1559 W. 4th St.
PO Box 3638   Phone: (717)327-1400
Williamsport, PA 17701   Fax: (717)327-8156

🎤 **3694 WRAK-AM - 1400**
1559 W. 4th St.
PO Box 3638   Phone: (717)327-1400
Williamsport, PA 17701   Fax: (717)327-8156

🎤 **3695 WWAS-FM - 88.1**
                                  Phone: (717)326-3761
1 College Ave.   x7214
Williamsport, PA 17701   **Fax: (717)327-4503**

WILLOW GROVE

🎤 **3696 Comcast Cablevision**
29 York Rd.   Phone: (215)657-6990
Willow Grove, PA 19090   Fax: (215)657-7096
Owner: Comcast Corp. **Founded:** 1979. **Cities Served:** Montgomery
County, PA.

YARDLEY

📖 **3697 Yardley News**
Inter County Publishing Co.
PO Box 334   Phone: (215)493-2794
Yardley, PA 19067   **Fax: (215)321-0527**

🎤 **3698 WCHR-FM - 94.5**
Woodside Rd.
Yardley, PA 19067   Phone: (215)493-4252

YORK

📖 **3699 York Daily Record**
1750 Industrial Hwy.   Phone: (717)840-4000
York, PA 17402   **Fax: (717)840-2009**

🎤 **3700 Cable TV of York**
1050 E. King St.   Phone: (717)846-4551
York, PA 17403   Fax: (717)843-5400
Owner: Susquehanna Cable Co. **Founded:** 1967. **Cities Served:** York
County, PA.

PUERTO RICO

AGUADILLA

🎙 **3701 Cable TV del Noroeste**
Hwy. 465 at Hwy. 110
Box 5229   Phone: (809)882-7040
Aguadilla, PR 00605   Fax: (809)882-3404
Owner: Cable Systems USA Partners, Rte. 66 N., Crown, PA 16220.
Founded: 1986. **Key Personnel:** Ricardo Ruiz, Pres./Gen. Mgr.; Ivan
Rosa, Plant Mgr. **Cities Served:** Aguada, Isabela, Moca, Aguadilla, and
Quebradillas, PR: 23,000 subscribing households; 53 channels; 1
community access channel.

ARECIBO

🎙 **3702 WCMN-AM - 1280**
PO Box 436   Phone: (809)878-0070
Arecibo, PR 00613   **Fax: (809)880-1112**

LUQUILLO

🎙 **3703 TCI Cable of Puerto Rico**
Box 719
Luquillo, PR 00773-0719   Phone: (809)889-3470
Owner: Tele-Communications, Inc. **Founded:** 1985. **Cities Served:**
Carnovanas, Ceiba, Fajardo, Loiza, Naguabo, and Rio Grande, PR.

SAN JUAN

🎙 **3704 Century ML Cable Corp.**
1 Manuel Camunas St.
Box 192296   Phone: (809)766-0909
San Juan, PR 00919-2296   Fax: (809)250-6532
Owner: Century Communications Corp. **Founded:** 1972. **Key Personnel:** Francisco Toste Santana, Gen. Mgr.; Guillermo Schwarz, Operations Dir. **Cities Served:** Bayamon, Carolina, Guaynabo, San Juan,
and Trujillo Alto, PR: 99,000 subscribing households; 52 channels; 1
community access channel.

RHODE ISLAND

CRANSTON

3705 Cranston Herald
Beacon Communications of Rhode Island
789 Park Ave.
Cranston, RI 02910
Phone: (401)732-3100
Fax: (401)732-3110

3706 Cox Cable Rhode Island, Inc.
111 Comstock Pkwy.
Cranston, RI 02920
Phone: (401)946-3830
Fax: (401)946-3830
Owner: Cox Cable Communications. **Founded:** 1981. **Cities Served:** Providence County, Burrillville, Glocester, Johnston, and Scituate, RI.

LINCOLN

3707 Heritage Communications, Inc.
Box 518
Lincoln, RI 02865-0518
Phone: (401)765-3802
Fax: (401)765-1003
Owner: Tele-Communications, Inc. **Founded:** 1982. **Cities Served:** Providence County, RI and Bristol, Norfolk, and Worcester counties, MA.

NEWPORT

3708 The Newport Navalog
Edward A. Sherman Publishing Co.
101 Malbone Rd.
PO Box 420
Newport, RI 02840
Phone: (401)849-3300
Fax: (401)841-2265

PROVIDENCE

3709 Providence Business News
300 Richmond St, Ste. 202
Providence, RI 02903
Phone: (401)273-2201
Fax: (401)274-0670

3710 Steamboat Bill
Steamship Historical Society of America, Inc.
300 Ray Dr., Ste. 4
Providence, RI 02906
Phone: (401)274-0805
Fax: (401)274-0836

3711 Blessing, Inc.
PO Box 41000
Providence, RI 02940-1000
Phone: (401)781-7134
Format: Religious. **Founded:** 1983. **Key Personnel:** Raymond Dempsey, Jr., Pres. **Cities Served:** Rhode Island and communities in Massachusetts: 5 channels; 5 community access channels; 1.5 hours per week of community access programming. **Ad Rates:** Noncommercial.

3712 WLKW-AM - 790
78 Oxford St., Ste. 401
Providence, RI 02905
Phone: (401)831-7979
Fax: (401)781-7822

3713 WWLI-FM - 105
75 Oxford St.
Providence, RI 02905
Phone: (401)272-1105
Fax: (401)781-7822

SMITHFIELD

3714 The Archway
Bryant College
PO Box 7
Smithfield, RI 02917-1284
Phone: (401)232-6028
Fax: (401)232-6710

WARWICK

3715 Warwick Beacon
Beacon Communications of Rhode Island
1944 Warwick Ave.
Warwick, RI 02889-5000
Phone: (401)732-3100
Fax: (401)732-3110

3716 WWRX-FM - 103.7
55 Alless Rd.
Warwick, RI 02886
Phone: (401)732-5690
Fax: (401)738-9329

WEST WARWICK

3717 Dimension Cable
9 J.P. Murphy Hwy.
West Warwick, RI 02893-2381
Phone: (401)828-2288
Fax: (401)828-3835
Owner: Times Mirror Cable TV. **Founded:** 1982. **Key Personnel:** Denise D. Farley, Gen. Mgr.; Don Layher, Sales and Mktg. Dir.; James DiSalle, Operations Dir.; John Linton, Technical Operations Dir. **Cities Served:** Kent County, Providence County, East Greenwich, North Providence, Providence, Coventry, West Warwick, and Warwick, RI: 86,000 subscribing households; 52 channels; 1 community access channel; 20 hours per week of community access programming.

SOUTH CAROLINA

ABBEVILLE

🎙 **3718 Cencom of Abbeville**
306 S. Main St.
Abbeville, SC 29620

Phone: (803)459-9646
Fax: (803)459-5963

AIKEN

🎙 **3719 Aiken Cablevision Ltd.**
3060 Cablevision Rd.
Box 151
Aiken, SC 29801

Phone: (803)648-8361
Fax: (803)648-8361

Owner: InterMedia Partners. **Founded:** 1968. **Cities Served:** Aiken and Barnwell counties, SC.

ANDERSON

🎙 **3720 Anderson Cablevision Associates**
1103 N. Fant St.
Anderson, SC 29621

Phone: (803)225-3156
Fax: (803)225-3301

Owner: Booth American Co. **Founded:** 1972. **Cities Served:** Anderson County, SC.

BARNWELL

🎙 **3721 WBAW-AM - 740**
PO Box 447
Barnwell, SC 29812

Phone: (803)259-3507
Fax: (803)259-2691

Format: Adult Contemporary; Urban Contemporary; News; Sports. Simulcasts WBAW-FM. **Network(s):** Mutual Broadcasting System; South Carolina News. **Owner:** Radio WBAW Inc. **Founded:** 1965. **Operating Hours:** Sunrise-sunset. **Key Personnel:** Joe Wilder, Pres.; Drew Wilder, Gen. Mgr.; Steve Brown, Program Dir.; B.J. Funderburk, Traffic Dir. **Ad Rates:** $3-$5 for 15 seconds; $5-$9 for 30 seconds; $8.75-$16.50 for 60 seconds.

🎙 **3722 WBAW-FM - 99.1**
PO Box 447
Barnwell, SC 29812

Phone: (803)259-3507
Fax: (803)259-2691

Format: Adult Contemporary. **Network(s):** Mutual Broadcasting System; South Carolina News. **Owner:** Radio WBAW Inc. **Founded:** 1966. **Operating Hours:** 5 a.m.-midnight. **Key Personnel:** Joe Wilder, Pres.; Drew Wilder, Gen. Mgr.; Steve Brown, Program Dir.; B.J. Funderburk, Traffic Dir. **Wattage:** 25,000. **Ad Rates:** $3-$5 for 15 seconds; $5-$9 for 30 seconds; $8.75-$16.50 for 60 seconds.

BEAUFORT

🎙 **3723 WOCW-FM - 92.1**
2617 Boundary St., Ste. 104
Beaufort, SC 29902

Phone: (803)524-9236
Fax: (803)524-1120

BENNETTSVILLE

🎙 **3724 WBSC-AM - 1550**
226 Radio Rd.
Bennettsville, SC 29512

Phone: (803)479-7121

Format: Oldies. **Owner:** Big Bend Broadcasting Corp. **Founded:** 1947. **Operating Hours:** 5 a.m.-midnight. **Key Personnel:** Ken Harman, Gen. Mgr. **Wattage:** 10,000. **Ad Rates:** $3.75-$3.95 for 15 seconds; $5-$5.60 for 30 seconds; $8.35-$8.75 for 60 seconds.

CHARLESTON

📖 **3725 Good Dog!**
Good Dog Magazine
2945 H Dove Haven Ct.
Charleston, SC 29414

Phone: (803)763-8750
Fax: (803)763-1788

Magazine for dog lovers. **Subtitle:** The Consumer Magazine for Dog Owners. **Founded:** 1988. **Frequency:** 6x/yr. **Printing Method:** Web offset. **Trim Size:** 8 3/8 x 10 7/8. **Cols./Page:** 3. **Col. Width:** 2 1/4 in. **Col. Depth:** 10 in. **Key Personnel:** Ross Becker, Publisher. **ISSN:** 0899-6024. **Subscription:** $18.97. $3 single issue.

| Ad Rates: | BW: | $975 | Circulation: | Paid ‡30,000 |
| | 4C: | $2,500 | | Non-paid ‡5,000 |

📖 **3726 The Post and Courier**
Evening Post Publishing Co.
134 Columbus St.
Charleston, SC 29403-4800

Phone: (803)577-7111
Fax: (803)723-4893

📖 **3727 South Carolina Historical Magazine**
South Carolina Historical Society
Fireproof Bldg.
100 Meeting St.
Charleston, SC 29401

Phone: (803)723-3225
Fax: (803)723-8584

🎙 **3728 WITV-TV - Channel 7**
c/o South Carolina Educational
Television
PO Box 11000
1101 George Rogers Blvd.
Columbia, SC 29211

Phone: (803)737-3200

🎙 **3729 WYBB-FM - 98.1**
59 Windermere Blvd.
Charleston, SC 29407-7411

Phone: (803)769-4799
Fax: (803)769-4797

Ad Rates: GLR = general line rate; BW = one-time black & white page rate; 4C = one-time four color page rate; SAU = standard advertising unit rate; CNU = Canadian newspaper advertising unit rate; PCI = per column inch rate.
Circulation: ★ = ABC; △ = BPA; ◆ = CAC; ● = CCAB; □ = VAC; ⊕ = PO Statement; ‡ = Publisher's Report; Boldface figures = sworn; Light figures = estimated.
Entry type: 📖 = Print; 🎙 = Broadcast.

251

CLEMSON

⚓ 3730 WCCP-AM - 1560
Laurence Rd.
Box 1560   Phone: (803)654-5400
Clemson, SC 29631   Fax: (803)654-9328
Format: Talk. **Owner:** Golden Corners Broadcasting Inc. **Founded:**
1967. **Formerly:** WBES. **Operating Hours:** Sunrise-sunset. **Key Person-**
nel: George W. Clement, Pres.; Faye Clement, V.P.; Tommy Powell,
Program Dir. **Wattage:** 1000. **Ad Rates:** $5-$7.50 30-second; $8-$10
for 60 seconds.

COLUMBIA

📖 3731 Economics of Education Review
Department of Economics
University of South Carolina   Phone: (803)777-2714
Columbia, SC 29208   Fax: (803)777-6876
Academic journal. **Founded:** 1981. **Frequency:** Quarterly. **Trim Size:** 7
1/2 x 10. **Cols./Page:** 2. **Col. Width:** 2 3/4 in. **Col. Depth:** 7 1/2 in. **Key**
Personnel: Elchanan Cohn, Editor. **ISSN:** 0272-7757. **Subscription:**
$200 institutions.
                                       Circulation: (Not Reported)
Advertising accepted; contact publisher for rates. Individual subscrip-
tion rates are available upon request.

📖 3732 Essays in International Business
University of South Carolina
College of Business Administration   Phone: (803)777-6942
Columbia, SC 29208   Fax: (803)777-3609
Journal publishing original manuscripts in the area of internationl
business. **Founded:** 1980. **Frequency:** 1x/yr. **Key Personnel:** Brian
Toyne, Editor-in-Chief; Douglas Nigh, Assoc. Editor-in-Chief. **Sub-**
scription: $7.50 single issue.
                                       Circulation: (Not Reported)
Advertising not accepted.

📖 3733 Journalism Quarterly
Assn. for Education in Journalism and Mass Communication
University of South Carolina
College of Journalism
1621 College St.   Phone: (803)777-2005
Columbia, SC 29208-0251   **Fax: (803)777-4728**

📖 3734 The South Carolina Policy Forum
Institute of Public Affairs
University of South Carolina
Gabrell Hall
Columbia, SC 29208   Phone: (803)777-8156
Journal focusing on public policy and governmental administration in
South Carolina. **Subtitle:** A Review of Public Affairs in South
Carolina. **Founded:** January 1990. **Frequency:** Quarterly. **Printing**
Method: Offset lithography. **Trim Size:** 8 1/2 x 11. **Cols./Page:** 2 or 3.
Col. Width: 3 1/2 or 2 1/4 in. **Col. Depth:** 9 1/8 in. **Key Personnel:**
Charlie B. Tyler, Mng. Editor; Douglas Dobson, Publisher. **ISSN:**
1055-2901. **Subscription:** $18.75. $6 single issue.
                                       Circulation: Paid 315
                                                    Non-paid 510
Advertising not accepted. **Formerly:** The South Carolina Forum.

⚓ 3735 Communication Systems, Inc.
2712 Middleburg Dr., Ste. 211
Columbia, SC 29204   Phone: (803)799-6460
Owner: Communication Systems, Inc. **Cities Served:** Richland County
and Lexington County, SC.

⚓ 3736 Star Cable Associates
101 W. Park Blvd.
Columbia, SC 29210   Phone: (803)750-0050
Owner: Star Cable Associates. **Cities Served:** Richland County, SC.

⚓ 3737 WQXL-AM - 1470
PO Box 3277   **Phone: (803)742-1470**
Columbia, SC 29230-3277   **Fax: (803)799-7911**

⚓ 3738 WTGH-AM - 620
PO Box 620   Phone: (803)796-9533
Columbia, SC 29202   **Fax: (803)796-7706**

CONWAY

📖 3739 The Chanticleer
Coastal Carolina College
PO Box 1954   Phone: (803)349-2330
Conway, SC 29526   **Fax: (803)349-2316**

⚓ 3740 WHMC-TV - Channel 23
c/o South Carolina Educational
  Television
PO Box 11000
1101 George Rogers Blvd.
Columbia, SC 29211   **Phone: (803)737-3200**

DILLON

📖 3741 The Dillon Herald
The Herald Publishing Co.
PO Drawer 1288   Phone: (803)774-3311
Dillon, SC 29536   **Fax: (803)841-1930**

EDGEFIELD

📖 3742 The Citizen-News
PO Box 448   Phone: (803)637-5306
Edgefield, SC 29824   **Fax: (803)637-6066**

FLORENCE

⚓ 3743 Vision Cable of South Carolina
3232 Bryson Dr.   Phone: (803)662-8191
Florence, SC 29501   Fax: (803)665-5483
Owner: Vision Cable Communications, Inc. **Founded:** 1963. **Cities**
Served: Darlington and Florence counties, SC.

⚓ 3744 WJMX-AM - 970
PO Box 103000   Phone: (803)667-9569
Florence, SC 29501-3000   Fax: (803)664-2869

⚓ 3745 WJMX-FM - 103.3
PO Box 103000   Phone: (803)667-9569
Florence, SC 29501-3000   **Fax: (803)664-2869**

⚓ 3746 WJPM-TV - Channel 33
c/o South Carolina Educational
  Television
401 George Rogers Blvd.
Columbia, SC 29211   **Phone: (803)737-3200**

⚓ 3747 WPDE-TV - Channel 15
3215 Cashua Dr.   Phone: (803)665-1515
Florence, SC 29501-6303   Fax: (803)665-4079

FORT MILL

⚓ 3748 Palmetto Cable TV
PO Box 1418
Fort Mill, SC 29715   **Phone: (803)548-6000**

GAFFNEY

⚓ 3749 WFGN-AM - 1180
Box 1388
Gaffney, SC 29342   **Phone: (803)489-9430**

GOOSE CREEK

📖 3750 The Goose Creek Gazette
PO Box 304   Phone: (803)572-0511
Goose Creek, SC 29445   **Fax: (803)572-0312**

GREENVILLE

📖 3751 The Paladin
Furman University
Box 28584   Phone: (803)294-2077
Greenville, SC 29613   **Fax: (803)294-3001**

⚲ 3752 WANS-AM - 1280
403 Woods Lake Dr.   Phone: (803)458-9267
Greenville, SC 29607   Fax: (803)297-8490

⚲ 3753 WESC-AM - 660
223 W. Stone Ave.   Phone: (803)242-4660
Greenville, SC 29609   **Fax: (803)271-5029**

⚲ 3754 WMUU-AM - 1260
920 Wade Hampton Blvd.   Phone: (803)242-6240
Greenville, SC 29609   **Fax: (803)370-3829**

⚲ 3755 WMUU-FM - 94.5
920 Wade Hampton Blvd.   Phone: (803)242-6240
Greenville, SC 29609   **Fax: (803)370-3829**

⚲ 3756 WNTV-TV - Channel 29
c/o South Carolina Educational
  Television
PO Box 11000
1101 George Rogers Blvd.
Columbia, SC 29211   **Phone: (803)737-3200**

⚲ 3757 WPLS-FM - 96.5
Furman University
Box 28573   Phone: (803)294-3045
Greenville, SC 29613   **Fax: (803)294-3001**

GREENWOOD

⚲ 3758 WNEH-TV - Channel 38
c/o South Carolina Educational
  Television
PO Box 11000
1101 George Rogers Blvd.
Columbia, SC 29211   **Phone: (803)737-3200**

GREER

⚲ 3759 WPJM-AM - 800
305 N. Tryon St.
Greer, SC 29651   **Phone: (803)877-1112**

INMAN

⚏ 3760 Inman Times
PO Drawer 7
Inman, SC 29349   **Phone: (803)472-9548**
Former Title: Times

JOHNSTON

⚲ 3761 WJES-AM - 1190
Drawer I   Phone: (803)275-4444
Johnston, SC 29832   **Fax: (803)275-3185**

⚲ 3762 WKSX-FM - 92.7
Drawer I   Phone: (803)275-4444
Johnston, SC 28852   Fax: (803)275-3185
Format: Oldies. **Network(s):** ABC; South Carolina. **Owner:** Edgefield-
Saluda Radio Co., at above address. **Operating Hours:** Continuous.
Key Personnel: Mike Casey, Pres./Gen. Mgr.; Frank Davis, Opera-
tions Mgr. **Wattage:** 6000.

KINGSTREE

⚲ 3763 Farmers Telephone Cooperative Inc.
1101 E. Main St.
PO Box 588   Phone: (803)382-2333
Kingstree, SC 29556   **Fax: (803)382-3909**

LADSON

⚲ 3764 WKCL-FM - 91.5
362 College Park Rd.
PO Box 809   Phone: (803)553-8740
Ladson, SC 29456   **Fax: (803)553-1525**

LAKE CITY

⚲ 3765 WVLC-AM - 1260
Box 1177   Phone: (803)394-2088
Lake City, SC 29560   **Fax: (803)665-8786**

MONCKS CORNER

⚲ 3766 WMCJ-AM - 950
314 Rembert Dennis Blvd.
PO Box 67   Phone: (803)761-6010
Moncks Corner, SC 29461   **Fax: (803)761-6979**

MOUNT PLEASANT

⚏ 3767 Vital Speeches of the Day
City News Publishing Co.
PO Box 1247   Phone: (803)881-8733
Mount Pleasant, SC 29465-1247   **Fax: (803)881-8733**

MURRELLS INLET

⚲ 3768 WDZA-FM - 94.5
PO Box 1630   Phone: (803)357-0348
Murrells Inlet, SC 29576   Fax: (803)357-1931
Format: Eclectic. **Owner:** Radio Systems Inc., at above address.
Founded: 1991. **Operating Hours:** Continuous. **ADI:** Florence-Myrtle
Beach, SC. **Key Personnel:** Robert E. Johnson, Pres. **Wattage:** 6000.

MYRTLE BEACH

⚏ 3769 Pee Dee Magazine
Pee Dee Magazine, Inc.
PO Box 1888   Phone: (803)448-9141
Myrtle Beach, SC 29578   Fax: (803)626-8887
Subtitle: Celebrating the History, Lifestyle and Culture of the Pee Dee
Region. **Founded:** 1988. **Frequency:** Bimonthly. **Printing Method:** Web
offset. **Trim Size:** 8 1/2 x 11. **Key Personnel:** Rod Gragg, Exec. Editor;
Beth Rodgers, Mng. Editor; Jim Creel, Jr., Advertising Dir. **Subscrip-
tion:** $18.90. $3.50 single issue.
Ad Rates: BW: $1,100   **Circulation:** Paid ‡3,000
    4C: $1,495   Controlled ‡7,000

⚲ 3770 Cox Cable South Carolina
1901 Oak St.   Phone: (803)448-7196
Myrtle Beach, SC 29577   Fax: (803)626-2922
Owner: Cox Cable Communications. **Founded:** 1962. **Cities Served:**
Horry County, Briarcliffe Acres, Conway, and Forestbrook, SC.

NORTH CHARLESTON

⚲ 3771 Storer Cable of Carolina, Inc.
4151 Spruill Ave.
North Charleston, SC 29406   Phone: (803)747-0546
Owner: Storer Cable Communications. **Founded:** 1973. **Cities Served:**
Berkeley County, Charleston County, Dorchester County, Goose
Creek, Hanahan, Hunley Park, Isle of Palms, Mount Pleasant, North
Charleston, Sullivan's Island, and Summerville, SC.

PAGELAND

⚏ 3772 The Pageland Progressive-Journal
Progressive Publishers
PO Box 218   Phone: (803)672-2358
Pageland, SC 29728   **Fax: (803)672-5593**

ROCK HILL

🎤 **3773 Catawba Services Inc.**
PO Box 11703
Rock Hill, SC 29731-1703   **Phone: (803)329-9000**

SAINT GEORGE

📖 **3774 Dorchester Eagle-Record**
5549 Memorial Blvd.
PO Drawer 278
Saint George, SC 29477   Phone: (803)563-3121

🎤 **3775 WQIZ-AM - 810**
Box 903   **Phone: (803)566-1100**
St. George, SC 29477   **Fax: (803)529-1933**

SALUDA

🎤 **3776 Palmetto Cablevision (Saluda Cablevision)**
Box 518   Phone: (803)445-8108
Saluda, SC 29138   **Fax: (803)445-7935**

SUMMERVILLE

🎤 **3777 WAZS-AM - 980**
Box 859
Summerville, SC 29484   Phone: (803)875-4411
Format: Country; Southern Gospel. **Network(s):** NBC. **Owner:** Radio Summerville Inc. **Founded:** 1962. **Operating Hours:** 6 a.m.-midnight Mon., 6 a.m.-9 p.m. Tues.-Sat., 6 a.m.-6 p.m. Sun. **Key Personnel:** Wayne Phillips, Pres.; Becky Snipes, Program Dir.; James Snipes, Sales Mgr. **Additional Contact Information:** Alt. telephone (803)871-9171.

SUMTER

🎤 **3778 Vision Cable of Sumter**
1170 N. Guignard Dr.   Phone: (803)469-2423
Sumter, SC 29150   Fax: (803)469-3700
Owner: Vision Cable Communications, Inc. **Founded:** 1964. **Cities Served:** Sumter County, SC.

WALHALLA

🎤 **3779 WGOG-AM - 1000**
PO Box 10   Phone: (803)638-3616
Walhalla, SC 29691   **Fax: (803)638-7975**

🎤 **3780 WGOG-FM - 96.3**
PO Box 10   Phone: (803)638-3616
Walhalla, SC 29691   Fax: (803)638-7975
Format: Adult Contemporary; Oldies. **Network(s):** NBC; South Carolina News. **Owner:** Luzanne Griffith. **Founded:** 1959. **Operating Hours:** Continuous. **Key Personnel:** Marvin Hill, Station Mgr. **Wattage:** 6000. **Ad Rates:** $4-$10.45 for 30 seconds; $6-$15.75 for 60 seconds.

WALTERBORO

📖 **3781 Colleton Shopper**
724 S. Jeffries Blvd.   Phone: (803)549-1543
Walterboro, SC 29488   **Fax: (803)549-2711**

📖 **3782 Weekend**
The Press and Standard, Inc.
PO Box 1248
113 Washington St.   Phone: (803)549-2586
Walterboro, SC 29488   Fax: (803)549-2446
Shopping guide. **Founded:** 1989. **Frequency:** Weekly (Fri.). **Printing Method:** Web offset. **Trim Size:** 11 1/2 x 17. **Cols./Page:** 5. **Col. Width:** 2 1/8 in. **Col. Depth:** 16 in. **Key Personnel:**P Dan Johnson, Editor; Harold R. Lubs, Publisher; J.R. Addison, Advertising and Circulation Mgr. **Subscription:** Free; $25 outside area.
Ad Rates: BW: $360   **Circulation:** 100
         4C: $600   Free 22,265
         PCI: $5.50

🎤 **3783 WALD-AM - 1080**
PO Box 1397
Walterboro, SC 29488   Phone: (803)538-4000
Format: Gospel; Country. **Network(s):** USA Radio. **Owner:** Holiday Communications, Inc. **Founded:** 1942. **Operating Hours:** Continuous. **Key Personnel:** D. Holiday, Gen. Mgr.; Sherrie Smith, Pres. **Wattage:** 2500. **Ad Rates:** $9 for 30 seconds; $17 for 60 seconds. **Additional Contact Information:** Alternate telephone (803)538-3789.

WEST COLUMBIA

🎤 **3784 Cablevision Industries**
1125 B Ave.   Phone: (803)791-4650
West Columbia, SC 29169   Fax: (803)794-4399
Owner: Cablevision Industries, Inc. **Founded:** 1977. **Key Personnel:** Jim Carey, Regional V.P.; Dale Ordoyne, Regional Mktg. Dir.; Bill Hauman, Regional Engineer; Bud Tibshrany, Govt. Relations; Rick Keyser, Asst. Gen. Mgr. **Cities Served:** Lexington County, Newberry County, Richland County, Arcadia Lakes, Cayce, Chapin, Eastover, Harvison, Irmo, Lexington, Little Mountain, Newberry, Pineridge, South Congaree, Springdale, and West Columbia, SC: 60 channels; 1 community access channel.

SOUTH DAKOTA

ABERDEEN

♣ 3785 Aberdeen Cable TV
24 1st Ave., NE
Box 910   Phone: (605)229-1775
Aberdeen, SD 57402   Fax: (605)229-0478
Owner: Douglas Communications Corp. **Founded:** 1970. **Cities Served:**
Brown County, SD. **Additional Contact Information:** Toll-free: 800-
456-0564.

BROOKINGS

⚐ 3786 Town and Country Shopper
PO Box 466   Phone: (605)692-9311
Brookings, SD 57006   **Fax: (605)692-6750**

DE SMET

⚐ 3787 The De Smet News
Blegen Publishing, Inc.
Box 69   Phone: (605)854-3331
De Smet, SD 57231   **Fax: (605)854-3332**

DEADWOOD

⚐ 3788 The Lawrence County Centennial
Allison Publications, Inc.
68 Sherman St.
PO Box 512   Phone: (605)578-3305
Deadwood, SD 57732   Fax: (605)578-3308

GROTON

♣ 3789 James Valley Co-op Telephone Co.
Box 260   Phone: (605)397-2323
Groton, SD 57445   Fax: (605)397-2350

MITCHELL

⚐ 3790 Advisor
Box 1343
Mitchell, SD 57301   Phone: (605)996-8916

RAPID CITY

⚐ 3791 The Antique Lable Collector Magazine
D.W. King & Associates, Publishers
PO Box 412
Rapid City, SD 57701-0412   Phone: (813)888-8057
Founded: 1986. **Frequency:** Quarterly. **Printing Method:** Web offset.
Trim Size: 11 x 17. **Cols./Page:** 3. **Subscription:** $25.
Ad Rates: BW: $160   **Circulation:** (Not Reported)

♣ 3792 KCLO-TV - Channel 15
2497 W. Chicago   Phone: (605)341-1500
Rapid City, SD 57702-2467   Fax: (605)348-5518

♣ 3793 TCI Cablevision of South Dakota
Box 537
Rapid City, SD 57701-1729   Phone: (605)343-3402
Owner: Tele-Communications, Inc. **Founded:** 1958. **Cities Served:**
Meade County, Pennington County, and Box Elder, SD.

ROSHOLT

⚐ 3794 The Rosholt Review
PO Box 136   Phone: (605)537-4276
Rosholt, SD 57260-0136   **Fax: (605)537-4276**

SIOUX FALLS

⚐ 3795 Tri-State Neighbor
Dakota Publishing, Inc.
2701 S. Minnesota Ave.   Phone: (605)335-7300
Sioux Falls, SD 57105   Fax: (605)335-8141

♣ 3796 Sioux Falls Cable TV
3507 S. Duluth   Phone: (605)339-3339
Sioux Falls, SD 57105   Fax: (605)335-1987
Owner: Midcontinent Cable Co. **Founded:** 1971. **Cities Served:**
Minnehaha County, SD.

SPEARFISH

♣ 3797 KSLT-FM - 107.3
2910 4th Ave.   Phone: (605)642-7792
Spearfish, SD 57783   Fax: (605)642-8872

WAGNER

⚐ 3798 The Wagner Post Advertizer
PO Box 100
Wagner, SD 57380   Phone: (605)384-5555
Ceased publication.

WATERTOWN

♣ 3799   Watertown Cable TV
15 S. Broadway St.
Box 1234   Phone: (605)886-7990
Watertown, SD 57201   Fax: (605)886-9327
Owner: Booth American Co. **Founded:** 1973. **Cities Served:** Codington County, SD.

WILMOT

▦ 3800   The Wilmot Enterprise
PO Box 37   Phone: (605)938-4651
Wilmot, SD 57279   **Fax: (605)938-4683**

YANKTON

♣ 3801   KYNT-AM - 1450
Box 628   Phone: (605)665-7892
Yankton, SD 57078-0628   **Fax: (605)665-0818**

TENNESSEE

BYRDSTOWN

♩ 3802 WSBI-AM - 1210
PO Box 316
Byrdstown, TN 38549
Phone: (606)387-6625
Fax: (606)387-8000

CARTHAGE

▥ 3803 Carthage Courier
504 Main
PO Box 239
Carthage, TN 37030
Phone: (615)735-1110
Fax: (615)735-0635

CHATTANOOGA

▥ 3804 Chattanooga Life and Leisure Magazine
PO Box 6009
Chattanooga, TN 37401
Phone: (615)629-5375
Fax: (615)629-5379
Ceased publication.

▥ 3805 East Brainerd Journal
Journal Publishing Inc.
PO Box 729
Ooltewah, TN 37363
Phone: (615)629-0472
Local newspaper. **Founded:** 1990. **Frequency:** 2x/mo. **Printing Method:** Web offset. **Cols./Page:** 4. **Col. Width:** 2 1/4 in. **Col. Depth:** 14 in. **Key Personnel:** Ted Betts, Publisher; F. Carmen French, Editor.
Ad Rates: BW: $400   **Circulation:** ‡16,000
Combined advertising rates available with The East Hamilton County Journal for a combined circulation of 25,000.

▥ 3806 National Knife Magazine
National Knife Collectors Assn.
PO Box 21070
Chattanooga, TN 37421
Phone: (615)892-5007
Fax: (615)899-9456

♩ 3807 TeleScripps Cable Co.
325 Market St.
Box 303
Chattanooga, TN 37402
Phone: (615)756-2000
Owner: Scripps Howard Cable Co. **Founded:** 1977. **Cities Served:** Walker County and Lookout Mountain, GA; Hamilton County, Sequatchie County, Collegedale, East Ridge, Lakesite, Lookout Mountain, Red Bank, Ridgeside, Signal Mountain, and Walden, TN.

♩ 3808 WAWL-FM - 91.5
4501 Amnicola Hwy.
Chattanooga, TN 37406
Phone: (615)697-4470
Fax: (615)697-4740

♩ 3809 WDYN-FM - 89.7
1815 Union Ave.
Chattanooga, TN 37404
Phone: (615)493-4382

♩ 3810 WFXS-FM - 102.3
1200 Mountain Creek Rd., Ste. 102
Chattanooga, TN 37405
Phone: (615)875-0659
Fax: (615)875-3306

CLARKSVILLE

▥ 3811 The Peddler
341 Union St.
Clarksville, TN 37040
Phone: (615)552-1160
Fax: (615)552-1777

CLEVELAND

▥ 3812 The Cleveland Daily Banner
Cleveland Newspapers, Inc.
1505 25th St. NW
PO Box 3600
Cleveland, TN 37320-3600
Phone: (615)472-5041
Fax: (615)476-1046

♩ 3813 WBAC-AM - 1340
1701-M S. Lee Hwy.
Box 1059
CLeveland, TN 37364-1059
Phone: (615)476-7593
Fax: (615)472-5290

COLLEGEDALE

▥ 3814 East Hamilton County Journal
Journal Publishing Inc.
PO Box 729
Ooltewah, TN 37363
Phone: (615)629-0472
Local newspaper serving Ooletewah, Collegedale, and Apison communities. **Founded:** 1989. **Frequency:** 2x/mo. **Printing Method:** Web offset. **Cols./Page:** 4. **Col. Width:** 2 1/4 in. **Col. Depth:** 14 1/2 in. **Key Personnel:** Ted Betts, Publisher; F. Carmen French, Editor.
Ad Rates: BW: $800   **Circulation:** ‡8,228
Dual advertising rates available with The East Brainerd Journal.

COLLIERVILLE

▥ 3815 Modern Woodworking
Target Magazine Group
PO Box 640
Collierville, TN 38017
Phone: (901)853-7720
Fax: (901)853-6437

COLUMBIA

◫ **3816 Middle Tennessee Shopper**
PO Box 1424
Columbia, TN 38402

Phone: (615)381-4990
Fax: (615)381-1017

COOKEVILLE

◱ **3817 WHUB-FM - 98.5**
136 E. Spring St.
PO Box 1420
Cookeville, TN 38503

Phone: (615)526-2131
Fax: (615)528-3635

◱ **3818 WTTU-FM - 88.5**
Box 5113
Cookeville, TN 38505

Phone: (615)372-3169
Fax: (615)372-6138

COWAN

◱ **3819 WZYX-AM - 1440**
540 W. Cumberland St.
Box 398
Cowan, TN 37318

Phone: (615)967-7471
Fax: (615)962-1440

DICKSON

◱ **3820 WQZQ-FM - 102.5**
PO Box 171097
Nashville, TN 37217

Phone: (615)399-1029
Fax: (615)399-1023

DONELSON

◱ **3821 WAMB-FM - 106.7**
1617 Lebanon Rd.
Nashville, TN 37210

Phone: (615)889-1960

Format: Middle-of-the-Road (MOR); Big Band/Nostalgia. **Network(s):** Mutual Broadcasting System. **Owner:** Great Southern Broadcasting Co., Inc.; (615)889-1960. **Founded:** 1990. **Operating Hours:** Continuous. **Key Personnel:** William O. Barry, Pres./Gen. Mgr.; Harry P. Stephenson, Gen. Sales Mgr.; Kenneth R. Bramming, Program Dir. **Wattage:** 75.

ELIZABETHTON

◱ **3822 WBEJ-AM - 1240**
626 1/2 Elk Ave.
Elizabethton, TN 37643

Phone: (615)542-2184
Fax: (615)542-2185

FRANKLIN

◫ **3823 The Williamson Leader**
The Williamson Leader, Inc.
121 Royal Oaks Trade Center
PO Box 729
Franklin, TN 37065

Phone: (615)794-4564
Fax: (615)794-9581

◱ **3824 WAKM-AM - 950**
Box 469
Franklin, TN 37065

Phone: (615)794-1594
Fax: (615)794-1595

HARROGATE

◫ **3825 Lincoln Herald**
Lincoln Memorial University Press
Box 2006
Harrogate, TN 37752-0901

Phone: (615)869-6235
Fax: (615)869-6370

JACKSON

◱ **3826 Tennessee Cablevision Systems**
2177 Christmasville Rd.
Jackson, TN 38305

Phone: (901)424-3213
Fax: (901)424-4257

Owner: Cablevision Industries, Inc. **Founded:** 1968. **Cities Served:** Madison County, TN.

JOHNSON CITY

◱ **3827 WETS-FM - 89.5**
East Tennessee State University
Box 70630
Johnson City, TN 37614-0630

Phone: (615)929-6440
Fax: (615)929-6449

KINGSPORT

◱ **3828 Warner Cable Communications, Inc.**
1221 N. Eastman Rd.
Box 809
Kingsport, TN 37660

Phone: (615)247-2183
Fax: (615)247-1807

Owner: Warner Cable Communications, Inc. **Founded:** 1980. **Cities Served:** Hawkins and Sullivan counties, TN.

KNOXVILLE

◱ **3829 TeleScripps Cable Co.**
614 N. Central Ave.
Box 27905
Knoxville, TN 37927

Phone: (615)637-5411
Fax: (615)637-8805

Owner: Scripps Howard Cable Co. **Founded:** 1975. **Cities Served:** Blount County, Greene County, Knox County, Afton, Halls, Powell, and Rockford, TN.

◱ **3830 WKOP-TV - Channel 15**
209 Communications Bldg.
University of Tennessee
Knoxville, TN 37996-0321

Phone: (615)974-5281
Fax: (615)974-4472

Format: Public TV. **Network(s):** Public Broadcasting Service (PBS). **Owner:** East Tennessee Public Communications Corp. **Founded:** 1990. **Operating Hours:** 9 a.m.-11 p.m. **ADI:** Knoxville (Crossville), TN. **Key Personnel:** E.A. Curtis, Jr., Pres./Gen. Mgr.; Jim Tindell, Asst. Gen. Mgr.; Elaine Tomber, Production Mgr.; Edward Horde, Program Mgr. **Local Programs:** *Scholar's Bowl. ET Horizons. The Branson Report.*

LEBANON

◫ **3831 The Star-Shopper**
PO Box 857
Lebanon, TN 37088
Ceased publication.

Phone: (615)444-6008
Fax: (615)444-4562

LENOIR CITY

◫ **3832 News-Herald**
Box 310
508 E. Broadway
Lenoir City, TN 37771

Phone: (615)986-6581
Fax: (615)988-3261

LEWISBURG

◱ **3833 WAXO-AM - 1220**
217 W. Commerce St.
Lewisburg, TN 37901

Phone: (615)359-6641

Format: Adult Contemporary. **Owner:** Marshall County Radio Corp. **Founded:** 1981. **Operating Hours:** 6 a.m.- midnight. **Key Personnel:** Bob Smartt, Gen. Mgr.; Kevin Knight, Program Dir.; Jennifer Jones, News and Promotions Dir. **Wattage:** 1000.

LUTTRELL

◫ **3834 Marine Fish Monthly**
Publishing Concepts Corp.
3243 Hwy. 61 E.
Luttrell, TN 37779

Phone: (615)992-3892
Fax: (615)992-5259

MEMPHIS

◫ **3835 Shake, Rattle and Roll**
Moonbeam Press
1725 B Madison, Ste. 3
Memphis, TN 38104

Magazine reporting on the music scene in Memphis, TN. **Frequency:** Monthly. **Key Personnel:** Cara McCastlain, Co-Editor; Sandy Heiss, Co-Editor; C.P.J. Mooney IV, Publisher. **Subscription:** $12.
Circulation: (Not Reported)

🎙 **3836 Memphis Cablevision**
5450 Winchester Rd.   Phone: (901)365-1770
Memphis, TN 38115   Fax: (901)369-4515
Owner: American TV & Communications Corp. **Founded:** 1976.
Cities Served: De Soto County and Southaven, MS; Shelby County,
TN.

MILLINGTON

📖 **3837 The Millington Star**
PO Box 305   Phone: (901)872-2286
Millington, TN 38083   **Fax: (901)872-2956**

📖 **3838 Star Shoppers' Aid**
PO Box 305   Phone: (901)872-2286
Millington, TN 38083   **Fax: (901)872-2956**

MORRISTOWN

🎙 **3839 WCRK-AM - 1150**
204 Brown Ave.
Box 220
Morristown, TN 37815-0220   Phone: (615)586-9101
Format: Adult Contemporary; Oldies. **Network(s):** AP. **Owner:** WCRK
Inc. **Founded:** 1947. **Operating Hours:** 5 a.m.-11 p.m. Mon.-Sat.; 6:30
a.m.-11 p.m. Sun. **Key Personnel:** Mark Ashford, Gen. Mgr.; Rick
Brooks, News Dir. **Wattage:** 5000 day; 500 night. **Ad Rates:** $2.65-
$4.50 for 10 seconds; $4.25-$6.35 for 30 seconds; $6.65-$10.30 for 60
seconds.

MURFREESBORO

🎙 **3840 WMTS-AM - 810**
201 W. Main St., Ste. 203   Phone: (615)893-6611
Murfreesboro, TN 37130   **Fax: (615)895-2633**

NASHVILLE

📖 **3841 The Babbler**
David Lipscomb University
Box 4126   Phone: (800)333-4358
Nashville, TN 37204-3951   **Fax: (615)269-1799**

📖 **3842 The Baptist Program**
Southern Baptist Convention Executive Committee
901 Commerce, Ste. 750   Phone: (615)244-2355
Nashville, TN 37203   **Fax: (615)742-8919**

📖 **3843 Blast! Magazine**
810 Division St.   Phone: (615)256-6556
Nashville, TN 37203   Fax: (615)256-1752
General interest magazine for young adults, aged 16-24, in the
metropolitan Nashville area. **Founded:** 1992. **Frequency:** Monthly.
Printing Method: Web offset. **Trim Size:** 11 x 13. **Key Personnel:**
Kristi Hinchman, Editor; Stewart Day, Publisher; Charly Monroe,
Assoc. Editor. **Subscription:** Free (in select secondary schools); $18
(mail).
Ad Rates: BW: $1,500   **Circulation:** Free 40,000
           4C: $1,810

📖 **3844 Christian Single**
The Sunday School Board of the Southern Baptist Convention
127 9th Ave. N.   Phone: (615)251-2277
Nashville, TN 37234   **Fax: (615)251-3866**

📖 **3845 Home Life**
Baptist Sunday School Board
127 9th Ave. N.
Nashville, TN 37234   Phone: (615)251-2271

📖 **3846 Journal of Health Care for the Poor and
Underserved**
Meharry Medical College
1005 D.B. Todd Blvd.   Phone: (615)327-6819
Nashville, TN 37208   Fax: (615)327-6362
Journal covering the health problems of poor, elderly, rural and inner-
city residents. **Founded:** 1990. **Frequency:** Quarterly. **Trim Size:** 6 x 9.
Cols./Page: 1. **Col. Width:** 4 3/4 in. **Col. Depth:** 7 1/4 in. **Key
Personnel:** Kirk A. Johnson, Editor; Amy Cato, Publisher. **ISSN:**
1049-2089. **Subscription:** $60.
                                       Circulation: Paid ‡281
                                                 Non-paid ‡1,167
Advertising not accepted. **Additional Contact Information:** Toll-free
800-669-1269.

📖 **3847 Journal of Special Education Technology**
Vanderbilt University
Peabody College
Box 328   **Phone: (615)322-8150**
Nashville, TN 37203   **Fax: (615)343-1570**

📖 **3848 Leader in the Church School Today**
Cokesbury/United Methodist Publishing House
201 8th Ave. S.
PO Box 801   Phone: (615)749-6000
Nashville, TN 37202   Fax: (615)749-6079

📖 **3849 The Magazine for Christian Youth!**
The United Methodist Publishing House
201 8th Ave. S.
PO Box 801   **Phone: (615)749-6319**
Nashville, TN 37202   **Fax: (615)749-6079**

📖 **3850 The News Beacon**
PO Box 140628   Phone: (615)889-1860
Nashville, TN 37214   Fax: (615)883-8500
Community newspaper. **Founded:** 1986. **Frequency:** Weekly (Wed./
Thurs.). **Printing Method:** Offset. **Trim Size:** 11 1/2 x 15. **Cols./Page:**
5. **Col. Width:** 11.5 picas. **Col. Depth:** 14 in. **Key Personnel:** Jack
Soodhalter, Editor and Publisher; Beverly Soodhalter, Gen. Mgr.
Subscription: $20.
Ad Rates: BW: $735   **Circulation:** Free ‡28,000
           4C: $1,085

📖 **3851 The News Herald**
PO Box 140628   Phone: (615)889-1860
Nashville, TN 37214   Fax: (615)883-8500
Community newspaper. **Founded:** 1984. **Frequency:** Weekly (Wed./
Thurs.). **Founded:** 1984. **Printing Method:** Offset. **Trim Size:** 11 1/2 x
15. **Cols./Page:** 5. **Col. Width:** 11.5 picas. **Col. Depth:** 14 in. **Key
Personnel:** Jack Soodhalter, Editor and Publisher; Beverly Soodhalter,
Gen. Mgr. **Subscription:** $20.
Ad Rates: BW: $735   **Circulation:** ‡26,000
           4C: $1,085

📖 **3852 Teacher in the Church Today**
Graded Press/United Methodist Publishing House
201 8th Ave., S.
PO Box 801   Phone: (615)749-6468
Nashville, TN 37202   Fax: (615)749-6079

📖 **3853 Youth!**
Cokesbury Publishing
201 8th Ave. S.
PO Box 801   Phone: (615)749-6463
Nashville, TN 37202   Fax: (615)749-6079
Magazine for Christian teens. **Subtitle:** The Magazine For Christian
Youth! **Founded:** 1985. **Frequency:** Monthly. **Trim Size:** 8 1/2 x 11.
Key Personnel: Tracy S. Ritchie, Contact. **Subscription:** $18. $2 single
issue.
                                       Circulation: ‡35,000
Advertising not accepted.

Ad Rates: GLR = general line rate; BW = one-time black & white page rate; 4C = one-time four color page rate; SAU = standard advertising unit rate;
CNU = Canadian newspaper advertising unit rate; PCI = per column inch rate.
Circulation: ★ = ABC; △ = BPA; ◆ = CAC; ● = CCAB; □ = VAC; ⊕ = PO Statement; ‡ = Publisher's Report; Boldface figures = sworn; Light figures = estimated.
Entry type: 📖 = Print; 🎙 = Broadcast.

259

♣ **3854 Viacom Cablevision**
660 Mainstream Dr.
Box 80570, Metro Center   Phone: (615)244-7462
Nashville, TN 37208-0570   Fax: (615)255-6528
Owner: Viacom Cable. **Founded:** 1979. **Cities Served:** Davidson County, TN.

♣ **3855 WNAH-AM - 1360**
44 Music Sq. E.   Phone: (615)254-7611
Nashville, TN 37203   **Fax: (615)254-4565**

♣ **3856 WNAH-FM - 92.5**
44 Music Sq. E.
Nashville, TN 37203   Phone: (615)254-7611
Format: Gospel. **Network(s):** Mutual Broadcasting System. **Owner:** Hermitage Broadcasting Co. **Founded:** 1949. **Operating Hours:** Continuous. **Key Personnel:** Hoyt Carter, Jr., Gen. Mgr./Program Dir. **Ad Rates:** $6-$12 for ten seconds; $8-$16 for 30 seconds; $10-$20 for 60 seconds.

♣ **3857 WSIX-FM - 97.9**
21 Music Sq. W.   **Phone: (615)664-2400**
Nashville, TN 37203   **Fax: (615)664-2457**

NEWPORT

♣ **3858 WLIK-AM - 1270**
640 West Hwy. 25170
Newport, TN 37821   Phone: (615)623-3095

OAK RIDGE

▥ **3859 Acid Precipitation**
U.S. Dept. of Energy, OSTI
PO Box 62   **Phone: (615)576-9374**
Oak Ridge, TN 37831   Fax: (615)576-2865

▥ **3860 Nuclear Reactors and Technology**
U.S. Dept. of Energy, OSTI
PO Box 62   Phone: (615)576-8401
Oak Ridge, TN 37831   Fax: (615)576-2865
Frequency: Monthly. **Subscription:** Sandra C. Hicks, Mng. Editor.
          Circulation: (Not Reported)
Advertising not accepted.

▥ **3861 Radioactive Waste Management**
U.S. Dept. of Energy, OSTI
PO Box 62   **Phone: (615)576-9374**
Oak Ridge, TN 37831   Fax: (615)576-2865

SAVANNAH

♣ **3862 WDNX-FM - 89.1**
Rte. 2
Lonesome Pine Rd.
Savannah, TN 38372   Phone: (901)925-9236

SEYMOUR

▥ **3863 Tri-County News**
PO Box 130   Phone: (615)577-5935
Seymour, TN 37865   **Fax: (615)525-5756**

SOMERVILLE

▥ **3864 Mid-South Horse Review**
Box 423   Phone: (901)465-4042
Somerville, TN 38068   Fax: (901)465-5493
Magazine covering horses. **Founded:** April 1992. **Frequency:** Monthly. **Printing Method:** Offset. **Cols./Page:** 4. **Col. Width:** 2 3/8 in. **Col. Depth:** 13 in. **Key Personnel:** Don L. Dowdle, Editor and Publisher; Hope Yarbo, Advertising Mgr. **Subscription:** $15.
Ad Rates: BW: $395   **Circulation:** Free 10,000
          4C: $575

WAVERLY

▥ **3865 The Shopper's Guide**
Kennedy Newspapers, Inc.
302-A W. Main
PO Box 626   Phone: (615)296-2426
Waverly, TN 37185-0111   Fax: (615)296-5156
Shopper. **Founded:** 1976. **Frequency:** Weekly. **Printing Method:** Offset. **Cols./Page:** 6. **Col. Width:** 2 in. **Col. Depth:** 13 in. **Key Personnel:** Bill Ridings, Publisher; Ward Phillips, Advertising Mgr. **Subscription:** Free.
Ad Rates: BW: $273   **Circulation:** Free ⊕6,803
          4C: $473
          PCI: $4.20

WAYNESBORO

▥ **3866 The Wayne County News**
The Wayne County News, Inc.
PO Box 156   Phone: (615)722-5429
Waynesboro, TN 38485   **Fax: same**

WINCHESTER

♣ **3867 WCDT-AM - 1340**
1201 S. College St.   Phone: (615)967-2201
Winchester, TN 37398   Fax: (615)967-2246

TEXAS

ABILENE

📖 3868 American Airgunner
PO Box 1459
Abilene, TX 79604-1459
Phone: (915)673-6538
Fax: (915)673-0404

📖 3869 War-Whoop
McMurry University
Box 248, McMurry Sta.
Abilene, TX 79697
Phone: (915)691-6375
Fax: (915)691-6599

🎙 3870 KACU-FM - 89.7
Box 7568, ACU Sta.
Abilene, TX 79699
Phone: (915)674-2441
Fax: (915)674-2417

🎙 3871 KGNZ-FM - 88.1
542 Butternut
Abilene, TX 79602
Phone: (915)673-3045
Fax: (915)672-7938

🎙 3872 UAE
1441 Woodard St.
Abilene, TX 79605
Phone: (915)698-3585
Fax: (915)698-0319
Owner: Tele-Communications, Inc. **Founded:** 1965, **Cities Served:** Taylor County and Tye, TX. **Additional Contact Information:** telephone (915)698-1510.

ALEDO

🎙 3873 Willow Park Cable T.V.
Box 595
Aledo, TX 76008
Phone: (817)441-8073

AMARILLO

🎙 3874 KAKS-FM - 107.9
Box 8580
Amarillo, TX 79114
Phone: (806)353-3500
Fax: (806)353-1142

🎙 3875 TV Cable of Amarillo
5800 W. 45th Dr.
Amarillo, TX 79109
Phone: (806)358-4801
Owner: TCA Cable TV, Inc. **Founded:** 1970. **Cities Served:** Potter County, and Rolling Hills, TX.

AMHERST

📖 3876 Amherst Press
PO Box 370
Amherst, TX 79312
Phone: (806)385-6444

ARLINGTON

🎙 3877 Arlington TeleCable, Inc.
2421 Matloch Rd.
Box 120
Arlington, TX 76015
Phone: (817)265-7766
Owner: TeleCable Corp. **Founded:** 1981. **Cities Served:** Tarrant County, Dalworthington Gardens, and Pantego, TX.

ATLANTA

🎙 3878 KALT-AM - 900
PO Box 1166
Atlanta, TX 75551
Phone: (903)796-2817
Fax: (903)796-6400

🎙 3879 KPYN-FM - 99.3
PO Box 1166
Atlanta, TX 75551
Phone: (903)796-2817
Fax: (903)796-6400

AUSTIN

📖 3880 American Short Fiction
University of Texas Press
PO Box 7819
Austin, TX 78713
Phone: (512)471-4531
Fax: (512)320-0668
Journal publishing original stories by the masters of today and tomorrow. **Founded:** 1991. **Frequency:** Quarterly. **Printing Method:** Offset. **Trim Size:** 5 3/4 x 9 1/4. **Key Personnel:** Laura Furman, Editor; Leah Dixon, Advertising Mgr. ISSN: 1051-4813. **Subscription:** $24; $36 institutions. $7.95 single issue.
Ad Rates: BW: $250
Circulation: 1,500

📖 3881 Austin Chronicle
PO Box 49066
Austin, TX 78765
Phone: (512)454-5766
Fax: (512)458-6910

📖 3882 The Bulletin
Publications and Communications, Inc.
12416 Hymeadow Dr., No. 2
Austin, TX 78750
Phone: (512)250-9203
Fax: (512)331-3900

📖 3883 DG Review
Data Base Publications
9390 Research Blvd., Ste. II 300
Austin, TX 78759
Phone: (512)343-9066
Fax: (512)345-1935
Ceased publication.

3884 Focus on Autistic Behavior
Pro-Ed Journals
8700 Shoal Creek Blvd.   Phone: (512)451-3246
Austin, TX 78758-6897   Fax: (512)451-8542
Journal provides practical management, treatment, and planning strategies for professionals working with people with autism and developmental disabilities. **Founded:** 1986. **Frequency:** 6x/yr. **Printing Method:** Offset. **Trim Size:** 8 1/2 x 11. **Cols./Page:** 1. **Col. Width:** 5 in. **Col. Depth:** 7 9/16 in. **Key Personnel:** Richard Simpson, Editor; Donald D. Hammill, Publisher; Judith K. Voress, Periodicals Dir. **ISSN:** 0887-1566. **Subscription:** $20; $40 institutions; $65 other countries.
Ad Rates: BW: $75   Circulation: Paid ‡826
                                   Non-paid ‡22

3885 Individual Psychology
University of Texas Press
PO Box 7819   Phone: (512)471-4531
Austin, TX 78713   Fax: (512)320-0668
Journal covering research concerning the theory founded by Alfred Adler. **Founded:** 1944. **Frequency:** Quarterly. **Printing Method:** Offset. **Trim Size:** 6 x 9. **Key Personnel:** Guy Manaster, Editor; Leah Dixon, Advertising Mgr. **ISSN:** 0277-7010. **Subscription:** $25; $49 institutions. $7 single issue.
Ad Rates: BW: $200   Circulation: 1,900

3886 Journal of Learning Disabilities
PRO-ED Publishers
8700 Shoal Creek Blvd.   Phone: (512)451-3246
Austin, TX 78758   Fax: (512)451-8542

3887 Journal of Politics
University of Texas Press
PO Box 7819   Phone: (512)471-4531
Austin, TX 78713   Fax: (512)320-0668
Journal covering American politics, political theory, and international politics. **Founded:** 1938. **Frequency:** Quarterly. **Printing Method:** Offset. **Trim Size:** 6 x 9. **Key Personnel:** Cecil Eubanks, Editor; Leah Dixon, Advertising Mgr. **ISSN:** 0022-3816. **Subscription:** $25; $50 institutions. $10 single issue.
                                   Circulation: 4,000
Advertising accepted; contact publisher for rates.

3888 The Journal of Special Education
Pro-Ed Journals
8700 Shoal Creek Blvd.   Phone: (512)451-3246
Austin, TX 78758-6897   Fax: (512)451-8542
Journal presents research findings in the field of special education. **Founded:** 1966. **Frequency:** Quarterly. **Printing Method:** Offset. **Trim Size:** 7 x 10. **Cols./Page:** 1. **Col. Width:** 4 13/16 in. **Col. Depth:** 7 1/2 in. **Key Personnel:** Lynn Fuchs, Editor; Douglas Fuchs, Editor; Donald D. Hammill, Publisher; Judith K. Voress, Periodicals Dir. **ISSN:** 0022-4669. **Subscription:** $35; $70 institutions; $85 other countries. $10 single issue.
Ad Rates: BW: $150   Circulation: Paid 3,077
                                   Non-paid 99

3889 Remedial and Special Education (RASE)
Pro-Ed Journals
8700 Shoal Creek Blvd.   Phone: (512)451-3246
Austin, TX 78758-6897   Fax: (512)451-8542
Journal interprets research and makes recommendations for practice in the fields of remedial and special education. **Founded:** 1984. **Frequency:** 6x/yr. **Printing Method:** Offset. **Trim Size:** 8 3/8 x 10 7/8. **Cols./Page:** 2. **Col. Width:** 3 5/16. **Col. Depth:** 9 5/8. **Key Personnel:** Lorna Idol, Editor; Donald D. Hammill, Publisher; Judith K. Voress, Periodicals Dir. **ISSN:** 0741-9325. **Subscription:** $35; $80 institutions; $95 other countries. $10 single issue.
Ad Rates: BW: $200   Circulation: Paid 2,587
                                   Non-paid 97

3890 Sociological Inquiry
University of Texas Press
PO Box 7819   Phone: (512)471-4531
Austin, TX 78713   Fax: (512)320-0668
Journal covering sociological research. **Founded:** 1930. **Frequency:** Quarterly. **Printing Method:** Offset. **Trim Size:** 6 x 9. **Key Personnel:** Dennis Pelk, Editor; Leah Dixon, Advertising Mgr. **ISSN:** 0038-0245. **Subscription:** $20; $40 institutions. $7 single issue.
Ad Rates: BW: $225   Circulation: 3,000

3891 Technical Employment News
Publications and Communications, Inc.
12416 Hymeadow Dr.   Phone: (512)250-9023
Austin, TX 78750   Fax: (512)331-3900
Former Title: The PD News

3892 Texas Alcade
Ex-Students' Assn. of The University of Texas at Austin
PO Box 7278   Phone: (512)471-3799
Austin, TX 78713   Fax: (512)471-8088

3893 Texas Propane
Texas Propane Gas Association
8408 N. Interegional Hwy.
PO Box 149735   Phone: (512)836-8620
Austin, TX 78714-0735   Fax: (512)834-0758
Former Title: Texas LP Gas News

3894 The Texas Surveyor
Texas Society of Professional Surveyors
400 E. Anderson, Ste. 340   Phone: (512)834-1275
Austin, TX 78752   **Fax: (512)834-1277**

3895 Texas Tribune
PO Box 15405
Austin, TX 78761   **Phone: (903)597-1124**

3896 Topics in Early Childhood Special Education
Pro-Ed Journals
8700 Shoal Creek Blvd.   Phone: (512)451-3246
Austin, TX 78758-6897   Fax: (512)451-8542
Magazine for special education professionals. Provides information on assessment, special programs, social policies, and developmental aids. **Founded:** 1981. **Frequency:** Quarterly. **Printing Method:** Offset. **Trim Size:** 6 x 9. **Cols./Page:** 1. **Col. Width:** 4 1/2 in. **Col. Depth:** 7 1/2 in. **Key Personnel:** Mark Wolery, Editor; Donald D. Hammill, Publisher; Judith K. Voress, Periodicals Dir. **ISSN:** 0271-1214. **Subscription:** $35; $70 institutions; $85 other countries.
Ad Rates: BW: $100   Circulation: Paid 2,263
                                   Non-paid 132

3897 KAZI-FM - 88.7
4700 Loyola Ln., No. 104   Phone: (512)926-0275
Austin, TX 78723   Fax: (512)929-0115
Format: Urban Contemporary; Contemporary Jazz; Gospel; Rap; Reggae. **Owner:** Austin Community Radio, Inc. **Founded:** 1982. **Operating Hours:** Continuous. **Key Personnel:** Marion Nickerson, Acting Gen. Mgr./Program Dir.; J. Hunt, Music Dir.; JoAnn Williams, Traffic Dir.; Sharon Jones, PSA Dir. **Wattage:** 1620. **Ad Rates:** $30 per unit. **Additional Contact Information:** Chairperson's phone: (512)250-5164.

3898 KRGT-FM - 92.1
2908 Overdale Rd.
Austin, TX 78723   **Phone: (512)759-5050**

3899 Prime Cable
600 Congress Ave., Ste. 3000   Phone: (512)476-7888
Austin, TX 78701   **Fax: (512)476-4869**

BAY CITY

3900 KMKS-FM - 102.5
PO Box 789   Phone: (409)244-4242
Bay City, TX 77404   **Fax: (409)245-0107**

BAYTOWN

3901 KWWJ-AM - 1360
4638 Decker Dr.   Phone: (713)424-7000
Baytown, TX 77520   **Fax: (713)424-7588**

BEAUMONT

3902 TCI Cablevision of Texas, Inc.
1460 Calder Ave.   Phone: (409)839-4601
Beaumont, TX 77701-1746   Fax: (409)839-4215
Owner: Tele-Communications, Inc. **Founded:** 1973. **Cities Served:** Jefferson County, TX.

BENBROOK

📖 **3903 Benbrook News**
Suburban Newspapers, Inc.
7820 Wyatt Dr.   Phone: (817)246-2473
Fort Worth, TX 76108   **Fax: (817)246-2474**

BIG SANDY

📖 **3904 Crochet Home**
The Needlecraft Shop, Inc.
23 Old Pecan Rd.   Phone: (903)636-4011
Big Sandy, TX 75755   **Fax: (903)636-4099**

📖 **3905 Cross Stitch! Magazine**
Jerry Gentry, Inc.
23 Old Pecan Rd.   Phone: (903)636-4011
Big Sandy, TX 75755   Fax: (903)636-2288
Magazine devoted to needlecraft. **Founded:** 1991. **Frequency:** Bi-monthly. **Printing Method:** Web offset. **Trim Size:** 8 1/2 x 11. **Cols./Page:** 3. **Col. Width:** 13.5 picas. **Col. Depth:** 58.5 picas. **Key Personnel:** Jerry Gentry, Pres.; Donna Robertson, V.P., Publishing; Carolyn Christmas, Editorial Dir. **ISSN:** 1048-5341. **Subscription:** $12.95; $18 other countries. $2.95 single issue.
Circulation: 90,000
Advertising not accepted. **Additional Contact Information:** 206 West St., Big Sandy, TX 75755.

📖 **3906 Hooked on Crochet**
Jerry Gentry, Inc.
23 Old Pecan Rd.   Phone: (903)636-4011
Big Sandy, TX 75755   Fax: (903)636-2288
Magazine devoted to crochet crafts. **Founded:** 1986. **Frequency:** Bimonthly. **Printing Method:** Web offset. **Trim Size:** 5 1/2 x 8. **Cols./Page:** 2. **Col. Width:** 2 1/8 in. **Col. Depth:** 7 in. **Key Personnel:** Jerry Gentry, Pres.; Donna Robertson V.P., Publishing; Carolyn Christmas, Editorial Dir. **ISSN:** 0893-1879. **Subscription:** $12.95; $18 other countries. $2.95 single issue.
Circulation: ‡140,000
Advertising not accepted. **Additional Contact Information:** 206 West St., Big Sandy, TX 75755.

📖 **3907 Plastic Canvas! Magazine**
The Needlecraft Shop, Inc.
23 Old Pecan Rd.   Phone: (903)636-4011
Big Sandy, TX 75755   **Fax: (903)636-4099**

📖 **3908 Quick & Easy Needlecraft**
Jerry Gentry, Inc.
23 Old Pecan Rd.   Phone: (903)636-4011
Big Sandy, TX 75755   Fax: (903)636-2288
Needlecraft magazine. **Founded:** 1992. **Frequency:** Bimonthly. **Printing Method:** Web offset. **Trim Size:** 8 1/2 x 11. **Cols./Page:** 3. **Col. Width:** 13.5 picas. **Col. Depth:** 58.5 picas. **Key Personnel:** Jerry Gentry, Pres.; Donna Robertson, V.P., Publishing; Carolyn Christmas, Editorial Dir. **Subscription:** $12.95; $18 other countries. $2.95 single issue.
Circulation: ‡40,000
Advertising not accepted. **Additional Contact Information:** 206 West St., Big Sandy, TX 75755.

📖 **3909 Simply Cross Stitch**
Jerry Gentry, Inc.
23 Old Pecan Rd.   Phone: (903)636-4011
Big Sandy, TX 75755   Fax: (903)636-2288
Crafts magazine. **Founded:** 1991. **Frequency:** 6x/yr. **Printing Method:** Web offset. **Trim Size:** 8 1/2 x 11. **Cols./Page:** 3. **Col. Width:** 13.5 picas. **Col. Depth:** 58.5 picas. **Key Personnel:** Jerry Gentry, Pres.; Donna Robertson, V.P., Publishing; Carolyn Christmas, Editorial Dir. **Subscription:** $12.95; $18 other countries. $2.95 single issue.
Circulation: ‡50,000
Advertising not accepted. **Additional Contact Information:** 206 West St., Big Sandy, TX 75755.

BISHOP

🎙 **3910 KFLZ-FM - 107.1**
110 E. Main St.
PO Box 66   Phone: (512)584-3800
Bishop, TX 78343   **Fax: (512)584-3959**

BLANCO

📖 **3911 Blanco County News**
PO Box 429   Phone: (512)833-4812
Blanco, TX 78606   **Fax: (512)833-4246**

BOERNE

📖 **3912 Hill Country Recorder**
PO Box 905   **Phone: (210)249-9524**
Boerne, TX 78006   **Fax: (210)698-3209**

BORGER

🎙 **3913 KQTY-AM - 1490**
Box 165   Phone: (806)273-7533
Borger, TX 79008-0165   **Fax: (806)273-3727**

BRADY

🎙 **3914 KIXV-FM - 95.3**
117 S. Blackburn
Box 630   Phone: (915)597-2119
Brady, TX 76825   **Fax: (915)597-1925**

🎙 **3915 KNEL-AM - 1490**
117 S. Blackburn
Box 630   Phone: (915)597-2119
Brady, TX 76825   **Fax: (915)597-1925**

BRIDGE CITY

🎙 **3916 KTFA-FM - 92.5**
2000 Roundbunch
PO Box 820   Phone: (409)735-7174
Bridge City, TX 77611   **Fax: (409)735-7177**

BROWNSVILLE

📖 **3917 Bargain Book**
Valley Media, Inc.
PO Box 4195   **Phone: (210)546-5113**
Brownsville, TX 78520   **Fax: (210)546-0903**

BROWNWOOD

📖 **3918 Brownwood Bulletin**
Brownwood Newspapers, Inc.
PO Box 1188   Phone: (915)646-2541
Brownwood, TX 76804   Fax: (915)646-6835

🎙 **3919 KBUB-FM - 90.3**
1113 La Monte Dr.
Brownwood, TX 76801   Phone: (915)643-2868
Format: Religious (Christian). **Owner:** Criswell Center for Biblical Studies. **Operating Hours:** Continuous. **Key Personnel:** Loretta Silvus, Coordinator. **Wattage:** 550. **Additional Contact Information:** Station address: 107 Draham St., Brownwood, TX 76801. Alt. phone (915)646-3364.

🎙 **3920 KBWD-AM - 1380**
Box 280   Phone: (915)646-3505
Brownwood, TX 76801   Fax: (915)646-2220
Format: Adult Contemporary. **Network(s):** ABC. **Owner:** Brown County Broadcasting, 801 Carnegie, Brownwood, TX 76801. **Found-**

Ad Rates: GLR = general line rate; BW = one-time black & white page rate; 4C = one-time four color page rate; SAU = standard advertising unit rate; CNU = Canadian newspaper advertising unit rate; PCI = per column inch rate.
Circulation: ★ = ABC; △ = BPA; ◆ = CAC; ● = CCAB; □ = VAC; ⊕ = PO Statement; ‡ = Publisher's Report; Boldface figures = sworn; Light figures = estimated.
Entry type: 📖 = Print; 🎙 = Broadcast.

263

ed: 1941. **Operating Hours:** 6 a.m.-midnight. **Key Personnel:** Don Dillard, Gen. Mgr. **Wattage:** 1000. **Ad Rates:** $11 per unit.

BRYAN

♨ 3921 TCA Cable TV
3609 Texas Ave.
Box TV   Phone: (409)846-2229
Bryan, TX 77805   Fax: (409)268-0139
Owner: TCA Cable TV, Inc. **Founded:** 1954. **Cities Served:** Brazos County, TX.

CARTHAGE

♨ 3922 KGAS-AM - 1590
226 S. Shelby St.   Phone: (903)693-6668
Carthage, TX 75633   **Fax: (903)693-7188**

♨ 3923 KGAS-FM - 104.3
226 S. Shelby St.   Phone: (903)693-6668
Carthage, TX 75633   Fax: (903)693-7188
Format: Country. **Owner:** KGAS Radio, at above address. **Founded:** 1992. **Operating Hours:** Continuous. **Key Personnel:** Jerry T. Hanszen, Owner/Gen. Mgr./News Dir.; Wanda J. Hanszen, Program Dir./Office Mgr./Owner. **Wattage:** 6000. **Ad Rates:** Combined rates available with KGAS-AM: $11 for 30 seconds; $13 for 60 seconds.

COLLEGE STATION

▣ 3924 Bulletin: Committee on South Asian Women
Texas A & M University
Dept. of Psychology   Phone: (409)845-2576
College Station, TX 77843   Fax: (409)845-4727
Periodical containing essays, reports, interview, reviews, and creative works by and about South Asian women. **Founded:** 1983. **Frequency:** 2x/yr. **Key Personnel:** J. Vaid, Editor. **ISSN:** 0885-4319. **Subscription:** $16; $12 students; $25 institutions.
                              Circulation: (Not Reported)
Advertising accepted; contact publisher for rates.

▣ 3925 Journal of Geography
National Council of Geography Education
Department of Geography
Texas A & M University   Phone: (409)845-5553
College Station, TX 77843   **Fax: (409)845-0056**

CORPUS CHRISTI

▣ 3926 Caller-Times
820 Lower N. Broadway
PO Box 9136   Phone: (512)884-2011
Corpus Christi, TX 78469   **Fax: (512)886-3732**

▣ 3927 Corpus Christi Lawyer
Woolford Publishing
400 Mann St., Ste. 700
Corpus Christi, TX 78401   Phone: (512)883-8833
Legal journal for Corpus Christi Bar Association members. **Founded:** 1981. **Frequency:** Quarterly. **Printing Method:** Offset. **Trim Size:** 8 1/2 x 11. **Cols./Page:** 3. **Col. Width:** 2 3/16 in. **Col. Depth:** 10 in. **Key Personnel:** Andrew J. Lehrman, Mng. Editor; Leah Woolford, Publisher/Creative Dir.; Jeff Woolford, Exec. Editor.
Ad Rates: BW: $650   **Circulation:** Non-paid ‡2,000

♨ 3928 KLUX-FM - 89.5
1200 Lantana
Corpus Christi, TX 78407   **Phone: (512)289-6831**

♨ 3929 TCI Cablevision of Texas, Inc.
Box 6607
Corpus Christi, TX 78411-4477   Phone: (512)857-5000
Owner: Tele-Communications, Inc. **Founded:** 1972. **Cities Served:** Nueces County, Agua Dulce, Driscoll, and Robstown, TX.

CRANE

▣ 3930 The Crane News
401 S. Gaston   Phone: (915)558-3541
Crane, TX 79731-2621   Fax: (915)558-2676

CROSBYTON

▣ 3931 Crosby County News & Chronicle
109 W. Aspen   Phone: (806)675-2881
Crosbyton, TX 79322   **Fax: (806)675-2619**

DAINGERFIELD

♨ 3932 KEGG-AM - 1560
Box 600
Daingerfield, TX 75638   Phone: (214)645-3928
Format: Oldies. **Network(s):** Satellite Music. **Operating Hours:** Sunrise-sunset. **Key Personnel:** Ruth Allen Ollison, CEO. **Wattage:** 100. **Ad Rates:** $5-$18 per unit.

DALLAS

▣ 3933 Auto Revista
Auto Revista
PO Box 670592   Phone: (214)386-0040
Dallas, TX 75367-0592   Fax: (214)386-4255
Bilingual (English/Spanish) automotive newspaper. **Founded:** 1989. **Frequency:** 2x/mo. **Printing Method:** Web offset. **Trim Size:** 11 1/4 x 13 1/2. **Cols./Page:** 4. **Col. Width:** 2 3/8 in. **Col. Depth:** 12 3/8 in. **Key Personnel:** Ray Lozano, III, Publisher; Jacob Lozano, Deputy Publisher. **Subscription:** Free; $26.
Ad Rates: BW: $640   **Circulation:** Free ‡34,859
             4C: $910

▣ 3934 Clements' International Report
Political Research, Inc.
16850 Dallas Pkwy.   Phone: (214)931-8827
Dallas, TX **75248-1970**   Fax: (214)248-7159

▣ 3935 Confectioner
American Publishing Corp.
17400 Dallas Pkwy., No. 121   **Phone: (214)250-3630**
Dallas, TX 75287-7305   **Fax: (214)250-3733**

▣ 3936 Contingency Journal
Thomas Publications, Inc.
10935 Estate Ln., Ste. 375   Phone: (214)343-3717
Dallas, TX 75238   Fax: (214)553-5603
Ceased publication.

▣ 3937 Future Stars
Statabase, Inc.
4887 Alpha Rd., Ste. 200
Dallas, TX 75244
Sports magazine highlighting future NBA, NFL, and major league baseball stars. **Frequency:** Monthly. **Key Personnel:** Dr. James Beckett, Editor and Publisher. **Subscription:** $19.95. $2.95 single issue.
                              Circulation: (Not Reported)

▣ 3938 Journal of Air Law and Commerce
School of Law
Southern Methodist University   Phone: (214)692-2570
Dallas, TX 75275   **Fax: (214)692-3946**

▣ 3939 Notes on Linguistics
Summer Institute of Linguistics
7500 W. Camp Wisdom Rd.   Phone: (214)709-2400
Dallas, TX 75236   Fax: (214)704-2433
Journal for liguists. **Subtitle:** Articles for Linguistic Field Workers. **Frequency:** Quarterly. **Printing Method:** Offset. **Trim Size:** 5 1/4 x 8 1/2. **Cols./Page:** 1. **Col. Width:** 4 1/8 in. **Col. Depth:** 6 3/4 in. **Key Personnel:** Eugene E. Loos, Editor; David Payne, Editor. **Subscription:** $20.
                              Circulation: (Not Reported)
Advertising not accepted. **Additional Contact Information:** Alternate phone; (214)709-3387.

▣ 3940 The Shopping News
4808 S. Buckner Blvd.   Phone: (214)388-3431
Dallas, TX 75227   **Fax: (214)388-1194**

▣ 3941 Southwest Review
307 Fondren Library W.   Phone: (214)373-7440
Dallas, TX 75275   **Fax: (214)373-7441**

◫ **3942 Sprinkler Age**
American Fire Sprinkler Association
12959 Jupiter Rd., Ste. 142   Phone: (214)349-5965
Dallas, TX 75238   Fax: (214)343-8898
Magazine for members of the American Fire Sprinkler Association. **Subtitle:** Official Publication of the American Fire Sprinkler Assoication. **Founded:** 1982. **Frequency:** Monthly. **Trim Size:** 8 1/2 x 11. **Cols./ Page:** 3. **Col. Width:** 2 1/4 in. **Col. Depth:** 10 in. **Key Personnel:** Janet K. Rend, Publisher. **ISSN:** 0896-2685. **Subscription:** $75.
Ad Rates: BW: $875   **Circulation:** Non-paid ‡3,926
           4C: $1,325

◫ **3943 Texas Contractor**
Peters Publishing Co. of Texas
PO Box 551359   Phone: (214)271-2693
Dallas, TX 75355-1359   Fax: (214)278-4652

◫ **3944 World of Politics**
Political Research, Inc.
16850 Dallas Pkwy.   Phone: (214)931-8827
Dallas, TX 75248-1970   Fax: (214)248-7159

⚓ **3945 KCMZ-AM - 1480**
5956 Sherry Ln., No. 2000   Phone: (214)691-1075
Dallas, TX 75225   **Fax: (214)368-1075**

⚓ **3946 KDTN-TV - Channel 2**
3000 Harry Hines Blvd.   Phone: (214)871-1390
Dallas, TX 75201   **Fax: (214)754-0635**

⚓ **3947 TCI Cablevision of Dallas, Inc.**
1565 Chenault St.
Dallas, TX 75228-5499   Phone: (214)328-2882
Owner: Tele-Communications, Inc. **Founded:** 1982. **Key Personnel:** Steve Crawford, Gen. Mgr.; Ronda Dorchester, Marketing Mgr.; Ken Reske, Operations Mgr.; Bennie Wilcox, Plant Mgr. **Cities Served:** Dallas County, Mesquite, and Farmers Branch, TX: 136,000 subscribing households; 65 channels; 13 community access channels.

DEL RIO

⚓ **3948 KDLK-FM - 94.3**
PO Box 1489   Phone: (512)775-9583
Del Rio, TX 78841-1489   **Fax: (512)774-4009**

⚓ **3949 KLKE-AM - 1230**
PO Box 1489   Phone: (512)775-9583
Del Rio, TX 78841-1489   **Fax: (512)774-4009**

DENISON

⚓ **3950 KTEN-TV - Channel 10**
Box 1450   Phone: (903)465-5836
Denison, TX 75050   **Fax: (903)465-5859**

DENTON

◫ **3951 The Bulletin of the Assn. for Business Communication**
Dept. of Management
College of Business Administration
University of North Texas   Phone: (817)565-4423
Denton, TX 76203   **Fax: (817)565-4930**

◫ **3952 The Clarinet**
International Clarinet Association
University of North Texas
College of Music
PO Box 13887   Phone: (817)565-4096
Denton, TX 76203   Fax: (817)565-4919

◫ **3953 Daily Lasso**
Texas Woman's University
Box 23866 TWU Sta.   Phone: (817)898-2191
Denton, TX 76204-1866   **Fax: (817)898-3198**

DIMMITT

⚓ **3954 KDHN-AM - 1470**
Box 608
Dimmitt, TX 79027   Phone: (806)647-4161
Format: Contemporary Country; Hispanic; Religious. **Owner:** Collins Communications Co. **Founded:** 1963. **Operating Hours:** 6 a.m.-10 p.m. **Key Personnel:** Wayne Collins, Gen. Mgr.; Terry Todd, Sales Mgr. **Wattage:** 500.

DUNCANVILLE

◫ **3955 Suburban Today**
Today Newspapers, Inc.
606 Oriole Blvd., Ste. 101
PO Box 381029   Phone: (214)298-4211
Duncanville, TX 75138   Fax: (214)298-6369

EAGLE PASS

⚓ **3956 XEMU-AM - 580**
PO Box 196   Phone: (512)773-3459
Eagle Pass, TX 78852   Fax: (512)773-3459
Format: Ethnic (Spanish); Country. **Owner:** Claudio M. Bres. **Founded:** 1937. **Operating Hours:** Continuous. **Key Personnel:** Martha Pope, Gen. Mgr.; Juventino Botello, Sales Mgr. **Wattage:** 5000. **Additional Contact Information:** 352 Rio Grande, Eagle Pass, TX, 78852, (512)773-3459.

EASTLAND

⚓ **3957 KEAS-AM - 1590**
306 S. Seamen
Eastland, TX 76448   Phone: (817)629-2621
Format: Country. Simulcasts KEAS-FM. **Network(s):** Mutual Broadcasting System. **Owner:** WDS Broadcasting Co., at above address. **Founded:** 1953. **Operating Hours:** Sunrise-sunset. **Key Personnel:** Dan Staggs, Owner/Gen. Mgr.; Michael Cogswin, Program and News Dir.; Diane Staggs, Music and Sales Dir. **Wattage:** 500. **Ad Rates:** $5.50-$9 for 30 seconds; $7-$11 for 60 seconds.

⚓ **3958 KEAS-FM - 97.7**
306 S. Seamen
Eastland, TX 76448   Phone: (817)629-2621
Format: Country. Simulcasts KEAS-AM. **Network(s):** Mutual Broadcasting System. **Owner:** WDS Broadcasting Co., at above address. **Founded:** 1953. **Operating Hours:** Continuous. **Key Personnel:** Dan Staggs, Owner/Gen. Mgr.; Michael Cogswin, Program and News Dir.; Diane Staggs, Music and Sales Dir. **Wattage:** 3000. **Ad Rates:** $5.50-$9 for 30 seconds; $7-$11 for 60 seconds.

EDINBURG

◫ **3959 UT Pan American**
Pan-American University
Student Publications EH100   Phone: (512)381-2541
Edinburg, TX 78539   **Fax: (512)381-2512**

EL PASO

◫ **3960 El Paso Shopping Guide**
10737 Gateway W., Ste. 250   Phone: (915)594-3910
El Paso, TX 79935-4906   Fax: (915)592-8996

⚓ **3961 Paragon Communications**
7010 Airport Rd.
El Paso, TX 79906-4943   Phone: (915)772-1123
Owner: Paragon Communications. **Founded:** 1972. **Cities Served:** El Paso County, Canutillo, Fabens, and Socorro, TX.

EMORY

📖 **3962 Rains County Leader**
PO Box 127   Phone: (903)473-2653
Emory, TX 75440   **Fax: (903)473-2653**

FARWELL

📖 **3963 State Line Tribune**
Box 255   Phone: (806)481-3681
Farwell, TX 79325   **Fax: (806)481-3681**

FLATONIA

📖 **3964 Argus**
214 S. Penn St.
Flatonia, TX 78941   **Phone: (512)865-3510**

FORNEY

📖 **3965 Forney Messenger**
Forney Messenger Inc.
201 W. Broad St.
PO Box 936   Phone: (214)564-3121
Forney, TX 75126   Fax: (214)552-3599

FORT WORTH

📖 **3966 Knowledge Magazine**
Knowledge, Inc.
3863 SW Loop 820, Ste. 100   Phone: (817)292-4272
Fort Worth, TX 76133-2063   Fax: (817)924-2893

🎙 **3967 Sammons Cable Services**
4528 W. Vickery St.   Phone: (817)737-4731
Fort Worth, TX 76107   Fax: (817)738-7472
Owner: Sammons Communications, Inc. **Founded:** 1982. **Cities Served:** Johnson County, Tarrant County, Benbrook, Blue Mound, Burleson, Crowley, Everman, Forest Hill, Haltom City, Hurst, Keller, Kennedale, Lake Worth, North Richland Hills, Richland Hills, Saginaw, Watauga, Westover Hills, and White Settlement, TX.

FREER

📖 **3968 The Freer Press**
205 S. Main
Box 567   Phone: (512)394-7402
Freer, TX 78357   **Fax: (512)394-5672**

GALVESTON

📖 **3969 International Journal of Developmental Neuroscience**
Department of Human Biological Chemistry and Genetics
Gail Borden Bldg.
Rm. 436 (F52), UTMB   Phone: (409)772-3667
Galveston, TX 77555-0652   Fax: (409)772-8028
Scientific journal. **Founded:** 1983. **Frequency:** 6x/yr.
Circulation: (Not Reported)
Advertising accepted; contact publisher for rates.

🎙 **3970 TCI Cablevision of Texas, Inc.**
Box 1050
Galveston, TX 77550-7315   Phone: (409)763-5321
Owner: Tele-Communications, Inc. **Founded:** 1969. **Cities Served:** Galveston County, TX.

GARLAND

🎙 **3971 Storer Cable TV of Texas, Inc.**
934 E. Centerville Rd.   Phone: (214)840-2388
Garland, TX 75041   Fax: (214)271-4535
Owner: Storer Cable Communications. **Founded:** 1973. **Cities Served:** Dallas County, Harris County, Rockwall County, Rowlett, and Sunnyvale, TX.

GREENVILLE

🎙 **3972 KIKT-FM - 93.5**
PO Box 1015   Phone: (214)455-1400
Greenville, TX 75403   Fax: (214)455-5485

HALLSVILLE

📖 **3973 Hallsville Herald**
121 W. Main
PO Box 930   **Phone: (800)247-9878**
Hallsville, TX 75650   Fax: (214)687-3291

HARLINGEN

🎙 **3974 KMBH-FM - 88.9**
Box 2147
Harlingen, TX 78551   Phone: (512)421-4111
Format: News; Classical; Jazz. **Network(s):** National Public Radio (NPR). **Owner:** RGV Educational Broadcasting, Inc. **Founded:** 1991. **Operating Hours:** 6 a.m.-midnight. **Key Personnel:** Darrell Rowlett, Pres./Gen. Mgr.; John Harris III, V.P./Asst. Gen. Mgr.; Bobbie Baraias, Program Mgr.; Thelma Comacho, Marketing Dir. **Wattage:** 3000. **Ad Rates:** Noncommercial.

HART

📖 **3975 The Hart Beat**
Wall Publications
Box 350   Phone: (806)938-2640
Hart, TX 79043-0350   **Fax: (806)938-2216**

HONDO

🎙 **3976 KRME-AM - 1460**
PO Box 447   **Phone: (210)426-3367**
Hondo, TX 78861-0447   **Fax: (210)426-3348**

HOUSTON

📖 **3977 Airports International**
SKC Communication Services Ltd.
1635 W. Alabama   Phone: (713)529-1616
Houston, TX 77006   Fax: (713)529-0936

📖 **3978 Facility Management Journal**
International Facility Management Association
1 E. Greenway Plaza, 11th Fl.   Phone: (713)623-4362
Houston, TX 77046-0194   Fax: (713)623-6124
Subtitle: Official Publication of the International Facility Management Association. **Founded:** 1989. **Frequency:** 6x/yr. **Printing Method:** Offset. **Trim Size:** 8 1/2 x 11. **Key Personnel:** Suzanne M. Pearson, EDP. **ISSN:** 1059-3667. **Subscription:** Free to members; $75 to nonmembers; $100 to nonmembers outside the U.S.
Ad Rates: BW: $1,650   **Circulation:** 12,000
               4C: $2,850
Formerly: IFMA Journal. **Additional Contact Information:** Alternate phone (713)871-2378.

📖 **3979 HEC Forum**
Center for Ethics, Medicine, and Public Issues
Baylor College of Medicine
1 Baylor Plaza   Phone: (505)867-0440
Houston, TX 77030   Fax: (505)867-0450
Journal for healthcare professionals. **Subtitle:** An Interprofessional Journal on Healthcare Institutions' Ethical and Legal Issues. **Founded:** 1989. **Frequency:** Quarterly. **Subscription:** Free; $90.50 institutions.
Circulation: (Not Reported)
Also known as Healthcare Ethics Committee Forum. **Formerly:** Hospital Ethics Committee Forum.

📖 **3980 Hola Magazine**
Spanish Publications, Inc.
6802 Bintliff St.   Phone: (713)774-4652
Houston, TX 77074   Fax: (713)774-4666
Founded: 1987. **Frequency:** Weekly (Thurs.). **Printing Method:** Web

offset. **Trim Size:** 8 1/2 x 11. **Cols./Page:** 5. **Col. Width:** 1 1/2 in. **Col. Depth:** 10 in. **Subscription:** Free.
Ad Rates: BW: $1,020   **Circulation:** Free ▢**49,024**
                4C: $1,400
                PCI: $24

⌸ **3981 Houston Press**
New Houston Press, Ltd.
2000 W. Loop S., No. 1900   **Phone:** (713)961-0300
Houston, TX **77027**   **Fax:** (713)961-3719

⌸ **3982 Houston Symphony Magazine**
Houston Metropolitan Ltd.
5615 Kirby Dr., No. 600   **Phone:** (713)524-3000
Houston, TX 77005   **Fax:** (713)524-8213

⌸ **3983 Houston Woman**
1702 S. Post Oak Ln.   **Phone:** (713)961-0599
Houston, TX 77056   **Fax:** (713)523-8915
Periodical for professional women. Includes articles on finance, health and fitness, legal issues, career strategies, personal issues, profiles, and calendar of business and professional events for women in and near Houston, TX. **Founded:** 1984. **Frequency:** Monthly. **Printing Method:** Web offset. **Trim Size:** 10 x 13. **Cols./Page:** 4. **Col. Width:** 2 1/4 in. **Subscription:** $15.
Ad Rates: BW: $2,057   **Circulation:** (Not Reported)
                4C: $2,657
                PCI: $60

⌸ **3984 La Subasta**
PO Box 740800   **Phone:** (713)777-1010
Houston, TX 77274-0800   **Fax:** (713)271-7523
Newspaper (Spanish tabloid) for the Hispanic community in Houston. **Subtitle:** El Periodico de las Oportunidades. **Founded:** 1981. **Frequency:** 3x/wk. (Wed., Thurs., Fri.). **Printing Method:** Offset. **Trim Size:** 10 x 14. **Cols./Page:** 6. **Col. Width:** 1 5/8 in. **Col. Depth:** 14 in. **Key Personnel:** Orlando R. Budini, Editor.
Ad Rates: PCI: $12.40   **Circulation:** Free **117,000**
Additional Contact Information: 6100 Hillcroft, Ste. 105, Houston, TX 77081.

⌸ **3985 MRI Banker's Guide to Foreign Currency**
Monetary Research International
PO Box 3174   **Phone:** (713)827-1796
Houston, TX 77253-3174   **Fax:** (713)827-8665
Publication providing a listing of all current bank notes of the world. **Founded:** 1990. **Frequency:** Quarterly. **Printing Method:** Offset. **Trim Size:** 8 3/8 x 11. **Cols./Page:** 3. **Col. Width:** 2 7/16 in. **Col. Depth:** 9 1/2. **Key Personnel:** Arnoldo Efron, Dir. **ISSN:** 1055-3851 **Subscription:** $200; $120 libraries. $50 single issue; $40 single issue libraries.
Ad Rates: BW: $300   **Circulation:** Paid 550
                PCI: $15   Non-paid 200
Color advertising not accepted.

⌸ **3986 North Texas Golfer**
Golfer Magazines, Inc.
9182 Old Katy Rd., #212   **Phone:** (713)464-0308
Houston, TX 77055   **Fax:** (713)464-0129

♣ **3987 KJZF-FM - 106.9**
6161 Savoy
No. 1100
Houston, TX 77036   **Phone:** (713)367-0107
Format: Jazz. **Network(s):** Unistar. **Owner:** US Radio. **Founded:** 1990. **Formerly:** KJOJ-FM(1991). **Operating Hours:** Continuous. **Key Personnel:** Don Peterson, V.P. and Gen. Mgr.; Gary Teaney, Gen. Sales Mgr.; Mike Ryan, Program Dir.; Denise Whiffill, Business Mgr.; Harold Riley, Chief Engineer. **Wattage:** 100,000.

♣ **3988 KKBQ-AM - 790**
11 Greenway Plaza, Ste. 2022
Houston, TX 77046   **Phone:** (713)961-0093
                            Fax: (713)963-1293

♣ **3989 KKBQ-FM - 92.9**
11 Greenway Plaza, Ste. 2022   **Phone:** (713)961-0093
Houston, TX 77046   **Fax:** (713)963-1293

♣ **3990 KLVL-AM - 1480**
111 N. Ennis   **Phone:** (713)225-3207
Houston, TX 77003   **Fax:** (713)225-2824

♣ **3991 KUHF-FM - 88.7**
University of Houston   **Phone:** (713)743-0887
Houston, TX 77204-4061   **Fax:** (713)743-1818

♣ **3992 KUHT-TV - Channel 8**
4513 Cullen Blvd.   **Phone:** (713)748-8888
Houston, TX 77004   **Fax:** (713)749-8216

♣ **3993 Phonoscope Cable TV**
6013 Westline Dr.
Houston, TX 77036   **Phone:** (713)271-0077
Owner: Phonoscope Cable TV. **Founded:** 1987. **Cities Served:** Harris County, TX.

♣ **3994 Storer Cable TV of Houston**
2505 Bisbee   **Phone:** (713)645-3738
Houston, TX 77017   **Fax:** (713)645-3821
Owner: Storer Cable Communications. **Founded:** 1980. **Cities Served:** Harris County, Clear Lake City, Sage Glen, Sage Meadow, and Scarsdale, TX.

♣ **3995 VCA TeleCable, Inc.**
4647 Pine Timber, Ste. 110
Houston, TX 77041   **Phone:** (713)460-9800
Owner: Horizon Cablevision, Inc. **Founded:** 1971. **Cities Served:** Harris County, TX.

♣ **3996 Warner Cable Communications, Inc.**
8400 W. Tidwell   **Phone:** (713)462-1900
Houston, TX 77040   **Fax:** (713)895-2611
Owner: Warner Cable Communications, Inc. **Founded:** 1979. **Cities Served:** Fort Bend County, Harris County, Bellaire, Missouri City, Staford, and West University Place, TX.

HUNTSVILLE

⌸ **3997 The Houstonian**
Sam Houston State University
PO Box 2178   **Phone:** (409)294-1495
Huntsville, TX 77341   **Fax:** (409)294-1598

INGLESIDE

⌸ **3998 The Biblical Evangelist**
Biblical Evangelism
PO Drawer 940   **Phone:** (512)776-2867
Ingleside, TX 78362-0940   **Fax:** (512)776-4903

IRVING

⌸ **3999 Exploring**
Boy Scouts of America
1325 W. Walnut Hill Ln.
PO Box 152079   **Phone:** (214)580-2365
Irving, TX 75015-2079   Fax: (214)580-2079

⌸ **4000 Las Colinas People**
4201 Wingren, Ste. 101   **Phone:** (214)717-0880
Irving, TX 75062   **Fax:** (214)717-9432

♣ **4001 KHVN-AM - 970**
545 E. John Carpenter Fwy., Ste. 1700   **Phone:** (214)988-7525
Irving, TX 75062   **Fax:** (214)988-1003

✇ **4002 Paragon Communications**
209 S. Rogers Rd.   Phone: (214)221-6531
Irving, TX 75060   Fax: (214)254-1075
Owner: Paragon Communications. **Founded:** 1981. **Cities Served:**
Dallas County, TX.

JACKSONVILLE

✇ **4003 KEBE-AM - 1400**
Box 1648
Jacksonville, TX 75766   Phone: (214)586-2527
Format: Contemporary Country. **Network(s):** ABC; Unistar. **Owner:**
Waller Broadcasting, Inc. **Founded:** 1947. **Operating Hours:** Continuous. **Key Personnel:** Dudley Waller, Pres./Gen. Mgr.; Jack Beazley,
Program Dir.; Gary Lesniewski, News Dir.; Jamie Rhodes, Public
Service Dir.; Alan Mather, Production Dir. **Wattage:** 1000. **Ad Rates:**
$13 for 30 seconds; $17 for 60 seconds.

JOHNSON CITY

▥ **4004 Johnson City Record Courier**
Box 205
Johnson City, TX 78636   Phone: (512)868-7181
Former Title: Record Courier

✇ **4005 KFAN-FM - 107.9**
Box 311   Phone: (512)997-2197
Fredericksburg, TX 78624   Fax: (512)997-2198
Format: Alternative/Independent/Progressive. **Network(s):** Texas
State. **Owner:** Fritz Broadcasting Co., Inc. **Founded:** 1991. **Operating
Hours:** Continuous. **Key Personnel:** Jayson Fritz, Gen. Mgr.; J.D.
Rose, Program Dir.; Jan Fritz, Gen. Sales Mgr. **Wattage:** 37,200. **Ad
Rates:** $7-$17 for 30 seconds; $11.25-$20 for 60 seconds.

✇ **4006 KNAF-AM - 910**
Box 311   Phone: (512)997-2197
Fredericksburg, TX 78624   Fax: (512)997-2198
Format: Contemporary Country. **Network(s):** Texas State. **Owner:**
Fritz Broadcasting Co., Inc. **Founded:** 1947. **Operating Hours:** 6 a.m.-
midnight. **Key Personnel:** Jayson Fritz, Gen. Mgr.; Duane Weinheimer, Program and Music Dir.; Jan Fritz, Gen. Sales Mgr.; Cody
Goodnight, News Dir. **Wattage:** 1000 day; 174 night. **Ad Rates:** $2.75-
$7.50 for 15 seconds; $2.65-$11 for 30 seconds; $3.65-$14 for 60
seconds.

KATY

▥ **4007 The Times (Katy)**
Hartman Newspapers, Inc.
PO Box 678   Phone: (713)391-3141
Katy, TX 77449   Fax: (713)391-2030
Community newspaper. **Frequency:** 2x/wk. **Cols./Page:** 6. **Col. Width:**
12 picas. **Col. Depth:** 21 in. **Subscription:** $21 (carrier); $25 (mail).
Ad Rates: SAU: $5.50   **Circulation:** Paid □6,862
                                                  Controlled □115

KEENE

✇ **4008 KJCR-FM - 88.3**
300 N. College Dr.   Phone: (817)556-4788
Keene, TX 76059   **Fax: (817)556-4744**

KENNEDALE

▥ **4009 Kennedale News**
B & B Publishing, Inc.
PO Box 406
Kennedale, TX 76060   Phone: (817)478-4661

KILLEEN

✇ **4010 KNCT-FM - 91.3**
Central Texas College
Hwy. 190 W.   **Phone: (817)526-1385**
Killeen, TX 76541   Fax: (817)526-4000

KIRBYVILLE

▥ **4011 East Texas Banner**
PO Drawer B   Phone: (409)423-2696
Kirbyville, TX 75956   **Fax: (409)423-4793**

LAMPASAS

✇ **4012 KCYL-AM - 1450**
PO Box 889   Phone: (512)556-3671
Lampasas, TX 76550   **Fax: (512)556-2166**

LAREDO

✇ **4013 KGNS-TV - Channel 8**
120 W. Delmar
PO Box 2829   Phone: (512)727-8888
Laredo, TX 78044   Fax: (512)727-5336

✇ **4014 Paragon Cable**
1313 W. Calton Rd.   Phone: (512)721-0607
Laredo, TX 78041   Fax: (512)721-0612
Owner: KBLCOM, Inc. **Founded:** 1961. **Cities Served:** Webb County
and Rio Bravo, TX.

LEVELLAND

▥ **4015 Levelland & Hockley County News Press**
Drawer 1628   Phone: (806)894-3121
Levelland, TX 79336   **Fax: (806)894-7957**

LIBERTY

▥ **4016 The Liberty Gazette**
PO Box 1908   Phone: (409)336-6416
Liberty, TX 77575   **Fax: (409)336-9400**

▥ **4017 Pony Express Mail**
PO Box 1908   Phone: (409)336-6416
Liberty, TX 77575   **Fax: (409)336-9400**

✇ **4018 KPXE-AM - 1050**
517 N. Travis   Phone: (409)336-5793
Liberty, TX 77575   Fax: (409)336-5250
Format: News; Sports; Adult Contemporary. **Network(s):** Texas State.
Owner: Trinity River Valley Broadcasting Corp., at above address.
Founded: 1968. **Operating Hours:** Sunrise-sunset; 10% network, 90%
local. **Key Personnel:** William Buchanan, Pres./Gen. Mgr.; Don
Norman, News Dir.; Allen Wayne, Program and Music Dir. **Wattage:**
250. **Ad Rates:** $8-$12 for 30 seconds; $11-$15 for 60 seconds.
Additional Contact Information: Toll-free: 800-375-1999.

✇ **4019 KSHN-FM - 99.9**
517 N. Travis   Phone: (409)336-5793
Liberty, TX 77575   Fax: (409)336-5250
Format: News; Sports; Adult Contemporary. **Network(s):** Texas State.
Owner: Trinity River Valley Broadcasting Corp., at above address.
Founded: 1968. **Operating Hours:** 5:30 a.m.-12 a.m.; 10 % network,
90% local. **Key Personnel:** William Buchanan, Pres./Gen. Mgr.; Gary
Underwood, News Dir.; Allen Wayne, Program and Music Dir.
Wattage: 50,000. **Ad Rates:** $8-$12 for 30 seconds; $11-$15 for 60
seconds.

LIVINGSTON

▥ **4020 Polk County Enterprise**
PO Box 1276   Phone: (409)327-4357
Livingston, TX 77351   **Fax: (409)327-7156**

✇ **4021 KETX-AM - 1440**
Drawer 1236
US 59 N.   Phone: (409)327-8916
Livingston, TX 77351   Fax: (409)327-8916
Format: Contemporary Country. Simulcasts KETX-FM. **Network(s):**
USA Radio. **Owner:** Polk County Broadcasting Co. **Founded:** 1957.
Operating Hours: 6 a.m.-midnight. **Key Personnel:** Hal Haley, Pres./
Chief Executive Officer. **Wattage:** 5000. **Ad Rates:** Combined rates
available with KETX-FM: $12-$15 for 30 seconds. **Additional Contact
Information:** (409)327-5389.

🎙 4022 KETX-FM - 92.3
Drawer 1236
US 59 N.   Phone: (409)327-8916
Livingston, TX 77351   Fax: (409)327-8916
Format: Contemporary Country. **Network(s):** USA Radio. **Owner:** Polk County Broadcasting Co. **Founded:** 1970. **Operating Hours:** 6 a.m.-midnight. **Key Personnel:** Hal Haley, Pres./CEO. **Wattage:** 50,000. **Ad Rates:** Combined rates available with KETX-AM: $12-$15 for 30 seconds. **Additional Contact Information:** (409)327-5389.

🎙 4023 KETX-TV - Channel 5
Drawer 1236
US 59 N.   Phone: (409)327-8916
Livingston, TX 77351   Fax: (409)327-8916
Format: Alternative/Independent/Progressive. **Network(s):** Independent. **Owner:** Polk County Broadcasting Co. **Founded:** 1985. **Operating Hours:** Continuous. **ADI:** Houston, TX. **Key Personnel:** Hal Haley, Pres./CEO. **Ad Rates:** $30 per unit.

LONGVIEW

🎙 4024 KYKX-FM - 105.7
1618 Judson Rd.
Box 5818   Phone: (903)757-2662
Longview, TX **75608-5818**   Fax: (903)757-2684

LUBBOCK

🎙 4025 Cox Cable Lubbock
6710 Hartford Ave.   Phone: (806)793-2222
Lubbock, TX 79413   Fax: (806)793-7818
Owner: Cox Cable Communications. **Founded:** 1965. **Cities Served:** Lubbock County, TX.

🎙 4026 KFMX-AM - 1340
5613 Villa Dr.   Phone: (806)747-1224
Lubbock, TX 79412   Fax: (806)747-2288
Format: Big Band/Nostalgia. **Owner:** Delier Broadcasting Ltd. **Operating Hours:** Continuous. **Key Personnel:** Scott Parsons, Gen. Mgr.; Barbara Lambert, Gen. Sales Mgr.; Wes Nessmann, Program Dir. **Wattage:** 1000.

🎙 4027 KKCL-FM - 98.1
1617 27th St.   **Phone: (806)763-2856**
Lubbock, TX 79405   **Fax: (806)763-5922**

🎙 4028 USA Cablesystems, Inc.
7240 Brittmoore Rd., Ste. 115
Houston, TX 77041   Phone: (713)849-4245
Owner: USA Cablesystems, Inc. **Cities Served:** Lubbock County, TX.
Additional Contact Information: Toll-free: 800-448-2816.

MATHIS

📖 4029 The Mathis News
San Patricio Publishing Co., Inc.
620 E. San Patricio   Phone: (512)547-3274
Mathis, TX 78368   Fax: (512)547-3275

MCKINNEY

🎙 4030 KSSA-FM - 106.9
3500 Maple Ave., Ste. 1310   Phone: (214)528-1600
Dallas, TX 75219   Fax: (214)528-4667
Format: Hispanic (Contemporary). **Owner:** Tony Rodriguez. **Founded:** 1947. **Operating Hours:** Continuous. **Key Personnel:** Mike Bradley, Gen. Mgr.; Fernando Gonzalez, Sales Mgr.; Katherine Castio, Office Mgr.; Florentino Garcia, News and Program Dir. **Wattage:** 3000.

MIDLAND

🎙 4031 Dimension Cable Services
2530 S. Midkiff
Midland, TX 79701   Phone: (915)694-7721
Owner: Times Mirror Cable TV. **Founded:** 1968. **Cities Served:** Midland County, TX.

🎙 4032 KTPX-TV - Channel 9
PO Box 60150   **Phone: (915)567-9999**
Midland, TX 79711   Fax: (915)561-5136

MISSION

📖 4033 South Texas Agri-News
PO Box 353   **Phone: (210)585-2787**
Mission, TX 78572-0353   **Fax: (210)585-2304**

MOODY

📖 4034 The Moody Courier
PO Box 38
502 Ave. E.   Phone: (817)853-2801
Moody, TX 76557-0038   **Fax: (817)754-3511**

NACOGDOCHES

🎙 4035 KEEE-AM - 1230
910 North St.
PO Box 631111   Phone: (409)564-4444
Nacogdoches, TX 75963-1111   Fax: (409)564-3392

🎙 4036 KJCS-FM - 103.3
910 North St.
PO Box 631111   Phone: (409)564-4444
Nacogdoches, TX 75963   Fax: (409)564-3392

NEDERLAND

📖 4037 Mid County Chronicle
PO Box 2140   Phone: (409)722-0479
Nederland, TX 77627   **Fax: (409)838-2857**

NEW BRAUNFELS

🎙 4038 New Braunfels Cable TV
160 Hwy. 81 W.   Phone: (512)625-3408
New Braunfels, TX 78130   **Fax: (512)629-7811**

NORMANGEE

📖 4039 The Normangee Star
PO Box 249   **Phone: (409)396-6649**
Normangee, TX 77871   **Fax: (409)396-6651**

ODESSA

🎙 4040 KCDQ-FM - 102
700 N. Grant, Ste. 404   Phone: (915)563-9102
Odessa, TX 79761   **Fax: (915)580-9102**

ORANGE

🎙 4041 KOGT-AM - 1600
PO Box 1667
Orange, TX 77630   Phone: (409)883-4381

PALESTINE

🎙 4042 KNET-AM - 1450
PO Box 649   **Phone: (903)729-6077**
Palestine, TX 75802   **Fax: (903)729-4742**

PANOLA

📖 **4043 Panola Watchman**
109 W. Panola
PO Box 518　　　　　　　　　Phone: (903)693-7888
Carthage, TX 75633　　　　　　**Fax: (903)693-5857**

PARIS

📻 **4044 KPLT-FM - 107.7**
2305 SE 3rd St.
PO Box 9　　　　　　　　　　Phone: (903)784-3311
Paris, TX 75460　　　　　　　　Fax: (903)784-5758

PERRYTON

📻 **4045 KEYE-AM - 1400**
Box 630　　　　　　　　　　　Phone: (806)435-5458
Perryton, TX 79070　　　　　　Fax: (806)435-5393
Format: Contemporary Country. **Network(s):** Texas State. **Owner:** Perryton Radio, Inc. **Founded:** 1948. **Operating Hours:** 5:30 a.m.-midnight. **Key Personnel:** Levita Joyner, Gen. Mgr.; Christopher Samples, Sales Mgr.; David Schwalk, News Dir.; Jerry Williams, Program Dir.; Steve Lile, PSA Dir. **Wattage:** 1000. **Ad Rates:** $4-$7.75 for 30 seconds;$5-$9.50 for 60 seconds.

PLANO

📻 **4046 TeleCable of Richardson-Plano**
1414 Summit Ave.
Plano, TX 75074　　　　　　　Phone: (214)578-7573
Owner: TeleCable Corp. **Founded:** 1984. **Cities Served:** Collin County, TX.

PLEASANTON

📻 **4047 KBOP-AM - 1380**
215 N. Main　　　　　　　　　Phone: (512)569-2194
Pleasanton, TX 78064　　　　　**Fax: (512)569-2196**

📻 **4048 KBOP-FM - 98.3**
215 N. Main　　　　　　　　　Phone: (512)621-2194
Pleasanton, TX 78064　　　　　**Fax: (512)569-2196**

RIVER OAKS

📖 **4049 River Oaks News**
Suburban Newspapers, Inc.
7820 Wyatt Dr.　　　　　　　Phone: (817)246-2473
Fort Worth, TX 76108　　　　　**Fax: (817)246-2474**

RUSK

📻 **4050 KTLU-AM - 1580**
618 N. Main
Box 475　　　　　　　　　　　Phone: (903)683-5305
Rusk, TX 75785　　　　　　　　**Fax: (903)683-5104**

📻 **4051 KWRW-FM - 97.7**
618 N. Main
Box 475　　　　　　　　　　　Phone: (903)683-5305
Rusk, TX 75785　　　　　　　　**Fax: (903)683-5104**

SAN ANGELO

📖 **4052 San Angelo City Lites Magazine**
Mikeska Inc.
PO Box 5500　　　　　　　　　Phone: (915)658-8367
San Angelo, TX 76902　　　　　Fax: (915)658-3180
Community cultural magazine and TV listing guide. **Founded:** 1985. **Frequency:** Bimonthly. **Printing Method:** Web offset. **Trim Size:** 10 3/4 x 8. **Cols./Page:** 6. **Col. Width:** 6 in. **Key Personnel:** Terry Mikeska, Publisher. **Subscription:** Free; $16 (mail).

Ad Rates:	BW:	$375	Circulation: Free ‡8,000
	4C:	$575	
	PCI:	$6.40	

SAN ANTONIO

📖 **4053 The Baby Connection News Journal**
Parent Education for Infant Development
PO Box 13320　　　　　　　　Phone: (512)493-6278
San Antonio, TX 78213-0320　　**Fax: (512)493-6278**

📖 **4054 The Beefmaster Cowman**
Gulf Coast Publishing Corp.
11201 Morning Ct.　　　　　　**Phone: (210)344-8300**
San Antonio, TX 78213-1300　　**Fax: (210)344-4258**

📖 **4055 Neuroscience and Biobehavioral Reviews**
Pergamon Press
University of Texas at San Antonio
Division of Life Sciences　　　　Phone: (512)691-4481
San Antonio, TX 78285　　　　　Fax: (512)691-4510
Neuroscience review journal. **Founded:** 1977. **Frequency:** Quarterly. **Printing Method:** Offset. **Trim Size:** 8 1/2 x 11. **Cols./Page:** 2. **Key Personnel:** Matthew J. Wayner, Editor-in-Chief. **ISSN:** 0149-7634.
Circulation: (Not Reported)
Advertising accepted; contact publisher for rates. Publisher's address: 660 White Plains Rd., Tarrytown, NY 10591-5153; phone (914)524-9200.

📖 **4056 Pharmacology Biochemistry and Behavior**
Division of Life Sciences
The University of Texas At San Antonio
San Antonio, TX 78285
Medical journal. **Founded:** 1966. **Frequency:** Monthly. **Trim Size:** 8 1/2 x 11. **Cols./Page:** 2. **Key Personnel:** Matthew J. Wayner, Editor-in-Chief. **ISSN:** 0091-3057. **Subscription:** $1,305 institutions.
Circulation: (Not Reported)
Advertising accepted; contact publisher for rates. **Additional Contact Information:** Publishing, subscription, and advertising offices Pergamon Press Inc., 660 White Plains Rd., Tarrytown, NY 10591-5153.

📖 **4057 Physiology & Behavior**
Division of Life Sciences
The University of Texas at San Antonio
San Antonio, TX 78285
Medical journal. **Founded:** 1973. **Frequency:** Monthly. **Trim Size:** 8 1/2 x 11. **Cols./Page:** 2. **Key Personnel:** Matthew J. Wayner, Editor-in-Chief. **ISSN:** 0031-9384. **Subscription:** $1,225 institutions.
Circulation: (Not Reported)
Advertising accepted; contact publisher for rates. **Additional Contact Information:** Publishing, subscription and advertising offices Pergamon Press, Inc., 660 White Plains Rd., Tarrytown, NY 10591-5153.

📖 **4058 The San Antonio Business Journal**
American City Business Journals
8200IH 10 W., Ste. 300　　　　Phone: (512)341-3202
San Antonio, TX 78230-4819　　**Fax: (512)341-3031**

📖 **4059 San Antonio Current**
2566 Boardwalk　　　　　　　Phone: (512)828-7660
San Antonio, TX 78217　　　　　Fax: (512)828-7883
Community newspaper. **Founded:** 1986. **Frequency:** Weekly. **Printing Method:** Offset. **Trim Size:** 10 x 13. **Cols./Page:** 4. **Col. Width:** 2 3/8 in. **Col. Depth:** 10 in. **Key Personnel:** Linda Cummings, Advertising Mgr. **Subscription:** Free.

Ad Rates:	BW:	$995	Circulation: Non-paid ‡32,000
	4C:	$1,520	

📖 **4060 San Antonio Register**
PO Box 1598
San Antonio, TX 78296-1598　　Phone: (512)222-1721
African-American community newspaper. **Founded:** 1931. **Frequency:** Weekly. **Printing Method:** Web offset. **Trim Size:** 13 1/2 X 22 3/4. **Cols./Page:** 6. **Col. Width:** 12 picas. **Col. Depth:** 21 in. **Key Personnel:** Kathy Little, Editor/Advertising Mgr. **Subscription:** $22.

Ad Rates:	BW:	$450	Circulation: Paid ‡7,800
	4C:	$850	Non-paid ‡200
	SAU:	$5.30	

4061 The Times Newspapers
Fisher Publications, Inc.
8603 Botts Ln.
PO Box 17947   Phone: (512)828-3321
San Antonio, TX 78217   **Fax: (512)828-3287**

4062 Today's Catholic
PO Box 28410   Phone: (512)734-2620
San Antonio, TX 78228-0410   **Fax: (512)734-2939**

4063 KBUC-AM - 830
BOX 18003
San Antonio, TX 78218   Phone: (512)656-7937
Format: English Oldies. **Owner:** Raquel Mendoza. **Founded:** 1990.
Operating Hours: Sunrise-sunset. **Wattage:** 250.

4064 KSAQ-FM - 96.1
217 Alamo Plaza, Ste. 200   **Phone: (210)271-9600**
San Antonio, TX 78205   **Fax: (210)271-0489**

4065 Paragon Cable
415 N. Main Ave.
Box 761   Phone: (512)222-0500
San Antonio, TX 78205   Fax: (512)222-2402
Owner: KBLCOM, Inc. **Founded:** 1979. **Cities Served:** Bexar County,
Comal County, Guadalupe County, Alamo Heights, Balcones Heights,
Castle Hills, Cibolo, Converse, Hollywood Park, Kirby, Live Oak,
Olmos Park, Schertz, Selma, Terrell Hills, Universal City, and
Windrest, TX.

SAN MARCOS

4066 The University Star
Southwest Texas State University
Journalism Dept.
Rm. 102, Old Main   **Phone: (512)245-3487**
San Marcos, TX 78666   **Fax: (512)245-3708**

SWEETWATER

4067 Nolan County Shopper
112 W. 3rd St.
PO Box 750   Phone: (915)236-6677
Sweetwater, TX 79556   **Fax: (915)235-4967**

TERRELL

4068 KPYK-AM - 1570
1412-C West Moore Ave.
PO Box 157   **Phone: (214)524-5795**
Terrell, TX 75160   **Fax: (214)524-5795**

TEXARKANA

4069 Dimension Cable Services
221 Texas Blvd.
Texarkana, TX 75501   Phone: (214)794-3426
Owner: Bob Tips. **Founded:** 1974. **Cities Served:** Bowie County, Nash,
and Wake Village, TX and Miller County, AR.

TYLER

4070 Both Sides Now
Free People Press
10547 State Hwy. 110 N
Tyler, TX 75704-9537   Phone: (903)592-4263

4071 Tyler Morning Telegraph
410 W. Erwin St.
PO Box 2030   Phone: (903)597-8111
Tyler, TX 75710   **Fax: (903)595-0335**

UNIVERSAL CITY

4072 Herald
Prime Time Publishing Co.
122 E. Byrd
PO Box 2789   Phone: (512)658-7424
Universal City, TX 78148   Fax: (512)658-0390

WACO

4073 KNFO-FM - 95.5
4949 Franklin Ave.
PO Box 23495   Phone: (817)776-3900
Waco, TX 76702-3495   **Fax: (817)776-3917**

4074 Waco Cablevision
4300-A W. Waco Dr.
Box 7852   Phone: (817)776-1141
Waco, TX 76714-7852   Fax: (817)776-2651
Owner: MetroVision, Inc. **Founded:** 1965. **Cities Served:** McLennan
County, Bellmead, Beverly Hills, McGregor, Northcrest, Robinson,
and Woodway, TX.

WHITE SETTLEMENT

4075 White Settlement Bomber News
Suburban Newspapers, Inc.
7820 Wyatt Dr.   Phone: (817)246-2473
Fort Worth, TX 76108   **Fax: (817)246-2474**

WICHITA FALLS

4076 Vista Cablevision, Inc.
3225 Maurine St.
Wichita Falls, TX 76305   Phone: (817)855-5700
Owner: American TV & Communications Corp. **Founded:** 1979.
Cities Served: Archer County, Wichita County, and Lakeside City,
TX.

Ad Rates: GLR = general line rate; BW = one-time black & white page rate; 4C = one-time four color page rate; SAU = standard advertising unit rate;
CNU = Canadian newspaper advertising unit rate; PCI = per column inch rate.
Circulation: ★ = ABC; △ = BPA; ◆ = CAC; ● = CCAB; □ = VAC; ⊕ = PO Statement; ‡ = Publisher's Report; Boldface figures = sworn; Light figures = estimated.
Entry type: ▢ = Print; ♣ = Broadcast.

271

UTAH

BRIGHAM CITY

🎙 4077 Insight Communications, Inc.
45 East 200 South
Brigham City, UT 84302
Phone: (801)723-8559
Fax: (801)723-8548
Owner: Insight Communications Co. **Founded:** 1987. **Cities Served:** Davis County, Weber County, Clearfield, Clinton, Farr West, Layton, Ogden, Plain City, Pleasant View, Syracuse, West Haven, and West Point, UT.

KANAB

📖 4078 Color Country Shopper
40 E. Center St.
Kanab, UT 84741
Phone: (801)644-2339
Shopping guide. **Founded:** 1988. **Frequency:** Weekly. **Printing Method:** Web offset. **Trim Size:** 14 x 22 1/2. **Cols./Page:** 5. **Col. Width:** 2 in. **Col. Depth:** 13 in. **Key Personnel:** Matt Brown, Publisher. **Subscription:** Free.
Ad Rates: BW: $260
PCI: $4
Circulation: Free ‡1,800

LAYTON

🎙 4079 TCI Cablevision of Utah
1596 North 400 West, Ste. A
Layton, UT 84041
Phone: (801)776-0600
Owner: Tele-Communications, Inc. **Founded:** 1981. **Cities Served:** Davis County, UT.

LOGAN

📖 4080 Utah Science
UAES (Agriculture Experimental Sta.
Information Office)
Utah State University
Logan, UT 84322-4845
Phone: (801)750-2189
Fax: (801)750-3321

🎙 4081 Sonic Cable Television of Utah
1350 North 200 West
Box 488
Logan, UT 84321
Phone: (801)752-9731
Fax: (801)753-6099
Owner: Sonic Communications. **Founded:** 1971. **Cities Served:** Cache County, UT.

MONTICELLO

🎙 4082 American Televenture of Utah, Inc.
Box 1175
Monticello, UT 84535
Phone: (801)587-2051
Owner: George Lee. **Formerly:** Blue Mountain Cable. **Key Personnel:**

Dennis Lee, Gen. Mgr.; Audrey Lee, Office Mgr. **Cities Served:** 17: 3,879 subscribing households; 22 channels. **Additional Contact Information:** Toll-free: 800-367-4799.

OGDEN

📖 4083 Accent and Travelog
Meridian International
1720 Washington Blvd.
PO Box 10010
Ogden, UT 84409
Phone: (801)394-9446
Magazine profiling international travel and tourist locations. **Frequency:** Monthly.
Circulation: Paid 12,839

📖 4084 Bridal Trends
Meridian International
1720 Washington Blvd.
PO Box 10010
Ogden, UT 84409
Phone: (801)394-9446
Magazine featuring modern and traditional approaches to weddings, receptions, and honeymoons. **Frequency:** Monthly.
Circulation: Paid 9,679

📖 4085 People In Action and Sports Parade
Meridian International
1720 Washington Blvd.
PO Box 10010
Ogden, UT 84409
Phone: (801)394-9446
Magazine profiling celebrities in sports, entertainment, and fine arts, who make a "positive contribution to society." **Frequency:** Monthly.
Circulation: Paid 26,665

📖 4086 Your Health
Meridian International
1720 Washington Blvd.
PO Box 10010
Ogden, UT 84409
Phone: (801)394-9446
Magazine profiling health care, fitness, and nutritional needs of senior citizens. **Frequency:** Monthly.
Circulation: Paid 13,182

📖 4087 Your Home, Indoors & Out and Better Living
Meridian International
1720 Washington Blvd.
PO Box 10010
Ogden, UT 84409
Phone: (801)394-9446
Magazine offering ideas in home decor, construction, landscaping, and management. **Frequency:** Monthly.
Circulation: Paid 47,922

♣ **4088 TCI Cablevision of Utah, Inc.**
3585 Harrison Blvd., Ste. 100
Ogden, UT 84403-2048   Phone: (801)621-8844
Owner: Tele-Communications, Inc. **Founded:** 1975. **Cities Served:**
Davis County, Uintah County, Weber County, Harrisville, North
Ogden, Ogden Canyon, Riverdale, Roy, South Ogden, South Weber,
and Uintah City, UT.

PARK CITY

♣ **4089 TCI Cable**
Box 1755
Park City, UT 84060   **Phone: (801)649-4020**

PROVO

📖 **4090 The American**
American Party of the United States
PO Box 597
Provo, UT 84112
Political journal. **Founded:** 1969. **Frequency:** 6x/yr. **Printing Method:**
Offset. **Trim Size:** 8.5 x 11. **Cols./Page:** 2. **Col. Width:** 3 3/8 in. **Col.**
Depth: 9.5 in. **Key Personnel:** Robert Smith, Editor; Jefferson
LeCates, Assoc. Editor; Eric Liebelt, Research Editor. **Subscription:**
$20.
Ad Rates: BW: $40   **Circulation:** Paid 400
              PCI: $1   Non-paid 200
Formerly: The American Eagle (1972); The American Voice (1976).

📖 **4091 BYU Studies**
Brigham Young University
1102 JKHB   Phone: (801)378-6691
Provo, UT 84602   **Fax: (801)378-4649**

📖 **4092 Journal of Microcolumn Separations**
Brigham Young University
Dept. of Chemistry
Provo, UT 84602-1022
Journal. **Founded:** 1989. **Frequency:** 6x/yr. **Key Personnel:** Cecil D.
Hill, Sub Mgr. **Subscription:** $210; $250 institutions.
                              Circulation: Paid ‡348
                                          Controlled ‡51

Advertising not accepted.

♣ **4093 KBYU-TV - Channel 11**
Brigham Young University
C-302   Phone: (801)378-0050
Provo, UT 84602   **Fax: (801)378-0309**

♣ **4094 TCI Cablevision of Utah, Inc.**
Box 2027
Provo, UT 84604   Phone: (801)377-8600
Owner: Tele-Communications, Inc. **Founded:** 1975. **Cities Served:**
Utah County, UT.

RICHFIELD

📖 **4095 The Richfield Reaper**
65 W. Center
PO Box 730   Phone: (801)896-5476
Richfield, UT 84701   Fax: (801)896-8123

♣ **4096 KKWZ-FM - 93.7**
450 East 400 South
PO Box 848   **Phone: (801)896-4456**
Richfield, UT 84701   Fax: (801)896-9333

SALT LAKE CITY

📖 **4097 New Era**
Church of Jesus Christ of Latter-Day Saints
50 E. North Temple St., 23rd Fl.   Phone: (801)240-2951
Salt Lake City, UT 84150   **Fax: (801)240-1727**

♣ **4098 KBER-FM - 101.1**
19 East 200 South   Phone: (801)322-3311
Salt Lake City, UT 84111   **Fax: (801)355-2117**

♣ **4099 KISN-AM - 570**
4001 South 700 East, Ste. 800   Phone: (801)262-9797
Salt Lake City, UT 84107   **Fax: (801)262-9772**

♣ **4100 KISN-FM - 97.1**
4001 South 177 E., Ste. 800   Phone: (801)262-9797
Salt Lake City, UT 84107   **Fax: (801)262-9772**

♣ **4101 KKAT-FM - 101.9**
PO Box 45150   Phone: (801)533-0102
Salt Lake City, UT 84145   **Fax: (801)521-5018**

♣ **4102 KKDS-AM - 1060**
PO Box 57760   **Phone: (801)262-5624**
Salt Lake City, UT 84157   **Fax: (801)266-1510**

♣ **4103 KLZX-FM - 93.3**
434 Bearcat Dr.   Phone: (801)533-9305
Salt Lake City, UT **84115**   Fax: (801)533-9103

♣ **4104 TCI Cablevision of Utah, Inc.**
1369 E. 10600 South
Sandy, UT 84092   Phone: (801)485-0500
Owner: Tele-Communications, Inc. **Founded:** 1970. **Cities Served:** Salt
Lake County, Draper, Midvale, Murray, Riverton, Sandy, South
Jordan, South Salt Lake City, and West Valley City, UT.

SANDY

♣ **4105 Insight Communications, Inc.**
9075 South 700 West   Phone: (801)561-9275
Sandy, UT 84070   Fax: (801)255-2711
Owner: Insight Communications Co. **Founded:** 1980. **Cities Served:**
Salt Lake and Utah counties, UT.

TROPIC

📖 **4106 Garfield County News**
120 N. Main
PO Box 127   **Phone: (801)679-8730**
Tropic, UT **84776**   **Fax: (801)679-8847**

WEST JORDAN

📖 **4107 The Utah AMERICAN EAGLE**
American Publishing
1811 West 9000 South   Phone: (801)255-8011
West Jordan, UT 84088   Fax: (801)255-8068
Ceased publication.

VERMONT

BENNINGTON

♣ 4108 Adelphia Cable
107 McKinley St.
Box 169   Phone: (802)442-9395
Bennington, VT 05201   Fax: (802)442-2063
Owner: Adelphia Communications Corp. **Founded:** 1962. **Cities Served:** Rensselaer County, Hoosick, Hoosick Falls, and North Hoosick, NY; Bennington County, North Bennington, Old Bennington, Pownal, Shaftsbury, and Woodford, VT.

BRADFORD

◻ 4109 Journal-Opinion
Main St.
PO Box 378   Phone: (802)222-5281
Bradford, VT 05033   **Fax: (802)222-5438**

BURLINGTON

◻ 4110 Women and Therapy
Haworth Press
John Dewey Hall
Dept. of Psychology
University of Vermont   Phone: (802)656-2680
Burlington, VT 05405   Fax: (802)656-8783
Periodical covering mental health problems affecting women, women's roles in society, the special needs of minority women, lesbians, older women, and alternatives to traditional mental health treatment.
Founded: 1982. **Frequency:** Quarterly. **Subscription:** $30.
Circulation: (Not Reported)
Published by Haworth Press.

CHARLOTTE

◻ 4111 Eating Well
Telemedia Eating Well, Inc.
Ferry Rd.   Phone: (802)425-3961
Charlotte, VT 05445   Fax: (802)425-3675

◻ 4112 Harrowsmith Country Life
Telemedia U.S.
Ferry Rd.   Phone: (802)425-3961
Charlotte, VT 05445   Fax: (802)425-3307
A country lifestyle magazine. **Founded:** 1986. **Frequency:** 6x/yr.
Printing Method: Web offset. **Trim Size:** 8 1/8 x 10 7/8. **Cols./Page:** 2 and 3. **Col. Width:** 20 and 13.6 picas. **Col. Depth:** 63 agate lines.
ISSN: 1049-4618. **Subscription:** $15.97. $2.95 single issue.
Ad Rates: BW: $6,741   **Circulation:** Paid ‡242,874
             4C: $9,907
Formerly: Harrowsmith.

PLAINFIELD

♣ 4113 WGDR-FM - 91.1
Program Director
PO Box 336
Plainfield, VT 05667   Phone: (802)454-7762
Format: Alternative/Independent/Progressive. **Key Personnel:** Laura Paris, Music Dir. **Ad Rates:** Noncommercial.

PLYMOUTH

◻ 4114 Earthtreks Digest
Five Corners Publications, Ltd.
Vermont Rte. 100
HCR 70, Box 7A
Plymouth, VT 05056
Ceased publication.

POULTNEY

♣ 4115 WNYV-FM - 94.1
Box 210   **Phone: (802)287-9031**
Poultney, VT 05764   **Fax: (802)287-9030**

RANDOLPH CENTER

♣ 4116 WCVR-FM - 102.1
PO Box 249   Phone: (802)728-4411
Randolph Center, VT 05061   **Fax: (802)728-4013**

♣ 4117 WWWT-AM - 1320
PO Box 249   Phone: (802)728-4411
Randolph Center, VT 05061   **Fax: (802)728-4013**

RUTLAND

◻ 4118 The Rutland Shopper
98 Allen St.   Phone: (802)775-4221
Rutland, VT 05701   **Fax: (802)775-9535**

♣ 4119 Rutland Cablevision
7 Pine St.
Rutland, VT 05701   Phone: (802)773-2755
Owner: Adelphia Communications Corp. **Founded:** 1962. **Cities Served:** Rutland County, Mendon, Proctor, and West Rutland, VT.

♣ 4120 WHWB-AM - 970
Box 945   Phone: (802)747-4700
Rutland, VT 05702   Fax: (802)747-1400

♣ 4121   WYOY-FM - 94.5
Box 945
Rutland, VT 05702

Phone: (802)747-4700
Fax: (802)747-1400

ST. JOHNSBURY

♣ 4122   WSTJ-AM - 1340
PO Box 249
Concord Ave.
St. Johnsbury, VT 05819

Phone: (802)748-2344
Fax: (802)748-2361

Format: Contemporary Country. **Network(s):** Satellite Music. **Owner:** Northeast Kingdom Broadcasting , Inc., at above address. **Founded:** 1948. **Formerly:** WTWN-AM. **Operating Hours:** Continuous. **Key Personnel:** Thomas Field, Operations Mgr.; Rick DeFabio, Gen. Sales Mgr.; Chris Keach, Program Dir.; Cheryl Staton, Office Mgr. **Wattage:** 3000 ERP. **Ad Rates:** $8.50-$12.50 for 30 seconds; $11-$15 for 60 seconds. **Additional Contact Information:** Alt. telephone (802)748-2345.

SPRINGFIELD

♣ 4123   First Carolina Cable TV
Box 520
Springfield, VT 05156

Phone: (802)885-4592
Fax: (802)885-8590

Owner: First Carolina Communications, Inc. **Founded:** 1953. **Key Personnel:** Robert Snowdon, Gen. Mgr.; Henry Hryckiewicz, Plant Mgr.; David Gunzinger, Construction Mgr./Technical Supervisor. **Cities Served:** Peterborough, New Ipswich, Jaffrey, Alstead, Campton, and Grafton, NH; Hancock, Bennington, Pittsford, Manchester, Killington, Fair Haven, Mount Ascutney, Weston, and Londonderry, VT. **Additional Contact Information:** Toll-free: 800-356-2966.

VERGENNES

♣ 4124   WIZN-FM - 106.7
PO Box 1067
Burlington, VT 05402

Phone: (802)860-1818

WOODSTOCK

♣ 4125   WMXR-FM - 93.9
Box 404
Woodstock, VT 05091

Phone: (802)457-9494
Fax: (802)457-9496

VIRGINIA

ALEXANDRIA

🕮 4126 Aviation, Space, and Environmental Medicine
Aerospace Medical Assn.
320 S. Henry St. Phone: (703)739-2240
Alexandria, VA 22314-3524 **Fax: (703)734-9652**

🕮 4127 Clinical Management
American Physical Therapy Assn.
1111 N. Fairfax St. Phone: (703)684-2782
Alexandria, VA 22314-1488 Fax: (703)684-7343
Ceased publication.

🕮 4128 The Consultant Pharmacist
American Society of Consultant Pharmacists
1321 Duke St. **Phone: (703)739-1300**
Alexandria, VA **22314-3563** **Fax: (703)739-1500**

🕮 4129 INFO-LINE
American Society for Training and Development
1640 King St.
Box 1443 Phone: (703)683-8100
Alexandria, VA 22313-2043 Fax: (703)683-8103
Magazine offering how-to information for training and development professionals. **Founded:** 1984. **Frequency:** Monthly. **Printing Method:** Offset. **Trim Size:** 8 1/2 x 11. **Cols./Page:** 3. **Col. Width:** 2 1/4 in. **Col. Depth:** 9 in. **Key Personnel:** Barbara Darraugh, Editor. **Subscription:** $79. $10 single issue.
Circulation: 3,500
Advertising not accepted.

🕮 4130 Jane's Defence Weekly
Jane's Information Group
1340 Braddock Pl., Ste. 300
Alexandria, VA 22314 Phone: (703)683-3700
Report addressing global defense issues. **Frequency:** Weekly. **ISSN:** 0265-3818. **Subscription:** $163.
Circulation: Paid ‡10,057
Non-paid ‡16,097
Advertising accepted; contact publisher for rates.

🕮 4131 The NSBE Bridge
The National Society of Black Engineers
1454 Duke St. Phone: (703)549-2207
Alexandria, VA 22314 Fax: (703)683-5312
Magazine for high school students devoted to raising interest in the technical disciplines among minority students. **Founded:** 1990. **Frequency:** Quarterly. **Key Personnel:** Norris Hite, Jr., Publisher/Managing Editor.
Ad Rates: BW: $3,000 **Circulation:** Non-paid **100,000**
4C: $4,000

🕮 4132 PT, Magazine of Physical Therapy
American Physical Therapy Association
1111 N. Fairfax St. Phone: (703)684-2782
Alexandria, VA 22314 Fax: (703)706-3169
Magazine for physical therapy professionals. **Founded:** 1993. **Frequency:** Monthly. **Printing Method:** Offset. **Trim Size:** 8 1/4 x 10 7/8. **Key Personnel:** Julie Hilgenberg, Advertising Mgr. **Subscription:** $30.
Circulation: (Not Reported)

🕮 4133 Technical & Skills Training
American Society for Training and Development
1640 King St.
Box 1443 Phone: (703)683-8100
Alexandria, VA 22313-2043 Fax: (703)683-9203
Magazine providing information on technical training programs, methods, and strategies. **Founded:** 1990. **Frequency:** 8x/yr. **Printing Method:** Web offset. **Trim Size:** 8 1/4 x 10 7/8. **Cols./Page:** 2 or 3. **Col. Width:** 21 picas or 14 picas. **Col. Depth:** 58 picas. **Key Personnel:** Ellen S. Carnevale, Editor. **ISSN:** 1047-8388. **Subscription:** $59.
Ad Rates: BW: $1,750 **Circulation:** Paid ‡5,000
4C: $2,600 Non-paid ‡15,000

🕮 4134 Transport Topics
American Trucking Assn., Inc.
2200 Mill Rd. Phone: (703)838-1770
Alexandria, VA 22314 **Fax: (703)548-3662**

🎙 4135 Jones Intercable, Inc.
617 A S. Pickett St. Phone: (703)751-7710
Alexandria, VA 22304 Fax: (703)823-3061
Owner: Jones Intercable, Inc. **Founded:** 1980. **Cities Served:** Arlington County, VA.

ALTAVISTA

🎙 4136 WKDE-AM - 1000
PO Box 390 Phone: (804)369-5588
Altavista, VA 24517 **Fax: (804)369-1632**

🎙 4137 WKDE-FM - 105.5
PO Box 390 Phone: (804)369-5588
Altavista, VA 24517 **Fax: (804)369-1632**

ARLINGTON

🕮 4138 American Gas
American Gas Assn.
1515 Wilson Blvd. Phone: (703)841-8686
Arlington, VA 22209 **Fax: (703)841-8687**

Ad Rates: GLR = general line rate; BW = one-time black & white page rate; 4C = one-time four color page rate; SAU = standard advertising unit rate; CNU = Canadian newspaper advertising unit rate; PCI = per column inch rate.
Circulation: ★ = ABC; △ = BPA; ◆ = CAC; ● = CCAB; □ = VAC; ⊕ = PO Statement; ‡ = Publisher's Report; Boldface figures = sworn; Light figures = estimated.
Entry type: 🕮 = Print; 🎙 = Broadcast.

4139 Army Reserve Magazine
1815 N. Fort Myer Dr., Rm. 501
Arlington, VA 22209
Phone: (703)696-3962
Fax: (703)696-3745

4140 Medical Device Patents Letter
Washington Business Information, Inc.
1117 N. 19th St.
Arlington, VA 22209-1798   Phone: (703)247-3433
Ceased publication.

4141 Parks and Recreation Magazine
National Recreation and Park Assn.
2775 S. Quincy St., Ste 300   Phone: (703)820-4940
Arlington, VA 22206   Fax: (703)671-6772

4142 Plastic Waste Strategies
Washington Business Information, Inc.
1117 N. 19th St.
Arlington, VA 22209-1798   Phone: (703)247-3433
Ceased publication.

4143 Urban Broadcasting Corp.
3565 Lee Hwy.
Arlington, VA 22201   Phone: (703)528-0051
Owner: Theodore M. White; (703)528-0051. Founded: 1989. Key Personnel: Theodore M. White, Pres./Gen. Mgr.; Page E. Silver, V.P./Business Mgr.; Gia Hinton, Production Mgr. Cities Served: Arlington, VA.

BRIDGEWATER

4144 WGMB-AM - 640
402 E. College St.
Bridgewater, VA 22812   Phone: (703)828-2501
Format: Alternative/Independent/Progressive. Key Personnel: Glenn Fitzgerald, Music Dir. Ad Rates: Noncommercial.

BRUNSWICK

4145 Brunswick Times-Gazette
PO Box 250   Phone: (804)848-2114
Lawrenceville, VA 23868   Fax: (804)848-0504

CASTLEWOOD

4146 WSPC-AM - 1140
PO Box 250   Phone: (703)762-5595
Castlewood, VA 24224   Fax: (703)762-5596

4147 WXLZ-FM - 107.3
PO Box 250   Phone: (703)762-5595
Castlewood, VA 24224   Fax: (703)762-5596
Format: Contemporary Country. Network(s): CBS. Owner: Yeary Broadcasting, Inc., at above address. Founded: 1992. Operating Hours: Continuous. Wattage: 3000.

CEDAR BLUFF

4148 WJHT-FM - 107.7
PO Box 1206
Cedar Bluff, VA 24609-1206   Phone: (703)964-9610
Format: Contemporary Country. Owner: Raslor Corp., at above address. Founded: 1988. Operating Hours: Continuous. Key Personnel: H. David Taylor, Gen. Mgr. Wattage: 3000. Additional Contact Information: $3.50-$5 for 30 seconds; $5-$7 for 60 seconds.

4149 WYRV-AM - 770
PO Box 1206
Cedar Bluff, VA 24609-1206   Phone: (703)964-9619
                                     Fax: (703)964-9610
Format: Southern Gospel. Owner: Raslor Corp., at above address. Founded: 1984. Operating Hours: Sunrise-sunset. Key Personnel: H. David Taylor, Gen. Mgr. Wattage: 5000. Ad Rates: $2.50-$4 for 15 seconds; $3.50-$5 for 30 seconds; $5-$7 for 60 seconds.

CHARLOTTESVILLE

4150 Journal of Artificial Intelligence in Education
Assn. for the Advancement of Computing in Education
Box 2966   Phone: (804)973-3987
Charlottesville, VA 22902   Fax: (804)978-7449

4151 Journal of Computers in Math and Science Teaching
Assn. for the Advancement of Computing in Education
Box 2966   Phone: (804)973-3987
Charlottesville, VA 22902   Fax: (804)978-7449

4152 Journal of Computing in Childhood Education
Assn. for the Advancement of Computing in Education
Box 2966   Phone: (804)973-3987
Charlottesville, VA 22902   Fax: (804)978-7449

4153 Journal of Educational Multimedia and Hypermedia
Association for the Advancement of Computing in Education
PO Box 2996   Phone: (803)973-3987
Charlottesville, VA 22902   Fax: (804)978-7449
Journal covering the technologies of multimedia/hypermedia for learning. Founded: 1991. Frequency: Quarterly. ISSN: 1055-8896. Subscription: $65; $78 institutions; $80 other countries.
Ad Rates: BW: $195   Circulation: Paid ‡4,000

4154 Adelphia Cable
324 W. Main St.
Charlottesville, VA 22901   Fax: (804)293-9263
Owner: Adelphia Communications Corp. Founded: 1963. Cities Served: Albemarle County and Lake Monticello, VA. Additional Contact Information: Toll-free: 800-835-4949.

CHATHAM

4155 WKBY-AM - 1080
Rte. 2, Box 105A   Phone: (804)432-8108
Chatham, VA 24531   Fax: (804)432-95290

CHESAPEAKE

4156 TCI of Virginia, Inc.
Box 2186
Chesapeake, VA 23320   Phone: (804)424-6660
Owner: Tele-Communications, Inc. Founded: 1982. Cities Served: Chesapeake, VA.

CHRISTIANSBURG

4157 WFNR-AM - 710
485 Tower Rd.   Phone: (703)382-6106
Christiansburg, VA 24073   Fax: (703)381-2932

4158 WFNR-FM - 100.7
485 Tower Rd.   Phone: (703)382-6106
Christiansburg, VA 24073   Fax: (703)381-2932
Format: Adult Contemporary. Owner: Travis Broadcasting Corp. Operating Hours: Continuous. Key Personnel: Bill Lineberry, Operations Mgr./Sales Mgr.; Nelson Walters, PSA Mgr.; Karen Travis, V.P./Gen. Mgr. Ad Rates: $.60-$4.40 for 30 seconds; $3-$22 for 60 seconds. Combined rates available with WFNR-AM.

CLARKSVILLE

4159 The News Progress
329 Virginia Ave.
Box 1015   Phone: (804)374-2451
Clarksville, VA 23927   Fax: (804)374-2074

COLLINSVILLE

4160 WFIC-AM - 1530
PO Box 475   Phone: (703)647-1530
Collinsville, VA 24078   Fax: (703)297-2780

COVINGTON

📖 4161 Alleghany Highlander
PO Box 271   **Phone: (703)962-2121**
Covington, VA 24426   **Fax: (703)962-5072**

DANVILLE

🎙 4162 WAKG-FM - 103.3
PO Box 1629   Phone: (804)797-4290
Danville, VA 24543   Fax: (804)797-3918

🎙 4163 WBTM-AM - 1330
PO Box 1629   Phone: (804)793-4411
Danville, VA 24543   Fax: (804)797-3918

ELKTON

📖 4164 The Valley Banner
Rockingham Publishing Co., Inc.
403 W. Spotswood Trail
PO Box 126   Phone: (703)298-9444
Elkton, VA 22827   **Fax: (703)298-2560**

EXMORE

🎙 4165 WKRE-FM - 107.5
PO Box 220   Phone: (804)442-5000
Exmore, VA 23350   **Fax: (804)442-4500**

FAIRFAX

📖 4166 Direction
National Moving & Storage Assn.
11150 Main St., Ste. 402   **Phone: (703)934-9111**
Fairfax, VA 22030   **Fax: (703)934-9712**

📖 4167 M & S Times
National Moving & Storage Assn.
11150 Main St.   **Phone: (703)934-9111**
Fairfax, VA 22030   **Fax: (703)934-9712**

FARMVILLE

📖 4168 The Rotunda
Longwood College
Box 2901   Phone: (804)395-2120
Farmville, VA **23909**   Fax: (804)395-2237

FINCASTLE

📖 4169 The Fincastle Herald and Botetourt County News
PO Box 127   Phone: (703)473-2741
Fincastle, VA 24090   **Fax: (703)473-2741**

FORT BELVOIR

📖 4170 Belvoir Eagle
Comprint, Inc.
Bldg. 269, Stop 196   **Phone: (703)805-2583**
Fort Belvoir, VA 22060-5196   Fax: (703)780-6145
Former Title: Fort Belvoir Castle

FREDERICKSBURG

🎙 4171 WFLS-AM - 1350
616 Amelia St.   Phone: (703)373-1500
Fredericksburg, VA 22401   **Fax: (703)373-8450**

FRONT ROYAL

📖 4172 Faith & Reason
Christendom Press
2101 Shenandoah Shores Rd.   Phone: (703)636-2900
Front Royal, VA 22630   **Fax: (703)636-1655**

GLEN ALLEN

📖 4173 Goochland Gazette
Richmond Suburban Newspapers
PO Box 1249   Phone: (804)747-1031
Glen Allen, VA 23060   Fax: (804)273-9929
Community newspaper. **Founded:** 1956. **Frequency:** Weekly. **Printing Method:** Offset. **Trim Size:** 14 1/2 x 23. **Cols./Page:** 6. **Col. Width:** 12.3 picas. **Col. Depth:** 21 1/2 in. **Key Personnel:** Sarah Douclege, Editor; Harry Benne, Publisher; Debbie Beck, Advertising Exec.; Brenda Gillon, Circulation Mgr. **Subscription:** $18; $28 (out of county).

Ad Rates:	GLR:	$2.50	Circulation: ‡3,100
	BW:	$960	
	4C:	$1,360	
	PCI:	$7.62	

📖 4174 Henrico Gazette
Richmond Suburban Newspapers
PO Box 1249   Phone: (804)747-1031
Glen Allen, VA 23060   Fax: (804)273-9929

GREAT FALLS

📖 4175 Great Falls Current
Dear Communications Inc.
PO Box 580   **Phone: (703)356-3320**
McLean, VA 22101   **Fax: (703)556-0825**

GRETNA

🎙 4176 WMNA-FM - 106.3
Box 730   Phone: (804)656-1234
Gretna, VA 24557   **Fax: (804)656-6003**

GROTTOES

📖 4177 Living
Shalom Foundation, Inc.
Rte. 2, Box 656   Phone: (703)249-3177
Grottoes, VA 24441   Fax: (703)249-3177
Family magazine. **Founded:** 1991. **Frequency:** Quarterly. **Printing Method:** Offset. **Trim Size:** 11 1/2 x 13 3/4. **Cols./Page:** 6. **Col. Width:** 1 5/8 in. **Col. Depth:** 12 3/4 in. **Key Personnel:** Eugene K. Souder, Editor. **Subscription:** Free.

Circulation: Non-paid 100,000
Advertising accepted; contact publisher for rates.

HAMPDEN-SYDNEY

🎙 4178 WWHS-FM - 92.1
Box 606
Hampden-Sydney College
Hampden-Sydney, VA 23943   **Phone: (804)223-6809**

HAMPTON

📖 4179 The Flyer
Military Newspapers of Virginia
2509 Walmer Ave.   Phone: (804)857-1212
Norfolk, VA 23513   Fax: (804)853-1634
Ceased publication.

🎙 4180 Warner Cable of Hampton
1323 W. Pembroke Ave.   Phone: (804)722-2851
Hampton, VA 23661   Fax: (804)728-0515
Owner: Warner Cable Communications, Inc. **Founded:** 1966. **Cities**

Ad Rates: GLR = general line rate; BW = one-time black & white page rate; 4C = one-time four color page rate; SAU = standard advertising unit rate; CNU = Canadian newspaper advertising unit rate; PCI = per column inch rate.
Circulation: ★ = ABC; △ = BPA; ◆ = CAC; ● = CCAB; □ = VAC; ⊕ = PO Statement; ‡ = Publisher's Report; Boldface figures = sworn; Light figures = estimated.
Entry type: 📖 = Print; 🎙 = Broadcast.

279

Served: Hampton, James City, and York counties, Poquoson, and Williamsburg, VA.

HAMPTON ROADS

♨ 4181 Cox Cable of Hampton Roads
5200 Cleveland St.
Box 62549   Phone: (804)497-1071
Virginia Beach, VA 23462   Fax: (804)671-1501
Owner: Cox Cable Communications. **Founded:** 1978. **Cities Served:** Currituck County, NC; Hampton County, Norfolk County, Virginia Beach County, Chesapeake, Fort Story, Norfolk, Portsmouth, and Virginia Beach, VA.

HARRISONBURG

▢ 4182 Daily News-Record
Rockingham Publishing Co., Inc.
231 S. Liberty St.
PO Box 193   Phone: (703)433-2702
Harrisonburg, VA 22801   **Fax: (703)433-9112**

▢ 4183 Journal of Accounting Education
Pergamon Press
James Madison University
School of Accounting
Harrisonburg, VA 22807   Phone: (703)568-3091
Accounting education journal. **Founded:** 1983. **Frequency:** 2x/yr. **Key Personnel:** Kent St. Pierre, contact. **Subscription:** $58; $152 institutions.

     Circulation: 1,100
Publisher's address: 660 White Plains Rd., Tarrytown, NY 10591-5153; phone (914)524-9200.

♨ 4184 WXJM-FM - 88
James Madison
Anthony Seagal
800 S. Main St.
Harrisonburg, VA 22807   Phone: (703)568-3559
Format: Alternative/Independent/Progressive. **Key Personnel:** Bill Rouck, Music Dir.; Kim Lay, Music Dir. **Ad Rates:** Noncommercial.

KINGWOOD

♨ 4185 WFSP-FM - 107.7
Rte. 7 W.
PO Box 567   Phone: (304)329-1780
Kingwood, VA 26537-0567   Fax: (304)329-1780
Format: Oldies; Adult Contemporary. **Network(s):** AP; Meadows Racing. **Owner:** Arthur W. George, at above address; (304)329-1784. **Founded:** 1991. **Operating Hours:** 5 a.m.-12 a.m. Mon.-Thurs.; 5 a.m.-2 a.m. Fri.; 6 a.m.-2 a.m. Sat; 6 a.m.-12 a.m. Sun. **Key Personnel:** Arthur W. George, Gen. Mgr./Owner; Dave Price, Station and Sales Mgr.; Ronda Smith, Traffic Mgr.; David Wills, Program Dir. **Wattage:** 3000. **Ad Rates:** $3-$3.75 for 15 seconds; $5-$8 for 30 seconds; $7.50-$11 for 60 seconds.

LEESBURG

▢ 4186 Leesburg Today
112 Q South St.   Phone: (703)771-8800
Leesburg, VA 22075   Fax: (703)771-8833
Newspaper covering all facets of life in Loudoun County. **Founded:** 1988. **Frequency:** Weekly. **Cols./Page:** 4. **Col. Width:** 2 7/16 in. **Col. Depth:** 13 in. **Key Personnel:** Brett Phillips, Editor and Publisher; Cathie Browning, Advertising Mgr. **Subscription:** Free.
Ad Rates: BW: $800   **Circulation:** Controlled □23,227
            4C: $1,175

▢ 4187 The New Federalist
PO Box 889   Phone: (703)777-9451
Leesburg, VA 22075   Fax: (703)771-3099
National newspaper. **Founded:** 1987. **Frequency:** Weekly. **Printing Method:** Web offset. **Trim Size:** 14 3/4 x 23. **Cols./Page:** 6. **Col. Width:** 2 in. **Key Personnel:** Nancy Spannaus, Editor-in-Chief ; Christina Huth, Managing Editor; Alan Yue, Assoc. Editor; Stuart Lewis, Photography Editor. **Subscription:** $20.
Ad Rates: BW: $2,800   **Circulation:** Paid ⊕117,378
            PCI: $30   Non-paid ⊕1,105

▢ 4188 VICA Professional: VP
Vocational Industrial Clubs of America
PO Box 3000   Phone: (703)777-8810
Leesburg, VA 22075   Fax: (703)777-8999
Magazine for vocational-technical educators and administrators. **Founded:** 1965. **Frequency:** 8x/year. **Printing Method:** Offset. **Trim Size:** 8 1/4 x 11 1/4. **Cols./Page:** 6. **Col. Width:** 1 11/16 in. **Col. Depth:** 5 in. **Key Personnel:** E. Thomas Hall, Editor; Heidi S. Ambrose, Advertising Mgr. **USPS:** 414-450. **Subscription:** $9.50. $1 single issue.
Ad Rates: BW: $1,080   **Circulation:** Paid ⊕15,903
            4C: $1,680   Non-paid ⊕696
Quarterly VICA Journal included with annual subscription rate.

LEXINGTON

▢ 4189 Shenandoah
Washington & Lee University
PO Box 722   Phone: (703)463-8765
Lexington, VA 24450   **Fax: (703)463-8945**

♨ 4190 WLUR-FM - 91.5
Washington & Lee University
Reid Hall   Phone: (703)463-8443
Lexington, VA 24450   **Fax: (703)463-8024**

LYNCHBURG

▢ 4191 Randolph-Macon Woman's College Alumnae Bulletin
Randolph-Macon Woman's College
     Phone: (804)947-8000
Lynchburg, VA 24503   **Fax: (804)947-8138**

♨ 4192 WBRG-AM - 1050
PO Box 1079   Phone: (804)845-5916
Lynchburg, VA 24505   **Fax: (804)845-5917**

♨ 4193 WLLL-AM - 930
1 Radio Ln.   **Phone: (804)385-9300**
Lynchburg, VA 24501   Fax: (804)385-9466

♨ 4194 WLVA-AM - 590
4119 Boonsboro Rd., Ste. 220   **Phone: (804)384-5936**
Lynchburg, VA 24503-2333   **Fax: (804)384-2203**

♨ 4195 WVLR-FM - 102.7
801 Court St.   **Phone: (804)846-5267**
Lynchburg, VA 24504   Fax: (804)845-8160

♨ 4196 WWOD-AM - 1390
2020 Mimosa   Phone: (804)384-1211
Lynchburg, VA 24503   Fax: (804)384-0397
Format: News. **Owner:** Bahakel Communications. **Founded:** 1947. **Operating Hours:** Continuous. **Key Personnel:** Wanda Burns, Gen. Mgr. **Wattage:** 3000. **Additional Contact Information:** Mailing address: PO Box 1390, Lynchburg, VA 24505.

MARION

♨ 4197 WOLD-AM - 1330
Box 31
Marion, VA 24354   **Phone: (703)783-7109**

♨ 4198 WOLD-FM - 102.5
Box 31
Marion, VA 24354   **Phone: (703)783-7100**

MCLEAN

▢ 4199 Environment Today
1483 Chain Bridge Rd., Ste. 202   Phone: (703)448-0322
McLean, VA 22101-4599   **Fax: (703)448-0270**

NEWPORT NEWS

⚓ 4200 UAE
179 Louise Dr.   Phone: (804)595-6969
Newport News, VA 23601   Fax: (804)595-2396
Owner: Tele-Communications, Inc. **Founded:** 1967. **Cities Served:**
York County and Newport News, VA.

NORFOLK

⚓ 4201 WAFX-FM - 106.9
700 Monticello Ave., Ste. 555   Phone: (804)624-9759
Norfolk, VA 23510   Fax: (804)627-3291
Format: Classic Rock. **Formerly:** WSKX-FM (1988). **Operating Hours:**
Continuous. **Key Personnel:** Jack Collins, Gen. Mgr.; Linda McCullough, Gen. Sales Mgr.; John Roberts, Program Dir.; Keith Kaufman, Promotions Dir.; Joe Wetherbee, Engineering Dir. **Wattage:** 100,000 ERP.

ORANGE

⚟ 4202 Orange County Review
Central Virginia Newspapers, Inc.
Box 589   Phone: (703)672-1266
Orange, VA 22960   **Fax: (703)672-5831**

QUANTICO

⚟ 4203 Quantico Sentry
PAO MCCDC
Public Affairs Office
Bldg. 3098 Range Rd.   Phone: (703)640-2741
Quantico, VA 22134-5126   Fax: (703)640-3527

QUINTON

⚓ 4204 WDCK-FM - 96.5
PO Box 100   **Phone: (804)320-9696**
Quinton, VA 23141   Fax: (804)932-9600

RADFORD

⚓ 4205 WVRU-FM - 89.9
PO Box 6973, Radford University Sta.   Phone: (703)831-5171
Radford, VA 24142   **Fax: (703)831-5893**

RESTON

⚟ 4206 The American Biology Teacher
National Assn. of Biology Teachers
11250 Roger Bacon Dr., No. 19   Phone: (703)471-1134
Reston, VA 22090   **Fax: (703)435-5582**

⚟ 4207 Journal for Research in Mathematics Education
National Council of Teachers of Mathematics
1906 Association Dr.   Phone: (703)620-9840
Reston, VA 22091-1593   Fax: (703)476-2970

⚟ 4208 Journal for Research in Music Education
Music Educators National Conference
1806 Robert Fulton Dr.   Phone: (703)860-4000
Reston, VA 22091-4348   Fax: (703)860-1531

⚟ 4209 Presstime
Newspaper Assn. of America
11600 Sunrise Valley Dr.   Phone: (703)648-1000
Reston, VA 22091   Fax: (703)620-4557

⚟ 4210 Studies in Art Education
National Art Education Assn.
1916 Association Dr.   Phone: (703)860-8000
Reston, VA 22091   **Fax: (703)860-2960**

⚟ 4211 The Weekly Messenger
DCI Publishing, Inc.
12040 S. Lakes Dr.   **Phone: (703)648-9100**
Reston, VA 22091   Fax: (703)648-3266

RICHMOND

⚟ 4212 The Presbyterian Outlook
The Presbyterian Outlook Foundation, Inc.
Box 85623   Phone: (804)359-8442
Richmond, VA **23285-5623**   Fax: (804)353-6369

⚟ 4213 Richmond Surroundings
Target Communications, Inc.
7814 Carousel Ln., Ste. 110   Phone: (804)346-4130
Richmond, VA 23294   **Fax: (804)965-0083**

⚟ 4214 Tuff Stuff jr.
Tuff Stuff Publications, Inc.
2309 Hungary Rd.
Richmond, VA 23228
Ceased publication.

⚟ 4215 VCU Magazine
Virginia Commonwealth University
Office of University Communications
826 W. Franklin St.
PO Box 2036   Phone: (804)367-1219
Richmond, VA 23284   Fax: (804)367-2018

⚟ 4216 Virginia Lawyers Weekly
106 North 8th St.   Phone: (804)783-0770
Richmond, VA 23219   **Fax: (804)788-1932**

⚓ 4217 Chesterfield Cablevision
6510 Ironbridge Rd.   Phone: (804)743-1171
Richmond, VA 23234   Fax: (804)743-1613
Owner: Storer Cable Communications. **Founded:** 1980. **Cities Served:**
Chesterfield County, VA.

⚓ 4218 Continental Cablevision of Richmond
918 North Blvd.   Phone: (804)355-2124
Richmond, VA 23230-4687   Fax: (804)353-0285
Owner: Continental Cablevision, Inc. **Founded:** 1980. **Cities Served:**
Henrico County, VA.

⚓ 4219 Continental Cablevision System
3914 Wistar Rd.   Phone: (804)262-4004
Richmond, VA 23228   Fax: (804)264-8435
Owner: Continental Cablevision, Inc. **Founded:** 1979. **Key Personnel:**
David R. Lee, District Mgr.; Bill Watson, Technical Mgr.; George
Weltmer, Sales Mgr. **Cities Served:** Henrico County, Hanover County,
Goochland County, and Ashland, VA: 75,000 subscribing households;
37 channels; 1 community access channel; 60 hours per week of
community access programming.

⚓ 4220 WCDX-FM - 92.7
2809 Emerywood Pkwy., Ste. 300   Phone: (804)672-9300
Richmond, VA **23294**   Fax: (804)672-9314

⚓ 4221 WKXO-AM - 1500
107 S. 1st St.   Phone: (606)986-9321
Richmond, VA 40475   **Fax: (606)986-8675**

⚓ 4222 WPLZ-FM - 99.3
2809 Emerywood Pkwy., No. 300
Richmond, VA 23294   **Phone: (804)672-9300**

ROANOKE

⚓ 4223 Cox Cable Roanoke
1909 Salem Ave.
Box 13726   Phone: (703)982-1110
Roanoke, VA 24036   Fax: (703)981-9067
Owner: Cox Cable Communications. **Founded:** 1976.

♠ **4224 WBRA-TV - Channel 15**
Box 13246
Roanoke, VA 24032   Phone: (703)344-0991
                                     Fax: (703)344-2148

SMITHFIELD

📖 **4225 The Times**
Times Publishing Co.
228 Main St.
PO Box 366   Phone: (804)357-3288
Smithfield, VA 23430   **Fax: (804)357-0404**

SUFFOLK

📖 **4226 Suffolk News-Herald**
PO Box 1220   Phone: (804)539-3437
Suffolk, VA 23434   **Fax: (804)539-8804**

VIENNA

📖 **4227 National Wildlife**
National Wildlife Federation
8925 Leesburg Pike   **Phone: (703)790-4510**
Vienna, VA 22180   **Fax: (703)442-7332**

WARRENTON

📖 **4228 Fauquier Times-Democrat**
ArCom Newspapers
39 Culpeper St.
PO Box 631   Phone: (703)347-4222
Warrenton, VA 22186-0631   Fax: (703)471-9596

♠ **4229 WPRZ-AM - 1250**
PO Box 3220   Phone: (703)349-1250
Warrenton, VA 22186   **Fax: (703)349-2726**

WARSAW

📖 **4230 Northern Neck News**
5 Court St.
PO Box 8   Phone: (804)333-3655
Warsaw, VA 22572   **Fax: (804)333-0033**

WILLIAMSBURG

📖 **4231 The Flat Hat**
College of William and Mary
PO Box 320   Phone: (804)221-3281
Williamsburg, VA 23185   **Fax: (804)221-3451**

WYTHEVILLE

📖 **4232 The Pennysaver**
Family Community Newspapers
460 W. Main St.   Phone: (703)228-6611
Wytheville, VA 24382   Fax: (703)228-7260

YORKTOWN

📖 **4233 The Flyer**
Worrell Enterprises, Inc.
PO Box 978   Phone: (804)898-7225
Yorktown, VA 23692   Fax: (804)890-0119
Weekly military newspaper. **Frequency:** Weekly. **Printing Method:**
Web offset. **Trim Size:** 11 1/2 x 15. **Cols./Page:** 5. **Col. Width:** 1 7/8 in.
Col. Depth: 13 1/2 in. **Key Personnel:** Carolyn M. Suz, Gen. Mgr.;
Peggy A. Brown, Advertising Mgr. **Subscription:** Free to military
personnel at Langley Air Force Base, VA.
Ad Rates: BW: $546   **Circulation:** Controlled ‡13,200
              4C: $996
              PCI: $7.80

WASHINGTON

BAINBRIDGE ISLAND

📖 **4234 In Context: A Quarterly of Humane Sustainable Culture**
Context Institute
Box 11470   Phone: (206)842-0216
Bainbridge Island, WA 98110   Fax: (206)842-5208
Magazine exploring pragmatic utopian community development.
Founded: 1983. **Frequency:** Quarterly. **Printing Method:** Photo offset.
Trim Size: 8 1/2 x 11. **Cols./Page:** 2. **Col. Width:** 3 in. **Col. Depth:** 9 1/4 in. **Key Personnel:** Robert Gilman, Editor; Sarah van Gelder, Managing Editor; Carla Cole, Circulation Mgr. **ISSN:** 0741-6180.
Subscription: $24.

                       Circulation: Paid ‡8,000
                               Non-paid ‡8,200

Advertising not accepted.

BELLEVUE

📖 **4235 Journal American**
1705 132nd Ave. NE
PO Box 90130   Phone: (206)455-2222
Bellevue, WA 98009   **Fax: (206)635-0603**

🎙 **4236 KASB-FM - 89.3**
10416 SE Kilmarnock
Bellevue, WA 98004-6698   Phone: (206)455-6154

🎙 **4237 KRPM-FM - 106.1**
15375 SE 30th Pl., No. 300   **Phone: (206)649-0106**
Bellevue, WA 98007-6500   **Fax: (206)649-9246**

🎙 **4238 KULL-AM - 770**
15375 SE 30th Pl., No. 300   **Phone: (206)649-0106**
Bellevue, WA 98007-6500   **Fax: (206)649-9246**

BELLINGHAM

📖 **4239 New Age Retailer**
Continuity Publishing, Inc.
114 W. Magnolia St., No. 204 **Phone: (206)676-0789**
Bellingham, WA 98225   **Fax: (206)676-0932**

🎙 **4240 KAFE-FM - 104.3**
2340 E. Sunset Dr.   **Phone: (206)734-5233**
Bellingham, WA 98226   **Fax: (206)734-5697**

🎙 **4241 TCI Cablevision of Washington**
Box 460
Bellingham, WA 98225   Phone: (206)734-5522
Owner: Tele-Communications, Inc. **Founded:** 1949. **Cities Served:** Whatcom County, WA.

CHELAN

📖 **4242 Lake Chelan Mirror**
315 E. Woodin Ave.
PO Box 296
Chelan, WA 98816   Phone: (509)682-2213
Former Title: Chelan Valley Mirror

COLFAX

🎙 **4243 KCLX-AM - 1450**
Box 710   **Phone: (509)397-4109**
Colfax, WA 99111   **Fax: (509)397-4752**

🎙 **4244 KZZL-FM - 99.5**
Box 710   **Phone: (509)397-4109**
Colfax, WA 99111   **Fax: (509)397-4752**
Format: Country. Simulcasts KCLX-AM. **Network(s):** Mutual Broadcasting System. **Owner:** Dakota Communications, at above address. **Founded:** 1991. **Formerly:** KCLX-FM. **Operating Hours:** Continuous. **Key Personnel:** Robert G. Hauser, Owner/Mgr. **Wattage:** 15,000 ERP. **Ad Rates:** Available upon request.

DEER PARK

🎙 **4245 KAZZ-FM - 107.1**
518 S. Fir
Box 1369   Phone: (509)276-8816
Deer Park, WA 99006   **Fax: (509)276-2790**

EDMONDS

🎙 **4246 Chambers Cable of Edmonds**
533 Main St.
Edmonds, WA 98020   Phone: (206)774-5146
Owner: Chambers Communications Corp. **Founded:** 1966. **Cities Served:** King County, Snohomish County, Richmond Beach, and Woodway, WA.

GOLDENDALE

🎙 **4247 KLCK-AM - 1400**
514 S. Columbus   **Phone: (509)773-3301**
Goldendale, WA 98620   **Fax: (509)773-3300**

ISSAQUAH

📖 **4248 Issaquah Valley Shopper**
Pacific Media Group, Inc.
PO Box 1328
Issaquah, WA 98027-1328   Phone: (206)392-6434

KELSO

🎤 **4249 KUKN-FM - 94.5**
506 Cowlitz Way W.
PO Box 90   Phone: (206)636-0110
Kelso, WA 98626   Fax: (206)577-6949
Format: Country. **Owner:** Washington Interstate Broadcasting Co. **Founded:** 1991. **Operating Hours:** Continuous. **Key Personnel:** Steve Hanson, Pres./Gen. Mgr.; Rick Roberts, Local Sales Mgr.; Bill Dodd, Program Dir.; Tim Burr, Music and Promotions Dir. **Wattage:** 6000. **Ad Rates:** $10-$15 for 30 seconds; $13.50-$20.25 for 60 seconds.

KENNEWICK

🎤 **4250 KOTY-FM - 106.5**
830 N. Columbia Center Blvd., No. 2-
B   **Phone: (509)783-0783**
Kennewick, WA 99336-7713   Fax: (509)735-8627

🎤 **4251 KTCR-AM - 1340**
830 N. Columbia Center Blvd., No. 2-
B   **Phone: (509)783-0783**
Kennewick, WA 99336-7713   Fax: (509)735-8627

🎤 **4252 KVEW-TV - Channel 42**
601 N. Edison   Phone: (509)735-8369
Kennewick, WA 99336   **Fax: (509)735-7889**

KIRKLAND

📖 **4253 Eastsideweek**
Sasquatch Publishing Co., Inc.
123 Lake St. S, Ste. B-1   Phone: (206)827-5550
Kirkland, WA 98033   Fax: (206)827-0952
Newsmagazine covering civic affairs, entertainment, and lifestyles in an "alternative voice." **Founded:** 1990. **Frequency:** Weekly. **Printing Method:** Offset. **Trim Size:** 11 x 15. **Cols./Page:** 4. **Col. Width:** 14 picas. **Col. Depth:** 13 1/2 in. **Key Personnel:** Knute Berger, Editor and Publisher; Ellen Cole, Advertising Mgr.; Mary Anne Christy, Circulation Mgr.
Ad Rates: BW: $1,487   **Circulation:** Paid 100
          4C: $1,887   Controlled 26,000
          PCI: $34.25
Combination advertising rates available with The Seattle Weekly.

LYNDEN

📖 **4254 Skagit Farmer**
Lewis Publishing Co., Inc.
PO Box 153   Phone: (206)354-4444
Lynden, WA 98264   Fax: (206)734-0575
Agricultural newspaper. **Subtitle:** Serving The Agricultural Communities in Skagit, Snohomish, San Juan, & Island Counties Since 1965. **Founded:** 1965. **Frequency:** Monthly. **Printing Method:** Offset. **Cols./Page:** 5. **Col. Width:** 2 1/16 in. **Col. Depth:** 14 in. **Key Personnel:** Michael D. Lewis, Publisher; Pam Richardson, Advertising Mgr. **Subscription:** Free; $7 donation in county; $10 out of area.
Ad Rates: BW: $630.50   **Circulation:** Free ‡4,500
          4C: $900.50
          PCI: $9.70

MORTON

🎤 **4255 Mike's TV Inc.**
Box J   Phone: (206)496-5635
Morton, WA 98356   **Fax: (206)496-5635**

NEWPORT

🎤 **4256 Pacific Northwest Cable**
Box 68   Phone: (509)447-2474
Newport, WA 99156   Fax: (509)447-4677
Owner: Pacific Northwest Cable Partners Ltd. **Cities Served:** Spokane County, WA.

OLALLA

📖 **4257 Business Opportunities Journal**
Business Service Corporation
PO Box 990   **Phone: (206)857-7444**
Olalla, WA 98359   **Fax: (206)857-3720**

OLYMPIA

📖 **4258 The Thurston-Mason Senior News**
Thurston County Council on Aging
529 W. 4th Ave.   Phone: (206)786-5595
Olympia, WA 98501   **Fax: (206)754-3362**

🎤 **4259 TCI Cablevision of Washington**
Box 129
Olympia, WA 98502-4577   Phone: (206)357-3364
Owner: Tele-Communications, Inc. **Founded:** 1966. **Cities Served:** Pierce and Thurston Counties, WA.

OTHELLO

🎤 **4260 KZLN-FM - 97.5**
Box 2869
Othello, WA 99344   **Phone: (509)488-6089**

PORT ORCHARD

📖 **4261 Business Ventures**
Business Service Corp.
569-F Division St.   **Phone: (206)876-0204**
Port Orchard, WA 98366   **Fax: (206)876-0795**
Ceased publication.

PROSSER

🎤 **4262 KARY-FM - 100.9**
PO Box 1310
Prosser, WA 99350   Phone: (509)786-1310
Format: Country; Ethnic (Spanish). **Network(s):** CNN Radio. **Owner:** Prosser-Grandview Broadcasters, Inc., at above address. **Founded:** 1989. **Operating Hours:** 5 a.m.-10p.m.; 7p.m.-10 p.m. Spanish. **Key Personnel:** Sidney Lee Roach, Operations Mgr./Sports Dir.; Judith Rae Roach, Office Mgr.; David Frechtn, Program and Music Dir.; Karl Wyckoff, Promotion and Sales Mgr. **Wattage:** 6000 ERP. **Ad Rates:** Available upon request.

🎤 **4263 KZXR-FM - 101.7**
1227 Hillcrest Dr.   Phone: (509)786-1017
Prosser, WA 99350   Fax: (509)786-1181

PUGET SOUND

🎤 **4264 Viacom Cablevision**
900 132nd St.
Box 5187   Phone: (206)745-8400
Everett, WA 98206   Fax: (206)745-8360
Owner: Viacom Cable. **Founded:** 1952. **Cities Served:** Island County, King County, Snohomish County, Bellevue, Bothell, Brier, Everette, Granite Falls, Kirkland, Lake Stevens, Mercer Island, Monroe, Mukilteo, Oak Harbor, Redmond, Seattle, Snohomish, Startup, and Sultan, WA.

QUINCY

🎤 **4265 Sun Country Cable Inc.**
Box 127   Phone: (509)787-3543
Quincy, WA 98848   **Fax: (509)787-3884**

RICHLAND

♣ 4266 KTNW-TV - Channel 31
c/o KWSU-TV
Washington State University
Edward R. Murrow Communications
  Center   Phone: (509)355-6511
Pullman, WA 99164-2530   Fax: (509)335-3772

SEATTLE

◫ 4267 Chinese Business Journal
PO Box 3041   Phone: (206)624-8781
Seattle, WA 98114-3041   Fax: (206)624-7437

◫ 4268 Chinese News
412 7th Ave., S.
Seattle, WA 98104
Ceased publication.

◫ 4269 Greater Seattle
Pacific Northwest Media Inc.
701 Dexter Ave. N., No. 101   Phone: (206)284-1750
Seattle, WA 98109   Fax: (206)284-2550
Seattle metropolitan area guide to contemporary living. **Founded:**
1992. **Frequency:** 6x/yr. **Trim Size:** 8 1/8 x 10 7/8. **Cols./Page:** 3. **Key
Personnel:** Giselle Smith, Editor; Keith Askenasi, Publisher. **Subscription:** $9.95. $1.95 single issue.
Ad Rates: BW: $2,900   **Circulation:** Non-paid ‡34,600
             4C: $3,500

◫ 4270 Inside WaU
University of Washington Libraries
Mail Stop 25   Phone: (206)543-1760
Seattle, WA 98195   Fax: (206)685-8727
Ceased publication.

◫ 4271 International Examiner
622 S. Washington   Phone: (206)624-3925
Seattle, WA 98104   Fax: (206)624-3046
Community newspaper. **Founded:** 1974. **Frequency:** 2x/mo. **Trim Size:**
11 1/2 x 16. **Key Personnel:** Danny Howe, Editor. **ISSN:** 1065-1500.
Subscription: Free; $18 (mail).
Ad Rates: PCI: $8.25   **Circulation:** Paid 600
                                                  Free 7,500

◫ 4272 The Jewish Transcript
Jewish Federation
2031 3rd Ave., Ste. 200   Phone: (206)441-4553
Seattle, WA 98121   Fax: (206)441-2736

◫ 4273 Northwest Kitchen and Bath Quarterly
Quarterly Publishing
Box 58866   Phone: (206)248-2064
Seattle, WA 98138   Fax: (206)852-4854
Consumer magazine containing articles on kitchen and bath decor
and remodeling ideas. **Founded:** 1988. **Frequency:** 3x/yr. **Printing
Method:** Web offset. **Trim Size:** 10 1/2 x 13. **Key Personnel:** Dave
Cockrill, Publisher/Sales Dir. **Subscription:** $4. $2.50 single issue.
Ad Rates: 4C: $1,250   **Circulation:** Paid ‡1,085
                                                  Non-paid ‡112,000

Accepts 1/4 page ads only.

◫ 4274 Seattle's Police Beat
Pacific Media Group
2314 3rd Ave.
Seattle, WA 98121   **Phone: (206)461-1300**

◫ 4275 Spectrum Newspapers Monthly, Seattle
Spectrum Newspapers
11171 Sun Center Dr., Ste. 110   Phone: (916)852-6222
Rancho Cordova, CA 95670   Fax: (916)852-6397
Newspapers serving active senior citizens, 55 and older, in Seattle.
Founded: 1975. **Frequency:** Monthly. **Printing Method:** Web offset.

Key Personnel: Bob Carney, Editor; Jacqueline Lucido, Gen. Mgr.;
Ridge Eagan, Advertising Dir. **USPS:** 980-481. **Subscription:** $12.
                                          Circulation: 75,000

◫ 4276 Technical Analysis of Stocks & Commodities
Technical Analysis, Inc.
3517 SW Alaska St.
PO Box 46518   Phone: (206)938-0570
Seattle, WA 98126   **Fax: (206)938-1307**

♣ 4277 KNDD-FM - 107.7
1100 Oliver St. 1550
Seattle, WA 98101   Phone: (206)622-3251
Format: Alternative/Independent/Progressive. **Key Personnel:** Marco
Collins, Music Dir.

♣ 4278 KOMO-TV - Channel 4
100 4th Ave. N.   Phone: (206)443-4000
Seattle, WA 98109   **Fax: (206)443-4014**

♣ 4279 KUOW-FM - 94.9
DS-50
University of Washington   Phone: (206)543-2710
Seattle, WA 98195   **Fax: (206)543-2720**

♣ 4280 SeaCom
3633 136th Pl. SE, Ste. 107   Phone: (206)433-3401
Seattle, WA 98103   Fax: (206)939-1902
Owner: Summit Communications, Inc. **Founded:** 1951. **Cities Served:**
King County, WA.

♣ 4281 TCI of Seattle, Inc.
1140 N. 94th St.
Seattle, WA 98103   Phone: (206)433-3401
Owner: Tele-Communications, Inc. **Founded:** 1951. **Cities Served:**
King County, Pierce County, Algona, Auburn, Black Diamond,
Buckley, Des Moines, Enumclaw, Issaquah, Kent, Maple Valley,
Medina, Orting, Pacific, Renton, Tukwila, and Wilkeson, WA.
Additional Contact Information: telephone (206)939-1902.

SEQUIM

◫ 4282 Peninsula Business Journal
Olympic View Publishing, Inc.
147 1/2 W. Washington St.
PO Box 1750   Phone: (206)683-3205
Sequim, WA 98382   Fax: (206)683-6670

SNOHOMISH

◫ 4283 Country Living
127 Ave. C
PO Box 499
Snohomish, WA 98290   Phone: (206)568-4121
Magazine. **Founded:** 1988. **Frequency:** Quarterly. **Key Personnel:**
Leslie Hynes, Editor; Susan Pierce, Advertising Mgr.
Ad Rates: BW: $959.40   **Circulation:** Non-paid ‡15,500
             4C: $1,700
             PCI: $16.66

SPOKANE

◫ 4284 The Reporter
Spokane Community College
Mail Stop 2010
N 1810 Greene St.   Phone: (509)533-7171
Spokane, WA 99207   **Fax: (509)533-7276**

♣ 4285 Cox Cable Spokane
1717 Buckeye
Box Hay C-1   Phone: (509)484-4931
Spokane, WA 99207   Fax: (509)483-7502
Owner: Cox Cable Communications. **Founded:** 1976. **Cities Served:**
Spokane County and Millwood, WA.

♣ **4286　KCDA-FM - 103.1**
450 University City Shopping Center　　Phone: (509)962-1111
Spokane, WA 99206　　　　　　　　　Fax: (509)926-1137

♣ **4287　KPBX-FM - 91.1**
2319 N. Monroe St.　　　　　　　　　Phone: (509)328-5729
Spokane, WA 99205　　　　　　　　　**Fax: (509)328-5764**

♣ **4288　KSBN-AM - 1230**
2211 E. Sprague Ave.　　　　　　　　Phone: (509)535-7272
Spokane, WA 99202-3930　　　　　　　**Fax: (509)535-7388**

♣ **4289　KWRS-FM - 90.3**
Station 40
Hardwick Union Bldg.
Whitworth College　　　　　　　　　Phone: (509)466-3278
Spokane, WA 99251　　　　　　　　　**Fax: (509)466-3221**

TACOMA

♣ **4290　KPLU-FM - 88.5**
121st & Park　　　　　　　　　　　Phone: (206)535-7758
Tacoma, WA 98447　　　　　　　　　**Fax: (206)535-8332**

♣ **4291　TCI Cablevision of Tacoma, Inc.**
Box 11209
Tacoma, WA 98409　　　　　　　　　Phone: (206)383-4311
Owner: Tele-Communications, Inc. **Founded:** 1971. **Cities Served:**
Pierce County and Ruston, WA.

♣ **4292　Viacom Cable**
2316 S. State St.　　　　　　　　　Phone: (206)597-7800
Tacoma, WA 98405　　　　　　　　　Fax: (206)272-4062
Owner: Viacom Cable. **Founded:** 1967. **Key Personnel:** Ed Hauge,
Producer/Dir.; Terry Bonagofsky, Production Tech. **Cities Served:**
Pierce County, WA: 139,000 subscribing households; 34 channels.
Additional Contact Information: Ext. 7109.

TOPPENISH

◫ **4293　Viva**
PO Box 511　　　　　　　　　　　Phone: (509)865-4055
Toppenish, WA 98948　　　　　　　　Fax: (509)865-2655
Spanish newspaper. **Frequency:** Weekly. **Cols./Page:** 5. **Col. Width:** 1
7/8 in. **Key Personnel:** Ted Escobar, Editor; Linda Layman, Office
Mgr. **Subscription:** Free.
Ad Rates:　PCI:　　$6　　　　　**Circulation:** Non-paid 10,000

◫ **4294　Wapato Independent**
PO Box 511　　　　　　　　　　　Phone: (509)877-3322
Toppenish, WA 98948　　　　　　　　Fax: (509)865-2655
Community newspaper. **Frequency:** Weekly. **Cols./Page:** 6. **Col.
Width:** 2 in. **Key Personnel:** John Livingston, Editor; Linda Layman,
Office Mgr. **Subscription:** $15; $20 out of area.
Ad Rates:　PCI:　　$4.50　　　　**Circulation:** 1,700

VANCOUVER

◫ **4295　Senior Messenger**
City of Vancouver
PO Box 1995　　　　　　　　　　　**Phone: (206)696-8222**
Vancouver, WA 98668　　　　　　　　**Fax: (206)696-8942**

♣ **4296　Columbia Cable of Washington**
6916 NE 40th St.　　　　　　　　　Phone: (206)892-6303
Vancouver, WA 98661　　　　　　　　Fax: (206)892-8744
Owner: Columbia International, Inc. **Founded:** 1982. **Cities Served:**
Clark County, WA and Multnomah, OR.

WENATCHEE

♣ **4297　KPQ-AM - 560**
32 N. Mission St.　　　　　　　　　Phone: (509)663-5121
Wenatchee, WA 98801　　　　　　　　**Fax: (509)664-6799**

♣ **4298　KPQ-FM - 102.1**
32 N. Mission　　　　　　　　　　Phone: (509)663-5121
Wenatchee, WA 98801　　　　　　　　**Fax: (509)664-6799**

YAKIMA

◫ **4299　Good Fruit Grower**
Washington State Fruit Commission
1005 Tieton Dr.
PO Box 9219　　　　　　　　　　　**Phone: (509)575-2315**
Yakima, WA 98909　　　　　　　　　Fax: (509)453-4880

♣ **4300　KYVE-TV - Channel 47**
1105 S. 15th Ave.　　　　　　　　　Phone: (509)452-4700
Yakima, WA 98902　　　　　　　　　**Fax: (509)452-4704**

YELM

◫ **4301　Nisqually Valley News**
207 Yelm Ave. W.
Box 597　　　　　　　　　　　　　Phone: (206)458-2681
Yelm, WA 98597　　　　　　　　　　**Fax: (206)458-5741**

WEST VIRGINIA

ARBOVALE

📖 **4302 American Journal of EEG Technology**
American Society of Electroneurodiagnostic Technologists, Inc.
PO Box 100 Phone: (304)456-4893
Arbovale, WV 24915 Fax: (304)456-3298
Subtitle: Journal of the American Society of Electroneurodiagnostic Technologists, Inc. **Founded:** 1961. **Frequency:** Quarterly. **Printing Method:** Offset. **Trim Size:** 6 x 9. **Cols./Page:** 1. **Key Personnel:** Janet Ghigo, Editor/Advertising Mgr. **ISSN:** 0002-9238. **Subscription:** $35; $45 other countries.

Ad Rates:			
BW:	$275	**Circulation:** Paid	‡3,379
4C:	$800	Non-paid	‡68

BECKLEY

♨ **4303 Beckley TeleCable**
113 1st Ave.
Box 1447
Beckley, WV 25802 Phone: (304)252-6358
Owner: TeleCable Corp. **Founded:** 1964. **Cities Served:** Fayette and Raleigh counties.

♨ **4304 WAXS-FM - 94.1**
PO Box 1127 **Phone: (304)877-5592**
Beckley, WV **25802-1127** **Fax: (304)877-5289**

♨ **4305 WJLS-FM - 99.5**
Box A-B Phone: (304)253-7311
Beckley, WV 25801 **Fax: (304)253-3466**

♨ **4306 WTNJ-FM - 105.9**
PO Box 1127 **Phone: (304)255-5221**
Beckley, WV 25801-1127 Fax: (304)877-5289

CHARLESTON

♨ **4307 Capital Cablevision**
209 Broad St.
Box 2673 Phone: (304)345-8483
Charleston, WV 25301 Fax: (304)357-6737
Owner: American TV & Communications Corp. **Founded:** 1966. **Cities Served:** Kanawha County, Dunbar, Institute, Ruthdale, and South Charleston, WV.

♨ **4308 WVEP-FM - 88.9**
600 Capitol St.
Charleston, WV 25301 Phone: (304)348-3239
Format: Classical;News;Jazz. **Network(s):** National Public Radio (NPR); American Public Radio (APR). **Owner:** West Virginia Educational Broadcasting Authority. **Founded:** 1987. **Operating Hours:** Continuous. **Key Personnel:** Barbara S. Herrick, Gen. Mgr.; Jeanne Fisher, Program Dir.; Francis Fisher, Engineering Dir.; Andy Ridenour, Exec. Producer; Keith E. Davis, Business Mgr. **Wattage:** 3600. **Ad Rates:** Noncommercial. **Additional Contact Information:** (304)348-3000.

♨ **4309 WVNP-FM - 89.9**
600 Capitol St.
Charleston, WV 25301 Phone: (304)348-3239
Format: Classical;News;Jazz. **Network(s):** National Public Radio (NPR); American Public Radio (APR). **Owner:** West Virginia Educational Broadcasting Authority. **Founded:** 1981. **Operating Hours:** Continuous. **Key Personnel:** Barbara S. Herrick, Gen. Mgr.; Jeanne Fisher, Program Dir.; Francis Fisher, Engineering Dir.; Andy Ridenour, Exec. Producer; Keith E. Davis, Business Mgr. **Wattage:** 2500. **Ad Rates:** Noncommercial. **Additional Contact Information:** (304)348-3000.

♨ **4310 WVPB-FM - 91.7**
600 Capitol St.
Charleston, WV 25301 Phone: (304)348-3239
Format: Classical;News;Jazz. **Network(s):** National Public Radio (NPR); American Public Radio (APR). **Owner:** West Virginia Educational Broadcasting Authority. **Founded:** 1974. **Operating Hours:** Continuous. **Key Personnel:** Barbara S. Herrick, Gen. Mgr.; Jeanne Fisher, Program Dir.; Francis Fisher, Engineering Dir.; Andy Ridenour, Exec. Producer; Keith E. Davis, Business Mgr. **Wattage:** 10,500. **Ad Rates:** Noncommercial. **Additional Contact Information:** (304)348-3000.

ELKINS

♨ **4311 WDNE-AM - 1240**
Washington & Davis Sts.
PO Box 1337 Phone: (304)636-1300
Elkins, WV 26241 **Fax: (203)636-1300**

GRAFTON

♨ **4312 WTBZ-AM - 1260**
PO Box 2 Phone: (304)265-2000
Grafton, WV 26354 **Fax: (304)265-0972**

♨ **4313 WTBZ-FM - 95.9**
PO Box 2 Phone: (304)265-2200
Grafton, WV 26354 **Fax: (304)265-0972**

Ad Rates: GLR = general line rate; BW = one-time black & white page rate; 4C = one-time four color page rate; SAU = standard advertising unit rate; CNU = Canadian newspaper advertising unit rate; PCI = per column inch rate.
Circulation: ★ = ABC; △ = BPA; ◆ = CAC; ● = CCAB; □ = VAC; ⊕ = PO Statement; ‡ = Publisher's Report; Boldface figures = sworn; Light figures = estimated.
Entry type: 📖 = Print; ♨ = Broadcast.

HUNTINGTON

4314 Century Huntington Co.
31 W. 6th Ave.
Box 7638   Phone: (304)522-8226
Huntington, WV 25777   Fax: (304)523-5493
Owner: Century Communications Corp. **Founded:** 1972. **Cities Served:** Cabell County, Barboursville, East Pea Ridge, Lesage, and West Pea Ridge, WV.

4315 WMUL-FM - 88.1
Marshall University
400 Hal Greer Blvd.   Phone: (304)696-6640
Huntington, WV 25755-2635   **Fax: (304)696-3333**

KINGWOOD

4316 WFSP-AM - 1560
Rte. 7 W.
PO Box 567   Phone: (304)329-1780
Kingwood, WV 26537-0567   **Fax: (304)329-1781**

MILTON

4317 Triax Cablevision USA
PO Box 400   Phone: (304)743-8176
Milton, WV 25541   Fax: (304)743-8035
Owner: Triax Communications Corp., 100 Fillmore, Ste. 600, Denver, CO 80206; (303)333-2424. **Founded:** 1982. **Formerly:** Cable Systems, USA; Charter Cable, Inc.. **Key Personnel:** Bob Legg, Regional Mgr.; Garry Lucas, Plant Mgr.; Maureen Minerd, Office Mgr.; Skip James, Construction Mgr.; Mary Shultz, Corporate CSR Trainer. **Cities Served:** Wayne, Mingo, Lincoln, Logan, McDowell, Mercer, Monroe, Cabell, Putnam and Nicholas, WV; Lawrence, Greenup, Pike, Martin, Letcher and Harlan, KY; Wise and Giles, VA: 42,330 subscribing households; 42 channels; 3 community access channels. **Additional Contact Information:** Toll-free: 800-874-2955; Toll-free billing 800-458-7429.

MORGANTOWN

4318 COST ENGINEERING
American Assn. of Cost Engineers
PO Box 1557   Phone: (304)296-8444
Morgantown, WV 26507-1557   **Fax: (304)296-5281**

4319 WNPB-TV - Channel 24
Box TV-24   Phone: (304)293-6511
Morgantown, WV 26507-1316   **Fax: (304)293-2642**

MULLENS

4320 WPMW-FM - 92.7
14 Moran Ave.
PO Box 488   Phone: (304)294-4405
Mullens, WV 25882-0014   **Fax: (304)294-0520**

PHILIPPI

4321 WQAB-FM - 91.3
Withers-Branddon hall
Alderson-Broaddus College
Box 1428   **Phone: (304)457-2916**
Philippi, WV 26416   **Fax: (304)457-1700**

PRINCETON

4322 Princeton Times
Lincoln Publishing West Virginia, Inc.
850 Mercer St.
PO Box 1199   Phone: (304)425-8191
Princeton, WV 24740   **Fax: (304)487-1632**

RANSON

4323 C/R TV Cable Inc.
302 N. Mildred St.   Phone: (304)725-9185
Ranson, WV 25438   **Fax: (304)725-0930**

RIPLEY

4324 WCEF-FM - 98.3
Box 798   Phone: (304)372-9800
Ripley, WV 25271   Fax: (304)372-9811
Format: Contemporary Country. **Owner:** McWhorter Communications Corp. **Founded:** 1981. **Operating Hours:** Continuous. **Key Personnel:** Ric Shannon, Gen. Mgr.; Rich Lacey, Program Dir.; Lois Casto, Gen. Sales Mgr. **Wattage:** 3000. **Ad Rates:** $5-$9.25 for 30 seconds; $6-$11.50 for 60 seconds.

SISTERSVILLE

4325 Tyler County Journal & Sports Review
Ogden Newspapers, Inc.
720 Wells St.
PO Box 191   Phone: (304)652-4141
Sistersville, WV 26175   **Fax: (304)652-1454**

4326 Tyler Star-News
Ogden Newspapers, Inc.
720 Wells St.
PO Box 191   Phone: (304)652-4141
Sistersville, WV 26175   **Fax: (304)652-1454**

SUMMERSVILLE

4327 WCWV-FM - 92.9
713 Main St.   Phone: (304)872-5202
Summersville, WV 26651   **Fax: (304)872-6904**

SUTTON

4328 WCKA-FM - 97.1
189A Main St.
Sutton, WV 26601   Phone: (304)765-7373
Format: Middle-of-the-Road (MOR). **Owner:** Mid-State Broadcasting Corp. **Founded:** 1987. **Operating Hours:** Continuous. **Key Personnel:** Jim Milliken, Gen.; Lisa Mace, Station Mgr. **Wattage:** 25,000.

4329 WSGB-AM - 1490
189A Main St.
Sutton, WV 26601   Phone: (304)765-7373
Format: Country. **Owner:** Mid-State Broadcasting Corp. **Founded:** 1964. **Operating Hours:** Continuous. **Key Personnel:** Lisa Mace, Station Mgr. **Wattage:** 1000.

WEIRTON

4330 WEIR-AM - 1430
PO Box 1430   Phone: (304)723-1430
Weirton, WV 26062   **Fax: (614)266-6648**

WEST LIBERTY

4331 The Trumpet
West Liberty State College
                                           Phone: (304)336-8213
West Liberty, WV 26074   **Fax: (304)336-8323**

WEST UNION

4332 Blues Revue Quarterly
Rte. 2, Box 118
West Union, WV 26456   Phone: (304)782-1971
Magazine reporting on acoustic and traditional blues. **Founded:** 1991. **Frequency:** Quarterly. **Trim Size:** 8 1/2 x 11. **Cols./Page:** 3. **Key Personnel:** Bob Vorel, Editor and Publisher. **Subscription:** $16. $4 single issue.
Ad Rates: BW: $445   **Circulation:** Paid 8,000

WHEELING

4333 TCI of West Virginia, Inc.
2184 National Rd.
Box 2078
Wheeling, WV 26003-5297   Phone: (304)242-5600
Owner: Tele-Communications, Inc. **Founded:** 1952. **Cities Served:** Marshall and Ohio counties, WV and Belmont County, OH.

WISCONSIN

AMERY

♨ 4334 WXCE-AM - 1260
Rte. 4, Box 1260
Amery, WI 54001
Phone: (715)268-7185
Fax: (715)268-7187

ANTIGO

♨ 4335 WATK-AM - 900
Hwy. 45 S., Box 509
Antigo, WI 54409
Phone: (715)623-4124
Format: Country. **Network(s):** Unistar. **Owner:** Ad-Mark Communications, at above address. **Founded:** 1948. **Operating Hours:** Continuous. **Key Personnel:** Jeff Wagner, V.P./Gen. Mgr.; Shaughn Novy, Sales and Marketing Dir.; Bill Berg, Sales Mgr.; Jim Greve, News Dir.; Al Higgins, Program Dir. **Wattage:** 250 day; 203 night. **Ad Rates:** $3.75-$9 for 30 seconds; $5.25-$12.60 for 60 seconds.

APPLETON

♨ 4336 Cablevision of Appleton
1620 Lawe St.
Box 2759
Appleton, WI 54913
Phone: (414)738-3160
Fax: (414)749-0618
Owner: American TV & Communications Corp. **Founded:** 1973. **Cities Served:** Calumet, Outagamie, and Winnebago counties.

♨ 4337 WEMI-FM - 100.1
1909 W. 2nd St.
Appleton, WI 54914
Phone: (414)749-9456
Fax: (414)749-0474

BELOIT

♨ 4338 Beloit Cablevision
1837 Park Ave.
Box 779
Beloit, WI 53511
Phone: (608)365-9555
Owner: American TV & Communications Corp. **Founded:** 1968. **Cities Served:** Winnebago County, Rockton, and South Beloit, IL; Rock County and Beloit Twp., WI.

BRODHEAD

▢ 4339 Independent-Register
922 Exchange St.
Brodhead, WI 53520
Phone: (608)897-2193
Fax: (608)897-4137

CADOTT

▢ 4340 Cadott Sentinel
Box 76
Cadott, WI 54727
Phone: (715)289-4978
Fax: (715)239-6688

CHILTON

▢ 4341 The Badger Sportsman
19 E. Main St.
Chilton, WI 53014
Phone: (414)849-7036
Fax: (414)849-4651

▢ 4342 Calumet County Shopper
19 E. Main St.
Chilton, WI 53014
Phone: (414)849-7036
Fax: (414)849-4651

♨ 4343 WMBE-AM - 1530
PO Box 30
205 E. Grand St.
Chilton, WI 53014
Phone: (414)849-7186

CLINTONVILLE

▢ 4344 Clintonville Shopper's Guide
17 9th St.
PO Box 330
Clintonville, WI 54929
Phone: (715)823-3107
Fax: (715)823-1364

♨ 4345 WFCL-AM - 1380
33 E. 3rd St.
Clintonville, WI 54929
Phone: (715)823-5128
Fax: (715)823-1367

♨ 4346 WJMQ-FM - 92.3
33 E. 3rd St.
Clintonville, WI 54929
Phone: (715)823-5128
Fax: (715)823-1367

CORNELL

▢ 4347 T.J.'s Community Bulletin
121 Main St.
PO Box 546
Cornell, WI 54732
Phone: (715)239-6688
Fax: (715)239-6200
Ceased publication.

CUBA CITY

▢ 4348 Tri-County Press
Tri-County Press Inc.
301 S. Main St.
PO Box 869
Cuba City, WI 53807-0869
Phone: (608)744-2107
Fax: (608)744-2151

DE PERE

♒ **4349 WJLW-FM - 95.9**
133 N. Superior St.
De Pere, WI 54115   Phone: (414)336-3696

DODGEVILLE

♒ **4350 WDMP-AM - 810**
PO Box 58   Phone: (608)935-2302
Dodgeville, WI 53533   **Fax: (608)935-3464**

♒ **4351 WDMP-FM - 99.3**
PO Box 58   Phone: (608)935-2302
Dodgeville, WI 53533   **Fax: (608)935-3464**

DURAND

♒ **4352 WRDN-AM - 1430**
300 W. Main
Box 208   Phone: (715)672-8989
Durand, WI 54736   **Fax: (715)672-4622**

EAU CLAIRE

♒ **4353 Wisconsin CATV**
2207 Heimstead Rd.
Box 125   Phone: (715)834-3151
Eau Claire, WI 54703   Fax: (715)836-8591
Owner: Northern Lakes Cable TV. **Founded:** 1961. **Cities Served:**
Chippewa, Dunn, Eau Claire, and Outagamie counties, WI.

ELROY

📖 **4354 Tribune Keystone**
249 Main St.   Phone: (608)462-8224
Elroy, WI 53929   **Fax: (608)847-6224**

FOND DU LAC

📖 **4355 Cooking For Profit**
C P Publishing, Inc.
104 S. Main St., Ste. 717
PO Box 267   Phone: (414)923-3700
Fond du Lac, WI 54936-0267   Fax: (414)923-6805

♒ **4356 Star Cablevision**
254 Winnebago Dr.
Box 1167   Phone: (414)923-4390
Fond du Lac, WI 54935   Fax: (414)923-4369
Owner: Star Cablevision Group. **Founded:** 1979. **Cities Served:** Fond
du Lac County, WI.

FORT ATKINSON

📖 **4357 Equipment Today**
Johnson Hill Press, Inc.
1233 Janesville Ave.   Phone: (414)563-6388
Fort Atkinson, WI 53538   **Fax: (414)563-1699**

📖 **4358 Pro**
Johnson Hill Press, Inc.
1233 Janesville Ave.   Phone: (414)563-6388
Fort Atkinson, WI 53538   **Fax: (414)563-1701**

GAYS MILLS

📖 **4359 Crawford County Independent Scout**
Kirkland Newpapers, Inc.
PO Box 188   Phone: (608)375-4458
Gays Mills, WI 54631   Fax: (608)375-2369

GREEN BAY

📖 **4360 Green Bay Press-Gazette**
435 E. Walnut
PO Box 19430   Phone: (414)435-4411
Green Bay, WI 54307-9430   **Fax: (414)431-8499**

📖 **4361 Musky Hunter**
ESOX Publishing, Inc.
2632 S. Packerland Dr., Ste. 10   Phone: (414)496-0334
Green Bay, WI 54313   **Fax: (414)496-0332**

♒ **4362 WPNE-TV - Channel 38**
3319 W. Beltline Hwy.   **Phone: (608)264-9600**
Madison, WI 53711   **Fax: (608)264-9622**

GREENDALE

📖 **4363 Country Woman**
Reiman Publications
5400 S. 60 St.
Greendale, WI 53129   Phone: (414)423-0100

📖 **4364 Woman Bowler**
Women's International Bowling Congress
5301 S. 76th St.   Phone: (414)421-9000
Greendale, WI 53129-1191   **Fax: (414)421-3013**

GREENFIELD

♒ **4365 Viacom Cablevision**
5475 W. Abbott Ave.
Greenfield, WI 53220   Phone: (414)282-6300
Owner: Viacom Cable. **Founded:** 1982. **Cities Served:** Milwaukee
County, WI.

HAYWARD

📖 **4366 News from Indian Country**
Indian Country Communications, Inc.
Rte. 2, Box 2900 A   Phone: (715)634-5226
Hayward, WI 54843   **Fax: (715)634-3243**

HUDSON

📖 **4367 Hot Sheet Shopper**
226 Locust St.
PO Box 147   Phone: (715)386-9333
Hudson, WI 54016   **Fax: (715)386-9891**

📖 **4368 Hudson Star-Observer**
226 Locust St.
PO Box 147   Phone: (715)386-9333
Hudson, WI 54016   **Fax: (715)386-9891**

IOLA

📖 **4369 Camping and RV Magazine**
PO Box 36
Iola, WI 54945-0036   **Phone: (715)445-4306**

📖 **4370 Muscle Car and Truck Buyer's Guide**
Krause Publications, Inc.
700 E. State St.
Iola, WI 54900
Ceased publication.

📖 **4371 Superstar and Rookie Special**
Krause Publications, Inc.
700 E. State St.
Iola, WI 10020-1393
Sports magazine. **Frequency:** 6x/yr. **Key Personnel:** Steve Ellingboe,
Editor; Kit Kiefer, Publisher. **Subscription:** $3.50 single issue.
Circulation: (Not Reported)

JANESVILLE

📖 **4372 The Janesville Sunday Messenger**
Community Shoppers, Inc.
1506 Creston Park Dr.   Phone: (608)752-0777
Janesville, WI 53545   Fax: (608)752-1007
Former Title: Messenger-Weekend

♣ **4373 Crown Cable**
Box 1127   Phone: (608)754-3644
Janesville, WI 53547   Fax: (608)756-8077
Owner: Crown Cable, Inc. **Founded:** 1966. **Cities Served:** Dane and Rock counties, Afton, Albion, Bradford, Clinton, Edgerton, Evansville, Fulton, Harmony, Indianford, Milton, Rock and Union townships, WI.

KENOSHA

♣ **4374 Jones Spacelink Ltd.**
Box 309   Phone: (414)656-8460
Kenosha, WI 53141-0309   Fax: (414)656-8490
Owner: Jones Spacelink, Inc., 9697 E. Mineral Ave., Englewood, CO 80112; (303)792-3111. **Founded:** 1984. **Formerly:** Cable TV Joint Fund 11; Total TV of Kenosha. **Key Personnel:** Jana L. Henthorn, Gen. Mgr.; Michael Love, Operations Mgr.; Scott Durand, Marketing Mgr.; Jeff Mitka, Advertising Sales Mgr.; Tori Oberdorf, Customer Sales Mgr.; Shane Wagner, Engineering Mgr. **Cities Served:** Kenosha, WI: 22,000 subscribing households; 55 channels; 4 community access channels; 20 hours per week of community access programming. Lake Geneva, WI: 2,500 subscribing households; 37 channels. Ripon, WI: 2,200 subscribing households; 37 channels; 1 community access channel. Also serves Somers, Pleasant Prairie, Geneva, Linn, and Lyons, WI.

KIEL

📖 **4375 Kiel Tri-County Record**
DELTA Publications
627 7th St.   Phone: (414)894-2828
Kiel, WI 53042   Fax: (414)894-2161

LA CROSSE

♣ **4376 WestMarc Cable Group**
620 Cass St.
Box 758
La Crosse, WI 54602-0758   Phone: (608)784-9200
Owner: Tele-Communications, Inc. **Founded:** 1961. **Cities Served:** LaCrosse County, WI and Houston County, MN.

♣ **4377 WKBH-FM - 105.5**
PO Box 1624   **Phone: (608)784-1570**
La Crosse, WI 54602-1624   Fax: (608)526-6813

♣ **4378 WLSU-FM - 88.9**
1725 State St.   Phone: (608)785-8380
La Crosse, WI 54601   **Fax: (608)782-5575**

LADYSMITH

♣ **4379 WLDY-AM - 1340**
PO Box 351
Ladysmith, WI 54848-0351   Phone: (715)532-5588

♣ **4380 WLDY-FM - 93.1**
PO Box 351
Ladysmith, WI 54848-0351   Phone: (715)532-5588

LITTLE CHUTE

📖 **4381 The Tattler**
530 Pine St.   **Phone: (414)788-2929**
Little Chute, WI 54140-1895   Fax: (414)766-4736

MADISON

📖 **4382 Athletic Business**
Athletic Business Publications, Inc.
1846 Hoffman St.   Phone: (608)249-0186
Madison, WI 53704   Fax: (608)249-1153

📖 **4383 Hardwood Floors**
Athletic Business Publications, Inc.
1846 Hoffman St.   Phone: (608)249-0186
Madison, WI 53704   Fax: (608)249-1153

📖 **4384 Isthmus**
101 King St.   Phone: (608)251-5627
Madison, WI 53703   Fax: (608)251-2165

📖 **4385 Italica**
American Assn. of Teachers of Italian
University of Wisconsin   Phone: (608)262-4076
Madison, WI 53706   **Fax: (608)262-4747**

📖 **4386 The Journal of Aesthetics and Art Criticism**
University of Wisconsin Press
114 N. Murray St.   **Phone: (608)262-4952**
Madison, WI 53715   Fax: (608)262-7560

📖 **4387 Journal of Extension**
Extension Journal, Inc.
432 N. Lake St.   Phone: (608)262-1974
Madison, WI 53706   **Fax: (608)265-3459**

📖 **4388 Land Economics**
University of Wisconsin Press
University of Wisconsin
427 Lorch St., Rm. 109   Phone: (608)262-2480
Madison, WI 53706   Fax: (608)262-4376

📖 **4389 Monatshefte**
University of Wisconsin Press
114 N. Murray St.   **Phone: (608)262-4952**
Madison, WI 53715   Fax: (608)262-7560

📖 **4390 Of A Like Mind**
Reformed Congregation
Box 6021
Madison, WI 53716   Phone: (608)255-5092
Newspaper for "spiritual womyn." Contains articles, reviews, and networking section. **Frequency:** Quarterly. **Key Personnel:** Lynnie Levy, Editor. **ISSN:** 0892-5984. **Subscription:** $13-$33; $21 institutions; $23-$43 other countries. $3 single issue.
Circulation: (Not Reported)

📖 **4391 Restoration and Management Notes**
114 N. Murray St.   Phone: (608)262-4952
Madison, WI 53715   Fax: (608)262-7560
Journal covering ecological restoration. **Founded:** 1981. **Frequency:** 2x/yr. **Trim Size:** 8 1/2 x 11. **ISSN:** 0733-0707. **Subscription:** $17; $48 institutions.
Circulation: Paid 2,400
Advertising accepted; contact publisher for rates.

📖 **4392 Today's Music Educator**
Drum Corps Sights and Sounds, Inc.
2802 International Ln., Ste. 112
PO Box 8052   Phone: (608)241-2292
Madison, WI 53708-8052   Fax: (608)241-4974
Specialized music magazine. **Founded:** 1988. **Frequency:** Quarterly. **Printing Method:** Web offset. **Trim Size:** 8 3/8 x 10 7/8. **Cols./Page:** 3. **Col. Width:** 2 1/4 in. **Col. Depth:** 10 in. **Key Personnel:** Steve Vickers, Editor and Publisher. **Subscription:** $12. $4 single issue.
Ad Rates: BW: $1,350   **Circulation:** ‡25,000
              4C: $1,750

📖 **4393 Wisconsin Architect**
Wisconsin Society of Architects
321 S. Hamilton   Phone: (608)257-8477
Madison, WI 53703-3606   **Fax: (608)257-0242**

📖 **4394 Wisconsin Professional Engineer**
Wisconsin Society of Professional Engineers
6425 Odana Rd., Ste. D   Phone: (608)274-8555
Madison, WI 53719-1199   **Fax: (608)274-8494**

◫ **4395 Wisconsin Restaurateur**
Wisconsin Restaurant Assn.
31 S. Henry, Ste. 300   Phone: (608)251-3663
Madison, WI 53703   Fax: (608)251-3666

◫ **4396 The Wisconsin Taxpayer**
Wisconsin Taxpayer Alliance
335 W. Wilson St.
Madison, WI 53703-3694   Phone: (608)255-4581
Magazine providing information on state and local governments and taxation.**Founded:** 1933. **Frequency:** 6x/yr. **Printing Method:** Offset press. **Trim Size:** 6 x 9. **Cols./Page:** 1. **Col. Width:** 13 picas. **Col. Depth:** 42 or 45 picas. **Key Personnel:** James R. Morgan, Pres.; Beulah M. Poulter, Operations Dir. **USPS:** 688-800. **Subscription:** $6.50.
           Circulation: ‡9,000
           Non-paid ‡700

Advertising not accepted.

♣ **4397 TCI Cablevision of Wisconsin**
5723 Tokay Blvd.
Madison, WI 53719-1284   Phone: (608)274-3822
Owner: Tele-Communications, Inc. **Founded:** 1973. **Cities Served:** Columbia County, Dane County, Jefferson County, Arlington, Blooming Grove, Cambridge, Christiana, Cross Plains, De Forest, Deerfield, Dunkirk, Dunn, Madison, Madison University, Maple Bluff, McFarland, Medina, Middleton, Monona, Oakland, Shorewood Hills, Stoughton, Sun Prairie, University of Wisconsin, Westport, and Windsor, WI.

MANITOWOC

♣ **4398 WCUB-AM - 980**
1915 Mirro Dr.
PO Box 1990   **Phone: (414)683-6800**
Manitowoc, WI 54221-1990   **Fax: (414)683-6807**

♣ **4399 WLTU-FM - 92.1**
1915 Mirro Dr.
PO Box 1990   **Phone: (414)683-6800**
Manitowoc, WI 54221-1990   **Fax: (414)683-6807**

MARINETTE

♣ **4400 WCJL-AM - 1300**
844 Pierce Ave.
PO Box 689   Phone: (715)732-4444
Marinette, WI 54143   Fax: (715)732-4446
Format: Country. **Network(s):** Independent. **Owner:** CJL Broadcasting, Inc., at above address. **Founded:** 1969. **Formerly:** WLOT-AM (1978). **Operating Hours:** Continuous. **Key Personnel:** Jim Callow, Gen. Mgr.; Ken Fronsee, Program Dir. **Wattage:** 1000. **Ad Rates:** $3.75-$6.75 for 30 seconds.

MAYVILLE

◫ **4401 Ad Power**
Wisconsin Free Press
PO Box 271   Phone: (414)387-2211
Mayville, WI 53050-0271   Fax: (414)387-5515
Shopping guide. **Founded:** 1990. **Frequency:** Monthly. **Printing Method:** Web offset. **Trim Size:** 11 1/4 x 17. **Cols./Page:** 6. **Col. Width:** 10 picas. **Col. Depth:** 16 in. **Subscription:** Free.
Ad Rates: BW: $199   **Circulation:** Free 11,100
        PCI: $4.30

MIDDLETON

◫ **4402 Cheese Market News**
Delta Communications
PO Box 244   **Phone: (608)831-6002**
Middleton, WI 53562   **Fax: (608)831-1004**

◫ **4403 Journal of the Wisconsin Optometric Association**
Wisconsin Optometric Assn.
PO Box 584   Phone: (608)836-0678
Middleton, WI 53562   Fax: (608)836-0858
Ceased publication.

MILWAUKEE

◫ **4404 American Academy of Allergy and Immunology–News and Notes**
American Academy of Allergy and Immunology
611 E. Wells St.   Phone: (414)272-6071
Milwaukee, WI 53202   Fax: (414)276-3349
Magazine for members of the American Academy of Allergy and Immunology. **Frequency:** Quarterly. **Printing Method:** Offset. **Key Personnel:** Sara E. Kaluzny, Managing Editor. **ISSN:** 0899-7489.
Ad Rates: BW: $670   **Circulation:** 5,000

◫ **4405 Families in Society**
Families International, Inc.
11700 W. Lake Park Dr.   Phone: (414)359-1040
Milwaukee, WI 53224   Fax: (414)359-1074

◫ **4406 Hag Rag**
PO Box 93243
Milwaukee, WI 53203   Phone: (414)372-3330
Journal containing radical lesbian feminist news, analysis, reviews, political commentary, theory, letters, and calendar of events. **Subtitle:** Intergalactic Lesbian Feminist Press. **Founded:** 1986. **Frequency:** 6x/yr. **Trim Size:** 8 3/8 x 10 3/4. **Cols./Page:** 2. **Col. Width:** 3 3/8 in. **Col. Depth:** 9 1/2 in. **Subscription:** $10; $15 Canada and Mexico; $20 institutions; $25 other countries.
Ad Rates: GLR: $1   Circulation: ‡700
        BW: $100

◫ **4407 Living Church**
Living Church Foundation, Inc.
816 E. Juneau Ave.   Phone: (414)276-5420
Milwaukee, WI 53202   **Fax: (414)276-7483**

◫ **4408 Marquette Magazine**
Marquette University
1212 W. Wisconsin Ave   Phone: (414)288-6712
Milwaukee, WI 53233   Fax: (414)288-6519
Alumni magazine. **Frequency:** Quarterly. **Printing Method:** Web offset. **Key Personnel:** Cathy Jakicic, Editor. **Subscription:** Free.
           Circulation: Non-paid ‡92,000

Advertising not accepted.

◫ **4409 Obscure Publications & Video**
Jim Romenesko
PO Box 1334
Milwaukee, WI 53201   Phone: (414)257-2339
Review magazine. **Founded:** 1989. **Frequency:** 6x/yr. **Printing Method:** Offset. **Trim Size:** 8 1/2 x 11. **Key Personnel:** Jim Romenesko, Editor and Publisher. **Subscription:** $2 single issue.
           Circulation: 500

◫ **4410 Outpost Exchange**
102 E. Capitol Dr.   Phone: (414)964-7789
Milwaukee, WI 53212   **Fax: (414)961-1961**

◫ **4411 Renascence**
Marquette University
Brooks Hall, Rm. 200   **Phone: (414)288-1564**
Milwaukee, WI 53233   **Fax: (414)288-7444**

◫ **4412 Reunions Magazine**
PO Box 11727   Phone: (414)263-4567
Milwaukee, WI 53211-0727   Fax: (414)263-6331
Magazine. **Founded:** 1990. **Frequency:** Quarterly. **Printing Method:** Offset. **Trim Size:** 8 1/2 x 11. **Key Personnel:** Edith Wagner, Publisher; Cynthia Crigler, Art Dir.; Carol Burns, Copy Editor. **Subscription:** $24.
Ad Rates: BW: $1,000   Circulation: Paid ‡2,000
        4C: $1,500   Non-paid ‡2,000

◫ **4413 Shepherd Express**
Alternative Publications, Inc.
1123 N. Water St.   Phone: (414)276-2222
Milwaukee, WI 53202   Fax: (414)276-3312
Community newspaper. **Founded:** 1982. **Frequency:** Weekly (Thurs.). **Printing Method:** Offset. **Trim Size:** 10 x 14 3/4. **Cols./Page:** 4. **Col. Width:** 2 3/8 in. **Key Personnel:** Doug Hissom, Editor; Martin Genz,

Publisher; Dane Claussen, Assoc. Publisher/Advertising Dir.; Joe Porubcan, Gen. Mgr. **Subscription:** Free; $25 (mail).

Ad Rates:	BW:	$1,000	Circulation: Free □33,319
	4C:	$1,375	Paid □241
	PCI:	$12.20	

MINERAL POINT

📖 4414 Democrat-Tribune
334 High St.   Phone: (608)987-2141
Mineral Point, WI 53565   **Fax: (608)935-9531**

MINOCQUA

🎤 4415 WMQA-AM - 1570
PO Box 96   **Phone: (715)356-9696**
Minocqua, WI 54548   Fax: (715)356-1977

🎤 4416 WMQA-FM - 96
PO Box 96   **Phone: (715)356-9696**
Minocqua, WI 54548   Fax: (715)356-1977

MUKWONAGO

📖 4417 Big Bend/Vernon Bulletin
Chief Publications
PO Box 204
Mukwonago, WI 53149   Phone: (414)363-4045
Shopper. **Frequency:** Weekly. **Printing Method:** Web offset. **Trim Size:** 17 1/2 x 11 1/2. **Cols./Page:** 6. **Col. Width:** 9.5 picas. **Col. Depth:** 16 1/4 in. **Key Personnel:** Ray DeVisser, Publisher; Ron Wirtz, Editor; Virginiz Kranz, Advertising Mgr. **Subscription:** Free.

Ad Rates:	BW:	$507.87	Circulation: Free ‡3,860
	4C:	$687.87	
	PCI:	$5.13	

📖 4418 HALES Corners Sunrise
Chief Publications
PO Box 204
Mukwonago, WI 53149   Phone: (414)363-4045
Ceased publication.

📖 4419 KMA Chief II
Chief Publications
PO Box 204
Mukwonago, WI 53149   Phone: (414)363-4045
Shopper. **Frequency:** Weekly. **Printing Method:** Web offset. **Trim Size:** 17 1/2 x 11 1/2. **Cols./Page:** 6. **Col. Width:** 9.5 picas. **Col. Depth:** 16 1/4 in. **Key Personnel:** Ray DeVisser, Publisher; Ron Wirtz, Editor; Virginia Kranz, Advertising Mgr. **Subscription:** Free.

Ad Rates:	BW:	$507.87	Circulation: Free ‡8,390
	4C:	$687.87	
	PCI:	$5.13	

Formerly: Kettle Moraine Advertiser.

📖 4420 Muskego Times Record
Chief Publications
PO Box 204
Mukwonago, WI 53149   Phone: (414)363-4045
Shopping guide. **Frequency:** Weekly. **Printing Method:** Web offset. **Trim Size:** 17 1/2 x 11 1/2. **Cols./Page:** 6. **Col. Width:** 9.5 picas. **Col. Depth:** 16 1/4 in.

Ad Rates:	BW:	$507.87	Circulation: Free ‡8,400
	4C:	$687.87	
	PCI:	$5.13	

NEILLSVILLE

🎤 4421 WCCN-AM - 1370
1201 Division St.   Phone: (715)743-2222
Neillsville, WI 54456   Fax: (715)743-2288
Format: Middle-of-the-Road (MOR). **Network(s):** AP; Satellite Music. **Owner:** Central Wisconsin Broadcasting Inc. **Founded:** 1957. **Operating Hours:** Sunrise-sunset. **Key Personnel:** J. Kevin Grad, Pres./Gen.

Mgr./Sales Mgr.; Peggy Grad, V.P. **Wattage:** 5000. **Ad Rates:** $5.60-$8.40 for 30 seconds;$7.50-$9.50 for 60 seconds.

🎤 4422 WCCN-FM - 107.5
1201 Division St.   Phone: (715)743-2222
Neillsville, WI 54446   Fax: (715)743-2288
Format: Classic Rock. **Network(s):** AP; Satellite Music. **Owner:** Central Wisconsin Broadcasting Inc. **Founded:** 1964. **Operating Hours:** Continuous. **Key Personnel:** J. Kevin Grad, Pres./Gen. Mgr./Sales Mgr.; Peggy Grad, V.P. **Wattage:** 100,000. **Ad Rates:** $5.60-$8.40 for 30 seconds; $7.50-$9.50 for 60 seconds.

NEW HOLSTEIN

📖 4423 Tempo
Delta Publications, Inc.
1803 Park Ave.   Phone: (414)898-4276
New Holstein, WI 53061   Fax: (414)894-2161
Shopping guide. **Founded:** 1987. **Frequency:** Weekly. **Printing Method:** Web offset. **Trim Size:** 15 x 21 1/4. **Cols./Page:** 9. **Col. Width:** 1 5/8 in. **Key Personnel:** Mark Sherry Publisher; Mike Mathes, Publisher; Joe Mathes, Advertising Mgr.

Ad Rates:	BW:	$351	Circulation: Free ‡18,200
	4C:	$650	
	PCI:	$4.40	

OCONTO FALLS

📖 4424 The Bonus Paper
PO Box 128   Phone: (414)846-3427
Oconto Falls, WI 54154   **Fax: (414)846-3430**

📖 4425 Oconto County Times-Herald
PO Box 128   Phone: (414)846-3427
Oconto Falls, WI 54154   **Fax: (414)846-3430**

ONALASKA

🎤 4426 Crown Cable Wisconsin, Inc.
314 Main St.
Box 279   Phone: (608)783-5255
Onalaska, WI 54650   Fax: (608)783-7033
Owner: Crown Cable Inc. **Founded:** 1973. **Cities Served:** La Cross County, Bangor, Barre, Campbell, Hamilton, Holland, Holmen, La Cross, Medary, Onalaska, and West Salem, WI.

ORFORDVILLE

📖 4427 Orfordville Journal and Footville News
124 E. Spring St.   Phone: (608)879-2211
Orfordville, WI 53576-0248   Fax: (608)879-2211

PALMYRA

📖 4428 Palmyra Enterprise
Coe Printers and Publishers
106 W. Main St.
PO Box M   **Phone: (414)495-2171**
Palmyra, WI 53156   Fax: (414)473-5635

PHILLIPS

📖 4429 The Extra Shopper
PO Box 170   Phone: (715)339-3036
Phillips, WI 54555   **Fax: (715)339-4300**

📖 4430 Phillips Bee
PO Box 170   Phone: (715)339-3036
Phillips, WI 54555   **Fax: (715)339-4300**

PLYMOUTH

📖 **4431 Sheboygan Falls News**
504 Broadway
PO Box 317   Phone: (414)467-6591
Plymouth, WI 53073   Fax: (414)893-5505

PORTAGE

📖 **4432 Daily Register**
Register Publishing Corp.
PO Box 470   Phone: (608)742-2111
Portage, WI 53901   Fax: (608)742-8346

POYNETTE

📖 **4433 Poynette Press**
125 N. Main   Phone: (608)635-2565
Poynette, WI 53955-0037   Fax: (608)846-9664

PRAIRIE DU CHIEN

🎙 **4434 Star Cablevision**
115 S. Marquette Rd.
Box 58
Prairie du Chien, WI 53821   Phone: (608)326-2211
Owner: Star Cablevision Group. **Founded:** 1968. **Cities Served:**
Allamakee County and Harper's Ferry, IA; Crawford County, Essman
Island, and Prairie du Chien Twp., WI.

PULASKI

📖 **4435 Miesiecznik Franciszkanski**
Franciscan Fathers
165 E. Pulaski St.   Phone: (414)822-5833
Pulaski, WI 54162   Fax: (414)822-5423

RACINE

🎙 **4436 Racine TeleCable Corp.**
5812 21st St.
Box 188
Racine, WI 53401   Phone: (414)637-9637
Owner: TeleCable Corp. **Founded:** 1970. **Cities Served:** Racine County, WI.

RANDOLPH

🎙 **4437 Peoples Broadband Communications System**
121 Williams St.   Phone: (414)326-5808
Randolph, WI 53956-0098   Fax: (414)326-4125

REEDSBURG

📖 **4438 Reedsburg Times-Press**
Sauk County Publishing
PO Box 269   Phone: (608)524-4336
Reedsburg, WI 53959-0269   Fax: (608)524-4337

RICHLAND CENTER

🎙 **4439 WRCO-AM - 1450**
2111 Bohmann Dr.
Box 529   Phone: (608)647-2111
Richland Center, WI 53581   Fax: (608)647-8025

🎙 **4440 WRCO-FM - 100.9**
2111 Bohmann Dr.
Box 529   Phone: (608)647-2111
Richland Center, WI 53581   Fax: (608)647-8025

RIVER FALLS

📖 **4441 River Falls Journal**
PO Box 25   Phone: (715)425-1561
River Falls, WI 54022   Fax: (715)425-5666

SHAWANO

🎙 **4442 WOWN-FM - 99.3**
1456 E. Green Bay St.   Phone: (715)524-2194
Shawano, WI 54166   Fax: (715)524-2196

🎙 **4443 WTCH-AM - 960**
1456 E. Green Bay St.   Phone: (715)524-2194
Shawano, WI 54166   Fax: (715)524-2196

SHEBOYGAN

🎙 **4444 Star Cablevision**
1623 Broadway
Sheboygan, WI 53081-5727   Phone: (414)457-9218
Owner: Star Cablevision Group. **Founded:** 1982. **Cities Served:**
Sheboygan County, WI.

🎙 **4445 WKTS-AM - 950**
1156 Union Ave.
Box 1045   Phone: (414)457-5561
Sheboygan, WI 53082-1045   Fax: (414)457-0950

SOUTH MILWAUKEE

📖 **4446 South Milwaukee Voice Graphic**
Community Newspapers
640 E. Ryan Rd.
PO Box 7   Phone: (414)768-5800
Oak Creek, WI 53154   Fax: (414)768-5837

SPARTA

📖 **4447 Monroe County Democrat**
Monroe County Publishers, Inc.
114 W. Oak St.   Phone: (608)269-3186
Sparta, WI 54656   Fax: (608)269-6876

📖 **4448 The Sparta Herald**
Monroe County Publishers, Inc.
114 W. Oak St.   Phone: (608)269-3186
Sparta, WI 54656   Fax: (608)269-6876

🎙 **4449 Marcus Cable Partners, LP**
PO Box 426
Sparta, WI 54660   Phone: (608)269-6776

🎙 **4450 WCOW-FM - 97.1**
113 W. Oak St.
PO Box 539   Phone: (608)269-3307
Sparta, WI 54656   Fax: (608)269-5170

🎙 **4451 WKLJ-AM - 1290**
113 W. Oak St.
PO Box 539   Phone: (608)269-3307
Sparta, WI 54656   Fax: (608)269-5170

STEVENS POINT

📖 **4452 Buyers' Guide**
71 Sunset Blvd.   Phone: (715)344-4700
Stevens Point, WI 54481   Fax: (715)344-5117
Shopper. **Founded:** 1981. **Frequency:** Weekly (Tues.). **Printing Method:**
Web offset. **Trim Size:** 10 1/4 x 14. **Cols./Page:** 4. **Col. Width:** 2 3/8 in.
Col. Depth: 196 agate lines. **Key Personnel:** Carl Ferrer, Gen. Mgr.;
Jim Anderson, Sales Rep. **Subscription:** Free.
Ad Rates: GLR: $1   **Circulation:** Free ‡23,000
                  BW: $547
                  4C: $917
                  PCI: $9.50
Circulation audited by CPVS.

📖 **4453 Horyzonty Weekly**
Artex Publishing Inc.
PO Box 202   Phone: (715)341-6959
Stevens Point, WI 54481   Fax: (715)341-6959

STRUM

☐ **4454 Ad-Delite**
Preston Press
17 5th Ave. N.
PO Box 278   Phone: (715)695-3401
Strum, WI 54770   **Fax: (715)695-3401**

SUN PRAIRIE

☐ **4455 The Advertiser**
112 Market St.   Phone: (608)837-2521
Sun Prairie, WI 53590   **Fax: (608)825-3053**

☐ **4456 The Star**
112 Market St.   Phone: (608)837-5161
Sun Prairie, WI 53590   **Fax: (608)825-3053**

SUSSEX

☐ **4457 Sports Card Review & Value Line**
William Paul Publishing, Inc.
PO Box 267   Phone: (414)246-7236
Sussex, WI 53089-0267   Fax: (414)246-9074
Magazine offering insider information. **Founded:** 1991. **Frequency:**
10x/yr. **Printing Method:** Web offset. **Trim Size:** 8 1/2 x 11 1/8. **Key
Personnel:** Jon Brecka, Editor and Publisher. **Subscription:** $19.95;
$14.95 (discounts subscription). $2.95 single issue.
Circulation: Non-paid 190,000
Advertising accepted; contact publisher for rates.

TOMAH

♠ **4458 WVCX-FM - 98.9**
PO Box 187   Phone: (608)372-2323
Tomah, WI 54660   **Fax: (414)935-3015**

WATERFORD

☐ **4459 The Waterford Post**
224A N. Milwaukee St.
PO Box 210   Phone: (414)534-4668
Waterford, WI 53185   Fax: (414)763-2238

WAUPUN

☐ **4460 Monday Marketeer**
PO Box 111   Phone: (414)398-2334
Waupun, WI 53963   **Fax: (414)324-8582**

WAUSAU

♠ **4461 WIFC-FM - 95.5**
602 Jefferson St.
PO Box 5595   Phone: (715)842-1672
Wausau, WI 54402-5595   **Fax: (715)848-3158**

♠ **4462 WSAU-AM - 550**
602 Jefferson St.
PO Box 5595   Phone: (715)842-1672
Wausau, WI 54402-5595   **Fax: (715)848-3158**

WAUWATOSA

☐ **4463 Bay Viewer**
Community News
PO Box 13155   Phone: (414)768-5800
Wauwatosa, WI 53213   **Fax: (414)768-5837**

WEST BEND

♠ **4464 WBWI-FM - 92.5**
303 E. Decorah Rd.
PO Box 933   Phone: (414)334-2344
West Bend, WI 53095   **Fax: (414)334-1512**

WHITEHALL

☐ **4465 Tri-County Tab**
1410 Main St.
Whitehall, WI 54773-0095   Phone: (715)538-4765
Shopping guide. **Founded:** 1977. **Frequency:** Weekly. **Printing Method:**
Web offset. **Trim Size:** 11 1/2 x 17. **Cols./Page:** 5. **Col. Width:** 11
picas. **Col. Depth:** 16 in. **Key Personnel:** Charles Gauger, Mgr.
Subscription: Free.
Ad Rates: BW: $356   **Circulation:** Free ‡13,980
                PCI: $4.45
Advertising accepted; contact publisher for rates.

WISCONSIN RAPIDS

☐ **4466 Wisconsin Rapids Buyers' Guide**
Buyers' Guide Group
PO Box 609   **Phone: (715)424-1230**
Waupaca, WI 54981   **Fax: (715)423-5070**

WYOMING

CASPER

♩ 4467 KCSP-FM - 90.3
1400 Kati Ln.
Casper, WY 82601   Phone: (307)265-5414

♩ 4468 TCI Cablevision of Casper
451 S. Durbin   Phone: (307)265-3136
Casper, WY 82601   Fax: (307)266-6821
Owner: Tele-Communications, Inc. **Founded:** 1953. **Key Personnel:**
Jeff Frankenberger, Mgr.; Brad Moore, Office Mgr.; John Miller,
Chief Engineer. **Cities Served:** Natrona County, Bar Nunn, Evansville,
Mills, Mountain View, and Paradise Valley, WY. 16,500 subscribing
households; 36 channels.

CHEYENNE

▦ 4469 Trader's Shopper's Guide
Graphic Media, Inc.
1001 E. Lincolnway   Phone: (307)634-8895
Cheyenne, WY 82001-4843   **Fax: (307)634-8530**

▦ 4470 Wingspan
Laramie County Community College
1400 E. College Dr.   Phone: (307)778-1304
Cheyenne, WY 82007   **Fax: (307)778-1399**

EVANSTON

▦ 4471 Uinta County Herald Shoppers Guide
PO Box 210   Phone: (307)789-6560
Evanston, WY 82930-0021   Fax: (307)789-2700
Shopping guide. **Founded:** 1989. **Frequency:** Weekly. **Printing Method:**
Offset. **Cols./Page:** 6. **Col. Width:** 12 picas. **Col. Depth:** 21 1/2 in. **Key**
Personnel: Keith R. Cerny, Publisher.
Ad Rates: BW: $890.10   **Circulation:** Free ‡7,700
          4C: $1,340.10
          SAU: $6.90

JACKSON

♩ 4472 KZJH-FM - 95.3
475 N. Cache St.
PO Box 2620   Phone: (307)733-1770
Jackson, WY 83001   **Fax: (307)733-4760**

LARAMIE

♩ 4473 KIMX-FM - 105.5
302 S. 2nd St., Ste. 202   Phone: (307)745-5208
Laramie, WY 82070   Fax: (307)745-3315

♩ 4474 TCI Cablevision of Wyoming
Box 640
Laramie, WY 82070-0640   Phone: (307)745-7333
Owner: Tele-Communication, Inc. **Founded:** 1954. **Cities Served:**
Albany County, WY.

LYMAN

▦ 4475 Home Office Opportunities
Deneb Publishing
PO Box 780   Phone: (307)786-4513
Lyman, WY 82937   Fax: (307)786-4513
Magazine for home business owners. **Founded:** 1989. **Frequency:** 6x/
yr. **Printing Method:** Web press. **Trim Size:** 6 1/2 x 10. **Cols./Page:** 2.
Col. Width: 2 6/8 in. **Col. Depth:** 9 in. **Key Personnel:** Diane
Wolverton, Editor. **ISSN:** 1059-0039. **Subscription:** $18. $2 single
issue.
Ad Rates: BW: $75   **Circulation:** Paid 300
          PCI: $6   Non-paid 200

MEDICINE BOW

▦ 4476 The Medicine Bow Post
PO Box 36   Phone: (307)379-2255
Medicine Bow, WY 82329   **Fax: (307)766-3812**

POWELL

♩ 4477 KPOW-AM - 1260
PO Box 968   **Phone: (307)754-5183**
Powell, WY 82435   **Fax: (307)754-9667**

RAWLINS

▦ 4478 Daily Times
Rawlins Newspapers, Inc.
6th & Buffalo
PO Box 370   Phone: (307)324-3411
Rawlins, WY 82301   **Fax: (307)324-2797**

SHERIDAN

♩ 4479 KWYO-AM - 1410
2 N. Main St., Ste. 207
PO Box 727
Sheridan, WY 82801   Phone: (307)674-4461

TORRINGTON

♟ 4480 KERM-FM - 98.3
R.R. 2, Box 40   Phone: (307)532-2158
Torrington, WY 82240   Fax: (307)532-2641

♟ 4481 KGOS-AM - 1490
Radio Rd.
R.R. No. 2, Box 40   Phone: (307)532-2158
Torrington, WY 82240   Fax: (307)532-2641

ALBERTA

AIRDRIE

4482 Calgary Rural Times
Box 3820
Airdrie, AB, Canada T4B 2B9
Phone: (403)948-7280
Fax: (403)233-7226
Community newspaper. **Frequency:** Weekly. **Subscription:** $27.
Circulation: (Not Reported)
Advertising accepted; contact publisher for rates. **Formerly:** Rocky View Times.

4483 Didsbury Chronicle
Box 3820
Airdrie, AB, Canada T4B 2B9
Phone: (403)335-4260
Ceased publication.

BANFF

4484 Bow Valley This Week
c/o Banff Crag & Canyon
223 Bear St.
Box 129
Banff, AB, Canada T0L 0C0
Phone: (403)762-2453
Fax: (403)762-5274

CALGARY

4485 Breakthrough! Quarterly Magazine
Aardvark Enterprises
204 Millbank Dr. SW
Calgary, AB, Canada T2Y 2H9
Phone: (403)256-4639

4486 Energy Processing/Canada
Nothern Star Communications Ltd.
1600-700 4 Ave. SW
Calgary, AB, Canada T2P 3J4
Phone: (403)263-6881
Fax: (403)263-6886

4487 Helicopters
Corvus Publishing Group Ltd.
158-1224 Aviation Pk. NE
Calgary, AB, Canada T2E 7E2
Phone: (403)275-9457
Fax: (403)275-3925

4488 Kerby News for Seniors
Trend Publications Ltd.
1324 11th Ave. SW, Ste. 309
Calgary, AB, Canada T3C 0M6
Phone: (403)228-9121
Fax: (403)229-3708
Magazine for mature consumers. **Founded:** 1984. **Frequency:** Monthly.
Printing Method: Web offset. **Trim Size:** 11 x 16. **Cols./Page:** 5. **Key**

Personnel: Elsie Hawksworth, Contact; Denis Burns, Contact. **Subscription:** $24.

Ad Rates:	GLR:	$2.59	**Circulation:** Paid ‡6,800
	BW:	$1,250	Non-paid ‡15,200
	4C:	$1,750	
	PCI:	$60	

4489 News for Seniors
Trend Publications Ltd.
1324 11th Ave. SW, Ste. 309
Calgary, AB, Canada T3C 0M6
Phone: (403)228-9121
Fax: (403)229-3708
Magazine for mature consumers. **Founded:** 1984. **Frequency:** Monthly.
Printing Method: Web offset. **Trim Size:** 11 x 16. **Cols./Page:** 5. **Col. Width:** 2 in. **Col. Depth:** 15 1/2 in. **Key Personnel:** Molly Good, Contact; Stephen Burns, Contact.

Ad Rates:	GLR:	$2.59	**Circulation:** Paid ‡6,500
	BW:	$1,250	Non-paid ‡18,500
	4C:	$1,750	
	PCI:	$60	

4490 Propane/Canada
Northern Star Communications Ltd.
1600-700 4th Ave. SW
Calgary, AB, Canada T2P 3J4
Phone: (403)263-6881
Fax: (403)263-2886

4491 Spirit of Ability
Trend Publications
1324 11th Ave. SW, Ste. 309
Calgary, AB, Canada T3C 0M6
Phone: (403)228-9121
Ceased publication.

4492 Wings Newsmagazine
Corvus Publishing Group Ltd.
158-1224 Aviation Pk. NE
Calgary, AB, Canada T2E 7E2
Phone: (403)275-9457
Fax: (403)275-3925

4493 CFCN-AM - 1060
Broadcast House
PO Box 7060, Sta. E
Calgary, AB, Canada T3C 3L9
Phone: (403)240-5800
Fax: (403)240-5801

4494 CFFR-AM - 660
2723 - 37th Ave. NE
Calgary, AB, Canada T1Y 5R8
Phone: (403)291-0000
Fax: (403)252-6690

4495 CJAY-FM - 92.1
Broadcast House
PO Box 2750, Sta. M
Calgary, AB, Canada T2P 4P8
Phone: (403)240-5850
Fax: (403)240-5801

4496 CJSW-FM - 90.9
MacEwan Hall, Rm. 127
2500 University Dr. NW
Calgary, AB, Canada T2N 1N4   **Phone: (403)220-3904**

CARDSTON

4497 Cardston Chronicle
PO Box 8   **Phone: (403)653-2222**
Cardston, AB, Canada T0K 0K0   **Fax: (403)653-2240**
Community newspaper. **Founded:** 1983. **Frequency:** Weekly. **Printing Method:** Web press. **Cols./Page:** 5. **Col. Width:** 11 picas. **Col. Depth:** 16 in. **Key Personnel:** Brad Flickinger, Owner. **Subscription:** $15; $32 in province; $64 other countries.

Ad Rates:	GLR:	$.53	Circulation: 1,503
	BW:	$590	
	PCI:	$7.42	

EDMONTON

4498 The ATA News
Alberta Teachers' Assn.
Barnett House
11010 142nd St.   **Phone: (403)453-2411**
Edmonton, AB, Canada T5N 2R1   **Fax: (403)455-6481**
Newspaper for the teachers' association in Alberta. **Founded:** 1965.
Frequency: 2x/mo. **Printing Method:** Web offset. **Trim Size:** 11 x 17.
Cols./Page: 5. **Col. Width:** 2 in. **ISSN:** 0001-267X.
    Circulation: Paid 40,500
Advertising accepted; contact publisher for rates.

4499 Canadian Slavonic Papers/Revue Canadienne des Slavistes
University of Alberta
Department of Comparative Literature
347 Arts Bldg.   **Phone: (403)492-2566**
Edmonton, AB, Canada T6G 2E6   **Fax: (403)492-5086**

4500 The Edmonton Sun
The Toronto Sun Publishing Corp.
250, 4990-92nd Ave.   **Phone: (403)468-0100**
Edmonton, AB, Canada T6B 3A1   **Fax: (403)468-0139**

4501 CFBR-FM - 100.3
18520 Stony Plain Rd., No. 100
Postal Sta. E.   **Phone: (403)486-2800**
Edmonton, AB, Canada T5A 2E2   **Fax: (403)489-6927**

4502 CFRN-AM - 1260
18520 Stony Plain Rd., Ste. 100   **Phone: (403)428-2600**
Edmonton, AB, Canada T5S 2E2   **Fax: (403)484-8739**

4503 CISN-FM - 103.9
10550 102nd St., No. 200   **Phone: (403)428-1104**
Edmonton, AB, Canada T5H 2T3   **Fax: (403)426-6502**

4504 CJSR-FM - 88.5
University of Alberta
Rm. 224 Sub
Edmonton, AB, Canada T66 2J7   **Phone: (403)492-5244**
Format: Alternative/Independent/Progressive. **Ad Rates:** Noncommercial.

HIGH RIVER

4505 High River Times
618 Center St S   **Phone: (403)652-2034**
High River, AB, Canada T1V 1E9   **Fax: (403)652-3962**

INNISFAIL

4506 Innisfail Booster
4932 49th St.
Box 262   **Phone: (403)227-3477**
Innisfail, AB, Canada T0M 1A0   **Fax: (403)227-3330**

LEDUC

4507 Leduc Representative
Webco Publishers
4504-61 Ave.
Bag 220   **Phone: (403)986-2271**
Leduc, AB, Canada T9E 2Y1   **Fax: (403)986-6397**
Former Title: Leduc Pennypower

4508 The Representative
Bowes Publishers Ltd.
Bag 220   **Phone: (403)986-2271**
Leduc, AB, Canada T9E 2Y1   **Fax: (403)986-6397**

LETHBRIDGE

4509 CISA-TV - Channel 7
PO Box 1120   **Phone: (403)327-1521**
Lethbridge, AB, Canada T1J 4A4   **Fax: (403)320-2620**

MANNING

4510 The Northern Pioneer
PO Box 571
La Crete, AB, Canada T0H 2H0   **Phone: (403)928-4000**

MANNVILLE

4511 Mannville Reflections
PO Box 90
Mannville, AB, Canada T0B 2W0   **Phone: (403)763-3066**
Ceased publication.

MAYERTHORPE

4512 Mayerthorpe Freelancer
Bowes Publishers Ltd.
Box 599   **Phone: (403)786-2602**
Mayerthorpe, AB, Canada T0E 1N0   **Fax: (403)786-2662**

MEDICINE HAT

4513 CHAT-TV - Channel 6
PO Box 1270
Medicine Hat, AB, Canada T1A 7H5   Phone: (403)529-1270
Format: Commercial TV. **Network(s):** Canadian Broadcasting Corporation (CBC)/Societe Radio-Canada (SRC). **Owner:** Monarch Broadcasting. **Founded:** 1947. **Operating Hours:** 6 a.m.-2 a.m. **Key Personnel:** Bryan Ellis, Gen. Mgr.; Brian Konrad, News Dir.; Gary Rathwell, Program Dir.; Tina Milley, Traffic Mgr.; Bob Werre, Chief Engineer. **Local Programs:** *News Plus. Talk of the Town.* **Ad Rates:** Available upon request.

MEDLEY

4514 CFB Cold Lake Courier
Box 3190   **Phone: (403)594-5206**
Medley, AB, Canada T0A 2M0   **Fax: (403)594-2139**
Community newspaper. **Founded:** November, 1967. **Frequency:** Weekly. **Printing Method:** Web press. **Trim Size:** 11 x 17. **Cols./Page:** 5. **Col. Width:** 2 in. **Col. Depth:** 16 in. **Key Personnel:** Debbie Lawrence, Contact; Laura Saueracker, Contact. **Subscription:** $21.40.
Ad Rates: PCI: $5   **Circulation:** Paid ◆4,000

PONOKA

4515 Ponoka Herald
Box 4308
5210 50th St.   **Phone: (403)783-3074**
Ponoka, AB, Canada T4J 1R7   **Fax: (403)783-5350**

RED DEER

4516 Central Alberta Adviser
Adviser Publications Ltd.
Bag 5012, Main PO Box
5929 48 Ave.   **Phone: (403)346-3356**
Red Deer, AB, Canada T4N 6R4   **Fax: (403)347-6620**

♣ **4517 CKRD-TV - Channel 6**
2840 Bremner Ave.　　　　　　　　　Phone: (403)346-2573
Red Deer, AB, Canada T4R 1M9　　　　　Fax: (403)346-9980
Format: Commercial TV. **Network(s):** Canadian Broadcasting Corporation (CBC)/Societe Radio-Canada (SRC). **Owner:** Western International Communications Ltd., 1960-505 Burrard St., Vancouver, BC, Canada; (604)687-2844. **Founded:** 1956. **Operating Hours:** 6 a.m.-2 a.m. **Key Personnel:** Barry Duggan, Gen. Mgr.; Frank Thibault, Program Dir.; Neill Fitzpatrick, News Dir.; Gerald Cherepuschak, Chief Engineer; Norm Michaels, Operations Mgr. **Local Programs:** *First at 5 News. Live with Kevin O'Connell. This Business of Farming.*

SEDGEWICK

📖 **4518 Sedgewick Community Press**
Box 99　　　　　　　　　　　　　Phone: (403)384-3641
Sedgewick, AB, Canada T0B 4C0　　　　Fax: (403)384-2244
Community newspaper. **Founded:** 1908. **Frequency:** Weekly. **Printing Method:** Offset. **Cols./Page:** 5. **Col. Width:** 11.5 picas. **Col. Depth:** 15 3/4 in. **Key Personnel:** Kerry Anderson, Publisher; Rick Truss, Publisher. **Subscription:** $12.28.
Ad Rates:　GLR:　　$.47　　　　　　**Circulation:** ★3,577
　　　　　　PCI:　　$4.60

BRITISH COLUMBIA

BURNABY

4519 Grocer Magazine
Canada Wide Magazines Ltd.
401-4180 Lougheed Hwy.   Phone: (604)299-7311
Burnaby, BC, Canada V5C 6A7   Fax: (604)299-9188
Food industry publication serving western Canada and Thunder Bay.
Founded: 1987. **Frequency:** 10x/yr. **Printing Method:** Sheetfed offset.
Trim Size: 8 1/8 x 10 7/8. **Key Personnel:** Peter Legge, Pres./Publisher;
Nancy Ryder, Editor. **Subscription:** Free to qualified subscribers; $27.
Ad Rates: BW: $1,950   **Circulation:** (Not Reported)
              4C: $2,575
Formerly: B.C. & Alberta Grocer.

4520 CJSF-FM - 93.9
TC-216
Simon Fraser Univ.   Phone: (604)291-3727
Burnaby, BC, Canada V5A 1S6   Fax: (604)291-4455

CAMPBELL RIVER

4521 CFWB-AM - 1490
909 Ironwood Rd.   Phone: (604)287-7106
Campbell River, BC, Canada V9W 3E5   **Fax: (604)287-7170**

COURTENAY

4522 North Island News
Thomson Newspapers
Box 3013   Phone: (604)334-4446
Courtenay, BC, Canada V9N 5N3   Fax: (604)334-4983

CRANBROOK

4523 Kootenay Business Magazine
Koocanusa Publications, Inc.
1510 2nd St. N.   Phone: (604)489-3455
Cranbrook, BC, Canada V1C 3L2   Fax: (604)489-3743

CRESTON

4524 CFKC-AM - 1340
c/o Four Seasons Radio Ltd.
1560 2nd Ave.   Phone: (604)368-5510
Trail, BC, Canada V1R 1M4   **Fax: (604)368-8471**

DAWSON CREEK

4525 CJDC-FM - 92.7
Tumbler Ridge   Phone: (604)782-3341
Dawson Creek, BC, Canada V1G 2B6   Fax: (604)782-3154
Format: Contemporary Hit Radio (CHR); Contemporary Country.
Network(s): Sun Radio. **Owner:** Mega Communications Ltd. **Founded:**
1989. **Operating Hours:** Continuous. **Key Personnel:** Mike Michaud,
Mgr.; Grant Mitton, News Dir. **Wattage:** 1000.

DUNCAN

4526 Cowichan News Leader
Island Publishers Ltd.
2742 James St.   Phone: (604)746-4471
Duncan, BC, Canada V9L 2X9   **Fax: (604)746-8529**

4527 The Pictorial
Island Publishers Ltd.
2742 James St.   Phone: (604)746-4471
Duncan, BC, Canada V9L 2X9   **Fax: (604)746-8529**

FERNIE

4528 Kootenay Cable Ltd.
Box 1769   Phone: (604)423-6442
Fernie, BC, Canada V0B 1M0   **Fax: (604)423-3855**

FORT ST. JAMES

4529 CIFJ-AM - 1480
c/o CIVH-AM
150 W. Columbia
PO Box 1370   Phone: (604)567-4914
Vanderhoof, BC, Canada V0J 3A0   Fax: (604)567-4982
Format: Country. **Owner:** Cariboo Central Interior Radio Inc., 1940
3rd Ave., Prince George, BC, Canada V2M 1G7; (604)564-2524.
Founded: 1974. **Operating Hours:** 6-9 a.m.; 3-6 p.m. **Key Personnel:**
Sandie Ziegler, Office and Traffic Mgr.; T.C. Bulmer, Program Dir.
and Sales Mgr.; Mike Monroe, Music Dir./Promotions and Operations Mgr. **Ad Rates:** $9-$19.75 for 30 seconds; $10-$24 for 60
seconds.

FRASER LAKE

4530 CIFL-AM - 1450
c/o CIVH-AM
150 W. Columbia
PO Box 1370   Phone: (604)567-4914
Vanderhoof, BC, Canada V0J 3A0   Fax: (604)567-4982
Format: Country. **Owner:** Cariboo Central Interior Radio Inc., 1940

3rd Ave., Prince George, BC, Canada V2M 1G7; (604)564-2524. **Founded:** 1974. **Operating Hours:** 6-9 a.m.; 3-6 p.m. **Key Personnel:** Sandie Ziegler, Office and Traffic Mgr.; T.C. Bulmer, Program Dir. and Sales Mgr.; Mike Monroe, Music Dir./Promotions and Operations Mgr. **Ad Rates:** $9-$19.75 for 30 seconds; $10-$24 for 60 seconds.

GILLIES BAY

★ 4531 Gillies Bay Community Television Assoc.
Box 219
Gillies Bay, BC, Canada V0N 1W0   **Phone: (604)486-7682**

GOLD RIVER

★ 4532 CJGR-FM - 100
909 Ironwood St.   Phone: (604)287-7106
Campbell River, BC, Canada V9W 3E5   Fax: (604)287-7170
Format: Adult Contemporary; Oldies. **Network(s):** Western Information (WIN); Sun Radio. **Owner:** Norma Brown. **Operating Hours:** 6 a.m.-midnight. **Key Personnel:** Brian Langston, Gen. Mgr. **Wattage:** 1000.

GOLDEN

★ 4533 CKGR-AM - 1400
825 10th Ave. S.
PO Box 1403   Phone: (604)344-7177
Golden, BC, Canada V0A 1H0   **Fax: (604)344-7233**

★ 4534 CKIR-AM - 870
825 10th Ave. S.
PO Box 1403   **Phone: (604)344-7177**
Golden, BC, Canada V0E 2T0   **Fax: (604)344-7233**

KAMLOOPS

★ 4535 CFJC-TV - Channel 4
460 Pemberton Terr.   Phone: (604)372-3323
Kamloops, BC, Canada V2C 1T5   Fax: (604)374-0445
Format: Commercial TV. **Network(s):** Canadian Broadcasting Corporation (CBC)/Societe Radio-Canada (SRC). **Owner:** Jim Pattison Industries Ltd. **Founded:** 1957. **Operating Hours:** 18 hours daily. **Key Personnel:** Rick Arnish, V.P.; Bill Dinicol, Controller; Bryan White, Gen. Sales Mgr.; Gordon Honey, Operations Mgr.; Dave Sommerton, Production Mgr. **Local Programs:** *CFJC Evening News. CFJC TV Midday. Probe.* **Additional Contact Information:** News fax: (604)372-5229.

KELOWNA

▢ 4536 Okanagan Life Magazine
248684 Alberta Ltd.
PO Box 1479, Sta. A   **Phone: (604)861-5399**
Kelowna, BC, Canada V1Y 7V8   **Fax: (604)868-3040**

★ 4537 CKOV-AM - 630
3805 Lakeshore Rd.   Phone: (604)762-3331
Kelowna, BC, Canada V1W 3K6   Fax: (604)762-2141

NANAIMO

★ 4538 CKEG-AM - 1350
4550 Wellington Rd.   Phone: (604)758-1131
Nanaimo, BC, Canada V9T 2H3   Fax: (604)758-4644

OLIVER

★ 4539 Oliver Tele-Vue Ltd.
Box 790   Phone: (604)498-3630
Oliver, BC, Canada V0H 1T0   **Fax: (604)498-8810**

PENTICTON

★ 4540 CIGV-FM - 100.7
125 Nanaimo Ave. W.   **Phone: (604)493-6767**
Penticton, BC, Canada V2A 1N2   **Fax: (604)493-0098**

★ 4541 CJMG-FM - 97.1
33 Carmi Ave.   Phone: (604)492-2800
Penticton, BC, Canada V2A 3G4   **Fax: (604)493-0370**

RICHMOND

★ 4542 CKZZ-FM - 95.3
11151 Horseshoe Way, No. 20   Phone: (604)280-0953
Richmond, BC, Canada V7A 4S5   Fax: (604)272-0917
Format: Dance; Rhythm and Blues. **Owner:** South Fraser Broadcasting Ltd., at above address. **Founded:** 1991. **Operating Hours:** Continuous. **Key Personnel:** Michael Dickinson, Pres./Gen. Mgr.; Brad Phillips, Program Dir.; Bill Waddington, Gen. Sales Mgr. **Wattage:** 75,000. **Ad Rates:** $110-$170 for 30 seconds; $154-$238 for 60 seconds.; Combined rates available with CISL-AM: $140-$235 for 30 seconds; $195-$329 for 60 seconds.

SUMMERLAND

★ 4543 CHOR-AM - 1450
Box 1170   Phone: (604)494-0333
Summerland, BC, Canada V0H 1Z0   **Fax: (604)493-0444**

SURREY

▢ 4544 Canada Poultryman/L'Aviculteur Canadien
Farm Papers Ltd.
9547 152nd St., Ste. 105B   Phone: (604)585-3131
Surrey, BC, Canada V3R 5Y5   Fax: (604)585-1504

TRAIL

★ 4545 CJAT-AM - 610
c/o Four Seasons Radio Ltd.
1560 2nd Ave.   Phone: (604)368-5510
Trail, BC, Canada V1R 1M4   **Fax: (604)368-8471**

VANCOUVER

▢ 4546 Adbusters
Media Foundation
1243 W. 7th Ave.
Vancouver, BC, Canada V6H 1B7   Phone: (604)736-9401
Environmentally conscious consumer magazine focusing on the media. **Subtitle:** Journal of the Mental Environment. **Founded:** 1989. **Frequency:** Quarterly. **Printing Method:** Lithography. **Trim Size:** 10 1/2 x 8. **Key Personnel:** Kalle Lasn, Editor and Publisher; Bill Schmalz, Publisher; Cat Simril, Editor. **Subscription:** $16; $32 institutions. $4.75 single issue.

                                          Circulation: Paid ‡3,000
                                                      Non-paid ‡2,000

Advertising not accepted.

▢ 4547 BC Studies
The University of British Columbia
2029 W. Mall   Phone: (604)822-3727
Vancouver, BC, Canada V6T 1Z2   **Fax: (604)822-9452**

▢ 4548 New Directions
Pacific New Directions Publishing Society
PO Box 34279 Sta. D   **Phone: (604)438-3149**
Vancouver, BC, Canada V6J 4P2   **Fax: (604)438-3149**

▢ 4549 Pacific Affairs
The University of British Columbia
Pacific Affairs   **Phone: (604)822-6508**
Vancouver, BC, Canada V6T 1Z2   **Fax: (604)822-9452**

★ 4550 CITR-FM - 101.9
University of British Columbia
Student Union Bldg., Rm. 233
6138 SUB Blvd.   Phone: (604)822-3017
Vancouver, BC, Canada V6T 1Z1   **Fax: (604)822-9364**

★ 4551 CJJR-FM - 93.7
1401 W. 8th Ave.   Phone: (604)731-7772
Vancouver, BC, Canada V6H 1C9   Fax: (604)731-0493

⬤ 4552 CKST-AM - 1040
1199 W. Pender St.   Phone: (604)669-1040
Vancouver, BC, Canada V6E 2R1   **Fax: (604)684-6949**

VANDERHOOF

⬤ 4553 CIRX-FM - 95.9
1940 3rd Ave.   Phone: (604)562-2236
Vanderhoof, BC, Canada V2M 1G7   Fax: (604)567-4982
Owner: Cariboo Central Interior Radio Inc. **Founded:** 1985.

VICTORIA

▢ 4554 Living Here Victoria
Key Pacific Publishers Co. Ltd.
1001 Wharf St., 3rd Fl.   Phone: (604)388-4324
Victoria, BC, Canada V8W 1T6   Fax: (604)388-6166
Ceased publication.

▢ 4555 The Trumpeter
Lightstar Press
PO Box 5853, Sta. B   Phone: (604)598-7004
Victoria, BC, Canada V8R 6S8   **Fax: (604)595-8265**

⬤ 4556 CFVU-FM - 101.9
PO Box 3035   Phone: (604)721-8607
Victoria, BC, Canada **V8W 3P3**   **Fax: (604)721-8728**

WILLIAMS LAKE

▢ 4557 The Tribune Weekender
188 N. 1st Ave.   Phone: (604)392-2331
Williams Lake, BC, Canada V2G 1Y8   Fax: (604)392-7253
Shopper. **Founded:** 1989. **Frequency:** Weekly (Sunday). **Printing
Method:** Web offset/ **Trim Size:** 11 1/4 x 16 3/4. **Cols./Page:** 5. **Col.
Width:** 12.4 picas. **Col. Depth:** 16 in. **Key Personnel:** Gary Crosina,
Publisher. **Subscription:** Free.
Ad Rates: GLR: $.95   **Circulation:** Non-paid **9,800**
            BW:
            $1,715.70
            4C: $2,045.70
            PCI: $13.30
Formerly: Super Sunday Shopper.

⬤ 4558 CFFM-FM - 97.5
83 S. 1st Ave.   Phone: (604)398-2336
Williams Lake, BC, Canada **V2G 1H4**   **Fax: (604)392-4142**

Ad Rates: GLR = general line rate; BW = one-time black & white page rate; 4C = one-time four color page rate; SAU = standard advertising unit rate;
CNU = Canadian newspaper advertising unit rate; PCI = per column inch rate.
Circulation: ★ = ABC; △ = BPA; ◆ = CAC; ● = CCAB; □ = VAC; ⊕ = PO Statement; ‡ = Publisher's Report; Boldface figures = sworn; Light figures = estimated.
Entry type: ▢ = Print; ⬤ = Broadcast.

305

MANITOBA

BRANDON

4559 The Quill
Brandon University Students' Union
270-18th St. Phone: (204)727-9667
Brandon, MB, Canada R7A 6A9 Fax: (204)727-3498

4560 Western Manitoba Profile on Business
The Sun Publishing Co. Ltd.
501 Rosser Ave. Phone: (204)727-2451
Brandon, MB, Canada R7A 5Z6 Fax: (204)725-0976
Magazine. **Frequency:** Quarterly. **Printing Method:** Offset. **Trim Size:**
44.6 picas x 65 picas. **Cols./Page:** 4. **Col. Width:** 10 picas. **Col. Depth:**
60 picas. **Key Personnel:** Brian D. Marshall, Mng. Editor; Rob Forbes,
Publisher.
Ad Rates: BW: $505 **Circulation:** (Not Reported)
  4C: $649

4561 CKLQ-AM - 880
624 14th St. E. Phone: (204)726-8888
Brandon, MB, Canada R7A 7E1 Fax: (204)726-1270

CARTWRIGHT

4562 Southern Manitoba Review
Box 249 Phone: (204)529-2342
Cartwright, MB, Canada R0K 0L0 Fax: (204)529-2029

FLIN FLON

4563 The Reminder
10 North Ave. Phone: (204)687-3454
Flin Flon, MB, Canada R8A 0T2 Fax: (204)687-4473

STEINBACH

4564 Die Mennonitische Post
Publishing Board
Box 1120 Phone: (204)326-6790
Steinbach, MB, Canada R0A 2A0 Fax: (204)326-4860

WINNIPEG

4565 The Canadian Appraiser
Appraisal Institute of Canada
1111 Portage Ave. Phone: (204)783-2224
Winnipeg, MB, Canada R3G 0S8 Fax: (204)783-5575

4566 Cattlemen
Farm Business Communications
Box 6600 Phone: (204)944-5763
Winnipeg, MB, Canada R3C 3A7 Fax: (204)942-8463

4567 Dairy Guide
Farm Business Communications
Box 6600 Phone: (204)944-5760
Winnipeg, MB, Canada R3C 3A7 Fax: (204)942-8463

4568 The Herald (Visnyk)
Ecclesia Publishing Co., Ltd.
9 St. Johns Ave. Phone: (204)586-3093
Winnipeg, MB, Canada R2W 1G8 Fax: (204)582-5241

4569 Manitoba Restaurant News
Mercury Publications Ltd.
945 King Edward St. Phone: (204)775-0387
Winnipeg, MB, Canada R3H 0P8 Fax: (204)775-7830
Founded: 1989. **Frequency:** Quarterly. **Printing Method:** Offset. **Trim
Size:** 8 1/4 x 11. **Cols./Page:** 3. **Col. Width:** 13 picas. **Col. Depth:** 140
agate lines. **Key Personnel:** Kelly Gray, Editor; Frank Yeo, Mktg. Dir.
Subscription: $25. $4 single issue.
Ad Rates: BW: $1,125 **Circulation:** 2,220
  4C: $1,825

4570 WRLA Yardstick
3C-2020 Portage Ave. Phone: (204)885-7798
Winnipeg, MB, Canada R3J 0K4 Fax: (204)889-3576
The official publication of the Western Regional Lumbermans
Association. **Frequency:** 6x/yr. **Printing Method:** Offset. **Trim Size:** 8
1/4 x 10 3/4. **Cols./Page:** 3. **Col. Width:** 13 picas. **Col. Depth:** 57 picas.
Key Personnel: Jim E. Watson, Editor; Craig Kelman, Publisher;
Gerry Lepine, Ad. Rep.
Ad Rates: BW: $675 **Circulation:** (Not Reported)
  4C: $1,075
Advertising for members: BW: $600; 4C: $1,000.

4571 CBW-AM - 990
541 Portage Ave.
PO Box 160 Phone: (204)788-3222
Winnipeg, MB, Canada R3C 2H1 Fax: (204)788-3635
Format: Jazz; Blues; Classical. **Network(s):** Canadian Broadcasting
Corporation (CBC)/Societe Radio-Canada (SRC). **Owner:** Canadian
Broadcasting Corp. **Key Personnel:** John Coutanche, Dir. **Ad Rates:**
Noncommercial.

4572 CBW-FM - 98.3
541 Portage Ave.
PO Box 160
Winnipeg, MB, Canada R3C 2H1 Phone: (204)788-3222
Format: Jazz; Blues; Classical. **Network(s):** Canadian Broadcasting

Ad Rates: GLR = general line rate; BW = one-time black & white page rate; 4C = one-time four color page rate; SAU = standard advertising unit rate;
CNU = Canadian newspaper advertising unit rate; PCI = per column inch rate.
Circulation: ★ = ABC; △ = BPA; ◆ = CAC; ● = CCAB; □ = VAC; ⊕ = PO Statement; ‡ = Publisher's Report; Boldface figures = sworn; Light figures = estimated.
Entry type: ▣ = Print; ♣ = Broadcast.

307

Corporation (CBC)/Societe Radio-Canada (SRC). **Owner:** Canadian Broadcasting Corp. **Key Personnel:** John Coutanche, Dir. **Ad Rates:** Noncommercial.

♟ 4573 CKND-TV - Channel 9
603 St. Mary's Rd.   Phone: (204)233-3304
Winnipeg, MB, Canada **R2M 3L8**   Fax: (204)233-5615

♟ 4574 CKY-AM - 580
Polo Park   Phone: (204)786-6181
Winnipeg, MB, Canada **R3G 0L7**   **Fax: (204)775-5978**

NEW BRUNSWICK

CURTIS PARK

📖 **4575 Chatair**
CFB Chatham
Curtis Park, NB, Canada E0C 2E0   Phone: (506)778-5600

FREDERICTON

🎙 **4576 CIHI-AM - 1260**
206 Rockwood Ave.   Phone: (506)451-9111
Fredericton, NB, Canada E3B 2M2   Fax: (506)453-9024

🎙 **4577 CKHJ-FM - 105.3**
206 Rockwood Ave.   Phone: (503)451-9111
Fredericton, NB, Canada E3B 2M2   Fax: (506)453-9024

MONCTON

📖 **4578 Atlantic Business Report**
Laurentian Publishing Group
140 Baig Blvd.   Phone: (506)857-9696
Moncton, NB, Canada E1E 1C8   Fax: (506)859-7395
Magazine reporting business news in the Atlantic provinces. **Founded:** 1990. **Frequency:** 5x/year. **Printing Method:** Offset. **Cols./Page:** 5. **Col. Width:** 2 in. **Col. Depth:** 15 in. **Key Personnel:** Raymond Matthews, Publisher/Gen. Mgr.; Lynda MacGibbon, Managing Editor. **ISSN:** 1192-0203. **Subscription:** $25. $2 single issue.

Ad Rates:	GLR:	$2.35	Circulation:	Paid **1,100**
	BW:	$2,549		Non-paid **12,900**
	4C:	$3,049		
	PCI:	$32.90		

Formerly: Maritime Report (1992).

📖 **4579 The Brunswick Business Journal**
Laurentian Publishing Group
140 Baig Blvd.   Phone: (506)857-9696
Moncton, NB, Canada **E1G 1C8**   Fax: (506)859-7395

ST. JOHN

🎙 **4580 CHSJ-TV - Channel 4**
335 Union St.
PO Box 2000   Phone: (506)632-2222
St. John, NB, Canada E2L 3T4   Fax: (506)632-3485
Network(s): Canadian Broadcasting Corporation (CBC)/Societe Radio-Canada (SRC). **Key Personnel:** L.M. Nichols, Pres.; Mel Johnston, Operations Mgr.; Ken Hauschildt, Chief Engineer; Dave Merzetti, Program Mgr.; Gary Murphy, Sales Mgr. **Local Programs:** *Maritimes Today. Blue Rainbow. All About Travel.*

WOODSTOCK

🎙 **4581 CJCJ-AM - 920**
PO Box 920   Phone: (506)325-3030
Woodstock, NB, Canada E0J 2B0   Fax: (506)325-3031

Ad Rates: GLR = general line rate; BW = one-time black & white page rate; 4C = one-time four color page rate; SAU = standard advertising unit rate; CNU = Canadian newspaper advertising unit rate; PCI = per column inch rate.
Circulation: ★ = ABC; △ = BPA; ◆ = CAC; ● = CCAB; □ = VAC; ⊕ = PO Statement; ‡ = Publisher's Report; Boldface figures = sworn; Light figures = estimated.
Entry type: 📖 = Print; 🎙 = Broadcast.

NEWFOUNDLAND

CORNER BROOK

🎤 **4582 CBY-AM - 990**
162 Premier Dr.
PO Box 610   Phone: (709)634-3141
Corner Brook, NF, Canada A2H 6G1   Fax: (709)634-8506
Format: Information; News; Sports. **Network(s):** Canadian Broadcasting Corporation (CBC)/Societe Radio-Canada (SRC). **Owner:** Canadian Broadcasting Corp. **Key Personnel:** W.S. Sheppard, Location Mgr.; Austin Batten, Administration Officer; Larry O'Brien, Technical Mgr.; Charlie Veitch, Exec. Producer.

🎤 **4583 CBYT-TV - Channel 5**
162 Premier Dr.
PO Box 610   Phone: (709)634-3141
Corner Brook, NF, Canada A2H 6G1   Fax: (709)634-8506
Format: News; Sports. **Network(s):** Canadian Broadcasting Corporation (CBC)/Societe Radio-Canada (SRC). **Owner:** Canadian Broadcasting Corp. **Operating Hours:** 3:30 p.m.-midnight. **Key Personnel:** W.S. Sheppard, Location Mgr.; Austin Batten, Administration Officer; Larry O'Brien, Technical Mgr.; Gus Kenny, Sales Mgr.

GRAND BANK

🎤 **4584 CKXJ-AM - 610**
PO Box 189   Phone: (709)832-2650
Grand Bank, NF, Canada A0E 1W0   Fax: (709)832-1353
Format: Country. **Network(s):** Independent. **Owner:** Newcap Broadcasting Ltd., Box 6180, Saint John's, NF, Canada A1C 5X8. **Operating Hours:** Continuous.

HAPPY VALLEY

🎤 **4585 CFGB-AM - 1340**
171 Hamilton River Rd.
PO Box 3015, Sta. B
Happy Valley, NF, Canada A0P 1E0   Phone: (709)896-2911
Format: Middle-of-the-Road (MOR). **Network(s):** Canadian Broadcasting Corporation (CBC)/Societe Radio-Canada (SRC). **Owner:** Canadian Broadcasting Corp. **Operating Hours:** 5:30 a.m.-1:30 a.m. **Key Personnel:** John Fleet, Operations Mgr.; Lorne Burry, Supervising Technician; Don Lockhart, Producer.

SAINT JOHN'S

🎤 **4586 CFIQ-AM - 970**
8010 Stn. A   Phone: (709)753-4040
Saint John's, NF, Canada A1B 3M7   Fax: (709)753-4420
Format: Oldies. **Network(s):** Independent. **Owner:** New Cap Broadcasting. **Founded:** 1983. **Operating Hours:** 6 a.m.-6 p.m. **Key Personnel:** Kathy Hicks, News Dir.; Brenda Kinsella, Traffic Dir.; Fred Trainor, Gen. Mgr.; Hilary Montborwcarwh, Program Dir.; Craig Jackson, Sports Dir. **Wattage:** 1000 day; 500 night.

NORTHWEST TERRITORIES

YELLOWKNIFE

♪ 4587 CKNM-FM - 101.9
5120 49th St.
PO Box 1919
Yellowknife, NT, Canada X1A 2P4

Phone: (403)920-2277
Fax: (403)920-4205

NOVA SCOTIA

ANTIGONISH

♣ 4588 CFXU-AM - 690
St. Francis State University
PO Box 948
Antigonish, NS, Canada B2G 1C0   Phone: (902)867-2410
Format: Alternative/Independent/Progressive. **Key Personnel:** Bob
Sexton, Music Dir. **Ad Rates:** Noncommercial.

DARTMOUTH

📖 4589 The Nova Scotia Medical Journal
Medical Society of Nova Scotia
City of Lakes Business Park
5 Spectacle Lake Dr.   Phone: (902)468-1866
Dartmouth, NS, Canada B3B 1X7   **Fax: (902)468-6578**

HALIFAX

📖 4590 The Clansman
Clansman Publishing Limited
PO Box 8805, Sta. A   Phone: (902)835-6244
Halifax, NS, Canada B3K 5M4   Fax: (902)835-0080
Ethnic publication covering subjects of interest to Scots. **Founded:**
1987. **Frequency:** Bimonthly. **Printing Method:** Offset. **Trim Size:** 11
1/4 x 14 1/2. **Cols./Page:** 5. **Col. Width:** 1 7/8 in. **Col. Depth:** 13 in.
Key Personnel: Angus M. Macquarrie, Publisher. ISSN: 0832-5189.
Subscription: $14.25; $25 other countries. $2.25 single issue.
Ad Rates: GLR: $1.52   **Circulation:** Paid ‡7,091
         BW: $1,090   Non-paid ‡10,000
         4C: $1,490
         PCI: $21.28

📖 4591 TRIDENT: The Maritime Command Newspaper
PO Box 3308   Phone: (902)427-2347
Halifax, NS, Canada B3J 3J1   **Fax: (902)427-2539**

📖 4592 Visual Arts News
Visual Arts Nova Scotia
1809 Barrington St., Ste. 901   Phone: (902)423-4694
Halifax, NS, Canada **B3J 3K8**   **Fax: (902)422-0881**

♣ 4593 CHFX-FM - 101.9
1313 Barrington St.
PO Box 400   Phone: (902)422-1651
Halifax, NS, Canada B3J 2R2   **Fax: (902)422-5330**

KENTVILLE

♣ 4594 Kings Kable Ltd.
Box 4000   **Phone: (902)681-0300**
Kentville, NS, Canada B4N 4S8   **Fax: (902)681-6470**

SHEARWATER

📖 4595 The Warrior
PO Box 190
CFB Shearwater   Phone: (902)463-5111
Shearwater, NS, Canada B0J 3A0   **Fax: (902)466-1796**

WINDSOR

♣ 4596 CFAB-AM - 1450
Box 278   Phone: (902)798-2111
Windsor, NS, Canada B0N 2T0   Fax: (902)798-8140
Format: Contemporary Country. **Owner:** Neil McMullen. **Founded:**
1945. **Key Personnel:** Dave Bannerman, Station Mgr. **Wattage:** 1000.

ONTARIO

AURORA

📖 **4597 Punch Digest for Canadian Doctors**
Punch Digest for Canadian Doctors Inc.
14845 Yonge St., Ste. 300   Phone: (416)841-5607
Aurora, ON, Canada L4G 6H8   Fax: (416)841-5688

AYLMER

🎙 **4598 East Elgin Cable TV Ltd.**
555 Talbot St. E.   Phone: (519)773-3162
Aylmer, ON, Canada N5H 2W1   **Fax: (519)765-2198**

BALA

📖 **4599 Antique Showcase**
Amis-Gibbs Publications, LTD.
PO Box 260   Phone: (705)762-5631
Bala, ON, Canada P0C 1A0   **Fax: (705)762-5640**

BRANTFORD

📖 **4600 Brant News**
Newfoundland Capital Corp.
446 Grey St., Ste. 301   Phone: (519)759-5550
Brantford, ON, Canada N3S 7L6   Fax: (519)759-8425

BROCKVILLE

🎙 **4601 CFJR-AM - 830**
Box 666   Phone: (613)345-1666
Brockville, ON, Canada K6V 5V9   Fax: (613)342-2438
Format: Classic Rock. **Owner:** St. Lawrence Broadcasting Ltd., at above address. **Founded:** 1926. **Operating Hours:** Continuous. **Key Personnel:** Linda Benoit, General and Sales Mgr.; Greg Hinton, Program Dir.; Gaetanne Masson, News Dir.; John Wright, V.P.; James A. Waters, Pres. **Wattage:** 5000 day; 1000 night. **Ad Rates:** $24-$63 for 30 seconds; $29-$79 for 60 seconds. Combined rates available with CHXL-FM.

CHATHAM

🎙 **4602 CFCO-AM - 630**
21 Keil Dr. S.
PO Box 630   Phone: (519)352-3000
Chatham, ON, Canada N7M 5K9   **Fax: (519)352-9690**

CLINTON

🎙 **4603 Bluewater TV Cable Ltd.**
RR 2   Phone: (519)482-9233
Clinton, ON, Canada N0M 1L0   **Fax: (519)482-7098**

🎙 **4604 Ex-Cen Cablevision Ltd.**
RR 2   Phone: (519)482-9233
Clinton, ON, Canada N0M 1L0   **Fax: (519)482-7098**

COBOURG

📖 **4605 Cobourg-Port Hope Shoppers Market**
319 Division St.   Phone: (416)372-2181
Cobourg, ON, Canada K9A 3R4   **Fax: (416)372-1763**

COLLINGWOOD

🎙 **4606 CKCB-AM - 1400**
Box 1400   Phone: (705)444-1400
Collingwood, ON, Canada L9Y 3Z3   **Fax: (705)444-6776**

CORNWALL

📖 **4607 Writer's Lifeline**
PO Box 32   Phone: (613)932-2135
Cornwall, ON, Canada K6H 5R9   **Fax: (613)932-7735**

DON MILLS

📖 **4608 Automotive Marketer**
Southam Business Information and Communications Group, Inc.
1450 Don Mills Rd.   Phone: (416)445-6641
Don Mills, ON, Canada M3B 2X7   Fax: (416)442-2077
Ceased publication.

📖 **4609 Business Computer News**
Moorshead Publications Ltd.
797 Don Mills Rd., 10th Fl.   Phone: (416)696-5488
Don Mills, ON, Canada M3C 3S5   **Fax: (416)696-7395**

📖 **4610 Canadian Auto Review**
Southam Business Information and Communications Group, Inc.
1450 Don Mills Rd.   Phone: (416)445-6641
Don Mills, ON, Canada M3B 2X7   Fax: (416)442-2077
Ceased publication.

📖 **4611 Canadian Consulting Engineer**
Southam Business Communications Inc.
1450 Don Mills Rd.   Phone: (416)445-6641
Don Mills, ON, Canada M3B 2X7   **Fax: (416)442-2214**

☐ **4612 Canadian Mining Journal**
Southam North American Magazine Group
1450 Don Mills Rd.   Phone: (416)445-6641
Don Mills, ON, Canada M3B 2X7   Fax: (416)442-2272

☐ **4613 Canadian Occupational Health and Safety News**
Southam Information and Technology Group
1450 Don Mills Rd.   Phone: (416)445-6641
Don Mills, ON, Canada M3B 2X7   Fax: (416)442-2200

☐ **4614 Gifts & Tablewares**
Southam Business Communications Inc.
1450 Don Mills Rd.   Phone: (416)445-6641
Don Mills, ON, Canada M3B 2X7   **Fax: (416)442-2213**

☐ **4615 Glad Tidings**
Women's Missionary Society (W.D.)
50 Wynford Dr.   **Phone: (416)441-1111**
Don Mills, ON, Canada M3C 1J7   Fax: (416)441-2825

☐ **4616 Laboratory Product News**
Southam Business Communications Inc.
1450 Don Mills Rd.   **Phone: (416)442-2052**
Don Mills, ON, Canada M3B 2X7   **Fax: (416)442-2201**

☐ **4617 OH&S Canada**
Southam Information & Technology Group
1450 Don Mills Rd.   Phone: (416)445-6641
Don Mills, ON, Canada M3B 2X7   Fax: (416)442-2200

☐ **4618 Plastics Business**
Southam Business Communications Inc.
1450 Don Mills Rd.   **Phone: (416)445-6641**
Don Mills, ON, Canada M3B 2X7   Fax: (416)442-2213

☐ **4619 Tribute Goes to the Movies**
Tribute Publications Ltd.
900A Don Mills Rd., Ste. 1000   Phone: (416)445-0544
Don Mills, ON, Canada M3C 1V6   Fax: (416)445-2894

DOWNSVIEW

☐ **4620 Graduate Computerworld**
Laurentian Technomedia Inc.
501 Oakdale Rd.   Phone: (416)746-7360
Downsview, ON, Canada M3N 1W7   Fax: (416)746-1421
Consumer Magazine covering careers in computers for college
students. **Founded:** 1990. **Frequency:** Quarterly. **Printing Method:** Web
offset. **Trim Size:** 8 7/8 x 12 1/4. **Key Personnel:** John Pickett, Editor;
Andy White, Publisher; Virginia Hutton, Assoc. Publisher. **Subscription:** $15; Free for post secondary institutes in Canada.
Ad Rates: BW: $4,950   **Circulation:** Non-paid ☐50,000
              4C: $5,750

DUBLIN

♠ **4621 Mitchell Seaforth Cable TV Ltd.**
123 Ontario St.
Dublin, ON, Canada N0K 1E0   Phone: (519)345-2341

DURHAM

☐ **4622 Saugeen City Life**
Insight Publications
PO Box 130
105 Garafraxa   Phone: (519)369-5155
Durham, ON, Canada N0G 1R0   Fax: (519)369-5096
Ceased publication.

ELLIOT LAKE

♠ **4623 CKNR-AM - 1340**
15 Charles Walk   Phone: (705)848-3608
Elliot Lake, ON, Canada P5A 2A2   Fax: (705)848-1378
Format: Adult Contemporary. **Network(s):** Standard Broadcast News.
Owner: Pelmorex Broadcasting Inc. **Founded:** 1967. **Operating Hours:**
Continuous. **Key Personnel:** Pierre Morrisseite, Pres.; Walter Hulme,
Mktg. Mgr.; Bob Alexander, Public Relations Dir. **Wattage:** 1000. **Ad
Rates:** $12-$30 for 30 seconds; $18-$40 for 60 seconds. **Additional
Contact Information:** Toll-free: 800-565-7359.

ELMIRA

☐ **4624 KW Real Estate News**
North Waterloo Publishing Ltd.
15 King St.   Phone: (519)669-5155
Elmira, ON, Canada N3B 2R1   Fax: (519)669-5928
Shopping guide. **Frequency:** Weekly. **Printing Method:** Offset. **Cols./
Page:** 4. **Col. Depth:** 16 in. **Subscription:** Free.
                                    Circulation: Free 10,000

GLOUCESTER

☐ **4625 Recreation Canada**
Canadian Parks & Recreation Assn. National Office Siege Social
  ACL/P
1600 James Naismith Dr.   Phone: (613)748-5651
Gloucester, ON, Canada K1B 5N4   **Fax: (613)748-5854**

GRAVENHURST

♠ **4626 Gravenhurst Cable System Ltd.**
205 Jones Rd.   Phone: (705)687-3765
Gravenhurst, ON, Canada P1P 1M8   Fax: (705)687-4789

HAMILTON

☐ **4627 The American Journal of Otology**
1 James St. S
PO Box 620, LCD1   Phone: (416)522-7017
Hamilton, ON, Canada L8N 3K7   Fax: (416)522-7839

☐ **4628 Dental Study Club**
Decker Periodicals, Inc.
PO Box 620LCD1
One James St. S.   Phone: (416)522-7017
Hamilton, ON, Canada L8N 3K7   Fax: (416)522-7839
Subtitle: Journal of Continuing Dental Education. **Founded:** 1991.
Frequency: Bimonthly. **Trim Size:** 8 1/8 x 10 7/8. **Key Personnel:** Liz
Rodjkovic, Publisher; Isabel Wrotkowski, Production Mgr. **Subscription:** $129; $179 institutions. $20 single issue.
Ad Rates: BW: $500   **Circulation:** Paid ‡1,000
              4C: $1,495   Non-paid ‡120

☐ **4629 International Journal of Dermatology**
Decker Periodicals
1 James St. S.
PO Box 620
LCD 1   Phone: (416)522-7017
Hamilton, ON, Canada L8N 3K7   **Fax: (416)522-7839**

HANOVER

☐ **4630 The Advertisers News**
413 18th Ave.   Phone: (519)364-2002
Hanover, ON, Canada N4N 3S5   Fax: (519)364-6950

☐ **4631 PostScripts**
413 18th Ave.   Phone: (519)364-2002
Hanover, ON, Canada N4N 3S5   Fax: (519)364-6950

KAPUSKASING

☐ **4632 Le Nord de Kapuskasing**
22 Byng   Phone: (705)335-8464
Kapuskasing, ON, Canada P4N 1W4   Fax: (705)335-6730

KINCARDINE

☐ **4633 The Independent**
Box 1240
840 Queen St.   Phone: (519)396-3111
Kincardine, ON, Canada N2Z 2Z4   **Fax: (519)396-3899**

LINDSAY

♠ **4634 CKLY-AM - 910**
249 Kent St. W   Phone: (705)324-9103
Lindsay, ON, Canada K9V 2Z3   Fax: (705)324-4149

LONDON

⊞ 4635 London Magazine
The Blackburn Group Inc.
203-231 Dundas St.   Phone: (519)679-4901
London, ON, Canada N6A 1H1   Fax: (519)434-7842

⊞ 4636 London Pennysaver
244 Adelaide St. S.   Phone: (519)685-2020
London, ON, Canada N5Z 3L1   **Fax: (519)649-0908**

♣ 4637 CHRW-FM - 94.7
UCC University Western Ontario
London, ON, Canada N6A 3K7   Phone: (519)661-3601
Format: Alternative/Independent/Progressive. **Key Personnel:** Rose
Vasti, Music Dir. **Ad Rates:** Noncommercial.

♣ 4638 CJBX-FM - 92.7
743 Wellington Rd. S.   **Phone: (519)686-2525**
London, ON, Canada N6C 4R5   Fax: (519)686-9067

MARKHAM

⊞ 4639 Canadian Gardering
Camar Publicaitons Ltd.
130 Spy Ct.   Phone: (416)475-8440
Markham, ON, Canada N3R 5H6   Fax: (416)475-9246
Canadian gardening magazine. **Founded:** 1990. **Frequency:** Bimonthly.
Trim Size: 8 1/8 x 10 7/8. **Cols./Page:** 3. **Col. Width:** 13 picas. **Key**
Personnel: John van Velzen, Publisher; Liz Primeau, Editor.
Ad Rates: BW: $3,965   **Circulation:** Paid ★75,000
            4C: $4,950   Non-paid ★1,400

⊞ 4640 Snow Goer
Camar Publications Ltd.
130 Spy Ct.   Phone: (416)475-8440
Markham, ON, Canada L3R 5H6   Fax: (416)475-9246
Subtitle: The Magazine for Canadian Snowmobilers. **Founded:** 1978.
Frequency: Quarterly. **Printing Method:** Web offset. **Trim Size:** 8 1/8 x
10 7/8. **Key Personnel:** Jacqueline Howe, Editor. **ISSN:** 0711-6454.
Subscription: $9.99. $3.50 single issue.
Ad Rates: BW: $9,700   **Circulation:** Paid ●25,000
            4C: $13,285   Non-paid ●100,000

MISSISSAUGA

⊞ 4641 CAD Systems
Kerrwil Publications Ltd.
395 Matheson Blvd. E.   Phone: (416)890-1846
Mississauga, ON, Canada L4Z 2H2   Fax: (416)890-5769
Magazine covering product and technology resourses for CAD
professionals. **Founded:** 1991. **Frequency:** 6x/yr. **Printing Method:**
Offset. **Trim Size:** 10 3/4 x 16. **Key Personnel:** Graham Pitcher,
Editor; Bob Erickson, Publisher. **ISSN:** 1183-9414. **Subscription:**
$32.10; $20 students; $61 other countries.
Ad Rates: BW: $3,995   **Circulation:** Non-paid ‡20,000
            4C: $4,935
Title result of merger of CAD/CAM Systems and AEC Canada.

⊞ 4642 The Canadian Journal of Infectious Diseases
Pulsus Group Inc.
2160 Dunwin Dr., Unit 1   Phone: (416)829-4770
Mississauga, ON, Canada L5L 1C7   Fax: (416)829-4799
Medical journal. **Founded:** 1990. **Frequency:** Bimonthly. **Printing**
Method: Web offset. **Trim Size:** 8 1/8 x 10 7/8. **Cols./Page:** 2. **Col.**
Width: 20 picas. **Col. Depth:** 57 picas. **Key Personnel:** Dr. L.E. Nicolle,
Editor-in-Chief; R.B. Kalina, Publisher; J. O'Flaherty, Mng. Editor.
Subscription: $40; $48 institutions; $46 U.S. $7.50 single issue.
Ad Rates: BW: $2,165   **Circulation:** Non-paid 20,500
            4C: $3,815

⊞ 4643 Engineering Digest
Canadian Engineering Publications Ltd.
5080 Timberlea Blvd., Ste. 8   Phone: (416)602-0814
Mississauga, ON, Canada L4W 5C1   Fax: (416)602-0818
Ceased publication.

NIAGARA FALLS

♣ 4644 Maclean Hunter Cable TV
7170 McLeod Rd.   Phone: (416)374-2334
Niagara Falls, ON, Canada L2G 3H2   Fax: (416)374-2398

NORTH YORK

♣ 4645 CILQ-FM - 107.1
5255 Yonge St.
Ste. 1400   Phone: (416)221-0107
North York, ON, Canada M2N 6P4   **Fax: (416)512-4810**

OAKVILLE

⊞ 4646 Carguide
Formula Publications Ltd.
447 Speers Rd., Ste. 4   Phone: (416)842-6591
Oakville, ON, Canada L6K 3S7   Fax: (416)842-6843
Consumer automobile guide. **Founded:** 1971. **Frequency:** Quarterly.
Printing Method: Web offset. **Trim Size:** 8 1/8 x 10 7/8. **Cols./Page:** 3.
Col. Width: 2 1/4 in. **Col. Depth:** 9 5/8 in. **Key Personnel:** J. Scott
Robinson, Publisher; Tracey Hanson, Circulation Mgr. **ISSN:** 0384-
9309. **Subscription:** $12.99. $4.00 single issue (Jan.); $2.95 single issue
(April, July, Oct.).
Ad Rates: BW: $3,800   **Circulation:** ‡55,000
            4C: $4,550
Published in two editions: Carguide (English) and Le Magazine
Carguide (French).Advertising rates for Le Magazine Carguide: Jan.
(Buyer's Guide): BW: $5,200; 4C: $6,300. Oct./April/July: BW:
$1,900; 4C: $2,650. Advertising rates for Carguide (Jan.–National
edition): BW: $7,825; 4C: $8,925.Circulation figures: Carguide (Jan.):
209,000; Le Magazine Carguide: Jan.: 91,952; Oct./April/July: 25,000
(French) 55,000 (English). **Formerly:** L'Annuaire de l'Auto.

OSHAWA

♣ 4647 CKDO-AM - 1350
360 King St. W.   Phone: (416)571-1350
Oshawa, ON, Canada L1J 2K2   Fax: (416)571-1150
Format: Oldies. **Network(s):** CTV. **Owner:** Power Broadcasting Inc.
Founded: 1946. **Formerly:** CKAR-AM (March 1992). **Operating**
Hours: Continuous. **Key Personnel:** David Lyman, Gen. Mgr.; Mari-
lyn Louw, Sales Mgr.; Lee Sterry, Program Mgr.; Mark Orton, News
Dir.; Martha McCain, Promotions Dir. **Wattage:** 10,000 day; 5000
night. **Ad Rates:** Available upon request.

♣ 4648 CKQT-FM - 94.9
360 King St., W.   Phone: (416)571-1350
Oshawa, ON, Canada L1J 2K2   Fax: (416)571-1150
Format: Easy Listening. **Network(s):** CTV. **Owner:** Power Broadcasting, Inc. **Founded:** 1957. **Operating Hours:** Continuous. **Key Person-**
nel: David Lyman, V.P./Gen. Mgr.; Marilyn Louw, V.P./Sales Mgr.;
Lee Sterry, V.P./Program Mgr.; Mark Orton, News Dir.; Martha
McCain, Promotions Dir. **Wattage:** 50,000. **Ad Rates:** Available upon
request.

OTTAWA

⊞ 4649 Au Courant
Public Affairs Division, Economic Council of Canada
PO Box 527   Phone: (613)952-1711
Ottawa, ON, Canada K1P 5V6   Fax: (613)952-2171
Ceased publication.

⊡ **4650 Biochemistry and Cell Biology (Biochimie et Biologie Cellulaire)**
The National Research Council of Canada
Research Journals
Bldg. M-55   Phone: (613)993-0362
Ottawa, ON, Canada K1A 0R6   Fax: (613)952-7656

⊡ **4651 Business and Professional Woman**
The Canadian Federation of Business and Professional Women's Clubs
56 Sparks St., Ste. 308   Phone: (613)234-7619
Ottawa, ON, Canada K1P 5A9   **Fax: same**

⊡ **4652 Canadian Association of Radiologists Journal**
Information Technology/Canadian Medical Assoc.
1867 Alta Vista Dr.
PO Box 8650   Phone: (613)731-9331
Ottawa, ON, Canada K1G 0G8   Fax: (613)731-4797
Radiology journal. **Founded:** 1949. **Frequency:** Bimonthly. **Printing Method:** Web offset. **Trim Size:** 8 1/8 x 10 7/8. **Cols./Page:** 3. **Col. Width:** 2 1/8 in. **Col. Depth:** 8 15/16 in. **Key Personnel:** E. Michel Azouz, Editor. **ISSN:** 0008-2902. **Subscription:** $110.
Ad Rates: BW: $710   **Circulation:** 2,000
              4C: $1,450

⊡ **4653 Canadian Geotechnical Journal (Revue Canadienne de Geotechnique)**
The National Research Council of Canada
Research Journals
Bldg. M-55   Phone: (613)993-0362
Ottawa, ON, Canada K1A 0R6   Fax: (613)952-7656

⊡ **4654 Canadian Journal of Agricultural Economics**
Agricultural Institute of Canada
151 Slater St., Ste. 907   Phone: (613)232-9459
Ottawa, ON, Canada K1P 5H4   Fax: (613)594-5190
Research journal publishing agricultural economics papers. **Frequency:** 5x/yr. **Printing Method:** Sheet offset. **Trim Size:** 6 x 9. **Cols./Page:** 1. **Col. Width:** 27 picas. **Col. Depth:** 43 picas. **Key Personnel:** Tim Fenton, Editor. **ISSN:** 0008-3976. **Subscription:** $95 individuals and institutions. $25 single issue.
                                   Circulation: Paid 1,200
Advertising not accepted.

⊡ **4655 Canadian Journal of Animal Science**
Agricultural Institute of Canada
151 Slater St., Ste. 907   Phone: (613)232-9459
Ottawa, ON, Canada K1P 5H4   Fax: (613)594-5190
Journal providing research on farm animals and animal products. **Founded:** 1951. **Frequency:** Quarterly. **Printing Method:** Sheet offset. **Trim Size:** 6 3/4 x 9 3/4. **Cols./Page:** 2. **Col. Width:** 15 picas. **Col. Depth:** 46 picas. **Key Personnel:** Tim Fenton, Editor. **ISSN:** 0008-3984. **Subscription:** $59; $107 institutions. $16 single issue.
Ad Rates: BW: $300   **Circulation:** Paid 1,300

⊡ **4656 Canadian Journal of Botany (Revue Canadienne de Botanique)**
The National Research Council of Canada
Research Journals
Bldg. M-55   Phone: (613)993-0362
Ottawa, ON, Canada K1A 0R6   Fax: (613)952-7656

⊡ **4657 Canadian Journal of Chemistry (Revue Canadienne de Chimie)**
The National Research Council of Canada
Research Journals
Bldg. M-55   Phone: (613)993-0362
Ottawa, ON, Canada K1A 0R6   Fax: (613)952-7656

⊡ **4658 Canadian Journal of Civil Engineering (Revue Canadienne de Genie Civil)**
The National Research Council of Canada
Research Journals
Bldg. M-55   Phone: (613)993-0362
Ottawa, ON, Canada K1A 0R6   Fax: (613)952-7656

⊡ **4659 Canadian Journal of Earth Sciences (Revue Canadienne des Sciences de la Terre)**
The National Research Council of Canada
Research Journals
Bldg. M-55   Phone: (613)993-0362
Ottawa, ON, Canada K1A 0R6   Fax: (613)952-7656

⊡ **4660 Canadian Journal of Forest Research (Revue Canadienne de Recherches Forestiere)**
The National Research Council of Canada
Research Journals
Bldg. M-55   Phone: (613)993-0362
Ottawa, ON, Canada K1A 0R6   Fax: (613)952-7656

⊡ **4661 Canadian Journal of Microbiology (Revue Canadienne de Microbiologie)**
The National Research Council of Canada
Research Journals
Bldg. M-55   Phone: (613)993-0362
Ottawa, ON, Canada K1A 0R6   Fax: (613)952-7656

⊡ **4662 Canadian Journal of Physiology and Pharmacology (Revue Canadienne de Physiologie et Pharmacologie)**
The National Research Council of Canada
Research Journals
Bldg. M-55   Phone: (613)993-0362
Ottawa, ON, Canada K1A 0R6   Fax: (613)952-7656

⊡ **4663 Canadian Journal of Respiratory Therapy**
Information Technology/Canadian Medical Assoc.
1867 Alta Vista Dr.
PO Box 8650   Phone: (613)731-9331
Ottawa, ON, Canada K1G 0G8   Fax: (613)731-4797
Journal covering respiratory therapy. **Founded:** 1964. **Frequency:** 5x/yr. **Printing Method:** Sheetfed offset. **Trim Size:** 8 1/8 x 10 7/8. **Cols./Page:** 2. **Col. Width:** 3 5/16 in. **Col. Depth:** 9 in. **Key Personnel:** Les Matthews, Editor; Cliff Seville, Editor. **ISSN:** 0831-2478. **Subscription:** $30.
Ad Rates: BW: $980   **Circulation:** 2,900
              4C: $1,525

⊡ **4664 Canadian Journal of Soil Science**
Agricultural Institute of Canada
151 Slater St., Ste. 907   Phone: (613)232-9459
Ottawa, ON, Canada K1P 5H4   Fax: (613)594-5190
Journal covering use, structure, management, and development of soils. **Founded:** 1957. **Frequency:** Quarterly. **Printing Method:** Sheet offset. **Trim Size:** 6 3/4 x 9 3/4. **Cols./Page:** 2. **Col. Width:** 15 picas. **Col. Depth:** 46 picas. **Key Personnel:** Tim Fenton, Editor. **ISSN:** 0008-4271. **Subscription:** $59; $107 institutions. $16 single issue.
Ad Rates: BW: $300   **Circulation:** Paid 1,250

⊡ **4665 Canadian Journal of Zoology (Revue Canadienne de Zoologie)**
The National Research Council of Canada
Research Journals
Bldg. M-55   Phone: (613)993-0362
Ottawa, ON, Canada K1A 0R6   Fax: (613)952-7656

⊡ **4666 Canadian Vocational Journal**
Canadian Vocational Assn.
PO Box 3435 Sta. D   Phone: (613)596-2515
Ottawa, ON, Canada K1P 6L4   **Fax: (613)596-2515**

⊡ **4667 Centretown News**
Carleton University School of Journalism
1231 Colonel By Dr.   **Phone: (613)788-7410**
Ottawa, ON, Canada KIS 5B6   Fax: (613)788-5604

⊡ **4668 Environmental Reviews (Dossiers environnement)**
National Research Council of Canada, Research Journals
                                   Phone: (613)993-9084
Ottawa, ON, Canada K1A 0R6   Fax: (613)952-7656
Environmental journal. **Founded:** 1993. **Frequency:** Quarterly. **Printing Method:** Offset. **Trim Size:** 8 1/2 x 11. **Cols./Page:** 2. **Col. Width:** 43 nonpareils. **Col. Depth:** 140 agate lines. **Key Personnel:** Dr. T.C. Hutchinson, Editor; Hoda Jabbour, Head of Promotions and Mktg.; Joan Hill, Mgr. **ISSN:** 1181-8700. **Subscription:** $160.
Ad Rates: BW: $550   **Circulation:** (Not Reported)
              4C: $1,000

Additional Contact Information: Marketing Dept. phone (613)993-9085.

📖 **4669 Genome**
The National Research Council of Canada
Research Journals
Bldg. M-55　　　　　　　　　　**Phone: (613)993-0362**
Ottawa, ON, Canada K1A 0R6　　　　**Fax: (613)952-7656**

📖 **4670 Humane Medicine**
Information Technology/Canadian Medical Assoc.
1867 Alta Vista Dr.
PO Box 8650　　　　　　　　　　**Phone: (613)731-9331**
Ottawa, ON, Canada K1G 0G8　　　　**Fax: (613)731-4797**
Journal covering the art and science of medicine. **Founded:** 1984.
Frequency: Quarterly. **Printing Method:** Web offset. **Trim Size:** 8 1/8 x
10 7/8. **Cols./Page:** 2 and 3. **Col. Width:** 3 5/16 in. **Col. Depth:** 9 5/8
in. **Key Personnel:** Dimitrios Oreopoulos, Editor; John Godden,
Editor. **ISSN:** 0828-7090. **Subscription:** $50; $60 other countries.
Ad Rates:　BW:　$2,310　　　　　**Circulation: 50,600**
　　　　　　4C:　$3,885

📖 **4671 Humanist in Canada**
Canadian Humanist Publications
PO Box 3769 Sta. C
Ottawa, ON, Canada K1Y 4J8　　　**Phone: (613)722-4652**

📖 **4672 Mediscan**
Canadian Medical Assoc.
1867 Alta Vista Dr.
PO Box 8650　　　　　　　　　　**Phone: (613)731-9331**
Ottawa, ON, Canada K1G 0G8　　　　**Fax: (613)523-0937**
Subtitle: Official Journal of the Canadian Federation of Medical
Students.**Founded:** 1988. **Frequency:** 3x/yr. **Trim Size:** 8 1/2 x 11.
Cols./Page: 2. **Col. Width:** 2 1/4 in. **Col. Depth:** 9 1/2 in. **Key
Personnel:** Debbie Rupert, Mng. Editor; Leesa Bruce, Asst. Dir. **ISSN:**
1188-0333. **Subscription:** Free to students.
Ad Rates:　BW:　$1,100　　　　　**Circulation: 5,900**
　　　　　　4C:　$2,000

📖 **4673 Outlook**
Canadian Council of the Blind
396 Cooper St.　　　　　　　　　**Phone: (613)567-0311**
Ottawa, ON, Canada K2P 2H7　　　　**Fax: (613)567-2728**
Ceased publication.

📻 **4674 CBOQ-FM - 103.3**
Box 3220, Sta. C　　　　　　　　**Phone: (613)724-1200**
Ottawa, ON, Canada K1Y 1E4　　　　**Fax: (613)598-3408**

📻 **4675 CHEZ-FM - 106.1**
126 York St., Ste. 509　　　　　　**Phone: (613)562-1061**
Ottawa, ON, Canada K1N 5T5　　　　**Fax: (613)562-1515**

📻 **4676 CHUO-FM - 89.1**
85 University, Ste. 227
Ottawa, ON, Canada T1N 6N5　　　**Phone: (613)564-2903**
Format: Alternative/Independent/Progressive. **Key Personnel:** Bob
McCarthy, Music Dir. **Ad Rates:** Noncommercial.

PEMBROKE

📻 **4677 CHVR-AM - 1350**
595 Pembroke St. E　　　　　　　**Phone: (613)735-1350**
Pembroke, ON, Canada K8A 3L7　　　**Fax: (613)735-7748**

PETERBOROUGH

📖 **4678 Arthur**
Trent University
　　　　　　　　　　　　　　　Phone: (705)748-1786
Peterborough, ON, Canada K9J 7B8　　**Fax: (705)748-1786**

📻 **4679 CKPT-AM - 1420**
340 George St. N
Box 177　　　　　　　　　　　**Phone: (705)742-8844**
Peterborough, ON, Canada K9J 6Y8　　**Fax: (705)742-1417**

REXDALE

📖 **4680 Motor Carrier Manager**
Ontario Trucking Association
555 Dixon Rd.　　　　　　　　　**Phone: (416)249-7401**
Rexdale, ON, Canada M9W 1H8　　　**Fax: (416)245-6152**
Ceased publication.

ST. CATHARINES

📖 **4681 Canadian Music Trade**
Norris Publications
23 Hannover Dr., Unit 7　　　　　**Phone: (416)641-3471**
St. Catharines, ON, Canada L2W 1A3　**Fax: (416)641-1648**

📖 **4682 Let's Talk Business**
Rannie Publications
91 Geneva St.　　　　　　　　　**Phone: (416)682-8323**
St. Catharines, ON, Canada L2R 4M9　**Fax: (416)682-3603**
Former Title: Niagara and Hamilton/Oakville

SAINT THOMAS

📖 **4683 The Times-Journal**
16 Hincks St.　　　　　　　　　**Phone: (519)631-2790**
Saint Thomas, ON, Canada N5R 5Z2　**Fax: (519)631-5653**

SCARBOROUGH

📖 **4684 Novy Domov (New Homeland)**
Masaryk Memorial Institute, Inc.
450 Scarborough Golf Club Rd.　　　**Phone: (416)439-4646**
Scarborough, ON, Canada M1G 1H1　　**Fax: (416)439-4646**

📖 **4685 The Underground**
Scarborough College Student Press
University of Toronto
1265 Military Trail, Rm. H213C　　　**Phone: (416)287-7054**
Scarborough, ON, Canada M1C 1A4　　**Fax: (416)287-7013**

SIOUX LOOKOUT

📖 **4686 The Explorer**
111 Meadwell Dr.
PO Box 989　　　　　　　　　　**Phone: (807)737-2959**
Sioux Lookout, ON, Canada P0V 2T0　**Fax: (807)737-3366**
Former Title: Northwest Explorer

SUDBURY

📻 **4687 CBCS-FM - 99.9**
15 MacKenzie St.　　　　　　　　**Phone: (705)688-3200**
Sudbury, ON, Canada P3C 4V1　　　**Fax: (705)688-3220**
Format: Information. **Network(s):** Canadian Broadcasting Corporation (CBC)/Societe Radio-Canada (SRC). **Owner:** Canadian Broadcasting Corp. **Key Personnel:** David Henley, Location Mgr. **Wattage:**
50,000.

TEESWATER

📖 **4688 The Clifford News**
Box 250　　　　　　　　　　　**Phone: (519)392-6175**
Teeswater, ON, Canada N0G 2S0　　**Fax: (519)392-8345**
Community newspaper. **Frequency:** Weekly.
Ad Rates:　PCI:　$4.50　　　　　**Circulation: 800**

Ad Rates:　GLR = general line rate; BW = one-time black & white page rate; 4C = one-time four color page rate; SAU = standard advertising unit rate;
CNU = Canadian newspaper advertising unit rate; PCI = per column inch rate.
Circulation: ★ = ABC; △ = BPA; ◆ = CAC; ● = CCAB; □ = VAC; ⊕ = PO Statement; ‡ = Publisher's Report; Boldface figures = sworn; Light figures = estimated.
Entry type: 📖 = Print; 📻 = Broadcast.

321

THUNDER BAY

♦ 4689 CKPR-TV - Channel 2
87 N. Hill St.   Phone: (807)344-9685
Thunder Bay, ON, Canada P7A 5V6   Fax: (807)345-9923
Format: Commercial TV. **Network(s):** Canadian Broadcasting Corporation (CBC)/Societe Radio-Canada (SRC). **Owner:** Thunder Bay Electronics Ltd. **Founded:** 1954. **Operating Hours:** 18. **Key Personnel:** H. Fraser Dougall, Pres.; A.H. Seuret, V.P./Gen. and Gen. Sales Mgr.; M.E. LaBelle, Program Dir./Promotions Mgr.; Gary Rinne, News Dir.; Manfred Volbracht, Chief Engineer. **Local Programs:** *Thunder Bay Television News Spectrum*.

TORONTO

📖 4690 Benefits Canada
Maclean Hunter Ltd.
777 Bay St.   **Phone: (416)596-5959**
Toronto, ON, Canada M5W 1A7   Fax: (416)593-3166

📖 4691 Borealis
Canadian Parks and Wilderness Society
160 Bloor St. E, Ste. 1335   Phone: (416)972-0868
Toronto, ON, Canada M4W 1E9   Fax: (416)972-0760
Magazine exploring Canadian parks and wilderness from an environmental perspective. **Subtitle:** The Magazine For Canadian Parks And Wilderness. **Founded:** 1989. **Frequency:** 3x/yr. **Subscription:** $35; $44 other countries. $3.95 single issue.
    Circulation: (Not Reported)
Formerly: Park News.

📖 4692 C.A.R.P. News (Canadian Association of Retired Persons)
Kemur Publishing Co. Ltd.
27 Queen St. E, Ste. 1304
Toronto, ON, Canada M5C 2M6   Phone: (416)594-3772
Newspaper for persons over 50. **Frequency:** Quarterly. **Key Personnel:** Isobel Warren, Editor.
    Circulation: (Not Reported)
Advertising accepted; contact publisher for rates. Editorial address: Box 867, Sta. F, Toronto, ON, M4Y 2N7.

📖 4693 Canadian Advertising Rates & Data
Maclean Hunter Ltd.
720 King St. W   Phone: (416)867-9500
Toronto, ON, Canada **M5V 2T3**   **Fax: (416)867-9330**

📖 4694 CineAction!
40 Alexander St., Ste. 705
Toronto, ON, Canada M4Y 1B5   **Phone: (416)964-3534**

📖 4695 Connexions
Connexions Information Sharing Services, Inc.
PO Box 158, Sta. D
Toronto, ON, Canada M6P 3J8   **Phone: (416)537-3949**

📖 4696 Cosmetiques
Maclean Hunter Ltd.
227 Front St. E., Ste. 402   Phone: (416)865-9362
Toronto, ON, Canada M5A 1E8   Fax: (416)865-1933
French edition of Cosmetics. **Subtitle:** Le magazine professionel quebecois de l'industrie de l'esthetique, des parfums et des produits de beaute. **Founded:** 1992. **Frequency:** Quarterly. **Printing Method:** Offset. **Trim Size:** 8 x 10 3/4. **Cols./Page:** 3. **Col. Width:** 26 nonpareils. **Col. Depth:** 140 agate lines. **Key Personnel:** Annie Lachaud, Editor; Ronald A. Wood, Editorial Dir.; Jim Hicks, Exec. Publisher. **Subscription:** $45; $33 Canada; $66 other countries.
Ad Rates: BW: $2,200   **Circulation:** Controlled ●5,000
             4C: $3,250

📖 4697 Dance in Canada (Danse au Canada)
Dance in Canada Assn.
35 McCaul St., Ste. 324C
Toronto, ON, Canada **M6C 2K2**   Phone: (416)595-0165

📖 4698 The Globe and Mail
444 Front St. W.   **Phone: (416)585-5000**
Toronto, ON, Canada M5V 2S9   **Fax: (416)585-5085**

📖 4699 Hazardous Materials Management
CHMM Inc.
401 Richmond St. W.   Phone: (416)348-9922
Toronto, ON, Canada M5V 1X3   Fax: (416)348-9744
Magazine covering the regulation of technology and environment in Canada. **Founded:** 1989. **Subtitle:** The Canadian Publication of Pollution Prevention and Control. **Frequency:** Bimonthly. **Printing Method:** Web offset. **Trim Size:** 8 1/8 x 10 7/8. **Cols./Page:** 3. **Col. Width:** 2 1/4 in. **Col. Depth:** 10 in. **Key Personnel:** Guy Crittenden, Editor; Todd Latham, Publisher. **ISSN:** 0843-9303. **Subscription:** $39.50. $10 single issue.
Ad Rates: BW: $2,450   **Circulation:** Paid ‡2,500
           4C: $3,565   Non-paid ‡15,500

📖 4700 The Imperial Quarterly
HBPO Box 75076
20 Bloor St. E
Toronto, ON, Canada M4W 3T3   Phone: (416)568-9681
Magazine. **Subtitle:** Memories of Old Russia. **Founded:** 1990. **Frequency:** Quarterly. **Printing Method:** Offset. **Key Personnel:** Paul Gilbert, Editor and Publisher. **ISSN:** 1188-0066. **Subscription:** $20 U.S.; $25 other countries. $6 single issue.
Ad Rates: BW: $150   **Circulation:** Paid 1,000
                          Non-paid 2,000

📖 4701 Impulse
Impulse Society for Cultural Presentation
16 Skey Ln.
Toronto, ON, Canada M6J 3S4   Phone: (416)537-9551
Ceased publication.

📖 4702 JW Plus
Jewellery World Ltd.
Canada Trust Tower, Ste. 1203
20 Eglinton Ave. W., Box 2021   Phone: (416)480-1450
Toronto, ON, Canada M4R 1K8   Fax: (416)480-2342
Jewelry trade publication. **Founded:** 1976. **Frequency:** Bimonthly. **Printing Method:** Sheetfed offset. **Trim Size:** 8 1/8 x 10 7/8. **Cols./Page:** 4/ **Col. Width:** 1 5/8 in. **Key Personnel:** Lorne Thorpe, Publisher. **Subscription:** $65; $100 other countries. (Includes Jewellery World Magazine.)
Ad Rates: BW: $325   **Circulation:** Non-paid ‡9,015
            PCI: $50

📖 4703 Kanadsky Slovak
Slovak Canadian Publishing, Inc.
1736 Dundas St. W.   Phone: (416)531-2055
Toronto, ON, Canada M6K 1V5   **Fax: (416)533-6924**

📖 4704 Kerala Express
PO Box 5, Sta. W
Toronto, ON, Canada **M6M 4Y9**   Phone: (416)654-0431

📖 4705 Kids Toronto
KidsCanada Publishing Corp.
540 Mt. Pleasant Rd., No. 201   Phone: (416)481-5696
Toronto, ON, Canada M4S 2M6   Fax: (416)481-3883

📖 4706 Leaside/Rosedale Town Crier
Town Crier, Inc.
1560 Bayview Ave., Ste.303
Toronto, ON, Canada M4G 3B8   Phone: (416)488-4779
Community newspaper. **Founded:** 1981. **Frequency:** Monthly. **Printing Method:** Offset. **Trim Size:** 11 3/8 x 17. **Cols./Page:** 5. **Col. Width:** 11.5 picas. **Col. Depth:** 94 picas.
    Circulation: (Not Reported)

📖 4707 LEISUREWAYS
Canada Wide Magazines Ltd.
2 Carlton St., Ste. 1707
Toronto, ON, Canada M5B 1J3   Phone: (416)595-5007

📖 4708 L'Express
17 Carlaw Rd., 2nd Fl.   Phone: (416)465-2107
Toronto, ON, Canada M4M 2R6   Fax: (416)465-3778
Former Title: L'Express de l'Ontario

4709 Magyar Elet (Hungarian Life)
Reform Hungaria Publishing Service Inc.
21 Vaughan Rd., Ste. 201   Phone: (416)652-6370
Toronto, ON, Canada M6G 2N2   Fax: (416)652-6370

4710 Materials Management & Distribution
Maclean Hunter Ltd.
777 Bay St.   Phone: (416)496-0220
Toronto, ON, Canada M5W 1A7   Fax: (416)496-7898

4711 The Mills Town Crier
Town Crier, Inc.
1560 Bayview Ave., Ste. 303   Phone: (416)488-4779
Toronto, ON, Canada M4G 3B8   Fax: (416)488-4918
Community newspaper (tabloid). **Founded:** 1991. **Frequency:** Monthly.
Printing Method: Offset **Trim Size:** 11 3/8 x 17. **Cols./Page:** 5. **Col. Width:** 11.5 picas. **Col. Depth:** 94 picas. **Key Personnel:** Malcolm Kelly, Editor; Harry Goldhar, Publisher; Ruth Goldhar, Advertising Mgr. **Subscription:** $18.
Ad Rates: GLR: $1.56   **Circulation:** Free 25,000
            BW: $1,185

4712 Orleans Xpress
1455 Youville Dr., Ste 209   Phone: (613)830-2000
Orleans, ON, Canada K1C 4R1   Fax: (613)830-1116

4713 Peritoneal Dialysis International
Multimed Inc.
1120 Finch Ave. W., Ste. 601
Toronto, ON, Canada M3J 3H7
Magazine for health professionals. **Frequency:** Quarterly. **Printing Method:** Offset. **Trim Size:** 8 1/2 x 11. **Key Personnel:** L. Cooper, Pres. **ISSN:** 0896-8608. **Subscription:** $110; $160 other.
Circulation: Paid ‡4,000

4714 Probe Post
The Pollution Probe Foundation
12 Madison Ave.   Phone: (416)926-1907
Toronto, ON, Canada M5R 2S1   Fax: (416)926-1601
Ceased publication.

4715 Quill & Quire
70 The Esplanade, 4th Fl.   Phone: (416)360-0044
Toronto, ON, Canada M5E 1R2   Fax: (416)360-8745

4716 Saturday Night
184 Front St. E., Ste. 400   Phone: (416)368-7237
Toronto, ON, Canada M5A 4N3   Fax: (416)368-5112

4717 TG Magazine
Teen Generation, Inc.
202 Cleveland St.   Phone: (416)487-3204
Toronto, ON, Canada M4S 2W6   Fax: (416)481-8226

4718 THEATRUM
PO Box 688 Sta. C   Phone: (416)493-5740
Toronto, ON, Canada M6J 3S1   Fax: (416)493-5740

4719 Toronto
The Globe and Mail
444 Front St. W.   Phone: (416)585-5411
Toronto, ON, Canada M5V 2S9   Fax: (416)585-5275
Ceased publication.

4720 TV Guide
Telemedia Publishing, Inc.
50 Holly St.   Phone: (416)482-8600
Toronto, ON, Canada M4S 3B3   Fax: (416)482-6054

4721 The World Affairs Canada Quarterly
World Affairs Canada
6 Hoskin Ave.   Phone: (416)599-8183
Toronto, ON, Canada M5S 1H8   Fax: (416)599-4752
Bilingual magazine for youth about world affairs (English/French).

Founded: 1992. **Frequency:** Quarterly. **Trim Size:** 8 1/2 x 11. **ISSN:** 1188-6870. **Subscription:** Free.
Circulation: (Not Reported)

4722 CBL-AM - 1927
Box 500, Terminal A   Phone: (416)975-7400
Toronto, ON, Canada M5W 1E6   Fax: (417)975-6336

4723 CFTO-TV - Channel 9
Box 9, Sta. O
Toronto, ON, Canada M4A 2M9   Phone: (416)299-2000

4724 CITY-TV - Channel 57
299 Queen St. W
Toronto, ON, Canada M5V 2Z5   Phone: (416)591-5757

4725 CJEZ-FM - 97.3
40 Eglinton E., 6th Fl.   Phone: (416)480-2097
Toronto, ON, Canada M4P 3B6   Fax: (416)480-0688
Format: Soft Adult Contemporary. **Owner:** Robert E. Redmond. **Founded:** 1987. **Operating Hours:** Continuous. **Key Personnel:** Robert E. Redmond, Pres.; Jay Jackson, Executive V.P.; J. Robert Wood, Gen. Mgr.; M. Mangialardo, Gen. Sales Mgr.; V. Delilla, Operations Mgr. **Wattage:** 4000 ERP. **Ad Rates:** $68-$160 $TSC;$85-$200 for 60 seconds.

4726 CKLN-FM - 88.1
380 Victoria St.
Toronto, ON, Canada M5B 1W7   Phone: (416)595-1477
Format: Alternative/Independent/Progressive. **Owner:** Ryerson University. **Founded:** 1970. **Formerly:** CRFM-FM. **Operating Hours:** Continuous. **Key Personnel:** Denise Benson, Music Dir.; Eun-Sook Lee, Station Mgr.; Nada El-Yassir, News Dir. **Wattage:** 250. **Ad Rates:** $30-$45 for 30 seconds; $45-$70 for 60 seconds. **Additional Contact Information:** News line (416)595-5068.

TRENTON

4727 CONTACT
CFB Trenton
PO Box 40   Phone: (613)965-7248
Astra, ON, Canada K0K 1B0   Fax: (613)965-7091

WATERLOO

4728 ALTERNATIVES
Alternatives, Inc.
University of Waterloo
c/o Faculty of Environmental Studies   Phone: (519)885-1211
Waterloo, ON, Canada N2L 3G1   Fax: (519)746-0292

4729 Biotechnology Advances
Institute for Biotechnology Research
University of Waterloo   Phone: (519)888-4006
Waterloo, ON, Canada N2L 3GI   Fax: (519)746-4979
Journal covering research, reviews and patent abstracts on biotechnology. **Founded:** 1981. **Frequency:** Quarterly. **Printing Method:** Camera-ready copy. **Trim Size:** 6 x 9. **Key Personnel:** M. Moo-Young, Exec. Editor; B.R. Glick, Editor. **ISSN:** 0734-9750. **Subscription:** $185.
Circulation: 500
Advertising not accepted.

WILLOWDALE

4730 Electronic Composition & Imaging
Youngblood Communications Corp.
505 Consumers Rd., Ste. 102   Phone: (416)299-6007
Willowdale, ON, Canada M2J 4V8   Fax: (416)299-6674

WINDSOR

♠ 4731 CBE-FM - 89.9
PO Box 1609   Phone: (519)255-3411
Windsor, ON, Canada N9A 1K7   Fax: (519)255-3573
Format: Classical. **Network(s):** Canadian Broadcasting Corporation (CBC)/Societe Radio-Canada (SRC). **Owner:** Canadian Broadcasting Corp. **Founded:** 1950. **Key Personnel:** Randall Barnard, Mgr.; Phil Peck, Exec. Producer. **Additional Contact Information:** Studio address: Security Bldg., 9th Fl., 267 Pelissier St., Windsor, ON N9A 4K5.

♠ 4732 CKLW-FM - 93.9
Box 480   Phone: (519)258-8888
Windsor, ON, Canada N9A 6M6   Fax: (519)258-0182
Format: Oldies. **Owner:** CUC Broadcasting Ltd. **Founded:** 1932. **Formerly:** CKMR-FM. **Operating Hours:** Continuous. **Key Personnel:** Terry Coles, Pres.; Dave Shafer, Operations Mgr.; Agnes Kerekes, Controller. **Wattage:** 100,000.

QUEBEC

ABITIBIENS

4733 Les Echos Abitibiens
1061, rue de l'Echo
PO Box 100   **Phone:** (819)825-3755
Val D'Or, PQ, Canada J9P 4P2 **Fax: (819)825-0361**

ASBESTOS

4734 CJAN-AM - 1340
Edifice Hotel de Ville
185 Du Roi, bureau 301 **Phone:** (819)879-5439
Asbestos, PQ, Canada J1T 1S4 **Fax: (819)879-9922**

COOKSHIRE

4735 Le Haut St-Francois
80 Est, rue Principale
PO Box 292 **Phone:** (819)875-5501
Cookshire, PQ, Canada J0B 1M0 **Fax: (819)875-5327**

DEGELIS

4736 CFVD-AM - 1370
654, 6ieme Rue
CP 670 **Phone:** (418)853-3370
Degelis, PQ, Canada G0L 1H0 **Fax: (418)853-3321**

4737 CFVD-FM - 102, 104 & 92
654, 6ieme Rue
CP 670 **Phone:** (418)853-3370
Degelis, PQ, Canada G0L 1H0 **Fax: (418)853-3321**

FARNHAM

4738 Le Producteur Plus
Les Editions L'Estampille Inc.
C.P. 147
455-A, St-Hillaire **Phone:** (514)293-8282
Farnham, PQ, Canada J2N 2R5 **Fax:** (514)293-8554
Farm magazine. **Founded:** 1991. **Frequency:** 10x/yr. **Printing Method:** Offset. **Trim Size:** 8 1/4 x 10 7/8. **Cols./Page:** 2, 3, or 4. **Col. Width:** 2 1/8 in. or 3 3/8 in. **Col. Depth:** 10 in. **Key Personnel:** Leonard Pigeon, Publisher. **ISSN:** 1183-9929. **Subscription:** $24.95.
Ad Rates: BW: $1,529 **Circulation:** ⊕12,353
   4C: $2,420 Non-paid ⊕3,522

FORT COULONGE

4739 CHIP-FM - 101.5
Box 820
La Radio du Pontiac **Phone:** (819)683-3155
Fort Coulonge, PQ, Canada J0X 1V0 **Fax: (819)683-3211**

JONQUIERE

4740 CFRS-TV - Channel 4
2303 rue Sir Wilfrid Laurier
Jonquiere, PQ, Canada G7X 7X3 **Phone:** (418)542-4551

KAHNAWAKE

4741 Kateri
Vice Postulation for the Cause of Canonization of Blessed Kateri
 Tekakwitha
PO Box 70
Kahnawake, PQ, Canada J0L 1B0 **Phone: (514)638-1546**

LAVAL

4742 Courrier des Moulins
Les Hebdos Telemedia Inc.
317 Montmorency **Phone:** (514)667-4360
Laval, PQ, Canada H7N 1X1 **Fax: (514)667-9498**

MANIWAKI

4743 CKMG-AM - 1340
175, Commerciale, Ste. 110 **Phone:** (819)449-1211
Maniwaki, PQ, Canada J9E 1P1 Fax: (819)449-7457

MONTREAL

4744 ADSUM
BFC Valcartier
Edifice 513, Ch. 140 **Phone:** (418)844-5598
Courcelette, PQ, Canada G0A 1R0 **Fax: (418)844-6643**

4745 Bulletin Voyages
Editions Acra Ltee.
Succursale E.
78 blvd. St. Joseph **Phone:** (514)287-9773
Montreal, PQ, Canada **H2T 2P4** Fax: (514)842-6180

Ad Rates: GLR = general line rate; BW = one-time black & white page rate; 4C = one-time four color page rate; SAU = standard advertising unit rate; CNU = Canadian newspaper advertising unit rate; PCI = per column inch rate.
Circulation: ★ = ABC; △ = BPA; ◆ = CAC; ● = CCAB; □ = VAC; ⊕ = PO Statement; ‡ = Publisher's Report; Boldface figures = sworn; Light figures = estimated.
Entry type: ▥ = Print; ♨ = Broadcast.

⊞ **4746 Electronique Industrielle et Commerciale (EIC)**
SERPRO International Inc.
8735 Lucien Plante   Phone: (514)383-7700
Montreal, PQ, Canada **H2M 2M7**   Fax: (514)383-7691

⊞ **4747 En Ville Montreal**
En Ville Publications, Inc.
8270 Mountain Sights, Ste. 201   Phone: (514)731-9471
Montreal, PQ, Canada H4P 2B7   Fax: (514)731-7459
Ceased publication.

⊞ **4748 Le Cooperateur Agricole**
La Cooperative Federee de Quebec
B.P. 500 Sta. Youville   Phone: (514)384-6450
Montreal, PQ, Canada H2P 2W2   **Fax: (514)858-2025**

⊞ **4749 Le Graffiti**
College Jean-de-Brebeuf
5625 Decelles   Phone: (514)342-3663
Montreal, PQ, Canada H3T 1W4   **Fax: (514)342-0130**

⊞ **4750 Le Magazine Affaires Plus**
Publications TRANSCONTINENTAL Inc.
1100 boul. Rene-Levesque ouest, 24
  etage   **Phone: (514)392-9000**
Montreal, PQ, Canada **H3B 4X9**   **Fax: (514)393-9430**

⊞ **4751 Le Mart**
Communications Vero Inc.
1600 Henry Bourassa W., No. 420   Phone: (514)332-8376
Montreal, PQ, Canada H3M 3E2   Fax: (514)744-2359
Ceased publication.

⊞ **4752 LES AFFAIRES**
Publications TRANSCONTINENTAL Inc.
1100, boul. Rene-Levesque Ouest, 24e
  Etage   **Phone: (514)392-9000**
Montreal, PQ, Canada **H3B 4X9**   **Fax: (514)392-4723**

⊞ **4753 The Link**
Link Publications Society Inc.
1455 de Maisonneuve W., Rm. H-649   Phone: (514)848-7405
Montreal, PQ, Canada H3G 1M8   **Fax: (514)848-3494**

⊞ **4754 MTL (English Edition)**
En Ville Publications Inc.
4984 Place de la Savane   Phone: (514)731-9517
Montreal, PQ, Canada **H4P 2M9**   **Fax: (514)731-6646**

⊞ **4755 MTL (French Edition)**
En Ville Publications
4984 Place de la Savane   Phone: (514)731-9517
Montreal, PQ, Canada **H4P 2M9**   **Fax: (514)731-6646**

⊞ **4756 Practical Allergy & Immunology**
Medicopea International Inc.
8200 Decarie Blvd., Ste. 212   Phone: (514)340-9157
Montreal, PQ, Canada H4P 2P5   Fax: (514)342-5783
Journal focusing on practical information for allergists and immunol-
ogists. **Frequency:** Quarterly. **ISSN:** 0831-0998. **Subscription:** $40; $60
other countries.
                                       Circulation: 3,195
Advertising accepted; contact publisher for rates.

⊞ **4757 Practical Optometry**
Medicopea International Inc.
8200 Decarie Blvd., Ste. 212   Phone: (514)340-9157
Montreal, PQ, Canada H4P 2P5   Fax: (514)342-5783
Journal for optometrists. **Frequency:** Quarterly. **ISSN:** 1181-6058.
Subscription: $40; $60 other countries.
                                       Circulation: 2,300
Advertising accepted; contact publisher for rates.

⊞ **4758 Quebec Yachting**
Publications TRANSCONTINENTAL Inc.
1100 boulevard Rene-Levesque Ouest,
  24e etage   **Phone: (514)392-9000**
Montreal, PQ, Canada **H3B 4X9**   **Fax: (514)392-4726**

⊞ **4759 RG**
CP 5245, Succursale C   Phone: (514)523-9463
Montreal, PQ, Canada H2X 3M4   Fax: (514)523-9463
Publication focusing on homosexual issues. **Founded:** 1982. **Frequen-
cy:** Monthly. **Printing Method:** Offset. **Trim Size:** 8 x 10. **Cols./Page:** 3.
Col. Width: 14 picas. **Key Personnel:** Alain Bouchard, Editor.
Subscription: $45; $50 U.S. $4 single issue.
Ad Rates: BW: $500   **Circulation:** Non-paid ‡10,500
               4C: $1,200
               PCI: $25

🎙 **4760 CKUT-FM - 90.3**
3480 McTavish
Ste. B 15   Phone: (514)398-6787
Montreal, PQ, Canada H3A 1X9   Fax: (514)398-8261
Format: Alternative/Independent/Progressive. **Founded:** 1987. **Operat-
ing Hours:** 9 a.m.-6 p.m. **Key Personnel:** Brian Zuraw, Music Dir.;
Louise Burns, Sales Mgr.; Rebecca Scott, Coordinator. **Wattage:** 5700.
Ad Rates: $12-$25 for 30 seconds; $24-$50 for 60 seconds.

🎙 **4761 Sorel-O-Vision Inc.**
1420 Sherbrooke St. W., Ste. 500   **Phone: (514)849-3711**
Montreal, PQ, Canada H3G 1K5   **Fax: (514)849-1855**

MOUNT ROYAL

⊞ **4762 Economic Planning In Free Societies**
Academic Publishing Co.
PO Box 145
Mount Royal, PQ, Canada H3P 3B9   **Phone: (514)738-5255**

QUEBEC

🎙 **4763 CKMI-TV - Channel 5**
1000 Myrand Ave.
Box 2026   Phone: (418)688-9330
Quebec, PQ, Canada G1V 2W3   **Fax: (418)688-4239**

RIMOUSKI

⊞ **4764 Le Havre**
73 St.-Germain Est
C.P. 710   Phone: (418)723-4800
Rimouski, PQ, Canada G5L 7C4   Fax: (418)722-4078

⊞ **4765 Le Pharillion Voyageur**
Les Editions Le Pharillion, Inc.
73 Est, rue St-Germain
C.P. 410   Phone: (418)723-4800
Rimouski, PQ, Canada G5L 7C4   Fax: (418)722-4078

⊞ **4766 Le Progres-Echo**
Echo du Bas St-Laurent
73 St.-Germain est
C.P. 710   Phone: (418)723-4800
Rimouski, PQ, Canada G5L 7C4   Fax: (418)722-4078

⊞ **4767 Le Rimouskois**
Les Editions Rimouskoises Inc.
156 Lepage
C.P. 460   Phone: (418)723-2571
Rimouski, PQ, Canada G5L 7C5   Fax: (418)723-1855

RIVIERE-DU-LOUP

🎙 **4768 CION-FM - 103.7**
279-A Lafontaine   Phone: (418)867-1037
Riviere-du-Loup, PQ, Canada G5R 3A9   Fax: (418)867-2829
Format: Album-Oriented Rock (AOR). **Owner:** CION FM Inc., at
above address. **Founded:** 1989. **Key Personnel:** Pierre Simon, Pres.;
Ghislain Morissette, Gen. Mgr./Program Dir. **Wattage:** 60,000.

🎙 **4769 Teledistribution Cablouis Inc.**
279A LaFontaine
Case Postale 1390   **Phone: (418)867-1478**
Riviere-du-Loup, PQ, Canada G5R 4L9 Fax: (418)867-2829

SAINT-LAURENT

📖 **4770 Canadian Wood Products**
Southam Business Communications Inc.
3300 Cote Vertu, Ste. 410   Phone: (514)339-1399
Saint-Laurent, PQ, Canada H4R 2B7   Fax: (514)339-1396
Magazine includes information on the sawmilling and remanufacturing industries. **Subtitle:** The Sawmilling and Remanufacturing Magazine. **Founded:** 1991. **Frequency:** Quarterly. **Printing Method:** Offset. **Cols./Page:** 3. **Col. Width:** 13 picas. **Col. Depth:** 60 picas. **Key Personnel:** Rollin Milroy, Editor; Tim Tolton, Publisher. **Subscription:** $15; $18 other countries. $4 single issue.
                    Circulation: Non-paid **6,256**
Advertising accepted; contact publisher for rates.

SASKATCHEWAN

CARNDUFF

4771 Triangle News
Box 689
Coronach, SK, Canada S0H 0Z0
Phone: (306)267-3381
Fax: (306)267-3381

KINDERSLEY

4772 West-Central Crossroads
Jamac Publishing Ltd.
909 Main St.
PO Box 1150
Kindersley, SK, Canada S0L 1S0
Phone: (306)463-4611
Fax: (306)463-6505
Shopping guide. **Frequency:** Weekly. **Printing Method:** Offset. **Trim Size:** 16 x 22 3/4. **Cols./Page:** 7. **Col. Depth:** 300 agate lines. **Key Personnel:** Tim Crump, Editor; Stewart Crump, Advertising Mgr. **Subscription:** Free.
Ad Rates: GLR: $.65 **Circulation:** Free ⊕8,500
BW: $1,365
PCI: $9.10

KIPLING

4773 Resort Weekly
PO Box 329
Kipling, SK, Canada S0G 2S0
Phone: (306)736-2535
Fax: (306)736-8445
Community newspaper covering the areas of Moose Mountain Provincial Park, White Bear Lake Resort, and Village of Kenosee Lake. **Founded:** 1989. **Frequency:** Weekly (May-Aug.). **Printing Method:** Offset. **Trim Size:** 11 1/2 x 14. **Cols./Page:** 5. **Col. Depth:** 207 agate lines. **Key Personnel:** G. Scott Kearns, Contact. **Subscription:** Free.
Ad Rates: GLR: $.43 **Circulation:** Non-paid 2,000
BW: $445
PCI: $6.02
Seasonal publication from May to mid-August.

MOOSE JAW

4774 Friday Magazine
Canadian Newspapers Co. Ltd.
44 Fairford St. W.
Moose Jaw, SK, Canada S6H 6E4
Phone: (306)692-6441
Fax: (306)692-2101
Community newspaper with TV listings. **Frequency:** 2x/mo. **Key Personnel:** John Strauss, Editor.
Circulation: Paid ‡10,000
Free ‡12,000
Advertising accepted; contact publisher for rates. Attention: David Singer. **Formerly:** TV Scene.

4775 Golden Years
Canadian Newspapers Co. Ltd.
44 Fairford St. W.
Moose Jaw, SK, Canada S6H 6E4
Phone: (306)692-6441
Fax: (306)692-2101
Publication for mature adults. **Founded:** 1989. **Frequency:** Quarterly. **Cols./Page:** 5. **Col. Width:** 2 in. **Col. Depth:** 13 in.
Circulation: Paid ‡10,000
Free ‡12,000
Advertising accepted; contact publisher for rates. Attention: Dave Singer.

4776 Money Saver
Canadian Newspapers Co. Ltd.
44 Fairford St., W.
Moose Jaw, SK, Canada S6H 6E4
Phone: (306)692-6441
Fax: (306)692-2101
Shopping guide providing local and syndicated news. **Frequency:** Weekly. **Cols./Page:** 5. **Col. Width:** 2 in. **Col. Depth:** 13 in. **Subscription:** Free.
Ad Rates: GLR: $.86 **Circulation:** Free ★12,000
BW: $782.60
4C: $1,257.60
PCI: $12.04

PRINCE ALBERT

♣ 4777 CIPA-TV - Channel 9
22 10th St. W.
Prince Albert, SK, Canada S6V 3A5
Phone: (306)922-6066
Fax: (306)763-3041

REGINA

4778 Grain
Saskatchewan Writers Guild
PO Box 1154
Regina, SK, Canada S4P 3B4
Phone: (306)757-6310
Fax: (306)565-8554

♣ 4779 CKCK-AM - 620
Box 6200
Regina, SK, Canada S4P 3H7
Phone: (306)569-6200
Fax: (306)352-5105

♣ 4780 CKIT-FM - 104.9
Box 1049
Regina, SK, Canada S4P 3B2
Phone: (306)924-1049
Fax: (306)352-5105

SASKATOON

♣ 4781 CBKS-FM - 105.5
CN Tower, 5th Fl.
Saskatoon, SK, Canada S7K 1J5
Phone: (306)956-7400
Fax: (306)956-7488
Format: News. Rebroadcasts CBKST-TV. **Network(s):** Canadian Broadcasting Corporation (CBC)/Societe Radio-Canada (SRC). **Own-**

er: Canadian Broadcasting Corp. **Key Personnel:** Gary Crippen, Operations Mgr.

4782 CBKST-TV - Channel 11
CN Tower, 5th Fl.   Phone: (306)956-7400
Saskatoon, SK, Canada S7K 1J5   Fax: (306)956-7488
Network(s): Canadian Broadcasting Corporation (CBC)/Societe Radio-Canada (SRC). **Owner:** Canadian Broadcasting Corp. **Founded:** 1971. **Key Personnel:** Gary Crippen, Operations Mgr.; Don Burdego, Sales Mgr.; Art Williams, Transmitter Supv.; Sheila Coles, Bureau TV Producer. **Local Programs:** *Newshour. CBC News First.*

WADENA

4783 The Wadena News
102 1st St. NE
PO Box 100
Wadena, SK, Canada S0A 4J0   Phone: (306)338-2231

WEYBURN

4784 Booster
Box 400
904 East Ave.   Phone: (306)842-7487
Weyburn, SK, Canada S4H 2K4   Fax: (306)842-0282
Shopper. **Founded:** 1972. **Frequency:** Weekly. **Printing Method:** Offset. **Trim Size:** 11 x 17. **Cols./Page:** 6. **Col. Width:** 9 1/2 in. **Col. Depth:** 15 in. **Key Personnel:** P. Ward, Editor; D. Ward Publisher. **Subscription:** Free.
Ad Rates: GLR: $.53   **Circulation:** Free ‡16,401
           PCI: $7.42

MASTER NAME AND KEYWORD INDEX

The Master Index is a comprehensive listing of all entries, both print and broadcast, included in this *Directory*. Citations in this index are interfiled alphabetically throughout regardless of media type. Publications are cited according to title and important keywords within titles; broadcast citations are by station call letters or cable company names. Indexed here also are: notices of recent cessations; former call letters or titles; foreign language and other alternate publication titles; other types of citations. Indexing is word-by-word rather than letter-by-letter, so that "New York" files before "News". Listings in the Master Index include geographic locations and entry numbers.

A

A. Magazine (New York, NY) **2827**
A Better Tomorrow (Washington, DC) **792**
A-R Cable Services, Inc. (Rockford, IL) **1391**
A-R Cable Services, Inc. (Auburn, ME) **1814**
A-R Cable Services, Inc. (Bangor, ME) **1815**
AAA Delaware Motorist (Philadelphia, PA) **3629**
AAA Maryland Motorist (Philadelphia, PA) **3630**
ABA Journal (Chicago, IL) **1242**
ABC Today (Washington, DC) **793**
Aberdeen Cable TV (Aberdeen, SD) **3785**
Ability Magazine (Irvine, CA) **308**
Abingdon Argus (Abingdon, IL) **1204**
Abitibiens; Les Echos (Abitibiens, PQ, Can.) **4733**
Aboriginal Science Fiction (Woburn, MA) **2020**
Abstracts; Gas (Chicago, IL) **1262**
Abstracts in Social Gerontology (Newbury Park, CA) **390**
Academic Questions (New Brunswick, NJ) **2573**
The Academy of Florida Trial Lawyers Journal (Tallahassee, FL) **1021**
Accent and Travelog (Ogden, UT) **4083**
Access! Manhattan (New York, NY) **2828**
Accountants; Taxation for (New York, NY) **3038**
Accounting, Management and Information Technologies (Tarrytown, NY) **3132**
Accounting Today (New York, NY) **2829**
Acid Precipitation (Oak Ridge, TN) **3859**
ACM Computing Surveys (New York, NY) **2830**
ACM Transactions on Database Systems (New York, NY) **2831**
ACM Transactions on Graphics (New York, NY) **2832**
ACM Transactions on Information Systems (New York, NY) **2833**
ACM Transactions on Mathematical Software (New York, NY) **2834**

ACM Transactions on Programming Languages and Systems (New York, NY) **2835**
Acoustical Physics (New York, NY) **2836**
Acquisition of Greater Dayton (Dayton, OH) **3394**
Across the Board (New York, NY) **2837**
Active Aging (Wichita, KS) **1690**
Activities, Adaptation and Aging (Binghamton, NY) **2691**
Acton Corp. North Arundel CATV (Millersville, MD) **1912**
Ad-Delite (Strum, WI) **4454**
Ad/Mag **2392**
Ad News (Greenfield, IN) **1462**
Ad Power (Mayville, WI) **4401**
Ad-Visor (Beulah, MI) **2042**
Adbusters (Vancouver, BC, Can.) **4546**
Addictions; American Journal of (Washington, DC) **795**
Adel News-Tribune (Adel, GA) **1049**
Adelphia Cable (West Seneca, NY) **3189**
Adelphia Cable (Bennington, VT) **4108**
Adelphia Cable (Charlottesville, VA) **4154**
Adelphia Cable Associates-South Dade (Princeton, FL) **1002**
Adelphia Cable Communications of Niagara (Niagara Falls, NY) **3080**
Adelphia Communications (Riviera Beach, FL) **1004**
Adhesives Age (Atlanta, GA) **1056**
Administration & Management; Library (Chicago, IL) **1277**
Administrative Law Review (Chicago, IL) **1243**
The Adobe Journal: Traditions Southwest (Albuquerque, NM) **2637**
Adolescence (San Diego, CA) **484**
ADSUM (Montreal, PQ, Can.) **4744**
The Advance (Holstein, IA) **1588**
Advance Leader (Ligonier, IN) **1497**
Advanced Systems News (Newton, MA) **1984**
Advances in Free Radical Biology & Medicine **3162**
The Advertiser (Ames, IA) **1531**
The Advertiser (Homer, LA) **1785**

Advertiser (Mora, MN) **2227**
The Advertiser (Sun Prairie, WI) **4455**
The Advertiser-Gleam (Guntersville, AL) **35**
The Advertisers News (Hanover, ON, Can.) **4630**
Advertising Age (New York, NY) **2838**
Advertising Rates & Data; Canadian (Toronto, ON, Can.) **4693**
Advertising Research; Journal of (New York, NY) **2931**
Advertising; St. Louis (Saint Louis, MO) **2392**
Adviser; Central Alberta (Red Deer, AB, Can.) **4516**
Advisor (Mitchell, SD) **3790**
The Advocate (San Pablo, CA) **551**
The Advocate (Williamstown, MA) **2018**
The Advocate-Tribune (Granite Falls, MN) **2190**
AdvocateMEN (Los Angeles, CA) **330**
Aero Magazine (Mission Viejo, CA) **382**
AERO Sun-Times (Helena, MT) **2436**
Aerosol Science; Journal of (Tarrytown, NY) **3166**
Aerospace Products (Morris Plains, NJ) **2568**
Aesthetics and Art Criticism; The Journal of (Madison, WI) **4386**
AFFAIRES; LES (Montreal, PQ, Can.) **4752**
Affaires Plus; Le Magazine (Montreal, PQ, Can.) **4750**
Affordable Aircraft (Canoga Park, CA) **242**
Afn Shvel (New York, NY) **2839**
Africa; Network **2745**
African Studies; Journal of Pan (Fresno, CA) **284**
Aftermarket Business (Cleveland, OH) **3359**
Ag Focus (Batavia, NY) **2689**
Ag Impact **2689**
Agent & Broker; American (Saint Louis, MO) **2377**
Aging; Active (Wichita, KS) **1690**
Aging; Activities, Adaptation and (Binghamton, NY) **2691**
Aging; Journal of Women and (Binghamton, NY) **2729**

Aging Research; Experimental (Washington, DC) **816**

Aging and Social Policy; Journal of (Binghamton, NY) **2694**

Agri-News; South Texas (Mission, TX) **4033**

Agricultural Economics; Canadian Journal of (Ottawa, ON, Can.) **4654**

Agriculture; California (Oakland, CA) **410**

Agriculture; Louisiana (Baton Rouge, LA) **1766**

AHIMA; Journal of (Chicago, IL) **1270**

AICHE Journal (New York, NY) **2840**

Aiken Cablevision Ltd. (Aiken, SC) **3719**

AIPE Facilities (Cincinnati, OH) **3342**

Air Cargo World (Atlanta, GA) **1057**

Air; Compressed (Washington, NJ) **2634**

Air Law and Commerce; Journal of (Dallas, TX) **3938**

The Air Pollution Consultant (Lakewood, CO) **686**

AirCapital Cablevision, Inc. (Wichita, KS) **1692**

Airgunner; American (Abilene, TX) **3868**

Airport Press (Jamaica, NY) **2797**

Airports International (Houston, TX) **3977**

Airpower Journal (Montgomery, AL) **58**

Akita World (Wheat Ridge, CO) **706**

Al Talib (Los Angeles, CA) **331**

Alabama Conservation (Montgomery, AL) **59**

Alabama School Journal (Montgomery, AL) **60**

Alabama, Inc.; TCI Cablevision of (Hoover, AL) **38**

The Alabamian (Montevallo, AL) **57**

Alameda; Senior Spectrum Monthly, (Sacramento, CA) **461**

The Alamosa News (Alamosa, CO) **627**

Alaska Geographic (Anchorage, AK) **79**

Alaskan Cable Network Inc. (Juneau, AK) **93**

Albion: A Quarterly Journal Concerned with British Studies (Boone, NC) **3207**

Albuquerque Woman (Albuquerque, NM) **2638**

Alcohol (Greenville, NC) **3248**

Alert Cable TV (Greensboro, NC) **3244**

All About Kids (Cincinnati, OH) **3343**

All-American Cablevision (Columbus, OH) **3391**

All Crosswords Special (Ambler, PA) **3550**

All Number-Finds (Ambler, PA) **3551**

Allan Kaye's Sports Cards News & Price Guides (St. Louis, MO) **2376**

Alleghany Highlander (Covington, VA) **4161**

The Alleghany News (Sparta, NC) **3283**

Allegheny Trucker (Indianapolis, IN) **1468**

Alma Times-Statesman (Alma, GA) **1050**

Alpha Epsilon Pi; The Lion of (Indianapolis, IN) **1477**

Alta Vista Journal (Alta Vista, KS) **1624**

Alternative Press (Cleveland, OH) **3360**

ALTERNATIVES (Waterloo, ON, Can.) **4728**

Altoona; Warner Cable Communications, Inc. of (Altoona, PA) **3549**

Alumnae Magazine **2011**

Alumnae Quarterly; Mount Holyoke (South Hadley, MA) **1998**

Alumni Magazine; Dartmouth (Hanover, NH) **2508**

Alzheimer Disease and Associated Disorders (New York, NY) **2841**

Amalgam (Dayton, OH) **3395**

Amarillo; TV Cable of (Amarillo, TX) **3875**

Amazon Times (Owings Mills, MD) **1920**

Ambiance (Portage, MI) **2135**

Amerasia Journal (Los Angeles, CA) **332**

The American (Provo, UT) **4090**

American Academy of Allergy and Immunology—News and Notes (Milwaukee, WI) **4404**

American Agent & Broker (Saint Louis, MO) **2377**

American Airgunner (Abilene, TX) **3868**

American-Arab Message (Detroit, MI) **2054**

American Bankers Association Banking Literature Index (Washington, DC) **794**

The American Biology Teacher (Reston, VA) **4206**

American Bookseller (Tarrytown, NY) **3133**

American Cable TV of St. Marys County (Hollywood, MD) **1907**

American Cablesystems **370**

American Cablesystems of South Central Los Angeles (Los Angeles, CA) **368**

American Cablevision (Thornton, CO) **702**

American Cablevision (Indianapolis, IN) **1486**

American Cablevision (Terre Haute, IN) **1523**

American Cablevision (Kansas City, MO) **2354**

American Cablevision of Queens (Flushing, NY) **2773**

American Cinematographer (Hollywood, CA) **302**

American Cinemeditor **276**

American College of Dentists; Journal of the (San Diego, CA) **494**

American Community Cablevision (Ithaca, NY) **2793**

American Country Collectibles (New York, NY) **2842**

The American Eagle **4090**

AMERICAN EAGLE; The Utah (West Jordan, UT) **4107**

American Ethnic History; Journal of (New Brunswick, NJ) **2582**

American Family Physician (Kansas City, MO) **2348**

American Fire Journal (Bellflower, CA) **219**

American Gas (Arlington, VA) **4138**

The American Genealogist (Demorest, GA) **1111**

American Hockey Magazine (Colorado Springs, CO) **638**

American Iron Magazine (Norwalk, CT) **756**

American Journal of Addictions (Washington, DC) **795**

American Journal of Clinical Oncology (New York, NY) **2843**

The American Journal of Dermatopathology (New York, NY) **2844**

American Journal of Education (Chicago, IL) **1244**

American Journal of EEG Technology (Arbovale, WV) **4302**

The American Journal of Forensic Medicine and Pathology (New York, NY) **2845**

The American Journal of Knee Surgery (Thorofare, NJ) **2629**

American Journal of Law & Medicine (Boston, MA) **1939**

The American Journal of Otology (Hamilton, ON, Can.) **4627**

The American Journal of Pediatric Hematology/Oncology (New York, NY) **2846**

American Journal of Psychology (Champaign, IL) **1234**

American Machinist (Cleveland, OH) **3361**

American Music (Champaign, IL) **1235**

The American Muslim (Saint Louis, MO) **2378**

American Pacific Co. (Desert Center, CA) **4090**

The American Patriot (New York, NY) **2847**

American Pharmacy (Washington, DC) **796**

American Potato Journal (Orono, ME) **1830**

American Premiere (Beverly Hills, CA) **228**

The American Senior (Los Angeles, CA) **333**

American Short Fiction (Austin, TX) **3880**

American Skating World (Pittsburgh, PA) **3647**

The American Sociologist (New Brunswick, NJ) **2574**

American Sokol Publication (Berwyn, IL) **1211**

American Squaredance (Salinas, CA) **474**

American Srbobran (Pittsburgh, PA) **3648**

American Televenture of Utah, Inc. (Monticello, UT) **4082**

The American Voice **4090**

American Voice (New York, NY) **2848**

American, Whitney Point Reporter, and Oxford Review Times; Chenango (Greene, NY) **2782**

Amherst Press (Amherst, TX) **3876**

Amphibian Magazine; Reptile & (Pottsville, PA) **3663**

Anaheim Hills Highlander (Santa Ana, CA) **558**

Analgesia; Anesthesia & (Baltimore, MD) **1843**

Analog Science Fiction & Fact (New York, NY) **2849**

Analytical and Quantitative Cytology and Histology (St. Louis, MO) **2379**

Anderson Cablevision Associates (Anderson, SC) **3720**

The Andover Journal Advocate (Andover, KS) **1625**

The Andrews Journal (Andrews, NC) **3200**

Anesthesia & Analgesia (Baltimore, MD) **1843**

Anesthesiology; Journal of Neurosurgical (New York, NY) **2951**

Anesthesiology Review (Belle Mead, NJ) **2531**

Angus Topics (Carmi, IL) **1225**

Animal Science; Canadian Journal of (Ottawa, ON, Can.) **4655**

The Ann Arbor News (Ann Arbor, MI) **2030**

The Annals of Applied Probability (Hayward, CA) **297**

Annals of Epidemiology (New York, NY) **2850**

The Annals of Probability (Hayward, CA) **298**

The Annals of Statistics (Hayward, CA) **299**

The Annals of Thoracic Surgery (New York, NY) **2851**

Anniston NewChannels (Anniston, AL) **4**

Annuaire de l'Auto; L' **4646**

Anthropological Research; Journal of (Albuquerque, NM) **2640**

Anthropology & Archeology of Eurasia (Armonk, NY) **2675**

Anthropology and Humanism Quarterly (Washington, DC) **797**

The Antique Lable Collector Magazine (Rapid City, SD) **3791**

Antique Showcase (Bala, ON, Can.) **4599**

Antiques; Art & (New York, NY) **2852**

Antiques & Auction News (Mount Joy, PA) **3616**

Antiques Journal; New England (Ware, MA) **2009**

Antrim County News (Bellaire, MI) **2039**

AOPA Pilot (Frederick, MD) **1899**

The Apache **102**

APCO BULLETIN (South Daytona, FL) **1017**

The Apostle (Birmingham, AL) **12**

Apparel (BFIA); Body Fashions/Intimate (New York, NY) **2859**

Bethany Republican-Clipper (Bethany, MO) 2313

Better Crops with Plant Food (Norcross, GA) 1138

Better Homes and Gardens Decorative Woodcrafts (Des Moines, IA) 1557

Better Vision Cable Co. (Roanoke, AL) 69

Beulah Beacon (Beulah, ND) 3299

Beverage Industry (Cleveland, OH) 3362

Beverage Journal; Kentucky (Frankfort, KY) 1710

Beverage Journal of Spirits, Wine and Beer Marketing in Iowa 1559

Beverage Media (New York, NY) 2858

Beverage Times; Golden State (Des Moines, IA) 1559

Beverages (Overland Park, KS) 1669

(BFIA); Body Fashions/Intimate Apparel (New York, NY) 2859

Bible Standard and Herald of Christ's Kingdom (Chester Springs, PA) 3569

Biblical Archaeologist (Atlanta, GA) 1063

The Biblical Evangelist (Ingleside, TX) 3998

Biblical Literature; Journal of (Atlanta, GA) 1072

Biblical Theology Bulletin (South Orange, NJ) 2627

Bibliography; Bulletin of (Westport, CT) 777

Bibliography; Inter-American Review of (Washington, DC) 824

Big Bend/Vernon Bulletin (Mukwonago, WI) 4417

The Big Reel (Madison, NC) 3259

Big Sandy Mountaineer (Big Sandy, MT) 2423

Big Sandy TV Cable, Inc. (Paintsville, KY) 1749

Bigfork Eagle (Bigfork, MT) 2424

Biker (Agoura Hills, CA) 198

Billings TCI/TCI Cablevision of Montana (Billings, MT) 2425

Binnewater Tides (Rosendale, NY) 3113

Biochemistry and Behavior; Pharmacology (San Antonio, TX) 4056

Biochemistry and Cell Biology (Biochimie et Biologie Cellulaire) (Ottawa, ON, Can.) 4650

Biochemistry and Molecular Biology; The Journal of Steroid (Tarrytown, NY) 3169

Biochemistry and Physiology: Part A: Comparative Physiology; Comparative (Tarrytown, NY) 3141

(Biochimie et Biologie Cellulaire); Biochemistry and Cell Biology (Ottawa, ON, Can.) 4650

Biocontrol Science and Technology (Dunnellon, FL) 908

Biodynamics (Kimberton, PA) 3602

Bioenergy; Biomass & (Tarrytown, NY) 3135

Biography; Current (Bronx, NY) 2741

Biologie Cellulaire); Biochemistry and Cell Biology (Biochimie et (Ottawa, ON, Can.) 4650

Biology (Biochimie et Biologie Cellulaire); Biochemistry and Cell (Ottawa, ON, Can.) 4650

Biology; Journal of Structural (San Diego, CA) 495

Biology; Journal of Thermal (Tarrytown, NY) 3171

Biology & Medicine; Advances in Free Radical 3162

Biology and Medicine; Computers in (Tarrytown, NY) 3145

Biology & Medicine; Free Radicals in 3162

Biology and Medicine; Perspectives in (Chicago, IL) 1286

Biology Reporter; Plant Molecular (New Brunswick, NJ) 2587

Biology Teacher; The American (Reston, VA) 4206

Biomass & Bioenergy (Tarrytown, NY) 3135

Biotechnology Advances (Waterloo, ON, Can.) 4729

Birmingham Cable Communications (Birmingham, AL) 16

Black Books Bulletin: Words Work (Chicago, IL) 1247

Black Lace (Los Angeles, CA) 334

Black Political Economy; The Review of (New Brunswick, NJ) 2589

The Black Scholar (Oakland, CA) 409

Blackburn Cable TV 1740

Blanco County News (Blanco, TX) 3911

Blast! Magazine (Nashville, TN) 3843

Blessing, Inc. (Providence, RI) 3711

Blitz (Los Angeles, CA) 335

Bloomingdale Press (Bloomingdale, IL) 1213

Bloomington-Normal; TeleCable of (Bloomington, IL) 1216

Blue Book Residual Values; Truck (Chicago, IL) 1300

Blue Book; Van Conversion (Chicago, IL) 1303

Blue Mountain Cable 4082

Blues Access (Boulder, CO) 631

Blues Revue Quarterly (West Union, WV) 4332

Bluewater TV Cable Ltd. (Clinton, ON, Can.) 4603

Boating & Sailing; Motor (New York, NY) 2972

Boatings Caribbean Sports & Travel Magazine; Pleasure (North Miami, FL) 977

Body Fashions/Intimate Apparel (BFIA) (New York, NY) 2859

Bodybuilding Lifestyles (Stamford, CT) 767

Bodywise Magazine (Eagan, MN) 2177

Bon Temps; Le (Boutte, LA) 1772

Bonsai Today (Sudbury, MA) 2004

The Bonus Paper (Oconto Falls, WI) 4424

Book Links: Connections Books, Libraries, and Classrooms (Chicago, IL) 1248

Book Marketing Update (Fairfield, IA) 1571

Books (San Diego, CA) 486

Books; The Women's Review of (Wellesley, MA) 2012

Bookseller; American (Tarrytown, NY) 3133

Booster (Weyburn, SK, Can.) 4784

Boothbay Register (Boothbay Harbor, ME) 1818

Borealis (Toronto, ON, Can.) 4691

The Borzoi Quarterly (Wheat Ridge, CO) 707

Boston; Cablevision of (Allston, MA) 1935

The Boston Quarterly (Wheat Ridge, CO) 708

Botanical Club; Bulletin of the Torrey (Bronx, NY) 2740

Botanique); Canadian Journal of Botany (Revue Canadienne de (Ottawa, ON, Can.) 4656

Botany (Revue Canadienne de Botanique); Canadian Journal of (Ottawa, ON, Can.) 4656

Botetourt County News; The Fincastle Herald and (Fincastle, VA) 4169

Both Sides Now (Tyler, TX) 4070

Bow Valley This Week (Banff, AB, Can.) 4484

Bowhunting World (Minnetonka, MN) 2220

Bowler; Woman (Greendale, WI) 4364

Bradford Journal 3615

Bradford Journal/Miner (Mount Jewett, PA) 3615

Brain Dysfunction 739

Brant News (Brantford, ON, Can.) 4600

Brea Highlander (Brea, CA) 234

Breakthrough (New York, NY) 2860

Breakthrough! Quarterly Magazine (Calgary, AB, Can.) 4485

The Breeze (Mathiston, MS) 2299

Bridal Trends (Ogden, UT) 4084

Bridgeport/Back of the Yards EXTRA (Chicago, IL) 1249

Bridgeport Times; Chittenango (Chittenango, NY) 2757

Bridgeview-Hills Reporter 1218

Briefing Charts; Conference Board (New York, NY) 2875

Brighton-Pittsford Shopper 3089

Bristol Bay News (Anchorage, AK) 81

British-American Communications (Los Angeles, CA) 369

British Car (Canoga Park, CA) 245

British-Telecom, Inc. 369

Brittany World (Wheat Ridge, CO) 709

The Broadcast (Vicksburg, MI) 2154

The Brookings Review (Washington, DC) 800

Brooklyn-Queens Cable TV (Flushing, NY) 2774

Broomstick (San Francisco, CA) 507

The Broward Informer (Sunrise, FL) 1020

Broward Review (Fort Lauderdale, FL) 911

The Broward-Sunrise Informer 1020

Brownton Bulletin 2168

Brownwood Bulletin (Brownwood, TX) 3918

The Brunswick Business Journal (Moncton, NB, Can.) 4579

Brunswick Times-Gazette (Brunswick, VA) 4145

Budgeting and Finance; Public (New Brunswick, NJ) 2588

Budgeting and Financial Management; Public (New York, NY) 3007

Builder News Extra (Westlake, LA) 1810

Building Management Hawaii (Honolulu, HI) 1164

Buildings (Cedar Rapids, IA) 1541

The Bull Terrier Quarterly (Wheat Ridge, CO) 710

The Bulletin (Brownton, MN) 2168

The Bulletin (Austin, TX) 3882

Bulletin of the American Society of Papyrologists (Atlanta, GA) 1064

The Bulletin of the Assn. for Business Communication (Denton, TX) 3951

Bulletin of the Atomic Scientists (Chicago, IL) 1250

Bulletin of Bibliography (Westport, CT) 777

The Bulletin of the Center for Children's Books (Champaign, IL) 1236

Bulletin: Committee on South Asian Women (College Station, TX) 3924

Bulletin of the Torrey Botanical Club (Bronx, NY) 2740

Bulletin Voyages (Montreal, PQ, Can.) 4745

Bullish On Crafts (Durango, CO) 666

Bus Fleet; School (Redondo Beach, CA) 443

Bus World (Woodland Hills, CA) 621

Business Air Today (Fort Dodge, IA) 1573

The Business Blanket (Bad Axe, MI) 2035

Business Computer News (Don Mills, ON, Can.) 4609

Business Concepts (Los Angeles, CA) 336

Business; Development (New York, NY) 2889

Business Documents (Philadelphia, PA) 3631

Business; Essays in International (Columbia, SC) 3732

Business Ethics (Chaska, MN) 2169

Business Exchange; Small (San Francisco, CA) 524

Business History Review (Boston, MA) 1940

Business Insurance (Chicago, IL) 1251

Business; Interactive Media (White Plains, NY) 3192

Chico New Voice Newspaper (Chico, CA) **256**

Chief Information Officer Journal (New York, NY) **2866**

Chiefland Shopper (Perry, IA) **1605**

Chiefland's Central Iowa Farm Magazine (Perry, IA) **1606**

CHILD (New York, NY) **2867**

Child Development; Monographs of the Society for Research in (Chicago, IL) **1281**

Child Welfare (New Brunswick, NJ) **2576**

Child Welfare League Newsletter: Children's Voice **803**

Children and Youth Services Review (Tarrytown, NY) **3137**

Children's Books; The Bulletin of the Center for (Champaign, IL) **1236**

Children's Digest (Indianapolis, IN) **1474**

Children's Literature Association Quarterly (Battle Creek, MI) **2036**

Children's Voice (Washington, DC) **803**

Chimes (Grand Rapids, MI) **2078**

Chimie); Canadian Journal of Chemistry (Revue Canadienne de (Ottawa, ON, Can.) **4657**

China Law Reporter (Chicago, IL) **1253**

Chinese Business Journal (Seattle, WA) **4267**

Chinese Education **2676**

Chinese Education & Society (Armonk, NY) **2676**

Chinese News (Seattle, WA) **4268**

Chinese Physics (New York, NY) **2868**

CHIP-FM - 101.5 (Fort Coulonge, PQ, Can.) **4739**

Chips-O-Wood (Mathiston, MS) **2300**

Chiropractic History (Pittsburgh, PA) **3649**

Chiropractic Products (Torrance, CA) **593**

Chittenango Bridgeport Times (Chittenango, NY) **2757**

Chocolate and Nut World (Santa Monica, CA) **573**

Choice TV (Riverside, CA) **449**

CHOR-AM - 1450 (Summerland, BC, Can.) **4543**

The Christian Index (Atlanta, GA) **1066**

Christian Psychology for Today **865**

Christian Single (Nashville, TN) **3844**

Christian Youth!; The Magazine for (Nashville, TN) **3849**

Christ's Epiphany; Present Truth and Herald of (Chester Springs, PA) **3570**

Christ's Kingdom; Bible Standard and Herald of (Chester Springs, PA) **3569**

Chromatographia (Tarrytown, NY) **3138**

Chromatographic Science; Journal of (Niles, IL) **1366**

The Chronicle (South Dartmouth, MA) **1997**

Chronicle News Magazine (Oxford, PA) **3627**

Chronobiology International (New York, NY) **2869**

CHRW-FM - 94.7 (London, ON, Can.) **4637**

CHSJ-TV - Channel 4 (St. John, NB, Can.) **4580**

CHUO-FM - 89.1 (Ottawa, ON, Can.) **4676**

Church Life; New (Bryn Athyn, PA) **3565**

Church; Living (Milwaukee, WI) **4407**

Church & Society (Louisville, KY) **1727**

Church; Your (Carol Stream, IL) **1227**

CHVR-AM - 1350 (Pembroke, ON, Can.) **4677**

CIFJ-AM - 1480 (Vanderhoof, BC, Can.) **4529**

CIFL-AM - 1450 (Vanderhoof, BC, Can.) **4530**

CIGV-FM - 100.7 (Penticton, BC, Can.) **4540**

CIHI-AM - 1260 (Fredericton, NB, Can.) **4576**

CILQ-FM - 107.1 (North York, ON, Can.) **4645**

Cincinnati Business Record; The Greater (Cincinnati, OH) **3346**

CineAction! (Toronto, ON, Can.) **4694**

Cinefex (Riverside, CA) **448**

Cinema, Video & Cable Movie Digest (Ambler, PA) **3552**

Cinematographer; American (Hollywood, CA) **302**

CIO (Framingham, MA) **1971**

CION-FM - 103.7 (Riviere-du-Loup, PQ, Can.) **4768**

CIPA-TV - Channel 9 (Prince Albert, SK, Can.) **4777**

Circulating Pines (Circle Pines, MN) **2170**

CIRX-FM - 95.9 (Vanderhoof, BC, Can.) **4553**

CISA-TV - Channel 7 (Lethbridge, AB, Can.) **4509**

CISN-FM - 103.9 (Edmonton, AB, Can.) **4503**

Cities; Minnesota (Saint Paul, MN) **2251**

Citizen (Laconia, NH) **2512**

Citizen-Journal (Osceola, AR) **184**

The Citizen-News (Edgefield, SC) **3742**

CITR-FM - 101.9 (Vancouver, BC, Can.) **4550**

City-County Magazine (Burlington, NC) **3210**

City of Covington CATV (Covington, GA) **1106**

City Reports (Cleveland, OH) **3365**

City & Society (Washington, DC) **804**

CITY-TV - Channel 57 (Toronto, ON, Can.) **4724**

City of Williamstown Cable (Williamstown, KY) **1758**

Civil); Canadian Journal of Civil Engineering (Revue Canadienne de Genie (Ottawa, ON, Can.) **4658**

Civil Engineering (Revue Canadienne de Genie Civil); Canadian Journal of (Ottawa, ON, Can.) **4658**

Civil War Chronicles (New York, NY) **2870**

CJAN-AM - 1340 (Asbestos, PQ, Can.) **4734**

CJAT-AM - 610 (Trail, BC, Can.) **4545**

CJAY-FM - 92.1 (Calgary, AB, Can.) **4495**

CJBX-FM - 92.7 (London, ON, Can.) **4638**

CJCJ-AM - 920 (Woodstock, NB, Can.) **4581**

CJDC-FM - 92.7 (Dawson Creek, BC, Can.) **4525**

CJEZ-FM - 97.3 (Toronto, ON, Can.) **4725**

CJGR-FM - 100 (Campbell River, BC, Can.) **4532**

CJJR-FM - 93.7 (Vancouver, BC, Can.) **4551**

CJMG-FM - 97.1 (Penticton, BC, Can.) **4541**

CJSF-FM - 93.9 (Burnaby, BC, Can.) **4520**

CJSR-FM - 88.5 (Edmonton, AB, Can.) **4504**

CJSW-FM - 90.9 (Calgary, AB, Can.) **4496**

CKAR-AM **4647**

CKCB-AM - 1400 (Collingwood, ON, Can.) **4606**

CKCK-AM - 620 (Regina, SK, Can.) **4779**

CKDO-AM - 1350 (Oshawa, ON, Can.) **4647**

CKEG-AM - 1350 (Nanaimo, BC, Can.) **4538**

CKGR-AM - 1400 (Golden, BC, Can.) **4533**

CKHJ-FM - 105.3 (Fredericton, NB, Can.) **4577**

CKIR-AM - 870 (Golden, BC, Can.) **4534**

CKIT-FM - 104.9 (Regina, SK, Can.) **4780**

CKLN-FM - 88.1 (Toronto, ON, Can.) **4726**

CKLQ-AM - 880 (Brandon, MB, Can.) **4561**

CKLW-FM - 93.9 (Windsor, ON, Can.) **4732**

CKLY-AM - 910 (Lindsay, ON, Can.) **4634**

CKMG-AM - 1340 (Maniwaki, PQ, Can.) **4743**

CKMI-TV - Channel 5 (Quebec, PQ, Can.) **4763**

CKMR-FM **4732**

CKND-TV - Channel 9 (Winnipeg, MB, Can.) **4573**

CKNM-FM - 101.9 (Yellowknife, NT, Can.) **4587**

CKNR-AM - 1340 (Elliot Lake, ON, Can.) **4623**

CKON-FM - 97.3 (Rooseveltown, NY) **3112**

CKOV-AM - 630 (Kelowna, BC, Can.) **4537**

CKPR-TV - Channel 2 (Thunder Bay, ON, Can.) **4689**

CKPT-AM - 1420 (Peterborough, ON, Can.) **4679**

CKQT-FM - 94.9 (Oshawa, ON, Can.) **4648**

CKRD-TV - Channel 6 (Red Deer, AB, Can.) **4517**

CKST-AM - 1040 (Vancouver, BC, Can.) **4552**

CKUT-FM - 90.3 (Montreal, PQ, Can.) **4760**

CKXJ-AM - 610 (Grand Bank, NF, Can.) **4584**

CKY-AM - 580 (Winnipeg, MB, Can.) **4574**

CKZZ-FM - 95.3 (Richmond, BC, Can.) **4542**

The Clansman (Halifax, NS, Can.) **4590**

Clarence-Lowden Sun News (Tipton, IA) **1616**

The Clarinet (Denton, TX) **3952**

Classic Trucks (Anaheim, CA) **203**

Classrooms; Book Links: Connections Books, Libraries, and (Chicago, IL) **1248**

Clause (Azusa, CA) **213**

Clavier (Northfield, IL) **1369**

The Clayton County Register (Elkader, IA) **1570**

Clear Picture Inc. (Wooster, OH) **3448**

Clear TV Cable (Toms River, NJ) **2631**

Clearview CATV Inc. (Bel Air, MD) **1874**

Clements' International Report (Dallas, TX) **3934**

Cleveland Area, Inc.; Cox Cable (Parma, OH) **3435**

Cleveland Clinic Journal of Medicine (Cleveland, OH) **3366**

The Cleveland Daily Banner (Cleveland, TN) **3812**

Client Magazine (Manhattan Beach, CA) **380**

The Clifford News (Teeswater, ON, Can.) **4688**

Clinical Hemorheology (Tarrytown, NY) **3139**

Clinical Infectious Diseases (Chicago, IL) **1254**

The Clinical Journal of Pain (New York, NY) **2871**

Clinical Journal of Sport Medicine (New York, NY) **2872**

Clinical Management (Alexandria, VA) **4127**

Clinical Neuropharmacology (New York, NY) **2873**

Clinical Psychology Review (Tarrytown, NY) **3140**

The Clinton County News (Saint Johns, MI) **2142**

The Clinton Daily News (Clinton, OK) **3456**

Clintonville Shopper's Guide (Clintonville, WI) **4344**

Clipper **2480**

Clipper Shopper (Blair, NE) **2446**

Cloverdale Reveille (Cloverdale, CA) **260**

The Coal Journal (Lexington, KY) **1717**

Coal Quality; The Journal of (Bowling Green, KY) **1699**

Coast Cable (San Jose, CA) **539**

Coast Press; Delaware (Rehoboth Beach, DE) **788**

Coastal Management (Washington, DC) **805**

Coastside Chronicle (San Mateo, CA) **548**

Cobblestone (Peterborough, NH) **2519**

Cobourg-Port Hope Shoppers Market (Cobourg, ON, Can.) **4605**

Collector Magazine; The Antique Lable (Rapid City, SD) **3791**

The Collectors Club Philatelist (New York, NY) **2874**

College; School and (Cleveland, OH) **3381**

College Student Psychotherapy; Journal of (Binghamton, NY) **2698**

College Teaching (Washington, DC) **806**

Collegian; The Daily (State College, PA) **3677**

Collegiate Insider (Skokie, IL) **1404**

Colleton Shopper (Walterboro, SC) **3781**

Collie Variety (Wheat Ridge, CO) **711**

Colony Communications, Inc. (Tujunga, CA) **600**

Colony Communications, Inc. (Brooklyn Park, MN) **2166**

Color Country Shopper (Kanab, UT) **4078**

Color Publishing (Westford, MA) **2015**

Colorado Business Magazine (Englewood, CO) **671**

Colorado Springs Cablevision (Colorado Springs, CO) **642**

Colorado; TCI Cablevision of (Boulder, CO) **636**

Colorado; TCI Cablevision of (Pueblo, CO) **697**

The Colorado Tribune (Pueblo, CO) **694**

Columbia Cable of Washington (Vancouver, WA) **4296**

Columbia Magazine (Columbia, MD) **1892**

Columbus, Inc.; TeleCable of (Columbus, GA) **1103**

Columbus; Warner Cable of (Columbus, OH) **3392**

Comcast Cablevision (Huntsville, AL) **39**

Comcast Cablevision (Fullerton, CA) **290**

Comcast Cablevision (Fort Wayne, IN) **1452**

Comcast Cablevision (Willow Grove, PA) **3696**

Comcast Cablevision of Baltimore County (Timonium, MD) **1932**

Comcast Cablevision of Flint (Flint, MI) **2071**

Comcast Cablevision of Indiana (Indianapolis, IN) **1487**

Comcast Cablevision of Mercer County (Trenton, NJ) **2632**

Comcast Cablevision of Meridian (Meridian, MS) **2301**

Comcast Cablevision of Middletown (Middletown, CT) **748**

Comcast Cablevision of Newport Beach (Newport Beach, CA) **405**

Comcast Cablevision of Paducah (Paducah, KY) **1747**

Comcast Cablevision of Philadelphia (Philadelphia, PA) **3642**

Comcast Cablevision of San Bernardino (San Bernardino, CA) **481**

Comcast Cablevision of Tuscaloosa (Tuscaloosa, AL) **76**

Comic Review; The Triangle (Chapel Hill, NC) **3213**

Command Magazine (San Luis Obispo, CA) **544**

The Commercial Record (South Windsor, CT) **766**

Commodities; Technical Analysis of Stocks & (Seattle, WA) **4276**

Common Lives/Lesbian Lives (Iowa City, IA) **1591**

Communication Systems, Inc. (Columbia, SC) **3735**

Communio-International Catholic Review (Washington, DC) **807**

Community Action Press **3650**

Community Bulletin; T.J.'s (Cornell, WI) **4347**

Community News South (Pittsburgh, PA) **3650**

The Community Press (Millbrook, AL) **49**

Community Times (Owings Mills, MD) **1921**

Commuter Air International (Atlanta, GA) **1067**

Companion Animal Practice (Santa Barbara, CA) **561**

Comparative Biochemistry and Physiology: Part A: Comparative Physiology (Tarrytown, NY) **3141**

Comparative Drama (Kalamazoo, MI) **2096**

Comparative Education Review (Chicago, IL) **1255**

Comparative Immunology, Microbiology and Infectious Diseases (Tarrytown, NY) **3142**

The Compass (Rochester, IN) **1515**

The Complete Smoker (Evanston, IL) **1331**

Compressed Air (Washington, NJ) **2634**

Computer-Aided Engineering (Cleveland, OH) **3367**

Computer Artist (Westford, MA) **2016**

Computer Game Review (Lombard, IL) **1349**

Computer Language (San Francisco, CA) **509**

Computer Languages (Tarrytown, NY) **3143**

Computer Listing Service's Machinery & Equipment Guide (Skokie, IL) **1405**

Computer News; Business (Don Mills, ON, Can.) **4609**

Computer Publishing Magazine (Santa Monica, CA) **574**

Computer Simulation; International Journal of (Norwood, NJ) **2598**

Computerized Investing (Chicago, IL) **1256**

Computerized Medical Imaging and Graphics (Tarrytown, NY) **3144**

Computers in Biology and Medicine (Tarrytown, NY) **3145**

Computers & Chemical Engineering (Tarrytown, NY) **3146**

Computers & Chemistry (Tarrytown, NY) **3147**

Computers & Education (Tarrytown, NY) **3148**

Computers & Electrical Engineering (Tarrytown, NY) **3149**

Computers & Fluids (Tarrytown, NY) **3150**

Computers & Geosciences (Tarrytown, NY) **3151**

Computers & Graphics (Tarrytown, NY) **3152**

Computers & Industrial Engineering (Tarrytown, NY) **3153**

Computers in Math and Science Teaching; Journal of (Charlottesville, VA) **4151**

Computers & Mathematics with Applications (Tarrytown, NY) **3154**

Computers & Operations Research (Tarrytown, NY) **3155**

Computers & Structures (Tarrytown, NY) **3156**

Computers & Users; Chicago (Chicago, IL) **1252**

Computing in Childhood Education; Journal of (Charlottesville, VA) **4152**

Computing Machinery; Journal of the Association for (New York, NY) **2932**

Computing Surveys; ACM (New York, NY) **2830**

Concept Cablevision (Sheridan, IN) **1519**

Concord Cable TV (Concord, CA) **263**

The Concrete Foundation Contractor **2362**

The Conejos County Citizen (La Jara, CO) **684**

Confectioner (Dallas, TX) **3935**

Conference Board Briefing Charts (New York, NY) **2875**

Configurations (Baltimore, MD) **1846**

Congressional Digest (Washington, DC) **808**

Connecticut; Cablevision of Southern (Bridgeport, CT) **735**

Connecticut, Inc.; Storer Cable TV of (New Haven, CT) **754**

Connexions (Toronto, ON, Can.) **4695**

ConnStruction (West Hartford, CT) **771**

Consciousness and Cognition: An International Journal (San Diego, CA) **487**

Conservation; Alabama (Montgomery, AL) **59**

Conservative Judaism (New York, NY) **2876**

The Constitution AM & PM **3465**

Construct Psychology; International Journal of Personal (Washington, DC) **826**

Construction Journal; Walker's Estimating & (Lisle, IL) **1348**

Construction & Modernization Report (Washington, DC) **809**

Construction Products (Des Plaines, IL) **1321**

CONSTRUCTOR (Washington, DC) **810**

The Consultant Pharmacist (Alexandria, VA) **4128**

Consumer Extra (Palatka, FL) **991**

Consumer Research; Journal of (Chicago, IL) **1271**

Consumers Market Bulletin; Farmers & (Atlanta, GA) **1070**

CONTACT (Trenton, ON, Can.) **4727**

Contemporary Management in Critical Care (New York, NY) **2877**

Contemporary Management in Internal Medicine (New York, NY) **2878**

Contemporary Management in Obstetrics and Gynecology (New York, NY) **2879**

Contemporary Management in Otolaryngology (New York, NY) **2880**

The Contemporary Management Series (New York, NY) **2881**

Contemporary Podiatric Physician (Torrance, CA) **594**

Contemporary South Asia (Dunnellon, FL) **909**

Continental Cablevision (Downey, CA) **270**

Continental Cablevision (Fresno, CA) **286**

Continental Cablevision (Los Angeles, CA) **370**

Continental Cablevision (Stockton, CA) **590**

Continental Cablevision (Jacksonville, FL) **942**

Continental Cablevision (Pompano Beach, FL) **999**

Continental Cablevision (Rolling Meadows, IL) **1397**

Continental Cablevision (Brockton, MA) **1954**

Continental Cablevision (Cambridge, MA) **1964**

Continental Cablevision (Quincy, MA) **1995**

Continental Cablevision (Westfield, MA) **2014**

Continental Cablevision (Dearborn Heights, MI) **2053**

Continental Cablevision (Lansing, MI) **2107**

Continental Cablevision (Southfield, MI) **2145**

Numbers cited in bold after listings are entry numbers rather than page numbers.

Master Index

European Finance and Trade; Russian and Eastern (Armonk, NY) **2680**

European Journal of Human Genetics (Farmington, CT) **740**

Evaluation Engineering; EE (Nokomis, FL) **975**

Evaluation Practice **393**

Evaluation and Program Planning (Tarrytown, NY) **3159**

Evaluation Review (Newbury Park, CA) **393**

The Evangelist (Baton Rouge, LA) **1765**

Evangelist; The Biblical (Ingleside, TX) **3998**

Evening Express (Portland, ME) **1831**

The Evening Star (Auburn, IN) **1426**

Ex-Cen Cablevision Ltd. (Clinton, ON, Can.) **4604**

The Excelsior (Lancaster, MO) **2356**

Exclusively Connecticut (New Haven, CT) **750**

Exclusively Women **750**

Executive Speeches (Dayton, OH) **3398**

Executive Suite Magazine (Silver Spring, MD) **1928**

Expeditions; Great (Raleigh, NC) **3271**

Experimental Aging Research (Washington, DC) **816**

Experimental Analysis of Behavior; Journal of the (Bloomington, IN) **1434**

Experimental Gerontology (Tarrytown, NY) **3160**

Experimental Nephrology (Farmington, CT) **741**

Expert Systems With Applications: An International Journal (Tarrytown, NY) **3161**

Explorer (Los Angeles, CA) **342**

The Explorer (Sioux Lookout, ON, Can.) **4686**

Exploring (Irving, TX) **3999**

The Exponent (Berea, OH) **3335**

Exposure Analysis and Environmental Epidemiology; Journal of (Princeton, NJ) **2608**

Extra (Valparaiso, IN) **1525**

The Extra Shopper (Phillips, WI) **4429**

Extraprize (Fallbrook, CA) **281**

Eye Toxicity Research; Lens and (New York, NY) **2961**

F

Facility Management Journal (Houston, TX) **3978**

Facts and Comparisons (Saint Louis, MO) **2381**

The Fairfax Forum (Fairfax, MO) **2336**

Fairfax Standard (Fairfax, MN) **2184**

Fairfield County Business Journal (Hawthorne, NY) **2785**

Fairmont Photo Press (Fairmont, MN) **2185**

Fairport Perinton Herald Mail (Fairport, NY) **2769**

Faith and Fellowship (Fergus Falls, MN) **2186**

Faith & Reason (Front Royal, VA) **4172**

Falcon Cable Systems Co. (Gilroy, CA) **293**

Falcon Cablevision (Big Bear Lake, CA) **232**

Falcon Video Communications (Weiser, ID) **1202**

The Falmouth Outlook (Falmouth, KY) **1708**

FAMA (Teaneck, NJ) **2628**

Families in Society (Milwaukee, WI) **4405**

Family Fun (New York, NY) **2897**

Family Law Quarterly (Chicago, IL) **1260**

Family; Marriage and (Saint Meinrad, IN) **1518**

Family Physician; American (Kansas City, MO) **2348**

Family Planning; Current Literature in (New York, NY) **2887**

Family Process (Waldwick, NJ) **2633**

Family Psychology; Journal of (Washington, DC) **831**

Family Psychotherapy; Journal of (Binghamton, NY) **2703**

Family Records, TODAY (Kansas City, MO) **2351**

Family Safety & Health (Itasca, IL) **1340**

Family Social Work; Journal of (Binghamton, NY) **2704**

Family Therapy (San Diego, CA) **492**

Family Times (Wilmington, DE) **791**

Family Word Seek Puzzles (Norwalk, CT) **758**

Fargo; Cablecom of (Fargo, ND) **3311**

Farm Bureau News; Arizona (Phoenix, AZ) **113**

Farm Bureau Press (Little Rock, AR) **172**

Farm Equipment Guide (Fort Dodge, IA) **1575**

Farm Finance News; National (New York, NY) **2975**

Farm Magazine; Chiefland's Central Iowa (Perry, IA) **1606**

Farm; The New (Emmaus, PA) **3580**

Farm News of Erie and Wyoming Counties (East Aurora, NY) **2763**

Farm News; Michigan (Lansing, MI) **2104**

Farm Press; Delta (Clarksdale, MS) **2278**

Farm Store (Minnetonka, MN) **2221**

Farm Today; Small (Clark, MO) **2322**

Farmer Today; Iowa (Cedar Rapids, IA) **1542**

Farmer & Wadley Herald; Louisville News & (Louisville, GA) **1129**

The Farmers' Advance (Camden, MI) **2046**

Farmers & Consumers Market Bulletin (Atlanta, GA) **1070**

Farmers Hot Line (Fort Dodge, IA) **1576**

Farmers Telephone Cooperative Inc. (Kingstree, SC) **3763**

Farmland News (Archbold, OH) **3331**

Farmville Enterprise (Farmville, NC) **3231**

FarmWeek (Bloomington, IL) **1214**

Fauquier Times-Democrat (Warrenton, VA) **4228**

Favorite Variety Puzzles and Games (Norwalk, CT) **759**

Favorite Westerns & Serial World (Vernon Center, MN) **2263**

Favorite Word Seek Puzzles (Norwalk, CT) **760**

Fayetteville; Cablevision of (Fayetteville, NC) **3232**

Fayetteville Eagle-Bulletin (Fayetteville, NY) **2771**

FDM (Furniture Design & Manufactuing) (Chicago, IL) **1261**

Feedstuffs Cattle Supplement (Minnetonka, MN) **2222**

Feline Practice (Santa Barbara, CA) **562**

Feminist Family Therapy; Journal of (Binghamton, NY) **2705**

Feminist Studies (College Park, MD) **1891**

Fiber and Integrated Optics (Washington, DC) **817**

Fiberoptic Product News (Morris Plains, NJ) **2569**

Fiction; American Short (Austin, TX) **3880**

Fiction; Critique: Studies in Contemporary (Washington, DC) **812**

Field & Stream (New York, NY) **2898**

Film Quarterly (Berkeley, CA) **220**

Film Threat (Beverly Hills, CA) **229**

Film and Video; Journal of (Atlanta, GA) **1073**

Finance; Mathematical (Cambridge, MA) **1960**

Finance News; National Farm (New York, NY) **2975**

Finance; Public Budgeting and (New Brunswick, NJ) **2588**

Finance; The Quarterly Review of Economics and (Champaign, IL) **1240**

Finance Today; Real Estate (Washington, DC) **855**

Finance and Trade; Russian and Eastern European (Armonk, NY) **2680**

Financial History; Friends of (New York, NY) **2904**

Financial Management (Tallahassee, FL) **1023**

Financial Management; Journal of Multinational (Binghamton, NY) **2715**

Financial Management; Public Budgeting and (New York, NY) **3007**

Financial Markets, Institutions and Money; Journal of International (Binghamton, NY) **2712**

Financial Review; Northwestern (Minneapolis, MN) **2211**

Financial Studies; The Review of (New York, NY) **3015**

Financial Technology News (New York, NY) **2899**

The Fincastle Herald and Botetourt County News (Fincastle, VA) **4169**

Fire Journal; American (Bellflower, CA) **219**

First Carolina Cable TV (Springfield, VT) **4123**

FIRST DAYS (Poughkeepsie, NY) **3097**

Firsts: Collecting Modern First Editions (Pasadena, CA) **427**

Fish Monthly; Marine (Luttrell, TN) **3834**

Fitness; Men's (Woodland Hills, CA) **622**

Fitness and Sports Review International (Escondido, CA) **277**

Fitness; Women's Sports & (Boulder, CO) **633**

Flagler/Palm Coast News-Tribune (Bunnell, FL) **886**

Flagpole Magazine (Athens, GA) **1051**

The Flame (Miami Shores, FL) **971**

Flashes Shopping Guide (Stuart, FL) **1019**

The Flat Hat (Williamsburg, VA) **4231**

Fleet Equipment (Palatine, IL) **1379**

Fleet Executive; NAFA (Iselin, NJ) **2562**

Flint; Comcast Cablevision of (Flint, MI) **2071**

Floors; Hardwood (Madison, WI) **4383**

Floral & Nursery Times (Northfield, IL) **1370**

Florida; Cablevision of Central (Lakeland, FL) **952**

Florida; Cablevision of Central (Orlando, FL) **985**

Florida Cattleman and Livestock Journal (Kissimmee, FL) **950**

Florida; Dynamic Cablevision of (Hialeah, FL) **933**

Florida Keys; Gibbons-Humm's Guide to the (Key Largo, FL) **947**

Florida Leader For High School Students (Gainesville, FL) **921**

Florida Living (Gainesville, FL) **922**

Florida Magazine; La (Boca Raton, FL) **883**

Florida Market Bulletin (Tallahassee, FL) **1024**

Florida Music Director (Tallahassee, FL) **1025**

Florida; Storer Cable TV of (Miami, FL) **969**

Florida; TCI Cablevision of (Daytona Beach, FL) **900**

Florida Underwriter (St. Petersburg, FL) **1007**

FloridAgriculture (Gainesville, FL) **923**

Numbers cited in bold after listings are entry numbers rather than page numbers.

K

KAAR-AM **3531**
KABC-AM - 790 (Los Angeles, CA) **371**
KACU-FM - 89.7 (Abilene, TX) **3870**
KADI-FM - 99.5 (Springfield, MO) **2410**
KADS-AM - 1240 (Elk City, OK) **3459**
KAET Magazine (Tempe, AZ) **135**
KAFA-FM - 104.5 (Colorado Springs, CO) **643**
KAFE-FM - 104.3 (Bellingham, WA) **4240**
KAFR-FM - 99.1 (Angel Fire, NM) **2646**
KAFT-TV - Channel 13 (Conway, AR) **160**
KAFY-AM - 970 (Bakersfield, CA) **214**
KAHR-FM - 96.7 (Poplar Bluff, MO) **2371**
Kaimin; Montana (Missoula, MT) **2441**
KAKN-FM - 100.9 (Naknek, AK) **94**
KAKS-FM - 107.9 (Amarillo, TX) **3874**
KALB-AM - 580 (Alexandria, LA) **1761**
Kaleidoscope (Birmingham, AL) **14**
Kaleidoscope Music (Chicago, IL) **1273**
Kalliope: A Journal of Women's Art (Jacksonville, FL) **941**
KALT-AM - 900 (Atlanta, TX) **3878**
KALW-FM - 91.7 (San Francisco, CA) **529**
Kamehameha Cablevision (Hawi, HI) **1163**
Kanadsky Slovak (Toronto, ON, Can.) **4703**
KANE-AM - 1240 (New Iberia, LA) **1793**
KANS-AM - 1510 (Larned, KS) **1647**
Kansas Monthly Employment Review (Topeka, KS) **1684**
Kansas Quarterly (Manhattan, KS) **1653**
Kansas, Inc.; TCI of (Manhattan, KS) **1655**
Kansas; TCI of (Newton, KS) **1663**
Kansas, Inc.; TCI of (Salina, KS) **1679**
Kansas, Inc.; TCI of (Topeka, KS) **1686**
KAOK-AM - 1400 (Westlake, LA) **1811**
KAPL-AM - 1550 (Apple Valley, CA) **209**
KAPR-AM - 930 (Douglas, AZ) **103**
Kapuskasing; Le Nord de (Kapuskasing, ON, Can.) **4632**
KARN-AM - 920 (Little Rock, AR) **173**
KARY-FM - 100.9 (Prosser, WA) **4262**
KASB-FM - 89.3 (Bellevue, WA) **4236**
Kashrus Faxletter (Brooklyn, NY) **2746**
KATE-AM - 1450 (Albert Lea, MN) **2161**
Kateri (Kahnawake, PQ, Can.) **4741**
KATU-TV - Channel 2 (Portland, OR) **3530**
KATY-AM **211**
Kauai CableVision (Puhi, HI) **1179**
KAVC-FM - 105.5 (Rosamond, CA) **451**
KAWL-AM - 1370 (York, NE) **2483**
KAWL-FM **2484**
KAWW-AM - 1370 (Heber Springs, AR) **166**
KAYN-FM - 98.3 (Nogales, AZ) **110**
KAZI-FM - 88.7 (Austin, TX) **3897**
KAZN-AM - 1300 (Pasadena, CA) **429**
KAZZ-FM - 107.1 (Deer Park, WA) **4245**
KBAY-FM - 100.3 (San Jose, CA) **541**
KBAZ-FM - 102.1 (Eunice, LA) **1781**
KBBE-FM - 101.7 (McPherson, KS) **1657**
KBBM-AM (Waldport, OR) **3546**
KBCC-FM - 88.5 (Bakersfield, CA) **215**
KBCH-AM - 1400 (Lincoln City, OR) **3514**
KBCU-FM - 88.1 (North Newton, KS) **1664**
KBCW-AM - 1470 (Brooklyn Park, MN) **2167**
KBDZ-FM - 93.1 (Perryville, MO) **2367**
KBER-FM - 101.1 (Salt Lake City, UT) **4098**
KBIF-AM - 900 (Fresno, CA) **287**
KBIM-TV - Channel 10 (Roswell, NM) **2659**
KBJ-TV - Channel 39 (Morgan City, LA) **1791**
KBLZ-FM - 89.9 (Omaha, NE) **2474**
KBME-TV - Channel 3 (Fargo, ND) **3303**
KBMS-AM - 1480 (Portland, OR) **3531**
KBMV-FM - 107.1 (Birch Tree, MO) **2315**

KBNO-AM - 1220 (Denver, CO) **657**
KBOE-FM - 104.9 (Oskaloosa, IA) **1604**
KBOL-AM - 1490 (Boulder, CO) **634**
KBOP-AM - 1380 (Pleasanton, TX) **4047**
KBOP-FM - 98.3 (Pleasanton, TX) **4048**
KBOY-FM - 95.7 (Medford, OR) **3516**
KBOZ-AM - 1090 (Bozeman, MT) **2427**
KBOZ-FM - 93.7 (Bozeman, MT) **2428**
KBPS-AM - 1450 (Portland, OR) **3532**
KBPS-FM - 89.9 (Portland, OR) **3533**
KBRF-AM - 1250 (Fergus Falls, MN) **2187**
KBRJ-FM - 104.1 (Anchorage, AK) **83**
KBRU-FM - 102 (Fort Morgan, CO) **676**
KBRX-AM - 1350 (O'Neill, NE) **2467**
KBRX-FM - 102.9 (O'Neill, NE) **2468**
KBSU-FM - 90.3 (Boise, ID) **1182**
KBTN-AM - 1420 (Neosho, MO) **2361**
KBUB-FM - 90.3 (Brownwood, TX) **3919**
KBUC-AM - 830 (San Antonio, TX) **4063**
KBUF-AM - 1030 (Garden City, KS) **1634**
KBWD-AM - 1380 (Brownwood, TX) **3920**
KBWH-FM - 106.3 (Blair, NE) **2447**
KBYU-TV - Channel 11 (Provo, UT) **4093**
KCAL-TV - Channel 9 (Los Angeles, CA) **372**
KCAW-FM - 104.7 (Sitka, AK) **96**
KCBQ-FM - 105.3 (San Diego, CA) **503**
KCBW-FM **2403**
KCBX-FM - 90.1 (San Luis Obispo, CA) **545**
KCCK-FM - 88.3 (Cedar Rapids, IA) **1544**
KCCM-FM - 91.1 (Moorhead, MN) **2225**
KCCU-FM - 89.3 (Lawton, OK) **3466**
KCDA-FM - 103.1 (Spokane, WA) **4286**
KCDQ-FM - 102 (Odessa, TX) **4040**
KCEM-AM **2647**
KCEM-FM **2648**
KCEV-FM **1630**
KCHA-AM - 1580 (Charles City, IA) **1547**
KCHA-FM - 95.9 (Charles City, IA) **1548**
KCHH-FM - 103.5 (Chico, CA) **258**
KCHK-AM - 1350 (New Prague, MN) **2228**
KCHU-FM - 88.1 (Valdez, AK) **98**
KCIL-FM - 107.5 (Houma, LA) **1786**
KCKY-AM - 1150 (Coolidge, AZ) **101**
KCLB-AM - 970 (Coachella, CA) **261**
KCLB-FM - 93.7 (Coachella, CA) **262**
KCLO-TV - Channel 15 (Rapid City, SD) **3792**
KCLT-FM - 104.9 (West Helena, AR) **194**
KCLX-AM - 1450 (Colfax, WA) **4243**
KCLX-FM **4244**
KCMA-FM - 92.1 (Tulsa, OK) **3487**
KCMB-FM - 104.7 (Baker, OR) **3493**
KCML-FM - 107.5 (Fresno, CA) **288**
KCMY-TV - Channel 29 (Sacramento, CA) **469**
KCMZ-AM - 1480 (Dallas, TX) **3945**
KCND-FM - 90.5 (Bismarck, ND) **3304**
KCOG-AM - 1400 (Centerville, IA) **1546**
KCPI-FM **2162**
KCQL-AM - 1340 (Aztec, NM) **2647**
KCQR-FM - 94.5 (Santa Barbara, CA) **566**
KCRF-FM - 96.7 (Lincoln City, OR) **3515**
KCRT-AM - 1240 (Trinidad, CO) **703**
KCRT-FM - 92.7 (Trinidad, CO) **704**
KCRV-FM **2320**
KCRX-AM - 1430 (Roswell, NM) **2660**
KCSC-FM - 90.1 (Edmond, OK) **3458**
KCSN-FM - 88.5 (Northridge, CA) **408**
KCSP-FM - 90.3 (Casper, WY) **4467**
KCSR-AM - 610 (Chadron, NE) **2449**
KCST-AM - 1250 (Florence, OR) **3508**
KCTO-AM - 1540 (Columbia, LA) **1775**
KCYL-AM - 1450 (Lampasas, TX) **4012**
KCZE-FM - 95.1 (Charles City, IA) **1549**
KCZQ-FM - 102.3 (Charles City, IA) **1550**
KCZY-FM - 92.7 (Osage, IA) **1603**
KDAB-FM - 94.9 (Prairie Grove, AR) **190**
KDAK-AM - 1600 (Carrington, ND) **3307**
KDEN-AM - 1340 (Aurora, CO) **629**

KDEX-AM - 1590 (Dexter, MO) **2332**
KDGO-AM - 1240 (Durango, CO) **667**
KDHN-AM - 1470 (Dimmitt, TX) **3954**
KDKK-FM - 97.5 (Park Rapids, MN) **2232**
KDLK-FM - 94.3 (Del Rio, TX) **3948**
KDLX-FM - 106 (Maryville, MO) **2358**
KDMD-TV - Channel 33 & 22 (Anchorage, AK) **84**
KDON-FM - 102.5 (Salinas, CA) **477**
KDPR-FM - 89.9 (Bismarck, ND) **3305**
KDR-TV - Channel 64 (Phoenix, AZ) **119**
KDRS-AM - 1490 (Paragould, AR) **186**
KDSE-TV - Channel 9 (Fargo, ND) **3308**
KDTN-TV - Channel 2 (Dallas, TX) **3946**
KDUP-AM - 860 (Portland, OR) **3534**
KDUR-FM - 91.9 (Durango, CO) **668**
KDWA-AM - 1460 (Hastings, MN) **2193**
KDXT-FM - 93.3 (Missoula, MT) **2442**
KDYN-AM - 1540 (Ozark, AR) **185**
KEAS-AM - 1590 (Eastland, TX) **3957**
KEAS-FM - 97.7 (Eastland, TX) **3958**
KEBE-AM - 1400 (Jacksonville, TX) **4003**
KEBR-FM - 89.3 (Sacramento, CA) **470**
KEDG-AM - 530 (Sacramento, CA) **471**
KEEE-AM - 1230 (Nacogdoches, TX) **4035**
KEGG-AM - 1560 (Daingerfield, TX) **3932**
KEGS-FM - 101.7 (Emporia, KS) **1632**
KEKB-FM - 99.9 (Grand Junction, CO) **679**
KEMV-TV - Channel 6 (Conway, AR) **182**
KENA-AM - 1450 (Mena, AR) **178**
KENA-FM - 101.7 (Mena, AR) **179**
Kennedale News (Kennedale, TX) **4009**
Kennedy Institute of Ethics Journal (Baltimore, MD) **1854**
Kent County News (Chestertown, MD) **1890**
Kentucky Beverage Journal (Frankfort, KY) **1710**
The Kentucky Journal (Lexington, KY) **1718**
Kerala Express (Toronto, ON, Can.) **4704**
Kerby News for Seniors (Calgary, AB, Can.) **4488**
KERM-FM - 98.3 (Torrington, WY) **4480**
KERP-FM - 91.9 (Pueblo, CO) **695**
KESM-AM - 1580 (El Dorado Springs, MO) **2334**
KETG-TV - Channel 9 (Conway, AR) **151**
Kettle Moraine Advertiser **4419**
KETX-AM - 1440 (Livingston, TX) **4021**
KETX-FM - 92.3 (Livingston, TX) **4022**
KETX-TV - Channel 5 (Livingston, TX) **4023**
KEXS-AM - 1090 (Excelsior Springs, MO) **2335**
KEYA-FM - 88.5 (Belcourt, ND) **3298**
KEYE-AM - 1400 (Perryton, TX) **4045**
KEYL-AM - 1400 (Long Prairie, MN) **2197**
KEYN-FM - 103.7 (Wichita, KS) **1693**
The Keys Advertiser (Marathon Shores, FL) **958**
Keys; Gibbons-Humm's Guide to the Florida (Key Largo, FL) **947**
Keystone/Jersey Truck Exchange (Indianapolis, IN) **1476**
Keystone; Tribune (Elroy, WI) **4354**
KEZI-TV - Channel 9 (Eugene, OR) **3503**
KFAN-FM - 107.9 (Fredricksburg, TX) **4005**
KFCR-FM - 93.5 (Fullerton, CA) **291**
KFFA-AM - 1360 (Helena, AR) **167**
KFFN-FM - 100.9 (Sierra Vista, AZ) **133**
KFGE-FM - 105.3 (Lincoln, NE) **2463**
KFIL-FM - 103.1 (Preston, MN) **2234**
KFLA-AM - 1310 (Scott City, KS) **1681**
KFLR-FM - 90.3 (Phoenix, AZ) **120**
KFLZ-FM - 107.1 (Bishop, TX) **3910**
KFMA-FM - 93.7 (Wickenburg, AZ) **148**
KFME-TV - Channel 13 (Fargo, ND) **3312**
KFMM-FM - 99.1 (Safford, AZ) **129**
KFMN-FM - 96.9 (Lihue, HI) **1176**

Numbers cited in bold after listings are entry numbers rather than page numbers.

L

Messenger; The Caldwell (Caldwell, KS) **1627**

Messenger-Weekend **4372**

Metabolism; Journal of Cerebral Blood Flow and (New York, NY) **2937**

Metal Collectors Edition (Hollywood, CA) **304**

Metals; Modern (Chicago, IL) **1280**

Meteorological & Geoastrophysical Abstracts (Littleton, MA) **1975**

Metro County Courier **1090**

The Metro Courier (Augusta, GA) **1090**

Metro EXTRA (Chicago, IL) **1279**

Metro Times **3236**

Metrokids Magazine (Philadelphia, PA) **3637**

The Metropolitan (Denver, CO) **652**

Metroten Cablevision, Inc. (Brooklyn Heights, OH) **3337**

MetroVision Inc. (Atlanta, GA) **1084**

MetroVision of Livonia, Inc. (Livonia, MI) **2111**

MetroVision of Oakland County (Farmington Hills, MI) **2069**

MetroWest Jewish News (Whippany, NJ) **2636**

Miami; New Times of (Miami, FL) **965**

Miami Tele-Communications, Inc. (Miami, FL) **968**

Miami Valley Business News (Dayton, OH) **3399**

Miami Valley's New Business **3399**

Miata Magazine (Roswell, GA) **1144**

Michigan Banker (Lansing, MI) **2103**

Michigan Farm News (Lansing, MI) **2104**

Michigan Hospitals (Lansing, MI) **2105**

Michigan Overseas Veteran (Lansing, MI) **2106**

Michigan Snowmobiler (East Jordan, MI) **2063**

Michigan Truck Exchange (Indianapolis, IN) **1478**

Microbiologie); Canadian Journal of Microbiology (Revue Canadienne de (Ottawa, ON, Can.) **4661**

Microbiology and Infectious Diseases; Comparative Immunology, (Tarrytown, NY) **3142**

Microbiology (Revue Canadienne de Microbiologie); Canadian Journal of (Ottawa, ON, Can.) **4661**

Microgravity Quarterly (Tarrytown, NY) **3176**

Microsoft Networking Journal (Louisville, KY) **1735**

Mid-America Weekly Trucking (Fort Dodge, IA) **1580**

Mid-Atlantic Tech **3687**

Mid County Chronicle (Nederland, TX) **4037**

Mid-Missouri Business (Columbia, MO) **2326**

Mid-South Horse Review (Somerville, TN) **3864**

Mid-South Sociological Association; Sociological Spectrum: The Official Journal of the (Washington, DC) **862**

Middle Tennessee Shopper (Columbia, TN) **3816**

Middlebury Independent (Middlebury, IN) **1503**

The Middletown Valley Citizen (Middletown, MD) **1910**

Midwest CableVision (Preston, MN) **2235**

Midwest Truck Trader **1580**

Miesiecznik Franciszkanski (Pulaski, WI) **4435**

Mifflinburg Telegraph (Mifflinburg, PA) **3612**

Mike's TV Inc. (Morton, WA) **4255**

Mile Hi Cablevision Associates Ltd. (Denver, CO) **664**

Military Forum (Washington, DC) **840**

Military Review (Fort Leavenworth, KS) **1633**

Mill Creek Cable TV, Inc. (Salem, OR) **3543**

The Millington Star (Millington, TN) **3837**

The Mills Town Crier (Toronto, ON, Can.) **4711**

The Minden Courier (Minden, NE) **2465**

Miner; Bradford Journal/ (Mount Jewett, PA) **3615**

Miner; McKean County (Bradford, PA) **3563**

Mineralogical Record (Tucson, AZ) **139**

Minerals Today (Washington, DC) **841**

Miner's News (Boise, ID) **1181**

Miniature Collector (Livonia, MI) **2110**

Miniature Quilts (Montrose, PA) **3613**

Mining Journal; Canadian (Don Mills, ON, Can.) **4612**

Minn/Dakota Truck Merchandiser (Indianapolis, IN) **1479**

(Minneapolis) Northeaster (Minneapolis, MN) **2207**

Minnesota (Minneapolis, MN) **2208**

Minnesota Cities (Saint Paul, MN) **2251**

Minnesota History (Saint Paul, MN) **2252**

Minnesota Legionnaire (Saint Paul, MN) **2253**

Minnesota Women's Press (Saint Paul, MN) **2254**

Miramar (Hollywood, FL) **936**

Mirror; Lake Chelan (Chelan, WA) **4242**

MIS Quarterly (Minneapolis, MN) **2209**

Mission Cable Co. (Mesa, AZ) **109**

Mission Cable Co. (Fort Gibson, OK) **3462**

Missionary Monthly (Grand Rapids, MI) **2079**

Mississippi; Cablesystems of (Hattiesburg, MS) **2291**

Mississippi Pharmacist (Jackson, MS) **2294**

Mississippi, Inc.; Sammons Communications of (Pascagoula, MS) **2306**

Mississippi State University Alumnus (Mississippi State, MS) **2303**

Missouri Business; Mid- (Columbia, MO) **2326**

Missouri Farm **2322**

Missouri Grocer (Springfield, MO) **2406**

Missouri Historical Review (Columbia, MO) **2327**

Missouri Lawyers Weekly (Jefferson City, MO) **2342**

Missouri; Rural (Jefferson City, MO) **2343**

Missouri; TCI Cablevision of (Columbia, MO) **2331**

Missouri; TCI Cablevision of (Peters, MO) **2368**

Missouri Valley Merchandiser (Missouri Valley, IA) **1602**

Missourian (Columbia, MO) **2328**

Missourian Weekly **2328**

Mitchell News Journal (Spruce Pine, NC) **3284**

Mitchell Seaforth Cable TV Ltd. (Dublin, ON, Can.) **4621**

Mobile Homes Courier (Vista, CA) **609**

Mobile Office (Woodland Hills, CA) **623**

Mobile Office Magazine's Quarterly Cellular Buyers' Guide (Woodland Hills, CA) **624**

Model Call (Los Angeles, CA) **352**

Model News (New York, NY) **2971**

Modelling of Geo-Biosphere Processes (Lawrence, KS) **1651**

Models & Talent **3023**

Modern Judaism (Baltimore, MD) **1858**

Modern Logic: International Journal of the History of Mathematical Logic, Set Theory, and Foundation of Mathematics (Ames, IA) **1532**

Modern Maturity (Lakewood, CA) **319**

Modern Metals (Chicago, IL) **1280**

The Modern News (Harrisburg, AR) **165**

Modern Woodworking (Collierville, TN) **3815**

The Modesto Bee (Modesto, CA) **383**

Modesto; Spectrum Newspapers Monthly, (Modesto, CA) **384**

Modoc County Record (Alturas, CA) **202**

Molecular Pathology; Diagnostic (New York, NY) **2890**

Monatshefte (Madison, WI) **4389**

Monday Marketeer (Waupun, WI) **4460**

Money; Journal of International Financial Markets, Institutions and (Binghamton, NY) **2712**

Money Saver (Moose Jaw, SK, Can.) **4776**

Moneytalk (Larksville, PA) **3604**

The Monitor-Herald (Calhoun City, MS) **2277**

Monitor; Mayville (Mayville, MI) **2116**

Monmouth Cablevision Associates (Belmar, NJ) **2532**

Monographs of the Society for Research in Child Development (Chicago, IL) **1281**

Monroe County Democrat (Sparta, WI) **4447**

Montachusett Times (Ayer, MA) **1938**

Montage (Stanford, CA) **588**

Montana Kaimin (Missoula, MT) **2441**

Montana; TCI Cablevision of (Helena, MT) **2439**

Monterey Peninsula Cable TV (Monterey, CA) **387**

Monterey; Senior Spectrum Monthly, Salinas/ (Sacramento, CA) **465**

Monterey; Spectrum Newspapers Monthly, Santa Clara/ (Santa Clara, CA) **567**

Montezuma Press (Montezuma, KS) **1662**

Montgomery; Cable TV of (Rockville, MD) **1913**

The Moody Courier (Moody, TX) **4034**

Mora Advertiser **2227**

The Morenci Observer (Morenci, MI) **2120**

Morgan County Press (Stover, MO) **2414**

Morton Grove Champion (Morton Grove, IL) **1361**

Motor Boating & Sailing (New York, NY) **2972**

Motor Carrier Manager (Rexdale, ON, Can.) **4680**

Motor World (Los Angeles, CA) **353**

Moulins; Courrier des (Laval, PQ, Can.) **4742**

Mound City News-Independent (Mound City, MO) **2360**

Mt. Aukum Review (Mount Aukum, CA) **388**

Mount Evans Cable and Video (Denver, CO) **665**

Mount Holyoke Alumnae Quarterly (South Hadley, MA) **1998**

Mountain America Truck Trader (Indianapolis, IN) **1480**

Mountain Brook Cablevision, Inc. (Mountain Brook, AL) **63**

Mountain Cable TV (Meta, KY) **1740**

The Mountain Messenger (Downieville, CA) **271**

Mountain Research and Development (Berkeley, CA) **222**

Mountaineer; Big Sandy (Big Sandy, MT) **2423**

Movement Disorders (New York, NY) **2973**

Moves (Salinas, CA) **475**

Movie Marketplace (Evanston, IL) **1333**

Movies; Tribute Goes to the (Don Mills, ON, Can.) **4619**

MPC World **516**

O

OS/2 Magazine **2816**
OS/2 and Windows Magazine **2816**
Osage County Chronicle (Osage City, KS) **1665**
Osage County Journal (Osage City, KS) **1666**
The Other Side of the Lake (Three Oaks, MI) **2150**
Otolaryngology; Contemporary Management in (New York, NY) **2880**
Otology; The American Journal of (Hamilton, ON, Can.) **4627**
Our California Environment (Fort Dodge, IA) **1581**
Our Right to Know (New York, NY) **2991**
Our Town (Pearl River, NY) **3087**
Our World (Daytona Beach, FL) **899**
Out (New York, NY) **2992**
Outdoor Beacon; Ohio's (Port Clinton, OH) **3436**
Outdoors; North Dakota (Bismarck, ND) **3302**
Outlook (Redwood City, CA) **445**
Outlook (Ottawa, ON, Can.) **4673**
Outpost Exchange (Milwaukee, WI) **4410**
Outside (Chicago, IL) **1285**
Outstate Business (Boyne City, MI) **2045**
Outweek Magazine (New York, NY) **2993**
Overland Park, Inc.; TeleCable of (Overland Park, KS) **1673**
Owensboro Cablevision (Owensboro, KY) **1746**
Oxford Review Times; Chenango American, Whitney Point Reporter, and (Greene, NY) **2782**

P

P.A.C. (Mount Joy, PA) **3617**
Pacific Affairs (Vancouver, BC, Can.) **4549**
Pacific/Asia Edition; OAG Travel Planner - (Oak Brook, IL) **1373**
Pacific/Asia Edition OAG Travel Planner Hotel & Motel RedBook **1373**
Pacific Citizen (Los Angeles, CA) **357**
Pacific Northwest Cable (Newport, WA) **4256**
Pacific Tech **3687**
Pacific Ties (Los Angeles, CA) **358**
Pacific West Cable Co. (Sacramento, CA) **473**
Paddle Sports (Soquel, CA) **585**
Paducah; Comcast Cablevision of (Paducah, KY) **1747**
The Pageland Progressive-Journal (Pageland, SC) **3772**
PageMarker In-Depth (Concord, MA) **1965**
Paint Works (Newton, NJ) **2597**
Paintball Magazine (Burbank, CA) **238**
The Paladin (Greenville, SC) **3751**
Palm Beach Illustrated (West Palm Beach, FL) **1042**
Palm Beach Jewish Journal **905**
Palm Beach Jewish Journal **1043**
Palm Beach Jewish Journal North (Deerfield Beach, FL) **905**
Palm Beach Jewish Journal South (West Palm Beach, FL) **1043**
Palmer Cablevision (Naples, FL) **973**
Palmetto Cable TV (Fort Mill, SC) **3748**
Palmetto Cablevision (Saluda Cablevision) (Saluda, SC) **3776**
Palmyra Enterprise (Palmyra, WI) **4428**
Palos Hills-Hickory Hills Reporter (Bridgeview, IL) **1218**
Pancreas (New York, NY) **2994**
Panola Watchman (Panola, TX) **4043**
The Paper (Sierra Vista, AZ) **131**
Papyrologists; Bulletin of the American Society of (Atlanta, GA) **1064**

Paragon Cable (Minneapolis, MN) **2217**
Paragon Cable (Portland, OR) **3536**
Paragon Cable (Laredo, TX) **4014**
Paragon Cable (San Antonio, TX) **4065**
Paragon Cable Manhattan (New York, NY) **3070**
Paragon Cable TV (Garden Grove, CA) **292**
Paragon Communications (Torrance, CA) **599**
Paragon Communications (Bradenton, FL) **885**
Paragon Communications (El Paso, TX) **3961**
Paragon Communications (Irving, TX) **4002**
Parametrics; Journal of (Germantown, MD) **1904**
Paraplegia News (Phoenix, AZ) **116**
Parapsychology; Journal of (Durham, NC) **3221**
Parent; Atlanta (Atlanta, GA) **1060**
Parenting; Passionate (Tucson, AZ) **140**
Parent's Digest (Des Moines, IA) **1560**
Parents Express (Philadelphia, PA) **3638**
Parents); Ser Padres (Being (New York, NY) **3019**
Park News **4691**
Parks; Plants Sites & (Coral Springs, FL) **897**
Parks and Recreation Magazine (Arlington, VA) **4141**
The Parma News (Parma, MI) **2132**
Particles and Nuclei; Physics of (New York, NY) **2997**
Partners (Monrovia, CA) **385**
Partners in Communications-Alabama (Mobile, AL) **53**
Passionate Parenting (Tucson, AZ) **140**
Pastoral Life (Canfield, OH) **3339**
Pathology; Ultrastructural (Washington, DC) **867**
Patriot-Citizen (Buena Vista, GA) **1099**
The Pavlovian Journal of Biological Science **2580**
PBC Federal Tax Guide (Los Angeles, CA) **359**
PC Games (Peterborough, NH) **2521**
PCR Methods and Applications (Cold Spring Harbor, NY) **2759**
The PD News **3891**
The Peddler (Clarksville, TN) **3811**
Pediatric Nursing; Issues in Comprehensive (Washington, DC) **828**
Pee Dee Magazine (Myrtle Beach, SC) **3769**
The Pelham Sun (Yonkers, NY) **3197**
Pelican Press (Sarasota, FL) **1013**
Pembroke Pines Sun (Hollywood, FL) **937**
Peninsula Beacon (San Diego, CA) **496**
Peninsula Business Journal (Sequim, WA) **4282**
Pennsylvania, Inc.; TCI of (Pittsburgh, PA) **3658**
Pennysaver (Marshalltown, IA) **1600**
Pennysaver (Hanover, MD) **1906**
The Pennysaver (Wytheville, VA) **4232**
Pennysaver (Oneida Edition) (Oneida, NY) **3085**
Pensacola; Cox Cable TV of (Pensacola, FL) **995**
The Pentecostal Messenger (Joplin, MO) **2347**
People and Education (Newbury Park, CA) **395**
People; Food (Acworth, GA) **1048**
People In Action and Sports Parade (Ogden, UT) **4085**
People & Places (High Point Edition) (Greensboro, NC) **3240**
Peoples Broadband Communications System (Randolph, WI) **4437**
Pep Talk - Group Marriage News **1162**
Peptides (New Orleans, LA) **1796**

Performing Arts Journal (Baltimore, MD) **1859**
Perido Pelican (Pensacola, FL) **994**
Perinton Herald Mail; Fairport (Fairport, NY) **2769**
Peritoneal Dialysis International (Toronto, ON, Can.) **4713**
Perry County/Petit Jean Country Headlight (Perryville, AR) **188**
The Perry Township Weekly (Beech Grove, IN) **1427**
Perryville Sun Times (Genevieve, MO) **2338**
The Persian Quarterly (Wheat Ridge, CO) **723**
Personal Construct Psychology; International Journal of (Washington, DC) **826**
Perspectives in Biology and Medicine (Chicago, IL) **1286**
Perspectives in Religious Studies (Macon, GA) **1130**
Perspectives on Science (Chicago, IL) **1287**
Pest Control (Cleveland, OH) **3378**
The Pet Dealer (Elizabeth, NJ) **2554**
Petit Jean Country Headlight; Perry County/ (Perryville, AR) **188**
Petroleum Marketer (Rockville, MD) **1926**
Petrology; Journal of Sedimentary (Tulsa, OK) **3485**
Pharillion Voyageur; Le (Rimouski, PQ, Can.) **4765**
Pharmacist; The Consultant (Alexandria, VA) **4128**
Pharmacist; Mississippi (Jackson, MS) **2294**
Pharmacoepidemiology; Journal of (Binghamton, NY) **2719**
Pharmacological and Toxicological Methods; Journal of (New York, NY) **2953**
Pharmacologie); Canadian Journal of Physiology and Pharmacology (Revue Canadienne de Physiologie et (Ottawa, ON, Can.) **4662**
Pharmacology Biochemistry and Behavior (San Antonio, TX) **4056**
Pharmacology; Journal of Cardiovascular (New York, NY) **2935**
Pharmacology (Revue Canadienne de Physiologie et Pharmacologie); Canadian Journal of Physiology and (Ottawa, ON, Can.) **4662**
Pharmacy; American (Washington, DC) **796**
Pharmacy Journal; Southern (Englewood, CO) **672**
Philadelphia American; South (Philadelphia, PA) **3641**
Philadelphia Cablevision, Inc.; Greater (Philadelphia, PA) **3643**
Philadelphia; Comcast Cablevision of (Philadelphia, PA) **3642**
Philadelphia Golf Magazine (Paoli, PA) **3628**
Philatelist; The Collectors Club (New York, NY) **2874**
Phillies Report (Springfield, PA) **3676**
Phillips Bee (Phillips, WI) **4430**
Philosophical Quarterly; International (Bronx, NY) **2742**
Philosophical Review (Ithaca, NY) **2792**
Philosophy; The Journal of Speculative (University Park, PA) **3685**
Philosophy and Literature (Baltimore, MD) **1860**
Philosophy; Russian Studies in (Armonk, NY) **2686**
The Phoenix (Westminster, MD) **1934**
The Phoenix (Swarthmore, PA) **3681**
Phonoscope Cable TV (Houston, TX) **3993**
Photo Press; Fairmont (Fairmont, MN) **2185**
Photochemistry and Photobiology (Lincoln, NE) **2461**
PhotoPro (Titusville, FL) **1041**

Numbers cited in bold after listings are entry numbers rather than page numbers.

Psychology; Current (New Brunswick, NJ) **2577**
Psychology and Human Sexuality; Journal of (Binghamton, NY) **2721**
Psychology; Individual (Austin, TX) **3885**
Psychology; International Journal of Personal Construct (Washington, DC) **826**
Psychology; Journal of Family (Washington, DC) **831**
Psychology; Journal of Russian and East European (Armonk, NY) **2678**
Psychology Review; Clinical (Tarrytown, NY) **3140**
Psychology and Theology; Journal of (La Mirada, CA) **313**
Psychology for Today; Christian **865**
Psychotherapy; Journal of Family (Binghamton, NY) **2703**
Psychotherapy; Journal of Gay and Lesbian (Binghamton, NY) **2707**
Psychotherapy; Journal of Religion in (Binghamton, NY) **2722**
The Psychotherapy Patient (Binghamton, NY) **2735**
Psychotherapy Practice and Research; Journal of (Washington, DC) **834**
Psychotherapy in Private Practice (Binghamton, NY) **2736**
PsycSCAN: PSYCHOANALYSIS (Washington, DC) **850**
PT, Magazine of Physical Therapy (Alexandria, VA) **4132**
PTI Journal (Costa Mesa, CA) **264**
Public Budgeting and Finance (New Brunswick, NJ) **2588**
Public Budgeting and Financial Management (New York, NY) **3007**
Public Cable Co. (Portland, ME) **1832**
Public Contract Law Journal (Chicago, IL) **1293**
The Public Employee Magazine (Washington, DC) **851**
The Public Historian (Berkeley, CA) **223**
Public Opinion (Decorah, IA) **1556**
Public Opinion Quarterly (Chicago, IL) **1294**
Public Power (Washington, DC) **852**
Public Productivity & Management Review (San Francisco, CA) **522**
Publications & Video; Obscure (Milwaukee, WI) **4409**
Publishing; Color (Westford, MA) **2015**
Puente Highlander; La (La Puente, CA) **314**
Puerto Rico; TCI Cable of (Luquillo, PR) **3703**
The Pullman Herald (San Mateo, CA) **550**
Punch Digest for Canadian Doctors (Aurora, ON, Can.) **4597**
Purchasing; Electronics (Newton, MA) **1987**
Putnam County Journal; Unionville Republican & (Unionville, MO) **2419**

Q

Qigong (San Francisco, CA) **523**
Quality Cities (Tallahassee, FL) **1026**
Quality Cities '91 **1026**
Quality Digest (Red Bluff, CA) **441**
Quality and Participation; The Journal for (Cincinnati, OH) **3348**
Quantico Sentry (Quantico, VA) **4203**
Quantum Electronics (New York, NY) **3008**
Quarry; Pit & (Cleveland, OH) **3379**
Quarter Horse Journal; Eastern/Western (Middleboro, MA) **1980**
The Quarterly Review of Economics and Finance (Champaign, IL) **1240**
The Quayle Quarterly (Bridgeport, CT) **734**
Quebec Yachting (Montreal, PQ, Can.) **4758**

Queens; American Cablevision of (Flushing, NY) **2773**
Queens Inner Unity Cable Systems (Queens, NY) **3099**
Quick & Easy Needlecraft (Big Sandy, TX) **3908**
The Quill (Brandon, MB, Can.) **4559**
Quill & Quire (Toronto, ON, Can.) **4715**
Quilt Craft (New York, NY) **3009**
Quilter's Newsletter Magazine (Wheat Ridge, CO) **724**
Quirk's Marketing Research Review (Minneapolis, MN) **2213**

R

R & D Magazine (Newton, MA) **1989**
R.E.P. (Overland Park, KS) **1671**
Racine TeleCable Corp. (Racine, WI) **4436**
Racing Collectibles Price Guide (Orlando, FL) **984**
The Racing Times (New York, NY) **3010**
Radical America (Somerville, MA) **1996**
Radical Teacher (Cambridge, MA) **1963**
Radio-Electronics **2770**
The Radio Ranks (New York, NY) **3011**
Radio Resource (Denver, CO) **653**
The Radio Sweep **3011**
Radioactive Waste Management (Oak Ridge, TN) **3861**
Radiologists Journal; Canadian Association of (Ottawa, ON, Can.) **4652**
Radiology; Urologic (New York, NY) **3056**
Railroad Information (Wolfeboro, NH) **2530**
Railway Track & Structures (New York, NY) **3012**
Rain Magazine (Eugene, OR) **3501**
Rains County Leader (Emory, TX) **3962**
Raleigh; Cablevision of (Raleigh, NC) **3276**
Randallstown News **1921**
Randolph-Macon Woman's College Alumnae Bulletin (Lynchburg, VA) **4191**
RCDA (New York, NY) **3013**
RCDA-Religion in Communist Dominated Areas **3013**
Reader (Los Angeles, CA) **361**
Reading Psychology: An International Quarterly (Washington, DC) **853**
Reading and Writing Quarterly: Overcoming Learning Difficulties (Washington, DC) **854**
Real Estate Finance Today (Washington, DC) **855**
Real Estate Quarterly (New Haven, CT) **752**
Real Estate Taxation; Journal of (New York, NY) **2955**
Realtor News (All Member Issue) (Washington, DC) **856**
Rebekah; California Odd Fellow and (Linden, CA) **322**
Record (Lompoc, CA) **324**
Record-Courier (Ravenna, OH) **3437**
The Record-Courier (Baker, OR) **3492**
Record Courier **4004**
The Record Farmer and Ranch-Statewide (Gainesville, FL) **926**
The Record-Local (Gainesville, FL) **927**
Recorder (East Brunswick, NJ) **2549**
Recreation Canada (Gloucester, ON, Can.) **4625**
Recreation Magazine; Parks and (Arlington, VA) **4141**
Red Cloud Chief (Red Cloud, NE) **2477**
Reedsburg Times-Press (Reedsburg, WI) **4438**
Reference & Research Book News (Portland, OR) **3527**
Reference Services Review (Ann Arbor, MI) **2033**

Rehabilitation Education (Champaign, IL) **1241**
Rehabilitation; Journal of Offender (Binghamton, NY) **2718**
Rehabilitation; Journal of Vision (Lincoln, NE) **2458**
Religion in Psychotherapy; Journal of (Binghamton, NY) **2722**
Religious Gerontology; Journal of (Binghamton, NY) **2723**
Religious; Review for (Saint Louis, MO) **2391**
Religious Studies; Perspectives in (Macon, GA) **1130**
REMark (Benton Harbor, MI) **2041**
Remarriage; Journal of Divorce and (Binghamton, NY) **2699**
Remedial and Special Education (RASE) (Austin, TX) **3889**
The Reminder (Flin Flon, MB, Can.) **4563**
Remington Press (Remington, IN) **1514**
Remnant Christian Magazine (Crowley, LA) **1776**
Renascence (Milwaukee, WI) **4411**
Renewable Energy: An International Journal (Tarrytown, NY) **3178**
Reno; Spectrum Newspapers Monthly, (Reno, NV) **2491**
Rental Dealer News (Costa Mesa, CA) **265**
Report on Urologic Techniques (New York, NY) **3014**
Reporter **2452**
The Reporter (Spokane, WA) **4284**
Reporter; The Voice & The (Huron, OH) **3420**
The Representative (Leduc, AB, Can.) **4508**
Reproductive and Genetic Engineering (Elmsford, NY) **2767**
Reptile & Amphibian Magazine (Pottsville, PA) **3663**
The Republican (Danville, IN) **1443**
The Republican Journal (Belfast, ME) **1817**
Research and Development; Industrial **1989**
Research in Music Education; Journal for (Reston, VA) **4208**
Research News Reporter (Washington, DC) **857**
Reseller Management (Morris Plains, NJ) **2570**
Resolution (Camden, ME) **1821**
Resort TV Cable Co., Inc. (Hot Springs, AR) **168**
Resort Weekly (Kipling, SK, Can.) **4773**
The Resource Center Bulletin (Albuquerque, NM) **2642**
Restaurant Administration Quarterly; The Cornell Hotel and (Ithaca, NY) **2790**
Restaurateur; Wisconsin (Madison, WI) **4395**
Restoration and Management Notes (Madison, WI) **4391**
Resurrection Magazine (Oxon Hill, MD) **1922**
Retailer; New Age (Bellingham, WA) **4239**
Retailing; Journal of (New York, NY) **2956**
Reunions Magazine (Milwaukee, WI) **4412**
Reveille; Cloverdale (Cloverdale, CA) **260**
The Review (Newark, DE) **786**
The Review (Liverpool, NY) **2809**
The Review of Black Political Economy (New Brunswick, NJ) **2589**
The Review of Financial Studies (New York, NY) **3015**
Review of International Affairs (Albuquerque, NM) **2643**
Review of Politics (Notre Dame, IN) **1510**
Review for Religious (Saint Louis, MO) **2391**
(Revue Canadienne de Botanique); Canadian Journal of Botany (Ottawa, ON, Can.) **4656**

Sonoma; Spectrum Newspapers Monthly, (Sonoma, CA) **584**

Sooland Cablecom Corp. (Sioux City, IA) **1614**

Sorel-O-Vision Inc. (Montreal, PQ, Can.) **4761**

The Soroptimists of the Americas (Philadelphia, PA) **3640**

Soundtrack (Ringwood, NJ) **2614**

The Source (New York, NY) **3029**

Sourdough Sentinel (Anchorage, AK) **82**

South Asia; Contemporary (Dunnellon, FL) **909**

South Asia Journal (Newbury Park, CA) **397**

The South Atlantic Quarterly (Durham, NC) **3223**

South Atlantic Review (Tuscaloosa, AL) **75**

South Bend Tribune (South Bend, IN) **1520**

South Benton Cablevision, Inc. (Keystone, IA) **1596**

South Benton Star-Press (Belle Plaine, IA) **1535**

South Carolina; Cox Cable (Myrtle Beach, SC) **3770**

The South Carolina Forum **3734**

South Carolina Historical Magazine (Charleston, SC) **3727**

The South Carolina Policy Forum (Columbia, SC) **3734**

South Carolina; Vision Cable of (Florence, SC) **3743**

South Central Los Angeles; American Cablesystems of (Los Angeles, CA) **368**

South County News-Times **2394**

South County Times (Saint Louis, MO) **2394**

South Dakota; TCI Cablevision of (Rapid City, SD) **3793**

South Florida Home Buyer's Guide (Deerfield Beach, FL) **906**

South Hills Record (Pittsburgh, PA) **3656**

South Lake Press (Clermont, FL) **890**

South Milwaukee Voice Graphic (South Milwaukee, WI) **4446**

South Philadelphia American (Philadelphia, PA) **3641**

South Texas Agri-News (Mission, TX) **4033**

South-Western Cable TV, Ltd. **1353**

Southampton Press (Southampton, NY) **3124**

Southern Baptist; The California (Fresno, CA) **283**

Southern Cable View (Eatonton, GA) **1116**

Southern California Construction Journal **524**

Southern Connection (Dawson, GA) **1109**

Southern Exposure (Durham, NC) **3224**

Southern Folklore Quarterly (Lexington, KY) **1719**

Southern Living (Birmingham, AL) **15**

Southern Manitoba Review (Cartwright, MB, Can.) **4562**

Southern Nebraska Register (Lincoln, NE) **2462**

Southern Pharmacy Journal (Englewood, CO) **672**

Southern Plumbing, Heating, Cooling (Greensboro, NC) **3241**

Southwest EXTRA (Chicago, IL) **1295**

Southwest Review (Dallas, TX) **3941**

Southwestern Cable TV/San Diego Division (San Diego, CA) **506**

The Southwestern Sportsman Magazine (Winkelman, AZ) **150**

Soviet Anthropology & Archeology **2675**

Soviet Astronomy **2854**

Soviet & Eastern European Foreign Trade **2680**

Soviet Education **2681**

Soviet Journal of Low Temperature Physics **2965**

Soviet Journal of Nuclear Physics **2995**

Soviet Journal of Optical Technology (New York, NY) **3030**

Soviet Journal of Particles and Nuclei **2997**

Soviet Journal of Plasma Physics **3001**

Soviet Journal of Quantum Electronics **3008**

Soviet Law and Government **2682**

Soviet Neurology & Psychiatry **2677**

Soviet Physics-Acoustics **2836**

Soviet Physics-Crystallography **2885**

Soviet Physics-Doklady **2996**

Soviet Physics-JETP **2928**

Soviet Physics-Semiconductors **3018**

Soviet Physics-Solid State **2998**

Soviet Physics-Technical Physics **3040**

Soviet Physics **2999**

Soviet Psychology **2678**

Soviet Review **2683**

Soviet Sociology **2687**

Soviet Sports Review **277**

Soviet Statutes and Decisions **2688**

Soviet Studies in History **2684**

Soviet Studies in Literature **2685**

Soviet Studies in Philosopy **2686**

Space, and Environmental Medicine; Aviation, (Alexandria, VA) **4126**

Spark! (Cincinnati, OH) **3350**

The Sparta Herald (Sparta, WI) **4448**

Special Collections **2734**

Spectrochimica Acta (Elmsford, NY) **2768**

Spectroscopy; Optics and (New York, NY) **2990**

The Spectrum (Buffalo, NY) **2749**

Spectrum Newspapers Monthly, Contra Costa/Tri Valley (Bishop, CA) **233**

Spectrum Newspapers Monthly, Denver (Denver, CO) **655**

Spectrum Newspapers Monthly, Fresno/Bakersfield (Fresno, CA) **285**

Spectrum Newspapers Monthly, Greater Sacramento (Sacramento, CA) **468**

Spectrum Newspapers Monthly, Las Vegas (Las Vegas, NV) **2488**

Spectrum Newspapers Monthly, Modesto (Modesto, CA) **384**

Spectrum Newspapers Monthly, Portland (Portland, OR) **3529**

Spectrum Newspapers Monthly, Reno (Reno, NV) **2491**

Spectrum Newspapers Monthly, San Francisco/Marin/San Mateo (San Francisco, CA) **525**

Spectrum Newspapers Monthly, Santa Clara/Monterey (Santa Clara, CA) **567**

Spectrum Newspapers Monthly, Seattle (Seattle, WA) **4275**

Spectrum Newspapers Monthly, Sonoma (Sonoma, CA) **584**

Spectrum Newspapers Weekly, Sacramento (Rancho Cordova, CA) **440**

Spectrum Newspapers Weekly, Stockton (Stockton, CA) **589**

Speculative Philosophy; The Journal of (University Park, PA) **3685**

Spinal Disorders; Journal of (New York, NY) **2957**

Spirit of Ability (Calgary, AB, Can.) **4491**

Spiritual Life (Washington, DC) **863**

Spirituality of Jesuits; Studies in the (Saint Louis, MO) **2397**

Spokane; Cox Cable (Spokane, WA) **4285**

Sport Cycling Freewheelin' (Canoga Park, CA) **248**

Sport Medicine; Clinical Journal of (New York, NY) **2872**

Sporting Goods Dealer (New York, NY) **3031**

Sporting Guns (Ocala, FL) **980**

Sporting Journal; Gray's (Augusta, GA) **1089**

Sports Card Review & Value Line (Sussex, WI) **4457**

Sports & Fitness; Women's (Boulder, CO) **633**

Sports Focus Magazine (Gaithersburg, MD) **1902**

Sports 'n Spokes (Phoenix, AZ) **117**

Sports Parade; People In Action and (Ogden, UT) **4085**

Sports Review; Tyler County Journal & (Sistersville, WV) **4325**

Sports Spectrum (Wayzata, MN) **2266**

Sportsman; The Badger (Chilton, WI) **4341**

Sportsman Magazine; The Southwestern (Winkelman, AZ) **150**

Spotlight Casting (Hollywood, CA) **305**

The Spring Hill New Era (Gardner, KS) **1636**

Spring Valley's Bureau County Republican (Spring Valley, IL) **1410**

Springfield Advance-Press (Springfield, MN) **2258**

Springfield Business Journal (Springfield, MO) **2407**

Springfield; Continental Cablevision, Inc. of (Springfield, MA) **1999**

Springfield Parent (Springfield, MO) **2408**

Springfield; TeleCable of (Springfield, MO) **2413**

Springfield; Times Mirror Cable TV of (Springfield, IL) **1411**

Sprinkler Age (Dallas, TX) **3942**

Squaredance; American (Salinas, CA) **474**

Srbobran; American (Pittsburgh, PA) **3648**

SRW Inc. (Hershey, PA) **3595**

St-Francois; Le Haut (Cookshire, PQ, Can.) **4735**

Stage Directions (West Sacramento, CA) **615**

Stagebill Group (Chicago, IL) **1296**

Stamps Auction News (Hornell, NY) **2788**

The Standard (Springfield, MO) **2409**

Standard Corporation Records (New York, NY) **3032**

Staplreview (Greenwood, MS) **2287**

The Star (Sun Prairie, WI) **4456**

Star Cable Associates (Columbia, SC) **3736**

Star Cablevision (Fond du Lac, WI) **4356**

Star Cablevision (Prairie du Chien, WI) **4434**

Star Cablevision (Sheboygan, WI) **4444**

Star-Democrat (Easton, MD) **1897**

Star-Gazette (Moose Lake, MN) **2226**

Star & Lamp (Charlotte, NC) **3217**

The Star & Lamp of Pi Kappa Phi **3217**

The Star-Shopper (Lebanon, TN) **3831**

Star Shoppers' Aid (Millington, TN) **3838**

State Line Tribune (Farwell, TX) **3963**

The State News (East Lansing, MI) **2065**

State Notary Bulletin (Canoga Park, CA) **249**

Staten Island Cable (Staten Island, NY) **3125**

Statistical Science (Hayward, CA) **301**

Statistics; The Annals of (Hayward, CA) **299**

Statutes and Decisions: Laws of the USSR and Its Successor States (Armonk, NY) **2688**

Steamboat Bill (Providence, RI) **3710**

The Steamboat Whistle (Steamboat Springs, CO) **700**

Steelabor (Pittsburgh, PA) **3657**

Stereo Review; Car (New York, NY) **2863**

Sterling Bulletin (Sterling, KS) **1683**

Steroid Biochemistry and Molecular Biology; The Journal of (Tarrytown, NY) **3169**

STL (Saint Louis, MO) **2395**

Stockton; Spectrum Newspapers Weekly, (Stockton, CA) **589**

Stone Through the Ages (Farmington, MI) **2068**

The Stoneham Independent (Stoneham, MA) **2002**

Stoneham News Weekender (Stoneham, MA) **2003**

Stoneham Shopper News **2003**

Storer Cable (Eatontown, NJ) **2552**

Storer Cable of Carolina, Inc. (North Charleston, SC) **3771**

Storer Cable Communications (North Little Rock, AR) **183**

Storer Cable Communications of Southern Kentucky (Bowling Green, KY) **1700**

Storer Cable TV of Connecticut, Inc. (New Haven, CT) **754**

Storer Cable TV of Florida (Miami, FL) **969**

Storer Cable TV of Florida, Inc. (Sarasota, FL) **1014**

Storer Cable TV of Houston (Houston, TX) **3994**

Storer Cable TV of Texas, Inc. (Garland, TX) **3971**

Storer Communications (Covington, KY) **1704**

Storer Communications of Jefferson County (Louisville, KY) **1737**

Straight Talk: A Magazine for Teens (Pleasantville, NY) **3092**

Strange Days (Worcester, MA) **2024**

Street Cruzin Magazine (Anaheim, CA) **206**

Street Rod Pickups (Canoga Park, CA) **250**

Strictly Somerset (Bridgewater, NJ) **2537**

STRINGS (San Anselmo, CA) **480**

Student Lawyer (Chicago, IL) **1297**

Student Life (Saint Louis, MO) **2396**

Studies in Art Education (Reston, VA) **4210**

Studies in Comparative International Development (New Brunswick, NJ) **2591**

Studies in the Spirituality of Jesuits (Saint Louis, MO) **2397**

The Stute (Hoboken, NJ) **2559**

Subasta; La (Houston, TX) **3984**

Suburban Cable TV (Coatesville, PA) **3574**

Suburban Cable TV (Lancaster, PA) **3603**

Suburban Cable TV (Upper Darby, PA) **3686**

Suburban Cablevision (East Orange, NJ) **2551**

Suburban Life-Press (Cincinnati, OH) **3351**

Suburban Today (Duncanville, TX) **3955**

Suffolk News-Herald (Suffolk, VA) **4226**

Summary of Labor Arbitration Awards (New York, NY) **3033**

Summer Fun (San Francisco, CA) **526**

The Summerville News (Summerville, GA) **1151**

The Summit (North Easton, MA) **1991**

Summit Cable Services (Winston-Salem, NC) **3294**

Sumter; Vision Cable of (Sumter, SC) **3778**

Sun (Trenton, IL) **1417**

Sun (Mount Pleasant, MI) **2122**

Sun Country Cable (Groveland, CA) **296**

Sun Country Cable Inc. (Quincy, WA) **4265**

Sun-Journal (Delphi, IN) **1444**

Sun News (De Land, FL) **903**

Sun-Sentinel (Fort Lauderdale, FL) **912**

Sunday Journal **2538**

Sunday Square Shooter (Staples, MN) **2259**

Sunset Magazine (Menlo Park, CA) **381**

Suntech Journal **527**

Sunworld (San Francisco, CA) **527**

Super Easy-To-Do (New York, NY) **3034**

Super Gaming (Lombard, IL) **1350**

Super Stars (New York, NY) **3035**

Super Sunday Shopper **4557**

Superfly (New York, NY) **3036**

Superior Fill-Ins (Ambler, PA) **3556**

Superstar and Rookie Special (Iola, WI) **4371**

Supertrax Magazine (Excelsior, MN) **2183**

Supervisor; Today's (Itasca, IL) **1342**

Surgery; The Annals of Thoracic (New York, NY) **2851**

Surgical Laparoscopy & Endoscopy (New York, NY) **3037**

Surveyor; The Texas (Austin, TX) **3894**

SV Entertainment (Chicago, IL) **1298**

Swampscott Reporter (Swampscott, MA) **2006**

Swimsuit Spectacular (Tarrytown, NY) **3179**

The Sylva Herald & Ruralite (Sylva, NC) **3285**

Symphony Magazine; Houston (Houston, TX) **3982**

The Symphony User's Journal (Louisville, KY) **1736**

Syracuse NewChannels Corp. (Syracuse, NY) **3130**

Systems Automation: Research & Applications (SARA); International Journal of (Bloomfield Hills, MI) **2043**

T

T & B **1404**

T.J.'s Community Bulletin (Cornell, WI) **4347**

Tacoma, Inc.; TCI Cablevision of (Tacoma, WA) **4291**

Tahoe Action (South Lake Tahoe, CA) **586**

Tantra: The Magazine (Torreon, NM) **2667**

Taos Magazine (Taos, NM) **2666**

Tarheel Banker (Raleigh, NC) **3274**

Tarpon Springs (Tarpon Springs, FL) **1038**

The Tattler (Little Chute, WI) **4381**

Taxation for Accountants (New York, NY) **3038**

Taxation; Journal of Corporate (New York, NY) **2941**

Taxation; Journal of Real Estate (New York, NY) **2955**

Taxation for Lawyers (New York, NY) **3039**

TCA Cable TV (Bentonville, AR) **153**

TCA Cable TV (Greenville, MS) **2285**

TCA Cable TV (Bryan, TX) **3921**

TCI of Arkansas (CSI), Inc. (Fort Smith, AR) **164**

TCI Cable (Park City, UT) **4089**

TCI Cable of New Mexico (Farmington, NM) **2651**

TCI Cable of Puerto Rico (Luquillo, PR) **3703**

TCI Cablevision of Alabama, Inc. (Hoover, AL) **38**

TCI Cablevision of Alabama (Piedmont, AL) **68**

TCI Cablevision of Casper (Casper, WY) **4468**

TCI Cablevision of Central Illinois (Peoria, IL) **1382**

TCI Cablevision of Colorado (Boulder, CO) **636**

TCI Cablevision of Colorado (Pueblo, CO) **697**

TCI Cablevision of Dallas, Inc. (Dallas, TX) **3947**

TCI Cablevision of Florida (Daytona Beach, FL) **900**

TCI Cablevision of Georgia (Athens, GA) **1053**

TCI Cablevision of Georgia (Columbus, GA) **1102**

TCI Cablevision of Great Falls (Great Falls, MT) **2432**

TCI Cablevision of Idaho (Pocatello, ID) **1200**

TCI Cablevision of Missouri (Columbia, MO) **2331**

TCI Cablevision of Missouri (Peters, MO) **2368**

TCI Cablevision of Montana (Helena, MT) **2439**

TCI Cablevision of Nevada, Inc. (Carson City, NV) **2485**

TCI Cablevision of New Castle County (New Castle, DE) **785**

TCI Cablevision of Ohio (Warren, OH) **3444**

TCI Cablevision of Oklahoma (Enid, OK) **3461**

TCI Cablevision of Oregon, Inc. (Burns, OR) **3494**

TCI Cablevision of Oregon (Eugene, OR) **3507**

TCI Cablevision of Oregon (Klamath Falls, OR) **3512**

TCI Cablevision of Oregon (Medford, OR) **3518**

TCI Cablevision of Oregon (Portland, OR) **3537**

TCI Cablevision of South Dakota (Rapid City, SD) **3793**

TCI Cablevision of Tacoma, Inc. (Tacoma, WA) **4291**

TCI Cablevision of Texas, Inc. (Beaumont, TX) **3902**

TCI Cablevision of Texas, Inc. (Corpus Christi, TX) **3929**

TCI Cablevision of Texas, Inc. (Galveston, TX) **3970**

TCI Cablevision of Utah (Layton, UT) **4079**

TCI Cablevision of Utah, Inc. (Ogden, UT) **4088**

TCI Cablevision of Utah, Inc. (Provo, UT) **4094**

TCI Cablevision of Utah, Inc. (Sandy, UT) **4104**

TCI Cablevision of Washington (Bellingham, WA) **4241**

TCI Cablevision of Washington (Olympia, WA) **4259**

TCI Cablevision of Wisconsin (Madison, WI) **4397**

TCI Cablevision of Wyoming (Laramie, WY) **4474**

TCI of Florida (Miami, FL) **970**

TCI of Greensburg (Greensburg, PA) **3588**

TCI of Indiana, Inc. (Bloomington, IN) **1436**

TCI of Iowa (Dubuque, IA) **1565**

TCI of Kansas, Inc. (Manhattan, KS) **1655**

TCI of Kansas (Newton, KS) **1663**

TCI of Kansas, Inc. (Salina, KS) **1679**

TCI of Kansas, Inc. (Topeka, KS) **1686**

TCI of Louisiana (Lake Charles, LA) **1789**

TCI of Nevada, Inc. (Reno, NV) **2495**

TCI of New York (Buffalo, NY) **2752**

TCI of North Dakota, Inc. (Grand Forks, ND) **3316**

TCI of North Dakota (Minot, ND) **3324**

TCI of Pennsylvania, Inc. (Pittsburgh, PA) **3658**

TCI of Seattle, Inc. (Seattle, WA) **4281**

TCI of Virginia, Inc. (Chesapeake, VA) **4156**

TCI of West Virginia, Inc. (Wheeling, WV) **4333**

Teacher; The American Biology (Reston, VA) **4206**

Teacher in the Church Today (Nashville, TN) **3852**

Teacher Education Quarterly (San Francisco, CA) **528**

Teacher; Today's Catholic (Dayton, OH) **3400**

Master Index

Visual Arts News (Halifax, NS, Can.) **4592**

Vital Speeches of the Day (Mount Pleasant, SC) **3767**

Viva (Toppenish, WA) **4293**

Viva Petites! (Newport Beach, CA) **404**

Vocational Journal; Canadian (Ottawa, ON, Can.) **4666**

Vogue Knitting Magazine (New York, NY) **3060**

The Voice **959**

Voice **2064**

The Voice (New Baltimore, MI) **2128**

The VOICE for Education (Harrisburg, PA) **3591**

The Voice of Florida (Margate, FL) **959**

The Voice of the Southwest (Gallup, NM) **2652**

The Voice & The Reporter (Huron, OH) **3420**

The Volta Review (Washington, DC) **870**

Voyages; Bulletin (Montreal, PQ, Can.) **4745**

Voyageur; Le Pharillion (Rimouski, PQ, Can.) **4765**

Voz; La (Cupertino, CA) **267**

W

W & J Magazine (Washington, PA) **3688**

WAAO-FM - 103.7 (Andalusia, AL) **2**

WABG-AM - 960 (Greenwood, MS) **2288**

WABL-AM - 1570 (Amite, LA) **1763**

WABX-AM - 990 (Mount Pleasant, MI) **2123**

WABY-AM - 1400 (Albany, NY) **2672**

Waco Cablevision (Waco, TX) **4074**

WACQ-FM - 99.9 (Tallassee, AL) **72**

WACR-FM - 103.9 & 95.7 (Columbus, MS) **2282**

WACX-TV - Channel 55 (Orlando, FL) **986**

Wade Cablevision (Philadelphia, PA) **3644**

The Wadena News (Wadena, SK, Can.) **4783**

WADI-FM - 95.3 (Corinth, MS) **2283**

Wadley Herald; Louisville News & Farmer & (Louisville, GA) **1129**

WAFM-FM - 95.3 (Amory, MS) **2271**

WAFS-AM - 920 (Atlanta, GA) **1085**

WAFX-FM - 106.9 (Norfolk, VA) **4201**

WAFY-FM - 103.1 (Braddock Heights, MD) **1911**

The Wagner Post Advertizer (Wagner, SD) **3798**

WAGY-AM - 1320 (Forest City, NC) **3233**

Wahoo Newspaper (Wahoo, NE) **2482**

WAID-FM - 106 (Clarksdale, MS) **2279**

WAIT-AM **1313**

WAJL-AM - 1190 (Orlando, FL) **987**

WAJO-AM - 1310 (Marion, AL) **47**

WAKE-FM - 89.5 (Winston-Salem, NC) **3295**

WAKG-FM - 103.3 (Danville, VA) **4162**

WAKM-AM - 950 (Franklin, TN) **3824**

WAKY-AM - 1550 (Greensburg, KY) **1714**

WALD-AM - 1080 (Walterboro, SC) **3783**

WALH-AM - 1340 (Mountain City, GA) **1137**

Walker's Estimating & Construction Journal (Lisle, IL) **1348**

Wallkill Valley Times (Walden, NY) **3187**

WAMB-FM - 106.7 (Nashville, TN) **3821**

WAMI-FM - 102.3 (Opp, AL) **66**

WANC-FM - 103.9 (Albany, NY) **3180**

WANM-AM - 1070 (Tallahassee, FL) **1027**

WANO-AM - 1230 (Pineville, KY) **1750**

WANS-AM - 1280 (Greenville, SC) **3752**

Wapato Independent (Toppenish, WA) **4294**

WAPI-FM - 94.5 (Birmingham, AL) **17**

WAQP-TV - Channel 49 (Saginaw, MI) **2140**

War-Whoop (Abilene, TX) **3869**

Warner Cable (Flagstaff, AZ) **105**

Warner Cable (Bakersfield, CA) **217**

Warner Cable of Canton (Canton, OH) **3340**

Warner Cable of Columbus (Columbus, OH) **3392**

Warner Cable Communications, Inc. (Fayetteville, AR) **161**

Warner Cable Communications, Inc. (Lynn, MA) **1977**

Warner Cable Communications, Inc. (Medford, MA) **1979**

Warner Cable Communications (Berlin, NH) **2497**

Warner Cable Communications, Inc. (Akron, OH) **3330**

Warner Cable Communications, Inc. (Cincinnati, OH) **3354**

Warner Cable Communications, Inc. (Youngstown, OH) **3450**

Warner Cable Communications, Inc. (Kingsport, TN) **3828**

Warner Cable Communications, Inc. (Houston, TX) **3996**

Warner Cable Communications, Inc. of Altoona (Altoona, PA) **3549**

Warner Cable of Danville (Danville, IL) **1316**

Warner Cable of De Kalb (De Kalb, IL) **1319**

Warner Cable of Hampton (Hampton, VA) **4180**

Warner Cable of Nashua (Nashua, NH) **2516**

The Warrior (Shearwater, NS, Can.) **4595**

Warship International (Toledo, OH) **3443**

Warwick Beacon (Warwick, RI) **3715**

The Washington Blade (Washington, DC) **871**

Washington; Columbia Cable of (Vancouver, WA) **4296**

Washington; Proceedings of the Entomological Society of (Washington, DC) **848**

Washington; TCI Cablevision of (Bellingham, WA) **4241**

Washington; TCI Cablevision of (Olympia, WA) **4259**

Waste Management; Radioactive (Oak Ridge, TN) **3861**

WASZ-FM - 95.3 (Ashland, AL) **6**

Watchman; Panola (Panola, TX) **4043**

Water; Land and (Fort Dodge, IA) **1579**

Water Resources Planning and Management; Journal of (New York, NY) **2958**

Water Utilities Association Journal; Maine (Readfield, ME) **1833**

Water Well Journal (Dublin, OH) **3407**

The Waterford Post (Waterford, WI) **4459**

WaterSki Magazine (Winter Park, FL) **1045**

Watertown Cable TV (Watertown, SD) **3799**

WATJ-AM - 1560 (Geneva, OH) **3416**

WATK-AM - 900 (Antigo, WI) **4335**

Watonwan County Shoppers Guide (Saint James, MN) **2245**

WaU; Inside (Seattle, WA) **4270**

WAUD-AM - 1230 (Auburn, AL) **9**

Waves (Spring Valley, CA) **587**

WAVJ-AM - 1350 (Black Mountain, NC) **3206**

WAVV-FM - 101.1 (Naples, FL) **974**

WAWL-FM - 91.5 (Chattanooga, TN) **3808**

WAXO-AM - 1220 (Lewisburg, TN) **3833**

WAXS-FM - 94.1 (Beckley, WV) **4304**

WAXT-FM - 96.7 (Anderson, IN) **1425**

The Waybill (Hyde Park, MA) **1974**

WAYJ-FM - 88.7 (Fort Myers, FL) **916**

The Wayne County News (Waynesboro, TN) **3866**

WAYT-AM - 1510 (Wabash, IN) **1527**

WAZS-AM - 980 (Summerville, SC) **3777**

WBAC-AM - 1340 (CLeveland, TN) **3813**

WBAI-FM - 95.5 (New York, NY) **3071**

WBAI Folio (New York, NY) **3061**

WBAL-TV - Channel 11 (Baltimore, MD) **1867**

WBAQ-FM - 97.9 (Greenville, MS) **2286**

WBAT-AM - 1400 (Marion, IN) **1500**

WBAW-AM - 740 (Barnwell, SC) **3721**

WBAW-FM - 99.1 (Barnwell, SC) **3722**

WBBQ-FM - 104.3 (Augusta, GA) **1091**

WBCA-AM - 1110 (Bay Minette, AL) **10**

WBCH-AM - 1220 (Hastings, MI) **2092**

WBCH-FM - 100.1 (Hastings, MI) **2093**

WBCX-FM - 89.1 (Gainesville, GA) **1120**

WBDC-FM - 100.9 (Jasper, IN) **1494**

WBEJ-AM - 1240 (Elizabethton, TN) **3822**

WBFH-FM - 88.1 (Bloomfield Hills, MI) **2044**

WBFN-AM - 1500 (Quitman, MS) **2308**

WBFO-FM - 88.7 (Buffalo, NY) **2753**

WBGR-AM - 860 (Baltimore, MD) **1868**

WBHN-AM - 1590 (Bryson City, NC) **3209**

WBHV-FM - 103.1 (State College, PA) **3678**

WBHY-AM - 840 (Mobile, AL) **54**

WBHY-FM - 88.5 (Mobile, AL) **55**

WBIQ-TV - Channel 10 (Birmingham, AL) **18**

WBIV-AM - 1060 (Boston, MA) **1947**

WBJB-FM - 90.5 (Lincroft, NJ) **2565**

WBKE-FM - 89.5 (North Manchester, IN) **1509**

WBKI-AM - 1440 (Bremen, GA) **1098**

WBKN-FM - 92.1 (Brookhaven, MS) **2275**

WBLN-FM - 103.7 (Murray, KY) **1745**

WBMB-AM - 590 (New York, NY) **3072**

WBNH-FM - 88.5 (Pekin, IL) **1380**

WBNJ-FM - 105.5 (Cape May Court House, NJ) **2540**

WBNX-TV - Channel 55 (Cuyahoga Falls, OH) **3393**

WBPM-FM - 94.3 (Kingston, NY) **2801**

WBRA-TV - Channel 15 (Roanoke, VA) **4224**

WBRC-TV - Channel 6 (Birmingham, AL) **19**

WBRG-AM - 1050 (Lynchburg, VA) **4192**

WBSC-AM - 1550 (Bennettsville, SC) **3724**

WBSN-FM - 89.1 (New Orleans, LA) **1798**

WBTB-AM - 1400 (Beaufort, NC) **3204**

WBTM-AM - 1330 (Danville, VA) **4163**

WBTY-FM - 105.5 (Homerville, GA) **1125**

WBUR-FM - 90.9 (Boston, MA) **1948**

WBUT-AM - 1050 (Butler, PA) **3566**

WBVN-FM - 104.5 (Marion, IL) **1352**

WBWB-FM - 96.7 (Bloomington, IN) **1437**

WBWI-FM - 92.5 (West Bend, WI) **4464**

WBXB-FM - 100.1 (Edenton, NC) **3227**

WBXX-FM - 95.3 (Battle Creek, MI) **2037**

WBYS-AM - 1560 (Canton, IL) **1220**

WBYS-FM - 98.3 (Canton, IL) **1221**

WBYZ-FM - 94.5 (Baxley, GA) **1095**

WBZA-AM - 1230 (Glen Falls, NY) **2778**

WBZR-AM (Shaker Heights, OH) **3440**

WCAL-FM - 89.3 (Northfield, MN) **2231**

WCAT-FM - 99.9 (Orange, MA) **1993**

WCAU-TV - Channel 10 (Philadelphia, PA) **3645**

WCAZ-AM - 990 (Carthage, IL) **1230**

WCAZ-FM - 92.1 (Carthage, IL) **1231**

WCBB-TV - Channel 10 (Lewiston, ME) **1827**

WCCB-AM - 640 (Clarion, PA) **3571**

WCCM-AM - 820 (Randolph, NJ) **2612**

WCCN-AM - 1370 (Neillsville, WI) **4421**

WCCN-FM - 107.5 (Neillsville, WI) **4422**

WCCP-AM - 1560 (Clemson, SC) **3730**

WCCZ-FM - 97.3 (Spangler, PA) **3675**

WCDQ-FM - 92.1 (Sanford, ME) **1835**

WCDT-AM - 1340 (Winchester, TN) **3867**

WCDX-FM - 92.7 (Richmond, VA) **4220**
WCEF-FM - 98.3 (Ripley, WV) **4324**
WCFE-FM - 91.9 (Plattsburgh, NY) **3090**
WCFJ-AM - 1470 (Ford Heights, IL) **1336**
WCGW-AM - 770 (Lexington, KY) **1721**
WCHC-FM - 89.1 (Worcester, MA) **2026**
WCHI-AM - 1350 (Chillicothe, OH) **3341**
WCHJ-AM - 1470 (Brookhaven, MS) **2276**
WCHR-FM - 94.5 (Yardley, PA) **3698**
WCIC-FM - 91.5 (Pekin, IL) **1381**
WCJC-FM - 99.3 (Marion, IN) **1501**
WCJL-AM - 1300 (Marinette, WI) **4400**
WCKA-FM - 97.1 (Sutton, WV) **4328**
WCLL-FM - 90.7 (Wesson, MS) **2312**
WCMM-FM - 94.7 (Manistique, MI) **2115**
WCMN-AM - 1280 (Arecibo, PR) **3702**
WCNC-AM - 1240 (Elizabeth City, NC) **3229**
WCNL-FM - 96.7 (Carlinville, IL) **1224**
WCON-FM - 99.3 (Cornelia, GA) **1105**
WCOW-FM - 97.1 (Sparta, WI) **4450**
WCOX-AM - 1450 (Camden, AL) **22**
WCOX-FM - 102.3 (Camden, AL) **23**
WCPS-AM - 760 (Tarboro, NC) **3286**
WCQS-FM - 88.1 (Asheville, NC) **3202**
WCRD-AM - 540 (Muncie, IN) **1505**
WCRK-AM - 1150 (Morristown, TN) **3839**
WCRM-AM - 1350 (Fort Myers, FL) **917**
WCRQ-FM - 92.7 (Arab, AL) **5**
WCRW-AM - 1240 (Chicago, IL) **1310**
WCRX-FM - 88.1 (Chicago, IL) **1311**
WCRZ-FM - 107.9 (Flint, MI) **2072**
WCSI-AM - 1010 (Columbus, IN) **1440**
WCUB-AM - 980 (Manitowoc, WI) **4398**
WCVL-AM - 1550 (Crawfordsville, IN) **1441**
WCVO-FM - 104.9 (New Albany, OH) **3415**
WCVR-FM - 102.1 (Randolph Center, VT) **4116**
WCW Magazine (Rockville Centre, NY) **3110**
WCWV-FM - 92.9 (Summersville, WV) **4327**
WDAC-FM - 94.5 (New Providence, PA) **3621**
WDAD-AM - 1450 (Indiana, PA) **3599**
WDCA-TV - Channel 20 (Bethesda, MD) **876**
WDCK-FM - 96.5 (Quinton, VA) **4204**
WDCR-AM - 1340 (Hanover, NH) **2509**
WDEE-AM - 1500 (Harrison, MI) **2091**
WDER-AM - 1320 (Derry, NH) **2504**
WDEX-AM - 1430 (Monroe, NC) **3263**
WDHA-FM - 105.5 (Cedar Knolls, NJ) **2541**
WDIQ-TV - Channel 2 (Birmingham, AL) **28**
WDMG-AM - 860 (Douglas, GA) **1113**
WDMP-AM - 810 (Dodgeville, WI) **4350**
WDMP-FM - 99.3 (Dodgeville, WI) **4351**
WDNE-AM - 1240 (Elkins, WV) **4311**
WDNR-FM - 89.5 (Chester, PA) **3568**
WDNX-FM - 89.1 (Savannah, TN) **3862**
WDOH-FM - 107.1 (Delphos, OH) **3404**
WDRK-FM - 103.5 (Panama City, FL) **887**
WDRP-FM - 98.9 (Windsor, NC) **3291**
WDSL-AM - 1520 (Mocksville, NC) **3262**
WDTS-AM - 620 (Georgetown, DE) **780**
WDYN-FM - 89.7 (Chattanooga, TN) **3809**
WDZA-FM - 94.5 (Murrells Inlet, SC) **3768**
WEAA-FM - 88.9 (Baltimore, MD) **1869**
WEBE-FM - 107.9 (Bridgeport, CT) **736**
WEBI-FM **1835**
WEBN-FM - 102.7 (Cincinnati, OH) **3355**
WECC-AM - 1190 (Saint Mary's, GA) **1146**
WECR-AM - 550 (St. Petersburg, FL) **1009**
WECW-FM - 95.5 (Elmira, NY) **2765**
WEEB-AM - 990 (Southern Pines, NC) **3280**
Weekend (Walterboro, SC) **3782**

The Weekender (Seward, NE) **2479**
Weekender (Erie, PA) **3582**
The Weekly (Rolla, MO) **2374**
The Weekly Messenger (Reston, VA) **4211**
Weekly Scene (Fort Lauderdale, FL) **913**
The Weekly Terre Haute (Terre Haute, IN) **1522**
WEEO-AM - 1130 (Waynesboro, PA) **3689**
WEFG-AM - 1490 (Whitehall, MI) **2157**
WEFG-FM - 97.5 (Whitehall, MI) **2158**
WEIQ-TV - Channel 42 (Birmingham, AL) **56**
WEIR-AM - 1430 (Weirton, WV) **4330**
WEJY-FM - 97.5 (Monroe, MI) **2119**
Wellesley Magazine (Wellesley, MA) **2011**
The Wellston Telegram (Wellston, OH) **3445**
WELS-AM - 1010 (Kinston, NC) **3254**
WELZ-AM - 1460 (Belzoni, MS) **2272**
WEMI-FM - 100.1 (Appleton, WI) **4337**
WEMJ-AM - 1490 (Laconia, NH) **2513**
WEMU-FM - 89.1 (Ypsilanti, MI) **2159**
WERH-AM - 970 (Hamilton, AL) **36**
WERX-FM - 102.3 (Edenton, NC) **3228**
WESC-AM - 660 (Greenville, SC) **3753**
The Wesleyan Advocate (Indianapolis, IN) **1485**
WESS-FM - 90.3 (East Stroudsburg, PA) **3577**
West Branch Times (West Branch, IA) **1621**
West-Central Crossroads (Kindersley, SK, Can.) **4772**
West Coast Lifestyle Magazine (Van Nuys, CA) **607**
West County Journal (Saint Louis, MO) **2398**
West Covina Highlander (West Covina, CA) **613**
West Orange Chronicle (Orange, NJ) **2603**
West Proviso Herald (Proviso, IL) **1383**
West Side **1464**
West Valley Cablevision (Chatsworth, CA) **255**
West Virginia, Inc.; TCI of (Wheeling, WV) **4333**
Westchester County Business Journal (Hawthorne, NY) **2787**
Westchester Herald (Westchester, IL) **1422**
Western CATV Inc. (Canyon County, CA) **251**
Western Manitoba Profile on Business (Brandon, MB, Can.) **4560**
Western New York Health Magazine and Hospital News (Buffalo, NY) **2750**
Western Roofing/Insulation/Siding (Reno, NV) **2492**
Westlake/Moss Bluff News Buyer's Guide **1810**
WestMarc Cable (Burlington, IA) **1537**
WestMarc Cable (Muskegon, MI) **2126**
WestMarc Cable (Rochester, MN) **2240**
WestMarc Cable Group (La Crosse, WI) **4376**
WestMarc Cable TV (Waterloo, IA) **1620**
The Weston Forum (Weston, CT) **776**
Westside Enterprise (Greenfield, IN) **1464**
The Westville Reporter (Lincoln, AR) **171**
WETL-FM - 91.7 (South Bend, IN) **1521**
WETS-FM - 89.5 (Johnson City, TN) **3827**
WEUP-AM - 1600 (Huntsville, AL) **40**
WEVS-FM - 92.7 (Saugatuck, MI) **2143**
WEVU-TV - Channel 26 (Bonita Springs, FL) **884**
WEWO-AM - 1460 (Laurinburg, NC) **3256**
WEXA Cable, Inc. (Conyers, GA) **1104**
WEYY-FM - 92.7 (Talladega, AL) **71**
WFAM-AM - 1050 (Augusta, GA) **1092**
WFCC-FM - 107.5 (Brewster, MA) **1952**
WFCL-AM - 1380 (Clintonville, WI) **4345**
WFEL-AM - 1570 (Towson, MD) **1933**

WFFT-TV - Channel 55 (Fort Wayne, IN) **1453**
WFGN-AM - 1180 (Gaffney, SC) **3749**
WFIC-AM - 1530 (Collinsville, VA) **4160**
WFIN-AM - 650 (Jacksonville, FL) **943**
WFIQ-TV - Channel 36 (Birmingham, AL) **32**
WFIT-AM - 530 (New York, NY) **3073**
WFKZ-FM - 103.1 (Tavernier, FL) **1039**
WFLQ-FM - 100.1 (French Lick, IN) **1455**
WFLS-AM - 1350 (Fredericksburg, VA) **4171**
WFLW-AM - 1360 (Monticello, KY) **1742**
WFLW-FM **1743**
WFNP-FM - 88.7 (New Paltz, NY) **2825**
WFNR-AM - 710 (Christiansburg, VA) **4157**
WFNR-FM - 100.7 (Christiansburg, VA) **4158**
WFOB-AM - 1430 (Fostoria, OH) **3409**
WFPA-AM - 1400 (Fort Payne, AL) **33**
WFPR-AM - 640 (Rindge, NH) **2526**
WFQS-FM - 91.3 (Asheville, NC) **3203**
WFSG-TV - Channel 56 (Tallahassee, FL) **993**
WFSP-AM - 1560 (Kingwood, WV) **4316**
WFSP-FM - 107.7 (Kingwood, VA) **4185**
WFSQ-FM - 91.5 (Tallahassee, FL) **1028**
WFSU-FM **1028**
WFSU-TV - Channel 11 (Tallahassee, FL) **1029**
WFTG-AM - 1400 (London, KY) **1724**
WFWM-FM - 91.7 (Frostburg, MD) **1900**
WFXS-FM - 102.3 (Chattanooga, TN) **3810**
WGAB-AM - 1180 (Newburgh, IN) **1507**
WGAR-FM - 99.5 (Cleveland, OH) **3384**
WGBF-FM - 103.1 (Evansville, IN) **1448**
WGBH-FM - 89.7 (Boston, MA) **1949**
WGCI-AM - 1390 (Chicago, IL) **1312**
WGCS-FM - 91.1 (Goshen, IN) **1459**
WGDR-FM - 91.1 (Plainfield, VT) **4113**
WGEV-FM - 88.3 (Beaver Falls, PA) **3557**
WGFB-FM - 99.9 (Peru, NY) **3088**
WGFP-AM - 940 (Webster, MA) **2010**
WGFR-FM - 92.1 (Queensbury, NY) **3100**
WGGA-AM - 1240 (Gainesville, GA) **1121**
WGGA-FM - 101.9 (Gainesville, GA) **1122**
WGHQ-AM - 920 (Kingston, NY) **2802**
WGIA-AM - 1350 (Blackshear, GA) **1096**
WGKR-AM - 540 (Jersey City, NJ) **2564**
WGKY-FM - 95.9 (Wickliffe, KY) **1756**
WGLS-FM - 89.7 (Glassboro, NJ) **2558**
WGMB-AM - 640 (Bridgewater, VA) **4144**
WGMC-FM - 90.1 (North Greece, NY) **3082**
WGMZ-FM - 101.7 (Frankenmuth, MI) **2074**
WGNC-AM - 1450 (Gastonia, NC) **3235**
WGOG-AM - 1000 (Walhalla, SC) **3779**
WGOG-FM - 96.3 (Walhalla, SC) **3780**
WGRD-FM - 97.9 (Grand Rapids, MI) **2081**
WGRE-FM - 91.5 (Greencastle, IN) **1461**
WGRK-AM **1714**
WGRY-AM - 1230 (Grayling, MI) **2089**
WGRY-FM - 101.1 (Grayling, MI) **2090**
WGTA-AM - 950 (Summerville, GA) **1152**
WGTO-AM - 540 (Ocoee, FL) **982**
WGTX-AM - 1280 (De Funiak Springs, FL) **901**
WGTY-FM - 107.7 (Gettysburg, PA) **3586**
WGVK-TV - Channel 52 (Grand Rapids, MI) **2082**
WGVU-AM - 1480 (Grand Rapids, MI) **2083**
WGVU-FM - 88.5 (Grand Rapids, MI) **2084**
WGVU-TV - Channel 35 (Grand Rapids, MI) **2085**
WGYJ-AM - 1590 (Atmore, AL) **7**
Whaling City Cable TV (New Bedford, MA) **1983**

WLVA-AM - 590 (Lynchburg, VA) **4194**
WLVF-AM - 930 (Haines City, FL) **931**
WLVR-FM - 91.3 (Bethlehem, PA) **3560**
WLVX-AM - 1550 (Bloomfield, CT) **730**
WMAK-AM - 980 (Pittsburg, KY) **1725**
WMAX-AM **2083**
WMAZ-TV - Channel 13 (Macon, GA) **1132**
WMBE-AM - 1530 (Chilton, WI) **4343**
WMBL-AM - 740 (Morehead City, NC) **3265**
WMCG-FM - 104.9 (Rochelle, GA) **1142**
WMCJ-AM - 950 (Moncks Corner, SC) **3766**
WMCR-AM - 640 (Monmouth, IL) **1359**
WMCR-FM **2100**
WMDH-FM - 102.5 (New Castle, IN) **1506**
WMEC-TV - Channel 22 (Springfield, IL) **1351**
WMEE-FM - 97.3 (Fort Wayne, IN) **1454**
WMER-AM - 1390 (Meridian, MS) **2302**
WMEX-FM **3386**
WMFD-AM - 630 (Wilmington, NC) **3290**
WMGA-AM - 580 (Moultrie, GA) **1136**
WMGR-AM - 930 (Bainbridge, GA) **1094**
WMHR-FM - 102.9 (Syracuse, NY) **3131**
WMHT-FM - 89.1 (Schenectady, NY) **3116**
WMLX-AM - 1180 (Cincinnati, OH) **3356**
WMMG-AM - 1140 (Brandenburg, KY) **1701**
WMMG-FM - 93.5 (Brandenburg, KY) **1702**
WMMR-FM - 96.3 (Minneapolis, MN) **2218**
WMMR-FM - 93.3 (Philadelphia, PA) **3646**
WMNA-FM - 106.3 (Gretna, VA) **4176**
WMQA-AM - 1570 (Minocqua, WI) **4415**
WMQA-FM - 96 (Minocqua, WI) **4416**
WMSG-AM - 1050 (Oakland, MD) **1916**
WMTC-AM - 730 (Vancleve, KY) **1753**
WMTC-FM - 99.9 (Vancleve, KY) **1754**
WMTE-FM - 97.7 (Manistee, MI) **2114**
WMTS-AM - 810 (Murfreesboro, TN) **3840**
WMUK-FM - 102.1 (Kalamazoo, MI) **2100**
WMUL-FM - 88.1 (Huntington, WV) **4315**
WMUU-AM - 1260 (Greenville, SC) **3754**
WMUU-FM - 94.5 (Greenville, SC) **3755**
WMVB-AM - 890 (Pittsburg, PA) **3659**
WMVG-AM - 1450 (Milledgeville, GA) **1135**
WMVR-AM - 1080 (Sidney, OH) **3441**
WMXR-FM - 93.9 (Woodstock, VT) **4125**
WMYN-AM - 1420 (Madison, NC) **3260**
WNAH-AM - 1360 (Nashville, TN) **3855**
WNAH-FM - 92.5 (Nashville, TN) **3856**
WNAV-AM - 1430 (Annapolis, MD) **1842**
WNDC-AM - 910 (Baton Rouge, LA) **1768**
WNDE-AM - 1260 (Indianapolis, IN) **1490**
WNDZ-AM - 750 (Portage, IN) **1513**
WNEH-TV - Channel 38 (Columbia, SC) **3758**
WNEK-FM - 105.1 (Springfield, MA) **2000**
WNFK-FM - 105.5 (Perry, FL) **996**
WNGG-FM - 100.9 (Clyde, OH) **3386**
WNGO-AM - 1320 (Mayfield, KY) **1739**
WNIJ-FM - 90.5 (Rockford, IL) **1395**
WNJC-AM - 1360 (Deptford, NJ) **2547**
WNKR-FM - 101.1 (Dania, FL) **898**
WNNY-AM - 1390 (Charlotte, MI) **2048**
WNPB-TV - Channel 24 (Morgantown, WV) **4319**
WNTK-FM - 100.5 (New London, NH) **2517**
WNTV-TV - Channel 29 (Columbia, SC) **3756**
WNUC-FM - 107.7 (Williamsville, NY) **3195**
WNUR-FM - 89.6 (Evanston, IL) **1334**
WNUV-TV - Channel 54 (Baltimore, MD) **1871**
WNYT-AM - 550 (Old Westbury, NY) **3084**
WNYU-FM - 89.1 (New York, NY) **3076**

WNYV-FM - 94.1 (White Hall, NY) **3190**
WNYV-FM - 94.1 (Poultney, VT) **4115**
WOAS-FM - 88.5 (Ontonagon, MI) **2130**
WOCG-FM - 90.1 (Huntsville, AL) **41**
WOCW-FM - 92.1 (Beaufort, SC) **3723**
WOES-FM - 91.3 (Elsie, MI) **2066**
WOKW-FM - 102.9 (Clearfield, PA) **3573**
WOLD-AM - 1330 (Marion, VA) **4197**
WOLD-FM - 102.5 (Marion, VA) **4198**
WOLF-FM - 97.7 (Houghton, MI) **2094**
WOLY-AM - 1500 (Battle Creek, MI) **2038**
Woman Bowler (Greendale, WI) **4364**
Woman; Business and Professional (Ottawa, ON, Can.) **4651**
The Woman Conductor (West Lafayette, IN) **1528**
Woman; Country (Greendale, WI) **4363**
Woman Entrepreneur (New York, NY) **3062**
Woman of Power (Orleans, MA) **1994**
Womanews (New York, NY) **3063**
Woman's Art Journal (Laverock, PA) **3605**
Woman's Day Crosswords (New York, NY) **3064**
The Woman's Pulpit (Stroudsburg, PA) **3680**
Women and Aging; Journal of (Binghamton, NY) **2729**
Women and Guns (Buffalo, NY) **2751**
Women and Health (Brooklyn, NY) **2747**
Women Lawyers Journal (Chicago, IL) **1307**
Women in Natural Resources (Moscow, ID) **1195**
Women and Therapy (Binghamton, NY) **2739**
Women and Therapy (Burlington, VT) **4110**
Women's Circle Counted Cross-Stitch **1428**
Women's Health Issues (New York, NY) **3065**
Women's Press; Minnesota (Saint Paul, MN) **2254**
The Women's Review of Books (Wellesley, MA) **2012**
Women's Sports & Fitness (Boulder, CO) **633**
Women's Studies Abstracts (New Brunswick, NJ) **2593**
Women's Times (San Diego, CA) **502**
WomenWise (Concord, NH) **2501**
Wometco Cable (Jonesboro, GA) **1126**
Wometco of Gwinnett (Snellville, GA) **1149**
Womyn's Press (Eugene, OR) **3502**
WONQ-AM - 1140 (Casselberry, FL) **888**
WOOD-FM - EZ-105.7 (Grand Rapids, MI) **2087**
Woodlands; Ohio (Columbus, OH) **3388**
Woodswomen News (Minneapolis, MN) **2215**
The Woodworker's Journal (New Milford, CT) **755**
Woodworking; Modern (Collierville, TN) **3815**
WOOZ-FM - 99.9 (Carbondale, IL) **1222**
WORB-FM - 90.3 (Farmington Hills, MI) **2070**
Workbench (Kansas City, MO) **2353**
The World (Boston, MA) **1946**
The World Affairs Canada Quarterly (Toronto, ON, Can.) **4721**
World of Politics (Dallas, TX) **3944**
The World & Science (Los Angeles, CA) **366**
World Wrestling Federation Battlemania (New York, NY) **3066**
WOUX-FM - 90.1 (Rochester, MI) **2137**
WOWB-FM - 105.5 (Utica, NY) **3185**
WOWN-FM - 99.3 (Shawano, WI) **4442**
WOXR-AM - 1580 (Oxford, AL) **67**
WOYS-FM - 100.9 (Eastpoint, FL) **879**
WOZN-FM - 98.7 (Tallahassee, FL) **949**
WPBA-TV - Channel 30 (Atlanta, GA) **1086**
WPCR-FM - 91.7 (Plymouth, NH) **2524**

WPDE-TV - Channel 15 (Florence, SC) **3747**
WPDJ-AM - 1300 (Huntington, IN) **1467**
WPDM-AM - 1470 (Potsdam, NY) **3095**
WPDQ-AM - 690 (Orange Park, FL) **983**
WPGC-AM - 1580 (Greenbelt, MD) **877**
WPHS-FM - 89.1 (Warren, MI) **2156**
WPIX-TV - Channel 11 (New York, NY) **3077**
WPJM-AM - 800 (Greer, SC) **3759**
WPKM-FM - 106.3 (Scarborough, ME) **1837**
WPLR-FM - 99.1 (Hamden, CT) **745**
WPLS-FM - 96.5 (Greenville, SC) **3757**
WPLT-FM - 93.9 (Plattsburgh, NY) **3091**
WPLW-AM - 1590 (Pittsburgh, PA) **3660**
WPLZ-FM - 99.3 (Richmond, VA) **4222**
WPMR-AM - 960 (Mount Pocono, PA) **3618**
WPMW-FM - 92.7 (Mullens, WV) **4320**
WPNE-TV - Channel 38 (Madison, WI) **4362**
WPNT-AM **1313**
WPPJ-AM - 670 (Pittsburgh, PA) **3661**
WPRY-AM - 1400 (Perry, FL) **997**
WPRZ-AM - 1250 (Warrenton, VA) **4229**
WPSC-FM - 88.7 (Wayne, NJ) **2635**
WPSR-FM - 90.7 (Evansville, IN) **1449**
WPTD-TV - Channel 16 (Dayton, OH) **3403**
WPUB-AM - 640 (New York, NY) **3078**
WPUP-FM - 103.7 (Athens, GA) **1054**
WQAB-FM - 91.3 (Philippi, WV) **4321**
WQCK-FM - 92.7 (Baker, LA) **1764**
WQCY-FM - 99.5 (Quincy, IL) **1384**
WQDR-FM - 94.7 (Raleigh, NC) **3277**
WQEC-TV - Channel 27 (Springfield, IL) **1385**
WQHH-FM - 96.5 (Lansing, MI) **2050**
WQHL-AM - 1250 (Live Oak, FL) **956**
WQHL-FM - 98.1 (Live Oak, FL) **957**
WQIZ-AM - 810 (St. George, SC) **3775**
WQLR-FM - 106.5 (Kalamazoo, MI) **2101**
WQNS-FM - 104.9 (Waynesville, NC) **3287**
WQRX-AM - 870 (Valley Head, AL) **77**
WQSR-FM - 105.7 (Baltimore, MD) **1872**
WQWQ-AM - 1520 (Muskegon, MI) **2127**
WQXL-AM - 1470 (Columbia, SC) **3737**
WQXO-AM - 1400 (Munising, MI) **2125**
WQXX-FM - 92.1 (Morganton, NC) **3266**
WQZQ-FM - 102.5 (Nashville, TN) **3820**
WRAK-AM - 1400 (Williamsport, PA) **3694**
WRBR-FM - 103.9 (Granger, IN) **1460**
WRBT-FM - 94.9 (Mount Carmel, IL) **1362**
WRCC-AM - 1600 (Warner Robins, GA) **1160**
WRCC-FM - 101.7 (Warner Robins, GA) **1161**
WRCO-AM - 1450 (Richland Center, WI) **4439**
WRCO-FM - 100.9 (Richland Center, WI) **4440**
WRDL-FM - 88.9 (Ashland, OH) **3332**
WRDN-AM - 1430 (Durand, WI) **4352**
WRDZ-AM - 1260 (Cleveland, OH) **3385**
WREE-View (New York, NY) **3067**
WREK-FM - 91.1 (Atlanta, GA) **1087**
Wrestling Confidential (New York, NY) **3068**
WRFC-AM - 960 (Athens, GA) **1055**
WRFR-FM - 96.7 (Franklin, NC) **3234**
WRGM-AM - 1440 (Mansfield, OH) **3426**
WRGR-FM - 102.3 (Tupper Lake, NY) **3183**
WRHP-FM - 107.9 (Liverpool, NY) **2810**
WRHV-FM - 88.7 (Schenectady, NY) **3117**
WRIE-AM - 1260 (Erie, PA) **3584**
WRIF-FM - 101.1 (Southfield, MI) **2061**
Wright County Shopper's Guide (Eagle Grove, IA) **1568**
WRIJ-FM - 106.9 (Grantsville, MD) **3610**

Writer's Guidelines Magazine (Pittsburg, MO) **2370**

Writer's Lifeline (Cornwall, ON, Can.) **4607**

WRLA Yardstick (Winnipeg, MB, Can.) **4570**

WRLD-AM - 1490 (Lanett, AL) **46**

WROI-FM - 92.1 (Rochester, IN) **1517**

WROS-AM - 1050 (Jacksonville, FL) **945**

WROX-AM - 1450 (Clarksdale, MS) **2280**

WRQI-FM - 95.1 & 95.5 (East Rochester, NY) **2764**

WRRK-FM **2114**

WRSA-FM - 96.9 (Huntsville, AL) **42**

WRSC-AM - 1390 (State College, PA) **3679**

WRXB-AM - 1590 (Saint Petersburg, FL) **1010**

WRZN-AM - 720 (Hernando, FL) **932**

WSAU-AM - 550 (Wausau, WI) **4462**

WSBI-AM - 1210 (Byrdstown, TN) **3802**

WSCR-AM - 820 (Chicago, IL) **1313**

WSEC-TV - Channel 14/65 (Springfield, IL) **1412**

WSFL-FM - 106.5 (New Bern, NC) **3269**

WSFP-FM - 90.1 (Fort Myers, FL) **918**

WSFW-AM - 1110 (Seneca Falls, NY) **3121**

WSFW-FM - 99.3 (Seneca Falls, NY) **3122**

WSGB-AM - 1490 (Sutton, WV) **4329**

WSGH-AM - 1040 (Winston-Salem, NC) **3296**

WSGR-FM - 91.3 (Port Huron, MI) **2134**

WSGY-FM - 100.3 (Tifton, GA) **1158**

WSHN-AM - 1550 (Fremont, MI) **2075**

WSHN-FM - 100.1 (Fremont, MI) **2076**

WSIX-FM - 97.9 (Nashville, TN) **3857**

WSKX-FM **4201**

WSLI-AM - 930 (Jackson, MS) **2297**

WSME-AM - 1220 (Sanford, ME) **1836**

WSNJ-FM - 107.7 (Bridgeton, NJ) **2536**

WSNN-FM - 99.3 (Potsdam, NY) **3096**

WSPB-AM - 1450 (Sarasota, FL) **1016**

WSPC-AM - 1140 (Castlewood, VA) **4146**

WSRD-FM - 104.9 (Johnstown, NY) **2800**

WSTH-FM - 106.1 (Columbus, GA) **1**

WSTJ-AM - 1340 (St. Johnsbury, VT) **4122**

WSWO-FM - 102.3 (Wilmington, OH) **3446**

WSYC-FM - 88.7 (Shippensburg, PA) **3673**

WSYD-AM - 1300 (Mount Airy, NC) **3267**

WTAD-AM - 930 (Quincy, IL) **1386**

WTAZ-FM - 102.3 (Morton, IL) **1360**

WTBZ-AM - 1260 (Grafton, WV) **4312**

WTBZ-FM - 95.9 (Grafton, WV) **4313**

WTCH-AM - 960 (Shawano, WI) **4443**

WTCN-AM - 1220 (Clearwater, MN) **2171**

WTGA-FM - 95.3 (Thomaston, GA) **1156**

WTGE-FM - 100.7 (Baton Rouge, LA) **1769**

WTGH-AM - 620 (Columbia, SC) **3738**

WTIM-AM - 1410 (Taylorville, IL) **1415**

WTIV-AM - 1230 (Titusville, PA) **3682**

WTMC-AM - 1290 (Ocala, FL) **981**

WTMP-AM - 1150 (Tampa, FL) **1035**

WTNJ-FM - 105.9 (Beckley, WV) **4306**

WTOT-AM - 980 (Marianna, FL) **963**

WTRP-AM - 620 (La Grange, GA) **1127**

WTRR-AM - 1400 (Sanford, FL) **1011**

WTRY-FM - 98.3 (Schenectady, NY) **3114**

WTSJ-AM - 1050 (Cincinnati, OH) **3357**

WTTA-TV - Channel 38 (Tampa, FL) **1036**

WTTC-AM - 1550 (Towanda, PA) **3683**

WTTU-FM - 88.5 (Cookeville, TN) **3818**

WTTV-TV - Channel 4 (Indianapolis, IN) **1491**

WTUZ-FM - 99.9 (New Philadelphia, OH) **3431**

WTVW-TV - Channel 7 (Evansville, IN) **1450**

WTWN-AM **4122**

WTXT-FM - 98.1 (Northport, AL) **31**

WUAG-FM - 103.1 (Greensboro, NC) **3247**

WUCF-FM - 89.9 (Orlando, FL) **988**

WUCM-TV - Channel 19 (University Center, MI) **2152**

WUCX-TV - Channel 35 (University Center, MI) **2153**

WUFL-AM - 1030 (Clinton Township, MI) **2148**

WUFT-FM - 89.1 (Gainesville, FL) **930**

WUGO-FM - 102.3 (Grayson, KY) **1713**

WUKY-FM - 91.3 (Lexington, KY) **1722**

WUMD-FM - 560 (Catonsville, MD) **1889**

WUSR-AM - 550 (Scranton, PA) **3671**

WUSR-FM - 107.9 (Scranton, PA) **3672**

WUTZ-AM - 1075 (Tampa, FL) **1037**

WVAC-FM - 107.9 (Adrian, MI) **2028**

WVAZ-FM - 102.7 (Chicago, IL) **1314**

WVCX-FM - 98.9 (Tomah, WI) **4458**

WVEP-FM - 88.9 (Charleston, WV) **4308**

WVIA-FM - 89.9 (Pittston, PA) **3662**

WVIM-FM - 95.3 (Hernando, MS) **2292**

WVIP-FM - 106.3 (Mount Kisco, NY) **2822**

WVIV-FM - 105.9 (Ithaca, NY) **2795**

WVKZ-AM - 1240 (Schenectady, NY) **3118**

WVLC-AM - 1260 (Lake City, SC) **3765**

WVLR-FM - 102.7 (Lynchburg, VA) **4195**

WVMC-FM - 90.7 (Mansfield, OH) **3427**

WVNC-FM - 96.7 (Canton, NY) **2755**

WVNO-FM - 106.1 (Mansfield, OH) **3428**

WVNP-FM - 89.9 (Charleston, WV) **4309**

WVOB-FM - 91.3 (Dothan, AL) **27**

WVOJ-AM - 970 (Jacksonville, FL) **946**

WVOR-FM - 100.5 (Rochester, NY) **3107**

WVPB-FM - 91.7 (Charleston, WV) **4310**

WVPE-FM - 88.1 (Elkhart, IN) **1446**

WVRD-FM - 107.1 (Belzoni, MS) **2273**

WVRU-FM - 89.9 (Radford, VA) **4205**

WVXU-FM - 91.7 (Cincinnati, OH) **3358**

WWAS-FM - 88.1 (Williamsport, PA) **3695**

WWBF-AM - 1130 (Bartow, FL) **882**

WWBK-FM - 98.3 (Fredericktown, OH) **3412**

WWCH-AM - 1300 (Clarion, PA) **3572**

WWCP-FM - 96.7 (Schenectady, NY) **3119**

WWEL-FM - 104 (London, KY) **1726**

WWHS-FM - 92.1 (Hampden-Sydney, VA) **4178**

WWKC-FM - 104.9 (Cambridge, OH) **3338**

WWKO-AM - 860 (Cocoa, FL) **891**

WWLI-FM - 105 (Providence, RI) **3713**

WWNO-FM - 89.9 (New Orleans, LA) **1800**

WWNZ-AM - 740 (Orlando, FL) **989**

WWNZ-FM - 104.1 (Orlando, FL) **990**

WWOD-AM - 1390 (Lynchburg, VA) **4196**

WWOK-AM - 1280 (Evansville, IN) **1451**

WWPH-FM - 107.9 (Princeton Junction, NJ) **2611**

WWRC-AM - 980 (Silver Spring, MD) **1931**

WWRK-FM - 92.1 (Elberton, GA) **1117**

WWRX-FM - 103.7 (Warwick, RI) **3716**

WWUH-FM - 91.3 (West Hartford, CT) **775**

WWVR-FM - 105.5 (West Terre Haute, IN) **1529**

WWWT-AM - 1320 (Randolph Center, VT) **4117**

WXAV-FM - 88.3 (Chicago, IL) **1315**

WXBC-AM - 540 (Annadale-On-Hudson, NY) **2674**

WXCE-AM - 1260 (Amery, WI) **4334**

WXIA-TV - Channel 11 (Atlanta, GA) **1088**

WXIE-FM - 92.3 (Oakland, MD) **1917**

WXIN-TV - Channel 59 (Indianapolis, IN) **1492**

WXJM-FM - 88 (Harrisonburg, VA) **4184**

WXKC-FM - 99.9 (Erie, PA) **3585**

WXLR-FM **3678**

WXLZ-FM - 107.3 (Castlewood, VA) **4147**

WXON-TV - Channel 20 (Southfield, MI) **2062**

WXPZ-FM - 101.3 (Milford, DE) **783**

WXRL-AM - 1300 (Lancaster, NY) **2806**

WXXK-FM - 101.7 (Claremont, NH) **2499**

WXXP-FM - 97.9 (Indianapolis, IN) **1493**

WXXQ-FM - 98.5 (Rockford, IL) **1396**

WXYC-FM - 89.3 (Chapel Hill, NC) **3214**

WXYT-AM - 1270 (Southfield, MI) **2147**

WXYV-FM - 102.7 (Baltimore, MD) **1873**

WYAM-FM - 106.1 (Hartselle, AL) **37**

WYBB-FM - 98.1 (Charleston, SC) **3729**

WYFE-FM - 88.9 (Hudson, FL) **939**

WYKK-FM - 98.3 (Quitman, MS) **2309**

WYLL-FM - 106.7 (Elk Grove Village, IL) **1327**

WYLS-AM - 670 (York, AL) **78**

Wynne Progress (Wynne, AR) **196**

Wyoming Counties; Farm News of Erie and (East Aurora, NY) **2763**

Wyoming; TCI Cablevision of (Laramie, WY) **4474**

WYOY-FM - 94.5 (Rutland, VT) **4121**

WYRV-AM - 770 (Cedar Bluff, VA) **4149**

WYXL-FM - 97.3 (Ithaca, NY) **2796**

WZBH-FM - 93.5 (Georgetown, DE) **781**

WZCC-AM - 1570 (Jeffersonville, IN) **1495**

WZKO-FM - 106.3 (Pineville, KY) **1751**

WZLB-AM - 1450 (Rome, NY) **3111**

WZLQ-FM - 98.5 (Tupelo, MS) **2311**

WZLX-FM - 100.7 (Boston, MA) **1951**

WZPQ-AM - 1360 (Jasper, AL) **44**

WZRQ-FM - 102.3 (Schenectady, NY) **3120**

WZYX-AM - 1440 (Cowan, TN) **3819**

WZZJ-AM - 1580 (Pascagoula, MS) **2307**

X

The X Journal (Denville, NJ) **2546**

X-TRA (Prineville, OR) **3538**

XEMU-AM - 580 (Eagle Pass, TX) **3956**

Y

Yachting; Quebec (Montreal, PQ, Can.) **4758**

Yadkin Ripple (Yadkinville, NC) **3297**

Yale Journal of Law and Feminism (New Haven, CT) **753**

The Yancey Journal (Burnsville, NC) **3211**

Yardley News (Yardley, PA) **3697**

Yesterdaze Toys (Otisville, MI) **2131**

Yorba Linda Star (Yorba Linda, CA) **626**

York; Cable TV of (York, PA) **3700**

York Daily Record (York, PA) **3699**

Your Church (Carol Stream, IL) **1227**

Your Health (Ogden, UT) **4086**

Your Home, Indoors & Out and Better Living (Ogden, UT) **4087**

"Youth Awareness Press" **141**

Youth Connections; NYC/New (New York, NY) **2985**

Youth Services Review; Children and (Tarrytown, NY) **3137**

Youth Today (Washington, DC) **873**

Youth! (Nashville, TN) **3853**

Youth!; The Magazine for Christian (Nashville, TN) **3849**

YSB (Washington, DC) **874**

Z

Zephyrhills News (Zephyrhills, FL) **1047**

Zillions (Yonkers, NY) **3198**

Zoo View (Los Angeles, CA) **367**

Zoologie); Canadian Journal of Zoology (Revue Canadienne de (Ottawa, ON, Can.) **4665**

Zoology (Revue Canadienne de Zoologie); Canadian Journal of (Ottawa, N, Can.) **4665**